National Library
of Canada

Bibliothèque nationale
du Canada

Doctoral Research On Canada And Canadians

Thèses de doctorat concernant le Canada et les Canadiens

1884 ~ 1983

by/par
Jesse J. Dossick

Ottawa 1986

Canadian Cataloguing in Publication Data

Dossick, Jesse J. (Jesse John), 1911-
  Doctoral research on Canada and Canadians,
1884-1983 = Thèses de doctorat concernant le
Canada et les Canadiens, 1884-1983

Text in English and French.
Includes index.
ISBN 0-660-53227-1
DSS Cat. no. SN3-223/1986

1. Canada--Bibliography. 2. Dissertations,
Academic--Canada--Bibliography. 3. Dissertations,
Academic--Bibliography. I. National Library of
Canada. II. Title. III. Title: Thèses de
doctorat concernant le Canada et les Canadiens,
1884-1983.

Z1365.D68 1986   016.971   C86-090126-2E

Données de catalogage avant publication (Canada)

Dossick, Jesse J. (Jesse John), 1911-
  Doctoral research on Canada and Canadians,
1884-1983 = Thèses de doctorat concernant le
Canada et les Canadiens, 1884-1983

Texte en anglais et en français.
Comprend un index.
ISBN 0-660-53227-1
Cat. MAS no. SN3-223/1986

1. Canada--Bibliographie. 2. Thèses et écrits
académiques--Canada--Bibliographie. 3. Thèses
et écrits académiques--Bibliographie.
I. Bibliothèque nationale du Canada. II. Titre.
III. Titre: Thèses de doctorat concernant le
Canada et les Canadiens, 1884-1983.

Z1365.D68 1986   016.971   C86-090126-2F

FOREWORD

Doctoral Research on Canada and Canadians, 1884-1983 is an important addition to the growing literature on Canadian theses. For some twenty years, the National Library, in collaboration with the Canadian university community, has contributed to the identification and availability of Canadian theses in several ways: by microfilming masters' and doctoral theses that are sent for reproduction by Canadian universities; by listing theses accepted at Canadian universities in the following serial publications: Canadiana (1953-   ), Canadian Theses, a printed bibliography covering the period from 1947 to 1979/80, and Canadian Theses (Microfiche), a biannual bibliography (cumulated every five years) that includes theses completed in Canada since 1980 and identifies foreign theses written by Canadians or of Canadian interest; and, by making copies of theses filmed by the National Library available for purchase and on-site consultation, and through interlibrary loan. Theses microfilmed by the National Library have been identified in this bibliography in the Index of Names and appear in the following format:

Smith, Gary John   10331
(MIC.F.TC-21973)

With the publication of this bibliography, the National Library reinforces, in a distinctive way, its commitment to provide support to members of the research community, particularly those engaged in Canadian Studies, and to acquire, preserve, and make accessible the national published heritage.

Marianne Scott
Marianne Scott
National Librarian

AVANT-PROPOS

Thèses de doctorat concernant le Canada et les Canadiens, 1884-1983 est un important complément à l'ensemble de la documentation portant sur les thèses canadiennes. Depuis environ vingt ans, la Bibliothèque nationale du Canada, en collaboration avec les universités canadiennes, a contribué à l'identification et à l'accessibilité des thèses canadiennes de plusieurs façons. Notamment, la Bibliothèque nationale a reproduit sur microfilm les thèses de maîtrise et de doctorat provenant des universités canadiennes; elle a répertorié des thèses acceptées par les universités canadiennes dans les publications en série suivantes: Canadiana (1953-   ), Thèses canadiennes, bibliographie sous forme imprimée comprenant les thèses parues de 1947 à 1979-1980, et Thèses canadiennes (Microfiche) bibliographie biennale, cumulative à tous les 5 ans, comportant les thèses écrites au Canada depuis 1980 et répertoriant les thèses étrangères rédigées par des Canadiens ou dignes d'intérêt pour le Canada. La Bibliothèque nationale a également filmé des thèses afin que les usagers puissent les acheter, les utiliser sur place ou les emprunter par le biais du prêt entre bibliothèques. Les thèses microfilmées par la Bibliothèque nationale ont été répertoriées dans cette bibliographie dans l'Index des noms de la façon suivante:

Fournier, Pierre   8753
(MIC.F.TC-31218)

Grâce à la publication de cette bibliographie, la Bibliothèque nationale consolide ses engagements et son appui aux chercheurs canadiens et tout particulièrement, à ceux qui sont impliqués dans les études canadiennes; ainsi, elle acquiert, conserve et rend accessible le patrimoine national publié.

Directeur général
de la Bibliothèque nationale

Marianne Scott
Marianne Scott

PREFACE

This bibliography was compiled, copied, corrected, and recopied by the author over an eight-year period. The statistical accounting, numbering, and indexing was also done by the author and he assumes total responsibility for any errors or omissions. The bibliography includes dissertations accepted through to the spring of 1983 and every effort has been put forth to make it as complete and accurate as possible. Apologies are extended to those scholars whose dissertations may have been omitted inadvertently or classified improperly.

The author wishes to express his appreciation for the cooperation extended to him by the personnel responsible for the dissertation collections at the universities of Alberta, British Columbia, Carleton, Laval, McGill, Montreal, Ottawa, Simon Fraser, and Toronto, all of which he visited. He extends his special thanks also to the staff of the National Library of Canada, particularly to Gwynneth Evans for making this project possible and to members of the Publications Section: Wendy Neumann, English editor, Marie Duhamel, French editor, Gynette Lacasse, layout, and Linda L'Heureux and Roseanne Ducharme, word processors.

The author also expresses his gratitude to the Academic Relations Office of the Canadian Embassy in Washington, D.C., for the small grant that enabled this work to be completed.

JD
Ottawa, 1986

PRÉFACE

Cette bibliographie a été préparée, transcrite, corrigée et retranscrite par l'auteur pendant plus de huit ans. La numérotation et la création de l'index ont également été effectuées par l'auteur qui assume l'entière responsabilité en ce qui a trait aux erreurs et aux omissions. Le nombre de thèses effectuées dans telle ou telle université est donné dans les introductions de chacune des sections. La bibliographie comprend les thèses acceptées jusqu'au printemps de 1983; tous les efforts possibles ont été mis dans ce projet afin de le rendre le plus complet et le plus exhaustif qui soit. L'auteur s'excuse auprès des personnes dont la thèse aurait été omise ou classifiée au mauvais endroit.

L'auteur souligne la grande coopération des employés responsables de la compilation des thèses aux universités de l'Alberta, de la Colombie-Britannique, de Montréal, d'Ottawa et de Toronto ainsi que les universités Carleton, Laval, McGill et Simon Fraser, endroits où il a effectué des recherches. L'auteur tient tout particulièrement à exprimer sa profonde reconnaissance aux employés de la Bibliothèque nationale, particulièrement à Gwynneth Evans qui a rendu ce projet possible et au personnel de la section des publications dont: Wendy Neumann, réviseur anglais, Marie Duhamel, réviseur français, Gynette Lacasse, responsable de la mise en page, Linda L'Heureux et Roseanne Ducharme, responsables du traitement de textes.

L'auteur désire également témoigner sa gratitude au Bureau des relations académiques de l'ambassade du Canada à Washington (D.C.), organisme qui lui a aidé dans l'élaboration de ses recherches.

JD
Ottawa, 1986

CONTENT

SOMMAIRE

INTRODUCTION

As a result of the advances achieved in Canadian graduate schools over the last 15 years, the output of doctoral research has grown tremendously. The total number of dissertations on a wide range of subject areas has reached a point where a classified bibliography is necessary to establish an inventory of doctoral dissertations on Canadian subjects. The present work attempts to fill that need.

It must be emphasized that the inventory in this particular study does not present a total picture of doctoral research completed in Canadian universities. It deals only with dissertations concerned with Canada and Canadians. What is not listed is the vast amount of doctoral research done in Canada and abroad which does not specifically relate to Canada.

The potential uses for this bibliography are endless. It provides information on the extent of graduate school research on Canada in three countries, Canada, the United States and Great Britain. Reference librarians and scholars researching Canada now have access to a central, permanent, bibliographical list. To further facilitate the sale, interlibrary loan and on-site use of doctoral dissertations, the National Library has incorporated in the Index of Names microfiche numbers of theses for which it holds copies on microform. These copies are available for sale from the Library's Canadian Theses on Microfiche Service. Scholars and specialists such as agronomists, economists, and policy-makers in governmental agencies will have access through this bibliography to data hitherto unknown to them. Professors may take advantage of the additional information to prepare lectures and, in their capacity as doctoral advisers, will find the list invaluable in discussing the selection of research topics with doctoral candidates. Unnecessary duplication will be avoided. The list will provide new leads, and point the way for future research by indicating the need for current surveys, encouraging the reexamination of controversial issues, and indicating gaps in our knowledge in various subject areas.

Two thirds of the total output listed in this bibliography was completed at Canadian universities, with most of the doctoral research approved in the last 15 years. One third was produced in American universities. Great Britain's contribution is considerably smaller, but numbers approximately 350 dissertations on Canadian subjects.

Doctoral research in Canada prior to 1970 was limited to a few older, well-established universities. The University of Toronto, the oldest doctorate-granting institution and chief contributor prior to 1970, emerges as the major producer, with almost 25 percent of the total number of doctorates approved in Canadian universities on Canadian subjects. The University of Toronto is also the leading contributor among Canadian universities in the areas of art, anthropology, communications, drama and theatre, economics, education, and geography, (it is a close second to McGill University in geology), geophysics,

INTRODUCTION

À la suite des progrès réalisés dans les établissements canadiens d'enseignement supérieur au cours des 15 dernières années, les résultats des recherches en vue du doctorat se sont multipliés de façon remarquable. Le nombre total des thèses dans une vaste gamme de sujets a augmenté à un tel point qu'une bibliographie classée est nécessaire pour avoir un inventaire des thèses traitant du Canada. Cet ouvrage tente de répondre à ce besoin.

Il faut insister sur le fait que l'inventaire établi dans cette étude n'offre pas une image complète des thèses de doctorat effectuées dans les universités canadiennes. Cet ouvrage n'énumère que les thèses concernant le Canada et les Canadiens. Seules les thèses de doctorat acceptées au Canada ou à l'étranger qui ne se rapportent pas directement au Canada ne sont pas répertoriées dans cet ouvrage.

Une telle bibliographie peut servir à de multiples usages. Elle fournit des renseignements sur l'ampleur des recherches effectuées sur le Canada dans les établissements d'enseignement supérieur de trois pays: le Canada, les États-Unis et la Grande-Bretagne. Les bibliothécaires de référence et les chercheurs qui font des travaux sur le Canada ont désormais accès à une liste bibliographique centrale, permanente et exhaustive. Afin de faciliter la vente, le prêt entre bibliothèques et l'utilisation sur place des thèses de doctorat, la Bibliothèque nationale a incorporé, dans l'Index des noms, les numéros des thèses sur microfiche quand elle en possède des exemplaires sur microforme. Les usagers peuvent acheter des exemplaires de ces thèses au Service des thèses sur microfiche. Des chercheurs et des spécialistes tels que des agronomes, des économistes et des responsables de l'établissement des politiques dans des agences gouvernementales auront accès, par cette bibliographie, à des données qui, jusque-là, leur étaient inconnues. Des professeurs peuvent recourir à des renseignements supplémentaires pour préparer leurs conférences et, en tant que directeurs de thèses, apprécieront l'utilité de la liste lorsqu'ils auront à discuter du choix des thèmes de recherches avec les candidats au doctorat. Il sera alors possible d'éviter de faire deux fois un même travail. La liste fournira de nouveaux fils conducteurs et ouvrira la voie à d'autres recherches en signalant les besoins des études actuelles; elle favorisera l'étude des questions génératrices de controverses et indiquera les lacunes que présentent nos connaissances dans différents sujets.

Les deux tiers de l'ensemble des ouvrages énumérés dans cette bibliographie ont été rédigés dans les universités canadiennes et la plus grande partie de ces thèses ont été approuvées dans les 15 dernières années. Un tiers des thèses a été produit dans les universités américaines. La contribution de la Grande-Bretagne est plus petite avec environ 350 thèses ayant trait au Canada.

Avant 1970, au Canada, la recherche en vue du doctorat était limitée à quelques universités anciennes bien

paleontology, health sciences, language, library studies, politics, psychology (with York University a close second), religion and sociology. It is also a major contributor in science studies. Toronto's doctoral output is more than twice that of the University of Alberta, the second-largest producer of dissertations on Canadian subjects. Alberta's major output is in education (second to Toronto), engineering, sports, and physical education. The universities of McGill and British Columbia follow with approximately equal output. McGill is first in geological studies, climate and meteorology, and third in scientific studies. The University of British Columbia is first in scientific studies mainly due to its large output in botany and forestry. The universities of Montreal and Ottawa are a close fifth and sixth in terms of doctoral output. Montreal along with Laval University is strong in law. Montreal is also a force in music and psychology but ranks third in literature. The University of Ottawa is second in literature, (Laval is number one) and religion while the University of Western Ontario, Laval, and Queen's follow in that order. The University of Manitoba is first in agriculture, the University of Waterloo is first in urban and regional planning, and the University of Calgary ranks first in doctoral output in the field of archaeology.

Although the primary purpose of this project is to list the dissertations with a brief statistical analysis of each classification, a secondary purpose is to encourage research in those areas in which little doctoral work has been done. No attempt has been made to present judgments on the overall picture of doctoral work in Canada.

Over the last decade the number of women engaged in doctoral research has increased dramatically. This trend is reflected in doctoral research on Canada, primarily in the fields of education, psychology, literature and languages, anthropology, and sociology. However, there does not seem to have been a large increase in the number of women pursuing doctoral research in scientific studies.

A statistical review of American dissertations shows that almost every graduate school in the United States has produced at least one dissertation dealing with Canada and Canadians. Of the 184 American universities listed, 14 have produced over 100 dissertations on Canada, with Harvard University at the top of the list. Columbia University is a close second, followed by the universities of Michigan, Wisconsin, Chicago, Washington (Seattle), Princeton, Cornell, Yale, Minnesota, Illinois, California (Berkeley), Ohio State, and Michigan State. The subject areas in which most research was completed are geology, economics, education, scientific studies.

Twenty-nine universities in the United Kingdom produced 339 doctoral dissertations on Canada and Canadians over a 70-year period, with the first thesis being accepted in 1914, in the field of economics, at the University of London. During the 1920's, eight dissertations were completed, four at the University of Edinburgh. Three times as many studies were

connues. L'Université de Toronto, le plus ancien établissement à avoir accordé des doctorats et le plus grand producteur de thèses avant 1970, a fourni le plus grand nombre de thèses avec presque 25 pour cent du nombre total des thèses de doctorat approuvées par les universités canadiennes. L'Université de Toronto vient en tête de l'ensemble des universités canadiennes dans les domaines de l'art, de l'anthropologie, des communications, de l'art dramatique et du théâtre, de l'économie, de l'éducation et de la géographie; elle suit McGill en géologie, en géophysique, en paléontologie, en sciences de la santé, en langues, en bibliothéconomie, en politique, en psychologie (où York la suit de très près), en religion et en sociologie; enfin, Toronto fournit une importante contribution en études scientifiques. La production de thèses de Toronto peut se comparer avec celle de l'Université de l'Alberta, qui est le second plus grand producteur de thèses portant sur des sujets canadiens. Les points forts de l'Alberta portent sur l'éducation (seconde université après Toronto), l'ingénierie, les sports et l'éducation physique. Les universités McGill et de la Colombie-Britannique suivent avec des résultats à peu près égaux. McGill est la première université pour les études de géologie, sur le climat et la météorologie, et la troisième pour les études scientifiques. La Colombie-Britannique est la première pour les études scientifiques en raison de sa vaste contribution en botanique et en foresterie. Montréal et Ottawa sont très près l'une de l'autre, aux cinquième et sixième rangs. Montréal se distingue dans le domaine du droit, comme Laval; elle se tient au troisième rang en littérature, et occupe une solide position en musique et en psychologie. Ottawa est deuxième en littérature (Laval est la première) et religion. Les universités Western Ontario, Laval et Queen's suivent, dans l'ordre, puis viennent les universités du Manitoba (première en agriculture), de Waterloo (première en planification urbaine et régionale) et de Calgary (première en archéologie).

Bien que le principal but de ce projet soit d'établir une liste de ces thèses avec une brève analyse statistique de chaque classification, il en existe un second qui est d'encourager la recherche dans les domaines où peu de thèses de doctorat ont été faites jusqu'ici. Aucune tentative n'avait encore été faite, pour permettre d'examiner une image d'ensemble des thèses de doctorat au Canada.

Depuis une dizaine d'années, le nombre de femmes qui font de la recherche en vue d'un doctorat s'est accru de façon marquée. Cette tendance s'est reflétée dans la recherche sur le Canada, surtout en matière d'éducation, de psychologie, de littérature et de langues, d'anthropologie et de sociologie. Il ne semble pas que les femmes aient fait une brèche spectaculaire dans les études scientifiques.

Un examen statistique des thèses américaines montre que presque tous les établissements d'enseignement supérieur aux États-Unis ont produit au moins une thèse portant sur le Canada et les Canadiens. Des 184 universités américaines énumérées, 14 ont produit cent thèses ou plus sur le Canada; Harvard est en tête

approved in the 1930's, with one third of that number coming from the University of London. Although the 1940's saw a drop to 15 studies, due to World War II, the number more than doubled in the 1950's to 33 dissertations (29 from London and Oxford). During the 1960's the number doubled again to a total of 78 titles.

The 1970's witnessed a very large increase to a total of 148 titles, and the 1980's thus far, have produced 32 theses. For the first half of the century, research on Canada was mostly carried out by the universities of London, Edinburgh, Oxford, and Cambridge. In the 1960's while several more universities approved dissertations on Canadian topics, the same four universities were dominant. In the 1970's however, as many as 25 universities produced dissertations on Canada. Reviewing the statistics, we find that the University of London has a commanding lead, with a total of 135 doctoral dissertations; Oxford University produced 69 titles, Cambridge University 40 titles, and the University of Edinburgh 23 titles. No attempt has been made to determine how many of the British dissertations were completed by Canadians studying for doctorates abroad.

The following is a review of subject areas studied by students of British universities, in order of output: history (74 titles), politics (46), geology (38), law (29), geography (26), immigration (17), literature (16), education (13), anthropology (13), health sciences (12), religion (10), science studies (9), paleontology (8) agriculture (9), language (3), urban and regional planning (2), architecture (1), publishing (1), library studies (1), climate (1), and no studies in the Canadian arts, communications, archaeology, geophysics, engineering, sports, and psychology. The University of London dominates all of the categories with the exception of religion, geology and scientific studies.

The book contains a small number of dissertations in English from European Schools, the universities of Dublin and Cork in Ireland, and New South Wales in Australia, which the compiler found during the course of his research. These have been included so that they may be helpful to future researchers.

de liste, Columbia la suit de près, puis se classent les universités du Michigan, de Wisconsin, de Chicago, de Washington (Seattle), de Princeton, Cornell, Yale, du Minnesota, de l'Illinois, de Californie (Berkeley), d'Ohio State et de Michigan State. La plupart des thèses portaient sur la géologie, l'économie, l'éducation et les études scientifiques.

Vingt-neuf universités du Royaume-Uni ont produit 339 thèses de doctorat sur le Canada et les Canadiens tout au long d'une période de 70 ans, la première thèse ayant été acceptée en 1914 en économie, à l'Université de Londres. Dans les années 1920, huit thèses ont paru, dont quatre à Édimbourg. Trois fois autant d'études ont été approuvées dans les années 1930, avec un tiers provenant de l'Université de Londres. La Deuxième Guerre mondiale, dans les années 1940, a amené une baisse du nombre des thèses de doctorat, qui est tombé à 15, chiffre qui a plus que doublé dans les années 1950 avec un total de 33 thèses (dont 29 pour Londres et Oxford seulement). Dans les années 1960, les chiffres ont encore plus que doublé pour atteindre 78 thèses.

Les années 1970 ont vu monter à 148 titres le total des thèses, et les années 1980, jusqu'à maintenant, en ont produit 32. Pendant la première moitié du siècle, ce sont les universités de Londres, Édimbourg, Oxford et Cambridge qui se sont intéressées aux recherches sur le Canada. Dans les années 1960, tandis qu'un plus grand nombre d'universités approuvaient des thèses sur des sujets canadiens, les mêmes quatre universités ont continué de se maintenir au premier rang. Dans les années 1970, cependant, il y eut jusqu'à 25 universités qui produisirent des thèses sur le Canada. Selon les statistiques, l'Université de Londres vient en tête avec un total de 135 thèses, celle d'Oxford vient ensuite avec 69, Cambridge s'inscrit en troisième place avec 40 titres, et Édimbourg suit avec 23. On n'a pas cherché à déterminer combien de thèses britanniques ont été présentées par des Canadiens poursuivant des études de doctorat à l'étranger.

Voici une liste détaillée des sujets de thèses choisis par les étudiants des universités britanniques: histoire (74 titres), politique (46), géologie (38), droit (29), géographie (26), immigration (17), littérature (16), éducation (13), anthropologie (13), sciences de la santé (12), religion (10), études scientifiques (9), paléontologie (8), agriculture (9), langues (3), planification urbaine et régionale (2), architecture (1), édition (1), bibliothéconomie (1), climat (1); il n'y a pas eu d'études sur l'art canadien, non plus que sur les communications, l'archéologie, la géophysique, l'ingénierie, les sports et la psychologie au Canada. L'Université de Londres compte le plus grand nombre de thèses dans toutes les catégories, à l'exception de la religion, de la géologie et des études scientifiques.

Le livre contient un petit nombre de thèses en anglais produites par des universités européennes, Dublin et Cork en Irlande, et New South Wales en Australie; le compilateur les a découvertes au cours de ses recherches. Comme ces ouvrages peuvent être utiles à de futurs chercheurs, ils ont été indiqués dans cette bibliographie.

AGRICULTURE/AGRICULTURE

During the last 15 years there has been a large increase in the amount of doctoral research done in the field of Canadian agriculture. Major research has been done in agricultural economics, agricultural engineering, Canadian agricultural products, agricultural geography, and agricultural history. The University of Manitoba leads the way in output of dissertations in these subjects areas, followed by the University of Toronto. In research on soil science, the University of Alberta is first, with the University of British Columbia a close second. The University of Guelph has completed the majority of research in plant culture and pathology. American universities produced twice as much in these three areas in the first 60 years of this century, but in the last 15 years, Canadian universities more than doubled the American output. Great Britain, from the 1940's through the 1970's, produced only nine dissertations, four of which came from the University of London.

In addition to the Canadian universities mentioned earlier, McGill University and the University of Saskatchewan, produced a respectable number of agricultural studies. Of the 31 American universities with dissertations in this classification, the universities of Minnesota, Cornell, Harvard, and Wisconsin produced the greatest number.

———

Au cours des 15 dernières années il y a eu un spectaculaire accroissement du nombre des thèses de doctorat dans le domaine de l'agriculture canadienne. La plus grande partie des recherches a porté sur l'économie agricole, l'ingénierie agricole, les différents produits de l'agriculture canadienne, la géographie agricole et l'histoire de l'agriculture. L'Université du Manitoba est celle qui a fourni le plus de thèses dans ces domaines, suivie par l'Université de Toronto. Dans les recherches sur la science des sols, l'Université de l'Alberta s'inscrit au premier rang, suivie de très près par celle de la Colombie-Britannique. L'Université Guelph se distingue par ses recherches sur la culture et la pathologie des plantes. Au cours des 60 premières années de ce siècle, les universités américaines, en ces trois domaines (sol, culture et pathologie des plantes), ont fourni deux fois plus de thèses que les universités canadiennes, mais l'inverse s'est produit dans les 15 dernières années où la production canadienne a plus que doublé la production américaine. La Grande-Bretagne, de 1940 à la fin de 1970, n'a présenté que 9 thèses, dont 4 à l'Université de Londres.

Il faut ajouter aux universités canadiennes mentionnées plus haut, l'Université McGill et celle de la Saskatchewan, qui ont fourni un nombre respectable d'études sur l'agriculture. Parmi les 31 universités américaines qui figurent dans cette classification, outre l'Université du Minnesota, il faut noter les universités Cornell, Harvard et du Wisconsin qui se sont placées au premier rang.

GENERAL ITEMS/OUVRAGES GÉNÉRAUX

1
Baker, Harold Reid. "An Opinion Survey of Agricultural Extension Work in Ontario." Cornell, 1959.

2
Bartell, Marvin. "The Performance Effectiveness of Research and Development Scientists: Agricultural Research in Canada." Northwestern, 1972.

3
Michaels, Patrick Joseph. "Atmospheric Anomalies and Crop Yields in North America." Wisconsin, 1979.

4
Sawer, Barbara Jean. "Predictors of the Wife's Involvement in Farm Decision Making." British Columbia, 1972. [Fraser Valley/Vallée du Fraser]

5
Williams, W. Blair. "The Canadian Federation of Agriculture: The Problem of a General Political Interest Group." Carleton, 1974.

AGRICULTURAL CHEMISTRY/CHIMIE AGRICOLE

6
Muir, Derek C.G. "The Determination of Triazine Herbicides and Their Degradation Products in Soils and Water from Quebec Agricultural Regions." McGill, 1977.
See also Soil Science/Voir aussi Science des sols

AGRICULTURAL ECONOMICS/ ÉCONOMIE AGRICOLE

General Items/Ouvrages généraux

Altobellow, M.A. See No./Voir no 1864

7
Anderson, Walton J. "The Efficiency of British Columbian and Canadian Agriculture." Chicago, 1953.
Ba-Angood, Saeed A.S. See No./Voir no 11302
Barichello, Richard R. See No./Voir no 2402

8
Bjarnason, Harold Frederick. "An Economic Analysis of 1980 International Trade in Feed Grains." Wisconsin, 1967.

9
Bollman, Raymond Douglas. "Off-Farm Work by Farmers: A Study with a Kinked Demand for Labour Curve." Toronto, 1978.

10
Brownstone, Meyer. "Farm Income: A Study in Agricultural Policy." Harvard, 1961.

11
Burton, Gordon L. "A Price Policy for Canadian Agriculture." Iowa State, 1947.

12
Collins, Keith James. "An Economic Analysis of Export Competition in the World Coarse Grain Market: A Short-Run Constant Elasticity of Substitution Approach." North Carolina State, 1977.

13
Cutler, Garnet Homer. "Canada's Foreign Trade in Agricultural Products." Wisconsin, 1928.

14
Easterbrook, William Thomas James. "Farm Credit in Canada." Toronto, 1938.

15
Floyd, John Earl. "The Distribution Effects of Farm Policy: A Comparison of the Experience of Canada and the United States in the Northern Great Plains." Chicago, 1964.

16
Glover, David James. "Contract Farming and the Trans-nationals." Toronto, 1983.

17
Griffith, Garry Richard. "An Econometric Simulation of Alternative Domestic and Trade Policies in the World Markets for Rapeseed, Soybeans and Their Products." Guelph, 1980.

18
Harling, Kenneth Foster. "An International Comparison of Agricultural Policy: Canada, the Federal Republic of Germany, and the United Kingdom." Purdue, 1981.

19
Heads, John. "Transport Subsidies and Regional Development." Manitoba, 1976.

20
Hedley, Max Joseph. "The Social Conditions of Production and the Dynamics of Tradition: Independent Commodity Production in Canadian Agriculture." Alberta, 1976.

21
Islam, Tariq Saiful. "Input Substitution and Productivity Change in Canadian Agriculture." Alberta, 1982.

22
Jaeger, Martin Jerome. "An Enquiry into the Feasibility of Using Production Control as a Means of Raising Agricultural Incomes in Canada." Manitoba, 1963.

23
Jolly, Robert William. "An Econometric Analysis of the Grain-Livestock Economy in Canada, with a Special Emphasis on Commercial Agricultural Policy." Minnesota, 1976.

24
Li, Lew King and/et Yeh, Martin H. "Technological Change in Canadian Agriculture." Manitoba, 1968.

25
Lier, John. "The Impact of the Rural Economy on Urban Structure and Form in the Canadian Wheat Belt." California, Berkeley, 1968.

26
Lok, Siepko Hendrik. "An Enquiry into the Relationships Between Changes in Over-all Productivity and Real Net Return Per Farm, and Between Changes in Total Output and Real Gross Return, Canadian Agriculture, 1926 to 1957." Michigan State, 1962.

27
Lopez, Ramon Eugenio. "Economic Behaviour of Self-Employed Farm Producers." British Columbia, 1981.

28
Lu, Wen-Fong. "An Integrated Supply and Demand Analysis of Canadian Rapeseed and Vegetable Oil Products." Manitoba, 1978.

29
Lyon, Noel Adversé. "The Economic Development of the Canadian Indians." Harvard, 1969.

30
Manuel, Paciencia Castello. "A Spatial Equilibrium Analysis of the Impact of Cargo Preference in the World and U.S. Grain Trade." Idaho, 1980.

Murray, John Wayne. See No./Voir no 168

Oleson, Brian Thomas. See No./Voir no 169

Pemberton, Carlisle Andrew. See No./Voir no 54

31
Phillips, William Gregory. "The Agricultural Implement Industry in Canada: A Study in the Development of Competition." Toronto, 1953.

32
Rigaux, L.R. "Education Inputs and Economic Growth in Canadian Agriculture." London, 1970.

Séguin, Maurice. See No./Voir no 115

33
Singh, Ranjit Harry. "Agricultural Drainage Development: A Simulation Approach for Public Expenditure Decisions." Manitoba, 1979.

Smit, Barry Edward. See No./Voir no 2197

34
Soe, Lin. "A Macro Policy Simulation Model of the Canadian Agricultural System." Carleton, 1980.

Stier, Jeffrey Charles. See No./Voir no 10817

35
Sun, Shih-Ping. "An Evaluation of the Actuarial Structure of the Crop Insurance Program in Canada." Manitoba, 1976.

36
Ware, Dennis William. "The Economic Implications of Free Trade in Agricultural Products Between Canada and the United States." Ohio State, 1965.

37
Washavosky, Jacob. "Agricultural Marketing Boards: A Conceptual Taxonomy of Their Basic Goal Areas -An Empirical Approach." Toronto, 1982.

Wilbberley, G.P. See No./Voir no 182

38
Williams, Gary Wayne. "The U.S. and World Oilseeds and Derivative Markets: Economic Structure and Policy Interventions." Purdue, 1981.

Wilson, Charles F. See No./Voir no 116

39
Yorgason, Vernon Wayne. "Agriculture in Canadian Economic Development: An Econometric Approach." Kansas State, 1971.

40
Zasada, Donald. "The Regulation of Handling and Storage Tariffs in the Canadian Country Grain Elevator Industry." Manitoba, 1982.

Eastern Canada/Est du Canada

41
Haythorne, George V. "Agriculture and the Farm Worker: An Analysis of Labour in Farming Based on a Study of Eastern Canada." Harvard, 1949. [Ontario and Quebec/Ontario et Québec]

Wilson, Harold Fisher. See No./Voir no 840

Western Canada/Ouest du Canada

42
Tosterud, Robert James. "A Simulation Model for Rationalizing the Grain Transportation and Handling System in Western Canada on a Regional Basis." Manitoba, 1973.

Alberta

Famure, Oluwole Dada. See No./Voir no 187
43
Garrow, Patrick. "The Status and Anticipated Manpower Requirements by Selected Sectors of the Agricultural Industry in Alberta." Calgary, 1970.
44
Graham, James Benjamin. "An Empirical Test of a Theory of Consumer Behavior in a Shortage Situation." Western Ontario, 1978. [Shortage of Fertilizer/Pénurie de fertilisant]
45
Marothia, Dinesh Kumar. "An Economic and Institutional Analysis of Soil Erosion on Agricultural Land." Alberta, 1981. [Peace River region/ Région de la rivière Peace]
46
Petersen, Thomas Alfred Steenberg. "An Analysis of Thirteen Years of Commercial Hail Suppression in Central Alberta." Washington State, 1971.
47
Pluta, Leonard Andrew. "A Study of Acreage Allocation Decision in Alberta and Saskatchewan." Queen's, 1967.
48
Wood, V. Alfred. "Public Land Policy for Alberta." Minnesota, 1954.

British Columbia/Colombie-Britannique

Anderson, Walton J. See No./Voir no 7
49
Dobie, James. "Economies of Scale in Sawmilling in British Columbia." Oregon State, 1971.
Hull, Dale Lester. See No./Voir no 11690

Manitoba

50
Ahmad, Bashir. "A Model to Determine the Impact of Improved Agricultural Efficiency in Manitoba." Manitoba, 1978.
Anim-Appiah, John. See No./Voir no 163
Floyd, John Earl. See No./Voir no 15
Glick, Harvey Leonard. See No./Voir no 145
51
Iga, Masaaki. "Economic Evaluation of On-Farm Irrigation in the Morden-Winkler Area of Southern Manitoba." Manitoba, 1970.
Lier, John. See No./Voir no 25
52
McBride, William Allan. "A Multiperiod Linear Programming Model for Farm Planning Under Uncertainty: A Dryland Irrigated Situation." Manitoba, 1976.

53
Nelson, Gary Stewart. "An Exploratory Use of Group Decision Theories in Evaluating Farm Planning Programming Models." Manitoba, 1964.
54
Pemberton, Carlisle Alexander. "Goals and Aspirations and the Low Income Farm Problem." Manitoba, 1976.
Ryan, John. See No./Voir no 88
55
Sahi, Ram Kumar. "Recursive Programming Analysis of Prairie Land Utilization Patterns." Manitoba, 1972.
56
Tung, Fu-Lai. "A Dynamic Model for Simulating Resource Development Program Impacts in the Interlake Area of Manitoba." Manitoba, 1975.
57
Walker, H.V.H. "Economies of Farm Size in the Carman Areas of Manitoba." Manitoba, 1964.

Newfoundland/Terre-Neuve

58
Crabb, P. "Agriculture in Newfoundland: A Study in Development." Hull, 1976.

Nova Scotia/Nouvelle-Écosse

59
Blackmer, Hugh Allison. "Agricultural Transformation in a Regional System: The Annapolis Valley, Nova Scotia." Stanford, 1976.

Ontario

60
Baird, Andrew Falconor. "The Role of Directors of Local Cooperatives in Ontario, Canada, in Continuity and Change." Cornell, 1961.
61
Davidson, Gary. "Agricultural Land Use Planning Policy in Ontario". Western Ontario, 1982.
Haythorne, George V. See No./Voir no 41
Lier, John. See No./Voir no 25
62
Lovering, James Herbert. "Agricultural Development Possibilities, Southeastern Renfrew County, Ontario." Cornell, 1967.
63
MacDougall, Edward Bruce. "Farm Number Changes in Relation to Land Capability and Alternative Employment Opportunity in the North Part of Central Ontario." Toronto, 1967.
64
Rust, Ronald Stuart. "Producer Benefits from the Operations of the Ontario Sugar Beet Growers Marketing Board." Illinois, 1959.

Prince Edward Island/Île-du-Prince-Édouard

65
Millerd, Francis Webb. "An Evaluation System for the Natural Resource Sectors of the Prince Edward Island Development Plan." Cornell, 1972.

Quebec/Québec

Ba-Angood, Saeed. See No./Voir no 11302

66
Ghorayshi, Fatemeh Parvin. "Agricultural Development in Quebec: An analysis of Production Units in the Agrarian Class Structure." Toronto, 1983.

Haythorne, George V. See No./Voir no 41

67
Lemelin, Charles. "Agricultural Development and Industrialization of Quebec." Harvard, 1952.

Saskatchewan

68
Hudson, Samuel C. "A Statistical Analysis of Long-Term Mortgage Financing by the Saskatchewan Farm Loan Board." Cornell, 1939.

AGRICULTURAL EDUCATION/ ENSEIGNEMENT AGRICOLE

See also Education: Agricultural Education/Voir aussi Éducation: Enseignement agricole

AGRICULTURAL ENGINEERING/GÉNIE AGRICOLE

Arinze, Edwin A. See No./Voir no 4581

69
Bello, Richard Laurence." Evapotranspiration in Greenhouses." McMaster, 1982. [Ontario]

Brook, Roger Charles. See No./Voir no 4539

70
Igwe, Okay Cyril. "Optimal Long-Term Development and Operation of Irrigation Systems with Storage Under Hydrological Uncertainty." British Columbia, 1977. [Nicola Valley Irrigation District/District d'irrigation de la vallée Nicola]

71
Ijioma, Chibueze Ibegbu. "The Effect of Tillage Tool Geometry on Soil Structural Behaviour." McGill, 1982.

72
Lal, Radkey. "A Laboratory Study of Effect of Agricultural Land Packers on Soil." Saskatchewan, 1968.

73
Macaulay, James Donald. "Mechanical Seed Extraction of Lodgepole Pine." British Columbia, 1975.

74
Mollard, John D.A. "Aerial Photographic Studies on the Central Saskatchewan Irrigation Project." Cornell, 1952.

75
Muir, William Ernest. "Studies of Fire Spread Between Buildings." Saskatchewan, 1967.

76
Nyborg, Erling Orvald. "Mechanical Raspberry Harvesting." British Columbia, 1970. [British Columbia/Colombie-Britannique]

77
Paroschy, John Henry. "Mechanical Winter Injury in Grapevine Trunks." Guelph, 1979. [Simcoe Experimental Station/Station expérimentale de Simcoe]

Pluta, Leonard Andrew. See No./Voir no 47

78
Prasher, Shiv Om. "Examination of the Design Procedures for Drainage/Subirrigation Systems in the Lower Fraser Valley, British Columbia." British Columbia, 1982.

Salloum, John Duane. See No./Voir no 340

Yaciuk, Gordon. See No./Voir no 4487

AGRICULTURAL GEOGRAPHY/ GÉOGRAPHIE AGRICOLE

General Items/Ouvrages généraux

79
Kaye, Barry. "The Historical Geography of Agriculture and Agricultural Settlements in the Canadian Northwest, 1774-Ca. 1830." London, 1977.

80
Reitsma, Hendrik-Jan. "Crop and Livestock Differences on Opposite Sides of the United States-Canada Boundary." Wisconsin, 1967.

81
Wells, T.A.G. "An Economic Geography of Commercialized Agriculture with Special Reference to North America." London, 1947.

Alberta

Brewster, Gordon Ross. See No./Voir no 220

82
Irby, Charles Claude. "Northeast Alberta: A Marginal Agricultural Situation." Simon Fraser, 1979.

83
Lupton, Austin Albert. "An Analysis of Some Factors Affecting the Areal Variability of Farm Size in Alberta." Alberta, 1969.

84
Tracie, Carl Joseph. "An Analysis of Three Variables Affecting Farm Location in the Process of Agricultural Settlement: The South Peace River Area." Alberta, 1970.

British Columbia/Colombie-Britannique

Chapman, John Doneric. See No./Voir no 4607

85
O'Riordan, Jonathan. "Efficiency in Irrigation Water-Use: A Case Study in the Okanagan Valley, British Columbia." British Columbia, 1969.

86
Weir, Thomas R. "A Geographic Survey of the Ranching Industry Within the Interior Plateau of British Columbia." Wisconsin, 1951.

Manitoba

87
De Lisle, David De Garis. "The Spatial Organization and Intensity of Agriculture in the Mennonite Villages of Southern Manitoba." McGill, 1975.

88
Ryan, John. "The Agricultural Operations of Manitoba Hutterite Colonies." McGill, 1973.

89
Tyman, John Langton. "Historical Geography: The Disposition of Farm Lands in Western Manitoba." Oxford, 1970.

New Brunswick/Nouveau-Brunswick

90
Lloyd, Donald Loftus. "The Patterns and Problems of Agriculture within Kent and Northumberland Counties, New Brunswick, Canada, 1961-1968." Maryland, 1971.

Newfoundland/Terre-Neuve

Crabb, P. See No./Voir no 58

Ontario

91
Ball, Norman Roger. "The Technology of Settlement and Land Clearing in Upper Canada Prior to 1840." Toronto, 1979.

92
Keddie, Philip Desmond. "The Expansion of Corn for Grain in Southern Ontario and Its Effects on the Farm Enterprise with Specific Reference to the Mid-Western Ontario Region." Waterloo, 1976.

93
Kelly, Kenneth. "The Agricultural Geography of Simcoe County, Ontario, 1820-1880." Toronto, 1968.

94
Mage, Julius Arnold. "Part-Time Farming in Southern Ontario with Specific Reference to Waterloo County." Waterloo, 1974.

95
McDermott, George Louis. "Advancing and Retreating Frontiers of Agricultural Settlement in the Great Clay Belt of Ontario and Quebec." Wisconsin, 1959.

96
McDonald, Geoffrey Thomas. "Agricultural Land Use Forecasting: An Example of Field Crops in Ontario, 1940-1968." Toronto, 1972.
Morgan, Christopher Lewellyn. See No./Voir no 263
97
Reeds, Lloyd George. "The Agricultural Geography of Southern Ontario." Toronto, 1956.

Quebec/Québec

98
Bureau, Luc. "Regional Perception of the Farm in Quebec." Minnesota, 1973.
99
McCardell, Nora E. "Agricultural Success: An Exploratory Study of Man, Land and Interrelationships." Waterloo, 1975. [Southwestern Quebec/Sud-ouest du Québec]
McDermott, George Louis. See No./Voir no 95
100
Pelletier, Raymond. "L'utilisation agricole du sol de l'Île Jésus." Montréal, 1962.

101
Smith, William. "Geographical Perspectives on Food Marketing Linkages Between Producers and Consumers: A Quebec Case." McGill, 1981.
102
Timofeeff, Nicolay Peter. "A Method of Establishing Agricultural Regions in the Lake St. John Lowland of Quebec, Canada." Columbia, 1968.

Saskatchewan

Sahir, Abul Hasan. See No./Voir no 171

AGRICULTURAL HISTORY/HISTOIRE AGRICOLE

General Items/Ouvrages généraux

103
Bicha, Karel Denis. "Canadian Immigration Policy and the American Farmer, 1896-1914." Minnesota, 1963.
104
Burbridge, Kenneth J. "The Cooperative Movement." Ottawa, 1945.
105
Choquette, Raymond. "Les potagers de guerre des centres urbains du Canada." Ottawa, 1945.
Churchill, Anthony Aylward. See No./Voir no 1263
Conway, John Frederick. See No./Voir no 10024
106
Courville, Serge. "L'habitant canadien et le système seigneurial, de 1627-1854." Montréal, 1979.
107
Farrell, Marvin W. "Land Tenure in Canadian Agriculture." Harvard, 1948.
108
Fowke, Vernon Clifford. "Government Aid to Canadian Agriculture to 1930: An Historical Introduction." Washington (Seattle) 1943.
Green, Stanton William. See No./Voir no 909
109
Herwig, Aletha Marguerite. "The Farmer and Canadian-American Reciprocity, 1911." Minnesota, 1943.
110
Jones, Robert L. "History of Agriculture in the Province of Canada, 1841-1867." Harvard, 1938.
111
Lattimer, John Ernest. "Land Tenure in Canada." Wisconsin, 1926.
112
Lemieux, Omer Adrien. "The Development of Agriculture in Canada During the Sixteenth and Seventeenth Centuries." Ottawa, 1940.
Macdonald, Norman. See No./Voir no 7466
Morrison, Hugh M. See No./Voir no 7096
Patton, Harald Smith. See No./Voir no 119
113
Perron, Marc A. "Un grand éducateur agricole Édouard A. Bernard (1835-1898); essai historique sur l'agriculture, 1760-1900." Laval, 1954.

114
Pomfret, Richard William Thomas. "The Introduction of the Mechanical Reaper in Canada, 1850-70: A Case Study in the Diffusion of Embodied Technical Change." Simon Fraser, 1974.

115
Séguin, Maurice. "L'agriculture et la vie économique des Canadiens (1760-1850)." Montréal, 1948.

116
Wilson, Charles F. "Agricultural Adjustment in Canada." Harvard, 1937.

Eastern Canada/Est du Canada

Haythorne, George V. See No./Voir no 41

Western Canada/Ouest du Canada

Kaye, Barry. See No./Voir no 79

117
Knuttila, Kenneth Murray. "The Impact of the Western Canadian Agrarian Movement on Federal Government Policy, 1900-1930: An Assessment and Analysis." Toronto, 1982.

118
Mackintosh, William Archibald. "Agricultural Cooperation in Western Canada." Queen's University, 1924.

119
Patton, Harald Smith. "Grain Growers' Cooperation in Western Canada." Harvard, 1925.

Sharp, Paul Frederick. See No./Voir no 7550

Alberta

120
Kristjanson, Baldur H. "Land Settlement in Northeastern Alberta." Wisconsin, 1949.

121
Stone, Donald Norman George. "Alberta's and British Columbia's Crown Lands Policies (1931-1973): Some Attitudinal and Behavioural Responses by Frontier Agriculturalists Towards these Policies." Saskatchewan, 1980.

Manitoba

122
Gracie, Bruce Alan. "The Agrarian Response in Prairie Canada to Industrialization and Urbanization: 1900-1935." McMaster, 1976.

123
Murchie, Robert Welch. "Unused Lands of Manitoba: A Report of a Survey of the Lands Not in Agricultural Use, with an Analysis of the Physical, Economic and Social Factors Affecting the Settlement of Such Lands." Minnesota, 1927.

124
Murray, Stanley Norman. "A History of Agriculture in the Valley of the Red River of the North, 1812 to 1920." Wisconsin, 1963.

125
Sommerfield, Howard Bruno. "Farm Power in Manitoba: A Study of the Production of Horses and Comparative Utilization of Animal and Mechanical Power." Minnesota, 1932.

Newfoundland/Terre-Neuve

126
Drummond, William M. "Agriculture in Newfoundland." Harvard, 1955.

Nova Scotia/Nouvelle-Écosse

127
Gentilcore, R. Louis. "Land Use and Agricultural Production in Antigonish County, Nova Scotia." Maryland, 1950.

Ontario

Ball, Norman Roger. See No./Voir no 91

128
Bucknam, Roland Franklin. "An Economic Study of Farm Electrification in New York, with a Discussion of Rural Electrification in the Provinces of Quebec and Ontario, Canada." Cornell, 1929.

129
Gates, Lillian F. "The Land Policies of Upper Canada." Radcliffe, 1956.

130
MacLeod, Marion J. "Agriculture and Politics in Ontario Since 1867." London, 1962.

131
Mays, Herbert Joseph. "Families and Land in Toronto, Gore Township, Peel County, Ontario, 1820-1890." McMaster, 1979.

132
Norton, William. "Agricultural Settlement Patterns in Upper Canada, 1782-1851: A Simulation Analysis." McMaster, 1923.

133
Sinclair, Peter Wilson. "Strategies of Development on an Agricultural Frontier: The Great Clay Belt, 1900-1950." Toronto, 1980.

134
Skey, Boris Peter. "Cooperative Marketing of Agricultural Products in Ontario." Toronto, 1933.

Quebec/Québec

Bucknam, Roland Franklin. See No./Voir no 128

135
Frankton, Clarence. "Agronomical and Ecological Research with Special Reference to the Pastures of the Eastern Townships of Quebec." McGill, 1940.

McCallum, John C.P. See No./Voir no 1247

136
McGuigan, Gerald Frederick. "Land Policy and Land Disposal under Tenure of Free and Common Socage, Quebec and Lower Canada, 1763-1809." Laval, 1963.

137
Migner, Robert-Maurice. "Le monde agricole québécois et les premières années de l'Union catholique des cultivateurs (1918-1930)." Montréal, 1975.

138
Pilon, Lise. "L'endettement des cultivateurs québécois: une analyse socio-historique de la rente foncière (1670-1904)." Montréal, 1979.

Saskatchewan

139
Britnell, George Edwin. "A Sudy of the Economic and Social Development of Saskatchewan." Toronto, 1938. [The wheat economy/Économie du blé]

140
McCrorie, James Napier. "The Saskatchewan Farmers' Movement: A Case Study." Illinois, 1972.

141
Ross, Arthur Larry. "National Development and Sectional Politics: Social Conflict and the Rise of a Protest Movement." Toronto, 1979. [Saskatchewan Grain Growers' Association-SGGA/Association des producteurs de grain de la Saskatchewan-SGGA]

AGRICULTURAL PRODUCTS - FARM SPECIALTIES/PRODUITS AGRICOLES - SPÉCIALITÉS DE LA FERME

Dairy farming/Fermes laitières

142
Anandajayasekeram, Ponniah. "Economics of a Milk Transportation Firm." Guelph, 1979.

143
Esan, Benjamin Olatunji. "Analysis of Variation Due to Genetic and Environmental Factors in Gross Milk Constituents in Quebec Dairy Cattle." McGill, 1972.

144
Garvin, Wilfred James. "Some Factors Affecting the Supply of Milk and Milk Products in Nova Scotia." Catholic, 1941.

Gilbert, Frederick Franklin. See No./Voir no 10590

145
Glick, Harvey Leonard. "The Use of Densitometric Data from Aerial Photographs for Field Crop Classification and Identification in Manitoba." Manitoba, 1983.

146
McIntosh, Curtis Emmanuel. "The Demand for Meat and Dairy Products in Canada with Projections for 1980." Alberta, 1972.

147
Patterson, Howard L. "An Economic Study of Dairy Farms in the Province of Alberta, Canada, 1939-1943." Cornell, 1946.

148
Rae, Robert Cameron. "The Effect of Dietary Crude Protein Level, Formaldehyde Treated Rapeseed (Canola) Meal and Dietary Tyrosine Supplementation on the Performance of Lactating Dairy Cows." Manitoba, 1983.

149
Robertson, Peter S. "Comparative Studies of Cheddar Cheese from Australia, Great Britain, Canada and New Zealand, with Special Reference to Tallowy Discoloration." Reading, 1961.

150
St. Louis, Robert. "A Simulation Analysis of Planned Dairy Farm Development in Eastern Quebec." Michigan State, 1970.

151
Sivarajasingam, Sittampalam. "Dairy Sire Evaluation for Total Economic Merit." Guelph, 1980.

Sundstrom, Marvin Thomas. See No./Voir no 1806

152
Williams, Chistopher John. "A Study of within Herd Variability in Milk Fat, Protein and Lactose Content of Bulk Milks in British Columbia and Factors Affecting the Design of Herd Milk Sampling Programs." British Columbia, 1973.

Willms, Walter David. See No./Voir no 10628

153
Wirick, Ronald Guy. "Price Supports Versus Direct Subsidies: A Simulation Test of the Federal Dairy Support Program, 1962-1972." Western Ontario, 1978.

154
Young, Gerald Loren. "Dairying in the Fraser-Whatcom Lowland: A Comparative Study of Public Policy and Rural Economy." Indiana, 1968.

155
Yungblut, Douglas Harold. "The Development and Application of Feed Intake Prediction Equations for Lactating Dairy Cattle." Guelph, 1979. [19 Commercial Dairy Farms/19 fermes laitières commerciales]

Fruit/Fruits

156
Krueger, Ralph Ray. "Changing Land-Use Patterns in the Niagara Fruit Belt." Indiana, 1959. [Ontario]

157
Short, Frederick W. "Fruit Marketing with Special Reference to the Niagara Peninsula of Ontario." Minnesota, 1948.

Apples/Pommes

158
Longley, Willard Victor. "Some Economic Aspects of the Apple Industry in Nova Scotia." Minnesota, 1931.

159
Morse, Norman Harding. "An Economic History of the Apple Industry of the Annapolis Valley in Nova Scotia." Toronto, 1952.

160
Richards, Albert E. "Prices and Returns for Nova Scotia Apples." Cornell, 1939.

161
Wilcox, John Carman. "The Determination of Some Factors Limiting Apple Production in British Columbia." Washington State, 1944.

Corn/Maïs

162
Dorling, Michael John. "Spatial Equilibrium Conditions for the Canadian Corn Economy in the 1961-1962 Crop Year." McGill, 1965.

Grapes/Raisins

Paroschy, John Henry. See No./Voir no 77

Wheat/Blé

163
Anim-Appiah, John. "Aggregate Versus Disaggregate Acreage Supply Response Models for Prairie Wheat and Barley." Manitoba, 1972.

Churchill, Anthony Aylward. See No./Voir no 1263

Britnell, George Edwin. See No./Voir no 139

164
Dunne, William. "Theoretical and Practical Considerations in the Segregation of Canadian Wheat by Protein Content." Manitoba, 1973.

165
Grindley, Thomas William. "The Economic Aspects of Single Cropping in Western Canada (Wheat)." Minnesota, 1929.

166
Huff, Harry Bruce. "Marketing of Canadian Wheat: An Economic Analysis with Projections for 1975 and 1980." Michigan State, 1969.

167
Marchylo, Brian Alexander. "The d-Amylase Isoenzyme System of Immature Canadian Grown Wheat." Manitoba, 1978.

168
Murray, John Wayne. "Wheat Policies of Major Exporting Countries, 1920-1973." Illinois, 1976. [United States, Canada, Australia and Argentina/États-Unis, Canada, Australie et Argentine]

169
Oleson, Brian Thomas. "Price Determination and Market Share Formation in the International Wheat Market." Minnesota, 1979.

170
Olfert, Owen Orton. "Quantitative Evaluation of Grasshopper Defoliation of Wheat in Saskatchewan." Saskatchewan, 1979.

171
Sahir, Abul Hasan. "Residential Pattern of Wheat Farmers in Southern Saskatchewan: A Case Study." Minnesota, 1973.

172
Schwartz, Nancy Eileen. "An Econometric Analysis of Potential Price Variability in the World Wheat Market." Cornell, 1983.

173
Simons, Richard Glyn. "Tiller and Ear Production Relation to Yield of Winter Wheat." Guelph, 1981. [Elora Research Station, Elora, Ontario/Station de recherche Elora, Elora, Ontario]

Slater, John Morton. See No./Voir no 2369

174
Song, Dae Hee. "An Economic Analysis of a World Wheat Cartel Among Trading Countries." Pennsylvania State, 1980.

175
Taplin, John Harold Eaton. "Demand in the World Wheat Market and the Export Policies of the United States, Canada, and Australia." Cornell, 1969.

176
Urich, Max Albert. "Sources of Genetic Variability in Kaw 61 and Ottawa Wheats." Kansas State, 1966.

177
Zentner, Robert Paul. "An Economic Evaluation of Public Wheat Research Expenditures in Canada." Minnesota, 1982.

Rapeseed and Soybean/Graines de colza et de soya

Griffith, Garry Richard. See No./Voir no 17

Tobacco/Tabac

178
Hall, Robert Burnett, Jr. "The Introduction of Flue-Cured Tobacco as a Commercial Crop in Norfolk County, Ontario." Michigan, 1952.

179
Haviland, William E. "The Economies of Tobacco Farming in Ontario." Harvard, 1950.

Livestock/Bétail

General Items/Ouvrages généraux

Benjamin, Bontha Rathnakumar. See No./Voir no 10639

Jolly, Robert William. See No./Voir no 23

180
Lin, Leon Chin-Shin. "Livestock Industry in Canada: An Input-Output Analysis, 1941-1975." Manitoba, 1967.

Reitsma, Hendrik-Jan. See No./Voir no 80

181
Schrader, Frederick Mallory. "The Demand for Meat in Canada." Illinois, 1951.

182
Wibberley, G.P. "Some Aspects of Livestock Marketing in Great Britain and North America." Wales, 1941.

183
Wilson, Arthur Grenville. "The Impact of the Feed Freight Subsidy on the Location of Livestock Production." Manitoba, 1968.

Wood, Benjamin William. See No./Voir no 11407

Cattle/Troupeaux

184
Acres, Stephen Douglas. "The Epidemiology of Acute Undifferentiated Neonatal Diarrhea of Beef Calves in Western Canada." Saskatchewan, 1977.

185
Dawson, Oliver Glenn. "An Economic Evaluation of Yield Grade Standards for Canadian Carcass Beef." Oregon State, 1982.

186
Edwards, Linnell M. "The Natural Resource Factors of Nevis and their Role in Beef Production Systems with Special Emphasis on Fodder Supplies." McGill, 1975.

187
Famure, Oluwole Dada. "An Economic Analysis of Institutional Buying Patterns for Meats in Edmonton and Surroundings." Alberta, 1978.

188
Garcia de Siles, José Luis. "Beef Carcass Characteristics as Related to Quality Attributes and Grading Standards." Pennsylvania State, 1975.

189
Goonewardene, Laksiri Anura. "Analysis and Application of Growth Models to Beef Cattle." Alberta, 1978.

190
Hoque, Mozzamel. "Estimation of Genetic and Environmental Parameters of Lifetime Production Traits and Longevity in Holstein-Friesean Cows." British Columbia, 1980. [Based on Canadian Record of Performance Data of 51 599 Cows/ D'après une étude canadienne des données du rendement de 51 599 vaches]

191
Kennedy, Brian Wayne. "Estimates of Genetic Environmental and Phenotypic Parameters in the Canadian Record of Performance Beef Cattle Population." Cornell, 1974.

192
Kerr, William Alexander. "Micro Economic Approaches to Technical Change in the Canadian Beef Cattle Industry: Two Studies of Crossbreeding as an Innovation." British Columbia, 1981.

193
Leigh, Abisogun Olubode. "Choice of Crossbreeding Systems for Commercial Beef Cattle Production." Guelph, 1973.

194
Macaulay, Thomas Gordon. "A Recursive Spatial Equilibrium Model of the North American Beef Industry for Policy Analysis." Guelph, 1976.

195
MacHardy, Fenton V. "An Investigation of the Application of Programming Techniques to Farm Management Problems with Special Reference to Beef Cattle Feeding in the Lothians of Scotland and in Alberta." Edinburgh, 1965.

196
Mack, Friedrich Georg. "The Impact of Transfer Cost and Trade Policies on International Trade in Beef, 1967-1980." Texas A and M, 1973.

McIntosh, Curtis Emmanuel. See No./Voir no 146

197
Meek, John James. "Simulation of the Cattle-Calves Sub-Sector in a Developed Economy with Special Reference to the Canadian Cattle Herd." Michigan State, 1975.

198
Stonehouse, David Peter. "An Enquiry into Risk Aspects of Beef Farming in Crop District Number Three, Manitoba." Manitoba, 1976.

Sheep/Moutons

199
Kindt, Lawrence E. "The Sheep Ranching Industry of Canada." American, 1940.

200
Rock, Terrence Walter. "An Evaluation of Seasonal Coyote Control Techniques and Sheep Losses in Saskatchewan." Nevada, 1978.

Swine/Porcs

201
Fredeen, Howard T. "Genetic Aspects of Canadian Bacon Production." Iowa State, 1952.

202
Newell, Jorge Alfredo. "Comparison of Boars, Barrows and Gilts as Meat Producing Animals." Alberta, 1973.

203
Shapiro, Stanley Jack. "Decision Making, Survival and the Organized Behaviour System: A Case Study of the Ontario Hog Producers Organizations." Pennsylvania, 1961.

SOIL SCIENCE/SCIENCE DES SOLS

General Items/Ouvrages généraux

204
Appiah, Michael Roy. "Phosphatase Activity of Soils and Its Relationship to Mineralization of Inositol Phosphates." Guelph, 1979. [Canadian and Ghanian Soils Compared/Comparaison entre le sol canadien et le sol ghanéen]

205
Campbell, James Alfred. "Nutrient Losses and Related Processes in a Seasonally-Operated Septic Bed Soil Under Favourable Conditions." McMaster, 1979.

206
De Jong, Reinder. "Energy Exchange at the Soil Surface and the Soil Temperature Regime." Manitoba, 1978.

207
Dumanski, Julian. "A Micromorphological Investigation on the Genesis of Soils Developed on Calcareous Aeolian Material." Alberta, 1970.

208
Hoffman, Douglas Weir. "Crop Yields of Soil Capability Classes and Their Uses in Planning for Agriculture." Waterloo, 1973.

209
Khan, Shahamat Ullah. "Some Aspects of Equilibrium Solutions for a Solonetizic and a Chernozemic Soil." Alberta, 1968.

210
Kloosterman, Bruce. "Using a Computer Soil Data File in the Development of Statistical Techniques for the Evaluation of Soil Suitability for Land Use." British Columbia, 1971.

211
Malhi, Sukhdev Singh. "Losses of Mineral Nitrogen Over the Winter in Chernozinic and Luvisolic Soils." Alberta, 1978.

212
Mathieu, Alfred L. "The Mineralogy of the Clay Fraction in Relation to the Genesis of Solodized Solonetz Soils." Saskatchewan, 1960.

213
Millette, Jean François Gérard. "Loess and Loess-Like Deposits of the Susquehanna River Valley of Pennsylvania and a Section of the Laurentians in Canada." Pennsylvania State, 1955.

214
Patil, Arvind Shankar. "Ion-Migration in Soil." Alberta, 1965.

215
Sheppard, Marsha Isabell. "A Computer Simulation of Freezing Soil Development and Validation Using Experimental Data." Guelph, 1977.

Eastern Canada/Est du Canada

216
Soper, Robert Joseph. "Characteristic of Soil Leachates Collected Under Eastern Hemlock (Tsuga canadensis)." McGill, 1959.

217
Wicklund, Reuben Edward. "Characteristics of a Toposequence of Soils, the Caribou Catena, in the Podzol Region of Eastern Canada." Michigan State, 1955.

Alberta

218
Alexander, Thundathilthekkethil George. "Inorganic and Extractable Phosphorus of Some Solonetzic Soils of Alberta." Alberta, 1973.

219
Beke, Gerard Johannes. "Soils of Three Experimental Watersheds in Alberta and Their Hydrologic Significance." Alberta, 1969.

220
Brewster, Gordon Ross. "Genesis of Volcanic Ash-Charged Soils having Podzolic Morphologies, Banff and Jasper National Parks, Alberta." Western Ontario, 1979.

Corns, Ian George William. See No./Voir no 11656

221
Crown, Peter Herbert. "Spectral Reflectance and Emittance and Associated Photographic and Non-Photographic Imagery in Relation to Soils of the Edmonton-Vegreville Region, Alberta." Alberta, 1977.

222
Helgeland, Joseph Douglas. "Characterization of Ah Humic Acids Obtained from Several Selected Soil Series." Alberta, 1975.

223
Khan, Mohammad Fasahat Ali. "Volatile Nitrogen Losses from Some Alberta Soils." Alberta, 1965.

224
Lousier, Joseph Daniel. "Population Ecology of Testacea (Protozoa rhizopoda) in an Aspen Woodland Soil." Calgary, 1979. [Kananaskis Valley/ Vallée de Kananaskis]

225
Luk, Shiu Hung. "Soil Erodibility and Erosion in Part of the Bow River Basin, Alberta." Alberta, 1975.

226
MacLean, Adrian Henry. "Soil Genesis in Relation to Groundwater and Soil Moisture Regimes Near Vegreville, Alberta." Alberta, 1974.

227
McKenzie, Rodney Collin. "Root Development and Crop Growth as Influenced by Subsoil Acidity in Soils of Alberta and Northeastern British Columbia." Alberta, 1973.

Marothia, Dinesh Kumar. See No./Voir no 45

228
Omanwar, Pandurang Keraba. "Available Phosphorus in Relation to the Physical and Chemical Characteristics of Phosphorus of Some Alberta Soils." Alberta, 1970.

229
Reid, Arthur Selbourne Jelf. "Some Factors Affecting Nitrogen Movement Transformations and Uptake in Alberta Soils." Alberta, 1965.

230
Synghal, Krishnan N. "Assessing Nitrogen Requirements of Some Alberta Soils." Alberta, 1958.

231
Verma, Tika Ram. "Moisture Balance in Soils of the Edmonton Area." Alberta, 1969.

British Columbia/Colombie-Britannique

232
Baker, Ted Edgar. "The Major Soils of the Tofino Area of Vancouver Island and Implications for Land Use Planning and Management." British Columbia, 1974.

Beil, Charles Edward. See No./Voir no 11451

233
Bhoojedhur, Seewant. "Adsorption and Heavy Metal Partitioning in Soils and Sediments of the Salmon River Area, British Columbia." British Columbia, 1975.

234
Chae, Yeh Moon. "The Distribution of Lipid Sulfur in Soils of British Columbia." British Columbia, 1979.

235
Hendershot, William Hamilton. "Surface Charge Properties of Selected Soils." British Columbia, 1978.

236
Keser, Nurettin. "Soils and Forest Growth in the Sayward Forest, British Columbia." British Columbia, 1970.

237
Lewis, Terence. "The Till-Derived Podzols of Vancouver Island." British Columbia, 1976.

McKenzie, Rodney Collin. See No./Voir no 227

238
Moon, David Earl. "The Genesis of Three Podzol-Like Soils Occurring Over a Climatic Gradient of Vancouver Island." British Columbia, 1982.

239
Nnyamah, Joseph Ugbogu. "Root Water Uptake in Douglas Fir Forest." British Columbia, 1977.

240
Novak, Michael David. "The Moisture and Thermal Regimes of a Bare Soil in the Lower Fraser Valley During Spring." British Columbia, 1981.

241
Otchere-Boateng, Jacob K. "Effect of Urea Fertilizer on Leaching in Some Forest Soils." British Columbia, 1976.

242
Paul, Compton Lawrence. "Prediction of Trafficability of Tile-Drained Farmland." British Columbia, 1978. [Lower Fraser Valley/Vallée du bas Fraser]

243
Sneddon, James Ian. "A Study of Two Soils Derived from Volcanic Ash in Southwestern British Columbia and a Review and Determination of Ash Distribution in Western Canada." British Columbia, 1974.

244
Tan, Chin-Sheng. "A Study of Stomatal Diffusion Resistance in a Douglas Fir Forest." British Columbia, 1977. [Vancouver Island/Île de Vancouver]

245
Van Ryswyk, Albert Leonard. "Forest and Alpine Soils of South Central British Columbia." Washington State, 1969.

Manitoba

246
Al-Taweel, Bashir Hashim. "Soil Genesis in Relation to Groundwater Regimes in a Hummocky Ground Moraine Area near Hamiota, Manitoba." Manitoba, 1983.

247
Anderson, Jonathan Robert. "The Activity of Triazine Herbicides in Manitoba and Ontario Soils." Guelph, 1971.

248
Christianson, Carlyle Bruce. "Chemodentrification in Frozen Soils." Manitoba, 1981.

249
Ehrlich, Walter Arnold. "Pedalogical Processes of Some Manitoba Soils." Minnesota, 1954.

250
Michalyna, Walter. "Influence of Drainage Regime with Chemistry and Morphology of Chernozemic Soils in Manitoba." Minnesota, 1974.

251
Obi, Adeniyi Olubunmi. "Isotope Studies on Crop Utilization and Soil Fixation of Nitrogen from Calcium Nitrate Ammonium Sulphate and Urea in Several Manitoba Soils." Manitoba, 1982.

252
Pang, Patrick Chi-Kee. "Transformation and Movement of Band-Applied Nitrogen Fertilizers in Several Manitoba Soils." Manitoba, 1974.

253
Sheppard, Stephen Charles." Plant Phosphorous Requirements and Soil Phosphorous Reactions as Influenced by Temperature." Manitoba, 1982.

Smeiris, Fred Eldon. See No./Voir no 328
254
Weir, Collin Coke. "Behaviour of Phosphates in Some Calcareous Manitoba Soils." Manitoba, 1962.

Nova Scotia/Nouvelle-Écosse

255
Wright, James R. "The Effect of Certain Soil Treatments in the Cobalt Supplying Power of Some Nova Scotian Soils." Michigan State, 1953.

256
Acton, Clifford John. "Micropedology and Electron Probe Analysis in a Genesis-Study of Lacustrine Soils of Grant County, Ontario." Guelph, 1970.

Anderson, Jonathan Robert. See No./Voir no 247
Anderson, Terry Ross. See No./Voir no 329
257
Asamoa, Godfried Kofi. "Discontinuity Location and Micromorphological Analysis in a Genesis Study of the Soils of the Honeywood Catena." Guelph, 1969.

258
Bailey, Loraine Dolar. "The Effect of Temperature Moisture and Roots on Nitrogen Transformation and Redox Potential in Surface and Subsurface Soil Samples." Guelph, 1971.

259
Banerjee, Ajit Kumar. "A Study of the Morphogenesis of Gray-Brown Podzolic Soils in Southern Ontario." Toronto, 1969.

Campbell, James Alfred. See No./Voir no 205
260
Freedman, William. "Effects of Smelter Pollution Near Sudbury, Ontario, Canada, on Surrounding Forested Ecosystems." Toronto, 1978.

261
Ketcheson, John William. "Studies of Soil Phosphorus Forms in Two Non-Calcareous Ontario Soils." Illinois, 1957.

262
Laryea, Kofi Budu. "Solute Dispersion in Soil." Guelph, 1979. [Brookston Clay of the Huron Catena/Argile Brookston de la chaîne Huron]

MacClean, Alister J. See No./Voir no 336
263
Morgan, Christopher Llewellyn. "Field and Laboratory Examination of Soil Erosion as a Function of Erosivity and Erodibility for Selected Hillslope Soils from Southern Ontario." Toronto, 1979.

264
Neilson, Gerald Henry. "Soluble and Sediment Nutrients Lost from Agricultural Watersheds." McGill, 1977.

265
Raad, Awni Tewfiq Saleh. "Genetic Development of Youthful Soils Derived from Dolomitic Materials in the Blue Springs Drainage Basin." Guelph, 1970.

266
Stobbe, Peter C. "Comparative Study of the Grey-Brown Podzolic, Brown Podzolic and Brown Forest Soils of Southern Ontario and Southern Quebec." McGill, 1950.

267
Venkataraman, Sundaram. "Clay Materials and Discontinuities in Nine Southern Ontario Soil Profiles." Guelph, 1971.

268
Willis, Arthur L. "Clay Minerals Present in Eight Representative Ontario Soils." Wisconsin, 1950.

Prince Edward Island/Île-du-Prince-Édouard

269
Bishop, Robert Frederick. "The Effect of Lime on the Chemical Composition of a Charlottetown Fine Sandy Foam and the Effect of Several Amendments in its Content of Water-Soluble Boron as Shown by Soil and Plant Analyses." Michigan State, 1953.

Quebec/Québec

270
Broughton, Robert Stephen. "The Performance of Subsurface Drainage Systems on Two Saint Lawrence Lowland Soils." McGill, 1972.

271
Couture, Michel. "Étude de la dynamique de la dégradation de la matière ligneuse dans les sols de différents écosystèmes forestiers du Québec méridional: rôle de la pédofaune et influence de la fertilisation à l'N-urée." Laval, 1980.

272
Knutti, Hans Jakob. "The Influence of Certain Environmental Factors, Particularly Soil Types on the Sward Cover of Permanent Pastures in Selected Areas of the St. Lawrence Lowland, Eastern Podzol, and Laurentian Upland Regions of Quebec." McGill, 1962.

273
Lepage, Ernest. "Études des lichens, des mousses et des hépatiques du Québec et leur rôle dans la formation du sol arabe dans la région du bas de Québec, de Lévis à Gaspé." Laval, 1943.

274
Lowe, Lawrence Edward. "The Sulphur Status of Quebec Soils with Particular Reference to the Amount of Organically Combined Sulphur and the Nature of Its Combination." McGill, 1963.

275
Murshid, Abu Hassan. "A Proposed New Method for Classifying Land Capability of Marginal and Prime Agricultural Land in the St. Lawrence Lowlands of Quebec." Laval, 1983.

Neilsen, Gerald Henry. See No./Voir no 264

276
Schnitzer, Morris. "Investigations on the Interactions of Catons with Extracts and Leachates from Forest Trees." McGill, 1955.

277
Seddyk, Esam Abdul-Sattar. "A Study of the Development of the Agric Horizons in Quebec Soils." McGill, 1980.

278
Shaykewich, Carl Francis. "Availability of Water for Plant Growth in Three Quebec Soils." McGill, 1968.

Stobbe, Peter C. See No./Voir no 266

279
Van Lierop, William. "La fertilisation des sols organiques acides du Québec." Laval, 1980.

280
Warnaars, Benjamin Caspar. "Soil Factors Affecting Corn (Zea mays L.) Root Growth, Fertilizer Nitrogen Uptake and Nitrogen Leaching Losses in Three Quebec Soils." McGill, 1973.

Saskatchewan

281
Acton, Donald Findlay. "Factors Influencing the Developments of Black Chernozemic Soils: Comparisons Within and Between Four Sites in a Lithologic Sequence in Saskatchewan, Canada." Illinois, 1971.

282
Anderson, Darwin Wayne. "The Characteristics of the Organic Matter of Grassland Transitional and Forest Soils." Saskatchewan, 1972.

283
Bentley, Charles F. "A Study of Some Solovetz Soil Complexes in Saskatchewan." Minnesota, 1946.

284
Bettamy, Jeffrey Roger. "The Studies of Sulfur in Saskatchewan Soils." Saskatchewan, 1973.

Dodd, James Dale. See No./Voir no 350

285
Halm, Benjamin Jackson. "The Phosphorus Cycle in a Native Grassland Ecosystem." Saskatchewan, 1972.

Hulett, Gary K. See No./Voir no 352

286
Kucey, Reginald Mathew Nicholas. "V.A. Mycorrhizal Fungi in Saskatchewan Soils and Their Effect on the Growth of Faba Beans." Saskatchewan, 1981.

287
Lutwick, Laurence E. "The Nature and Distribution of Free Iron in the Grey Wooded (Podzolic) Soils of Saskatchewan." Saskatchewan, 1960.

288
Pettapiece, William Wayne. "Pedological Investigations in the Front Ranges of the Rocky Mountains Along the North Saskatchewan River Valley." Alberta, 1970.

289
Sadler, John Mountford. "Influences of Applied Phosphorus on the Nature of and Availability of Inorganic Phosphorus in a Catenary Sequence of Saskatchewan Soils." Saskatchewan, 1973.

290
Saggar, Surinder Kumar. "Studies of Sulphur in Relationship to Carbon and Nitrogen in Soil Organic Matter." Saskatchewan, 1981.

291
St-Arnaud, Roland Joseph. "The Pedogenesis of a Black-Grey Wooded Sequence of Soils in Saskatchewan, Canada." Michigan, 1961.

292
Tiessen, Holm. "Changes in Soil Organic Matter and Phosphorus During Cultivation of Grassland Soils". Saskatchewan, 1982.

Arctic, Northwest Territories and the Yukon/ Arctique, Territoires du Nord-Ouest et Yukon

293
Fox, Catherine Anne. "The Soil Micromorphology and Genesis of the Turbic Cryosols from the Mackenzie River Valley and Yukon Coastal Plain." Guelph, 1979.

Kerby, Norma Joann. See No./Voir no 11541

294
Paeth, Robert Carl. "Genetic and Stability Relationships of Four Western Cascade Soils." Oregon State, 1970.
295
Rencz, Andrew Nicholas. "The Relationship Between Heavy Metals in the Soil and Their Accumulation in Various Organs of Plants Growing in the Arctic." New Brunswick, 1978.
296
Walton, Grant Fontain. "The High Arctic Environment and Polar Desert Soils." Rutgers, 1972. [Canadian Arctic Archipelago/Archipel arctique canadien]

PLANT CULTURE SCIENCE AND PATHOLOGY/ SCIENCE ET PATHOLOGIE DE LA CULTURE VÉGÉTALE

Studies and Experiments and Physiology/ Études, expériences et physiologie

General Items/Ouvrages généraux

297
Ahmed, Shabir. "Lengthening of the Filling-Period in Soybeans (Glycine max (L.) Merrill)." Guelph, 1969.
298
Baron, Vernon Samuel. "Evaluation of Early-Maturing European and Canadian Corn Hybrids for Grain and Forage Production in Canada." Guelph, 1983.
299
Brewer, Robert Franklin Ross. "Studies in Ascochyta pisi, Lib." Toronto, 1955.
300
Dhanavantari, Bobberjung N. "A Study of Strawberry Leaf Scotch Disease Caused by Diplocarpon earliana (Ell. and Ev.) Wolf." Toronto, 1964.
301
Fletcher, Ronald Austin. "Photomorphogenetic Effects of Regions in the Visible Spectrum on Certain Plant Species." Alberta, 1964.
302
Hutchinson, Aleck. "Bio-chemical and Physiological Studies of Malus Rootstocks." McGill, 1959.
303
Jones, Rogers. "Studies in Metabolic Changes Accompanying Inhibition and Vernalization of a Spring and a Winter Wheat." Ottawa, 1967.
304
Li, Shin-Chai. "Genetic Studies of Earliness and Growth Stages of Lycopersicon esculentum Mill." British Columbia, 1975.
305
MacLeod, Donald J. "The Mosaic Types of Viruses Affecting Potatoes in Canada and Great Britain." Cambridge, 1945.
McDonald, Howard. See No./Voir no 11341
306
Meier, Henry Frederick August. "Effect of Direct Current on Cells of Root Tip of Canada Field Pea." Columbia, 1921.
Pottinger, Robert Peter. See No./Voir no 11327

307
Prucha, Martin John. "Physiological Studies of Bacillus Rodicicola of Canada Field Pea." Cornell, 1913.
308
Rahn, James Jacob. "Air and Plant Temperatures in a Corn Canopy." Guelph, 1970.
309
Rai, Rama Kant. "Hybrid Wheat Potential and Studies on Male Sterility in Wheat (Triticum aestiviem L.)." Guelph, 1970.
310
Sim, Soon-Liang. "The Influence of Certain Environmental and Physiological Factors in Seed Yield in Avena sativa L." McGill, 1971.

Eastern Canada/Est du Canada

311
Daily, Gavin Thomas. "Vegetation Succession and Soil Change in Developing Lowland Ecosystems of Eastern Canada." McGill, 1966.
312
Field, Tony Richard Osgood. "Analysis and Simulation of the Effect of Temperature on the Growth and Development of Alfalfa (Medicago sativa L.)." Guelph, 1974. [Southeastern Canada/Sud-est du Canada]
313
Wells, Bertram Whittier. "The Zoocecidia of Northeastern United States and Eastern Canada." Chicago, 1917.

Western Canada/Ouest du Canada

314
Broadfoot, William Craig. "Studies on Foot and Root Rot of Wheat in Western Canada." Minnesota, 1932.
315
Cairns, Robert Ross. "A Study of Alfalfa Response to Applied Sulphur and the Soil and Plant Sulphur Relationships on Two Gray Wooded Soils in Northwestern Canada." Pennsylvania State, 1958.

Alberta

316
Hawn, Elmer Joseph. "Studies on Crown Bird Rot of Alfalfa in Southern Alberta." Minnesota, 1957.
McKenzie, Rodney Collin. See No./Voir no 227
317
Powell, John Martin. "The Aerobiology of the Aecial State of the Comandra Blister Rust, Cronartium comandrae Peck in Alberta." British Columbia, 1969.

British Columbia/Colombie-Britannique

318
Douglas, George Wayne. "Alpine Plant Communities of the North Cascades Range, Washington and British Columbia." Alberta, 1973.
Gillespie, David Roy. See No./Voir no 11211

319
Granger, Raymond Laurent. "Factors Associated with Spartan Breakdown of Apple." McGill, 1979.
320
Johnson, Daniel Lloyd. "Predation, Dispersal and Weather in an Orchard Mite System." British Columbia, 1983.
321
Leggett, Mary Elizabeth. "Potential for Biological Control of Onion White Rot in the Fraser Valley of British Columbia." Simon Fraser, 1983.
McKenzie, Rodney Collin. See No./Voir no 227
322
Yamanaka, Koji. "The Role of Grass-Legume Communities in Revegetation of a Subalpine Mine Site in British Columbia." British Columbia 1982.
323
Ziller, Wolf Gunther. "Life History Studies of British Columbia Tree Rusts." Toronto, 1955.

Manitoba

324
Donaghy, David Ian. "Zero Tillage Crop Productions in Manitoba." Manitoba, 1973.
325
Gutek, Larry Henry. "Studies Toward a Breeding Program in Wild Rice. "Manitoba, 1975. [Paddy Production in Manitoba/Production des rizières au Manitoba]
326
McVetty, Peter Barclay Edgar. "Determination of Characters for Yield Selection in Spring Wheat Breeding Programs." Manitoba, 1978.
Neill, Garnet Bruce. See No./Voir no 11249
327
Rashid, Khalid Youssef. "Inheritance of Specific Resistance to Rust (Uromyces vicia-fabae) in Faba Bean (Vicia fabae) and Evaluation of Slow-Rusting Resistance." Manitoba, 1983.
Sheppard, Stephen C. See No./Voir no 253
328
Smeiris, Fred Eldon. "The Wetland Vegetation of the Red River Valley and Drift Prairie Regions of Minnesota, North Dakota and Manitoba." Saskatchewan, 1967.
Ure, George Brian. See No./Voir no 11254

Ontario

329
Anderson, Terry Ross. "Mycophagous Vampyrellidae from Soil That Perforated Spores of Thielaviopsis basicola and Cochliobolus sativus." Toronto, 1979.
330
Azu, John Nene-Osom. "Growth and Development of Spanish Peanuts (Arachis hypogaea L.) in Southern Ontario." Guelph, 1979.
331
Benedict, Winfred Gerald. "Studies on Sweet Clover Failures in Western Ontario." Toronto, 1952.
332
Brown, Donald Murray. "A Phenological Study of Soybeans in Iowa and Ontario, Canada." Iowa State, 1958.

333
Bruin, Gerardus Cornelis Anna. "Resistance in Peronosporales to Acylanine-Type Fungicides." Guelph, 1980. [Blue mold epidemic in tobacco/Épidémie de mildiou dans le tabac]
334
Chew, Poon Sian. "Significance and Chemical Control of Bean Root Disease in Ontario." Guelph, 1978.
Devine, Malcolm David. See No./Voir no 11579
335
Koch, Lyle Ward. "Spur Blight of Raspberries in Ontario Caused by Didymella applanata." Toronto, 1931.
336
MacClean, Alister J. "The Effect of Soil pH as Modified by Liming, on the Availability of Phosphorus and Potassium for Alfalfa in Some Eastern Ontario Soils." Michigan State, 1954.
337
McKeen, Wilbert Ezekiel. "A Study of Sugar Beet Root Rot in Southern Ontario." Toronto, 1949.
Neill, Garnet Bruce. See No./Voir no 11240
338
Poysa, Vaino Wilhelm. "The Response of Some Facultative Triticale (X Triticosecale Wittmack) to Vernalization and Autumn and Spring Sowing." Guelph, 1981.
339
Quashie-Sam, Semion James. "Ecological Studies on Rhizobium japonicum and Inoculation of Soybeans in the Soybean Growing Areas of Ontario." Guelph, 1979.
340
Salloum, John Duane. "Land disposal of newsprint mill effluents." McGill, 1973.
341
Smith, David William. "Studies in the Taxonomy and Ecology of Blueberries (Vaccinium, Subgenus Cyanoccus) in Ontario." Toronto, 1967.
342
Smith, Richard Byron. "Maturity Indices for Ontario Apples." Guelph, 1969.
343
Tollenaar, Matthijs. "Sink-Source Relationship During Reproductive Development in Maize." Guelph, 1976. [Elora Research Station in Guelph/Station de recherche Elora à Guelph]
344
Wright Philip Alan. "An Economic Analysis of Potato Yields on Certain Ontario Mineral Soils in Controlled Fertilizer Experiments, 1954-1956." Michigan State, 1962.
345
Zimmer, Ramon Clemence. "Carrot Blight in Southwestern Ontario and the Importance of Radiation and Temperature in the Sporulation of Alternaria danci." Western Ontario, 1968.

Prince Edward Island/Île-du-Prince-Édouard

Bishop, Robert Frederick. See No./Voir no 269

Quebec/Québec

346
Cameron, Peter James. "The Bionomics of the Apple Maggot, Rhagoletis pomonella." McGill, 1973.

347
Finn, Basil J. "A Study of the Comparative Merits of Rock Phosphates and Superphosphate on a Grain Crop Seeded to a Hay Mixture on Three Major Soil Types of the Eastern Townships of Quebec, Canada." Michigan State, 1955.

Granger, Raymond Laurent. See No./Voir no 319

348
Olthorf, Theodorius Hendrikus Antonius. "Studies in Certain Nematopagous Fungi." McGill, 1963.

Saskatchewan

349
Ayyad, Mohamed A.G. "An Analysis of the Vegetation-Microenvironmental Complex on Prairie Slopes in Saskatchewan." Saskatchewan, 1963.

350
Dodd, James Dale. "Plant Succession in Saline Areas of Saskatchewan." Saskatchewan, 1960.

351
Gebeyehou, Getinet. "The Relationships Between the Vegetative and Grain Filling Periods and Grain Yield in Durum Cultivars and Lines (Triticum turgidum L.)." Saskatchewan, 1980. [Experiments at Saskatoon/Expériences à Saskatoon]

352
Hulett, Gary K. "Species Distributional Patterns in Dune Sand Areas in the Grasslands of Saskatchewan." Saskatchewan, 1963.

353
Irvine, Rendel Byron. "Growth of Roots and Shoots of Semidwarf and Tall Genotypes of Hordeum vulgare L." Saskatchewan, 1978.

354
Johnson, Ross Eugene. "Rooting Characteristics of Prairie Species in Saskatchewan." Saskatchewan, 1960.

Kucey, Reginald Mathew Nicholas. See No./Voir no 286

355
Limin, Allan Edward. "Cold Hardness Potential in the Wheat Relatives and Its Expression in Triticum and Triticum secala amphiploids." Saskatchewan, 1981.

Arctic/Arctique

See also Botany/Voir aussi Botanique

ANTHROPOLOGY/ ANTHROPOLOGIE

The major sub-classifications in anthropology deal with Native peoples of Canada, and cultural and urban anthropology. Very little doctoral research on Canadian anthropology came out of Canadian universities during the first 60 years of this century. Five times as many studies were produced in American universities. During the 1970's Canadian output increased dramatically and this trend continues into the 1980's.

Eighteen Canadian universities were responsible for the dissertations listed in Anthropology. The University of Toronto produced one-third of the total, and the Universities of British Columbia, Alberta, and McGill University placed second, third, and fourth respectively.

In the section on Native people, studies of the Metis, and of Indians in different provinces are presented. In the section on cultural anthropology, almost 30 ethnic and religious groups are examined through doctoral research.

————

Les principales sous-classifications en anthropologie portent sur les nombreux peuples autochtones du Canada et sur l'anthropologie culturelle et urbaine. Au cours des 60 premières années de ce siècle, très peu de thèses universitaires canadiennes ont abordé le thème de l'anthropologie canadienne. Pendant ce temps, les universités américaines faisaient cinq fois plus d'études à ce sujet. Les années 1970 ont vu un remarquable tournant en ce domaine et cette tendance s'est poursuivie dans les années 1980.

Les thèses d'anthropologie viennent de 18 universités canadiennes; l'Université de Toronto a fourni un tiers du total, suivie de l'Université de la Colombie-Britannique, l'Université de l'Alberta et l'Université McGill.

Dans la section des études sur les Autochtones, l'ouvrage présente des thèses sur les Métis et sur des Indiens de différentes provinces. En anthropologie culturelle, les thèses de doctorat traitent presque de 30 groupes ethniques et religieux.

GENERAL ITEMS/OUVRAGES GÉNÉRAUX

356
Bonnichsen, Robson. "Models for Deriving Cultural Information from Stone Tools." Alberta, 1974.

357
Down, Mary Margaret. "A Cross-Cultural Analysis of the Concept of Money Management." Cornell, 1965.

358
Engle, Ronald Crim. "Value Differences and Comparative Rates of Socio-Cultural Change in Four English-Speaking Democracies." Florida State, 1966.

359
Ferland, Madeleine. "Ethnographie canadienne: des jeux canadiens à la connaissance de l'homme." Laval, 1963.

360
Field, Lanora Leigh. "Immunoglobulin Allotypes in Jewish Populations: A Study of the Diversity of Jewish Peoples and the Nature of the Gm System." Toronto, 1980.

361
Katz, Bruce Allen. "The Production of an Ethnography: Some Methodological and Substantive Issues for Analyzing Social Settings." British Columbia, 1975.

362
Lamy, Paul. "Language and Ethnicity: A Study of Bilingualism, Ethnic Identity, and Ethnic Attitudes." Mc Master, 1976.

363
Maxey, Alva Beatrice. "A Probe into the Dimensionality of Racial and Ethnic Stereotyping." Saskatchewan, 1972.

364
Minore, James Bruce. "Socio-Cultural Ecosystems in Rural Canada." Florida, 1976.
Spiess, Arthur Eliot. See No./Voir no 846

365
Taylor, Donald Maclean. "A Cross-Cultural Investigation of Ethnic Stereotypes and Communication." Western Ontario, 1969.

366
Van Dyke, Edward William. "Bluemenort: A Study of Persistence in a Sect." Alberta, 1972.

367
Wong, Yuwa. "Ethnicity and State Policy: The Canadian Case." Simon Fraser, 1981.

ANTHROPOLOGICAL STUDIES IN SPECIFIC REGIONS/ÉTUDES ANTHROPOLOGIQUES DE RÉGIONS PARTICULIÈRES

General Items/Ouvrages généraux

368
Brown, Jennifer. "Company Men and Native Families: Fur Trade Social and Domestic Relations in Canada's Old Northwest." Chicago, 1977.

Eastern Canada/Est du Canada

369
Ross, Hazel Miriam. "Women and Wellness: Defining, Attaining, and Maintaining Health in Eastern Canada." Washington, Seattle, 1981.

370
Young, Frank Wilbur. "Integration and Urban Influence: A Study of Two Canadian Fishing Villages Undergoing a Natural Experiment." Cornell, 1957.

Western Canada/Ouest du Canada

371
Young, Mary McPherson. "Boundary Maintenance in a Religious Minority Group in Western Canada." Alberta, 1974.

Great Lakes Region/Région des Grands Lacs

372
Kolar, J.C. "Hungry Hall and Late Woodland Populations of the Upper Great Lakes." Toronto, 1983.

373
Pfeiffer, Susan Kay Gosker. "The Skeletal Biology of Archaic Populations of the Great Lakes Region." Toronto, 1976.

Alberta

374
Beaujot, Roderic Paul. "Ethnic Fertility Differentials in Edmonton." Alberta, 1975.

375
Morrison, Robert Bruce. "Stress and Socio-Cultural Change in a New Town." Alberta, 1977. [Grande Cache]

376
Reshetylo, Daniel Allan. "Reconciling Identity and Diversity in an Outlaw Motor Cycle Club." Alberta, 1981. [Edmonton]

British Columbia/Colombie-Britannique

377
Barnett, Homer Garner. "The Nature and Function of the Potlatch." California, Berkeley, 1938.

378
Cove, John James. "A Comparative Approach to Decision-Making: Risk Taking by Fishing Boat Captains in Two Canadian Fleets." British Columbia, 1971.

379
Folan, William J. "The Community Settlements and Subsistence Patterns of the Nootka Sound Area: A Diachronic Model." Southern Illinois, 1972.

380
Grabert, Garland Frederick. "Prehistoric Cultural Stability in the Okanogan Valley of Washington and British Columbia." Washington, Seattle, 1970.

381
Hall, John Laurence. "Anahim Lake, British Columbia: A Study of Indian/White Interaction in a Western Canadian Ranching Community." Toronto, 1981.

382
Hewes, Gordon W. "Aboriginal Use of Fishery Resources in Northwestern North America." California, Berkeley, 1947.

383
Houlihan, Patrick Thomas. "Art and Social Structure on the Northwest Coast." Wisconsin, 1972.

384
Indra, Doreen Marie. "Ethnicity, Social Stratification and Opinion Formation; an Analysis of Ethnic Portrayal in the Vancouver Newspaper Press, 1905-1975." Simon Fraser, 1980.

385
Kleiber, Nancy Ruth Lewis. "Family Size and Family Organization in Selected Subcultural Groups in Vancouver, British Columbia." California, Davis, 1972.

386
Laforet, Andrea Lynne. "Folk History in a Small Canadian Community." British Columbia, 1974. [Yale, British Columbia/Yale, Colombie-Britannique]

387
Miller, Philip Carl. "A British Columbian Fishing Village." British Columbia, 1978.

388
Pokotylo, David Leslie. "Lithic Technology and Settlement Patterns in Upper Hat Creek Valley, B.C.." British Columbia, 1978.

389
Prattis, James Ian. "Dilemmas of Decision-Making: A Methodological Test Case in Economic Anthropology." British Columbia, 1970.

390
Ray, Verne Frederick. "Cultural Relations in the Plateau of Northwestern America." Yale, 1939.

391
Simmons, Terry Allan. "But We Must Cultivate Our Garden: Twentieth Century Pioneering in Rural British Columbia." Minnesota, 1979.

392
Sloane, Morton Joseph. "The Interrelationship of Economics, Class and Leadership on the Northwest Coast." New Mexico, 1956.

393
Smith, Douglas Wilson. "Quicksilver Utopias: The Counterculture as a Social Field in British Columbia." McGill, 1978.

Maritime Provinces/Provinces maritimes

Blackmer, Hugh Allison. See No./Voir no 59
394
De Roche, Constance Pennacchio. "Macroeconomic and Microsocial Processes; Social Change in a Nova Scotian Village." Washington, St. Louis, 1982.

Mayer, Francine-M. See no./Voir no 442
395
Medjuck, Beth Sheva. "Wooden Ships and Iron People: The Lives of the People of Moncton, New Brunswick, 1851-1871." York, 1979.

396
Mertz, Elizabeth Ellen. " 'No Burden to Carry': Cape Breton Pragmatics and Metapragmatics." Duke, 1982.

Newfoundland and Labrador/Terre-Neuve et Labrador

397
Antler, Ellen Pildes. "Fisherman, Fisherwoman, Rural Proletariat: Capitalist Commodity Production in the Newfoundland Fishery." Connecticut, 1982.

398
Britan, Gerald Mark. "Fisherman and Workers; the Processes of Stability and Change in a Rural Newfoundland Community." Columbia, 1974.

399
Cox, Steven L. "Prehistoric Settlement and Culture Change at Okak, Labrador." Harvard, 1977.

400
Davis, Dona Lee. "Women's Experience of Menopause in a Newfoundland Fishing Village." North Carolina, 1980.

401
Faris, James Chester. "Cat Harbour: A Newfoundland Fishing Settlement." Cambridge, 1966.

402
Firestone, Melvin M. "Social Structure of a Northern Newfoundland Fishing Settlement." Washington, Seattle, 1966.

403
Gaffney, Michael Edward. "Crosshanded: Work Organization and Values in a Newfoundland Fishery." Ohio State, 1982.

404
Kodish, Debora Gail. " 'Never Had a Word between Us.' Pattern in the Verbal Art of a Newfoundland Woman." Texas, 1981.

405
Mars, Gould. "An Anthropological Study of Longshoremen and of Industrial Relations in the Port of St. John's, Newfoundland, Canada." London, 1972.

406
Mc Cay, Bonnie Jean. " 'Appropriate Technology' and Coastal Fishermen of Newfoundland." Columbia, 1976. [Fogo Island/Île de Fogo]

407
Nemec, Thomas Francis. "An Ethnohistorical and Ethnographic Study of the Cod Fishery at St. Shotts, Newfoundland." Michigan, 1980.

408
Ness, Robert Conrad. "Illness and Adaptation in a Newfoundland Outport." Connecticut, 1977.

409
Pocius, Gerald Lewis. "Calvert: a Study of Artifacts and Spatial Usage in a Newfoundland Community." Pennsylvania, 1979.

Richling, Barnett Edward. See No./Voir no 621
410
Robbins, Edward Herschell. "Class and Ethnicity: Social Relations in Wabush, Newfoundland-Labrador." Michigan, 1974.

411
Small, Lawrence George. "The Interrelationship of Work and Talk in a Newfoundland Fishing Community." Memorial University of Newfoundland, 1966.

412
Szwed, John Francis. "Private Cultures and Public Imagery: Interpersonal Relations in a Newfoundland Peasant Society." Ohio State, 1965.

413
Wareham, Wilfred William. "Towards an Ethnography of 'Times'. Newfoundland Party Traditions, Past and Present." Pennsylvania, 1982. [Fishing village/Village de pêche]

414
Zimmerly, David William. "Cain's Land Revisited: Culture Change in Central Labrador, 1775-1972." Colorado, 1973.

Northwest Territories/Territoires du Nord-Ouest

415
Hurlich, Marshall Gerald. "Environmental Adaptation: Biological and Behavioral Response to Cold in the Canadian Subarctic." SUNY, Buffalo, 1976.

416
Krech, Shepard, III. "Changing Trapping Patterns in Fort McPherson, Northwest Territories." Harvard, 1974.

417
Morrison, D.A. "Thule Culture in Western Coronation Gulf, N.W.T." Toronto, 1983.

Prairie Provinces/Provinces des Prairies

418
Anderson, Alan Betts. "Assimilation in the Bloc Settlements of North Central Saskatchewan: A Comparative Study of Identity Change among Seven Ethno-Religious Groups in a Canadian Prairie Region." Saskatchewan, 1972.

419
Blakeslee, Donald John. "The Plains Interband Trade System: An Ethnohistoric and Archaeological Investigation." Wisconsin, Milwaukee, 1975.

420
Dyck, Ian George. "The Harder Site: A Middle Period Bison Hunters' Campsite in the Northern Great Plains." Alberta, 1976.

421
Elias, Peter Douglas. "Metropolis and Hinterland in Northern Manitoba." Toronto, 1974.

Hufferd, James. See No./Voir no 4845

422
Luxton, Margaret Joan. "Why Women's Work is Never Done: A Case Study from Flin Flon, Manitoba, of Domestic Labour in Industrialist Capitalist Society." Toronto, 1978.

423
Stubbs, G.M. "The Geography of Cultural Assimilation in the Prairie Provinces." Oxford, 1966.

424
Syms, Edward Leigh. "Indigenous Ceramics and Ecological Dynamics of Southwestern Manitoba 500 B.C. - A.D. 1800." Alberta, 1976.

Ontario

425
Davies, Joan Anne Moreland. "Ethnic Demand Hierarchies in the Market Place: Economic and Social Exchange in Kensington Market (Toronto)." Toronto, 1977.

426
Kelner, Merrijoy Sharon. "The Elite Structure of Toronto: Ethnic Composition and Patterns of Recruitment." Toronto, 1969.

427
Sieciechowicz, Krystyna Z. " 'We Are All Related Here': The Social Relations of Land Utilization in Winnummin Lake, Northwestern Ontario." Toronto, 1982.

428
Stymeist, Davis Harold. "The Permanent Resident-Outsider Distinction in Sioux Lookout, Ontario: An Analysis of a Local Social System." Toronto, 1976.

Quebec/Québec

429
Arbess, Saul E. "Values and Socio-Economic Change: The George River Case." McGill, 1968.

430
Bariteau, Claude. "Liens de dépendance et stratégies de développement: le cas de Havre aux Maisons (Îles de la Madeleine)." McGill, 1979.

431
Basham, Richard Dalton. "Crisis in Blanc and White: Urbanization and Ethnic Identity in French Canada." California, Berkeley, 1972.

432
Bouchard, Claude. "Univariate and Multivariate Genetic Analysis of Anthropometric and Physique Characteristics of French Canadian Families." Texas, 1977. [Montreal/Montréal]

433
Bouchard, Serge. "Nous autres, les gars de truck: essai sur la culture et l'idéologie des camionneurs de longue-distance dans le nord-ouest québécois." McGill, 1981.

434
Conklin, Elizabeth Nancy. "Women's Voluntary Associations in French Montreal: A Study of Changing Institutions and Attitudes." Illinois, 1972.

435
Dawson, Nora. "La vie matérielle de la paroisse de St-Pierre de l'Île d'Orléans." Laval, 1954.

436
Deshaies-Lafontaine, D. "A Socio-Phonetic Study of a Quebec French Community: Trois-Rivières." London, 1975.

437
Felt, Paula Chegwidden. "The Environmental Movement in Montreal: The Social Organization of Problem-Solving Voluntary Associations." Northwestern, 1973.

438
Gold, Gerald Louis. "The Emergence of a Commercial Bourgeoisie in a French Canadian Town." Minnesota, 1972.

439
Handler, Richard. "My Country is Winter: An Ethnography of Nationalism in Quebec." Chicago, 1979.

440
Handrick, Philip James. "Institutions, Ideology and Power: Social Change in the Eastern Townships of Quebec." Michigan State, 1981.

441
Leavy, Normand. "Les réseaux d'influence à Sainte-Perpétue: une analyse par la méthode de la théorie des graphies." Laval, 1981.

442
Mayer, Francine M. "Évolution de la structure génétique d'une population ouverte: la serpentine." Montréal, 1977.

443
Petherbridge, Douglas Lawrence. "A Description of the Society and Culture of the Province of Quebec, 1966." Alberta, 1967.

444
Philippe, Pierre. "Étude des effets de la consanguinité sur quelques facteurs de la fécondité (Contribution à l'analyse anthrobiologique du Canada français)." Montréal, 1972.

Pilon, Lise. See No./Voir no 138

445
Stewart, Donald Alexander, Jr. "Social Identity and Commitment: Migration and Settlement in New Northern Towns." McGill, 1980.

446
Umoren, Uduakobong E., Rev. "Symbols, Process and Pilgrimage: A Processional Symbolic Analysis of the Ahearn Memorial Pilgrimage to the Shrine of Sainte-Anne de Beaupré." Catholic, 1982.

NATIVE PEOPLES/PEUPLES AUTOCHTONES

General Items/Ouvrages généraux

Arbess, Saul E. See No./Voir no 429

447
Boldt, Menno. "Indian Leaders in Canada: Attitudes Toward Equality, Identity and Political Status." Yale, 1973.

448
Byles, Robert Hal. "A Study of the Relationship Between Biological and Cultural Diversity in North American Indians." New Mexico, 1971.

449
Callaway, Donald Goodwin. "Raiding and Feuding Among Western North American Indians." Michigan, 1978.

450
Cauthers, Janet Helen. "The North American Indian as Portrayed by American and Canadian Historians 1830-1930." Washington, Seattle, 1974.

451
Chard, Chester Steven. "Kamchada Culture and Its Relationships in the Old and New World." California, Berkeley, 1953.

452
Coffin, James Larry. "A Statistical Analysis of Driver's and Massey's 1957 Monograph, Comparative Studies of North American Indians." Indiana, 1973.

453
Denton, Trevor Davies. "Strangers in Their Land: A Study of Migration from a Canadian Indian Reserve." Toronto, 1970.

454
Detwiler, Frederick Emrey, Jr. "The Sun Dance of the Oglala: A Case Study in Religion, Ritual and Ethics." Pennsylvania State, 1983.

Dosman, Edgar Joseph Edward. See No./Voir no 733

Down, Mary Margaret. See No./Voir no 357

455
Drucker, Philip. "Diffusion in Northwest Culture in the Light of Some Distributions." California, Berkeley, 1936.

456
Dyck, N.E. "Advocacy of Brokerage and Leadership: An Examination of Inter-Band Political Organization Among Saskatchewan Indians." Manchester, 1976.

457
England, Raymond Edward. "The Planning and Development Process in Indian Reserve Communities." Waterloo, 1970.

458
Erickson, Edwin Erich. "The Song Trace: Song Styles and the Ethnohistory of Aboriginal America." Columbia, 1969.

459
Evers, Susan Eleanor. "Weight Status and Morbidity of Canadian Indian and Non-Indian Children during the First Two Years of Life." Western Ontario, 1980.

Fernandez, Marco Antonio. See No./Voir no 2056

460
Fishman, Laura Schrager. "How Noble the Savage? The Image of the American Indian in French and English Travel Accounts, CA 1550-1680." CUNY, 1979.

461
Franstead, Dennis Lee. "Culture Change and the Response to Acculturative Pressures Among the Indian Population of the Western Great Lakes; A Psychosocial Study." Northwestern, 1981.

462
Gillies, E.L. "The Indigenous Tribes of British Columbia and European Influence upon Them." Edinburgh, 1923.

Hall, John Laurence. See No./Voir no 381

463
Hallowell, Alfred I. "Bear Ceremonialism in the Northern Hemisphere." Pennsylvania, 1924.

464
Haywood, Charles. "Bibliography of North American Folklore and Folksong." Columbia, 1951.

465
Heizer, Robert F. "Aboriginal Whaling in the Old and New Worlds." California, Berkeley, 1941.

466
Herman, Mary W. "Indian Fur Trade of New France in the Seventeenth Century." California, Berkeley, 1953.

Hewes, Gordon W. See No./Voir no 382

Houlihan, Patrick Thomas. See No./Voir no 383

467
Howell, Benita Jankle. "Native American Trickster Mythology from the Northwest Coast: A Computer-Aided Comparison of Content." Kentucky, 1978.

468
Hudson, Herschel C. "Cultural and Social Dimensions of North American Indians." Indiana, 1979.

469
Hummelin Remmelt Carel Reinder. "The Arts and Native People: The Awareness of the Arts in Ontario Native Communities." Toronto, 1982.

470
Inglis, Gordon Bahan. "The Canadian Indian Reserve Community, Population, and Social System." British Columbia, 1971.

471
James, E.O. "The Cult of the Dead in North America." London, 1925.

472
King, Arden R. "Aboriginal Skin Dressing in Western North America." California, Berkeley, 1947.

473
Lal, Ravindra. "Indians of the Eastern Canadian Parklands: An Economic Ethnohistory, 1800-1930." McMaster, 1982.

474
Leechman, John Douglas. "The 'Red Indian' of Literature: A Study in the Perpetuation of Error." Ottawa, 1941.

475
Lowry, R.B. "Genetic Studies of Cleft Lip and Cleft Palate in the North American Indians of British Columbia." Queen's, Belfast, 1979.

Lyon, Noel Adversé. See No./Voir no 29

476
McCaskill, Donald Neil. "The Urbanization of Canadian Indians in Winnipeg, Toronto, Edmonton, and Vancouver: A Comparative Analysis." York, 1979.

477
Nettl, Bruno. "American Indian Music North of Mexico: Its Styles and Areas." Indiana, 1953.

478
Nichols, Claude Andrew. "Moral Education Among the North American Indians." Teachers College, Columbia, 1930.

479
Nicks, Gertrude Cecilia. "Demographic Anthropology of Native Populations in Western Canada, 1800-1975." Alberta, 1980.

480
Patterson, E. Palmer, II. "Andrew Paull and Canadian Indian Resurgence." Washington, Seattle, 1962. [1892-1958]

481
Piper, Edward Harry. "A Dialogical Study of the North American Trickster Figure and the Phenomenon of Play." Chicago, 1975.

482
Ricketts, Mac Linscott. "The Structure and Religious Significance of the Trickster-Tranformer-Culture Hero in the Mythology of the North American Indian." Chicago, 1965.

483
Rostlund, Erhard. "A Distribution Study of Fresh-Water Fish and Fishing in Aboriginal America, North of Mexico." California, Berkeley, 1951.

Rothman, Mark David. See No./Voir no 4128

484
Ruhly, Sharon Kay. "The Communication of Culture Through Film." Ohio State, 1972. [Indian culture/Culture indienne]

485
Salter, Michael Albert. "Games in Ritual: A Study of Selected North American Indian Tribes." Alberta, 1972.

Sherzer, Joel F. See No./Voir no 7785

486
Shkelnyk, Anastasia Maria. "Pathogenesis in a Social Order: A Case Study of Social Breakdown in a Canadian Indian Community." Massachusetts Institute of Technology, 1982.

487
Thomas, Prentice M., Jr. "Ecological and Social Correlates of Religions among North American Indians." Tulane, 1972.

488
Turner, Christy Gentry, II. "The Dentition of Arctic Peoples." Wisconsin, 1967.

Ullman, Stephen Hayes. See No./Voir no 722

489
Vastokas, Joan Marie. "Architecture of the Northwest Coast Indians of America." Columbia, 1966.

490
Weightman, Barbara Ann. "The Musqueam Reserve: A Case Study of the Indian Social Milieu in an Urban Environment." Washington, Seattle, 1972. [Vancouver]

491
Weitz, Jacqueline Marie. "Cultural Change and Field Dependence in Two Native Canadian Linguistic Families." Ottawa, 1971.

492
Wike, Joyce Annabel. "The Effect of the Maritime Fur Trade on the Northwest Coast Indian Society." Columbia, 1951.

Wong-Rieger, Durhane. See No./Voir no 9765

493
Woods, Carter. "Criticism of Wissler's North American Culture Areas." Yale, 1931.

Métis

494
Driben, Paul. "We are Métis: The Ethnography of a Halfbreed Community in Northern Alberta." Minnesota, 1975.

Fernandez, Marco. See No./Voir no 2056

495
Hatt, Fred Kenneth. "The Response to Directed Social Change of a Alberta Métis Colony." Alberta, 1969.

Morrison, Robert Bruce. See No./Voir no 375

496
Peterson, Jacqueline Louise. "The People In Between: Indian - White Marriage and the Genesis of a Métis Society and Culture in the Great Lakes Region, 1680 - 1830." Illinois at Chicago Circle, 1981.

Smith, Derek George. See No./Voir no 625

497
Spaulding, Philip Taft. "The Métis of Île-à-La-Crosse." Washington, Seattle, 1970. [Saskatchewan]

Algonquian Linguistic Family/ Famille linguistique algonquienne

General Item/Ouvrage général

498
Bailey, Alfred Goldsworthy. "The Conflict of European and East Algonkian Cultures, 1504-1700: A Study in Canadian Civilization." Toronto, 1934.

Algonquin/Algonquins

499
Black, Meredith Jean. "Algonquin Ethnobotany; An Interpretation of Aboriginal Adaptation in Southwestern Quebec." Michigan, 1973.

500
Callender, Charles. "Central Algonkian Social Organization." Chicago, 1958.

501
Flannery Regina. "An Analysis of Coastal Algonquian Culture." Catholic, 1938.

Blackfoot/Pieds-Noirs

502
Fisher, Anthony Dwight. "The Perception of Instrumental Values Among the Young Blood Indians of Alberta." Stanford, 1966.

503
Lewis, Oscar. "The Effects of White Contact upon Blackfoot Culture with Special Reference to the Role of the Fur Trade." Columbia, 1942.

504
Parry, Keith William John. " 'To Raise These People Up': An Examination of a Mormon Mission to an Indian Community as an Agent of Social Change." Rochester, 1972. [Blood Indian Reserve/Réserve des Indiens du Sang, Alberta]

Chippewa (See also/Voir aussi Ojibwai)
Saulteux

505
Bishop, Charles Aldrich. "The Northern Chippewa: Ethnohistorical Study." SUNY, Buffalo, 1969.

506
Christie, Thomas Laird. "Reserve Colonialism and Sociocultural Change." Toronto, 1976. [Southern Ontario, Indian Reserve Community/Sud de l'Ontario, communauté de la réserve indienne]

507
Friedl, Ernestine. "An Attempt at Directed Culture Change: Leadership Among the Chippewa, 1640-1948." Columbia, 1950.

Cree/Cris

Barger, Walter Kenneth. See No./Voir no 583

508
Feit, Harvey Allan. "Waswanipi Realities and Adaptations: Resource Management and Cognitive Structure." McGill, 1979.

509
Hoffmann, Hans. "Assessment of Cultural Homogeneity Among the James Bay Cree." Yale, 1957.

510
Mandelbaum, David Goodman. "Changes in an Aboriginal Culture Following a Change in Environment as Exemplified by the Plains Cree." Yale, 1936.

511
Meyer, David Alexander. "The Red Earth Crees and the Marriage Isolate, 1860-1960." McMaster, 1982. [Saskatchewan].

512
Morantz, Toby Elaine. "The Impact of the Fur Trade on Eighteenth and Nineteenth Century Algonquian Social Organization: An Ethnographic Ethnohistoric Study of the Eastern James Bay Cree from 1700-1850." Toronto, 1981.

513
Preston, Richard Joseph, III. "Cree Narration: An Expression of the Personal Meanings of Events." North Carolina, 1971.

514
Scott, Colin H. "The Semiotics of Material Life Among Wemindji Cree Hunters." McGill, 1983.

Sieciechowicz, Krystynaz. See No./Voir no 427

515
Sikand, Jagpal Singh. "Acculturation and Psychological Stress among the Northern Cree and Saulteaux of Manitoba with Reference to Group Identification and Differentation." Regina, 1980.

Smith, Derek George. See No./Voir no 625

Stewart, Donald Alexander, Jr. See No./Voir no 445

516
Trudeau, Jean. "Culture Change among the Swampy Cree Indians of Winisk, Ontario." Catholic, 1966.

517
Urion, Carl Armand. "Control of Topic in a Bilingual (Cree-English) Speech Event." Alberta, 1978.

518
Winterhalder, Bruce Paul. "Foraging Strategy Adaptations of the Boreal Forest Cree." Cornell, 1977. [Northern Ontario/Nord de l'Ontario]

Malecite/Malécites

519
Mechling, William Hubbs. "The Social and Religious Life of the Malecites and Micmacs." Harvard, 1917.

Micmac/Micmacs

520
Bock, Philip Karl. "The Social Structure of a Canadian Indian Reserve." Harvard, 1963.

521
Fidelholtz, James Lawrence. "Micmac Morphophonemics." Massachusetts Institute of Technology, 1968.

522
Gonzalez, Ellice Becker. "The Changing Economic Roles of Micmac Men and Women: An Ethnohistorical Analysis." SUNY, Stony Brook, 1979.

Guillemin, Jeanne E. See No./Voir no 832

523
Hoffman, Bernard Gilbert. "The Historical Ethnography of the Micmac of the Sixteenth and Seventeenth Centuries." California, Berkeley, 1955.

524
McGee, Harold Franklin, Jr. "Ethnic Boundaries and Strategies of Ethnic Interaction: A History of Micmac – White Relations in Nova Scotia." Southern Illinois, 1974.

Mechling, William Hubbs. See No./Voir no 519

Moore, Dorothy Emma. See No./Voir no 9980

525
Nietfeld, Patricia Kathleen Linskey. "Determinants of Aboriginal Micmac Political Structure." New Mexico, 1981.

Trudel, François. See No./Voir no 629

526
Van Horn, Lawrence Franklin. "Differential Language Use at Burnt Church, a Bilingual Micmac Indian Community of Eastern Canada." CUNY, 1977. [New Brunswick/Nouveau-Brunswick]

Mississauga/Mississaugas

Chamberlain, Alexander Francis. See No./Voir no 7794

527
Smith, Donald Boyd. "The Mississauga, Peter Jones and the White Man: The Algonkians' Adjustment to the Europeans on the North Shore of Lake Ontario to 1860." Toronto, 1975.

Montagnais

528
Barriault, Yvette. "Mythes et rites chez les Montagnais de la Côte Nord." Ottawa, 1970.

529
Leacock, Eleanor Burke. "The Montagnais 'Hunting Territory' and the Fur Trade." Columbia, 1953.

530
McGee, John Thomas. "Cultural Stability and Change Among the Montagnais Indians of the Lake Melville Region of Labrador." Catholic, 1962.

Trudel, François. See No./Voir no 629

Naskapi/Naskapis

Ballad, Charles Guthrie. See No./Voir no 8320

531
Robbins, Richard Howard. "Drinking Behavior and Identity Resolution." North Carolina, 1970. [Quebec/Québec]

Trudel, François. See No./Voir no 629

Ojibwa (See also/Voir aussi Chippewa)

532
Boggs, Stephen Taylor. "Ojibwa Socialization: Some Aspects of Parent-Child Interaction in a Changing Culture." Washington, St. Louis, 1955.

Callender, Charles. See No./Voir no 500

533
Dunning, Robert William. "Social and Economic Change Among the Northern Ojibwa (Canada) with Special Reference to Kinship and Marriage." Cambridge, 1957.

534
Echlin, Kimberly Ann. "The Translation of Ojibwa: The Nanabush Myths." York, 1982.

535
Graham, Elizabeth Jane. "Strategies and Souls." Toronto, 1973. [South Ontario/Sud de l'Ontario]

536
Greenberg, Adolph Morris. "Adaptive Responses by an Ojibway Band to Northern Development." Wayne State, 1978. [Loon Lake Ojibwa/Lac Ojibwa, Ontario]

537
Grim, John Allen. "The Shaman: An Interpretation of the Religious Personality Based on Ethnographic Data from the Siberian Tribes and the Woodland Ojibway of North America." Fordham, 1980.

538
Hay, Thomas Hamilton. "Ojibwa Emotional Restraint and the Socialization Process." Michigan State, 1968. [Manitoba]

539
Hedican, Edward James. "Transaction and Exchange Dynamics in a Northern Ojibway Village: A Microtheoretical Approach to Political Development and Economic Change." McGill, 1978.

540
Landes, Ruth. "Ojibwa Sociology." Columbia, 1937.

541
Mortimore, Richard George Ernest. "The Road to Eagle Bay: Structure, Process and Power in a Highly Acculturated Ojibwa Band." Toronto, 1975.

Sieciechowicz, Krystyna. See No./Voir no 427

542
Smith, James G.E. "Kindred, Clan and Conflict: Continuity and Change Among the Southwestern Ojibwa." Chicago, 1974.

543
Szathmary, Emoke Jolan Erzsebet. "Genetic Studies on Two Ontario Ojibwa Indian Communities." Toronto, 1974.

544
Vecsey, Christopher Thomas. "Traditional Ojibwa Religion and Its Historical Changes." Northwestern, 1977.

545
Vennum, Thomas. "Southwestern Ojibwa Music." Harvard, 1975.

Windigo

546
Marano, Louis Anthony. "Windigo Psychosis: The Anatomy of an EMIC-ETIC Confusion." Florida, 1981.

547
Teicher, Morton Irving. "Windigo Psychosis: A Study of Relationship Between Belief and Behaviour Among the Indians of Northwestern Canada." Toronto, 1956.

Athapaskan Linguistic Family/ Famille linguistique athapaskane

General Items/Ouvrages généraux

548
Duncan, Kate Corbin. "Bead Embroidery of the Northern Athapaskans: Style, Design, Evolution and Transfer." Washington, Seattle, 1982.

James, Robert W. See No./Voir no 2331

549
Libby, Dorothy Lee Rainier. "Girls Puberty Observances Among Northern Athabascans." California, Berkeley, 1952.

550
MacNeish, June H. "The Lynx Point People: A Northern Athabascan Band." Chicago, 1959.

McKennan, Robert Addison. See No./Voir no 616

551
Milan, Frederick Arthur. "An Experimental Study of Thermoregulation in Two Arctic Races." Wisconsin, 1963.

552
Mishler, Craig Wallace. "Gwich'in Athapaskan Music and Dance: An Ethnography and Ethnohistory." Texas, 1981. [Northwestern Canada/Nord-ouest du Canada]

553
Rushforth, Everett Scott. "Kinship and Social Organization Among the Great Bear Lake Indians: A Cultural Decision-Making Model." Arizona, 1977. [Northwest Territories/Territoires du Nord-Ouest]

Tsuchiyama, Tamie. See No./Voir no 8334

554
Yerbury, John Collin. "The Social Organization of the Subarctic Athapaskan Indians: An Ethnohistorical Reconstruction." Simon Fraser, 1980.

Beaver/Castors

555
Mills, Antonia Curtze. "The Beaver Indian Prophet Dance and Related Movements Among North American Indians." Harvard, 1982.

556
Ridington, William Robbins, Jr. "The Environmental Context of Beaver Indian Behavior." Harvard, 1968.

Carrier

557
Goldman, Irving. "The Alkatcho Carrier: Historical Background of Crest Prerogatives." Columbia, 1941.

558
Kobrinsky, Vernon Harris. "Ethnohistory and Ceremonial Representation of Carrier Social Structure." British Columbia, 1973.

559
MacDonald, Joseph Lorne. "A Study of Stress in the Social Structure of the Moricetown Indians as a Factor in Reserve Housing Development." Brandeis, 1967. [Hwitsiwaten of British Columbia/Hwitsiwaten de la Colombie-Britannique]

560
Munro, John B. "Language, Legends and Lore of the Carrier Indians." Ottawa, 1945.

Chilcotin/Chilcotins

561
Lane, Robert Brockstedt. "Cultural Relations of the Chilcotin Indians of West Central British Columbia." Washington, Seattle, 1953.

Chipewyan

Carter, Robin Michael. See No./Voir no 7802

562
Irimoto, Tokashi. "Ecological Anthropology of the Caribou – Eater Chipewyan on the Woolaston Lake Region of Northern Saskatchewan." Simon Fraser, 1980.

563
Jarvenpa, Robert Warren. "The People of Patuanak: The Ecology and Spatial Organization of a Southern Chipewyan Band." Minnesota, 1975. [Saskatchewan]

564
Koolage, William W., Jr. "Adaptation of Chipewyan Indians and Other Persons of Native Background in Churchill, Manitoba." North Carolina, 1971.

565
Sharp, Henry Stephen. "The Kinship System of the Black Lake Chipewyan." Duke, 1973.

566
South, David Merrill. "Fort Resolution People: An Historical Study of Ecological Change." Minnesota, 1975.

Déné/Dénés

Dyer, Aldrich James. See No./Voir no 596

567
Osgood, Conelius Berrien. "The Ethnology of the Northern Déné." Chicago, 1930.

568
Singer, Charles. "Constraint and Buffering in Communal Survival with Special Reference to the Déné." Toronto, 1980. [NWT/Territoires du Nord-Ouest]

Wahn, Michael Brian. See No./Voir no 1194

Yerbury, John Collin. See No./Voir no 554

Dogrib/Flanc-de-Chien

569
Schmidt, Richard Conrad. "The Integration of Subsistence Life in a Broader Socio-Economic System: A Subarctic Community." Toronto, 1971.

Hare/Lièvres

570
Durgin, Edward Charles. "Brewing and Boozing: A Study of Drinking Patterns Among the Hare Indians." Oregon, 1974. [Northwest Territories/Territoires du Nord-Ouest]

571
Savishinsky, Joel Stephen. "Stress and Mobility in an Arctic Community: The Hare Indians of Colville Lake, Northwest Territories." Cornell, 1970.

572
Sue, Hiroko. "Ethnography of the Hare Indians, Northwest Territories, Canada." Bryn Mawr, 1964.

Kasini/Kasinis

573
McDonnell, Roger Francis. "Kasini Society: Some Aspects of the Social Organization of an Athapaskan Culture Between 1900-1950." British Columbia, 1975. [Yukon]

Kutchin/Kutchins

574
Acheson, Ann Welsh. "Nomads in Town: The Kutchin of Old Crow, Yukon Territory." Cornell, 1977.

575
Hadleigh-West, Frederick. "The Netsi Kutchin: An Essay in Human Ecology." Louisiana State, 1963.

576
Legros, Dominique. "Structure socio-culturelle et rapports de domination chez les Indiens Tutchone septentrionaux du Yukon au dix-neuvième siècle." Colombie-Britannique, 1981.

577
Roth, Eric Abella. "Historic Demography and Population Structure of a Subarctic Isolate: Old Crow Village, Yukon Territory." Toronto, 1980.

578
Slobodin, Richard. "Band Organization of the Peel River Kutchin." Columbia, 1959.

Slavery/Esclaves

579
Asch, Michael Ira. "A Social Behavioral Approach to Music Analysis: The Case of the Slavey Drum Dance." Columbia, 1972. [Northwest Territories/Territoires du Nord-Ouest]

Inuit Linguistic Family/Famille linguistique inuite

Eskimo Bands/Bandes esquimaudes

580
Andrade, James Edward. "The Economic, Social and Cosmological Dimensions of the Preoccupation with Short-Term Ends in Three Hunting and Gathering Societies: The Mibuti Pygmies of Zaire, the Kung San of Namibia and Botswana and the Netsilik Eskimos of Northern Canada." London, 1980.

581
Arima, Eugene Yuji. "A Contextual Study of the Caribou Eskimo Kayak." Toronto, 1972. [Northwest Territories/Territoires du Nord-Ouest]

582
Balikci, Asen. "Development of Basic Socio-Economic Units in Two Eskimo Communities." Columbia, 1962. [Netsilik and/et Povungnituk]

583
Barger, Walter Kenneth. "Great Whale River: Integration and Adjustment in the Canadian North." North Carolina, 1974.

584
Ben-Dor, Shmuel. "Eskimos and Settlers in a Labrador Community." Memorial, 1966.

585
Blake, Elizabeth Anarye. "Negotiating Health and Illness: An Inuit Example." Alberta, 1978.

586
Briggs, Jean Louise. "Utkuhiksalingmiut Eskimo Emotional Expression: The Patterning of Affection and Hostility." Harvard, 1967. [Northwest Territories/Territoires du Nord-Ouest]

587
Buchler, Ira Richard. "A Formal Theory of Kinship Reckoning." Pittsburgh, 1964.

588
Burch, Ernest S., Jr. "Authority, Aid, and Affection: The Structure of Eskimo Kin Relationships." Chicago, 1966.

589
Caron, André-H. "Television in the North: Its Effect on the Cultural 'Images' Inuit Children Have of Their Own and Other Groups." Harvard, 1976.

590
Cavanagh, Beverley Anne. "Music of the Netsilik Eskimo: A Study of Stability and Change." Toronto, 1979.

591
Charron, Claude-Yves. "Quelques mythes et récits de tradition orale inuite: essai d'analyse semi-culturelle." Montréal, 1977.

592
Condon, Richard Guy. "Inuit Behavior and Seasonal Change: A Study of Behavioral Ecology in the Central Canadian Arctic." Pittsburgh, 1981.

593
Coperthwaite, William Sherman. "A Travelling Museum of Eskimo Culture." Harvard, 1972.

594
Damas, David. "The Structure of Igluligmiut: Local Groupings." Chicago, 1962. [Northwest Territories/Territoires du Nord-Ouest]

Dekin, Albert Arch, Jr. See No./Voir no 889

De Laguna, Frederica Annis. See No./Voir no 952

595
Doyle, William John. "A Functions-Anatomic Description of Eustachian Tribe Vector Relations in Four Ethnic Populations: An Osteologic Study." Pittsburgh, 1977. [Black, Caucasian, Eskimo and American Indian/Noirs, Caucasiens, Esquimaux et Indiens de l'Amérique]

596
Dyer, Aldrich James. "Images of Inuit and Déné Dramatic personae Portrayed in the Journals of Expeditions to the Northwest Territories Area Prior to 1880." Alberta, 1980.

597
Ekblaw, Walter Elmer. "The Material Response of the Polar Eskimo to Their Far Arctic Environment." Clark, 1926.

598
Ellis, Robert Sydney. "The Attitude Toward Death and the Types of Belief in Immortality; A Study in the Psychology of Religion." Clark, 1914.

599
Essene, Frank J., Jr. "A Comparative Study of Eskimo Mythology." California, Berkeley, 1947.

600
Findlay, Marjorie Craven. "The Means of Improving the Economic Situation of the Ungava Bay Eskimos." McGill, 1956.

601
Gilbertson, Albert Nicolay. "Some Ethical Phases of Eskimo Culture." Clark, 1913.

602
Glassford, Robert Gerald. "Application of a Theory of Games to the Transitional Eskimo Culture." Illinois, 1970. [Mackenzie River/Rivière Mackenzie]

Graburn, Nelson H. See No./Voir no 7833

603
Guemple, Donald Lee. "Kinship Reckoning Among the Belcher Island Eskimo." Chicago, 1966.

604
Harp, Elmer, Jr. "The Cultural Affinities of the Newfoundland Dorset Eskimo." Harvard, 1953.

605
Heinrich, Albert C. "Eskimo Type Kinship and Eskimo Kinship: An Evaluation and a Provisional Model for Presenting Data Pertaining to Inupiaq Kinship Systems." Washington, Seattle, 1964.

606
Hoag, Peter Lochrie. "Acculturating Eskimo Arts: The Diffusion of Government Sponsored Production Facilities in Alaska and Canada." Michigan, 1981. [Quebec Eskimo region/Région esquimaude du Québec]

607
Hodgkins, Gael Atherton. "The Sea Spirit of the Central Eskimo: Mistress of Sea Animals and Supreme Deity." Chicago, 1977.

608
Hylander, William Leroy. "The Adaptive Significance of Eskimo Cranofacial Morphology." Chicago, 1972.

609
Jansen, William Hugh, II. "Eskimo Economics: An Aspect of Culture Change at Rankin Inlet." Wisconsin, 1975.

610
Jensen, Kenneth Delane. "A Cultural Historical Study of Domination, Exploitation, and Co-operation in the Canadian Arctic." Michigan State, 1975.

Jordan, Richard Heath. See No./Voir no 721

611
Kennedy, John Charles. "Holding the Line: Ethnic Process in a Northern Labrador Community." Michigan State, 1978.

Lester, Geoffrey Standish. See No./Voir no 7839

Loree, Donald James. See No./Voir no 731

612
Matthiasson, John Stephen. "Eskimo Legal Acculturation: The Adjustment of Baffin Island Eskimos to Canadian Law." Cornell, 1967. [Tununermiut]

613
Mayes, Robert Gregory. "The Creation of a Dependent People: The Inuit of Cumberland Sound, Northwest Territories." McGill, 1978.

Massenet, Jean-Marie. See No./Voir no 7834

614
Mayhall, John T. "The Morphology of the Permanent Dentition of Prehistoric and Modern Central Arctic Eskimoid Peoples: A Study of Their Biological Relationships." Chicago, 1977.

615
McElroy, Ann Pulver. "Modernization and Cultural Identities: Baffin Island Inuit Strategies of Adaptation." North Carolina, 1973.

616
McKennan, Robert Addison. "Indians of the Upper Tanana, Alaska." Harvard, 1933. [Comparison with Canadian Counterparts - Athabaskan and Eskimo/Comparaison avec les contreparties canadiennes - Athapaskanes et Esquimaux]

617
Merbs, Charles Francis. "Patterns of Activity - Induced Pathology in Canadian Eskimo Isolate." Wisconsin, 1969. [Sadlermiut - Northwest Territories/Territoires du Nord-Ouest]

Minor, N. Kathleen Mary. See No./Voir no 4167

618
Nusbaum, D. "Cold: Its Demands and Suggestions: A Study of the Importance of Environment in the Development of Eskimo Culture." Oxford, 1939.

619
Poole, Peter. "Conservation and Inuit Hunting, Conflict or Compatibility." McGill, 1981.

620
Riches, D.J. "A Study of Social Change Amongst the Killinirngmiut Eskimos of Canada's East Arctic." London, 1975.

621
Richling, Barnett Edward. "Hard Times Them Times: An Interpretive Ethnohistory of Inuit and Settlers in the Hopedale District of Northern Labrador, 1752-1977." McGill 1979.

622
Rode, Andris. "Some Factors Influencing the Fitness of a Small Eskimo Community." Toronto, 1972.

623
Russell, Frank. "A Study of a Collection of Eskimo Crania from Labrador with Observations on the Prevailing System of Craniometry." Harvard, 1898.

624
Simard, Jean-Jacques. "La révolution congelée: coopération et développement au Nouveau-Québec Inuit." Laval, 1983.

625
Smith, Derek George. "Natives and Outsiders: Pluralism in the Mackenzie River Delta, Northwest Territories, Canada." Harvard, 1972.

626
Smith, Eric Alden. "Evolutionary Ecology and the Analysis of Human Foraging Behavior: An Inuit Example from the East Coast of Hudson Bay." Cornell, 1980.

627
Stevenson, David. "The Social Organization of the Clyde Inlet Eskimos." British Columbia, 1972. [Northeast Baffin Island/Nord-est de l'Île de Baffin]

628
Taylor, James Garth. "An Analysis of the Size of Eskimo Settlements on the Coast of Labrador During the Early Contact Period." Toronto, 1968.
629
Trudel, François. "Inuit, Amerindians and Europeans: A Study of Interethnic Economic Relations in the Canadian Southeastern Seaboard (1500-1800)." Connecticut, 1981.

Valaskakis, Gail Guthrie. See No./Voir no 1054

Wahn, Michael Brian. See No./Voir no 1194
630
Way, Jacob Edson, III. "An Osteological Analysis of a Late Thule: Early Historic Labrador Eskimo Population." Toronto, 1978.
631
Wells, James Ralph. "The Origin of Immunity to Diphtheria in Isolated Communities of Polar Eskimos." Washington, St. Louis, 1932.
632
Wenzel, George William. "Social Organization as an Adaptive Referent in Inuit Cultural Ecology: The Case of Clyde River and Aqvigtiuk." McGill, 1980.
633
Weyer, Edward Moffat, Jr. "The Eskimos: A Study in Adaptation to Environment." Yale, 1930.
634
Wiget, Andrew O. "The Oral Literature of Native North America: A Critical Anthology." Utah, 1977.
635
Zegura, Stephen Luke. "A Multivariate Analysis of the Inter - and Intra - Population Variation Exhibited by Eskimo Crania." Wisconsin, 1971.

Haida Linguistic Family/Famille linguistique haida

Anker, Daniel Ezra. See No./Voir no 7804
636
Blackman, Margaret Berlin. "The Northern and Kaigani Haida: A Study in Photographic Ethnohistory." Ohio State, 1973.
637
Henderson, John R. "Haida Culture Change: A Geographical Analysis." Michigan State, 1972.
638
Kaufmann, Carole Natalie. "Changes in Haida Indian Argillite Carvings, 1820 to 1910." California, Los Angeles, 1969.
639
Stearns, Mary Lee. "Culture in Custody: Adaptation in a Canadian Indian Community." California, Los Angeles, 1973.

Iroquoian Linguistic Family/ Famille linguistique iroquoise

Huron/Hurons

640
Anderson, Karen Lee. "Huron Women and Huron Men: The Effect of Demography, Kinship and the Social Division of Labour on Male/Female Relations Among the 17th Century Huron." Toronto, 1982.

641
Jerkic, Sonja Maria. "An Analysis of Huron Skeletal Biology and Mortuary Practices: The Maurice Ossuary." Toronto, 1975.
642
Ramsden, Peter George. "A Refinement of Some Aspects of Huron Ceramic Analysis." Toronto, 1975.

Iroquois

643
Bradley, James Wesley. "The Onondaga Iroquois: 1500-1655; A Study in Acculturative Change and Its Consequences." Syracuse, 1979.
644
Carpenter, Edmund Snow. "Intermediate Period Influences in the Northeast." Pennsylvania, 1950.
645
Foley, Denis. "An Ethnohistoric and Ethnographic Analysis of the Iroquois from the Aboriginal Era to the Present Suburban Era." SUNY, Albany, 1975.
646
Foster, Michael Kirk. "From the Earth to Beyond the Sky: An Ethnographic Approach to Four Longhouse Iroquois Speech Events." Pennsylvania, 1974. [Ontario]
647
Herrick, James William. "Iroquois Medical Botany." SUNY, Albany, 1977.
648
Kapches, Mima Cora Grant Brown. "The Middleport Pattern in Ontario Iroquois Prehistory." Toronto, 1981.
649
Krieg, Robert Edward. "Forest Theatre: A Study of the Six Nations Pageant Plays in the Grand River Reserve." Western Ontario, 1978.

Latta, Martha Ann. See No./Voir no 916

Mulvey, Mary Doris. See No./Voir no 6980
650
Noble, William Charles. "Iroquois Archaeology and the Development of Iroquois Social Organization (1100-1650 A.D.): A Study in Culture Change Based on Archaeology, Ethnohistory and Ethnology." Calgary, 1968.
651
Noon, John Alfred. "The League of the Iroquois on the Grand River: An Acculturation Study in Government and Law." Pennsylvania, 1943.

Reynolds, Wynn Robert. See No./Voir no 7441
652
St.John, Donald Patrick. "The Dream-Vision Experience of the Iroquois: Its Religious Meaning." Fordham, 1981.
653
Scheele, Raymond. "Warfare of the Iroquois and Their Northern Neighbors (Hurons, Algonquins, and Montagnais)." Columbia, 1950.
654
Selden, Sherman Ward. "The Legend, Myth and Code of Deganaweda and Their Significance to Iroquois Cultural History." Indiana, 1966.

655
Snyderman, George S. "Behind the Tree of Peace: A Sociological Analysis of Iroquois Warfare." Pennsylvania, 1949.

656
Stites, Sara Henry. "The Economics of the Iroquois." Bryn Mawr, 1904.

657
Strawn, Robertson L. "Public Speaking in the Iroquois League." Michigan, 1941.

658
Weaver, Sally Mae. "Health, Culture and Dilemma: A Study of the Non-Conservative Iroquois, Six Nations Reserve, Ontario." Toronto, 1967.

659
Weber, Joann Cynthia. "Types and Attributes in the Study of Iroquois Pipes." Harvard, 1970.

660
Webster, Gary Stewart. "Northern Iroquoian Hunting: An Optimization Approach." Pennsylvania State, 1983.

661
Wolf, Morris. "Iroquois Religion and Its Relation to Their Morals." Columbia, 1919.

662
Wright, James Valliere. "The Ontario Iroquois Tradition." Wisconsin, 1964.

Mohawk/Mohawks

Bonvillain, Nancy Lee. See No./Voir no 7812

663
Frisch, Jack Aaron. "Revitalization, Nativism and Tribalism among the St. Regis Mohawks." Indiana, 1970.

664
Hamori-Torok, Charles. "The Acculturation of the Mohawks of the Bay of Quinte." Toronto, 1966.

665
Katzer, Bruce. "The Caughnawaga Mohawks: Occupations, Residence, and the Maintenance of Community Membership." Columbia, 1972.

666
Mathur, Mary Elaine. "The Iroquois in Time and Space: A Native American Nationalistic Movement." Wisconsin, 1971. [St. Regis Mohawks in New York, Ontario and Quebec/Mohawks de St-Regis à New York, en Ontario et au Québec]

Postal, Paul M. See No./Voir no 7814

Oneida/Oneidas

667
Campisi, Jack. "Ethnic Identity and Boundary Maintenance in Three Oneida Communities." SUNY, Albany, 1974.

668
Ricciardelli, Alex Frank. "Factionalism at Oneida, an Iroquois Indian Community." Pennsylvania, 1961. [Ontario]

669
Ricciardelli, Catherine Hinckle. "Kinship Systems of the Oneida Indians." Pennsylvania, 1966.

Kootenayan Linguistic Family/ Famille linguistique kootenayenne

Kootenay

670
Brunton, Bill Biozz. "The Stick Game in Kutenai Culture." Washington State, 1974.

Garvin, Paul Lucian. See No./Voir no 7801

671
Schaeffer, Claude Everett. "The Subsistence Quest of the Kutenai: A Study of the Interaction of Culture and Environment." Pennsylvania, 1940.

Salishan Linguistic Family/ Famille linguistique salishane

General Items/Ouvrages généraux

672
Bell, Joy Florence. "Rock Art of the Coast Salish Territory: An Analysis of Style, Form and Function." Washington, Seattle, 1982.

673
Ham, Leonard Charles. "Seasonality, Shell Midden Layers, and Coast Salish Subsistence Activities at the Crescent Beach Site Dg Rr 1." British Columbia, 1983.

674
Holden, Madronna. "The Myth of Dokwebal: A Dialogue in the Sense of History." New School for Social Research, 1974.

675
Kew, John Edward Michael. "Coast Salish Ceremonial Life: Status and Identity in a Modern Village." Washington, Seattle, 1970.

676
Levy, Richard Stephen. "A Cross-Cultural Assessment of Similarities in Interior Salish Myth Contest." British Columbia, 1974.

677
Lewis, Claudia Louise. "A Study of the Impact of Modern Life on a Canadian Indian Band." Columbia, 1959.

678
Mitchell, Marjorie Ruth. "Women, Poverty, and Housing: Some Consequences of Hinterland Status for a Coast Salish Indian Reserve in Metropolitan Canada." British Columbia, 1976.

679
Robinson, Sarah Ann. "Spirit Dancing Among the Salish Indians of Vancouver Island, British Columbia." Chicago, 1963.

680
Suttles, Wayne. "Economic Life of the Coast Salish of Haro and Rosario Straits." Washington, Seattle, 1951.

681
Wingert, Paul Stover. "American Indian Sculpture: A Study of the Northwest Coast." Columbia, 1949. [Salish]

Cowichan/Cowichans

682
Lane, Barbara Savadkin. "A Comparative and Analytic Study of Some Aspects of Northwest Coast Religion (Cowichan Indians of Southern British Columbia)." Washington, Seattle, 1953.

Squamish/Squamishs

683
Ryan, Joan. "Squamish Socialization." British Columbia, 1973. [Capilano Reserve/Réserve Capilano]

Siouan Linguistic Family/ Famille linguistique siouenne

Dakota/Dakotas

684
Corrigan, Samuel Walter. "Politics and Social Structure in a Canadian Dakota Band: A Study of the Formation of Political Groups Amongst the Standing Buffalo Dakota." Cambridge, 1970.

Tlingit Linguistic Family/Famille linguistique tlingite

Durlach, Theresa Mayer. See No./Voir no 686

Tsimshian Linguistic Family/ Famille linguistique tsimshiane

Niska/Nishgas

685
McNeary, Stephen A. "Where Fire Came Down: Social and Economic Life of the Niska." Bryn Mawr, 1976.

Tsimshian/Tsimshians

Dunn, John Asher. See No./Voir no 7829
686
Durlach, Theresa Mayer. "The Relationship Systems of the Tlingit, Haida and Tsimshian." Columbia, 1929.
687
Garfield, Viola Edmundson. "Tsimshian Clan and Society." Columbia, 1939.
688
Halpin, Marjorie Myers. "The Tsimshian Crest System: A Study Based on Museum Specimens and the Marius Barbeau and William Beynon Field Notes." British Columbia, 1973.

Wakashan Linguistic Family/ Famille linguistique wakashane

Haisla/Haislas

689
Pritchard, John Charles. "Economic Development and the Disintegration of Traditional Culture among the Haisla." British Columbia, 1977.

Kwakiutl

690
Aycock, Daniel Alan. "Property, Patrons and Risk: The Exploitation of Human Labor in General Evolutionary Perspective." Toronto, 1974.
Barnett, Homer Garner. See No./Voir no 377
691
Codere, Helen Frances. "Fighting with Property: A Study of Kwakiutl Potlatching and Warfare, 1792-1930." Columbia, 1950.
Grigsby, Jefferson Eugene, Jr. See No./Voir no 953
692
Michaelson, David Rubin. "From Ethnography to Ethnology: A Study of the Conflict of Interpretations of the Southern Kwakiutl Potlatch." New School for Social Research, 1980.
693
Reid, Katerina Susanne. "The Origins of the Tsetseqa in the Baxus: A Study of Kwakiutl Prayers, Myths and Ritual." British Columbia, 1976.
694
Reid, Martine Jeanne. "La cérémonie Hamatsa des Kwagul: approche structuraliste des rapports mythe-rituel." Colombie-Britannique, 1981.
695
Rohner, Ronald Preston. "Ethnography of a Contemporary Kwakiutl Village: Gilford Island Band." Stanford, 1964.
696
Sommer, Frank Henry, III. "Kwakiutl Iconography." Yale, 1950.
697
Spradley, James Phillips. "James Sewid: A Social Cultural and Psychological Analysis of a Bicultural Innovator." Washington, Seattle, 1967.
698
Wallens, Stanley Gerald. "Metaphor and Morality in a Nineteenth Century Kwakiutl Culture." Northwestern, 1977.
699
Wolcott, Harry Fletcher. "A Kwakiutl Village and Its School: Cultural Barriers to Classroom Performance." Stanford, 1964.

Nootka/Nootkas

700
Kenyon, Susan Mary. "The Kyuquot Way: A Study of a West Coast (Nootkan) Community." Bryn Mawr, 1977.
701
Moore, Turrall Adcock. "The Emergence of Ethnic Roles and the Beginning of Nootkan Native Overseas European Relations, 1774-1789." Oregon, 1977.
Swadesh, Morris. See No./Voir no 7831

Other Bands/Autres groupes

Clayoquot/Clayoquots

702
Koppert, Vincent Aloysius. "Contributions to Clayoquot Ethnology." Catholic, 1930. [Nootka Tribe of Vancouver Island]

Itama/Itamas

703
Irwin, Henry Thomas Johnson. "The Itama: Late Pleistocene Inhabitants of the Plains of the United States and Canada and the American Southwest." Harvard, 1968.

Kaska/Kaskas

704
Honigmann, John Joseph. "Kaska Ethos: A Study in Methodology." Yale, 1946.

Mistassini/Mistassinis

705
Rogers, Edward S. "Mistassini Hunting Groups and Hunting Territories." New Mexico, 1958. [Quebec/Québec]

706
Tanner, Adrian. "Bringing Home Animals: Religious Ideology and Mode of Production of the Mistassini Cree Hunters." Toronto, 1976.

Stoney/Assiniboines

707
Andersen, Raoul Randall. "An Inquiry into the Political and Economic Structure of the Alexis Band of Wood Stoney Indians, 1880-1964." Missouri, 1968. [Alberta]

708
Notzke, Claudia. "The Development of Canadian Indian Reserves: As Illustrated by the Example of the Stoney and Peigan Reserves." Calgary, 1982.

Wabanaki/Wabanakis

709
Morrison, Alvin Hamblen. "Dawnland Decisions: Seventeenth-Century Wabanaki Leaders and Their Responses to the Differential Contact Stimuli in the Overlap Area of New France and New England." SUNY, Buffalo, 1974.

INDIANS IN THE REGIONAL STUDIES/ INDIENS DES PROVINCES ET DES RÉGIONS

Western Canada/Ouest du Canada

710
Braroe, Neils Winther. "Change and Identity: Patterns of Interaction in an Indian-White Community." Illinois, 1970.
Vastokas, Joan Marie. See No./Voir no 489

Alberta

Beaujot, Roderic Paul. See No./Voir no 374
711
Gue, Leslie Robb. "A Comparative Study of Value Orientations in an Alberta Indian Community." Alberta, 1967.

British Columbia/Colombie-Britannique

712
Cybulski, Jerome Stanley. "Skeletal Variability in British Columbia Coastal Populations: A Descriptive and Comparative Assessment of Cranial Morphology." Toronto, 1973.

713
Daywalt, William E. "A Critical Study of Contemporary Mexican Indian Pottery." California, Los Angeles, 1948. [Includes a corollary study of work at Indian reservations in British Columbia/Inclus une étude corollaire du travail dans des réserves indiennes en Colombie-Britannique]

714
Finnegan, Michael John. "Population Definition on the Northwest Coast by Analysis of Discrete Character Variation." Colorado, 1972.

715
Jones, Joan Megan. "Northwest Coast Indian Basketry: A Stylistic Analysis." Washington, Seattle, 1976.

716
Mills, John Edwin. "The Ethnohistory of Nootka Sound, Vancouver Island." Washington, Seattle, 1955.

717
Shankel, George Edgar. "The Development of Indian Policy in British Columbia." Washington, Seattle, 1945. [1840-1940]

Great Lakes/Grands Lacs

718
Altuna, Linda. "The Distribution of Burial Goods in the Western and Upper Great Lakes Region during Middle Woodland Times." Toronto, 1979.

719
Vastokas, Romas. "Aboriginal Use of Copper in the Great Lakes Area." Columbia, 1970.

720
Yarnell, Richard Asa. "Aboriginal Relationships Between Culture and Plant Life in the Upper Great Lakes Region." Michigan, 1963.

Labrador

721
Jordan, Richard Heath. "Pollen Studies at Hamilton Inlet, Labrador, Canada, and Implications for Environmental Prehistory." Minnesota, 1975.

Nova Scotia/Nouvelle-Écosse

722
Ullman, Stephen Hayes. "Cross-Cultural and Sub-Cultural Variations in Political Socialization: A Study of Caucasian and Indian Canadians." Minnesota, 1973. [Cape Breton Island/Île du Cap Breton]

Ontario

Graham, Elizabeth Jane. See No./Voir no 535
723
Jamieson, Elmer. "The Mental Capacity of Southern Ontario Indians." Toronto, 1928.
724
Molto, Joseph Eldon. "Biological Relationships of Southern Ontario Woodland Peoples: The Evidence of Discontinuous Cranial Morphology." Toronto, 1980.
725
Stothers, David Marvyn. "The Princess Point Complex." Case Western Reserve, 1974.

Prairie Provinces/Provinces des Prairies

726
Dailey, Robert Clifton. "Medical Practices Among the Plains Indians. A Study in Culture Pattern." Toronto, 1957.
727
Kerri, James Nwannukwu. "Urban Native Canadians: The Adjustment of Amerindians to the City of Winnipeg (Canada)." Washington, Seattle, 1973.

Northwest Territories and Yukon/ Territoires du Nord-Ouest et Yukon

728
Fedirchuk, Gloria Joyce. "Functional Analysis of the Julian Technology Fisherman Lake, Northwest Territories." New Mexico, 1975.
729
King, Richard Alfred. "A Case Study of an Indian Residential School." Stanford, 1964.
730
Lambert, Carmen. "Identification et intégration ethnique à l'intérieur d'une ville nordique, White-horse, Yukon." McGill, 1974.
731
Loree, Donald James. "Power and the Marginal Situation: Indian Relations in the Yellowknife-Fort Rae Area of the Northwest Territories." Alberta, 1974.
732
McClellan, Catherine. "Culture Change and Native Trade in Southern Yukon Territory." California, Berkeley, 1950.
Turner, Christy Gentry, II. See No./Voir no 488

Saskatchewan

733
Dosman, Edgar Joseph Edward. "The Urban Dimension of the Indian Problem in Canada." Harvard, 1971.

734
Kehoe, Alice Beck. "The Ghost Dance Religion in Saskatchewan: A Functional Analysis." Harvard, 1964.

CULTURAL AND URBAN ANTHROPOLOGY/ ANTHROPOLOGIE CULTURELLE ET URBAINE

General Items/Ouvrages généraux

Beaujot, Roderic Paul. See No./Voir no 374
Bouchard, Serge. See No./Voir no 433
735
Brien-Dandurand, Renée. "Famille monoparentalé et responsibilité maternelle. Contribution à l'étude des rapports sociaux de sexes." Montréal, 1983.
736
Helling, Rudolf Anton. "A Comparison of the Acculturation of Immigrants in Toronto, Ontario and Detroit, Michigan." Wayne State, 1962.
737
Kliewer, Erich Victor. "Factors Influencing the Life Expectancy of Immigrants in Canada and Australia." British Columbia, 1979.
738
Layton, Monique Jacqueline Berthe. "Street Women and Their Verbal Transactions: Some Aspects of the Oral Culture of Female Prostitute Drug Addicts." British Columbia, 1978.
739
Marchant, Cosmo Kenningham. "A Hierarchy of Rights: Linguistic, Religious, Racial and Ethnic Minorities in Canada." York, 1981.
Morrison, Robert Bruce. See No./Voir no 375
Stymeist, David Harold. See No./Voir no 428

Africans/Africains

740
Moeno, Sylvia Ntlantla. "The 'Non-White' South Africans in Toronto: A Study of the Effects of Institutionalized Apartheid in a Multicultural Society." York, 1981.

African-Asians/Africains-Asiatiques

741
Moudgil, Ranvir. "From Stranger to Refugee: A Study of the Integration of Ugandan Asians in Canada." SUNY, Buffalo, 1977.

Americans/Américains

742
Salsedo, André Joseph. "American Migration to Toronto: Influences on the Motivation to Emigrate." Syracuse, 1975.

Blacks/Noirs

743
Austin, Bobby William. "The Social Status of Blacks in Toronto." McMaster, 1972.
Farrell, John Kevin Anthony. See No./Voir no 7214

744
Hill, Daniel Grafton. "Negroes in Toronto: A Sociological Study of a Minority Group." Toronto, 1960.
Lewis, George Kinsman. See No./Voir no 747
Moore, Dorothy Emma. See No./Voir no 9980
Simpson, Donald George. See No./Voir no 7208

Caribbeans and West Indians/Caraïbes Antillais

745
Akoodie, Mohammed Ally. "Immigrant Students: A Comparative Assessment of Ethnic Identity, Self-Concept and Focus of Control Amongst West Indian, East Indian and Canadian Students." Toronto, 1980.
Assam, Ann Padmore. See No./Voir no 7713
746
Frechette, Errol James. "Attitudes of French and English Speaking Canadians Toward West Indian Immigrants: A Guttman Facet Analysis." Michigan State, 1970.
747
Lewis, George Kinsman. "The Acculturation of Barbados Agriculture Workers in Canada." Ball State, 1975.
748
Ramcharan, Subhas. "The Adaptation of West Indians in Canada." York, 1974.
749
Vuorinen, Saara Sofia. "Ethnic Identification of the Caribbean Immigrants in the Kitchener-Waterloo Area." Waterloo, 1974.

Chinese/Chinois

750
Chow, Wing-Sam. "A Chinese Community in a Prairie City: A Historic Perspective of Its Class and Ethnic Relations." Michigan State, 1981.
751
Fisher, Stephen Frederick. "Changing Patterns of Social Organization Among the Chinese in Ottawa: A Study of Internal and External Determinants." Carleton, 1979.
752
Hoe, Ban Seng. "Structural Changes of Two Chinese Communities in Alberta, Canada." Vanderbilt, 1974.
753
Mandel, Dorothy E. "Aspects of the Adaptive Process in Migration: The Chinese in Canada." United States International, 1982.
754
Smye, Marti Diane. "A Study of the Relationship Between the Proficiency in English and Cultural Background of Chinese Immigrant Students and Their Educational and Social Development." Toronto, 1977.
755
Thompson, Richard Henry. "The State and the Ethnic Community: The Changing Social Organization of Toronto's Chinatown." Michigan, 1979.
756
Yeh, Ming-che. "Canadian vs. Chinese Cross-Cultural Developmental Study of Moral Judgment." Toronto, 1980.

Czechs/Tchèques

757
Adolf, Jacek Zugmunt. "Adaptation of East European Refugees and Political Émigrés in Toronto, with Special Reference to Immigrants from Poland and Czechoslavakia." York, 1977.

Doukhobors

Anderson, Alan Betts. See No./Voir no 418
758
Frantz, Charles Eugene. "The Doukhobor Political System: Social Structure and Social Organization in a Sectarian Society." Chicago, 1959.
759
Hirabayashi, Gordon K. "The Russian Doukhobors of British Columbia: A Study of Social Adjustment of Conflict." Washington, Seattle, 1952.

East Indians/Indiens (Inde)

Akoodie, Mohammed Ally. See No./Voir no 745
760
Buchignani, Norma Leroy. "Immigration, Adaptation and the Management of Ethnic Identity: An Examination of Fijian East Indians in British Columbia." Simon Fraser, 1978.
761
Subramandiam, Indira Anne. "Identity-Shift: Post Migration Changes in the Identity among First Generation East Indian Immigrants in Toronto." Toronto, 1978.

English/Anglais

762
Iutcovich, Mark. "French and English Canadians in 'Milltown': A Pilot Study of the Organizational and Interactional Aspects of a Bicultural and Bilingual Town." Case Western Reserve, 1970.
763
Price, Kenneth Arthur. "The Social Construction of Ethnicity: The Case of English Montrealers." York, 1980.

Europeans/Européens

764
Stearns-Seidner, Anna. "L'intellectuel européen et le problème de son intégration culturelle au Canada." Montréal, 1954.

French Canadians/Canadiens-français

Colman, Rosalie Marson. See No./Voir no 824
Dennis, Herbert Knight. See No./Voir no 825
Deshaies-Lafontaine, D. See No./Voir no 436
Dexter, Robert Cloutman. See No./Voir no 826
Grosmaire, Jean-Louis. See No./Voir no 4760
765
Hautecoeur, Jean-Paul. "L'Acadie: idéologies et société." Laval, 1974.
Hodges, David Julian. See No./Voir no 835
Iutcovitch, Mark. See No./Voir no 762
Kelley, Henry Edward. See No./Voir no 7745

766
Laberge, Suzanne. "Étude de la variation des pronoms sujets définis et indéfinis dans le français parlé à Montréal." Montréal, 1978.

Lamy, Jean-Paul. See No./Voir no 8214

767
MacLean, Annie Marion. "The Acadian Element in the Population of Nova Scotia." Chicago, 1900.

768
Maxwell, Thomas Robert. "The French Population of Metropolitan Toronto: A Study of Ethnic Participation and Ethnic Identity." Toronto, 1971.

McQuillan, David A. See No./Voir no 4850

769
Miner, Horace Mitchell. "St-Denis: A French-Canadian Parish: Changes in Rural French-Canadian Culture" Chicago, 1937.

Mover, Joel Leonard. See No./Voir no 10230

770
Olzak, Susan Maria Grumich. "An Ecological-Competitive Model of the Emergence of Ethnicity: The French-Canadian Example." Stanford, 1978.

771
Robertson, Barbara Mae. "The Socio-Cultural Determiners of French Language Maintenance: The Case of Niagara Falls, Ontario." SUNY, Buffalo, 1980.

772
Ross, Aileen D. "Ethnic Relations and Social Structure: A Study of the Invasion of French Speaking Canadians into an English-Canadian District." Chicago, 1951.

773
Sanderson, Mary Hildegarde. "A Comparative Study of French Canadian Loggers and Their Families." Boston University, 1967.

Santerre, Richard. See No./Voir no 8235

774
Sealy, Nanciellen Davis. "Ethnicity and Ethnic Group Persistence in an Acadian Village in Martime Canada." Southern Illinois, 1975. [Ste. Marie-sur-Mer, New Brunswick/Nouveau-Brunswick]

Stewart, Donald Alexander, Jr.. See No./Voir no 445

Vicero, Ralph Dominic. See No./Voir no 4852

Germans/Allemands

775
Crooks, William R. "The Effectiveness of Culture-Free Tests in Measuring the Intellectual Characteristics of German Immigrants in Canada." Oregon State, 1956.

Currie, Albert Wayne. See No./Voir no 10227

776
Grenke, Arthur. "The Formation and Early Development of an Urban Ethnic Community - A Case Study of the Germans in Winnipeg, 1872-1919." Manitoba, 1975.

Greeks/Grecs

777
Bredimas-Assimopoulos, Constantina. "Relation entre mobilité socio-professionnelle et intégration des immigrants: les grecs de Montréal." Montréal, 1975.

778
Gavaki, Efrosini. "The Integration of Greeks in Canada." Indiana, 1975.

779
Orlowski, Duane Edmund. "Unstable Urban Bilingualism: The Mother Tongue Socialization of the Children of Greek Immigrants in Toronto, Canada." Illinois, 1977.

780
Polyzoi, Eleoussa. "An Examination of the Experience of Immigration: A Movement from a Familiar to a Strange Frame of Reference." Toronto, 1982.

Hutterites/Huttérites

Anderson, Alan Betts. See No./Voir no 418

Baden, John A. See No./Voir no 8695

781
Baum, Ruth Elizabeth. "The Ethnohistory of Law: The Hutterite Case." SUNY, Albany, 1979.

782
Heiken, Diane Ellen Bray. "The Hutterites: A Comparative Analysis of Viability." California, Santa Barbara, 1978.

Mann, George Adolphe. See No./Voir no 10233

783
Peter, Karl Andreas. "Factors of Social Change and Social Dynamics in the Communal Settlements of Hutterites: 1527-1967." Alberta, 1971.

Ryan, John. See No./Voir no 88

784
Serl, Vernon Claude. "Stability and Change in Hutterite Society." Oregon, 1964.

785
Shenker, B. "The Persistence of Intentional Communities: A Comparison of Hutterite Colonies, The Kibbutzim and Therapeutic Communities." London, 1978.

786
Stephenson, Peter Hayford. "A Dying of the Old Man and a Putting on of the New: The Cybernetics of Ritual Metanoia in the Life of the Hutterian Commune." Toronto, 1978.

Indians (Asiatic)/Indiens (Asiatiques)

787
Chadney, James Gaylord. "The Vancouver Sikhs: An Ethnic Community in Canada." Michigan State, 1976.

788
Joy, Annamma. "Accommodation and Cultural Persistence: The Case of the Sikhs and the Portuguese in the Okanogan Valley of British Columbia." British Columbia, 1982.

789
Nasser-Bush, Merun Hussein. "Differential Adjustment Between Two Indian Immigrant Communities in Toronto: Sikhs and Ismailies." Colorado, 1974.

Irish/Irlandais

Mannion, John Joseph. See No./Voir no 4849

790
See, Katherine O'Sullivan. "Toward a Theory of Ethnic Nationalism: A Comparison of Northern Ireland and Quebec." Chicago, 1979.

Italians/Italiens

791
Castelli, Guiseppe. "Étude sur le rôle de l'Église dans l'intégration des immigrés d'origine italienne dans la société montréalaise." Montréal, 1981.

792
Colalillo, Guiliana Giovanna. "Value Structures within Italian Immigrant Families: Continuity or Conflict." Toronto, 1981.

793
Duce, Graciela E. "The Process of Integration of Immigrants: The Case of Italians in Montreal." Montreal, 1977.

794
Ribordy, François-Xavier. "Immigration: conflit de culture et criminalité des Italiens à Montréal." Montréal, 1970.

Weinfeld, Morton Irwin. See No./Voir no 805

Japanese/Japonais

795
Hockin, Margaret L. "A Study of the Process of Acculturation as Revealed in Canadian Japanese Family Life." Cornell, 1950.

796
Makabe, Tomoko. "Ethnic Group Identity: Canadian-Born Japanese in Metropolitan Toronto." Toronto, 1976.

Jews/Juifs

797
Chiel, Arthur A. "Jews in Manitoba." Jewish Theological Seminary of America, 1960.

798
Evans, Kenneth Charles. "The Foreigner: A Study in Semitic Social Relationships." Toronto, 1932.

799
Latowsky, Evelyn Kallen. "Three Toronto Synagogues: A Comparative Study of Religious Systems in Transition." Toronto, 1969.

800
Mastai, Judith Anne F. "Adaptation Tasks of Israeli Immigrants to Vancouver." British Columbia, 1981.

801
Pirie, Margaret Cameron. "Patterns of Mobility and Assimilation: A Study of the Toronto Jewish Community." Yale, 1957.

802
Shaffir, William B.Z. "Life in an Urban Chassidic Community: Insulation and Proselytization." McGill, 1972.

803
Siemens, Gerhard J. "A Study of the Dermatoglyphics of Jewish People of Toronto and Chicago." Toronto, 1947.

804
Speisman, Stephen Alan. "The Jews of Toronto: A History to 1937." Toronto, 1975.

805
Weinfeld, Morton Irwin. "Determinants of Ethnic Identification of Slavs, Jews, and Italians in Toronto." Harvard, 1977.

Zeitz, Mordecai E. See No./Voir no 7274

Mennonites

806
Appavoo, Muthiak David. "Religion and Family Among the Markham Mennonites." Yale, 1978. [Ontario]

807
Berg, Wesley Peter. "Choral Festivals and Choral Workshops among the Mennonites of Manitoba and Saskatchewan, 1900-1960, with an Account of Early Developments in Russia." Washington, Seattle, 1979.

808
Laurence, Hugh Getty. "Change in Religion, Economics, and Boundary Conditions Among Amish Mennonites in Southwestern Ontario." McGill, 1980.

809
Martens, Hildegard Margo. "The Relationship of Religious to Socio-Economic Divisions Among the Mennonites of Dutch-Prussian-Russian Descent in Canada." Toronto, 1977.

810
Thielman, George G. "The Canadian Mennonites." Case Western Reserve, 1955.

Van Dyke, Edward William. See No./Voir no 366
Young, Mary McPherson. See No./Voir no 371

Muslims/Musulmans

811
Razaul, Haque M. "Cultural Assimilation and Consumer Decision-Making Among Muslim Couples in Windsor, Ontario." Wayne State, 1978.

Netherlandic Canadians/Canadiens néerlandais

812
Wentholt, H. "Studies in Social Life." University of the Hague, Holland, 1961.

Adolf, Jacek Zugmunt. See No./Voir no 757

813
Radecki, Henry. "Ethnic Organizational Dynamics: A Study of the Polish Group in Canada." York, 1975.

Portuguese/Portuguais

814
Fernandez, Ronald Louis. "A Logic of Ethnicity; A Study of the Significance and Classification of Ethnic Identity Among Montreal Portuguese." McGill, 1978.

815
Jida-Miranda, Maria-Lia. "La relation entre les changements récents et les maladies chez les immigrants portugais à Montréal." Montréal, 1975.

33

Joy, Annamma. See No./Voir no 788

816
Lavigne, Gilles. "La formation d'un quartier ethnique: les Portugais à Montréal." Montréal, 1979.

Lipman, Marvin Harold. See No./Voir no 10033

Slavs/Slaves

Weinfeld, Morton Irwin. See No./Voir no 805

Ukrainians/Ukrainiens

Currie, Albert Wayne. See No./Voir no 10227

Yugoslavs/Yougoslaves

Godler, Zlata. See No./Voir no 7649

817
Herman, Harry Vjekoslar. "Ethnicity and Occupation: Comparative Analysis of the Occupational Choices of Croation and Macedonian Immigrants to Ontario (Canada)." Toronto, 1978.

818
Vrsic, Gabriel. "Contributions of the Yugoslavs to the North American Continent." Montreal, 1958.

Canadians in the United States/Canadiens des États-Unis

819
Anctil, Pierre. "Aspects of Class Ideology in a New England Ethnic Minority: The Franco-Americans of Woonsocket, Rhode Island (1865-1929)." New School for Social Research, 1980.

820
Arceneaux, Maureen G. "Acadian to Cajun: Population, Family, and Wealth in Southwest Louisiana, 1765-1854." Brigham Young, 1982. [These Acadians were refugees rather than exiles, who spent the French and Indian war in Nova Scotia fighting the British/Ces Acadiens sont des réfugiés plutôt que des exilés, qui ont passé la guerre française-indienne en combattant contre les anglais dans la Nouvelle-Écosse]

821
Bellemare, Marcel J. "Social Networks in an Inner-City Neighborhood; Woonsocket, Rhode Island." Catholic, 1974.

822
Brandon, Elizabeth. "Moeurs et langue à la paroisse Vermillan en Louisiane." Laval, 1955.

823
Coehlo, Anthony. "A Row of Nationalities: Life in a Working Class Community: The Irish, English and French Canadians of Fall River, Massachusetts, 1850-1890." Brown, 1980.

824
Colman, Rosalie Marson. "An Historical Analysis of the French English Bilingual Programs Conducted in Connecticut by the Daughters of the Holy Spirit." Connecticut, 1978.

825
Dennis, Herbert Knight. "The French Canadians: A Study in Group Traits with Special Reference to the French Canadians of New England." Harvard, 1918.

826
Dexter, Robert Cloutman. "The Habitant Transplanted: A Study of the French Canadian in New England." Clark, 1923.

827
Early, Frances Horn. "French-Canadian Beginnings in an American Community: Lowell, Massachusetts, 1868-1886." Concordia, 1980.

828
Edwards, John Robert. "Growing up a Franco-American: The Social and Academic Effects of Bilingual Education in Northern Vermont." McGill, 1974.

829
Gerstle, Gary Lloyd. "The Rise of Industrial Unionism: Class, Ethnicity and Labor Organization in Woonsocket, Rhode Island, 1931-1941." Harvard, 1982.

830
Glauber, Robin Roth. "Ethnic Group and Social Class Variations in Households and Families of Nashwa, New Hampshire, 1850-1900." New School for Social Research, 1982.

831
Guignard, Michael James." Ethnic Survival in a New England Mill Town: The Franco-Americans of Biddeford, Maine." Syracuse, 1976.

832
Guillemin, Jeanne E. "The Micmac Indians in Boston: The Ethnography of an Urban Community." Brandeis, 1973. [Indian-White Relations/Relations indiennes-anglaises]

833
Guillet, Ernest Bernard. "French Ethnic Literature and Culture in an American City: Holyoke, Massachusetts." Massachusetts, 1978.

834
Haebler, Peter. "Habitants in Holyoke: The Development of the French-Canadian Community in a Massachusetts City, 1865-1910." New Hampshire, 1976.

835
Hodges, David Julian. "The Cajun Culture of Southwestern Louisiana: A Study of Cultural Isolation and Role Adaptation as Factors in the Fusion of Black African and French Acadian Culture Traits." New York, 1972.

Kovacik, Charles Frank. See No./Voir no 4848

836
Liptak, Dolores Ann. "European Immigrants and the Catholic Church in Connecticut, 1870-1920," Connecticut, 1979. [Also French Canadians/ Canadiens-français aussi]

McQuillan, David Aidan. See No./Voir no 4850

Parenton, Vernon J. See No./Voir no 9822

Santerre, Richard. See No./Voir no 8235

837
Schweda, Nancy Lee. "Goal Oriented Interaction in the French-Speaking St. John River Valley of Northern Maine: A Sociolinguistic and Ethnomethodological Study of the Use of Verbal Strategies by Professional Community Members Living in a Bilingual Society with a French-English Speech Continuum." Georgetown, 1979.

838
Sloan, William Neville. "A New Direction for the Anthropological Study of Social Change and Economic Development: A Case Study of Vermont, 1535-1870." McGill, 1982.

839
Sorg, Marcella Harnish. "Genetic Demography of Deme Formation in a Franco-American Population: 1830-1903." Ohio State, 1979. [Old Town, Maine]

Vicero, Ralph Dominic. See No./Voir no 4852

840
Wilson, Harold Fisher. "A Study in the Social History of Rural Northern New England, 1820-1930." Harvard, 1933.

ARCHAEOLOGY / ARCHÉOLOGIE

Apart from the recent studies in which the University of Calgary (27 titles) is the leader, followed by Toronto (12), only three other Canadian universities have produced doctoral studies in the field of Archaeology, Simon Fraser University, the University of British Columbia, and York University, make up the total of 47 titles. This has been matched by American universities who have produced 48 doctoral dissertations on this subject. Of the 26 universities involved, Wisconsin is first with six titles, followed by Washington, Seattle, Michigan, Michigan State, and Harvard with four titles each.

———

En dehors des récentes études pour lesquelles l'Université de Calgary (27 ouvrages) vient en tête, suivie par celle de Toronto (12), seulement trois autres universités canadiennes ont produit des thèses de doctorat en ce domaine, l'Université Simon Fraser (5), l'Université de la Colombie-Britannique (2) et l'Université York (1), ce qui fait un total de 47 ouvrages, qui rejoint à peu de chose près le total des universités américaines (48). Des 26 universités en cause, celle du Wisconsin est en tête avec 6 ouvrages suivie par Washington, Seattle, Michigan, Michigan State et Harvard, avec 4 ouvrages chacune.

REGIONAL STUDIES/ÉTUDES RÉGIONALES

North America/Amérique du Nord

841
Buchner, Anthony Paul. "Cultural Responses to Altithermal (Atlantic) Climate along the Eastern Margins of the North American Grasslands: 5500-3000 B.C." Calgary, 1980.

842
Del Bene, Terry Alan. "The Anangula Lithic Technological System: An Appraisal of Eastern Aleutian Technology Circa 8250-8750 B.P." Connecticut, 1982. [Some comparisons with Canadian sites/Quelques comparaisons avec des sites canadiens]

843
Fisher, Reginald G. "The Relation of North American Pre-History to Post-Glacial Climatic Fluctuations." Southern California, 1935.

844
Haynes, Gary Anthony. "Bone Modifications and Skeletal Disturbances by Natural Agencies: Studies in North America." Catholic, 1981.

845
Randahl, Frances Sylvia. "A Prehistory of the United States and Canada: An Archaeological Overview of Population and Adaptation in Pre-Columbian Times." Wayne State, 1979.

846
Spiess, Arthur Eliot. "Substance and Culture Change in Caribou-Hunting Peoples: Ethnography and Archaeology." Harvard, 1978.

847
Stout, Samuel Darrel. "Histomorphometric Analysis of Archaeological Bone." Washington, St. Louis, 1976. [Eskimo/Esquimau]

Western Canada/Ouest du Canada

848
Anderson, Patricia Marie. "Reconstructing the Past: The Synthesis of Archaeological and Palynological Data, Northern Alaska and Northwestern Canada." Brown, 1982.

849
Jensen, Peter Michael. "The Leaf-Shaped Projectile Point in Early Western American Prehistory." California, Davis, 1976.

Eastern Canada/Est du Canada

850
Blanchette, Jean-François. "The Role of Artifacts in the Study of Foodways in New France 1720-1760: Two Case Studies Based on the Analysis of Ceramic Artifacts." Brown, 1979.

851
Jordan, Douglas Frederick. "The Bull Brook Site in Relation to 'Fluted Point' Manifestations in Eastern North America." Harvard, 1960.

Noble, William Charles. See No./Voir no 650

852
Rothschild, Nan Askin. "Age and Sex Status and Role in Prehistoric Societies of Eastern North America." New York, 1975.

853
Weil, Edward Benjamin. ""Paleo-Indian Period in Northeastern North America." SUNY, Buffalo, 1978.

Alberta

854
Byrne, William John. "The Archaeology and Prehistory of Southern Alberta as Reflected by Ceramics: Late Prehistoric and Protohistoric Cultural Developments." Yale, 1973.

855
Driver, Jonathan Campbell. "Holocene Man and Environments in the Crowsnest Pass, Alberta." Calgary, 1978.

856
Duke, Philip George. "Systems Dynamics in Prehistoric Southern Alberta: 2000 B.P.-Historic Period." Calgary, 1982.

857
Losey, Timothy Campbell. "The Prehistoric Cultural Ecology of the Western Prairie - Forest Transition Zone, Alberta, Canada." Alberta, 1978.

858
Nance, Jack Dwain. "Classification and Analysis of Artifacts." Calgary, 1972.

859
Nesbitt, Paul Edward. "A stylistic Analysis of Aboriginal Plateau Rock Art and Its Relationship to the Intermontane Region." Calgary, 1972.

860
Wilson, Michael. "Once Upon a River: Archaeology and Geology of the Bow River Valley at Calgary, Alberta." Calgary, 1981.

British Columbia/Colombie-Britannique

861
Beattie, Owen Beverly. "An Analysis of Prehistoric Human Skeletal Material from the Gulf of Georgia Region of British Columbia." Simon Fraser, 1981.
Bell, Joy Florence. See No./Voir no 672

862
Burley, David Vincent. "Marpole: An Anthropological Reconstruction of a Prehistoric Northwest Coast Culture Type." Simon Fraser, 1979.

863
Calvert, Sheila Gay Cunningham. "A Cultural Analysis of Faunal Remains From Three Archaeological Sites in Hesquiat Harbour, B.C." British Columbia, 1980.

864
Donahue, Paul Francis. "4500 Years of Cultural Continuity on the Central Plateau of British Columbia." Wisconsin, 1977.

865
Fladmark, Knut Reidar. "Prehistoric Development of the Northwest Coast Cultural Pattern." Calgary, 1974.
Grabert, Garland Frederick. See No./Voir no 380

866
Haggarty, James Colton. "The Archaeology of Hesquiat Harbour: The Archaeological Utility of an Ethnographically Defined Social Unit." Washington State, 1982.

867
Mitchell, Donald Hector. "Archaeology of the Gulf of Georgia Area, a Natural Region and Its Culture Types." Oregon, 1968.

868
Monks, Gregory Gerald. "An Examination of Relationships Between Artifact Classes and Food Resource Remains at Deep Bay, Di Se 7." British Columbia, 1977. [Vancouver Island/Île de Vancouver]

869
Pomeroy, John Anthony. "Bella Bella Settlement and Subsistence." Simon Fraser, 1981.

870
Sanger, David. "The Archaeology of the Lochnore Nesikep Locality, British Columbia: Final Report." Washington, Seattle, 1967.

871
Stryd, Arnold Henri. "The Later Prehistory of the Lillooet Area, British Columbia." Calgary, 1973.

872
Thompson, Gail. "Prehistoric Settlement Changes in the Southern Northwest Coast: A Functional Approach." Washington, Seattle, 1978.

873
Turnbull, Christopher John. "Archaeology and Ethnohistory of the Arrow Lakes, Southeastern British Columbia." Calgary, 1973.

874
White, James Murray. "Late Quaternary Geochronology and Palaeoecology of the Upper Peace River District, Canada." Simon Fraser, 1983.

Great Lakes/Grands Lacs

875
Cleland, Charles Edward. "The Prehistoric Animal Ecology and Ethnozoology of the Upper Great Lakes Region." Michigan, 1966.

876
Fogel, Ira Lee. "The Dispersal of Copper Artifacts of the Archaic Tradition in Prehistoric North America." Chicago, 1963.

877
Hulse, Charles Allen. "A Spatial Analysis of Lake Superior Shipwrecks: A Study in the Formative Process of Archaeological Record." Michigan State, 1981.

878
Janzen, Donald Edward. "The Naomikong Point Site and the Dimensions of Laurel in the Lake Superior Basin." Michigan, 1968.

879
McPherson, Alan Locke. "The Juntunen Site and the Late Woodland Prehistory of the Upper Great Lakes Area." Michigan, 1966.

880
Melbye, Floyd Jerome. "An Analysis of a Late Woodland Population in the Upper Great Lakes." Toronto, 1969.
Pfeiffer, Susan Kay Gosher. See No./Voir no 373
Pratt, Gary Michael. See No./Voir no 918

881
Roberts, Arthur Cecil Batt. "Preceramic Occupations along the North Shore of Lake Ontario". York, 1982.
Vastokas, Romas. See No./Voir no 719

New Brunswick/Nouveau-Brunswick

882
Barka, Norman Forthun. "Historic Sites Archaeology at Portland Point, New Brunswick, Canada: 1631-1850." Harvard, 1965.

Newfoundland and Labrador/Terre-Neuve et Labrador

883
Fitzhugh, William Wyvill, IV. "Environmental Archaeology and Cultural Systems in Hamilton Inlet, Labrador: A Survey of the Central Labrador Coast from 3000 B.C. to the Present." Harvard, 1970.

884
Linnamae, Urve. "Dorset Culture in Newfoundland and the Arctic." Calgary, 1973.

Way, Jacob Edson, III. See No./Voir no 630

Northwest Territories and the Yukon/ Territoires du Nord-Ouest et Yukon

Anderson, Patricia Marie. See No./Voir no 848

885
Arnold, Charles Duncan. "The Lagoon Site (OjRl-3): Implications for Paleoeskimo Interactions." Calgary, 1978. [Southern coast of Banks Island, Northwest Territories/Côte du sud de l'île Banks, Territoires du Nord Ouest]

886
Arundale, Wendy Hanford. "The Archaeology of the Nanook Site: An Explanatory Approach." Michigan State, 1976.

887
Bielawski, Ellen Eileen. "Space and Season: A Study of the Spatial Behavior of Prehistoric Arctic Hunters." Calgary, 1981.

888
Corbin, James E. "Aniganigaruk: A Study in Nunamiut Eskimo Archaeology." Washington State, 1975.

889
Dekin, Albert Arch, Jr. "Models of Pre-Dorset Culture: Towards an Explicit Methodology." Michigan State, 1975.

890
Gordon, Bryan Herbert Copp. "Of Men and Herds in Barrenland Prehistory." Calgary, 1974.

891
Helmer, James Walter. "Climate Change and Dorset Culture Change in the Crozier Strait Region, N.W.T.: A Test of the Hypothesis." Calgary, 1982.

892
Janes, Robert Roy. "Dispersion and Nucleation Among Nineteenth Century McKenzie Basin Athapaskans: Archaeological, Ethnohistorical and Ethnographic Interpretations." Calgary, 1976.

893
LeBlanc, Raymond Joseph. "The Rat Indian Creek Site and the Late Prehistoric Period in the Interior Northern Yukon." Toronto, 1983.

894
McCartney, Allen Papin. "Thule Eskimo Prehistory Along Northwestern Hudson Bay." Wisconsin, 1971.

895
McCartney, Nancy Glover. "Effects of Eskimos on Soils and Vegetation at Two Northern Archaeological Sites." Wisconsin, 1976.

896
McGhee, Robert John. "Copper Eskimo Prehistory." Calgary, 1968.

897
Millar, James F.V. "Archaeology of Fisherman Lake, Western District of Mackenzie, N.W.T.". Calgary, 1968.

898
Morlan, Richard Eugene. "The Later Prehistory of the Middle Porcupine Drainage, Northern Yukon Territory." Wisconsin, 1971.

899
Sabo, George, III. "Thule Culture Adaptations on the South Coast of Baffin Island, N.W.T.". Michigan State, 1981.

900
Schlederman, Peter. "Thule Eskimo Prehistory of Cumberland Sound, Baffin Island, Canada." Calgary, 1975.

901
Shinkwin, Anne Dolores. "Dakah De'nin's Village and the Dixthada Site: A Contribution to Northern Athapaskan Prehistory." Wisconsin, 1975. [Yukon]

902
Smith, Jason Wallace. "The Northeast Asian—Northwest American Microblade Tradition and the Ice Mountain Microblade and Core Industry." Calgary, 1974.

903
Taylor, William Ewart, Jr. "The Arnapik and Tyara Site: An Archaeological Study of Dorset Culture Origins." Michigan, 1965.

904
Workman, William Bates. "Prehistory of the Aishihik - Kluane Area, Southwest Yukon Territory, Canada." Wisconsin, 1974.

Nova Scotia/Nouvelle-Écosse

905
MacDonald, George Frederick. "Excavations at Debert, Nova Scotia: A Study of Lithic Technology and Settlement Pattern at a Fluted Point Site." Yale, 1966.

Ontario

906
Clabeaux-Striegel, Marie Kathryn. "Paleopathology of the Orchard Site, Fort Erie, Ontario." SUNY, Buffalo, 1967.

907
Emerson, John N. "The Archaeology of the Ontario Iroquois." Chicago, 1954.

908
Finlayson, William David. "The Saugeen Culture: A Middle Woodland Manifestation in Southwestern Ontario." Toronto, 1976.

909
Green, Stanton William. "The Agricultural Coloniza- tion of Temperate Forest Habitats: An Ecological Model." Massachusetts, 1977. [Including 18th century upper canada/Inclus le Haut-Canada du XVIIIe siècle]

910
Hartney, Patrick Cooper. "Palaeopathology of Ar- chaeological Aboriginal Populations from Southern Ontario and Adjacent Regions." Toronto, 1978.

911
Jackes, Mary Katheryn. "The Huron Spine: A Study Based on the Kleinburg Ossuary Vertebrae." Toronto, 1977.

912
Johnston, Richard Barnett. "Southern Ontario Point Peninsula Woodland in Northeastern Prehistory." Indiana, 1962.

913
Keenlyside, David Lane. "Late Prehistory of Point Pelee, Ontario and Environs." Calgary, 1978.

914
Kenyon, Walter Andrew. "The Miller Site: An Archaeological Report." Toronto, 1967.

915
Knight, Dean Humphrey. "The Montreal River and Shield Archaic." Toronto, 1977.

916
Latta, Martha Ann. "The Iroquoian Culture of Huronia: A Study of Acculturation Through Ar- chaeology." Toronto, 1977.
Noble, William Charles. See No./Voir no 650

917
Patterson, David Kingsworth, Jr. "A Diachronic Study of Dental Palaeopathology and Attritional Status of Prehistoric Ontario Pre-Iroquois and Iroquois Populations." Toronto, 1983.

918
Pratt, Gary Michael. "The Western Basin Tradition: Changing Settlement-Substance Adaptation in the Western Lake Erie Basin Region." Case Western Reserve, 1981. [Southwestern Ontario/Sud-ouest de l'Ontario]

919
Sykes, Clark Mansfield. "An Archaeological and Ethnohistorical Analysis of Huron Intra-Community Exchange Systems." Toronto, 1983.

920
Wall, Robert David. "The Preceramic Period in the Southwest Canadian Shield: An Initial Model For- mulation." Catholic, 1981. [Lake of the Woods, Northwest Ontario/Nord-Ouest de l'Ontario]

Prairie Provinces/Provinces des Prairies

921
Arthur, George William. "An Introduction to the Ecology of Early Historic Communal Bison Hunting Among the Northern Plains Indians." Calgary, 1974.

922
Davis, Leslie Beryl. "The Prehistoric Use of Obsidian in the Northwestern Plains." Calgary, 1972.
Dyck, Ian George. See No./Voir no 420

923
Foor, Thomas Allyn. "Cultural Continuity on the Northwestern Great Plains - 1300 B.C. to A.D. 200, The Pelican Lake Culture." California, Santa Barbara, 1982.

924
Nash, Ronald John Thomas. "The Arctic Small Tool Tradition in Manitoba." Calgary, 1968.

925
Reeves, Brian O.K. "Culture Change in the Northern Plains, 1000 B.C. - A.D. 1000." Calgary, 1970.

926
Tamplin, Morgan John. "Prehistoric Occupation and Resource Exploitation on the Saskatchewan River at the Pas, Manitoba." Arizona, 1977.

927
Walker, Ernest Gordon. "The Gowen Site: An Early Archaic Site on the Northern Plains." Texas, 1980. [Central Saskatchewan/Centre de la Saskat- chewan]

Quebec/Québec

928
Benmouyal, Joseph. "North Gaspé-Prehistory: A Contribution to Quebec Archaeology." Simon Fraser, 1981.

929
Marois, Roger Joseph-Maurice. "Settlement Patterns in the Late Prehistory and Early History: Southern Quebec." Calgary, 1973.

ARCHITECTURE/ARCHITECTURE

This is another area where very little doctoral research has been pursued. Three Canadian univer- sities have produced only five titles in the last seven years: Laval University (3), the University of Toronto (1), and Simon Fraser University (1). Five American universities have produced six titles, with Cornell responsible for two, and Columbia, Michigan, Oregon and Princeton, one each. Great Britain produced one title at the University of Edinburgh in 1975.

————

Il existe un autre domaine où très peu de thèses de doctorat ont été produites. Trois universités cana- diennes ont fourni 5 ouvrages en tout au cours des 7 dernières années: l'Université Laval (3), l'Université de Toronto (1) et l'Université Simon Fraser (1). Six autres ouvrages sont redevables à 5 universités améri- caines: Cornell (2), Colombia, Michigan, Oregon et Princeton (un ouvrage chacune). La Grande-Bretagne a produit une thèse à l'Université d'Édimbourg en 1975.

GENERAL ITEMS/OUVRAGES GÉNÉRAUX

930
Cameron, Christina. "Charles Baillairge, Architect (1826-1906)." Laval, 1983.

931
Coffey, Brian Lee. "The Pioneer House in Southern Ontario, Canada: Construction Material Use and Resultant Forms to 1850." Oregon, 1982.

932
Cross, Kevin James. "Urban Redevelopment in Canada." Cornell, 1958.

933
Fortier, Yvan. "Trois habitations rurales du XVIIIe siècle à Sainte-Foy. Étude sur le terrain et documents notariés." Laval, 1979.

934
Gifford, Robert Durrell. "Personal and Situational Factors in Judgments of Typical Architecture." Simon Fraser, 1976. [North Burnaby, British Columbia/Burnaby Nord, Colombie-Britannique]

935
Gowans, Alan Wilbert. "A History of Church Architecture in New France." Princeton, 1950.

936
Lahaise, Georges-Pierre. "Origine et évolution des principaux types d'architecture rurale au Québec et le cas de la région de Charlevoix." Laval, 1981.

937
Marsan, Jean-Claude. "Montreal in Evolution: Historical Account of the Development of Montreal's Architecture and Environment." Edinburgh, 1975.

938
McKinnon, Sarah Morgan. "Traditional Rural Architecture in Northwest France and Quebec, 1600-1800." Toronto, 1976.

Oostendorp, Anke. See No./Voir no 9732

939
Shimizu, Kaien Masaru. "A New Generation of Northern Communities." Michigan, 1976. [Faro, Kitimat, Churchill Falls, and/et Inuvik]

940
Thompson, William Paul. "Hutterite Community: Artefact Ark: An Historical Study of the Architecture and Planning of a Communal Society." Cornell, 1977.

Vastokas, Joan Marie. See No./Voir no 489

ARTS/ARTS

Surprisingly, for a nation that has much to be proud of in the production of artistic works, very little doctoral research has been completed in this area. The Canadian and American universities are responsible for 11 dissertations each. The first 13 items are general studies of Canadian art, and the final nine deal with art of the Native people of Canada. Six Canadian universities have produced a total of 11 dissertations, with the University of Toronto contributing four. Eight American universities have produced 11 dissertations; Columbia (3) and Washington (Seattle), (2) are the leaders.

Il est surprenant de constater qu'au sein d'une nation, pourtant si fière de la production de ses oeuvres d'art, on retrouve si peu de thèses de doctorat sur ce domaine. Les universités canadiennes n'ont présenté respectivement que 11 thèses sur le sujet. Les 13 premiers ouvrages traitent de l'art canadien en général et les 9 derniers, de l'art des autochtones du Canada. Six universités canadiennes ont produit au total 11 thèses, dont 4 viennent de l'Université de Toronto. Huit universités américaines en ont produit 11: l'Université Columbia (3) et l'Université de Washington (Seattle) (2) se classent en tête.

941
Cauchon, Michel. "L'iconographie de la légende québécoise." Laval, 1979.

942
Davison-Wood, Karen Margaret. "A Philistine Culture? Literature, Painting, and the Newspapers in Late Victorian Toronto." Concordia, 1982.

943
Eyford, Glen Allenby. "The Artist as Educator: A Philosophical Examination of the Communicative Function of the Arts." Toronto, 1975. [Includes 100 pages of Canadian artists views on art/Inclus 100 pages des points de vue des artistes canadiens sur l'art]

944
Gibbons, Jacqueline Anne. "Artists, Dealers and Hustlers: The Art of Business and the Business of Art." Toronto, 1979.

945
Hannibal, Emmeth Ronald. "Existential Challenges: The Confluence and Expression of Art Culture, and Education at the Winnipeg Art Gallery, 1975-1977." Harvard, 1978.

Hoag, Peter Lockrie. See No./Voir no 606

946
Hubbard, Robert Hamilton. "The Colonial Tradition in French Canadian Sculpture, 1670-1850." Wisconsin, 1942.

947
Porter, John Robert. "Un peintre et collectionneur québécois engagé dans son milieu: Joseph Légaré (1795-1855)." Montréal, 1981.

948
Rodrigue, Denise. "Le cycle de Pâques au Québec et dans l'ouest de la France." Laval, 1978.

949
Sorge, Walter Felix. "The Artist in the University: Problems and Personal Development." Columbia, 1963. [Vancouver]

Timleck, Derry Gray. See No./Voir no 4035

950
Van Wagner, Judy Kay Collischan. "Walter Murch." Iowa, 1972.

951
Wadland, John Henry. "Ernest Thompson Seton: Man in Nature and the Progressive Era (1880-1915)." York, 1977.

Wainwright, John Andrew. See No./Voir no 8045

Art of the Native Peoples of Canada/
Art des peuples autochtones du Canada

Bell, Joy Florence. <u>See No./Voir no</u> 672

952
DeLaguna, Frederica Annis. "A Comparison of Eskimo and Paleolithic Art." Columbia, 1933.

Duncan, Kate Corbin. <u>See No./Voir no</u> 548

953
Grigsby, Jefferson Eugene, Jr. "African and Indian Masks: A Comparative Study of Masks Produced by the Ba Kuba Tribe of the Congo and Masks Produced by the Kwakuitl Indians of the Northwest Coast of America." New York, 1963.

Houlihan, Patrick Thomas. <u>See No./Voir no</u> 383

954
Mathews, Zena Pearlstone. "The Relation of Seneca False Face Masks to Seneca and Ontario Archaeology." California, Los Angeles, 1977.

Nesbitt, Paul Edward. <u>See No./Voir no</u> 859

Wingert, Paul Stover. <u>See No./Voir no</u> 881

MUSIC/MUSIQUE

This classification is composed of a number of general topics, such as the history of music in Canada, folk songs, Indian music, religious music, Canadian music, musicians and composers, and music education. It has not proved to be a strong area for advanced graduate research. Of the 63 items, 19 are in the area of music education. It is interesting to note that of the 18 doctoral studies of nine Canadian musicians and composers, only two were completed at Canadian universities. It is possible, of course, that a number of the studies completed in American universities may have been done by Canadians who elected to study music at American universities. Of the 27 American universities represented, Rochester (7), Columbia (6), and Indiana (4) were the leaders. Of the eight Canadian universities represented, Montreal (4) and Toronto (3) were the leaders. The bulk of research for all universities was completed in the 1970's and 1980's. The first American study, entitled "The Folk Songs of Canada," was produced at Harvard University in 1909. It was not until 1932, that another study was produced at Laval University on the evolution of religious music in French Canada.

Cette classification se compose d'un certain nombre d'études générales comme l'évolution de l'art musical au Canada, les chansons folkloriques, la musique indienne, la musique religieuse, la musique canadienne, les musiciens et les compositeurs ainsi que l'enseignement de la musique. Ce sujet ne tient pas une place très importante dans les études de doctorat. Avec 63 thèses, 19 d'entre elles portent sur l'enseignement de la musique. Il est intéressant de noter que, des 18 thèses de doctorat présentées par neuf musiciens et compositeurs canadiens, seulement deux ont été faites dans des universités canadiennes. Il est possible, naturellement, que certains Canadiens aient choisit d'étudier la musique dans des universités américaines. Des 27 universités américaines représentées,

Rochester (7 thèses), Columbia (6) et Indiana (4) se sont révélées des chefs de file. De même, l'Université de Montréal (4 thèses) et l'Université de Toronto (3) se placent en tête des 8 universités canadiennes. Pour toutes les universités, la masse de recherche se situe dans les années 1970 à 1980. La première étude américaine intitulée "The Folk Songs of Canada" a été faite à l'Université Harvard en 1909. Ce n'est qu'en 1932 que l'Université Laval a produit une autre étude sur l'évolution de la musique religieuse au Canada français.

General Items/Ouvrages généraux

Beal, Audrey Lynne. <u>See No./Voir no</u> 9500

955
Gruson, Linda Margaret. "What Distinguishes Competence? An Investigation of Piano Practicing." Waterloo, 1981. [Music grade one to concert pianist/Du 1er niveau en musique au pianiste de concert]

956
Holz, Ronald Walker. "A History of the Hymn Tune Meditation and Related Forms in Salvation Army Instrumental Music in Great Britain and North America, 1880-1980." Connecticut, 1981.

957
Howell, Gordon P. "The Development of Music in Canada." Rochester, 1960.

958
Huard, Michael. "Les processus primaires et secondaires chez les musiciens de jazz professionnel." Montréal, 1971.

Kendrick, Margaret Joan. <u>See No./Voir no</u> 9016

Maher, Timothy Francis. <u>See No./Voir no</u> 9556

959
Owen, Stephanie Olive. "The Piano Concerts in Canada Since 1955." Washington, St. Louis, 1969.

960
Pouinard, Alfred Antonin. "Recherches sur la musique d'origine française en Amérique du Nord: Canada et Louisiane." Laval, 1951.

961
Zenger, Dixie Robison. "Violin Techniques and Traditions Useful in Identifying and Playing North American Fiddle Styles." Stanford, 1980. [United States and Canada/États-Unis et Canada]

Folk Songs/Chansons folkloriques

Haywood, Charles. <u>See No./Voir no</u> 464

962
Macmillan, Cyrus John. "The Folk-Songs of Canada." Harvard, 1909.

963
Wenker, Jerome Richard. "A Computer-Aided Analysis of Anglo-Canadian Folktunes." Indiana, 1978. [Ontario]

Wilson, Mary Louise Lewis. <u>See No./Voir no</u> 8336

Music of Native Peoples/
Musique des peuples autochtones

Asch, Michael Ira. <u>See No./Voir no</u> 579

Cavanagh, Beverley Anne. <u>See No./Voir no</u> 590

964
Lutz, Maija M. "The Effects of Acculturation on Eskimo Music of Cumberland Peninsula." Wisconsin, 1977. [Baffin Island/Île de Baffin]

Mishler, Craig Wallace. See No./Voir no 552

Nettl, Bruno. See No./Voir no 477

Vennum, Thomas. See No./Voir no 545

965
Whittinger, Julius Edward. "Hymnody of Early American Indian Missions." Catholic, 1971.

Religious Music/Musique religieuse

Berg, Wesley Peter. See No./Voir no 807

966
Garner, Stephen Warren. "A Pedagogic Guide to Twentieth-Century Sacred Art Song in the United States, Great Britain and Canada." Southwestern Baptist Theological Seminary, 1979.

967
Lock, William Rowland. "Ontario Church Choirs and Choral Societies, 1819-1918." Southern California, 1972.

Mealing, Francis Mark. See No./Voir no 8323

968
Pelletier, J.R. "L'évolution de la musique religieuse au Canada français." Laval, 1932.

Whittinger, Julius Edward. See No./Voir no 965

Canadian Music, Musicians and Composers/ Musique canadienne, musiciens et compositeurs

General Items/Ouvrages généraux

969
Chapman, Norman Belfield. "Piano Music by Canadian Composers, 1940-1965." Case Western Reserve, 1973.

970
Hanson, Frank K. "Symphony in Canada." McGill, 1947.

971
Hepner, Lee Alfred. "An Analytical Study of Selected Canadian Orchestral Compositions at the Mid-Twentieth Century." New York, 1971.

972
Lister, William Warwick. "The Contemporary Sonata for Violin and Piano by Canadian Composers." Boston University, 1970.

973
Skelton, Robert Allen. "Joseph Joachim's Hungarian Concerto in D Minor, Opus II; Weinzweig, Gould, Schafer: Three Canadian String Quartets." Indiana, 1976.

Archer, Violet Balestreri (1913-   )

974
Huiner, Harvey Don. "The Choral Music of Violet Archer." Iowa, 1980.

Carignan, Jean (1916-   )

975
Begin, Carmelle. "La musique traditionnelle pour violon: Jean Carignan." Montréal, 1979.

Champagne, Claude (1891-1965)

976
Walsh, Anne. "The Life and Works of Claude Adonai Champagne." Catholic, 1972. [Dean of French-Canadian composers/Doyen des compositeurs canadiens-français]

Coulthard, Jean (1900-   )

977
Rowley, Vivienne Wilda. "The Solo Piano Music of the Canadian Composer Jean Coulthard." Boston University, 1973.

Forte, Allen (1926-   )

978
McNeal, Horace Pitman, Jr. "A Method of Analysis Based on Concepts and Procedures Developed by Allen Forte and Applied to Selected Canadian String Quartets, 1953-1962." Ohio State, 1979.

Freedman, Harry (1922-   )

979
Nichols, Kenneth Hugh. "The Orchestral Compositions of Harry Freedman: A Parametric Analysis of Major Works Written Between 1952-1967." Minnesota, 1981.

Garant, Serge (1929-   )

980
Lefebvre, Marie-Thérèse. "Nouvelle approche de la conception de matériaux sonores dans les oeuvres post-sérielles: une analyse du Quintette de Serge Garant." Montréal, 1981.

Gorman, Larry (1900-   )

981
Ives, Edward Dawson. "The Satirical Song Tradition in Maine and the Maritime Provinces of Canada with Particular Reference to Larry Gorman." Indiana, 1962.

Mathieu, Rodolphe (1890-1962)

982
Bourassa-Trépanier, Juliette. "Rodolphe Mathieu, musicien canadien (1890-1962)." Laval, 1972.

Naylor, Bernard (1907-   )

983
Baerg, William John. "A Study of the Unaccompanied Choral Works of Canadian Composer Bernard Naylor." Johns Hopkins, 1980.

Somers, Harry Stewart (1925-)

984
Butler, Edward Gregory. "The Five Piano Sonatas of Harry Somers." Rochester, 1974.

985
Enns, Leonard Jacob. "The Sacred Choral Music of Harry Somers: An Analytical Study." Northwestern, 1982.

986
Houghton, Diane. "The Solo Vocal Works of Harry Somers." Missouri, Kansas City, 1980.

Weinzweig, John Jacob (1913-)

987
Webb, Douglas John. "Serial Techniques in John Weinzweig's Divertimentos and Concertos (1945-1968)." Rochester, 1977.

Willan, Healey (1880-1968)

988
Campbell-Yukl, Joylin. "Healey Willan: The Independant Organ Works." Missouri, Kansas City, 1976.

989
Johnson, Norman Gary. "Healey Willan (1880-1968): His Life and Influences Important to His Music." Southern Baptist Theological Seminary, 1979.

990
Marwick, William Edward. "The Sacred Choral Music of Healey Willan." Michigan State, 1970.

991
Telschow Frederick H. "The Sacred Music of Healey Willan." Rochester, 1970.

Music Education/Enseignement musical

992
Abbott, Eric Oscar. "The Evolution of the Canadian Music Festival as an Instrument of Musical Education." Boston University, 1969.

993
Bates, Duane Adair. "The Status of Music Education in 1969-70 in the Cities of Southern Ontario Having a Population in Excess of 100 000." Illinois, 1972.

994
Brault, Diana Victoria. "A History of the Ontario Music Educators' Association (1919-1974)." Rochester, 1977.

995
Brown, Alfred Malcolm. "A Study of Teacher Education and Certification for the Teaching of Music in Canadian Public Schools." Florida State, 1960.

996
Churchley, Franklin Eugene. "The Piano in Canadian Music Education." Teachers College, Columbia, 1959.

997
Fraser, Arthur McNutt. "Music in Canadian Public Schools Survey and Recommendations." Teachers College, Columbia, 1951.

998
Green, James Paul. "A Proposed Doctoral Program in Music for Canadian Universities with Specific Recommendations for Specialization in Music Education." Rochester, Eastman School of Music, 1974.

Gruson, Linda Margaret. See No./Voir no 955

999
Hinton, Dallas Edward. "The Effect of Different Musical Timbres on Students Identification of Melodic Intervals." British Columbia, 1982.

Hochheimer, Laura. See No./Voir no 3855

1000
Hrestak, Hrvoje Joseph. "The Nature and Effectiveness of Music in Nova Scotia Public Schools." Dalhousie, 1983.

1001
Mills, Isabelle Margaret. "Canadian Music: A Listening Program for Intermediate Grades with Teaching Guide." Teachers College, Columbia, 1971.

1002
O'Neill, Mary Elizabeth. "A Plan for the Development of a Curriculum in Music for Marianopolis College, Montreal, Canada." Teachers College, Columbia, 1968.

1003
Paganelli, Yolanda Rafaela. "A Comparison of Curricula Requirements for a Student Majoring in Piano in Selected Conservatories and Universities in the Americas." Ball State, 1980. [Chapter 2 deals with canadian universities/Le chapitre 2 traite des universités canadiennes]

1004
Patterson, Lawrence William Alexander. "Undergraduate Programs for Music Teacher Preparation in Canadian Colleges and Universities." Illinois, 1972.

Ringuette, Raymond. See No./Voir no 3728

1005
Sanduss, Joachim. "A Study of the Musical Preferences, Interests, and Activities of Parents as Factors in Their Attitude Toward the Musical Education of Their Children." British Columbia, 1969.

1006
Trowsdale, George Campbell. "A History of Public School Music in Ontario." Toronto, 1962.

1007
Trudeau, Nicole. "Les programmes d'éducation musicale à l'école québécoise et à l'école française." Montréal, 1983.

1008
Vogan, Nancy Fraser. "The History of Public School Music in the Province of New Brunswick, 1872-1939." Rochester, 1979.

1009
Weeks, Peter Alan Donald. "An Ethnomethodological Study of Collective Music-Making." Toronto, 1982.

DANCE/DANSE

General Items/Ouvrages généraux

Mishler, Craig Wallace. See No./Voir no 552

1010
Mitchell, Lillian Leonora. "Boris Volkoff: Dancer, Teacher, Choreographer." Texas Women's, 1982.

Folk Dance/Danse folklorique

Silver, Judith Alta. See No./Voir no 9473

Native Dances/Danses autochtones

See also Anthropology/Voir aussi Anthropologie

DRAMA AND THEATRE/
ART DRAMATIQUE ET THÉÂTRE

Interest in Canadian drama and theatre has suddenly
come alive. In 1932, a pioneering effort was produced
at McGill University, entitled "The French Theatre in
Montreal, 1878-1931." Despite this, no other studies
were completed until the 1970's which produced six.
In the first four years of the 1980's, seven studies have
been completed. The University of Toronto has
dominated this field with a total of nine studies
compared to one each by five other universities.
American interest has also grown. After one study in
the 1940's, seven were produced in the 1960's, eight in
the 1970's and four thus far in the 1980's, making a
total of 20. Of the 15 American universities producing
dissertations in this area, Michigan (3), Wayne State
(3), and Louisiana State (2) are the leaders, with the
remaining 12 universities producing one dissertation
each.

———

L'intérêt pour l'art dramatique et le théâtre canadien
s'est soudainement éveillé. En 1932, un effort a été
fait pour la première fois à l'Université McGill avec
une thèse intitulée "The French Theatre in Montreal,
1878-1981". Depuis, il n'y en a pas eu jusque dans les
années 1970, années au cours desquelles il en a paru
six. De 1980 à 1984, il y a déjà eu 7 études.
L'Université de Toronto s'est distinguée par un total de
9 thèses tandis que chacun des 5 autres établissements
n'en présentait qu'une. Aux États-Unis, l'intérêt pour
ce domaine a suivi la même courbe ascendante. Après
une seule étude au cours des années 1940, il y en a eu
7 au cours des années 1960, 8 au cours des années 1970
et jusqu'à présent 4, de 1980 à 1984, ce qui fait un
total de 20 études. Quinze universités américaines ont
abordé ce sujet; Michigan (3 thèses) Wayne State (3) et
Louisiana State (2) tiennent la tête du groupe, chacune
des 12 universités restantes n'ayant produit qu'une
thèse.

1011
Aikens, James Russell. "The Rival Operas, Toronto
Theatre, 1874-84." Toronto, 1975.

1012
Beauchamp, Hélène. "L'histoire et les conditions du
théâtre pour enfants au Québec, 1950-1980."
Sherbrooke, 1983.

1013
Behl, Dennis Lorman. "Tanya Moisewitsch: Her Con-
tribution to Theatre Arts from 1935-1980." Kent
State, 1981. [Stratford, Ontario]

1014
Bisson, Margaret Mary. "Le théâtre français à
Montréal, 1878-1931." McGill, 1932.

1015
Campbell, Nora Rene. "The Stratford Shakespeare
Festival of Canada: Evolution of an Artistic Policy
(1953-1980) as a Basis for Its Success." Wisconsin,
1982.

1016
Day, Arthur R. "The Shaw Festival at Niagara-on-the
Lake in Ontario, Canada, 1962-1981: A History."
Bowling Green State, 1982.

1017
Edwards, Murray Dallas. "The English Speaking
Theatre in Canada, 1820-1914." Columbia, 1963.

1018
Elliott, Craig Clifford. "Annals of the Legitimate
Theatre in Victoria, Canada from the Beginning to
1900." Washington, Seattle, 1969.

1019
Elliott, Hilary Mary. "Images of Society in English
Canadian Drama 1919-1975." Toronto, 1982.

Ferguson, Tamara Jocelyn. See No./Voir no 9290

1020
Gardner, David Emmett. "An Analytic History of the
Theatre in Canada: The European Beginnings to
1760." Toronto, 1983.

Gould, Allen Mendel. See No./Voir no 8085

1021
Gustafson, David Axel. "The Canadian Regional
Theatre Movement." Michigan State, 1971.

1022
Hamblett, Edwin Clifford. "Marcel Dubé and the
Renaissance of the Theatre in Montreal." Pennsyl-
vania, 1963.

1023
Haynes, Nancy Jane. "A History of the Royal
Alexandra Theatre, Toronto, Ontario, Canada:
1914-1918." Colorado, 1973.

Krieg, Robert Edward. See No./Voir no 649

1024
MacKinnon, Therese Lucina. "Theatre for Young
Audiences in Canada." New York, 1974.

1025
Macklin, Evangeline L. "Educational Dramatics in the
Maritime Universities in Canada." Teachers
College, Columbia, 1942.

1026
McGill, Robert Emmet. "Stratford, 55: The Estabish-
ment of Convention." Michigan, 1972. [The
Stratford Shakespearean Festival of Ontario,
Canada/Festival shakespearien de Stratford,
Ontario, Canada]

1027
O'Dell, Leslie Anne. "Theatrical Events in Kingston,
Ontario: 1879-1897." Toronto, 1982.

1028
O'Neill, Mora Dianne Guthrie." A Partial History of
the Royal Alexandra Theatre, Toronto, Canada
1907-1939." Louisiana State, 1976.

1029
O'Neill, Patrick Bernard Anthony. "A History of
Theatrical Activity in Toronto, Canada from Its
Beginnings to 1858." Louisiana State, 1973.

1030

Plant, Richard Lester. "Leaving Home: A Thematic Study of Canadian Literature with Special Emphasis on Drama 1606 to 1977." Toronto, 1979.

1031

Pope, Karl Theodore. "An Historical Study of the Stratford, Ontario Festival Theatre." Wayne State, 1966.

1032

Rickett, Olla Goewey. "The French-Speaking Theatre of Montreal, 1937-1963." Cornell, 1964.

1033

Rudakoff, Judith Debra. "Characterization and Interactions in the Plays of David French, David Freeman, Michael Tremblay and David Fennario." Toronto, 1983.

1034

Saint-Pierre, Annette A. "Le théâtre au Manitoba français." Ottawa, 1979.

1035

Seaver, Richard Everett. "Douglas Campbell: A Study of His Artistic Accomplishment as an Actor and Director of Selected Theatres in England, Canada, and the United States to 1979." Wayne State, 1981.

1036

Skene, R.R. "Theatre and Community Development Toward a Professional Theatre in Winnipeg, 1897-1958." Toronto, 1983.

1037

Spensley, Philip John. "A Description and Evaluation of the Training Methods of the National Theatre School of Canada, English Acting Course, 1960-1968." Wayne State, 1970.

1038

Stillwell, LeVern Henry. "An Analysis and Evaluation of the Major Examples of the Open Stage Concept as Initiated at Stratford, Ontario to 1964." Michigan, 1969.

1039

Stuart, Euan Ross. "An Analysis of Productions on the Open Stage at Stratford, Ontario." Toronto, 1974.

1040

Trudeau, Claudette Suzanne Marie. "Le théâtre canadien-français à Montréal, 1867-1914: historique, dramaturgie, idéologie." Toronto, 1981.

1041

Van Zyl, François David Wallace. "Planning Criteria for Locating Professional Performing Arts Facilities in the Central City Core of a Metropolitan Region with Special Reference to the City of Toronto." Waterloo, 1974.

1042

Whuittaker, Walter Leslie. "The Canada Council for the Encouragement of the Arts, Humanities and Social Sciences: Its Origins, Formation, Operation and Influence upon Theatre in Canada, 1957-1963." Michigan, 1965.

1043

Young, William Curtis. "A Guide to Manuscripts and Special Collections in the Theatrical Arts in the United States and Canada." Kansas, 1970.

COMMUNICATIONS/ COMMUNICATIONS

This comparatively new field has just begun to capture the interest of Canadian and American students American universities produced two dissertations concerning Canada in the 1960's, 13 in the 1970's, and only one so far in the 1980's, Canadian universities produced seven in the 1970's, and have already produced eight in the first four years of the 1980's.

In addition to general items, communication theory through the works of Harold Innis and Marshall McLuhan is examined, followed by public opinion and propaganda in Canada. Ten Canadian universities have produced dissertations in this field, the University of Toronto and McGill University are the leaders with three each.

———

Ce domaine relativement nouveau vient de commencer à retenir l'intérêt des étudiants canadiens et américains. Tandis que les universités américaines produisaient 2 thèses sur le Canada dans les années 1960, 13 dans les années 1970, et seulement une jusqu'à présent dans les années 1980, les universités canadiennes en ont produit 7 dans les années 1970, et ont déjà dépassé ce nombre dans l'actuelle décennie avec 8 thèses de 1980 à 1984.

Aux ouvrages d'intérêt général, il faut ajouter les études sur la théorie de la communication, avec les travaux d'Harold Innis et Marshall McLuhan, suivies par des travaux sur l'opinion publique et la propagande au Canada. Dix universités canadiennes ont aussi produit des thèses en ce domaine. L'Université de Toronto et l'Université McGill avec 3 thèses chacune se classent en tête du groupe.

GENERAL ITEMS/OUVRAGES GÉNÉRAUX

1044

Bogdanowicz, M.S. "Reader Response to Technical Writing." Toronto, 1983.

Charlebois, Carol Ann. See No./Voir no 1082

Foote, John Allen. See No./Voir no 8520

1045

Fortner, Robert Steven. "Messiahs and Monopolists: A Cultural History of Canadian Communications Systems, 1846-1914." Illinois, 1978.

1046

Hayes, Bonnie Jean. "Generalization of Treatment Effects in Training Public Speakers." Queen's, 1983.

Indra, Doreen Marie. See No./Voir no 384

Jones, Vernon James. See No./Voir no 1086

1047

Lemieux, André. "La communication par le langage comme moyen de transmission d'information: dialectique orientée vers la présentation d'un modèle et de ses implications pédagogiques." Ottawa, 1976.

1048

McIlwraith, Robert Douglas. "Fantasy Life and Media Use Patterns of Adults and Children." Manitoba, 1981.

1049

Mills, Michael Irwin. "On Fitting Cartoon-Strips to Descriptions: A Study of Some Relations Between Perception and Language." McGill, 1980.

1050

Moir, Robert Oliphant Mathieu. "Talking to Strangers: Self-Disclosure Sequency Patterns." McGill, 1979. [Canadian Bell Telephone - interpersonal communication/Communication interpersonnelle-téléphone canadien Bell]

Ollivier, Emile. See No./Voir no 10001

1051

Ravault, René Jean Jacques. "Some Possible Economic Dysfunctions of the Anglo-American Practice of International Communications (A Theoretical Approach)." Iowa, 1980. [Canada, the United States, United Kingdom., Australia and New Zealand/Canada, États-Unis, Royaume-Uni, Australie et Nouvelle-Zélande]

1052

Rydant, Albert Louis. "Regional Information Systems and the Diffusion of Social Innovations in British Columbia." Victoria, 1979.

Siller, Frederick Howard. See No./Voir no 1104

Singh, Indu Bhushan. See No./Voir no 8856

1053

Tamilia, Robert Dominique. "A Cross-Cultural Analysis of Selected Source Effects on Information Processing in an Advertising Context: An Empirical Study of French and Canadian Consumers." Ohio State, 1977. [Montréal]

1054

Valaskakis, Gail Guthrie. "A Communicational Analysis of Interaction Patterns: Southern Baffin, Eastern Arctic." McGill, 1979.

COMMUNICATION THEORY/ THÉORIE DE LA COMMUNICATION

Innis, Harold Adams (1894-1952)

1055

Cooper, Thomas William. "Pioneers in Communication: The Lives and Thought of Harold Innis and Marshall McLuhan." Toronto, 1980.

1056

Czitrom, Daniel Joseph. "Media and the American Mind: The Intellectual and Cultural Reception of Modern Communication, 1838-1965." Wisconsin, 1979.

1057

Davidowitz, Moshe. "Time and Space Bias in Media: Clarifying a Communication Theory of Harold Adams Innis." New York, 1977.

Keast, Ronald Gordon. See No./Voir no 9772

1058

Persky, Joel. "The Relationship Between the Writings of Harold Adams Innis and Marshall McLuhan." New York, 1975.

Striegel, James Finley. See No./Voir no 1068

1059

Thomas, Alan Miller. "The Work of Harold A. Innis with Respect to Its Application to the Development of Broadcasting." Columbia, 1969.

Valaskakis, Gail Guthrie. See No./Voir no 1054

1060

Watson, Alexander John. "Marginal Man: Harold Innis' Communications Works in Context." Toronto, 1981.

McLuhan, Marshall (1911-1980)

Cooper, Thomas William. See No./Voir no 1055

Czitrom, Daniel Joseph. See No./Voir no 1056

1061

Goldberg, Toby. "An Examination, Critique and Evaluation of the Mass Communications Theories of Marshall McLuhan." Wisconsin, 1971.

1062

Kingsley, Jack Calvin. "The Effect of Marshall McLuhan's Concept of Perception on the Oral Interpretation of Literature." California, Los Angeles, 1972.

Lynch, Mary Agnes. See No./Voir no 8469

1063

Maruyama, Allen. "A Theological Critique of Marshall McLuhan's New Man of the Electric Age." Aquinas Institute of Theology, 1972.

Meskill, Michael Francis. See No./Voir no 2579

1064

Norvell, George Michael. "A Reference Dictionary of Terms in the Published Works of Herbert Marshall McLuhan." Maryland, 1979.

Penta, Gerard Charles. See No./Voir no 2584

Persky, Joel. See No./Voir no 1058

1065

Quinn, James Joseph. "An Examination of the Evolution of Jazz as It Relates to the Pre-Literate and Post-Literate Percepts of Marshall McLuhan." Northwestern, 1971.

1066

Séguin, Pierre. "Marshall McLuhan, le fou du village planétaire: lecture religiologique et théologique." Montréal, 1980.

1067

Stone, Blair Francis. "Marshall McLuhan and the Humanist Tradition: Media Theory and Encyclopedic Learning." Massachusetts, 1974.

1068

Striegel, James Finley. "Marshall McLuhan on Media." Union Graduate School (Ohio), 1978.

Valaskakis, Gail Guthrie. See No./Voir no 1054

COMMUNICATIONS IN EDUCATION/ COMMUNICATIONS EN ÉDUCATION

See also Education Communications in Education/Voir aussi Éducation. Communications en éducation

PUBLIC OPINION AND PROPAGANDA/ OPINION PUBLIQUE ET PROPAGANDE

Beadle, Gordon Bruce. See No./Voir no 1078

Coughlin, Richard Maurice. See No./Voir no 9972

1069

Gow, James Iain. "The Opinions of French Canadians in Quebec on the Problems of War and Peace, 1945-1960." Laval, 1970.

1070

Kyle, Jack Leslie. "The Effect of Incentives on Mail Survey Response Rate and Content." Victoria, 1981. [Mail survey examining public opinion of community health activities/Enquête postale au sujet de l'opinion publique de la santé communautaire]

1071

Moore, Robert John. "An Investigation of Public Opinion about Seat Belts in the City of Regina Saskatchewan, Canada: A Case Study in the Application of a Clinical Quantitative Research Strategy for Public Opinion Research." Regina, 1975.

1072

Schwartz, Mildred Anne. "Canadian National Identity as Seen Through Public Opinion Polls, 1941-1963." Columbia, 1965.

1073

Young, William Robert. "Making the Truth Graphic: The Canadian Government's Home Front Information Structure and Programmes During World War II." British Columbia, 1978.

PUBLISHING/ÉDITION

1074

Fleming, Erin Patricia Lockhart. "A History of Publishing in Toronto, 1978-1841, with a Descriptive Bibliography of Imprints." London, 1980.

1075

Parker, George Lawrence. "A History of a Canadian Publishing House: A Study of the Relation Between Publishing and the Profession of Writing, 1890-1940." Toronto, 1969.

INFORMATION SERVICES/SERVICES D'INFORMATION

1076

Thirkettle, Frank William. "A Data System for the Isis-II Optical Experiments." York, 1975. [Data processing at York University/Traitement des données à l'Université York]

JOURNALISM, THE PRESS, PERIODICALS, HISTORY OF THE PRESS/ JOURNALISME, PRESSE, PÉRIODIQUES ET HISTOIRE DE LA PRESSE

Thirty dissertations are found in this classification, with 20 from 12 Canadian universities, and ten from seven American universities. Fifteen of the Canadian titles were produced between 1970 and 1980. McGill University is the leader, and the University of Toronto, York University and the universities of Montreal and Ottawa follow with two dissertations each. Of the seven American universities, Minnesota produced four studies, and six other universities each produced one.

Dans cette classification, il y a 30 thèses, dont 20 proviennent de 12 universités canadiennes et 10, de 7 universités américaines. Quinze des thèses canadiennes ont paru dans les années 1970 et 1980. L'Université McGill est en tête du mouvement; les universités de Toronto, York, de Montréal et d'Ottawa suivent avec des thèses chacune. Des 7 universités américaines, celle du Minnesota est responsable de 4 études et les 6 autres universités d'une chacune.

1077

Angers, Gérard." Un siècle de journalisme canadien." Ottawa, 1941.

1078

Beadle, Gordon Bruce. "The Canadian Press Reaction to the Abdication of Edward the VIII." Syracuse, 1966.

Binger, Jane Louise. See No./Voir no 6913

1079

Black, Hawley Lisle. "The Role of the Canadian Press News Agency in Gatekeeping Canada's News." McGill, 1979.

Borzo, Henry. See No./Voir no 7455

1080

Brunskill, Ronald. "A Newspaper Content Analysis Study of Canadian Political Integration, 1845-1895." Carleton, 1976.

1081

Careless, James M.S. "George Brown and the Toronto Globe, 1850-1867: A Study in Opinion." Harvard, 1950.

1082

Charlebois, Carol Ann. "The Structure of Federal-Provincial News." York, 1977. [A content analysis of Canadian dailies/Analyse de contenu des quotidiens canadiens]

Church, John Halcot. See No./Voir no 1825

1083

Davies, Gwendolyn. "A Literary Study of Selected Periodicals from Maritime Canada, 1789-1872." York, 1980.

Davison-Wood, Karen Margaret. See No./Voir no 942

1084

Epp, Frank Henry. "An Analysis of Germanism and National Socialism in the Immigrant Newspaper of a Canadian Minority Group, the Mennonites, in the 1930's." Minnesota, 1965.

1085

Fortin, Gérald-Adélard. "An Analysis of the Ideology of a French Canadian Nationalist Magazine: 1917-1954: A Contribution to the Sociology of Knowledge." Cornell, 1956.

Hamel, Réginald. See No./Voir no 8302

Indra, Doreen Marie. See No./Voir no 384

1086

Jones, Vernon James. "A Factor Analytic Search for Dimensions of Audience Exposure to a Mass Medium." British Columbia, 1975.

1087

Kalbfleisch, Herbert Karl. "The History of the German Newspapers of Ontario, Canada, 1835-1918." Michigan, 1953.

Lacasse, Madeleine Ladouceur. See No./Voir no 8211

1088
Lalande, Jean-Guy. "Russia and the Soviets as Seen in Canada: une recherche de l'opinion politique de la presse canadienne, de 1914 à 1921." McGill, 1981.

1089
Lefebvre, André. "Le 'Montreal Gazette' et le nationalisme canadien, 1835-1842." Montréal, 1967.

Macdonald, Helen Grace. See No./Voir no 7456

1090
McDougall, Robert Law. "A Study of Canadian Periodical Literature of the Nineteenth Century." Toronto, 1950.

1091
McLean, Elizabeth M.M. "Newspaper Reaction to Issues of Domestic and Foreign Policy in Canada." Alberta, 1978.

Mills, Michael Irwin. See No./Voir no 1049

1092
Nish, Margaret Elizabeth. "Canadian Hansard: Interpreting the Canadian Parliamentary Press During the Period of the Canadian Union." McGill, 1971.

1093
Nostbakken, David Vinge. "The Concept of Mimesis in Television Learning: A Study of the Television Learner as Participant." Toronto, 1980.

1094
Obeng-Quaidoo, Isaac. "Hutterite Land Expansion and the Canadian Press." Minnesota, 1977.

1095
Paine, Frederick Karl. "Magazine Journalism Education in British, Canada and the United States." Minnesota, 1977.

Poon, Wei Keung. See No./Voir no 2795

1096
Pride, Cletis Graden. "How Seven Commonwealth Papers Reported Foreign Affairs, 1956-1968: A Content Analysis." North Carolina, 1970. [Toronto Globe and Mail]

Proulx, Jean-Pierre. See No./Voir no 9824

1097
Reid, Philippe. "Représentations idéologiques et société globale: le journal Le Canadien (1806-1842)." Laval, 1980.

1098
Rose, Mary J. "A History of School Broadcasting in Canada." Northwestern, 1951.

Ross, Vincent. See No./Voir no 4091

1099
Saint-George, Jean. "Histoire des relations de la presse et de la radio au Canada." Montréal, 1945.

1100
Saint-Germain, Yves. "The Genesis of the French Language Business Press and Journalists in Quebec, 1871-1914." Delaware, 1975.

1101
Schiele, Bernard Eugène. "Incidence télévisuelle sur la diffusion des connaissances scientifiques vulgarisées." Montréal, 1979.

1102
Schwass, Rodger Daniel. "National Farm Radio Forum: The History of an Educational Institution in Rural Canada." Toronto, 1972.

1103
Siegel, Arthur. "Canadian Newspaper Coverage of the F.L.Q. Crisis: A Study of the Impact of the Press on Politics." McGill, 1974.

1104
Siller, Frederick Howard. "Newspaper Reading: A Study in Selective Effects." Western Ontario, 1972.

1105
Sister, Mary Julia. "The Toronto Globe and the Slavery Issues, 1850-1860." Ottawa, 1957.

Smith, Allan Charles Lethbridge. See No./Voir no 7500

Waniewicz, Ignacy. See No./Voir no 4081

1106
Wilson, Susannah Jane Foster. "The Relationship Between Mass Media Content and Social Change in Canada: An Examination of the Image of Women in Mass Circulating Canadian Magazines of 1930-1970." Toronto, 1977.

1107
Wright, Donald Kenneth. "An Analysis of the Training and Professionalization of Canadian Journalists." Minnesota, 1974.

FILM: COMMERCIAL AND EDUCATIONAL/ FILM COMMERCIAL ET ÉDUCATIF

Since doctoral research on films has grown considerably in the United States in recent years, it was thought advisable to provide a separate section for film even though the total number of studies is small. Of the ten dissertations listed, six are from four Canadian universities: McGill (2), Montreal (2), Alberta (1), and Simon Fraser (1). All were completed within the last five years. The four dissertations from the United States are from Ohio State (2), University of Southern California (1), and Stanford University (1).

———

Étant donné que les recherches sur les films se sont considérablement développées aux États-Unis ces dernières années, on a pensé qu'il était raisonnable de prévoir une section séparée pour les films, même si le nombre modeste des thèses sur ce sujet est peu élevé. Des 10 thèses énumérées, 6 sont dues à 4 universités canadiennes: l'Université McGill (2), l'Université de Montréal (2), l'Université de l'Alberta (1) et l'Université Simon Fraser (1). Toutes les thèses ont été terminées au cours des 5 dernières années. Les 4 thèses des États-Unis viennent des universités d'Ohio State (2), de Southern California (1) et de l'Université Stanford (1).

Chatwin, Arthur Edgar. See No./Voir no 4218

1108
Eley, David Roche. "Notre Pays: The Signification of the Wilderness Image in the Quebec Cinema During the Quiet Revolution." McGill, 1979.

1109
Ezekiel, Jeremiah William. "Political Content in Contemporary Commercial Films." Alberta, 1978.

Howard, Louis Wayne. See No./Voir no 10260

1110
James, Clifford Rodney. "The National Film Board of Canada: Its Task of Communication." Ohio State, 1968.

1111
James, David Barker. "The National Film Board of Canada: The Development of Its Documentary Achievement." Stanford, 1977.

1112
Miller, Robert Edwin. "The Canadian Film Development Corporation Promoting the Feature Film Industry in Canada." Southern California, 1980.

1113
Nash, M. Teresa. "Images of Women in National Film Board of Canada Films During World War II and the Post-War Years (1939-1949)." McGill, 1983.

1114
Pendakur, Manjunath. "Canadian Feature Film Industry: Monopoly and Competition." Simon Fraser, 1980.

Ruhly, Sharon Kay. See No./Voir no 484

1115
Tremblay, Christianne. "Structures sociales et idéologiques dans la pré-histoire du cinéma québécois (1942-1953)." Montréal, 1979.

1116
Véroneau, Denise. "Analyse de l'effet d'un document cinématographique sur l'attitude de citoyens québécois concernant le rôle et le statut de la femme au Québec." Montréal, 1976.

RADIO AND TELEVISION/RADIO ET TÉLÉVISION

This sector of the communications industry is divided into two sub-classifications: commercial and educational. It has been a recent subject for research, with the bulk of the dissertations appearing in the 1970's and 1980's. Of the 24 Canadian dissertations produced by 14 universities, the University of Toronto is the leader (8), followed by the University of Montreal (4), University of Western Ontario (3) and the University of British Columbia (2). The remaining ten schools produced one dissertation each. Of the 20 studies produced by 16 American universities, Stanford approved three, Michigan, Michigan State, and Wayne State approved two each, and the remaining 12 universities account for one each. Canada's increase in dissertations in the 1980's enabled it to exceed the United States in total output, 27 to 22. Twenty-nine of the total number were in the commercial area, and 20 in the educational. Canada produced 13 of that number, five from the University of Toronto.

———

Ce partie de l'industrie des communications se divise en deux sous-secteurs: commercial et éducatif. C'est là aussi un sujet de recherche récent, la majorité des études apparaissant dans les années 1970 et se poursuivant dans les années 1980. L'Université de Toronto avec 8 thèses, vient en tête des 14 universités ayant produit 24 thèses canadiennes sur le sujet; suivent dans l'ordre, l'Université de Montréal (4), l'Université Western Ontario (3) et l'Université de la Colombie-Britannique (2). Les dix autres universités du groupe comptent une thèse chacune. Aux États-Unis, 20 thèses ont été produites par 16 universités; l'Université de Stanford en a approuvé trois, celles de Michigan, de Michigan State et Wayne State chacune deux et enfin les 12 autres universités peuvent se prévaloir d'une thèse chacune. L'augmentation des thèses au Canada, de 1980 à 1984, a permis de surpasser le total des productions américaines, avec 27 thèses contre 22. Sur l'ensemble des thèses, 29 couvraient le domaine commercial et 20, celui de l'éducation. La contribution du Canada a été de 13, dont 5 pour l'Université de Toronto seulement.

Commercial/Commercial

1117
Ahmed, Sadrudin Abdulmalek. "The Relationship of Personality Characteristics and Television Programme Preference and Viewing Behaviour: A Study of London, Ontario Housewives." Western Ontario, 1974.

1118
Babe, Robert Elwood. "The Economics of the Canadian Cable Television Industry." Michigan State, 1972.

1119
Bass, Marian Helen. "Sex-Role Stereotyping on Television Programmes Popular with Children." York, 1980.

1120
Blakley, Stewart William. "Canadian Private Broadcasters and the Reestablishment of a Private Broadcasting Network." Michigan, 1979.

1121
Bourque, Paul-André. "L'écriture dramatique pour la télévision, fiction, réflexion et essai." Sherbrooke, 1982.

Caron, André-H. See No./Voir no 589

1122
Caron, Margaret Ann Bjornson. "Sex Stereotyping in Canadian Television." Regina, 1979.

1123
Cieply, Alfred. "A Multivariate Analysis of Perceptions and Attitudes Towards Violence as a Function of Television Viewing and Mental Disorder." Toronto, 1979. [Metropolitan Toronto/Toronto métropolitain]

1124
Cohen, Mitchell Evans. "The Public Television Audience: The Phantom Elite." Michigan, 1982. [728 television viewers in Ontario/728 téléspectateurs de l'Ontario]

1125
Elliott, Kim Andrew. "An Alternative Programming Strategy for International Radio Broadcasting." Minnesota, 1979.

Faris, Ronald Lyle. See No./Voir no 4022

1126
Gillespie, Gilbert Abraham. "The Apparent Viability of the Public Access (Community) Cable Television Idea in Urban North America." Kansas, 1973.

Goldberg, Gerald Elliott. See No./Voir no 9681

1127
Good, Leonard McRae. "An Econometric Model of the Canadian Cable Television Industry and the Effects of CRTC Regulation." Western Ontario, 1974.

1128
Guité, Jean Charles Michel. "Requiem for Rabbit Ears: Cable Television Policy in Canada." Stanford, 1973.

1129
Hackett, Robert Anthony. " 'Bias' in Television News: A Content Analysis of CBC and CTV National Evening Newscasts, with Special Emphasis on Labour and Business Coverage." Queen's, 1983.

1130
Hall, James Larry. "The History and Policies of the Canadian Broadcasting Corporation's International Service." Ohio University, 1973.

Hudson, Heather Elizabeth. See No./Voir no 1154

1131
Hull, William Henry Miller. "A Comparative Study of the Problems of Ministerial Responsibility in Australian and Canadian Broadcasting." Duke, 1959.

1132
Jackson, Roger Lee. "An Historical and Analytical Study of the Origin, Development and Impact of the Dramatic Programs Produced for the English Language Networks of the Canadian Broadcasting Corporation." Wayne State, 1966.

1133
Josephson, Wendy Louise. "The Effects of Violent Television upon Children's Aggression: Elicitation, Disinhibition, or Catharsis?" Manitoba, 1983.

1134
Laurence, Gérard. "Histoire des programmes de télévision. Essai méthodologique appliqué aux cinq premières années de CBFT-Montréal." Laval, 1979.

McGechaen, Alexander. See No./Voir no 1158

1135
McKay, R. Bruce. "The CBC and the Public: Management Decision Making in the English Television Service of the Canadian Broadcasting Corporation, 1970-1974." Stanford, 1976.

Miller, Robert Edward. See No./Voir no 1159
Minaudo, Vito S. See No./Voir no 1160

1136
Nolan, Michael Joseph. "Alan Plaunt and Canadian Broadcasting." Western Ontario, 1983.

1137
O'Brien, John Egli. "A History of the Canadian Radio League, 1930-1936." Southern California, 1964.

1138
Peers, Frank Wayne. "The Politics of Canadian Broadcasting: 1920-1939." Toronto, 1966.

1139
Preshing, William Anthony. "The Canadian Broadcasting Corporation's Commercial Activities, and their Interrelationship to the Corporation's Objectives and Development." Illinois, 1965.

1140
Rickwood, Roger Ronson. "Canadian Broadcasting Policy and the Private Broadcasters: 1936-1968." Toronto, 1976.

1141
Romanow, Walter Ivan. "The Canadian Content Regulations in Canadian Broadcasting: An Historical and Critical Study." Wayne State, 1974.

Rothenberg, Stuart. See No./Voir no 8853
Saint-George, Jean. See No./Voir no 1099

1142
Spector, Norman. "Communications and Sovereignty: The Regulation of Cable Television in Canada, 1968-1973." Columbia, 1977.

1143
Toogood, Alexander Featherston. "Canadian Broadcasting: A Problem of Control." Ohio State, 1969.

1144
Yates, Alan. "W.O. Mitchell's Jake and the Kid: The Canadian Popular Radio Play as Art and Social Comment." McGill, 1979.

Educational/Éducatif

1145
Bouchard, André. "Étude comparative et qualitative de l'image télévisuelle dans le processus d'acquisition de la langue maternelle (le français) chez des enfants de 5 à 7 ans." Montréal, 1978.

1146
Bushe, Cornelius. "Television Modes of Presentation and Their Implications for Learning." Toronto, 1981

1147
Dansereau, Stéphanie. "Les structures narratives et les signes économiques détenteurs de sens chez les enfants âgés de six et huit ans: étude de récits obtenus à partir d'une conte télévisuel pour enfants en lecture semi-analytique." Montréal, 1978.

1148
Ditzel, Thomas Mervyn. "Developmental Problems in Establishing an Educational Television Station: A Case Study of the Organization, Programming, Finances and Evaluation Aspects of Canada's First ETV Broadcasting Service." Ohio State, 1971.

Faris, Ronald Lyle. See No./Voir no 4022

1149
Gailey, Richard Willard. "Qualifications of Canadian Broadcast Education Faculty: A Comparison to Model Qualifications as Recommended by Two Juries of Experts." Brigham Young, 1980.

1150
Gillis, Lynette Marie. "Using Questions to Facilitate Learning in Children's Educational Television." Toronto, 1982.

1151
Harrison, Linda Faye. "The Relationship Between Television Viewing and School Children's Performance: A Measures of Ideational Fluency and Intelligence: A Field Study." British Columbia, 1977.

1152
Higgins, Christopher Alan. "Analysis of a Remote Health Care System with Telemedicine." Waterloo, 1981.

1153
Hodapp, Timothy Victor. "The Use of Television as a Modelling Agent for Problem-Solving Strategies." Toronto, 1976.

1154
Hudson, Heather Elizabeth. "Community Communication and Development: A Canadian Case Study." Stanford, 1974. [Northwestern Ontario and central Arctic/Nord-Ouest de l'Ontario et centre de l'Arctique]

1155
Kingson, Walter Krulevitch. "National School Broadcasts of the Canadian Broadcasting Corporation." New York, 1949.

1156
Klos, Frank William, Jr. "A Study of the Origin, Development and Impact of the Davey and Goliath Television Series, 1959-1977 and Its Present Effectiveness in Teaching Religious Values to Children." Temple, 1979.

1157
Knutson, Franklin Albert. "A Survey of Religious Radio Broadcasting in St. John's, Newfoundland." Michigan State, 1969.

Mandel, Alan Rudolf. See No./Voir no 9113

1158
McGechaen, Alexander. "The Role of Television in Adult Education." British Columbia, 1978.

1159
Miller, Robert Edward. "An Investigation into the Treatment of Visual Information Through the Television Medium." Calgary, 1971.

1160
Minaudo, Vita S. "Schématisme intellectuel et récognition de messages télévisés." Ottawa, 1971. [Secondary school seniors/Étudiants de 2e cycle du secondaire]

(8), Manchester (4), Liverpool (2), and four other universities.

———

Les études en économie au Canada ont eu beaucoup de succès et constituent la quatrième plus importante classification. Les travaux en ce domaine ont été plus abondants dans les universités américaines dans les années 1970 et 1980; la recherche dans les universités canadiennes a également pris de l'extension. En 1894 en effet, l'Université Columbia faisait paraître la première thèse sur l'économie canadienne, et, en 1897 c'était le tour de l'Université de Chicago. Avant les années 1970, la production américaine avait surpassé celle du Canada. Cependant, de 1970 à 1974, le nombre des thèses canadiennes a augmenté grâce à l'Université de Toronto qui a produit environ un quart du nombre total des études canadiennes. Les universités McGill et Western Ontario, l'Université de la Colombie-Britannique et l'Université Queen suivent dans l'ordre. Quant aux universités américaines, l'Université Harvard mène le mouvement, l'Université de Chicago vient en seconde place, à bonne distance et ensuite les universités California (Berkeley) Michigan, Pennsylvania et Columbia, chacune à son rang. L'économie canadienne occupe la seconde place parmi les sujets d'études de quelque importance sur le Canada, auxquels s'intéressent les universités britanniques avec un total de 72 thèses en ce domaine. Des 9 universités britanniques, l'Université de Londres mène le jeu avec un total de 44 thèses, suivi par Oxford (1), Cambridge (8), Manchester (4), Liverpool (2) et 4 autres universités (une thèse chacune).

ECONOMICS/ÉCONOMIE

The study of Canadian economics has been very popular, making it the fourth largest classification. Work on the subject was more prolific in American universities until the 1970's and 1980's, when graduate research in Canadian universities increased dramatically. In 1894, Columbia University produced the first dissertation, and in 1897, the University of Chicago produced the second dissertation on Canadian economics. In each of the decades prior to the 1970's, the American output exceeded the Canadian. However, in the first four years of the 1970's, the number of dissertations from Canadian universities increased with the University of Toronto producing one quarter of the Canadian total. McGill University, the universities of Western Ontario, British Columbia, and Queen's follow in that order. Among the American universities, Harvard is the leader with Chicago a distant second, and the University of California (Berkeley), the University of Michigan, Pennsylvania, and Columbia following in that order. Canadian economics is the second-largest area of Canadiana studied in British universities, with a total of 72 dissertations. Of the nine British universities represented in this area, London is the leader with a total of 44 studies, followed by Oxford (1), Cambridge

GENERAL ITEMS/OUVRAGES GÉNÉRAUX

1161
Ahking, Francis Wilson. "Testing for Neutrality and Rationality with an Open-Economy Model: The Case of Canada." Virginia Polytechnic and State University, 1981.

1162
Aziz, Rashid. "The Regional Distribution Pattern of Economic Activity in Canada: A Linear Programming Exercise." McMaster, 1981.

1163
Bannister, Geoffrey. "Modes of Change in the Ontario Economy." Toronto, 1974.

1164
Beaucage, André. "Idéologie, solidarité et politique salariale syndicale: l'expérience des fronts communs du secteur public québécois, de 1971 à 1975." Montréal, 1982.

1165
Bourdeau de Fontenay, Alain Jean-Marie Daniel. "A Contribution to the Foundations of Seasonal Analysis." Vanderbilt, 1979.

1166
Cuddy, J.D.A. "The Optimization of Micro-Economic Policy: A Canadian Study." Cambridge, 1975.

1167
Dungan, Douglas Peter. "An Empirical, Multi-Sectoral, Walrasian-Keynesian Model of the Canadian Economy." Princeton, 1980.

1168
Fernandez-Suarez, Antonio. "La demande des actifs risqués dans un contexte canadien." Montréal, 1980.

Gillen, David William. See No./Voir no 4928

1169
Goulding, James Wray. "The Last Outport: Newfoundland in Crisis." York, 1981.

1170
Hafez, Bahjat Mohammad. "The Design and Estimation of Regional Economic Accounts in Ontario." McMaster, 1979.

1171
Harel-Giasson, Francine. "Perception et actualisation des facteurs de promotion chez les femmes, cadres des grandes entreprises québécoises francophones du secteur privé." Montréal, 1982.

1172
Hobbs J.-Brian. "Les transformations dans le discours du développement organisationnel sur les organisations: une étude empirique de la production théorique." Laval, 1983.

1173
Hotson, John Hargrove. "An International Comparison of the Stability of Wage Cost Markup and Gross Income Velocity of Circulation." Pennsylvania, 1964.

1174
Irvine, Ian Joseph. "An Analysis of the Distribution of Lifetime Purchasing Power in Canada." Western Ontario, 1979.

1175
Keeley, James Francis. "Constraints on Canadian International Economic Policy." Stanford, 1980.

1176
Lasserre, Pierre. "Factor Demands and Output Supply by the Extractive Firm: Theory and Estimation." British Columbia, 1982.

1177
Latham, Allan Brockway. "Some Economic and Social Aspects of Roman Catholicism in French Canada." Harvard, 1931.

1178
Lloyd, Cynthia Brown. "The Effect of Child Subsidies on Fertility: An International Study." Columbia, 1972.

1179
Lowry, Douglas Bradley. "Economic Motivation among Canadian Calvinists." Massachusetts Institute of Technology, 1970.

1180
Matossian, Nicholas V. "The Economic Allocation of Government Expenditures in Canada and the Role of Social Rate of Return Analyses." McGill, 1981.

1181
McLeod, Alexander N. "Maintaining Employment and Incomes in Canada: A Study of the Special Difficulties Faced by a Country that is Dependent on International Trade and is Committed to the Maintenance of Domestic Employment and Incomes." Harvard, 1949.

1182
Morefield, Roger Dale. "Economic Planning and the Economic Council of Canada." Duke, 1977.

Morey, Edward Rockendorf. See No./Voir no 10445

1183
Nehlawi, Joseph. "Consistent and Efficient Estimation of Real Econometric Models with Undersized Samples: A Study of the Trace Economic Model of the Canadian Economy." Dalhousie, 1975.

1184
O'Neill, Timothy John. "The Role of Private Non-Profit Research Organizations in Policy Formation: A Case Study of the Atlantic Provinces Economic Council and the Institute of Public Affairs." Duke, 1979.

1185
Raynauld, Jacques. "An Aggregate Short-Run Canadian Macro Model: Multiple Time Series, Analysis and Rational Expectations." Queen's, 1982.

1186
Reid, Roger Thomas. "The Effective Protection of Canadian Production by Tariffs, Trade Costs, Taxes and Subsidies." Queen's, 1976.

1187
Sabourin, Conrad. "Économie des langues: aspects théoriques et applications." Concordia, 1980.

1188
Sallows, Sharon Heather. "An Organizational Analysis of the Use of the Crown Corporation as a Tool of Public Policy." Pennsylvania, 1978.

1189
Schroeder, Harold John. "Corporate Social Performance in Canada: Reasons and Remedies for the Expectations-Reality Gap." Southern California, 1981.

1190
Seccareccia, Mario Sebastiano. "Price Changes and Movements in the Composition of Output and Employment in Canada: Theoretical Framework and Empirical Analysis." McGill, 1983.

1191
Sugges, Peter R. Jr. "Beliefs about the Multinational Enterprise: A Factor Analytic Study of British, Canadian, French and Mexican Elites." New York, 1976.

1192
Syed, Aftab Ali. "Structural Change, Key Sectors and Linkage-Balanced Growth: An Input-Output Analysis of the Canadian Economy." Simon Fraser, 1976.

1193
Thachenkary, Cherian Sebastian. "An Empirical Evaluation of Some Determinants of Organizational Communication." Waterloo, 1981.

1194
Wahn, Michael Brian. "Economic Development and Native Health in the Northwest Territories." Alberta, 1980.

1195
Wilson, Thomas Frederick. "Energy Price Policies in Canada and Mexico." Stanford, 1982.

1196
Winter, George Robert. "External Economies and Diseconomies in Economic Development with Reference to Canada." Iowa State, 1962.

Young, John Geoffrey. See No./Voir no 1776

1197
Young, J.H. "Some Aspects of Canadian Economic Development." Oxford, 1955.

1198
Zandi, Farokh-Reza. "The Effects of an Oil Price Rise on Inflation, Output and the Exchange Rate in the Case of Subsidization Policy." Carleton, 1982.

ECONOMIC HISTORY/HISTOIRE DE L'ÉCONOMIE

See also Agricultural History, Financial History, Labor History, Tariffs and Trade/Voir aussi Histoire de l'agriculture, Histoire des finances, Histoire du travail, Tarifs et commerce

General Items/Ouvrages généraux

1199
Bellemare, Diane. "La sécurité du revenu au Canada: une analyse économique de l'avénement de l'état-providence." McGill, 1981. [Colonial period to the present/De la période coloniale à aujourd'hui]

Britnell, George Edwin. See No./Voir no 139

1200
Clark, Samuel Delbert. "The Canadian Manufacturers' Association: A Political and Social Study." Toronto, 1938.

1201
Corbett, David C. "Immigration, Population Growth, and Canadian Economic Development." McGill, 1955.

1202
Cousineau, Rosario. "Histoire de la politique commerciale extérieure du Canada de 1602 à 1951." Ottawa, 1952.

Dawson, Nora. See No./Voir no 435

1203
Epp, Abram Ernest. "Cooperation Among Capitalists: The Canadian Merger Movement." Johns Hopkins, 1973.

1204
Goodwin, Craufurd David Wycliffe. "Canadian Economic Thought: The Political Economy of a Developing Nation, 1814-1914." Duke, 1958.

1205
James, Hugh Mackenzie. "Monopoly Relations in the Canadian State, 1939-1957." British Columbia, 1983.

1206
Jones, Clarence Fielden. "The Port of Montreal." Chicago, 1923.

1207
Kelley, George Thomas. "Early Canadian Industrialization: A Case Study in Relative Backwardness." Clark, 1971.

1208
Kraft, Calvin T. "The Financial Relationship Between the Provinces and the Dominion of Canada." Harvard, 1937.

Lesage, Germain. See No./Voir no 4816

1209
Lithwick, Irwin. "The Growth of Urban Population in Canada to 1976: An Economic Model." Western Ontario, 1974.

1210
Lithwick, Norman Harvey. "Economic Growth in Canada: A Quantitative Analysis." Harvard, 1964.

Lyon, Noël Adversé. See No./Voir no 29

1211
Macleod, Betty Belle Robinson. "A History of Canadian Economic Development with Special Reference to Immigration." Duke, 1967.

1212
McCarty, John Myron. "Economic Aspects in the Evolution of the Great Lakes Freighter." Southern California, 1971.

Morantz, Toby Elaine. See No./Voir no 512

Neill, Robert Foliet. See No./Voir no 6950

1213
Partin, Charles Arthur. "Roots of State Entrepreneurship in Australia, Canada, and the United States: A Comparative Study." Texas, 1961.

1214
Petersen, James Otto. "The Origins of Canadian Mining: The Part Played by Labor in the Transition from Tool Production to Machine Production." Toronto, 1978.

1215
Rakhra, Amrik S. "The Economic Development of the Eastern Ontario Region: An Historical Analysis." Ottawa, 1982.

1216
Rotstein, Abraham. "Fur Trade and Empire: An Institutional Analysis." Toronto, 1967.

Stites, Sara Henry. See No./Voir no 656

1217
Taylor, Norman William. "A Study of French Canadians as Industrial Entrepreneurs." Yale, 1958.

1218
Woodsworth, Glenn James. "The Influence of the Far East on Canadian Social and Economic History." London, 1940.

- 1763

1219
Allaire, Gratien. "Les engagés de la fourrure, 1701-1745: une étude de leur motivation." Concordia, 1981.

1220
Comeau, Roger. "Pêche et traite en Acadie jusqu'en 1713." Ottawa, 1949.

1221
Daigle, Jean. "Nos amis les ennemis: relations commerciales de l'Acadie avec le Massachussetts, 1670-1711." Maine, 1975.

1222
Davies, G.J. "England and Newfoundland: Policy and Trade, 1660-1783." Southampton, 1979.

1223
Fuller, George Newman. "Economic and Social Beginnings of Michigan." Michigan, 1916.

Herman, Mary W. See No./Voir no 466

1224
Igartua, José Eduardo. "The Merchants and Negociantes of Montréal, 1750-1775: A Study in Socio-Economic History." Michigan State, 1974.

1225
Johnson, Amanda. "The Michigan Fur Trade." Chicago, 1925.

Kupp, Theodorius Johannes. See No./Voir no 6979

1226
Lawson, Murray Grant. "A Study in English Mercantilism, 1700-1775." California, Berkeley, 1943.

1227
Lounsbury, Ralph Greenlee. "The British Fishery of Newfoundland in the British Commercial and Colonial System, 1660-1763." Yale, 1928.

1228
Lunn, Alice Jean. "Economic Development in New France, 1713-1760." McGill, 1942.

1229
Matthews, K. "The West Country-Newfoundland Fisheries (Chiefly in the Seventeenth and Eighteenth Centuries)." Oxford, 1968.

1230
Miquelon, Dale Bernard. "Robert Dugard and the Societé au Canada of Rouen, 1729-1770." Toronto, 1973.

Munro, William Bennett. See No./Voir no 6970

1231
Murray, Jean E. "The Fur Trade in New France and New Netherlands Prior to 1645." Chicago, 1937.

Ott, Edward R. See No./Voir no 7007

1232
Pritchard, James Stewart. "Ships, Men and Commerce: A Study of Maritime Activity in New France." Toronto, 1971.

1763-1849

1233
Aitken, Hugh G.J. "W.H. Merritt and the Welland Canal Company: A Study in the Entrepreneurial Approach to Economic History." Harvard, 1951.

1234
Antler, Steven David. "Colonial Exploitation and Economic Stagnation in Nineteenth Century Newfoundland." Connecticut, 1975.

1235
Bain, Colin M. "The Social Impact of Kirkaldy's Industrial Revolution." Guelph, 1973.

1236
Bell, Herbert Clifford. "Studies in the Trade Relations of British West Indies and North America, 1763-1773, 1783-1793." Pennsylvania, 1909.

1237
Bridgewater, William R. "The American Fur Company." Yale, 1938.

1238
Brown, George Williams. "The St. Lawrence Waterway as a Factor in International Trade and Politics, 1783-1854." Chicago, 1924.

1239
Carlos, Ann Martina. "The North American Fur Trade, 1804-1821: A Study in the Life-Cycle of Duopoly." Western Ontario, 1980.

1240
Cross, Michael Sean. "The Dark Druidical Groves: The Lumber Community and the Commercial Frontier in British North America to 1854." Toronto, 1968.

1241
Davidson, Gordon Charles. "The Northwest Company." California, Berkeley, 1916.

Davies, G.J. See No./Voir no 1222

1242
Forster, John Jakob Benjamin. "Tariffs and Politics: The Genesis of the National Policy, 1842-1879." Toronto, 1982.

1243
Hall, Roger Denis. "The Canada Company, 1826-1843." Cambridge, 1974.

1244
Jenks, Leland Hamilton. "The Migration of British Capital to 1875." Columbia, 1927.

1245
Karamanski, Theodore John. "The Last Divide: The Fur Trade and the Exploration of the Far Northwest 1821-1852." Loyola, Chicago, 1980. [Hudson's Bay Company/Compagnie de la Baie d'Hudson]

Krech, Shepard, III. See No./Voir no 416

Lal, Ravindra. See No./Voir no 473

1246
Leader, Herman Alexander. "The Hudson's Bay Company in California, 1830-1846." California, Berkeley, 1927.

Mays, Herbert Joseph. See No./Voir no 131

1247
McCallum, John C.P. "Agriculture and Economic Development in Quebec and Ontario to 1870." McGill, 1977.

McGuigan, Gerald Frederick. See No./Voir no 136

1248
Muller, Henry N., III. "The Commercial History of the Lake Champlain - Richelieu River Route, 1760-1815." Rochester, 1969.

1249
O'Leary, Wayne M. "The Maine Sea Fisheries, 1830-1896: The Rise and Fall of a Native Industry." Maine, 1981. [Important references to the Nova Scotia cod fisheries/Importantes références à la pêche à la morue en Nouvelle-Écosse]

1250
Ommer, Rosemary Elizabeth. "From Outpost to Outpost: The Jersey Merchant Triangle in the Nineteenth Century." McGill, 1979.

1251
O'Neil, Marion. "The Northwest Company on the Pacific Slope." California, Berkeley, 1941.

1252
Ouellet, Fernand. "Histoire économique et sociale du Québec, 1760-1850, structures et conjonctures." Laval, 1965.

1253
Rice, J.R.E. "Shipbuilding in British America, 1787-1890: an Introductory Study." Liverpool, 1978.

1254
Rothney, G.O. "British Policy in the North American Cod Fisheries with Special Reference to Foreign Competition, 1776-1819." London, 1939.

1255
Ryan, S.P. "Newfoundland's Saltfish Markets, 1814-1914." London, 1982.

Séguin, Maurice. See No./Voir no 115

Setzer, Vernon G. See No./Voir no 2348

Sirridge, Agnes T. See No./Voir no 7047

Sutherland, David Alexander. See No./Voir no 7181

Swan, G.R. See No./Voir no 7264

1256
Tucker, Gilbert N. "The Economic History of the Province of Canada, 1845-1851." Cambridge, 1930.

1257
Tulchinsky, Gerald Jacob Joseph. "Studies of Businessmen in the Development of Transportation and Industry in Montréal, 1837-1853." Toronto, 1971.

1850-1930

Antler, Steven David. See No./Voir no 1234

1258
Armstrong, Robert. "The Asbestos Industry in Quebec, 1878-1929." Laval, 1979.

Babcock, Robert Harper. See No./Voir no 2091

Belfield, Robert Blake. See No./Voir no 1782

1259
Blain, Lawrence Alexander. "Regional Cyclical Behaviour and Sensitivity in Canada, 1919-1973." British Columbia, 1977.

1260
Bliss, John William Michael. "A Living Profit: Studies in the Social History of Canadian Business, 1883-1911." Toronto, 1972.

1261
Buckley, Suzann Caroline. "Attempts at Imperial Economic Planning, 1887-1919: The Canadian Response." Duke, 1972.

1262
Burton, A.M. "The Influence of the Treasury on the Making of British Colonial Policy, 1868-1880." Oxford, 1960.

1263
Churchill, Anthony Aylward. "The Staple and Economic Growth: The Canadian Wheat Boom, 1900-1914." Washington, Seattle, 1967.

1264
Common, Sarah. "The Economics of the Settlement of the Prairie Provinces of Canada 1900-1931." London, 1933.

1265
Craven, Paul. "An Impartial Umpire: Industrial Relations and the Canadian State, 1900-1911." Toronto, 1980.

Cummins, John Gaylord. See No./Voir no 1815

Dales, John Harkness. See No./Voir no 1784

1266
Degen, Robert Arthur. "Some Major Factors in the Development of the Canadian Economy, 1900-1950." Wisconsin, 1956.

1267
Delmas, Paul Julian George. "Mergers in Canadian Industry, 1890-1914." Columbia, 1973.

1268
Donald, William John Alexander. "The Canadian Iron and Steel History: A Study in the Economic History of a Protected Industry." Chicago, 1914.

1269
Dow, Alexander Carmichael. "The Canadian Base Metal Mining Industry (Non-Ferrous) and Its Impact on Economic Development in Canada, 1918-1955." Manitoba, 1980.

1270
Drummond, Ian MacDonald. "Capital Markets in Australia and Canada, 1895-1914: A Study in Colonial Economic History." Yale, 1959.

1271
Eaton, Albert Kenneth. "Canada and the Gold Standard, 1926-1931." Harvard, 1933.

Farrar, Floyd Alvin. See No./Voir no 7655

Forster, John Jacob Benjamin. See No./Voir no 1242

Forbes, Ernest R. See No./Voir no 2280

1272
Gallacher, Daniel Thomas. "Men, Money, Machines: Studies Comparing Colliery Operations and Factors of Production in British Columbia's Coal Industry to 1891." British Columbia, 1979.

Gervais, Gaétan S. See No./Voir no 2303

1273
Gutzke, David William. "The Brewing Industry as a Pressure Group, 1875-1914." Toronto, 1982.

Hall, Carl Ansel St. Clair. See No./Voir no 1786

Haslett, Earl Allan. See No./Voir no 1802

Holmes, James M. See No./Voir no 2013

1274
Jessop, David. "Anglo-Canadian Commercial Relations, 1896-1911." Dalhousie, 1974.

1275
Jestin, Warren James. "Provincial Policy and the Development of the Metallic Mining Industry in Northern Ontario: 1845-1920." Toronto, 1977.

Krech, Shepard, III. See No./Voir no 416

Lal, Ravindra. See No./Voir no 473

1276
Lautard, Emile Hugh. "Occupational Segregation by Sex and Industrialization in Canada: 1891-1971." British Columbia, 1978.

1277
Laxer, Gordon David. "The Social Origins of Canada's Branch Plant Economy, 1837-1914." Toronto, 1981.

1278
Lowe, Graham Stanley. "The Administrative Revolution: The Growth of Clerical Occupations and the Development of the Modern Office in Canada, 1911-1931." Toronto, 1979.

1279
Lower, Arthur Reginald M. "Lumbering in Canada: A Study in Economics and Social History." Harvard, 1929.

1280
MacLeod, Donald Eric. "Miners, Mining Men and Mining Reform: Changing the Technology of Nova Scotian Gold Mines and Collieries, 1858-1910." Toronto, 1982.

1281
MacPherson, Hector. "Cooperative Credit Associations in the Province of Quebec." Chicago, 1910.

1282
Main, Oscar Warren. "The Canadian Nickel Industry, 1885-1939: A Study in Market Control and Public Policy." Toronto, 1953.

1283
Masters, D.C. "The Reciprocity Treaty of 1854: Its History and Its Relations to British Colonial and Foreign Policy and to the Development of Canadian Fiscal Autonomy." Oxford, 1935.

Mattson, Margaret Solveig. See No./Voir no 2273

1284
Maule, C.J. "Mergers in Canadian Industry, 1900-1963." London, 1966.
Mays, Herbert Joseph. See No./Voir no 131
McCallum, John C.P. See No./Voir no 1247
1285
McCarty, J.W. "British Investment in Overseas Mining, 1880-1914." Cambridge, 1961.
1286
McClelland, Peter Dean. "The New Brunswick Economy in the Nineteenth Century." Harvard, 1967.
1287
McDonald, Robert Arthur John. "Business Leaders in Early Vancouver 1886-1914." British Columbia, 1977.
1288
McDougall, Duncan Michael. "The Economic Growth of Canada and the U.S., 1870-1955: A Quantitative Analysis of Selected Aspects." Johns Hopkins, 1958.
1289
McDowall, Duncan L. "Steel at the Sault: Sir James Dunn and the Algoma Steel Corporation, 1906-1956." Carleton, 1978.
1290
McGahan, Elizabeth Moore Walsh. "The Port in the City: Saint John, N.B. (1867-1911) and the Process of Integration." New Brunswick, 1979.
1291
McInnis, Robert Marvin. "Regional Income Differentials in Canada 1911 to 1961." Pennsylvania, 1966.
Meany, Edmond Stephen, Jr. See No./Voir no 1834
1292
Mifflen, Francis James. "The Antigonish Movement: A Revitalization Movement in Eastern Nova Scotia." Boston College, 1974.
Naylor, R.T. See No./Voir no 1518
1293
Noble, Edward James. "Men and Circumstances: Entrepreneurs and Community Growth: A Case Study of Orillia, Ontario, 1867-1898." Guelph, 1980.
O'Leary, Wayne M. See No./Voir no 1249
Ommer, Rosemary Elizabeth. See No./Voir no 1250
Paquette, Pierre Jean. See No./Voir no 1880
1294
Parker, Keith Alfred. "The Staple Industries and Economic Development, Canada, 1841-1867." Maryland, 1966.
Patton, Arald Smith. See No./Voir no 119
1295
Piedalue, Gilles. "La bourgeoisie canadienne et le problème de la réalisation du profit au Canada, 1900-1930." Montréal, 1930.
Pinchin, Hugh McAlester. See No./Voir no 1997
1296
Pulker, Edward A. "The Role of Anglicans in Reform of the Economic Order in Canada, 1914-1945." Ottawa, 1974.
Rea, James E. See No./Voir no 7325
1297
Rea, K.J. "The Canadian Northwest: A Study in Sub-Arctic Economic Development, 1898-1958." London, 1959.
Rice, J.R.E. See No./Voir no 1253

1298
Rosenfeld, Barry David. "Canadian Government Expenditures, 1871-1966." Pennsylvania, 1972.
1299
Ross, William Gillies. "Hudson Bay Whaling, 1860-1915." Cambridge, 1971.
Ryan, S.P. See No./Voir no 1255
1300
Ryan, William Francis. "Economic Development and the Church in French Canada, 1896-1914." Harvard, 1914.
1301
Schwartzman, David. "Mergers in the Nova Scotia Coal Fields: A History of the Dominion Coal Company, 1893-1940." California, Berkeley, 1953.
1302
Stabler, Jack Carr. "Regional Development Theory and the Growth of the Canadian Prairie Region, 1870-1961." Utah, 1969.
1303
Stanbury, William Thomas. "Changes in the Size and Structure of Government Expenditure in Canada, 1867-1968." California, Berkeley, 1972.
1304
Steele, Marion Louise. "Dwelling Starts in Canada, 1921-1940." Toronto, 1972.
Struthers, James Edward. See No./Voir no 2198
1305
Swiger, Ernest Cullimore, Jr. "The Big Markets of the Old World: Canadian Commercial Relations with Europe, 1896-1914." Duke, 1975.
1306
Traves, Thomas Donald. "Security and Enterprise-Canadian Manufacturers and the State, 1917-1931." York, 1976. [Newsprint, sugar refining, automobiles and primary iron and steel/Papier-journal, raffinerie de sucre, automobile, fer et acier bruts]
1307
Trimble, William Joseph. "The Mining Advance into the Inland Empire: A Comparative Study of the Beginnings of the Mining Industry in Idaho and Montana, Eastern Washington and Oregon, and the Southern Interior of British Columbia and of Institutions and Laws Based upon that Industry." Wisconsin, 1909.
1308
Whetten, Nathan Laselle. "Social and Economic Structures of the Trade Centers in the Canadian Prairie Provinces, with Special Reference to Its Changes, 1910-1930." Harvard, 1932.
Williams, Glen Sutherland. See No./Voir no 1398
1309
Woroby, Tamara M. "Changes in Wage Inequality: The Canadian Experience, 1901-1921." Queen's, 1981.

1930 - 1983

1310
Alexandrin, Glen Gleb. "A Study of Investment, Employment and Growth in Newfoundland with a Statistical Analysis of the Period 1949-1961." Clark, 1967.

1311
Anderson, Barry Lowell. "Royal Commissions, Economists and Policy: A Study of the Economic Advisory Process in Post War Canada." Duke, 1978.

Ansari, Salmuddin. See No./Voir no 4779

Aronsen, Lawrence Robert. See No./Voir no 2385

Blain, Lawrence Alexander. See No./Voir no 1259

1312
Blauer, Rosalind. "Inflation and the Redistribution of Income and Net Worth of Canadian Households, 1950-1967." McGill, 1971.

1313
Brodie, Henry. "Selective Price Control in Canada, World War II." New York, 1943.

Campbell, Robert Malcolm. See No./Voir no 1374

1314
Chambers, Fergus James. "Interrelationships of Canadian Economic Policies, 1945-1950." Toronto, 1959.

Cummins, John Gaylord. See No./Voir no 1815

Dales, John Harkness. See No./Voir no 1784

Degen, Robert Arthur. See No./Voir no 1266

Dow, Alexander Carmichael. See No./Voir no 1269

Farrar, Floyd Alvin. See No./Voir no 7655

1315
Finkel, Alvin. "Canadian Business and the 'Reform' Process in the 1930's." Toronto, 1976.

1316
Finlay, John Robert. "Structural and Dynamic Change in Grocery Retailing in Canada, 1930-1970." Queen's, 1970.

1317
George, Ronald Edison. "Nova Scotia's Post-War Industrial Development." London, 1967.

1318
Goodman, Isaac B. "Some Aspects of Canadian Commercial Policy, 1930-1949." California, Berkeley, 1950.

1319
Grey, R.Y. "Canadian Federal Institutions and Economic Policy, 1939-1950." London, 1953.

1320
Hart, Douglas John. "State Economic Management in Wartime: A Study of the 'Regimentation' of Industry in the Canadian Industrial Mobilization." York, 1981.

1321
Hill, Edmund Russell. "A Comparative Study of the United States and Canadian Economies Based on Selected Key Indicators, 1929 to 1956." Pittsburgh, 1961.

Johnston, Robert Alexander. See No./Voir no 1618

1322
Khemani, R.K. "Concentration in Canadian Manufacturing Industries, 1948-1972: A Sample Study." London, 1979.

1323
Kitchen, Brigitte. "Canadian Controversy over Family Income Support, Policies - 1928-1976." London, 1977.

Krech, Shepard, III. See No./Voir no 416

1324
Marcus, Edward. "Economic Fluctuations in Canada, 1927-1939." Princeton, 1950.

Maule, C.J. See No./Voir no 1284

1325
McCready, Douglas Jackson. See No./Voir no 1325

McDougall, Duncan Michael. See No./Voir no 1288

McDowall, Duncan L. See No./Voir no 1289, 1897

McInnis, Robert Marvin. See No./Voir no 1291

1326
Mellish, Gordon Hartley. "Official Intervention and the Canadian Dollar, 1950-1962." Virginia, 1965.

1327
Mhun, Henry. "L'influence de la guerre sur la production et la distribution au Canada." Montréal, 1950.

1328
Mings, Turley Ray. "An Inter-Country Comparison of the Factors Determining Cyclical Behavior in Sweden, Canada, Austria and Belgium, 1929-1937." California, Berkeley, 1966.

Paquette, Pierre Jean. See No./Voir no 1880

Pilcher, Dalton Jefferson. See No./Voir no 2374

Pinchin, Hugh McAlester. See No./Voir no 1997

1329
Poulin-Simon, Lise. "Le loisir industriel et le chômage au Canada: une histoire économique." McGill, 1977.

Pulker, Edward A. See No./Voir no 1296

Rea, K.J. See No./Voir no 1297

1330
Rege, Udayan Purushottama. "Domestic and Foreign Takeovers of Canadian Business Corporations, 1962-1973." Western Ontario, 1978.

1331
Rose, Albert. "Cyclical Problems in Canadian Post-War Readjustment." Illinois, 1942.

Rosenberg, Mark Warren. See No./Voir no 6696

Rosenfeld, Barry David. See No./Voir no 1298

Rowland, Benjamin Moore. See No./Voir no 7572

1332
Safarian, Albert Edward. "The Canadian Economy in the Great Depression." California, Berkeley, 1956.

Schwartzman, David. See No./Voir no 1301

1333
Sharpe, Donald Andrew. "The Structure of the Canadian Economy, 1961-1976: A Marxian Input-Output Analysis." McGill, 1982.

1334
Sievwright, Eric Colville. "The Effect of Petroleum Development on the Alberta Economy, 1947-1957." McGill, 1961.

1335
Spence, Ernest J.H. "Canadian War-Time Price Control, 1941-1947." Northwestern, 1947.

Stabler, Jack Carr. See No./Voir no 1302

Stanbury, William Thomas. See No./Voir no 1303

Steele, Marion Louise. See No./Voir no 1304

1336
Stewart, Ian Affleck. "A Quarterly Econometric Model of the Canadian Model, 1951-1962." Cornell, 1966.

1337
Waddell, Christopher Robb. "The Wartime Prices and Trade Board: Price Control in Canada in World War II." York, 1981.

1338
Wold, Ivor Peterson. "Economic Change in Canada, Pre-War to Recent, Emphasizing Aggregates." Texas, 1960.

CANADIAN ECONOMIC THEORY/ THÉORIE SUR L'ÉCONOMIE CANADIENNE

Alexander, Malcolm Laurence. See No./Voir no 1367

Baba, Vishwanath Venkataraman. See No./Voir no 1926

1339
Bakony, Leo Irwin. "A Quarterly Econometric Model of the Canadian Economy." Washington, Seattle, 1959.

1340
Barber, Clarence Lyle. "Inventories and the Business Cycle, with Special Reference to Canada." Minnesota, 1952.

1341
Beare, J.B. "A Theoretical and Empirical Analysis of the Determination of the Price-Level with Special Reference to Canada." London, 1970.

1342
Burton, David Anthony Travis. "Expectations and a Small Open Economy." Western Ontario, 1979.

Campbell, Robert Malcolm. See No./Voir no 1374

1343
Canzoneri, Matthew Buford. "An Econometric Model of Canada Incorporating Rational Expectations and Designed for Control Theory Applications." Minnesota, 1975.

Clarke, Phyllis Esphere. See No./Voir no 1376

1344
Daub, Mervin Austin. "An Appraisal of Canadian Short-Term Aggregate Economic Forecasts." Chicago, 1972.

1345
Davies, Gordon Wilson. "An Economic-Demographic Simulation Model Designed to Test the Effects of Changes in the Rate and Skill Composition of Net Immigration on the Canadian Economy from 1952-1968." Michigan, 1972.

1346
Davis, Thomas Edward. "An Econometric Model of the Current Account of the Canadian Balance of Payments." Michigan, 1965.

1347
Dino, Richard Nicholas. "An Econometric Test of the Purchasing Power Parity Theory: Canada 1870-1975." SUNY, Buffalo, 1977.

Dungan, Douglas Peter. See No./Voir no 1167

Fortin, Bernard Fernand. See No./Voir no 2057

Goodwin, Craufurd David Wycliffe. See No./Voir no 1204

1348
Gorbet, Frederick William. "Formula Flexibility and the Performance of the Canadian Economy: A Simulation Study Using the RDX2 Econometric Model." Duke, 1972.

Goulding, James Wray. See No./Voir no 1169

1349
Gregory, Allan Walter. "The Demand for Money in Canada: An Econometric Evaluation of the Conventional Specification." Queen's, 1982.

1350
Hartwick, John Martin. "Regional Analysis by Means of Interregional Input-Output Models and Linear Programming with Application to Eastern Canada." Johns Hopkins, 1969.

Holmes, James M. See No./Voir no 2013

1351
Lau, Honkan K. "Adaptive Optimal Regulation of the Canadian Economy Using Optional Control Theory." Toronto, 1974.

Lazaridis, Pavagiotis. See No./Voir no 1754

Mathieu, Nicolas Jean. See No./Voir no 1482

1352
McFarland, Joan Murray. "Linder and Demand-Led Theories of the Pattern of Trade: A Review in the Canadian Context." McGill, 1971.

Morin, Roger-André. See No./Voir no 1485

Neill, Robert Foliet. See No./Voir no 6950

1353
Nobbs, Richard Albert. "A Computerized Organization Model: Its Development and the Measurement of Its Benefits in a Strategic Planning Situation." Western Ontario, 1972.

Penner, Norman. See No./Voir no 8460

1354
Pett, H. Gregory. "Imported Inflation: The Role of Traded Goods: The Canadian Experience." Wayne State, 1980.

Poddar, Arun Kumar. See No./Voir no 2212

Rousseau, Henry Paul. See No./Voir no 1505

1355
Schaefer, Gordon Peter. "The Urban Area Production Function and the Urban Hierarchy: The Case of Saskatchewan." Western Ontario, 1975.

1356
Seldon, James Ralph. "Some Aspects of Canadian Immigration Policy in Theory and in Practice." Duke, 1969.

1357
Shaffer, Marvin Harold. "The Role of Competition in Macro Models." British Columbia, 1974.

Sharpe, Donald Andrew. See No./Voir no 1333

1358
Southey, Clive. "Studies in Fishery Economics." British Columbia, 1969.

Stabler, Jack Carr. See No./Voir no 1302

1359
Steinhorson, Dallas H. "Problems in Input-Output Analysis of the Canadian Economy." Harvard, 1954.

Stollery, Kenneth Robert. See No./Voir no 1903

1360
Tahir, Sayyid. "Testing for the Existence of Distribution Effects in the Aggregate Consumption Function." McMaster, 1981.

1361
Tremblay, Louis-Marie. "La théorie de Selig Perlman et le syndicalisme canadien." Laval, 1965.

Tsai, Hiu Liang. See No./Voir no 1564

1362
Turtle, John Patrick. "A Theoretical Model of Housing Markets with Empirical Tests Using Canadian Data." Washington, Seattle, 1974.

1363
Vanderkamp, J. "A Theoretical Model of Wage and Price Level Determination with an Empirical Application to the Canadian Economy." London, 1964.

Van Lierop, Johannes Henricus. See No./Voir no 1583

1364
Victor, Peter Alan. "Input-Output Analysis and the Analysis of Economic and Environmental Interactions." British Columbia, 1971.

1365
Walker, Michael Angus. "A Long Term Econometric Model of the Canadian Economy with Emphasis on the Financial Sector: A Simulation Study of Some Alternative Policy Rules." Western Ontario, 1971.

1366
Watts, Martin John. "Discrimination and Job Search in Imperfect Labour Markets." British Columbia, 1976.

POLITICAL ECONOMY/ÉCONOMIE POLITIQUE

General Items/Ouvrages généraux

1367
Alexander, Malcolm Laurence. "The Political Economy of Semi-Industrial Capitalism: A Comparative Study of Argentina, Australia and Canada, 1950-1970." McGill, 1979.

1368
Andrew, Caroline Parkin. "Federal Policy Development and Tri-Level Relations in the 1960's." Toronto, 1975.

1369
Archibald, Robert William. "Scanning the Canadian Business Environment: The Government Sector." Western Ontario, 1976.

1370
Berry, Glyn R. "Bureaucratic Politics and Canadian Economic Policies Affecting the Developing Countries - The Case of the Strategy for International Development Cooperation 1975-1980." Dalhousie, 1981.

1371
Brice, Max O. "Dépenses en travaux publics et décisions budgétaires municipales: le cas des municipalités de l'Ontario." Ottawa, 1979.

1372
Brooks, Joel Elliott. "Socio-Economic Inequality in Developed Democracies: Politico-Economic Determinants and Consequences." Carleton, 1981.

1373
Brown, Matthew Paul. "The Political Economy and Public Administration of Rural Lands in Canada - New Brunswick and Nova Scotia Perspectives." Toronto, 1982.

Burman, Patrick Walsh. See No./Voir no 8563
1374
Campbell, Robert Malcolm. "The Keynesian Politico-Economic Synthesis: Canadian Economic Policy 1945-1968." London, 1980.

1375
Caragata, Patrick James. "Non Fuel Minerals and Canadian Foreign Policy: Negotiating from Strength and Weakness." Toronto, 1981.

1376
Clarke, Phyllis Esphere. "Application of Marxist Thought to Canada." Toronto, 1977.

1377
Cox, Joseph Christopher. "The Interregional Impact of Federal Grants to Provincial Governments." McMaster, 1979.

1378
Crommelin, Brian Michael L. "Studies in Government Management of Oil and Gas Resources in Canada." British Columbia, 1975.

Curtis, Bruce Malcolm. See No./Voir no 2485
Dagher, Joseph H. See No./Voir no 1910
1379
Darville, Richard Tulloss. "Political Economy and Higher Education in the Nineteenth Century Maritime Provinces." British Columbia, 1978.

Dewar, Kenneth Cameron. See No./Voir no 1785
DeWilde, James Frederick. See No./Voir no 1743
Downey, Terrence James. See No./Voir no 1906
1380
Ferguson, Barry Glen. "The New Political Economy and Canadian Liberal Democratic Thought: Queen's University 1890-1925." York, 1982.

1381
Finkle, Peter Zach Ross. "Fisheries Management in the Northwest Atlantic: Canadian Perspectives." Toronto, 1975.

Granger, Isabelle Alix. See No./Voir no 1454
Grey, R.Y. See No./Voir no 1319
1382
Hampson, Fen Osler. "Fraught with Risk: The Political Economy of Petroleum Policies in Canada and Mexico." Harvard, 1982.

Hart, Douglas John. See No./Voir no 1320

1383
Hudon, Raymond Paul Joseph. "De la gérance de l'intégration continentale, au redéploiement de l'économie canadienne: politique, économique et constitutionnelle des années soixante-dix au Canada." Queen's, 1982.

1384
Kurtz, Larry Robert. "Public Policy and the Housing Problem: Goals, Programs, and Policy Constraints." Toronto, 1977.

1385
Lawrie, Neil John. "The Canadian Construction Association: An Interest-Group Organization and Its Environment." Toronto, 1976.

Laxer, Gordon David. See No./Voir no 1277
1386
Layton, Jack G. "Capital and the Canadian State: Foreign Investment Policy, 1957-1983." York, 1983.

Le Goff, Jean-Pierre. See No./Voir no 1755
Levant, Avrom Victor. See No./Voir no 8891
1387
Leyton-Brown, David Robert. "Governments of Developed Countries as Hosts in Multinational Enterprise: The Canadian, British, and French Policy Experience." Harvard, 1973.

Lithwick, Irwin. See No./Voir no 1209
1388
Mahon, Paule Rianne. "Canada's Textile Policy: A Case Study of the Politics of Industrial Policy Formation in Canada." Toronto, 1977.

Maley, Jean McCanns. See No./Voir no 1480

1389

Mason, Gregory Creswell. "The Regulation of the Market for Information in Rental Housing: A Simulation Study." British Columbia, 1975.

Massami, Bryan Haglewood. See No./Voir no 179

Matossian, Nicholas V. See No./Voir no 1180

Morrissey, Frederic Patric. See No./Voir no 1793

1390

Owen, Brian Edward. "Business Manager's Influence on Government: Case Study of Participation in Three Processes of Government Policy Formulation in Manitoba." Western Ontario, 1976.

Pal, Leslie Alexander. See No./Voir no 1486

1391

Paragg, Ralph Ramsarup. "Canada and the Commonwealth Caribbean: The Political Economy of a Relationship in Transition." Queen's, 1979.

1392

Racette, Daniel. "Monetary Aspects of the Interwar Period in Canada and the United States: An Econometric Model." Toronto, 1980.

1393

Resnick, Philip. "The Land of Cain: The Political Economy of English Canadian Nationalism, 1945-1975." Toronto, 1976.

1394

Riddle, Bruce Lee. "Political Elements in Exchange Rate Change: A Quantitative Study of Domestic Objective Versus International Obligations, 1960-1971." Syracuse, 1977. [A study of 14 nations of which Canada is one/Une étude sur 14 pays dont le Canada]

Riley, Richard Brinton. See No./Voir no 1795

Rosenfeld, Barry David. See No./Voir no 1298

Sallows, Sharon Heather. See No./Voir no 1188

1395

Schmidt, David Albert. "U.S. Foreign Direct Investment and Political Risk: An Inquiry into the Recipient Investment Policies of Canada." Indiana, 1982.

1396

Schwartz, Lawrence Phillip. "An Empirical Study of Provincial-Local Grants in Canada." Pennsylvania, 1977. [British Columbia/Colombie-Britannique]

Stanbury, William Thomas. See No./Voir no 1303

Stykolt, Stefan. See No./Voir no 1971

1397

Watson, Kenneth Frank. "An Evaluation of the Canadian Program for Export Market Development." Harvard, 1981.

1398

Williams, Glen Sutherland. "The Political Economy of Canadian Manufactured Exports: The Problem, Its Origins and the Department of Trade and Commerce, 1885-1930." York, 1978.

1399

Wintsobe, Ronald Stephen. "The Economics of Bureaucracy." Toronto, 1976.

1400

Wolfe, David Allan. "The Delicate Balance: The Changing Economic Role of the State in Canada." Toronto, 1980.

Woodside, Kenneth E. B. See No./Voir no 1732

Brown, Ronald Duncan. See No./Voir no 1675

Dennis-Escoffir, Shirley. See No./Voir no 1923

1401

De Ridder, Jerome J. "Comparison of Seven Fundamental Features of the Statement of Changes in Financial Position in the United States, Canada, the United Kingdom, New Zealand and Australia." Nebraska, 1980.

Dodge, David Allison. See No./Voir no 1653

1402

Drury, Donald Hazen. "An Examination of Differences in Financial Reporting Between Canada and the United States: An Empirical Analysis." Northwestern, 1976.

1403

Duncan, Carson Michael. "Forecasts of Earnings: Empirical Studies of Effects on Investment Analysts and Incidence in Canadian Annual Reports." Western Ontario, 1978.

1404

Haberer, John Frederick. "Some Conceptual Problems in Moneyflows Accounting: United States and Canada." Duke, 1960.

1405

Henderson, Murray Scott. "Some Factors Influencing the Annual Reports of North American Corporations." California, Los Angeles, 1969.

1406

Johnson, Alan Packard. "A Comparative Study of Auditing Standards in Australia, Canada, England and the United States." Illinois, 1969.

1407

Kudar, Randolph Parris. "Centralized Control in a Varied Environment: A Test for Contingency Theory." Western Ontario, 1978.

1408

Lam, Wai Ping. "Corporate Audit Committees in Ontario, Canada: An Empirical Study." Michigan State, 1974.

Lanfranconi, Claude Peter. See No./Voir no 1458

1409

Langevin, Marcel. "Corporate Social Responsibility Accounting: A Canadian Empirical Study." Syracuse, 1982.

1410

Mann, Harvey. "The Evolution of Accounting in Canada." New York, 1973.

1411

Murphy, George Joseph. "The Evolution of Selected Annual Corporate Financial Reporting Practices in Canada: 1900-1970." Michigan State, 1970.

Nollet, Jean. See No./Voir no 1946

1412

Nourallah, Fayez Salim. "Accounting under Nationalization in Britain, Canada and France." Illinois, 1966.

Reese, Craig Eugene. See No./Voir no 1724

1413

Sbrocchi, Frank Lloyd. "A Survey of Registered Industrial Accountants on the Importance of Selected Management Accounting Topics." Concordia, 1982.

1414
Schoch, Herbert Paul. "A Comparative Study of Selected Reporting Practices in Four Countries." American, 1974. [Canada, United Kingdom, Australia and the United States/Canada, Royaume-Uni, Australie et États-Unis]

1415
Stolar, Robert William. "A Proposed Flow of Resources Model with Particular Reference to the National Accounts of the United States and Canada." Florida, 1978.

1416
Taylor, Martin Edward. "The Formulation of Accounting Standards: A Comparison of Six Countries." Texas, 1974.

1417
Wolf, Frank Michael. "A Positive Theory of Manager's Decisional Behaviour in Public Accounting Firms." British Columbia, 1980.

1418
Zin, Michael. "An Evaluation of the Accounting Provisions in the Companies Act, Canada, and the Corporations Act, Ontario." Michigan State, 1962.

BANKING AND FINANCE/ OPÉRATIONS BANCAIRES ET FINANCE

Banking/Opérations bancaires

1419
Alley, William E. "The Nationalization of Central Banks with Particular Reference to Developments in Canada, England, France, and the United States." Illinois, 1941.

1420
Andersen, Peter Russell. "Discretionary and Contractual Saving in Canada: A Cross-Sectional Study." Harvard, 1967.

1421
Benson, John N. "Cash and Short-Term Liquid Asset Management in Canadian Chartered Banks 1962-1968." Queen's, 1973.

1422
Breckenridge, Rocliff Morton. "The Canadian Banking System, 1817-1890." Columbia, 1894.

1423
Brodt, Abraham Isaac. "A Dynamic Balance Sheet Management Model for a Canadian Chartered Bank." New York, 1976.

1424
Coombs, H.C. "Dominion Exchanges and Central Bank Problems Arising Therefrom." London, 1934.

1425
Couture, Gaétan Yves. "The Marketing Concept: Its Implementation and Influence on the Organizational Structure of the Canadian Chartered Banks." Illinois, 1972.

1426
Curtis, Clifford Austin. "The Canadian Banking System, 1910-1925." Chicago, 1926.

1427
Fortin, Pierre. "A Study of Bank of Canada Behavior: 1962-1973." California, Berkeley, 1975.

1428
Galbraith, John Alexander. "The Economics of Canadian Banking: An Analysis of Banking Operations and Transactions." McGill, 1959.

Goldberg, Simon Abraham. See No./Voir no 1637

1429
Holladay, James. "History of Banking in Canada, 1907-1927." Iowa, 1927.

1430
Inman, Mark K. "Experience in Banking, 1929-1934." Harvard, 1938.

1431
Italiano, Joseph Angelo. "Canadian Chartered Banks - Deposit Rate Setting and Portfolio Selection." Queen's, 1981.

1432
Julien, Yves Benoit. "An Econometric Model of the Financial Behavior of the Caisses Populaires." Rensselaer Polytechnic Institute, 1975.

1433
Kusy, Martin. "Bank Asset and Liability Management." British Columbia, 1978. [Vancouver City Saving Credit Union/Coopérative de crédit et d'épargne de Vancouver]

1434
Lafrance, Robert Rolland. "Optimal Portfolio Behaviour in Imperfect Financial Markets: An Econometric Study of Canadian Chartered Banks 1961-1973." London, 1977.

1435
Miles, Peter Lomer. "Assets and Liabilities of Chartered Banks: An Econometric Analysis." McGill, 1968.

1436
Moore, Basil John. "The Effects of Counter-Cyclical Monetary Policy on the Canadian Chartered Banks, 1935-1957." Johns Hopkins, 1959.

1437
Neufeld, E.P. "Bank of Canada Operations, 1935-1952." London, 1954.

1438
Olakampo, J.O.W. "Central Banking Problems in Commonwealth Countries: A Review of Experiences Since 1945." London, 1961.

1439
Pattison, John Charles. "An Econometric Analysis of Asset Selection by Individual Canadian Banks, 1967-1970." London, 1972.

1440
Picard, R.I.C. "Canadian Banking in Wartime." Ottawa, 1945.

1441
Redish, Angela. "The Optimal Supply of Bank Money: Upper Canada's Experience on and off the Specie Standard." Western Ontario, 1982.

1442
Salyzyn, Vladimir. "The Competition for Personal Savings Deposits in Canada." Illinois, 1965.

1443
Simpson, Thomas McNider, III. "Government and Central Bank: A Comparative Study (Canada, the United States, and the United Kingdom)." Johns Hopkins, 1965.

1444
Singh, Ranbir. "Rural Cooperative Banking Systems for Short-Term and Intermediate Credit in Canada, United States, and the Union of South Africa." Illinois, 1933.

1445
Stokes, Milton Lonsdale. "The Bank of Canada: The Development and Present Position of Central Banking in Canada." Pennsylvania, 1938.

1446
Sussman, Edmond. "The Role of Mortgage Banking in the Canadian Economy." McGill, 1963.

1447
Théoret, Raymond. "Étude du comportement des banques à charte canadiennes dans la perspective de la théorie des contrats implicites." Montréal, 1979.

1448
Trimnell, Frank Owen. "A Two-Tier Model of Canadian Chartered Bank Rate-Setting Behaviour and The Implications for Identifying Demands for Loans and Deposits Equations." McMaster, 1982.

1449
Winakor, Arthur H. "Branch Banking in the United States with Comparative Studies of Scotland, England and Canada." Illinois, 1934.

Finance

General Items/Ouvrages généraux

1450
Boyce, Raymond William. "Fiscal Zoning in Canadian Cities." Carleton, 1983.

1451
Campbell, Harry F. "A Benefit/Cost Rule for an Additional Public Project in Canada." Queen's, 1973.

Fernandez, Marco Antonio. See No./Voir no 2056

1452
Gainer, Walter Dunham. "Regional Income Leakages and the Multiplier; Alberta, 1948-1956." Massachusetts Institute of Technology, 1960.

1453
Gould, Lawrence Irwin. "An Evaluation of Alternative Models for Predicting Security Returns." Toronto, 1975.

1454
Granger, Isabelle Alix. "The Regulation of Trust Companies and Finance Companies in British Columbia." Simon Fraser, 1967.

1455
Haritos, Zissis. "Rational Road Pricing Policies in Canada." Toronto, 1972.

1456
Herring, Richard John. "International Financial Integration: Capital Flows and Interest Rate Relationships Among Six Industrial Nations." Princeton, 1973.

1457
Laiken, Stanley Norman. "An Analysis of Financial Performance and the Level of External Growth Through Merger." Western Ontario, 1972.

1458
Lanfranconi, Claude Peter. "Change in Corporate Financial Disclosure in Canada: An Empirical Study of the Use of Notes to Financial Statements and Supplementary Financial Data Schedules for Disclosure in Corporate Annual Reports in Canada." Western Ontario, 1976.

1459
Lynn, James Hugh. "Towards the Evaluation of Regional Balance Policies with an Interregional Simulation Model." Toronto, 1976.

1460
Millen, Ronald Harold Vincent. "Automatic Rate Adjustments and Short-Term Productivity Objectives for Bell Canada." Concordia, 1975.

1461
Terry, Christopher Stephen. "General Purpose Grants in the U.S.A., Canada and Australia." New York, 1975.

1462
Turnbull, Stuart McLean. "The Capital Asset Pricing Model and the Probability of Bankruptcy: Theory and Empirical Tests." British Columbia, 1974.

1463
Yagil, Joseph. "Financial Effects of Pure Conglomerate Mergers." Toronto, 1980.

Federal Monetary and Fiscal Thought and Policy/ Politiques monétaires et financières fédérales

1464
Baguley, Robert Wayne. "International Capital Flows and Canadian Monetary and Fiscal Policies, 1951-1962." Harvard, 1969.

1465
Brault, Florent. "The Fiscal Policy of Canada Since Confederation." St. Louis, 1952.

1466
Brazer, Harvey Elliot. "Coordination in Canadian Federal Finance." Columbia, 1951.

1467
Brecher, Irving. "Monetary and Fiscal Thought and Policy in Canada, 1919-1939." Harvard, 1951.

1468
Carter, George Edward. "Canadian Conditional Grants Postwar." Clark, 1969.

1469
Comeau, Robert Lyons. "Financial Intermediaries and Canadian Monetary Policy." Brown, 1966.

1470
Dean, James Woodburn. "Aspects of Instrument/Target Links in Canadian Monetary Policy." Harvard, 1973.

1471
Dewhirst, John Frederick. "A Flow-of-Funds Analysis of the Timing of Canadian Corporate Investment and Financial Policies and Implications for the Effectiveness of Monetary Policy, 1950-1963." Michigan, 1968.

1472
Dingle, James Frederic. "Effect of Monetary Policies on the Purchases of Consumer Durable Goods in Canada." Massachusetts Institute of Technology, 1968.

1473
Doak, Ervin John. "Financial Intermediation by Government Theory and Canadian Experience Since 1867." Toronto, 1970.

1474

Eapen, Arakkal Thomas. "A Study of Fiscal Federalism in the United States, Canada, Australia, and India in Terms of Objectives of Federal Finance." Michigan, 1962.

1475

Eastman, Harry C.M. "Canadian Commercial Policy Since the War." Chicago, 1952.

1476

Garner, Clyde Alan. "Capital Flows and Canadian Monetary Policy: An Empirical Study." Harvard, 1977.

1477

Kennedy, Michael Edward. "Monetary Policy in a Monetarist Framework: The Canadian Experience from 1963 to 1969." Queen's, 1976.

1478

Kwon, Oh Yul. "Optimal Fiscal Strategy for Economic Stabilization: An Econometric Study with Illustrative Application to Canada." McMaster, 1972.

1479

MacDonald, Rae M.; Moss, H. Richard. "Some Differential Effects of Canadian Monetary Policy upon the Atlantic Region." Dalhousie, 1976.

1480

Maley, Jean McCanns. "The Impact of Federal Grants on Provincial Budgets: Canada." Rochester, 1972.

1481

Maris, Brian Alan. "Application of a Monetarist Model for Economic Stabilization to Canada." Kansas State, 1974.

1482

Mathieu, Nicolas Jean. "An Application of Control Theory to Microeconomic Policies in the Canadian Economy." Pennsylvania, 1976.

Matossian, Nicolas V. See No./Voir no 1180

1483

May, J. "An Econometric Study into the Effects of Postwar Fiscal Policy on Investment Expenditure in Canadian Manufacturing." York, 1972.

1484

Miller, Frederick Carl. "Canadian Fiscal and Monetary Policy, 1945-1955." Clark, 1958.

1485

Morin, Roger-André. "Capital Asset Pricing Theory: The Canadian Experience." Pennsylvania, 1976.

1486

Pal, Leslie Alexander. "Keynesian Commitment, Keynesian Illusion: The Politics of Canadian Fiscal Policy, 1943-1963." Queen's, 1981.

1487

Phidd, Richard W. "The Economic Council and Economic Policy Formulation in Canada." Queen's, 1972.

Rabeau, Yves. See No./Voir no 1503

1488

Selody, Jack George. "A Monetary Model of Canadian Price and Output Fluctuation." Western Ontario, 1979.

1489

Shapiro, Harold Tafler. "The Canadian Monetary Sector: An Econometric Analysis." Princeton, 1964.

1490

Smith, David Chadwick. "Monetary Policy and Economic Growth in an Open Economy: The Canadian Experience, 1950-1956." Harvard, 1959.

1491

Strick, John Charles. "Government Expenditures and Fiscal Policy: An Approach to Analysis." Alberta, 1966.

1492

Stringer, Y. "A Quantitative Appraisal of Canadian Federal Fiscal Policy, 1955-1970." York (Great Britain), 1978.

1493

Tarasofsky, Abraham. "Monetary Policy and the Sales Finance Industry: The Canadian Experience, 1953-1962." McGill, 1968.

Turnbull, Stuart McLean. See No./Voir no 1462

Waddell, Christopher Robb. See No./Voir no 1337

Walker, Michael Angus. See No./Voir no 1365

1494

Wenzlau, Thomas Eugene. "Canadian Postwar Monetary Policy, 1946-1951." Illinois, 1953.

1495

Winer, Stanley Lewis. "Monetary - Fiscal Influences in Federal States: With Application to the Post-War Canadian Economy." Johns Hopkins, 1975.

Provincial and Municipal Fiscal Relations and Policy/Relations et politiques financières provinciales et municipales

1496

Birch, A.H. "Problems of Public Finance and Social Legislation in Federal States." London, 1951.

Cox, Joseph Christopher. See No./Voir no 1377

1497

Dupré, Joseph Stefan. "Fiscal Policy in Newfoundland." Harvard, 1958.

1498

Graham, John Finlayson. "Provincial-Municipal Fiscal Relations and Economic Development in a Low-Income Province: Nova Scotia." Columbia, 1959.

1499

Jack, Lawrence B. "Control of Municipal Finance in Three Federal Countries: Canada, the United States, and Australia." McGill, 1943.

Jestin, Warren James. See No./Voir no 1275

1500

Larin, Gilles Normand. "Le financement des services métropolitains et l'usage de la tarification, particulièrement dans le cas du service de la police dans la communauté urbaine de Montréal." McGill, 1979. [Financing collective services of a community like Montréal/Services financiers collectifs d'une communauté telle que Montréal]

MacDonald, Rae M.; Moss, H. Richard. See No./Voir no 1479

Maley, Jean McCans. See No./Voir no 1480

1501

McFadyen, Stuart Malcolm. "Home Owner Grants: The British Columbia Experience." California, Berkeley, 1969.

1502

Michas, Nicholas. "Variations in the Level of Provincial-Municipal Expenditures in Canada: An Econometric Analysis." Illinois, 1967.

1503
Rabeau, Yves. "The Federal-Provincial Fiscal Policies: A Short Term Analysis with Application to
the Quebec Economy." Massachusetts Institute of
Technology, 1970.
1504
Rivard, Jean Yves. "Determinants of City Expendi-
tures in Canada." Michigan, 1967.
1505
Rousseau, Henri Paul. "Application of the Theory of
Markets to Provincial Finance: A Theoretical and
Econometric Analysis of Alberta Budgetary Real-
ization Process." Western Ontario, 1974.
1506
Stocks, Anthony Howarth. "Some Problems in the
Finance and Organization of Metropolitan Government with Particular Reference to the Toronto
Federation." SUNY, Buffalo, 1963.

Financial History/Histoire financière

General Items/Ouvrages généraux

1507
Ammerman, Howard K. "Canadian Devaluation,
1949." Chicago, 1957.
Bellemare, Diane. See No./Voir no 1199
1508
Boreham, Gordon Francis. "Changes in the Financial
Structure of Canada: 1953-1958." Columbia, 1962.
Carter, George Edward. See No./Voir no 1468
1509
Chisholm, Derek. "Canadian Monetary Policy 1914-
1934: The Enduring Glitter of the Gold Standard."
Cambridge, 1980.
1510
Currie, L.B. "Monetary History of Canada, 1914-
1926." Harvard, 1931.
1511
Fitzgerald, Vincent William John. "The Inflationary
Process in an Open Economy: Canada 1961-1974."
Harvard, 1976.
1512
Graddy, Duane B. "The Empirics of the Equilibrium
Balanced Growth Model." Lehigh, 1974.
Hamada, Koichi. See No./Voir no 1531
1513
Harnarine, Harold. "Monetary Conditions and the
Demand and Supply of Consumer Credit in Canada,
1948-1972." Dalhousie, 1977.
1514
Hyde, Duncan Clark. "The War Finance of the Domi-
nion of Canada." Harvard, 1921.
Kraft, Calvin T. See No./Voir no 1208
Lafrance, Robert Rolland. See No./Voir no 1434
1515
MacKenzie, H.M. "Mutual Assistance: The Finance of
British Requirements in Canada During the Second
World War." Oxford, 1981.
Masters, D.C. See No./Voir no 1283

1516
McIvor, N.S. "The Impact of International Economic
Fluctuations on Employment and Incomes in New
Zealand, 1929-1939, and the Nature and Effects of
Public Policy Towards It, with Some Comparative
Study of Australia and Canada in the Same Period."
London, 1949.
1517
McIvor, R. Craig. "Monetary Expansion and Canadian
War Finance, 1939-1945." Chicago, 1948.
Mellish, Gordon Hartley. See No./Voir no 1326
Murphy, George Joseph. See No./Voir no 1411
1518
Naylor, R.T. "Foreign and Domestic Investment in
Canada: Institutions and Policy, 1867-1914."
Cambridge, 1978.
1519
Norton, Margaret T. "Canadian Economic and
Financial Growth after World War II." New York,
1963.
Pal, Leslie Alexander. See No./Voir no 1486
Picard, R.I.C. See No./Voir no 1440
1520
Ridpath, John Bruce. "An Econometric and Historical
Study of the Freely-Floating Canadian Dollar,
1931-1939." Virginia, 1975.
Selody, Jack George. See No./Voir no 1488
Waddell, Christopher Robb. See No./Voir no 1337
1521
Wang, Hong-Cheng. "On Monetarist Models and their
Applications to the Canadian Economy, 1957-
1974." McGill, 1980.

Provincial Financial History/
Histoire financière provinciale

Alberta

1522
Hanson, Eric J. "A Financial History of Alberta, 1905-
1950." Clark, 1952.

British Columbia/Colombie-Britannique

1523
Carlsen, Alfred Edgar. "Major Developments in Public
Finance in British Columbia, 1920-1960." Toronto,
1961.
1524
Palmer, Peter F. "A Fiscal History of British Columbia in the Colonial Period." Stanford, 1932.

Nova Scotia/Nouvelle-Écosse

1525
Maxwell, James Ackley. "A Financial History of Nova
Scotia, 1848-1899." Harvard, 1927.

Quebec/Québec

1526
Bauer, Milton F. " 'Caisse Populaire' Movement in
Quebec: 1932-1950." Chicago, 1968.
1527
Faribault, Marcel. "La fiducie dans la province de
Québec." Montréal, 1936.

MacPherson, Hector. See No./Voir no 1281

1528
Vallières, Marc Georges. "La gestion des opérations financières du gouvernement québécois, 1867-1920." Laval, 1981.

Capital/Capitaux

Amoako-Adu, Benjamin. See No./Voir no 1697
Baguley, Robert Wayne. See No./Voir no 1464
Carroll, William Kingsley. See No./Voir no 10019

1529
Connelly, Dennis Eugene. "Comparative Study of Capital Structures: Selected Industries – Canada and the United States." Illinois, 1971.

Carter, William Harrison, Jr. See No./Voir no 2387

1530
Frankel, Allen Barry. "A Borrower-Oriented Model of U.S. - Canadian Long Term Fixed-Interest Capital Flows." Oregon, 1973.

Garner, Clyde Alan. See No./Voir no 1476

1531
Hamada, Koichi. "Economic Growth and Long-Term International Capital Movements." Yale, 1965. [Canada 1900-1930]

Herring, Richard John. See No./Voir no 1456

1532
Islam, Nurul. "Studies in Foreign Capital and Economic Development: Some Aspects of Absorption of Foreign Capital in Canada, India, and Japan." Harvard, 1956.

1533
Jenkins, Glenn P. "Analysis of Rates of Return from Capital in Canada." Chicago, 1972.

Kryzanowski, Lawrence. See No./Voir no 1692

1534
Leipziger, Danny Melvin. "Long-Term Capital Movement and Economic Policy: Canada (1953-1961)." Brown, 1973.

1535
Naqib, Fadle Mustafa. "The Impact of Public Pensions on Capital Formation and the Supply of Labor." Queen's, 1982.

1536
Parr, Philip Clayton. "The Small British Columbia Firm and the Long-Term Capital Market: An Investigation of Some Interactions." Washington, Seattle, 1967.

1537
Rashid, Muhammad. "The Theory and Measurement of the Cost of Capital to the Canadian Economy." Queen's, 1978.

Rhomberg, Rudolph Robert. See No./Voir no 1613

1538
Rogstad, Barry Kent. "Long Run International Capital Movements: Impact on the Canadian Economy." Brown, 1968.

1539
Stewart-Patterson, Cleveland. "An Empirical Investigation of the Determinants of Corporate Capital Structure Decisions." McGill, 1980.

1540
Tam, Cham-Kan. "An Econometric Study of Canadian Capital Formation by Industry." Toronto, 1976.

.541
Upson, Roger Ballard. "The Usage of Foreign Capital Markets by United States International Companies." Michigan, 1965.

Money and Income/Argent et revenu

1542
Arango, Sebastian. "A Portfolio Approach to the Demand for Money in an Open Economy." New York, 1977. [Canada, Germany, the United Kingdom and the United States/Canada, Allemagne, Royaume-Uni et États-Unis]

Blauer, Rosalind. See No./Voir no 1312

1543
Breton, Albert Antoine. "The Demand for Money in Canada, 1900-1959." Columbia, 1965.

1544
Brown, Malcolm Clarence. "An Analysis of the Demand for Money in Canada, 1926 to 1966." Cornell, 1969.

1545
Cavanaugh, Kenneth Lankford. "The Efficiency of Futures Markets for Foreign Currency." Washington, Seattle, 1983. [Canadian dollars/Dollars canadiens]

1546
Cherneff, Robert Vincent. "The Determinants and Money Supply Effects of Variations in the Relative Demand for Currency in Canada 1955-1963." Washington, Seattle, 1970.

1547
Clark, Carolyn. "The Permanent Income Hypothesis of the Demand for Money in Canada, 1926-1965." California, Berkeley, 1970.

1548
Cockerline, Jon Phillip. "Econometrics of Money Demand with Applications to the Canadian Economy." McGill, 1981.

1549
Davies, James B. "Life-Cycle Savings, Inheritance, and the Distribution of Personal Income and Wealth in Canada." London, 1979.

1550
Donovan, Donal John. "Consumption, Leisure and the Demand for Money and Money Substitutes." British Columbia, 1977.

1551
Dy Reyes, Felix Robles, Jr. "A Test of the Direction of Causation Between Money and Income in Canada, Japan and the United States." Iowa State, 1974.

Gardner, William Ray, Jr. See No./Voir no 1601
Gasser, William John. See No./Voir no 1602

1552
Gerland, Daniel Raymond. "Foreign Currency Futures: An Empirical Examination of Tracer Performance." Wisconsin, 1981. [Six currencies: Canadian dollar, Japanese yen, British pound, West German deutschemark, Swiss franc, and Mexican peso and their associated contrasts were examined/Six devises ont été étudiées: le dollar canadien, le yen japonais, la livre sterling britannique, le deutche mark de la RFA, le franc suisse, le peso mexicain et leurs équivalents monétaires]

1553
Goveia, John Charles. "Demand for Money in Canada, 1947 to 1970." Northern Illinois, 1972.

Gregory, Allan Walter. See No./Voir no 1349

1554
Guest, D.T. "The Development of Income Maintenance Programmes in Canada, 1945-1967." London, 1968.

Hartigan, James Christopher. See No./Voir no 2365

1555
Haulman, Clyde Austin. "Determinants of the Money Supply in Canada: 1875-1964." Florida State, 1969.

1556
House, William James. "Per Capita Income Differentials in the Provinces of Canada." Brown, 1970.

Kamp, Robert Cornelius. See No./Voir no 1977

1557
Kelly, Alexander Kenneth. "The Money Multiplier and the Canadian Money Supply (1955-65)." Western Ontario, 1968.

1558
MacLaury, Bruce King, Jr. "The Canadian Money Market, Its Development and Its Impact." Harvard, 1961.

1559
Malik, Muhammad Hussain. "Macro-Economic Influences on the Distribution of Income: A Case Study of Canada." McMaster, 1983.

McInnis, Robert Marvin. See No./Voir no 1291

1560
McLeod, Donald. "Some Aspects of the Development of the Market for Canadian Treasury Bills, 1953-1962." Columbia, 1965.

1561
Poloz, Stephen Shawn. "Unstable Velocity, Volatile Exchange Rates, and Currency Substitution: The Demand for Money in a Multicurrency World." Western Ontario, 1982.

1562
Polzin, Paul Elmer. "The Canadian Money Supply." Michigan State, 1968.

1563
Shedd, Stanford. "Factors in Interregional Income Differences in Canada." Southern Illinois, 1972.

1564
Tsai, Hui-Liang. "Demand for and Supply of Money: A Comparative Analysis of Canada, Taiwan, Yugoslavia and the United States." Florida State, 1976.

1565
Weber, Gerald Irwin. "An Econometric Study of the Money Supply of Canada." California, Los Angeles, 1964.

1566
Wonnacott, Gordon Paul. "The Canadian Dollar, 1948-1957." Princeton, 1959.

Credit/Crédit

MacPherson, Hector. See No./Voir no 1281

1567
Sears, John Tulloch. "The Availability of Institutional Credit for Small Businesses in Nova Scotia with Special References to Small Manufacturing Firms." Harvard, 1966.

Debt/Dette

1568
Baban, R.C.N. "Debt Management and Monetary Policy: A Comparison of Experience in the United Kingdom, United States and Canada, 1940-1968." Manchester, 1972.

1569
Berney, Robert Edward. "Debt Management: A Comparative Study of Canadian and United States Experience." Wisconsin, 1963.

1570
Bishop, George Archibald. "Debt Management as an Instrument of Compensatory Policy in Canada: World War II to 1960." Toronto, 1961.

1571
Christofides, Loizos Nicolaou. "The Canadian Conversion Loan of 1958: A Study in Debt Management." British Columbia, 1973.

1572
Fookey, D.E. "Canadian Federal Debt Management, 1931-1951." London, 1953.

1573
Johnson, Ivan Charles. "Provincial and Municipal Debt in Canada 1946-66." Western Ontario, 1971.

1574
Murphy, Lawrence Joseph. "An Analysis of the Demand for Government of Canada Marketable Debt." McMaster, 1973.

1575
Speagle, Richard Ernest. "Comparative Public Debt Management: Canada and the United States, 1939-1946." Princeton, 1958.

Housing/Logement

General Items/Ouvrages généraux

1576
Bajic, Vladimir P. "Transportation System Changes and the Structure of Housing Prices: The Effect of a New Subway Line in Metropolitan Toronto." Toronto, 1981.

Harris, Simon Richard. See No./Voir no 2240

1577
Johnston, Kevin James. "Quantification of the Cost of Alternative Forms of Housing Market Intervention in Canada." British Columbia, 1983.

Kurtz, Larry Robert. See No./Voir no 1384

1578
Li, Si-Ming. "Stock Variability and Housing Choice: An Analysis of Individual Housing Choice Behaviour in Twenty-Three Canadian Cities." Queen's, 1981.

Mason, Gregory Creswell. See No./Voir no 1389

McFadyen, Stuart Malcolm. See No./Voir no 1501

1579
Munro, Hugh James. "The Effects of Information on Consumers' Decisions to Retrofit Their Homes." Western Ontario, 1982.

1580
Preston, Valerie Ann. "Life Cycle Effects on Residential Area Evaluation." McMaster, 1978. [Hamilton, Ontario]

Saccomanno, Fedel Frank Mario. See No./Voir no 2262

1581
Santos y de Regla, Benjamin. "Property Taxation and Housing Market Analysis." Manitoba, 1975.

1582
Stokes, Ernest Ball. "Housing Markets in Canada: An Econometric Analysis Using Regional Panel Data." Queen's, 1979.

1583
Van Lierop, Johannes Henricus. "The Determination of Relative House Prices." Toronto, 1981.

Housing: Mortgage Loans/
Logement: prêts hypothécaires

1584
Askari-Rankouhi, Mostafa. "A Disequilibrium Econometric Model of the Canadian Institutional Mortgage Market." Queen's, 1981.

1585
Chung, Joseph Hee-Soo. "Housing and Mortgage Loans: Postwar Canadian Experience." Toronto, 1967.

1586
D'Andrea, John Joseph. "The Mortgage, Housing and Deposit Sectors of the Canadian Economy." Princeton, 1978.

1587
Eger, Albert Frederic. "Financing the Market for Existing Housing: An Alternate Source of Funds." British Columbia, 1977.

1588
Smith, Lawrence Berk. "The Postwar Canadian and Residential Mortgage Market and the Role of Government." Harvard, 1966.

1589
Trevithick, Morris Henry. "Central Mortgage and Housing Corporation as a Strategic Factor in Canadian Federal Housing Policy: A Historical Case Study." Pittsburgh, 1976.

Interest Rates/Taux d'intérêt

1590
Agranove, Larry Melvyn. "The Effect of Interest Rate Disclosure on Consumer Installment Purchase Behavior." Western Ontario, 1971.

1591
Banaga, Abdul Raouf Sulaiman. "Time Series Analysis of Canadian Interest Rates." California, Santa Barbara, 1981.

1592
Chua, Anthony Q. "The Relationship Between United States and Foreign Interest Rates: A Study of Financial Market Integration." Michigan State, 1981. [Short term and long term interest rates of Canada, West Germany, United Kingdom, France, Netherlands, and Switzerland/Les taux d'intérêts à court et à long terme au Canada, en Allemagne de l'Ouest, au Royaume-Uni, en France, aux Pays-Bas et en Suisse]

1593
Gestrin, Bengt Victor. "The Structure of Interest Rates in Canada." Toronto, 1966.

Herring, Richard John. See No./Voir no 1456

1594
McCollum, James Freeman. "Interest Rates and Inflation in Canada." Rice, 1974.

1595
Scarth, William Marshall. "Interest Rates and Macroeconomic Models." Toronto, 1971.

Exchange Rates/Taux de change

1596
Boothe, Paul Michael. "Estimating the Structure and Efficiency of the Canadian Foreign Exchange Market: 1971-1978." British Columbia, 1981.

1597
Callier, Philippe. "The Covered Interest Arbitrage Margin: An Investigation into the Relevance of the Modern Theory of the Forward Foreign Exchange Rate." Simon Fraser, 1979.

1598
Cornell, Peter McCaul. "Flexible Exchange Rates: The Canadian Case." Harvard, 1956.

1599
Duong, Ba Tien. "Effects of Exchange Rate Changes on Prices, Wages and Employment in Canada." Western Ontario, 1977.

1600
Frederick, James R. "Rational Expectations and the Modern Theory of Forward Exchange Markets: Some New Consistent Estimates from the Canadian Experience." Wayne State, 1983.

1601
Gardner, William Ray, Jr. "The Canadian Dollar; 1950-57: A Study of Rate Stabilizing Factors in Flexible Exchange Market." Indiana, 1959.

1602
Gasser, William John. "The Canadian Money Supply under Fixed and Flexible Exchange Rates." Ohio State, 1976.

1603
Ginman, Peter John. "The Relative Effects of Uncertainty on Import Volume under Flexible and Pegged Exchange Rates: The Canadian Experience 1951-1964." Michigan State, 1969.

1604
Gorman, Linda Grace. "The Distributed Lag Effect of Exchange Rate Changes on Selected Canadian Commodity Imports: Cotton, Cocoa, Sugar and Frozen Concentrated Orange Juice." Pittsburgh, 1982.

1605
Hawkins, Robert Garvin. "Canadian Economic Stagnation, the Flexible Exchange Rate and Economic Policy, 1957-1961." New York, 1966.

Kim, Chul-Hwan. See No./Voir no 2342

1606
Kim, Jin-Woo. "Monetary Policy and Exchange Rate Under Managed Floating: A Study of US $/Canadian $ Rate." Kentucky, 1982.

1607
Lande, Eric Paul. "A Market Structure Approach to the Impact of Exchange Rate Changes on Exports and the Balance of Trade: Canada in the 1960's and 1970's." McGill, 1978.

London, Anselm Lullellyn. See No./Voir no 2344

1608
Longworth, David John. "Floating Exchange Rates: The Canadian Experience." Masschusetts Institute of Technology, 1979.

1609
McTeer, Robert Doyal, Jr. "Flexible Exchange Rates and Domestic Policy: The Canadian Case." Georgia, 1971.

1610
Officer, Lawrence Howard. "An Econometric Model of the Canadian Economy under the Fluctuating Exchange Rate." Harvard, 1965.

Poloz, Stephen Shawn. See No./Voir no 1561

1611
Poole, William, Jr. "The Canadian Experiment with the Flexible Exchange Rates, 1950-62." Chicago, 1966.

1612
Rafati, Mohammad Reza. "Exchange Rate Risk and the Long Term Borrowing Behaviour of Canadian Provincial Governments and Private Corporations under Different Exchange Rate Regimes." Queen's, 1980.

1613
Rhomberg, Rudolph Robert. "Fluctuating Exchange Rates in Canada: Short Term Capital Movements and Domestic Stability." Yale, 1959.

Riddle, Bruce Lee. See No./Voir no 1394

1614
Rogers, Kenneth Douglas. "A Refutation of the Case for Floating Exchange Rates: The Canadian Experience 1950-1962." New York, 1967.

1615
Rosen, Harvey Stuart. "Monetary and Fiscal Policy under a Fluctuating Exchange Rate: Canada." Case Western Reserve, 1969.

1616
Sarlo, Christopher A. "Reduced Form Models of the Canadian Economy: Fixed and Flexible Exchange Rates." Queen's, 1981.

Stewart, Ian Affleck. See No./Voir no 1336
Wallace, Myles Stuart. See No./Voir no 2351
Zandi, Farokh-Reza. See No./Voir no 1198

Floating Discount Rate/Flottement du taux d'escompte

1617
Cage, William Edwin. "The Canadian Discount Mechanism: 1955-1965." Virginia, 1966.

1618
Johnston, Robert Alexander. "The Canadian Experience with the Floating Discount Rate, 1952-1962." Yale, 1965.

Insurance/Assurance

General Items/Ouvrages généraux

Anderson, Peter Russell. See No./Voir no 1420

1619
Tremblay, Doris. "Financial Statements of Insurance Companies in the United States and in Canada." Illinois, 1966.

Automobile

1620
Kennedy, Kenneth Francis. "A Case Study in Private vs. Public Enterprise: The Manitoba Experience With Automobile Insurance." Illinois, 1976.

Health (Medical and Hospital)/ Santé (médecine et hospitalisation)

1621
Coyte, Peter Christopher. "The Economics of Medicare: Equilibrium within the Medical Community." Western Ontario, 1982.

1622
Cudmore, James Sedley. "Comparative Study of Health Insurance and Public Medical Care Schemes in Germany, Great Britain, the United States of America and Canada." Toronto, 1951.

1623
Goldberg, Theodore Irving. "Trade Union Interest in Medical Care and Voluntary Insurance: A Study of Two Collectively Bargained Programmes." Toronto, 1963.

1624
Hammond, Joseph Angus Bernard. "Differential Utilization Patterns and Public Evaluation of Physicians' Services in a Medically Insured Public: The Case of Ontario." York, 1975.

1625
Hamovitch, Maurice B. "Compulsory Health Insurance in the United States and Canada." Chicago, 1951.

1626
Hetherington, Rober William. "Medical Care and a Social System: An Historical Analysis of the Evolution of North America's First Comprehensive Compulsory State Sponsored Medical Care Program." Yale, 1966. [Saskatchewan]

1627
Honda, Steven Takao. "Distributional Effects of the Canadian National Health Insurance Program: A Long Run Locational Approach." California, Los Angeles, 1981.

1628
Horne, John MacGregor. "Copayment and Utilization of Publicly Insured Hospital Services in Saskatchewan: An Empirical Analysis." Carleton, 1978.

1629
Lindenfield, Rita Graham. "The Hospital Insurance and Diagnostic Services Act: Its Federal, Provincial Aspects." Chicago, 1964.

1630
Manga, Pranlal. "A Benefit Incidence Analysis of the Public Medical and Hospital Insurance Programs in Ontario." Toronto, 1976.

1631
Naylor, C.D. "The Canadian Medical Profession and State Medical Care Insurance: Key Developments." Oxford, 1983.

1632
Patriquin, James Douglas. "Economics of Inter-Governmental Grants, with Special Reference to Hospital Insurance in Canada." London, 1979.

1633
Spekkens, André. "The Canadian Experience with Government Hospital Insurance Plans." Iowa, 1978.
1634
Taylor, Malcolm G. "The Saskatchewan Hospital Services Plan: A Study in Compulsory Health Insurance." California, Berkeley, 1949.
1635
Zycher, Benjamin. "Substitution in Public Spending: The Budgetary Incidence of Canadian National Health Insurance." California, Los Angeles, 1979.

Life Insurance/Assurance-vie

1636
Fleck, James Douglas. "Canadian Life Insurance Investment Policy with Particular Reference to the Period 1952-1961." Harvard, 1964.
1637
Goldberg, Simon Abraham. "Institutional Savings and Investments in Canada, with Special Reference to Life Insurance." Harvard, 1954.
1638
Graham, Robert Edward. "The Effect of Regulation on the Common Stock Holdings of Canadian Life Insurance Companies." Toronto, 1975.
1639
Krinsky, Itzhak. "Investment Behaviour of Canadian Life Insurance Companies: A Mean-Variance Approach." McMaster, 1983.

Retirement Savings, Old Age Insurance and Pensions/ Épargne-retraite, pensions de vieillesse et autres pensions

1640
Ascah, Louis Gordon. "Government and Private Pensions in Canada." McGill, 1979.
Brooks-Hill, Frederick James. See No./Voir no 1650
1641
Daly, Michael Joseph. "An Analysis of Registered Retirement Savings Plans and their Role in Canada's Retirement Income System." Queen's, 1982.
1642
Edwards, Adrian Charles. "Canadian Private Pension Plans: A Study of their History, Trends, Taxation, and Investments." Ohio State, 1967.
1643
Schoplein, Robert Nicholas. "Tax Incentives to Induce Savings for Retirement." Wisconsin, 1965.
1644
Somers, Bertram Alexander. "The Economic Effects of Public Pension Plans in Canada: A theoretical and Empirical Analysis." McGill, 1983.

Unemployment Insurance/Assurance-chômage

1645
Hanvelt, Robin Alden. "Unemployment Insurance and the Distribution of Workers Between Labour Force States." British Columbia, 1980.
1646
Johnson, Andrew Frank. "Political Leadership and the Process of Policy-Making: The Case of Unemployment Insurance in the 1970's." McGill, 1983.

1647
Kelly, Lawrence Alexander. "Unemployed Insurance in Canada: Economic, Social and Financial Aspects." Queen's, 1967.
1648
Smitkin, John Nichols. "The Incidence and Economic Effect of the Financing of Unemployment Insurance." McMaster, 1982.

Investment/Investissement

Alexandrin, Glen Gleb. See No./Voir no 1310
1649
Braithwaite, Fitzwarren Carlton. "An Economic Analysis of the Determinants of Investment in Canadian Manufacturing." Queen's, 1971.
1650
Brooks-Hill, Frederick James. "The Investment Performance of Trusted Canadian Pension Funds." Pennsylvania, 1973.
1651
Buckley, K.A.H. "Real Investment in Canada 1900 to 1930." London, 1951.
1652
Conerly, William Booth. "Investment and Uncertainty in Canada and the United States." Duke, 1980.
Dewhurst, John Frederick. See No./Voir no 1471
1653
Dodge, David Allison. "The Structure of Earnings of Canadian Accountants, Engineers and Scientists and the Implications for Returns to Investment in University Education." Princeton, 1972.
1654
Dudley, Carlton Lewis, Jr. "A Theoretical Financial Analysis of the Long Term Subsidy Value of the Regional Development Incentives Program in Canada, and a Related Paper on Corporate Investment Theory." California, Berkeley, 1974.
Duncan, Carson Michael. See No./Voir no 1403
Edwards, Adrian Charles. See No./Voir no 1642
1655
Empey, William Franklin. "Regional Investment in Canada." Boston College, 1978.
Forde, Penelope Allison. See No./Voir no 1748
1656
Gérin-Lajoie Jean. "Internal Financing of Post-War Investments in Canadian Primary Textiles." McGill, 1953.
Goldberg, Simon Abraham. See No./Voir no 1637
1657
Goodale, Denis. "An Empirical Study of the Initial Public Financing of Selected Small Canadian Corporations." Washington, Seattle, 1973.
1658
Hampton, Peter. "Foreign Investment and the Theory of Economic Growth: Examined within the Framework of Canadian Economic Development." Ottawa, 1963.
1659
Harman, Francis James. "An Analysis of Investment Incentive Policies in Canada." McMaster, 1977.

1660
Helliwell, J.F. "The Investment Process: A Study of Capital Expenditure and the Effects on Them of Fiscal and Monetary Policies, with Special Reference to Large Canadian Corporations, 1954-62." Oxford, 1966.

1661
Holmes, Richard Arthur. "The Canadian Survey of Manufacturers' Investment: A Statistical Study." Indiana, 1960.

Lazaridis, Panagiotis. See No./Voir no 1754
Le Goff, Jean-Pierre. See No./Voir no 1755

1662
Lusztig, Peter Alfred. "An Analysis of the Concentration of Economic Power in the Hands of Institutional Investors - The Canadian Perspective." Stanford, 1965.

1663
Marton, Katherin. "Attitudes Toward Foreign Investments: A Case Study of the Canadian Blue Collar Worker Employed at Ford Canada." New York, 1973.

May, J. See No./Voir no 1483

1664
McDonough, Lawrence Cecil. "A Forward Looking Model of Neo-Classical Investment Behavior with Application to Five Canadian Manufacturing Industries." Queen's, 1981.

Murray, John David. See No./Voir no 2347
Naylor, R.T. See No./Voir no 1518

1665
Paterson, Donald G. "British Direct Investment in Canada, 1890-1914." Sussex, 1971.

1666
Penner, Rudolph Gerhard. "Foreign Investment and Canadian Economic Growth, 1950-1960." Johns Hopkins, 1963.

1667
Shapiro, Daniel Mark. "Multinational Investment and the Canadian Economy." Cornell, 1974.

1668
Shearer, Ronald Alexander. "International Investment, Economic Growth and the Case of Canada." Ohio State, 1959.

1669
Springate, David John Victor. "Regional Development Incentive Grants and Private Investment in Canada: A Case Study of the Effect of Regional Development Incentives on the Investment Decisions of Manufacturing Firms." Harvard, 1972.

1670
Thiessen, G.G. "Federal Government Lending as an Instrument of Economic Policy in Canada, 1954-1964." London, 1972.

1671
Van Loo, Mary Frances. "The Effect of Direct Investment on Canadian Investment." California, Berkeley, 1971.

1672
Wahab, Abdul. "Foreign Investment Decisions of Western Canadian Firms." British Columbia, 1978.

Stocks, Bonds, Equities, Securities and Portfolio Behaviour/Valeurs, obligations, actions, titres mobiliers et valeurs en portefeuille

Stocks/Valeurs

Allan, John Richard. See No./Voir no 1696

1673
Bart, John Telesephore. "The Expectations of Stock Market Participants for Selected Stocks." Western Ontario, 1974.

1674
Boeckh, John Anthony. "Long-Run Stockmarket in Canada: Performance Implications for Allocational Efficiency." Pennsylvania, 1968.

1675
Brown, Ronald Duncan. "The Usefulness of Financial Ratios for Predicting Common Stock Performance of Canadian Manufacturing Firms." Syracuse, 1978.

1676
Gordon, Irene Malinda. "Unfunded Past Service Obligations: An Efficient Markets Hypothesis." Simon Fraser, 1981.

Graham, Robert Edward. See No./Voir no 1638

1677
Johnson, Byron Oliver Simpson. "The Vancouver Stock Exchange, 1945 to 1969." Santa Clara, 1972.

1678
Kilbride, Bernard James. "Listing Requirements of the Leading Stock Exchanges in Canada." Texas, 1962.

1679
Lawson, William Morse. "Market Efficiency and the Interaction among Three Classes of Participants Trading on the Toronto Stock Exchange." York, 1974.

Mitchell, Carlyle L. See No./Voir no 1868
Morin, Roger-André. See No./Voir no 1485

1680
Rabinovitch, Robert. "Characteristics of Stock Ownership in Canada." Pennsylvania, 1972.

Bonds/Obligations

1681
Ananthanarayanan, A.L. "Parameter Estimation of Stochastic Interest Rate Models and Applications to Bond Pricing." British Columbia, 1978. [Bonds and Treasury bills/Obligations et bons du trésor]

1682
Caron, Y. "The Trust for Bond-Holders in the Province of Quebec." Queen's, 1965.

1683
Dipchand, Cecil Ramnarine. "The Determinants of Risk Premiums on Publicly Traded Canadian Corporate Bonds: An Empirical Study." Western Ontario, 1973.

1684
Garant, Jean Pierre. "The Floating Charge in Canadian Bond Market." Illinois, 1971.

1685
McCallum, John Stuart. "The Expected Holding Period Return, the Term Structure of Interest Rates and Investment in the Government of Canada Bond Market." Toronto, 1973.

1686
Peters, John Ross. "The Economics of Private Placements in Canada." McGill, 1968. [Corporate bond market/Marché des obligations enregistrées]

Equities/Actions

1687
Close, Nicholas. "The Reaction of the Canadian Secondary Market in Equities to Large Value Transactions." Western Ontario, 1973.

1688
Conway, Geoffrey Robert. "The Supply of, and Demand for Canadian Equities." Harvard, 1973.

1689
Masson, Paul Robert Leo. "Risk and Return in Financial Matters with an Application to Canadian Equities." London, 1973.

1690
Shaw, David Carvell. "The Market for New Equity Issues in Canada." Pennsylvania, 1968.

Securities/Titres mobiliers

1691
Gram, Harold Albert. "The Canadian Government Securities Market." Syracuse, 1963.

1692
Kryzanowski, Lawrence. "Some Tests of the Efficacy of Security Regulation in Canadian Capital Markets." British Columbia, 1976.

1693
Williamson, John Peter. "Effects of Securities Regulation on Canadian Corporate Financing." Harvard, 1961.

Portfolio Behaviour and Selection/ Valeur et choix de portefeuille

Arango, Sebastian. See No./Voir no 1542
1694
Clinton, Kevin James. "Portfolio Behaviour of the Trust and Mortgage Loan Companies of Canada, 1967-1972: A Theoretical and Econometric Analysis." Western Ontario, 1973.

Italiano, Joseph Angelo. See No./Voir no 1431
1695
Kirkham, Peter G. "The Portfolio Behaviour of Selected Canadian Financial Intermediaries: An Econometric Analysis." Princeton, 1970.

Lafrance, Robert Rolland. See No./Voir no 1434

Taxes/Impôt

1696
Allan, John Richard. "The Income Tax Burden on Canadian Stockholders." Princeton, 1965.

1697
Amoako-Adu, Benjamin. "The Effect of the Canadian Tax Reforms on the Capital Markets." Toronto, 1981.

1698
Bancroft, Donald Asa. "Variation of Property Tax Assessments in Alberta." Syracuse, 1971.

1699
Barber, Lloyd Ingram. "The Influence of Federal Income Tax on the Growth of Cooperative Merchandising in Canada." Washington, Seattle, 1964.

1700
Bernardinucci, Don A. "The Effect on Corporate Equity Holdings of a Comprehensive and Integrated Tax Base and the Implications for Investment." McGill, 1974.

1701
Boote, Maurice John. "Income Retention and Fixed Capital Expansion: A Group of Canadian Manufacturing Corporations, 1932-1953." McGill, 1959.

1702
Boucher, Michel. "Analyse de deux propriétés de l'impôt québécois sur le revenu des particuliers." Laval, 1978.

1703
Bucovetsky, Meyer Wilfred. "Tax Reform in Canada: A Case Study of the Mining Industry." Toronto, 1971.

1704
Clark, Robert M. "Some Aspects of the Development of Personal Income Tax in the Provinces and Municipalities of Canada up to 1930." Harvard, 1947.

1705
Clayton, Francis Alfred. "Distribution of Urban Residential Property Tax Burdens and Expenditure Benefits in Canada." Queen's, 1967.

1706
Daly, Donald. "Estimating Collections from the Canadian Personal Income Tax." Chicago, 1953.

1707
Dean, James Michael. "Income Tax Adjustments for Inflation - with Special Emphasis on Canada." Virginia Polytechnic Institute and State University, 1974.

Dennis-Escoffier, Shirley. See No./Voir no 1923
Downie, Felix Philip. See No./Voir no 2782
Forde, Penelope Allison. See No./Voir no 1748
1708
Fulton, Patricia. "Homeowner Imputed Rent and Capital Gains: Implications for Equity Within the Tax System." Western Ontario, 1980.

1709
Gardner, Robert John Logie. "The Politics of Reform: Class Interests and Tax Reform in Canada, 1960-1971." McMaster, 1983.

1710
Ghaeli, Reza. "A Macroeconometric Analysis of the Incidence and Economic Effects of the Corporation Income Tax in Canada." McMaster, 1982.

1711
Goffman, Irving Jay. "Erosion of the Personal Income Tax Base in Canada and the United States." Duke, 1959.

1712
Good, David Allen. "The Politics of Anticipation: Making Tax Policy in Canada." California, Berkeley, 1979.

1713
Hindle, Colin James. "Negative Income Taxation and Poverty in Ontario." Toronto, 1970.

1714
Johnson, Daniel. "Tax Avoidance in Canada, with Comparative Reference to Australia and the United Kingdom." London, 1971.

1715
Johnston, James Wilson. "Succession Duties in Canada." Indiana, 1958.

1716
Jutlah, Clifford Benjamin. "Income Tax Relationships: Estimation and Role in Economic Stabilization." Toronto, 1970.

1717
LaForest, Gerard Vincent. "The Allocation of Taxing Power under the Canadian Constitution." Yale, 1966.

Larin, Gilles. See No./Voir no 2571

1718
MacNaughton, Alan Robert. "Taxation and the Financial Policy of Canadian Closely-Held Corporation." British Columbia, 1983.

1719
Mendels, Roger Pierre. "Economics of Accelerated Depreciation: The Canadian Experience." Wisconsin, 1963.

Michas, Nicholas. See No./Voir no 1502

Murray, John David. See No./Voir no 2347

1720
Owen, Clifford Frank. "Business Financing and Taxation Policies." Toronto, 1958.

1721
Peterson, James Scott. "The International Aspects of Canadian Income Taxation." McGill, 1970.

1722
Petrie, J. Richards. "The Tax Systems of Canada: A Description and Analysis of the Major Federal, Provincial and Municipal Tax Bases." McGill, 1941.

1723
Poe, Weyland Douglas. "Local Sales Taxes in the United States and Canada." Indiana, 1959.

1724
Reese, Craig Eugene. "The Use of Tax Policy to Control Pollution: A Comparative Analysis of the Major Industrialized Countries in North America and Eastern Europe." Texas, 1979. [United States, Canada, France, Germany, Sweden and the United Kingdom/États-Unis, Canada, France, Allemagne, Suède et Royaume-Uni]

Santos y de Regla, Benjamin. See No./Voir no 1581

Schoplein, Robert Nicholas. See No./Voir no 1643

1725
Soroka, Lewis Arthur. "The Canadian Personal Income Tax: The Response of Revenue to Income Changes." McGill, 1970.

1726
Sparks, Jared, Jr. "Excise Taxes and Inflation Control: The Canadian Experience, 1939-1957." Illinois, 1958.

1727
Spencer, Byron Grant. "Shifting of the Corporation Income Tax: The Canadian Experience." Rice, 1967.

1728
Strauss, Hans Ernst Hermann. "The Burden of Property Tax Exemptions in Ontario." McGill, 1976.

Todres, Elaine Meller. See No./Voir no 8500

1729
Vineberg, Solomon. "Provincial and Local Taxation in Canada." Columbia, 1912.

1730
Watson, William George. "Taxation and Public Expenditure in the OECD Countries, 1945-1975, with Emphasis on the United Kingdom, Canada, and Sweden." Yale, 1980.

1731
Woods, Marvyn J. "Federal Taxation of Income of Cooperative Trading Corporations in the United States and Canada." New York University, Law, 1962.

1732
Woodside, Kenneth E. B. "The Politics of Redistributive Taxation in Canada and Britain 1945-1971." Chicago, 1977.

See also Tax Laws/Voir aussi Lois fiscales

INDUSTRY/INDUSTRIE

General Items/Ouvrages généraux

1733
Acheson, Thomas William. "The Social Origins of Canadian Industrialism: A Study in the Structure of Entrepreneurship." Toronto, 1971.

1734
Baetz, Mark Conrad. "The Purposes and Influence of a Canadian Exercise in a Formal Consultative Industrial Planning." Western Ontario, 1981.

1735
Beattie, David. "An Analysis of Conglomerate Diversification and Performance." Queen's, 1976.

1736
Bellicha, Yoram. "Estimating Returns to Scale in Selected Manufacturing Industries in Canada." McGill, 1979.

1737
Boston, Ralph Emerson. "A Basis for an Industrial Development Program for British Columbia." Michigan, 1962.

1738
Cannon, James Bernard. "An Analysis of Manufacturing as an Instrument of Public Policy in Regional Economic Development: Canadian Area Development Agency Program 1963-1968." Washington, Seattle, 1970.

1739
Carrington, Peter John. "Horizontal Co-optation Through Corporate Interlocks." Toronto, 1981.

Clark, Samuel Delbert. See No./Voir no 1200

Conlon, Robert Maxwell. See No./Voir no 2003

1740
Cooper, Robert Gravlin. "Market Assessment Expenditures in Industrial New Product Ventures." Western Ontario, 1973.

1741
Courchene, Thomas Joseph. "Inventory Behavior and the Stock-Order Distinction: An Analysis by Industry and by State of Fabrication with Empirical Applications to the Canadian Manufacturing Sectors." Princeton, 1967.

Cox, Joseph Christopher. See No./Voir no 1377

1742
Dalto, Guy Calvin. "Size, Technology and Administrative Intensity: A Longitudinal and Cross-Sectional Analysis." Chicago, 1975. [156 Canadian industries, 1961-1972/156 industries canadiennes, 1961-1972]

1743
DeWilde, James Frederick. "Modern Capitalist Planning and Canadian Federalism: The Case of High Technology Industries." McGill, 1979.

1744
Dickson, Vaughan Andrew. "Scale Efficiency in Canadian Manufacturing." Western Ontario, 1977.

1745
Dimma, William Andrew. "The Canadian Development Corporation: Diffident Experiment on a Large Scale." Harvard, 1973.

1746
Drennon, Herbert Neal. "The Industrial Relations Policy of the Canadian Dominion Government, 1939-1948." Duke, 1951.

1747
Ebel, Bernd. "Interindustry Linkages and the Agglomeration of Manufacturing Industries in the Canadian Economy." Alberta, 1974.

Foote, Raymond Leslie. See No./Voir no 10164

1748
Forde, Penelope Allison. "Tax Incentives and Investment in Two Canadian Manufacturing Industries." McGill, 1981.

1749
Gladwin, Thomas Neil. "The Role of Ecological Considerations in the Multinational Corporate Project Planning Process: A Comparative Study of North American and Western European Based Petroleum, Chemicals, and Metal Firms." Michigan, 1975.

1750
Gupta, Vinod Kumar. "Structure, Conduct and Performance in Canadian Manufacturing Industries: A Simultaneous Equations Approach." Toronto, 1977.

Hart, Douglas John. See No./Voir no 1320

1751
Hodgins, Cyril D. "On Estimating the Economies of Large-Scale Production: Some Tests in Data for the Canadian Manufacturing Sector." Chicago, 1968.

Johnson, Neil Alexander. See No./Voir no 2059

1752
Killing, John Peter. "Manufacturing Under License in Canada." Western Ontario, 1975.

1753
Kotowitz, Yehuda. "Production Functions in Canadian Manufacturing, 1926-1961." Chicago, 1970.

1754
Lazaridis, Panagiotis. "Foreign Direct Investment in Canadian Manufacturing: Technological Differences Between Foreign and Domestic Firms." Concordia, 1981.

1755
LeGoff, Jean-Pierre. "Effectiveness of the Canadian Government Investment Incentives for Manufacturing Sector from 1965 to 1974." Cornell, 1977.

1756
Lemelin, André. "Patterns of Interindustry Diversification in Canadian Manufacturing Enterprises." Harvard, 1979.

Lemelin, Charles. See No./Voir no 67

1757
MacCharles, Donald Clare. "The Cost of Administrative Organizations in Canadian Secondary Manufacturing Industries." Toronto, 1978.

1758
McDiarmid, Orville J. "Protection and Canadian Industrial Development." Harvard, 1936.

McDonough, Lawrence Cecil. See No./Voir no 1664

McFarland, Joan Murray. See No./Voir no 1352

1759
McFetridge, Donald Grant. "Market Structure and Price Behaviour: Empirical Studies of the Canadian Manufacturing Sector." Toronto, 1972.

1760
McGuinness, Norman William. "The Impact of Technology and Product Characteristics on the International Sales of New Canadian Products: A Diffusion Analysis." Western Ontario, 1978.

1761
Montmarquette, Claude. "A Model of Inventory Holdings with Empirical Application to Canadian Manufacturing Industries." Chicago, 1973.

1762
Moussette, Marcel. "Le chauffage domestique au Canada des origines à l'industrialisation." Laval, 1981.

1763
Murty, Grandhi, V.R. "A Statistical Study of Concentration in the Manufacturing Industries of Canada." McGill, 1955.

1764
Olley, Robert Edward. "Movements of Factor Costs Per Unit in Canadian and American Manufacturing Industries, 1947-1964." Queen's, 1969.

Paquin, Jean-Paul. See No./Voir no 2190

1765
Perret, Marie-Solange. "The Impact of Cultural Differences on Budgeting in a Multinational Company." Western Ontario, 1982.

1766
Pincus, John Alexis. "Primary Industry and the Economic Development of Canada." Harvard, 1964.

1767
Post, George Richard. "Capital Expenditures in Canadian Manufacturing." Northwestern, 1963.

1768
Postner, Harry Haskell. "Estimation of the Elasticity of Capital-Labour Substitution in Postwar Canadian Manufacturing Industries." Minnesota, 1970.

1769
Purchase, Bryne Brock. "Acquisitions, Intangible Assets and the Growth of the Firm: An Interindustry Analysis." Toronto, 1981.

1770
Reddy, Jammula Mahenda. "Statistical Estimation of the Elasticities of Demand for Nondurable Goods in the Canadian Economy." Alberta, 1971.

Riddell, William Craig. See No./Voir no 2122

1771
Rosenbluth, Gideon. "Concentration in Canadian Manufacturing Industries." Columbia, 1953.

1772
Sakellariou, Dimitri M. "Industrial Linkage: A Case Study." Alberta, 1972.

Saunders, Ronald Stanley. See No./Voir no 2377

1773
Sexty, Robert William. "The Relationship Between Rates Return and Concentration Growth, Capital and Trade in Canadian Manufacturing Industries." Colorado, 1974.

Sims, William Allen. See No./Voir no 2239

Taylor, Norman William. See No./Voir no 1217

1774
Williams, John. "A Comparative Study of the Industrial Relations System and Law of Great Britain, Canada and Australia." Nebraska, 1975.

1775
Wilson, David Thomas. "An Exploratory Study of the Effect of Personality and Problem Elements Upon Purchasing Agent Decision Styles." Western Ontario, 1970.

1776
Young, John Geoffrey. "A Cost-Benefit Analysis of the Area Development Incentives Act Program in the Atlantic Provinces." Harvard, 1974.

Zollo, Tancredi. See No./Voir no 4793

Specific Industries/Industries particulières

Agricultural/Agriculture

See also Agricultural Economics/Voir aussi Économie agricole

Chemical/Chimie

Gladwin, Thomas Neil. See No./Voir no 1749

Communications

1777
Khadem, Ramin. "An Econometric Model of the Demand for International Voice Telecommunication from Canada." McGill, 1975.

Millen, Ronald Harold Vincent. See No./Voir no 1460

1778
O'Brien, John Wilfred. "Publicly and Privately Owned Telephone Systems: An Economic Comparison." McGill, 1962.

Construction

1779
Binhammer, Helmut Herbert. "A Study of the Residential Construction Sector in the Canadian Economy." McGill, 1961.

1780
Harvey, Jean Lucien. "Competitive Bidding on Canadian Public Construction Contracts: Stochastic Analysis for Optimization." Western Ontario, 1979.

Hogg, William Alfred. See No./Voir no 5089

Kurtz, Larry Robert. See No./Voir no 1384

Lawrie, Neil John. See No./Voir no 1385

Distributive/Distribution

Ma, Sylvia See-Wai. See No./Voir no 2230

Maister, David Hilton. See No./Voir no 1803

Drug/Produits pharmaceutiques

1781
Pazderka, Bohumir. "Promotion and Competition in the Canadian Prescription Drug Industry." Queen's, 1976.

Electric Power Industry/Industrie de l'énergie électrique

1782
Belfield, Robert Blake. "The Niagara Frontier: The Evolution of Electric Power Systems in New York and Ontario, 1880-1935." Pennsylvania, 1981.

1783
Boyle, Lawrence James. "The Development of the Hydro-Electric Industry in Quebec." Maryland, 1973.

1784
Dales, John Harkness. "The Hydro-Electric Industry in Quebec, 1898-1940." Harvard, 1953.

1785
Dewar, Kenneth Cameron. "State Ownership in Canada: The Origins of Ontario Hydro." Toronto, 1975.

DeYoung, John H., Jr. See No./Voir no 4472

1786
Hall, Carl Ansel St. Clair. "Electrical Utilities in Ontario Under Private Ownership, 1890-1914." Toronto, 1968.

1787
Hanna, Allan Alexander. "Settlement and Energy Policy in Perspective: A Theoretical Framework for the Evaluation of Public Policy." Western Ontario, 1980.

Hardy-Roch, Marcelle. See no./Voir no 10013

1788
Horne, Gilbert Richard. "The Receivership and Reorganization of the Abitibi Power and Paper Company Limited." Michigan, 1954.

1789
Howard, Jane Mary. "Economic Aspects of the St. Lawrence Power and Navigation Project." Catholic, 1950.

1790
Hyndman, Richard McCrae. "Residential Demand for Energy in Canada." Toronto, 1975.

Mamandur, Rangaiah Chetty. See No./Voir no 4584

1791
Massam, Bryan Hazlewood. "An Approach to the Analysis of Spatial Administrative Patterns: Ontario Hydro-Electric Power Commission." McMaster, 1969.

1792
McIntyre, Wallace E. "Niagara Falls Hydro-Electric Industry." Clark, 1951.

1793
Morrissey, Frederick Patric. "A Study of the Hydro-Electric Power Commission of Ontario." Columbia, 1951.

1794
Mountain, Dean Clarence. "Interfuel Substitution in the Electricity Industry." Western Ontario, 1979. [Nova Scotia, New Brunswick and Ontario/Nouvelle-Écosse, Nouveau-Brunswick et Ontario]

Newkirk, Ross Thomas. See No./Voir no 4558

1795
Riley, Richard Brinton. "Public Policy and the Electric Power Industry in Canada: A Comparative Political Analysis of Power Development in Three Western Provinces." Duke, 1975.

1796
Rioux, Albert. "L'électrification rurale du Québec." Laval, 1942.

1797
Smith, L. Graham. "Public Participation at a Normative Level: Electric Power Planning in Ontario." Western Ontario, 1982.

Electrical Products and Electronics/ Produits électriques et électroniques

Baba, Vishwanath Venkataraman. See No./Voir no 1926

1798
Clarke, Stephen Glenn. "Diversification, Product Mix Change and Competition: A Study of Firms in Electrical Manufacturing." Queen's, 1972.

1799
Kardasz, Stanley W. "Foreign Control and Investment Behaviour: A Case Study of Two Firms in the Canadian Electrical Products Industries." Queen's, 1976.

Food and Drink/Nourriture et breuvage

1800
Bronson, Harold Emory. "The Developing Structure of the Meat Packing Industry in Saskatchewan: A Study in Economic Welfare." Saskatchewan, 1965.

1801
Chan, Man-Wah Luke. "A Model of the Canadian Beef and Dairy Cattle Industry Based on Markov Chain Techniques." McMaster, 1978.

Finlay, John Robert. See No./Voir no 1316

Gutzke, David William. See No./Voir no 1273

1802
Haslett, Earl Allen. "Factors in the Growth and Decline of the Cheese Industry in Ontario." Toronto, 1969.

Lin, Leon Chin-Shin. See No./Voir no 180

Ma, Sylvia See-Wai. See No./Voir no 2230

1803
Maister, David Hilton. "Barriers to Change in Distributive Industries: The Canadian Grain Delivery System." Harvard, 1976.

Patton, Harald Smith. See No./Voir no 119

1804
Roseman, Frank. "The Canadian Brewing Industry: The Effect of Mergers and Provincial Regulation on Economic Conduct and Performance." Northwestern, 1968.

1805
Sherbaniuk, James Alexander. "Regina V. Canadian Breweries Limited: An Analysis of a Merger Case." Washington, Seattle, 1964.

1806
Sundstrom, Marvin Thomas. "Regional and Farm Level Adjustments in Southern Ontario's Dairy Industry, 1968-1974." McMaster, 1975.

1807
Taylor, Reed David. "Characteristics of the United States Producer Maple Syrup Markets." Pennsylvania State, 1965.

Zasada, Donald. See No./Voir no 40

Film Industry/Industrie cinématographique

Pendakur, Manjunath. See No./Voir no 1114

Forest Products Industries/ Industries des produits forestiers

General Items/Ouvrages généraux

1808
Brakel, Pieter. "Production Relationships, Market Structure, Firm Behaviour and the Supply of Exports: An Application to the Canadian Forest Products Industries." Toronto, 1977.

1809
Hardwick, Walter Gordon. "The Forest Industries of Coastal British Columbia: A Geographic Study of Place and Circulation." Minnesota, 1963.

1810
Hayter, Roger. "An Examination of Growth Patterns and Locational Behaviour of Multi-Plant Forest Product Corporations in British Columbia." Washington, Seattle, 1973.

Shore, Terence Leckie. See No./Voir no 11230

Pulp and Paper/Pulpe et papier

1811
Bélanger, Gérard. "Structural and Locational Determinants of Regional Employment Growth: A Case Study of the Canadian Pulp and Paper Industry." Western Ontario, 1978.

1812
Birch, John Worth. "The Changing Location of the North American Pulp Industry, 1880 to 1955." Johns Hopkins, 1962.

1813
Clemente, Ricardo Ama. "Interregional Competition in the Pulpwood Industry of the United States and Canada." Pennsylvania State, 1970.

1814
Côté, Serge. "Les voies de la monopolisation: le cas de l'usine de papier de Bathurst." Montréal, 1979.

Cottell, Philip Leroy. See No./Voir no 2052

Cross, Michael Sean. See No./Voir no 1240

1815
Cummins, John Gaylord. "Concentration and Mergers in the Pulp and Paper Industries of the United States and Canada, 1895-1955." Johns Hopkins, 1961.

1816
Hayes, Francis Joseph. "The Pulp and Paper Industry in Canada: An Analysis of the Restrictions on Competition." McGill, 1960.

Horne, Gilbert Richard. See No./Voir no 1788

1817
Jain, Hem Chand. "Industrial Relations in the Pulp and Paper Industry in the Atlantic Region." Illinois, 1968. [1953-1963]

1818
Lachance, Paul Émile. "A Study of the Pulp and Paper Industry of the Province of Quebec in Relation to Its Present and Future Wood Supplies." Michigan, 1954.

1819
Legendre, Camille George. "Organizational Technology, Structure and Environment: The Pulp and Paper Logging Industry." Michigan State, 1977.

1820
Mehta, Nitin Tarachand. "Policy Formation and Declining Industry: The Case of the Canadian Dissolving Pulp Industry." Harvard, 1978.

1821
Muller, Robert Andrew. "Simulation of Adjustment to Pollution Control Costs in the Pulp and Paper Industry." Toronto, 1975.

Nokoe, Tertius Sagary. See No./Voir no 11705

1822
Reinertsen, Philip J. "The Pulp and Paper Industries in Sweden and Canada." Chicago, 1959.

1823
Roberge, Roger Adrian. "The Timing, Type, and Location of Adaptive Inventive Activity in the Eastern Canadian Pulp and Paper Industry, 1806-1940." Clark, 1972.

1824
Thevenon, Michael Jean. "An Economic Analysis of Pulp and Paper and Board Exports from the Pacific Northwest." Oregon State, 1972.

Newsprint/Papier-journal

1825
Church, John Halcot. "Determinants of the Performance and Development of the Canadian Newsprint Industry, 1920 to 1970." Western Ontario, 1978.

1826
Dagenais, Marcel Gilles. "The Determination of the Output and Price Levels in the North American Newsprint Paper Industry." Yale, 1964.

1827
Islam, Muhammed Nurul. "Interregional Competition and Comparative Location Advantages of North American Newsprint Industry." McGill, 1973.

1828
Le, Can Duy. "An Econometric Analysis of the Canadian Newsprint Market 1950-1972." Toronto, 1979.

1829
Singer, Jacques Joachim. "Postwar Development and Future of the North American Newsprint Industry." Massachusetts Institute of Technology, 1961.

Saw-Mill/Scierie

1830
Nadeau, Jean-Paul. "An Economic Study of Quebec's Saw-Mill Industry." Syracuse, 1969.

Timber/Bois d'oeuvre

1831
Bessom, Richard Moody. "Competitive Marketing Strategies of Major American and Canadian Softwood Plywood Firms." Washington, Seattle, 1965.

1832
Cauvin, Dennis Mederic. "Measurement of a Forest's Contribution to the Economy of Alberta." Washington, Seattle, 1972.

1833
Gray, John Andrew. "Pricing and Sale of Public Timber: A Case Study of the Province of Manitoba." Michigan, 1971.

Lower, Arthur Reginald M. See No./Voir no 1279

1834
Meany, Edmond Stephen. "The History of the Lumber Industry in the Pacific Northwest to 1917." Harvard, 1936. [Includes British Columbia/Inclut la Colombie-Britannique]

1835
Raghavendra, Bangalore Gururajachar. "Some Mathematical Programming Models in the Design and Manufacture of Plywood." British Columbia, 1982.

1836
Wilson, David A. "An Analysis of Lumbering Exports from the Coast Region of British Columbia to the United Kingdom and the United States, 1920-1952." California, Berkeley, 1955.

Wooden Match/Allumettes de bois

1837
Stewart, Max Douglas. "Some Economic Aspects of the Canadian Wooden Match Industry and Public Policy." Michigan State, 1960.

Fuel and Heating Industries/ Industries des carburants et du chauffage

Moussette, Marcel. See No./Voir no 1762

Machinery/Machinerie

1838
Perkett, William Oliver. "An Analysis of the Obstacles to Increased Foreign Trade which Confront British Columbia Industrial Machinery Manufacturers." Washington, Seattle, 1964.

Motor Vehicles/Véhicules motorisés

1839
Appana, Mohan. "Product-Plant Assignment in North American Automobile Assembly." Ottawa, 1981.

1840
Coates, Norman. "Industrial Relations Implications of Canadian - United States Economic Integration: The Automobile Industry as a Case Study." Cornell, 1967.

1841
Connidis, Ingegjerd L.A. "The Canadian Motor Vehicle Assembly Industry: A Study of Protection and Productivity Under the Auto Pact." Queen's, 1979.

1842
Flynn, David Michael. "The Rationalization of the United States and Canadian Automobile Industry." Massachusetts, 1979.

1843
Helmers, Henrik Olaf. "Some Effects of the United States-Canadian Automobile Agreement." Michigan, 1967.
Kim, Moshe. See No./Voir no 2325

1844
Lau, Hung-Hay. "An Evaluation of the Economic Impact of Continental Free Trade in Used Cars on Employment in the Canadian Automobile Industry." Toronto, 1973.

1845
Neisser, Albert C. "The Impact of the Canada-United States Automotive Agreement on Canada's Motor Vehicle Industry: A Study in Economies of Scale." New School, 1966.
Phillips, William Gregory. See No./Voir no 31

1846
Robertson, Robert Allen. "An Analysis of the Motor Vehicle Industry as a Factor in the Economic Life of Canada." Illinois, 1960.

1847
Shaw, Donald Elliott. "An Empirical Study of Seller Concentration and Profits in the New Motor Vehicle Retailing Industry of Eight Canadian Prairie Cities." Saskatchewan, 1975.

1848
Smith, Victor E. "An Application and Critique of Certain Methods for the Determination of a Statistical Production Function for the Canadian Automobile Industry, 1917-1930." Northwestern, 1941.
Stykolt, Stefan. See No./Voir no 1971

1849
Wilton, David Arthur. "An Econometric Model of the Canadian Automobile Manufacturing Industry." Massachusetts Institute of Technology, 1969.

Watches/Montres

1850
Hostettler, Pierre. "The Future of the 'World Watch Industry': A Comparative Study Using Delphi." Texas Tech, 1976. [United States, Japan, Switzerland, Germany, France and Canada/États-Unis, Japon, Suisse, Allemagne, France et Canada]

Commercial Fishing/Pêche commerciale

General Items/Ouvrages généraux

1851
Charles, Anthony Trevor. "Optimal Fisheries Investment." British Columbia, 1982.

1852
Lamb, Charles William, Jr. "An Analysis of Marketing Systems for Canadian Freshwater Fish in Two Time Periods." Kentucky State, 1974.

1853
McGaw, R.L. "An Econometric Model of the North American Scallop Industry." Manchester, 1978.

1854
Morgan, R.L.R. "Sea Fisheries: A Geographical Study." London, 1954.
Rostlund, Erhard. See No./Voir no 483
Southey, Clive. See No./Voir no 1358

1855
Swygard, Kline Ruthven. "The International Halibut and Sockeye Salmon Fisheries Commissions: A Study in International Administration." Washington, Seattle, 1948.

Western Canada/Ouest du Canada

1856
Capalbo, Susan Marie. "Bioeconomic Supply and Imperfect Competition: The Case of the North Pacific Halibut Industry." California, Davis, 1982.

1857
Judson, Thomas Andrew. "The Freshwater Commercial Fishing Industry of Western Canada." Toronto, 1961.

1858
Koh, Kwang-Lim. "International Regulation of Fisheries with Special Reference to Those in the North Pacific Ocean." Rutgers, 1953.

1859
Southward, Glen Morris. "A Simulation Study of Management Regulatory Policies in the Pacific Halibut Fishery." Washington, Seattle, 1966.

1860
Wang, Der-Hsiung. "An Econometric Study of the Canadian Sockeye Salmon Market." Oregon State, 1976.

British Columbia/Colombie-Britannique

1861
Gardner, Peter Nigel. "Optimal Management of the Fraser River Sockeye Salmon." British Columbia, 1980.

1862
Loose, Verne William. "Optimal Exploitation of a Salmon Fishery: A Simulation Approach." British Columbia, 1978. [Skeena River Fishery/Pêche sur la rivière Skeena]
Miller, Philip Carl. See No./Voir no 387

1863
Robinson, Gilbert Adrian. "A Study of the Pacific Ocean Perch Fisheries of the Northwestern Pacific Ocean." Seattle, 1972.

Atlantic Provinces/Provinces de l'Atlantique

1864
Altobello, Marilyn Agnes. "Optimal Control Theory as Applied to the Management of a Replenishable Natural Resource: The Atlantic Sea Scallop." Massachusetts, 1976.

1865
Brewer, Keith John. "The Canadian East Coast Groundfish Industry." McGill, 1973.

1866
Cayley, Charles E. "The North Atlantic Fisheries in the United States-Canadian Relations." Chicago, 1931.

Finkle, Peter Zack Ross. See No./Voir no 1381

Gaffney, Michael Edward. See No./Voir no 403

1867
Jansen, Janni Margaretha. "Regional Socio-Economic Development: The Case of Fishing in Atlantic Canada." Rutgers, 1981.

MacInnes, Daniel William. See No./Voir no 2115

1868
Mitchell, Carlyle L. "Stock Adjustment Models, Canada's East Coast Groundfish Fisheries." Ottawa, 1979.

1869
Stenger, Alfred. "A Study of Certain Economic and Social Problems Related to the North Atlantic Fisheries Industries." Ottawa, 1948.

1870
Tugwell, Stephen Maurice. "Production and Efficiency in the Maritime Lobster Fishery." Queen's, 1974.

Wolfgang, Robert W. See No./Voir no 11350

Newfoundland/Terre-Neuve

Antler, Ellen Pildes. See No./Voir no 397

1871
Daggett, Athern Park. "Fishery Rights in Territorial Waters Secured by International Agreements." Harvard, 1931.

McCay, Bonnie Jean. See No./Voir no 406

Ryan, S.P. See No./Voir no 1255

Small, Lawrence George. See No./Voir no 411

1872
Stiles, Ralph Geoffrey. "Reluctant Entrepreneurs: Organizational Change and Capital Management in a Newfoundland Fishery." McGill, 1973.

Ontario

1873
Hyde, Martin James. "Indian Commercial Fisheries in the Patricia District of Ontario: An Economic Analysis." McGill, 1963.

Quebec/Québec

1874
Larocque, Paul. "Pêche et coopération en Gaspésie (1938-1964)." Concordia, 1978. [Cooperative Federation of United Fishers of Québec/Fédération coopérative des pêcheurs unis du Québec]

Metals, Minerals and Mining/ Métaux, minéraux et industrie minière

Bucovetsky, Mayer Wilfred. See No./Voir no 1703

1875
Choksi, Shehrnaz. "Pricing Policies in the Canadian Copper, Aluminium, Nickel and Steel Industries." McGill, 1980.

1876
Cranstone, Donald Alfred. "An Analysis of Ore Discovery Costs and Rates of Ore Discovery in Canada Over the Period 1946 to 1977." Harvard, 1982.

1877
Gelman, Robert M. "Economic Development of the Mining Industries of the Northern Frontier under a Planned and Free Economy: The Soviet Union and Canada." Catholic, 1964.

Gladwin, Thomas Neil. See No./Voir no 1749

Jestin, Warren James. See No./Voir no 1275

Lasserre, Pierre. See No./Voir no 1176

Lepore, Giuseppe. See No./Voir no 2238

McCarty, J.W. See No./Voir no 1285

1878
Moore, Patrick Albert. "The Administration of Pollution Control in British Columbia: A Focus on the Mining Industry." British Columbia, 1974.

1879
Nemetz, Peter Newman. "The Economics of Water Pollution Control in the British Columbia Metal Mining Industry." Harvard, 1973.

Newell, Dianne Charlotte Elizabeth. See No./Voir no 10508

1880
Paquette, Pierre Jean. "L'extraction de matières premières et la politique minière de l'état: une analyse de leur évolution et de leur contribution au développement économique du Québec: 1867-1973." McGill, 1983.

Petersen, James Otto. See No./Voir no 1214

1881
Richardson, Peter Rodney. "The Acquisition of New Process Technology by Firms in the Canadian Mineral Industries." Western Ontario, 1975.

1882
Werner, Antony Boris Tracey. "The Financing of the Canadian Metal Mining Industry, 1945-1960." Pennsylvania State, 1973.

Aluminum/Aluminium

Choksi, Shehrnaz. See No./Voir no 1875

1883
Hollbach, Arthur Reiner. "The Canadian Primary Aluminium Industry." McGill, 1958.

Asbestos/Amiante

Armstrong, Robert. See No./Voir no 1258

1884
Parent, Robert. "La bourgeoisie canadienne et le capital étranger dans le développement de l'industrie de l'amiante au Canada." Montréal, 1982.

Coal/Charbon

1885
Freyman, Andrew Jack. "Analysis of an Industrial Sector: The Coal Mining Industry in Nova Scotia." Columbia School of Mines, 1967.
Gallacher, Daniel Thomas. See No./Voir no 1272
Hyndman, Richard McCrae. See No./Voir no 1790
Schwartzman, David. See No./Voir no 1301

Copper and Zinc/Cuivre et zinc

Choksi, Shehrnaz. See No./Voir no 1875
1886
Gupta, Satyadeo. "Market Structure and Econometric Modeling: A Case Study of the World Zinc Industry." McMaster, 1980.
1887
Mahalingasivam, Rasiah. "Market for Canadian Refined Copper: An Econometric Study." Toronto, 1969.
1888
Wittier, Glen Eric. "Domestic Processing of Mine Output in Canada with Case Studies on Zinc and Copper Refining." Pennsylvania State, 1974.

Gold/Or

MacLeod, Donald Eric. See No./Voir no 1280

Iron and Steel/Fer et acier

1889
Barnett, Donald Frederick. "The Import Shares of Rolled and Tubed Steel Products in Canada." Queen's, 1969.
1890
Baumann, Harold G. "The Diffusion of Technology and International Competitiveness: A Case Study of the Canadian Primary Iron and Steel Industry." Queen's, 1972.
Choksi, Shehrnaz. See No./Voir no 1875
1891
DeMelto, Dennis P. "The Effect of Foreign Competition on the Canadian Primary Steel Industry: 1950-1966." McGill, 1970.
Donald, William John Alexander. See No./Voir no 1268
1892
Eldon, Walter D.R.. "American Influence in the Canadian Iron and Steel Industry." Harvard, 1952.
1893
Elver, Robert Bruce. "Competition in the Canadian Primary Steel Industry, 1945-1966." Pennsylvania State, 1967.
1894
Jonish, James Edward. "Collective Wage Determination and International Trade: The U.S. and Canadian Steel Industries." Michigan, 1969.
1895
Ker, Sin Tze. "Technological Change in the Canadian Iron and Steel Mills Industry, 1946-1969." Manitoba, 1973.
1896
Kirpalani, Vishnu. "Prévisions de production et d'exportations du minerai de fer canadien en 1980." Montréal, 1970.

1897
McDowall, Duncan L. "Steel at the Sault: Sir James Dunn and the Algoma Steel Corporation, 1906-1956." Carleton, 1978.
1898
Russell, Terence Michael. "Retention, Financing Investment, Dividends and Share Prices: A Case Study of the Canadian Primary Iron and Steel Industry, 1947-1961." Toronto, 1966.
1899
Saunders, George S. "The Movement of Union and Non-Union Wage Rates in the Ontario Iron and Steel Products Industries, 1946-1954." Wisconsin, 1959.
1900
Smith, Philip Marvin. "An Econometric Study of Short-Term Behavior in the Canadian Steel Industry." Queen's, 1976.
Wardell, Nancy Needham. See No./Voir no 2371

Nickel

1901
Cairns, Robert Douglas. "Rents in the Canadian Nickel Industry." Massachusetts Institute of Technology, 1978.
Choksi, Shehrnaz. See No./Voir no 1875
Griffen, Peter J. See No./Voir no 1907
1902
Kowalski, George Jerzy. "Pricing, Entry and Performance in the Nickel Industry." Queen's, 1978.
Main, Oscar Warren. See No./Voir no 1282
1903
Stollery, Kenneth Robert. "A Theory of the Exploration and Production of Minerals." Queen's, 1980. [International nickel/Nickel international]

Potash/Potasse

1904
Richards, John Guyon. "Primary Industry and Regional Development: Potash in Saskatchewan." Washington, St. Louis, 1982.

Sulfur/Soufre

1905
Beukes, Theodorus Ernst. "The Impact of Recovered Sulfur on the Structure and Performance of the North American Sulfur Industry." Pennsylvania State, 1978.

Uranium

1906
Downey, Terrence James. "Canadian Government Involvement in the Development of the Uranium Industry, 1930 to 1963." Western Ontario, 1977.

Vanadium

1907
Griffin, Peter J. "Extraction of Vanadium and Nickel from Athabasca Oil Sands Fly Ash." Alberta, 1981.

Petroleum and Natural Gaz/Pétrole et gaz naturel

Aronoff, Stanley. See No./Voir no 1924

1908
Brown, Si. "Technology, Pipelines and Environment: The Role and Effects of Applied Technologies on the Planning and Construction of Ontario Oil Pipelines." Waterloo, 1978.

1909
Campbell, Duncan Robert. "The Impact of Seller Concentration on Market Performance: A Comparative Study of the Canadian and American Petroleum Refining and Marketing Industries." Cornell, 1966.

Crommelin, Brian Michael L. See No./Voir no 1378

1910
Dagher, Joseph H. "Effect of the National Oil Policy on the Ontario Petroleum Refining Industry." McGill, 1968.

1911
Debanné, Joseph Gabriel. "A Regional Techno-Economic Energy Supply-Distribution Model." Waterloo, 1976.

1912
Eglington, Peter Cheston. "The Economics of Industry Petroleum Exploration." British Columbia, 1975.

1913
Etienne, Eisenhower Celse. "The Acquisition of Physical Facilities by Subsidiaries of Multinational Corporations: The Case of the Canadian Petroleum Refining Industry." Western Ontario, 1982.

Gladwin, Thomas Neil. See No./Voir no 1749

Hyndman, Richard McCrae. See No./Voir no 1790

1914
Jung, Bong Seo. "An Economic Model of Petroleum Exploration." Toronto, 1976.

1915
McRae, Robert Norman. "A Quantitative Analysis of Some Policy Alternatives Affecting Canadian Natural Gas and Crude Oil Demand and Supply." British Columbia, 1977.

1916
Patton, Donald John. "The Effect of Foreign Ownership and Control in Government-Business Relations in the Host Country: The Petroleum and Natural Gas Industry in Canada." Indiana, 1973.

1917
Plotnick, Alan Ralph. "Economic and Commercial Policy Aspects of Marketing Western Canadian Petroleum in Canada and the United States." Pennsylvania, 1960.

1918
Prince, John Philip. "The Economic Potential of Enhanced Oil Recovery in Canada." Alberta, 1980.

Sallows, Sharon Heather. See No./Voir no 1188

Sievwright, Eric Colville. See No./Voir no 1334

Waterhouse, Michael Francis. See No./Voir no 10475

Wilson, Thomas Frederick. See No./Voir no 1195

Textile

1919
Curtis, Douglas C.A. "Producer Behaviour in the Canadian Man-Made Fibre and Yarn Industry, 1950-1968." McGill, 1972.

Gérin-Lajoie, Jean. See No./Voir no 1656

1920
Kelly, Donald Wright. "The Development of a New Textile Policy for Canada: A Case Study of Government-Industry Relations in Canada." Harvard, 1974.

1921
Kim, Sang Yoong. "An Econometric Model of the Canadian Clothing and Textile Industry." McMaster, 1981.

1922
Lazer, William. "An Analysis and Evaluation of the Marketing of Textile Clothing by Western Canadian Manufacturers." Ohio State, 1956.

Mahon, Paule Rianne. See No./Voir no 1388

Ryant, Joseph Charles. See No./Voir no 2080

Leisure and Recreation Industries, Hotels and Tourism/ Industries des loisirs et de la récréation, hôtels et tourisme

1923
Dennis-Escoffier, Shirley. "The Impact of Federal Income Tax on Capital Budgeting Equipment Decisions: A Comparative Study of Hotels in Selected Resort Cities of the United States, Canada and the Bahamas." University of Miami, 1981.

Plumb, Jon Michael. See No./Voir no 10462

MANAGEMENT AND EXECUTIVE/ GESTION ET ADMINISTRATEURS

1924
Aronoff, Stanley. "Remote Sensing Technology Transfer in Environmental Management: Application of a Theory of Information: A Case Study of Moose Habitat Assessment for Gas Field Development Planning in Alberta, Canada." California, Berkeley, 1982.

1925
Atkinson, Mary Helen Elizabeth. "Power Management in a Team Organization." Alberta, 1980.

1926
Baba, Vishwanath Venkataraman. "On the Nature of Job Involvement: An Enquiry into Its Antecedent and Consequent Conditions." British Columbia, 1979. [Greater Montreal/Montréal métropolitain]

1927
Bachand, Raymond C. "Boards of Directors in Canadian Government Enterprises: An Exploratory Research." Harvard, 1981.

1928
Baird, Andrew Falconor. "The Role of Directors of Local Cooperatives in Ontario Canada, in Continuity and Change." Cornell, 1961.

1929
Bélanger, Laurent. "Occupational Mobility of French and English Canadian Business Leaders in the Province of Quebec." Michigan State, 1967.

1930
Brookbank, Carman Roy. "The Effects of a Development Program Versus Bureaucratic Constraints on a Personal Growth and Autonomy: An Empirical Study of Management Development." Toronto, 1976.

1931

Cahoon, Allan Ray. "Managerial Behavior under Conditions of Mandated Change in a Canadian Bureaucracy: An Empirical Study of the Relationships Among Organizational Climate, Job Satisfaction and Leadership Change Style." Syracuse, 1974.

1932

Carruth, Thomas Paige. "An Analysis of Training Programs for Executive and Operations Personnel in Selected Businesses and Industries in the United States and Canada." Texas Technological, 1960.

Coupal, Michel. See No./Voir no 9285

1933

D'Amboise, Gérald Robert. "Personnel Characteristics, Organizational Practices, and Managerial Effectiveness: A Comparative Study of French and English-Speaking Chief Executives in Quebec." California, Los Angeles, 1974.

1934

De Brentani, Ulrike. "Evaluation of New Industrial Product Ideas: An Empirical Study of the New Product Screening Model and an Analysis of Managers' Screening Behaviour." McGill, 1983.

De Camprieu, Renaud Marc. See No./Voir no 2226

Dundas, Kenneth Ninian Melville. See No./Voir no 2373

Duxbury, Linda Elizabeth. See No./Voir no 6683

1935

Field, Richard Harold George. "A Test of the Vroom-Yetton Contingency Model of Leadership Behavior." Toronto, 1981. [276 university business administration students/276 étudiants universitaires en administration des affaires]

Fielder, John William. See No./Voir no 4062

Frey, Kenneth David. See No./Voir no 4024

1936

Gardner, Eldon J. "Trust and Loan Company Operations and the Valuation of Their Shares." Toronto, 1983.

Garnier, Bernard. See No./Voir no 3625

George, Ronald Edison. See No./Voir no 1317

1937

Gephart, Robert Paul. "Making Sense of Organizational Succession." British Columbia, 1979.

Hafen, Greg A. See No./Voir no 9005

1938

Hanel, Frank Joseph. "Field Testing the Effectiveness of a Self-Instruction Time Management Manual with Managerial Staff in an Institutional Setting." Manitoba, 1981.

1939

Johnson, Alan Anthony. "Contextual Correlates of Executive Uncertainty." York, 1980. [95 executives of Canadian public corporations/95 administrateurs de corporations publiques canadiennes]

Kanchier, Carol Joyce. See No./Voir no 9446

Kirudja, Charles Mugambi. See No./Voir no 6780

Kleinschmidt, Elko J. See No./Voir no 2016

1940

Kothari, Vinay B. "The Extent of Obsolescence of Selected Canadian Business Managers." North Texas State, 1970.

Lavigne, Gilles. See No./Voir no 816

1941

Levin, Benjamin Ruvin. "The Experience of Managing: People's Accounts of Their Work." Toronto, 1982.

Lowry, Douglas Bradley. See No./Voir no 1179

Lundy, Katherine Lillian Pauline. See No./Voir no 10212

1942

McKie, Donald Craig. "An Ontario Industrial Elite: The Senior Executive in Manufacturing Industry." Toronto, 1974.

1943

Migneron, Jean-Gabriel. "Méthodes d'analyse et de mesure de l'environnement acoustique urbain et leur application à l'aménagement." Montréal, 1977.

1944

Nag, Chowdhury Deb Kumar. "An Exploratory Study of Manager-Developed Decision Support Systems." Simon Fraser, 1983.

1945

Newman, Michael. "Managerial Access to Information." British Columbia, 1981.

Noël, Guy. See No./Voir no 2737

1946

Nollet, Jean. "Client Strategies in the Management of the Audit Process." Western Ontario, 1983.

1947

Oppenheimer, Robert Jonathon. "Testing Three Way Interactions Among Leader Behaviours, Task Structure and Personal Characteristics of Subordinate as Indicated by the Path-Goal Theory of Leadership." Toronto, 1981. [269 managers, supervisors, etc./269 directeurs, gestionnaires, etc.]

Owen, Brian Edward. See No./Voir no 1390

1948

Pickard, Lynette Elizabeth. "Management of Laboratories: Examining Symbolic and Substantive Outcomes." British Columbia, 1982.

1949

Pilette, Danielle. "Les promoteurs au Québec: les secteurs foncier et immobilier résidentiel." Montréal, 1981.

1950

Ross, Gerald Howard Barney. "Work Activities and Physiological Stress: Monitoring Managers on the Job." Western Ontario, 1979.

1951

Rothwell, Donald Stuart. "An Enquiry into the Factors that Combine to Explain Managerial Achievement." McGill, 1973.

1952

Schaupp, Dietrich Ludwig. "A Cross-Cultural Study of a Multinational Company: Attitudes of Satisfactions, Needs and Values Affecting Participative Management." Kentucky, 1974.

1953

Schier, Lewis. "A Study of the Occupational Mobility of the Managerial Elite of the Province of Ontario, Canada." New York, 1971.

1954

Slutsky, B.V. "Duties and Powers of Management in the Company Law of Canada and England." London, 1972.

1955

Smart, Carolyne Faith. "A Study of Executives' Perceptions of Corporate Crises." British Columbia, 1980. [Senior executives from 94 firms in Canada and the United States/Cadres de 94 organismes au Canada et aux États-Unis]

1956
Smetanka, John Andrew. "International Business and the Dialectics of Global Integration: A Study of Canadian Corporate Executives." Harvard, 1977.
1957
Smith, Archibald Ian. "The Effects of Alcohol on Aspects of Business Decision Making." Western Ontario, 1980.
1958
Smith, Bryan James. "An Initial Test of a Theory of Charismatic Leadership Based on the Responses of Subordinates." Toronto, 1982.
Soubrier, Robert. See No./Voir no 10466
1959
Summers, Randal William. "The Relationship Between Position and Power Base Preference in Management." Alberta, 1980. [York University/Université York]
1960
Wilson, Christopher Richard M. "Continuing Learning Activities of Managers in Industry." Toronto, 1977.
Wolf, Frank Michael. See No./Voir no 1417
Yule, David Lloyd George. See No./Voir no 4042
Zins, Michel A. See No./Voir no 2234

MARKETING/ÉTUDE DES MARCHÉS

Alexander, Judith Ann. See No./Voir no 2222
Anderson, Charles Dennis. See No./Voir no 2223
1961
Angevine, Gerald Edwin. "Explaining and Forecasting Consumer Expenditures with Canadian Consumer Sentiment Measures." Michigan, 1973.
1962
Barnes, James Gordon. "The Communications Effect of Selected Retail Price Promotional Advertising Cues." Toronto, 1975.
Bessom, Richard Moody. See No./Voir no 1831
1963
Bourgeois, Jacques Charlemagne. "Market Definition: A Theory and Application." Toronto, 1981.
1964
Bozinoff, Lorne. "The Perceptual Structure of Products/Services." Toronto, 1980.
1965
Claxton, John David. "Prepurchase Information Gathering by Household Durable Buyers: An Exploratory Study Using Numerical Taxonomic Analysis." Western Ontario, 1971.
Huff, Harry Bruce. See No./Voir no 166
Kirpalani, Vishnu. See No./Voir no 1896
Lamb, Charles William, Jr. See No./Voir no 1852
Lande, Eric Paul. See No./Voir no 1607
1966
Lefebvre, Jean-Marie. "Types of Minority Responses as Predictors of Preferences for Two Socially and Two Privately Consumed Consumer Goods: An Experiment with French-Canadians." Syracuse, 1976.
Ma, Sylvia. See No./Voir no 2230
McCabe, Robert Wylie. See No./Voir no 4905
1967
McDougall, Gordon Hedley George. "Credibility of Comparative Price Retail Advertising." Western Ontario, 1971.

Meredith, Lindsay Norman. See No./Voir no 2392
Muller, Thomas Edward. See No./Voir no 2231
1968
Mundie, John Duncan. "The Perfecting of Marketing Information for Industries in a Developing Industrial Economy with Reference to the Province of Manitoba." Stanford, 1966.
1969
Murray, John Alexander. "An Evaluation of Consumer Buying Intentions in Canada as a Predictive Device." Illinois, 1967.
1970
Ritchie, John Raymond Brent. "The Identification of Market Segments Through the Application of an Individual Differences Multidimensional Scaling Model." Western Ontario, 1972.
Rousseau, Henry Paul. See No./Voir no 1505
Smith, William. See No./Voir no 101
1971
Stykolt, Stefan. "Economic Analysis and Combines Policy: A Study of Intervention into the Canadian Market for Tires." Harvard, 1958.
1972
Thomas, Dwight Robert. "Culture and Consumption Behaviour in English and French Canada." Colorado, 1975.
1973
West, Douglas Scott. "Market Preemption as a Barrier to Entry in a Growing, Spatially Extended Market." British Columbia, 1979. [Supermarkets in British Columbia/Supermarchés en Colombie-Britannique]
Wilson, David Thomas. See No./Voir no 1775
Zins, Michel A. See No./Voir no 2234

TRADE AND TARIFFS/COMMERCE ET TARIFS

Balance of Payments/Balance des paiements

1974
Arndt, Sven William. "Disequilibrium in an Open Economy: Canada, 1950-1962." California, Berkeley, 1964.
1975
Chugh, Ram Lal. "Short-Term Capital Movements in the Canadian Balance of Payments: A Theoretical and Empirical Analysis." Wayne State, 1970.
Davis, Thomas Edward. See No./Voir no 1346
1976
Greenwood, Hans P. "Forces of Adjustment in the Canadian Balance of International Payments, 1926-1938." Cornell, 1949.
1977
Kamp, Robert Cornelius. "The Impact of the Balance of Payments on the Canadian Money Supply (1962-70)." Carleton, 1973.
1978
Laber, Gene Earl. "International Travel in the Canadian Balance of Payments, 1949-1964." Maryland, 1967.
1979
Malach, Vernon Walter. "International Cycles and Canada's Balance of Payments of 1921-33." London, 1948.
1980
Ogram, Ernest William, Jr. "Canada's Post War Balance of Payments Adjustments, 1946-1954." Illinois, 1957.

1981
Powrie, T.L. "Some Aspects of the Canadian Balance of Payments 1950-1958, with Special Reference to the Mechanism of Adjustment." Oxford, 1962.

1982
Singh, Karnail. "The Monetary View of the Balance of Payments: An Empirical Investigation." Western Ontario, 1973.

1983
Sirken, Irving A. "Fluctuations in Canadian Foreign Exchange Reserves 1946-50: A Study in Balance of Payment Adjustments and Foreign Economic Policy." Harvard, 1953.

1984
Stovel, John A. "Canada in the World Economy: A Study of the Changes in the Canadian Balance of Trade and Balance of Payments from Confederation to World War II, with a Critique of Viner's Canada's Balance of International Indebtedness, 1900-1913." Harvard, 1949.

1985
Thompson, R.W. "The Balance of Payments and the National Income in a Dependent Economy: Canada, 1926-38." London, 1961.

1986
Viner, Jacob. "Canada's Balance of International Indebtedness, 1900-1913: An Inductive Study in the Theory of International Trade." Harvard, 1922.

1987
Wilson, Arlene E. Lange. "Inflation and United States Exports of Manufactured Goods, 1960-1971." New York, 1974.

1988
Woodley, William John Richard. "Canada's Post-War Balance of Payments: A Case Study of Remedies for Balance of Payments Disequilibrium." Cornell, 1949.

1989
Zaremba, Alois Louis. "Canadian Balance of Payments, 1946-59: Foreign Investment and Economic Development." Ohio State, 1960.

Tariffs/Tarifs

1990
Annett, Douglas R. "British Imperial Preference in Canadian Commercial Policy." Harvard, 1947.

1991
Annis, Charles A. "A Study of Canadian Tariffs and Trade Agreements." Cornell, 1936.

1992
Blake, George Gordon. "Customs Administration in Canada, an Essay in Tariff Technology." Toronto, 1954.
Conlon, Robert Maxwell. See No./Voir no 2003
Forster, John Jakob Benjamin. See No./Voir no 1242

1993
Fortune, John Neill. "Effects of Change in Canadian Tariffs on Imports of Appliances from the United States." Indiana, 1968.

1994
Francis, Jonathan Hervey. "Some General Equilibrium Effects of Tariff Changes on Wages and Incomes in Canada." Michigan, 1975.
Masters, D.C. See No./Voir no 1283
McDiarmid, Orville J. See No./Voir no 1758

1995
McLaren, Walter Wallace. "The Tariff History of Canada." Harvard, 1908.
Murphy, Brendan A. See No./Voir no 2026

1996
Overman, William D. "Tariff Relations Between the United States and Canada, 1867-1900." Ohio State, 1931.

1997
Pinchin, Hugh McAlester. "Canadian Tariff Levels 1870-1959." Yale, 1970.

1998
Pollack, Gerald A. "The Effects on Imports from Canada of United States Tariff Reductions Under the Reciprocal Trade Agreements Program." Princeton, 1958.

1999
Singh, Harshendra Kumar. "The Canadian Tariff and Productivity of Canadian Manufacturing Industries." Manitoba, 1973.

2000
Snyder, Richard C. "The Most-Favored-Nation Clause: An Analysis with Particular Reference to Recent Treaty Practice and Tariffs." Columbia, 1949.

Trade/Commerce

Annis, Charles A. See No./Voir no 1991
Barnett, Donald Frederick. See No./Voir no 1889

2001
Birrell, J.H. "British Post-War Trade with the British Commonwealth Nations, Especially in Its Geographical Aspects." Edinburgh, 1927.

2002
Bowman, Donald Fox. "The Influence and Implications of Containerization upon the Use of the Great Lakes-St. Lawrence Seaway in International Trade." Michigan, 1972.
Brown, George Williams. See No./Voir no 1238

2003
Conlon, Robert Maxwell. "Internal Transport Costs and Tariffs as Barriers to Trade and Influences on Structure and Performance of Australian and Canadian Manufacturing." New South Wales, 1980.

2004
Daigle, Benoit Ludovic. "The Possibility of Trade Between Canada and Latin America." Catholic, 1969.

2005
Dartnell, Albert Loyd. "Economic Consequences of Closer Union Between Canada and the West Indies." McGill, 1963.

2006
Dixon, Frederick Thomas. "The Impact of Foreign and Domestic Business Cycles on United States Exports to Japan, Canada, and the United Kingdom." Temple, 1974.

2007
Drinkwater, David Alan. "Some Economic Characteristics of Canadian Exporting Firms." Western Ontario, 1971.

2008
Dunn, Robert Martin Jr. "Flexible Exchange Rates and the Prices of Traded Goods: A Study of Canadian Markets." Stanford, 1967.

2009
English, Harry Edward. "The Role of International Trade in Canadian Economic Development Since the 1920's." California, Berkeley, 1957.
2010
Forward, Charles Nelson. "The Shipping Trade of Newfoundland." Clark, 1958.
Ginman, Peter John. See No./Voir no 1603
2011
Glenday, Graham. "Labor Adjustment and Trade Liberalization: Costs and Adjustment Policies in the Canadian Context." Harvard, 1983.
Hartigan, James Christopher. See No./Voir no 2365
2012
Hodges, Dorothy Jacobsen. "An International Comparison of Industry Production Functions: Implications for International Trade Theory." Wisconsin, 1966.
2013
Holmes, James M. "An Econometric Test of Some Modern International Trade Theories: Canada, 1870-1960." Chicago, 1967.
Huff, Harry Bruce. See No./Voir no 166
2014
Hynes, Cecil Vernon. "An Analysis of Michigan and Ontario Trade and Transport Reciprocity." Michigan State, 1965.
2015
Ingledew, William Albert. "The Influence of Major Departmental Chains on Adoption Rates and Developing Patterns of Trade Inflows of New Consumer Products to the Canadian Market." Western Ontario, 1975.
Jonish, James Edward. See No./Voir no 1894
2016
Kleinschmidt, Elko J. "Export Strategies, Firm Internal Factors and Export Performance of Industrial Firms: A Canadian Empirical Analysis." McGill, 1983.
2017
Kohli, Ulrich Johann Robert. "Canadian Technology and Derived Import Demand and Export Supply Functions." British Columbia, 1976.
Lande, Eric Paul. See No./Voir no 1607
2018
Landuyt, Bernard F. "Reciprocity in the Foreign Trade Policy of the United States." Iowa State, 1938.
2019
Litvak, Isaiah. "Obstacles to Imports from Communist Countries: A Canadian Study." Columbia, 1969.
2020
Loken, Mark Keith. "The Impact of Effective Commercial Policy on Patterns of Canadian Exports." Duke, 1972.
2021
MacFadyen, Alan James. "Instability of Canadian Foreign Trade, 1946-1965." Pennsylvania State, 1970.
Mack, Friedrick Georg. See No./Voir no 196
2022
McCalla, Peter Douglas Whitby. "The Buchanan Businesses, 1834-72: A Study in the Organization and Development of Canadian Trade." Oxford, 1972.
McFarland, Joan Murray. See No./Voir no 1352

2023
McIlwraith, Thomas Forsyth. "The Logistical Geography of the Great Lakes Grain Trade, 1820-1850." Washington, Seattle, 1973.
2024
McKinley, Donald F. "Business Abroad: The Canadian Case." Ottawa, 1972.
2025
McKinnon, Thomas Roy. "The Effect of Changes in National Income on Exports for Federal Republic of Germany, Japan, and Canada." Mississippi, 1972.
2026
Murphy, Brendan A. "Canadian Import Demand, and the Effects of Tariffs on the Prices of Domestic Factors." Western Ontario, 1982.
2027
Nappi, Carmine. "Des méthodes quantitatives appliquées au commerce international et interprovincial du Québec." McGill, 1974.
2028
O'Brien, Gregory Charles. "The Life of Robert Dollar: 1844-1932." Claremont, 1969.
2029
Parizeau, J. "The Terms of Trade with Canada, 1869-1952." London, 1955.
Perkett, William Oliver. See No./Voir no 1838
Pett, H. Gregory. See No./Voir no 1354
2030
Rabiega, William Albert. "Methodologies for the Prediction of Cargo Tonnage over the St. Lawrence Seaway." Southern Illinois, 1973.
2031
Reid, Stanley Douglas. "Export Behaviour in the Small Canadian-owned Manufacturing Enterprise — An Empirical Investigation." York, 1981.
2032
Reuber, Grant Louis. "Britain's Export Trade with Canada." Harvard, 1957.
2033
Roberts, Guy H. "The Foreign Commerce of the United States During the Confederation." Harvard, 1904.
2034
Robinson, Thomas Russell. "Foreign Trade and Economic Stability: The Canadian Case." Yale, 1967.
2035
Sawyer, John Arthur. "Forecasting Industry Output and Imports in an Open Economy: Some Experiments for Canada, 1950-58." Chicago, 1966.
2036
Sedjo, Roger Andrew. "Price Trends, Economic Growth, and the Canadian Balance of Trade. A Three Country Model." Washington, Seattle, 1969.
2037
Séguin-Dulude, Louise. "Analyse de la structure et de l'évolution des exportations de pays industrialisés: 1963-1969." Montréal, 1975.
2038
Slater, David Walker. "The Growth and Structure of Canadian Imports 1926-1955." Chicago, 1958.
Snyder, Richard C. See No./Voir no 2000

2039
Stryker, Josiah Dirck. "United States and Canadian Manufacturing Production and Exports." Columbia, 1967.

Swiger, Ernest Cullimore, Jr. See No./Voir no 1305

2040
Tempalski, Jerry. "An Analysis of Structural Change in the Demand for Imports and Exports in the Major Industrial Countries." Michigan, 1981. [United States, Canada, Japan, West Germany and the United Kingdom/États-Unis, Canada, Japon, Allemagne de l'Ouest et Royaume-Uni]

Thevenon, Michael Jean. See No/Voir no 1824

2041
Triantis, Stephen George. "Cyclical Changes in the Merchandise Balance of Countries Exporting Chiefly Primary Products, 1927 to 1933." Toronto, 1956.

2042
Vaughan, Michael Bryan. "An Economic Analysis of Canadian Restraints on Imports of Low-Cost Cotton Yarns." Toronto, 1976.

2043
Wahl, Donald Frederick. "Productivity and the Structure of Canada's Foreign Trade, 1924-1955." Harvard, 1959.

Ware, Dennis William. See No./Voir no 36

Watson, Kenneth Frank. See No./Voir no 1397

Williams, Glen Sutherland. See No./Voir no 1398

Wilson, Arlene E. Lange. See No./Voir no 1987

2044
Wilson, David A. "An Analysis of Lumbering Exports from the Coast Region of British Columbia to the United Kingdom and United States, 1920-1952." California, Berkeley, 1955.

2045
Yadav, Gopal Ji. "The Discriminatory Aspects of Canada's Imports of Manufactured Goods from the Less Developed and the Developed Countries." Queen's, 1970.

2046
Zarley, Arvid M. "The Impact of Economic Integration on Third Countries: A Case Study of Canadian Export Shares in the British Market under Alternative Courses of European Integration." Purdue, 1965.

LABOUR AND INDUSTRIAL RELATIONS/ TRAVAIL ET RELATIONS INDUSTRIELLES

General Items/Ouvrages généraux

2047
Barnes, Samuel Henry. "The Ideologies and Policies of Canadian Labor Organizations." Duke, 1957.

Baureiss, Guater A. See No./Voir no 10189

2048
Boyd, Archibald D. "Engineering and Scientific Manpower in Canada." Ottawa, 1967.

Butler, Peter Marshall. See No./Voir no 10029

2049
Campbell, Elizabeth Jane. "The Balance Wheel of the Industrial System: Maximum Hours, Minimum Wage and Workmen's Compensation Legislation in Ontario, 1900-1939." McMaster, 1981.

2050
Chen, Mervin Yaotsu. "The Influence of Social Structure, Technology and Background Factors on Supervisory Style in Industry." McMaster, 1975.

2051
Connelly, Mary Patricia. "Canadian Women as a Reserve Army of Labour." Toronto, 1976.

2052
Cottell, Philip Leroy. "Occupational Choice and Employment Stability Among Forest Workers." Yale, 1972. [British Columbia/Colombie-Britannique]

2053
Crysdale, Robert Cecil Stewart. "Occupational and Social Mobility in Riverdale, a Blue Collar Community." Toronto, 1968.

2054
Dupuis, Jean-Claude. "Les métiers de fer traditionnels du Canada français." Laval, 1968.

2055
Evans, John Charles. "The Social Opportunity Cost of Labour in Canada." Chicago, 1978.

2056
Fernandez, Marco Antonio. "Evaluation of Manpower Training Programs: The Interlake Manpower Corps." Manitoba, 1977. [Manitoba]

2057
Fortin, Bernard Fernand. "A Labor Supply Analysis of Low-Income Families in the Province of Quebec." California, Berkeley, 1979.

2058
Fox, Bonnie J. "Women's Domestic Labour and Their Involvement in Wage Work: Twentieth Century Changes in the Reproduction of Daily Life." Alberta, 1980.

Gaffney, Michael Edward. See No./Voir no 403

Glenday, Graham. See No./Voir no 2011

Goulding, James Wray. See No./Voir no 1169

Hanvelt, Robin Alden. See No./Voir no 1645

Haythorne, George V. See No./Voir no 41

2059
Johnson, Neil Alexander. "An Evaluation of the Paradox of Short-Run Increasing Returns to Labour with Empirical Analysis for Canadian Manufacturing Industries." Johns Hopkins, 1979.

Lundy, Katherine Lillian Pauline. See No./Voir no 10212

Luxton, Margaret Joan. See No./Voir no 422

MacKinnon, Malcolm Hector. See No./Voir no 10022

2060
Mayer, Janet Judith. "Ideological Practices and White Collar Domination: A Study of Labour Control in the Monopoly Sector." Carleton, 1982.

2061
McBride, Stephen Kenneth. "Organized Labour and Social Democracy in Britain and Canada." McMaster, 1980.

2062
Miller, Fern Audrey Rae. "The Radicalization of Quebec Labour." Yale, 1981.

Naqib, Fadle Mustafa. See No./Voir no 1535

2063
Plain, Richard Hayward McVicar. "Inter-Regional and Inter-Industry Differences in the Elasticity of Factor Substitution of Efficiency of Labour in Canada." Alberta, 1972.

2064
Schlesinger, R.C. "Jewish Women in Transition: Delayed Entry into the Workforce." Toronto, 1983.

2065
Schuster, E.J.E. "Industrial Conflict and Its Institutionalization: A Comparative Analysis of Sweden, Canada and the United States." Oregon, 1970.

Smit, Barry Edward. See No./Voir no 2197

Stewart, Ian Hampton. See No./Voir no 7934

2066
Tracy, Martin Booth. "The Earnings Test and Work Patterns: Experiences of Canada and the United States." Illinois, 1982. [Labour force participation-ages 65-67/Participation des travailleurs de 65 à 67 ans]

Watts, Martin John. See No./Voir no 1366

2067
White, Terrence Harold. "Power and Autonomy in Organizations." Toronto, 1972. [Labor relations in 11 manufacturing firms in Ontario/Relations de travail dans 11 manufactures de l'Ontario]

2068
Willox, P. "The Capital Crisis and Labour: Perspective on the Dynamics of Working-Class Consciousness in Canada." Uppsala Universitet, (Sweden/Suède) 1980.

Individual Worker Problems/ Problèmes particuliers du travailleur

2069
Akl, Selim George. "An Analysis of Various Aspects of the Traveling Salesman Problem." McGill, 1978.

Derow, Ellan Odiorme. See No./Voir no 2177

2070
Fullan, Michael. "Workers' Receptivity to Industrial Change in Different Technological Settings." Toronto, 1969.

2071
Gandz, Jeffrey. "Employee Grievances: Incidence and Patterns of Resolution." York, 1978.

2072
Grisé, Jacques. "International Aspects of Workers' Achievement Needs with Trait Anxiety Levels and Their Relationships to Job Complexity, Job Tension, Job Performance, Job Satisfaction and Workers' Potential." Western Ontario, 1973.

2073
Jamal, Muhammad. "Need Fulfillment in Work and Non-Work as Related to Mental Health." British Columbia, 1976.

2074
Laplante, Serge André. "Displaced Workers: A Study of Reclassification Activities in Quebec." Harvard, 1973.

2075
Loucks, Kenneth Edmon. "Self-Fulfillment on the Job." Western Ontario, 1974. [A Canadian chartered bank/Banque à chartre canadienne]

Marton, Katherin. See No./Voir no 1663

2076
Newton, Keith. "Economic Aspects of Federal Government Sponsored Institutional and On-the-Job Training in Canada." Simon Fraser, 1976.

2077
Oliver, Avihai. "Job Design, Role Stress and Employees' Responses to Their Jobs: An Interactive Model." Toronto, 1979. [2 Canadian retail department stores/2 grands magasins canadiens]

2078
Piché, Louise. "La motivation au travail et l'orientation marriage-carrière de la femme selon son niveau hiérarchique." Montréal, 1978.

2079
Rencz, Donald Samuel. "An Analysis of Tasks Performed by Low-Ability Office Employees as Viewed by Office Supervisory Personnel in Alberta, Canada." Oregon State, 1978.

2080
Ryant, Joseph Charles. "Social Determinants of Job-Seeking Behaviour of the Youth in a One-Industry Town." McGill, 1974. [Textile]

2081
Schrank, William E. "Canadian Job Search-Labor Turnover Relations: An Empirical Study in the Use of Monthly Data." Wisconsin, 1973.

Schreck, David Donald. See No./Voir no 2244

2082
Sexton, Jean. "Blue Collar Workers Displaced by Complete and Permanent Plant Shutdowns: The Quebec Experience." Cornell, 1975.

2083
Siegel, Sanford Benjamin. "Towards an Analytical Model of the Situated Working Class Individual." Toronto, 1980. [Foxtown, Ontario]

Simas, Kathleen A. See No./Voir no 9615

2084
Theeuwes, Julius Jacobus Maria. "Family Labour Supply and Labor Force Participation Decisions." British Columbia, 1975.

2085
Whittingham, Frank J. "Additional and Discouraged Workers Among Married Women in Canada." Queen's, 1972.

2086
Wisniewski, Lawrence John. "Choosing a Man's Job: The Effect of Socialization on Female Occupational Entry." McMaster, 1977.

Labor History/Histoire du travail

General Items/Ouvrages généraux

2087
Gauvreau, Jean-M. "L'artisan dans la province de Québec." Montréal, 1943.

2088
Pentland, Harry Clare. "Labour and the Development of Industrial Capitalism in Canada." Toronto, 1961.

Rider, Peter Edward. See No./Voir no 7135

- 1763

2089
Moogh, Peter Nicholas. "The Craftsmen of New France." Toronto, 1973.

1763-1867

2090
Marlak, Charles F. "A Labor History of the Niagara Frontier (1846-1917) Containing an Introduction Consisting of Conditions Prior to 1846." Ottawa, 1947.

Zerker, Sally Friedberg. See No./Voir no 2151

1867-1918

2091
Babcock, Robert Harper. "The A.F.L. in Canada, 1896-1908: A Study in American Labor Imperialism." Duke, 1970.

2092
Bercuson, David Jay. "Labour in Winnipeg: The Great War and the General Strike." Toronto, 1971.

2093
Bradwin, Edmund William. "The Bunkhouse Man: A Study of Work and Pay in the Camps of Canada, 1903-1914." Columbia, 1928.

2094
Cherwinski, Walter Joseph. "Organized Labour in Saskatchewan: The T.L.C. Years, 1905-1945." Alberta, 1972.

2095
Coombs, David Grosvenor. "The Emergence of a White Collar Workforce in Toronto, 1895-1911." York, 1978.

Craven, Paul. See No./Voir no 1265

2096
Harvey, Fernand. "Les travailleurs québécois et la commission du travail, 1886-1889: étude d'un phénomène de révolution industrielle et de mutation sociale." Laval, 1977.

2097
Hayward, Percy Roy. "Compensation for Injuries to Canadian Workmen." Pennsylvania, 1918.

2098
Kealey, Gregory Sean. "The Working Class Response to Industrial Capitalism in Toronto, 1867-1892." Rochester, 1978.

2099
Logan, Harold Amos. "The Organized Labor Movement in Canada: A History of Trade Union Organization in Canada." Chicago, 1925.

Lowe, Graham Stanley. See No./Voir no 1278
Marlak, Charles F. See No./Voir no 2090

2100
McCormack, Andrew Ross. "The Origins and Extent of Western Labour Radicalism, 1896-1919." Western Ontario, 1973.

Palmer, Bryan Douglas. See No./Voir no 7203
Petersen, James Otto. See No./Voir no 1214

2101
Piva, Michael J. "The Condition of the Working Class in Toronto, 1900-1921." Concordia, 1975.

2102
Roberts, David Wayne. "Studies in the Toronto Labour Movement, 1896-1914." Toronto, 1978.

2103
Robin, Martin. "Radical Politics and Organized Labour in Canada, 1880-1930." Toronto, 1966.

2104
Rutherford, William Herbert. "The Industrial Worke in Ontario." Toronto, 1915.

2105
Seager, Charles Allen. "The Proletariat in Wild Ros Country: The Alberta Coal Miners, 1905-1945. York, 1982.

2106
Selekman, Ben Morris. "Postponing Strikes: A Stud of the Industrial Disputes Investigation Act o Canada." Columbia, 1927.

2107
Squires, Benjamin M. "Operation of the Industria Disputes Investigation Act of Canada. Columbia, 1921.

Struthers, James Edward. See No./Voir no 2198

2108
Tuck, Joseph Hugh. "Canadian Railways and th International Brotherhoods: Labour Organizatio in the Railway Running Trades in Canada, 1865 1914." Western Ontario, 1976.

Woroby, Tamara M. See No./Voir no 1309
Zerker, Sally Friedberg. See No/Voir no 2151

1919-1983

2109
Abella, Irving Martin. "The Struggle for Industria Unionism in Canada: The C.I.O., the Communis Party and the Canadian Congress of Labour, 1936 1956." Toronto, 1969.

Barnes, Samuel Henry. See No./Voir no 2047

2110
Casaday, Lauren Wilde. "Labor Unrest and the Labo Movement in the Salmon Industry of the Pacifi Coast." California, Berkeley, 1938. [Britis Columbia/Colombie-Britannique]

Cherwinski, Walter Joseph. See No./Voir no 2094

2111
Couper, Walter J. "Wages and Labor Conditions i Certain Selected Industries in Canada, 1933-1934 California, Berkeley, 1937.

Decore, Anne-Marie June. See No./Voir no 10178
Drennon, Herbert Neal. See No./Voir no 1746

2112
Horowitz, Gad. "Canadian Labour in Politics, 1937 1961." Harvard, 1965.

2113
Huxley, Christopher Victor. "The Institutionalizatio of Industrial Conflict: A Comparative Analysis o Strike Activity in Britain and Canada Since 1945. Toronto, 1980.

Legendre, Camille George. See No./Voir no 1819
Lithwick, Irwin. See No./Voir no 1209
Logan, Harold Amos. See No./Voir no 2099
Lowe, Graham Stanley. See No./Voir no 1278

2114
MacDowell, Laurel Sefton. " 'Remember Kirklan Lake': The Effects of the Kirkland Lake Gol Miners' Strike, 1941-42." Toronto, 1979.

2115
MacInnes, Daniel William. "Clerics, Fishermen, Fa mers and Workers: The Antigonish Movement an Identity in Eastern Nova Scotia, 1928-1939 McMaster, 1978.

2116
Marsh, Leonard C. "The Canadian Working Population: An Analysis of Occupational Status-Divisions and the Incidence of Unemployment - 1939." McGill, 1940.

2117
McAllister, Barbara Heather. "Labour and the State: The Canadian Labour Congress, Consultative Forums, and Income Policies, 1960-1978." Toronto, 1982.

2118
Meltz, Noah Moshe. "Changes in the Occupational Composition of the Canadian Labor Force, 1931-1961." Princeton, 1964.

2119
Millar, Frederick David. "Shapes of Power: The Ontario Labour Relations Board, 1944 to 1950." York, 1981.

Miller, Fern Audrey Rae. See No./Voir no 2062

2120
Petryshyn, Jaroslav. "A.E. Smith and the Canadian Labour Defence League." Western Ontario, 1977.

2121
Phillips, Paul Arthur. "The British Columbia Labour Movement in the Inter-War Period: A Study of Its Social Political Aspects." London, 1967.

2122
Riddell, William Craig. "The Determinants of Negotiated Wage Changes in Canadian Industry, 1953-1973: A Study Based on Wage Contract Data." Queen's, 1977.

Seager, Charles Allen. See No./Voir no 2105

2123
Speirs, Rosemary Ellen Jane. "Technological Change and the Railway Unions, 1945-1972." Toronto, 1974.

Stewart, Bryce Morrison. See No./Voir no 2174

2124
Storey, Robert Henry. "Workers, Unions and Steel: The Shaping of the Hamilton Working Class, 1935-1948." Toronto, 1982.

Struthers, James Edward. See No./Voir no 2198

2125
Williams, Charles Brian. "Canadian-American Trade Union Relations - A Study of the Development of Binational Unionism." Cornell, 1964.

2126
Young, James Walton. "Structural Unemployment, Migration and Growth During an Expansionary Phase: Canada, 1961-1965." McGill, 1975.

Catholic Labor Unions/Syndicats catholiques

2127
Barrett, Francis D. "Ecological Analysis of the National and Catholic Labor Movement in Quebec." Massachusetts Institute of Technology, 1953.

2128
Boucher, Paul. "L'union catholique des cultivateurs." Montréal, 1935.

2129
Isbester, Alexander Fraser. "A History of the National Catholic Unions in Canada, 1901-1965." Cornell, 1968.

2130
Maltais, Marie Ludovic. "Les syndicats catholiques canadiens: étude socio-économique." Catholic, 1925.

2131
Rouillard, Jacques. "Les syndicats nationaux au Québec, 1900-1930." Ottawa, 1976.

2132
Têtu, Michel. "Les premiers syndicats catholiques canadiens (1900-1921)." Laval, 1961.

Studies of Individual Labor Unions or Associations/ Études des syndicats particuliers ou des associations

General Item/Ouvrage général

2133
Forsyth, George Robert. "Private Sector White Collar Workers: Examining Their Propensity for Unionism." Western Ontario, 1976.

Civil and Public Service/Fonction civile et publique

2134
Caiden, G.E. "A Comparative Study of the Federal Civil Service of Canada and the Commonwealth Public Service of Australia." London, 1959.

2135
Crispo, John Herbert Gillespie. "Collective Bargaining in the Public Service: A Study of Union-Management Relations in Ontario Hydro and TVA." Massachusetts Institute of Technology, 1960.

2136
Frankel, Saul Jacob. "Staff Relations in the Canadian Civil Service." McGill, 1958.

Highland, Jeffrey Ray. See No./Voir no 2161

2137
Lemelin, Maurice. "The Public Service Alliance of Canada: A Look at a Union in the Public Sector." California, Los Angeles, 1976.

2138
Prives, Moshe Zalman. "Career in the Civil Service: Canada, Great Britain and the United States." McGill, 1958.

Construction

2139
Hébert, Gérard J. "L'extension juridique des conventions collectives dans l'industrie de la construction dans la province de Québec, 1934-1962." McGill, 1963.

Baba, Vishwanath Venkataraman. See No./Voir no 1926

Fishermen/Pêcheurs

2140
McDonald, D.H.I. "W.F. Coaker and the Fishermen's Protective Union in Newfoundland Politics, 1908-15." London, 1971.

Steinberg, Charles. See No./Voir no 2171

Hospital Workers/Travailleurs hospitaliers

2141
Sethi, A.S. "A Framework for the Study of Hospital Labour Relations in Canada and the U.K." Manchester, 1976.

Iron and Steel/Fer et acier

2142
Bozzini, Luciano. "Formes et genèse de la conscience ouvrière chez les ouvrières de la sidérurgie." Montréal, 1975.

2143
Freeman, William Bradford. "Oligarchy and Democracy: A Study of the Political Life of a Local Union." McMaster, 1979. [Local 1005 Steelworkers' Union of Hamilton, Ontario/Union des métallurgistes, Local 1005 de Hamilton, Ontario]

Kruger, Arthur Martin. See No./Voir no 2164

Longshore/Débardeurs

2144
Bjarnason, Emil Grover. "Mechanisation and Collective Bargaining in the British Columbia Longshore Industry." Simon Fraser, 1976.

2145
Khan, Emamuddeen. "Industrial Relations in the Canadian Longshore Industry: A Case Study of Collective Bargaining in the Ports of Montreal and Vancouver." London, 1972.

Meat Packing/Conservation de la viande

2146
Montague, John Tait. "Trade Unionism in the Canadian Meat Packing Industry." Toronto, 1950.

Office Workers/Employés de bureau

Lowe, Graham Stanley. See No./Voir no 1278

2147
Wood, William Donald. "An Analysis of Office Unionism in Canadian Manufacturing Industries." Princeton, 1950.

Postal Workers/Travailleurs postaux

2148
Gonnsen, August. "Labor Conflict in the Canadian Post Office: An Investigation of Factors Contributing to Its Persistence and Intensity." SUNY, Buffalo, 1981.

Pulp and Paper/Pulpe et papier

Legendre, Camille George. See No./Voir no 1819

2149
Schonning, Egil. "Union-Management in the Pulp and Paper Industry of Ontario and Quebec, 1914-1950." Toronto, 1950.

Railway Brotherhoods/Fraternités des employés de chemins de fer

Reynolds, Roy R. See No./Voir no 2167
Tuck, Joseph Hugh. See No./Voir no 2108

Teachers/Professeurs

See also Education: Teachers/Voir aussi Éducation Professeurs

Theatrical Stage Employees and Motion Picture Machine Operators/Employés du théatre et projectionistes

2150
Baker, Robert Osborne. "The International Alliance of Theatrical Stage Employees and Moving Picture Machine Operators of the United States and Canada." Kansas, 1933.

Typographers/Typographes

2151
Zerker, Sally Friedberg. "A History of the Toronto Typographical Union 1832-1925." Toronto, 1972.

Woodworkers/Travailleurs du bois

2152
Lembeke, Jerry Lee. "The International Woodworkers of America: An Internal Comparative Study of Two Regions." Oregon, 1978. [United States and Canada/États-Unis et Canada]

Labor and Politics/Travail et politiques

Arbitration, Collective Bargaining, Conciliation, Strikes/Arbitrage, conventions collectives, conciliations, grèves

2153
Anton, Frank Robert. "The Role of Government in the Settlement of Industrial Disputes in Canada, with Special Reference to Conciliation in Ontario and Supervised Strike Voting in Alberta and British Columbia." London, 1962.

Bjarnason, Emil Grover. See No./Voir no 2144

2154
Boivin, Jean. "The Evolution of Bargaining Power in the Province of Quebec Public Sector (1964-1972)." Cornell, 1975.

2155
Carrothers, Alfred William Rooke. "Collective Bargaining Law in Canada." Harvard Law, 1966.

2156
Craig, Alton Westwood. "The Consequences of Provincial Jurisdiction for the Process of Company-Wide Collective Bargaining in Canada: A Study of the Packinghouse Industry." Cornell, 1964.

Crispo, John Herbert Gillespie. See No./Voir no 2135

2157
Cunningham, William Bannerman. "Compulsory Conciliation and Collective Bargaining: The New Brunswick Experience." Brown, 1957.

2158
Eastman, Sheila Baldwin MacQueen. "Multiple-Employer Collective Bargaining: Three Case Studies." Toronto, 1952.

Fisher, Edward George. See No./Voir no 2172

Goldberg, Theodore Irving. See No./Voir no 1623

2159
Herlihy, H. Murray. "The Collective Bargaining Policies of the UAW-C10 in Canada." Chicago, 1955.

2160
Herman, Emil Edward. "The Problem of Determination of the Appropriate Bargaining Units by Labour Relations Boards in Canada." McGill, 1965.

2161
Highland, Jeffrey Ray. "Collective Bargaining in the Federal Public Services of Canada and the United States." Washington State, 1977.

Huxley, Christopher Victor. See No./Voir no 2113

2162
Kinsley, Brian Leslie. "Strike Activity and the Industrial Relations System in Canada." Carleton, 1979.

2163
Ko, Ting Tsz. "Governmental Methods of Adjusting Labor Disputes in North America and Australia." Columbia, 1926.

2164
Kruger, Arthur Martin. "Labour Organization and Collective Bargaining in the Canadian Basic Steel Industry." Massachusetts Institute of Technology, 1960.

2165
Logan, John Edwin. "An Analysis of the Effects of Compulsory Conciliation in Canada on Collective Bargaining and Strikes." Columbia, 1969.

MacDowell, Laurel Sefton. See No./Voir no 2114

2166
Marchak, Maureen Patricia. "Bargaining Strategies of White-Collar Workers in British Columbia." British Columbia, 1970.

Ponak, Allen M. See No./Voir no 6918

2167
Reynolds, Roy R. "Public Policy with Respect to the Settlement of Labor Disputes in the Canadian Railway Industry." Massachusetts Institute of Technology, 1951.

Riddell, William Craig. See No./Voir no 2122

2168
Robins, Patrick James. "The Nature and Effect on Bargaining of Occupational Stereotyping in a Labour Relations Context." Manitoba, 1983.

2169
Sawatzky, Aron. "An Analysis of the Relationships Between Arbitration Board Awards and Selected Independent Variables in the Province of Manitoba." North Dakota, 1973.

2170
Siklos, Pierre Leslie. "Choosing the Employment Contract: Individual versus Collective Arrangements." Carleton, 1981.

2171
Steinberg, Charles. "Collective Bargaining Rights in the Canadian Sea Fisheries: A Case Study of Nova Scotia." Columbia, 1973.

Labour Legislation/Droit de travail

2172
Fisher, Edward George. "The Effects of Changes in Labor Legislation on Strike Activity in British Columbia: 1945-75." British Columbia, 1979.

2173
Martin, William Steward Arnold. "A Study of Legislation Designed to Foster Industrial Peace in the Common Law Jurisdictions of Canada." Toronto, 1954.

2174
Stewart, Bryce Morrison. "Canadian Labor Laws and the Treaty." Columbia, 1926.

2175
Underhill, Harold F. "Labor Legislation in British Columbia." California, Berkeley, 1936.

Employment and Unemployment/Emploi et chômage

Alexandrin, Glen Gleb. See No./Voir no 1310

2176
Bate Boerop, John Leonard Daniel. "Psychological Impact of Employment and Unemployment in Profile." York, 1982.

Cadden, Patrick Guthrie. See No./Voir no 4794

2177
Derow, Ellan Odiorne. "Married Women's Employment and Domestic Labor." Toronto, 1977.

2178
Farrell, John Terrence. "Five Programs in Search of Policy: An Analysis of the Programs of the Job Creation Branch and Community Employment Strategy, Department of Manpower and of Immigration." McMaster, 1981.

2179
Frank, James Godfrey. "Labour Supply Estimates: The Case of Single Individuals in Canada." Queen's, 1979.

2180
Fric, Lawrence. "The Role of Commercial Employment Agencies in the Canadian Labour Market." Toronto, 1973.

2181
Gonick, Cyril Wolfe. "Aspects of Unemployment in Canada." California, Berkeley, 1965.

2182
Gross, Andrew Charles. "Engineering Manpower in Canada." Ohio State, 1968.

Hanveit, Robin Alden. See No./Voir no 1645

2183
Hartie, Douglas G. "Employment Forecasting in Canada." Duke, 1957.

2184
Kapsalis, Constantine. "An Econometric Estimation of Labour Supply Functions in Canada." Rochester, 1975.

Kelly, Lawrence Alexander. See No./Voir no 1647

2185
Ketchum, Edward John Davison. "The Short-Run Demand for Labor in Canadian Manufacturing Industries." Princeton, 1972.

2186
Leaper, Richard John. "Female Labor Force Attachment: An Analysis of Unemployment Rates in the United States and Canada." Duke, 1976.

2187
Lightman, Ernie Stanley. "The Economics of Military Manpower Supply in Canada." California, Berkeley, 1972.

2188
Mehmet, Ozay. "Optimum Choice Between Institutional and On-the-Job Adult Manpower Training Activities in the Province of Ontario." Toronto, 1968.

2189
Niemi, Beth. "Sex Differentials in Unemployment in the United States and Canada, 1947-1966." Columbia, 1970.

2190
Paquin, Jean-Paul. "Structure industrielle: croissance et cycles de l'emploi régional au Canada." Ottawa, 1979.

2191
Pieroni, Rita Maria. "Factors and Predictors Underlying Psychological Distress During Unemployment." York, 1980.

Poddar, Arun Kumar. See No./Voir no 2212

2192
Ralston, Helen. "Career Aspirations and the Migration Process in a Longitudinal Study Among Young Adults of Nova Scotia." Carleton, 1973.

2193
Riediger, Alfred J. "Employee Assistance Program: The Supervisor's Perspective." Alberta, 1979.

2194
Runcie, N. "A Study of Hire Purchase in the United Kingdom and Three Dominions, Australia, Canada and New Zealand, Since 1945." London, 1960.

Seccareccea, Mario Sebastiano. See No./Voir no 1190

Siklos, Pierre Leslie. See No./Voir no 2170

2195
Sinclair, Donald Michael. "Public Policy to Improve the Employability of Young People: The Ontario Career Action Program." Toronto, 1979.

2196
Skoulas, Nicholas. "Determinants of the Participation Rate of Married Women in the Canadian Labour Force: An Econometric Analysis." Simon Fraser, 1973.

2197
Smit, Barry Edward. "A Regional Analysis of Employment Changes in Canadian Agriculture." McMaster, 1977.

Sommer, Daniel. See No./Voir no 9107

2198
Struthers, James Edward. "No Fault of their Own: Unemployment and the Canadian Welfare State, 1914-1941." Toronto, 1979.

2199
Swidinsky, Robert. "Unemployment and Labor Force Participation: The Canadian Experience." Minnesota, 1969.

Tracy, Martin Booth. See No./Voir no 2066

Watts, Martin John. See No./Voir no 1366

Young, James Walton. See No./Voir no 2126

Young, John Geoffrey. See No./Voir no 1776

See also Unemployment Insurance/Voir aussi Assurance-chômage

Wages/Rémunération

2200
Albright, Wilfred Paul. "The Impact of Unions on Wages of Supermarket Cashiers in Southern Ontario." SUNY, Buffalo, 1970.

2201
Bradfield, Frederick Michael. "The Sources of Wages and Labour Efficiency Differences Between Ontario and Quebec." Brown, 1971.

2202
Brody, Bernard. "The Canadian Government Geographic Public Service Wage Policy and the Letter Carrier Case (1972-73)." McGill, 1979.

2203
Chernick, Sidney Earl. "Studies in the Structure of Canadian Wages." Massachusetts Institute of Technology, 1956.

2204
Chinta, Nagireddy P. "An Empirical Study of Wage and Price Controls in Canada: 1975-1978." Dalhousie, 1982.

Francis, Jonathan Hervey. See No./Voir no 1994

2205
Hall, L.G. "An Historical Study of Salary Payments to Teachers and of the Emergence Principles of Salary Scheduling in Alberta." Toronto, 1967.

2206
Hasan, Muhammad A. "Employment and Wage Structure Effects of Canadian Federal Minimum Wage." Queen's, 1976.

2207
Henry, Zin A. "An Economic Analysis of the Guaranteed Wage and Its Application to the Canadian Economy." McGill, 1957.

2208
Johnson, Gilbert Gerald. "Non-Union Wage Changes in Canada." Yale, 1977.

Jonish, James Edward. See No./Voir no 1894

2209
Kumar, Pradeep. "Relative Wage Differentials in Canadian Industries." Queen's, 1974.

Markovich, Denise Elizabeth. See No./Voir no 2345

2210
Migue, Jean-Luc. "The Theory of the Occupational Wage Structure: An Application to the Canadian Experience." American, 1968.

2211
Peitchinis, S.G. "The Determination of the Wages of Railwaymen: A Study of Canadian, omission Since 1914." London, 1960.

2212
Poddar, Arun Kumar. "Labour Supply Behaviour of a Selected Youth Group with Implications of a Guaranteed Annual Income Scheme." Western Ontario, 1976.

2213
Puckett, T.C. "Wage Garnishment: A Study of the Problem in a Canadian Metropolis." London, 1978.

Riddell, William Craig. See No./Voir no 2122

2214
Roy, Paul Martel. "L'instauration d'une seule échelle de salaires pour les enseignants du secteur public au Québec: une étude en politique de ressources humaines." McGill, 1974.

Saunders, George S. See No./Voir no 1899
2215
Schenk, Christopher Robert. "Massey Workers and Wage Controls: A Case Study of Mobilization and Coercive Integration." Toronto, 1983.
2216
Scott, Richard Donald. "Schooling, Experience, Hours of Work, and Earnings in Canada." British Columbia, 1979.
2217
Starr, Gerald Frank. "Union-Nonunion Wage Differentials: A Cross-Sectional Analysis." Toronto, 1973.
2218
Tandon, Bankey Behari. "An Empirical Analysis of Earnings of Foreign-Born and Native-Born Canadians." Queen's, 1977.

Tracy, Martin Booth. See No./Voir no 2066
2219
Vaillancourt, François. "Differences in Earnings by Language Groups in Quebec, 1970: A Study of the Determinants of the Labour Earnings of Males in Quebec in 1970." Queen's, 1978.

Vanderkamp, J. See No./Voir no 1363
2220
Williamson, David Robert. "Wage Change Determinants in the Construction Industry: Ontario, 1960-1970." Western Ontario, 1973.

Woroby, Tamara M. See No./Voir no 1309
2221
Zaidi, Mahmood Ahmed. "The Determinants of Wage Rate Changes in Canada: An Empirical Study." California, Berkeley, 1966.

IMMIGRATION AND MIGRATION AND THE ECONOMY/ IMMIGRATION, ÉMIGRATION ET ÉCONOMIE

See also Immigration and Migration/Voir aussi Immigration et migration

CONSUMER BEHAVIOR, ECONOMICS AND RESEARCH/COMPORTEMENT DES CONSOMMATEURS, L'ÉCONOMIE POLITIQUE ET LA RECHERCHE

Agranove, Larry Melvyn. See No./Voir no 1590
2222
Alexander, Judith Ann. "Some Aspects of Consumer Behaviour When Goods are Interrelated." Simon Fraser, 1974.
2223
Anderson, Charles Dennis. "Consumer Information Seeking for a Durable Product." Western Ontario, 1977.

Angevine, Gerald Edwin. See No./Voir no 1961
2224
Bring, Gordon. "Consumer Space Preferences." McMaster, 1971.

Claxton, John David. See No./Voir no 1965

2225
Davies, Ivor Garth. "Service Provision and Consumer Behaviour in a Frontier Area: Northwestern Ontario." Edinburgh, 1972.
2226
De Camprieu, Renaud Marc. "Personal Values as a Potential Basis for Cross-Cultural Segmentation." Toronto, 1979.
2227
Dionne, Georges E. "Le risque moral et le furetage des consommateurs." Montréal, 1980.
2228
Filiatrault, Pierre. "L'influence des situations sur l'évaluation des critères de décision des consommateurs." Laval, 1979. [Restaurants in Quebec/ Restaurants au Québec]

Harnarine, Harold. See No./Voir no 1513
2229
Heslop, Louise Annette. "An Experimental Study of the Effects of Premium Advertising on Cereal Choices by Parents and Children." Western Ontario, 1977.

Irvine, Ian Joseph. See No./Voir no 1174

Lefebvre, Jean-Marie. See No./Voir no 1966
2230
Ma, Sylvia See-Wai. "Retail Patronage Behavior in the Supermarket Industry." Toronto, 1981.

MacPherson, Hector. See No./Voir no 1281
2231
Muller, Thomas Edward. "The Impact of Consumer Information on Brand Sales: A Field Experiment with Point-of-Purchase Nutritional Information Load." British Columbia, 1982.

Munro, Hugh James. See No./Voir no 1579

Murray, John Alexander. See No./Voir no 1969

2232
Thirkell, Peter Creswell. "Consumers Expectations Disconfirmation and Satisfaction." Western Ontario, 1981. [Mail survey of 985 Canadian consumers/Enquête par correspondance adressée à 985 consommateurs canadiens]

Thomas, Dwight Robert. See No./Voir no 1972
2233
Windal, Pierre Bernard Marie. "On Some Analytical Approaches to the Study of Consumer Brand Switching Behavior." British Columbia, 1978.
2234
Zins, Michel A. "Facteurs influençant les stratégies de traitement de l'information utilisées par les consommateurs." Laval, 1981.

ECOLOGICAL PROBLEMS/ PROBLÈMES ÉCOLOGIQUES

2235
Bardecki, Michael James. "Wetlands in Southern Ontario: A Policy Science Approach." York, 1981.

Brown, Si. See No./Voir no 1908

Campbell, James Alfred. See No./Voir no 205
2236
Donnelly, Brian Eugene. "International Law: Canada's Effort to Protect Itself from Marine Pollution." Georgia, 1977.

Gladwin, Thomas Neil. See No./Voir no 1749

2237
Landsberger, Sheldon. "Characterization of Trace Elemental Pollutants in Urban Snow Using Proton-Induced X-Ray Emission and Instrumental-Neutron Activation Analysis." Toronto, 1982. [Snow from Island of Montreal and Toronto/Neige à Montréal et à Toronto]

2238
Lepore, Giuseppe. "The Economics of Air Pollution with Special Reference to the Control of Sulphur-Oxides Emissions in Canada." McGill, 1974.

Middleton, John David. See No./Voir no 11645
Moore, Patrick Albert. See No./Voir no 1878
Muller, Robert Andrew. See No./Voir no 1821
Nemetz, Peter Newman. See No./Voir no 1879
Reese, Craig Eugene. See No./Voir no 1724

2239
Sims, William Allen. "The Economics of Sewer Effluent Charges." Toronto, 1978. [Sewage treatment pollution, waste-industry/Pollution par usines de traitement, industrie de traitement de déchets]

Tufuor, Joseph Kwame. See No./Voir no 3730

SOCIO-ECONOMIC AFFAIRS AND STUDIES/ AFFAIRES ET ÉTUDES SOCIO-ÉCONOMIQUES

Burbridge, Kenneth J. See No./Voir no 104
Findlay, Marjorie Craven. See No./Voir no 600
Goulding, James Wray. See No./Voir no 1169

2240
Harris, Simon Richard. "Class Struggle in the Domain of Social Production: The Political Significance of Residential Segregation in Kingston, Ontario, 1961-1976." Queen's, 1981.

Jansen, Janni Margaretha. See No./Voir no 1867

2241
Jenkins, Harry P.B. "Financing Adequate Public Services in Nova Scotia." Chicago, 1949.

Kitchen, Brigitte. See No./Voir no 1323

2242
Kunin, Roslyn. "Labour Force Participation Rates and Poverty in Canadian Metropolitan Areas." British Columbia, 1970.

Lautard, Emile Hugh. See No./Voir no 1276
Lowry, Douglas Bradley. See No./Voir no 1179
MacInnes, Daniel William. See No./Voir no 2115
McFadyen, Stuart Malcolm. See No./Voir no 1501

2243
Schirber, Martin Edward. "The Cooperative Movement of Antigonish, Nova Scotia." Harvard, 1940.

2244
Schreck, David Donald. "Occupational Segregation by Sex." British Columbia, 1978.

Stenger, Alfred. See No./Voir no 1869
Watts, Martin John. See No./Voir no 1366

2245
Weir, John Angus. "An Economic Study of the Program in Rural Reconstruction in Prince Edward Island in Canada: An Evaluation." Notre Dame, 1964.

Whittingham, Frank J. See No./Voir no 2085

TRANSPORTATION/TRANSPORT

General Items/Ouvrages généraux

2246
Baass, Karsten Goetz. "A Procedure to Determine a Good Zonal System in the Transportation Planning Process." Waterloo, 1979. [Montreal/Montréal]

2247
Bryan, Ingrid Arvidsdotter. "Essays on Transportation and Trade." Alberta, 1972.

Conlon, Robert Maxwell. See No./Voir no 2003

2248
Craven, Jack Wolfe. "The Role of Transportation in Regional Development: Impacts on Industrial Location." Manitoba, 1980.

2249
DeCea Chicano, Joaquin. "Modèles d'affectation de réseau de transport collectif urbain: traitement de l'accès et de la diversion entre les chemins." Montréal, 1982.

2250
Dionne, René. "Une analyse théorique et numérique du problème du choix optimal d'un réseau de transport sans congestion." Montréal, 1975.

2251
Dunn, Michael James. "A Statistical Analysis of the Demand for Domestic and Passenger Transportation in Canada, 1960-1969." Oregon, 1972.

2252
Fleming, Daryl Stanley. "The Significance of Transport Costs for Selected Commodity Movements Between the Maritime Provinces, New England and Middle Atlantic States." New Brunswick, 1983.

2253
Gaudry, Marc J.I. "The Demand for Public Transit in Montreal and Its Implications for Transportation Planning and Cost-Benefit Analysis." Princeton, 1974.

Haritos, Zissis. See No./Voir no 1455
Heads, John. See No./Voir no 19

2254
Heaver, Trevor David. "The Evaluation of Transportation Projects in Northern British Columbia." Indiana, 1966.

2255
Hodgson, Michael John. "Highway Network Development and Optimal Accessibility Change in the Toronto Centered Region." Toronto, 1973.

2256
Khajavi, Shokooh. "Optimal Peak-Load Pricing Investment and Service Levels for Urban Streets." Toronto, 1980. [Bus Transportation/Transport par autobus]

2257
Kissling, Christopher Charles. "Transportation Networks Accessibility and Urban Functions: An Empirical and Theoretical Analysis." McGill, 1967.

2258
Langford, John W. "The Reorganization of the Federal Transport Folio: The Application of a Ministry System." McGill, 1973.

2259
McComb, Lloyd Alexander. "Simplified Urban Transportation Planning Procedures Using Census Data." Toronto, 1982.

Morrall, John Franklin. See No./Voir no 4557

Mundy, Ray Allen. See No./Voir no 2376

2260
Oum, Tae Hoon. "Demand for Freight Transportation with a Special Emphasis on Mode Choice in Canada." British Columbia, 1979.

2261
Pearson, Philip Michael Lee. "The Planning and Evaluation of Intercity Travel Systems." Waterloo, 1969.

Robinson, John Bertram L. See No./Voir no 4562

2262
Saccomanno, Fedel Frank Mario. "A Wage-Based Model of Residential Site Value Transfer." Toronto, 1978.

2263
Said, Galal Mostafa. "An Urban Systems Model for the Toronto Region." Waterloo, 1980.

2264
Schultz, Richard John. "Federalism, Bureaucracy and Public Policy: A Case Study of the Making of Transportation Policy." York, 1976.

Shallal, Louis A.Y. See No./Voir no 4485

Skuba, Michael. See No./Voir no 2999

2265
Smith, William Randy. "Transport Improvements and Urban Network Evolution: Southern Ontario 1851-1921." York, 1978.

2266
Sullivan, Brian Edward. "An Analysis of the Demand for and Supply of Rural Public Transportation: The Case of Alberta." Stanford, 1974.

2267
Westmacott, Martin William. "Western Canada and the National Transportation Act: A Case Study in Cooperative Federalism." Alberta, 1972.

Air Transport/Transport aérien

2268
Baldwin, John Russell. "A Positive Theory of Regulation and the 'Public' Corporation in the Context of the Canadian Air Transport Industry." Harvard, 1973.

2269
Borins, Sandford Frederick. "The Economics of Airport Planning: The Case of Toronto." Harvard, 1976.

2270
Briaud, Jean-Louis Charles. "The Pressuremeter: Application to Pavement Design." Ottawa, 1979. [Airport pavement to be able to carry heavy planes/Piste d'atterissage pouvant supporter des avions lourds]

2271
Haanappel, Peter P.C. "Ratemaking and International Air Transport: A Legal Analysis of International Air Fares and Rates." McGill, 1976.

Hamzawi, Salah Gonda. See No./Voir no 4475

2272
Marks, C.J.A. "Air Transport in the British Commonwealth: A Study in Economic Geography." London, 1970.

2273
Mattson, Margaret Solveig. "The Growth and Protection of Canadian Civil and Commercial Aviation, 1918-1930." Western Ontario, 1979.

2274
Reukema, Barbara Ann. "Discriminatory Refusal of Carriage in North America." McGill, 1981.

2275
Seldon, Zena Katherine. "The Economic Implications of Alternative Air Transport Regulatory Practices: A Canada-United States Comparison." Manitoba, 1979.

2276
Studnicki-Gizbert, Konrad W. "Economics of Canadian Air Transport Industry." McGill, 1964.

2277
Truavskis, Boris. "Passenger Demand for a 1976 QSTOL Aircraft System in the Calgary-Edmonton Corridor." Calgary, 1974.

2278
Wallace, Reginald Stanley. "A Domestic Multi-Model Goods Distribution Model with Emphasis on Air Cargo." Waterloo, 1971.

Maritime

Aitken, Hugh G.J. See No./Voir no 1233

Bowman, Donald Fox. See No./Voir no 2002

Brown, G.W. See No./Voir no 1238

Ellis, David William Henry. See No./Voir no 4530

2279
Fletcher, Daniel O. "A Study of Package Freight Carriers on the Great Lakes." Michigan, 1960.

2280
Forbes, Ernest R. "The Maritime Rights Movement 1919-1927: A Study of Canadian Regionalism." Queen's, 1975.

Forward, Charles Nelson. See No./Voir no 2010

2281
Hartley, Joseph R. "The Effect of the St. Lawrence Seaway on Grain Movements." Indiana, 1957.

2282
Harvey, Jacqueline. "Le trafic maritime de la côte-nord, étude géographique." Laval, 1973.

Howard, Jane M. See No./Voir no 1789

2283
Johnson, Arthur L. "Boston and the Maritime: A Century of Steam Navigation." Maine, 1971. [1836-1954]

Jones, Clarence Fielden. See No./Voir no 1206

2284
Laing, Lionel H. "Merchant Shipping Legislation and Admiralty Jurisdiction in Canada." Harvard, 1935.

McArthur, N.M. See No./Voir no 4704

McCarty, John Myron. See No./Voir no 1212

McGahan, Elizabeth Moore Walsh. See No./Voir no 1290

McIlwraith, Thomas Forsyth. See No./Voir no 2023

2285
McIntyre, Geoffrey R. "A Comparative Analysis of Federal Port Policy in the United States and Canada." New York, 1978.

93

2286
Mellen, Frances Nordlinger. "The Development of the Toronto Waterfront During the Railway Expansion Era, 1850-1912." Toronto, 1974.

2287
Opheim, Lee Alfred. "Twentieth Century Shipwrecks in Lake Superior." St. Louis, 1971.

Pritchard, James Stewart. See No./Voir no 1232

Rabiega, William Albert. See No./Voir no 2030

2288
Rice, R.E. "The Rise of Shipbuilding in British North America, 1787-1890." Liverpool, 1978.

2289
Ricklefs, John Edward. "Regional Port Programming and the Great Lakes, St. Lawrence Seaway System." Columbia, 1982.

2290
Riendeau, Bruno. "A Port Choice Model of the Carrier, the Shipper and the Consignee: An Application to Container Transport Between the North and South Atlantic, and Selected Quebec, East Coast and Great Lakes Ports in Canada and the United States." Pennsylvania, 1977.

2291
Robinson, Ross. "Spatial Structuring of Port-Linked Flows: The Port of Vancouver, Canada, 1965." British Columbia, 1969.

2292
Slack, Brian. "A Geographical Analysis of the System of Ports on the South Shore of the Lower St. Lawrence River." McGill, 1972.

2293
Sydor, Leon Paul. "The St. Lawrence Seaway: National Shares in Primary Seaway Benefits." Princeton, 1970.

Tulchinsky, Gerald Jacob Joseph. See No./Voir no 1257

2294
Tunell, George G. "Transportation on the Great Lakes of North America." Chicago, 1897.

Pipelines

Brown, Si. See No./Voir no 1908

Railways and Freight/Chemins de fer et transport des marchandises

2295
Baskerville, Peter A. "The Boardroom and Beyond Aspects of a Study of the Upper Canadian Railroad Community." Queen's, 1973.

2296
Crainic, Teodor Gabriel. "Un modèle de planification tactique pour le transport ferroviaire des marchandises." Montréal, 1982.

2297
Currie, Archibald William. "The Canadian Railway Problem, with Special Reference to Freight Rates on Grain." Harvard, 1938.

2298
Dougall, Herbert Edward. "Government Influences on the Canadian Railway Industry." Northwestern, 1950.

2299
Dunford, Fraser Edwin Frank. "Spinality in Regional Transportation Networks." Queen's, 1975.

2300
Fleming, Howard A. "A History of the Hudson Bay Railway." California, Los Angeles, 1952.

2301
Fournier, Leslie Thomas. "The Canadian National Railways: A Study of the Nationalization of Railways in Canada." California, Berkeley, 1928.

2302
George, Peter James. "A Benefit-Cost Analysis of the Canadian Pacific Railway." Toronto, 1967.

2303
Gervais, Gaétan S. "L'expansion du réseau ferroviaire québécois (1875-1895)." Ottawa, 1979.

2304
Ghoneim, Nadia Sobhi Abdel-Nour Mohamed. "Schedule Evaluation and Zone Structuring for Urban Rail Commuter Service on Planned and Existing Routes." Calgary, 1982.

Hamzaivi, Salah Gouda. See No./Voir no 4475

2305
Harries, Hubert W. "Canadian Freight Rate Control by Statute." Iowa State, 1955.

2306
Hewetson, Henry W. "The Distance Principle in Railway Freight Rates with Particular Reference to Canada." Chicago, 1951.

2307
Innis, Harold Adams. "History of the Canadian Pacific Railway." Chicago, 1920.

2308
Irwin, Leonard B. "Pacific Railways and Nationalism in the Canadian-American Northwest, 1845-1873." Pennsylvania, 1939.

2309
Leclerc, Wilbrod. "Pricing Railway Freight Services in Canada." McGill, 1964.

2310
MacDonald, James Andrew. "Post-1945 Branch Line Railways in Canada: An Analysis of the Carrier Benefits." Stanford, 1973.

2311
MacGibbon, Duncan Alexander. "Railway Rates and the Canadian Railway Commission." Chicago, 1915.

2312
McLean, Simon James. "The Railway Policy of Canada." Chicago, 1897.

Mellen, Frances Nordlinger. See No./Voir no 2286

2313
Poon, Chung Lam. "Urban Railway Relocation: An Economic Evaluation." Western Ontario, 1976.

2314
Rao, Ponugoti Someswar. "Forecasting the Demand for Railway Freight Transportation Services: An Integration of Econometric Modelling and Input Output Analysis." Queen's, 1976.

2315
Regehr, Theodore David. "The Canadian Northern Railway: Agent of National Growth, 1896-1911." Alberta, 1967.

2316
Rollit, John Buchanan. "Transportation as a National Problem." McGill, 1934.

2317
Roman, D.W. "The Contribution of Imperial Guarantees for Colonial Railway Loans to the Consolidation of British North America, 1847-65." Oxford, 1978.

2318
Roy, Patricia Elizabeth. "The British Columbia Electric Railway Company, 1897-1928: A British Company in British Columbia." British Columbia, 1970.

2319
Samaha, Mohamed Aly. "Dynamic response and optimization of a railroad freight car under periodic and stochastic excitations." Concordia, 1978.

Tuck, Joseph Hugh. See No./Voir no 2108

Tulchinsky, Gerald Jacob Joseph. See No./Voir no 1257

2320
Weaver, Robert Kent. "The Politics of State Enterprise: Railroad Nationalization in the United States and Canada." Harvard, 1982.

2321
Webb, Ross Allan. "The Mechanization of Transport in Nova Scotia, 1825-1867." Pittsburgh, 1956.

2322
Wilson, William Warren. "Financing the Operation and Rehabilitation of Rail Branch Lines." Manitoba, 1980.

2323
Young, Brian J. "The North Shore Railways: A Study of the Montreal Colonization Railroad and the North Shore Railway, 1854-1885." Queen's, 1973.

Bus and Subway/Autobus et métro

2324
Bajic, Vladimir P. "Transportation System Changes and the Structure of Housing Prices: The Effect of a New Subway Line in Metropolitan Toronto." Toronto, 1981.

Khajavi, Shokooh. See No./Voir no 2256

Trucking/Camionage

Anandajayasekeram, Ponniah. See No./Voir no 142
Bouchard, Serge. See No./Voir no 433

Dartnell, Albert Lloyd. See No./Voir no 2005
2325
Kim, Moshe. "The Structure of Technology of the Canadian Trucking Industry." Toronto, 1982.

CANADIAN - UNITED STATES ECONOMIC RELATIONS AND COMPARISONS/ COMPARAISONS ET RELATIONS ÉCONOMIQUES, CANADA - ÉTATS-UNIS

General Items/Ouvrages généraux

2326
Anderson, Richard Svend. "The North American Market for Beef: Analysis of Future Market Dimensions and Competitive Relationships." Ohio State, 1975.

2327
Berengaut, Julian. "International Commodity Arbitrage and the Relationships Between Foreign and Domestic Prices in Canada and the United States." Wisconsin, 1978.

2328
Clement, Wallace. "Continental Capitalism: Corporate Power Relations Between Canada and the U.S." Carleton, 1976.

2329
Due, Jean Margaret Lucinda Mann. "Consumption Levels in Canada and the United States, 1947 to 1950." Illinois, 1953.

2330
Gusen, Peter. "The International Transmission of Business Cycles and Foreign Industrial Control: Canada and the United States." Duke, 1976.

2331
James, Robert W. "Wartime Economic Cooperation: A Study of Relations Between Canada and the United States." Chicago, 1950.

2332
Jensen, Jon Michael. "Temporal and Inter-Temporal Equilibrium in the Foreign Exchange Market: Theory and Evidence from the U.S.-Canadian Dollar Market, 1965-1973." Wisconsin, 1976.

Keeley, James Francis. See No./Voir no 1175
Mc Intyre, Geoffrey R. See No./Voir no 2287

2333
Moffett, Samuel Erasmus. "The Americanization of Canada." Columbia, 1907.

Partin, Charles Arthur. See No./Voir no 1213

2334
Reekie, Charles Ian Maxwell. "Some Aspects of Foreign Demand for United States Wheat." North Carolina State, 1967.

Seldon, Zena Katherine. See No./Voir no 2275

2335
Smith, Alexander. "The Commerce Power in the United States: A Canadian Translation." Stanford, 1957.

Tracy, Martin Booth. See No./Voir no 2066
Wilson, Harold Fisher. See No./Voir no 840

2336
Wonnacott, Ronald Johnston. "An Input-Output Relationship of the Canadian and U.S. Economies." Harvard, 1959.

Finance

Alley, William E. See No./Voir no 1419
Baban, R.C.N. See No./Voir no 1568
Connelly, Dennis Eugene. See No./Voir no 1529

2337
Colella, Francis J. "An Econometric Study of United States-Canada Short-Term Capital Flows (1959-1970)." Fordham, 1973.

Cudmore, James Seeley. See No./Voir no 1622
Drury, Donald Hazen. See No./Voir no 1402
Frankel, Allen Barry. See No./Voir no 1530

2338
Freedman, Charles. "Long-Term Capital Flows Between the United States and Canada." Massachusetts Institute of Technology, 1970.

2339
Grady, Patrick Michael. "The Canadian Exemption from the United States Interest Equalization Tax." Toronto, 1973.

Haberer, John Frederick. See No./Voir no 1404

Hamovitch, Maurice B. See No./Voir no 1625

2340
Hawley, James P. "U.S. Restriction of the Export of Capital 1961-1971: State Policy and Long-Term Economic Perspectives." McGill, 1977.

2341
Helleiner, Gerald Karl. "Interconnection Between Canadian and United States Capital Markets, 1952-60." Yale, 1962.

Jack, Lawrence B. See No./Voir no 1499

2342
Kim, Chul-Hwan. "The Deviations of Exchange Rates from Purchasing Power Parity: An Empirical Test of the PPP Doctrine." California, Santa Barbara, 1982.

2343
Lee, Chung Hoon. "The Demand for Foreign Securities and International Long-Term Capital Movements: The United States-Canadian Case." California, Berkeley, 1967.

2344
London, Anselm Lullellyn. "The Informational Efficiency of the Canada-U.S. Foreign Exchange Market." Queen's, 1978.

2345
Markovich, Denise Elizabeth. "Incomes Policy and the Rate of Wage Increase: A Comparison of Canada and the United States, 1956-76." Manitoba, 1979.

2346
Molot, Maureen Appel. "A Common Market for Capital: Indicator of Canada-United States Integration." California, Berkeley, 1972.

2347
Murray, John David. "Tax Differentials and International Capital Flows: The Canadian-United States Experience." Princeton, 1978.

Schoch, Herbert Paul. See No./Voir no 1414

2348
Setzer, Vernon G. "The Commercial Reciprocity of the United States, 1774-1829." Pennsylvania, 1936.

Simpson, Thomas McNider, III. See No./Voir no 1443

Singh, Ranbir. See No./Voir no 1444

Stolar, Robert William. See No./Voir no 1415

2349
Stroetmann, Karl Antonius. "The Theory of Long-Term International Capital Flows and Canadian Corporate Debt Issues in the United States." British Columbia, 1974.

2350
Trinh, Hieu Nghia. "Internal Financing Policy of Canadian Manufacturing Firms with Emphasis on the Role of U.S. Subsidiaries in the Canadian Economy." Illinois, 1973.

Tsai, Hiu Liang. See No./Voir no 1564

Upson, Roger Ballard. See No./Voir no 1541

2351
Wallace, Myles Stuart. "The Monetary Approach: An Examination of Some Theoretical and Empirical Aspects of Flexible Exchange Rates: Canada-United States, 1950 IV-1961 I." Colorado, 1976.

Winakor, Arthur H. See No./Voir no 1449

2352
Wright, Gerald Campbell Vaughan. "Canada's Management of Financial Relations with the United States, 1963-1968." Johns Hopkins, 1976.

2353
Zenoff, David Brossell. "The Determinants of Diversified Remittance Practices of Wholly-Earned European and Canadian Subsidiaries of American Multi-National Corporations." Harvard, 1967.

Trade and Tariffs/Commerce et tarifs

Anderson, Richard Svend. See No./Voir no 2326

Aronsen, Laurence Robert. See No./Voir no 2385

2354
Baker, Richard C. "The Tariff under Roosevelt and Taft." Columbia, 1942.

2355
Brandes, Hans-Gunther. "An Investigation of the Canada-United States Trade in Newsprint." Syracuse (New York State University, College of Forestry), 1955.

2356
Cowan, Ralph Keith. "Effects of the United States-Canadian Automotive Agreement on Canada's Manufacturing Trade and Price Structure." Michigan, 1972.

2357
Crookell, Harold. "The Role of Product Innovation in Trade Flows of Household Appliances Between Canada and the U.S.A." Western Ontario, 1970.

2358
Detomasi, Don Dunford. "The Exchange Rate Elasticity of Canadian Exports to the United States: An Econometric Analysis." Utah, 1968.

2359
Elchibegoff, Ivan M. "United States International Timber Trade with the Pacific Countries (Land Utilization and Forest Resources in the Pacific Countries." New School, 1942.

Francis, Jonathan Hervey. See No./Voir no 1994

2360
Gandhi, Prem Parkash. "Free Trade Between United States and Canada: Its Potential Economic Effects on Northern New York." New School, 1973.

2361
Ganong, Carey Kierstead. "The Canadian Reaction to the American Tariff Policy." Wisconsin, 1931.

2362
Gernant, Paul Leonard. "The International Trade Effects of the 1965 United States-Canadian Automotive Agreement." Michigan, 1977.

2363
Gold, Marc Hilary. "The 1965 Canadian-American Automotive Trade Agreement: An Econometric Evaluation." Wayne State, 1976.

2364
Halstead, Donald Paul. "An Analysis of the Economic Effects of Free Trade Between Canada and the United States." Florida State, 1974.

2365
Hartigan, James Christopher. "Trade Policy and Income Distribution in the United States and Canada." Duke, 1979.

2366
Hastings, Paul G. "A Canada-United States Customs Union." Pennsylvania, 1950.
Herwig, Aletha Marguerite. See No./Voir no 109
Hynes, Cecil Vernon. See No./Voir no 2014
Jonish, James Edward. See No./Voir no 1894
2367
Kilduff, Vera R.R. "An Analysis of the Development of Canadian-American Trade." Brown, 1939.
Landuyt, Bernard F. See No./Voir no 2018
Masters, D.C. See No./Voir no 1283
2368
Netschert, Bruce C. "The Mineral Foreign Trade of the United States in the Twentieth Century: A Study in Mineral Economics." Cornell, 1950.
Overman, William D.. See No./Voir no 1996
Plotnick, Alan Ralph. See No./Voir no 1917
Pollack, Gerald A. See No./Voir no 1998
Roberts, Guy H. See No./Voir no 2033
Rothenberg, Stuart. See No./Voir no 8853
Rowland, Benjamin Moore. See No./Voir no 7572
Setzer, Vernon G. See No./Voir no 2348
2369
Slater, John Morton. "The World Wheat Economy: Implications for the Consumption and Trade of United States Wheat." Illinois, 1966.
Stryker, Joseah B. See No./Voir no 2039
2370
Talarico, Joseph Frank. "A Study of the Postwar Pattern of Commerce and Finance Between the United States and Canada, 1946-1953." Rutgers, 1958.
Thevenon, Michael Jean. See No./Voir no 1824
2371
Wardell, Nancy Needham. "United States Iron Ore Imports: Sourcing Strategies for United States Steel Companies." Harvard, 1978.
Ware, Dennis William. See No./Voir no 36
Wilson, David A. See No./Voir no 2044

Industries

2372
Carlisle, Arthur Elliott. "The Effect of Cultural Differences on Managerial and Industrial Relations, Policies and Practices: A Study of U.S.- Controlled Companies Operating in English and French Canada." Michigan, 1966.
Carter, William Harrison, Jr. See No./Voir no 2387
Cayley, Charles E. See No./Voir no 1866
Clemente, Ricardo Ama. See No./Voir no 1813
2373
Dundas, Kenneth Ninian Melville. "The Management of U.S. Subsidiaries in Canada." Western Ontario, 1979.
Eldon, Walter D.R. See No./Voir no 1892
Flynn, David Michael. See No./Voir no 1842
Gladwin, Thomas Neil. See No./Voir no 1749
Helmers, Henrik Olaf. See No./Voir no 1843
Jonish, James Edward. See No./Voir no 1894
Meredith, Lindsay Norman. See No./Voir no 2392
Neisser, Albert C. See No./Voir no 1845
2374
Pilcher, Dalton Jefferson. "American Factories in Canada." Virginia, 1931.

Productivity Comparisons/ Comparaisons de la productivité

Bessom, Richard Moody. See No./Voir no 1831
2375
Fowler, David John. "A Comparison of the Performance of Canadian and U.S. Manufacturing and Mining Industries." Toronto, 1976.
Hill, Edmund Russell. See No./Voir no 1321
Lithwick, Norman Harvey. See No./Voir no 1210
2376
Mundy, Ray Allen. "U.S. and Canadian Urban Mass Transportation Systems: A Comparative Empirical Analysis." Pennsylvania State, 1974.
2377
Saunders, Ronald Stanley. "The Determinants of the Productivity of Canadian Manufacturing Industries Relative to that of Counterpart Industries in the United States." Harvard, 1978.
2378
Scheppach, Raymond Carl, Jr. "A Canadian-United States Productivity Comparison." Connecticut, 1970.
Stryker, Josiah Dirck. See No./Voir no 2039

Labor and Wages/Travail et rémunération

2379
Blandy, Richard John. "Migration and Skills: A Comparative Quantitative Analysis of the Migration of Professional and Blue-Collar Workers to the United States from Great Britain, France and Canada, and to Canada from Great Britain, France and the United States." Columbia, 1969.
2380
Comay, Peter Yochanan. "International Migration of Professional Manpower: The Canada-U.S. Case." Princeton, 1969.
2381
Curtis, John Margeson. "Direct United States Influence on Canadian Prices and Wages." Harvard, 1969.
Francis, Jonathan Hervey. See No./Voir no 1994
Jonish, James Edward. See No./Voir no 1894
2382
Langley, Paul Christopher. "Migration, Earnings Differentials and Past Migratory Experience: Canada and the United States." Queen's, 1977.
2383
Meyer, Benjamin. "U.S.-Canadian Wage Differentials: A Look at the Possibility of Parity and Its Problems." SUNY, Buffalo, 1973.
Niemi, Beth. See No./Voir no 2189
2384
Smith, Douglas Allister. "An Econometric Analysis of the United States Impact on Manufacturing Wages in Canada." Massachusetts Institute of Technology, 1973.
Williams, Charles Brian. See No./Voir no 2125

American Investments in Canada/
Investissements américains au Canada

2385
Aronsen, Lawrence Robert. "The Northern Frontier: United States Trade and Investment in Canada 1945-1953." Toronto, 1980.

2386
Barg, Benjamin. "A Study of United States Economical Control in Canadian Secondary Industry." Columbia, 1960.

2387
Carter, William Harrison, Jr. "American Branch Plants in Canada: One Phase of the International Movement of Capital." Harvard, 1932.

Coates, Norman. See No./Voir no 1840

Flowers, Edward Brown. See No. / Voir no 2396

2388
French, Robert W. "American Direct Investments in Canada." Michigan, 1937.

2389
Hitchin, David Edward. "Canadianization of United States Controlled Corporations in Canada: Authority Relationships and Conflict Resolution." California, Los Angeles, 1965.

2390
Knapp, Robert Whelan. "United States Direct Investment in Canada, 1950-1960." Michigan, 1963.

2391
Lubitz, Raymond. "United States Direct Investment in Canada and Canadian Capital Formation, 1950-1962." Harvard, 1967.

Marton, Katherin. See No./Voir no 1663

2392
Meredith, Lindsay Norman. "Marketing Determinants of U.S. Multinational Corporate Investment in Canadian Industries." Simon Fraser, 1981.

Pilcher, Dalton Jefferson. See No./Voir no 2374

2393
Ripley, Eleanor Duncan. "United States Investment in Canadian Securities, 1958-1965." Harvard, 1969.

2394
Roby, Yves. "Réactions des Québécois aux investissements américains." Rochester, 1975.

Canadian Investments in the United States/
Investissements canadiens aux États-Unis

2395
Blais, Jeffrey Peter. "Theoretical and Empirical Investigation of Canadian and British Direct Foreign Investment in Manufacturing in the United States." Pittsburgh, 1975.

2396
Flowers, Edward Brown. "Oligopolistic Reaction in European Direct Investment in the United States." Georgia State, 1975.

2397
Oh, Jeung Hoon. "The Determinants of Foreign Direct Investment in the United States: Some Empirical Evidence." Northern Illinois, 1982. [Canada among others/Le Canada parmi d'autres]

EDUCATION/ÉDUCATION

More doctoral dissertations have been produced in this classification than in any other subject area. The University of Toronto, which accounts for 31 percent of the total, produced the first doctorate in this field in 1903, followed in 1907 by Teachers College, Columbia. The 1970's and 1980's witnessed the heaviest growth in doctoral work, quadrupling the output of the previous 60 years. The statistics for the first four years of the 1980's promise another period of growth. Five universities in Great Britain produced 14 titles, with the University of London the leader.

Il y a eu plus d'études de doctorat dans ce domaine que dans aucun autre. L'Université de Toronto qui compte 31 pour 100 du total a été la première université à accorder un doctorat en ce domaine en 1903, suivie en 1907 par Teachers College et Columbia. Les années 1970 et 1980 ont connu la plus grande poussée, quadruplant la production des 60 années précédentes. Les statistiques de 1980 à 1984 promettent dix autres années brillantes. Cinq universités en Grande-Bretagne ont produit 14 thèses, l'Université de Londres venant en tête.

General Items/Ouvrages généraux

2398
Beaudet, Joseph Edward. "Parents dans l'éducation." Ottawa, 1927.

2399
Francis, Mary Ethel Annexstad. "The Role of Values Education in Multicultural Education." Toronto, 1980.

Hannibal, Emmett Ronald. See No./Voir no 945

2400
Norris, Kenneth Everett. "The Permanence of School Learning as Indicated by a Study of Unemployed Men." McGill, 1939.

2401
Sparham, Donald Cauthers. "Education in Transition. An Organizational Analysis." York, 1977.

National/Échelle nationale

2402
Barichello, Richard Ralph. "The Schooling of Farm Youth in Canada." Chicago, 1979.

2403
Burke, Mavis E. "An Analysis of Canadian Educational Assistance to the Commonwealth Caribbean Leeward and Windward Islands, 1960-1970." Ottawa, 1975.

2404
Edwardh, Melvin Oscar. "Essential Concepts Regarding Canada." Northern Colorado, 1961.

2405
Hauck, Arthur Andrew. "Some Educational Factors Affecting the Relations Between Canada and the United States." Teachers College, Columbia, 1932.

2406
Hoy, C.H. "Education and Minority Groups in the United Kingdom and Canada: A Comparative Study of Policies and Objectives." London, 1975.

2407
Orlikow, Lionel. "Dominion - Provincial Partnerships in Canadian Education, 1960-1967." Chicago, 1970.

Provincial/Échelle provinciale

2408
Blum, William D. "Opinion Toward Education in Montreal, Canada." Wisconsin, 1947.

2409
Cheal, John Ernest. "Canadian Provincial School Systems: Their Input-Ouput Differences." Chicago, 1962.

2410
Danis, Claudia. "Les modèles d'intervention en éducation populaire extra-institutionnelle dans le Québec actuel." Montréal, 1981.

2411
Gélinas, Jean-Paul. "Les motivations politiques des étudiants du Cegep de Sainte-Foy." Laval, 1979.

2412
Kistler, Ruth Barthold. "Religion, Education and Language as Factors in French-Canadian Cultural Survival." New York, 1947.

2413
Lambert, Pierre D. "Contemporary Pattern of French-Canadian Education in the Province of Quebec." Iowa, 1955.

2414
McKenna, Mary Olga. "The Impact of Cultural Forces on Commitment to Education in the Province of Prince Edward Island." Boston College, 1964.

Orlikow, Lionel. See No./Voir no 2407

2415
Podmore, Christopher John. "Private Schooling in English Canada." McMaster, 1976.

2416
Sloan, Leroy Vincent. "A Policy Analysis of Legislation Permitting Public - Private School Agreements for the Provision of Educational Services." Alberta, 1980.

HISTORY OF EDUCATION/ HISTOIRE DE L'ÉDUCATION

General Items/Ouvrages généraux

2417
Angrave, James. "Scottish Masters: The Influence of the Scottish Enlightenment in Canada Since 1745." Sheffield, 1973.

2418
Barry, J.K. "An Examination of the Emergence of a National System of Education in Canada, 1791 to 1970." National University of Ireland (Cork), 1975.

2419
Best, Ernest Maurice. "Social Reconstruction in Canada." New York, 1920.

2420
Bizier, Jeanne. "L'éducation chrétienne à l'école: perspective du Rapport Parent et perspective de l'église." Ottawa, 1968.

Colman, Rosalie Marson. See No./Voir no 824

2421
Currie, Allister Blaine. "A Comparison of Forms of Public Provision for Secondary Education in English-Speaking North America with Those of England, and an Historical Interpretation of Some Differences that Emerge." London, 1937.

2422
Dyde, Walters Farrell. "Public Secondary Education in Canada." Teachers College, Columbia, 1929.

2423
Goulson, Carolyn Floyd. "An Historical Survey of Royal Commissions and Other Major Governmental Inquiries in Canadian Education." Toronto, 1966.

2424
Johnstone, Paul Anthony. "Some Implications of Current Canadian Concepts of the Just Society for Education in Canada." Ottawa, 1973.

Kennedy, John Robinson. See No./Voir no 10363

2425
Lyons, John Edward. "In Pursuit of an Ideal: A History of the National Council of Education." Alberta, 1980.

2426
Parks-Trusz, Sandra Lynn. "A Sociological Study of Knowledge Production and Control: Comparative Education in North America, 1945-1975." SUNY, Buffalo, 1979.

Runge, Janis Margaret. See No./Voir no 2589

2427
Scholes, A.G. "Education for Empire Settlement: A Study in Juvenile Migration." Edinburgh, 1931.

2428
Wernecke, Hans Bertram. "Interprovincial Cooperation in Education in West Germany and Canada, 1945-1969: The West German Conference of Ministers of Education and the Council of Ministers of Education (Canada)." Pennsylvania, 1971.

1763-1867

2429
Adams, Howard Joseph. "The Role of Church and State in Canadian Education 1800-1867." California, Berkeley, 1966.

2430
Boulianne, Réal Gérard. "The Royal Institution for the Advancement of Learning: The Correspondence, 1820-1829, a Historical and Analytical Study." McGill, 1970.

2431
Jobling, Keith Bertram. "The Role of the Superintendency in the Development of Education in Upper and Lower Canada, 1842-1867." Ottawa, 1971.

2432
Spencer, Hildreth Houston. "To Nestle in the Mane of the British Lion: A History of Canadian Black Education, 1820 to 1870." Northwestern, 1970.

2433
Spragge, George Warburton. "Monitorial Schools in the Canadas, 1810-1845." Toronto, 1935.

2434
Anderson, James Thomas Milton. "The Education of the New Canadian: A Treatise on Canada's Greatest Educational Problem." Toronto, 1918.

2435
Andrews, Bruce Alfred. "The Federal Government and Education: Canadian and American Perspectives." British Columbia, 1978. [1867-1970]

2436
Japp, Robert. "Education as a Political Issue under the Union." McGill, 1937.

2437
Linask, Kersti Luhaäär. "An Historical Study of Selected Estonian Supplementary Schools in the United States and Canada from 1950 to the Present." Connecticut, 1978.

Lyons, John Edward. See No./Voir no 2425

2438
Sutherland, John Neil. "Children in English-Canadian Society: Framing the Twentieth Century Consensus." Minnesota, 1973.

History of Education in the Provinces/ Histoire de l'éducation dans les provinces

Alberta

2439
Byrne, Timothy Clarke. "The Historical Development and an Evaluation of Provincial Leadership in the Field of High School Instruction for the Province of Alberta." Colorado, 1956.

2440
Hodgson, Ernest Daniel. "The Nature and Purpose of the Public School in Northwest Territories (1885-1905) and Alberta (1905-1963)." Alberta, 1964.

2441
Patterson, Robert Steven. "The Establishment of Progressive Education in Alberta." Michigan State, 1968.

2442
Reeves, Arthur W. "The Equalization of Educational Opportunity in the Province of Alberta." Stanford, 1949.

2443
Sayers, Graham Frederick. "Educational Policy Formation within the County System of Alberta: A Study of Influence." Calgary, 1981.

2444
Sheehan, Nancy Mary. "Temperance, the WCTU, and Education in Alberta, 1905-1930." Alberta, 1980.

2445
Sparby, Harry Theodore A. "A History of the Alberta School System to 1925." Stanford, 1958.

2446
Walker, Bernal Ernest. "Public Secondary Education in Alberta: Organization and Curriculum, 1889-1951." Stanford, 1955.

2447
Wolfe, Norbert. "A Case Study of the Historical and Contemporary Events and Forces Leading to the Establishment of a Fourth Category of Private Schools in Alberta." Calgary, 1980.

2448
Barman, Jean. "Growing Up British in British Columbia: Boys in Private School, 1900-1950." British Columbia, 1982.

2449
Gross, Carl Henry. "Education in British Columbia, with Particular Consideration of the Natural and Social Factors." Ohio State, 1939.

2450
Hindle, George. "The Educational System of British Columbia." Toronto, 1918.

2451
Jones, David Charles. "Agriculture: The Land and Education: British Columbia, 1914-1929." British Columbia, 1978.

2452
MacLaurin, Donald L. "The History of Education in the Crown Colonies of Vancouver Island and British Columbia and in the Province of British Columbia." Washington, Seattle, 1936.

2453
Peters, Mary Alice. "A Study of Recent Developments in Secondary Education in British Columbia, 1957-1967." Leeds, 1968.

2454
Sharpe, Robert Friend. "An Objective Study of the Junior High School in Vancouver." Toronto, 1940.

2455
Wormsbecker, John Henry. "The Development of Secondary Education in Vancouver." Toronto, 1961.

Manitoba

2456
Crunican, Paul Eugene. "The Manitoba School Question and Canadian Federal Politics, 1890-1896: A Study in Church-State Relations." Toronto, 1968.

2457
Glinz, Leslie Albert. "The Development of Public Secondary Education in Manitoba." Stanford, 1931.

2458
Rusak, Stephen Thaddeus. "Archbishop Adelard Langevin and the Manitoba School Question, 1895-1915." Alberta, 1975.

2459
Sherrill, Peter Thomas. "The Imperial Factor in the Manitoba School Question." Vanderbilt, 1970.

2460
Van Camp, Keven Robert. "A History of the Frontier School Division with Emphasis on Centralization and Decentralization in the Organization and Administration of the Division." Manitoba, 1981.

2461
Wilson, Keith. "The Development of Education in Manitoba." Michigan State, 1967.

Maritime Provinces/Provinces maritimes

General Items/Ouvrages généraux

2462
Netten, John Wilfred. "The Influence of the Anglican Church in the Development of Education in the Maritime Provinces from 1727 to 1900." Toronto, 1969.

New Brunswick/Nouveau-Brunswick

2463
Anderson, Amos McIntyre. "The History of Elementary Education in the Province of New Brunswick." New York, 1941.

2464
Fitch, James Harold. "A Century of Educational Progress in New Brunswick, 1800-1900." Toronto, 1930.

2465
Hody, Maud Hazel. "The Development of the Bilingual Schools of New Brunswick." Toronto, 1964.

McCready, Douglas Jackson. See No./Voir no 1325

Newfoundland/Terre-Neuve

2466
Barnes, Arthur. "The History of Education in Newfoundland." New York, 1917.

2467
Bruce, Mary Jane (Sister Mary Teresina). "An Historical Study of Family, Church and State Relations in Newfoundland Education." Ottawa, 1963.

2468
Burke, Vincent P. "History of Catholic Education, Newfoundland, the Oldest British Colony." Ottawa, 1914.

2469
Cramm, Frank. "A Historical Examination of Educational Change in Newfoundland, 1949-1969." Boston University, 1981.

2470
Rowe, Frederick William. "The History of Education in Newfoundland." Toronto, 1951.

Nova Scotia/Nouvelle-Écosse

2471
Davis, David Gray. "Reorganization of Secondary Education in Nova Scotia." Harvard, 1927.

2472
Hamilton, William Baillie. "Education, Politics and Reform in Nova Scotia, 1800-1848." Western Ontario, 1970.

2473
Thibeau, Patrick Wilfred. "Education in Nova Scotia Before 1811." Catholic, 1921.

2474
Verma, Dhirendra. "Technical-Vocational Education in Nova Scotia within the Context of Social, Economic and Political Change, 1880-1975." Atlantic Institute of Education, 1978.

Prince Edward Island/Île-du-Prince-Édouard

2475
McGuigan, Derrill Ignatius. "The Historical Antecedents of the Free School Act and the Public School Act of Prince Edward Island." Ottawa, 1956.

Northwest Territories/Territoires du Nord-Ouest

Hodgson, Ernest Daniel. See No./Voir no 2440

2476
McLeod, Keith Alwyn. "Education and the Assimilation of the New Canadians in the Northwest Territories and Saskatchewan, 1885-1934." Toronto, 1975.

2477
Toombs, Morley Preston. "The Control and Support of Public Education in Rupert's Land and the Northwest Territories to 1905 and Saskatchewan to 1960." Minnesota, 1962.

Ontario

2478
Abbott, John Robin. "Educational Policy Formation and Implementation on the Ontario Primary Resource Frontier: The Case of the District of Algoma, 1903-1922." Toronto, 1983.

2479
Althouse, John George. "The Ontario Teacher: An Historical Sketch of Progress, 1800-1910." Toronto, 1929.

2480
Arend, Sylvie Marie Jacqueline. "Of Mosaics and Colonial Men: Elite and Education in Ontario and Quebec, 1910-1913." York, 1982.

2481
Bannister, John Arthur. "Early Educational History of the County of Norfolk." Toronto, 1926.

2482
Bella, Walter Nehemiah. "The Development of the Ontario High School." Toronto, 1918.

2483
Coleman, Herbert Thomas John. "Public Education in Upper Canada (Ontario), with Special Reference to the Period Between 1791 and 1841." Teachers College, Columbia, 1907.

2484
Corbett, Barbara Elizabeth. "The Public School Kindergarten in Ontario, 1883 to 1967." Toronto, 1969.

2485
Curtis, Bruce Malcolm. "The Political Economy of Elementary Educational Development: Comparative Perspectives on State Schooling in Upper Canada." Toronto, 1981. [Elementary education development up to 1850/Développement de l'enseignement primaire depuis 1850]

2486
Davey, Ian Elliott. "Educational Reform and the Working Class: School Attendance in Hamilton, Ontario, 1851-1891." Toronto, 1975.

2487
Dixon, Robert Thomas. "The Ontario Separate School System and Section 93 of the 'BNA' Act." Toronto, 1976.

2488
Downes, Walter. "The Effect of British Colonial Policy on Public Educational Institutions in Upper Canada, 1784-1840." Ottawa, 1974.

2489
Easson, McGregor. "The Intermediate School in Ottawa." Toronto, 1934.

2490
Gaffield, Charles Mitchell. "Cultural Challenge in Eastern Ontario: Land, Family and Education in the Nineteenth Century." Toronto, 1979.

2491
Godbout, Arthur J.E. "Les francophones du Haut-Canada et leurs écoles avant l'acte de l'union." Ottawa, 1969.

2492
Graff, Harvey Jay. "Literacy and Social Structure in the Nineteenth Century City." Toronto, 1975.

2493
Hackett, Gerald Thomas. "The History of Public Education for Mentally Retarded Children in the Province of Ontario, 1867-1964." Toronto, 1969.

2494
Hardy, John Howard. "Teachers' Organizations in Ontario: An Historical Account of Their Part in Ontario Educational Development, and Their Influence on the Teacher and Teaching 1840-1938." Toronto, 1939.

2495
Hardy, John Stewart. "Training Third Class Teachers: A Study of the Ontario County Model School System, 1877-1907." Toronto, 1981.

2496
High, Norman Hervey. "A Study of Educational Opportunity in the Provincially Controlled Schools of Haldimand County, Ontario." Cornell, 1950.

2497
Jain, Geneviève Laloux. "Canadian History Textbooks and Nationalism in Ontario and Quebec 1867-1914." McGill, 1970.

2498
Ketchum, John Anthony Cheyne. "'The Most Perfect System': Official Policy in the First Century of Ontario's Government Secondary Schools and Its Impact on Students Between 1871 and 1910." Toronto, 1979.

2499
Love, James Hume. "Social Stress and Education Reform in Mid-Nineteenth Century Upper Canada." Toronto, 1978.

2500
MacDonald, Peter Ian. "The Transformation of a Pre-Capitalist Educational Formation: The Development of Education in Nineteenth Century Ontario." Toronto, 1980.

2501
MacDougall, James Brown. "Building the North (New Ontario)." Toronto, 1919.

2502
Mark, Clarence Ellsworth. "The Public Schools of Ottawa: A Survey." Toronto, 1919.

2503
Matthews, William David Edison. "The History of th Religious Factor in Ontario Elementary Education." Toronto, 1950.

2504
McDonald, Neil Gerard. "Forming the Nationa Character: Political Socialization in Ontari Schools, 1867-1914." Toronto, 1980.

McMillan, George. See No./Voir no 4102

2505
Miller, Albert Herman. "The Theory and Practice o Education in Ontario in the 1860's." Britis Columbia, 1968.

2506
Moorcraft, K. "Character Builders: Women an Education in Whitby, Ontario, 1900 to 1920. Toronto, 1983.

Morrow, Leslie Donald. See No./Voir no 2635

2507
Moynes, Riley Elgin. "Teachers and Pteranodons: Th Origins and Development of the Education Depart ment of the Royal Ontario Museum (1914-1974). Toronto, 1978.

2508
O'Driscoll, Denis Christopher. "Ontario Attitude Towards American and British Education, 1792 1950: A Comparative Study of Internationa Images." Michigan, 1974.

2509
Prentice, Alison Leeds. "The School Promoters: Edu cation and Social Class in Mid-Nineteenth Centur Upper Canada." Toronto, 1974.

2510
Robinson, George Carlton. "A Historical and Critica Account of Public Secondary Education in th Province of Ontario, 1792-1916." Harvard, 1918.

2511
Spence, Ruth Elizabeth. "Education as Growth, It Significance for the Secondary Schools of Ontario. Teachers College, Columbia, 1925.

2512
Stamp, Robert Miles. "The Campaign for Technica Education in Ontario, 1876-1914." Wester Ontario, 1970.

2513
Waide, Frederick Gordon. "A History of Primar Education in Ontario and Quebec." New York 1912.

2514
Wilson, John Donald. "Foreign and Local Influences o Popular Education in Upper Canada, 1815-1844. Western Ontario, 1971.

Winzer, Margaret Ann. See No./Voir no 2647

Quebec/Québec

Arend, Sylvie Marie Jacqueline. See No./Voir no 2480

2515
Audet, Louis Phillippe. "Le système scolaire de l province de Québec, tome III; l'institution royale ses débuts: 1800-1825." Laval, 1953.

Blum, William D. See No./Voir no 2408

Boland, Francis J. See No./Voir no 3553

2516
Bounadère, René. "Justification historique des petits séminaires de la province de Québec." Laval, 1945.

2517
Bousquet, Marie-Elizabeth. "Les maîtres de Québec: leur valeur et leur formation, 1608-1858." Montréal, 1970.

2518
Burgess, Donald Arthur. "Education and Social Change: A Quebec Case Study." Harvard, 1978. [New France to the present/De la Nouvelle-France à aujourd'hui]

2519
Charland, Jean-Pierre. "L'enseignement spécialisé au Québec, 1867 à 1965." Laval, 1982.

2520
Cook, Harold Sterling. "Improving Educational Opportunity for Quebec Youth." Teachers College, Columbia, 1951.

2521
Croteau, Georges. "Les frères éducateurs au service de la promotion des étudiants dans l'enseignement public au Québec, 1920 à 1960." Ottawa, 1971.

2522
Désilets, Jean-Paul (Frère Donatien-Marie). "L'évolution des structures de la jeunesse étudiante catholique canadienne de 1935 à 1961." Ottawa, 1962.

2523
Drolet, Jean-Yves. "A Study of the Impact of Demographic and Socio-Economic Factors on School Attendance Rates in the Province of Quebec from 1901 to 1959." Alberta, 1961.

2524
Dubé, Clairette. "Évolution des politiques de perfectionnement du personnel enseignant français de la C.E.C.M. de 1964 à 1970, d'après les documents officiels." Montréal, 1979.

2525
Finley, Eric Gault. "The Bi-Religious Basis of Quebec's Public School System: Its Origins and Subsequent Development." Teachers College, Columbia, 1960.

2526
Fleurent, Maurice. "L'éducation morale au petit séminaire de Québec 1668-1857." Laval, 1977.

2527
Goyette, Gabriel. "L'idéologie scolaire proposée par une reine pédagogique québécoise, 1927-1964." Ottawa, 1971.

2528
Groulx, Abbé Lionel. "L'enseignement français dans le Québec." Montréal, 1932.

2529
Hunte, Keith Donnerson. "The Ministry of Public Instruction in Quebec, 1867-1875: A Historical Study." McGill, 1965.

Jain, Geneviève Laloux. See No./Voir no 2497

2530
Labarrère-Paule, André. "Les instituteurs et les institutrices laï'ques catholiques au Canada français (1836-1900)." Laval, 1961.

Lambert, Pierre D. See No./Voir no 2413

2531
Lamonde, Yvan. "L'enseignement de la philosophie au Québec, 1665-1920." Laval, 1978.

2532
Laville, Christian. "Conception réalisation et expérimentation d'un cours de formation historique et sociale de travailleurs adultes: histoire du Québec d'aujourd'hui." Carnegie Mellon, 1980.

2533
Lessard, Victrice. "L'instruction obligatoire dans la province de Québec, de 1875 à 1943." Ottawa, 1962.

2534
Létourneau, Jeannette. "Les écoles normales de jeunes filles au Québec (1836-1974)." Ottawa, 1979.

Levine, Marc Veblen. See No./Voir no 2793

2535
Majerus, Yvette V. "L'éducation dans le diocèse de Montréal d'après la correspondence de ses deux premiers évêques, Mgr J.J. Lartigue et Mgr I. Bourget, de 1820 à 1867." McGill, 1971.

2536
Matthews, Barbara Lee. "The Growth of Disagreement Among Teachers over the Dual School System in the Province of Quebec." Michigan, 1973.

2537
Plante, Lucienne. "L'enseignement classique à la congrégation de Notre-Dame 1908-1971." Laval, 1971.

2538
Stringer, Guy. "Évolution de l'autonomie des commissaires d'écoles de la province de Québec de 1846 à 1967." Ottawa, 1969.

2539
Thivierge, Nicole. "L'enseignement ménager - familial au Québec, 1880-1970." Laval, 1982.

2540
Thwaites, James Douglas. "The Origins and the Development of the 'Fédération des commissions scolaires catholiques du Québec,' 1936-1967." Laval, 1976.

Touchette, Claude René. See No./Voir no 4095
Waide, Frederick Gordon. See No./Voir no 2513

Saskatchewan

Blenkinsop, Padraig John. See No./Voir no 4096

2541
Denny, James Davidson. "The Organization of Public Education in Saskatchewan." Toronto, 1930.

2542
Foght, Harold Waldstein. "A Study of Education in Saskatchewan." American, 1918.

2543
Gadzella, Bernadette M. "The Growth and Development of the Large School Administrative Units in Saskatchewan (1905-1960)." Ottawa, 1960.

2544
Langley, Gerald James. "Saskatchewan's Separate School System: A Study of One Pattern of Adjustment to the Problem of Education in a Multi-Religion Democratic Society." Columbia, 1950.

2545
McKague, Ormond Knight. "Socialist Education in Saskatchewan, 1942-1948: A Study in Ideology and Bureaucracy." Oregon, 1981. [Educational policies of the C.C.F./Politique dans l'enseignement de la C.C.F.]

McLeod, Keith Alwyn. See No./Voir no 2476

Toombs, Morley Preston. See No./Voir no 2477

2546
Wiggin, Gladys A. "A History of Elementary and Secondary Schools in Saskatchewan." Maryland, 1947.

See also History of Curriculum. History of Higher Education. History of Religious Education/Voir aussi Histoire du plan d'étude. Histoire de l'enseignement supérieur. Histoire de l'enseignement religieux.

Canadian Educators/Enseignants canadiens

2547
Carlton, Sylvia. "Egerton Ryerson and Education in Ontario, 1844-1877." Pennsylvania, 1950.

2548
Carter, Bruce Northleigh. "James L. Hughes and the Gospel of Education: A Study of the Work and Thought of a Nineteenth Century Canadian Educator." Toronto, 1967.

Cook, Terry Gordon. See No./Voir no 7372

2549
Dhillon, Pritam Singh. "The Educational Thought of J.G. Althouse." Toronto, 1970.

2550
Fiorino, Albert Francis. "The Philosophical Roots of Egerton Ryerson's Idea of Education as Elaborated in His Writings Preceding and Including the Report of 1846." Toronto, 1975.

2551
Homel, Gene Howard. "James Simpson and the Origins of Canadian Social Democracy." Toronto, 1978.

2552
Malloy, Brenda Margaret. "Henry Foss Hall, A Canadian Educator, 1897-1971: The Interaction Between a Man and a Developing Institution." Florida State, 1975.

2553
Near, Hubert L. "The Educational Theories of Stephen Leacock." George Peabody, 1963.

2554
Norman, Jane Margaret. "Loran Arthur de Wolfe and Rural Educational Reform in Nova Scotia." Calgary, 1970.

2555
Purdy, Judson Douglas. "John Strachan and Education in Canada, 1800-1851." Toronto, 1962.

Regan, Ross H. See No./Voir no 2703

Rusak, Stephen Thaddeus. See No./Voir no 2458

Segin, J.J. See No./Voir no 2695

2556
Thomson, Colin Argyle. "W.P. Oliver, Black Educator." Alberta, 1972.

2557
Wood, Anne. "John Harold Putman and the Roots of Progressive Education in the Ottawa Public Schools, 1911-1923." Ottawa, 1973.

EDUCATIONAL PHILOSOPHY/ PHILOSOPHIE ÉDUCATIVE

Atkinson, Donald Robert. See No./Voir no 10110

Carter, Bruce N. See No./Voir no 2548

Dhillon, Pritam Singh. See No./Voir no 2549

Dupuis, Jean Claude. See No./Voir no 2054

Fiorino, Albert Francis. See No./Voir no 2550

2558
Giroux, Aline. "Étude des fondements philosophiques de valeurs humaines. Programme d'éducation morale." Ottawa, 1983.

McKague, Ormond Knight. See No./Voir no 2545

Near, Hubert L. See No./Voir no 2553

Poupard, Danielle. See No./Voir no 4441

EDUCATION THEORY AND PRACTICE/ THÉORIE ET PRATIQUE EN ENSEIGNEMENT

General Items/Ouvrages généraux

2559
Anderson, Barry Douglas. "Bureaucratization and Student Alienation from School." Toronto, 1970.

2560
Bachor, Patricia Angelica Cranton. "The Interaction of Learner Characteristics and Degree of Learner Control in CAI." Toronto, 1976.

2561
Bancroft, George Winston. "Occupational Status, Mobility and Educational Achievement of 572 Males in Southern Ontario." Toronto, 1961.

Bizier, Jeanne. See No./Voir no 2420

2562
Bledsoe, James Barry. "The Autobiography of Inquiry: Reflexive Comparisons Between Children's Culture and the Culture of Science." Toronto, 1979.

2563
Brophy, Beverly Isabel. "Semestering and the Teaching Learning Situation." Toronto, 1975. [Secondary education/Enseignement secondaire]

2564
Bunn, Helen H. "The Relationship Between Helper Set Type and Ability to Communicate Facilitative Conditions." Ottawa, 1978.

2565
Case, Robert Thomas. "Information Processing, Social Class, and Instruction: A Developmental Investigation." Toronto, 1971.

2566
Cooper, Deborah L. "Fact Inference Distinction Training: A Method for Developing Alternative Conclusions in Grade 4 and Grade 6 Children." Toronto, 1976.

Creed, Philip John. See No./Voir no 2679

Datey, Blaise. See No./Voir no 2971

2567
De Angelo, Rosalind Frances. "A Test of Congruence of Aspects of Jurgen Habermas' Theory of Legitimation Crisis with Recent Developments in Education in the Province of Ontario, Canada." SUNY, Buffalo, 1978.

2568
Gehlbach, Roger Dale. "Verbal Correlates of Instructional Effectiveness with Young Children." Toronto, 1974.

Graham, Evelyn Elizabeth. See No./Voir no 3297

Greenglass, David Irwin. See No./Voir no 4064

2569
Hardy, Timothy Ashley. "Teacher-Student Dyadic Relationships in the Elementary Classroom: A Participant Observation Study." Toronto, 1974.

Henninger, Polly Johnson. See No./Voir no 9442

Hewitt, Jean Dorothy. See No./Voir no 2991

2570
Jomphe, Gérald E. "Vers une théorie de l'interaction individuelle et sociale, et essai descriptif de l'action individuelle au sein d'une institution universitaire." Ottawa, 1972.

Kansky, Robert James. See No./Voir no 3162

2571
Larin, Gilles. "L'approche 'Learners Verification and Revision' appliquée au matériel d'enseignement formel en cinquième année." Montréal, 1982.

2572
Larose, Réal. "Recherche évaluative sur l'élaboration de projets éducatifs." Montréal, 1976.

2573
Larter, Sylvia Joan. "The Measurement and Comparison of Small Group Skills and Sociability in Schools Differing in Program and Architectural Openness." Toronto, 1977.

2574
Laver, Alfred Bryan. "The Effects of Drive Task Difficulty and Orienting Procedure on Incidental Learning." Ottawa, 1962.

2575
Lavigne, J. Albert C. "An Empirical Investigation of the Effects on Learning and Retention of a Multiple Channel Presentation of an Advance Organizer." Montréal, 1981.

2576
Leblanc, Simone. "Évaluation des effets d'une application de la théorie de De Charms sur l'apprentissage du français chez un groupe d'élèves acadiens." Montréal, 1982.

2577
Marjoribanks, Kevin McLeod. "Ethnic and Environmental Influences on Levels and Profiles of Mental Abilities." Toronto, 1970.

Marshall, David George. See No./Voir no 2665

Matheson, Helen. See No./Voir no 2666

Mays, Annabelle M.M. See No./Voir no 3505

2578
McCatty, Cressy Alexander Mayo. "Patterns of Learning Projects Among Professional Men." Toronto, 1973.

2579
Meskill, Michael Francis. "Holistic Educational Theory in Vico, Joyce, and McLuhan Applied to American Higher Education." Claremont, 1979.

2580
Mock, Karen Rochelle. "The Relationship of Audiovisual Attention Factors and Reading Ability to Children's Television Viewing Strategies." Toronto, 1975.

2581
Munro, Barry. "Meaning and Learning." Alberta, 1959.

2582
Parducci, Ronald Edmond. "The Psychosocial Stressors Affecting the Aged's Phenomenological Self as Studied Through the Self-Report Relative to Learning." Toronto, 1978.

2583
Parrott, Eric George. "The Relation of Cognitive Abilities, Stimulus Variation, and Instructions to Concept Identification." Toronto, 1975.

2584
Penta, Gerard Charles. "Marshall McLuhan and Educational Theory: An Inquiry into the Epistemological and Aesthetic Foundations of Learning Style." Michigan State, 1974.

2585
Pratt, David. "An Instrument for Measuring Evaluative Assertions Concerning Minority Groups and Its Application in an Analysis of History Textbooks Approved for Ontario Schools." Toronto, 1969.

2586
Racette, Geneviève. "Une pédagogie nouvelle pour favoriser l'apprentissage de la démarche historique chez l'élève du secondaire II." Montréal, 1977.

2587
Rauf, Abdur. "A Study of Objective Social Classes and Their Expectations Towards Personal and Societal Futures." Toronto, 1979. [Ontario]

2588
Rix, Marion Elizabeth Ann Hill. "Understanding Changing Promotion Criteria Through Understanding Personal Contructs." Toronto, 1980.

2589
Runge, Janis Margaret. "Progressive Educational Reform in Comparative Perspective." Toronto, 1979.

2590
Sackett, Leroy Walter. "The Canadian Porcupine: A Study of the Learning Process." Clark, 1910.

2591
Tremblay, Jean. "L'expérience québécoise en éducation sexuelle, à la lumière d'expériences étrangères." Montréal, 1980.

2592
Wilensky, Marshall Shimon. "Theory-Practice Incongruence in an Alternative Secondary School." Toronto, 1979.

2593
Zuk, William Michael. "A Comparative Study of Graphic Modes of Conceptualization of Indian, Métis and White Students." Oregon, 1973. [Manitoba]

Teaching Methods in Subject Areas/
Méthodes d'enseignement par sujets

Mathematics/Mathématiques

2594
Colette, Jean-Paul. "L'histoire des mathématiques dans l'enseignement des mathématiques: historique de la gestion et attitude des professeurs des collèges québécois francophones." Montréal, 1974.

2595
Lukasevich, Ann. "A Study of Relationships Among Instructional Style (Open vs. Non-Open), Architectural Design (Open Space vs. Non-Open Space) and Measures of Self Concept and Reading and Mathematics Achievement of Third Grade Children." British Columbia, 1976.

2596
Pallascio, Richard. "Étude de l'évolution des interactions élèves-professeurs reliée à l'implantation d'un nouveau modèle de perfectionnement en enseignement des mathématiques." Montréal, 1979.

Music/Musique

Mills, Isabelle M. See No./Voir no 1001

Nursing Sciences/Sciences infirmières

Glass, Helen Preston. See No./Voir no 6890

Physical Education/Éducation physique

Leblanc, Hughes. See No./Voir no 10416

Reading/Lecture

Janes, Ethel Mary. See No./Voir no 3963
Koerber, Walter Frederick. See No./Voir no 3996

Science

2597
Green, Edgar D., Jr. "An Assessment of the Influence of an Elementary School Science Teaching Methods Course and Instructor in the Science Classroom Role Concept of Prospective Elementary School Teachers." Florida State, 1972.

Social Studies/Sciences sociales

2598
Piscione, Joseph Anthony. "A Field Evaluation of Social Problem Solving Training with Junior High School Aged Children." Toronto, 1981.
Pratt, David. See No./Voir no 2585

2599
Roberts, Albert Henry. "A Study of the Methods and Techniques Used by Elementary Teachers in the Province of Newfoundland and Labrador, Canada, in Their Teaching of Social Studies." Indiana, 1970.

Curriculum Development, Implementation and Program Evaluation/ Plan d'étude, application et évaluation du programme

General Items/Ouvrages généraux

2600
Dukacz, A.S. "In-Service as a Vehicle for Curriculum Implementation: A Comparison of Two Models." Toronto, 1983.
Frankcombe, Brian James. See No./Voir no 3180

2601
Goulet, Georges. "Analyse comparative des note attribuées au curriculum par un groupe d'auteu choisis et ébauche d'une théorie générale Ottawa, 1976.

2602
Hathaway, Warren Elkanah. "A Feasibility Study the Network-Based Approach to Curriculum Deve opment." Alberta, 1974.

2603
Higgins, John Michael. "A Determination of Soci Science Generalizations Basic to the Social Studi Curriculum, Organizing and Governing in Canada Toronto, 1968.

2604
Jeffares, David. "A Descriptive Study of Teach Decisions in Curriculum Development." Albert 1973.

2605
McPherson, Alfred Angus Murray. "An Analysis Selected Perceptions of Curriculum Developme as Expressed by Pupils and Instructional Personn in Manitoba." Michigan State, 1975.

2606
Miller, Thomas William. "An Analysis of Teach Participation in Curriculum Development for Pr ject Canada West." Saskatchewan, 1972. [El mentary and secondary education/Enregistreme au primaire et au secondaire]

2607
Oberg, Antoinette Alexander. "Information Referen and Patterns in the Curriculum Planning of Clas room Teachers." Alberta, 1975.

2608
Ohan, Farid Emil. "Moral Education: Its Possibility the Schools." Toronto, 1976.

2609
Orpwood, Graham W.F. "The Logic of Curriculu Policy Deliberation: An Analytical Study fro Science Education." Toronto, 1982.
Oviatt, Delmer T. See No./Voir no 3112

2610
Podrebarac, George R. "Practitioners' Perceptions Curriculum Implementation." Toronto, 19 [Ontario elementary schools/Écoles primaires Ontario]

2611
Pylypiw, James Alexander. "A Description of Clas room Curriculum Development." Alberta, 1974.

2612
Warren, Wendy Kaye. "A Conceptual Framework f Examining Learning Group Discourse in Relation Phase of Activity." Toronto, 1982. [Gra eleven/Onzième année]

2613
White, Ivan Floyd. "Development of Procedures f Planned Curriculum Change." Toronto, 1981. [keeping with the objectives of the current Ontar Ministry of Education guidelines/Conforméme aux objectives des directrices courantes du mini tère de l'Éducation de l'Ontario]

2614
White, William Gar. "Toward an Analytical Model f the Evaluation of Curriculum Guidelines." Ottaw 1982.

2615

Winter, Carol Florence. "Conceptualizing the Practice of Educational Consultancy from the Perspective of Curriculum and Instruction." Toronto, 1979.

2616

Woodburn, Robert Harrison. "The Development of a Leisure Education Resource Book for Teachers of Grade K-13 in the Province of Ontario." Northern Colorado, 1977.

2617

Wright, Ruth Lynne. "A Contextual Model of Curriculum Implementation." Ottawa, 1982.

History of Curriculum and Instruction/ Histoire du plan d'étude et enseignement

General Items/Ouvrages généraux

2618

Green, George Henry Ebenezer. "The Development of Curriculum in the Secondary Schools of British Columbia." Toronto, 1944.

2619

Larson, Vernon Carl. "A Survey of Short-Course Programs in the United States and Canada." Michigan State, 1955.

2620

Sheane, George Kennedy. "The History and Development of the Curriculum of the Elementary School in Alberta." Toronto, 1948.

Art

2621

Tait, George Edward. "A History of Art Education in the Elementary Schools of Ontario." Toronto, 1957.

Biology/Biologie

2622

Taylor, Stanley James. "An Account of the Changes in Biology Education in Ontario High Schools (1871-1978)." British Columbia, 1981.

English and Literature/Anglais et littérature

2623

Phillips, Charles Edward. "The History of Teaching English in Ontario, 1800-1900." Toronto, 1935.

2624

Schloss, Brigitte. "The Uneasy Status of Literature in Second Language Teaching at the School Level: A Historical Perspective." Toronto, 1980.

French/Français

2625

Comeau, Joseph Edward. "L'enseignement du français dans les écoles publiques de la Nouvelle-Écosse depuis 1900." Montréal, 1949.

Geography/Géographie

2626

Quick, Edison. "The Development of Geography and History Curriculum in the Elementary Schools of Ontario, 1846-1966." Toronto, 1967.

History/Histoire

Quick, Edison. See No./Voir no 2626

Home Economics/Économie domestique

2627

Chaput, Jeanne S. "L'évolution de l'enseignement des sciences familiales dans le contexte social et éducatif du Québec." Ottawa, 1968.

2628

Rowles, Edith. "A Brief History of Some Early Canadian Developments in Home Economics." Teachers College, Columbia, 1957.

Mathematics/Mathématiques

2629

Allen, Harold Don. "The Teaching of Trigonometry in the United States and Canada: A Consideration of Elementary Course Content and Approach and Factors Influencing Change, 1890-1970." Rutgers, 1977.

2630

Gray, William Barrisdale. "The Teaching of Mathematics in Ontario, 1800-1941." Toronto, 1948.

2631

Partlow, Hugh Russell. "A Comparison of St. Catherine's Public School Standards in Arithmetic and Reading, 1933-1938 and 1952-1954." Toronto, 1955.

2632

Weinstein, Pauline Smith. "An Analysis of Methodology in the Teaching of Arithmetic Concepts as Reflected in Textbooks Used in Canadian Schools Prior to 1890." Oregon, 1973.

Modern Languages/Langues modernes

2633

Goldstick, Isidore. "Modern Languages in the Ontario High School: A Historical Study." Toronto, 1928.

Music/Musique

2634

Spell, Lota M.H. "Musical Education in North America During the Sixteenth and Seventeenth Centuries." Texas, 1923.

Trowsdale, George Campbell. See No./Voir no 1006

Physical Education/Éducation physique

2635

Morrow, Leslie Donald. "Selected Topics in the History of Physical Education in Ontario: From Dr. Egerton Ryerson to the Strathcona Trust 1844-1939." Alberta, 1975.

Science

2636
Croal, Albert George. "The History of the Teaching of Science in Ontario, 1800-1900." Toronto, 1940.

2637
Engel, Barney. "The Science Curriculum in the Public Schools of Manitoba, Canada, 1890-1961." Chicago, 1964.

2638
Gough, Ruby Louise. "An Historical Study of Science Education in Newfoundland." Boston University, 1973.

Social Studies/Sciences sociales

Dhand, Hargopal. See No./Voir no 3179

Technical and Vocational Subjects/ Sujets techniques et professionnels

2639
Bryce, Robert Curry. "The Technical and Vocational Training Assistance Act of 1961-67: An Historical Survey and Documentary Analysis." Alberta, 1971.

2640
Grywalski, Stanley. "A History of Technical - Vocational Education in the Secondary Schools of Alberta, 1900-1969." Oregon, 1973.

Special Education/Enseignement spécialisé

2641
Borthwick, Burton Lloyd. "Auxiliary Education for Orthopaedically Handicapped Students, 1911-1974." Ottawa, 1979.

2642
Drewe, Fred Harold. "A Comparative Survey of the Provision of Public Education for Slow-Learning and Mentally Handicapped Children in North Dakota and Manitoba from 1900 to 1940." Michigan State, 1976.

Hackett, Gerald Thomas. See No./Voir no 2493

2643
Johnston, Marion Campbell. "The Development of Special Class Programmes for Gifted Children in the Elementary Schools of Ontario from 1910 to 1962." Toronto, 1964.

2644
Levesque, Denis R. "Évolution des services à l'enfance exceptionnelle dans les écoles séparées françaises d'Ottawa, 1934-1973." Ottawa, 1975.

2645
MacDonald, Donald D. "Sight-Saving Classes in the Public Schools." Toronto, 1923.

2646
Radcliffe, Samuel John. "Retardation in the Schools of Ontario." Toronto, 1922.

2647
Winzer, Margaret Ann. "An Examination of Some Selected Factors That Affected the Education and Socialization of the Deaf in Ontario, 1870-1900." Toronto, 1982.

Curriculum of Early Childhood and Elementary Education/ Plan d'étude au niveau de la maternelle et de l'enseignement primaire

See also Curriculum Development and Instruction/Voi aussi Plan d'étude et enseignement

Curriculum of Secondary Schools and Education of Youth/ Plan d'étude au niveau secondaire et enseignement de la jeunesse

See also Curriculum Development and Instruction/Voi aussi Plan d'étude et enseignement

Curriculum of Higher Education/ Plan d'étude au niveau de l'enseignement supérieur

See also Curriculum Development and Education/Vo aussi Plan d'étude et enseignement

Curriculum for the Education and Rehabilitation of the Exceptional/Plan d'étude en enseignement et réhabilitation

See also Curriculum Development and Education/Vo aussi Plan d'étude et enseignement

Curriculum for Reading/Plan d'étude en lecture

See also Curriculum Development and Education/Vo aussi Plan d'étude et enseignement

Curriculum for Physical Education/ Plan d'étude en éducation physique

See also Curriculum Development and Education/Vo aussi Plan d'étude et enseignement.

ADMINISTRATION

General Items/Ouvrages généraux

2648
Adams, William Arthur. "Communication Patterns i Formal Organizations." Alberta, 1973.

2649
Bailey, C.L. "The Beginnings of Organized Educational Administration in the Empire." London 1933.

2650
Berghofer, Desmond Edward. "The Futures Perspective in Educational Policy Development." Alberta 1972.

2651
Bird, A.C. "A Practicum Associate: An Ethnographi Account." Alberta, 1982.

2652
Boswell, David M. "A Study of the Recently Established Provincial Government Youth Department and Agencies in Seven Provinces of Canada Brigham Young, 1971.

2653
Chapman, Robin James. "Regionalization of the Administration of Public Education in Canada." Alberta, 1974.

Cheal, John Ernest. See No./Voir no 2409

2654
Colvin, Alfred Cephus. "Federal-Provincial Manpower Policies and Mechanisms Used in Their Implementation." Alberta, 1975.

2655
Daignault, Jacques. "Prolégonènes à toute pédagogie future qui pourra se présenter comme art véritable." Laval, 1983.

2656
Fortin, Donald. "Fondement des attitudes à l'égard d'une action visant à faire participer davantage les enseignants à la prise de décision." Montréal, 1976.

2657
Fortin, Paul Arthur. "Le processus décisionnel et le comportement d'achat des organisations. Une application du choix des sites de congrès par des associations nord-américaines." Laval, 1976.

2658
Gélinas, Arthur. "A Systems Conceptual Model of Special Education Administration." Alberta, 1978.

2659
Hill Rix, Marion Elizabeth Ann. "Understanding Changing Promotion Criteria Through Understanding." Toronto, 1980.

2660
Hurlbert, Earl Leroy. "Conflict Management in Schools." Alberta, 1973.

2661
Husby, Philip James. "The Relationship Between Education and Earnings Among the Canadian Provinces." Alberta, 1969.

2662
Hyde, William Paul. "The Use of Small Groups for Identifying Problems in a Formal Organization." British Columbia, 1977.

Levin, Benjamin Ruvin. See No./Voir no 1941

2663
MacKillican, William S. "An Empirical Study of the Relationship Between School Management Patterns and the Change Toward Classroom Openness." Ottawa, 1976.

2664
March, Milton Edgar. "Variations in Degree of Control over Educational Decisions." Alberta, 1981. [Four western provinces/Quatre provinces de l'Ouest]

2665
Marshall, David George. "Project Leader Developmental Ethnocentricity, Position Power, and Perceptions of Development Project Effectiveness." Alberta, 1980.

2666
Matheson, Helen. "Information Seeking Behaviors and Attitude to Information Among Educational Practitioners." British Columbia, 1979. [British Columbia/Colombie-Britannique]

McCallum, Mary Aletha. See No./Voir no 4354

2667
Miller, James Collins. "Rural Schools in Canada: Their Organization, Administration and Supervision." Teachers College, Columbia, 1913.

2668
Montgometrie, Thomas Craig. "Instructional Department Computer Support Systems: A Strategy and an Implementation." Alberta, 1981.

2669
Mullin, D.D. "Perceptions of Consultative Services Held by Teachers, Principals, Consultants and Superintendents." Toronto, 1983.

Onuoha, Alphonse R.A. See No./Voir no 6809

2670
Poirier, Yves. "Une analyse de facteurs administratifs au moyen d'une étude comparative des perceptions de ces facteurs par quinze théoriciens de l'organisation et de l'administration scolaire." Ottawa, 1971.

2671
Richardson, William Leeds. "The Administration of Schools in the Cities of the Dominion of Canada." Chicago, 1919.

2672
Ricker, Harold Owen. "A Consideration of Some Administrative and Planning Implications of Gradeless Schools." Waterloo, 1979.

2673
Schneider, Louis Francis. "A Study of the Graduate Education of Planners in North America: A Competency-Based Program for the 1980's and Beyond." Florida State, 1981.

2674
Siddiqui, Mohammad Fariduddin. "Manpower Information System for Educational Planning." Toronto, 1974.

2675
Sinclair, Glenn William. "The Development of a Program in Moral Reasoning for Educational Administration." Alberta, 1978.

Sloan, Leroy Vincent. See No./Voir no 2416

2676
Stryde, Sherman James. "The Development of an Instrument for Describing Dimensions of the Teacher-Learning Process." Alberta, 1973.

2677
Woolner, Paul Allan. "The Power Processes of a Public Sector Organizational Change: Towards a Grounded Theory." Toronto, 1982.

Alberta

2678
Cosgrove, Ronald Michael. "An Investigation of Country-School Division Differences in Alberta with Respect to Selected Aspects of Local School Operation." Calgary, 1972.

2679
Creed, Philip John. "Satisfaction with Leader Behavior: A Test of Selected Aspects of the Path-Goal Theory of Leadership." Alberta, 1978.

2680
Deverell, Alfred F. "Educational Needs of the Rocky Mountain School Division, Alberta, Canada." Stanford, 1950.

Garrow, Patrick. See No./Voir no 43

2681
Hambly, John Robert Stanley. "A Survey of County School Administration in Alberta." Toronto, 1960.

2682
Harrison, Robin Christopher J.L. "Consultative Needs and Practices in Selected Junior High Schools in Alberta." Alberta, 1978.

2683
Haughey, Margaret L. "Consultative Practices in Elementary Schools." Alberta, 1976.

2684
Hopkirk, Gerald A. "Temporary Systems in Education." Alberta, 1977.

2685
Jonason, Jonas Christian. "The Large Units of School Administration in Alberta." Oregon, 1951.

2686
Keoyte, Sen. "Educational Planning in Alberta: A Case Study." Alberta, 1973.

Kolesar, Henry. See No./Voir no 2856

2687
Kozakewich, Edward James. "The Cameron Commission, Interest Groups and Policy-Making." Alberta, 1980.

2688
Kunjbehari, Lalta Lloyd. "Politics and Expertise in Policymaking: A Model and Case Study." Alberta, 1981. [Junior high school - Sherwood Park/Septième et huitième année - Parc Sherwood]

2689
Lazaruk, Walter Andrew. "A Comparative Analysis of Selected Designated Community Schools and Non-Designated Schools in Alberta." Oregon, 1982.

2690
Lorincz, Louis Michael. "A Study of Moral Development: Concepts and Potential Educational Applications." Calgary, 1980. [Calgary Catholic high school system/Système des écoles secondaires catholiques de Calgary]

2691
McLellan, James Layton. "Sage Analysis of the Instructional Process: A Study of Schools in the Calgary Public School System 1979-1980." Brigham Young, 1980.

2692
Millikan, Ross Hamilton. "Consultative Needs and Practices in Selected Senior High Schools in Alberta." Alberta, 1979.

2693
Okello, Lekoboam O. "Planning Practices of Planning and Research Branch, Alberta Department of Planning." Alberta, 1979.

Pomfret, Denis Alan. See No./Voir no 10003

2694
Seaton, Ean Charles. "Selected Preparation Program Needs for Educational Administrators in the Province of Alberta." Calgary, 1979.

2695
Séguin, Jean Joseph. "Public Policy Planning in Education: A Case Study of Policy Formation for the Early Childhood Services Program in Alberta." Alberta, 1977.

2696
Symyrozum, L.E. "A Study of the Relationship Between Educational Program Levels in Alberta School Systems and Selected Measures of Fiscal and Non-Fiscal Variables." Alberta, 1981.

2697
Treleaven, Harvey Leroy. "Private Schools in Alberta: A Delphi Study." Utah, 1981.

2698
Williams, Lowell Leavitt. "Educator Attitudes Toward Ten Selected Sub-Concepts of Planning, Programming, Budgetary System in One Large Urban School Jurisdiction in Alberta." Calgary, 1972.

2699
Wood, Jack Maxwell. "A Study of the Effects of Alterations in the Workweek upon an Educational Organization." Alberta, 1977.

British Columbia/Colombie-Britannique

2700
Child, Alan Herbert. "The Historical Development of the Large Administrative Educational Unit in British Columbia Prior to 1947, with Special Reference to the Introductory Phase, 1933-1937." Alberta, 1972.

2701
English, John Frederick Kerr. "An Evaluation of the Reorganized System of Local School Administration in British Columbia." Toronto, 1956.

2702
Marshall, Michael Anthony. "Dimensions and Determinants of School Workflow Structure." British Columbia, 1978.

Plenderleith, W. See No./Voir no 2908

2703
Regan, Ross H. "Goals of Vocational Education for British Columbia: Comparative Views of Personnel from Business, Labor, and Education." Washington State, 1978.

2704
Smith, Denis C. "A Study of the Origin and Development of Administrative Organization in the Educational System of British Columbia." California, Los Angeles, 1953.

2705
Tindill, Arthur Sidney. "A Model for the Development of a District Administrators' Training Program in the Province of British Columbia." Seattle, 1981.

2706
Weeks, Harold L. "Organization, Administration and Supervision of Business Education in British Columbia." Harvard, 1943.

2707
Woodrow, James. "Authority and Power in the Governance of Public Education: A Study of the Administrative Structure of the British Columbia Education System." British Columbia, 1974.

Manitoba

2708
Bergen, John Jacob. "School District Reorganization in Rural Manitoba." Alberta, 1967.

2709
Bjarnason, Carl. "The Preparation of Educational Administrators in Manitoba." Michigan State, 1971.

710
oore, Andrew. "Educational Administration in Manitoba with Special Reference to the Statutes and Regulations Concerned." Toronto, 1944.

711
alph, Edwin George. "French-Programming Policy Issues in a School Jurisdiction: A Case Study." Manitoba, 1979.

awatzky, Aron. See No./Voir no 2169

New Brunswick/Nouveau-Brunswick

712
lacKenzie, William H. "A Plan of Procedures for the Reorganization of the School Administrative Units in the Province of New Brunswick." Teachers College, Columbia, 1942.

Newfoundland/Terre-Neuve

713
arrett, Charles Raymond. "Direction of the Organization and Implementation of a Regional High School District to Serve the Clarenville, Newfoundland Area." Harvard, 1961.

714
uy, Allan Roy. "A General Systems Example of Educational Planning: An Application to the Province of Newfoundland." Toronto, 1977.

Northwest Territories/Territoires du Nord-Ouest

715
ucker, Otto George. "The Administration of Publicly Supported Schools in the Northwest Territories of Canada Since 1905." Toronto, 1972.

Nova Scotia/Nouvelle-Écosse

716
lunter, James Jamison, Jr. "The Organization and Administration of the Public School System in the Province of Nova Scotia." Syracuse, 1942.

717
lorrison, Allan B. "A Proposal for Reorganizing Intermediate Administrative Districts in the Province of Nova Scotia." Columbia, 1948.

Ontario

718
llen, Howard Clarence. "The Organization and Administration of the Educational System of the Provinces of Quebec and Ontario." Syracuse, 1937.

719
luster, Ethel W. "Educational Information Consultants: Case Studies of Part-Time Knowledge Linkers." Toronto, 1978. [North Bay area/Région de North Bay]

720
wender, Michael A.B.J. "An Empirical Study of Consolidation and Equal Educational Opportunity in Ontario, Canada." Claremont, 1978.

Brown, John Douglas. See No./Voir no 2862

2721
Fox, James Harold. "The Centralized Control of Secondary Education in the Province of Ontario: An Evaluation of the Administrative Control Exercized by the Central Educational Authority, with Suggestions Regarding Desirable and Practical Adjustments." Harvard, 1937.

2722
Guillet, Raymond D. "The Status of Women in Administrative Positions in the Province of Ontario." Wayne State, 1982.

Harris, Joseph John. See No./Voir no 2867

Hill Rix, Marion E.A. See No./Voir no 2659

2723
Jakes, Harold Edward. "Regional Office Autonomy: A Study Within the Ontario Ministry of Education." Toronto, 1980.

2724
Larson, Kenneth Louis. "Metropolitan School Government: Its Development and Operation in Toronto." California, Berkeley, 1964.

Lenchyshin, David Arthur. See No./Voir no 2982

2725
McLean, Walter Robert. "A Study of the Perceptions of Administrators in Alternative Education in Selected Cities within the United States and the Province of Ontario, Canada." Wayne State, 1978.

2726
McReynolds, William Peter. "A Model for the Ontario Educational System." Toronto, 1969.

2727
Rachlis, L. "The Effects of Adult Daytime Students on the Administration of Some Ontario Schools." Toronto, 1983.

2728
Robinson, Roosevelt Macdonald. "Communications and Power Within the York Region System of Education During the Period of Transition, 1969-1974." Toronto, 1975.

2729
Roncari, Jean Isobel Dawson. "Negotiation: A Case Study of the Creative Process." Toronto, 1980.

2730
Scott, Douglas Malcolm. "A Workshop Approach to Developing Interpersonal Skills Learning Projects." Toronto, 1981.

2731
Seasay, Alieu. "The Role of Multicultural Community Officers in the Ontario School System: A Case Study." Toronto, 1982.

2732
Selby, John. "Local Autonomy and Central Control in Ontario Education: A Study of Inter-Organizational Relationships." McMaster, 1973.

Stapleton, John James. See No./Voir no 2798

2733
Thom, Douglas John. "Hockey Participation as a Factor in the Secondary School Performance of Ontario Students: An Effects Study for Administrators." Toronto, 1979.

Trask, Maxwell. See No./Voir no 2879

Quebec/Québec

Allen, Howard Clarence. See No./Voir no 2718

2734
Assal, Georges. "Développement d'un modèle de gestion d'un programme de formation professionnelle au Québec selon le système Planification - Programmation - Budgétisation - Évaluation (PPBE)." Montréal, 1982.

Burgess, Donald A. See No./Voir no 2518

2735
Laurin, Paul. "Description des emplois de l'équipe de gestion au sein des écoles secondaires polyvalentes de la province de Québec." Montréal, 1974.

2736
Nault, Aimé. "Redefining Role and Function of Regional Offices in Quebec Education System." Harvard, 1971.

2737
Noël, Guy. "Exploration des dimensions connotatives de la pensée gestionnelle chez des cadres québécois et français." Montréal, 1977.

2738
Shannon, Isabelle Louise. "The Role of School Committees and Parents' Committees in Education in Quebec." Michigan, 1977.

2739
Simon, Pierre. "Analyse de l'influence d'un cours de perfectionnement des cadres." Montréal, 1975.

Saskatchewan

2740
Foster, John E. "The Administrative Means of Extending the Use of Audio-Visual Materials in Saskatchewan." Indiana, 1951.

2741
Gillespie, Edgar Dean. "A Study of Some Emerging Practices in Larger School Units of Administration in Saskatchewan." Teachers College, Columbia, 1950.

2742
Hicks, Douglas Leonard. "Upward Communication in Educational Hierarchies." Saskatchewan, 1972.

Ricker, Harold Owen. See No./Voir no 2672

School Finance and Economics of Education/
Finances scolaires et économie de l'éducation

General Items/Ouvrages généraux

Andrews, Bruce Alfred. See No./Voir no 2435
Bharath, Ramachandran. See No./Voir no 3608

2743
Boynton, Arthur John. "Income Elasticities of Educational and Non-Educational Government Revenue Among Canadian Provinces." Illinois, 1976. [1950-1972]

2744
Brown, Wilfred John. "Redistributive Implications of Federal-Provincial Fiscal Arrangements for Elementary and Secondary Education in Canada." Toronto, 1974.

Cameron, David Murray. See No./Voir no 2777

2745
Chidekel, Samuel J. "An Analysis of Some Aspects o Federal Support of Education in the United State and Canada." Loyola, 1961.

2746
Crean, J.F.M. "Costs, Rates of Return and th Demand for Education in Canada since 1945. London, 1969.

2747
Glendenning, Donald Ernest Malcolm. "Impact o Federal Financial Support on Vocational Educatio in Canada." Indiana, 1964.

2748
Kurialocherry, Anthony J. "The Financing of Privat Education in Certain Democratic Countries (A Comparative Study of the Systems in the Unite States, Canada and India)." Loyola, 1962.

2749
LeSieur, Antonio. "Facteurs militaires qui ont amen le gouvernement fédéral à aider financièrement le institutions d'enseignement supérieure au Canada. Ottawa, 1961.

2750
Meek, James Collins. "Local School Board Revenue and Expenditures in a Period of Declining Enrol ments." Alberta, 1979.

2751
Paterson, Ian Wilson. "An Analysis of Determinants o Education Expenditures Among the Provinces o Canada, Decenially, 1941-1961." Alberta, 1967.

Philippon, Donald Joseph. See No./Voir no 6708

2752
Robbins, John E. "A Study of Some of the Essential in the Financing of Education in Canada. Ottawa, 1935.

Roy, Paul Martel. See No./Voir no 2214

2753
Sharples, Brian. "An Analysis of the Responsiveness o Public Education Financial Support of Economi Growth in the Provinces of Canada 1930-1966 an the Implications for the Financing of Education i the Decade 1971-1981." Alberta, 1971.

2754
Toombs, Wilbert Nelson. "An Analysis of Parliamen tary Debate on Federal Financial Participation i Education in Canada, 1867-1960." Alberta, 1967.

2755
Wilkinson, Bruce William. "Some Economic Aspects o Education in Canada." Massachusetts Institute o Technology, 1965.

Alberta

2756
Atherton, Peter John. "The Impact of Rising Price Levels on Expenditures for School Operation i Alberta." Alberta, 1969.

2757
Caldwell, Brian John. "Decentralized School Budget ing in Alberta: An Analysis of Objectives, Adop tion, Operation and Perceived Outcomes in Selec ted School Systems." Alberta, 1977.

2758
Deiseach, Donal Fiontain. "Fiscal Equalization o School System Revenues Under the Alberta Schoo Foundation Program 1961-1971." Alberta, 1974.

2759
Duke, William Richard. "A Cost Analysis of Selected Schools in an Urban School System." Alberta, 1971.
2760
Gillis, John Hugh. "An Exploratory Study of the Relationship Between Educational Expenditure and Certain Measures of Academic Achievement in a Sample of Alberta Schools." Alberta, 1972.
2761
Henry, Ralph M. "Monetary Return to Educational Programs: The Engineering Technologies in Alberta." Alberta, 1972.
2762
Kulba, John William. "Equity in Taxation and School Finance: A Relationship Between Property and Income Bases in Alberta Census Regions." Oregon, 1974.
2763
Maliyankino, Thadeo Lutatina. "Economic Benefits of Manpower Training Programmes at the Alberta Vocational Centre, Edmonton." Alberta, 1975.
2764
Miller, Herbert E. "Scholarships for Alberta." Teachers College, Columbia, 1947.
2765
Shapiro, David. "Three Aspects of the Economics of Education in Alberta." Princeton, 1972.
2766
Uhlman, H.J. "A Study of the Impact of Demographic and Economic Changes in Rural Alberta on the Financing of Education." Alberta, 1959.
2767
Wilson, Kevin Arthur. "Private Monetary Returns to Baccalaureate Education." Alberta, 1970.

British Columbia/Colombie-Britannique

2768
Armstrong, Henry Graham. "An Output Adjusted Price Index for Public School Expenditures in British Columbia (1961-1969)." British Columbia, 1972.
2769
King, Herbert B. "The Financing of Education in British Columbia." Washington, Seattle, 1936.

Manitoba

Coleman, Peter Edward F. See No./Voir no 2812
Duncan, Deirdre Jean. See No./Voir no 2838
2770
Nicholls, Glenn Harvey. "An Inquiry into the Implications of Full Provincial Funding as an Alternative for Financing the Public Schools of Manitoba." Manitoba, 1980.
2771
Woods, David S. "Financing the Schools of Rural Manitoba." Chicago, 1935.

Maritime Provinces/Provinces maritimes

General Items/Ouvrages généraux

Currie, Allister Blaine. See No./Voir no 2421

2772
Lake, Philip. "Expenditure Equity in the Public Schools of Atlantic Canada." Illinois State, 1982.

New Brunswick/Nouveau-Brunswick

McCready, Douglas Jackson. See No./Voir no 1325
2773
Wallschlaeger, Michael John. "Potential Organizational Problems Associated with a Full State Funding Plan for Financing Public Education." Wisconsin, 1973.

Newfoundland/Terre-Neuve

2774
Warren, Philip John. "Financing Education in Newfoundland." Alberta, 1963.

Ontario

2775
Baird, Norman Barnes. "Educational Finance and Administration for Ontario." Toronto, 1946.
2776
Benson, Ralph. "Determinants of Expenditure for Public Secondary Education in the Province of Ontario." Toronto, 1946.
2777
Cameron, David Murray. "The Politics of Education in Ontario, with Special Reference to the Financial Structure." Toronto, 1969.
2778
Cameron, Maxwell A. "The Financing of Education in Ontario." Toronto, 1935.
2779
Carmone, Frank Joseph. "An Investigation of Subjective Evaluation Functions in the Context of University Budgeting." Waterloo, 1971.
2780
Cook, Gail Carol Annabel. "Effect of Federation on Education Expenditures in Metropolitan Toronto." Michigan, 1968.
2781
Dawson, Donald Allan. "Economies of Scale in the Secondary Education Sector in the Province of Ontario." Western Ontario, 1970.
2782
Downie, Felix Philip. "A Study of the Feasibility of Alternative Methods of Financing Elementary and Secondary Education in Ontario Through Property Tax Reform from a Survey of Opinions of School Officials." St. Johns, 1978.
2783
Lagroix, Earl Joseph. "The Senior School Business Official in Ontario, Canada: The Job and Involvement." Toronto, 1977.
2784
Treddenick, John Macauley. "An Econometric Analysis of Public Education Activity in Ontario 1947-1965." Queen's, 1969.

Quebec/Québec

2785
Bezeau, Lawrence Manning. "A Mathematical Optimization Model of Education and Income Utility in the Province of Quebec." Stanford, 1974.

2786
Trueman, George Johnstone. "School Funds in the Province of Quebec." Teachers College, Columbia, 1970.

Saskatchewan

2787
Guy, Alexander John Young. "Unit Cost Analysis of the Saskatchewan Comprehensive High School." Alberta, 1972.

2788
Langlois, Hervé Oscar. "Tax Equity in School Finance Programs in Relation to the Income and Property Bases in Nine Saskatchewan Cities." Oregon, 1972.

Toombs, Morley Preston. See No./Voir no 2477

Northwest Territories/Territoires du Nord-Ouest

Toombs, Morley Preston. See No./Voir no 2477

Politics of Education/Politique en enseignement

2789
Anderson, Robert Newton. "The Role of Government in Canadian Education: An Analysis of Bureaucratic Structure." Minnesota, 1964.

Andrews, Bruce Alfred. See No./Voir no 2435

2790
Ayre, David John. "Universities and the Legislature: Political Aspects of the Ontario University Question 1806-1906." Toronto, 1981.

Cameron, David Murray. See No./Voir no 2777

Datey, Blaise. See No./Voir no 2971

2791
Dickson, William Rushworth. "Involvement by Decree: Citizen Involvement in Education by Legislative Mandate." Ohio State, 1978.

Gélinas, Jean-Paul. See No./Voir no 2411

Goulson, Carolyn Floyd. See No./Voir no 2423

2792
Haché, Jean-Baptiste. "Language and Religious Factors in Canadian Ethnic Politics of Education: A Case Study in Power Mobilization." Toronto, 1976.

2793
Levine, Marc Veblen. "Public Policy and Social Conflict in Multicultural Societies: Case Studies of the Politics of Education in Philadelphia, 1800-1860, and Montreal, 1960-1981." Pennsylvania, 1982.

Long, John Clifford Anthony. See No./Voir no 3530

2794
Lucas, Barry Gillespie. "Federal Relations to Education in Canada, 1970: An Investigation of Programs, Policies and Directions." Michigan, 1971.

Orlikow, Lionel. See No./Voir no 2407

2795
Poon, Wai-Keung. "The Student Newspaper: A Political Perspective." Toronto, 1976. [University of Toronto and provincial educational legislation/ Université de Toronto et loi provinciale sur l'éducation]

2796
Ricker, Eric William. "Teachers, Trustees and Policy: The Politics of Education in Ontario, 1945-1975." Toronto, 1981.

2797
Selinger, Alphonse Daniel. "Politics and Education Policy in Alberta." Oregon, 1967.

2798
Stapleton, John James. "The Politics of Educational Innovation: A Case Study of the Credit System in Ontario." Toronto, 1975.

2799
Stringham, Bryant Louis. "The School Act of 1970: A Case Study in Public Policymaking in Education." Alberta, 1974.

2800
Trottier, Claude René. "Teachers as Agents of Political Socialization." Toronto, 1980.

2801
Wright, Annette Eileen. "The Nature of Legislated Policy: A Comparative Analysis of Selected Educational Legislation." British Columbia, 1979.

Law and Education/Droit et éducation

2802
Bargen, P.F. "The Legal Status of the Canadian Public School Pupil." Alberta, 1959.

2803
Daniels, Edwin Robert. "The Legal Context of Indian Education in Canada." Alberta, 1974.

2804
Enns, Frederick. "The Legal Status of the Canadian Public School Board." Alberta, 1961.

2805
Fenske, Milton Reinhold. "The Evolution of the Formal Legal Structure of Separate Schools in the Prairie Provinces." Alberta, 1969.

2806
Keith, M. Virginia. "The Legal Status of the School Board in the Province of New Brunswick." Ottawa, 1961.

2807
Krivy, Gary Joseph Paul. "The Legal Rights and Responsibilities of University Students in Canada." Arizona, 1982.

2808
Lamb, Robert Lee. "The School Trustee In and At Law." Toronto, 1963.

2809
MacLean, Donald Alexander. "Catholic Schools in Western Canada; Their Legal Status." Catholic, 1923.

2810
McCurdy, Sherburne Graham. "The Legal Status of the Canadian Teacher." Alberta, 1965.

2811
Ross, George J. "The Courts and the Canadian Public Schools." Chicago, 1949.

The Community and Education/
Le public et l'enseignement

Barron, Robert Frederick John. See No./Voir no 2989

2812
Coleman, Peter Edward Fowler. "The Distribution of Educational Services in Manitoba: An Analysis of the Effects of Provincial Policies, with Proposals for Change." British Columbia, 1974.

2813
Disney, David Michael. "Determining Community Expectations: A Case Study." Toronto, 1975. [West Lynde, Ontario]

2814
Figur, Berthold. "Processing Citizens' Proposals for Educational Change in a Canadian Province." Stanford, 1968.

2815
Hanna, Carolyn Linda. "Community Schools in Manitoba." Manitoba, 1980.

2816
Kidd, James R. "A Study to Formulate a Plan for the Work of the Canadian Citizenship Council." Teachers College, Columbia, 1947.

2817
Langford, Howard David. "Educational Service: Its Functions and Possibilities (Ontario)." Teachers College, Columbia, 1932.

Laperrière-Nguyen, Anne. See No./Voir no 3087

Lazaruk, Walter Andrew. See No./Voir no 2689

Pickard, Brent William. See No./Voir no 3580

2818
Prout, Peter Francis. "General and Specific Environmental Conditions in Relation to Community Educational Developments in Canada's Provinces and Territories." Alberta, 1977.

Ryckman, Robert M. See No./Voir no 4420

Séguin, J.J. See No./Voir no 2695

Shannon, Isabelle Louise. See No./Voir no 2738

2819
Shuttleworth, Dale Edwin. "The Learning Exchange System (Learnxs): Analysis of a Demonstration Project in Community Education." Toronto, 1978.

Siegel, Sanford Benjamin. See No./Voir no 2083

2820
Westwater, Robert. "A Study of the Work in Canada and Newfoundland of Canadian Legion Educational Services." Toronto, 1949.

2821
Wybourn, Edbrooke Sidney. "The Canadian YMCA as an Agent of International Understanding." Teachers College, Columbia, 1961.

Study and Evaluation of Schools, School Districts and Programs/Étude et évaluation des écoles, des institutions de districts et des programmes

2822
Collett, D.J. "Testing a Model for Monitoring an Educational System." Alberta, 1981.

2823
Doherty, Maryanne. "An Evaluation of Modularized Systems." Alberta, 1981.

2824
Dryden, Louis James. "Educational Program Evaluation: An Effectiveness Model." Calgary, 1976.

2825
Fagbamiye, Olukayode Emmanuel. "Conflict and School District Reorganization in Thirty-Eight Southern Ontario Counties." Toronto, 1971.

2826
Fisher, Harry King. "The Application of a System Evaluation Model to the Department of National Defence Schools Overseas: A Case Study." Toronto, 1975. [SCESS - The Service for the Co-operative Evaluation of School Systems/SCESS - Service coopératif d'évaluation des systèmes scolaires]

Goulson, Carolyn Floyd. See No./Voir no 2423

2827
Graham, John Ronald. "Administering Follow-Up Activities to School System Evaluation: A Case Study." Toronto, 1979.

2828
Hamwood, John Alban. "Productivity and Efficiency in Secondary School Systems." Toronto, 1973.

2829
Hawkesworth, Earle Kitchener. "Initiating Change in Alberta High Schools Through Team Evaluation." Colorado, 1969.

2830
Horovatin, Joseph Daniel. "Theory-Based and Field-Tested Guidelines for the Design and Implementation of Program-Evaluation Studies." Calgary, 1977.

2831
Lécuyer, Joseph Edmond André. "Analyzing, Reporting, and Validating a Design to Evaluate Developmental Agencies in the Field of Education." Toronto, 1976.

2832
Matthews, John C. "The Report of the Survey of the Public Schools of Charlottetown, Prince Edward Island." Teachers College, Columbia, 1954.

2833
Morrow, Robert George. "A Longitudinal Follow-Up of High School Graduates and Their Evaluation of the Program in an Alberta School District." Oregon, 1980.

2834
Nygaard, Marvin Hector. "Macro Program Evaluation: A Study of a Provincial Program of Compensatory Education." Calgary, 1977.

2835
Whitehead, LeRoy Ezra. "The Personal Value Orientation of Educational Program Evaluators as a Variable in Educational Program Evaluation." Calgary, 1977.

2836
Wilson, Allan Cecil. "A Plan for Evaluating the Adequacy of City-School Systems." Toronto, 1950.

School Organization/Organisation scolaire

Anwar, Muhammad. See No./Voir no 2988

Batchler, Mervyn William. See No./Voir no 2916

2837
Bullen, Edward Lester. "A Study of Some Ecological Effects of Internal Organization in Two Secondary Schools: A House System Compared with a Centralized Organization." Toronto, 1981.

115

2838
Duncan, Deirdre Jean. "A Study of Organizational Change: High School Budgeting." Manitoba, 1976.

2839
Dyck, Merla Helene. "The Effect of Organizational and Group Characteristics on Perception of Climate." Alberta, 1978.

2840
Eddy, Wesley Percy. "The Relationship of Local-Cosmopolitan Role Orientation to Organizational Characteristics of Schools." Alberta, 1968.

2841
Hall, Francine Marian. "Organizational Goal Determination in Public Schools." Toronto, 1975.

2842
Harvey, Ray F.E. "School Organizational Climate and Teacher Classroom Behavior." Alberta, 1965.

2843
Hersom, Naomi Louise. " Dimensions of Organizational Structure and Organizational Behavior." Alberta, 1969.

2844
Hodgkinson, Christopher Edward. "Values and Perceptions in Organizations: A Study of Value Orientations and Social Interaction Perceptions in Education Organizations." British Columbia, 1968. [Vancouver]

2845
House, John Hamilton. "An Analysis of Interpersonal Influence Relationships within a School Organization." Alberta, 1967.

Knoop, Robert. See No./Voir no 4314

2846
Mansfield, Earl Arthur. "Administrative Communication and the Organizational Structure of the School." Alberta, 1967.

Marshall, David George. See No./Voir no 2665

2847
Martin, Robert Angus. "Selected Aspects of Elementary School Structure and Students' Acceptance of the Norm of Universalism." Toronto, 1971.

2848
Ochitwa, Orest Paul. "A Study of the Organizational Climate of High and Low Adopter Elementary Schools in the Province of Saskatchewan, Canada." Indiana, 1973.

2849
Sackney, Lawrence Ernest. "The Relationship Between Organizational Structure and Behavior in Secondary Schools." Alberta, 1976.

Stapleton, John James. See No./Voir no 2798

2850
Sullivan, Keith Charles. "Community Schools: An Analysis of Organizational and Environmental Characteristics." Alberta, 1976.

Treslan, Dennis L. See No./Voir no 3357

2851
Wilks, Arthur Garland. "Identifying the Degree of Compatibility Between Members' Values and Organizational Characteristics as a Basis for Organization Improvement." Calgary, 1980.

School Management/Gestion scolaire

2852
Donnelly, Bert J. "The Relationship Between School Management Patterns and Environmental Press on Students in Grade Seven and Eight." Ottawa, 1980.

2853
Ladouceur, Jean. "School Management Profile and Capacity for Change." Toronto, 1973.

MacKillican, William S. See No./Voir no 2663

Bureaucracy in the Schools/ Bureaucratie dans les écoles

2854
Allison, Derek John. "An Analysis of the Congruency Between a Model of Public Schools and Max Weber's Model of Bureaucracy." Alberta, 1980.

Anderson, Robert Newton. See No./Voir no 2789

2855
Faulkner, Raymond T. "Least Preferred Co-Worker Score of the Principal and Degree of Bureaucratization in Open and Traditional Schools." Ottawa, 1981.

2856
Kolesar, Henry. "An Empirical Study of Client Alienation in the Bureaucratic Organization." Alberta, 1967. [20 Alberta high schools/20 écoles secondaires d'Alberta]

2857
MacKay, David Allister. "An Empirical Study of Bureaucratic Dimensions and Their Relation to Other Characteristics of School Organizations." Alberta, 1965.

McKague, Ormond Knight. See No./Voir no 2545

2858
McKague, Terence Russell. "A Study of the Relationship Between School Organizational Behavior and the Variables of Bureaucratization and Leader Attitudes." Alberta, 1968.

2859
Punch, Keith Francis. "Bureaucratic Structure in Schools and Its Relationship to Leader Behavior: An Empirical Study." Toronto, 1967.

Robinson, Norman. See No./Voir no 2943

School Boards and Trustees/ Conseils et administrateurs scolaires

Barone, Anthony John. See No./Voir no 2957
Birkenstock, David. See No./Voir no 3618

2860
Brayne, Robin Charles. "A Political System Approach to the Study of Demands of an Urban School Board." British Columbia, 1979. [Pacific School Board/Conseil scolaire du Pacifique]

2861
Brosseau, John Francis. "Opinions of the Public School Trustees, and Professional Educators on Current Educational Practices." Alberta, 1973. [Edmonton]

2862
Brown, John Douglas. "An Exploration of the Construction of Recommendations for Policy for a Board of Education: Investigating the Culture of Administration." Toronto, 1982.

2863
Cameron, Ian Julian. "School-Board Public Conflict in British Columbia." British Columbia, 1981.

2864
Denholm, James Johnstone. "An Historical Study of Relations Between the Board of School Trustees of the City of Vancouver and the Government of the Province of British Columbia." California, Berkeley, 1962.

Enns, Frederick. See No./Voir no 2804

2865
Epp, Ernest John. "A Study of Urban School Trustee Decision-Making." Toronto, 1979.

2866
Falusi, Arnold Joseph. "An Empirical Investigation of the Effects of Organization Development on Task Group Processes in Education." Toronto, 1972.

2867
Harris, Joseph John. "An Analysis of the Application of the Metropolitan School Governance Concept: An Exploratory Study." Michigan, 1972.

2868
Hodgson, William Robert. "A Study of the Factors in the Acceptance or Non-Acceptance of Nomination for School Board Election in British Columbia." Northern Colorado, 1964.

Keith, M. Virginia. See No./Voir no 2806

Lamb, Robert Lee. See No./Voir no 2808

2869
Leonard, George Albert. "A Descriptive Study of a Superintendent's Perception of In-Service Training Programs for School Board Members in the United States and Canada." Wayne State, 1978.

2870
Lewis, Edward Dale. "The Process of Re-Organization of the Academic Administrative Staff of the Toronto Board of Education." Colorado, 1977.

March, Milton E. See No./Voir no 2664

2871
Matthews, Neville Osborn. "A Study of the Decision-Making Process of Two School Boards in an Alberta Community." Alberta, 1968.

2872
McLeod, Gerald Thomas. "Educational Governance as Theatre: A Study of Interaction Underlying Alberta School Boards' Collective Agreements with Teachers." Alberta, 1976.

Meek, James Collins. See No./Voir no 2750

2873
O'Toole, Padraig. "Analyzing the Perspective of a Roman Catholic Separate School Board." Toronto, 1982.

2874
Proudfoot, Alexander James. "A Study of the Socio-Economic Status of Influential School Board Members in Alberta as Related to Their Attitudes Toward Certain Common Problems Confronting School Boards." Oregon, 1962.

Ralph, Edwin George. See No./Voir no 2711

2875
Renihan, Patrick Joseph. "Control Dimensions and School Board Decision Emphasis." Alberta, 1977.

2876
Roberts, William Glyndwr. "The Alberta School Trustees' Association: A Study of the Activity of a Social Organization in the Alberta Educational System." Alberta, 1967.

2877
St. James, Alice Margaret. "An Investigation of Participation by Community Groups in the Decision Making Process in Elected, Partly Elected, and Appointed School Boards." Alberta, 1967.

Scott, Douglas Malcolm. See No./Voir no 2730

2878
Tennant, Paul. "The Influence of Local School Boards in Central Education Authorities in British Columbia." Chicago, 1963.

2879
Trask, Maxwell. "An Examination of the Relationships Among the Variables Organizational Size, Complexity, and the Administrative Component of Ontario School Boards." Ottawa, 1978.

Ukaga, Gabriel Chidi. See No./Voir no 2952

2880
Viney, Bonnie. "The Relationship Between Organizational Structure and Effectiveness in School Board Program Departments." Ottawa, 1981.

Supervision/Direction

2881
Anderson, Henrietta Alexandrina Ramage. "Supervision of Rural Schools in British Columbia: A Review of the Present System and a Plan of Reorganization." Washington, Seattle, 1931.

Boulet, F.X. See No./Voir no 2918

2882
Brown, Corbin Alexander. "Elementary School Supervision in Ontario: An Evaluation of Certain Aspects of the Supervisory Programme." Toronto, 1948.

2883
Buffett, Frederick. "A Study of Existing and Desired Supervisory Practices in Newfoundland." Boston University, 1967.

2884
DeWitt, Kilby A. "The Effects of Two Supervisory Focuses on Ratings of Classroom Situations Judged from Videotape Segments." McGill, 1983.

Fradsham, Boyce Tennyson. See No./Voir no 2926

2885
Margules, Morton. "A Comparison of Supervisors' Ratings of Most Effective and Least Effective Industrial Arts Teachers on Three Competency Dimensions." Ottawa, 1968.

2886
Martin, Victor Leo. "A Study of the Task Expectations for Elementary School Supervisors of Instruction in the Province of British Columbia as Perceived by Supervisors and Teachers." Idaho, 1979.

2887
Martin, Yvonne Marjorie. "Supervisor Verbal Behaviour, Teacher Belief Systems, and Teacher Behaviour Modification." McGill, 1977.

2888
McCall, Horace Fillmore. "Organization and Procedures of Supervision in the Alberta Public Schools." Oregon State, 1956.

2889

Miller, Selwyn Archibald. "A Comparative Study of Supervision in the Various Canadian Provinces, with a View to Determining the Optimum Load for Supervisors of Each Type." Toronto, 1946.

2890

Parsons, George Llewellyn. "Teacher Perceptions of Supervisory Effectiveness: An Analysis of Supervisory Roles in Secondary Systems." Toronto, 1971.

2891

Savoie, André. "La relation de confiance et les comportements de supervision des cadres scolaires." Montréal, 1978.

School Administrative Personnel/ Personnel administratif scolaire

General Items/Ouvrages généraux

McLean, Walter Robert. See No./Voir no 2725

2892

Nixon, Mary Theresa. "Women Administrators and Women Teachers: A Comparative Study." Alberta, 1975.

2893

Powell, Keith Raymond. "The Role of the Coordinating Secretary in Organizations Affiliated with the Association of School Business Officials of the United States and Canada." Ball State, 1976.

2894

Von Fange, Erick Alvin. "Implications for School Administration of the Personality Structure of Educational Personnel." Alberta, 1962.

Superintendents and Inspectors/ Directeurs et inspecteurs

2895

Barnabe, Clermont. "A Study of the Relations Between Differential Values and Role Expectations for the Role of the School Superintendent in Quebec." SUNY, Buffalo, 1973.

2896

Collins, Cecil Patrick. "The Role of the Provincially Appointed Superintendent of Schools in Larger Units of Administration in Canada." Alberta, 1958.

2897

Constant, Raymond Albert Fernand. "An Analysis of Superintendent Turnover in Unitary School Divisions in the Province of Manitoba and the Relationship to Methods of Selection and Process of Employment." North Dakota, 1973.

2898

Cormier, Roger Armand. "Information in Each Operational Area for Important Divisions of School Superintendents." Alberta, 1971.

2899

Duignan, Patrick Augustine. "Administrative Behavior of School Superintendents: A Descriptive Study." Alberta, 1979.

2900

Earle, John Alfred. "Sources of Influence for Instructional Innovations in Canada Urban School Systems as Perceived by Superintendents." Alberta, 1969.

2901

Elliott, Charles Martyn. "Proposals for the Improvement of the Instructional Leadership Provided [ ] Elementary School Inspectors in Northern Ontari[ ] Teachers College, Columbia, 1954.

2902

Fast, Raymond Gary. "Perceptions, Expectations a[ ] Effectiveness of School Superintendents in Albe[ ] and Pennsylvania as Reported by Principals a[ ] Board Members." Pennsylvania State, 1968.

2903

Gannon, Neil Cecil. "A Study to Determine the N[ ] Role of the County and Divisional Superintende[ ] in the Province of Alberta, Canada." Monta[ ] 1973.

2904

Gathercole, Frederick James. "The Role of the Loc[ ] ly-Employed Superintendent of Schools in Alber[ ] Saskatchewan and Manitoba." Toronto, 1964.

2905

Howsam, Robert Basil. "The City Superintendent [ ] Schools in Canada." California, Berkeley, 1956.

2906

Lall, Bernard Mohan. "Role Expectations of [ ] School Superintendent as Perceived by Superinte[ ] dents, Principals, Teachers, and Board Members [ ] the Province of Saskatchewan." Oregon, 1968.

Leonard, George Albert. See No./Voir no 2869

March, Milton E. See No./Voir no 2664

2907

Marshall, Lionel George. "The Classroom Role [ ] Saskatchewan Teachers as Ascribed by Repo[ ] Written by Superintendents of Schools." Oreg[ ] 1972.

Parry, Robert John. See No./Voir no 2940

2908

Plenderleith, William Alexander. "An Experiment [ ] the Reorganization and Administration of a Ru[ ] Inspectoral Unit in British Columbia." Toron[ ] 1937.

2909

Pope, Thomas. "An Empirical Study of the Relatio[ ] ships Between Adherence to Formal Norms, Co[ ] petencies in Fulfilling Formal Norms and Leade[ ] ship Effectiveness." Ottawa, 1976. [33 sch[ ] superintendents in Newfoundland/33 directeu[ ] d'école de Terre-Neuve]

Porter, Gerald Robert. See No./Voir no 2941

2910

Ready, Lawrence Maxwell. "The Preparation Needs [ ] Superintendents in Large Administrative Units [ ] Saskatchewan." Alberta, 1962.

2911

Rees, Robert E. "Superintendent of Schools in Rel[ ] tion to School Division Boards in the Province [ ] Alberta." Northwestern, 1947.

2912

Sampson, Leonard Patrick. "A Survey of the Metho[ ] of Selection and the Conditions of Employment [ ] Provincially Employed Superintendents and Inspe[ ] tors of Schools in the English Speaking Provinces [ ] Canada." Alberta, 1965.

2913

Sherk, Harry Gordon. "The Role of the Inspector [ ] High Schools in Alberta - New Dimension: Tea[ ] Evaluations." Colorado, 1971.

2914
Stothers, C.E. "The Technique of Investigation in a Rural Inspectorate." Toronto, 1934.

Stringer, Guy. See No./Voir no 2538

2915
Thomas, Robert Francis. "The Role of an Area Superintendent in Ontario School Systems." Toronto, 1977.

Principals and Vice-Principals/
Directeurs et directeurs-adjoints

2916
Batchler, Mervyn William. "A Study of Relationships Between Organizational Climates and the Administrative Behavior of School Administrators." Alberta, 1977.

2917
Blumell, Richard Emerson. "A Study of Administrative Leadership of Alberta High School Principals." Montana State, 1964.

2918
Boulet, F.X. "Clinical Supervision as an Alternative for Classroom Observation by School Principals." Alberta, 1981.

2919
Danyluk, Joseph John. "Interrelationship Between Secondary School Principals' Level of Self-Actualization Leadership Attitude, and Teacher Perception of Principal Leadership Behavior." Alberta, 1981.

2920
Didyk, John. "The Relationship of Personal Characteristics and Organizational Conditions to Principals' Career Experiences of Psychological Success." Manitoba, 1981.

2921
Dow, Ian. "An Experimental Study of the Relationship Between Administrative Atmosphere and Supervisory Expectations Held by Teachers for the Principal." Ottawa, 1971.

2922
Dufresne, Donald Joseph. "The Role of the Elementary School Principal in the Teacher Training Practicum." Toronto, 1981.

2923
Egnatoff, John George. "The Nature and Extent of Changes in the Conceptual and Functional Status of the Saskatchewan School Principal Between 1954 and 1965." Toronto, 1968.

Faulkner, Raymond T. See No./Voir no 2855

2924
Flannigan, Terrance Roden. "A Comparison of Role Expectations of Secondary School Vice-Principals in Ohio and Saskatchewan." Bowling Green State, 1970.

2925
Flynn, John Joseph. "Development and Implementation of Performance-Based Evaluation of Elementary School Principals." Toronto, 1975.

2926
Fradsham, Boyce Tennyson. "A Study of Newfoundland Principals' Perceptions of District Supervisors' Services." Indiana, 1978.

2927
Friss, Edward. "The Elementary School Assistant Principal in the Edmonton, Alberta, Public Schools." Oregon, 1980.

2928
Girard, Donald Archie. "Dual Leadership: A Study of Instrumental and Expressive Dimensions of Principal and Vice-Principal Leader Behavior." Alberta, 1968.

2929
Gould, Edgar Nathan. "An Analysis of Role Expectations for the High School Principal Held by Principals and Teachers in Selected Suburban School Districts in Quebec." SUNY, Albany, 1972.

2930
Haliburton, Roy Edward. "Factors Influencing Principals' Ratings of Administrative Potential Among Junior High School Chairmen." Toronto, 1971.

House, John Hamilton. See No./Voir no 2845

2931
Keeler, Bernard Trueman. "Dimensions of the Leader Behavior of Principals, Staff Morale and Productivity." Alberta, 1962.

2932
Lavery, Robert Emmett. "Principal Leadership Style and School Effectiveness in English and French Elementary Schools." Alberta, 1973.

2933
Louden, Lindsay Warren. "Administrative Decision Making in Schools." Alberta, 1980.

2934
Lowery, Robert Eugene. "An Analysis of the Present Administrative Policy of Principals and Vice Principals in the Calgary Public and Separate School Systems." Montana, 1966.

2935
MacMillan, Michael Roderick. "Pupil Control Ideology and Status Obeisance of Teachers and Principals in Elementary Schools." Alberta, 1973.

March, Milton E. See No./Voir no 2664

2936
Miklos, Erwin. "Dimensions of Conflicting Expectations and the Leader Behavior of Principals." Alberta, 1963.

2937
Newberry, Alan John Hesson. "Practices and Criteria Employed in the Selection of Elementary School Principals in British Columbia." Indiana, 1975.

2938
Oss, John Anthony. "The Interaction Between the Principal and Influential Citizens in the Educational Policy Making Process in the Province of Quebec." SUNY, Albany, 1978.

2939
Palmer, Frederick Cornelius T. "The Relationships Among Dogmatism, Autonomy, Administrative Style and Decision-Making of Aspiring and Practicing School Principals." Toronto, 1974.

2940
Parry, Robert John. "Elementary School Principal Effectiveness: Perceptions of Principals and Superintendents." Toronto, 1978.

2941
Porter, Gerald Robert. "Stewardship Theory and Principal Effectiveness: Perceived by Teachers and Superintendents in Alberta, Canada." Brigham Young, 1980.
2942
Rice, Alan William. "Individual and Work Variables Associated with Principal Job Satisfaction." Alberta, 1978.
2943
Robinson, Norman. "A Study of the Professional Role Orientation of Teacher and Principals and Their Relationship to Bureaucratic Characteristics of School Organizations." Alberta, 1967.
Roncari, Jean Isobel Dawson. See No./Voir no 2729
2944
Ryan, Richard Michael. "A Study of the Role of the Elementary Principal in the Province of Quebec." Utah State, 1973.
2945
Schwartz, Arthur Mark. "The Principal as Boundary Administrator: A Field Study of Inner-City Schools." Toronto, 1981.
2946
Scott, John Glenn. "The Urban Elementary School Principal in Ontario - His Status According to the Expressed View of Principals and Senior Administrative Officials." Toronto, 1965.
2947
Sheehan, Carmel Antoinette. "Role Conflict and Value Divergence in Sister Administrators." Toronto, 1972.
2948
Singhawisal, Wilars. "An Analysis of Degrees of Consensus on Role Expectations of the District High School Principal in Ontario as Perceived by the Principals Themselves, the Board Members and the Teachers." Toronto, 1964.
2949
Stockton, Donald Alan. "Design of an In-Service Program for Assistant Principals of the English Schools of the Montreal Catholic School Commission." Massachusetts, 1971.
2950
Storey, Vernon James. "Work-Related Learning Efforts of School Principals: An Exploratory Study." British Columbia, 1978.
2951
Thomson, John Gray. "An Empirical Study of the Relationship Between Ontario Secondary Principals' Leadership Effectiveness and Helping Relationship in Ontario Secondary Teachers." Ottawa, 1972.
2952
Ukaga, Gabriel Chidi. "An Examination of Operational Problems in a Developmental Project: A Systems Approach." Calgary, 1975. [A project for the improvement of the planning competencies of school principals Calgary School Board of Education, District 19/Un projet en vue du perfectionnement des compétences de planification des directeurs d'écoles du Conseil scolaire de Calgary, District 19]

2953
Virgin, Albert Edward. "Communication Effectiveness Related to Leadership and Personality Characteristics of School Principals." Toronto, 1968.
2954
Watson, Glenn Aubrey. "The Development, Implementation and Evaluation of an In-Service Training Program Evaluation for Elementary School Principals." Toronto, 1977.
2955
Williams, Leonard Edward. "The Impact of Collective Bargaining on the Instructional Leadership Role of the Newfoundland School Principal." Boston University, 1983.

Secretary-Treasurer/Secrétaire-Trésorier

2956
Giles, Thomas Edward. "A Study of the Role of the Secretary-Treasurer in School Divisions and Counties in Alberta." Oregon, 1965.
Lagroix, Earl Joseph. See No./Voir no 2783

School Plant/Architecture scolaire

2957
Barone, Anthony John. "The Process of Planning for Changing Elementary School Accommodation Needs: Sharing of School Buildings - Ontario Public and Separate School Boards." Toronto, 1977.
2958
Doan, Arthur Wallace Ross. "The Evaluation of Elementary School Buildings and Grounds (Toronto and the County of York)." Toronto, 1932.
2959
Fisher, Charles Wilfred. "Educational Environments in Elementary Schools Differing in Architecture and Program Openness." Toronto, 1973.
2960
Touzin-St-Pierre, Lloyd Cécile. "Un modèle d'éducateur apte à oeuvrer en éducation ouverte dans une architecture à aires ouvertes." Montréal, 1981. [Secondary level/Niveau secondaire]

Decision Making/Prise de décision

Carmone, Frank Joseph. See No./Voir no 2779
2961
Eastcott, Leslie Raymond. "Faculty Perceptions of and Preferences for Participation in Decision Making." Alberta, 1975.
Epp, Ernest John. See No./Voir no 2865
Fortin, Donald. See No./Voir no 2656
Fortin, Paul Arthur. See No./Voir no 2657
2962
Hoen, Robert Randolph. "Participation in School Level Program Decision-Making: A Case Study." British Columbia, 1975.
2963
Housego, Ian Edward. "How a Decision Was Made: A Study of the Teacher Training Issue in Saskatchewan." Alberta, 1965.

2964
Kirouac, Jacques. "Relations de deux structures administratives différentes sur le profil décisionnel dans les régionales scolaires du Québec." Ottawa, 1977.

Kyle, Neil John. See No./Voir no 8921

Ledgerwood, Charles Douglas. See No./Voir no 3366

Louden, Lindsay Warren. See No./Voir no 2933

March, Milton E. See No./Voir no 2664

Marshall, Anthony R. See No./Voir no 3632

Matthews, Neville Osborn. See No./Voir no 2871

2965
McBeath, Arthur Groat. "A Survey of the Perceptions of the Levels of Decision-Making in Educational Program in the Elementary and Secondary Schools of Saskatchewan." Illinois, 1969.

2966
Plaxton, Robert Piercy. "The Relationships of Decision-Rule to Interaction Patterns, Satisfaction and Commitment in Small Groups." Alberta, 1970.

2967
Ponder, Arthur Aubrey. "The Effects of Involvement in Decision-Making on the Productivity of Three-Man Laboratory Groups." British Columbia, 1973.

2968
Shields, Gerald Bruce. "Equality in Decision-Making Power." Oregon, 1980. [Physical education secondary school teachers/Professeurs d'éducation physique au secondaire]

2969
Stewart, Alfred Neil. "The Fort Vermilion Case: A Study of the Decision-Making Process." Alberta, 1968.

Educational Innovation/
Changements dans l'enseignement

2970
Clinton, Alfred. "A Study of Attributes of Educational Innovations as Factors in Diffusion." Toronto, 1972.

2971
Datey, Blaise. "The Socio-Political Process of Innovation and Planning as Demonstrated by the Introduction of CEGEP's in Quebec's Education System." Toronto, 1973.

Doherty, Maryanne. See No./Voir no 2823

Earle, John Alfred. See No./Voir no 2900

2972
Fish, James. "An Empirical Study of the Effect of Dogmatism and Tenure Status in Educational Innovativeness." Ottawa, 1975.

2973
Henderson, Florence Irene. "Organizational Structure and the Adoption of Educational Innovations." Toronto, 1975. [Elementary education/Enseignement primaire]

Ladouceur, Jean. See No./Voir no 2853

Larose, René. See No./Voir no 2572

MacKallican, William S. See No./Voir no 2663

2974
Mwasa, Joseph. "Some Factors that Influence the Process of Implementation of Educational Innovations: A Study of the Individualized System in Ontario, the School Improvement Program in California and the Namutamba Project in Uganda." Toronto, 1982.

2975
Prebble, Thomas Kenneth. "The Jordan Plan: A Case Study in Educational Change." Alberta, 1975.

Roncari, Jean Isobel Dawson. See No./Voir no 2729

Simms, Jeremy J. See No./Voir no 3138

2976
Taylor, Gilbert Frederick. "A Case Study of an Innovation in the Educational Policy Area." Toronto, 1982.

2977
Tushingham, Gary Warren. "A Study of Some Factors Affecting Implementation of Organizational Innovations in Ontario Public Secondary Schools." Wayne State, 1974.

2978
Wiens, John. "Attitude, Influence and Innovativeness in Educational Organization." Alberta, 1968.

Accreditation, Admissions, Attendance and Prediction
of Success/Crédits, admissions, présence et
chances de succès

2979
Birnie, Howard Harry. "The Development of a Philosophy and Plan of School Accreditation for the Province of Saskatchewan, Canada." North Dakota, 1967.

2980
Cammarat, Salvatore. "Mass Screening Technique for the Prediction of Adjustment to the First Grade." Ottawa, 1962.

Drolet, Jean-Yves. See No./Voir no 2523

Flaherty, Mary Josephine. See No./Voir no 4063

Gauthier, Gaston. See No./Voir no 3472

Isabelle, Laurent A. See No./Voir no 3735

2981
Keddy, John Arthur. "Selection of Candidates for Entrance to the Ontario College of Education." Toronto, 1950.

2982
Lenchyskyn, David Arthur. "The Design of an Attendance Information System for Ontario Secondary Schools." SUNY, Buffalo, 1981.

2983
Massot, Alain. "Structures décisionnelles dans le processus de qualification - distribution du secondaire V à l'université." Montréal, 1978.

2984
Rusnack, Terrence Anthony. "Accreditation in Alberta Education." Calgary, 1977.

2985
Tymko, Joseph Lawrence. "Accreditation of Alberta Senior High Schools: A Case Study of Public Policy Implementation." Alberta, 1979.

2986
Vaillancourt, Raymond F. "Manifest Structure Analysis in Academic Prediction." Ottawa, 1961.

2987
Williston, Robert Horace. "Admission of Adult Students to University Programs: The Use of Predictors." Toronto, 1981.

Pupil Personnel/Personnel étudiant

2988
Anwar, Muhammad. "Students' Desired Performance in School Government in Ontario." Toronto, 1978.

2989
Barron, Robert Frederick John. "Attitudes of Members of Educational Interest Groups Towards the School Placement of Exceptional Children." Alberta, 1979.

Drolet, Jean-Yves. See No./Voir no 2523

2990
Herman, Albert. "A Comparison of the Self-Concepts and the Ideal Self-Concepts of Grade Ten Matriculation and Non-Matriculation Students in the County of Lacombe, Alberta." Montana, 1968.

2991
Hewitt, Jean Dorothy. "Corporal Punishment in Education: The Tip of the Authoritarian Iceberg." Toronto, 1981.

2992
Macleod, Alan Ross. "Students' Union Power and Influence Structures." Alberta, 1972.

2993
Page, Gordon Graham. "The Classification of Students to Facilitate Decisions on Instruction Directed Toward Affective Goals." British Columbia, 1974.

2994
Read, Edwin Albert. "Promotion Policies and Practices in the Schools of Alberta." Oregon, 1956.

2995
Sly, Hildreth Francis. "An Analysis of Sex Differences in an Alberta School Population." Alberta, 1960.

2996
Smyth, William John. "An Ecological Analysis of Pupil Use of Academic Learning Time." Alberta, 1979.

Pupil Transportation/Transport des étudiants

2997
Bardock, Edison Frederick. "Pupil Transportation in Alberta." Montana, 1975.

2998
Mowat, Gordon Leslie. "A Plan for Recognizing the Costs of Pupil Transportation in Alberta for Purposes of Equalizing Educational Opportunity." Stanford, 1953.

Regan, Ross H. See No./Voir no 2703

Séguin, J.J. See No./Voir no 2695

2999
Skuba, Michael. "Population Density and Pupil Transportation Costs." Alberta, 1965. [Alberta]

General Items/Ouvrages généraux

3000
Alapini, Hippolytus Olukayode. "What the Elementar Schools Should be Doing: Blueprints from Thre Canadian Provinces-Ontario, Alberta and Britis Columbia." British Columbia, 1981.

3001
Blowers, Thomas Anthony. "Personnel Utilization Elementary and Secondary Education in Alberta Alberta, 1972.

3002
Brassard, Jean. "Étude de la relation entre l'efficaci des ateliers pédagogiques des écoles primaires (Québec et les orientations d'action des part naires." Ottawa, 1971.

3003
Brown, James Anthony. "The Social Decentration ar Cultural Understanding of Canadian Children Alberta, 1975.

Cammarat, Salvatore. See No./Voir no 2980

3004
Canning, Patricia M. "Canadian Children's Unde standing of Their Political System." Windsor, 197

3005
Cleghorn, Ailie. "Patterns of Teacher Interaction an Immersion School in Montreal." McGill, 1981.

3006
Davis, John Earl. "The Political Socialization Children in Remote Areas of Canada." Toront 1971.

3007
Gagné, Jacques Réal. "Personalizing the Education Experience and the Hall-Dennis Report Michigan, 1972.

3008
Hambleton, Alixe Elizabeth. "The Elementary Scho Librarian in Ontario: A Study of Role, Ro Perception, Role Conflict and Effectivenes: Toronto, 1980.

3009
Hedges, Henry George. "Volunteer Parental Assi tance in Elementary Schools." Toronto, 1972.

3010
Kapoor, Surinder Kumar. "A Comparative Study Writings in Periodical Publications Concerni Public Elementary and Secondary Education Canada." Montana, 1972.

3011
Khan, Nasim Ullah. "Systems Based Individualiz Learning in Early Childhood." Toronto, 1978.

3012
Ntunaguza, Gabriel. "La généralisation de l'ense gnement primaire et l'utilisation de resources no traditionnelles." Montréal, 1981.

Séguin, Jean-Joseph. See No./Voir no 2695

3013
Van Dromme, Huguette Ruimy. "Les déterminants la réussite et de l'échec scolaire au niveau de 6e année." Montréal, 1972.

History of Elementary Education/ Histoire de l'enseignement au primaire

See also History of Canadian Education/Voir aussi Histoire de l'enseignement canadien

Early Childhood/Première enfance

General Items/Ouvrages généraux

3014
Boorman, Joyce Lilian. "Imagination and Children: Implications for a Theory of Imagination in Children's Learning." Alberta, 1980. [three years to eight years through a creative dance program at the University of Alberta/Programme de danse créative chez des enfants de 3 à 8 ans à l'Université de l'Alberta]

Dickson, William Rushworth. See No./Voir no 2791

3015
Preston, Charles Franklyn. "The Development of Moral Judgement in Young People." Toronto, 1962.

Séguin, Jean-Joseph. See No./Voir no 2695

Pre-School - Pre-Kindergarten/ Pré-scolaire - Pré-maternelle

3016
Baker, Lois Josephine. "The Adult Role in Early Child Language Acquisition: A Study of the Dialogue of Two Mother-Child Pairs." Simon Fraser, 1981.

3017
Betasalel-Paesser, Raquel. "Centre de jour éducatif: implications psycho-pédagogiques d'un programme destiné aux enfants de moins de deux ans." Montréal, 1974.

Birnbaum, Dava Wolfe. See No./Voir no 9354

3018
Church, Edward John Maxwell. "An Evaluation of Pre-School Education in Canada." Toronto, 1950.

3019
Connolly, Jennifer Anne. "The Relationship Between Social Pretend Play and Social Competence in Pre-Schoolers: Correlational and Experimental Studies." Concordia, 1981.

Dart, Richard James. See No./Voir no 6832

3020
Duchesne, Hermann. "Étude d'un instrument d'évaluation des compétences personnelles et sociales au pré-scolaire." Montréal, 1983.

3021
Eaton, Philip. "A Multisensory Computer Assisted Learning Investigation of the Acquisition of Visual Discrimination Skills in Pre-Schoolers and the Mentally Retarded." Calgary, 1975.

3022
Gazan, Sonja Chava. "A Strategy for Stimulation of Representational Skills in the Preschooler." Toronto, 1976.

3023
Goodman, Sherryl Hope. "The Integration of Verbal and Motor Behavior in Preschool Children." Waterloo, 1978.

3024
Goodz, Naomi Susan Sugarman. "Young Children's Comprehension of Words Referring to Temporal Sequence." McGill, 1977.

3025
Hore, Terence. "Social Class Differences in Some Aspects of the Verbal and Non-Verbal Communication Between Mother and Preschool Child." Alberta, 1969.

3026
Johnston, C. Celeste Smith. "The Promotion of Social Competencies in Toddlers Through Peer Modeling." McGill, 1979. [Montreal day care center from 18 to 42 months old/Garderie à Montréal, de 18 à 42 mois]

3027
Johnston, Nancy Mary Elizabeth. "An Experimental Investigation into the Role of Language in Discrimination, Memory and Transfer in Pre-School Children." Toronto, 1969.

3028
Krasnor, Linda Doreen Rose. "An Observational Study of Social Problem Solving in Preschoolers." Waterloo, 1982.

Lai, William Louis. See No./Voir no 3237

3029
Liu, Peter Andrew. "An Investigation of the Relationship Between Qualitative and Quantitative Advances in the Cognitive Development of Pre-school Children." Toronto, 1981.

3030
Miezitis, Solveiga Ausma. "An Exploratory Study of Divergent Production in Preschoolers." Toronto, 1968.

3031
Partridge, Mary Janice. "The Role of Physical Structure in the Control of Social Contingencies to Produce Prosocial Behaviour and Play Setting." Simon Fraser, 1980. [Five year olds/Cinq ans]

Pinkus, Joan. See No./Voir no 9346

3032
Polowy, Hannah S. "Day Care Supervisors Interaction with Three and Four Year Old Children Perceived as Behaviourally Different in a Natural Day Care Setting." British Columbia, 1981.

3033
Segal, Melvyn. "The Relationship Between the Cognitive Style of Reflection, Impulsivity and the Free Play Behaviors of Nursery School Boys." Montréal, 1974.

Tari, Andor Joseph. See No./Voir no 3101

3034
Thériault-Pitre, Jacqueline. "Étude comparative du phénomène d'accélération dans l'apprentissage du nom et du son des lettres de l'alphabet chez des enfants de quatre ans." Laval, 1978.

3035
Verriour, Patrick St. George. "The Literary Language of Selected Four Year Old Children." Alberta, 1979.

3036
Wargny, Nancy J. "Cognitive Aspects of Language Learning in Infants: What Two-Year Olds Understand of Proper, Common and Superordinate Nouns." McGill, 1977.

3037
Waterman, Larry William. "An Evaluation of Variables Affecting the Communication Performance of Preschool Children." Windsor, 1980.

3038
Watson, Russell A.M. "The Interrelationships Among Various Aspects of Language Development in Two Year Olds." Toronto, 1983.

3039
Wintre, Maxine Ann Gallander. "The Development of Social Participation Skills of Preschool Children." York, 1978.

3040
Wright, Kathleen L. "A Naturalistic Study of Social Behaviours of Children in a Preschool." Carleton, 1977.

Kindergarten/Maternelle

3041
Blakey, Janis Marie. "An Investigation of the Relationship Between Children's Key Vocabulary Responses and Certain Piagetian Concepts." British Columbia, 1980.

3042
Bruck, Margaret Ellen. "The Influence of Kindergarten Experience on the Language Acquisition of Children from Different Socioeconomic Backgrounds." McGill, 1972.

Cosgrove, Gregory Tracey. See No./Voir no 3091

Dilley, Marcia Grace. See No./Voir no 3206

Ezrin, Sharyn A. See No./Voir no 4422

Gignac, Leonard Joseph. See No./Voir no 3214

3043
Grunau, Ruth Veronica Elizabeth. "Effects of Elaborative Prompt Condition and Developmental Level on Performance of Addition Problems by Kindergarten Children." British Columbia, 1975.

3044
Ingle, Robert Alexander. "An Experimental Study of the Relationship of Learning Style and Type of Word-Recognition Training to Differentially-Elicited Responses at the Kindergarten Level." Calgary, 1973.

3045
Jensen, Peter Kenneth. "Increasing Cooperative Social Interactions Between Kindergarten Children in a Free Play Setting." Alberta, 1979.

3046
Kariuki, Priscilla Wanjiru. "Training and Transfer of Class Inclusion in Young Children." Alberta, 1980.

Karniol, Rachel. See No./Voir no 3232

3047
Kavanagh, Oliver F. "A Study of Dependency Behavior in Kindergarten Children in Relation to Teacher Style." Toronto, 1973.

Klein, Gerard. See No./Voir no 3787

Lall, G.R. See No./Voir no 4121

Lamb, Eila Mary. See No./Voir no 3121

3048
McConaghy, Gerald Manford. "The Implementation of a New Kindergarten Programme: A Case Study." Toronto, 1981.

3049
O'Neill, Marie José. "An Evaluation of a Method for Developing Learning Strategies in Kindergarten Children with Potential Learning Disabilities." Toronto, 1975.

Rice, Marnie Elizabeth. See No./Voir no 9571

Sanders, Beverly Jean. See No./Voir no 3265

Child Development/Développement de l'enfant

General Items/Ouvrages généraux

Priddle, Ruth Evelyn. See No./Voir no 9384

Achievement/Réalisation

3050
Asarnow, Joan Rosenbaum. "Interpersonal Competence in Preadolescent Boys: An Analysis of Peer Assessment Measures and Social Interaction." Waterloo, 1980. [Grades four, five and six/Quatrième, cinquième et sixième année]

3051
Battle, James. "The Effects of a Tutoring Problem on the Self-Esteem and Academic Achievement of Elementary Students." Alberta, 1972.

3052
Baumal, Ruth. "Learned Helplessness in Children: Development and Reversibility." Toronto, 1980. [Grades one, three and six/Première, troisième et sixième année]

3053
Berens, Anne Elizabeth. "The Socialization of Achievement Motives in Boys and Girls." York, 1973. [Grade five/Cinquième année]

3054
Blackmore, David E. "A Latent Trait Study of Item Bias and Achievement Differences." Alberta, 1980.

3055
Chapman, James William. "Affective Characteristics of Learning Disabled and Normally Achieving Elementary School Children: A Comparative Study." Alberta, 1979.

3056
Cullen, Joy Lauren. "Learning to Cope with Failure." Alberta, 1979. [Grade four/Quatrième année]

3057
Danley, Raymond Roger. "A Study of Relationship Between Environments and Student Achievement." Toronto, 1982. [Grade five/Cinquième année]

Day, Victor Hugh. See No./Voir no 3156

Eggert, Wallace Victor. See No./Voir no 3103

3058
Greenfield, Thomas Barr. "Systems Analysis in Education: A Factor Analysis and Analysis Variance of Pupil Achievement." Alberta, 1964.

3059
Hutson, R. Leighton. "An Exploratory Study of Parents-Child Relationship and Academic Achievement." Montréal, 1969.

Jones, Frisell Wagner. See No./Voir no 3086

3060
Jones, Pauline Alice. "Person-Situation Congruence Relative to Sex Differences in Elementary School Achievement." Alberta, 1969.

3061
King, Leonard Henry. "An Attributional Analysis of Student Achievement-Related Behavior and the Expectancy Effect." Alberta, 1979.

3062
Madak, Paul Richard. "The Effect of Past School Mobility on School Performance of Grade Six Students." Manitoba, 1982.

Moore, Joyce Elaine. See No./Voir no 9456

3063
Morris, Julius Richard. "A Longitudinal Investigation of Early Evaluation and Teacher Consultation on Children's Performance in the Primary Grades." Toronto, 1979.

3064
Smithman, Harold Henry. "Student Achievement as a Measure of Teacher Performance." California, Los Angeles, 1970.

3065
Speare, Allen Denley. "Student Mobility and Academic Achievement." Toronto, 1971.

3066
Sunday, E.P.M. "The Assignment of Skills Related to Peer Acceptance in Grade Four Children." Toronto, 1983.

Tari, Andor Joseph. See No./Voir no 3101

3067
Therrien, Susan Alice. "Teachers' Attributions of Student Ability." Alberta, 1975.

3068
Wagner, Rudolph. "The Relationships of Cognitive Style and Classroom Environment to Academic Achievement: An Exploratory Study." Ottawa, 1978.

Walters, Jean Elizabeth Maddox. See No./Voir no 3275

3069
Woodliffe, Helen Mae. "A Study of Change in the Creative Thinking Ability of Grade V Children." Toronto, 1970.

Behaviour/Comportement

Asarnow, Joan Rosenbaum. See No./Voir no 3050

3070
Batcher, Elaine. "Emotion in the Classroom: A Study of Children's Experience." Toronto, 1979.

Baumal, Ruth. See No./Voir no 3052

3071
Burstein, Samuel Benjamin. "Cognitive Behavioral Intervention with Agressive Children: A Comparative Study." Waterloo, 1980.

Howard, Theresa Coleen. See No./Voir no 3758

Kendall, Mary Ellen. See No./Voir no 3096

King, Leonard Henry. See No./Voir no 3061

3072
Loeber, Magda S. "The Relationship Between Classification and Consequences of Student Behaviour in Three Primary Classrooms." Queen's, 1979.

3073
Mahen, Robert Gordon. "Relationships Between Students' Classroom Behaviors and Selected Context, Process, and Product Variables." Alberta, 1977.

McDonald, Mary K. See No./Voir no 9381

3074
Morris, Mary Laverne. "A Study of Childhood Depression with Special Emphasis on Classroom Behaviour." Toronto, 1978.

Moyal, Barbara Ruth Roback. See No./Voir no 9197

3075
Petrimoulx, Catherine. "Cooperative Behavior in Boys in Relationship to Internal External Control, Modeling and Communication." Windsor, 1976. [Grade five/Cinquième année]

3076
Rudner, Howard Lawrence. "Effects of Modeling and Role-Playing on Assertive Behavior in Children." Alberta, 1976.

3077
Toker, Mia Beer. "Impulsivity, Teaching Strategies and Matching Behavior of Grade Two Children." McGill, 1976.

Walters, Jean M. See No./Voir no 3275

3078
Wood, H. Diane. "Predicting Behavioural Types in Preadolescent Girls from Psychosocial Development and Friendship Values." Windsor, 1976.

3079
Wright, Ian Michael. "Moral Reasoning and Conduct of Selected Elementary School Children." Alberta, 1975.

Race and Socioeconomic Status in Child Development/ Statut racial et socio-économique dans le développement de l'enfant

3080
Baillargeon, Madeleine. "La compréhension du langage de l'enseignant d'enfants de statuts socio-économiques différents." Laval, 1978.

Bruck, Margaret. See No./Voir no 3042

Buckridan, Rakib. See No./Voir no 3801

3081
Comeau, Judith. "Comparaison de language oral de sujets de dix ans et de seize ans issus de deux milieux socio-économiques." Montréal, 1976.

3082
Eley, Malcolm Gordon. "Socioeconomic Status Differences in Mother-Child Verbal Interaction Practices as Related to the Symbolic Mediatory Processes of the Child." Alberta, 1973.

3083
Graham, Thomas Francis. "Doll Play Phantasies of Negro and White Primary School Children." Ottawa, 1952.

Greenberg, Corin Merle. See No./Voir no 9003

Hore, Terence. See No./Voir no 3025

3084
Horth, Raynald. "Analyse de quelques éléments du processus de marginalisation de perturbés affectifs graves." Montréal, 1978.

3085
Ijaz, Mian Ahmed. "Ethnic Attitudes of Elementary School Children Toward Blacks and East Indians and the Effect of a Cultural Program on These Attitudes." Toronto, 1980. [Grades five and six/Cinquième et sixième année]

3086
Jones, Frissell Wagner. "The Interrelation of Socio-economic Status and Academic Achievement in Nova Scotia, Pennsylvania, and Virginia." Pennsylvania State, 1964.

Keeton-Wilson, Anne. See No./Voir no 3233

3087
LaPerrière-Nguyen, Anne. "Le processus d'exclusion de l'école des réalités des classes populaires: une analyse des perceptions de l'école et de la communauté." Toronto, 1980. [Montreal/Montréal]

3088
Manos, James. "Children's Cognitive Abilities and Their Relation to Socio-Economic Status and Some Personality Characteristics." Alberta, 1975.

3089
Molloy, Geoffrey Neale. "Age, Socioeconomic Status and Patterns of Cognitive Ability." Alberta, 1973.

Roberts, Gloria B. See No./Voir no 3263

Weinzweig, Paul Alan. See No./Voir no 10008

Parent-Child Relations and Parent Education/ Relations parents-enfants et éducation des parents

Baker, Lois Josephine. See No./Voir no 3016

3090
Burke, Sharon Ogden. "Familial Strain and the Development of Normal and Handicapped Children in Single and Two Parent Families." Toronto, 1978.

3091
Cosgrove, Gregory Tracey. "Home Training of Parents of Culturally Different Junior Kindergarten Children." Toronto, 1982.

3092
Danziger, Flora. "Verbal Communication Between Mother and Child and Some Aspects of Cognitive Decentering." Toronto, 1975.

Eley, Malcolm Gordon. See No./Voir no 3082

3093
Fradkin, Barbara. "Premenstrual Tension, Expectancy and Mother-Child Relations." Ottawa, 1982.

Gyra, John C. See No./Voir no 9004

3094
Himes, Mavis Carole. "Language Development and Patterns of Mother-Child-Interaction." Toronto, 1978.

Hutson, R. Leighton. See No./Voir no 3059

3095
Kaplan, Faith Kinaler. "Parent Education Program: A Comparison of the Effects of Parent Effectiveness Training and Human Effectiveness Training in Parent Social Competence, Family Interaction and Child Behavior." Toronto, 1977.

3096
Kendall, Mary Ellen. "Maternal Influence on the Father-Absent Child: Childrearing Practices and Adjustment Associated with Two Patterns of Child Behavior." Alberta, 1977.

3097
Lewis, Norah Lillian. "Advising the Parents: Child Rearing in British Columbia during the Inter-War Years." British Columbia, 1980.

3098
McKim, Margaret Kathleen. "Mother and Child a Problem Solving Unit: An Analysis of the Characteristics and Determinants of Reflective and Impulsive Behaviour." Carleton, 1977.

3099
Muskat, J.S. "The Impact of Fatherhood: An Exploratory Study." Toronto, 1983.

Painter, Susan Lee. See No./Voir no 9387

Roberts, Gloria Bernadette. See No./Voir no 3263

Robertson, Sharon Elaine. See No./Voir no 3264

3100
Schneider, Barry Howard. "An Elaboration of the Relationship Between Parental Behaviour and Children's Moral Development." Toronto, 1977.

Steinert, Yvonne. See No./Voir no 4421

3101
Tari, Andor Joseph. "The Quality of Fathering and It Relation to the Achievement Motives of the Pre School Child." Alberta, 1971.

Tudiver, Judith Gail. See No./Voir no 9230

Teacher-Pupil Relations/Relations professeurs-élèves

3102
Bognar, Carl Joseph. "The Effect of Dissonant Feedback about Achievement on Teachers' Expectations." Toronto, 1980. [Grade six/Sixième année]

Cressman, Clare B. See No./Voir no 4304

3103
Eggert, Wallace Victor. "A Study of Teaching Behaviors as They Relate to Pupil Behaviors, Achievement and Attitudes." Alberta, 1977.

3104
Fasano, James H. "Pupil Characteristics and Teacher Pupil Dyadic Interaction." Alberta, 1977.

Hedges, Henry George. See No./Voir no 3009

3105
Johnson, Francis Henry. "Changing Conceptions o Discipline and Pupil-Teacher Relations in Canadia Schools." Toronto, 1952.

3106
MacDonald, I.F. "Teacher-Pupil Interaction and the Development of Moral Reasoning in Sixth Grade Children." Alberta, 1976.

3107
Moody, Peter Richard. "Descriptive Studies of Si Children in their Classroom Contexts." Alberta 1980.

Morris, Mary Laverne. See No./Voir no 3074

3108
Muttart, David Garth. "A Study of Teacher-Pupi Interaction as It Relates to Differential Teache Expectations and Selected Teacher Characteris tics." Alberta, 1977.

Steinert, Yvonne. See No./Voir no 4421

CURRICULUM DEVELOPMENT AND INSTRUCTION/ PLAN D'ÉTUDE ET ENSEIGNEMENT

General Items/Ouvrages généraux

3109
Boag, Noel Harvey. "Teacher Perception of Curricula Change." Alberta, 1980.

Dupuis, Jean-Claude. See No./Voir no 2054

3110
Irvine, Florence Gladys. "A Study of Some Curricular Problems of Selected Rural Elementary Schools in Ontario, with Particular Reference to the Occupational Mobility of Students." Toronto, 1972.

3111
Mallinson, Thomas John. "An Experimental Investigation of Group-Directed Discussion in the Classroom." Toronto, 1954. [From grades five to grade twelve/De la cinquième à la douzième année]

3112
Oviatt, Delmer T. "A Revision of the Program of Studies for the Elementary Schools of Alberta (Grades I-IV)." Stanford, 1949.

3113
Williams, Rosemary Janet. "Children's Perception of Foreign Countries and Foreign Peoples: Implications for Curriculum and Instruction." Toronto, 1982.

Art

3114
Boughton, Douglas Gordon. "Development and Validation of a Curriculum Evaluation Model for the Visual Arts." Alberta, 1976.

Cox, Marlene Joan. See No./Voir no 4112

3115
Moody, Margaret Mary. "An Analysis of the Goals and Activities Recommended by Canadian Provincial Elementary Art Curriculum Guides, Compared with Each Other, and with Recent Art Education Literature." Oregon, 1974.

Tait, George Edward. See No./Voir no 2621

Creative Dance/Danse créative

Boorman, Joyce Lilian. See No./Voir no 3014

French/Français

Bertrand, Frère. See No./Voir no 3123
Bradford, Florence Emily. See No./Voir no 7724

3116
Chidekel, Beatrice Vivian. "A Comparative Study of the French Curriculum in Selected Elementary School Systems of the United States and Canada." Loyola, 1961.

3117
Desjarlais, Lionel. "Le bilinguisme et la connaissance du vocabulaire à l'école primaire." Ottawa, 1954.

Gervais-Ranger, Flore. See No./Voir no 3129

3118
Léger, Raymond Joseph. "Critical Teaching Behaviors of the Ontario French-Language Elementary School Teachers Perceived by Pupils." Pennsylvania State, 1972.

Lemire, Soeur Antoinette. See No./Voir no 3132

3119
Richards, Merle Saundra Kazdan. "A Comparison of Classroom Climate in Regular and French Immersion Primary Classes." Toronto, 1978. [Teaching of French as a second language to English-speaking elementary education students/Enseignement du français langue seconde aux étudiants anglophones au primaire]

Suarez, Frère. See No./Voir no 3139
Tremaine, Ruth V. See No./Voir no 3142
Urbain, Frère Marie. See No./Voir no 3143

Health, Family Life/Santé, vie familiale

3120
Gray, Gerald Eldon. "The Development of an Elementary School Curriculum Guide, Division One and Two, for the Province of Saskatchewan." Oregon, 1976.

3121
Lamb, Eila Mary. "A Study of a Primary Preventive Intervention with Young Children." British Columbia, 1978.

Language Arts/Philologie

Arana, Milton Eulogio. See No./Voir no 4109

3122
Batstone, David Wilton. "The Use of Visual Recognition Testing in Spelling by Fourth Grade Children." Western Ontario, 1982.

3123
Bertrand, Frère. "Étude de vocabulaire compris par les enfants dans les livres écrits pour les adultes." Montréal, 1944.

Bouchard, André. See No./Voir no 1145

3124
Brown, Lloyd Raymond. "Imagination and Literary Theory: Implications for a Literature Program in the Elementary School." Alberta, 1971.

Clandinin, D.J. See No./Voir no 4303

3125
Cork, Elizabeth Fredericka. "The Effect of the Personality Variable Locus of Control on Imitation Learning." Ottawa, 1979.

Desjarlais, Lionel. See No./Voir no 3117
Durand, Marielle. See No./Voir no 3207

3126
Farrar, Mary Patricia Thomas. "Defining and Examining Instruction: An Analysis of Discourse in a Literature Lesson." Toronto, 1981.

3127
Fleming, David Russell. "The Effect of Audience on the Expressive Language of Working Class Children." Toronto, 1979. [Grades three and four/Troisième et quatrième année]

3128
Gambell, Trevor John. "The Occurrence and Analysis of a Repertoire of Situational Language in Grade Six Children." Alberta, 1978.

3129
Gervais-Ranger, Flore. "Quelques aspects de la subordination dans la langue d'enfants de sixième année." Montréal, 1974.

3130
Hambley, Janice Marie. "The Growth of Word Meaning during Middle Childhood." Toronto, 1978. [Grades three and six/Troisième et sixième année]

Himes, Mavis Carole. See No./Voir no 3094
Keller, Arnold. See No./Voir no 4251

3131
Kumar, Krishna. "Literature in the School Curriculum: A Comparative Study of the Literary Materials Approved for Use in Grades Four, Five, and Six in Madhya Pradesh, India, and Ontario, Canada." Toronto, 1981.

Labercane, George Donald. See No./Voir no 3933

3132
Lemire, Soeur Antoinette. "Structure syntaxique de la langue de l'enseignement en 5ᵉ année." Ottawa, 1968.

3133
Martyn, Harold George. "Grammar in Ontario Elementary Public Schools." Toronto, 1931.

3134
Mosha, Herme Joseph. "Curriculum Change in Language Arts in Alberta: A Case Study." Alberta, 1979.

3135
Nolan, Francis Michael. "Composing Processes of Grade 6 Able Writers." Alberta, 1978.

3136
Piya-Ajariya, Laeka. "Teacher Expectations of Beginning Grade One Pupils' Performance on Selected Language-Related Skill Tasks." Alberta, 1978.

3137
Sebastian, Robert Newbold. "The Effectiveness of Concomitant Instructional Materials in Elementary School Lunchrooms as a Means for Vocabulary Development." Toronto, 1977.

3138
Simms, Jeremy Joseph. "The Dynamics of the Implementation of Curriculum Innovations." Alberta, 1978. [Grades two and six/Deuxième et sixième année]

Strauss, H. Peter. See No./Voir no 3979

3139
Suarez, Frère. "Les fables du bonhomme (La Fontaine) au service de l'école canadienne." Ottawa, 1949.

3140
Sweeney, James Ernest. "Neuropsychological Significance of Phonetically Accurate and Phonetically Inaccurate Spelling Errors in Younger and Older Children." Windsor, 1977.

3141
Thomas, Veslof. "A Spelling Errors Analysis and an Appraisal of Its Usefulness in Improving the Spelling Achievement of Selected Alberta Students." Oregon, 1966.

3142
Tremaine, Ruth V. "Syntactic and Cognitive Development in English-Speaking Children Learning French in Primary School." Ottawa, 1974.

3143
Urbain, Frère Marie. "Pour une échelle d'orthographe-vocabulaire écrit des jeunes Canadiens-français." Montréal, 1937.

3144
Vinette, Roland. "Le vocabulaire des enfants de l'école primaire." Montréal, 1943.

3145
Watson, Rita Patricia May. "From Meaning to Definition: The Development of Word Meaning in the School-Aged Child." Toronto, 1982.

3146
Whale, Kathleen Bailie. "The Teaching of Writing in an Elementary School." Toronto, 1980.

3147
Zebroski, James Thomas. "Writing as 'Activity': Composition Development from the Perspective of the Vygotskian School." Ohio State, 1983.

Mathematics/Mathématiques

3148
Anderson, Alvin Leonard. "Testing and the Elementary Mathematics Program in Zone One: A School System Approach." Alberta, 1979.

Babcock, Gail Reichenbach. See No./Voir no 3418

3149
Bana, John Peter. "Distractions in Non-Verbal Mathematical Problems: Some Effects on the Problem-Solving Behavior and Performance of Young Children." Alberta, 1977.

3150
Bergeron, Jacques C. "Stratégies des enfants de 9 à 12 ans face à un problème de structures mathématiques." Montréal, 1976.

3151
Bourgeois, Roger Daniel. "Young Children's Behavior in Division Problems." Alberta, 1976.

3152
Campbell, John Duncan. "The Arithmetic of the Elementary Schools in Ontario." Toronto, 1943.

3153
Cathcart, William George. "The Relationship Between Primary Students' Rationalization of Conservation and Their Mathematical Ability and Achievement." Alberta, 1969.

3154
Cooper, Norma Colleen. "Information Processing by Teachers and Pupils During Mathematics Instruction." Alberta, 1979.

3155
Coron, Michel. "Initiation au calcul et raisonnement mathématique chez des enfants de huit et neuf ans." Montréal, 1967.

3156
Day, Victor Hugh. "Attribution Retraining and Academic Persistence." Queen's 1979. [Grades five and six/Cinquième et sixième année]

Drost, Dale R. See No./Voir no 3424

3157
Feavyour, Herman Eldon. "Problem Solving Ability in Arithmetic (Grade 3)." Toronto, 1957.

3158
Forget, Jacques. "Modification du rendement et des intérêts en mathématiques par l'utilisation systématique de jeux éducatifs." Montréal, 1981.

3159
Gaskill, James Leslie. "The Emotional Block in Mathematics: A Multivariate Study." British Columbia, 1979. [Grade six/Sixième année]

Greenberg, Norman Arthur. See No./Voir no 9530

Gruneau, Ruth Veronica Elizabeth. See No./Voir no 3043

3160
Haug, Elmer Joseph. "A Comparative Study of Mathematics Achievement in Two Types of Instructional Setting: Continuous Progress and Traditional." Toronto, 1973.

3161
Joyce, Lester D. "A Guide for Teachers of Arithmetic in Canadian Elementary Schools." Teachers College, Columbia, 1949.

3162
Kansky, Robert James. "An Analysis of Models Used in Australia, Canada, Europe, and the United States to Provide an Understanding of Addition and Multiplication over the Natural Numbers." Illinois, 1969.

King, Leonard Henry. See No./Voir no 3061

Lawson, Glen Allen. See No./Voir no 9550

3163
Little, John Irvine. "A Mathematical and Cognitive Analysis of Children's Behavior in Spatial Problems." Alberta, 1976.

Lukasevich, Ann. See No./Voir no 2595

Partlow, Hugh Russell. See No./Voir no 2631

3164
Phillips, Alexander James. "Discovery, Identification and Remedial Treatment of Difficulties in the Fundamental Operations in Elementary School Arithmetic." Toronto, 1945.

3165
Pothier, Yvonne Marie. "Partitioning: Construction of Rational Number in Young Children." Alberta, 1981.

3166
Roach, Paul J. "Evidence for Hemispheric Dominance in Children's Arithmetic Calculation Performance." Windsor, 1975.

3167
Seaton, Edward Thomas. "Practice in Arithmetic or the Arithmetic Scale for Ontario Public Schools." Toronto, 1924.

Smyth, William John. See No./Voir no 2996

3168
Sumagaysay, Lourdes S. "The Effects of Varying Practice Exercises and Relating Methods of Solution in Mathematics Problem-Solving." Toronto, 1970.

Tuokko, Holly Ann. See No./Voir no 9081

Physical Education/Éducation physique

See also Curriculum Development and Instruction/Voir aussi Plan d'étude et enseignement

Science

3169
Chakandua, Jimmy G. "Defining Characteristics of a New Elementary Science Curriculum: Variance Among Developers, Teachers and Practices in Classrooms." British Columbia, 1982.

Dupuis, Jean-Claude. See No./Voir no 2054

Finegold, Menahem. See No./Voir no 3448

3170
Kargbo, Dennis. "Operational Structures Applied by Children to Problems Related to Predator-Prey Interaction in Ecology and the Beliefs Held about This Phenomenon: A Comparison with Inheider and Piaget's Study of the Hydraulic Press Problem." British Columbia, 1980.

3171
Morrisey, James Thomas. "Factors That Influence Elementary Teachers in One School District of New Brunswick (Canada) to Use Outdoor Education as a Teaching Method." Maine, 1981.

3172
Pearson, David Arthur. "The Influence of the Reflective/Impulsive Dimension of Problem-Solving Skills in Elementary School Science." Alberta, 1976. [Grade six/Sixième année]

3173
Schoeneberger, Mary Margaret. "Hard as Rock: A Study of Children's Perceptions of Mineral Hardness." Alberta, 1981. [Geological understanding/Compréhension géologique]

3174
Trempe, Pierre-Léon. "La capacité à connaître certains phénomènes naturels chez des jeunes du primaire ayant complété le programme-cadre des sciences de la nature (Ministère de l'Éducation de Québec)." Montréal, 1981.

3175
Wolfe, L.F. "Toward Understanding the Ideas About Science Communicated by Elementary School Teachers." Toronto, 1983.

Social Studies/Études sociales

3176
Bailey, Gordon Archibald. "Education and the Social Construction of Reality: Canadian Identity as Portrayed in Elementary School Social Studies Textbooks." Oregon, 1975.

3177
Banda, Meinrad R. "Children's Political Perception and Attitudes Toward Democratic Values." Alberta, 1981. [Kindergarten and grades one and two/Maternelle, première et deuxième année]

Boag, Noel Harvey. See No./Voir no 3109

Canning, Patricia M. See No./Voir no 3004

3178
De Cotiis, Constant J. "A Study of Prevailing Practices in the Presentation of Contemporary Problems in Elementary Schools." Laval, 1951.

3179
Dhand, Hargopal. "A Value Analysis of Saskatchewan Social Studies Textbooks." Montana, 1967.

3180
Frankcombe, Brian James. "Comparative Curriculum Development in Elementary Social Studies/Social Science in Alberta and Tasmania." Michigan State, 1978.

Henslowe, Shirley Anne. See No./Voir no 3958

Korteweg, Laurens. See No./Voir no 3467

3181
Landes, Ronald George. "Socialization to Political Culture: A Comparative Study of English-Canadian and American School Children." York, 1973. [From grades four to grade eight/De la quatrième à la huitième année]
3182
Lattin, Richard Thomas. "An Evaluation of Elementary School Pupils Knowledge of Canada as Related to the Opinion of Authorities." Iowa, 1952.

3183
Newman, Warren Oscar. "A Study of the Relationship Between Time Understanding and Social Studies Achievement in Grade Six Children." Toronto, 1970.
3184
Odynak, Emily. "Kanata Kit One: A Classroom Experience." Alberta, 1981.
3185
Westermark, Tory I. "A Comparative Study of Selected Canadian and American Sixth-Grade Students' Knowledge of Certain Basic Concepts about Canada and the United States." Oregon, 1962.

Educational Psychology at the Elementary Education Level/ Psychologie éducative au niveau élémentaire

See also Special Education/Voir aussi Éducation spécialisée
3186
Amundson, Norman Edmund. "Transitional Analysis with Children." Alberta, 1975. [Grades 3 to 6/De la troisième à la sixième année]
3187
Anderson, Dianne Evelyn. "Psychosocial Correlates of Locus of Control Expectancies in Female Children." Alberta, 1976.
3188
Audy, Jacques. "La connaissance des résultats et les cédules de renforcement relativement à la performance motrice avec des garçons de 9 et 10 ans." Ottawa, 1971.
3189
Baugh, Elspeth Harcus Wallace. "The Relationship Between Performance on Laboratory Measures of Attention in Previously Identified High and Low-Risk Grade One Pupils." York, 1978.
Benezra, Esther. See No./Voir no 3885
Berens, Anne Elizabeth. See No./Voir no 3053
3190
Bernfeld, Gary Alan. "Dynamics and Correlates of Individual Differences in Social and Non-social Information Processing in Children." Queen's, 1982. [second grade/Deuxième année]
Bernstein, Deborah Ann. See No./Voir no 3943
3191
Beserve, Christopher Abilogun. "Relationship Between Home Environment and Cognitive and Personality Characteristics of Working-Class West Indian Pupils in Toronto: Consequences for Their Education." Toronto, 1976.
3192
Bhatty, Rajbir. "Motivation in Low-Achiever and Normal Children." Saskatchewan, 1977.

3193
Bickersteth, Patrick. "A Cross-Cultural Study c Memory and Reasoning." Alberta, 1979. [Canad and/et Sierra Leone]
3194
Bregen, Mary Sharon. "The Relationship of Self Esteem and Social Desirability Responding t Primary Grade Children's Classroom Adjustment. York, 1981.
3195
Borgen, William Alfred. "Relative Effects of a Seg mented Model Versus a Molar Model in Teachin Children Appropriate Group Discussion Skills. Alberta, 1976.
3196
Boutilier, Robert Gordon. "The Development c Understanding of Social Systems." Britis Columbia, 1981.
3197
Bradbury, Ola Hinton. "Patterns of Children's Prefer ences." Alberta, 1972.
3198
Brammer, Dennis Leslie. "Maladaptive Behaviors: Predictive and Follow-up Study." Alberta, 1977.
Burtis, Paul Judson. See No./Voir no 9355
3199
Chattaway, Erma Jean. "Learned Helplessness Elementary School Aged Children: The Effects c Noncontingency, Failure, and Reinforcement Res ponsibility on Training and Generalization Tas Performance." Manitoba, 1981.
3200
Coe, Karen Jamie Fraser. "A Developmental Study c Children's Picture-Word Recall and Recognitio Memory as a Function of Presentation Media. Calgary, 1979.
3201
Corlis, Carol Anne. "Curiosity in Open and Close Schooling Systems: A Developmental Investiga tion." Toronto, 1975.
3202
Coward, Teresa R. "The Effects of Match/Mismatc Between Reinforcement History and Success c Failure on Violence of Success or Failure and c Attribution of Responsibility for Success c Failure." York, 1975. [Toronto YMCA boys fror nine to thirteen years old/Garçons de 9 à 13 ans d YMCA de Toronto]
3203
Crozier, Marilyn Elizabeth. "Tutoring with Precisio in the Elementary School." Alberta, 1972.
Dansereau, Stéphanie. See No./Voir no 1147
3204
De Avila, Edward A. "Children's Transformation c Visual Information According to Non-Verba Syntactical Rules." York, 1974.
Derevensky, Jeffrey L. See No./Voir no 3805
Desbiens, Danielle. See No./Voir no 9661
3205
Desmarais, Gilles. "Différentiation et compétenc motrices en relation avec la prévalence manuell chez l'enfant droitier: une étude exploratoire. Ottawa, 1977.

3206
Dilley, Marcia Grace. "Verbal and Non-Verbal Memory in Children." Western Ontario, 1975.

3207
Durand, Marielle. "L'étude des manifestations du pouvoir de l'autorité de l'adulte sur l'enfant - personnage et ses réactions de celui-ci face à ce pouvoir dans la littérature enfantine." Montréal, 1975.

Esses, Lillian Marlene. See No./Voir no 9365

3208
Fagan, Michael John. "Student, Teacher, and Classroom Level Variables as Determinants of Self-Concept among Elementary School Students." Toronto, 1979.

3209
Flewelling, Robert William. "The Development of Habituation and Its Relation to Selective Attention in Elementary School Children." Carleton, 1976.

Flores, Miguela Bustos. See No./Voir no 3496

Forsberg, Lois Anne. See No./Voir no 9523

3210
Fu, Lewis Lean Wei. "An Experimental Investigation of the Interaction Between Resultant Achievement Motivation and Experimentally Induced Probability of Succeeding at a Task." Ottawa, 1975. [Grade six/Sixième année]

3211
Garson, Chrystelle. "Cognitive Impulsivity in Children and the Effects of Training." McGill, 1977.

3212
Getty, Gerald Ronald. "Stylistic and Methodological Considerations in the Description of School Children." Western Ontario, 1975.

3213
Giasson-Lachance, Jocelyne. "Utilisation de la couleur dans la mise en relief de graphèmes chez des enfants de classes maternelles." Laval, 1977.

3214
Gignac, Leonard Joseph. "Observation of Learning Style as a Means of Identifying and Treating Learning Failure in Young Children." Windsor, 1980. [627 children in kindergarten and first grade/627 enfants de maternelle et de première année]

3215
Goodman, Doba Rebecca. "Stage Transitions and the Developmental Trace of Constructive Operators: An Investigation of a Neopiagetian Theory of Cognitive Growth." York, 1979.

3216
Goyecke, John R.M. "The Development of Children's Reaction Time Set: The Significance of Time Estimation and Cardiac Activity." Waterloo, 1969.

3217
Grant, Marion Elder. "Memory and Forgetting: A Theoretical, Historical and Statistical Study." Toronto, 1931.

3218
Greckol, Sonja Ruth. "A Developmental Study of Children's Jokes: Descriptive and Structural Approaches." Alberta, 1978.

Greenberg, Corin Merle. See No./Voir no 9003

3219
Groenweg, Gerrit. "The Development of Comprehension: Some Linguistic and Cognitive Determinants of Sentence Verification." Toronto, 1983.

3220
Hallschmid, Claus A. "Intrinsic Motivation: The Effects of Task Choice, Reward Magnitude, and Reward Choice." Alberta, 1977.

Harrison, Linda Faye. See No./Voir no 1151

3221
Hartmann, Bryan Douglas. "A Review of Conceptual Tempo and an Examination of the Definition of This Construct in Relation to Intelligence, Problem Difficulty and Critical Alternative Instruction." Alberta, 1977. [Grade five students from St. John's, Newfoundland/Étudiants de cinquième année de Saint-Jean, Terre-Neuve]

3222
Herscovitch, Arthur Gary. "The Influence of a Model on the Development of Adaptive and Maladaptive Problem-Solving Behavior in Children." Manitoba, 1975.

3223
Hidi, Suzanne Erica. "Conditional Reasoning in Children: Inferred Versus Given Rules and Intrinsically Conditional Versus Intrinsically Predicative Relations." Toronto, 1976.

3224
Hildyard, Angela. "Children's Abilities to Produce Inferences from Written and Oral Material." Toronto, 1976.

Horth, Raynald. See No./Voir no 3084

3225
Hritzuk, John. "A Comparative and Experimental Study of Set." Alberta, 1968.

3226
Hundert, Joel Philip. "The Accuracy of Self-Rated Academic Performance in a Classroom Token Program." Western Ontario, 1976.

3227
Hundleby, Sigrid Anne. "Three Self-Instructional Videotape Communication Skill Programs." Alberta, 1977.

3228
Irvine, James William. "Handedness Preference, Manual Dexterity, Ear Asymmetry in Dichotic Listening and Grade Two Reading Proficiency." Alberta, 1972.

3229
Ives, Sumner William. "Children's Ability to Coordinate Spatial Perspectives Through Notational Descriptions." Toronto, 1976.

3230
Jamieson, M.S. "The Immigrant Child and Adjustment to Learning in a Second Culture." Alberta, 1982.

3231
Jones, Robert J. "Auditory and Visual Sense Modality Functioning and Reading in Primary Grade Boys." Waterloo, 1973.

Kariuki, Priscilla Wanjiru. See No./Voir no 3046

3232
Karniol, Rachel. "A Causal Attribution Interpretation of Immanent Justice Responses in Children." Waterloo, 1977.

3233
Keeton-Wilson, Anne. "Processes for Serial Recall Related to the Socio-Economic Status and Intelligence of Children in Grade One." Toronto, 1973.

Keller, Sandra M. See No./Voir no 10401

3234
Keschner, Dorothee Anna. "Dependence and Independence in Primary School Children." Toronto, 1957.

King, Michael Christopher. See No./Voir no 9019

3235
Kinkaide, Alexandra. "Children's Knowledge of Temporal Sequences: Spontaneous and Trained Responses." Alberta, 1979.

3236
Kurland, David Midian. "The Effect of Massive Practice on Children's Operational Efficiency and Short Term Memory Span." Toronto, 1981.

3237
Lai, William Louis. "The Effects of Discrimination - Acquisition with and without Errors on Reversal and Nonreversal Shifts in Preschool and Second Grade Children." Alberta, 1976.

3238
Langevin, Ronald Lindsay André. "A Study of Curiosity, Intelligence and Creativity." Toronto, 1970. [Grade six/Sixième année]

Larin, Gilles. See No./Voir no 2571

3239
Lawton, Murray Shaune. "The Development of Analytic Integrative, Cognitive Styles in Young Children." Toronto, 1977. [one, three and five year olds/1, 3 et 5 ans]

3240
L'Écuyer, René. "Les transformations des perceptions, de soi chez les enfants de trois, cinq et huit ans." Montréal, 1972.

3241
Leung, Jupian Jupchung. "Induction, Recipient Deservingness and Personality Attractiveness: Effects on Children's Helping Behaviors." British Columbia, 1981. [195 Grade five and six boys and girls/195 garçons et filles de la cinquième et sixième année]

3242
Lewis, Elmer N. "Memory: Learning, Retention and Forgetting of Public School Pupils." Toronto, 1934.

3243
Loeb, Nora. "The Psychological and Educational Significance of Social Acceptability and Its Approval in an Elementary School Setting." Toronto, 1941.

3244
Maas, Elizabeth. "Children's Understanding of Emotionally, Mentally and Physically Handicapped Behaviours, and Related Mental Health Concepts: A Developmental Study." British Columbia, 1976.

MacDonald, Irene France. See No./Voir no 3106

3245
Malloch, Lynette Rockwood. "Modified Cognitive Therapy and the Preadolescent: A Descriptive Exploratory Study." Toronto, 1979. [Grades five and six/Cinquième et sixième année]

3246
Martin, David Standish. "A Study of Pupil Ethno-Centrism Toward Pre-Western Eskimo Culture in Relation to Certain Learner Variables and Instructional Conditions." Boston College, 1971.

3247
McCarty, Mary Anne. "The Influence of Imaginativ Play Predisposition on the Learning of Socia Skills." Toronto, 1977. [Grade three/Troisièm année]

3248
McDonald, Linda Mary Olive. "A Validation of Thre Instructional Procedures for Early Language. Alberta, 1980.

3249
McLauchlan, Derek George. "Modifying the Tas Strategies of Impulsive Children." Alberta, 1977.

McLaughlin, Judith B. See No./Voir no 9033

Mock, Karen Rochelle. See No./Voir no 2580

Moore, Russell F. See No./Voir no 4325

Morris, Mary Laverne. See No./Voir no 3074

Moyal, Barbara Ruth Roback. See No./Voir no 9197

3250
Mulcahy, Robert Francis. "GSR, HR Responses an Vigilance Behaviour in Normal and Retarde Children." Alberta, 1975.

3251
Mwamwenda, Tuntufye Selemani. "A Relationshi Between Successive-Simultaneous Synthesis an Concrete Operational Thought." Alberta, 198] [Kindergarten and grades one and two/Maternelle première et deuxième année]

3252
Neufeld, Gordon Arthur. "The Relationship of Speech Sound Discrimination to the Development of Ea Asymmetries in Grade-School Children." Britis Columbia, 1975.

3253
Nicholl, George MacKenzie. "The Effect of Advance Organizers on a Cognitive Social Learning Group. Toronto, 1975. [from nine to thirteen years old/D 9 à 13 ans]

3254
Noyes, Barbara Ann. "The Effects of Seating Arrange ments on Performance in a Classroom Setting. York, 1971. [Grade six/Sixième année]

3255
Pasko, Stan Joseph. "The Effect of Varying th Number of Irrelevant Attributes on Area Conser vation Performance." Ottawa, 1976. [Grade two Deuxième année]

3256
Pelletier, Aurèle. "Étude de la différenciation psy chologique de Witkin en fonction de l'irradiation e de la généralisation du set de Uznadze." Ottawa 1982.

Peters, Kenneth Gordon. See No./Voir no 3889

3257
Pike, Ruth. "How Children Answer Questions Abou Perceived Events, Pictures and Statements. Toronto, 1973.

3258
Piper, David. "Syllogistic Reasoning in Varied Narra tive Frames: Aspects of Logico-Linguistic Deve opment." Alberta, 1981. [Grades four and six Quatrième et sixième année]

Pothier, Yvonne Marie. See No./Voir no 3165

3259
Price, Jeffrey L. "The Development and Evaluation an Affect Adjective Checklist for the Measure ment of Anxiety in Children." Windsor, 1976.

132

3260
Pulos, Steven Michael. "Developmental Cognitive Restraints on Structural Learning." York, 1979. [from seven to eleven year olds/7 à 11 ans]

3261
Reynaud, Aldéo. "La relation entre l'intégration tactile-visuelle, l'intelligence et le rendement en lecture en troisième, quatrième et cinquième année scolaire." Ottawa, 1969.

3262
Rich, Susan Ann. "Cognitive Restructuring in Children: The Prediction of Intelligence and Learning." Toronto, 1982.

3263
Roberts, Gloria Bernadette. "Early Experience and the Development of Cognitive Competencies and Language Skills: Teaching Low-Income and Afro-West Indian Immigrant Mothers Strategies for Enhancing Development." Toronto, 1982.

3264
Robertson, Sharon Elaine. "Parent Education: The Dreikurs Model." Alberta, 1976. [Edmonton]

3265
Sanders, Beverly Jean. "Experimental Analysis of Visual Matching-to-Sample in Children." McGill, 1969. [Kindergarten children/Enfants à la maternelle]

Shah, Hemendra. See No./Voir no 3920
Shoom-Kirsch, Donna Norma. See No./Voir no 3890

3266
Siperko, G.M.B. "Meaningful Learning and the Development of a Self-Concept." Alberta, 1976.

3267
Stairs, Arlene. "Local Action Research in an Early Childhood Education Program: Towards More Adequate Conceptualization and More Appropriate Methodology." Carleton, 1979.

Steinert, Yvonne. See No./Voir no 4421

3268
Stevens, Renée Paley. "The Failure-Disabled Student: Three Studies of the Student At-Risk for School Failure and a Suggested Remedial Model." McGill, 1979. [Grades six and seven/Sixième et septième année]

3269
Sutherland, E. Ann. "Teacher Expectancy Effects." McGill, 1973. [Montreal grades one and two/Première et deuxième année à Montréal]

Swaine, John Ronald. See No./Voir no 9075
Sykes, Donald Henry. See No./Voir no 3891
Taylor, Nancy Douglas. See No./Voir no 9585
Thibaudeau, Guy. See No./Voir no 4236

3270
Trigg, Linda Joyce. "Cognitive and Affective Self-Instructional Statements and Task Persistence." Manitoba, 1980. [Grades three and four/Élèves de troisième et quatrième année]

3271
Tsao, Fei. "Age and Grade as Functions of Variability." Toronto, 1942.

3272
Wagner, William James. "Reasoning by Analogy in the Young Child: A Study of Relationship Between the Development of Working Memory Capacity and the Ability of Children to Reason by Analogy on Figural Analogy Problems." Toronto, 1982.

3273
Walker, Laurence John. "Cognitive and Perspective-Taking Prerequisites for the Development of Moral Reasoning." Toronto, 1978. [From grade four to seven/De la quatrième à la septième année]

3274
Wallot, Albert. "Graphisme enfantin et influences culturelles: les caractéristiques visuelles du milieu géographique dans la représentation de la maison par le dessin chez les enfants de neuf ans." Montréal, 1982.

3275
Walters, Jean Elizabeth Maddox. "Social and Non-social Problem Solving of Aggressive and Non-agressive Elementary School Boys." Queen's, 1979.

3276
Warner, Alan. "A Social and Academic Assessment of the Outcomes and Experiential Education Trips with Elementary School Children." Dalhousie, 1983.

3277
Weinberger, Alex S. "The Effects of Problem-Solving Ability and Task Difficulty on the Pupil Response During Cognitive Tasks Employing Continuous Stimuli." Windsor, 1980.

3278
Wilkinson, Michael. "Relaxation Training: EMG Feedback with Children." Alberta, 1976. [Grade six/Sixième année]

3279
Wilson, Alexander Meade. "Differential Diagnosis of Brain-Damaged Children from Normal and Emotionally Disturbed Children Using Selected Neuropsychological Measures." Calgary, 1977.

3280
Wilson, Franklin. "Body Image and Personal Space: An Exploratory Investigation." Toronto, 1979. [Grades six, seven and eight in an urban Catholic school/Sixième, septième et huitième année dans une école catholique de Montréal]

3281
Wilson, Harold Alexander. "The Effects of Labeling and Activity on Disciplinary and Affective Response Tendencies to Children." Toronto, 1976.

Yewchuk, Carolyn Rose. See No./Voir no 3851

3282
Yu, Agnes Yinling. "The Implications of Language, Culture, Social Class and Cognitive Style in Higher Cognitive Processes: A Cross-Cultural Developmental Study." Alberta, 1981. [From six to eleven years old/6 à 11 ans]

INTERMEDIATE AND SECONDARY EDUCATION/ ÉCOLES INTERMÉDIAIRES ET SECONDAIRES

General Items/Ouvrages généraux

Bullen, Edward Lester. See No./Voir no 2837
Canning, Patricia M. See No./Voir no 3004

3283
Garland, Parnell. "The Effect of Principal-Teacher Interaction on Secondary School Environments: An Empirical Study." Ottawa, 1973.

3284

Palkiewicz, Jan. "L'étude d'un projet éducatif fondé sur la conception organique de l'éducation dans une école secondaire publique." Montréal, 1982.

3285

Ray, D.W. "Social Education in Secondary Schools of England, Canada and the United States: A Study of Factors." London, 1968.

3286

Spevack, Michael G. "Drugs and the Adolescent High School Student: A Three Year Survey Study." McGill, 1973.

3287

Wangerin, Walter Martin. "A Descriptive Study of the Minimum Requirements for Graduation from Secondary Education in the Provinces of Canada in 1958." Alberta, 1959.

Alberta

3288

Baergen, William Peter. "Public Support of Private Secondary Schools in Alberta, Canada: An Analysis of Relevant Policy Issues." Oregon, 1982.

Blowers, Thomas Anthony. See No./Voir no 3001
Harrison, Robin Christopher J.L. See No./Voir no 2682
Hawkesworth, Earle Kitchener. See No./Voir no 2829
Herman, Albert. See No./Voir no 2990

3289

Kelsey, John Graham Thornton. "Conceptualization and Instrumentation for the Comparative Study of Secondary School Structure and Operation." Alberta, 1973.

Lorincz, Louis Michael. See No./Voir no 2690

3290

Racha-Intra, Suparak. "Basic Inferential Statistics in Grade Nine." Alberta, 1977.

Newfoundland/Terre-Neuve

3291

England, Wilburne Stanley. "An Analytical Case Study of the Perceived Factors Which Aided or Impeded the Establishment of a Regional High School in a Newfoundland Community." Boston University, 1968.

3292

Gushire, William Joseph. "The Acceptability of Certain Principles of Secondary Education and the Implications for Newfoundland Education." Boston University, 1958.

Ontario

3293

Aim, Edward Mason. "Resources for Secondary Education in Ontario: Their Distribution and Relationship to Educational Outposts." Toronto, 1972.

3294

Box, Colin Edward. "Drug Education in Ontario, Canada Secondary Public Schools." Indiana, 1971.

3295

Corbett, Frederick Charles. "The Community Involvement Program: Social Service as a Factor in Adolescent Moral and Psychosocial Development." Toronto, 1977.

3296

Ducharme, David Joseph. "Program Organization in Ontario Public Alternative Secondary Schools." Toronto, 1981.

3297

Graham, Evelyn Elizabeth. "Feverstein's Instrumental Enrichment Used To Change Cognitive and Verbal Behaviour in a City-Core Multi-Ethnic Toronto Secondary School." Toronto, 1981.

3298

King, Alan John Campbell. "Social Class in a Secondary School Setting." Toronto, 1965.

Quebec/Québec

3299

Arzola, Sergio. "Situation de classe et idéologie éducationnelle chez les étudiants de secondaire V au Québec." Laval, 1981.

3300

Coesman, Norbert. "La relation entre l'interaction et le prestige des professeurs de divers secteurs de l'enseignement secondaire." Ottawa, 1975.

3301

Senneville, Donald Shipley. "Analysis of Selected Secondary School Student Learning Styles in Canada, Mexico, and the United States." Arizona, 1982. [Quebec City/Québec]

Saskatchewan

Dawson, Donald Allan. See No./Voir no 2781
Donnelly, Bert J. See No./Voir no 2852
Hoen, Robert Randolph. See No./Voir no 2962
House, John Hamilton. See No./Voir no 2845
Millikan, Ross Hamilton. See No./Voir no 2692
Pelletier, Guy. See No./Voir no 4283
Pomfret, Denis Alan. See No./Voir no 10003
Ryan, Sister Marie Margaret. See No./Voir no 4200
Sackney, Lawrence Ernest. See No./Voir no 2849
Shutteworth, Dale Edwin. See No./Voir no 2819
Tymko, Joseph Laurence. See No./Voir no 2985

3302

Wedel, George John. "The General Educational Development High School Equivalency Diploma in the Province of Saskatchewan." Northern Colorado, 1974.

History of Secondary Education/ Histoire de l'enseignement au secondaire

See also Education. History of Canadian Education/ Voir aussi Éducation. Histoire de l'enseignement canadien

Students/Étudiants

General Items/Ouvrages généraux

3303
Bevan, George Henry. "An Empirical Study of the Need for Independence in High School Students." Alberta, 1971.

3304
Blain, Robert. "A Comparison Between English and French Canadian Students in Terms of Social and Personal Desirability Perceptions." Montréal, 1960.

3305
Bryans, David Garth. "Education and Acculturation: The School in a Multicultural Setting." Alberta, 1972.

3306
Calliste, Agnes Miranda. "Educational and Occupational Expectations of High School Students: The Effects of Socioeconomic Background, Ethnicity and Sex." Toronto, 1980. [Ontario]

3307
Doerksen, Gerard Benjamin. "Religiosity, Values and Purpose in Life of High School Students." Alberta, 1978.

3308
Flowers, John Franklin. "The Viewpoints of Ontario Grade Twelve Students Toward Themselves and Toward Americans." Toronto, 1958.

3309
Friesen, David. "A Study of the Subculture of Students in Eight Selected Western Canadian High Schools." North Dakota, 1966.

Gfellner, Barbara Mary. See No./Voir no 9679

3310
Gilbert, Sidney Norman. "Educational and Occupational Aspirations of Ontario High School Students: A Multivariate Analysis." Carleton, 1973.

3311
Hanley, James A. "Quantitative Studies in Cigarette Smoking Behaviour." Waterloo, 1973. [78 000 Canadian school children, from grade eight to grade twelve/78 000 enfants des écoles canadiennes de la huitième à la douzième année]

3312
Hobbs, Edward Desmond. "Formal Operations in Secondary Students: A Test of the Idea of Intellectual Structural Limitations." Alberta, 1975.

3313
O'Neill, Gilbert Patrick. "Post-Secondary Aspirations of High School Seniors from Different Contextual Settings." Toronto, 1976.

3314
Pépin, Jean-Guy. "Health Interests of 2 552 Secondary School Students of La Commission des Écoles Catholiques de Montréal." Oregon, 1972.

3315
Raphael, Dennis. "An Investigation into Aspects of Identity Status of High School Females." Toronto, 1975.

3316
Sayer, Lynda Anne. "Career Awareness of Grade Nine Girls: Evaluation of Treatment Programs." Toronto, 1980.

Shiner, Sandra Miriam. See No./Voir no 3767

Sorochty, Roger W. See No./Voir no 4202

Taylor, Gerald Dale. See No./Voir no 4157

Student Achievement, Attitudes, Behavior, Personality, Skills and Values/ Réalisations, attitudes, comportement, personnalité, compétence et intérêts des étudiants

3317
Abrahamson, David Stephen. "Perceived Parent Behavior, Locus of Control Beliefs and Achievement Behavior in Adolescents." Manitoba, 1977.

Andrews, William A. See No./Voir no 4172

3318
Baker, Robert Andrew. "Educational Aspirations and Expectations and Perceived Educational Values." Toronto, 1980. [Grade eleven/Onzième année]

3319
Barrados, Maria. "The Progress Through Secondary School of a Grade 8 Cohort of Ontario Students." Carleton, 1978.

3320
Beggs, Donald William. "Improving Argument and Reasoning in Students of the Senior Secondary School (Using a Pre-College Philosophy Course)." Toronto, 1981.

3321
Behrens, Lot Ted. "Personality Correlates of Over-Achievement and Underachievement." Calgary, 1976. [Junior high school/Huitième et neuvième année]

3322
Boak, Ronald Terrance Robert. "Achievement and Anxiety of Junior High School Students as Functions of Teacher Interpersonal Skills." Calgary, 1974.

3323
Brown, Chesley Kenneth. "Pupil Personality Teaching Style and Achievement." Alberta, 1967.

3324
Cantarella, Claudette. "Valeurs de travail de l'étudiant de niveau collégial." Montréal, 1982.

3325
Chabassol, D.J. "Correlates of Academic Underachievement in Male Adolescents." Alberta, 1959.

Christensen, Douglas Harold. See No./Voir no 3364

Connell, Robert Bruce. See No./Voir no 4179

3326
Des Lierres, Thérèse. "Mesure des habiletés d'observation et d'interprétation chez les élèves de secondaires I, II et III." Montréal, 1980.

3327
Digout, Stanislaus Lawrence. "A Comparison of Values of Grade Twelve Students in Selected Public and Roman Catholic Separate Schools in Alberta." Alberta, 1979.

Dufresne, Raymond. See No./Voir no 3404

3328
Du Preez, Ingram Frank. "Moral and Religious Problems and Attitudes as Expressed by Students in Seventh Day Adventist Academies in the United States and Canada." Andrews, 1977.

3329
Ejeckam, Winifred C. "Personality Correlates of Fear of Success." Ottawa, 1980. [324 grade twelve students/324 étudiants de douzième année]

3330
Even, Alexander. "Patterns of Academic Achievement in Grade 12 Chemistry and Their Relationship to Personal Attitudinal and Environmental Factors." Toronto, 1968.

3331
Franklyn, Gaston J. "A Comparative Empirical Study of the Relationship Between Academic Achievement, Alienation from School and Ethnicity Among Grade IX Students in the MacKenzie District of the Northwest Territories." Ottawa, 1971.

Fullerton, John Timothy. See No./Voir no 9674

3332
Gill, Mohindra Pall. "Pattern of Achievement in Relation to Self-Concept and Self-Ideal Congruence of Grade 9 Students." Toronto, 1968.

Hartman, Lorne Michael. See No./Voir no 9009

3333
Herscovics, Nicolas. "Compréhension de la droite et de l'équation au niveau secondaire." Montréal, 1979.

Howley, Thomas Patrick. See No./Voir no 4227

3334
Katyal, Krishan L. "The Effect of the Work Experience Program on the Self-Concept, the Work Values, and School Interest of Selected Canadian High School Students." Montana, 1977. [Alberta]

3335
Kawecki, Alina. "An Investigation of Performance Under Contingent and One-Step Path Conditions." Ottawa, 1980. [Ontario]

3336
Kehoe, John William. "An Application of the Principle of Inconsistency to Strategies for Changing Attitudes Toward Culturally Diverse Groups." Toronto, 1972.

3337
Kim, Bo Kyung. "Attitudes, Parental Identification, and Locus of Control of Korean, New Korean-Canadians and Canadian Adolescents." Toronto, 1976.

3338
Kitchen, Hubert William. "Relationship Between the Value-Orientation of Grade Nine Pupils in Newfoundland and the Characteristics of Their Primary and Secondary Groups." Alberta, 1966.

Lalonde, Bernadette Irene D. See No./Voir no 4192

3339
Lambert, Roland A. "Cognition and Achievement: An Examination of Individual Differences Among Grade Ten Students." Alberta, 1962.

3340
Loranger, Michel. "L'évaluation des comportements en classe chez des élèves de secondaire II." Laval, 1978.

3341
MacDonald, John Angus. "A Study of the Relationshi Between Student Achievement of Process Skill and the Mode of Instruction in Junior High Schoo Sciences." Alberta, 1974.

3342
MacLellan, Haidee Patricia. "Differential Values Beliefs and Concerns of Achieving and Under achieving High School Students." Alberta, 1979.

3343
McKittrick, Edith Patricia. "Attitudes of High Schoo Students in Manitoba Toward the Use of Alcoholi Beverages." Ottawa, 1966.

3344
Morissette, Dominique. "Étude des causes de la déci sion que prennent les élèves du cours secondaire d continuer leurs études ou de les abandonner. Laval, 1981.

3345
Muller-Hehn, Anita. "Les collégiens québécois et l français, contribution à l'étude et à la mesure d l'attitude vis-à-vis de la langue maternelle. Montréal, 1982.

3346
Ouellet, Roland. "Influence de l'école sur les aspira tions scolaires des jeunes de niveau secondaire. Montréal, 1976.

3347
Peach, John Whitmore. "Achievement Expectation and Student Attitudes in Ten Selected Manitob Senior High Schools." Alberta, 1970.

3348
Penner, Wesley Jerry. "Some Comparisons of Lif Style Reflected in the Dress and Behavior of Hig School Students." Alberta, 1971.

3349
Peterson, Mayfield. "Study Methods and Attitude Toward School and Levels of Achievement o Adolescents in Grades Ten, Eleven and Twelve. Ottawa, 1970.

3350
Pucella, Pasquale. "L'histoire au niveau secondaire étude sur les attitudes des élèves." Montréal 1973.

3351
Richer, Stephen Irwin. "Programme Grouping an Educational Plans: A Study of Canadian Hig School Students." Johns Hopkins, 1968.

3352
Russell, Susan Jessie. "Sex Role Socialization in th High School: A Study of the Perpetuation o Patriarchal Culture." Toronto, 1978.

Ryan, Marie Margaret. See No./Voir no 4200

Spevack, Michael G. See No./Voir no 3286

3353
Treasure, Morris Ralph. "Inferring and Hypothesizin Abilities of Junior High School Students." Alberta 1975.

3354
Young, John Ernest McKim. "A Study in the Measure ment of Expressed Attitudes of English-Speakin Canadian High School Seniors Toward Americans. Toronto, 1952.

Student Activities, Decision-Making and Governance/Activités, prise de décision et conduite des étudiants

Anwar, Muhammad. See No./Voir no 2988

3355
Eastabrook, John Henry Glenn. "Student Participation in School-Wide Decision-Making: A Case Study of Secondary School Student Role Changing." Toronto, 1979.

3356
Jarrett, John W. "The Intermediate School Student Involvement in School Activities." Ottawa, 1978.

Macleod, Alan Ross. See No./Voir no 2992

Opp, Paul Franklin. See No./Voir no 3383

3357
Treslan, Dennis Liv. "Student Participation in Senior High School Governance: A Control Assembly Model." Calgary, 1977.

3358
Willis, Kenneth Richard. "Pupil Participation in the Activities of the Secondary School: An Analysis of Supporting Thought with a Subsidiary Examination of Actual Practice." Toronto, 1950.

3359
Wood, James Douglas. "Student Influence in Decision-Making in Secondary Schools." Toronto, 1977.

Teacher-Student Relations/ Relations entre professeurs et étudiants

3360
Doyon, Raymonde. "Rapport Parent et relations maître-élève au cours secondaire." Ottawa, 1966.

Fasano, James H. See No./Voir no 3104

3361
Guest, Gerald Richard. "The Teacher-Student Relationship and Student Response to Double Binds." Victoria, 1976. [Grade eight/Huitième année]

3362
Hanson, Raymond Lee. "A Tri-Dimensional Analysis of Teacher-Student Verbal Interaction During Evaluative Ventures." Alberta, 1975.

3363
Ricker, Léa-Marie. "Le dialogue enseignant-élève à l'école secondaire selon le rapport Parent." Ottawa, 1966.

Trottier, Claude R. See No./Voir no 2800

Curriculum and Instruction in the Secondary School/ Plan d'étude et enseignement dans les écoles secondaires

General Items/Ouvrages généraux

3364
Christensen, Douglas Harold. "A Comparative Study Between Department of Education Assigned Marks and Accredited High Schools' Assigned Marks in Alberta." Utah State, 1980.

Dupuis, Jean-Claude. See No./Voir no 2054

Green, George Henry Ebenezer. See No./Voir no 2618

3365
Hawkes, Norma Jeanne. "Analysis of Channel Selection by Junior Secondary School Students on the Reorganized Curriculum in British Columbia Schools." Oregon, 1967.

3366
Ledgerwood, Charles D. "Toward a Conceptualization of Ideal Styles of Curriculum Decision-Making in Small Groups." Alberta, 1975.

3367
MacDonald, G. "Uniformity in the Academic Subjects of the Industrial Course." Toronto, 1952.

Mallinson, Thomas John. See No./Voir no 3111

3368
McCarthy, Joseph P. "The Effectiveness of the Nova Scotia High School Curriculum in Preparing Urban High School Graduates for Vocation, for Citizenship, and for the Worthy Use of Leisure Time." Harvard, 1945.

Pépin, Jean-Guy. See No./Voir no 3314

3369
Pullen, Harry. "Secondary School Curriculum in Canada with Special Emphasis on an Ontario Experiment." Toronto, 1955.

3370
Rothe, John Peter. "An Exploration of Existential Phenomenology as an Approach to Curriculum Evaluation." British Columbia, 1979.

3371
Ryan, Alan G. "Development of a Model and Its Use in Aiding the Further Implementation of CRIB Project." Alberta, 1977. [Edmonton]

Shiner, Sandra Miriam. See No./Voir no 3767

Simms, Jeremy Joseph. See No./Voir no 3138

3372
Strauss, Dennis Lyle. "The Planning, Implementation, and Appraisal of an Independent Study Program at Bedford Road Collegiate, Saskatoon, Saskatchewan." Oregon, 1975.

Subject Areas/Matières

General Items/Ouvrages généraux

3373
Connelly, Desmond J. "A Descriptive and Comparative Study of the Instructional Objectives of Teachers of Chemistry, English, French, Geography, History, and Mathematics at Grade Twelve Level in English Speaking High Schools of the Ottawa Board of Education." Ottawa, 1972.

3374
Edwards, Peter. "A Computer Generated Corpus and Lexical Analysis of English Language Instructional Materials Prescribed for Use in British Columbia Junior Secondary Grades." British Columbia, 1974.

Agricultural Education/Enseignement en agriculture

See also Curriculum Development and Instruction/Voir aussi Plan d'étude et enseignement

Art

3375
Bourbeau-Poirier, Louise. "Art Attitude Investigation at the Junior High School Level in the Quebec Area." Ohio State, 1978.

3376
Clubine, Gordon Laverne. "A Plan for the Improvement and Extension of Art Education in Ontario Secondary Schools." Teachers College, Columbia, 1952.

3377
Clubine, Mary Helen. "Effective Procedures in the Teaching of Art in Ontario Secondary Schools." Teachers College, Columbia, 1952.

Cox, Marlene Joan. See No./Voir no 4112

3378
Gaitskell, Charles Dudley. "Art Education in the Province of Ontario." Toronto, 1947.

3379
Hawke, David Monro. "The Life-World of a Beginning Teacher of Art." Alberta, 1980.

Career Education/Plan de carrière

Glaze, Avis Elane. See No./Voir no 4182

Commercial Subjects/Domaine commercial

3380
Edward, Wesley Grafton. "Improvement Curves in the Learning of Typewriting." Toronto, 1923.

3381
White, Lloyd. "Some Aspects of Commercial Law in Ontario Secondary Schools." Toronto, 1942.

Dramatics/Art dramatique

3382
Assagba, Yao Ayékotan. "Rationalité et aspirations: la théorie de la rationalité de l'acteur dans l'analyse des aspirations scolaires au cours secondaire." Laval, 1983.

3383
Opp, Paul Franklin. "Dramatics in Secondary Schools: An Extracurricular Study in Participation and Practices." Toronto, 1933.

Earth Science/Science de la terre

3384
Schroeter, Elizabeth Arlene. "Earth Science in the Secondary Schools." Toronto, 1953.

Modern Languages/Langues modernes

General Item/Ouvrage général

3385
Caria, Antonio. "Attitudes of Students, Teachers, Administrators and Parents Regarding Modern Language Study in the Edmonton Separate School District." Oregon, 1981.

English Language and Literature/Anglais et littérature

Allen, Sheila Moreen. See No./Voir no 4448

3386
Bone, Georgina Mary. "Some Features of Langua[g] Used by Adolescents." Alberta, 1980.

3387
Chorny, Mirron. "A Survey of the Teaching of Engli[sh] Composition in Grades Nine, Eleven, and Twelve Alberta, 1960." Alberta, 1966.

3388
Corcoran, William Thomas. "A Study of the Respons[e] of Superior and Average Students in Grades Eig[ht] Ten, and Twelve to a Short Story and a Poem Alberta, 1978.

3389
Cragg, Edith Marion Catherine. "A Study of t[he] Content of Literature Text Books for Engli[sh] Speaking Students in Canadian High Schools Relation to International Understanding Betwe[en] the United States and Canada and Canadian Unit[y] Northwestern, 1950.

3390
Downie, David Alexander. "A Comparison of Tea[m] Teaching and Autonomous Teaching in High Sch[ool] English and Social Studies." Alberta, 1970.

3391
Galloway, Priscilla Anne. "Sexism and the Seni[or] English Literature Curriculum in Ontario Secon[d]ary Schools." Toronto, 1977.

3392
Godwin, Lois Ruth. "Suggested Procedures for t[he] Teaching of English Language 10 to 'C' and ' Students in Urban High Schools in the Province Alberta." Teachers College, Columbia, 1961.

3393
Jeroski, Sharon Frances. "Competence in Writt[en] Expression: Interactions Between Instruction a[nd] Individual Differences Among Junior High Sch[ool] Students." British Columbia, 1982.

3394
Josephson, Mundi Irving. "A Study of the Effects Instruction in Close Textual Analysis on the Abili[ty] of Secondary-School Students to Interpret Imagin[a]tive Literature Independently." Alberta, 1975.

3395
Klassen, Bernard Rodney. "Sentence-Combining Exe[r]cises as an Aid to Expediting Syntactic Fluency Learning English as a Second Language." Mi[n]nesota, 1976.

3396
Lampard, Dorothy Mary. "An Examination of t[he] Construction and Reconstruction of Meaning Seen in the Written Responses Made to Questio[ns] About What Has Been Read by Students in the Hi[gh] Schools of Alberta." Oregon, 1966.

3397
Lazar, Avrim D. "An Inquiry into the Process Grammar Concept Attainment in the Franc[o] Ontarian Junior School Child." Ottawa, 1976.

3398
Robinson, Samuel Dale. "The Response-Orient[ed] Literature Curriculum in the Secondary School: Critical Inquiry into the Effects of Two Teachi[ng] Methods." Alberta, 1973.

3399
Ross, Harry Campbell. "A Comparative Study of the Responses Made by Grade Eleven Vancouver Students to Canadian and New Zealand Poems." British Columbia, 1975.

3400
Sanford, Robert Morley. "An Investigation of the Response of High School Students to Poetic Language." Alberta, 1971.

Schloss, Brigitte. See No./Voir no 2624

3401
Tomkins, Muriel Winnifred. "Critical and Philosophical Theories of Metaphor and Their Implications for the Teaching of English: A Perspective on Canadian High School Textbooks." Harvard, 1968.

Warren, Wendy Kaye. See No./Voir no 2612

3402
Willinsky, John M. "The Well-Tempered Tongue: The Significance of Standard English in a Nova Scotia High School." Dalhousie, 1982.

French/Français

3403
Booth, Mary Joyce. "Expectations of French Proficiency, Bilingual Employment Services and Francophone Reaction." Alberta, 1978.

3404
Dufresne, Raymond. "L'attitude des élèves au secondaire à l'égard du français langue maternelle: élaboration et expérimentation d'une échelle." Montréal, 1979.

Hopkirk, Gerald A. See No./Voir no 2684

3405
McEwen, Nelly Zurcher. "An Exploratory Study of the Multidimensional Nature of Teacher-Student Verbal Interaction in Second Language Classrooms." Alberta, 1976. [Grade ten/Dixième année]

Muller-Hehn, Anita. See No./Voir no 3345

3406
Richards, Gerald Raymond. "The Development of a Conceptual Framework for the Teaching of the Cultural Components of Second Languages." Toronto, 1976. [Teaching of French as a second language in Ontario/Enseignement du français langue seconde en Ontario]

3407
Roy, Robert Roger. "Oral French Proficiency: Identification and Evaluation." Alberta, 1968.

Family Life/Vie familiale

3408
Guest, Henry Hewson. "Correlates of Readiness for Various Aspects of Family Life Education Among Secondary School Students of Winnipeg, Manitoba." Florida State, 1971.

3409
West, Norman William. "The Effect of Instruction in Family Planning on Knowledge, Attitudes and Behavior of London (Ontario) Senior Secondary School Students." Ohio State, 1976.

Geography/Géographie

3410
Aubin-La Pointe, Monique. "Construction et évaluation d'un cours programmé sur la représentation cartographique du relief en secondaire I." Montréal, 1975.

3411
Hromyk, William John. "An Evaluation of High School Seniors' Knowledge of Anglo-American Geographic Concepts." Oregon, 1972. [British Columbia and Saskatchewan/Colombie-Britannique et Saskatchewan]

3412
Mayo, William Leonard. "The Development of Secondary School Geography as an Independent Subject in the United States and Canada." Michigan, 1964.

3413
Scholer, Marc. "Comparaison de l'efficacité relative d'un livre 'brouille' et d'un terminal d'ordinateur comme modes d'administration d'un enseignement programmé en géographie." Montréal, 1977.

Home Economics/Économie familiale

3414
Dixon, Beverly Ruth. "An Investigation into the Use of Raths' Values Clarification Strategies with Grade Eight Pupils." Michigan State, 1978. [Vancouver, British Columbia/Vancouver, Colombie-Britannique]

3415
Hames, Patricia Jane. "Development of an Evaluation Model for Implementation of Home Economics Subject Matter in Selected Schools in Ontario, Canada." Texas Tech, 1980.

Mathematics/Mathématiques

3416
Aguirre, José M. "Students' Perceptions of Three Vector Quantities." British Columbia, 1981.

Allen, Harold Don. See No./Voir no 2629

3417
Auger, Jean. "Correction individuelle des difficultés d'apprentissage en mathématiques au niveau secondaire III, IV et V." Montréal, 1981.

3418
Babcock, Gail Reichenbach. "The Relationship Between Basal Measurement Ability and Rational Number Learning at Three Grade Levels." Alberta, 1978.

3419
Beaton, Mary Anne. "A Study of Underachievers in Mathematics at the Tenth Grade Level in Three Calgary High Schools." Northwestern, 1966.

3420
Boychuk, Halia Katherine. "Creative Problem-Solving in Junior High School Mathematics." Alberta, 1974. [Edmonton grade nine/Neuvième année à Edmonton]

3421
Brindley, Selwyn Robert William. "The Relative Effectiveness of a Concrete Process-Oriented Teaching Approach for Grade Seven Fractions and Ratios." Calgary, 1980.

3422
Broomes, Desmond Rodwell. "Psychological and Sociological Correlates of Mathematical Achievement and Ability Among Grade 9 Students." Toronto, 1971.

3423
Côté, Benoît. "Analyse d'une situation d'apprentissage d'opérations numériques au début du secondaire." McGill, 1981.

3424
Drost, Dale R. "Geometric Sectioning Ability and Geometry Achievement." Alberta, 1977.

3425
Giesbrecht, Edwin Cornelius. "The Attainment of Selected Mathematical Competencies by High School Students in Saskatchewan." Saskatchewan, 1977.

3426
Guirguis, Fayeh Shoukry. "Major Factors in the Evaluation of Modern Mathematics in Secondary Education in Quebec (1960-1977)." Montreal, 1981.

3427
Hanna, Gila. "A Critique of the Role of Rigorous Proof in the Secondary School Mathematics Curriculum." Toronto, 1981.

Hopkirk, Gerald A. See No./Voir no 2684

3428
Horne, Edgar Byron. "A Comparative Study of College Preparatory Mathematics Curricula in Canada in 1964-65." Illinois, 1966.

3429
Huang, Henry Chung-Chi. "A Study of Computer-Assisted Instruction in Junior High School Mathematics: An Individually Self-Progressive System." Calgary, 1980.

3430
Klopoushak, Edward L. "The Use of Hand-Held Calculators in Grade 8 Mathematics." Alberta, 1978.

3431
Lacasse, Raynald. "Les dimensions évaluatives des professeurs de mathématiques au secondaire." Montréal, 1980.

3432
Marsh, F.G. "Cognitive Style, Instructional Strategy and Mathematics Achievement." Alberta, 1980.

Munro, Barry Cartwright. See No./Voir no 2581

3433
Ong, Sit-Tui. A Curriculum Implementation of Creative Problem-Solving in Junior High School Mathematics." Alberta, 1976. [Edmonton]

3434
Pereira-Mendoza, Lionel. "The Effect of Teaching Heuristics on the Ability of Grade Ten Students to Solve Novel Mathematical Problems." British Columbia, 1975.

3435
Poisson, Yves. "Objectifs de comportement, conditions d'apprentissage et événements d'enseignement tels que décrits par Gagné et leurs effets sur l'acquisition de concepts et de règles concernant la fonction quadratique." Laval, 1974.

3436
Pozniak, Tadeusz D. "Broadening the Mathematical Aspect of the Concept Skill Correlation at One Grade Algebra Level." Ottawa, 1956.

Racha-Intra, Suparak. See No./Voir no 3290

3437
Rahim, Medhat Hishmat. "Piece-Wise Congruent Regions, Their Area Measure Structure, and Geometric Thinking Processes." Alberta, 1981.

3438
Sajid, Muhammad S. "The Effect of Remedial Instruction on Achievement in Seventh Grade Algebra Linear Equations." Toronto, 1959.

3439
Tweedle, Dean Frederick. "A Heuristic Approach Problem-Solving in Grade Eleven Mathematics Alberta, 1978.

3440
Vance, James Hinman. "The Effects of a Mathematics Laboratory Program in Grades 7 and 8: An Experimental Study." Alberta, 1970.

3441
Williams, Edgar Roland. "An Investigation of Senior High School Students': Understanding of the Nature of Mathematical Proof." Alberta, 1979.

Music/Musique

See also Arts. Musique/Voir aussi Arts. Musique

Philosophy/Philosophie

Beggs, Donald William. See No./Voir no 3320

Physical Education/Éducation physique

See also Sports/Physical Education and Leisure Time Activities/Voir aussi Éducation physique et activités de loisirs.

Science/Sciences

3442
Amoss, Harold Edwin. "Elementary Science in the Secondary Schools of Ontario." Toronto, 1916.

3443
Anamuah-Mensah, Jophus. "Student Difficulties with Volumetric Analysis." British Columbia, 198 [Grade twelve chemistry/Douzième année chimie]

3444
Anderson, Edward Charles. "Creation, Evolution and Science Teaching in the Secondary School Toronto, 1982.

3445
Bowers, Henry. "Transfer Values of Secondary School Science." Toronto, 1927.

3446
Cyr, Gérard J. "Les effets de la fréquence d'expérimentation en laboratoire de physique sur le développement d'habiletés intellectuelles chez les élèves du secondaire IV de la province de Québec en 1973." Montréal, 1975.

3447
Doucette, Andrew Leo. "A Science Program for Alberta Schools Based on Student Interests Stanford, 1949.

Dupuis, Jean-Claude. See No./Voir no 2054

Engel, Barney Mordecai. See No./Voir no 2637

3448

Finegold, Menahem. "The Character of Classroom Discussion of Original Research Reports as a Mode of Instruction in Physics." Toronto, 1974. [Grade eleven/Onzième année]

3449

Flather, Donald McIntosh. "An Evaluation of the Science Program in the High Schools of British Columbia." Washington, Seattle, 1950.

3450

Gay, Gary Robert. "Affective and Cognitive Behaviors of Students as Related to Teaching Mode Characteristics." Alberta, 1976.

3451

Grantham, Herbert Harris. "The Science Curriculum in British Columbia Schools, with Emphasis Upon the Secondary Levels." Stanford, 1951.

3452

Griffiths, Alan Keith. "The Mole Concept: Investigation of an Hierarchical Model." Alberta, 1979. [Chemistry in a Calgary high school/La chimie dans une école secondaire de Calgary]

3453

Hammond, Allan Robert. "Assessment Context in Relation to Physics Achievement and Cognitive Style." Alberta, 1976.

3454

Hedley, Robert Lloyd. "Student Attitude and Achievement in Science Courses in Manitoba Secondary Schools." Michigan State, 1966.

3455

Hofferd, George William. "Content and Methodology of Ontario Lower School Biology." Toronto, 1932.

Kargbo, Dennis Borboh. See No./Voir no 3170

3456

Llull, Georges. "Orientation vers les personnes et motivation intrinsèques des étudiants en sciences du niveau secondaire V (Commission scolaire régionale de Chambly)." Montréal, 1981.

MacDonald, John Angus. See No./Voir no 3341

3457

Routh, Charles Joseph. "A Comparison of the Concepts Taught in Secondary School Chemistry Courses in Selected Schools of Canada, Great Britain, New Zealand and the United States." Pittsburgh, 1961.

Russell, Thomas Lee. See No./Voir no 4427

Schoelneberger, Mary Margaret. See No./Voir no 3173

3458

Searles, William Edward. "An Investigation into the Types of Junior High School Science Curricula Produced Through the Utilization of MacDonald's Three Curriculum Development Models." Ottawa, 1979.

Taylor, Stanley James. See No./Voir no 2622

3459

Thibert, Gilles. "L'enseignement des sciences au secondaire et le développement des attitudes scientifiques." Montréal, 1981.

3460

Wheeler, Alan Edmund. "The Role of the Proportionality Schema in Introductory High School Chemistry." Alberta, 1976. [Edmonton]

3461

Williams, Richard Lee. "A Comparative Study of Metric Skills of Intermediate Students in Calgary, Alberta, and Spokane, Washington." Washington State, 1978.

Sex Education/Éducation sexuelle

3462

Bartoletti, Mario Dante. "Developing and Assessing Video-Taped Vignettes Focused on the Sexual Imagery and Feelings of Teen-Agers." Toronto, 1979.

Tremblay, Jean. See No./Voir no 2591

Social Studies/Sciences sociales

3463

Berry, Gerald Lloyd. "A Handbook for Teachers of Social Studies in the Secondary Schools of Alberta." Colorado, 1963.

3464

Cooke, Frank Albert. "A Descriptive Study of the Relationship Between the Social Premises Inherent in an Individualized Curriculum and Those Endorsed by Selected History Teachers and Its Significance upon Their Expressed Preferences for Implementing Such a Curriculum in the Public Secondary Schools in Hamilton, Ontario." SUNY, Buffalo, 1979.

Dhand, Hargopal. See No./Voir no 3179

3465

Finn, Theophilus George. "The Social Studies Program in the Province of Alberta." Stanford, 1950.

3466

Harasymiw, Elaine L. Verchomin. "Political Socialization and Education: Knowledge and the Generation of Political Support." Calgary, 1981.

3467

Korteweg, Laurens. "A Decade of Social Studies Curriculum Development in Alberta." Alberta, 1972.

3468

Lichtenberg, Mitchell Palmer. "A Model for the Use of Urban History in Social Studies Education." Carnegie-Mellon, 1972.

3469

Losier, Sister St. Michael. "An Evaluation of Education for Democracy in the Secondary Schools of the Maritime Provinces of Canada." Fordham, 1952.

Munro, Barry C. See No./Voir no 2581

Piscione, Joseph Anthony. See No./Voir no 2598

Pucella, Pasquale. See No./Voir no 3350

Rothe, John Peter. See No./Voir no 3370

Thexton, James D. See No./Voir no 4235

Trottier, Claude René. See No./Voir no 2800

3470

Walsh, Gerald. "Conceptions of World History in the World History Programmes of Canadian Secondary Schools: A Survey and Appraisal." British Columbia, 1966.

3471

Wilson, Donald Cathcart. "Emic-Evaluative Inquiry: An Approach for Evaluating School Programs." Alberta, 1976.

Social Skills/Compétences sociales

Schner, Joseph George. See No./Voir no 9322

Vocational and Technical Education/ Enseignement technique et professionnel

Ben-Dor, Tsilia Romm. See No./Voir no 4175

Bowd, Alan Douglas. See No./Voir no 4134

3472
Gauthier, Gaston. "Essai de prédiction du succès à l'école du meuble." Montréal, 1948.

3473
Green, Walter Henry H. "The Development of the Vocational School to Meet Community Needs (Fort William Vocational School)." Toronto, 1941.

3474
King, Robert John. "Personality and Behavioral Correlates of the Conceptual Level Matching Model with Vocational Secondary School Students." Toronto, 1974.

3475
Lawrence, T.H. "Methodology of Technical Education: An Evaluation of a Cooperative Education Programme for Secondary Schools in Ontario." Toronto, 1983.

MacDonald, George. See No./Voir no 3367

3476
McLeod, Heleen Julianna. "Trades and Services in Vocational and Composite High School Settings." Alberta, 1980.

3477
Pankiewicz, Gerald. "Assessment of Industrial Vocational Education Needs to Manitoba's Secondary Schools and Comparative Analysis with Responses to Similar Needs in West Germany and the United States of America." Manitoba, 1983.

Regan, Ross H. See No./Voir no 2703

3478
Ross, Campbell John. "An Assessment of the Alberta Industrial Arts Teacher Education Program." Alberta, 1976.

Work Experience Program/ Programme d'expérience de travail

Katyal, Krishan L. See No./Voir no 3334

Educational Psychology at the Secondary Level/ Psychologie pédagogique au niveau secondaire

3479
Avore, Joseph B., Jr. "A Comparison of the Effects of Conceptual Training and Tutoring on the Academic Skills of Disadvantaged Children." Windsor, 1975.

3480
Baulu, Mireille. "Les perspectives de soi d'étudiants forts, moyens et faibles, réussissant en milieu collégial." Montréal, 1982.

3481
Bennett, Carol-Anne. "Effective Interpersonal Coping Skills in Relation to Underachievement." Toronto, 1979.

3482
Blackwood, George E. "The Relationship Between Delayed Gratification and Torrance's Concept of Creative Thinking at the Grade Eight Level." Ottawa, 1981.

3483
Blake, Rick Nelson. "The Effects of Problem Context upon the Problem Solving Processes Used by Field Dependent and Independent Students: A Clinical Study." British Columbia, 1976.

3484
Blankstein, Kirk Robert. "Cognitive and Somatic Mediators and Exteroceptive Feedback: Effects of Training on Physiological Control and Self-Reported Fear During Rest and Stress." Waterloo, 1972.

Boutilier, Robert Gordon. See No./Voir no 3196

Brown, William Cecil. See No./Voir no 6739

3485
Bujold, Charles Eugene. "The Role of Self-Concepts, Occupational Concepts, and Reality Considerations in the Occupational Choice of French-Canadian Secondary School Boys." Columbia, 1972.

3486
Carbno, William Clifford. "The Development of Reasoning Ability to the Adolescent Years." Toronto, 1976.

3487
Chan, Randolph Maurice. "The Effect of Group Learning on Performance and Satisfaction Change as a Function of Need Affiliation." Toronto, 1975.

3488
Courval, Jean. "Élaboration et expérimentation d'un questionnaire de perceptions étudiantes sur le monde scolaire au niveau secondaire." Montréal, 1976.

3489
Cram, Ruby Victoria. "A Psycholinguistic Investigation of the Cloze Responses of Secondary School Students." British Columbia, 1980.

3490
Crawford, Douglas Gordon. "Family Interaction, Achievement Values and Motivation as Related to School Dropouts." Toronto, 1969.

3491
Deosaran, Ramesh Anthony. "Social Class, Self-Concept and Educational Expectations: A Social Psychological Study." Toronto, 1977. [Grade eight/Huitième année]

Doerksen, Gerard Benjamin. See No./Voir no 3307

3492
Doyle, Mother Hortense. "The Self-Concept Studied in Relation to the Culture of Teen-Age Boys and Girls in Canada, England and the United States." St. Louis, 1960.

3493
Dufour, Albert. "Étude comparative des effets de deux distributions différentes du temps consacré à une matière, sur le rendement scolaire et la satisfaction des besoins psychologiques fondamentaux d'étudiants du niveau secondaire." Laval, 1971.

3494
Fitzsimmons, George William. "Group Desensitization of Test Anxiety: The Contribution of Therapeutic Homework Assignments." Toronto, 1973.

495
Ieming, William Gerald. "Factors Affecting the Predictive Accuracy of Ontario Upper School Results." Toronto, 1954.

496
lores, Miguela Bustos. "Some Differences in Cognitive Abilities Between Canadian and Filipino Students." Toronto, 1969.

497
Garrett, William A. "Causal Attribution for the Performance of Self and Others as a Function of Locus of Control, Observer Empathy and Success-Failure." Windsor, 1975.

Glaze, Avis Elane. See No./Voir no 4182

498
Glynn, Edward Lewis. "Self-Determined and Externally Determined Token Reinforcement Schedule in Classroom Learning." Toronto, 1969.

Granville, Howard. See No./Voir no 4184

499
Greer, Ruth Nancy Elizabeth. "Spontaneous Elaboration of Paired Associates and Formal Operational Thinking: A Development Analysis." British Columbia, 1977.

3500
Hymmen, Phyllis Alice. "Formalized Group Guidance: Some Facilitating Activities and Inhibiting Factors." Toronto, 1976. [Junior high school/ Septième et huitième année]

3501
Kansup, Wanlop. "Student Perceptions of Occupational Characteristics: A Multi-Dimensional Approach." Alberta, 1977. [Edmonton]

Keown, Lauriston Livingston. See No./Voir no 6740

Kramer, Edwin Arthur. See No./Voir no 9023

3502
Lamothe, Pierre. "Relation entre concept de soi et participation de l'adolescent à des activités de groupe en milieu scolaire de niveau secondaire." Montréal, 1982.

3503
Lansdell, Clyde Edison. "Religious Convictions and Interpersonal Relations in a Christian Community." Toronto, 1980.

3504
Lorimer, Rowland Moore. "The Acquisition of Moral Judgements in Adolescence: The Effects of an Exposition of Basic Concepts Versus Exposure to and Discussion of a Filmed Dramatic Example." Toronto, 1968.

3505
Mays, Annabelle Marjorie Maude. "The Concept of Moral Atmosphere in Educational Settings." Toronto, 1979. [Grades seven and eight/Septième et huitième année]

3506
McDougall, Daniel. "Achievement and Learning Effects of a Computer-Assisted Simulation Game." Calgary, 1971. [Grades eight and nine/Huitième et neuvième année]

McLeod, Heleen Julianna. See No./Voir no 3476

3507
Mott, Terrance Roger. "A Study of a Career-Choice Problem: Indecision Versus Indecisiveness." Alberta, 1975.

Munro, Barry. See No./Voir no 2581

3508
Pajonas, Patricia Joan. "Obedience and Heterogeneity: Catholic Secondary Schools in Boston and Montreal." Harvard, 1970.

3509
Paris, Ginette. "Étude de la croissance de la compétence interpersonnelle des professeurs par l'utilisation conjointe de deux instruments de changement: le groupe de formation et le test Perpe." Montréal, 1975.

Pelletier, Guy. See No./Voir no 4283

3510
Perrault, Yvonne L. "Sex, Motivation, Extraversion and Neurotocism as Multiple Predictors and Moderators when Predicting Two Grade Nine Attainment Criteria." Ottawa, 1976.

3511
Pratt, Joyce Barbara. "The Development and Evaluation of an Extended Assertiveness Training Program." Toronto, 1978.

3512
Ramsay, Georges Lavis. "An Empirical Investigation into the Multidimensionality of the Trait Construct of Intrinsic Motivation." York, 1982. [1050 French-speaking senior high school students/1050 étudiants francophones de neuvième, dixième, onzième et douzième année]

3513
Salame, Ramzi F. L'auto-évaluation des performances chez deux groupes d'adolescents sur-productifs et sous-productifs: ses relations avec des variables de motivation scolaire." Montréal, 1979.

3514
Sanchez-Craig, Beatriz Martha. "Reappraisal Procedures in the Modification of Unsatisfactory Social Interactions." Toronto, 1973.

Taylor, Gerald Dale. See No./Voir no 4157

3515
Torbit, Gary Edward. "Interpersonal Attraction and Cognitive Complexity of High School Students." Alberta, 1973.

3516
Wasilewski, Bohdan Kazimierz. "Effect of Emphasis on Time-to-Solution and Verbal Versus Spatial Stimuli on Attribute Identification Performance." Victoria, 1974.

3517
Welbourne, Arthur James. "The Effectiveness of the Verdun Projective Battery as a Personality Screening Device at the High School Level." Ottawa, 1955.

3518
Wilcox, William Roy. "The Use of Relaxation and Suggestion with Anxious Underachieving Grade Eight Students." Alberta, 1973.

Wilensky, Marshall Shimon. See No./Voir no 2592

HIGHER EDUCATION/
ENSEIGNEMENT SUPÉRIEUR

General Items/Ouvrages généraux

Baker, Robert Andrew. See No./Voir no 3318

3519

Barkow, Ben. "Accountability in Higher Education: Student and Faculty Views Within a Psychology Department." York, 1975.

Cody, Howard Hugh. See No./Voir no 8487

3520

Hackshaw, Eugenia. "The Impact of Overseas Volunteer Programs on Developing Countries: A Case Study of Canadian University Service Overseas in the East Caribbean Region." New York, 1971.

3521

Josaitis, Marvin. "The Professionals in North American Higher Education Governing and Coordinating Agencies." Michigan, 1977.

3522

O'Malley, Denis Anthony. "The Market for Higher Degree Holders and the Graduate Education System in Canada." Alberta, 1975.

3523

Préfontaine, Marielle. "Women's Role Orientation in Three Types of French-Canadian Educational Institutions." Cornell, 1969.

3524

Sadighian, Masoud. "A Comparative Analysis of University Goals and Governments in North America and Iran." Alberta, 1975.

Schneider, Louis Francis. See No./Voir no 2673

3525

Shevenell, Raymond H. "L'enseignement supérieur en Amérique du Nord." Ottawa, 1949.

3526

Shute, James Carey Miller. "A Study of International Activity in Canadian Universities." Michigan State, 1967.

3527

Walker, Robert W. "Success and Failure in a Military College: A Test of Holland's Theory of Vocational Choice." Queen's, 1977-1978.

3528

Weinhauer, Carlin Eugene. "Church-Related College Environmental Relations." Alberta, 1979.

General Items for Provincial Higher Education/ Ouvrages généraux sur l'enseignement supérieur provincial

Alberta

3529

Farquhar, Hugh Ernest. "The Role of the College in the System of Higher Education in Alberta." Alberta, 1967.

3530

Long, John Clifford Anthony. "The Transferability Issue in Alberta: A Case Study in the Politics of Higher Education." Alberta, 1979.

3531

Maddocks, George Raymond. "A Comparative Analysis of Approaches to Planning Development in Post-Secondary Education." Alberta, 1972.

Marshall, Anthony R.A. See No./Voir no 3632

3532

Nussbaumer, Margaret. "The Worth Report and Developments in Alberta's Post-Secondary Policies and Structures, 1968 to 1976." Alberta, 1977.

3533

Small, James Matthew. "College Coordination Alberta: Social Development and Appraisal Michigan State, 1972.

3534

Small, Michael Willoughby. "A Case Study in Educational Policy Making: The Establishment of Athabasca University." Alberta, 1980. [Edmonton]

3535

Weleschuk, Marian Alfred. "A Study of the Need for Instructor Development as Perceived by Instructors and Administrators in Alberta Colleges." Alberta 1977.

3536

West, P.M. "The Formation of the Department of Advanced Education: A Case Study in Postsecondary Education, 1966-1973." Alberta, 1982.

Maritime Provinces/Provinces maritimes

3537

Clarke, Claude Reginald. "Coordination of Higher Education in Atlantic Canada." Alberta, 1975.

Laidlaw, Alexander Fraser. See No./Voir no 4054

Ontario

Maddocks, George Raymond. See No./Voir no 3531

3538

McLarty, James Kenneth. "Organization of Higher Education for Improved Access-Equity and Spatial Justice in Primary Resource Regions: The Case of Northern Ontario, Canada." Michigan State, 1979.

3539

Trusz, Andrew Richard. "The Activities of Governmental Education Bodies in Defining the Role of Post-Secondary Education Since 1945: A Comparative Case Study of the State of New York and the Province of Ontario, 1945-1972." SUNY, Buffalo, 1977.

Quebec/Québec

3540

Bellagamba, Anthony D. "A Project of Interinstitutional Cooperation: The Seminary of St. Augustin in Cap-Rouge, Quebec, Canada." SUNY, Buffalo, 1970.

3541

Gill, Robert Monroe. "Universities and Development in Quebec." Duke, 1975.

3542

Gordon, Robert Arthur. "The Development of Canadianism in the English Language Universities of Quebec 1960-1970." Massachusetts, 1971.

3543

Reid, André. "Étude des perceptions et des attentes de rôles de l'Université de Sherbrooke." Ottawa, 1982.

History of Higher Education/
Histoire de l'enseignement supérieur

General Items/Ouvrages généraux

Collette, Jean-Paul. See No./Voir no 2594

Delmas, Paul Julian George. See No./Voir no 1267

3544
De Pencier, Marni Frazer Lithgow. "Ideas of the English-Speaking University in Canada to 1920." Toronto, 1978.

Glazier, Kenneth MacLean. See No./Voir no 9958

Hughes, Norah L. See No./Voir no 9861

McKillop, Alexander Brian. See No./Voir no 7091

3545
Pilkington, Gwendoline. "A History of the National Conference of Canadian Universities 1911-1961." Toronto, 1974.

3546
Scarfe, Janet Christine. "Letters and Affection: The Recruitment and Responsibilities of Academics in English-Speaking Universities in British North America in the Mid Nineteenth Century." Toronto, 1982.

Alberta

Campbell, Gordon. See No./Voir no 3570

3547
McLeod, Norman Leslie. "Calgary College 1912-1915: A Study of an Attempt to Establish a Privately Financed University in Alberta." Calgary, 1970.

Small, Michael Willoughby. See No./Voir no 3534

Manitoba

3548
Gregor, Alexander Douglas. "The Federated University Structure in Manitoba." Michigan State, 1974.

Maritime Provinces/Provinces maritimes

Darville, Richard Tulloss. See No./Voir no 1379

3549
McMullin, Stanley G. "Thomas McCulloch: The Evolution of a Liberal Mind." Dalhousie, 1975. [b.1776-d. 1843/Né en 1776, mort en 1843]

3550
Newcomer, Richard S. "The Administration of the Extension Courses of the University of Maryland at Harmon Air Force Base in Newfoundland, 1951-1952." Duke, 1953.

3551
Zanes, John Page. "Where the Seddleheads Grow and the Wind Blows Blue: A Consideration of a Canadian Literary Tradition." Texas, 1979. [University of New Brunswick/Université du Nouveau-Brunswick]

Ontario

3552
Axelrod, Paul Douglas. "The Economy, Government and the Universities of Ontario: 1945-1973." York, 1980.

Ayre, David John. See No./Voir no 2790

3553
Boland, Francis J. "Problems of the Basilian Fathers in Establishing St. Michael's College in Toronto, Ontario." Ottawa, 1955.

3554
Bowker, Alan Franklin. "Truly Useful Men: Maurice Hutton, George Wrong, James Havor and the University of Toronto, 1880-1927." Toronto, 1975.

3555
Dunlop, Edward Alexander. "The Development of Extension Education at Queen's University 1889-1945." Toronto, 1981.

3556
Keane, David Ross. "Rediscovering Ontario University Students of the Mid Nineteenth Century: Sources for and Approaches to the Study of the Experience of Going to College and Personal, Family and Social Backgrounds of Students." Toronto, 1981.

3557
McNabb, George Gibbon. "The Development of Higher Education in Ontario." Queen's, 1924.

3558
Patrick, Glenda Marie. "The Establishment and Development of College of Applied Arts and Technology: A Study of Vocational and Technical Policy in the Province of Ontario, 1889-1979." Toronto, 1982.

3559
Ross, Peter Noble. "The Origins and Development of the Ph.D. Degree at the University of Toronto, 1871-1932." Toronto, 1972.

Ryckman, Robert M. See No./Voir no 4420

3560
Stewart, Edward Emslie. "The Role of the Provincial Government in the Development of the Universities of Ontario, 1791-1964." Toronto, 1970.

3561
Temple, Anna. "The Development of Higher Education for Women in Ontario 1867-1914." Wayne State, 1981.

Trusz, Andrew Richard. See No./Voir no 3539

Quebec/Québec

Audet, Louis-Philippe. See No./Voir no 2515

3562
Lavallée, André. "Le projet de création d'une université à Montréal (1878-1889): l'opposition entre Montréal et Québec, ultramontains et libéraux." Montréal, 1971.

Continuing Education (Post-Secondary)/
Éducation permanente (post-secondaire)

See also Adult Education/Voir aussi Éducation des adultes

Community and Junior Colleges/
Collèges communautaires (1er cycle)

General Items/Ouvrages généraux

Bacon, John Alan. See No./Voir no 3617

3563
Epstein, Maurry Hart. "Relationship Between Interpersonal Relations/Orientations and Leader Behavior of Canadian Community College Administrative Leaders." George Peabody, 1976.

Gelowitz, Arnold Charles. See No./Voir no 4162

3564
Havard, Ronald James. "The Philanthropic Support of Community Colleges in Canada." Indiana, 1975.

Howley, Thomas Patrick. See No./Voir no 4227

3565
Lazar, Morty Max. "A Comparative Analysis of Canadian and American Community College Students." York, 1975.

3566
Leduc, Ronald J. "Perceptions and Expectations of Behavior of Community, College Academic Deans: A Study of Canadian Community College Deans of Themselves, Their Superordinates and Subordinates." Brigham Young, 1982.

Parrott, Eric George. See No./Voir no 2583

3567
Tower, Gael Welles. "The International Transfer of Students from Community College to Senior Institutions: Canada and United States." Arizona, 1979.

Alberta

3568
Barrington, Gail Vallance. "The Impact of Environmental Forces on Alberta Community Colleges, 1980-1990." Alberta, 1981.

3569
Bosetti, Rino Angelo. "A Comparative Analysis of Functioning Post-Secondary Non-University Educational Institutions." Alberta, 1975.

3570
Campbell, Gordon. "History of the Alberta Community College System." Calgary, 1972.

3571
Clarke, Neil William James. "Organizational Design in a Community College: A Case Study." Alberta, 1977.

3572
Collin, Wilbur John. "A Model for the Analysis of Staff Development in a Post-Secondary Educational Institution." Alberta, 1977.

3573
Falkenberg, Eugene Edward. "A Study of the Success of Junior College Transfer Students to the University of Alberta, Edmonton and the University of Calgary from Public Junior Colleges in the Province of Alberta, Canada." Montana, 1969.

3574
Fisher, Harold Melvin. "A Study of Student Characteristics, Attitudes and Attrition from Secretarial Science Programs in Seven Selected Two-Year Post-Secondary Educational Institutions in Alberta." Oregon State, 1977.

Goodwin, John Robert. See No./Voir no 3628

Harrison, William George. See No./Voir no 4117

3575
Hassen, Matthew Robert. "Intraorganizational Relationships Between Work Technology, Structure and Organizational Effectiveness in a Community College." Alberta, 1976.

Heemsberger, Donald Bastiaan. See No./Voir no 9440

3576
Hollington, Kenneth Charles. "Fault-Free Approach to Management Development Programs: Alberta Community Colleges." Brigham Young, 1979.

3577
MacNeil, James Leo. "How Selected Groups Evaluate the Student Personnel Services at a Public Community College." Oregon State, 1976. [Lethbridge Community College, Lethbridge, Alberta/Collège communautaire de Lethbridge, Alberta]

3578
Morphy, David Raymond. "A Descriptive Study of the Professional Development Activities of Student Affairs Professionals in the Two Year Post Secondary Educational System of Alberta, Canada." Michigan State, 1978.

3579
Murphy, Peter James. "A Community College Programme Information System." Alberta, 1976.

3580
Pickard, Brent William. "The Role of Community College Community Services as Perceived by Community Organizations." Alberta, 1975.

British Columbia/Colombie-Britannique

3581
Gray, Robert William. "The Governance of Three Post-Secondary Two Year Colleges in British Columbia." British Columbia, 1975.

3582
Hendry, Andrew Munn. "Student Services in the Community College of British Columbia." Alberta, 1974.

3583
Hollick-Kenyon, Timothy Hugh. "An Analysis of the Coordination of Community Colleges in British Columbia." Oregon, 1979.

Rubidge, Nicholas Andrew. See No./Voir no 4049

3584
Williams, David Rees. "Structure and Perceived Adequacy of Performance in British Columbia Community Colleges." British Columbia, 1980.

3585
Workman, William Laurence. "Factors Associated with the Emergence of Selected Two Year Colleges in British Columbia." Alberta, 1975.

Ontario

Bachor, Patricia A.C. See No./Voir no 2560

3586
Bartram, Peter Edward Raven. "The Ontario College of Applied Arts and Technology: A Review and Analysis of Selected Literature, 1965-1976." Toronto, 1980.

3587
Calder, William Berry. "The Development and Future Directions of Student Services in Ontario Colleges of Applied Arts and Technology." Toronto, 1982.

3588
Cameron, Donald Alan. "An Examination of Social Service Programs in Ontario Community Colleges with Special Reference to Field Instruction." Toronto, 1975.

3589
Desroches, Jocelyn Jean-Yves. "The Concept Determinants of Job Satisfaction: An Exploratory Study in the Colleges of Applied Arts and Technology in Ontario." Toronto, 1976.

3590
Ellis, Maxyne Evelyn Dormer. "A Study of Personal Characteristics, Family Background and School Factors Associated with the Patterns of Progress Through the Grades of Grade 13 Students in Metropolitan Toronto." Toronto, 1968.

3591
Flynn, John David. "Structural Congruence of Community Colleges and Economic Development Areas in Ontario." Cornell, 1975.

3592
Goss, Anthony John. "The Effectiveness of the Colleges of Applied Arts and Technology of Ontario." SUNY, Buffalo, 1972.

Hartleib, Carl John. See No./Voir no 3681

3593
Kelly, Desmond Aylmer Gratten. "A Study of the Student Population at an Ontario College of Applied Arts and Technology Between 1967-1969 with an Analysis of Factors Relating to Academic Success." Toronto, 1970.

McLean, Ruth Winnifred. See No./Voir no 3658

3594
Murphy, Michael Neil. "An Analysis of the General Education Component in Curricula of the Ontario College of Applied Arts and Technology." Toronto, 1983.

3595
Noordeh, Ardeshir. "The Redistributional Effects of Investment in Post-Secondary Education in Ontario Community Colleges: A Life Cycle Analysis." Carleton, 1983.

3596
Okihiro, Norman Ryukichi. "Community Colleges and Early Job Outcomes: The Role of Colleges of Applied Arts and Technology in Ontario." York, 1981.

Patrick, Glenda M. See No./Voir no 3558

Peszat, Lucille Catharine. See No./Voir no 3721

Potvin, Robert John Michael. See No./Voir no 4418

3597
Robertson, George Hawthorne. "A Proposed In-Service Training Program for Academic Administrators in Ontario Community Colleges." Florida State, 1976.

3598
Stannard, Stanley Adam. "Ontario Colleges of Applied Arts and Technology in Transition." Wayne State, 1976.

3599
Weeks, Donald Ralph. "The Preparation and Selection of Community College Presidents in Ontario." Michigan State, 1979.

3600
Weinstein, Edwin Lawrence. "Student Selection and Admissions Decisions. Toronto, 1980. [Nursing program of Ontario College of Applied Arts and Technology/Programme de sciences infirmières au Collège Algonquin des arts appliqués et de technologie]

Quebec/Québec

3601
Aumont, Marcel. "The Relationship Between Early Withdrawals and Selected Institutional Factors in Colleges of the Montreal Metropolitan Area." Catholic, 1974. [Quebec community college/Collège communautaire du Québec]

3602
Girard, Hermann C. "A Conceptual Model for Implementing a New Decision-Making Process at the Saguenay and Lake St. John Community College in Quebec." Toledo, 1972.

3603
Webb, David Charles. "The Introduction of the Two-Year College in Quebec: A Case Study in Educational and Social Reform." Pittsburgh, 1972.

Manitoba

3604
Innes, Robert John. "Issues in the Design of a Program of Professional Preparation for Community College Instructors in Manitoba." Manitoba, 1980.

3605
Kolt, Stanley Ernest. "The Establishment and Financing of Junior Colleges in Rural Manitoba." North Dakota, 1969.

3606
Russell, Charles Neil. "Environmental Presses within an Academic Community of an Evolving Canadian Community College." Southern California, 1974. [Red River Community College, Winnipeg/Collège communautaire Red River à Winnipeg]

The Economics and Financing of Higher Education/ Économie et financement de l'enseignement supérieur

Axelrod, Paul Douglas. See No./Voir no 3552

3607
Bassyouni, Abdelrahman Ali Mohamed. "A Cost Effectiveness and Analysis of Individualized and Traditional Methods of Technical Learning." Calgary, 1979. [Southern Alberta Institute of Technology/ Institut de technologie du sud de l'Alberta]

3608
Bharath, Ramachandran. "The Income Redistribution Effects of Public Expenditure in Higher Education." Simon Fraser, 1976.

3609
Budd, Henry Harold. "The Financial Future of Canadian Bible Colleges." Oregon, 1980.

Carmone, Frank Joseph, Jr. See No./Voir no 2779

Dibski, Dennis John. See No./Voir no 4375

Dodge, David Allison. See No./Voir no 1653

Havard, Ronald James. See No./Voir no 3564

3610
Hyman, Charles. "An Analysis of Factors Associated with Variations in Canadian University Operating Expenditures in the Decade 1960/61 to 1969/70." Alberta, 1972.

Kolt, Stanley. See No./Voir no 3605

LeSieur, Antonio. See No./Voir no 2749

3611
Michaud, Lucien Fidèle. "Government Policies of Financial Support of Church-Related Colleges and Universities in Canada." Teachers College, Columbia, 1970.

O'Malley, Denis Anthony. See No./Voir no 3522

3612
Prakash, Brahm. "The Demand for and Financing of Higher Education in Canada." Toronto, 1976.

3613
Schaafsma, Joseph. "An Econometric Analysis of the Demand for Higher Education in Canada with Special Emphasis on the Investment and Consumption Aspects." Toronto, 1973.

3614
Stager, David Arnold Albert. "Monetary Returns to Post-Secondary Education in Ontario." Princeton, 1968.

3615
Tihanyi, Eva. "The Private Valuation of a University Degree with a Probabilistic View of Returns and Costs." Saskatchewan, 1971.

3616
Walkington, Albert Hodgson. "Budget Allocation and Program Approval in Non-University Post-Secondary Institutions." Alberta, 1975.

Wallace, Kenneth Walter Anthony. See No./Voir no 4383

Wilson, Kevin Arthur. See No./Voir no 2767

Organization and Administration/ Organisation et administration

3617
Bacon, John Alan. "Communications and Role Satisfaction in Post-Secondary Institutions." Alberta, 1971.

Bassyouni, Abdelrahman A.M. See No./Voir no 3607

3618
Birkenstock, David. "A Comparison of Values of Board Chairmen and Educational Administrators in Seventh-Day Adventist Residential Academies, Colleges and Universities in the United States of America and Canada." Andrews, 1976.

3619
Brunet, Luc. "Évaluation d'un cours de perfectionnement: le rôle du climat organisationel et du renforcement dans le transfert de l'apprentissage." Montréal, 1981.

3620
Campbell, Duncan Darroch. "An Empirical Approach to the Inference and Classification of University Goals: The University of Alberta, 1959-60 to 1968-69." Toronto, 1973.

Carmone, Frank J. See No./Voir no 2779

Clarke, Neil William James. See No./Voir no 3571

3621
Collins, Gary Walter. "An Investigation of the Environmental Image of Ottawa University." Utah, 1973.

3622
Cornish, David J. "The Impact of Participation and Information on Perception of College Goals." Alberta, 1977. [Red Deer College/Collège Red Deer]

3623
Day, Thomas Charles. "Administration-Faculty Conflict over the Distribution of Control in Policy Formulation in Alberta Colleges." Alberta, 1971.

Epstein, Maurry Hart. See No./Voir no 3563

Fialkoff, Steven Alan. See No./Voir no 9938

3624
Frederick, Nicholas Octave. "The Autonomy of Universities and Colleges: A Tentative Theory of Power Distribution Based on a Comparative Case Study of Government Relations with Universities and Colleges in Ontario." Toronto, 1979.

3625
Garnier, Bernard. "The Impact of Conflict - Handling Modes of Academic Deans on Their Perceived Managerial Effectiveness: An Empirical Study of Selected Canadian Universities." Western Ontario, 1981.

Gazard, Peter Robin. See No./Voir no 9957

3626
Gillies, Howard Earl. "Developing a Conceptual Framework for Analyzing Issues in the Governance of Professional Education in Ontario Universities." Toronto, 1981.

3627
Girard, André. "Étude comparée sur l'enseignement post-secondaire au premier cycle du point de vue de l'organisation et des structures." Laval, 1974.

3628
Goodwin, John Robert. "An Empirical Study of Bureaucratic Structural Dimensions and Their Relationship to the Variable Organizational Size." Ottawa, 1979.

Gray, Robert William. See No./Voir no 3581

Greenhill, Craig James. See No./Voir no 3652

Hannah, Kathryn J.N. See No./Voir no 6892

Hassen, Matthew R. See No./Voir no 3575

3629
Heron, Robert Peter. "Growth Stages in the Development of College Structures." Alberta, 1972.

Hyde, William Paul. See No./Voir no 2662

3630
Kelly, Gerald Oliver. "A Study of Participation in College Governance." Alberta, 1973.

3631

Kingstone, Alan. "The Polytechnical Institute President at Work: A Study of the Work of an Executive in Higher Education." Toronto, 1980. [Ryerson Polytechnical Institute/Institut polytechnique Ryerson]

Leduc, Ronald J. See No./Voir no 3566

3632

Marshall, Anthony Robert Alfred. "Judgement in Decision Making: The Evaluation of Proposals for New Instructional Programs in Higher Education." Alberta, 1976.

3633

Massey-Hicks, Mirvene George. "Relationship of Self-Theory to Organizational Theory in Administrative Appraisal." Calgary, 1975. [Alberta college system/Système collégial de l'Alberta]

Murphy, Peter James. See No./Voir no 3579

3634

Murray, Virginia Elizabeth. "The Library in the Organizational and Administrative Structure of the Canadian University." Teachers College, Columbia, 1966.

3635

Newberry, John Franklin. "A Comparative Analysis of the Organizational Structures of Selected Post-Secondary Educational Institutions." Alberta, 1972.

3636

Padfield, Clive A.F. "A Comparison of the Value Systems of Academic Administrators and Physical Educators in Seven Western Universities." Southern California, 1979.

3637

Pannu, Rajinder Singh. "Collegial Bureaucracy: A Study of Power and Conflict in Academic Self-Governance in a New Canadian University." Alberta, 1973.

Robertson, George Hawthorne. See No./Voir no 3597

Rose, Robert Arthur. See No./Voir no 9961

3638

Schieman, Ervin. "The Role of the Media Director at Selected Canadian Universities as Determined by a Delphi Survey." Indiana, 1980.

Sinclair, Glenn William. See No./Voir no 2675

Small, Michael Willoughby. See No./Voir no 3534

3639

Smyth, Delmar McCormack. "Structures for University Government to the Beginning of the Twentieth Century with Particular Reference to American, British and Canadian Institutions." Toronto, 1972.

Summers, Randal William. See No./Voir no 1959

3640

Taylor, William Harold. "The Evolution of a Policy-Making System: A Case in University Governance." Alberta, 1980. [University of Calgary/Université de Calgary]

3641

Van Raamsdonk, Renée Giselle. "University Language Centres in Canada: An Organizational Study." Calgary, 1980.

Weeks, Donald Ralph. See No./Voir no 3599

Williston, Robert Horace. See No./Voir no 2987

3642

Young, David George. "The Effectiveness of Temporary Adaptive Systems." Alberta, 1979.

3643

Zaharchuk, Ted Michael. "Some Aspects of Planning for Post-Secondary Vocational Institutions: A Case Study of the Ryerson Polytechnical Institute." Toronto, 1971.

Educational Planning/Planification de l'enseignement

3644

Lambert, Leah Rae. "Educational Planning for Manpower Needs in the Criminal Justice System: Issues in the Recruitment and Training of Essential Personnel." Toronto, 1979.

Educational Research in Universities/Recherche sur l'enseignement dans les universités

3645

Brehaut, Willard. "A Quarter Century of Educational Research in Canada: An Analysis of Dissertations (English) in Education Accepted by Canadian Universities, 1930-1955." Toronto, 1958.

3646

Cooper, Helen Elaine. "Factors in Thesis Development and Completion." Toronto, 1982. [University of Toronto/Université de Toronto]

3647

Goh, Swee Chua. "The Effects of Social Influence on Resource Allocation Decisions in Organizations. Some Theoretical Extensions and an Empirical Test." Toronto, 1980. [National Research Council/Conseil national de recherches]

3648

Markle, Glen Hugh. "Student and Supervision Interactions: A Model of the Thesis Completion Process." Toronto, 1976.

Faculty/Faculté

3649

Allan, David Hamilton. "An Explanatory Study of the Use of Resources to Control College Staff." Alberta, 1974.

Barkow, Ben. See No./Voir no 3519

3650

Bonneau, Gilles A. "Une analyse psycho-phénoménologique et contextuelle de perfectionnement universitaire tel que vécu par un groupe d'enseignants." Laval, 1980.

Collette, Jean-Paul. See No./Voir no 2594

3651

Gagné, Fernand. "Étude de la perception par des enseignants et des étudiants des divers éléments de compétence des enseignants du niveau collégial." Montréal, 1980.

Gailey, Richard Willard. See No./Voir no 1149

Garry, Carl. See No./Voir no 4347

3652

Greenhill, Craig James. "Analysis for Institutional Decision: The Problem of Faculty Rank Distribution." British Columbia, 1981.

Isabelle, Laurent A. See No./Voir no 3735

3653

Jennings, Daniel Edward. "An Exploratory Study of Characteristics of Faculty Members of Graduate Professional Schools of Social Work in the United States and Canada." Catholic, 1965.

3654

Lamontagne, Jacques. "Les professeurs de collège pendant la réforme scolaire des années soixante au Québec, analyse psycho-sociologique d'un changement social." Montréal, 1974.

3655

Landry, Simon. "Impacts of University Professors' Unionization on Roles and Role Perceptions of a Group of Selected Participants: The Case of the University of Ottawa." Toronto, 1979.

3656

MacFarland, Gertrude Cecile. "Certain Factors Affecting Mobility and the Relationship between Spatial and Social Mobility of University Faculty, Particularly Scientists - Ontario, 1967-1968." Michigan State, 1969.

3657

Maloney, Timothy Lawrence. "Job Satisfaction among Physical Educators at English-Speaking Canadian Universities." Alberta, 1974.

3658

McLean, Ruth Winnifred. "The First Semester: How New Part-Time Continuing Education College Instructors Learn How to Teach." Toronto, 1980.

Parent, Richard. See No./Voir no 9461

Scarfe, Janet Christine. See No./Voir no 3546

Taylor, William David. See No./Voir no 11875

3659

Von Zur-Muehlen, Max. "University Faculty in Canadian Schools of Business." Oregon, 1970.

Students/Étudiants

3660

Abram, Philip Charles. "Student Personality Characteristics, Teacher Ratings and Student Achievement." Manitoba, 1978.

3661

Asper, Linda Barker. "Attitudes of Graduate Students Toward the Master of Education, University of Manitoba." Manitoba, 1975.

3662

Banerjee, Nipa. "Students from India in Canadian Universities." Toronto, 1977.

3663

Binette, André. "Travail et loisir: Comparaison selon le sexe, des valeurs d'étudiants en psychologie." Montréal, 1975.

3664

Boonyawiroj, Somsak. "Adjustment of Foreign Graduate Students: Nine Case Studies." Toronto, 1983.

3665

Butler, Lenora Frances. "Matching Technique to Student Needs as Measured by the Stern Activities Index." Toronto, 1976.

Calder, William Berry. See No./Voir no 3587

3666

Clarke, David Edward. "The Effects of Orientation, Feedback, and Motivation on Persistence, Performance, and Satisfaction in a Study Skills Program." York, 1970. [A study of 310 college students/Enquête touchant 310 étudiants de collèges]

3667

Clifton, Rodney Alfred. "The Socialization of Graduate Students in the Social and Natural Sciences." Toronto, 1976.

3668

Conrad, Sister Greta. "Clothing Values and their Relation to Personality Factors and to Selected Demographic Variables for Two Groups of Canadian University Women." Pennsylvania State, 1970.

3669

Crossley, Thane Robert. "A Comparison of the Relative Effectiveness of Role Playing and Imagery in Teaching Male Undergraduates Effective Dating Skills." Toronto, 1980.

3670

Cust, Marlene A. "Self-Actualization and Psychological Androgyny in a Sampling of University Women." Alberta, 1978.

3671

Davis, Roger Allen. "General Anxiety Desensitization and the Hierarchy." Alberta, 1976.

3672

Dick, William W. "Clarity of Self-Concepts in the Vocational Development of Male Liberal Arts Students." Ottawa, 1966.

3673

Doucet, Alfred. "The Implications of Rank Ordering on the Clark-Trow Typology of University Students." Ottawa, 1976.

3674

Dumais, Louise. "A Study of Married Students, Numbers, Problems, Policies, and Programs in Selected French Universities in the Province of Quebec, the Context of the Quebec Educational Reform." New York, 1973.

3675

Dupont, Robert. "Valeurs de travail d'étudiants en droit, en génie et en psychologie." Montréal, 1975.

Ellis, Maxyne E.D. See No./Voir no 3590

3676

El Senoussi, Veronica. "The UCLA Foreign Alumni Study, 1945-70." California, Los Angeles, 1973.

3677

Ferguson, Marianne. "The Religious Identity of College Students and the Holding Power of Church Denominations." McMaster, 1980.

3678

Finnigan, Bryan. "A Comparative Study of Some Social, Economic and Political Attitudes of French-Canadian, English-Canadian and American University Students." Laval, 1970.

Fisher, Harold Melvin. See No./Voir no 3574

Gélinas, Jean-Paul. See No./Voir no 2411

3679

Grady, William Ellis. "Selected Variables Related to Academic Achievement of American and Canadian Male Freshmen at the University of North Dakota." North Dakota, 1969.

3680
Guérin, Gilles. "Élaboration d'un modèle de prévision des effectifs étudiants au niveau universitaire." Montréal, 1973.

3681
Hartleib, Carl John. "The Impact of an I.O.S.P. on the Personal Competencies and Self-Actualization Levels of Social-Service Students." Toronto, 1978.

3682
Hitchman, Gladys Symons. "The Professional Socialization of Women and Men in Two Canadian Graduate Schools." York, 1976.

3683
Janzen, Henry Lawrence. "A Factor Analytic Investigation of the Soviet Concept of Set." Calgary, 1971.

Kelly, Desmond Aylmer Gratten. See No./Voir no 3593

3684
Kelsey, Ian Bruce. "A Comparative Study of Values of Students Attending the University of British Columbia in 1963 as Measured by the Allport-Vernon Test for Personal Values." Washington, Seattle, 1963.

Krivy, Gary Joseph Paul. See No./Voir no 2807

3685
Landry, Michel. "L'adaptation française d'un questionnaire d'anxiété, fidélité, validité et normalisation avec une population étudiante de niveau collégial." Montréal, 1976.

3686
Lavallée, Alain. "L'incidence du dogmatisme et des valeurs d'éducation sur le comportement contestataire d'étudiants de niveau collégial." Montréal, 1977.

Lazar, Morty Max. See No./Voir no 3565

3687
Le Bel, Louis. "L'effet des couleurs rouge-bleu sur la fluidité et l'originalité de la pensée divergente chez les introvertis." Ottawa, 1976.

3688
Loken, Joel Obert. "A Multivariate Analysis of Student Activism at the University of Alberta." Alberta, 1971.

3689
Loughton, Albert John. "People and Change: Multicultural Projects at a Canadian University." Michigan, 1971. [Brandon]

3690
Luce, Sally R. "Sex Differences in Achievement Attributions: Patterns and Processes." Carleton, 1979. [132 students in a computing course/132 étudiants d'informatique]

MacLeod, Alan Ross. See No./Voir no 2992

3691
McGrath, Patrick John. "The Measurement of Social Inadequacy." Queen's, 1979.

3692
McIntosh, Herman Whitefield. "A Study of Normal School Students: Teacher Selection and Appraisal." Toronto, 1937.

3693
Meyers, Gordon Peterson. "Student Strategies for Adaptation in the Academic Arena: A Description of Collective Behavior at One University." Toronto, 1979.

3694
Pettem, Marie Odette Leblanc. "The Relationship Between Depressive Dispositions and Responses to Stressful Life Events in College Students." Calgary, 1981.

3695
Ping, Benjamin Leung Kai. "A Developmental Profile of the Student Activist." York, 1983.

Poon, Wei Keung. See No./Voir no 2795

3696
Proulx, Monique Cécile. "Personal Family and Institutional Factors Associated with Attitudes Toward Women's Roles Among French Canadian College Students." Waterloo, 1976.

3697
Quarter, Jack Joel. "The Student Movement of the 1960's: A Social Psychological Analysis." Toronto, 1970.

3698
Robinson, Barrie William. "Love Counts: Romanticism in Canadian Undergraduate Students." Alberta, 1980.

3699
Rose, George Raymond. "The Meaning of Work for Alberta Post-Secondary Occupational Students." Washington, Seattle, 1971.

3700
St-Onge, Louise. "Représentations axiologiques du travail et biculturalisme québécois: profils d'étudiants de niveau collégial." Montréal, 1980.

3701
Sheridan, Donald Patrick. "The Effects of Feedback on Test Achievement in CAI." Alberta, 1979.

3702
Smyth, Frances E. "Relationship of Maternal Employment and Current Field of Study to Certain Sex-Role Attitudes of Male and Female University Students." Ottawa, 1979.

3703
Strasburger, Erich Leopold. "A Multidimensional Model of Inferential Judgement." Western Ontario, 1980.

3704
Sutherland, S.L. "An Empirical Study of Political Ideologies: Their Incidence and Activity and Background Correlates Among Students at the University of Alberta." Essex, 1976.

Szalai, John Paul. See No./Voir no 9076

Tam, Chung Ngoh-Isaac. See No./Voir no 9202

3705
Toews, Laurette Kathleen Woolsly. "Self-Hatred in College Women: Sex Role Stereotypes and Some Sex Affiliation." Alberta, 1973.

3706
Travis, Leroy Douglas. "Political Economy, Social Learning and Activism: Toward a Theory of Educational Turmoil." Alberta, 1975.

3707
Trenton, Thomas Norman. "Canadian Identity and Nationalism Among University Students: An Exploratory Analysis of the Applicability of Current Theory on Student Protest." Toronto, 1976.

Tufuor, Joseph K. See No./Voir no 3730

3708

Villagonzalo, Paulino Iriarte. "Predicting Training Outcomes for Students in a Technological Institute." Alberta, 1970.

3709

Vraa, Calvin Woodrow. "The Relation of Selected Academic Biographical and Personality Factors to the Achievement of Canadian College Freshmen." North Dakota, 1969.

3710

Wagner, Roy M.K. "The Relationship of Geographic Distance and Five Other Home Area Variables to University Participation." Alberta, 1981.

3711

Yingst, Larry Ronald. "The Academic and Social Images of the University of Calgary as Perceived by the Freshmen Students." Calgary, 1973.

Amin Shukri. See No./Voir no 9638

Annis, Helen Marie. See No./Voir no 8948

Arnold, Larry Sherwood. See No./Voir no 8949

Barkow, Ben. See No./Voir no 3519

Beattie, Margaret E. See No./Voir no 8603

Beer, Anne Maria. See No./Voir no 4057

Bell, Ronald Gordon. See No./Voir no 8898

Brickman, Julia Ruth Rogers. See No./Voir no 9217

Brown, William Cecil. See No./Voir no 6739

Campbell, Douglas F. See No./Voir no 9955

Charlesworth, Maxine Anne. See No./Voir no 9653

Fischer, Donald George. See No./Voir no 9672

Friedmann-Winsberg, Suzanne. See No./Voir no 3734

Gfellner, Barbara Marie. See No./Voir no 9679

Gilmor, Timothy McLeod. See No./Voir no 8914

Gorn, Michael Herman. See No./Voir no 7296

Grimes, Catherine. See No./Voir no 9128

Hallman, David William. See No./Voir no 9534

Hallschmid, Claus A. See No./Voir no 3220

Harvey, Michael Dobbs. See No./Voir no 9689

Henshaw, David Charles. See No./Voir no 9010

Isabelle, Laurent A. See No./Voir no 3735

Josefwvitz, Nina. See No./Voir no 9444

Keane, David Ross. See No./Voir no 3556

Kee, Herbert William. See No./Voir no 9697

Kimmis, Richard Clark. See No./Voir no 9300

Kobayashi, Nobako. See No./Voir no 9020

Leigh, Gillian Mary. See No./Voir no 9551

Leiper, Robert Neil. See No./Voir no 9709

Lesko, Wayne A. See No./Voir no 9711

McCormack, James. See No./Voir no 9717

Merrill, Lesly I. See No./Voir no 9036

Moore, Joseph A.L. See No./Voir no 8926

Mothersill, Kerry James. See No./Voir no 9196

Morphy, David Raymond. See No./Voir no 3578

Munro, John B. See No./Voir no 560

Phillips, Dorothy Anne. See No./Voir no 9735

Plate, David R. See No./Voir no 9159

Ridley, Clifford Keith. See No./Voir no 9228

Schwartz, Geraldine Jerri. See No./Voir no 4000

Sexton, David Lorne. See No./Voir no 9060

Shedletsky, Ralph. See No./Voir no 8940

Stephens, William Eldon. See No./Voir no 8858

Thompson, Edward Gerald. See No./Voir no 4365

Thompson J. Wayne. See No./Voir no 9479

Tilby, Penelope Jean. See No./Voir no 9078

Van der Merwe, Marina Suzanne. See No./Voir no 6736

Williston, Robert Horace. See No./Voir no 2987

Wilson, Kevin Arthur. See No./Voir no 2767

Yackulic, Richard Alan. See No./Voir no 9484

Yates, Elizabeth Presvitt. See No./Voir no 9232

Curriculum and Instruction in Higher Education/ Plan d'étude et enseignement en éducation supérieur

General Items/Ouvrages généraux

Marshall, Anthony Robert Alfred. See No./Voir no 3632

3712

Tyler, Thomas Lee. "A Readability Study of English Student Materials Used in the Home Study Program of the Department of Seminaries and Institutes of Religion Compared with the Reading Abilities of Sample of the Youth Enrolled in That Program in the United States and Canada." Brigham Young 1974.

Art

Hannibal, Emmett Ronald. See No./Voir no 945

Sinclair, Glenn William. See No./Voir no 2675

Sorge, Walter Felix. See No./Voir no 949

3713

Verniero, Sharon Anne. "The Development of Measures of Ego Regression in the Study of Creativity in University Art Students." Windsor, 1982.

3714

Zicha, Victor George. "Guidelines for an Adequate Program of Studies for Preparing Art Teachers at the St-Joseph Teachers College, Montreal, Quebec Canada." New York, 1968.

Business/Affaires

3715

Mullings, Gloria Elizabeth. "The Effects of Learner Program Control in Computer Assisted Instruction." Toronto, 1981.

Dental Education/Enseignement dentaire

See also Curriculum Development and Instruction/Voir aussi Plan d'étude et d'enseignement

Dramatics/Dramatique

3716

Gardner, R. "The Dramatic Script and Procedural Knowledge: A Key to the Understanding of Dramatic Structure and a Foundation for the Development of Effective Curriculum Design in Dramatic Instruction at the Tertiary Level." Toronto, 1983.

3717

Machlin, Evangeline L. "Educational Dramatics in the Maritime Universities in Canada." Teachers College, Columbia, 1942.

Engineering/Ingénierie

Dupont, Robert. See No./Voir no 3675

English/Anglais

3718
Harris, Ronald Sutton. "The Place of English Studies in a University Program of General Education: A Study Based on the Practices of the English-Speaking Universities and Colleges of Canada in 1951-1952." Michigan, 1953.

Forestry/Foresterie

3719
Blenis, Henry Willard, Jr. "The Forest Technician in the Atlantic Provinces of Canada." Pennsylvania State, 1969.

Health Science/Science de la santé

3720
Andrews, Michael Bruce Barrington. "Interorganizational Relationships and Effectiveness in a Program for the Preparation of Allied Health Professionals." Alberta, 1978.

3721
Peszat, Lucille Catharine. "The Development of Health Sciences Education Programs in Metropolitan Toronto Region Colleges of Applied Arts and Technology, 1967-1977: A Study of Selected Factors Influencing This Development." Toronto, 1979.

History/Histoire

3722
Meikle, William Duncan. "And Gladly Teach: G.M. Wrong and the Department of History at the University of Toronto." Michigan State, 1977.

Home Economics/Économie domestique

3723
Burge, Sister Irene. "Prediction of Performance of Students in College Clothing Construction Courses." Iowa State, 1974. [Five Universities of the Maritime Provinces/Cinq universités des Provinces maritimes]

3724
Cormier, Rosilda Ghislaine. "Development of a Home Economics Curriculum for the Université de Moncton." Michigan State, 1970.

3725
Crown, Elizabeth Marie. "Institutional Renewal in Degree-Granting Units of Home Economics in Canada." Alberta, 1978.

3726
Morley, Mary Louise. "Home Economics in Canada, 1960-1970." Columbia, 1973.

Préfontaine, Marielle. See No./Voir no 3523
Rowles, Edith. See No./Voir no 2628

Home and Family Life/Vie familiale

Chaput, Jeanne S. See No./Voir no 2627

3727
LaCroix, Sister Alida-Marie. "An Evaluation of the Curriculum of the Institut de Pédagogie Familiale Montréal, for the Purpose of Strengthening the Program of Home and Family Life." Teachers College, Columbia, 1965.

Languages/Langues

Van Raamsdonk, Renée. See No./Voir no 3641

Law/Droit

Dupont, Robert. See No./Voir no 3675

Mathematics/Mathématiques

Collette, Jean-Paul. See No./Voir no 2594

Music Education/Enseignement musical

Brown, Alfred Malcolm. See No./Voir no 995
Green, James Paul. See No./Voir no 988
O'Neill, Mary Elizabeth. See No./Voir no 1002

3728
Ringuette, Raymond. "Considérations théoriques sur l'organisation et la direction d'un programme de formation des musiciens éducateurs à l'Université Laval." Illinois, 1980. [A theoretical basis for the music teacher education program at Laval University/Base théorique au programme de formation des maîtres en musique de l'Université Laval]

Outdoor Education/Enseignement hors campus

3729
Nadeau, Georges-André. "Outdoor Education as Seen Through a Delphi Survey of Selected Groups of Experts in the Province of Quebec, Canada, U.S.A., and Overseas and Implications for the Outdoor Education Curriculum At Laval University, Quebec." Michigan State, 1976.

3730
Tufuor, Joseph Kwame. "Changes in Students' Attitudes Towards Conservation Resulting from Outdoor Education: A Case Study." British Columbia, 1982.

Philosophy/Philosophie

3731
Saucier, Jean. "La participation de l'enseignant à l'apprentissage philosophique de l'apprenant." Montréal, 1980.

Physical Education/Éducation physique

See also Sports, Physical Education and Recreation/ Voir aussi Sports, éducation physique et loisirs

Psychology/Psychologie

Barkow, Ben. See No./Voir no 3519
Binette, André. See No./Voir no 3663

3732

Davison, James H. "Effects of Small Group Discussions on Personal Learning and Personality in an Educational Psychology Course." Waterloo, 1973.

Dupont, Robert. See No./Voir no 3675

3733

Saul, David John. "Toward a Consensual Model for the Redesign of Professional Curricula: The Development of a Relevant Course of Study in Educational Psychology for Teacher Preparation." Toronto, 1971.

Radio and Television/Radio et télévision

Gailly, Richard Willard. See No./Voir no 1149

Science

Clifton, Rodney Alfred. See No./Voir no 3667

Finegold, Menahem. See No./Voir no 3448

3734

Friedmann-Winsberg, Suzanne. "L'orientation des élèves vers les personnes, les programmes qu'ils suivent et l'intérêt qu'ils portent aux cours de physique." Montréal, 1977.

3735

Isabelle, Laurent A. "Actuarial versus Clinical Methods in Predicting Achievement in a Science Faculty." Ottawa, 1961.

3736

Packer, Katherine Helen. "Methods Used by Chemists and Clinical Engineers in Canadian Universities to Maintain Current Awareness with Special Reference to the Use of SDI System." Maryland, 1975.

3737

Pelletier, Marc-Lionel. "L'influence de deux types d'objectifs de comportement sur la performance et la retention en biologie 170-442." Montréal, 1982.

3738

Rouleau, Suzanne. "Influence de la fréquence des séances de laboratoires et de l'activité des étudiants au laboratoire sur leur satisfaction." Montréal, 1979.

Vaillancourt, Raymond F. See No./Voir no 2986

Social Science/Sciences sociales

Clifton, Rodney Alfred. See No./Voir no 3667

Social Work/Travail social

3739

Cummings, Joan Elizabeth. "Integration of Learning Graduate Social Work Education." Toronto, 1973.

Curtis, Hugh Jefferson. See No./Voir no 10077

Hansen, Forrest Carl. See No./Voir no 4249

Hartleib, Carl John. See No./Voir no 3681

3740

Hutton, Miriam Freda. "Using the Concept of Network to Rethink Education and Manpower Planning for the Social Services, with Special Reference to Canada." Toronto, 1978.

Jennings, Daniel Edward. See No./Voir no 3653

3741

Lundy, Lawrence Allan. "Learning the Ethical Norms of Practitioner-Client Relationships at a School of Social Work." Toronto, 1969.

3742

Marshall, Christine Mavis. "Social Work Students Perceptions of their Practicum Experience: A Study of Learning by Doing." Toronto, 1982.

3743

Munns, Violet Beatrice. "The Field Practicum in the Organizational Context." Toronto, 1977.

3744

Murase, Kenneth. "International Students in Education for Social Work: An Assessment of the Educational Experience by International Graduates of Schools of Social Work in North America, 1948-1957." Columbia, 1961.

3745

Stange, Karl Henry. "A Short Season of Reform: The Regina School of Social Work, 1971-1978." Wisconsin, 1979.

Sociology/Sociologie

3746

Tomović, Vadislav A. "Sociology in Canada: An Analysis of Its Growth in English Language Universities 1908-1972." Waterloo, 1976.

Spanish/Espagnol

3747

Valdés, Maria-Elena de. "A Conceptual Analysis of the Domain of Spanish Studies and Its Application in the Curriculum of University Education in Ontario." Toronto, 1976.

Speech/Discours

3748

Campbell, Pearl Read. "Speech Education in the English-Speaking Teacher Training Institutions of Canada." Wisconsin, 1957.

3749

Wilson, Llewellyn Lee. "Speech Education in Canada: Facilities, and Personnel." Northwestern, 1967.

Statistics/Statistiques

Hansen, Forrest Carl. See No./Voir no 4249

Thanatology/Thanatologie

3750

Anderson, Barbara Marlene. "Death Education: A Formative Assessment of a Thanatology Curriculum at the Tertiary Level of Education." Toronto, 1982.

Theology/Théologie

Cooper, Alvin John. See No./Voir no 9948

Wilson, Lon Erwin. See No./Voir no 9963

SPECIAL EDUCATION, REHABILITATION AND PSYCHOLOGY OF THE EXCEPTIONAL/ ENSEIGNEMENT SPÉCIALISÉ, RÉHABILITATION ET PSYCHOLOGIE DE L'ENFANCE EXCEPTIONNELLE

General Items/Ouvrages généraux

3751
Agard, Ralph Leonard. "Sociocultural Intelligence and Achievement Scores in a Black Toronto Population: An Analysis for Programming Decisions." Toronto, 1982.

3752
Baker, Laura Doris. "The Development of Special Educational Provisions for Exceptional Children in the City of Winnipeg." Toronto, 1967.

3753
Blowers, Elizabeth Anne. "Auditory, Visual and Intellectual Patterns in Grade One Children." Alberta, 1975.

Burke, Sharon Ogden. See No./Voir no 3090

Charland, Jean-Pierre. See No./Voir no 2519

3754
Clark, Isabelle Marie Forcier. "Achieving and Under-Achieving Students' Problem-Solving Performance: Detection of Linguistic Ambiguity, Reflection-Impulsivity, Tolerance-Intolerance of Ambiguity, and Hypothesis Testing." Saskatchewan, 1983.

3755
Cole, Peter George. "A Multivariate Analysis of the Personal Independence of Normal and Handicapped Children." Saskatchewan, 1974.

3756
Finnestad, Harvey L. "Development of Programs for the Sensory Multi-Handicapped in Alberta." Brigham Young, 1981.

3757
Foord, Esme Noreen. "Special Education in British Columbia." Toronto, 1959.

Gélinas, Arthur. See No./Voir no 2658

3758
Howard, Theresa Coleen. "A Comparison of Recommendations Made by Classroom Teachers and Teacher Diagnosticians for Children with Behaviour and Academic Problems." Toronto, 1982.

Levesque, Denis R. See No./Voir no 2644

3759
Moore, Jean Louise V. "A Sage Analysis of Special Education Curriculum Development in the Province of Alberta." Brigham Young, 1979.

3760
Morris, James Thomas. "Mainstreaming/Integration in the Province of Ontario." Oregon, 1977.

3761
North, Joseph. "Identification of Students with Learning Handicaps." Washington State, 1975. [Alberta]

3762
Rawlyk, Shirley Larson. "Delivery of Special Education Services in Saskatchewan." Illinois, 1974.

Willson, Stanley. See No./Voir no 4288

Education of the Gifted/

Barron, Robert Frederick John. See No./Voir no 2989

3763
Ewing, John Morton. "An Experimental Study of Two School Procedures as Applied to Superior Children." Toronto, 1931.

Johnston, Marion Campbell. See No./Voir no 2643

3764
Julien, Louise. "Étude de la compréhension d'un récit écrit ou filmique chez des enfants de classes régulières et de classes spéciales." Montréal, 1978.

Lang, Charles. See No./Voir no 4216

3765
McGillivray, Robert Hilher. "Differences in Home Background Between High-Achieving and Low-Achieving Gifted Children." Toronto, 1963.

O'Neill, Marie José. See No./Voir no 3049

3766
Pal, Hilda Indira. "Child Rearing Practices and Locus of Control in Gifted Adolescents." Toronto, 1977.

3767
Shiner, Sandra Miriam. "Curriculum Implications of the Profiles of Gifted High School Students." Toronto, 1979.

3768
Stoddart, William Brunton. "A Critical Analysis of the Provisions for the Gifted Child in the Forest Hill School System - A Case Study." Toronto, 1965.

3769
Taylor, Margaret Jane Whatman. "Effects of Instruction in Notetaking on Academically Gifted Children." Toronto, 1982.

3770
Worden, Otis Osborne. "A Comparative Experimental Study of Two Similar Groups of Super-Normal Elementary School Children." Toronto, 1936.

3771
Wright, Mary Jean. "A Follow-up Study of Superior Children from Special Classes." Toronto, 1949.

Slow-Learners/Apprenants lents

3772
Bachor, Daniel Gustave. "Information Processing Capacity and Teachability of Low-Achieving Students." Toronto, 1976.

Bain, David Alexander. See No./Voir no 3796

3773
Couturier, Thérèse Jacinthe. "Élaboration et application d'un programme de stimulation pour enfants lents en première année." Montréal, 1981.

Drewe, Fred Harold. See No./Voir no 2642

3774
Jampolsky, Murray. "Some Characteristics of Slow Learners in a Special School." Alberta, 1972.

Keller, Martha Perry Freese. See No./Voir no 3824

King, Clement Theodore. See No./Voir no 3785

3775
Klotz, Melvin. "A Comparison of Grade Nine Failures: Regular High School Programs vs. Special Vocational High School Programs in the Edmonton Separate School District." Oregon, 1974.

Stevens, Renée Paley. See No./Voir no 3268

3776

Waksman, Mary. "A Home Intervention Programme: Effects on Maternal Teaching Style and on Children's Cognitive Performance." Toronto, 1975. [Kindergarten/Maternelle]

Learning Disabled/Déficients mentaux

General Items/Ouvrages généraux

3777

Brooker, Barry H. "Selective Attentions in Normal and Learning Disabled Boys: An Evoked Potential and Behavioral Analysis." Queen's, 1981.

3778

Butkowsky, Irwin Sam. "On the Generality of Learned Helplessness in Children with Learning Difficulties." Waterloo, 1982.

Chapman, James William. See No./Voir no 3055

Cullen, Joy Lauren. See No./Voir no 3056

3779

Del Dotto, Jerel E. "Differential Subtypes of Sinistral Learning Disabled Children: A Neuropsychological Taxonomic Approach." Windsor, 1982.

3780

Fisk, John L. Identification of Subtypes of Learning Disabled Children: A Neurophychological, Multivariate Approach." Windsor, 1979. [Four age groups 7-8, 9-10, 11-12, 13-14/Quatre groupes de 7-8 ans, 9-10 ans, 11-12 ans et 13-14 ans]

3781

Frost, Ruth. "The Arithmetic Achievement of Learning Disabled Students: A Training Study." Calgary, 1982.

3782

Gates, Robert D. "Patterns of Neuropsychological Impairment in Learning-Disabled Children." Windsor, 1982.

3783

Joschko, Michael. "The Neuropsychological Significance of the 'ACID' Pattern on the WISC: A Multivariate Approach to Subtyping Learning Disabled Children." Windsor, 1981.

3784

Kaufman, David. "The Relation of Academic Performance to Strategy Training and Remedial Techniques: An Information Processing Approach." Alberta, 1978. [Grade four/Quatrième année]

3785

King, Clement Theodore. "Hyperactivity, Introversion-Extroversion and Strength of the Nervous System in Learning Disabled Children." Alberta, 1978.

3786

Kirkbride, Anna Joan. "The Development of Classification and Memory Ability in Achieving and Learning Disabled Children: Piagetian and Levels of Processing Approaches." Alberta, 1981.

3787

Klein, Gerard. "The Diagnostic Use of Geometric Form-Copying Tests: An Investigation of Normal Kindergarten and Learning Disabled Children's Error Production." Western Ontario, 1982.

3788

MacKenzie, Joan Phillips. "Some Characteristics of Two Learning Disabled Subgroups Identified from WISC/WISC-R Factor Score Patterns." McGill, 1981.

McDonald, Linda Mary Olive. See No./Voir no 3248

3789

Polatajko, Helene J. "Vestibular Function and Academic Learning: A Study of Normal Children and Children Identified as Learning Disabled." Toronto, 1982.

3790

Porter, James E. "Identification of Subtypes of Learning Disabled Children: A Multivariate Analysis of Patterns of Personality Functioning." Windsor, 1980.

3791

Strang, John Douglas. "Personality Dimensions of Learning Disabled Children: Age and Subtype Differences." Windsor, 1981.

3792

Warren, William John. "Placement of Learning Disabled Students." Calgary, 1980.

3793

Wilchesky, Marc H. "Recognition of Peer Facial Expressions by Learning-Disabled and Normal Children." York, 1980.

3794

Williams, Noel Henry. "Arousal and Information Processing in Learning Disabled Children." Alberta, 1976.

Retarded/Handicapés mentaux

3795

Baig, Kamal. "Home Training of Parents, and Their Trainable Mentally Retarded Children." Toronto, 1977.

3796

Bain, David Alexander. "Graphemic Discrimination by Educable Mentally Retarded and Slow-Learners." British Columbia, 1975.

3797

Baker, John Garry. "Methodological Factors Influencing Simultaneous Discrimination Acquisition and the Feature Positive Effect with Retarded Children." York, 1977.

3798

Biberdorf, John Robert. "An Investigation of Subject Experimenter Ratios: Verbal Training Session with One Retarded Child and with Two Simultaneously." Manitoba, 1975.

3799

Bouchard, Jean-Marie. "L'application d'un programme intégré d'éducation corporelle auprès de déficients mentaux et son influence sur l'acquisition des habilités motrices et préparatoires à l'apprentissage scolaire: perspective multidisciplinaire." Laval, 1976.

3800

Brailsford, Eugene D. "An Investigation into the Topology of Exogenous Feeble-Minded Children." Ottawa, 1965.

3801
Buckridan, Rakib. "Social Acceptance Enhancement of Low Socioeconomic Status Pupils in Special Classes." Ottawa, 1975.

3802
Burke, Harley Lorne. "Breadth of Attention of Moderately Retarded Children: An Investigation of the Concept and Its Susceptibility to Training." York, 1979.

3803
Carey, Robert Gene. "An Experimental Investigation of Positive Practice Overcorrection." Western Ontario, 1981.

3804
Carney, Philip Francis. "Increasing Retardates Academic Response Frequencies: Response-Response Analysis with Precision Teaching Techniques." Queen's, 1974.

Carruthers, Benjamin Carl. See No./Voir no 8974

3805
Derevensky, Jeffrey L. "A Developmental Study of Haptic Perception of Shape in Normal Young Children and Mentally Retarded Older Children." McGill, 1976.

3806
Dewson, Michael Richard James. "Sensory Reinforcement by the Operant Conditioning of Nonambulatory Profoundly Mentally Retarded Adolescents." Manitoba, 1981.

3807
Dion, Pierre. "Choix sociométriques de déficients mentaux." Ottawa, 1963.

3808
Dionne, Michel. "Étude sur la capacité d'abstraction conceptuelle des retardés mentaux éducables." Montréal, 1978.

3809
Dobson, Lois Ann. "A Comparison of Mentally Retarded Children to Normal Children and of Disabled Readers to Normal Readers: An Evaluation of a Similar Sequence Hypothesis and a Deficit Hypothesis." Windsor, 1981.

3810
Doherty, Gillian. "The Effects of Specific Perceptural-motor Training on the Physical Fitness, Perceptual motor skills, Academic Readiness, and Academic Functionning of Educable mentally Retarded Children." York, 1971.

3811
Doré, Robert. "Influence relative de modalités de rétroaction dans l'apprentissage chez des enfants déficients mentaux moyens." Montréal, 1982.

Drewe, Fred Harold. See No./Voir no 2642

Eaton, Philip. See No./Voir no 3021

3812
Elias, John Walter. "Computer Simulation of a Comprehensive Community Service System for the Mentally Retarded." York, 1976.

3813
Garneau, Jean. "Facteur de retard pédagogique dans un milieu rural." Montréal, 1951.

3814
Gibson, Barry John. "An Attributional Analysis of Performance Outcomes and the Alleviation of Learned Helplessness on Motor Performance Tasks: A Comparative Study of Educable Mentally Retarded and Non-Retarded Boys." Alberta, 1980.

3815
Gignac, Janine. "Vérification de l'efficacité d'un programme de stimulation de language chez l'enfant déficient mental." Montréal, 1979.

Hackett, Gerald Thomas. See No./Voir no 2493

3816
Hardwick, Claudia Shaw. "Mental Retardation and Eyelid Conditioning: Effects of Verbal Cues on Extinction." Western Ontario, 1980.

Hardy, Larry Michael. See No./Voir no 9537

3817
Hepburn, Donald Walter. "An Experimental Study of Two Language Modelling Procedures with Moderately Mentally Retarded Children." Alberta, 1977.

3818
Herbst, Diana Shawn. "A Study of X-Linked Mental Retardation in British Columbia." British Columbia, 1980.

3819
Hillyard, Alexander Leonard. "Stimulus Complexity During Original Learning and Generalization." Alberta, 1979. [Pre-school children/Enfants d'âge pré-scolaire]

3820
Hoy, Elizabeth Ann. "Programming, Labelling and Concept Learning in Retarded Children." McGill, 1969.

3821
Hughes, Maxfield Jeffry. "Small Group Behaviour of Educable Mentally Retarded Boys." Alberta, 1974.

3822
Joyce, S. Maureen. "Cognitive Controls and Field-Dependence-Independence: An Investigation of Their Development in 6-, 9-, and 12-year-old Normal and Retarded Readers." Windsor, 1974.

3823
Kaprowy, Eugene Anthony. "Primary Reinforcement, a Token System and Attention Criteria and Feedback Procedures with Profound Retardates in a Verbal Training Classroom." Manitoba, 1975.

3824
Keller, Martha Perry Freese. "An Experimental Analysis of the Relationship Between Receptive and Productive Language Acquisition in Developmentally Delayed Children." Western Ontario, 1977.

3825
Landino, John Edward. "Coding in the Mentally Retarded: Applications to Learning and Memory." Calgary, 1979.

3826
Leonhart, William Boyd. "Acquisition and Generalization of Prearithmetic Skills in Severely Retarded Men." Manitoba, 1980.

3827
Little, Donald Malcolm. "Teacher Behavior and Influence in EMR Classes: An Analysis of Interaction and Communication Patterns in Classes for the Mildly Retarded." Alberta, 1973.

3828
Lowther, Rachel Mary. "Additional Settings Versus Additional Trainers as Sufficient Stimulus Exemplars for Programming Generalization of a Greeting Response of Severely Retarded Persons." Manitoba, 1980.

3829
McCaw, William Ralph. "Non-Institutional Training of Retarded Children in Ontario." Northwestern, 1956.

3830
Mercier, Jocelyn. "L'acquisition d'une habilité psychomotrice chez les déficients mentaux éducables." Ottawa, 1982.

3831
Molino, Joseph. "Sensory Integration in Moderate and Mildly Retarded Adults." Ottawa, 1982.

3832
Morse-Chevrier, Jean. "Le diagnostic différentiel du retard mental en milieu défavorisé par une tâche d'apprentissage opératoire." Montréal, 1975.

3833
Mosk, Mark David. "A Comparative Analysis of Prompting and Stimulus Shaping Procedures for Teaching Visual-Motor Skills to Retarded Children." Western Ontario, 1982.

3834
Mosley, James Lawrence. "The Influence of Social Reinforcement of the Rectilinear Dot Progression Task Performance of Normal and Retarded Subjects." Western Ontario, 1970.

Mulcahy, Robert Francis. See No./Voir no 3250

Mullaly, R.P. See No./Voir no 10086

3835
Norrie, Beatrice Irene. "Verbal Skill as an Aid to Problem-Solving in the Retarded." Calgary, 1973. [Young adult males/Jeunes hommes]

3836
Olenick, Debra Lynn. "Differential Reinforcement and Trial-Initiation Procedures in Picture-Name Training with Severely Retarded Children." Manitoba, 1979.

3837
Pace, James B. "Operant Conditioning Procedures with Profoundly Retarded Children in the Acquisition of Concepts." Ottawa, 1971.

Pallota-Cornick, Maria Angela Carvalho. See No./Voir no 8928

Radcliffe, Samuel John. See No./Voir no 2646

3838
Ramayya, Penumaka D. "Some Aspects of Metamemory and Memory in Retarded and Nonretarded Children: A Developmental Study." Alberta, 1980.

3839
Rodgers, Denis Cyril. "An Investigation of the Auditory Memory Abilities of Grade 2 Retarded -Under-Achieving Readers and Competent-Achieving Readers under Conditions of Reinforcement and Non-Reinforcement." Toronto, 1969.

3840
Rodrigues, Myra Miliza. "The Nature of Self-Injurious Behaviour Among Visually Impaired Residents of Mental Retardation Facilities." Toronto, 1982.

3841
Sandals, Lauran Hayward. "Computer Assisted Learning with the Developmentally Handicapped." Calgary, 1973. [Adults/Adultes]

3842
Santin, Sylvia Euphrosyne Pegis. "The Language of Teachers to Young Mentally Retarded Children in the Classroom." Toronto, 1982.

3843
Simic, Joan Elaine. "Variables Affecting the Development and Maintenance of Spontaneous Verbal Manding in Functionally Nonverbal Retarded Children." Western Ontario, 1976.

3844
Stephens, Carl Edmund. "Effects of Sequential and Non-Sequential Conditioned Reinforcers in a Picture-Naming Task with Retarded Children." Manitoba, 1975.

3845
Strain, Allan Richard. "Coin Computation Task Analysis and a Computer Assisted Instruction Program for the Retarded." Calgary, 1980.

Sweeney, James Ernest. See No./Voir no 3140

3846
Tang, Fay C.F. "Cognitive Advancement in Mentally Retarded Adolescents and Adults." Ottawa, 1979.

3847
Valiquette, John Edmund. "A Study of Upper Extremity Strength and Endurance of Educable Mentally Retarded and Non-Retarded Boys in Selected Ontario Separate Schools." Indiana, 1982.

3848
Wall, Albert Edward. "The Reciprocal Topping Performance of Educable Mentally Retarded Boys." Alberta, 1978.

3849
Williams, Wilfred Lawrence. "The Effect of Cooperation Procedures on the Acquisition and Subsequent Generalization of a Sign Language Communication Repertoire in Severely and Profoundly Retarded Girls." Manitoba, 1977.

3850
Wray, Lyle Dwight. "A Comparison of Faded and Non Faded Echoic Prompts in Teaching Retarded Children to Name Pictures." Manitoba, 1980.

3851
Yewchuk, Carolyn Rose. "Eye-Movements of Normal and Educable Mentally Retarded Children During Discrimination Shift Learning." Alberta, 1972.

3852
Yitzhak, Varda. "The Effect of Feverstein's Instrumental Enrichment Program on the Cognitive Reasoning of Retarded Performers as Measured by Piaget's Conservation Tasks." Toronto, 1981.

Handicapped/Handicapés

General Item/Ouvrage général

3853
England, Gordon Douglas. "The Influence of a Computer Assisted Budgeting Program on Learning Performance of Developmentally Handicapped Individuals." Calgary, 1980.

Physically Handicapped/Handicapés physiques

General Items/Ouvrages généraux

Borthwick, Burton L. See No./Voir no 2641
3854
Harvey, Gilles. "Rééducation fonctionnelle et évaluation électromyographique de l'écriture du côté controlatéral à la dominance chez des hémiplégigues droits." Montréal, 1982.
3855
Hochheimer, Laura. "A Critical Comparison of Certain European and American Pedagogical Approaches to the Use of Music in the Rehabilitation of Physically Handicapped Children." Indiana, 1972.
Karaz, Valerie Lynne. See No./Voir no 4145
3856
Létourneau, Pierre. "Le rendement au Ottawa-Wechsler dans les cas d'hémiplégie non traumatique." Montréal, 1975.
MacKinnon, Joyce Roberta. See No./Voir no 6718
3857
Prueter, Herbert John. "Care and Education of Crippled Children in Ontario." Toronto, 1936.
3858
Pulton, Thomas William. "Interaction Strain and Social Encounters with the Physically Handicapped." Victoria, 1981.
3859
Roeher, Godfrey Allan. "A Study of Certain Public Attitudes Toward the Orthopedically Disabled." New York, 1959. [Saskatchewan]

Aphasia/Aphasie

3860
Bérubé, Louise. "La désintégration sémantique à l'origine des troubles de l'expression et de la compréhension chez les sujets aphasiques." Montréal, 1981.
3861
Gante, M. "The Development and Clinical Validation of a Psycholinguistic Test for Aphasia." Alberta, 1981.

Brain Damaged/Dommages au cerveau

Wilson, Alexander Meade. See No./Voir no 3279

Cerebral Palsy/Paralysie cérébrale

Junemann, Georgina. See No./Voir no 9134
3862
Ruth, Jean Bouma. "Achievement Motivation: A Follow-Up Study of Cerebral Palsy in Northern Alberta." Alberta, 1971.

Hearing and Hearing Impaired/ Audition et troubles de l'ouie

3863
Anderson, D.E. "Deafness and Mother-Child Interaction." Alberta, 1982.

3864
Bartholomeus, Bonnie Noreen. "Development of Auditory Naming Behavior." McGill, 1969.
3865
Bebko, James Mark. "Memory and Rehearsal Characteristics of Profoundly Deaf Children." York, 1980.
Blowers, Elizabeth Anne. See No./Voir no 3753
3866
Bunch, Gary Owen. "An Evaluation of Natural and Formal Language Programmes with Deaf Children." British Columbia, 1975.
3867
Conway, Clifford Bruce. "The Hearing Abilities of Children in Toronto Public Schools." Toronto, 1937.
3868
Dodds, Ronald Garrett. "Encoding Processes Used by Deaf Children when Reading Print Sentences." Toronto, 1982.
3869
Dominique, Frère. "Handicapped Children - Hard of Hearing." Montréal, 1946.
3870
Frankel, Barbara Gail. "Adult Onset Hearing Impairment: Social and Psychological Correlates of Adjustment." Western Ontario, 1981.
3871
Hoeppner, Jo-Ann Bentley. "Visual Perceptual Processes and Reading in Deaf and Hearing Children." Waterloo, 1973.
3872
Houldin, Barbara Klein. "A Non-Linguistic Test of Abstract Thinking for Deaf and Hearing Children." Toronto, 1980.
3873
Kargianis, Leslie Denis. "Language as a Mediational Variable in Hearing and Deaf Children." Toronto, 1968.
3874
Lake, Deborah. "Syntax and Sequential Memory in Deaf Children." Waterloo, 1981.
3875
Le François, Josette. "Effet d'un filtrage léger des fréquences aiguës sur la discrimination auditive de la parole de jeunes entendants (âge moyen 6 ans) et de jeunes déficients auditifs (âge moyen 7 ans)." McGill, 1980.
3876
Leong, W.-T. "A Study of the Interrelation of Variables Which Affect the Language Development of Deaf Preschool Children." Toronto, 1983.
3877
Leslie, Perry Thorold. "Selected Linguistic Skills in Young Deaf Children." British Columbia, 1972.
3878
Ling, Agnes Hamilton. "Identification of Auditory Sequences by Hearing-Impaired and Normal Hearing Children." McGill, 1973.
McMahon, James H. See No./Voir no 9311
3879
Mongeau, Jean-Claude. "L'intégration scolaire et sociale de l'enfance exceptionnelle: application à l'enfant sourd." Montréal, 1974.

3880
Regan, Joseph James. "An Attempt to Modify Cognitive Impulsivity in Deaf Children: Self-Instruction Versus Problem-Solving Strategies." Toronto, 1981.

3881
Springer, Stephen Alan. "A Study of the Performance of Deaf and Hearing Subjects on Piagetian and Neo-Piagetian Tasks." York, 1977.

3882
Stoker, Richard Glen. "Temporal Pattern Recognition and Speech Perception by the Hearing Impaired." McGill, 1980.

Winzer, Margret Ann. See No./Voir no 2647

Wolff, Anthony Bernard. See No./Voir no 9088

Hyperactive Children/Enfants hyperactifs

3883
Ain, Marilyn Esther. "The Effects of Stimulus Novelty on Viewing Time and Processing Efficiency of Hyperactive Children." McGill, 1981.

3884
Baldwin, M.A. "Activity Level Attention Span and Deviance: Hyperactive Boys in the Classroom." Waterloo, 1976.

3885
Benezra, Esther. Verbal and Non-Verbal Memory in Hyperactive, Reading Disabled and Normal Children." McGill, 1980.

3886
Chan, Mick Ying-Pui. "Analysis and Pharmacokintics of Methylphenidate (Ritalin): Studies in Hyperactive Children." Toronto, 1980.

3887
Conte, R.A. "A Behavioral and Psychophysiological Analysis of Hyperactive Children." Toronto, 1983.

3888
Goldman, Janice Olivia Babcock. "Serotonin Levels in Hyperactive Children." Windsor, 1976.

3889
Peters, Kenneth Gordon. "Selective Attention and Distractibility in Hyperactive and Normal Children." McGill, 1977.

3890
Shoom-Kirsch, Donna Norma. "The Effects of a Perceptual-Motor Programme and a Physical Education Type Programme on Hyperactive Children." York, 1976.

3891
Sykes, Donald. "Sustained Attention in Hyperactive Children." McGill, 1969.

3892
Tant, Judy Louise. "Problem Solving in Hyperactive and Reading Disabled Boys." McGill, 1978.

3893
Thompson, L. Marion. "The Effect of Methylphenidate on Self-Concept and Locus of Control of Hyperactive Children." Toronto, 1979.

3894
Vain, Marilyn Esther. See/Voir Ain, Marilyn Esther.

Hyperkinetic Children/Enfants hyperkinétiques

3895
Bambrick, James R. "Effect of Two Levels of Methylphenidate Hydrochloride for Hyperkinetic Children on Measures of Attention and Mother-Child Interaction." Windsor, 1979.

3896
Broad, James Charles. "Social Skills Training of Hyperkinetic Children." Queen's, 1982.

3897
Busby, Keith. "Sleep and Waking Ultradian Rhythms in Hyperkinetic Children." Ottawa, 1980.

3898
Freeman, Richard J. "The Effects of Methylphenidate on Avoidance Learning and Risk-Taking by Hyperkinetic Children." Waterloo, 1978.

Blind and Sight-Impaired/Aveugles et troubles de la vue

3899
Banwell, Gregory T. "Haptic Perception in the Blind and Sighted: A Perceptual Learning Hypothesis." Ottawa, 1979.

3900
Davidson, Iain Francis William Knowles. "Effects of Visual Impairment in Children's Verbal Creativity." Toronto, 1981.

3901
Fletcher, Janet Florence. "Spatial Representation in Blind School Children." Toronto, 1981.

3902
Goupil, Georgette. "Les conditions d'intégration de l'élève handicapé de la vue dans les écoles régulières du Québec." Montréal, 1981.

MacDonald, Donald D. See No./Voir no 2645

Rodrigues, Myra Miliza. See No./Voir no 3840

Dyslexia/Dyslexie

3903
Donner, Jeffrey Robert. "Audio-Psycho-Phonological Remedial Training in Relation to the Psycho-Social and Personality Adjustment of Five Dyslexia Boys." Ottawa, 1983.

Mamen, Margaret. See No./Voir no 9379

3904
Neysmith-Roy, Jean. "Cognitive Control Functioning and Spontaneous Speech: Intensive Case Studies of Audio-Psycho-Phonological Remedial Training with Five Dyslexia Boys." Ottawa, 1981.

3905
Roy, Robert. "Perceptual Processing Abilities and Academic Skills: Intensive Case Studies of Audio-Psycho-Phonological Remedial Training with Five Dyslexia Boys." Ottawa, 1981.

3906
Sutherland de Merlis, Doris. "The Effect of Phonetic Kinesthetic Training on the Measurable Reading Performance of Primary Pupils with Reversal and Inversion Difficulties." Ottawa, 1959.

Speech and Language Impairment/ Discours et troubles de language

3907
Abelson, Annalee. "Perception of Sentence Stress in Language Impaired Children." McGill, 1981.

3908
Boudreau, Léonie. "L'influence de l'aide sociale associée à la respiration régularisée sur la mesure et le traitement du bégaiement." Laval, 1981.

3909
Golick, Margaret. "Language Disorders in Children: A Linguistic Investigation." McGill, 1977.

3910
Hébert, Maria. "Les exercices extra-thérapie: leur rôle dans le traitement du bégaiement." Montréal, 1982.

3911
Patty, John M.V. "The Modification of Types of Stuttering Through Self-Monitoring." York, 1974. [Three experiments with adults/Trois expériences avec des adultes]

Petrunik, Michael G. See No./Voir no 10218

3912
Wolfus, Beverly Bella. "An Analysis of Lexical Acquisition in Children with Developmental Dysphasia." Toronto, 1981.

Emotionally Handicapped or Disturbed/ Personnes émotionnellement handicapées

3913
Bolus, Charles Robert. "A Proposed Model Treatment Programme for the Province of Ontario Based upon a Study of Maryvale - A Treatment Center for Emotionally Disturbed Adolescent Girls." Wayne State, 1975.

Brammer, Dennis Leslie. See No./Voir no 3198

3914
Caverzan, Raymond Cornelius. "Experimental Language Program for Non-Verbal Emotionally Disturbed Children." Toronto, 1971.

3915
Gelcer, Esther. "Social Decentration: Its Measurement and Training in Emotionally Disturbed Institutionalized Children." Toronto, 1977.

Gilmour-Barrett, Karen C. See No./Voir no 9126

Hammond, Leslie Leigh Gardner. See No./Voir no 4310

3916
Hurst, Paul Eugene. "A Comparison of Death Concept Development in Emotionally Disturbed and Non-Disturbed Children." Toronto, 1980. [160 boys between 4 years and 12 years for 11 months in Ontario/160 garçons entre 4 et 12 ans, pendant 11 mois en Ontario]

3917
Marcovitch, Howard David. "The Assessment and Training of Referent Communication Skills in Socially Deviant Children." Toronto, 1979.

3918
McCluskey, Kenneth Wilfred. "Vocal Communication of Emotion: A Program of Research." Manitoba, 1980.

Reker, Gary Theodore. See No./Voir no 9052

3919
Richardson, Wayne Ronald. "The Effects of Tokens, Praise and Tangibles on Academic and Conduct Behaviours." York, 1971. [Children at a centre for the disturbed/Enfants à un centre de personnes handicapées]

3920
Shah, Hemendra. "An Investigation into the Deductive Inferential Abilities of Young Normal and Behaviourally Disordered Boys." Toronto, 1979. [Six and nine year olds/6 et 9 ans]

Wilson, Alexander Meade. See No./Voir no 3279

Autistic Children/Enfants autistiques

3921
Bonta, James Louis. "Use of Signing in Delayed Matching-to-Sample with Language Deficient Children." Ottawa, 1979.

3922
Hung, David Wai-Kwong. "The Development and Maintenance of Cooperative Play in Austistic Children: An Experimental Analysis." Western Ontario, 1975.

3923
Kluck, Brian Lee. "Attentional Response Deficits of Autistic Children." Waterloo, 1980.

Mack, Judith Elaine. See No./Voir no 9030

3924
Masterton, Brooks Alan. "The Use of Visual Feedback by Autistic Children." Toronto, 1982.

3925
Oxman, Joel Allan. "Sign Language by Autistic Children: A Socio-Linguistic Analysis." York, 1981.

3926
Sherman, Jeffrey Stephen. "Stereotyped Behaviour: Dependence on Situation in Autistic Children." York, 1977.

READING/LECTURE

General Items/Ouvrages généraux

3927
Andrade, Teresa Manalad. "Growth Patterns in Reading Achievement." British Columbia, 1969.

3928
Backman, Joan Elizabeth. "The Role of Psycholinguistic Abilities in Reading Acquisition." Carleton, 1980.

3929
Beebe, M.J. "A Model of the Relationships Between Reading Strategies and Reading Comprehension." Alberta, 1981.

3930
Beniskas, Jean-Marie. "Wise Patterns and Reading Achievement." Ottawa, 1959.

3931
Boos, Robert W. "A Study of the Possible Distinction Between 'Controlling Eye and Dominant Eye' and the Relation of Both, with Hand Dominance to Reading Achievement." Ottawa, 1968.

Crausman, Bert. See No./Voir no 8976

3932

Halpern, Honey Gael. "An Investigation of Reading and Conceptual Tempo Measures." British Columbia, 1982.

3933

Labercane, George Donald. "Speech Acts and Reading Acts: An Investigation into the Relationship Between the Two Processes." Alberta, 1979.

3934

Loveridge, J.M. Young. "The Use of Orthographic Structure by More and Less Skilled Readers." Toronto, 1983.

3935

Phillips-Riggs, L. "The Relationship Between Reading Proficiency, Background Knowledge, and Influencing Strategies." Alberta, 1961.

Pre-School and Kindergarten/
Niveau pré-scolaire et maternelle

3936

Cleland, Patricia Anna. "Word Consciousness Meaning and Learning to Read." Toronto, 1981.

3937

Doake, D.B. "Book Experience and Emergent Reading Behaviour in Preschool Children." Alberta, 1981.

3938

Light, Martha Carolyn. "A Longitudinal Study of the Effects of a Kindergarten Reading Programme." Toronto, 1980.

3939

Picard-Gerber, Marilen Joy. "Verbal Mediational Factors in Visual Paired Associate Learning of Poor Readers." Concordia, 1980. [From two and a half to seven years/De 30 mois à 7 ans]

Elementary School Level/Niveau primaire

3940

Baker, Elaine Meredith. "An Analysis of Reading Comprehension in Canadian Reading Series: 1923-1979 for Grades Four, Five, and Six." Alberta, 1980.

3941

Baker, Janice Elizabeth. "The Interaction Between Selected Teaching Strategies and Content in a Piagetian – Based Reading Program." Toronto, 1980. [Grade four/Quatrième année]

3942

Baron, Lois. "The Eye Movement Patterns of Children Viewing Static Versus Moving Stimuli and the Relation of These Eye Movements to Field Articulation and Reading Ability." Toronto, 1978.

3943

Bernstein, Deborah Ann. "A Qualitative Investigation with the Effects of Realistic Content in Reading." Toronto, 1982.

3944

Board, Peter Emile. "Toward a Theory of Instructional Influence: Aspects of the Instructional Environment and Their Influence on Children's Acquisition of Reading." Toronto, 1982.

3945

Brackstone, Ross Daniel. "The Structure of Talk in Primary Reading Lessons." Toronto, 1981.

3946

Briggs, Elizabeth Joanne. "Reading Eye Movemen[t] and Instructional Television." Toronto, 197[?] [From grade three to grade six/De la troisième [à] la sixième année]

3947

Browne, Margaret Patricia Jane. "An Explorato[ry] Study of Teacher-Pupil Verbal Interaction in Pr[i]mary Reading Program." Alberta, 1971.

3948

Bruinsma, Robert Walter. "The Relationship Betwe[en] First Grade Children's Reading Achievement a[nd] Their Performance on Selected Metalinguist[ic] Tasks." British Columbia, 1982.

Clandinin, D.J. See No./Voir no 4303

3949

Craddock, Sonia May. "An Investigation of Physic[al] setting in Narrative Discourses and Its Influence [on] the Reading Conprehension and Reading Interest [of] Elementary School Students." British Columbi[a,] 1982.

3950

Denburg, Susan Myra. "The Interaction of Picture a[nd] Print in Reading Instruction." Toronto, 1975.

3951

Di Pasquale, Glenn William. "An Examination of t[he] Sequencing Difficulties of Poor Reading Childre[n.]" Western Ontario, 1979.

Dobson, Lois Ann. See No./Voir no 3809

Dodds, Ronald Garrett. See No./Voir no 3868

3952

Farrell, Mona. "The Predictive Relationship of S[e]lected Oral Language Variables to Readi[ng] Achievement in First Grade Inner City Childre[n.]" McGill, 1973.

3953

Forrest, Donna Lynn. "Cognitive and Meta-Cogniti[ve] Aspects of Reading." Waterloo, 1980. [Grad[e] three and six/Troisième et sixième année]

3954

Furniss, Elaine Rosemary. "Schemes for Reading a[nd] Recall of Story Narrative and Descriptive Inform[a]tional Texts: A Study of Sixth Grade Proficie[nt] Readers." Alberta, 1979.

3955

Goelman, Hillel. "Selective Attention in Langua[ge] Comprehension: A Study of Good, Average a[nd] Poor Readers." Toronto, 1979. [84 grade four st[u]dents/84 étudiants de quatrième année]

3956

Goldberg, Jack S. "Perceptual Abstraction and Sp[el]ling Pattern Acquisition in Relation to Deficie[nt] Reading in Children of the Third and Four[th] Grades." Montréal, 1975.

3957

Haines, Leonard Paul. "Visual and Phonologic[al] Coding in Word Processing by Grade 4, 6 and [8] Readers." Saskatchewan, 1978.

3958

Henslowe, Shirley Anne. "Development and Validati[on] of a Basic Library Locational Skills Model f[or] Elementary School Library Reading and Social St[u]dies Education." British Columbia, 1977.

Hoeppner, Jo-Ann B. See No./Voir no 3871

3959
Hogan, Timothy. "Second Language Acquisition and Maternal Language Reading Achievement in Grades 4, 5, 6." Ottawa, 1966.

3960
Holmes, Alfred. "Voluntary Reading of Toronto Public School Pupils." Toronto, 1932.

3961
Hughes, Margaret Ann. "Word Identification and Comprehension in Learning to Read." Toronto, 1977. [Grade two/Deuxième année]

Irvine, James William. See No./Voir no 3228

3962
James, Dorothy Mae Digdon. "A Study of Patterns of Prediction in Reading Comprehension in Grades Four and Six." Alberta, 1979.

3963
Janes, Ethel Mary. "A Bulletin on Problems in the Teaching of Beginning Reading for Teachers in Newfoundland: Proposed Procedures and Preparation." Teachers College, Columbia, 1970.

3964
Jarvis, Elizabeth Orysia. "Auditory Abilities of Primary School Children: A Study of the Relationship of Auditory Abilities to Each Other and to Reading Achievement, and an Investigation of the Relationships Among Selected Auditory Test Profiles." Toronto, 1973.

Jones, Robert J. See No./Voir no 3231

3965
Lamarre, Joseph Léo Paul André. "An Analysis of Oral Language Readiness for Reading of Selected Canadian Second-Grade Students in French and English Monolingual and Bilingual Programs." Georgia, 1976.

3966
Lancaster, M.K. "Field Dependence-Field Independence, Embedded Reading, and Reading Achievement in Second Grade Students." Toronto, 1983.

Light, Martha Carolyn. See No./Voir no 3938

3967
Lovett, Maureen Winnifred. "Early Reading Competence: The Perception and Memory of Sentential Information." McGill, 1977. [Grades one and two/Première et deuxième année]

3968
Lucas, Christine Wooledge. "Paced Reading for Disfluent Elementary Readers." McGill, 1975.

Mamen, Margaret. See No./Voir no 9379

3969
Mandziuk, Lucia Marie. "MFFT Reaction Time and Reading Performance of Elementary School Children." Windsor, 1981. [20 boys and 20 girls in grades four and six/20 garçons et 20 filles de quatrième et sixième année]

3970
Marshall, Malcolm Frederick. "Auditory-Visual and Spatial-Temporal Integration Abilities of Above Average and Below Average Readers." British Columbia, 1979. [Grade three/Troisième année]

3971
Mason, Patricia Lynn. "Children's Knowledge About Effective Reading: Study, Strategies and Its Relationship to Their Academic Performance." Windsor, 1979.

3972
McDermott, William Vincent. "Differential Interaction Patterns Within the Families of Reading Problem Boys." Windsor, 1977.

3973
McLeod, Roderick William. "An Exploratory Study of Inference and Cognitive Synthesis in Reading Comprehension with Selected Grade Four Readers." Alberta, 1978.

3974
Miller, Larry Arnold. "An Investigation into the Relationship of Anaphoric Reference and Reading Comprehension of Grade Two Pupils." Alberta, 1976.

3975
Minkler, Frederick William. "A Study of the Voluntary Reading Interest of Children in Canadian Elementary Schools." Toronto, 1946.

3976
Mitterer, John Otto. "There Are Two Kinds of Poor Readers." McMaster, 1981. [Grade three/Troisième année]

3977
Newman, Judith Marta. "Children's Reading Ability and Information Retrieval." Toronto, 1976.

Rodgers, Denis Cyril. See No./Voir no 3839

Smyth, William John. See No./Voir no 2996

3978
Stamm, Sharon Winston. "Encoding and Verification by Children at Three Levels of Reading Comprehension Proficiency." McGill, 1978.

3979
Strauss, H. Peter. "The Development of Sentence Comprehension Strategies in the Child." York, 1975. [Montessori school in the Toronto area/École Montessori dans la région de Toronto]

Sutherland de Merlis, Doris. See No./Voir no 3906

3980
Sweet, Robert Arthur. "An Investigation of the Relationship Between Teachers' Attitudes and Their Curriculum Planning Decisions in Primary Reading Instruction: An Application of the Fishbein Model." British Columbia, 1977.

3981
Tauran, Roulard Herman. "The Influences of Reading on the Attitudes of Third Graders Toward Eskimos." Maryland, 1967.

3982
Thomae, Richard Bruce. "Early Reading and Hemispheric Differentiation." Toronto, 1978.

3983
Van Hoff, Howard S. "Parental Participation in a Primary Reading Program." Ottawa, 1955.

3984
Wahlstrom, Wanda Louise. "Developing Self-Concept Through Bibliotherapy." Toronto, 1982.

3985
Weiss, David Shlomo. "The Effects of Text Segmentation on Reading." Toronto, 1981. [648 grade four and seven students - good, average and poor readers were tested/648 élèves de quatrième et de septième année ont été évalués bons, moyens et pauvres lecteurs]

3986
Whittle, Robert MacLean. "The Interactive Effect of Style of Short-Term Memory and Exposure to

Semantic and Alphabetic Materials on Achievement in First Grade Oral Reading." Ottawa, 1977.

3987
Willows, Dale Marjorie. "Reading Between the Lines: A Study of Selection Attention in Good and Poor Readers." Waterloo, 1972. [Grade six boys/Garçons de sixième année]

3988
Wyatt, Frank Leopold. "Functional M Space and Dual Processing in Beginning Reading." Toronto, 1983.

3989
Young, Gerald C. "A Comparison of Visual and Auditory Sequencing in Good and Poor Readers in Grades Two and Six." Windsor, 1974.

Intermediate and Secondary Education Level/ Enseignement de niveaux intermédiaire et secondaire

3990
Ahrendt, Kenneth Martin. "An Analysis of the Effects of an Experimental Remedial Reading Program on the Comprehension Skills of Potential School Dropouts." British Columbia, 1969. [Grade eight/Huitième année]

3991
Bird, Marlene Isabelle. "Reading Comprehension Strategies: A Direct Teaching Approach." Toronto, 1980. [Grade seven and eight readers/Lecteurs de septième et huitième année]

3992
Coutts, Herbert Thomas. "The Relation Between the Reading Competence of Alberta's Ninth Grade Pupils in Four Content Fields and Their Achievement in Those Fields." Minnesota, 1951.

Cram, Ruby Victoria. See No./Voir no 3489

3993
Crealock, Carol Marie. "Risk-Taking and Reading Test Performance." Toronto, 1973. [Grades seven, eight and nine/Septième, huitième et neuvième année]

3994
Crocker, Oswald Kitchener. "The Leisure Reading of High School Students in Newfoundland Library Facilities in the Schools, and Home Background as Related to Reading." Indiana, 1967.

3995
Jewell, Cedric Beresford. "A Reading Comprehension Test for Senior High School Students in Large Urban Areas in Alberta, Canada." Oregon, 1969.

3996
Koerber, Walter Frederick. "An Evaluation of Some Methods and Procedures in the Teaching of Reading to Non-Academic Adolescent Boys (Jarvis School)." Toronto, 1947.

3997
Logan, Bayne Stuart. "An Investigation of the Efficacy of a Child-Centered Approach to Reading at the Junior Grade Level: A Psycholinguistic Perspective." Ottawa, 1977.

3998
MacNeil, T.B. "The Effect of Sentence-Combining Practice on the Development of Reading Comprehension and the Written Syntactic Skills of Ninth Grade Students." Alberta, 1981.

3999
Mary Madeleine, Sister. "The Relative Effectivene of a Multi-Level Reading Program at the Inte mediate Grade Level." Ottawa, 1959.

4000
Schwartz, Geraldine Jerri. "College Students as Co tingency Managers for Adolescents in a Program Develop Reading Skills." McGill, 1976.

4001
Storey, Arthur George. "A Reading Comprehensic Test for Junior High School Pupils in Alberta Stanford, 1960.

4002
Truszka, Mary Gregory. "A Survey of the Readi Interests of Catholic High School Girls with Impl cations for Guidance Practices." Ottawa, 1961.

4003
Wilkins, Cecil J. "An Administrative Plan for th Improvement of Reading in the Toronto Seconda Schools." Teachers College, Columbia, 1953.

Higher Education Level/ Enseignement de niveau supérieur

4004
Ford, Barbara Cecile. "Factors Involved in th Reading Ability of Students in Ontario Colleges Applied Arts and Technology." Toronto, 1972.

4005
Geva, Esther. "Meta-Textual Notions and Readir Comprehension." Toronto, 1981. [Students fro two community colleges/Étudiants de deux collèg communautaires]

4006
Koe, George Gerald. "Experimental Investigation the Effects of Hypnotically Induced Suggestions Self-Concept and Reading Performance." Briti Columbia, 1981. [Volunteer University of Briti Columbia undergraduates/Les volontaires étaie des étudiants non diplômés de l'Université de Colombie-Britannique]

4007
Tolsma, Catherine Colette. "Relationships Betwe Two Methods of Vocabulary Instruction, Vocabula Achievement, Reading Attitude, and Focus of Co trol in a Community College Reading Course British Columbia, 1982.

Tyler, Thomas Lee. See No./Voir no 3712

Reading at the Adult Level/ Lecture au niveau adulte

4008
MacLean, Margaret Louise. "Reading Processes Skilled Older Adult Readers." McGill, 1982.

4009
O'Brien, M.A. "Four Adults Learning to Read Alberta, 1981.

The Reading Disabled/ Personnes ayant des problèmes de lecture

Allen, Sheilah M. See No./Voir no 4448
Benezra, Esther. See No./Voir no 3885
Boyce, Eleanor. See No./Voir no 4242

4010

Dalby, John Thomas. "Cerebral Organization in Reading-Disabled Children." Calgary, 1980.

Dobson, Lois Ann. See No./Voir no 3809

Favreau, Micheline. See No./Voir no 9520

Hambly, Janice Marie. See No./Voir no 3130

4011

Hardy, Madeline Isobel. "Clinical Follow-Up Study of Disabled Readers." Toronto, 1968.

Ingle, Robert Alexander. See No./Voir no 3044

Irvine, James W. See No./Voir no 3228

Jones, Robert J. See No./Voir no 3231

Lukasevich, Ann. See No./Voir no 2595

Partlow, Hugh Russell. See No./Voir no 2631

4012

Petraus Kas, Rymantas. "The Identification of Subtypes of Reading Retardates: A Neuropsychological Multivariate Approach." Windsor, 1978.

Steinert, Yvonne. See No./Voir no 4421

Waters, Gloria Sydna. See No./Voir no 9589

Wiedrick, Laurence George. See No./Voir no 7980

ADULT EDUCATION (CONTINUING EDUCATION)/ ÉDUCATION PERMANENTE

General Items/Ouvrages généraux

Abbott, Eric Oscar. See No./Voir no 992

4013

Armstrong, David Patrick. "Adult Learners of Low Educational Attainment: The Self-Concept, Backgrounds and Educated Behaviour of Average and High-Learning Adults of Low Educational Attainment." Toronto, 1971.

4014

Bates, Heather M. "A Phenomenological Study of Adult Learners: Participant's Experiences of a Learner-Centered Approach." Toronto, 1979.

4015

Blunt, Adrian. "Participation in Adult Learning Activities and the Relationship Between Social Stress and Health." British Columbia, 1982.

Brookbank, Carman Roy. See No./Voir no 1930

4016

Caron, Liliane. "Identification des compétences nécessaires au diététiste comme éducateur d'adultes." Montréal, 1981.

4017

Cole, James Randy. "Teaching Interpersonal Coping Skills to Adult Psychiatric Patients." Toronto, 1979.

4018

Con, Ronald Jonathan. "Government and Ethnic Minority Groups: A Case Study of the Relationships Between Federal Adult-Oriented Programs and Citizen Organizations of the Chinese in Canada." Boston University, 1974.

Darrach-Pearse, Shirley Anne. See No./Voir no 10078

4019

Davies, Leland John. "Energy Experiences of Adult Learners in Learning Groups." Toronto, 1979.

4020

Denis, Margaret Mary. "Toward the Development of a Theory of Intuitive Learning in Adults Based on a Descriptive Analysis." Toronto, 1979.

Douey, John Donald. See No./Voir no 10229

4021

Downing, George Leonard. "A Normative Study of Planetarium Directors in the United States and Canada to Determine Current Practices in Adult Education and Opinions Regarding Selected Adult Learning Principles." Wyoming, 1971.

4022

Faris, Ronald Lyle. "Adult Education for Social Action or Enlightenment: An Assessment of the Development of the Canadian Association for Adult Education and Its Radio Forums from 1935 to 1952." Toronto, 1971.

Fielding, David Wilson. See No./Voir no 6876

4023

Filson, Glen Charles. "Major Personal Changes in a Group of Canadians Working in Nigeria." Toronto, 1975.

4024

Frey, Kenneth David. "Learning System Description: A Method of Examining Organizational Learning." Toronto, 1980. [Two groups of managers in a large Canadian insurance firm/Deux groupes de gestionnaires d'une grande compagnie d'assurance canadienne]

4025

Greene, Ralph Irving. "Various Ways in which New Canadians Might Learn English Outside the Classroom without Formal Assistance." Toronto, 1972.

4026

Griffith, Gwyneth P. "Images of Interdependence, Meaning and Movement in Learning/Teaching." Toronto, 1982.

Hardwick, Claudia Shaw. See No./Voir no 3816

Hummelin, Remmelt C.R. See No./Voir no 469

4027

Jackson, Edward Thomas. "Adult Education for Community Participation in Water Supply and Sanitation Improvements in Rural Communities of Northern Ghana and Northern Canada: A Comparative Study of the Role of the Canadian State." Toronto, 1981.

Johnson, Peter Richard. See No./Voir no 4144

Karaz, Valerie Lynn. See No./Voir no 4145

4028

Kelley, Maurice Vernon. "Young Male Trainees in Program 5: A Study of A Priori Factors Associated with Early Withdrawal by Young Men from Program 5 Adult Training Centers." Toronto, 1969.

4029

Knoepfli, Heather Elizabeth Blaine. "The Origin of Women's Autonomous Learning Groups." Toronto, 1971.

Larson, Vernon Carl. See No./Voir no 2619

4030

MacKinnon, Neil Joseph. "Multivariate Explorations in Role Analysis: A Canadian Adult Education Center for the Unemployed." Illinois, 1970.

4031

Matusicky, Carol Ann. "In-Service Training for Family-Life Educators: An Institutional Model." Toronto, 1982.

McCatty, Cressy Alexander Mayo. See No./Voir no 2578

McGechaen, Alexander. See No./Voir no 1158

4032

McGinnis, Paul St. Clair. "Major Personal Changes in Forty Returning CUSO Volunteers." Toronto, 1975. [Canadian University Service Overseas/Service universitaire canadien outre-mer]

Nelson, John E. See No./Voir no 7703

Norris, Kenneth Everett. See No./Voir no 2400

Painchaud-Leblanc, Gisèle. See No./Voir no 7705

Scott, Anne. See No./Voir no 6734

4033

Singh, Raj Kumar. "Military Retirees' Perceptions of Their Transition from the Canadian Armed Forces to Civilian Life: Implications for Adult Learning." Toronto, 1980.

4034

Taylor, Marilyn Margaret. "Adult Learning in an Emergent Learning Group: Toward a Theory of Learning from the Learner's Perspective." Toronto, 1979.

Thomson, Colin Argyle. See No./Voir no 2556

4035

Timleck, Derry Gray. "A Literature Study on the Extension of Aesthetic Decision-Making for Institutionalized Elderly in Eastern Canada." Oregon, 1981.

4036

Torrance, Robert Joseph. "An Investigation to Determine Optimal Conditions for Adult Learning through Multimedia Programs." Toronto, 1979.

4037

Tremblay, Nicole. "L'aide à l'apprentissage en situation d'autodidaxie." Montréal, 1981.

4938

Trussler, Terrence Andrew. "The Discovery of Critical Experience in the Social Invention of Everyday Life." Toronto, 1982.

4039

Wickett, Reginald Ernest Yeatman. "Adult Learning Projects Related to Spiritual Growth." Toronto, 1978.

Wilson, Christopher Richard M. See No./Voir no 1960

Alberta

Krysowaty, J.B. See No./Voir no 4456

4040

Manuel, Donald Winsor. "Meta-Evaluation of an In-Service Program for Adult Education." Alberta, 1976.

Nicol, Andrew James. See No./Voir no 4124

O'Brien, Margaret Anne. See No./Voir no 4009

Pitsel, Patricia Lynne. See No./Voir no 9318

4041

Wasserman, D.A. "An Evaluation of Two Career Development Programs for Adults." Alberta, 1982.

Wilson, Christopher Richard Maclean. See No./Voir no 1960

4042

Yule, David Lloyd George. "Management of Learning in Work Settings." Toronto, 1979.

4043

Zelmer, Amy Elliott. "The Adult Part-Time Student Role as Experienced by Some Students in Extension Programs at the University of Alberta, 1970-1971." Michigan State, 1973.

British Columbia/Colombie-Britannique

4044

Anderson, Darrell Vail. "The Adoption of Recommended Administrative Practices by Directors of Public School Adult Education in the Province of British Columbia." British Columbia, 1975.

4045

Davison, Catherine Val. "The Effects of Goal Specifications and Instructor Behaviour on Information Acquisition by Adult Learners." British Columbia, 1972. [Vancouver]

4046

Dickinson, James Gary. "An Analytical Study of the Pemberton Valley in British Columbia, with Special Reference to Adult Education." British Columbia, 1968.

4047

Lamoureux, Marvin Eugene. "Threshold Pricing in University Continuing Education." British Columbia, 1976.

Mastai, Judith Anne F. See No./Voir no 800

4048

McKinnon, Donald Peter. "The Adoption of Innovations as a Measure of Participation in Adult Education." British Columbia, 1977. [Surrey, British Columbia/Colombie-Britannique]

4049

Rubidge, Nicholas Andrew. "The Effects of Learning and Instructional Style Congruence in an Adult Education Learning Environment." British Columbia, 1979. [Two adult education centres of Vancouver Community College/Deux centres d'éducation permanente du Vancouver Community College]

4050

Rusnell, Albert Dale. "Development of an Index of Quality for the Planning of Management Training Programs." British Columbia, 1974. [Vancouver]

4051

Seah, Hong Ghee. "Contrastive Analysis, Error Analysis and Interlanguage in Relation to Adult Chinese Speakers Learning English as a Second Language." Simon Fraser, 1981. [Vancouver Community College/Collège communautaire de Vancouver]

4052

Wales, Bertram Edwards. "The Development of Adult Education in British Columbia." Oregon State, 1958.

Manitoba

Pallota-Cornick, Maria Angela Carvalho. See No./Voir no 8928

Newfoundland/Terre-Neuve

4053

O'Neil, Florence M. "A Plan for the Development of an Adult Education Program for Rural Newfoundland." Columbia, 1944.

Nova Scotia/Nouvelle-Écosse

Gillen, Marie A. See No./Voir no 9817

4054
Laidlaw, Alexander Fraser. "The Campus and the Community, A Study of the Adult Education Program of St. Francis Xavier University, Antigonish, Nova Scotia." Toronto, 1958.

4055
Lowder, Ellie Mae. "The Present Status of the Antigonish Movement in Nova Scotia." George Peabody, 1967.

Ontario

4056
Ansley, Sylvia Lorraine. "Edgar, an Institution in Evolution: Management by Function Versus Management by Structure." York, 1971. [Ontario Department for Health Occupational Centre (Edgar) for Mildly Retarded Adults/Centre rééducatif (Edgar) de déficients légers adultes du ministère de la santé de l'Ontario]

Baker, Harold Reid. See No./Voir no 1

4057
Beer, Anne Maria. "Adult Education: Why Adults Continue their Education in Ontario, with Particular Emphasis on the Experiences of Part-Time Students of Atkinson College, York University." York, 1980.

4058
Blackwell, David McClaughry. "Major Institutional Changes among Adult Males in King Township." Toronto, 1981.

Braid, Andrew Falconor. See No./Voir no 1929

4059
Brooke, Wilfrid Michael. An Investigation of Certain Factors Contributing to Dropping Out in an Ontario Adult Basic Education Program." Toronto, 1973.

4060
Cochrane, Nancy Joan Hutchison. "The Meanings that Some Adults Derive from their Personal Withdrawal Experiences: A Dialogical Inquiry." Toronto, 1981.

4061
Cowley, Richard William V. "The Change Process in Community Development: A Descriptive Model." Toronto, 1979.

Denis, Margaret Mary. See No./Voir no 4020

4062
Fielder, John William. "Evaluation as a Consultation Process at a Telephone Distress Center." Toronto, 1978.

4063
Flaherty, Mary Josephine. "The Prediction of College Level Academic Achievement in Adult Extension Students." Toronto, 1968.

Francoeur, Mary Ellen. See No./Voir no 8994

Garke, Mary Elaine. See No./Voir no 8998

4064
Greenglass, David Irwin. "Interaction Between Cognitive Level and Structure of Presentation on Performance: An Adult Learning Situation Involving Museum Artifacts." Toronto, 1979.

4065
Griffith, Charles Arthur. "A Study of Ontario Municipal Recreation Personnel with Implications for Continuing Education." Indiana, 1969.

Hardwick, Claudia Shaw. See No./Voir no 3816

4066
Hawkins, Terrance Clifford. "The Identification and Comparison of Needs of Adults in an Ontario School System." Toronto, 1977.

4067
MacRae, Donald Lachlan. "The Development and Field Testing of the Effective Communicator Model." Toronto, 1979.

4068
McKenzie, Thomas Ross. "Past and Present Status of the Teaching of English to Non-English Speaking Immigrants to Canada, with Special Reference to Ontario." Toronto, 1954.

Mehmet, Ozay. See No./Voir no 2188

4069
Munro, Ronald Joseph. "The Development of an Effective Teaching – Learning Model To Meet the Motivational Needs of Learners Engaged in a Leaderless Task Activity." Toronto, 1979.

4070
Nacke, Margaret D'Arc. "Life after the Workshop: Effects of the Survey of Resources for Development in Ministry Workshop." Toronto, 1979. [Toronto, Peterborough and/et Buffalo]

4071
Neehall, J. "Degree of Intentionality of Adult Change." Toronto, 1983.

4072
Orton, Larry James. "A Study of Interaction Between Organizations Providing Adult Education." Toronto, 1982.

Parducci, Ronald E. See No./Voir no 2582

Peszat, Lucille C. See No./Voir no 3721

4073
Posluns, Elaine. "The Change Process of Women Becoming Liberated from Sex-Role Stereotypes." Toronto, 1981.

4074
Poudrier, Lucien Mark. "Impaired Drivers: An Educational Alternative to Incarceration." Toronto, 1978. [North Bay]

Savoie, Mary Leona. See No./Voir no 6908

4075
Shorey, Leonard Ludwig. "Teacher Participation in Continuing Education." Toronto, 1969. [Windsor]

4076
Strong, Frederick Blakeney. "Manpower Training in Adult Training Centres and the Adult Training Counselling Centre in Toronto as Viewed by Staff Involved, 1960-1969." Toronto, 1977.

4077
Thomas, Paul French. "The Influence of Dreams in the Personal Changes of Forty Adults." Toronto, 1978.

4078
Vernon, Foster. "The Development of Adult Education in Ontario, 1790-1900." Toronto, 1969.

4079
Vigoda, Deborah V.F. "Some Factors Influencing Participation in Educational Activities by Older Ontario Men." Toronto, 1980.

4080
Voege, Marion Penrice. "An Exploratory Study of Attitudes and Behavior During Retirement." Toronto, 1983.

4081
Waniewicz, Ignacy. "The Clientele for Adult Part-Time Learning and Obstacles to Learning in Ontario." Toronto, 1979.

4082
Webster, Loyola Cathleen. "Effects of a Multi-Modality Treatment Program on the Institution-alized Functionally Impaired Aged." Toronto, 1981.

4083
Wesche, Marjorie Anne Birgham. "The Good Adult Language Learner: A Study of Learning Strategies and Personality Factors in an Intensive Course." Toronto, 1975.

4084
Wong, Angelina Teresa. "A Study of the Relationship Between the Proficiency in English and Cultural Background of Chinese Immigrant Students and their Educational and Social Development." Toronto, 1977. [University of Toronto students/ Étudiants de l'Université de Toronto]

4085
Ziv, Liora. "Current Learning Activities of Some Older Adults and Those They Recall from Twenty Years Ago." Toronto, 1982.

Quebec/Québec

4086
Bernard, Jean-Louis. "Perceived Constraints Opera-ting in CEGEPs of Quebec Regarding the Adoption of New Practices in Adult Education." Boston University, 1972.

4087
Cantin, Gabrielle. "Les orientations des éducateurs d'adultes au Québec." Montréal, 1974.

Coupal, Michel. See No./Voir no 9285

4088
Dallaire, Hélène. "L'influence d'un programme de conditionnement physique sur la perception de soi de personnes agées." Montréal, 1980.

4089
Driscoll, Alma. "Rural Teachers: Rural Leaders." Laval, 1945.

4090
Robineault, Pierre G. "Les motifs d'inscription des adultes de la famille formation maîtres de l'UQAM." Montréal, 1982.

4091
Ross, Vincent. "Communications scolaires de masse et solidarités microsociales: la mobilisation et le soutien de la participation des adultes inscrits à Tévec." Laval, 1980.

4092
Sarrasin, Joanne. "L'influence d'un programme de conditionnement physique sur le concept de soi d'adultes." Montréal, 1983.

4093
Serre, Fernand. "L'importance d'apprendre seul ou les objets et les processus des projets éducatifs et autodidactes des adultes de la classe dite défavo-risée." Montréal, 1978.

4094
Thibault, André. "Perceptions du rôle du CEGEP, en formation socio-culturelle des adultes et en ser-vices à la communauté." Montréal, 1976.

4095
Touchette, Claude Joseph René. "Evaluation of Objectives and Programmes in Adult Education at the University of Montreal, 1876-1950." Toronto, 1973.

Saskatchewan

4096
Blenkinsop, Padraig John. "A History of Adult Educa-tion in the Prairies: Learning to Live in Agrarian Saskatchewan, 1870-1944." Toronto, 1979.

Wiggin, Gladys A. See No./Voir no 2546

AGRICULTURAL EDUCATION/ ENSEIGNEMENT AGRICOLE

Barichello, Richard R. See No./Voir no 2402

Baker, Harold Reid. See No./Voir no 1

4097
Bouchard, André Joseph. "Training Needs of County Agricultural Extension Agents in Quebec, Canada." Ohio State, 1966.

4098
Lawr, Douglas Archie. "Development of Agricultural Education in Ontario, 1870-1910." Toronto, 1972.

4099
MacGregor, Hugh A. "A Proposal for Canadian Federal-Provincial Participation in Vocational Agriculture." Oregon State, 1951.

4100
Madill, Alonzo James. "A History of Agricultural Education in Ontario." Toronto, 1930.

4101
McCutcheon, Wilfrid W. "Some Factors for Considera-tion in the Establishment of Departments of Agri-culture in the Protestant Rural Secondary Schools of Quebec; and the Rural Secondary Schools of New Brunswick and Nova Scotia." Cornell, 1951.

4102
McMillan, George. "The Agricultural High School in Ontario." Toronto, 1924.

Schwass, Rodger Daniel. See No./Voir no 1102

Wiggin, Gladys A. See No./Voir no 2546

4103
Wilson, Le Roy John. "The Education of the Farmer: The Educational Objectives and Activities of the United Farmers of Alberta and the Saskatchewan Grain Growers' Association, 1920-1930." Alberta, 1975.

ARMED SERVICES AND EDUCATION/ SERVICES ARMÉS ET ENSEIGNEMENT

4104
Ayers, John Douglas L. "The Development of a Selection and Classification Program for the Cana-dian Armed Services." Toronto, 1951.

4105
Brazeau, Ernest Jacques. "The Training of French Canadian Groundcrew Personnel in the Royal Canadian Air Force (1953-1957)." Chicago, 1961.

4106
Crowe, Herman Albert. "The Effect of Certain Atti-tudes on the Grading of Army Officer Cadets." Toronto, 1956.

4107
Hedley, Harold Whitfield. "A Study of the Education of Illiterates in the Canadian Army." Toronto, 1949.

4108
Howard, James W. "A Study of Cadet Training in the Dominion of Canada." Cornell, 1936.

Singh, Raj Kumar. See No./Voir no 4033

EDUCATION OF NATIVE PEOPLES/
ENSEIGNEMENT DONNÉ AUX AUTOCHTONES

4109
Arana, Multon Eulogio. "The Oral English Syntax of Five - and Six-Year-Old Bilingual Indian Children in Manitoba." St. Louis, 1979.

Brown, James Anthony. See No./Voir no 3003

4110
Burnaby, Barbara Jane. "Roles of Languages in Education for Native Children in Ontario." Toronto, 1979.

4111
Cook, Thelma Lillian Sharp. "Producing Equal Status Interaction Between Indian and White Boys at British Columbia: An Application of Expectation Training." Stanford, 1975.

4112
Cox, Marlene Joan. "A Cross-Cultural Study of Sex Differences Found in Drawings by Canadian Inuit and American Children." Illinois State, 1979.

Daniels, Edwin Robert. See No./Voir no 2803

4113
Dilling, Harold John. "Educational Achievement and Social Acceptance of Indian Pupils Integrated in Non-Indian Schools of Southern Ontario." Toronto, 1965.

Dyer, Aldrich James. See No./Voir no 596

Franklyn, Gaston J. See No./Voir no 3331

4114
Gibson, George D. "Jesuit Education of the Indians in New France, 1611 to 1658." California, Berkeley, 1940.

4115
Gorlick, Carolyne Ann. "Cultural Hegemony and Planned School Change." Toronto, 1981. [Inuit]

4116
Graham, Dorothy Marguerite. "A Comparison Between the Indian and Non-Indian Children in Southern Saskatchewan Based on Listening Comprehension, Reading Comprehension, Auditory Discrimination and I.Q." Northern Colorado, 1972.

4117
Harrison, William George. "A Survey of Indian Education in Five Selected Alberta Community Colleges: Some Models and Recommendations." Washington State, 1977.

4118
King, Alfred Richard. "A Case Study of an Indian Residential School (Yukon)." Stanford, 1964.

4119
Knowles, Donald Wilson. "A Comparative Study of Mediational Task Performance of Indian and Middle Class Children." Alberta, 1968.

4120
Koenig, Dolores Mary. "Cognitive Styles of Indians, Métis, Inuit and Non-Natives of Northern Canada and Alaska and Implications for Education." Saskatchewan, 1981.

4121
Lall, Geeta Rani. "Role-Expectations of Indian Teacher-Aides Employed in the Kindergartens of Saskatchewan Reserves as Perceived by Six Status Groups." Oregon, 1974.

4122
Mallett, W. Graham. "A Comparative Study of the Language Experience Approach with Junior High Native-Indian Students." Arizona State, 1975. [British Columbia/Colombie-Britannique]

McCombs, Arthur Rae. See No./Voir no 4415

4123
McDowell, Marilyn Eleanor. "Diagnosis of Behavior of Eskimo Students During Prevocational Training." Iowa State, 1973.

Nichols, Claude Andrew. See No./Voir no 478

4124
Nicol, Andrew James. "Self-Concept and Perceptions of Skilled Occupations of Selected Adult Métis in Rural Northern Alberta." Oregon State, 1979.

4125
Persson, Diane Iona. "Blue Quills: A Case Study of Indian Residential Schooling." Alberta, 1980.

4126
Pettit, George A. "Primitive Education in North America: Its Processes and Effects." California, Berkeley, 1940.

4127
Porter, Eric Ronald. "The Anglican Church and Native Education Residential Schools and Assimilation." Toronto, 1981.

4128
Rothman, Mark David. "The Response of the National Indian Brotherhood of Canada to the Indian Education Policy of the Canadian National Government." New York, 1977.

Salter, Michael Albert. See No./Voir no 485

4129
Schotte, Frederick. "Native Education in Northwestern Ontario: The Ontario Northern Corps and Formal Schooling in Isolated Ojibwa Communities." Toronto, 1977.

4130
Scrimshaw, Ronald Thomas. "Educational Dropout Among Blackfoot Indians in Alberta: A Sage Analysis 1979." Brigham Young, 1980. [Secondary education/Enseignement au secondaire]

4131
Whyte, Kenneth James. "A Study of the Value Orientations of People of the Inuit and Eurocanadian Cultures Within a School Setting in the Northwest Territories." Oregon, 1976.

4132
Williams, Constance Elaine Jayne. "Indian Control of Indian Education in Ontario, Canada: Success or Failure?" Michigan State, 1982.

Wolcott, Harry Fletcher. See No./Voir no 699

4133
Zielinski, Wasyl Gregory. "Achievement of Grade VII Compound and Coordinate Cree and English-Speaking Bilinguals in Northland School, Division 61." Montana, 1971. [Northern Alberta/Nord de l'Alberta]

Zuk, William Michael. See No./Voir no 2593

The Educational Psychology of Native Youths/ Psychologie éducative des jeunes autochtones

4134
Bowd, Alan Douglas. "A Cross-Cultural Study of Environmental Influences and Mechanical Aptitude in Several Indian Groups." Calgary, 1971. [British Columbia and Alberta/Colombie-Britannique et Alberta]

4135
Couture, Joseph Ernest. "Alberta Indian Youth: A Study in Cree and Blood Student Conflict." Alberta, 1972.

4136
Herman, Frederick Douglas Grant. "The Proximity of Personality and Cognitive Factors in Indian Students." Toronto, 1971.

Jamieson, Elmer. See No./Voir no 723

4137
Simonson, David Alan. "A Multivariate Analysis of Indian and Non-Indian Student Alienation." Alberta, 1973.

4138
Steinberg, Rhona Hinda. "Psychometric and Operative Intelligence in an Indian School Population." Saskatchewan, Regina, 1974.

Whyte, Kenneth James. See No./Voir no 4131
Zuk, William Michael. See No./Voir no 2593

GUIDANCE AND COUNSELING/ ORIENTATION ET CONSULTATION

General Items/Ouvrages généraux

4139
Allard, Pierre. "The Parent Report and Guidance and Counseling in the Province of Quebec." Michigan, 1971.

4140
Boniferro, Thomas Joseph. "An Exploratory Study in the Use of Teacher Ratings in the Early Identification of Children with Learning Difficulties." Alberta, 1975.

Branch, Edward Beverly. See No./Voir no 9427

4141
Brown, Thomas Harry Joshua. "An Application of Role Theory in Determining the Present and Preferred Functions for Canadian Counsellors." Alberta, 1974.

Coupal, Michael. See No./Voir no 9285
Davis, Gerald Albert. See No./Voir no 9286

4142
Dunlop, Florence S. "Subsequent Careers of Non-Academic Boys." Teachers College, Columbia, 1935.

Gilbert, Sidney Norman. See No./Voir no 3310
Hindmarch, Brian. See No./Voir no 9296
Howard, Louis Wayne. See No./Voir no 10260

4143
Jevne, Ronna Fay. "Counsellor Competencies a Selected Issues in Canadian Counsellor Education Calgary, 1979.

4144
Johnson, Peter Richard. "Group Sexuality Counsell for Developmentally Handicapped Adults." Ca gary, 1979.

4145
Karaz, Valerie Lynne. "Aspects of Communication Physically and Mentally Handicapped Adults." Ca gary, 1979.

4146
Keys, George Eric Maxwell. "Certain Aspects Guidance in Western Australia, New South Wal and Ontario." Toronto, 1959.

4147
Kincaid, Patricia Jean. "The Omitted Reali Husband-Wife Violence in Ontario and Policy Imp cations for Education." Toronto, 1981.

Klarreich, Samuel Henry. See No./Voir no 4166

4148
Klug, Leo F. "An Empirical Investigation of t Relationship Between Self-Actualization a Reconciliation with Death." Ottawa, 1976.

4149
Lippman-Hand, Abby. "Genetic Counseling: Paren Responses to Uncertainty." McGill, 1978.

4150
Marshall, Elizabeth Anne. "An Investigation of t Relationship Between Client Learning Style a Preference for Counsellor Approach." Toron 1981.

4151
McAndrew, Joan Kathleen. "A Study of the Expe ences of Families Receiving Genetic Counsellin Toronto, 1978.

4152
McConnell, Lawrence G. "Counsellor Education in t Treatment of Sexual Problems: Programme Dev opment and Evaluation." McGill, 1975.

4153
Meade, Edward Simon. "A Study of the Orientatic and Attitudes of Marriage Counsellors Who Hanc Marital Separation Cases." Toronto, 1980.

4154
Oakes, Jocelyn Diane. "The Establishment of a Cc sultation Relationship." Toronto, 1982.

4155
O'Brien, C.C. "A Philosophy of Guidance." Ottaw 1944.

4156
Peters, Neil M. "An Experimental Application of t Concepts of Image and Plans to the Counseli Setting." Alberta, 1961.

Phillipson-Price, Adrienne. See No./Voir no 6723
Riediger, Alfred J. See No./Voir no 2193

4157
Taylor, Gerald Dale. "Social Factors and the Educ tional and Occupational Ambition of Youth Ontario." Toronto, 1979.

Tucker, David Harold. See No./Voir no 9325

4158
Van Hesteren, Francis Nicholas. "Foundations of t Guidance Movement in Canada." Alberta, 1971.

4159
Young, Richard Anthony. "Career Development: Values, Attitudes, and Behavior in Rural Adolescent Males." McGill, 1977.

Training in Guidance and Counseling/ Formation en orientation et en consultation

4160
Boyd, Evelyn Marie. "Reflection in Experiential Learning: Case Studies of Counsellors." Toronto, 1982.

4161
Christensen, Carole Cecile Pigler. "Effects of Dissimilarity in Initial Interviews: An Experimental Evaluation of Cross-Cultural Training." McGill, 1980.

4162
Gelowitz, Arnold Charles. "A Proposal for Professional Preparation in College Student Personnel Work for Western Canada." Oregon State, 1979.

4163
Graub, Sup Mei. "An Exploratory Experimental Study of the Effects of Autogenic Training on Therapist-Trainees' Anxiety and Performance." McGill, 1974.

Hardy, James Roger. See No./Voir no 4185

4164
Hearn, Margaret Therese. "Three Modes of Training Counsellors: A Comparative Study." Western Ontario, 1976.

4165
Hum, Andrew. "Language Laboratory Use in the Training of Counsellors: An Exploratory Comparative Study." Alberta, 1973.

4166
Klarreich, Samuel Henry. "A Comparison of Group Training in Problem Solving Skills and Short-Term Group Counselling in the Treatment of Adolescent Offenders on Probation." Toronto, 1975.

4167
Minor, N. Kathleen Mary. "A Review of Counseling Among Cultures with Emphasis upon Culture Specific Counseling Within the Inuit Society: A Method and Training Program." Massachusetts, 1983.

4168
Morris, Raymond Martin. "The Significance of Trainee Personally Relevant Self-Expression on Empathy and Congruence in a Pre-Practicum Counsellor Training Program." Toronto, 1973.

4169
Pachal, Doreen Mae. "Empathy Training for Adolescent Peer Counselling." British Columbia, 1982.

4170
Usher, Brian Robert. "The Teaching and Training of Interpersonal Skills and Cognitions in a Counsellor Education Program." Toronto, 1974.

4171
Welch, Cecil Allan. "Counsellor Training in Interviewing Skills: Interpersonal Process Recall in a Microcounselling Model." McGill, 1976.

Guidance in the Elementary and Secondary Schools/ Orientation dans les écoles primaires et secondaires

4172
Andrews, William Robinson. "Behavioral and Client Centered Counseling of High School Underachievers." Alberta, 1969.

4173
Appell, Julian. "Joint Effect of Counsellor-Mode and Student Personality on Outcome." Calgary, 1977.

4174
Banmen, John. "An Exploratory Study of Guidance Services in the High Schools of Manitoba." Wyoming, 1970.

4175
Ben‐Dor, Tsilia Romm. "Career Development of Teenage Girls as a Process of Integrating the Vocational Career Concept with Family Plans." Toronto, 1979.

Bujold, Charles E. See No./Voir no 3485

4176
Burns, George Emmett. "Change Process in Relation to the Implementation of the Ministry of Education Senior Guidance Guideline: A Case Study." Toronto, 1979.

4177
Cassie, James Robert Bruce. "An Assessment of the Effects of a Computer - Assisted Career Information Service on the Career Maturity of Ontario Students in Grades Nine, Ten and Eleven." SUNY, Buffalo, 1976.

4178
Chiu, Clifton Ya-Lam. "Differential Programming and Implementation of Self-Concept Through Vocational Choice." British Columbia, 1977. [Grade ten/ Dixième année]

4179
Connell, Robert Bruce. "A Dyadic Interaction Approach to the Implementation of an Interpersonal Coping Skills Program with Adolescents." Toronto, 1978.

4180
Crowder, Thomas H. "The Effect of Audiovisual Tape Self-Confrontation on the Self-Concept of High Anxiety Twelfth-Grade Students Within a Client-Centered Counseling Situation." Ottawa, 1978.

Davis, Melvin Peter. See No./Voir no 9287

4181
Devinante, S. "Le counseling du groupe avec les enseignants. Effet du 'C Group' sur le self-concept de l'étudiant." Ottawa, 1977.

Gilbert, Sidney Norman. See No./Voir no 3310

4182
Glaze, Avis Elane. "Factors Which Influence Career Choice and Future Orientation of Females: Implications for Career Education." Toronto, 1980.

Grabb, Edward George. See No./Voir no 9994

4183
Grant, Harold Embree. "A Plan for a Guidance Program in the Montreal Protestant Central School System." Teachers College, Columbia, 1950.

4184
Granville, Howard. "The Contribution of Homework to Counselling Outcome." Toronto, 1978.

4185

Hardy, James Roger. "A Comparison of Three Methods of Training Peer Counsellors at the Secondary School Level." Ottawa, 1979.

4186

Harris, Justine Garwood. "Approachability of Adults in Secondary Schools, as Selected by Students." British Columbia, 1969.

4187

Hassard, James Harvey. "Perceptions of Ideal Counsellor Role Held by Secondary School Principals in Southwestern Ontario." Michigan State, 1976.

4188

Hester, Gerald LeRoy. "A Study to Help Develop a Guidance Program in the Yorkton Public School System, Yorkton, Saskatchewan, Canada." Teachers College, Columbia, 1964.

4189

Johns, Harold Percival. "Curriculum Planning and Guidance Services in British Columbia." Ottawa, 1950.

Kansup, Wanlop. See No./Voir no 3501

4190

Klempay, Mary Janet. "The Effectiveness of Various Responses to Students' Expressed Needs of Counseling on Measures of Self-Concept." Ottawa, 1964.

4191

Kristjanson, G. Albert. "An Analysis of Relationships Between Selected Factors and Level of Occupational Aspirations of Some Manitoba High School Youth." Wisconsin, 1967.

4192

Lalonde, Bernadette Irene Dierdre. "The Construction and Validation of a Measure of Academic Self-Efficacy." Toronto, 1979. [Secondary school level/École de niveau secondaire]

4193

Massey, Barbara Jane. "A Survey of Counselor, Student, Teacher, Administrator, Parent and School Trustee Attitudes and Factors Influencing Attitudes Toward Present High School Counseling Services." Alberta, 1973.

4194

McIntosh, William John. "A Study in Shop Guidance at Jarvis School for Boys, Toronto." Toronto, 1946.

McKittrick, Edith Patricia. See No./Voir no 3343

McLeod, Heleen Julianna. See No./Voir no 3476

4195

Merchant, David Francis. "Elementary School Guidance in Canadian Urban Areas: A Study of Present and Preferred Counsellor Functions." Alberta, 1973.

Morissette, Dominique. See No./Voir no 3344

Mott, Terrance Roger. See No./Voir no 3507

4196

Nichols, Marie A. "A Plan for the Development of Guidance Based on Evidences of Needs Obtained from Pupils and School Staff." Teachers College, Columbia, 1944.

4197

Pope, Glen Robin. "Attitude Change From a Guidance Teaching Method Using Videotaped Peer Models." Victoria, 1974.

4198

Quily, Peter Louis. "Introduction of Development Group Counselling and Its Effects in an Urban School System." Alberta, 1973.

4199

Richard, Marc M.J. "La relation entre le climat organisationel des écoles secondaires et le degré de consensus sur les attentes de rôle du conseiller une recherche expérimentale." Ottawa, 1976.

4200

Ryan, Sister Marie Margaret. "An Analysis of the Differential Effects of Coeducational and Single Sex Schools on Self-Actualization and Academic Achievement." Boston College, 1974.

Sayer, Lynda Anne. See No./Voir no 3316

4201

Seville, Saturno T. "A Study of the Guidance Functions Performed and Preferred by Grades 7 and 8 Teachers in the Separate Schools of Ottawa." Ottawa, 1970.

4202

Sorochty, Roger W. "Clarifying the Concept of Vocational Maturity Through the Use of a Career Development Program with High School Freshmen and Seniors." Ottawa, 1976.

4203

Walker, John Roger. "Teaching Job Seeking Skills High School Students: Traditional and Behavior Methods Compared." Manitoba, 1980.

Warren, William John. See No./Voir no 3792

4204

Webster, Edward. "Vocational Guidance in Relation School Training and the Distribution of Mental Abilities." McGill, 1936.

4205

Wilson, John A.R. "The Counselor in Canadian Secondary Schools." Oregon State, 1952.

4206

Yellin, Carole Susan. "The Role of Evaluative Feedback in Counseling and Counseling Supervision." Toronto, 1975.

Young, Richard Anthony. See No./Voir no 4159

4207

Young, Robert Hume. "Current Practices in Guidance Services in the Secondary Schools of British Columbia." Oregon State, 1969.

Guidance in Colleges and Universities/ Orientation dans les collèges et les universités

4208

Barnes, David Benton. "Analysis of Student, Faculty and Administrators' Perceptions of the Role of the Acadia University Counseling Centre." Rutgers, 1970.

4209

Burnett, Edward. "Vocational Counselling and Linear Model of Attitude." McGill, 1979. [McGill University students/Étudiants de l'Université McGill]

4210

Johnston, Edwin Frederick. "The Effects of Independent Densensitization and Study Skills Instruction On Anxiety, Study Behaviours and Academic Performance." McGill, 1974.

4211

Kennedy, Margaret Sandra Lee. "The Effect of Persuasibility of the Client's Self-Esteem, His or Her Sex and the Sex of the Counsellor." McGill, 1975.

Kimmis, Richard Clark. See No./Voir no 9300

4212

Knoll, Alexander. "Guidance Personnel Worker Accuracy of Predicting College Freshmen Attitude Toward Drugs in Montreal C.E.G.E.P.s." Syracuse, 1975.

Marshall, Elizabeth Anne. See No./Voir no 4150

4213

Poirier, Pierre-Paul. "Niveau d'adaptation et concept de soi des clients et des non-clients des services universitaires de counseling." Montréal, 1975.

4214

Stirling, Alexander. "Academic Skill Training: A Multi-Modal Approach." McGill, 1981.

Usher, Brian Robert. See No./Voir no 4170

COMMUNICATIONS IN EDUCATION/ COMMUNICATIONS DANS L'ENSEIGNEMENT

General Items/Ouvrages généraux

Kapoor, Surinder Kumar. See No./Voir no 3010
Schieman, Ervin. See No./Voir no 3638

Audio-Visual/Audio-visuel

4215

Branscombe, Frederic Ray. "The Pre-Service Professional Training of Teachers in the Province of Ontario, as It Relates to Instruction in the Selection, Production and Utilization of Audio-Visual Instructional Materials." New York, 1969.

Foster, John E. See No./Voir no 2740

Hundleby, Sigrid Anne. See No./Voir no 3227

4216

Lang, Charles J. "A Study of the Use of Audio-Visual Instructional Materials in the Curriculum of Selected American, Mexican and Canadian Programs for the Gifted." California, Los Angeles, 1961.

4217

Ritchie, Myles Houston. "An Investigation of Audio-Visual Education with Emphasis on British Columbia." Oregon State, 1943.

Motion Pictures and Education/Film et enseignement

4218

Chatwin, Arthur Edgar. "An Experimental Study of the Motion Picture Film in the Teaching of Geography." Toronto, 1938.

4219

Jacob, Jean-Noël. "Compréhension du langage cinématographique au point de vue spatial et temporel par les garçons de 11 ans et de 9 ans." Ottawa, 1966.

Julien, Louise. See No./Voir no 3764

TESTS AND MEASUREMENTS/EVALUATION

Akoodie, Mohammed Ally. See No./Voir no 745
Anderson, Alvin Leonard. See No./Voir no 3148
Bowie, Gerald William. See No./Voir no 10414

4220

Brother, Charles. "An Adaptation of the Henmon-Nelson Test of Mental Ability to French-Speaking Children." Institut Pédagogique Saint-Georges, 1954.

Cieply, Alfred. See No./Voir no 1123

4221

Colquhoun, Dorothy Rebecca. "The Relationship and Evaluation Between Ontario Nurse Registration Examinations and Certain Criterion Measures." Teachers College, Columbia, 1967.

4222

Davis, Harold John. "An Evaluation of the Canadian Tests of Basic Skills Testing Program Presently Carried Out by the Department of Education, Yukon Territory, Canada." Oregon, 1982.

4223

Ellis, Edward Norman. "The Effectiveness of Culture Free Tests in Measuring the Intellectual Characteristics of German Immigrants to Canada." Oregon State, 1956.

Fielder, John William. See No./Voir no 4062

4224

Goldring, Cecil Charles. "Intelligence Testing in a Toronto Public School." Toronto, 1924.

4225

Halliwell, Stanley Thomas. "The Effects of Scoring Instructions and Stress upon Multiple-choice Test Behavior." Toronto, 1975.

4226

Holmes, Barbara Joyce. "Individually-Administered Intelligence Tests: An Application of Anchor Test Norming and Equating Procedures in British Columbia." British Columbia, 1981.

4227

Howley, Thomas Patrick. "A Faceted Operational Model for the Assessment of Creative Ability." Toronto, 1979.

4228

Jones, Edward Austin. "A Study of the Relationship between Objective Tests and Written Essays as Measures of the Writing Ability of Grade Ten Students." Alberta, 1969.

Kelsey, Ian Bruce. See No./Voir no 3684

Koziev, Roberta Louise. See No./Voir no 9448

Lalonde, Bernadette Irene Dierdre. See No./Voir no 4192

4229

McGill, G.W. "Objective Tests in Geography." Toronto, 1927.

4230

Merchant, Francis Walter. "The Ontario Examination Systems." Toronto, 1903.

4231

Moreau, G.Y. "Test d'orientation scolaire." Montréal, 1946.

4232
Paton, James McNidder. "Examinations in English, Survey of Examination Philosophy and Practice in High School English of British, American and Canadian Schools." Toronto, 1948.

Pratt, David. See No./Voir no 2585

Sheridan, Donald Patrick. See No./Voir no 3701

4233
Smith, Iola. "Estimating Total-Test Scores from Matrix Samples Using Latent Trait Theory." Toronto, 1980.

Storey, Arthur George. See No./Voir no 4001

4234
Surkes, Steven. "The Effects of Test Instructions on Children's Performance in a Verbal Divergent Thinking Test." Victoria, 1979. [Grade seven/Septième année]

4235
Thexton, James David. "The Development of a Test for Economic Achievement for Grades XII and XIII in Ontario." Ohio University, 1976.

4236
Thibaudeau, Guy. "Test projectif d'aptitude scolaire (T.A.S.)." Montréal, 1973.

4237
Thorn, Frank Molyneux. "Fundamental Techniques in the Construction of a Canadian Group Achievement Test." Toronto, 1933.

4238
Wardhaugh, Ronald. "An Investigation of Certain Uses of a Test Constructed According to Principles of Transformational Grammar." Alberta, 1965.

4239
Whitehead, Ritchie George. "Regression Analysis, Alberta Grade Nine Departmental Examinations, Predicting Success in Grade Twelve Departmental Examinations." Utah State, 1974.

4240
Willis, Charles Barwick. "The Practical Application of Mental Tests in the Elementary School." Toronto, 1928.

4241
Willoughby, Ernest Ross Floyd. "A General Chemistry Test for Canadian High Schools." Toronto, 1931.

Wood, Nancy L. See No./Voir no 10413

Young, John Ernest McKim. See No./Voir no 3354

TEXTBOOKS/MANUELS

Bailey, Gordon Archibald. See No./Voir no 3176

4242
Boyce, Eleanor. "Canadian Readers Since 1846: A Study of Their Merits and Weaknesses as Instruments of Education." Manitoba, 1949.

Dhand, Hargopal. See No./Voir no 3179

Jain, Geneviève Laloux. See No./Voir no 2497

4243
Kahn, Joan Yess. "Modes of Medical Instruction: A Semiotic Comparison of Textbooks of Medicine and Popular Home Medical Books." McGill, 1980.

4244
Parvin, Viola Elizabeth. "Authorization of Textbooks for the Elementary Schools of Ontario, 1846-1950." Toronto, 1961.

Pratt, David. See No./Voir no 2585

Weinstein, Pauline Smith. See No./Voir no 2632

4245
White, Edwin Theodore. "Public School Textbooks in Ontario." Toronto, 1922.

4246
Woolard, Louis Clyde. "Theistic Religion in British Columbia Public School Textbooks." Yale, 1959.

EDUCATIONAL TECHNOLOGY/ TECHNIQUE D'ENSEIGNEMENT

4247
Dienes, Zoltan Bertalan. "The Time Factor in Computer-Assisted Instruction." Toronto, 1972.

Edwards, Peter. See No./Voir no 3374

4248
Ephraty, N. "The Relationship Between an Educational Technology Program Innovation in a Teacher Education Institute and Teacher's Practical Knowledge." Toronto, 1983.

4249
Hansen, Forrest Carl. "An Evaluation of Computer Assisted Instruction (CAI) for Teaching Statistics to Social Work Students." Toronto, 1981.

Huang, Henry Chung Chi. See No./Voir no 3429

4250
Kearsley, Gregory Peter. "A Study of Learner-Control in Computer-Based Instruction." Alberta, 1978. [Secondary and higher education/Enseignement secondaire et supérieur]

4251
Keller, Arnold. "The Comma Converser: An Intelligent Computer-Assisted Learning Program To Teach the Use of the Comma." Concordia, 1982.

Klopoushak, Edward L. See No./Voir no 3430

4252
Lam, Yee Lay Jack. "School Structure and Educational Technology." Toronto, 1971. [Ontario County/Comté de l'Ontario]

4253
Ma, Shao Ngang. "A Study of Students' Learning of Logarithmic Functions Using an Adaptive Computer Assisted Instruction System." Calgary, 1981.

McDougall, Daniel. See No./Voir no 3506

Montgomerie, Thomas Craig. See No./Voir no 2668

4254
Moore, George Albert Baker. "The Development of Educational Technology in Canadian Universities." Syracuse, 1972.

Mullings, Gloria Elizabeth. See No./Voir no 3715

Sandals, Lauran Hayward. See No./Voir no 3841

Strain, Allan Richard. See No./Voir no 3845

4255
Taerum, Terry Verne. "A Teaching Procedure for Computer Assisted Instruction in Mathematics and Statistics." Calgary, 1978.

4256
Tunstall, Kenneth Wilfred J.R. "Computer Assisted Group Problem Solving." Toronto, 1970.

4257
Voyce, Stanley. "A Multilingual-Interpreter System for Languages Used in Computer Assisted Instruction." Toronto, 1979.

4258
Westrom, Marvin Lawton. "The Teacher-Authored Instruction Manager (TAIM): A Computer Managed Instruction System." Alberta, 1973.

259
illson, Katherine Joan. "A Survey of the Conditions Surrounding the Introduction and First-Year Utilization of Microcomputers in Fourteen Selected Elementary Schools of Edmonton, Alberta, Canada." Oregon, 1982.

TEACHERS/PROFESSEURS

General Items/Ouvrages généraux

260
ikenhead, John D. "To Teach, or Not to Teach." Oregon, 1954. [Alberta, Manitoba, Saskatchewan, British Columbia/Colombie-Britannique]

ousquet, Marie-Elizabeth. See No./Voir no 2517
261
rackstone, Demaris Darlene. "Negotiating a Change of Perspective in Teacher-Librarian Relationships Within a Secondary School." Toronto, 1981.

262
uck, Geoffrey J. "The Contribution of Teachers Associations to the Status of the Teaching Profession in Canada." Manitoba, 1949.

riscoll, Alma. See No./Voir no 4089
263
lumphreys, Edward Harold. "Interaction, Prestige and Occupational Concepts of Secondary School Teachers in the Province of Ontario." Toronto, 1968.

264
ngalls, Karen Ellen. "A Study to Determine Business Education Teachers' Perceptions of Professional Development/Growth Activities in the Province of Alberta." Washington State, 1978.

265
lcBurney, Campbell. "A Validation of the Hurder Model in Rural Resource Teacher Service Delivery." Ottawa, 1983.

266
Morissette, Robert. "Les habiletés d'enseignement des professeurs de la spécialité 'couture et habillement'." Montréal, 1977.

267
Murphy, Raymond John Joseph. "The Interpretation of Professionalism and Bureaucracy: The Case of Secondary School Teachers in Canada." Toronto, 1974.

268
)ster, John Edward. "The Image of the Teacher in Canadian Prairie Fiction, 1921-1971." Alberta, 1972.

269
ail, Barry Richard. "A Case Study in Assistance for Parent-Teacher Organizations: A Model for Improving Their Operation." Toronto, 1977.

Teacher Personnel and Problems/
Problèmes du personnel enseignant

270
lubine, Ivan Ward. "Teacher Load in the Secondary School of Ontario." New York, 1944.

271
Cooke, Geoffrey James. "Teachers' Roles and Structural Differentiation." Toronto, 1971.

4272
El-Masri, Waguih. "Le système de probation des enseignants au Québec pour les années 1972-1974." Montréal, 1976.

4273
Hamilton, John McLean Parsons. "Career Experiences of Teachers Released Due to Declining Enrolment." Toronto, 1982.

4274
Harman, William Gowans. "Policy Models for Planning Teacher Manpower." Toronto, 1971. [Ontario]

4275
Kirkwood, Kristian John. "An Examination of Some Correlates of Teacher Absenteeism." Toronto, 1980.

4276
Law, Norma R. "Problems of Permanently Appointed Winnipeg Teachers and Administrative Procedures to Meet These Problems." Northwestern, 1949.

4277
MacDougall, John Innes. "An Investigation into the Subject and Grade Level Factors in Teacher Load with Particular Reference to the Programme of Studies for the High Schools of British Columbia." Washington, Seattle, 1944.

4278
Naylor, George Charles. "Demographic and Personality Variables Associated with Persistence and Promotion in the Alberta Teaching Force." Alberta, 1972.

Nixon, Mary Theresa. See No./Voir no 2892
4279
Oades, Carolyn Diane. "Relationship of Teacher Motivation and Job Satisfaction." Manitoba, 1983.

4280
Pallesen, Leonard Carl. "Teacher Satisfaction with a Computer-Assisted Placement in the Secondary Schools of a Large Urban System." Calgary, 1970.

4281
Parry, Robert Scott. "Teaching Staff and Turnover and School Organization Structure." Calgary, 1970.

4282
Paul, Ross Henderson. "Organizational Structure and Professional Autonomy: A Comparative Study of Teacher Authority Conflict in Montreal and Outer London." London, 1973.

4283
Pelletier, Guy. "L'influence de l'école secondaire publique sur le sentiment d'aliénation des enseignants: une analyse stratégique." Montréal, 1980.

4284
Richards, Donald Marcus. "Availability and Requirements for Teachers in Alberta: 1971-1981." Alberta, 1972.

Robinson, Norman. See No./Voir no 2943
Roy, Paul Martel. See No./Voir no 2214
Thompson, Edward Gerald. See No./Voir no 4365
4285
Tindale, Joseph Arthur. "Generational Conflict: Class and Cohort Relations Among Ontario Public Secondary School Teachers." York, 1980.

4286
Tracey, Kevin. "A Study of Teacher Recruitment in the Province of Newfoundland." Catholic, 1969.

4287
Uhlman, Charles Clarence. "Staffing and Salary Ratios in School Districts in British Columbia." Alberta, 1972.

4288
Willson, Stanley. "Development of the School Contracting Manual: Teacher Version." Alberta, 1976. [Alberta elementary grades three through six/De la troisième à la sixième année en Alberta]

4289
Wolfe, William Brian. "An Analysis of the Labour Market Experiences of Recent Graduates of Ontario Teacher Training Institutions." Toronto, 1980.

Teachers and Teaching/Professeurs et enseignement

Attitudes, Behavior, Personality, Morale, Teacher-Student Relationships, and Teaching/ Attitudes, comportement, personnalité, morale, relations professeurs-étudiants et enseignement

4290
Akhtar, Muhammad Mumtaz. "Freedom of Work-Related Choices and Work-Attachment: An Exploratory Study of Secondary Teachers." British Columbia, 1975.

4291
Arikado, Marjorie Sadako. "Status Congruence and Consensus as They Relate to Teacher Satisfaction in the Open Plan School." Toronto, 1973. [Ontario]

4292
Attridge, Carolyn Bernice. "Teacher and Student Behavior and Its Environmental Context in Diverse Classroom Settings." Toronto, 1975.

4293
Awomolo, Amos Ademola. "Teacher Discussion Leadership Behaviour in a Public Issues Curriculum and Some Cognitive Personality Correlates." Toronto, 1973.

4294
Barakett, Joyce Brand. "Teachers' Theories and Methods in Structuring Routine Activities: Another View on How Social Inequality is Perpetuated in the Classroom." Montréal, 1979.

4295
Bateson, David John. "Changes in Student-Teacher Perceptions Following a Residential Outdoor Program." British Columbia, 1981.

4296
Beraneck, Michel. "Le maître dans trois modèles pédagogiques, vues francophones de 1960 à 1970, grille d'analyse et tableaux de synthèse." Ottawa, 1979.

4297
Blahey, Peter John. "The Effect of Selected Variables on Teachers' Path-Goal Cognition." Toronto, 1975.

Bonneau, Gilles A. See No./Voir no 3650

4298
Bride, Kenneth Wilbert. "A Study of Prestige and Attitude Differentials Among Practicing Alberta Teachers." Alberta, 1973.

4299
Buettner, Edwin George John. "The Socialization Teachers: Effects of Graduate School and Wor place upon Professional Role Orientation." Man toba, 1982.

Bunn, Helen Hoque. See No./Voir no 2564

4300
Cadotte, Robert. "La pédagogie progressiste Québec: fondements et méthodes." Montréa 1982.

4301
Campbell, Frank Gerard. "An Exploratory Study Teacher Attitudes Toward Work and Retiremen Calgary, 1982.

4302
Chalmers, John West. "Some Factors Conducive Correspondence-Teaching Success in Public Educ tion in Alberta." Stanford, 1947. [Teacher sele tion/Choix de professeur]

4303
Clandinin, Dorothy Jean. "A Conceptualization Image as a Component of Teacher Personal Pract cal Knowledge in Primary School Teacher Reading and Language Programs." Toronto, 1983.

Cleghorn, Ailie. See No./Voir no 3005

4304
Cressman, Clare B. "Teacher-Student Relationship Teacher Dogmatism, Student Self-Esteem and St dent Perception of Teacher Attitudes." Ottaw 1979.

4305
De Bagheera, Georgette. "L'influence d'un sta d'auto-analyse des comportements de maître s l'attitude des élèves envers la langue seconde Montréal, 1982.

Dubé, Clairette. See No./Voir no 2524
Eggert, Wallace Victor. See No./Voir no 3103

4306
Elbaz, Freema Luwiesh. "The Teacher's Practic Knowledge: A Case Study." Toronto, 1980.

4307
Ferguson, Robert Carlisle. "Teachers and Teach Aides: A Case Study of Innovation in an Eleme tary School." Toronto, 1976.

4308
Fournier, Jean-Pierre. "Utilisation de l'approche sy tématique: élaboration et validation d'un modè pour préparer un plan de leçon ou d'unité d'appre tissage." Montréal, 1980.

Gagné, Fernand. See No./Voir no 3651
Greenberg, Allan Morley. See No./Voir no 9529
Griffith, Gwyneth Proctor. See No./Voir no 4026

4309
Hall, John Raymond. "An Ethnography of Teacher Informal Assessment Practice in a Calgary El mentary School." Calgary, 1980.

4310
Hammond, Leslie Leigh Gardner. "Self-Monitoring the Modification of Teacher Behaviour and Perce tions of Their Behaviour." York, 1975.

Harvey, Ray F.E. See No./Voir no 2842

4311
Hayes, Helen Elizabeth. "Teacher Orientation: A Interview Study of Teachers of English." Toront 1980. [From grade seven to grade ten/De septième à la dixième année]

4312
Hellyer, Alan McIntyre. "Perceptions of Educational Experiences, Student Satisfaction and Teacher Morale." Alberta, 1974.

4313
Hickman, George A. "A Study of Teacher Evaluation Systems in the Province of Newfoundland and Labrador." Toronto, 1983.

4314
Knoop, Robert. "Dimensions of Job Satisfaction as Determinants of Organizational Effectiveness." Ottawa, 1976.

4315
Lavigne, Jean-Claude. "L'attitude des professeurs de dessin technique à l'égard des documents 'audio-vision' et l'influence de cette attitude sur le rendement de leurs étudiants." Montréal, 1973.

Léger, Raymond Joseph. See No./Voir no 3118

4316
Lithwick, Carol Louise Appel. "Effects of Process Consultation on Teaching-Student Interaction." Toronto, 1982.

4317
MacDonald, Roderick Andrew. "A Study of the Intrinsic Reward Structure of the Classroom for the Teacher." Toronto, 1978.

4318
Marland, Percy Wilson. "A Study of Teachers' Interactive Thoughts." Alberta, 1977.

Marshall, Lionel George. See No./Voir no 2907

Martin, Wilfred Benjamin Weldon. See No./Voir no 9998

Martin, Yvonne Marjorie. See No./Voir no 2887

4319
Masse, Denis. "Teacher Participation and Professional Attitudes." Alberta, 1969.

4320
McBride, Billie Eleanor Jean. "A Factorial Study of Student Assessments of Teaching Performance." Alberta, 1963.

4321
McDonald, J.F. "The Allocation of Instructional Time by the Elementary Teacher." Toronto, 1983.

McLean, Ruth Winnifred. See No./Voir no 3658

4322
Michaud, Pierre. "Une échelle d'attitudes des professeurs." Montréal, 1968. [Elementary and secondary school teachers/Enseignants aux niveaux primaire et secondaire]

4323
Milburn, Geoffrey. "Derivation and Application of a Dramatic Metaphor for the Assessment of Teaching." Toronto, 1982.

4324
Mireau, Laurie Jane. "Teacher Expectancy Effects and Student Attributes." Alberta, 1980. [Grade three/Troisième année]

Moase, Reginald B. See No./Voir no 4468

Moody, Peter R. See No./Voir no 3107

4325
Moore, Russell F. "Self-Nonself-Differentiation and Its Relation to Student-Teacher Interpersonal Perceptions, Academic Achievement and Self-Concern." Ottawa, 1977.

Muttart, David Garth. See No./Voir no 3108

4326
O'Reilly, Robert Richard. "A Study of Teacher-Attitudes Concerning Standardized Practices in Instructional Areas." Alberta, 1968.

4327
Peruniak, Geoffrey Stephen. "Effects of Complex Teaching Strategies on Teacher and Student Behaviour." Toronto, 1978.

4328
Pura, Sophie Kathryn. "A Study of Teachers' Attitudes Towards Parental Volunteers in the Classroom and Their Relationships to Professional Role Orientation and Situational Job Security." Ottawa, 1976.

4329
Ramsoomair, Henry Franklin. "Control in the Classroom: A Study of Individuals' Perspectives." Toronto, 1982.

4330
Richard, Bruno. "Le groupe restraint: instrument de développement de la personalité et de la relation éducative chez les futurs enseignants." Montréal, 1972.

4331
Robbins, Stuart G. "The Development of an Instrument to Analyze Teacher Behavior in Elementary School Physical Education." Alberta, 1973.

4332
Savage, Hubert William. "The Manifestation and Prediction of Authoritarianism in Classroom Control." Toronto, 1960.

4333
Seigel, Rhonda Sharon. "The Male Teacher in the Primary Classroom." Alberta, 1978.

4334
Silver, Faith M. "An Empirical Investigation of the Relationship Between Teacher Self-Actualization and Classroom Openness." Ottawa, 1976. [Elementary and Junio and Senior high school teachers in Eastern Ontario/Professeurs au secondaire dans l'est de l'Ontario]

Sweet, Robert Arthur. See No./Voir no 3980

4335
Tremblay, Bernard. "Les caractéristiques de la personne et du comportement du professeur de niveau collégial, favorisant un apprentissage existentiel par l'étudiant." Montréal, 1968.

4336
Trosky, Odarka Savella. "Modifications in Teachers' Questioning Behavior in the Development of Reading Comprehension and a Series of Supervisory Conferences." Toronto, 1971.

Trottier, Claude René. See No./Voir no 2800

4337
Tuckwell, Neil Brian. "A Study of the Impact of an Intervention Program on Teacher Thought Processes." Alberta, 1980.

4338
Turnbull, Sarah Louise. "A Case Study of an Overreactive Teacher." Toronto, 1982.

4339
Walsh, John A. "Student-Teacher Identification and Academic Achievement." Ottawa, 1966.

4340
Watson, Raymond Kevin. "Empathy and Teacher Relationships." Calgary, 1980. [Calgary schools/Écoles de Calgary]

4341
Williams, M.J. "Organizational Stress Experiences by Teachers." Alberta, 1981.

Wilson, Harry Alexander. See No./Voir no 3281

4342
Wodlinger, Michael George. "A Study of Teacher Interactive Decision Making." Alberta, 1980. [Grade six/Sixième année]

Teacher Associations, Organizations, Unions, Salaries and Collective Bargaining/Associations, organismes, syndicats, salaires et conventions collectives de professeurs

Adams, William Arthur. See No./Voir no 2648

4343
Bailey, Warren Stevenson. "The Influence of the Alberta Teachers' Association on Educational Legislation in Alberta, 1918-1948." Stanford, 1956.

4344
Blais, Gilles. "Collective Bargaining for Teachers in Canada: A Comparative Study." California, Los Angeles, 1972. [British Columbia, Ontario, Quebec/Colombie-Britannique, Ontario, Québec]

Buck, Geoffrey J. See No./Voir no 4262

4345
Charles, Lawrence Moses. "Implications of Collective Bargaining to the Achievement of Shared Decision-Making by Ontario Teachers." Toronto, 1982.

4346
Fris, Joe. "Professionalisation and Militancy Among Ontario Secondary School Teachers." Toronto, 1976.

4347
Garry, Carl. "A Sociological Theory of Industrial Relations as Illustrated by Case Study Investigations of the Unionization of University Faculty Members, Nurses and Social Workers." York, 1980.

Hall, L.G. See No./Voir no 2205

Hardy, John Howard. See No./Voir no 2494

4348
Harrison, A.K. "Procedures and Reasons for Termination of Teacher Contracts in Canada." Alberta, 1980.

4349
Hayes, Terrance Timothy. "Goal Achievement of the Alberta Teachers' Association: Perceptions of a Sub-Population of Its Membership." United States International, 1980.

4350
Ingram, Ernest John. "Member Involvement in the Alberta Teachers' Association." Alberta, 1965.

Johnson, Bruce Kilgour. See No./Voir no 4370

4351
Kratzmann, Arthur. "The Alberta Teachers' Association: A Documentary Analysis of the Dynamics of a Professional Organization." Chicago, 1964.

Landry, Simon. See No./Voir no 3655

4352
Lewis, Archibald Clifford. "Contracts and Tenure of Canadian Teachers." Toronto, 1940.

4353
Marcotte, William Arthur. "An Examination of Collective Bargaining Between Canadian Public School Teachers and Their Employers." Toronto, 1980.

4354
McCallum, Mary Aletha. "Power to Lead: A Case Study of the Rise and Fall of an Individual's Authority to Initiate Collective Action Within a Formal Organization." Toronto, 1976.

4355
McDowell, Clarence Stirling. "The Dynamics of the Saskatchewan Teachers' Federation." Alberta, 1966.

McLeod, Gerald Thomas. See No./Voir no 2872

4356
Muir, James Douglas. "Canadian School Teacher Salaries: Impact of Collective Bargaining and Other Factors." Cornell, 1970.

4357
Nason, Gerald. "The Canadian Teachers' Federation: A Study of Its Historical Development, Interests and Activities from 1919 to 1960." Toronto, 1964.

4358
Nelson, Michael Davidson. "Teacher Militancy: An Explorative Comparative Case Study of Four Teachers' Groups." Carleton, 1981.

4359
Odynak, Steve Nick. "The Alberta Teachers' Association as an Interest Group." Alberta, 1964.

4360
Roald, Jerry Bruce. "Pursuit of Status: Professionalism, Unionism, and Militancy in the Evolution of Canadian Teachers' Organizations, 1915-1955." British Columbia, 1970.

Roy, Paul Martel. See No./Voir no 2214

4361
Rozycki, Gaston Raymond. "The Scope of Bargained Items under Decentralized and Centralized Forms of Collective Bargaining." Alberta, 198. [Alberta Teachers' Association and Saskatchewan Teachers Federation/Association des professeurs de l'Alberta et fédération des professeurs de Saskatchewan]

4362
Scharf, Murray Patrick. "An Investigation of the Relationship Between the Professional Role Orientation and Social Structure of Teacher Groups. Alberta, 1968.

4363
Segall, William Edwin. "A Study of Collective Professionalism in Western Canada: The Alberta Teachers' Association." Arkansas, 1967.

4364
Skolrood, Arthur Harold. "The British Columbia Teachers' Federation: A Study of Its Historical Development, Interests and Activities from 1916 to 1963." Oregon, 1967.

4365
Thompson, Edward Gerald. "The Effects of the Metro Toronto Teachers' Strike on Students and Teachers." Toronto, 1979.

4366
Topley, Derrick Norman. "The Professional Policies of the Ontario Secondary School Teachers' Federation, 1919-1966." Toronto, 1970.

Vail, Barry Richard. See No./Voir no 4269

4367
Vintar, John. "The Experiences with the Fact Finding Process as it relates to Negotiated Settlements Under Bill 100 in Ontario." Toronto, 1981. [Teachers and school boards/Professeurs et conseils scolaires]

4368
Waters, Joseph St. Clair. "Boards of Reference in Ontario: Resolving Teacher-Board Contract Termination Disputes." Toronto, 1982.

4369
Watson, Roy Ernest Love. "The Nova Scotia Teachers' Union: A Study in the Sociology of Formal Organization." Toronto, 1960.

Teacher Welfare/Protection de l'enseignant

4370
Johnson, Bruce Kilgour. "An Investigation of Teachers' Salary and Working Conditions in Selected School Jurisdictions in Alberta 1960-1969." Alberta, 1972.

4371
Richardson, Ralph Percy. "Superannuation Schemes for Teachers." Toronto, 1922.

4372
Thomas, John Morris. "A Study of Teachers' Retirement Schemes in Canada, Including a Review of the Social Philosophy and General Principles Underlying a Sound Retirement Scheme." Toronto, 1942.

TEACHER EDUCATION/ FORMATION DES MAÎTRES

General Items/Ouvrages généraux

4373
Babin, Patrick. "Adaptation of Modeling Procedures and Their Effect on the Development of Higher-Order Questioning Behavior in an Elementary Teacher - Education Program." Ottawa, 1971.

Brown, Alfred Malcolm. See No./Voir no 995

4374
Chikombah, Cowden E.M. "The Extended Practicum in Alberta Teacher Education: A Case Study in Policy Development." Alberta, 1979.

4375
Dibski, Dennis John. "Private Returns to Teacher Education in Alberta." Alberta, 1971.

Ephraty, N. See No./Voir no 4248

4376
Gamache, Sister Margaret Theresa. "A Study of the Teacher Education Programs of Quebec Province: Their Implications to Graduate Study in the United States with Special Consideration of Sister Formation Colleges." Portland, 1965.

4377
Hopkins, David William Richard. "Survey Feedback and the Problem of Change in Teacher Education." Simon Fraser, 1981. [Education in Canadian teacher training institutions/Enseignement dans les institutions canadiennes de perfectionnement pour les professeurs]

Innes, Robert John. See No./Voir no 3604

4378
Kaplan, David Jay. "Teacher Education Viewed Internationally." Boston University, 1973.

4379
Létourneau, L.A. "Policy Implementation: The Creation of a French Teacher Training Institute in Manitoba." Alberta, 1981.

MacDougall, John Innes. See No./Voir no 4277

4380
Peck, Bryan Trevor. "A Comparative Study of Some Developments in the British Tradition of Teacher Education 1960-1970, with Particular Reference to the Colleges in England, Wales, Scotland and British Columbia." London, 1973.

4381
Sharma, Ram Rachhpal. "A Comparison of the Education of Secondary Teachers in Alberta (Canada), Kenya (East Africa) and Punjab (India)." Oregon, 1975.

4382
Sheridan, Harold Stanley. "The Development of Public Elementary Teacher Education in Ontario, New York, and Michigan: A Comparative Study." George Washington, 1971.

4383
Wallace, Kenneth Walter Anthony. "The Private Monetary Returns to Vocational Education Teacher Training in Alberta." Alberta, 1970.

4384
Watts, Howard Norman. "An Evaluation of the Objectives of an Elementary Teacher Education Program." Alberta, 1972.

History of Teacher Education/ Histoire de la formation des maîtres

4385
Andrews, Samuel Dalton. "Conceptual Influences in Teacher Education in the Province of Quebec, 1857 to 1961." Connecticut, 1972.

4386
Ault, Orvill E. "The Relation of Certain Problems to the Training of Teachers in the United States, Ontario, France, Scotland and Germany." Edinburgh, 1936.

Bailey, Alan W. See No./Voir no 4404

4387
Black, William Griffiths. "The Development and Present Status of Teacher Education in Western Canada, with Special Reference to the Curriculum." Chicago, 1937.

4388
Bujea, Eleanor. "The Development of Business Teacher Education in Canada, 1900-1970." North Dakota, 1973.

4389
Cann, Marjorie Mitchell. "An Historical Study of the Office of Coordinator of Teacher Education in the Canadian Provinces of New Brunswick, Ontario, Saskatchewan, Alberta and British Columbia." Michigan, 1957.

4390
Cheng, Chung-Sing. "The Main Factors That Led to the Establishment of the University of Ottawa Teachers' College." Ottawa, 1961.

4391
Cohen, S.W. "A Comparative Study of the Development of Teacher Training in Britain, the United States, and the British Dominions." London, 1950.

4392
Cook, John Thomas. "Teacher Training in the Province of New Brunswick: An Historical and Analytical Study of Its Evolution, Together with Proposed Measures of Practical Reform." Harvard, 1940.

4393
Graham, George Arthur. "A Study of Programs for Advanced Degrees in Schools of Education in Canada." Washington State, 1960.

4394
Halnon, William. "A Descriptive Critical and Constructive Study of the Control, Organization and Administration of Training Elementary Teachers in England, Canada and the United States." Indiana, 1925.

Hardy, John S. See No./Voir no 2495

4395
Hodgins, Thomas Arnold. "University Education for Elementary School Teachers of Ontario, 1950-1970." Syracuse, 1971.

4396
Hutton, Harry K. "French Canadian Normal Schools: An Historical, Interpretive and Evaluative Study." Pennsylvania State, 1952.

4397
Lorimer, Wesley C. "The Improvement of Teacher Education in the Normal School of Saskatchewan." Teachers College, Columbia, 1948.

4398
Marshall, Mortimer V. "An Evaluation of the Present Teacher-Training Program in Nova Scotia, with Recommendations for Improvement." Harvard, 1930.

4399
Melvin, Arthur Gordon. "The Professional Training of Teachers for the Ontario Public Schools." Teachers College, Columbia, 1923.

4400
Newcombe, Ervin Ernest. "The Development of Elementary School Teacher Education in Ontario Since 1900." Toronto, 1965.

4401
Piquette, Roland. "Les programmes de formation des maîtres dans les écoles normales françaises du Québec (1857-1970)." Montréal, 1973.

4402
Rogers, S. John. "The Organization, Control and Administration of the Teacher Training System of the Province of Ontario: 1900-1920." Ottawa, 1973.

4403
Shipley, Charles M. "Proposals for Developing the Curriculum for a Two-Year Program in Nova Scotia's Provincial Normal College." Teachers College, Columbia, 1948.

Teacher Training: Pre-Service Academic and Professional Preparation/Formation des maîtres: préparation pré-académique et professionnelle

4404
Bailey, Alan Westlake. "The Professional Preparation of Teachers for the Schools of the Province of New Brunswick, 1784 to 1964." Toronto, 1964.

4405
Barnett, Robert Claude. "A Comparison of Teacher Belief Systems Regarding the Classroom Teaching/Learning Experience of Students in Selected Concurrent and Consecutive Elementary Teacher-Training Programs in Ontario." Indiana, 1976.

4406
Boudreau, Berthe. "Curriculum Materials Centers in Teacher Education Institutions in Canada." Indiana, 1982.

Branscombe, Frederic Ray. See No./Voir no 4215

4407
Desilets, Germaine-Nicolas. "Professional Preparation, In-Service Activities and Job Satisfaction of the Teachers of English as a Second Language at the Secondary Level in the Province of Quebec." Michigan, 1970.

4408
Doxey, Isabel Marion. "Training Programme Effect on Selected Verbal Behaviours of Kindergarten Teachers." Toronto, 1977.

Dufresne, Donald Joseph. See No./Voir no 2922

4409
Gaydos, Andrew. "Vocational Teacher Preparation Needs in Ontario as Viewed by First Year Teachers, Fifth Year Teachers, Technical Coordinators and Teacher Educators." Ohio State, 1975.

Hickman, George A. See No./Voir no 4313
Housego, Ian Edward. See No./Voir no 2963

4410
Huot, Janine. "Éléments pour un modèle de la communication pédagogique." Montréal, 1979.

4411
Kennedy, Sister Mary Perpetua. "An Evaluative Study of the Preparation of Secondary School Teachers in the Province of Newfoundland, Canada." Catholic, 1968.

4412
Klostermann, Kerry Julian Wolfgang. "Occupational Cognition, Experience, Satisfaction and Self: Teacher Trainees Vocational Self Constructs." Western Ontario, 1978.

4413
MacDonald, Ronald. "The Opinions of College and University Teachers in the Atlantic Region of Canada Regarding the Preparation of College and University Teachers." Cornell, 1961.

4414
Masters, Bernard L. "Teacher Preparation for Open Space Schools." Alberta, 1973. [Elementary level/Niveau primaire]

4415
McCombs, Arthur Rae. "Village Based Teacher Education Project for Rural Canadians: A Study of the Brandon University Northern Teacher Education Project." Michigan State, 1979.

4416
Nephew, James Harold. "A Four Year Model for the Academic and Professional Preparation of Elementary School Teachers in Ontario." Wayne State, 1974.

4417
Park, James. "Effects of Direct and Vicarious Experiences in Learning Groups." Alberta, 1971. [University of Alberta/Université de l'Alberta]

4418
Potvin, Robert John Michael. "A Didactic Teaching Approach to the Implementation of Interpersonal Coping Skills." Toronto, 1974.

4419
Reid, Roma Marguerite. "Accessibility Characteristics in Individualizing Teacher Education Programs: Acquisition of Basic Teaching Skills." Toronto, 1975.

4420
Ryckman, Robert M. "Needs and Directions of Teacher Training in the Regional Municipality of Niagara as Perceived by Selected Publics of Brock College of Education." Bowling Green State, 1975.

4421
Steinert, Yvonne. "Mothers as Teachers: A Comparison of Maternal and Remedial Teacher Training Styles." Montréal, 1977.

Teacher Preparation in Subject Areas/ Formation des maîtres

Early Childhood/Jeunes enfants

4422
Ezrin, Sharyn A. "The Goals-Guide Behaviors Evaluation Strategy: A Formative Evaluation Plan for Teaching of Early Childhood Education Programmes." Carleton, 1977.

4423
McCann, R. "An Examination of Early Childhood Teacher Education: England and Newfoundland." Leicester, 1978.

English as a Second Language/Anglais, langue seconde

Desilets, Germaine-Nicolas. See No./Voir no 4407

Industrial Arts/Arts industriels

Ross, Campbell John. See No./Voir no 3478

4424
Vaughan, Maurice Stephen. "The Preparation and Certification of Industrial Arts Teachers in Canada." North Dakota, 1967.

Mathematics/Mathématiques

4425
Kapoor, Dharam V. "A Suggested Teacher Education Program for Saskatchewan Secondary School Mathematics Teachers." Oregon, 1975.

Poisson, Yves. See No./Voir no 3435

Music/Musique

Ricord, O. See No./Voir no 4444

Nursing/Sciences infirmières

4426
Griffin, Amy Elizabeth. "The Improvement of the Educational Preparation of Instructors in Preservice Programs in Nursing in Ontario." Columbia, 1963.

Reading/Lecture

Janes, Ethel Mary. See No./Voir no 3963

Science

4427
Russell, Thomas Lee. "On the Provision Made for Development of Views of Science and Teaching in Science Teacher Education." Toronto, 1976.

Social Studies/Sciences sociales

4428
Toews, Henry. "The Preparation of Senior High School Social Studies Teachers in Alberta." Montana, 1974.

Pre-Service Teachers, Student Teaching and Teacher Internship/Stagiaires en éducation

4429
Andrews, Helen Katherine. "A Study of Associate Teachers' Conference Practices with Student Teachers." Toronto, 1980.

4430
Bailey, Michael Roy. "The Effects of Guided Self-Analysis on the Verbal Teaching Behaviors and Attitudes of Student Teachers." Alberta, 1973.

Bateson, David John. See No./Voir no 4295

Branscombe, Frederic Roy. See No./Voir no 4215

4431
Cuff, Harry Alfred. "A Descriptive and Comparative Study of Student Teaching Practices in Canada, 1970-1971." Boston University, 1971.

4432
Dorner, John Nicholas. "Communication Skill Development in Student Teachers by the Use of Play Practice." Victoria, 1978.

4433
Earl, Samuel Aubrey. "An Examination of Selected Opinion on Teacher Internship in the Province of Alberta, 1964." Montana State, 1965.

4434
Franzoni, Edward Matthew. "Microtraining-Teaching Pre-Service Teachers More Effective Communication Skills." Alberta, 1978.

4435
Gregory, Alan. "The Effect of Student Teaching on the Professional Self-Concept of Student Teachers: A Study of Student Teachers in the Professional Development Program, Simon Fraser University." Simon Fraser, 1976.

4436
Hennessy, C. "Becoming a Teacher: How Eight Pre-Service Teachers Experience Practica." Toronto, 1983.

4437
Krecsy, James Patrick. "Personality Factors of Student Teachers and Faculty Supervisors as Related to Student Teachers' Perceptions of Success." Manitoba, 1975.

4438
Leclerc, Mariel. "Étude des changements du comportement verbal des stagiaires en fonction des caractéristiques de la relation maître de stage-stagiaire." Laval, 1973.

4439
Ludlow, Wayne Everett. "The Role of the Cooperating Teacher in the Field Experience Component of Teacher Education at Memorial University of Newfoundland, as Perceived by Incumbents of the Field Experience Triad." Northern Colorado, 1975.

4440
Marble, William Oscar. "Development of Student Teacher Effectiveness over an Extended Practicum." Simon Fraser, 1982.

Moore, Russell F. See No./Voir no 4325

4441
Poupard, Danielle. "Étude exploratoire des valeurs d'éducation, de la satisfaction et des expériences vécues chez deux groupes d'étudiants en formation des maîtres." Montréal, 1974.

4442
Preston, Raymond George. "Effects of Relationships Within the Student Teaching DYAD on Pupil Achievement." Alberta, 1975.

4443
Richard, Fernand. "Perceptions de soi des futures enseignantes." Montréal, 1971.

4444
Ricord, O. "Microteaching, Modelling and Feedback and Their Effects on Pre-Service Teachers in Music." Alberta, 1982.

4445
Scaldwell, William Arnold. "The Effects of Television Workshops in the Assessment of Student Teachers by Supervising Teachers." Toronto, 1972.

4446
Schmidt, Peter Karl. "The Effects of Two Methods of Interpersonal Skill Development with Preservice Elementary School Teachers on Attitude Toward Students." Toronto, 1981.

4447
Staples, Richard Brian. "The Professional Development Needs of Practicing Alberta Teachers." Montana, 1970.

Tremblay, Bernard. See No./Voir no 4335

Beginning Teachers, In-Service Training and the Improvement of Teaching/Professeurs débutants, stage et perfectionnement de l'enseignement

4448
Allen, Sheilah Moreen. "Inservice Education in Secondary Reading for English Teachers: A Conceptual Analysis." British Columbia, 1977.

4449
Burke, Gloria Victoria. "Experienced Teachers' Perceptions and Preferences Concerning Off-Campus University Courses and School District-Sponsored In-Service Education Activities in the Province of Alberta." Alberta, 1980.

4450
Cheatley, Alice Mary Elizabeth. "Teacher In-Service and Professional Development in the Urban School Divisions of Metropolitan Winnipeg." North Dakota, 1977.

Dubé, Clairette. See No./Voir no 2524

4451
Fair, James William. "Teachers as Learners: The Learning Projects of Beginning Elementary School Teachers." Toronto, 1973.

4452
Harris, Robert Clayton. "Group Counselling with Teachers: An Effective In-Service Education Technique." Toronto, 1969.

Hawke, David M. See No./Voir no 3379

4453
Hewitson, Malcolm Thomas. "The Professional Satisfaction of Beginning Teachers." Alberta, 1975.

4454
Hume, William Elliot. "Improvement of the Elementary Teacher in Service." Toronto, 1923.

4455
Kapuscinski, Sister Bernice Phyllis. "An In-Service Experience in Individualization of Instruction." Saskatchewan, 1977.

4456
Krysowaty, Joyce Bernice. "Adult Development in Relation to Teacher Professional Development." Alberta, 1979.

4457
Larson, Olaf Peter. "A Study of Inservice Education in the School Divisions and Counties of Alberta." Oregon, 1962.

4458
MacLeod, Nelson B. "A Plan for Teacher Education in Nova Scotia with Emphasis on In-Service Education." Teachers College, Columbia, 1949.

Matusicky, Carol. See No./Voir no 4031

4459
McDougall, William D. "Suggestions for the Improvement of Elementary Teacher Education in the Province of Alberta." Teachers College, Columbia, 1947.

4460
McIntosh, Janet Christina. "The First Year of Experience: Influences on Beginning Teachers." Toronto, 1976.

4461
Miller, John Pearse. "The Effects of Inservice Human Relations Training on Teacher Interpersonal Functioning." Toronto, 1971.

Moase, Reginald Beverly. See No./Voir no 4468

4462
Oliva, Frank Daniel. "A Study of the Orientation Programs for New Elementary Teachers in Selected City School Systems of Canada." Oregon, 1966.

4463
Perkins, Marjorie Morrison. "Evaluation of Two Variations of an In-Service Training Program on Appraisal of Oral Language." Toronto, 1979.

4464
Schreiber, Fred Oscar. "In-Service Education Preferences of Teachers and Administrators in the Province of Alberta." Manitoba, 1975.

Shorey, Leonard Ludwig. See No./Voir no 4075

4465
Stewart, Lorne Duncan. "A Study of the In-Service Educational Opportunities Available to Beginning Teachers in Alberta." Colorado, 1966.

4466
Wilson, Sybil Everesta. "Instructional Needs of Beginning Primary School Teachers and Expressed Satisfaction with In-College Training." Toronto, 1972.

4467
Wright, Aubrey Willis. "The Problems of Beginning Ele mentary Teachers in Newfoundland Schools and the Relationship of These Problems with Pre-Service and In-Service Programs." Northern Colorado, 1975.

Teacher Certification/Brevet d'enseignement

Brown, Alfred Malcolm. See No./Voir no 995
Hopkirk, Gerald A. See No./Voir no 2684

4468
Moase, Reginald Beverly. "A Study of Educational Attitudes of a Sample of Candidates Seeking Teacher Certification in Ontario." Toronto, 1978.

Vaughan, Maurice Stephen. See No./Voir no 4424

ENGINEERING/INGÉNIERIE

This section has been sub-classified by region rather than under headings.

The bulk of research in this area was produced in Canadian universities, and the major part was completed during the 1970's. The American output amounts to a little more than one-fifth (22) of the total (124). Of the 22 Canadian universities producing dissertations in engineering, Alberta, Toronto, Waterloo, and McGill are the leaders. Of the 17 American universities involved, most produced only one item. The University of Buffalo is the leader (4), with its research centering around Lake Erie (3) and Lake Ontario (1).

––––––––

Cette section est organisée par sous-classifications régionales plutôt que par vedettes.

La majorité des thèses en ce domaine vient des universités canadiennes et la plupart des thèses datent des années 1970. La production américaine est d'un peu plus d'un cinquième (22) du total (124). Des 22 universités canadiennes qui ont produit des thèses en ingénierie, les universités de l'Alberta, de Toronto, de Waterloo ainsi que McGill ont été les plus actives. Des 17 universités américaines qui se sont intéressées à ces études, la plupart n'ont produit qu'une seule thèse. L'Université de Buffalo vient en tête avec 4 thèses, dont trois traitent du lac Érié et une du lac Ontario.

See also Agricultural Engineering/Voir aussi Génie agricole

GENERAL ITEMS/OUVRAGES GÉNÉRAUX

Boyd, Archibald D. See No./Voir no 2048
Briaud, Jean-Louis Charles. See No./Voir no 2270

4469
Campbell, Gordon Donald. "An Analysis of Highway Finance and Road-User Imposts in Canada." Purdue, 1956.

4470
Carman, John Stanley. "The Mineral Position of Canada." Columbia, 1952.

4471
Chari, Tuppal Ramanuja. "Some Geotechnical Aspects of Iceberg Grounding." Memorial University of Newfoundland, 1975. [Canada's eastern seabord/ Côte de l'est du Canada]

De Cea Chicano, Joaquin. See No./Voir no 2252

4472
De Young, John H., Jr. "Technological Diffusion in the Electric Power Industry - Canada, Great Britain, and the United States, 1950-1973." Pennsylvania State, 1975.

4473
Elias, Demetrius. "Minimum Cost Design of Centralized Teleprocessing Networks Using Canadian Common Carrier Facilities." McGill, 1978.

Ghoneim, Nadia S. See No./Voir no 2304

4474
Gray, Andrew Ross. "The Effect of Weather on Airport Runway Operations." Toronto, 1977.

4475
Hamzawi, Salah Gouda. "An Optimization Methodology for Design and Evaluation of Intercity Passenger Transport Systems." Carleton, 1977.

4476
Henriquez, Luis Nelson. "An Economic Planning Framework for Mining Research and Development: The Case of Canada Centre for Mineral and Energy Technology." McGill, 1979.

4477
Hungr, Oldrich. "Dynamics of Rock Avalanches and Other Types of Slope Movements." Alberta, 1981.

4478
Lake, Richard Wallace. "An Economic Decision model for Mineral Development in Canada." Queen's, 1976.

4479
Millard, John Rodney Emmett. "The Development of the Engineering Profession in Canada 1880-1920." Toronto, 1982.

4480
Milne, William George. "Earthquake Risk in Canada." Western Ontario, 1966.

4481
Nassar, Mohamed Ahmed. "Gravity Field and Levelled Heights in Canada." New Brunswick, 1977.

4482
Ng, Kong Seng. "Detoxification of Bleached Kraft Mill Effluents by Foam Separation." British Columbia, 1978. [Ten Canadian mills/Dix usines canadiennes]

4483
Norris, Donald K. "Structural Conditions and Violent Stress Relief in Coal Mines of the Southern Canadian Cordillera." California Institute of Technology, 1953.

4484
Pennel, Douglas Gordon. "Residual Strength Analysis of Five Landslides." Alberta, 1969.

Samaha, Mohamed Aly. See No./Voir no 2319

4485
Shallal, Louis A.Y. "Peak Hour Ratios Estimation, Application and Cost-Effectiveness in the Urban Transportation Planning Process." Carleton, 1979.

4486
Watt, Theodore Marvin. "Studies of the Topside Ionosphere with the Alouette Satellite." Stanford, 1965.

4487
Yaciuk, Gordon. "Temperatures in Grain Storage Systems." Manitoba, 1973. [All of Canada/Tout le Canada]

REGIONAL STUDIES/ÉTUDES RÉGIONALES

Eastern Canada/Est du Canada

4488
Locat, Jacques. "Contribution à l'étude de l'origine de la structuration des argiles sensibles de l'est du Canada." Sherbrooke, 1982.

The Arctic, Northwest Territories and the Yukon/ Arctique, Territoires du Nord-Ouest et Yukon

4489
Elkhoraribi, Mohamed Cherif Eliman. "Volume Change of Frozen Soils." Carleton, 1975.

4490
Poulin, Ambrose O. "On the Thermal Nature and Sensing of Snow-Covered Arctic Terrain." McGill, 1972.

4491
Pufahl, Dennis Edward. "The Behavior of Thawing Slopes in Permafrost." Alberta, 1976.

4492
Roggensack, William Dale. "Geotechnical Properties of Fine-Grained Permafrost Soils." Alberta, 1977. [Northwest Territories/Territoires du Nord-Ouest]

4493
Savigny, K. Wayne. "In situ Analysis of Naturally Occurring Creep in Ice-Rich Permafrost Soil." Alberta, 1980.

4494
Sego, David Charles Cletus. "Deformation of Ice Under Low Stresses." Alberta, 1980.

4495
Weaver, Jeffrey Stephen. "Pile Foundations in Permafrost." Alberta, 1979.

Alberta

4496
Bardon, Michael Fredric Richard. "Tar Sand Fragments in Hot Gas Streams." Calgary, 1978.

4497
Bray, Dale Irving. "Generalized Regime-Type Analysis of Alberta Rivers." Alberta, 1972.

4498
De Medeiros, Luciano V. "Deep Excavations in Stiff Soils." Alberta, 1979. [Edmonton]

4499
Dusseault, Maurice Bernard. "The Geotechnical Characteristics of the Athabasca Oil Sands." Alberta, 1977.

4500
El-Nahhas, Fathalla Mohamed. "The Behaviour of Tunnels in Stiff Soils." Alberta, 1981. [Edmonton]

4501
Engmann, Jeremias Edwin Oko. "Transverse Mixing Characteristics of Open and Ice Covered Channel Flows." Alberta, 1974. [Lesser Slave River]

4502
Gomez-Bueno, C.O. "Recovery of Vanadium from Athabasca Tar Sands Fly Ash." Waterloo, 1979.

Griffin, P.J. See No./Voir no 1907

4503
Hayashitani, Masao. "Thermal Cracking of Athabasca Bitumen." Calgary, 1978.

4504
Iskander, Fadel Fawzi. "A Probabilistic Analysis of the Economics of Oil Recovery from the Athabasca Tar Sands." Tulsa, 1980.

4505
McRoberts, Edward Charles. "Stability of Slopes in Permafrost." Alberta, 1973.

British Columbia/Colombie-Britannique

4506
Brackhaus, Karl Heinz. "The Generation and Control of 1.5 Megawatts of RF Power for the Trium Cyclotron." British Columbia, 1975.

4507
Dawson, Graham Elliott. "A Dynamic Test Model for Power System Stability and Control Studies." British Columbia, 1970. [University of British Columbia station/Station de l'Université de Colombie-Britannique]

4508
Giovando, Lawrence Frank. "Some Aspects of the Optical Turbidity of British Columbia Inlet Waters." British Columbia, 1960.

4509
Joy, Christopher Stewart. "Water Quality Modelling in Estuaries." British Columbia, 1974. [Fraser River Estuary/Estuaire de la rivière Fraser]

4510
Keevil, Norman Bell, Jr. "Exploration at the Craigmont Mine, British Columbia." California, Berkeley, 1965.

4511
Koers, Dirk Antonie. "Studies of the Control and Operation of the Aerobic Digestion Process Applied to Waste Activated Sludges at Low Temperatures." British Columbia, 1979.

4512
Law, Tean Chie. "Deformations of Earth Dams During Construction." Alberta, 1975. [Mica Dam/Barrage de Mica]

4513
Nixon, Charles Donald. "The Design of Light Industrial Buildings." Alberta, 1979.

4514
Snead, David Edward. "Creep Rupture of Saturated Undisturbed Clays." British Columbia, 1970.

Great Lakes/Grands Lacs

4515
Chieh, Shih-Huang. "Development of an Ice Transport Simulation Model for the Ice Regime of Lake Erie." SUNY, Buffalo, 1981.

4516
Chien, Calvin Chih-Ching. "Chloride Build-Up and Control in Lake Erie." SUNY, Buffalo, 1974.

4517
Dischel, Robert S. "Longshore Currents and Diffusion at the Shore of Lake Ontario." New York, 1975.

4518
Gedney, Richard T. "Numerical Calculations of the Wind-Driven Currents in Lake Erie." Case Western Reserve, 1971.

4519
Gélinas, Pierre J. "Contributions to the Study of Erosion Along the North Shore of Lake Erie." Western Ontario, 1974.

4520
Hale, Alan MacDougall. "Thermal Oscillations at Douglas Point, Lake Huron." Waterloo, 1968.

4521
Li, Chih-Yen. "Hydraulic Model Study of Surface and Subsurface Wind-Driven Currents in Lake Ontario." SUNY, Buffalo, 1974.

4522
Lien, San-Lang. "Circulation Patterns in Lake Superior." Wisconsin, 1973.

4523
Quinn, Frank Hugh. "Quantitative Dynamic Mathematical Models for Great Lakes Research." Michigan, 1971.

4524
Stoughton, Herbert Warren. "Investigations of the Accuracy of Water Level Transfer to Determine Geodetic Elevations in Lake Ontario." Michigan, 1980.

4525
Wake, Akio. "Development of Thermodynamic Simulation Model for the Ice Regime of Lake Erie." SUNY, Buffalo, 1977.

4526
Yu, Shaw-Lei. "A Stochastic Approach to the Study of Evaporation from Lake Ontario." Cornell, 1968.

Manitoba

4527
Newbury, Robert William. "The Nelson River: A Study of Subarctic River Processes." Johns Hopkins, 1968.

4528
Sharma, Satish Chandra. "Models of Residential Location Distribution and Land Development Proposals." Manitoba, 1978.

4529
Valhappan, Palaniappan. "Non-Linear Stress-Deformation Analyses of Lake Agassiz Clays Using Finite Element Method." Manitoba, 1974.

Maritimes Provinces/Provinces maritimes

General Items/Ouvrages généraux

4530
Ellis, David William Henry. "Scheduling a Fleet of Vehicles to Maintain Inventories." Toronto, 1978.
Fleming, Daryl Stanley. See No./Voir no 2252

New Brunswick/Nouveau-Brunswick

4531
Goel, Madan Kumar. "Automated Photogrammetric Procedures for Location and Design of Highways." New Brunswick, 1975.

Newfoundland/Terre-Neuve

4532
Aboul-Ela, Mohamed Tawfik. "Towards a Methodology for Evaluating Transport Policies: A Case Study - The Newfoundland Link." New Brunswick, 1981.

4533
Benson, Raymond Philip. "Rock Mechanics Aspects in the Design of the Churchill Falls Underground Powerhouse, Labrador." Illinois, 1970.
Chari, Tuppal Ramanuja. See No./Voir no 4471

4534
Neff, Thomas Louis. "Rock Mechanics Observations Concerning the Behavior of the Churchill Falls Underground Powerhouse, Labrador." Illinois, 1972.

Nova Scotia/Nouvelle-Écosse

4535
Duncan, Michael A. "Correlation of Field and Laboratory Evidence of Alkali-Silica Reactivity in Nova Scotia Concrete." Nova Scotia Technical College, 1971.

4536
Notley, Keith Roger. "Analysis of the Springfield Mine Disaster (October 23, 1958)." Queen's, 1980.

Northwest Territories/Territoires du Nord-Ouest

4537
Freeman, Nelson Graham Stephen. "Measurement and Modelling of Fresh Water Plumes Under an Ice Cover." Waterloo, 1982. [Hudson Bay, La Grande Winter Plume and/et Great Whale Plume]

4538
Stolle, Dieter Franz Eugen. "The Finite Element Modelling of Flow and Instability of Large Ice Masses." McMaster, 1982. [Erebus Glacier]

Ontario

Bello, Richard Lawrence. See No./Voir no 69

4539
Brook, Roger Charles. "Design of Multistage Grain Dryers." Michigan State, 1977.

4540
De Martinecourt, Jean-Pierre. "A Critical Experimental and Numerical Analysis of the Performance of the Bore Hole Shear Technique in Sensitive clays." Carleton, 1981.

4541
Deschenes, Jean Hughes. "Bearing Capacity of Footings Close to Slopes of Cohesionless Soil." Ottawa, 1978.

4542
Dodds, Robert Brian. "Stress Wave Propagation in Prepared Clay Specimens Consultation at the University of Waterloo Library." Waterloo, 1969.

4543
Gill, Ajit Singh. "A Study of Cohesion in Terms of Effective Stresses for Some Ontario Clays." Toronto, 1968.

Gray, Andrew Ross. See No./Voir no 4474

4544
Haddad, Parviz. "A Multivariable-Statistical Approach to the Evaluation of the Undrained Behaviour of Clays." Toronto, 1977. [Willard, Ontario]

Hale, Alan Mac Dougall. See No./Voir no 4520

4545
Hashish, Mahmoud Galal. "Wind Response of Hyperbolic Cooling Towers." Western Ontario, 1973. [Experiment at University of Western Ontario/ Expérience à l'Université Western Ontario]

4546
Jackman, Harold William. "Scheduling of Construction Projects Under Conditions of Capital Rationing Using a Goal Programming Approach." Toronto, 1972. [Ontario Hospital Commission]

4547
Jenkins, Allan Laurence. "Optimal Location of Facilities for Recycling Municipal Solid Waste in Southern Ontario." Toronto, 1979.

4548
Joseph, Jacob R. "Probability Models of Outdoor Recreation in Ontario." Waterloo, 1972.

4549
Karan, Mehmet A. "Municipal Pavement Management System." Waterloo, 1977. [Waterloo]

4550
Kassem, Atef M. "Development and Application of Simultaneous Routing Model for Dual Drainag Systems." Ottawa, 1982.

4551
Kim, Yung Duk. "Deformation Characteristics of th St. Clair Clay Till." Western Ontario, 1970.

4552
Lau, Ka Ching. "Horizontal Drains in Clay Slopes. Toronto, 1983.

4553
Law, Kum Tim. "Analysis of Embankments in Sensi tive Clays." Western Ontario, 1975.

4554
Lin, Kwan-Chow. "Significance of Temperature in th Activated Sludge Process." Toronto, 1976 [Toronto]

Martell, David Leigh. See No./Voir no 11747

4555
Metge, Michel. "Thermal Cracks in Lake Ice. Queen's, 1977.

4556
Mohsen, Mohammed Farrukh Neyaz. "Gas Migratio from Sanitary Landfalls and Associated Problems. Waterloo, 1975.

4557
Morrall, John Frankland. "Work Trip Distribution an Modal Split in the Metropolitan Toronto Region. Waterloo, 1971.

4558
Newkirk, Ross Thomas. "A Computer-Based Plannir System to Optimize Environmental Resource Allc cations when Locating Utilities." Western Ontari 1976. [Ontario Hydro/Hydro Ontario]

Nixon, Charles Donald. See No./Voir no 4513

4559
Ogunbadejo, Tajudeen Adetayo. "Physico-Chemistr of Weathered Clay Crust Formation." Wester Ontario, 1973.

4560
Paciga, John Joseph. "Trace Element Characteriza tion and Size Distributions of Atmospheric Part culate Matter in Toronto." Toronto, 1975.

Paroschy, John Henry. See No./Voir no 77

4561
Parsons, Clifford Barry. "Experimental Investigatic of the Physical Mechanisms of Dryout in a Hig Pressure Steam-Water System." Waterloo, 197 [Chalk River Nuclear Laboratories of Atom Energy/Laboratoires nucléaires d'Énergie atomiqu Canada à Chalk River]

4562
Robinson, John Bertram Leonard. "Market Segmer Analysis of Worktrip Transport to the Ottaw Central Business District." New Brunswick, 1982.

Sharma, Satish Chandra. See No./Voir no 4528

4563
Sharma, Tribeni Chandra. "A Discrete Dynamic Mod of Watershed Sediment Yield." Guelph, 1977.

Said, Galal Mostafa. See No./Voir no 2263

4564
Surgenor, Brian William. "Development and Validatic of a Nuclear Simulator for Human Performanc Measurement in the Task of Fault Management Queen's, 1983.

4565
Tay, Joo-Hwa. "Study of Settling Characteristics of Physical-Chemical Flocs in Sedimentation Tanks." Toronto, 1976. [Research at University of Toronto Laboratories, Sarnia, West Windsor Treatment Plants and Burlington Canadian Center for Inland Waters Pilot Plant/Recherche aux laboratoires de l'Université de Toronto, aux usines de traitement de Sarnia et de l'ouest de Windsor et à l'usine pilote du Centre canadien des eaux intérieures à Burlington]

4566
Taylor, Iain Duncan Stewart. "A Priority Queuing Mode to Measure Performance in the Ontario Ambulance System." Toronto, 1976.

4567
Tywoniuk, Nick. "A Study of the Bed Load Transport of a Gravel-Bold River." Ottawa, 1979.

4568
Vivian, Robert Evans. "A Chemical Engineering Study of Sudbury Ore Processes." Columbia, 1933.

4569
Whiteley, Hugh Russell. "The Origins and Chemical Composition of Steamflow in Blue Springs Creek, Ontario." Guelph, 1975.

4570
Williams, David Robert. "Riverbank Stability at Ottawa." Queen's, 1979. [Ottawa River/Rivière Outaouais]

4571
Yuen, Clement Ming-Kai. "Rock-Structure Time Interaction in Lined Circular Tunnels in High Horizontal Stress Field." Western Ontario, 1979.

Quebec/Québec

Baass, Karsten Goetz. See No./Voir no 2246

4572
Bhattacharya Ashim Kumar. "Hydrologic and Economic Models for Subsurface Drainage." McGill, 1977.

4573
Djamgouz, Okay Tewfik. "Relationship Between Ferromagnetic Particles and Airborne Chrysotile Fibres in the Asbestos Mines and Mills of Quebec." McGill, 1983.

4574
Foroud, Nader. "A Flood Hydrograph Simulation Model for Watersheds in Southern Quebec." McGill, 1978.

4575
Hwang, Chung-Yung. "Size and Shape of Airborne Asbestos Fibres in Mining and Mineral Processing Environments." McGill, 1981.

4576
Julien, Pierre. "Prédiction d'apport solide pluvial et nival dans les cours d'eau nordiques à partir du ruissellement superficiel." Laval, 1983.

4577
Khosla, Vijay Kumar. "Behavior of Dry Ottawa Sand Under Cyclic Loading." Ohio State, 1972.

4578
Lauzier, Louis. "L'analyse polarographique et polaro-métrique de l'oxygène dissoue dans l'eau de mer et les eaux de rivières." Laval, 1946. [Baie des Chaleurs]

4579
Lee, Chack Fan. "Analysis of Progressive Failure in Clay Slopes." Western Ontario, 1972. [St. Lawrence and Ottawa valleys/Vallées du Saint-Laurent et de l'Outaouais]

4580
Tabba, Mohammad Myassar. "Risk Analysis of Slope Stability with Special Reference to Canadian Sensitive Clays." McGill, 1979. [Site of/Site de Saint-Jean Vianney]

Saskatchewan

4581
Arinze, Edwin A. "Simulation and Experimental Evaluation of a Solar Assisted Energy Conserving Greenhouse." Saskatchewan, 1981.

4582
Dyck, John Henry. "The Detection of Subsurface Resistive Zones: A Study in Groundwater Geophysics in Saskatchewan." Saskatchewan, 1969.

4583
Landine, Robert Charles. "Predictions of Dissolved Oxygen Levels in the South Saskatchewan River." Saskatchewan, 1970.

4584
Mamandur, Rangaiah Chetty. "Efficient Methods of Steady State Performance Analysis and Transmission Network Planning in Electric Power Systems." Calgary, 1977.

4585
Nasr, Mostafa Saeed. "Chemical Color Removal from the Caustic Extraction Effluent of a Pulp and Paper Mill Bleach Plant." Saskatchewan, 1976.

GEOGRAPHY/GÉOGRAPHIE

Geographical studies is one of the areas in which scholars have demonstrated a growing interest during the last 15 years. The University of Chicago approved the first doctorate in this discipline in 1914. Output from American universities grew slowly until the 1960's and 1970's. Similarly, dissertations from Canadian universities were limited until the 1970's, when a dramatic increase occured. Of the universities producing 20 titles or more, Toronto is the leader with British Columbia, McGill, Western Ontario, McMaster, and Alberta following in that order. In the United States, among the 37 universities producing dissertations in this classification, 17 produced only one title. the Universities of Michigan (15), Washington (Seattle) (13), Clark (13), and Chicago (12) are the major contributors. Twenty-six titles were produced in Great Britain from nine universities, with London approving nine. In addition to general items, regional geography, economic geography, historical geography, political geography, and urban geography are the main headings.

La géographie représente l'un des importants secteurs pour lesquels les chercheurs ont montré un intérêt au cours des 15 dernières années. L'Université de Chicago a accordé le premier doctorat en cette discipline en 1914. Dans les universités américaines, le nombre des thèses a augmenté lentement jusque vers les années 1960 et 1970. De même dans les universités canadiennes, il n'y a pas eu de progrès notable jusqu'aux années 1970, année à partir de laquelle la production a beaucoup augmenté. Parmi les universités produisant 20 ouvrages ou plus, celle de Toronto se distingue une fois encore, suivie, dans l'ordre, par les universités de la Colombie-Britannique, McGill, Western Ontario, McMaster et de l'Alberta. Aux États-Unis, des 37 universités qui ont produit des thèses en ce domaine, 17 n'ont qu'un seul ouvrage à faire valoir. Les universités du Michigan (15), de Washington (Seattle) (13), Clark (13) et de Chicago (12) sont celles qui ont le plus contribué à la production de thèses en géographie. Vingt-six thèses ont été présentées en Grande-Bretagne dans neuf universités; Londres, pour sa part, en a approuvé neuf. Aux études d'ordre général, il faut ajouter des travaux sur la géographie régionale, économique, historique, politique et urbaine.

CANADIAN GEOGRAPHERS/ GÉOGRAPHES CANADIENS

4586
Diubaldo, Richard Julio. "The Canadian Career of Vilhjalmur Stefansson." Western Ontario, 1973.
4587
Tomkins, George Strong. "Griffith Taylor and Canadian Geography." Washington, Seattle, 1966.

GENERAL ITEMS/OUVRAGES GÉNÉRAUX

4588
Barker, Mary Lynn. "The Structure and Content of Environmental Cognitions: An Exploratory Study of Evaluations of Air Pollution Among Five Professional and Disciplinary Student Groups." Toronto, 1972.
4589
Deshaies, Laurent. "Analyse spatiale de la croissance et de la décroissance des villes minières canadiennes." Laval, 1978.
4590
Gagnon, Pierre. "Theoretical Investigation on Step by Step Procedures for the Adjustment of Large Horizontal Geodetic Networks." New Brunswick, 1976. [Includes geodetic surveys of Canada/ Incluant des études géodésiques du Canada]
4591
Goodchild, Michael Frank. "The Generation of Small-scale Relief Features of Eroded Limestone: A Study of Erosional Scallops." McMaster, 1970.
4592
Pijawka, K. David. "A Comparative Study of the Regulation of Pesticide Hazards in Canada and the United States." Clark, 1983.

4593
Rowbotham, Peter Frederick. "Trespass Law and Territoriality: A Geographic and Evolutionary Perspective." Simon Fraser, 1979.
4594
Taruvinga, Peter Pangarirai. "Geomorphic Cartography: The Canadian Perspective: An Assessment of Selected Landform Mapping Approaches in Canada." Waterloo, 1982.
4595
Turner, Howard. "The Use of Shadows on Aerial Photographs to Obtain Ground Parameters of Buildings by Image Processing." Waterloo, 1975.
4596
Young, Gordon James. "Glacier Mass-Balance and Terrain Shape: A Methodological Study." McGill, 1974.

AGRICULTURAL GEOGRAPHY/ GÉOGRAPHIE AGRICOLE

See also Agricultural: Agricultural Geography/Voir aussi Agriculture: Géographie agricole

REGIONAL GEOGRAPHY/GÉOGRAPHIE RÉGIONALE

General Items/Ouvrages généraux

4597
Ewing, Gordon Orr. "An Analogy of Consumer Space Preferences Using the Method of Paired Comparisons." McMaster, 1971.
Langdon, George L. See No./Voir no 4697
Pijawka, K. David. See No./Voir no 4592
4598
Wood, Colin James Barry. "The Diffusion of Innovations Requiring Community Decisions: A Geographical Analysis." McMaster, 1971.
Young, Mary McPherson. See No./Voir no 371

Eastern Canada/Est du Canada

Catellier, Hubert. See No./Voir no 4990

Central Canada/Centre du Canada

Newbury, Robert William. See No./Voir no 4527
4599
Sorenson, Curtis James. "Interrelationships Between Soils and Climate and Between Paleosols and Paleoclimates: Forest/Tundra Ecotone, North Central Canada." Wisconsin, 1973.

Western Canada/Ouest du Canada

4600
Owens, Ian Francis. "Alpine Midflowers in the Niger Pass Area, Canadian Rocky Mountains." Toronto, 1973.

Great Lakes/Grands Lacs

4601
Kreutzwiser, Reid Douglas. "An Evaluation of Lake Erie Shoreline Flood and Erosion Hazard Policy." Western Ontario, 1978.

4602
Loy, William G. "The Coastal Geomorphology of Western Lake Superior." Chicago, 1963.

4603
Needham, Roger David. "Newspaper Response to the Coastal Zone Hazards of Lake Erie: A Canadian-American Comparison." Waterloo, 1982.

4604
Pease, Steven Robert. "Determination and Mapping of January Isolation Patterns over Lake Ontario: Testing a New Research Methodology." Wisconsin, Milwaukee, 1978.

British Columbia/Colombie-Britannique

4605
Archibold, Oliver William. "Vegetation Recovery Following Pollution Control at Trail, British Columbia." Simon Fraser, 1975.

4606
Cawker, Kenneth B. "Historical Dynamics of Artemisio tridentata Nutt, in Southern British Columbia." Simon Fraser, 1979.

4607
Chapman, John Doneric. "Land Classification in British Columbia: A Review and Appraisal of the Land Utilization Research and Survey Division." Washington, Seattle, 1958.

4608
Dearden, Philip. "Visual Landscape Quality: Some Problems in Landscape Perception and Evaluation of the Saanich Peninsula, British Columbia." Victoria, 1978.

4609
Evans, Ian Sylvester. "The Geomorphometry and Asymmetry of Glaciated Mountains, with Reference to the Bridge River District, British Columbia." Cambridge, 1974.

4610
Fitzharris, Brian Blair. "Some Accumulation and Deposition on a West Coast Midlatitude Mountain." British Columbia, 1975. [Mt. Seymour/Mont Seymour]

4611
Hamilton, William George. "Utilizing Humanistic Field Methods in Objectifying Sense of Place: A Scenic Landscape Analysis in the North Okanagan Valley, British Columbia." Oregon, 1980.

Hardwick, Walter Gordon. See No./Voir no 1809

Hayter, Roger. See No./Voir no 1810

Heaver, Trevor David. See No./Voir no 2254

4612
Jackson, Edgar Lionel. "Response to Earthquake Hazard: Factors Related to the Adoption of Adjustments by Residents of Three Earthquake Areas of the West Coast of North America." Toronto, 1974.

Kerr, Donald. See No./Voir no 4999

4613
Lake, David Wayne. "A Study of Landscape Evolution in the Crowsnest Pass Region, 1898-1921." Oklahoma, 1972.

4614
Marsh, John Stuart. "Man, Landscape, and Recreation in Glacier National Park, British Columbia, 1880 to Present." Calgary, 1972.

4615
Minghi, Julian Vincent. "Some Aspects of the Impact of an International Boundary on Spatial Patterns: An Analysis of the Pacific Coast Lowland Region on the Canada-United States Boundary." Washington, Seattle, 1962.

4616
Nanson, Gerald Charles. "Channel Migration, Floodplain Formation and Vegetation Succession on a Meandering River Floodplain in N.E. British Columbia, Canada." Simon Fraser, 1977.

O'Riordan, Jonathan. See No./Voir no 85

4617
Ross, William Michael. "Oil Pollution as a Developing International Problem: A Study of the Puget Sound and Strait of Georgia Regions of Washington and British Columbia." Washington, Seattle, 1972.

4618
Rothwell, David Colin. "Cognitive Mapping of the Home Environment." British Columbia, 1975.

Rydant, Albert Louis. See No./Voir no 1052

4619
Ryder, Jane Margaret. "Alluvial Fans of Post-Glacial Environments Within British Columbia." British Columbia, 1970.

4620
Schreier, Hanspeter. "Chemical Terrain, Variability: A Geomorphological Approach Using Numerical and Remote Sensing Techniques." British Columbia, 1976.

4621
Sewell, William Robert Derrick. "Economic and Institutional Aspects of Adjustment to Floods in the Lower Fraser Valley." Washington, Seattle, 1964.

4622
Suckling, Philip Wayne. "A Solar Radiation Model and an Analysis of Synoptic Solar Radiation Regimes in British Columbia." British Columbia, 1977.

4623
Taylor, Stuart Martin. "Alternative Approaches to the Analysis of Consumer Spatial Behaviour." British Columbia, 1974. [Vancouver]

4624
Wankiewicz, Anthony Cyril. "Water Percolation Within a Deep Snowpack-Field Investigation at a Site on Mt. Seymour, British Columbia." British Columbia, 1976.

4625
Waylen, Peter Robert. "Analysis of High Flow in the Fraser River Catchment, British Columbia." McMaster, 1982.

Weir, Thomas R. See No./Voir no 86

4626
Weirich, Frank A. "Sedimentation Processes in a High Altitude Proglacial Lake in Southwestern British Columbia." Toronto, 1982.

4627
Whitaker, Roy Alexander. "An Algorithm for Estimating the Medians of a Weighted Graph Subject to Side Constraints, and an Application to Rural Hospital Location in British Columbia." British Columbia, 1971.

4628
Yap, David Hamilton. "Sensible Heat Fluxes Measured in and near Vancouver, B.C." British Columbia, 1973.

Maritime Provinces/Provinces maritimes

New Brunswick/Nouveau-Brunswick

4629
Davidson-Arnott, Robin George Denison. "Form Movement and Sedimentological Characteristics of Wave-Formed Bars: A Study of Their Role in the Nearshore Equilibrium, Kouchibouquac Bay, New Brunswick." Toronto, 1975.

4630
De Jonge, Coen K. "Glacial Physiography of the St. John's River Valley, New Brunswick." Clark, 1951.

4631
Mittler, Peter Robert. "Storm Related Sediment Flux and Equilibrium in a Barred Nearshore Kouchibouquac Bay, New Brunswick, Canada." Toronto, 1981.

Nova Scotia/Nouvelle-Écosse

4632
Burman, Savitri G. "Geographical Problems of Land Use in Nova Scotia." Clark, 1951.

4633
Clarke, Roger Mervyn. "In Them Days: The Breakdown of a Traditional Fishing Economy in an English Village on the Gaspé Coast." McGill, 1973.

4634
Cox, Richard Edmund. "The Louisbourg Quay." Idaho, 1969.

4635
Jenkins, William Angus. "Land Use Study, Digby County, Nova Scotia." Harvard, 1961.

4636
Powell, Grace Lillian. "A Geography Analysis of Recent Trade Patterns of Halifax and Saint John." Pennsylvania State, 1968.

4637
Russell, H. Harrison. "Cape Breton Island: The Land and the People." Clark, 1926.

4638
Sitwell, Oswald Francis George. "Land Use and Settlement Patterns in Pictou County, Nova Scotia." Toronto, 1968.

Prince Edward Island/Île-du-Prince-Édouard

4639
Armon, John William. "The Dynamics of a Barrier Island Chain, Prince Edward Island, Canada." McMaster, 1975.

4640
Stilgenbauer, Floyd Adlai. "The Geography of Prince Edward Island." Michigan, 1929.

Newfoundland and Labrador/Terre-Neuve et Labrador

Newfoundland/Terre-Neuve

4641
Brookes, Ian Alfred. "The Glaciation of Southwestern Newfoundland." McGill, 1970.

Dean, Vera K. "Newfoundland." Clark, 1949.

Head, Clifford Grant. See No./Voir no 4858

Ibele, Oscar H., Jr. See No./Voir no 4887

4642
Mednis, Robert Janis. "A Phytogeographical Analysis of the Occurrence of Vegetation Patterns on Fogo Island, Newfoundland-Labrador, Canada." Boston University, 1971.

4643
Tucker, Christopher Marshall. "Late Quaternary Events on the Burin Peninsula, Newfoundland, with Reference to the Islands of St. Pierre et Miquelon (France)." McMaster, 1979.

Labrador

4644
Drummond, Robert Norman. "The Glacial Morphology of the Cambrian Lake Area, Labrador-Ungava." McGill, 1965.

4645
Johnson, John P. "Deglaciation and Emergence of the Webb Bayport Manvers Run Area of Labrador." McGill, 1964.

4646
Loeken, Olav H. "Deglaciation and Post-Glacial Emergence of Northernmost Labrador." McGill, 1962.

4647
Morrison, Alistair. "Glacial Geomorphology of the Churchill Falls Area, Labrador." McGill, 1967.

The Arctic, Northwest Territories and the Yukon/ Arctique, Territoires du Nord-Ouest et Yukon

The Arctic/Arctique

4648
Hodgson, J.M.D. "Arctic Consciousness in Nineteenth Century England: The Arctic Journals of John Franklin and the Franklin Searchers." Essex, 1974.

4649
Jenness, John L. "Oceanography and Physiography of the Canadian Western, Arctic." Clark, 1951.

4650
Parkinson, Claire Lucille. "A Numerical Simulation of the Annual Cycle of Sea Ice in the Arctic and Antarctic." Ohio State, 1977.

4651
Ridge, Frank G. "General Principles in the Planning (Development) of Sub-Arctic Settlements." McGill, 1962.

4652
Robinson, John L. "The Canadian Eastern Arctic: A Geographic Study." Clark, 1946.

4653
Walker, Harley Jesse. "The Changing Nature of Man's Quest for Food and Water as Related to Snow Ice and Permafrost in the American Arctic." Louisiana State, 1960.

Northwest Territories/Territoires du Nord-Ouest

4654
Adams, William Peter. "Studies of Ablation and Runoff in an Arctic Glacier." McGill, 1966.

4655
Andrews, J.T. "Glacial Geomorphological Studies in North Central Baffin Island, Northwest Territories, Canada." Nottingham, 1965.

4656
Banting, Douglas Ralph. "Characterization of Arctic Soils: Interrelationships with Site and Vegetation." Western Ontario, 1982.

4657
Barnett, David Martin. "Glacial Geomorphology in a Sub-Polar Proglacial Lake Basin: A Process-Response Model." Western Ontario, 1977.

Bone, Robert Martin. See No./Voir no 4813

4658
Brown, Anton. "Fracture Analysis in Opemiska Mine Area." Queen's, 1971.

4659
Brown, Roger James Evan. "Permafrost in Canada: Its Effects on Developments in a Region of Marginal Human Activity." Clark, 1961.

4660
Crane, Robert George. "Synoptic Analysis of Arctic Ice-Atmosphere Interactions Using Satellite Microwave Data." Colorado, 1981. [Beaufort-Chukchi Sea sectors and the Arctic/Secteurs de la mer de Beaufort-Chukchi et l'Arctique]

4661
Dyke, Arthur Silas. "Quaternary Geomorphology, Glacial Chronology and Climatic and Sea-Level History of Southwestern Cumberland Peninsula, Baffin Island, Northwest Territories, Canada." Colorado, 1977.

4662
Feldman, Uri. "Predicting the Motions of Detached Ice Floes." McMaster, 1978.

4663
Fraser, John Keith. "The Physiography of the Boothia Peninsula Area, Northwest Territories: A Study in Terrain Analysis and Air Photo Interpretation of an Arctic Area." Clark, 1964.

4664
Gell, William Alan. "Underground Ice in Permafrost, MacKenzie Delta-Tuktoyaktuk Peninsula, N.W.T." British Columbia, 1976.

4665
Gill, Donald Allen. "Vegetation and Environment in the MacKenzie River Delta, Northwest Territories: A Study in Sub-Arctic Ecology." British Columbia, 1971.

4666
Green, Jerry Edward. "A Functional Analysis of the Populated Places in Canada's Yukon Territory and the Mackenzie District of the Northwest Territories, 1898-1971: A Study in Settlement Persistence." North Carolina, 1976.

4667
Harry, David G. "Aspects of the Permafrost Geomorphology of Southwest Banks Island, Western Canadian Arctic." Ottawa, 1982.

4668
Kay, Paul Allan. "Post-Glacial History of Vegetation and Climate in the Forest-Tundra Transition Zone Dubawnt Lake Region, Northwest Territories, Canada." Wisconsin, 1976.

Kerby, Norma J. See No./Voir no 11550

4669
Kerfoot, Denis Edward. "The Geomorphology and Permafrost Conditions of Garry Island, N.W.T." British Columbia, 1970.

4670
Kidd, Desmond Fife. "Bear Lake-Coppermine River Area." Princeton, 1932.

4671
King, Roger Hutton. "Periglaciation on Devon Island, Northwest Territories." Saskatchewan, 1969.

4672
Lewkowicz, Antoni G. "A Study of Slopewash Processes in the Continuous Permafrost Zone, Banks Island, Western Canadian Arctic." Ottawa, 1981.

Mayes, Robert Gregory. See No./Voir no 613

4673
Mercer, John Hainsworth. "The Physiography and Glaciology of Southernmost Baffin Island." McGill, 1954.

4674
Pearson, Roger William. "Resource Management Strategies and Regional Viability: A Study of the Great Slave Lake Region, Canada." Illinois, 1970.

4675
Robitaille, Benoît. "Recherches sur la géomorphologie du sud-est de l'Île Cornwallis, Territoires du Nord-ouest, Recherches sur certains problèmes de la Péninsule Foxe, Île de Baffin, Territoires du Nord-Ouest." Laval, 1959.

4676
Sim, Victor W. "The Physiography of Melville Peninsula, N.W.T." McGill, 1962.

4677
Simpson, Samuel John. "The York Factory Area, Hudson Bay." Manitoba, 1972.

4678
Smith, Michael William. "Factors Affecting the Distribution of Permafrost Mackenzie Delta, N.W.T." British Columbia, 1973.

4679
Taylor, Andrew. "Physiography of the Queen Elizabeth Islands in the Canadian Arctic Archipelago." Montréal, 1956.

4680
Thompson, Hugh R. "Pangnirtung Pass, Baffin Island: An Exploratory Regional Geomorphology." McGill, 1954.

Usher, Peter Joseph, Jr. See No./Voir no 4818
Wenzel, George William. See No./Voir no 632

4681
Wolforth, John Raymond. "'Dual Allegiance' in the Mackenzie Delta, N.W.T.: Aspects of the Evolution and Contemporary Spatial Structure of a Northern Community." British Columbia, 1971.

Yukon

4682
Bryan, Merwyn Leonard. "Sedimentation in Glacially Fed Kluane Lake, Yukon Territory, Canada." Michigan, 1971.

Forbes, Donald Lawrence. See No./Voir no 11979

4683
Gray, James Telfer. "Processes and Rates of Development of Talus Slopes and Protalus Rock Glaciers in the Ogilvie and Wernecke Mountains, Yukon Territory." McGill, 1971.

Green, Jerry Edward. See No./Voir no 4666

4684
Koroscil, Paul Michael. "The Changing Landscape of the Yukon Territory and the Settlement of Whitehorse." Michigan, 1970.

4685
Laatsch, William Ganfield. "Yukon Mining Settlement: An Examination of Three Communities." Alberta, 1972.

4686
McCloy, James Murl. "Morphologic Characteristics of the Blow River Delta, Yukon Territory, Canada." Louisiana State, 1969.

4687
Nickling, William G. "Eolian Sediment Transport, Slime River Valley, Yukon Territory." Ottawa, 1976.

4688
Price, Larry Wayne. "Morphology and Ecology of Solifluction Lobe Development — Ruby Range, Yukon Territory." Illinois, 1970.

Ontario

Bowles, Jane Margaret. See No./Voir no 10459

4689
Dean, William George. "Physiography and Vegetation of the Albany River Map Area, Northern Ontario: An Aerial Photograph Reconnaissance." McGill, 1959.

4690
Duckworth, Peter Battersby. "Paleocurrent Trend in the Latest Outwash at the Western End of the Oak Ridge Moraine, Ontario." Toronto, 1975.

Grainger, Robert N. See No./Voir no 6776

4691
Hallman, Donald Emerson. "The Identification and Comparison of Preferences for Recreation Locations: The Example of Ontario Provincial Park Camps." Michigan State, 1973.

4692
Hathout, Salah Ahmed. "Physio-Chemical, Mineralogical and Micromorphological Studies on Alfisol and Spodosol Profiles from Southern Ontario." McMaster, 1972.

4693
Helleiner, Frederick Maria. "A Geographical Interpretation of Recreation Waterways, with Special Reference to the Trent-Severn Waterway." Western Ontario, 1972.

4694
Hewings, John Meredith. "Environmental Indices an Public Attitudes: The Case of the Ontario A Pollution Index." Toronto, 1975.

4695
Hope, Spencer Albert Charles. "Spatial Analysis Socio-Political Attributes: The Haldimand-Norfol Region in Southwestern Ontario." Western Ontario, 1977.

4696
Lam, Nina Siri-Ngan. "Methods and Problems of Are Interpolation." Western Ontario, 1980. [London]

4697
Langdon, George L. "The Mesabi Iron Ore District an the Northern Anthracite Field." Clark, 1952.

4698
Lee, Chun-Fen. "The Middle Grand River Valley Ontario: A Study in Regional Geography Toronto, 1943.

4699
Liu, Kam-Biu. "Postglacial Vegetational History Northern Ontario: A Palynological Study Toronto, 1982.

4700
Logan, Roderick MacKenzie. "The Geography Intermunicipal Relations: A Case Study in th Grimsby Area, Ontario." McMaster, 1973.

4701
Lucas, Robert Charles. "The Quetico-Superior Are Recreational Use in Relation to Capacity." Minn sota, 1962.

4702
MacIver, Ian. "Urban Water Supply Alternatives: Pe ception and Choice in the Grand Basin, Ontario Chicago, 1970.

4703
Marshall, John Urquhart. "The Analysis of Centr Place Systems: A Study of Geographic Metho ology." Toronto, 1968.

Massami, Bryan Hazlewood. See No./Voir no 179

4704
McArthur, Neil Max. "River To Seaway." Michiga 1955.

Morgan, Christopher L. See No./Voir no 263

4705
Morin, Fernand. "Utilité d'une banque de données gé scientifiques dans l'aménagement d'un territoir rôle de la cartographie géotechnique automatisée Ottawa, 1978.

4706
Morrison, Neil Farguharson. "Essex County, Provinc of Ontario: A Geographical Study." Michiga 1944.

4707
Paul, Alexander Humphrey. "Relationships of Weathe to Summer Attendance at Some Outdoor Recre tion Facilities in Canada." Alberta, 1971.

4708
Rees, David L. "Streamwater Solute Variations in Partially Urbanized Watershed at North Ba Ontario." Ottawa, 1982.

4709
Richards, John Howard Byron. "Land Use and Settl ment on the Fringe of the Shield in Souther Ontario." Toronto, 1954.

Roberts, Arthur Cecil Batt. See No./Voir no 881

4710
Rumney, George R. "The Settlement of the Nipissing Passageway." Michigan, 1947.

4711
Sangal, Beni Prasad. "Estimation of Evaporation and Evapotranspiration: A Comparative Study of the Budyko Approach with Special Reference to Southern Ontario." Western Ontario, 1973.

4712
Saunderson, Houston Clements. "Eskerine Sedimentation: An Analysis of Hypotheses and an Empirical Text." Toronto, 1974.

4713
Subins, Gunar. "Multivariate Analysis and Regional Hierarchies of Environmental Factors Influencing Streamflow in River Basins of Southern Ontario." Western Ontario, 1974.

4714
Tapper, Gerald Oscar. "Spatial Characteristics of Net Radiation and Its Components for Ontario." California, Riverside, 1978.

4715
Taylor, James Addison. "The Natural and Cultural Relationships of Tourist Outfitter's Camps in Northern Ontario." Illinois, 1962.

4716
Watson, James W. "The Geography of the Niagara Peninsula with Special Emphasis on Changes in Land Use and Settlement." Toronto, 1945.

4717
Welch, David Michael. "Slope Analysis and Evolution on Protected Lacustrine Bluffs." Western Ontario, Ontario, 1972. [Port Burwell-Lake Erie/Lac Érié]

4718
Wilkinson, Paul Frank. "Public Participation and Environmental Management: The Role of Public Participation and Public Interest Groups in Environmental Quality Management." Toronto, 1974.

4719
Wolfe, Roy Israel. "Recreational Land Use in Ontario." Toronto, 1956.

4720
Woodruff, James Frederick. "Present and Future Settlement in the Hearst-Nipigon Region." Michigan, 1952.

Prairie Provinces/Provinces des Prairies

General Items/Ouvrages généraux

4721
Oladipo, Emmanuel Olukayode. "On the Spatial and Temporal Characteristics of Drought in the Interior Plains of North America: A Statistical Analysis." Toronto, 1983.

4722
Spence, Edward Smith. "An Analysis of the Relationships of Selected Streamflow Characteristics to Physical Geographic Patterns in the Plains Area of the Canadian Prairie Provinces." Alberta, 1971.

Stubbs, G.M. See No./Voir no 423

4723
Vanderhill, Burke Gordon. "Settlement in the Forest Lands of Manitoba, Saskatchewan, and Alberta: A Geographical Analysis." Michigan, 1956.

Alberta

4724
Alley, Neville Foster. "The Quaternary History of Part of the Rocky Mountains, Foothills, Plains and Western Porcupine Hills, Southwestern Alberta." Calgary, 1972.

Barendregt, Rene W. See No./Voir no 5380

4725
Boydell, Anthony Nigel. "Multiple Glaciation in the Foothills, Rocky Mountain House Area, Alberta." Calgary, 1972.

Brewster, Gordon Ross. See No./Voir no 220

4726
Brown, Michael Joseph. "Karst Geomorphology and Hydrology of the Lower Maligne Basin, Jasper, Alberta." McMaster, 1970.

Cheng, Jacqueline Ruth. See No./Voir no 10449

4727
Jones, Stephen B. "Human Occupance of the Bow-Kicking Horse Region, Canadian Rocky Mountains." Harvard, 1934.

4728
Jost, Tadeusz P. "The Geographical Aspects of the North-Western Slopes of the Swan Hills." Montréal, 1956.

4729
Karlstrom, Eric Thor. "Late Cenozoic Soils of the Glacier and Waterton Parks Area, Northwestern Montana and Southwestern Alberta and Paleoclimatic Implications." Calgary, 1981.

4730
Keys, Charles Lawrence. "Spatial Reorganization in a Central Place System: An Alberta Case." Alberta, 1975.

4731
Laycock, Arleigh Howard. "A Physiographic Classification of Soils for Land Use Planning on the Eastern Slopes of the Canadian Rockies." Minnesota, 1957.

4732
Luckman, Brian Henry. "Scree Slope Characteristics and Associated Geomorphic Processes in Sunrise Valley, Jasper National Park, Alberta." McMaster, 1973.

Luk, Shiu-Hung. See No./Voir no 225

4733
McPherson, Harold James. "Morphology and Fluvial Processes of the Lower Red Deer Valley, Alberta." McGill, 1967.

4734
Rains, Robert Bruce. "Some Aspects of the Pluvial Geomorphology of the Whitemud Basin, Central Alberta." Alberta, 1969.

4735
Smith, Derald Glen. "Aggradation and Channel Braiding in the North Saskatchewan River, Alberta, Canada." Johns Hopkins, 1973.

4736

Stene, Lawrence Paul. "Holocene and Present Alluvial Investigations, Porcupine Hills, Southwestern Alberta." Western Ontario, 1976.

Manitoba

4737

Gill, Allison Margaret. "Residents' Images of Northern Canadian Resource Communities." Manitoba, 1982. [Thompson and/et Leaf Rapids]

4738

Lloyd, Trevor. "The Red River Valley of Manitoba: A Regional Study." Clark, 1940.

4739

Moehlman, Arthur Henry. "The Red River of the North." Michigan, 1932.

Newbury, Robert William. See No./Voir no 4527

4740

Pritchett, John P. "The Red River Settlement." Queen's, 1931.

4741

Ringrose, Susan Margaret. "The Sedimentology of Esker Deposits in Manitoba, with Particular Reference to Coarse Sediment Deposition, and Implications for the Late Glacial History of Manitoba." London, 1979.

Saskatchewan

4742

Bradwell, David. "The Sequence and Timing of Development of the Saskatchewan River Basin." Oregon, 1964.

4743

Duncan, Craig. "The Saskatchewan River Basin, Canada: A Geographical Appraisal of the Water Resources." Ohio State, 1955.

4744

Hodgins, Larry Edwin. "Morphology of the South Saskatchewan River Valley, Outlook to Saskatoon." Toronto, 1970.

4745

Linn, Hilareon Dewell. "Health Care in the Settled Portion of Saskatchewan: A Central Place System and Its Implications for Regionalization of Health Care Delivery." Saskatchewan, 1977.

4746

Rasid, Harunur. "The Effects of the Gardiner Dam on Geomorphic Processes and Morphology in the South Saskatchewan River Valley: Riverhurst to Outlook." Saskatchewan, 1975.

Quebec/Québec

4747

Allard, Michel. "Le rôle de la géomorphologue dans les inventaires bio-physiques: l'exemple de la région Gatineau-Lièvre." McGill, 1977.

4748

Bail, Pierre. "Problèmes géomorphologiques de l'englacement et de la transgression marine pléistocènes en Gaspésie sud-orientale." McGill, 1983.

4749

Beauregard, Ludger. "La Vallée du Richelieu." Montréal, 1957.

4750

Booth, John Derek. "Changing Forest Utilizati[on] Patterns in the Eastern Townships of Quebec, 18[ ] to 1930." McGill, 1972.

4751

Brière, Roger. "Géographie du tourisme au Québe[c] Montréal, 1967.

4752

Bussières, Paul. "Géographie de la côte-nord et de s[ ] arrière pays (province de Québec)." Laval, 1962.

4753

Clibbon, Peter. "Land Use Patterns in the Laurentia[ ] Between the Saint-Maurice and Rouge Valle[ ] (Quebec)." Laval, 1968.

4754

Cliche, Pierre. "Géographie de la pauvreté [ ] Québec." Laval, 1978.

4755

Dredge, Lynda Ann. "Quaternary Geomorphology [ ] the Quebec North Shore, Godbout to Sept-Ile[ ] Waterloo, 1977.

4756

Dubois, Jean-Marie. "Environnements quaternaires [ ] évolution postglaciaire d'une zone côtière en éme[r]sion en bordure sud du bouclier canadien: [ ] moyenne Côte-Nord du Saint-Laurent, Québe[c] Ottawa, 1980.

4757

Falaise, Noël. "Les Îles de la Madeleine, étude gé[o]graphique." Montréal, 1954.

4758

Fréchette, André B. "Étude sur les levés cadastra[ux] dans la province de Québec avec considérati[on] spéciale des méthodes photogrammétrique[ ] Laval, 1966.

4759

Glendinning, Robert Morton. "The Lake St. Je[an] Lowland, Province of Quebec." Michigan, 1933.

4760

Grosmaire, Jean-Louis. "L'immigration française [ ] Québec: essai de géographie sociale." Montré[al] 1982.

4761

Hardy, Léon H. "Contribution à l'étude géomorpho[lo]gique de la portion québécoise des basses terre[s] la baie de James." McGill, 1976.

Jones, Clarence Fielden. See No./Voir no 1206

4762

Lagarac, Daniel. "Étude géomorphologique Baises [ ] Hudsonie (Nouveau-Québec)." Laval, 1981.

4763

Lauriol, Bernard. "La géomorphologie quaternaire [ ] sud de l'Ungava." Montréal, 1982.

4764

MacPherson, Constance Joyce. "The Post-Champl[ain] Evolution of the Drainage Pattern of the Montr[eal] Lowland." McGill, 1966.

4765

Occhietti, Serge. "Le quaternaire de la région [ ] Trois-Rivières/Shawinigan, Québec: contributio[n] la paléogéographie de la vallée moyenne du Sai[nt] Laurent et corrélations stratigraphiques." Ottaw[a] 1979.

4766

Parry, John Trevor. "The Laurentians: A Study [ ] Geomorphological Development." McGill, 1963.

4767
Parson, Helen Edna. "Rural Land Use Change: A Study of the Gatineau Valley of Quebec." Kentucky, 1976.

4768
Peattie, Roderick. "Geographic Conditions of the Lower St. Lawrence Valley." Harvard, 1920.

4769
Pilon, Jean. "Étude de la couche active et du pergélisol dans la région de Baie aux Feuilles, Ungava." Montréal, 1983.

4770
Power, Graham Clifford. "Institutional Constraints on Water Resource Planning: Saskatchewan - 1965 to 1969." Western Ontario, 1975.

4771
Price, Anthony Glynne. "Snowmelt Runoff Processes in a Subarctic Area." McGill, 1976. [Schefferville]

Rasid, Harunur. See No./Voir no 4746

4772
Rajotte, Freda. "The Quebec City Recreational Highland." McGill, 1973.

4773
Ritchot, Gilles. "La morphologie des environs de Montréal (depuis la glaciation jusqu'à nos jours)." Montréal, 1969.

4774
Saint-Arnaud, Robert. "La carte fondamentale du Québec." Laval, 1969.

Slack, Brian. See No./Voir no 2292

4775
Tanghe, Raymond. "La géographie humaine de Montréal." Montréal, 1928.

4776
Taylor, Colin Hubert. "Sediment Discharge from the Eaton River Basin (Quebec) During Spring Runoff." McGill, 1972.

4777
Twidale, Charles Rowland. "Development of Slopes in Central New Quebec-Labrador." McGill, 1958.

ECONOMIC GEOGRAPHY/ GÉOGRAPHIE ÉCONOMIQUE

General Items/Ouvrages généraux

4778
Anderson, Thomas Dole. "The Geography of Christmas Tree Production and Marketing in Anglo-America: with Special Attention to Twelve Counties in Western Pennsylvania." Nebraska, 1966.

4779
Ansari, Salmudden. "The Impact of the Regional Development Incentives Act Programme in Selected Slow Growth Areas of Canada: An Analysis of Industrial Structural Change and Employment Growth: 1961-1978." Ottawa, 1983.

Appana, Mohan. See No./Voir no 1839

4780
Ballabon, Maurice B. "Areal Differentiation of the Manufacturing Belt in Central Canada." McGill, 1956.

4781
Brown, Sheila Ann. "An Investigation of Attitude as a Determinant of Consumer Spatial Behaviour." Alberta, 1975.

Cannon, James Bernard. See No./Voir no 1738

4782
Careless, A.G.S. "Canadian Federalism and Policies of Regional Economic Development." Oxford, 1972.

4783
Code, William Robert. "The Spatial Dynamics of Financial Intermediaries: An Interpretation of the Distribution of Financial Decision-Making in Canada." California, Berkeley, 1971.

Corbett, David C. See No./Voir no 1201

Craven, Jack Wolfe. See No./Voir no 2248

4784
Eagan, William Frank. "Industrial Location: The Possibility of Canadian Owned Firms Moving into Northern New York State." Syracuse, 1957.

4785
Green, Alan George. "Regional Aspects of Canada's Economic Growth." Harvard, 1966.

4786
Harrison, Wilks Douglas. "Geography of Iron Ore Pellets." North Carolina, 1970.

4787
Kulka, Terrence Barratt. "A Spatial Restructuring of Business Organizations: A Feasibility Study of Remote Work Arrangements." McGill, 1979.

4788
Mansell, Robert Leonard. "Canadian Regional Inequality: The Process of Adjustment." Alberta, 1975.

Marks, C.J.A. See No./Voir no 2272

Morgan, R.L.R. See No./Voir no 1854

4789
Robinson, Ira Miles. "New Industrial Towns on Canada's Resource Frontier." Chicago, 1962.

4790
Robinson, John Bridger. "Both Feet Planted Firmly in Mid-Air: An Investigation of Energy Policy and Conceptual Frameworks." Toronto, 1981. [National Energy Board forecasts of energy supply and demand/Prévisions de l'offre et de la demande énergique par l'Office national de l'énergie]

Smit, Barry Edward. See No./Voir no 2197

4791
Summers, Harold Angus Charles. "The Location of Distribution Centers in Canada." Indiana, 1969.

4792
Walker, David Frank. "An Adaptive Framework for the Study of Industrial Location Decisions." Toronto, 1971.

Wells, T.A.G. See No./Voir no 81

Young, James Walton. See No./Voir no 2126

4793
Zollo, Tancredi. "A Study of Locational Factors Determining an Optimal Interregional Distribution of Industries in Canada." Concordia, 1976.

Prairie Provinces/Provinces de Prairies

Alberta

4794
Cadden, Patrick Guthrie. "The Public Sector as Urban Employer: The Local Importance and Locational Distribution of Public Employment in Alberta." Calgary, 1980.

4795
Cook, Norman Alan. "Perceptual Variations of Retailing in Edmonton." Alberta, 1972.

4796
Earmme, Seung Young. "A Water Use Projection Model for the North Saskatchewan River Basin, Alberta 1980-1985: An Input-Output Approach." Alberta, 1979.

Eglinton, Peter Cheston. See No./Voir no 1912

4797
Omara-Ojungu, Peter Hastings. "Resource Management in Mountainous Environments, the Case of the East Slopes Region, Bow River Basin, Alberta, Canada." Waterloo, 1981.

Sievwright Eric Colville. See No./Voir no 1334

4798
Szplett, Elizabeth Schmehl. "Corporate Quaternary Linkages and Firm Characteristics: Analysis of Selected Petroleum Administrative Functions in Calgary, Canada." Calgary, 1982.

Thompson, Roderick Ross. See No./Voir no 4957

Manitoba

Bellan, Ruban C. See No./Voir no 4962
Craven, Jack Wolfe. See No./Voir no 2248

4799
Loft, Genivera Edmunds. "Geographical Influences on the Economic Development of Manitoba." Wisconsin, 1925.

Simpson, Samuel John. See No./Voir no 4677
Thompson, Roderick Ross. See No./Voir no 4957

Saskatchewan

4800
Hope, Ernest Charles. "An Economic Classification of Land in Seven Municipalities of South Central Saskatchewan, 1936." Cornell, 1940.

4801
McPherson, John Cecil. "The Economics of Central Place Hierarchies: Applications to the Great Plains Experience." Brown, 1973.

Richards, John Guyon. See No./Voir no 1904

4802
Scace, Robert Chaston. "The Management and Use of a Canadian Plains Oasis: The Cypress Hills Public Reserves." Calgary, 1972.

Thompson, Roderick Ross. See No./Voir no 4957

British Columbia/Colombie-Britannique

4803
Dawson, Ian N. "A Marketing Model of Transportation Demand at Industrial Sites." British Columbia, 1974.

4804
Draper, Dianne Louise. "Resources Management Socio-Economic Development and the Pacific North Coast Native Cooperative: A Case Study Waterloo, 1977.

Hardwick, Walter G. See No./Voir no 1809

4805
Keane, Michael John. "The Problem of Boundaries Regional Economic Planning: The Case of British Columbia." Simon Fraser, 1977.

4806
Liu, Juanita Ngit Wun. "The Economic Impact Tourism on an Island Economy: A Case Study Victoria, B.C." Simon Fraser, 1980.

Atlantic Provinces/Provinces de l'Atlantique

General Items/Ouvrages généraux

Harvey, Jacqueline. See No./Voir no 2282
Jansen, Janni M. See No./Voir no 1867

4807
Saunders, Stanley Alexander. "The Economic Welfare of the Maritime Provinces." Toronto, 1933.

Walker, David Frank. See No./Voir no 4792
Young, John Geoffrey. See No./Voir no 1776

New Brunswick/Nouveau-Brunswick

Watt, John Alexander. See No./Voir no 4857
Young, R.A. See No./Voir no 4159

Newfoundland/Terre-Neuve

4808
Bouchard, André Bernard. "Natural Resources Analysis of a Section of the Gros Morne National Park in Newfoundland, Canada." Cornell, 1975.

Crabb, P. See No./Voir no 58

4809
Philbrook, Thomas Vere. "Industrialization in the Small Community: A Study of Three Newfoundland Communities." Minnesota, 1964.

4810
Storey, Keith John. "Inter-Industry Relationships and Regional Development Strategies: An Analysis Industrial Groupings in the Newfoundland Space Economy." Western Ontario, 1977.

Nova Scotia/Nouvelle-Écosse

MacInnes, Daniel William. See No./Voir no 2115

4811
Todd, Daniel. "Polarization in a Peripheral Region Economy: A Spatial Analysis of Manufacturing Industry, with Reference to Nova Scotia, Canada London, 1976.

Prince Edward Island/Île-du-Prince-Édouard

Millerd, Francis Webb. See No./Voir no 65

The Arctic and Northwest Territories/ Arctique et Territoires du Nord-Ouest

4812
Anders, Gerhard. "On the Economic Development of Canada's Northwest Territories." Texas A & M, 1972.

4813
Bone, Robert Martin. "The Canadian Northwest: A Study of its Economic Development with Observations on the Comparative Development of the Siberian Northland." Nebraska, 1962.

4814
Iskander, Wasby Boulos. "The Economic Potential of Copper in the Canadian Arctic." Indiana, 1973.

Jensen, Kenneth Delane. See No./Voir no 610

4815
Lancaster, Jane. "Mineral Resources and Industries of the Northwestern Canadian Shield." Columbia, 1962.

4816
Lesage, Germain. "Évolution politique et économique au Keewatin." Ottawa, 1945.

4817
Raveson, Thomas Jay. "The Economy of the Northwest Territories of Canada: A Macroeconomic Estimation." Johns Hopkins, 1973.

4818
Usher, Peter Joseph, Jr. "The Bankslanders: Economy and Ecology of a Frontier Trapping Community." British Columbia, 1970.

4819
Zaslow, Morris. "The Development of the Mackenzie Basin, 1920-40." Toronto, 1959.

Ontario

4820
Blackbourn, Anthony. "Locational Patterns of American-Owned Industry in Southern Ontario." Toronto, 1968.

4821
Collins, Lyndhurst. "Markov Chains and Industrial Migration: Forecasting Aspects of Industrial Activity in Ontario." Toronto, 1970.

Craigie, David Edward. See No./Voir no 11010

4822
Ewing, R.G. "The Changing Retail Structure of Sault Ste. Marie, Ontario, 1901-1971." Edinburgh, 1975.

4823
Gilmour, James Muckle. "Structural and Spatial Change in Manufacturing Industry: South Ontario 1850-1890." Toronto, 1970.

4824
Kureth, Elwood John Clark. "The Geographic, History and Political Factors Influencing the Development of Canada's Chemical Valley." Michigan, 1971.

Mock, Dennis Ronald. See No./Voir no 4949

Newkirk, Ross Thomas. See No./Voir no 4558

4825
Norris, Darrell Alan. "Business Location and Consumer Behaviour 1882-1910: Eastern Grey County, Ontario." McMaster, 1977.

Olagbaiye, Joseph. See No./Voir no 4953

4826
Overgaard, Herman Olaf Johan. "Water Problems in Southwestern Ontario." Columbia, 1960.

4827
Ray, David Michael. "Market Potential and Economic Shadow: A Quantitative Analysis of Industrial Location in Southern Ontario." Chicago, 1966.

4828
Seifreid, Neil Robert Michael. "A Study of Changes in Manufacturing in Mid-Western Ontario, 1951-1964." Washington, Seattle, 1969.

4829
Silva, Wanniaratchige Percy Terrence. "The Southern Georgian Bay Region 1855-1961: A Study in Economic Geography." Toronto, 1966.

Smith, L. Graham. See No./Voir no 1797

4830
Sneddon, Richard. "The Central Business District of Peterborough, Ontario: Retail Function and Structure." Chicago, 1963.

Sundstrom, Marvin Thomas. See No./Voir no 1806

Taylor, James Addison. See No./Voir no 4715

4831
Ward, Harold B. "Hamilton, Ontario, as a Manufacturing Center." Chicago, 1935.

4832
Waters, John William. "The Locational Significance of Primary Steel Producer-Consumer Industry Relationships in Peninsular Ontario." Iowa, 1954.

4833
White, William Alan. "Chicago and Toronto: A Comparative Study in Early Growth." Northwestern, 1974.

Quebec/Québec

4834
Burrill, Meredith F. "Studies on the Industrial Geography of Montreal." Clark, 1930.

4835
Camu, Pierre. "L'axe économique du Saint-Laurent entre Kingston et Québec." Montréal, 1951.

Cliche, Pierre. See No./Voir no 4754

Findlay, Marjorie Craven Bursa. See No./Voir no 600

Hoag, Peter Lochrie. See No./Voir no 606

4836
Klein, Juan Luis. "Région, déploiement du capital et coût du travail. Contribution à l'analyse de la croissance manufacturière dans la région de Québec." Laval, 1982.

Lemelin, Charles. See No./Voir no 67

4837
Marchand, Claude Françoise. "Quebec and the Continental Economy: Spatio-Temporal Change, 1957-1975." Toronto, 1979.

Rabiega, William Albert. See No./Voir no 2030

Smith, William. See No./Voir no 101

HISTORICAL GEOGRAPHY/
GÉOGRAPHIE HISTORIQUE

General Items/Ouvrages généraux

Courville, Serge. See No./Voir no 106
Kellogg, James Eugene. See No./Voir no 4860

4838
Ray, Arthur Joseph Jr. "Indian Exploitation of the Forest-Grassland Transition Zone in Western Canada, 1650-1860: A Geographical View of Two Centuries of Change." Wisconsin, 1971.
Ryan, Jerry Bill. See No./Voir no 4892

Sixteenth, Seventeenth and Eighteenth Centuries/ Seizième, dix-septième et dix-huitième siècles

4839
Alwin, John Arnold. "Mode, Pattern, and Pulse: Hudson's Bay Company Transport, 1670 to 1821." Manitoba, 1978.

4840
Harris, Richard Colebrook. "A Geography of the Seigneurial System in Canada During the French Regime." Wisconsin, 1964.
Kaye, Barry. See No./Voir no 79

4841
Manhart, George Brown. "Studies in English Commerce and Exploration in the Reign of Elizabeth: The English Search for a Northwest Passage in the Time of Queen Elizabeth." Pennsylvania, 1923.

4842
Moodie, Donald Wayne. "An Historical Geography of Agricultural Patterns and Resource Appraisals in Rupert's Land, 1670-1774." Alberta, 1972.

4843
Ruggles, R.I. "The Historical Geography and Cartography of the Canadian West, 1670-1795: The Discovery, Exploration, Geographical Description and Cartographic Delineation of Western Canada to 1795." London, 1958.

4844
Williams, Glyndwr. "The British Search by Sea for the Northwest Passage, 1719-94." London, 1959.

Nineteenth Century/Dix-neuvième siècle

Birch, John Worth. See No./Voir no 1812
Hilts, Stewart Garvie. See No./Voir no 4930
Hodgson, J.M.D. See No./Voir no 4648

4845
Hufferd, James. "Pioneering Cultural Integration of the Canadian Prairie in the Pioneer Period." Minnesota, 1979.

4846
Johnson, Ronald Clifford Arthur. "The Effect of Contemporary Thought Upon Park Policy and Landscape Change in Canada's National Parks, 1885-1911." Minnesota, 1972.
Kaye, B. See No./Voir no 79

4847
Knight, David B. "A Capital for Canada: Conflict and Compromise in the Nineteenth Century." Chicago, 1977.

4848
Kovacik, Charles Frank. "A Geographical Analysis of the Foreign-Born in Huron, Similac, and St. Clair Counties of Michigan, with Particular Reference to Canadians, 1850-1880." Michigan State, 1970.

4849
Mannion, John Joseph. "Irish Imprints on the Landscape of Eastern Canada in the Nineteenth Century: A Study in Cultural Transfer and Adaptation." Toronto, 1971.

4850
McQuillan, David. "Adaptation of Three Immigrant Groups to Farming in Central Kansas, 1875-1925." Wisconsin, 1975. [French Canadians/Canadiens français]

4851
Ross, Eric D. "The Canadian Northwest in 1811: A Study in the Historical Geography of the Old Northwest of the Fur Trade on the Eve of the First Agricultural Settlement." Edinburgh, 1962.

4852
Vicero, Ralph Dominic. "Immigration of French Canadians, to New England, 1840-1900: A Geographical Analysis." Wisconsin, 1968.

4853
Wynn, Graeme Clifford. "The Assault on the New Brunswick Forest, 1780-1850." Toronto, 1974.

Twentieth Century/Vingtième siècle

Birch, John Worth. See No./Voir no 1812

4854
Carr, Edwin R. "Great Falls to Nome: The Inland Air Route to Alaska, 1940-1945." Minnesota, 1947.

4855
Hansen, J.A.G. "A Comparative Study of Land Use Structure and Change in Canada, in the United States and Britain, c.1951-1971." London, 1981.
Johnson, Ronald Clifford A. See No./Voir no 4846
McQuillan, David A. See No./Voir no 4850
Young, James Walton. See No/Voir no 2126

Great Lakes/Grands Lacs

McIlwraith, Thomas Forsyth. See No./Voir no 2023

British Columbia/Colombie-Britannique

Bradbury, John Henry. See No./Voir no 4915
Cawker, Kenneth B. See No./Voir no 4606

4856
Farley, Albert Leonard. "Historical Cartography of British Columbia, with a Separate Appendix of Maps." Wisconsin, 1960.
Holdsworth, Deryck W. See No./Voir no 4922

New Brunswick/Nouveau-Brunswick

4857
Watt, John Alexander. "Uneven Regional Development in Canada: A Study of Saint John, N.B. 1880-1910." Waterloo, 1981.
Wynn, Graeme Clifford. See No./Voir no 4853

Newfoundland/Terre-Neuve

4858
Head, Clifford Grant. "The Changing Geography of Newfoundland in the Eighteenth Century." Wisconsin, 1971.

4859
Thornton, Patricia. "Dynamic Equilibrium: Settlement Population and Ecology in the Strait of Belle Isle, Newfoundland, 1840-1940." Aberdeen, 1979.

Northwest Territories and Yukon/ Territoires du Nord-Ouest et Yukon

Green, Jerry Edward. See No./Voir no 4666

4860
Kellogg, James Eugene. "The Impact of the Railroad upon a Frontier Region: The Case of Alaska and the Yukon." Indiana State, 1975.

Moodie, Donald Wayne. See No./Voir no 4842

4861
Rae, George Ramsay. "The Settlement of the Great Slave Lake Frontier, Northwest Territories, Canada: From the Eighteenth to the Twentieth Century." Michigan, 1963.

4862
Stager, John K. "Historical Geography of the Mackenzie River Valley, 1750-1850." Edinburgh, 1962.

Zaslow, Morris. See No./Voir no 4819

Ontario

Ball, Norman Roger See No./Voir no 91

4863
Bland, Warren Roger. "The Changing Locational Patterns of Manufacturing in Southern Ontario from 1881 to 1932." Indiana, 1970.

4864
Brunger, Alan George. "A Spatial Analysis of Individual Settlement in Southern London District, Upper Canada, 1800-1836." Western Ontario, 1974.

4865
Cartwright, Donald Gordon. "French Canada Colonization in Eastern Ontario to 1910: A Study of Process and Pattern." Western Ontario, 1973.

4866
Clarke, John. "A Geographical Analysis of Colonial Settlement in the Western District of Upper Canada, 1788-1850." Western Ontario, 1970.

4867
Doucet, Michael John. "Building the Victorian City: The Process of Land Development in Hamilton, Ontario 1847-1881." Toronto, 1977.

4868
Ennals, Peter Morley. "Land and Society in Hamilton Township, Upper Canada, 1797-1861." Toronto, 1978.

Galois, Robert M. See No./Voir no 4918

4869
Goheen, Peter G. "Victorian Toronto, 1850-1900: Pattern and Process of Growth." Chicago, 1970.

4870
Heidenreich, Conrad Edmund. "The Historical Geography of Huronia, in the First Half of the Seventeenth Century." McMaster, 1971.

4871
Jackson, William A.D. "The Lands Along the Upper St. Lawrence Canadian-American Development During the Nineteenth Century." Maryland, 1953.

4872
Kirk, Donald W. "Southwestern Ontario: The Areal Pattern of Urban Settlement in 1850." Northwestern, 1949.

Levine, Gregory James. See No./Voir no 9798
Mellen, Frances Nordlinger. See No./Voir no 2286
Norris, Darrell Alan. See No/Voir no 4825

4873
Schmeider, Allen Arthur. "The Historical Geography of the Erie Triangle." Ohio State, 1963.

White, William Alan. See No./Voir no 4833

Prairie Provinces/Provinces des Prairies

General Items/Ouvrages généraux

4874
Barnett, Le Roy Gene. "An Historical Geography of the Nineteenth Century Buffalo Bone Commerce on the Northern Great Plains." Michigan State, 1979.

4875
Evans, Simon Malim. "The Passing of a Frontier: Ranching in the Canadian West, 1882-1912." Calgary, 1976.

4876
Lehr, John Campbell. "The Process and Pattern of Ukrainian Rural Settlement in Western Canada 1892-1914." Manitoba, 1978.

Stabler, Jack Carr. See No./Voir no 1302

Alberta

4877
Batchelor, Bruce Edward. "The Agrarian Frontier near Red Deer and Lacombe, Alberta, 1882-1914." Simon Fraser, 1978.

4878
Dale, Edmund Herbert. "The Role of Successive Town and City Councils in the Evolution of Edmonton, Alberta, 1892 to 1966." Alberta, 1969.

Manitoba

4879
Richtik, James Morton. "Manitoba Settlement: 1870 to 1886." Minnesota, 1971.

Tyman, J.L. See No./Voir no 89

4880
Warkentin, John Henry. "The Mennonite Settlements in Southern Manitoba: A Study in Historical Geography." Toronto, 1961.

Saskatchewan

4881
Fitzgerald, Denis Patrick. "Pioneer Settlement in Northern Saskatchewan." Minnesota, 1966.

Quebec/Québec

Booth, John Derek. <u>See No./Voir no</u> 4750

4882
Brouillette, Normand. "Le développement industriel d'une région du proche hinterland québécois: la Mauricie, 1900-1975." McGill, 1983.

Courville, Serge. <u>See No./Voir no</u> 106

4883
Grouse, Nellis Maynard. "Contributions of the Canadian Jesuits to the Geographical Knowledge of New France, 1632-1675." Cornell, 1924.

4884
Hodgson, Robert David. "The Champlain-Richelieu Lowland: A Study in Historical Geography." Michigan, 1951.

4885
Parker, W.H. "The Geography of the Province of Lower Canada in 1837." Oxford, 1958.

POLITICAL GEOGRAPHY/GÉOGRAPHIE POLITIQUE

Barlow, Ivor Maxton. <u>See No./Voir no</u> 4963

4886
Dean, Veva K. "Newfoundland: A Study in Political Geography." Clark, 1949.

4887
Ibele, Oscar H., Jr. "Geographic Influences and Political Problems in Newfoundland." Ohio State, 1947.

4888
Lindgren, David Treadwell. "The Interruptive Effect of the Maine-New Brunswick Boundary: A Study in Political Geography." Boston University, 1970.

Lloyd, Trevor. <u>See No./Voir no</u> 4738

4889
Nicholson, Norman Leon. "Canadian Boundaries, Their Evolution, Establishment and Significance." Ottawa, 1961.

4890
Perejda, Andrew Daniel. "The St. Clair River, A Study in Political Geography." Michigan, 1950.

4891
Rumley, Dennis. "Stability and Change in Electoral Patterns: The Case of the 1972 British Columbia Provincial Election in Vancouver." British Columbia, 1975.

4892
Ryan, Jerry Bill. "Geographic Rationalizations in American Expansion and Territorial Aggression: 1775-1920." Kansas, 1972.

4893
Simpson, Geoffrey Sedgwick. "Quebec and Paris: The French Search for the Western Sea in Canada, 1660-1760." Cambridge, 1972.

4894
Smith, Gordon Ward. "The Historical and Legal Background of Canada's Arctic Claims." Columbia, 1952.

4895
Whebel, C.F.J. "The Geographical Basis of Local Government in Southern Ontario." London, 1961.

4896
Wolfe, Jacqueline Susan. "Political Information Channels in an At-Large Municipal Electoral System (City of Guelph 1972 and 1974)." McMaster, 1976.

URBAN GEOGRAPHY/GÉOGRAPHIE URBAINE

General Items/Ouvrages généraux

4897
Beaman, Jay Gillmore. "A Framework for Modeling Geographic Mobility with Test Applications to the Analyses of Mobility Data for Thirteen Canadian Cities." Cornell, 1973.

Bring, Gordon. <u>See No./Voir no</u> 2224

4898
Brozowski, Roman Steve. "Revealed Preference in Intra-Urban Migration." Western Ontario, 1977.

4899
Brummell, Arden Craig. "A Theory of Intraurban Residential Mobility Behaviour." McMaster, 1977.

Goheen, Peter G. <u>See No./Voir no</u> 4869

4900
Golant, Stephen Myles. "The Residential Location and Spatial Behaviour of the Elderly: A Canadian Example." Washington, Seattle, 1972.

4901
Ichikawa, Hiroo. "A Comparative Study of Urban Form and its Spatial Characteristics for Japanese and North American Cities." Waterloo, 1982.

4902
Joseph, Alun Edward. "Relations Between the Diffusion of Innovations and Urban Growth." McMaster, 1976.

4903
Kuz, Tony John. "Cross-Sectional and Longitudinal Analyses of Canadian Urban Systems: 1951, 1961 and 1951-1961." Pennsylvania State, 1972.

4904
Lamarche, Rodolphe H. "Measurement of Interaction Properties in the Canadian Metropolitan System." Ottawa, 1979.

4905
McCabe, Robert Wylie. "Retail Location Models and Public Decisions." Toronto, 1977.

4906
McCann, Lawrence Douglas. "Changing Morphology of Residential Areas in Transition." Alberta, 1972.

4907
Mercer, John. "The Spatial Pattern of Urban Residential Blight." McMaster, 1971.

4908
Millward, Hugh Albert. "The Convergence of Urban Plan Features: A Comparative Examination of Trends in Canada and England." Western Ontario 1975.

4909
Mozersky, Kenneth Avrum. "Structural Differentiation of Community: An Analysis of Western Canadian Communities Undergoing Change." Cornell 1970. [Manitoba and/et Saskatchewan]

4910
O'Connor, Kevin Bernard. "Industrial Structure and Urban Growth of Canadian Cities, 1951-1961." McMaster, 1974.

Ray, Arthur Joseph Jr. <u>See No./Voir no</u> 4838

4911
Pierce, John T. "Urban Growth in Canada: A Study of Land Conversion, 1960-1971." London, 1976.

4912
Roberts, Ellis Noel Rees. "Environment, Community and Lifestyle: Components of Residential Preference for Cities." Toronto, 1976.

Shimizu, Kaien Maseru. See No./Voir no 939

4913
Underwood, Thomas Joseph. "A Spatial Analysis of Children's Preferences for City Streets and Travel Routes." Western Ontario, 1975.

4914
Ward, James Stanley. "Geographic Dynamics of Skid Rows in North America." Maryland, 1973.

British Columbia/Colombie-Britannique

General Items/Ouvrages généraux

4915
Bradbury, John Henry. "Instant Towns in British Columbia: 1964 to 1972." Simon Fraser, 1977.

4916
Chambers, Alan David. "Simulation of Cottage Lot Subdivision: A Synthesis of Social, Economic and Environmental Concerns." British Columbia, 1971.

4917
Villeneuve, Paul Yvon. "The Spatial Adjustment of Ethnic Minorities in the Urban Environment." Washington, Seattle, 1971.

Vancouver

Bottomley, John. See No./Voir no 10480

4918
Galois, Robert Michael. "Social Structure in Space: The Making of Vancouver, 1886-1901." Simon Fraser, 1980.

4919
Gayler, Hugh James. "Consumer Spatial Behaviour and its Relation to Social Class and Family Status in Metropolitan Vancouver, Canada." British Columbia, 1974.

4920
Gibson, Edward Mark Walter. "The Impact of Social Belief on Landscape Change: A Geographical Study of Vancouver." British Columbia, 1972.

4921
Gill, Warren George. "Mainstream Urban Life Styles: Indices and Determinants." British Columbia, 1981.

4922
Holdsworth, Deryck William. "House and Home in Vancouver: The Emergence of a West Coast Urban Landscape, 1886-1929." British Columbia, 1981.

4923
Joardar, Souro Dyuti. "Emotional and Behavioral Responses of People to Urban Plazas: A Case Study of Downtown Vancouver." British Columbia, 1977.

4924
Outcalt, Samuel Irvine. "A Study of Needle Ice Events at Vancouver, Canada, 1961-1968." British Columbia, 1970.

4925
Steyn, Douw Gerbrand. "Turbulence, Diffusion and the Daytime Mixed Layer Depth over a Coastal City." British Columbia, 1980. [Pollutants in the atmosphere over Vancouver/Contaminants dans l'atmosphère au-dessus de Vancouver]

Victoria

Liu, J.N.W. See No./Voir no 4806

4926
Robinson, Malcolm Emerson. "A Method for Investigating the Effects of Tourism on the Functional and Morphological Development of a City as Applied to Greater Victoria, British Columbia." Northwestern, 1957.

Robinson, Ross. See No./Voir no 2291

Weightman, Barbara Ann. See No./Voir no 490

4927
Wuorinen, Vilho. "A Methodology for Mapping Total Risk in Urban Areas." Victoria, 1979. [Tested in Victoria metropolitan area/Essayé dans la région de Victoria]

Ontario

General Items/Ouvrages généraux

4928
Gillen, David William. "An Economic Analysis of the Effects of Alternative Parking Policies on Model Choice and Congestion." Toronto, 1975."

4929
Grima, Angelo Paul. "Residential Water Demand: Alternative Choices for Management." Toronto, 1970.

Hansvick, Christine Louise. See No./Voir no 9688

4930
Hilts, Stewart Garvie. "In Praise of Progress: Attitudes to Urbanization in Southwestern Ontario, 1850-1900." Toronto, 1981.

Levine, Gregory James. See No./Voir no 9798

4931
Murray, Malcolm Arthur. "A Geographic Analysis for Selected Ontario and Ohio-Indiana Cities." Syracuse, 1955.

4932
Mutambirwa, Christopher C. "Modelling Differentials in Urban Growth with Applications to the Ontario Urban System." Western Ontario, 1974.

4933
Russwurm, Lorne Henry. "Expanding Urbanization in the London to Hamilton Area of Western Ontario, 1941-1961." Illinois, 1964.

4934
Semple, Robert Keith. "Regional Types of Viability Within a System of Urban Places." Ohio State, 1969.

Smith, William Randy. See No./Voir no 2265

Hamilton

Doucet, Michael John. See No./Voir no 4867

Ennals, Peter Worley. See No./Voir no 4868

4935

O'Kelly, Morton Edward John. "Impacts of Multipurpose Trip-Making on Spatial Interaction and Retail Facility Size." McMaster, 1981.

Preston, Valerie Ann. See No./Voir no 1580

Russwurm, Lorne Henry. See No./Voir no 4933

4936

Smith, Geoffrey Charles. "An Analysis of Intra-Urban Consumer Spatial Imagery Fields." McMaster, 1974.

Kitchener-Waterloo

4937

Bunting, Trudi Elizabeth. "Behaviour Systems in the City: A Conceptual and Analytical Approach to the Investigation of Household Activities." Toronto, 1975.

London

4938

Andress, Donald Douglas. "Spatial Patterns of Intra-Urban Population Age Structure Differentiation in London, Canada." Western Ontario, 1978.

Brozowski, Roman S. See No./Voir no 4898

4939

Khondakar, Nezamuddin." Some Changes in Socio-Economic and Spatial Characteristics of Ethnic Groups in London, Ontario, 1961-1971." Western Ontario, 1981.

4940

Muncaster, Russell Walter. "A Model for Mixed Urban-Place Hierarchies: An Application to the London, Ontario Urban Place System." Clark, 1972.

Russwurm, Lorne Henry. See No./Voir no 4933

4941

Waters, Nigel Michael. "Methodology for Servicing the Geography of Urban Fire: An Exploration, with Special Reference to London, Ontario." Western Ontario, 1977.

Toronto

4942

Barrett, Frank Alexander. "The Search Behavior of Recent House Movers: A Study of Intra-Urban Relocation in Toronto, Canada." Michigan State, 1973.

4943

Bourne, Larry Stuart. "Private Redevelopment of the Central City: Spatial Processes of Structural Change in the City of Toronto." Chicago, 1967.

4944

Gad, Gunter Helmut Karl. "Toronto's Central Office Complex: Growth, Structure and Linkages." Toronto, 1976.

4945

Gibson, Sarah Duane. "Sense of Place - Defence of Place: A Case Study of the Toronto Island." Toronto, 1981.

4946

Hill, Frederick Irvin. "The Integration of Periphe Towns into an Urban Field: The Toronto-Center Region." Toronto, 1976.

Hodgson, Michael John. See No./Voir no 2255

4047

Konrad, Victor Alexander. "Orientations Toward t Past in the Environment of the Present: Retr spect in Metropolitan Toronto." McMaster, 1978.

4948

Maher, Christopher Anthony. "Residential Change a the Filtering Process: Central Toronto, 1953-7 Toronto, 1972.

Mellen, Frances Nordlinger. See No./Voir no 2286

4949

Mock, Dennis Ronald. "Agglomeration and Industr Linkages: Case Studies of Metropolitan Toront Toronto, 1976.

4950

Moore, Peter William. "Zoning and Neighbourho Change in the Annex in Toronto, 1900-197 Toronto, 1978.

4951

Morrison, Philip Scott. "Residential Property Conve sion-Subdivision Merger and Quality Change in t Inner City Housing Stock, Metropolitan Toron 1958-1973." Toronto, 1978.

4952

Murdie, Robert Alexander. "Factorial Ecology Metropolitan Toronto, 1951-1961: An Essay on t Social Geography of the City." Chicago, 1969.

4953

Olagbaiye, Joseph Ajiboye. "Intra-Urban Industr Migration: A Simulation Model of Plant S Selection and Its Application to Metropolit Toronto." McMaster, 1972.

4954

Peddie, Richard. "Residential Mobility, Occupan Conversion and Neighbourhood Change." Toron 1978. [Alexandra Park/Parc Alexandra]

4955

Punter, John Vincent. "Urbanites in the Countrysi Case Studies of the Impact of Exurban Develo ment of the Landscape in the Toronto-Center Region, 1954-1971." Toronto, 1974.

Roberts, Ellis Noel Rees. See No./Voir no 4912

4956

Sharpe, Christopher Andrew. "Vacancy Chains a Residential Relocation: The Response to N Construction in the Toronto Housing Market Are Toronto, 1976.

White, William Alan. See No./Voir no 4833

Prairie Provinces/Provinces des Prairies

General Item/Ouvrage général

4957

Thompson, Roderick Ross. "Commodity Flows a Urban Structure: A Case Study in the Prai Provinces." Calgary, 1977.

Alberta

Calgary

4958
Payne, Robert John. "Children's Urban Landscapes in Huntington Hills, Calgary." Calgary, 1977.

4959
Zieber, George Henry. "Inter- and Intra-City Location Patterns of Oil Offices for Calgary and Edmonton 1950-1970." Alberta, 1972.

Edmonton

Brown, Sheila Ann. See No./Voir no 4781

4960
Carter, Thomas S. "A Profile of Tenants in Central Edmonton: Their Characteristics and Housing Preferences." Alberta, 1978.

McCann, Lawrence Douglas. See No./Voir no 4906

4961
McCracken, Kevin William John. "Patterns of Intra-Urban Migration in Edmonton and the Residential Relocation Process." Alberta, 1973.

Zieber, George Henry. See No./Voir no 4959

Manitoba

Winnipeg

4962
Bellan, Ruben C. "The Development of Winnipeg as a Metropolitan Centre." Columbia, 1958.

Sharma, Satish Chandra. See No./Voir no 4528

Quebec/Québec

General Item/Ouvrage général

Marois, Claude. See No./Voir no 10322

Montreal/Montréal

4963
Barlow, Ivor Maxton. "Political Fragmentation, Municipal Expenditures and Public Service Provision in the Montreal Metropolitan Area: A Study in Urban Political Geography." McGill, 1978. [1951-1971]

4964
Foggin, Peter Michael. "An Inductive Model of Changes in the Intra-Urban Land Value Surface: The Impact of Transportation, Land Use, and Socio-Economic Factors in Central Montreal." McGill, 1970.

4965
Langlois, André. "L'analyse factorielle à trois entrées: une application à l'espace ethnique montréalais." Laval, 1983.

4966
Ricour, Françoise. "Suburbanisation et structures urbaines de l'Île Jésus." Montréal, 1969.

New Brunswick/Nouveau-Brunswick

St. John/Saint-Jean

Watt, John Alexander. See No./Voir no 4857

Northwest Territories/Territoires du Nord-Ouest

Mayes, Robert Gregory. See No./Voir no 613

CLIMATE AND METEOROLOGY/ CLIMAT ET MÉTÉOROLOGIE

As with most of the other disciplines, the bulk of the research in this category was completed during the 1970's. The total number of studies is quite small, with American output slightly more than half of the Canadian number. Of the 13 universities working in this area, McGill is the major producer with almost two-fifths of the total to its credit. The Universities of Toronto, British Columbia, and McMaster, follow in that order. Among the 14 American universities, Wisconsin, Michigan, and Clark rank first, second and third, but with comparatively few titles to their credit. Great Britain can point to three titles in this classification, two from the University of London and one from the University of East Anglia.

Comme dans la plupart des autres disciplines, la grande partie des recherches en cette catégorie s'est effectué dans les années 1970. Le nombre total de thèses est assez réduit et la production américaine se tient légèrement au-dessus de la moitié du nombre canadien. L'Université McGill est la plus active des 13 établissements travaillant en ce domaine, avec presque deux cinquièmes du total à son crédit. Les universités de Toronto, de la Colombie-Britannique et McMaster suivent, loin derrière l'Université McGill. Parmi les 14 universités américaines, celles du Wisconsin, du Michigan et Clark occupent les trois premières places, mais avec comparativement peu de thèses à offrir. Dans cette classification, la Grande-Bretagne détient trois ouvrages, deux à l'Université de Londres et un à l'Université d'East Anglia.

GENERAL ITEMS/OUVRAGES GÉNÉRAUX

4967
Astling, Elford George. "A Study of the Atmospheric Energy Transport over North America." Wisconsin, 1970.

4968
Bellon, Aldo. "The Development, Operation and Evaluation of Two Years of Real-Time Short-Term Precipitation Forecasting Procedure." McGill, 1981.

4969
Blasing, Terence Jack. "Methods for Analyzing Climatic Variations in the North Pacific Sector and Western North America for the Last Few Centuries." Wisconsin, 1975.

4970
Boville, Byron Walter. "A Dynamical Study of the 1958-59 Stratospheric Polar Vortex." McGill, 1961.

4971
Carlson, Paul Erik. "Measurement of Snowfall by Radar." McGill, 1970.

4972
Chouinard, Clément B. "Simulation of East Coast Cyclogenesis Using a Primitive Equation Model Coupled with a Detailed Planetary Boundary Layer Formation." McGill, 1978.

4973
Dewey, Kenneth Frederic. "An Analytical Study of Lake-Effect Snowfall." Toronto, 1973.

4974
Hay, J.E. "Aspects of the Heat and Moisture Balance of Canada." London, 1970.

4975
Isyumov, Nicholas. "An Approach to the Prediction of Snow Loads." Western Ontario, 1971.

Kay, Paul Allan. See No./Voir no 4668

4976
Knox, John Lewis. "Atmospheric Blocking in the Northern Hemisphere." British Columbia, 1981.

4977
Koeppe, Clarence Eugene. "The Climate of Canada and Newfoundland." Clark, 1929.

4978
Kunz, Ernest Chen-Tsun. "Climatology of the Mechanical Energy Dissipation in the Lower Atmosphere over the Northern Hemisphere." Wisconsin, 1963.

4979
Marwitz, John. "The Structure and Motion of Some Severe Hailstorms." McGill, 1971.

4980
McKay, Donald Charles. "Measurements of the Structure of Atmospheric Turbulence and Energy Fluxes Involved in the Energy Budget of a Snow-Cover." Guelph, 1977.

4981
Pond, George Stephen. "Turbulence Spectra in the Atmospheric Boundary Layer over the Sea." British Columbia, 1966.

4982
Reitan, Clayton Harold. "An Assessment of the Role of Volcanic Dust in Determining Modern Changes in the Temperature of the Northern Hemisphere." Wisconsin, 1971.

4983
Rouse, Wayne R. "Aspects of a Forest Microclimate." McGill, 1965.

4984
Shaw, David Montgomery. "Thermodynamic Studies of Paleoclimates." Columbia, 1969.

Sorenson, Curtis James. See No./Voir no 4599

4985
Stewart, Robert Bruce. "The Evaporation from Three High Latitude Surfaces." McMaster, 1975. [Hudson Bay/Baie Hudson]

4986
Sumner, Alfred R. "Standard Deviation of Me[an] Monthly Temperature from the Long-Period Me[an] in Anglo-America." Clark, 1950.

4987
West, Kenneth Ernest. "H_2O^{18}/H_2O^{16} Variations [in] Ice and Snow of Mountainous Regions of Canad[a]." Alberta, 1972.

4988
Wilson, Richard Garth. "Evapotranspiration Estima[tes] from the Water Balance and Equilibrium Model[s]." McMaster, 1971.

Yu, Shaw-Lei. See No./Voir no 4526

4989
Zwack, Peter P. "Interrelated Mesoscale Squall Li[nes] and Continuous Precipitation." McGill, 1973.

REGIONAL STUDIES/ÉTUDES RÉGIONALES

Eastern Canada/Est du Canada

4990
Catellier, M. Hubert. "Le problème géographique [de] l'hiver dans les cantons de l'Est." Laval, 1953.

Central Canada/Centre du Canada

4991
McFadden, James Douglas. "Interrelationship of La[ke] Ice and Climate in Central Canada." Wiscons[in,] 1965.

Southern Canada/Sud du Canada

4992
Bartlein, Patrick John. "The Influence of Short Peri[od] Climatic Variations on Streamflow in the Unit[ed] States and Southern Canada 1951-1970." W[is]consin, 1978.

4993
McClain, Ernest Paul. "Some Effects of the Weste[rn] Cordilleras of North America in Cyclonic Activ[ity] in the United States and Southern Canad[a]." Florida State, 1958.

St. Lawrence River/Fleuve Saint-Laurent

4994
Greene, Gordon Mather. "Simulation of Ice-Cov[er] Growth and Thermal Decay on the Upper S[t.] Lawrence River." Michigan, 1981.

Western Canada/Ouest du Canada

4995
Hage, Keith Donald. "On Summer Cyclogenesis [in] Western Canada Associated with Upper Co[ld] Lows." Chicago, 1959.

4996
Rheumer, George Alfred. "Climate and Clima[tic] Regions of Western Canada." Illinois, 1953.

997

arnal, Brenton Murray. "The Relationship Between Synoptic Seale Atmospheric Circulation and Glacier Mass Balance in Southwestern Canada." Simon Fraser, 1983.

British Columbia/Colombie-Britannique

itzharris, Brian Blair. See No./Voir no 4610

998

argett, Ann Elizabeth. "Internal Waves in the Strait of Georgia." British Columbia, 1970.

999

Kerr, Donald Peter. "The Regional Climatology of Southern British Columbia." Toronto, 1950.

000

alway, Anthony Austen. "Statistical Estimation and Production of Avalanche Activity from Meteorological Data for the Rogers Pass Area of British Columbia." British Columbia, 1976.

uckling, Philip Wayne. See No./Voir no 4622

001

Walker, Edward Robert. "A Synoptic Climatology for British Columbia: Some Effects of Mountainous Terrain on Observed Weather." McGill, 1961.

Great Lakes/Grands Lacs

002

Clemens, Jerome McClain. "Estimates in the Mixed Space Time Domain of the Conversion of Kinetic Energy Between the Mean Flow and the Eddies in the Great Lakes Atmosphere." Ohio State, 1974.

Doan, Kenneth Henry. See No./Voir no 10911

5003

Gaskill, Daniel Wills. "Climatic Variability Around the Great Lakes Specific to the Problem of Ice Forecasting." Michigan, 1982.

5004

Granger, Orman Eloi. "The Evapotranspiration Climatonomy of the Lake Ontario Drainage Basin." Toronto, 1974.

5005

Haq, Aminul. "The Time-Dependent Flow in Large Lakes, with Application to Lake Erie." Case Western Reserve, 1974.

5006

Holroyd, Edmond William, III. "The Meso-and Microscale Structure of Great Lakes Snowstorm Bands - A Synthesis of Ground Measurements, Radar Data and Satellite Observations." SUNY, Albany, 1971.

5007

Kopec, Richard Joseph. "Areal Extent of the Great Lakes Significant Influence on Vicinal Temperature Regimes." Clark, 1965.

5008

Loucks, Ronald Harold. "Patricle Size Distribution of Chlorine and Bromine in Mid-Continent Aerosols from the Great Lakes Basin." Michigan, 1969.

5009

Neralla, Venkata Rao. "Incorporation of Convections in the Synoptic Study of Large Scale Effects of the Great Lakes." Waterloo, 1974.

Pease, Steven Robert. See No./Voir no 4604

5010

Robinson, Peter John. "Longwave Radiation Exchanges Over Lake Ontario." McMaster, 1972.

5011

Sanderson, Marie Elizabeth Lustig. "A Climatic Water Balance of the Lake Erie Basin, 1958-1963." Michigan, 1965.

5012

Wise, Daniel Lewis. "Techniques to Estimate the Surface Wind Field and Associated Wave Characteristics on Lake Erie." Ohio State, 1979.

Newfoundland/Terre-Neuve

Koeppe, Clarence Eugene. See No./Voir no 4977

Labrador

Petzold, Donald Emil. See No./Voir no 5015

The Arctic, Northwest Territories and the Yukon/ Arctique, Territoires du Nord-Ouest et Yukon

5013

Bates, Howard Francis. "An HF Sweep Frequency Study of the Arctic Ionosphere." Alaska, 1961.

5014

Belmont, Arthur David. "Lower Tropospheric Inversions at the Ice Island T-3." McGill, 1956.

5015

Benjey, William Grant. "Seasonal Energy Balance Trends in the Subarctic: The Microclimates of a Broken Spruce Forest and Clearing, Kluane Lake, Yukon, 1970-1971." Michigan, 1974.

5016

Braithwaite, Roger James. "Air Temperature and Glacier Ablation - A Parametric Approach." McGill, 1977. [White Glacier, Axel Heiberg Island/Glacier Blanc, Île Axel Heiberg]

5017

Cogley, John Graham. "Properties of Surface Runoff in the High Arctic." McMaster, 1975.

5018

Ghosh, Ranjit. "The Effect of Low Temperature on the Tensile, Impact and Fatigue Behavior of Four HSLA Steels Developed for Use in the Arctic." Laval, 1980.

5019

Hare, Frederick Kennet. "The Climate of the Eastern Canadian Arctic and Subarctic and Its Influence on Accessibility." Montréal, 1950.

5020

Havens, J.M. "Summer Climate in High Latitudes and Altitudes, with Special Reference to the Climate and Contemporary Sub-Polar Alpine Glaciation of Axel Heiberg Island, N.W.T., Canada." London, 1969.

5021

Herman, Gerald Francis. "Radiative-Diffusive Models of the Arctic Boundary Layer." Massachusetts Institute of Technology, 1976.

5022

Jacobs, John Douglas. "Synoptic Energy Budget Studies in the Eastern Baffin Island-Davis Strait Region." Colorado, 1973.

5023
Julian, Paul Rowland. "Tropospheric Behavior Associated with the Arctic Stratospheric Warming Phenomenon." Pennsylvania State, 1960.

5024
Kakela, Peter John. "Snow and the Thornthwaite Water Balance in a Subarctic Environment." Alberta, 1969.

5025
Kolberg, Donald Wayne. "Summer Synoptic Climatology of the St. Elias Mountains, Yukon and Alaska." Michigan, 1973.

5026
LeDrew, Ellsworth Frank. "Physical Mechanisms Responsible for the Major Synoptic Systems in the Eastern Canadian Arctic in the Winter and Summer of 1973." Colorado, 1976.

5027
Lettau, Bernhard. "The Use of Sub Arctic Bogs as Natural Climatic Indicators." Wisconsin, 1966.

5028
Orvig, Svenn. "Glacial Meteorological Observations on Icecaps in Baffin Island." McGill. 1954.

Pufahl, Dennis Edward. See No./Voir no 4491

5029
Taylor, Beatrice Elizabeth. "The Energy Balance Climate of Meighen Ice Cap, N.W.T." McGill, 1974.

5030
Thomson, Richard Edward. "Theoretical Studies of the Circulation of the Subarctic Pacific Region and the Generation of Kelvin Type Waves by Atmospheric Disturbances." British Columbia, 1971.

5031
Williams, L.D. "Investigation of the Onset of Glaciation in Northern Canada Using an Energy Balance Snow Model." East Anglia, 1978.

5032
Wonders, William Clare. "The Climate of the Canadian Arctic Archipelago." Toronto, 1951.

Nova Scotia/Nouvelle-Écosse

5033
Hart, William Charles. "Major Ions in Nova Scotian Precipitation." Dalhousie, 1977.

Rankin, Douglas Stewart. See No./Voir no 5673

The Prairie Provinces/Provinces des Prairies

General Items/Ouvrages généraux

5034
Dey, Balaram. "Synoptic Climatological Aspects of Summer Dry Spells in the Canadian Prairies." Saskatchewan, 1973.

5035
Pakiam, James Edwin. "The Role of Electrical Processes in the Thunderstorm of the Canadian Prairies." Saskatchewan, 1973.

5036
Villmow, Jack R. "Nature and Origin of the Canadian Dry Belt." Wisconsin, 1955. [Palliser Triangle/Triangle Palliser]

Alberta

5037
Chisholm, Alexander James. "Alberta Hailstorms: Radar Study and Model." McGill, 1970.

English, Marianne. See No./Voir no 5049

5038
Inkster, Don Robert. "A Radar Study of Seede[d] Alberta Hailstorms." McGill, 1977.

Karlstrom, Eric Thor. See No./Voir no 4729

5039
Munro, Donald Scott. "Energy Exchange on a Melti[ng] Glacier." McMaster, 1975. [Peyto Glacier/Glaci[er] Peyto]

5040
Pell, Jerry. "The Alberta Hailstorm as Observed [on] the Ground and by Radar." McGill, 1970.

5041
Warner, Charles. "Visual and Radar Aspects of Larg[e] Connective Storms." McGill, 1971. [Four Albert[a] storms/Quatre tempêtes en Alberta]

Manitoba

5042
Grenda, Robert Norman. "Rocket Measurements [of] Upper Atmosphere Density and Temperature ove[r] Fort Churchill, Manitoba." Toronto, 1966.

Saskatchewan

5043
Wolbeer, Hendrik Jan. "Experimental and Theoretic[al] Investigations of Evaporation from Small Reser[r]voirs." Saskatchewan, 1964.

Ontario

5044
De-Heer-Amissah, Adrian Nicholas. "Energy Budge[t] over an Inland Watershed." Toronto, 1965.

5045
Goodison, Barry Edward. "Snowfall and Snow Cover i[n] Southern Ontario: Principles and Techniques o[f] Assessment." Toronto, 1977.

5046
Pedro, Junior Mario José. "Relation of Leaf Surfac[e] Wetness Duration to Meteorological Parameters[.] Guelph, 1981. [Simcoe and Elora researc[h] station/Station des recherches Simcoe et Elora]

5047
Rahman, K.H. Shaf. "A Three Phase Temperatur[e] Density Model to Simulate and Compare Potentia[l] Snowmelt Runoff." Western Ontario, 198[2] [Medway Drainage Basin near London/Bassi[n] hydrographique Medway près de London]

Sangal, B.P. See No./Voir no 4711

Quebec/Québec

5048
Chyurlia, Jerome Paul. "Solute Load Variability i[n] Small Appalachian Watersheds During Sprin[g] Runoff: The Eaton Basin, 1971-1973." McGil[l] 1977.

5049
English, Marianne. "The Growth of Large Hail: Studies Derived from Alberta and Montreal Hailstorms." McGill, 1972.

5050
Fuggle, Richard Francis. "Nocturnal Atmospheric Infrared Radiation in Montreal." McGill, 1971.

5051
Petzold, Donald Emil. "Synoptic Investigations of the Summer Climate and Lake Evaporation in Quebec-Labrador." McGill, 1980.

5052
Shaw, Roderick Wallace. "Movement, Morphology and Circulation of Montreal Summer Storms." Toronto, 1970.

5053
Singh, Bhawan. "The Effect of Intercepted Rainfall on Evapotranspiration Rates over a Mixed Hardwood Forest in Southern Quebec." McGill, 1976.

5054
Walawender, Michael John. "A Study of the Charlevoix Structure, Quebec, Canada." Pennsylvania State, 1972.

5055
Wilson, Cynthia. "The Climate of the Province of Quebec, a Study in Applied Climatology." Laval, 1972.

GEOLOGY/GÉOLOGIE

This classification is one of the most thoroughly explored areas, ranking second only to education. John Hopkins University offered the first study in 1888, followed by the Universities of Columbia and Chicago in 1895, and Columbia again in 1899, (preceding the University of Toronto by five years). For the first half of this century, American universities produced considerably more research than Canadian schools, but from the 1960's on, the Canadian output increased markedly. In the United States, Princeton University is the leading contributor, with the Universities of Wisconsin, Yale, Harvard, Columbia, and Michigan following in that order. In Canada, McGill University is the outstanding contributor, with the University of Toronto a close second. Queen's University ranks third, ahead of the Universities of British Columbia, Alberta, McMaster, and Western Ontario, which occur in that order. Geology ranks fourth in output of British studies of Canada.

———

Cette catégorie est l'une des plus étudiées; elle vient au second rang, après l'éducation. C'est à l'Université Johns Hopkins que revient la première étude, en 1888; elle a été suivie par les universités Columbia et Chicago en 1895, et de nouveau Columbia en 1899 (précédant l'Université de Toronto de cinq ans). Dans la première moitié du siècle, les universités amé-

ricaines ont produit bien plus que les universités canadiennes, mais depuis 1960, la production canadienne a progressé de façon marquée. Aux États-Unis, l'Université Princeton vient en tête, suivie dans l'ordre, par les universités du Wisconsin, de Yale, de Harvard, de Columbia et du Michigan. Au Canada, l'Université McGill se classe bien avant les autres établissements; l'Université de Toronto suit d'assez près. L'Université Queen's reste au troisième rang, tout en distançant nettement les universités de la Colombie-Britannique, de l'Alberta, McMaster et Western Ontario, toutes citées dans l'ordre. La géologie occupe le quatrième rang des disciplines étudiées dans les ouvrages britanniques sur le Canada.

(Stratigraphy, geochemistry, glaciology, metallurgy, mineralogy, petrology, etc.)/ (Stratigraphie, géochimie, glaciologie métallurgie, minéralogie, pétrologie, etc.)

GENERAL ITEMS/OUVRAGES GÉNÉRAUX

5056
Armstrong, Calvert William. "Role of Replacement Processes in the Formation of Complex Lithium Pegmatites (Canada)." Western Ontario, 1970.

5057
Cameron-Schumann, Monique. "Electron Microprobe Study of Uranium Minerals and Its Application to Some Canadian Deposits." Alberta, 1978.

Carman, John Stanley. See No./Voir no 4470

Cranstone, Donald Alfred. See No./Voir no 1876

5058
Du Bois, Philip M. "Some Paleomagnetic Results from North America and Europe and Their Geological Significance." Cambridge, 1960.

5059
Fryer, Brian Jackson. "Canadian Precambrian Iron-Formations: Ages and Trace Element Compositions." Massachusetts Institute of Technology, 1972.

5060
Gascoyne, Melvyn. "Pleistocene Climates Determined from Stable Isotope and Geochronical Studies of Speleothem." McMaster, 1980.

5061
Gates, Todd Michael. "Improved Dating of Canadian Pre-Cambrian Dikes and a Revised Polar Wandering Curve." Massachussetts Institute of Technology, 1972.

5062
Gregory, G.P. "Geochemical and Dispersion Patterns Related to Kimberlite Intrusives in North America." London, 1970.

5063
Harmon, Russell Scott. "Late Pleistocene Paleoclimates in North America as Inferred from Isotopic Variations in Speleotherms." McMaster, 1976. [Alberta, British Columbia and Northwest Territories/Alberta, Colombie-Britannique et Territoires du Nord-Ouest]

5064
Hay, Peter William. "The Stability and Occurrence of Cordierite in Selected Gneisses from the Canadian Shield." Stanford, 1965.

5065
Hedden, William Jesse. "The Stratigraphy and Tectono-Depositional History of the Smithville and Black Rock Lithosomes (Canadian) of Northeastern Arkansas with Revisions of Upper Canadian Stratigraphy in the Ozarks." Missouri, Rolla, 1976.

5066
Julian, Bruce René. "Regional Variations in Upper Mantle Structure Beneath North America." California Institute of Technology, 1970.

5067
Kalogeropoulos, Stavros Ilia. "Chemical Sediments in the Hanging Wall of Volcanogenic Massive Sulfide Deposits." Toronto, 1982. [The Millenbach Mine/ Mine Millenbach]

5068
Kilburn, Lionel C. "The Nickel, Cobalt, Copper, Zinc, Lead and Sulphur Content of Some North American Base Metals Sulfide Ores." Manitoba, 1960.

5069
King, Elbert Aubrey. "Investigations of North American Tektites." Harvard, 1965.

5070
Kobluck, David Ronald. "Boring and Cavity Dwelling Algae: Effects on Cementation and Diagenesis in Marine Carbonates." McMaster, 1977. [Alberta, Ontario and Quebec/Alberta, Ontario et Québec]

5071
Labovitz, Mark Larry. "Unit Regional Value of the Dominion of Canada." Pennsylvania State, 1978.

5072
Laznicka, Petr. "Quantitative Aspects in the Distribution of Base and Precious Metal Deposits of the World." Manitoba, 1971.

5073
McGregor, Duncan Colin. "Spores and Other Plant Microfossils from Selected Devonian Sedimentary Formations of Canada." McMaster, 1957.

Milne, William George. See No./Voir no 4480

5074
Schindler, John Norman. "Rhenium and Osmium in Some Canadian Ores in Neutron Activation Analysis." McMaster, 1975.

5075
Sherwood, Herbert Gordon. "The Quantitative Mineralogy of Forty-Five Canadian Base Metal Sulphide Ore Deposits." Manitoba, 1968.

5076
Simmons, Edwin Craig. "Origins of Four Anorthsite Suites." SUNY, Stony Brook, 1976. [Canadian Shield/Bouclier canadien]

5077
Sopuck, Vladimir Joseph. "A Lithogeochemical Approach in the Search for Areas of Felsic Volcanic Rocks Associated with Mineralization in the Canadian Shield." Queen's, 1977.

5078
Steinthorsson, Sigurdur. "The Oxide Mineralogy, Initial Oxidation State, and Deuteric Alteration in Some Precambrian Diabase Dike Swarms in Canada." Princeton, 1974.

5079
Stephenson, Randell Alexander. "Continental Topography and Gravity." Dalhousie, 1982.

5080
Strangway, David William. "Magnetic Properties o Some Canadian Diabase Dike Swarms." Toront 1960.

5081
Suguitan, Lynda Santos. "Evaluation of Five Muske Landscape Patterns with Similar Types of Vegeta Cover Utilizing Pollen Analysis." McMaster, 1964

5082
Waiser, William Andrew. "Rambler Professor Joh Macoun's Career with the Geological Survey o Canada, 1882-1912." Saskatchewan, 1983.

5083
Walker, Wilfred. "Archean Magmatism and Meta logeny: Geological Sequences in Some Archea Orefields." Ottawa, 1977.

5084
Wren, Christopher D. "Examination of Environment Factors Affecting the Distribution of Mercury an Other Metals in Precambrian Shield Lake Ecosy tems." Guelph, 1983.

REGIONAL STUDIES/ÉTUDES RÉGIONALES

Eastern Canada/Est du Canada

5085
Beltagy, Ali Ibrahim Ali Mohammed. "The Geo chemistry of Some Recent Marine Sediments fro the Gulf of St. Lawrence: A Study of the Le Than 63 Micron Fraction." McGill, 1974.

5086
Buyce, Milton Raymond. "Significance of Authigen K-Feldspar in Cambrian-Ordovician Carbonat Rocks of the Proto-Atlantic Shelf in Nort America." Rensselaer Polytechnic Institute, 1975.

5087
Dainty, Anton Michael. "Crustal Studies in Easter Canada." Dalhousie, 1968.

5088
Geldsetzer, Helmut. "Tectonically Controlled Sed mentation During the Middle Paleozoic of North eastern North America." Queen's, 1971.

5089
Hogg, William Alfred. "Building and Industrial Ston of Eastern Canada." McGill, 1959.

5090
Mudie, Peta J. "Palynology of Later Quaternar Marine Sediments, Eastern Canada." Dalhousi 1981.

5091
Pitcher, Max Grow. "Evolution of Chazyan (Ord vician) Reefs of Eastern United States an Canada." Columbia, 1964.

5092
Pointon, C.R. "Palaeozoic Volcanogenic Minera Deposits at Parys Mountain, Avoca and S.E Canada." Aston, 1979.

5093
Scott, Gary Robert. "Paleomagnetism of Carbon ferous and Triassic Strata from Cratonic Nort America." Texas, Dallas, 1975.

5094
Simonson, Bruce Miller. "Sedimentology of Precambrian Iron-Formations with Special Reference to the Sokoman Formation and Associated Deposits of Northeastern Canada." Johns Hopkins, 1982.

5095
Tolderlund, Douglas Stanley. "Seasonal Distributional Patterns of Planktonic Foraminifera at Five Ocean Stations in the Western North Atlantic." Columbia, 1969. [Labrador Sea/Mer du Labrador]

Western Canada/Ouest du Canada

5096
Armstrong, Robert Clarke. "The Dispersion of Mercury and Other Metals Related to Mineral Deposits in the Canadian Cordillera." Queen's, 1975.

5097
Broughton, Paul Leonard. "Origin of Coal Basins by Salt Solution Tectonics in Western Canada." Cambridge, 1980.

5098
Carsola, Alfred J. "Marine Geology of the Arctic Ocean and Adjacent Seas of Alaska and Northwestern Canada." California, Los Angeles, 1953.

5099
Colquhoun, Donald John. "Triassic Stratigraphy of Western Central Canada." Illinois, 1960.

5100
Dick, Lawrence Allan. "A Comparative Study of the Geology, Mineralogy, and Conditions of Formation of Contact Metasomatic Mineral Deposits in the Northeast Canadian Cordilleras." Queen's, 1980.

5101
Drake, Julian John. "Hydrology and Karst Solution in the Southern Canadian Rockies." McMaster, 1974.

5102
Goodman, A.J. "The Interpretation of Petrographical and Other Evidence from Borings in Western Canada." Birmingham, 1934.

5103
Gunton, John E. "Geochemical Dispersion Associated with Porphyry-Type Mineralization in the Canadian Cordilleras." Queen's, 1974.

5104
Hanfield, Robert Charles. "Archaeocyatha from the Mackenzie and Cassiar Mountains, Western Canada." Princeton, 1970.

5105
Lichti-Federovich, Sigrid. "Problems on the Interpretation of Holocene Pollen Spectra from the Western Interior of Canada." Trent, 1968.

5106
Palonen, Pentti Arnold. "Sedimentology and Stratigraphy of Gog Group Sandstones in Southern Canadian Rockies." Calgary, 1976.

5107
Picklyk, Donald D. "Overthrust Faulting-Finite Element Models of the Initial Stages in the Development of the Southern Canadian Rockies, a Foreland Thrust and Fold Belt." Queen's, 1973.

5108
Pocock, Y.P. "Palynology of the Jurassic Sediments of Western Canada." London, 1965.

5109
Rapson, J.E. "The Petrography and Depositional Environment of the Permian Ranger Canyon and Mowitch Formations, Ishbel Group from the Southern Canadian Rocky Mountains." London, 1967.

5110
Sargent, Melville Wayne. "Depositional Patterns in the Upper Cambrian Lyell Formation, Southern Canadian Rockies." Calgary, 1976.

5111
Silver, Burr Arthur. "North American Mid-Jurassic Through Mid-Cretaceous Stratigraphic Patterns of Colorado Plateau, Rocky Mountains, and Great Plains." Washington, Seattle, 1966.

5112
Stronach, Nicholas John. "Sedimentology and Paleoecology of a Shale Basin: The Fernie Formation of the Southern Rocky Mountains, Canada." Calgary, 1982.

5113
Woodward, Harold W. "Insoluble Residues of the Devonian, Southern Rocky Mountains, Western Canada." Wisconsin, 1953.

Southern Canada/Sud du Canada

5114
Doyle, Patrick Joseph. "Regional Geochemical Reconnaissance and Compositional Variations in Grain and Forage Crops on the Southern Canadian Interior Plain." British Columbia, 1977.

5115
Nanz, Robert H., Jr. "Composition and Abundance of Finegrained Pre-Cambrian Sediments of the Southern Canadian Shield." Chicago, 1952.

The Great Lakes/Les Grands Lacs

General Items/Ouvrages généraux

5116
Berti, Albert Anthony. "Palynology and Stratigraphy of the Mid-Wisconsin in the Eastern Great Lakes Region, North America." Western Ontario, 1971.

5117
Cohn, Barry Phillip. "A Forecast Model for Great Lakes Water Levels." Syracuse, 1975.

5118
Gwyn, Quintin Hugh. "Heavy Mineral Assemblages in Tills and Their Use in Distinguishing Glacial Lobes in the Great Lakes Region." Western Ontario, 1971.

Krezoski, John Roman. See No./Voir no 11783

5119
Marshall, Ernest Willard. "The Geology of the Great Lakes Ice Cover." Michigan, 1977.

Lake Erie/Lac Érié

5120
Lewis, Charles Frederick Michael. "Sedimentation Studies of Unconsolidated Deposits in the Lake Erie Basin." Toronto, 1967.

Lake Huron/Lac Huron

5121
Bourbonnière, Richard Arthur. "Geochemistry of Humic Matter in Holocene Great Lakes Sediments." Michigan, 1979.

5122
Broster, Bruce E. "Compositional Variations in the St. Joseph Till Units in the Goderich Area." Western Ontario, 1982.

5123
McDowell, John Parmelee. "A Paleocurrent Study of the Mississagi Quartzite along the North Shore of Lake Huron." Johns Hopkins, 1963.

5124
Nwachukwu, Silas Ogo Okonkwo. "The Geologic Significance of Geomagnetic Measurements in the Lake Huron Basin and Adjacent Areas." Toronto, 1964.

5125
Ovenshine, Alexander Thomas. "Sedimentary Structures in Portions of the Gowganda Formation, North Shore of Lake Huron, Canada." California, Los Angeles, 1965.

5126
Parviainen, Esko Atso Nolevi. "The Sedimentation of the Huronian Ramsay Lake and Bruce Formations, North Shore of Lake Huron, Ontario." Western Ontario, 1973.

5127
Rice, William A. "Geology of the Blind River -Spragge Area, North Shore of Lake Huron." Yale, 1940.

Lake Superior/Lac Supérieur

5128
Bradshaw, Bennie Albert. "Petrological Comparison of Lake Superior Iron Formations." Toronto, 1957.

5129
Carlson, Thomas Warren. "Influence of Deep Water Currents on Sedimentation in Lake Superior." Minnesota, 1982.

5130
Dell, Carol Irene Green. "Late Quaternary Sedimentation in Lake Superior." Michigan, 1971.

5131
Farrand, William Richard. "Former Shorelines in Western and Northern Lake Superior Basin." Michigan, 1960.

5132
Halls, Henry Campbell. "Geological Interpretation of Geophysical Data from the Lake Superior Region." Toronto, 1970.

5133
La Berge, Gene Ludger. "Development of Magnetite in Iron Formations of the Lake Superior Region." Wisconsin, 1963.

5134
Marsden, Ralph W. "The Application of Accessory Mineral Methods to the Pre-Cambrian Rocks of the Lake Superior Region." Wisconsin, 1939.

5135
Mengel, Joseph Torbitt, Jr. "The Cherts of the Lake Superior Iron-Bearing Formations." Wisconsin, 1963.

5136
Merk, George Phillip. "Provenance and Tecton. Inferences Concerning the Keweenawan Interflo Sediments of the Lake Superior Region." Michiga State, 1972.

5137
Nussmann, David George. "Trace Elements in th Sediments of Lake Superior." Michigan, 1965.

5138
Symons, David Thorburn Arthur. "Paleomagnetic Stu dies of Lake Superior Iron Ore Deposits." Toront 1965.

Gulf of St. Lawrence/Golfe Saint-Laurent

5139
Rodrigues, Cyril Gerard. "Holocene Microfauna an Paleoceanography of the Gulf of St. Lawrence. Carleton, 1981.

British Columbia/Colombie-Britannique

5140
Aalto, Kenneth Rolf. "Glacial Marine Sedimentatio and Stratigraphy of the Toby Conglomerate (Uppe Proterozoic), Southeastern British Columbia Northwestern Idaho and Northeastern Washington Wisconsin, 1970.

5141
Aho, Aaro E. "Geology and Ore Deposits of th Property of Pacific Nickel Mines near Hop British Columbia." California, Berkeley, 1954.

5142
Aitken, James D. "Greenstones and Associated Ultra mafic Rocks of the Atlin Map Area, Britis Columbia." California, Los Angeles, 1954.

5143
Allan, John Andrew. "Geology of the Ice Rive District, British Columbia." Massachusetts Inst tute of Technology, 1912.

5144
Anderson, Franz Elmer. "Stratigraphy of Late Pleisto cene and Holocene Sediments from the Strait Juan de Fuca." Washington, Seattle, 1967.

5145
Archibald, Douglas Arthur. "Geochronology a Tectonic Implications of Magmatism and Metamo phism: Southern Kootenay Arc and Neighbourir Regions, Southeastern British Columbia." Queen 1983.

5146
Armstrong, John Edward. "Geology of the West Ha of the Fort Fraser Map Area British Columbia Toronto, 1939.

5147
Ashley, Gail Mowry. "Sedimentology of a Freshwat Tidal System, Pitt River-Pitt Lake, Briti Columbia." British Columbia, 1977.

5148
Asihene, Kwanie Anane Buahin. "The Texada Form tion of British Columbia and Its Associated Magn tite Concentrations." California, Los Angele 1970.

5149
Bacon, William Russell. "The Geology and Mineral Deposits of the Sechelt Peninsula-Jervis Inlet Area, British Columbia." Toronto, 1952.

5150
Bailey, David G. "The Geology of the Morehead Lake Area, South Central British Columbia." Queen's, 1978.

5151
Balkwill, Hugh Robert. "Structural Analysis of the Western Ranges, Rocky Mountains, near Golden, British Columbia." Texas, 1969.

5152
Bamber, Edward Wayne. "Mississippian Corals from Northeastern British Columbia, Canada." Princeton, 1962.

5153
Bancroft, Joseph A. "Preliminary Report on a Portion of the Coast of British Columbia and the Islands Adjacent Thereto in the Nanaimo District." McGill, 1910.

5154
Barr, Sandra Marie. "Geology of the Northern End of Juan de Fuca Ridge and Adjacent Continental Slope." British Columbia, 1973.

5155
Basinger, James French. "Structurally Preserved Metasequoia from the Middle Eocene of Southern British Columbia, Canada." Alberta, 1979.

5156
Bateman, Alan Mara. "Geology and Ore Deposits of Bridge River District, British Columbia." Yale, 1913.

5157
Beddoe-Stephens, B. "The Petrology and Geochemistry of the Rossland Volcanic Rocks of Southern British Columbia." Durham, 1978.

5158
Bell, Richard Thomas. "Precambrian Rocks of the Tuchodi Lakes Map Area, Northeastern British Columbia, Canada." Princeton, 1966.

5159
Benvenuto, Gary Louis. "Structural Evolution of the Hosmer Thrust Sheet, Southeastern British Columbia." Queen's, 1978.

5160
Bevier, Mary Lou. "Geology and Petrogenesis of Mio-Pleocene Chilcotin Group Basalts, British Columbia." California, Santa Barbara, 1982.

5161
Bishop, Donald Thomas. "Petrology and Geochemistry of the Purcell Sills, Boundary County, Idaho and Adjacent Areas." Idaho, 1976.

5162
Blome, Charles David. "Upper Triassic Radiolaria from Eastern Oregon and British Columbia." Texas, Dallas, 1981.

5163
Bolm, John Gary. "Structural and Petrographic Studies in the Shuswap Terrane." Idaho, 1975.

5164
Bostock, Hugh Samuel. "Geology and Ore Deposits of Nickel Plate Mountain, Hedley, British Columbia." Wisconsin, 1929.

5165
Brabec, Dragan. "A Geochemical Study of the Guichon Creek Batholith, British Columbia." British Columbia, 1971.

5166
Briskey, Joseph A., Jr. "Geology, Petrology, and Geochemistry of the Jersey, East Jersey, Huestis, and Iona Porphyry Copper-Molybdenum Deposits, Highland Valley, British Columbia." Oregon State, 1980.

5167
Brock, Byron B. "The So-Called Load Metamorphism of the Shuswap Terrane of British Columbia." Wisconsin, 1934.

5168
Bruce, Everend Lester. "Geology and Ore Deposits of Rossland, Victoria, British Columbia." Columbia, 1915.

5169
Bultman, Thomas Robert. "Geology and Tectonic History of the Whitehorse Trough West of Atlin, British Columbia." Yale, 1979.

5170
Burns, Robert Earle. "A Model of Sedimentation in Small Sill-Less Embayed Estuaries of the Pacific Northwest." Washington, Seattle, 1962. [Port San Juan, Vancouver Island/Port San Juan, Île de Vancouver]

5171
Burrus, Robert Carlton. "Analysis of Fluid Inclusions in Graphitic Metamorphic Rocks from Bryant Pond, Maine, and Khtada Lake, British Columbia: Thermodynamic Basis and Geologic Interpretation of Observed Fluid Compositions and Molar Volumes." Princeton, 1977.

5172
Burwash, Edward Moore Jackson. "The Geology of Vancouver and Vicinity." Chicago, 1915.

5173
Bustin, Robert Marc. "Structural Features of Coal Measures of the Kootenay Formation, Southeastern Canadian Rocky Mountains." British Columbia, 1980.

5174
Cairnes, Clive Elmore. "Geology of the Coquihalla Area, British Columbia." Princeton, 1922.

5175
Campbell, Charles D. "The Kruger Alkaline Syenites of Southern British Columbia." Stanford, 1934.

5176
Campbell, Kenneth Vincent. "Metamorphic Petrology and Structural Geology of the Crooked Lake Area, Cariboo Mountains, British Columbia." Washington, Seattle, 1971.

5177
Cargill, Donald George. "Geology of the 'Island Copper' Mine, Port Hardy, British Columbia." British Columbia, 1975.

5178
Carson, Bobb. "Stratigraphy and Depositional History of Quaternary Sediments in Northern Cascadia Basin and Juan de Fuca Abyssal Plain, Northeast Pacific Ocean." Washington, Seattle, 1971.

5179
Carson, David John Temple. "Metallogenic Study of Vancouver Island with Emphasis on the Relationship of Mineral Deposits to Plutonic Rocks." Carleton, 1968.

5180
Carswell, Henry Thomas. "Origin of the Sullivan Lead-Zinc-Silver Deposit, British Columbia." Queen's, 1961.

5181
Carter, Lionel. "Surficial Sediments of Barkley Sound and Adjacent Continental Shelf, Vancouver Island, British Columbia." British Columbia, 1971.

5182
Carter, Nicholas Charles. "Geology and Geochronology of Porphyry Copper and Molybdenum Deposits in West-Central British Columbia." British Columbia, 1974.

5183
Carvalho, Ilson Guimaraes. "Geology of the Western Mines District, Vancouver Island, British Columbia." Western Ontario, 1979.

5184
Cavanagh, Lorraine Marie Monnier. "Biostratigraphy of the Cache Creek Group Horsefeed Formation, Tagish and Tutshi Lakes Area, South Central Yukon Territory and Northwest British Columbia, Canada." Wisconsin, 1980.

5185
Christie, James Stanley. "Geology of Vaseaux Lake Area." British Columbia, 1973.

5186
Christie, Robert Loring. "Geology of the Plutonic Rocks of the Coast Mountains in the Vicinity of Bennett, British Columbia." Toronto, 1959.

5187
Christopher, Peter Allen. "Application of K-Ar and Fission-Track Dating to the Metallogeny of Porphyry and Related Mineral Deposits in the Canadian Cordillera." British Columbia, 1973.

5188
Church, Barry Neil. "Geology of the White Lake Area, British Columbia." British Columbia, 1967.

5189
Clague, John Joseph. "Late Cenozoic Geology of the Southern Rocky Mountain Trench, British Columbia." British Columbia, 1973.

5190
Clark, Thomas. "Geology of an Ultramafic Complex on the Turnagain River, North-Western British Columbia." Queen's, 1976.

5191
Cleveland, Courtney E. "The Geology of the Empire Mine, Bralorne, British Columbia." McGill, 1940.

5192
Cook, Donald George. "Structural Style Influenced by a Cambrian Regional Facies Change in the Mount Stephen-Mount Dennis Area, Alberta-British Columbia." Queen's, 1968.

5193
Couch, Richard William. "Gravity and Structures of the Crust and Subcrust in the Northeast Pacific Ocean West of Washington and British Columbia." Oregon State, 1969.

5194
Craig, Douglas B. "Structure and Petrology with Shuswap Metamorphic Complex, Revelstok British Columbia." Wisconsin, 1966.

5195
Crickmay, Colin H. "The Geology and Paleontology the Harrison Lake District, British Columbi Together with a General Review of the Jurass Faunas and Stratigraphy of Western Nor America." Stanford, 1925.

5196
Crosby, Percy. "Structure and Petrology of the Ce tral Kootenay Lake Area, British Columbia Harvard, 1960.

5197
Davies, Edward Julian Llewellyn. "Ordovician a Silu rian of the Northern Rocky Mountains Betwe Peace and Muskwa Rivers, British Columbia Alberta, 1966.

5198
Davis, Newton Fraser Gordon. "Clearwater La Area, British Columbia." Princeton, 1929.

5199
Dawson, Kenneth Murray. "Geology of Endako Mir British Columbia." British Columbia, 1972.

5200
Dolmage, Victor. "The Geology of the Telkwa Riv District, British Columbia." Massachussetts Ins tute of Technology, 1917.

5201
Douglas, Bruce James. "Structural and Stratigrapl Analysis of a Metasedimentary Inlier within Coast Plutonic Complex, British Columb Canada." Princeton, 1983.

5202
Drummond, Arthur Darryl. "Mineralogical a Chemical Study of Craigmont Mine, Merri British Columbia." California, Berkeley, 1966.

5203
Drysdale, Charles Wales. "The Geology of Franklin Mining Camp, British Columbia." Ya 1912.

5204
Duncan, Ian James. "The Evolution of the Thor-O Gneiss Dome and Related Geochronologi Studies." British Columbia, 1982. [Shusw Terrane]

5205
Eccles, John Kerby. "Textures of Lower Paleoz Rocks of Northeastern British Columbia." Illino 1958.

5206
Edmunds, Frederick Robin. "Multivariate Analysis Petrographic and Chemical Data from the Aldri Formation, Southern Purcell Mountain Ran British Columbia, Canada." Pennsylvania Sta 1977.

5207
Evans, Charles Sparling. "Geology of Brisco-Dogto Map-Area, British Columbia." Princeton, 1927.

5208
Ewing, Thomas Edward. "Geology and Tecto Setting of the Kamloops Group, South-Cent British Columbia." British Columbia, 1981.

5209
Fiesinger, Donald William. "Petrology of the Quaternary Volcanic Centers in the Quesnel Highlands and Garibaldi Provincial Park Areas, British Columbia." Calgary, 1975.

5210
Findlay, David Christopher. "Petrology of the Tulmeen Ultramafic Complex, Yale District, British Columbia." Queen's, 1963.

5211
Fletcher, Christopher John N. "Structure and Metamorphism of Penfold Creek Area, near Quesnel Lake, Central British Columbia." British Columbia, 1972.

5212
Fox, Peter Edward. "The Petrology of Adamant Pluton, British Columbia." Carleton, 1966.

5213
Freeze, Arthur Charles. "Geology of Pinchi Lake, British Columbia." Princeton, 1942.

5214
Fulton, Robert John. "Deglaciation of the Kamloops Region, British Columbia." Northwestern, 1963.

5215
Fyles, James T. "Geology of the Cowichan Lake Area, Vancouver Island, British Columbia." Columbia, 1955.

5216
Fyles, John Gladstone. "Surficial Geology of the Horne Lake and Parksville Map-Area, Vancouver Island, British Columbia." Ohio State, 1956.

5217
Gabrielse, Hubert. "Petrology and Structure of the McDame Ultramafic Belt, British Columbia." Columbia, 1955.

5218
Gallagher, Maureen Theresa. "Substrate Controlled Biofacies: Recent Foraminifera on the Continental Shelf and Slope of Vancouver Island, B.C." Calgary, 1979.

5219
Gardner, Douglas A.C. "Structural Geology and Metamorphism of Calcareous Lower Paleozoic States, Blueberry River-Redburn Creek Area, near Golden, British Columbia." Queen's, 1977.

5220
Gilbert, Robert. "Observations of Lacustrine Sedimentation at Lilloet Lake, British Columbia." British Columbia, 1974.

5221
Glover, Joseph K. "Geology of the Summit Creek Map Area, Southern Kootenay Arc, British Columbia." Queen's, 1978.

5222
Green, Lewis H. "Wall-Rock Alternation Associated with Certain Zinc and Lead Deposits Formed Through the Replacement of Limestone: Salmo Map-Area, British Columbia." Wisconsin, 1954.

5223
Green, Nathan Louis. "Multistage Andesite Genesis in the Garibaldi Lake Area, Southwestern British Columbia." British Columbia, 1978.

5224
Grove, Edward Willis. "Detailed Geological Studies in the Stewart Complex, Northwestern British Columbia." McGill, 1973.

5225
Gunning, H.C. "Economic Geology of the Lardeau Map-Area, British Columbia." Massachusetts Institute of Technology, 1929.

5226
Haimila, Norman Edward. "Contact Phenomenon of the Central Vancouver Island Intrusion." Michigan State, 1974.

5227
Hamilton, T.S. "Late Cenozoic Alkaline Volcanics of the Level Mountain Range, Northwestern British Columbia: Geology, Petrology and Paleomagnetism." Alberta, 1981.

5228
Hanson, William Bruce. "Stratigraphy and Sedimentology of the Cretaceous Nanaimo Group, Saltspring Island, British Columbia." Oregon State, 1976.

Hendershot, William Hamilton. See No./Voir no 235

5229
Henderson, Gerald Gordon Lewis. "Geology of the Stanford Range, British Columbia." Princeton, 1953.

5230
Hicock, Stephen Robert. "Pre-Fraser Pleistocene Stratigraphy, Geochronology, and Paleoecology of the Georgia Depression, British Columbia." Western Ontario, 1980.

5231
Hills, Leonard Vincent. "Palynology and Age of Early Tertiary Basins, Interior British Columbia." Alberta, 1966.

5232
Hoadley, John William. "Geology of the Zeballos Map-Area, Vancouver Island, British Columbia." Toronto, 1950.

5233
Hoffer, Jerry Martin. "Plagioclase Variations in a Porphyritic Flow of the Columbia River Basalt." Washington State, 1965.

5234
Hoffman, Stanley Joel. "Mineral Exploration of the Nechako Plateau, Central British Columbia, Using Lake Sediment Geochemistry." British Columbia, 1976.

5235
Holland, Stuart Sawden. "The Geology of the Western Half of the Vernon Map Area, British Columbia." Princeton, 1933.

5236
Hollister, Lincoln Steffens. "Electron Microprobe Investigations of Metamorphic Reactions and Mineral Growth Histories, Kwoiek Area, British Columbia." California Institute of Technology, 1966.

5237
Hopkins, William Stephen, Jr. "Palynology of the Tertiary Rocks of the Whatcom Basin, Southwestern British Columbia and Northwestern Washington." British Columbia, 1966.

5238
Hoy, Trygvie. "Structure and Metamorphism of Kootenay Arc Rocks Around Riondel, B.C." Queen's, 1974.

5239
Hughes, John E. "The Peace and Pine River Foothills (Structure and Tectonics)." McGill, 1964.

5240
Hunt, Graham Hugh. "The Purcell Eruptive Rocks." Alberta, 1962.

5241
Hyndman, Donald William. "Petrology and Structure of Nakusp Map-Area, British Columbia." California, Berkeley, 1964.

5242
Irwin, Arthur B. "Geology of the Howson Creek Area, Slocal Mining Division, British Columbia." McGill, 1950.

5243
James, Howard T. "Geology and Ore Deposits of the Brittannia Map-Area, British Columbia." Harvard, 1927.

5244
Johnson, Ronald Dwight. "Dispersal of Recent Sediments and Mine Tailing in a Shallow-Silled Fjord, Rupert Inlet, British Columbia." British Columbia, 1974.

5245
Jones, Alexander Gordon. "Vernon Map-Area, British Columbia." Harvard, 1960.

5246
Jones, Jonathan Wyn. "A Study of Some Low-Grade Regional Metamorphic Rocks from the Omineca Crystalline Belt, British Columbia." Calgary, 1972.

5247
Jones, Michael Baxter. "Hydrothermal Alteration and Mineralization of the Valley Copper Deposit, Highland Valley, British Columbia." Oregon State, 1975.

5248
Jones, Peter Barrett. "Geology of the Flathead Area, Southeastern British Columbia." Colorado School of Mines, 1966.

5249
Jones, Russell H.B. "Geology and Ore Deposits of Hudson Bay Mountain, Coast District, British Columbia." Wisconsin, 1926.

5250
Jure, Albert Edward. "The Petrography of the Purcell Sills." Wisconsin, 1930.

Keevil, Norman Bell, Jr. See No./Voir no 4510

5251
Kenah, Christopher. "Mechanism and Physical Conditions of Emplacement of the Quottoon Pluton, British Columbia." Princeton, 1979.

5252
Kingston, David Russell. "Paleozoic Stratigraphy of the Tetsa-Halfway Rivers Area, Northeastern British Columbia, Canada." Wisconsin, 1956.

5253
Kirkham, Rodney Victor. "A Mineralogical and Geochemical Study of the Zonal Distribution of Ores in the Hudson Bay Range, British Columbia." Wisconsin, 1969.

5254
Kleinspehn, Karen Lee. "Cretaceous Sedimentatic and Tectonics, Tyaughton-Methow Basin, Sout eastern British Columbia." Princeton, 1982.

5255
Kuniyoshi, Shingi. "Petrology of the Karmuts Group, Northeastern Vancouver Island, Briti Columbia." California, Los Angeles, 1972.

5256
Kwong, Yan-Tat John. "A New Look at the Aft Copper Mine in the Light of Mineral Distributior Host Rock Geochemistry and Irreversible Minera Solution Interactions." British Columbia, 198 [Kamloops]

5257
Lambert, Maurice Bernard. "The Bennett Lake Cat dron Subsidence Complex, British Columbia a Yukon Territory." Carleton, 1972.

5258
Lang, Arthur Hamilton. "Geology and Mineral Dep sits of the Owen Lake Mining Camp, Briti Columbia." Princeton, 1930.

5259
Lappin, Allen Ralph. "Partial Melting and the Gener tion of Quartz Dioritic Plutons at Crust Temperatures and Pressures within the Coa Range Batholithic Complex near the Khyex Riv British Columbia." Princeton, 1976.

5260
Leatherbarrow, Robert Wesley. "Metamorphism Pelitic Rocks from the Northern Selkirk Mountai Southeastern British Columbia." Carleton, 1981.

5261
Le Couteur, Peter Clifford. "A Study of Lead Isotor from Mineral Deposits in Southeastern Brit Columbia and from the Anvil Range, Yukon Ter tory." British Columbia, 1973.

5262
Lee, James W. "The Geology of Nickel Pla Mountain, British Columbia." Stanford, 1952.

5263
Leech, Geoffrey Bosdin. "Petrology of the Ultrama and Gabbroid Intrusive Rocks of the Shulaps Ran British Columbia." Princeton, 1949.

5264
Lett, Raymond E. W. "Secondary Dispersion of Tran tion Metals through a Copper-Rich Bog in t Cascade Mountains, British Columbia." Brit Columbia, 1979.

5265
Lincoln, Timothy Nye. "The Redistribution of Copp During Metamorphism of the Karmutsen Volcani Vancouver Island, British Columbia." Californ Los Angeles, 1978.

5266
Little, Heward Wallace. "The Ultrasonic and Asso ated Rocks of the Middle River Range, Brit Columbia." Toronto, 1947.

5267
Lowes, Brian Edward. "Metamorphic Petrology a Structural Geology of the Area East of Harri Lake, British Columbia." Washington, Seatt 1972.

5268
Lynott, William John. "Geology and Mineral Deposits of Warn Bay-Tofino Inlet Map-Area West Coast of Vancouver Island, British Columbia." Princeton, 1949.

5269
MacDonald, Alan Stratton. "The Salmo Lead-Zinc Deposits: A Study of Their Deformation and Metamorphic Features." British Columbia, 1973.

5270
MacIntyre, Donald George. "Evolution of Upper Cretaceous Volcanic and Plutonic Centers and Associated Porphyric Copper Occurrences, Tahtsa Lake Area, British Columbia." Western Ontario, 1977.

5271
MacKenzie, John David. "The Geology of Graham Island, British Columbia." Massachusetts Institute of Technology, 1916.

5272
Manns, Francis Tucker. "Stratigraphic Aspects of the Silurian-Devonian Sequence Hosting Zinc and Lead Mineralization near Robb Lake, Northwestern B.C." Toronto, 1982.

5273
Mathews, William H. "Geology of the Mount Garibaldi Map-Area, Southwestern British Columbia." California, Berkeley, 1948.

5274
McAllister, Arnold L. "The Geology of the Ymir Map-Area, British Columbia." McGill, 1950.

5275
McCann, William Sidney. "Geology and Mineral Deposits of the Bridge River Map-Area, British Columbia." Yale, 1920.

5276
McIlreath, Ian Alexander. "Stratigraphic and Sedimentary Relationships at the Western Edge of the Middle Cambrian Carbonate Facies Belt, Field, British Columbia." Calgary, 1977.

5277
McKinstry, Hugh Exton. "I. Supergene and Hypogene Mineralization in Certain Cordilleran Silver Deposits. II. Qualitative Microchemical and Magnetic Tests in the Identification of Opaque Minerals." Harvard, 1926. [Atlin and/et Beverdell]

5278
McMechan, Margaret Evaline. "Stratigraphy, Structure, and Tectonic Implications of the Middle Proterozoic Purcell Supergroup in the Mount Fisher Area, Southeastern British Columbia." Queen's, 1980.

5279
McMechan, Robert Douglas. "Stratigraphy, Sedimentology, Structure and Tectonic Implications of the Oligocene Kishenehn Formation, Flathead Valley Graben, Southeastern British Columbia." Queen's, 1981.

5280
McMillan, William John. "Petrology and Structure of the West Flank, Frenchman's Cap Dome, near Revelstoke, British Columbia." Carleton, 1972.

5281
McTaggart, Kenneth C. "The Belt of Lower Cretaceous Rocks Along Fraser River, Southwestern British Columbia." Yale, 1948.

5282
Meade, Harlan Donnelly. "Petrology and Metal Occurrences of the Takla Group and Hogem and Germansen Batholiths, North Central British Columbia." Western Ontario, 1977.

5283
Medford, Gary Allan. "Geology and Thermal History of an Area near Okanagan Lake, Southern British Columbia." British Columbia, 1976.

5284
Meloche, John Dennis. "Evolution of Biogeochemical Element Cycles with Emphasis on the Role of Metal-Organic Interactions in the Accumulation of Heavy Metals in Organic-Rich Sediments." Western Ontario, 1981.

5285
Monger, James William Heron. "The Stratigraphy and Structure of the Type-Area of the Chilliwack Group, Southwestern British Columbia." British Columbia, 1966.

5286
Montgomery, Joseph. "Petrology, Structure and Origin of the Copper Mountain Intrusion near Princeton, British Columbia." British Columbia, 1967.

5287
Morrison, Michael Lynn. "Structure and Petrology of the Southern Portion of the Malton Gneiss, British Columbia." Calgary, 1982.

5288
Morton, Ronald Lee. "Alkalic Volcanism and Copper Deposits of the Horsefly Area, Central British Columbia." Carleton, 1976.

5289
Mothersill, John Sydney. "The Halfway Formation of the Milligan Creek Area, British Columbia." Queen's, 1967.

5290
Mulligan, Robert. "Geology of the Nelson and Adjoining Part of Salmo Map Areas, British Columbia." McGill, 1951.

5291
Mutti, Lawrence J. "Structure and Metamorphism of the Cranberry Region, Thorodin Gneiss Dome, Shuswap Metamorphic Complex, British Columbia." Harvard, 1978.

5292
Newmarch, Charles Bell. "Geology of the Crowsnest Coal Basin, with Special Reference to the Fernie Coal Area (British Columbia)." Princeton, 1951.

5293
Nielsen, Kent Christopher. "Tectonic Setting of the Northern Okanagan Valley at Mara Lake, British Columbia." British Columbia, 1978.

5294
Norford, Brian Seeley. "Paleozoic Stratigraphy and Paleontology of the Lower Turnagain River Map-Area, Northern British Columbia." Yale, 1959.

5295
Northcote, Kenneth Eugene. "Geology and Geochronology of the Guichon Creek Batholith, B.C." British Columbia, 1968.

5296
Ohmoto, Hiroshi. "The Bluebell Mine, British Columbia, Canada." Princeton, 1969.

5297
Okulitch, Andrew Vladimir. "Geology of Mount Kobau." British Columbia, 1969.

5298
Olade, Moses A. D. "Bedrock Geochemistry of Porphyry Copper Deposits, Highland Valley, British Columbia." British Columbia, 1975.

5299
Oldham, Charles H. G. "Gravity and Magnetic Investigations Along the Alaskan Highway and in Southeastern Ontario." Toronto, 1954.

5300
Pacht, Jory Allen. "Sedimentology and Petrology of the Late Cretaceous Nanaimo Group in the Nanaimo Basin, Washington and British Columbia: Implications for Late Cretaceous Tectonics." Ohio State, 1980.

5301
Page, Richard James. "Sedimentology and Tectonic History of the Esowista and Ucluth Peninsulas, West Coast, Vancouver Island, British Columbia." Washington, Seattle, 1974.

5302
Panteleyev, Andrejs. "Geologic Setting, Mineralization, and Aspects of Zoning at the Berg Porphyry Copper-Molybdenum Deposit, Central British Columbia." British Columbia, 1976.

5303
Parrish, Randall Richardson. "Cenozoic Thermal and Tectonic History of the Coast Mountains of British Columbia as Revealed by Fusion Track and Geological Data and Quantitative Thermal Models." British Columbia, 1982.

5304
Paterson, Ian Arthur. "The Geology of the Pinchi Lake Area, Central British Columbia." British Columbia, 1973.

5305
Patmore, William Henry. "Pseudo-Pyrometasomatic Gold at Hedley, British Columbia." Princeton, 1941.

5306
Peatfield, Giles R. "Geologic History and Metallogeny of the 'Boundary District' Southern British Columbia and Northern Washington." Queen's, 1978.

5307
Pharo, Christopher Howard. "Sediments of the Central and Southern Strait of Georgia, British Columbia." British Columbia, 1973.

5308
Pigage, Lee Case. "Metamorphism and Deformation on the Northeast Margin of the Shuswap Metamorphic Complex, Azure Lake, British Columbia." British Columbia, 1979.

5309
Poole, William Hope. "Geology of the Cassiar Mountains in the Vicinity of the Yukon-British Columbia Boundary." Princeton, 1956.

5310
Potter, Christopher John. "Geology of the Bridge River Complex, Southern Shulaps Range, British Columbia: A Record of Mesozoic Convergent Tectonics." Washington, Seattle, 1983.

5311
Presley, Bobby Joe. "Chemistry of Interstitial Wat[er] from Marine Sediments." California, Los Angele[s], 1969.

5312
Preto, Vittorio A. G. "Structure and Petrography [of] the Grand Forks Group (Precambrian or Paleozo[ic] Shuswap Terrane) British Columbia." McGill, 196[ ].

5313
Price, Raymond Alex. "Structure and Stratigraphy [of] the Flathead North Map-Area (East Half), Briti[sh] Columbia and Alberta." Princeton, 1958.

5314
Raeside, Robert Pollock. "Structure, Metamorphis[m] and Magmatization of the Scrip Range, Mi[ca] Creek, British Columbia." Calgary, 1982.

5315
Read, Peter Burland. "Petrology and Structure [of] Poplar Creek Map-Area, British Columbia[.]" California, Berkeley, 1966.

5316
Reamsbottom, Stanley Baily. "Geology and Metamo[r]phism of the Mount Breckinridge Area, Harris[on] Lake, British Columbia." British Columbia, 1974.

5317
Reesor, John Elgin. "The White Creek Batholith a[nd] its Geological Environment in Dewar Creek Ma[p] Area, British Columbia." Princeton, 1952.

5318
Reinecke, Leopold. "The Geology and Ore Deposits [of] the Beaverdell Map-Area, British Columbia." Ya[le], 1914.

5319
Renault, Jacques Roland. "The Geological Conditio[ns] of Molybdenite Deposition as Deduced from Te[x]tural Analysis." Toronto, 1964.

5320
Rice, H.M.A. "The Geology and Economic Geology [of] the Cranbrook District, British Columbia[.]" California Institute of Technology, 1934.

5321
Richards, Thomas Albert. "Plutonic Rocks Betwe[en] Hope, B.C. and the 49th Parallel." Briti[sh] Columbia, 1971.

5322
Robinson, Malcolm Campbell. "The Geological Setti[ng] and Relationships of Ore Deposits in the We[st] Kootenay District, British Columbia." Princeto[n], 1951.

5323
Roddick, James Archibald. "The Plutonic Rocks in t[he] Vancouver North-Coquitlam Area in the Souther[n] Coast Mountains of British Columbia[.]" Washington, Seattle, 1955.

5324
Roots, Ernest Frederick. "Geology and Mineral Dep[o]sits of the Aiken Lake Map-Area, Briti[sh] Columbia." Princeton, 1949.

5325
Rose, Bruce. "Geology of Savona District, Briti[sh] Columbia." Yale, 1913.

5326
Roy, Kenneth James. "Stratigraphic Analysis and Environmental Reconstruction of the Boundary Member of the Charlie Lake Formation (Triassic) Northeastern British Columbia." Northwestern, 1968.

5327
Ryan, Barry Desmond. "Structural Geology and RB-SR Geochronology of the Anarchist Mountain Area, Southcentral British Columbia." British Columbia, 1974.

Ryder, June Margaret. See No./Voir no 4619

5328
Sanchez, Arthur Ledda. "Chemical Speciation and Adsorption Behavior of Plutonium in Natural Waters." Washington, Seattle, 1983.

5329
Sangster, Donald Frederick. "The Contact Metasomatic Magnetite Deposits of Southwestern British Columbia." British Columbia, 1964.

5330
Sargent, Thomas Edward Hartley. "Geology of the Bedwell River-Drinkwater Creek Area, British Columbia." Massachusetts Institute of Technology, 1942.

5331
Schau, Mikkel Paul. "Geology of the Upper Triassic Nicola Group in South Central British Columbia." British Columbia, 1969.

5332
Schofield, Stuart James. "Geology of East Kootenay, British Columbia, with Special Reference to the Origin of Granite in Sills." Massachusetts Institute of Technology, 1912.

Schreier, Hanspeter. See No./Voir no 4620

5333
Scott, Darcy Lon. "Stratigraphy of the Lower Rocky Mountains Supergroup in the Southern Canadian Rocky Mountains." British Columbia, 1964.

5334
Scott, James Alan Bryson. "Upper Cretaceous Foraminifera of the Haslam Qualicum, and Trent River Formations, Vancouver Island, British Columbia." Calgary, 1974.

5335
Sears, James Walter. "Geology of the Albert Peak Area, Western Selkirk Mountains, British Columbia." Queen's, 1979.

5336
Shaw, David Andrew. "Structural Setting of the Adamant Pluton, Northern Selkirk Mountains, British Columbia." Carleton, 1981.

5337
Shepard, Francis Parker. "The Structure and Stratigraphy of the Rocky Mountain Trench from Gateway to Golden (British Columbia)." Chicago, 1922.

5338
Simpson, David. "A Study of Certain Mineral Deposits at the Headwaters of the Spillimacheen River, British Columbia." McGill, 1952.

5339
Sinclair, Alastair James. "A Lead Isotope Study of Mineral Deposits in the Kootenay Arc." British Columbia, 1964.

5340
Singleton, Glen Allen. "Weathering in a Soil Chronosequence." British Columbia, 1979. [Cox Bay on Vancouver Island/Cox Bay sur l'Île de Vancouver]

Smith, Alexander. See No./Voir no 2335

5341
Smith, Donald Leigh. "The Tippicanoe Sequence in Western North America." Washington, Seattle, 1966.

5342
Smith, Geoffrey Wayne. "Surficial Geology of the Shuswap River Drainage, British Columbia." Ohio State, 1969.

5343
Smith, Roberta Katherine. "Glacio-Marine Foraminifera of British Columbia and Southeast Alaska." British Columbia, 1966.

5344
Soregaroli, Arthur Earl. "Geology of the Boss Mountain Mine, British Columbia." British Columbia, 1968.

5345
Souther, Jack Gordon. "The Geology of Terrace Area Coast District, British Columbia." Princeton, 1956.

5346
Stephens, George Christopher. "The Geology of the Salal Creek Pluton, Southwestern British Columbia." Lehigh, 1972.

5347
Struik, Lambertus Cornelis. "Geology of Barkerville-Cariboo River Area, Central British Columbia." Calgary, 1980.

5348
Stuart, Roy Armstrong. "Geology of the Kemano-Tahtsa Area, British Columbia." Princeton, 1956.

5349
Surdam, Ronald Clarence. "Low-Grade Metamorphism of the Karmutsen Group Buttle Lake Area, Vancouver Island, B.C." California, Los Angeles, 1967.

5350
Sutherland, Patrick K. "Carboniferous Stratigraphy of North-East British Columbia, with a Detailed Study of the Tetracoral Fauna." Cambridge, 1953.

5351
Sutherland-Brown, Atholl. "The Structure and Stratigraphy of the Antler Creek Area, British Columbia." Princeton, 1954.

5352
Swanson, Clarence Otto. "The Genesis of the Texada Island Magnetite Deposits." Wisconsin, 1924.

5353
Swinbanks, David Donald. "Environment Factors Controlling Floral Zonation and the Distribution of Burrowing and Tube-Dwelling Organisms on Fraser Delta Tidal Flats, British Columbia." British Columbia, 1979.

5354
Syvitski, James Patrick Michael. "Sedimentological Advances Concerning the Flocculation and Zooplankton Pelletization of Suspended Sediment in Howe Sound, British Columbia: A Fjord Receiving Glacial Meltwater." British Columbia, 1978.

5355
Tallman, Ann Marie. "The Glacial and Periglacial Geomorphology of the Fourth of July Creek Valley, Atlin Region, Cassiar District, Northwestern British Columbia." Michigan State, 1975.

5356
Tennyson, Marilyn Elizabeth. "Stratigraphy, Structure, and Tectonic Setting of Jurassic and Cretaceous Sedimentary Rocks in the West-Central Methow-Pasayten Area, Northwestern Cascade Range, Washington and British Columbia." Washington, Seattle, 1974.

5357
Thompson, Robert, I. "Geology of the Akolkolex River Area near Revelstoke, British Columbia." Queen's, 1972.

5358
Thompson, Thomas Luman. "Stratigraphy, Tectonics, Structure and Gravity in the Rocky Mountain Trench Area, Southeastern British Columbia, Canada." Stanford, 1962.

5359
Thorpe, Ralph Irving. "Controls of Hypogene Sulphide Zoning, Rossland, British Columbia." Wisconsin, 1967.

5360
Tipper, Howard W. "Revision of the (Jurassic) Hazleton and Takla Groups of Central British Columbia." Washington State, 1954.

5361
Trettin, Hans Peter. "Geology of the Fraser River Valley Between Lillooet and Big Bar Creek." British Columbia, 1960.

5362
Usher, John L. "The Stratigraphy and Paleontology of the Upper Cretaceous Rocks of Vancouver Island, British Columbia." McGill, 1950.

5363
Wagner, Frances Joan Estelle. "Paleontology and Stratigraphy of the Marine Pleistocene Deposits of Southwestern British Columbia." Stanford, 1954.

5364
Walker, John Fortune. "Geology and Mineral Deposits of Windermere Map-Area, British Columbia." Princeton, 1924.

5365
Ward, Peter Douglas. "Stratigraphy, Paleoecology and Functional Morphology of Heteromorph Ammonites of the Upper Cretaceous Nanaimo Group, British Columbia and Washington." McMaster, 1976.

5366
Westervelt, Thomas N. "Structural Superposition in the Lake O'Hara Region, Yoho and Kootenay National Parks, British Columbia, Canada." Wyoming, 1979.

5367
Williams, Thomas Bowerman. "The Comox Coal Area, Vancouver Island, Canada." Wisconsin, 1925.

5368
Winzer, Stephen Randolph. "Metamorphism and Chemical Equilibrium in Some Rocks from the Central Kootenay Arc." Alberta, 1973.

5369
Wolfe, William John. "Petrology, Mineralogy and Geochemistry of the Blue River Ultramafic Intrusion, Cassiar District, British Columbia." Yale, 1967.

Woodsworth, Glenn James. See No./Voir no 1218

Woodward, Harold W. See No./Voir no 5113

5370
Woolverton, Ralph S. "The Lumby Lake Greenstone Belt." McGill, 1954.

5371
Yale, Raymond William. "A Faunal and Stratigraphic Study of Upper Paleozoic Rocks of Vancouver Island, British Columbia." British Columbia, 1965.

5372
Young, Frederick Griffin. "Sedimentary Cycles and Facies in the Correlation and Interpretation of Lower Cambrian Rocks East-Central British Columbia." McGill, 1970.

5373
Zwanzig, Herman V. "Structural Transitions Between the Foreland Zone and the Core Zone of the Columbian Orogen Selkirk Mountains, British Columbia." Queen's, 1973.

Prairie Provinces/
Provinces des Prairies

General Items/Ouvrages généraux

5374
Harker, Stuart David. "Campanian Organic-Walled Microplankton from the Interior Plains of Canada, Wyoming and Texas." Saskatchewan, 1978.

5375
Wickenden, Robert Thomas Daubigny. "The Upper Creataceous Foraminifera of the Prairie Provinces (Canada)." Harvard, 1931.

Alberta

5376
Alcock, Frederick James. "The Geology of the Lake Athabaska Region." Yale, 1915.

5377
Amajor, L.C. "Chronostratigraphy, Depositional Patterns and Environmental Analysis of Sub-Surface Lower Cretaceous (Albian) Viking Reservoir Sandstones in Central Alberta and Part of Southwestern Saskatchewan." Alberta, 1980.

5378
Andrichuk, John M. "Regional Stratigraphic Analysis of the Devonian System in Wyoming, Montana, Southern Saskatchewan and Alberta." Northwestern, 1951.

5379
Badgley, Peter C. "Stratigraphy, Sedimentology and Gas and Oil Geology of the Lower Cretaceous of Central Alberta." Princeton, 1952.

5380
Barendregt, René William. "A Detailed Geomorphological Survey of the Pakowki-Pinhorn Area of Southeastern Alberta." Queen's, 1977.

5381
Bassett, Henry Gordon. "Correlation of Devonian Selections in Northern Alberta and Northwest Territories." Princeton, 1952.

5382
Bayrock, Luboslaw Antin. "Glacial Geology of the Alliance-Galahad-Hardisty-Brownfield Area, Alberta, Canada." Wisconsin, 1960.

5383
Beach, Hugh H. "The Geology of Moose Mountain Area, Alberta." Yale, 1940.

5384
Beales, Francis William. "The Sedimentation and Diagenesis of Certain Late Paleozoic Rocks of Southwest Alberta." Toronto, 1952.

5385
Bielenstein, Hans. "The Rundle Thrust Sheet, Banff, Alberta: A Structural Analysis." Queen's, 1970.

5386
Binda, Pier Luigi. "Sedimentology and Vegetal Micropaleontology of the Rocks Associated with the Cretaceous Kneehills Tuff of Alberta." Alberta, 1970.

5387
Brown, Michael Charles. "Karst Geomorphology and Hydrology of the Lower Maligne Basin, Jasper, Alberta." McMaster, 1970.

5388
Brown, Richard Arthur Cornelius. "Upper Paleozoic Stratigraphy and Paleontology in the Mt. Greenock Area, Alberta." Toronto, 1950.

5389
Buchwald, Caryl Edward. "Types and Distribution of Sandstones in the Belly River and Edmonton Formations (Uppermost Cretaceous) of the North Saskatchewan River Area, West Central Alberta." Kansas, 1966.

5390
Burden, Elliott Thomas. "Lower Cretaceous Terrestrial Palynomorph Biostratigraphy of the McMurray Formation, Northeastern Alberta." Calgary, 1982.

5391
Burnie, Stephen Wilbur. "A Sulphur and Carbon Isotope Study of Hydrocarbons from the Devonian of Alberta, Canada." Alberta, 1979.

5392
Burwash, Ronald Allan McLean. "A Reconnaissance of the Sub-Surface Pre-Cambrian of the Province of Alberta, Canada." Minnesota, 1955.

Collins, Jon A. See No./Voir no 5641
Cook, Donald G. See No./Voir no 5192

5393
Corrigan, Anthony Francis. "The Evolution of a Cratonic Basin from Carbonate to Evaporite Deposition, and the Resulting Stratigraphic and Diagenetic Changes, Upper Elk Point Subgroup, Northeastern Alberta." Calgary, 1975.

5394
Craig, Bruce Gordon. "Surficial Geology of the Drumheller Area, Alberta, Canada." Michigan, 1956.

5395
Das Gupta, Udayan. "A Study of Fracturer Reservoir Rocks, with Special Reference to Mississippian Carbonate Rocks of Southwest Alberta." Toronto, 1978.

5396
Denson, Norman MacLaren. "Late Middle Cambrian Trilobite Faunas and Stratigraphy of Alberta, Montana, Wyoming and Utah." Princeton, 1942.

5397
Dickie, Geoffrey James. "A Quantitative Geologic of Cretaceous and Jurassic Oil and Gas Pools in Alberta." Alberta, 1972.

5398
Douglas, Robert J.W. "Callum Creek, Langford Creek and Gap Map Area, Alberta." Columbia, 1950.

5399
Dunn, Darrel Eugene. "Hydrogeology of the Stettler Area, Alberta, Canada." Illinois, 1967.

El-Nahhas, Fathalla Mohamed. See No./Voir no 4500

5400
Ellwood, Robert Brian. "Surficial Geology of the Vermilion Area, Alberta, Canada." Illinois, 1961.

5401
Erdman, Oscar A. "Geology of Alexo and Saunders Map Areas, Alberta, Canada." Chicago, 1946.

5402
Fischbuch, Norman Robert. "The Devonian Swan Hills Reef Complexes of Central Alberta." Saskatchewan, 1968.

5403
Fox, Frederick G. "The Stratigraphy of the Devonian and Mississippian Rocks in the Foothills of Southern Alberta." Oklahoma, 1948.

5404
Gibson, David Whiteoak. "Triassic Stratigraphy and Petrology Between the Athabasca and Smoky Rivers of Alberta." Toronto, 1966.

5405
Glaister, Rowland Perry. "Lower Cretaceous of Southern Alberta and Adjoining Areas." Northwestern, 1957.

5406
Goble, Ronald James. "The Mineralogy Composition and Crystal Structure of Selected Copper Sulphides from the Belt Purcell Supergroup S.W. Alberta, Canada." Queen's, 1977.

5407
Gold, Christopher Malcolm. "Quantitative Methods in the Evaluation of the Quaternary Geology of the Sand River (73L) Map Sheet, Alberta, Canada." Alberta, 1978.

5408
Greggs, Robert George. "Upper Cambrian Biostratigraphy of the Southern Rocky Mountains, Alberta." British Columbia, 1962.

5409
Grey, Charles E. "Cyclic Sedimentation, Dessa Dawn and Rundle Formations, Banff and Jasper Parks, Alberta." Wisconsin, 1951.

5410
Hall, Hubert H. "Mississippian Stratigraphy in Southwestern Alberta and Northwestern Montana." Wisconsin, 1952.

5411
Harker, Peter. "Stratigraphy and Paleontology of the Banff and Associated Carboniferous Formations of Western Canada." Michigan, 1951.

5412
Harland, Rex. "Dinoflagellates and Acritarchs from the Bearpaw Formation, Southern Alberta." Alberta, 1971.

5413
Harvey, John F. "Mississippian Stratigraphy of Jasper Park, Alberta." Wisconsin, 1953.

Hayes, Bonnie Jean R. See No./Voir no 1046

5414
Henderson, Eric P. "Pleistocene Geology of the Watino Quadrangle, Alberta." Indiana, 1953.

5415
Hicks, Harold Smith. "The Geology of the Fitzgerald and Northern Portion of the Chipewyan Map Areas, Northern Alberta, Canada." Minnesota, 1932.

5416
Hopkins, John Charles. "Petrography, Distribution and Diagenesis of Foreslope, Nearslope and Basin Sediments, Miette and Ancient Wall Carbonate Complexes (Devonian), Alberta." McGill, 1972.

5417
Hughes, George Muggah. "The Glacial Geology of the Redwater and Morinville Areas, Alberta." Illinois, 1962.

5418
Hughes, Richard D. "Geology of Portions of Sunwapta and Southesk Map Areas, Jasper National Park, Alberta, Canada." Oklahoma, 1953.

5419
Irish, Ernest J.W. "The Geology of the Moon Creek Map-Area West Central Alberta." Illinois, 1949.

5420
Jackson, Lionel Eric. "Quaternary Stratigraphy and Terrain Inventory of the Alberta Portion of the Kananaskis Lakes 1:250,000 Sheet 82J." Calgary, 1977.

5421
Jarzen, David MacArthur. "Evolutionary and Paleoecological Significance of Albian to Campanian Angiosperm Pollen from the Amoco B-1 Youngstown Borehole, Southern Alberta." Toronto, 1973.

5422
Jones, Islwyn Wyn. "The Microscopical and Chemical Nature of Alberta Coals." Toronto, 1928.

Jure, Albert Edward. See No./Voir no 5250

Karlstrom, Eric Thor. See No./Voir no 4729

5423
Ketner, Keith Brindley. "Ordovician Siliceous Sediments of the Cordilleran Geosyncline." Wisconsin, 1968.

5424
Klovan, John Edward. "Facies Analysis of Redwater Reef Complex, Alberta, Canada." Columbia, 1963.

5425
Landes, Robert W. "Stratigraphy and Paleontology of the Marine Formations of the Montana Group, Southeastern Alberta." Princeton, 1937.

5426
Leavitt, Eugene Millidge. "The Petrology, Paleontology and Geochemistry of the Caison Creek, North Reef Complex, Alberta." Alberta, 1967.

5427
Leonard, Eric Michael. "Glaciolacustrine Sedimentation and Holocene Glacial History, Northern Banff National Park, Alberta." Colorado, 1981.

5428
Locker, John Gary. "The Petrographic and Engineering Properties of Fine Grained Sedimentary Rock of Central Alberta." Alberta, 1969.

5429
MacNeil, Donald J. "The Stratigraphy and Structure of the Hillcrest Coalfield, Alberta." Princeton, 1935.

5430
MacQueen, Roger Webb. "Stratigraphy and Sedimentology of the Mount Head Formation, Alberta, Canada." Princeton, 1965.

5431
McCrossan, Robert G. "Upper Devonian Inter-reef Calcareous Shales of Central Alberta, Canada." Chicago, 1957.

5432
McLaren, Digby Johns. "The Devonian Stratigraphy and Correlation of the Alberta Rocky Mountains with Descriptions of the Brachiopod Family, Rhynchonellidae." Michigan, 1951.

5433
Meier, Mark Frederick. "Mode of Flow of Saskatchewan Glacier, Alberta, Canada." California Institute of Technology, 1957.

5434
Mellon, George Barry. "The Petrology of the Blairmore Group, Alberta, Canada." Pennsylvania State, 1959.

5435
Meshri, Indurani Dayal. "Deposition and Diagenesis of Glauconite Sandstone, Berrymore-Lobstick-Bigoray Area, South-Central Alberta: A Study of Physical Chemistry of Cementation." Tulsa, 1981.

5436
Mills, Hugh Harrison. "Sediment Characteristics of Some Small Temperate Glaciers." Washington, Seattle, 1975. [Includes Athabasca Glacier Glacier Athabaska]

5437
Mountjoy, Eric Walter. "Structure and Stratigraphy of the Miette and Adjacent Areas, Eastern Jasper National Park, Alberta." Toronto, 1960.

5438
Murray, James Wolfe. "Some Stratigraphic and Paleoenvironmental Aspects of the Swan Hills and Waterways Formations, Judy Creek, Alberta, Canada." Princeton, 1964.

5439
Nauss, Arthur William. "Stratigraphy of the Vermilion Area, Alberta, Canada." Stanford, 1943.

5440
Nielsen, Grant Leroy. "Hydrogeology of the Irrigation Study Basin, Oldman River Drainage, Alberta, Canada." Brigham Young, 1970.

5441
Noble, James Peter Allison. "A Paleoecologic and Paleontologic Study of an Upper Devonian Reef in the Miette Area, Jasper National Park, Alberta, Canada." Case Western Reserve, 1966.

5442
Nowak, Robert Lars. "Application of the Liquid Limit Parameter to Subsurface Tile Correlation in the Vicinity of Calgary." Alberta, 1981.

5443
Paterson, William Stanley Bryce. "Observations on Athabaska Glacier and Their Relation to the Theory of Glacier Flow." British Columbia, 1962.

5444
Pawlowicz, Richard M. "Discrimination Among Depositional Environments Based on Element Abundance in Upper Cretaceous Rocks of Southern Alberta." New Mexico Institute of Mining and Technology, 1975.

5445
Peikert, Ernest William. "Petrological Study of a Group of Porphyroblastic Rocks in the Precambrian of Northeastern Alberta." Illinois, 1961.

5446
Pelzer, Ernest Edward. "Mineralogy, Geochemistry and Stratigraphy of the Besa River Shale." Alberta, 1965.

5447
Petryk, Allen Alexander. "Lower Carboniferous Foraminifera and Biostratigraphy of Southwestern Alberta." Saskatchewan, 1969.

5448
Pollock, C.A. "Devonian Conodonts from Alberta." Wales, 1966.

5449
Powers, Sidney. "The Acadian Triassic." Harvard, 1915.

Price, Raymond Alex. See No./Voir no 5313

5450
Rahmani, Ridyadh Abdul Rahim. "Heavy Mineral Analysis of Upper Cretaceous and Paleocene Sandstones in Alberta and Adjacent Areas of Saskatchewan." Alberta, 1973.

5451
Raymond, Charles Forest. "Flow in a Transverse Section of Athabasca Glacier, Alberta, Canada." California Institute of Technology, 1969.

5452
Reik, Gerhard Albert. "Joints, Microfractures and Remedial Strain in Cardium Siltstone, South Ram River Area, Alberta: A Field and Experimental Investigation of Factors That Contribute to Fracture Porosity and Permeability in Sedimentary Rock." Toronto, 1973.

5453
Richmond, William Oliver. "Paleozoic Stratigraphy and Sedimentation of the Slave Point Formation, Southern Northwest Territories and Northern Alberta." Stanford, 1965.

5454
Robinson, Joseph Edward. "Analysis by Spatial Filtering of Some Intermediate Scale Structures in Southern Alberta." Alberta, 1968.

5455
Roed, Murray Anderson. "Surficial Geology of the Edson-Hinton Area, Alberta." Alberta, 1969.

5456
Russell, Loris Shano. "Stratigraphy and Paleontology of the Uppermost Cretaceous and Lower Tertiary Formations of Alberta." Princeton, 1930.

5457
Rutter, Nathaniel Westlund. "The Surficial Geology of the Banff Area, Alberta." Alberta, 1966.

5458
Sanderson, James Owen Gresham. "The Geology of a Region Along the Red Deer River, Alberta, Canada." Toronto, 1928.

5459
Schmidt, Ronald G. "Joint Patterns in Relation to Regional and Local Structure in the Central Foothills Belt of the Rocky Mountains of Alberta." Cincinnati, 1957.

5460
Sikka, Desh Bandu. "A Radiometric Survey of Redwater Oilfield, Alberta, Canada." McGill, 1960.

5461
Singh, Chaitanya. "Palynology of the Manville Group, (Lower Cretaceous), Central Alberta." Alberta, 1964.

5462
Snead, Robert Garland. "Microfloral Diagnosis of the Cretaceous-Tertiary Boundary, Central Alberta." Alberta, 1968.

5463
Sophocleous, Marios. "Analysis of Heat and Water Transport in Unsaturated-Saturated Porous Media." Alberta, 1978.

5464
Spreng, Alfred C. "Cyclic Sedimentation in the Banff Formation, Alberta." Wisconsin, 1950.

5465
Srivastava, Satish Kumar. "Anglosperm Microflora of the Edmonton Formation, Alberta, Canada." Alberta, 1968.

5466
Stalker, Archibald M. "The Geology of the Red Deer Area, Alberta, with Particular Reference to the Geomorphology and Water Supply." McGill, 1950.

5467
Stanley, Alan David. "Relation Between Secondary Structures in Athabasca Glacier and Laboratory Deformed Ice." British Columbia, 1966.

5468
Stewart, James Smith. "The Geology of the Disturbed Belt of Southwestern Alberta." Yale, 1916.

5469
Stoakes, Franklin Arthur. "Sea Level Control of Carbonate-Shale Deposition During Progradational Basin-Filling: The Upper Devonian Duvernay and Ireton Formations of Alberta, Canada." Calgary, 1980.

5470
Stott, Donald Franklin. "The Alberta Group and Equivalent Rocks, Rocky Mountain Foothills, Alberta." Princeton, 1958.

5471
Sutterlin, Peter George. "Uppermost Devonian (Post Woodbend) Studies in Southern Alberta Areas." Northwestern, 1958.

5472
Tharin, James C. "Glacial Geology of the Calgary, Alberta Area." Illinois, 1960.

5473
Tovell, Walter Massey. "Some Aspects of the Geology of the Milk River and Pakowki Formations (Southern Alberta)." Toronto, 1956.

5474
Wagner, William Philip. "Correlation of Rocky Mountain and Laurentide Glacial Chronologies in Southwestern Alberta, Canada." Michigan, 1966.

5475
Walls, Richard Alan. "Cementation History and Porosity Development, Golden Spike Reef Complex (Devonian), Alberta." McGill, 1978.

5476
Walpole, Robert Leonard. "Microfacies Study of the Rundle Group, Front Ranges, Central Alberta." Illinois, 1961.

5477
Warren, Percival Sydney. "The Geology of the Banff Area (Alberta, Canada)." Toronto, 1924.

5478
Watanabe, Roy Yoshinobu. "Petrology of Cataclastic Rocks of Northeastern Alberta." Alberta, 1966.

5479
Weber, Wilfred William Louis. "The Geology of the Duverny Area with Particular Reference to the Granitic Intrusives." Toronto, 1950.

5480
Weiner, John Louis. "The Old Fort Point Formation, Jasper, Alberta." Alberta, 1967.

5481
Wendte, John Curtis. "Sedimentation and Diagenesis of the Cooking Lake Platform and Lower Leduc Reef Facies, Upper Devonian, Redwater, Alberta." California, Santa Cruz, 1974.

5482
Westgate, John Arthur. "The Surficial Geology of the Foremost-Cypress Hills Area, Alberta, Canada." Alberta, 1965.

5483
Williams, Edwin Philip. "Geology of the Cardston Area, Alberta, Canada." Harvard, 1956.

5484
Williams, Gordon Donald Clarence. "The Mannville Group, Central Alberta." Alberta, 1960.
Wilson, Michael. See No./Voir no 860

Manitoba

5485
Allan, John Donald. "Geological Studies of the Lynn Lake Area, North Manitoba." Massachusetts Institute of Technology, 1948.

5486
Ambrose, John W. "Geology of the Northeast Portion of the Flinflon Map-Area, Manitoba." Yale, 1935.

5487
Armstrong, Paul Frederic. "The Geology and Ore Deposits of Elbow Lake Mining Area, Northern Manitoba." Yale, 1923.

5488
Bailes, Alan Harvey. "Sedimentology and Metamorphism of a Proterozoic Volcaniclastic Tourbidite Suite that Crosses the Boundary Between the Flin Flon and Kisseynew Belts, File Lake, Manitoba, Canada." Manitoba, 1979.

5489
Beakhouse, Gary Philip. "Geological, Geochemical and Rb-Sr and U-Ph Zircon Geochronological Investigtions of Granitoid Rocks from the Winnipeg River Belt, Northwestern Ontario and Southeastern Manitoba." McMaster, 1982.

5490
Bliss, Neil W. "A Comparative Examination of Two Ultramafic Bodies at the S.W. End of the Manitoba Nickel Belt, with Special Reference to Chromite Mineralogy." McGill, 1973.

5491
Campbell, Frederick H.A. "Sedimentation and Stratigraphy of Part of the Rice Lake Group Manitoba." Manitoba, 1972.

5492
Coats, Colin J. A. "Serpentinized Ultramafic Rocks the Manitoba Nickel Belt." Manitoba, 1966.

5493
Davies, James Frederick. "Geology and Gold Deposits of the Rice Lake - Wanipigow River Area Toronto, 1963.

5494
Dwibedi, Kamalakanta. "Petrology of the English River Gneissic Belt, Northwestern Ontario and Southeastern Manitoba." Manitoba, 1967.

5495
Elphick, Stephen Conrad. "Chemical Reactions High-Grade Pelitic Gneisses from Manitoba Canada." Cambridge, 1978.

5496
Elson, John Albert. "Surficial Geology of the Tiger Hills Region, Manitoba, Canada." Yale, 1956.

5497
Emslie, Ronald Frank. "The Petrology and Economic Geology of Two Mafic Intrusions in the Lynn Lake Area, Northern Manitoba." Northwestern, 1961.

5498
Fabbri, Andrea Gabrielle. "Image Processing Geological Data." Ottawa, 1981.

5499
Fasola, Armando. "Biostratigraphy and Paleoecology of Dinoflagellate Cysts in Late Cenomanian Early Campaign Deposits in Southwestern Manitoba." Toronto, 1982.

5500
Fenton, Mark MacDonald. "The Quaternary Stratigraphy of a Portion of Southeastern Manitoba Canada." Western Ontario, 1974.

5501
Goetz, Peter Andrew. "Depositional Environment the Sherridon Group and Related Mineral Deposits near Sherridon, Manitoba." Carleton, 1980.

5502
Grice, Reginald Hugh. "Hydrogeology at a Hydro electric Installation on Paleozoic Dolomites Grand Rapids, Manitoba." Illinois, 1964.

5503
Henderson, James Fenwick. "The Geology of the Granville Lake District, Manitoba." Wisconsin 1933.

5504
Heywood, William Walter. "Precambrian Geology the Ledge Lake Area, Manitoba and Saskatchewan Canada." Washington, Seattle, 1959.

5505
Horwood, Hereward C. "The Cross Lake Map-Area, Manitoba." Massachusetts Institute of Technology, 1934.

Hughes, John E. See No./Voir no 5239

5506
Hunter, Hugh E. "Petrology of the Two Lake Cabbro, Barrington Lake Area, Northern Manitoba." California, Los Angeles, 1954.

5507
Hutcheon, Ian E. "The Metamorphism of Sulfide-Bearing Pelitic Rocks from Snow Lake, Manitoba." Carleton, 1977.

5508
Juhas, Allan Paul. "Geology and Origin of Copper-Nickel Sulphide Deposits of the Bird River Area of Manitoba." Manitoba, 1973.

5509
Kalliokoski, Jorma Osmo Kalervo. "Geology of the Weldon Bay Area, Manitoba." Princeton, 1951.

5510
Klassen, Rudolph Waldemar. "The Surficial Geology of the Riding Mountain Area, Manitoba-Saskatchewan." Saskatchewan, 1966.

5511
Koo, Jahak. "Origin and Metamorphism of the Flin Flon Copper-Zinc Sulfide Deposit, Northern Saskatchewan and Manitoba, Canada." Saskatchewan, 1973.

5512
Last, William Michael. "Sedimentology and Post-Glacial History of Lake Manitoba." Manitoba, 1980.

5513
Lord, Clifford S. "Geology in the Vicinity of Beresford Lake, Manitoba." Massachusetts Institute of Technology, 1938.

5514
McCammon, Helen Mary. "Fauna of the Manitoba Group from Manitoba, Canada." Indiana, 1959.

5515
McGinn, Roderick Alan. "Alluvial Fan Geomorphic Systems: The Riding Mountain Escarpment Model." Manitoba, 1979.

5516
McGlynn, John C. "Structural and Petrologic Studies of the Rocks of the Elbow-Heming Lake Areas, Manitoba." Chicago, 1954.

5517
McNeil, David Harvey. "The Cretaceous System in the Manitoba Escarpment." Saskatchewan, 1977.

5518
McPherson, Robert Andrew. "Pleistocene Geology of the Beausejour Area, Manitoba." Manitoba, 1970.

5519
Miller, Robert J.M. "Geology and Ore Deposits of the Cedar Bay Mine Area." Laval, 1959.

5520
Milligan, George Clinton. "Geology of the Lynn Lake District, Northern Manitoba." Harvard, 1961.

5521
Mukherjee, Amar Chandra. "The Precambrian Geology of the Flin Flon Area, Northern Saskatchewan and Manitoba, Canada." Saskatchewan, 1971.

5522
Mwanang'onze, Elimelech H.B. "Stratigraphy and Petrochemistry of the Host Rocks of Copper-Zinc Deposits in the Flin Flon-Snow Lake Greenstone Belt." Manitoba, 1978.

5523
Narbonne, Guy M. "Stratigraphy, Reef Development and Trace Fossils of the Upper Silurian Douro Formation in the Southeastern Canadian Arctic Islands." Ottawa, 1981.

5524
Nelson, Samuel J. "Ordovician Paleontology and Stratigraphy of the Churchill and Nelson Rivers, Manitoba." McGill, 1952.

5525
Oliver, Thomas A. "Geology of the McGavock Lake Area, Northern Manitoba." California, Los Angeles, 1952.

5526
Peterman, Edwin Z. "Precambrian Basement of Saskatchewan and Manitoba." Alberta, 1962.

5527
Rance, Hugh. "Superior-Churchill Structural Boundary Wabowden, Manitoba." Western Ontario, 1968.

5528
Robertson, David S. "The Petrology of the Kisseynew Gneiss of the Batty Lake Area, Manitoba." Columbia, 1953.

5529
Rousell, Don Herbert. "The Petrology of Archaean and Proterozoic Rocks at Cross Lake, Manitoba, and the Effects of the Hudsonian Orogeny." Manitoba, 1965.

5530
Sangameshwar, Salem R.R. "Trace-Element and Sulphur Isotope Geochemistry of Sulphide Deposits from the Flin Flon and Snow Lake Areas of Saskatchewan and Manitoba." Saskatchewan, 1972.

5531
Stearn, Colin W. "Stratigraphy and Coral Faunas of the Silurian of Southern Manitoba." Yale, 1952.

5532
Stephenson, John Francis. "Gold Deposits of the Rice Lake-Beresford Lake Area, Southeastern Manitoba." Manitoba, 1972.

5533
Stockwell, Clifford Howard. "The Pegmatite Dykes and Associated Rocks of Southeastern Manitoba, and Adjacent Portions of Ontario." Wisconsin, 1930.

5534
Stone, Denver Cedrill. "The Sydney Lake Fault Zone in Ontario and Manitoba, Canada." Toronto, 1982.

5535
Thiessen, Richard Leigh. "Theoretical and Computer Assisted Studies in Tectonics Structural Geology and Isotope Dating." SUNY, Albany, 1980. [Chisel Lake ore body/Masse minéralisée du Lac Chisel]

Tippett, Clinton Raymond. See No./Voir no 5903

5536
Trueman, David Lawrence. "Stratigraphy, Structure and Metamorphic Petrology of the Archean Greenstone Belt at Bird River, Manitoba." Manitoba, 1980.

5537
Williams, Harold. "A Petrographic Study of the Metamorphic Rocks of the Chisel Lake Area, Northern Manitoba." Toronto, 1961.
5538
Wright, Charles Malcolm. "Geology and Origin of the Pollucite-Bearing Montgary Pegmatite, Manitoba." Wisconsin, 1961.
5539
Young, Harvey Ray. "Petrology of the Virden Member of the Lodgepole Formation, Mississippian in Southwestern Manitoba." Queen's, 1973.

Saskatchewan

Alcock, Frederick James. See No./Voir no 5376
Amajor, Levi Chukwuemeka. See No./Voir no 5377
Andrichuk, John M. See No./Voir no 5378
5540
Beavan, Arthur Paul. "Geology and Gold Deposits of Goldfields, Lake Athabaska, Saskatchewan." Princeton, 1938.
5541
Beck, Leslie S. "Structural Environment and Genesis of Uranium Deposits in the Athabasca Region, Saskatchewan, Canada." Leeds, 1966.
5542
Blake, Donald A.W. "The Geology of the Forget Lake and Nevins Lake Map-Areas, Northern Saskatchewan." McGill, 1953.
5543
Brooke, Margaret Martha. "Jurassic Microfaunas and Biostratigraphy of Saskatchewan and North Central Montana." Saskatchewan, 1972.
5544
Cant, Douglas James. "Braided Stream Sedimentation in the South Saskatchewan River." McMaster, 1977.
5545
Chamberlain, Joseph Annandale. "Structural Control of Pitchblende Orebodies, Eldorado, Saskatchewan." Harvard, 1959.
5546
Cherry, John Anthony. "Geology of the Yorkton Area, Saskatchewan." Illinois, 1966.
5547
Christiansen, Earl Alfred. "Glacial Geology of the Swift Current Area, Saskatchewan." Illinois, 1959.
5548
Christie, Archibald M. "The Geology of the Goldfields Area, Saskatchewan." McGill, 1948.
5549
Conybeare, Charles E.B. "Structure and Metamorphism in the Goldfields Area, Saskatchewan, with Special Reference to the Pitchblende Deposits." Washington State, 1950.
5550
David, Peter Pascal. "Surficial Geology and Ground Water Resources of the Prelate Area (72-K), Saskatchewan." McGill, 1965.
5551
Dawson, Kenneth Ralph. "A Petrographic Description of Wall Rocks and Alteration Products Associated with Pitchblende-Bearing Veins in the Goldfields Region, Saskatchewan." Toronto, 1952.

5552
De Lury, Justin Sarsfield. "Geology, Topography, and Resources of the Wapawekka and Deschambaul Lake Area of Saskatchewan." Minnesota, 1925.
5553
Dudar, John Steve. "The Geology and Mineralogy of the Verna Uranium Deposit, Beaverlodge, Saskatchewan." Michigan, 1960.
5554
Eastwood, George E.P. "The Origin and Geologic History of the Snake Rapids Pluton, Saskatchewan." Minnesota, 1950.
5555
Edie, Ralph W. "Geological Studies in the Goldfields Area, Saskatchewan and the Genesis of Pitchblende." Massachusetts Institute of Technology, 1952.
5556
Evoy, Ernest Franklin. "Geology of the Gunnar Uranium Deposit, Beaverlodge Area, Saskatchewan." Wisconsin, 1961.
5557
Faulkner, Edward Leslie. "The Distribution of Cobalt and Nickel in Some Sulphide Deposits of the Flin Flon Area, Saskatchewan." Saskatchewan, 1964.
5558
Froese, Edgar. "Structural Geology and Metamorphic Petrology of the Coronation Map Area, Saskatchewan." Queen's, 1964.
5559
Fumerton, Stewart Lloyd. "Geology of the Reindeer Lake Area, Saskatchewan, with Emphasis on Granite Rock." Saskatchewan, 1979.
5560
Gaskarth, Joseph William. "Petrogenesis of Precambrian Rocks in the Hanson Lake Area, East-Central Saskatchewan." Saskatchewan, 1967.
5561
Gendzwill, Don John. "A Gravity Study in the Amisk Lake Area, Saskatchewan." Saskatchewan, 1969.
5562
Hale, W.E. "Geology of the Uranium City Area (West Half) with Special Reference to the Pitchblende Deposits." Queen's, 1953.
Heywood, William Walter. See No./Voir no 5504
5563
Howells, William C. "The Windrum Lake Area, Saskatchewan." McGill, 1940.
5564
Kent, Donald M.J. "The Geology of the Upper Devonian Saskatchewan Group and Equivalent Rocks in Western Saskatchewan and Adjacent Areas." Alberta, 1968.
5565
Kirkland, Samuel John Thomas. "A Study of the Tazin-Athabasca Unconformity, Northern Saskatchewan." Queen's, 1953.
Klassen, Rudolph Waldemar. See No./Voir no 5510
Koo, Jahak. See No./Voir no 5511
5566
MacDonald, Gilbert H. "The Mississippian of Saskatchewan." Toronto, 1953.
5567
MacKenzie, Warren Stuart. "The Geology of the Southesk Cairn Carbonate Complex." Toronto, 1965.

5568
McLean, James Ross. "The Upper Cretaceous Judith River Formation in the Canadian Great Plains: Its History and Lithostratigraphy." Saskatchewan, 1970.

5569
Meneley, William Allison. "Geology of the Melfort Area (73-A), Saskatchewan." Illinois, 1964.

5570
Money, Peter Lawrence. "The Precambrian Geology of the Needle Falls Area, Saskatchewan." Alberta, 1967.

5571
Moran, Stephen Royse. "Geology of the Hudson Bay Area, Saskatchewan." Illinois, 1969.

Mukerjee, Amar Chandra. See No./Voir no 5521

5572
Nautiyal, Avinash Chandra. "Frasnian Acritarcha and Biostratigraphy of the Interior Plains Region, Canada." Saskatchewan, 1972.

5573
Padgham, William Albert. "The Geological Structure of the Lac La Ronge Region, Saskatchewan." Wisconsin, 1969.

5574
Parizek, Richard Rudolph. "Glacial Geology of the Willow Bunch Lake Area, Saskatchewan." Illinois, 1961.

Peterman, Edwin Zell. See No./Voir no 5526

5575
Proctor, Richard Malcolm. "Quantitative Clay Mineralogy of the Vanguard and Blairmore Formations, Southwestern Saskatchewan." Kansas, 1960.

Rahmani, Ridyadh A.R. See No./Voir no 5450

Sangameshwar, Salem R. R. See No./Voir no 5530

5576
Sassano, Giampaolo. "The Nature and Origin of the Uranium Mineralization at the Fay Mine, Eldorado, Saskatchewan, Canada." Alberta, 1972.

5577
Satterly, Jack. "Geological Reconnaissance of the Pelican Narrows Area, Saskatchewan." Cambridge, 1931.

5578
Scott, John Stanley. "Surficial Geology of the Elbow-Outlook Area, Saskatchewan, Canada." Illinois, 1960.

5579
Smith, Edgar E.N. "Structure Wall Rock Alteration and Ore Deposits at Martin Lake, Saskatchewan." Harvard, 1952.

5580
Thiede, David Steven. "The Genesis of Metalliferous Brines from Evaporites — A Study Based upon the Middle Devonian Elk Point Group of Canada." Wisconsin, 1978.

5581
Trigg, Charles M. "The Petrology and Structural Geology of an Area Including the Verna Uranium Deposit, Beaverlodge, Saskatchewan." McGill, 1964.

5582
Vonhof, Jan Albert. "Tertiary Grades and Sands in the Canadian Great Plains." Saskatchewan, 1969.

5583
Wall, John Hallett. "Jurassic Microfaunas from Saskatchewan, Western Canada." Missouri, 1958.

5584
Whitaker, Sidney Hopkins. "Geology of the Wood Mountain Area (72-G) Saskatchewan." Illinois, 1965.

Wickenden, Robert Thomas Daubigny. See No./Voir no 5375

5585
Wyder, John Ernest. "Geophysical and Geological Study of Surficial Deposits near Frobisher, Saskatchewan." Saskatchewan, 1968.

Atlantic Provinces/Provinces de L'Atlantique

General Items/Ouvrages généraux

5586
Copeland, Murray John. "The Upper Carboniferous Arthropods from the Maritime Provinces of Canada." Michigan, 1955.

5587
Evans, Robert Douglas. "Studies in the Evaporites of the Maritime Provinces of Canada." Kansas, 1972.

5588
Grant, Douglas Roderick. "Recent Coastal Submergence of the Maritime Provinces, Canada." Cornell, 1970.

5589
Klein, George Devries. "Stratigraphy, Sedimentary Petrology and Structure of Triassic Sedimentary Rocks, Maritime Provinces, Canada." Yale, 1960.

Powers, Sidney. See No./Voir no 5449

5590
Rostoker, Mendel Davis. "The Geology of the Canso Group in the Maritime Provinces of Canada." Boston University, 1960.

5591
Smitheringale, William Vickers. "The Manganese Occurrences of the Maritime Provinces, Canada." Massachusetts Institute of Technology, 1928.

New Brunswick/Nouveau-Brunswick

5592
Anderson, Francis D. "The Geology of the Woodstock and Millville Areas, New Brunswick." McGill, 1956.

5593
Bamwoya, James Jasper. "Exploration Geochemistry in the Burnt Hill Area, New Brunswick: Distribution of Elements in Bedrock and in Heavy and Light Fractions of Stream Sediments." New Brunswick, 1978.

5594
Belyea, Helen Reynolds. "The Geology of the Musquash Area, New Brunswick." Northwestern, 1940.

5595
Benson, David Gwyn. "The Mineralogy of the New Brunswick Sulphide Deposits." McGill, 1959.

5596
Brown, Donald Dawson. "Hydrogeology of Taylor Island, New Brunswick." Western Ontario, 1971.

5597
Butt, Khurshid Alam. "Genesis of Granitic Stocks in Southwestern New Brunswick." New Brunswick, 1976.

5598
Carr, Peter Alexander. "Geology and Hydrogeology of the Moncton Map-Area, New Brunswick, Canada." Illinois, 1964.

5599
Cherry, Michael Edward. "The Petrogenesis of Granites in the St. George Batholith, Southwestern New Brunswick, Canada." New Brunswick, 1976.

5600
Chork, Chin Yoon. "The Application of Some Statistical and Computer Techniques to the Interpretation of Soil and Stream Sediment Geochemical Data." New Brunswick, 1978. [Key Anacon area/Région de Key Anacon]

5601
Cumming, Charles Linnaeus. "The Igneous Rocks of St. John, New Brunswick." Princeton, 1976.

5602
Dagger, G.W. "The Origin of the Mount Pleasant Tungsten-Molybdenum Deposit, N.B., Canada." Manchester, 1972.

5603
Davies, John Leslie. "The Geology and Geochemistry of the Austin Brook Area, Gloucester County, New Brunswick, with Special Emphasis on the Austin Brook Iron Formation." Carleton, 1972.

5604
Davis, George Herbert. "Structural Analysis of the Caribou Sulfide Deposit, Bathurst, New Brunswick, Canada." Michigan, 1971.

5605
Dechow, Ernest William Chatham. "The Geology of the Heath Steele Mine, Newcastle, New Brunswick, Canada." Yale, 1959.

5606
Donohoe, Howard Vane Jr. "Analysis of Structures in the St. George Area, Charlotte County, New Brunswick." New Brunswick, 1978.

5607
Doran, Jeffrey Bernard. "A New Species of Psilophyton from the Lower Devonian of Northern New Brunswick, Canada." Alberta, 1979.

5608
Flaherty, Gerard Francis. "Geology of Chignecto Area, New Brunswick." Massachusetts Institute of Technology, 1933.

5609
Gandhi, Subbaraja Mohandas. "Exploration Rock Geochemical Studies in and Around the Caribou Sulfide Deposit, New Brunswick, Canada." New Brunswick, 1978.

5610
Garnett, John Arthur. "Structural Analysis of Part of the Lubec-Bellisle Fault Zone, Southwestern New Brunswick." New Brunswick, 1973.

5611
Goodfellow, Wayne David. "Rock Geochemical Exploration and Ore Genesis at Brunswick No. 12 Deposit, New Brunswick." New Brunswick, 1975.

5612
Graf, Joseph Lucas, Jr. "Rare Earth Elements Hydrothermal Tracers During the Formation Massive Sulfide Deposits and Associated Iron Fo mations in New Brunswick." Yale, 1975.

5613
Helmstaedt, Herwart. "A Structural Analysis Beaver Harbour Area, Charlotte County, N.E New Brunswick, 1968.

5614
Howard, Waldorf V. "The Devonian Volcanic Series the Vicinity of Dalhousie, New Brunswick McGill, 1924.

5615
Jones, Robert Alan. "Geology and Petrography Ordovician Volcanic Rocks, Bathurst-Newcast District, New Brunswick." Cincinnati, 1964.

5616
Lee, Hurlbert A. "Two Phases of Till and Oth Glacial Problems in the Edmundston Grand Fa Region (New Brunswick, Quebec, and Maine Chicago, 1954.

5617
Loudon, John Russell. "The Origin of the Porphyry a Porphyry-Like Rocks of Elbow, New Brunswick Toronto, 1960.

5618
Lusk, John. "Sulphur Isotope Abundances and Ba Metal Zoning in the Heath Steele B-1 Oreboo Newcastle, New Brunswick." McMaster, 1968.

5619
Matthew, William Diller. "Effusive and Dyke Roc near St. John, New Brunswick." Columbia, 1895.

5620
McBride, Derek Ernest. "The Structure and Stratigr phy of the B-Zone, Heath Steele Mines, Newcast. New Brunswick." New Brunswick, 1976.

5621
Mercer, William. "Distribution of Gold and Palladiu in Massive Sulphide Deposits and Host Roc Bathurst-Newcastle District, New Brunswick McMaster, 1975.

5622
Naing, Win. "Photogeology of the Caledonia Area Southern New Brunswick." New Brunswick, 1977.

5623
Saif, Saiful Islam. "Identification, Correlation a Origin of the Key Anacon-Brunswick Mines O Horizon, Bathurst, New Brunswick." Ne Brunswick, 1978.

5624
Schluger, Paul Randolph. "Sedimentology of the Per Formation, New Brunswick, Canada, and Mair U.S.A." Illinois, 1972.

5625
Scratch, Richard Boyd. "Geologic, Structural, Flu Inclusion and Oxygen Isotope Study of the La George Antimony Deposit, Southern N Brunswick." Western Ontario, 1981.

5626
Skinner, Ralph. "Geology of the Tetagouche Bathur New Brunswick." McGill, 1956.

5627
Suensilpong, S. "The Geology and Mineralogy of Nigadoo River Mine, N.B., Canada." Manchester, 1969-70.

5628
Szabo, Nicholas Louis. "Dispersion of Indicators by Glacial Transportation at Mount Pleasant." New Brunswick, 1975.

5629
Tupper, William MacGregor. "Sulfur Isotopes and the Origin of the Sulfide Deposits of the Bathurst-Newcastle Area in New Brunswick." Massachusetts Institute of Technology, 1959.

5630
Uthe, Richard Edward. "Assessment of Soil Conductance and pH in Exploration Geochemistry for Selected Mining Areas of New Brunswick, Canada." New Brunswick, 1978.

5631
Wahl, John Lesslie. "Rock Geochemical Exploration at the Heath Steele and Key Anacon Deposits, New Brunswick." New Brunswick, 1978.

5632
Wardle, Richard Julian. "The Stratigraphy and Tectonics of the Greenhead Group: Its Relationship to Hadrynian and Paleozoic Rocks, Southern New Brunswick." New Brunswick, 1978.

5633
Whitehead, Robert Edgar. "Application of Rock Geochemistry to Problems of Mineral Exploration and Ore Genesis at Heath Steele Mines, New Brunswick." New Brunswick, 1973.

Nova Scotia/Nouvelle-Écosse

5634
Akande, Samuel Olusegun. "Genesis of the Lead-Zinc Mineralization at Gays River, Nova Scotia, Canada: A Geologic, Fluid Inclusion and Stable Isotopic Study." Dalhousie, 1983.

5635
Bell, Walter Andrew. "The Mississippian Formations of the Horton-Windsor District, Nova Scotia." Yale, 1920.

5636
Belt, Edward Scudder. "Stratigraphy and Sedimentology of the Mabou Group (Middle Carboniferous) Nova Scotia, Canada." Yale, 1963.

5637
Bourque, Pierre. "Stratigraphie du silurien et du dévonien basal du nord-est de la Gaspésie avec une illustration de la faune à brachiopodes." Montréal, 1973.

5638
Cameron, Alexander Rankin. "Some Petrological Aspects of the Harbour Seam, Sydney Coalfield, Nova Scotia." Pennsylvania State, 1961.

5639
Chatterjee, Aumlaya Kumar. "Mineralization and Associated Wall Rock Alteration in the George River Group, Cape Breton Island, Nova Scotia." Dalhousie, 1980.

5640
Clifton, H. Edward. "The Pembroke Breccia of Nova Scotia." Johns Hopkins, 1963.

5641
Collins, Jon A. "The Sedimentary Copper Universal; from Sedimentologic and Stratigraphic Syntheses of the Proterozoic of Icon, Quebec; Grinnell Formation, Alberta; Nonesuch Shale, Michigan and the Mississippian Horton-Windsor Formation of Nova Scotia." Queen's, 1975.

Côté, Philip Richard. See No./Voir no 5740

5642
Crosby, Donald G. Jr. "The Wolfville Map-Area, Kings and Hants Counties, Nova Scotia." Stanford, 1952.

5643
Dalrymple, Robert Walker. "Sediment Dynamics of Macrotidal Sand Bars, Bay of Fundy." McMaster, 1977.

5644
Eisbacher, Gerhard Heinz. "Tectonic Analysis in the Cobequid Mountains, Nova Scotia, Canada." Princeton, 1967.

5645
Gillis, John William. "Geology of Northwestern Pictou County, Nova Scotia, Canada." Pennsylvania State, 1964.

5646
Goranson, Edwin Alexander. "I. The Behavior of Ore Minerals in Polarized Light. II. Pre-Carboniferous Geology of the Bras d'Or, Sydney, and Glace Bay Map Sheets, Cape Breton, Nova Scotia." Harvard, 1933.

5647
Gray, Richard H. "The Sydney Coalfield." McGill, 1940.

5648
Griswold, Thomas Baldwin. "A Study of the Effects of a Mafic Dike on a Granite Front Georgeville, Antigonish County, Nova Scotia." Yale, 1977.

5649
Guernsey, Tarrant D. "The Geology of North Mountain, Cape Breton." Columbia, 1929.

5650
Harris, Ian McKittrick. "Geology of the Goldenville Formation, Taylor Head, Nova Scotia." Edinburgh, 1971.

5651
Herb, Gregor. "Diagenesis of Deeply Buried Sandstones on the Scotian Shelf." Dalhousie, 1975.

5652
Hickox, Charles Frederick Jr. "Geology of the Central Annapolis Valley, Nova Scotia." Yale, 1958.

5653
Hill, Philip R. "Detailed Morphology and Late Quaternary Sedimentation of the Nova Scotian Slope, South of Halifax." Dalhousie, 1982.

5654
Hutchinson, Robert D. "The Stratigraphy and Correlation of the Cambrian Sedimentary Rocks of Cape Breton Island, Nova Scotia, Canada." Wisconsin, 1950.

5655
Kaplan, Sanford Sandy. "The Sedimentology, Coal Petrology, and Trace Element Geochemistry of Coal Bearing Sequences from Joggins, Nova Scotia, Canada and Southeastern Nebraska, U.S.A." Pittsburgh, 1980.

5656
Kelley, Danford Greenfield. "Mississippian Stratigraphy and Geologic History of Central Cape Breton Island, Nova Scotia." Massachusetts Institute of Technology, 1959.

5657
King, Lewis H. "Studies on Spontaneous Combustion Using Nova Scotia Coals." Massachusetts Institute of Technology, 1955.

5658
Knight, Ronald John. "Sediments, Bedforms and Hydraulics in a Macrotidal Environment, Cobequid Bay, (Bay of Fundy) Nova Scotia." McMaster, 1977.

5659
Lambiase, Joseph John. "Sediment Dynamics in the Macrotidal Avon River Estuary, Nova Scotia." McMaster, 1977.

5660
Lucas, Margaret Jennifer. "Variation Studies of Non-Marine Pelecypods from the Upper Carboniferous of Eastern North America." Illinois, 1957.

5661
Lund, Richard Jacob. "Differentiation in the Cape Spencer Flow (Nova Scotia)." Wisconsin, 1930.

5662
Lyall, Anil Kumar. "A Study of Offshore Sediment Movement and Differentiation of Beach and Dune Sands in the Cape Sable Island Area, Nova Scotia." Dalhousie, 1970.

5663
Maehl, Richard Henry. "Silurian of Pictou County, Nova Scotia." Massachusetts Institute of Technology, 1961.

5664
McLearn, Frank Harris. "The Stratigraphy and Correlation of the Arisaig Silurian Series (Nova Scotia)." Yale, 1917.

5665
Moodie, Roy Lee. "A Contribution to a Monograph of the Extinct Amphibia of North America, New Forms from the Carboniferous." Chicago, 1908.

5666
Murphy, James Brendan. "Tectonics and Magnetism in the Northern Antigonish Highlands, Nova Scotia." McGill, 1982.

5667
Murray, Bruce Churchill. "Stratigraphy of the Horton Group in Parts of Nova Scotia." Massachusetts Institute of Technology, 1956.

5668
Newman, W.R. "Geology and Microscopic Features of the Phalen Seam, Sydney Coal Field, Sydney, Nova Scotia." Toronto, 1934.

5669
Newman, William Alexander. "Wisconsin Glaciation of Northern Cape Breton Island, Nova Scotia, Canada." Syracuse, 1971.

5670
Nielsen, Erick. "Composition and Origin of Wisconsinian Till in Mainland Nova Scotia." Dalhousie, 1976.

5671
Norman, George W.H. "Lake Ainslie Map-Area, N.S." Princeton, 1929.

5672
Phinney, William Charles. "Phase Equilibrium in the Metamorphic Rocks of St. Paul Island and Cape North, Nova Scotia." Massachusetts Institute of Technology, 1960.

5673
Rankin, Douglas Stewart. "Heat Flow-Heat Production Studies in Nova Scotia." Dalhousie, 1974.

5674
Sage, Nathaniel M., Jr. "Windsor Group Stratigraphy in the Antigonish and Mahone Bay Areas, Nova Scotia." Massachusetts Institute of Technology, 1953.

5675
Sarkar, Prasanta Kumar. "Petrology and Geochemistry of the White Rock Metavolcanic Suite, Yarmouth, Nova Scotia." Dalhousie, 1978.

5676
Schiller, Edward Alexander. "Mineralogy and Geology of the Guysborough Area, Nova Scotia, Canada." Utah, 1963.

5677
Scott, David Bruce. "Distributions and Population Dynamics of Marsh-Estuarine Foraminifera with Applications to Relocating Holocene Sea Levels." Dalhousie, 1977.

5678
Sinha, Ravindra Prasad. "Petrology of Volcanic Rocks of North Mountain, Nova Scotia." Dalhousie, 1971.

5679
Stacy, Maurice C. "Stratigraphy and Paleontology of the Windsor Group (Upper Mississippian) in Parts of Cape Breton Island, Nova Scotia." Massachusetts Institute of Technology, 1952.

5680
Stevenson, Ira M. "Geology of the Truro Map Area, Colchester and Hants Counties, Nova Scotia." McGill, 1954.

5681
Trescott, Peter Chapin. "An Investigation of the Ground Water Resources of the Annapolis-Cornwallis Valley, Nova Scotia." Illinois, 1967.

5682
Wightman, Daryl M. "Late Pleistocene Glaciofluvial and Glaciomarine Sediments on the North Side of the Minas Basin, Nova Scotia." Dalhousie, 1980.

5683
Williams, Merton Yarwood. "Geology of the Arisaig-Antigonish District, Nova Scotia." Yale, 1912.

5684
Wishart, James S. "Studies in the Chromite Group." Princeton, 1935.

5685
Woodman, Joseph Edmund. "Geology of the Moose River Gold District, Halifax County, Nova Scotia, Together with the Pre-Carboniferous History of the Meguma Series." Harvard, 1902.

5686
Wright, William Josiah. "Geology of the New Ross Map-Area, with an Introductory Chapter on the Goldbearing Series and the Granites of Southern Nova Scotia." Yale, 1915.

Newfoundland and Labrador/Terre-Neuve et Labrador

General Item/Ouvrage général

5687
Grant, Alan Carson. "The Continental Margin off Labrador and Eastern Newfoundland – Morphology and Geology." Dalhousie, 1971.

Labrador

5688
Baragar, William R.A. "A Study of the Basaltic Rocks in Part of the Labrador Trough." Columbia, 1959.

5689
Berg, Jonathan Henry. "Mineralogy and Petrology of the Contact Aureoles of the Anorthositic Nain Complex, Labrador." Massachusetts, 1976.

5690
Bergeron, Robert. "Study of the Quebec-Labrador Iron Belt Between Deny Lake and Larch River." Laval, 1954.

5691
Brand, Stephen Richard. "Geology, Petrology and Geochemistry of the Lower Kingurutik River Area, Labrador, Canada." Purdue, 1976.

5692
Callahan, John E. "A Regional Heavy Mineral Petrographic and Stream Sediment Geochemical Survey Applied to Mineral Exploration, Churchill Falls Area, Labrador." Queen's, 1973.

5693
Chough, Sung Kwun. "Morphology, Sedimentary Facies and Processes of the Northwest Atlantic Mid-Ocean Channel Between 61[and 52[N, Labrador Sea." McGill, 1978.

5694
Clark, Anthony M.S. "A Reinterpretation of the Stratigraphy and Deformation of the Aillik Group, Makkovik, Labrador." Memorial University of Newfoundland, 1974.

5695
Curtis, Lawrence Wilson. "Petrology of the Red Wine Complex, Central Labrador." Toronto, 1975.

5696
Donaldson, John Allan. "Geology of the Marion Lake Area, Quebec-Labrador." Johns Hopkins, 1960.

5697
Dufresne, Cyrille. "A Study of the Kaniapiskau System in the Burnt Creek-Goodward Area, New Quebec and Labrador, Newfoundland." McGill, 1952.

5698
Evans, Daniel Frederick. "Geology and Petrochemistry of the Kitts and Michelin Uranium Deposits and Related Prospects, Central Mineral Belt, Labrador." Queen's, 1980.

5699
Fahrig, Walter F. "The Petrology of the Ultramafic Rocks of the Labrador Trough." Chicago, 1954.

5700
Fawley, Allan P. "Geology and Iron Formation of the Petitsikapau Area, Labrador." California, Los Angeles, 1948.

5701
Frarey, Murray James. "Geology of the Willbob Lake Area, Northern Quebec and Western Labrador." Michigan, 1954.

5702
Geiger, Kenneth Warren. "Reconnaissance Geology and Mineral Deposits of the Wilson Lake-Winokapau Lake Area, Labrador." Cornell, 1961.

5703
Hashimoto, Tsutomu. "Mineral Assemblages and Phase Equilibria in the Metamorphosed Silicate Iron Formation of the Cape Smith Belt, New Quebec and the Labrador Trough." Laval, 1967.

5704
Howell, John E. "Silification in the Fleming Formation of the Knob Lake Group of the Labrador Iron Belt." Wisconsin, 1954.

5705
Huntington, Hope Davies. "Anorthositic and Related Rocks from Nukasorsuktokh Island, Labrador." Massachusetts, 1980.

5706
Hurst, Richard William. "Geochronologic Studies in the Precambrian Shield of Canada. Part I. The Archaean of Coastal Labrador. Part II. The Sudbury Basin: Sudbury, Ontario." California, Los Angeles, 1975.

5707
Jackson, Garth Digby. "The Geology of the Neal (Virot) Lake Area, West of Wabush Lake, Labrador, with Special Reference to the Iron Deposits." McGill, 1963.

5708
Klein, Cornelis. "Mineralogy and Petrology of the Wabash Iron Formation, Labrador City Area, Newfoundland." Harvard, 1965.

5709
Knowles, David Martin. "The Structural Development of Labrador Trough Formations in the Grenville Province, Wabush Lake Area, Labrador." Columbia, 1967.

5710
Lamb, Henry Francis. "Late Quaternary Vegetational History of the Forest-Tundra Ecotone in North Central Labrador." Cambridge, 1982.

5711
Lee, Burdett W. "Geology of the Red Wine Mountains, Labrador." McGill, 1954.

5712
Linder, Harold William. "The Origin of Copper-Nickel Mineralization in Gabbroic Rocks of the Northern Labrador Trough." Minnesota, 1966.

Loeken, Olav H. See No./Voir no 4646

5713
Mann, Ernest Leigh. "The Geology of the Seal Lake Area, Central Labrador." McGill, 1959.

5714
Marchand, Michael. "A Geochemical and Geochronologic Investigation of Meteorite Impact Melts at Mistastin Lake, Labrador and Sudbury, Ontario." McMaster, 1976.

5715
Marten, Brian Ernest. "The Relationship Between the Aillik Group and the Hopedale Complex, Kaipokok Bay, Labrador." Memorial University of Newfoundland, 1977.

5716
Morse, Stearns Anthony. "Geology of the Kiglapait Layered Intrusion, Coast of Labrador, Canada." McGill, 1962.

5717
Odell, Noel E. "A) The Geology of Northeast Greenland. B) The Glaciology and Geomorphology of Northeast Greenland. C) The Geomorphology of Northern Labrador." Cambridge, 1940.

5718
O'Leary, Jeffrey. "Application of Geology and Geostatistics at the Scully Mine, Ore Body, Wabush, Labrador." London, 1973.

5719
Perrault, Guy Gilles. "The Geology of the Western Margin of the Labrador Trough." Toronto, 1955.

5720
Ranson, William Albrecht. "Anorthosites of Diverse Magma Types in the Puttuaaluk Lake Area, Nain Complex, Labrador." Massachusetts, 1979.

5721
Rubins, Charles Curtis. "Structural Stratigraphic and Petrologic Relations of Rocks South of the Barth Island Layered Intrusion, Labrador." Syracuse, 1973.

5722
Singh, Sudesh Kumar. "Petrological and Mineralogical Studies of the Ivan Lake Agpaitic Complex, Central Labrador." Ottawa, 1972.

5723
Speer, John Alexander. "The Stratigraphy and Metamorphism of the Snyder Group, Labrador." Virginia Polytechnic Institute and State University, 1976.

5724
Vocke, Robert Donald. "Petrogenetic Modelling in an Archean Gneiss Terrain, Saglek Northern Labrador." SUNY, Stony Brook, 1983.

5725
Wheeler, Everett P. "A Study of Some Diabase Dikes of the Labrador Coast." Cornell, 1930.

5726
Whitmore, Duncan R. E. "The Proterozoic Rocks of the Squaw Lake - Woolett Lake Area, West Central Labrador." Princeton, 1943.

Newfoundland/Terre-Neuve

5727
Arnott, R.J. "Sedimentology, Structure and Stratigraphy of North East New World Island, Newfoundland." Oxford, 1983.

5728
Baird, David M. "Geology and Mineral Deposits of the Burlington Peninsula, Newfoundland." McGill, 1947.

5729
Betz, Frederick. "Geology and Mineral Deposits of the Canada Bay Area, Northern Newfoundland." Princeton, 1938.

5730
Bradley, Daniel Albert. "Geology of the Gisburn Lake-Terrenceville Area Fortune Bay Region, Southeastern Newfoundland." Michigan, 1954.

5731
Brown, Peter Alan. "Basement-Cover Relationships in Southwestern Newfoundland." Memorial University of Newfoundland, 1975.

5732
Buddington, Arthur Francis. "Pre-Columbian Rocks of Southeast Newfoundland." Princeton, 1916.

5733
Bursnall, John Treharne. "Stratigraphy, Structure and Metamorphism West of Baie Verte, Burlington Peninsula, Newfoundland." Cambridge, 1975.
Buyce, Milton Raymond. See No./Voir no 5086

5734
Casey, John Francis. "The Geology of the Southern Part of the North Arm Mountain Massif, Bay of Islands Ophiolite Complex, Western Newfoundland with Application to Ophiolite Obduction and the Genesis of the Plutonic Portions of Oceanic Crust and Upper Mantle." SUNY, Albany, 1980.

5735
Closs, Lloyd G. "An Evaluation of Selected Multivariate Mathematical Techniques as Aids in Interpretation of the Reconnaissance Geochemical Stream Sediment Data of the Halles Bay Concession, Newfoundland." Queen's, 1974.

5736
Coish, Raymond Alpheaus. "Igneous and Metamorphic Petrology of the Mafic Units of the Betts Cove and Blow-Me-Down Ophiolites, Newfoundland." Western Ontario, 1977.

5737
Colman-Saad, Stephen Peter. "The Geologic Development of the Bay D'Espoir Area, Southeastern Newfoundland." Memorial University of Newfoundland, 1974.

5738
Cooper, John R. "Geology of the Southern Half of the Bay of Islands Igneous Complex." Princeton, 1935.

5739
Coron, Cynthia Rose. "Facies Relations and Ore Genesis of the Newfoundland Zinc Mines Deposit, Daniel's Harbour, Western Newfoundland." Toronto, 1982.

5740
Côté, Philip Richard. "Lower Carboniferous Sedimentary Rocks of the Horton Group in Parts of Cape Breton Island, and Their Relation to Similar Strata of the Anguille Group in Southwestern Newfoundland." Ottawa, 1968.

5741
Dale, Nelson Clark. "The Cambrian Manganese Deposits of Conception and Trinity Bays, Newfoundland." Princeton, 1914.

5742
De Wit, Maarten Johan. "The Geology Around Bear Cove, Eastern White Bay, Newfoundland." Cambridge, 1973.
Dufresne, Cyrille. See No./Voir no 5697

5743
Eastler, Thomas Edward. "Geology of Silurian Rocks Change Islands and Easternmost Notre Dame Bay Newfoundland." Columbia, 1971.

744
ranks, Stephen Guest. "Stratigraphy, Sedimentology and Petrology of Early Paleozoic Island Arc Deposits, Newfoundland." Case Western Reserve, 1976.

745
uller, James O. "Geology and Mineral Deposits of the Fleur-de-Lys Area." Columbia, 1942.

746
Gale, G.H. "An Investigation of Some Sulfide Deposits of the Rambler Area, Newfoundland." Durham, 1972.

747
Gonzalez-Bonorino, Gustavo. "Sedimentology and Stratigraphy of the Curling Group, Humber Arm Supergroup, Central Western Newfoundland." McMaster, 1979.

Hashimoto, Tsutomu. See No./Voir no 5703

5748
Hayes, Albert Orion. "Geology of the Wabana Iron Ore of Newfoundland." Princeton, 1914.

5749
Hayes, John Jesse. "Geology of the Hodges-Hills-Marks Lake Area, Northern Newfoundland." Michigan, 1952.

5750
Helwig, James Anthony. "Stratigraphy and Structural History of the New Bay Area, North Central Newfoundland." Columbia, 1967.

5751
Heyl, George R. "Geology and Mineral Deposits of the Bay of Exploits Area, Notre Dame Bay, Newfoundland." Princeton, 1935.

5752
Higgins, Neville Charles. "The Genesis of the Grey River Tungsten Project: A Fluid Inclusion, Geochemical and Isotopic Study." Memorial University of Newfoundland, 1980.

5753
Horne, Gregory Stuart. "Stratigraphy and Structural Geology of Southwestern New World Island Area, Newfoundland." Columbia, 1968.

5754
Howell, Benjamin Franklin. "The Faunas of the Cambrian Paradoxides Beds at Manuels, Newfoundland." Princeton, 1920.

5755
Ingerson, Fred E. "Layered Peridotitic Laccoliths of the Trout River Area, Newfoundland." Yale, 1934.

5756
Jacobi, Robert Douglas. "Geology of Part of the Terrane North of Lukes Arm Fault North-Central Newfoundland (Part I). Modern Submarine Sediment Slides and Their Geological Implications." Columbia, 1980.

5757
Jamieson, Rebecca Anne. "The St. Anthony Complex, Northwestern Newfoundland: A Petrological Study of the Relationship Between a Peridotite Sheet and Its Dynothermal Aureole." Memorial University of Newfoundland, 1979.

5758
Jayasinghe, Nimal Ranjith. "Granitoids of the Wesleyville Area in Northeastern Newfoundland: A Study of Their Evolution and Geological Setting." Memorial University of Newfoundland, 1979.

5759
Jenness, Stuart E. "Geology of the Gander River Ultrabasic Belt, Newfoundland." Yale, 1934.

5760
Jones, C.M. "The Ballantrae Complex as Compared to the Ophiolites of Newfoundland." Cardiff, 1978.

5761
Karson, Jeffrey Alan. "Geology of the Northern Lewis Hills, Western Newfoundland." SUNY, Albany, 1977.

5762
Kidd, William Spencer Francis. "The Evolution of the Baie Verte Lineament, Burlington Peninsula, Newfoundland." Cambridge, 1974.

Klein, Cornelis. See No./Voir no 5708

5763
Kowalik, Joe. "Geological, Mineralogical and Stable Isotope Studies of a Polymetallic Massive Sulfide Deposit: Buchans, Newfoundland." Minnesota, 1979.

5764
Lock, Brian Edward. "The Lower Paleozoic Geology of Western White Bay, Newfoundland." Cambridge, 1969.

5765
MacDonald, Roderick Dickson. "The Geology of the Wintering River Area, Notre Dame Bay, Newfoundland." Princeton, 1940.

5766
MacLean, Hugh James. "Geology and Mineral Deposits of the Little Bay Area, Notre Dame Bay, Newfoundland." Princeton, 1940.

5767
McCartney, William Douglas. "Geology of the North Central Peninsula, Newfoundland." Harvard, 1959.

5768
Moll, Nancy Eileen. "The Structure and Petrology of the Gabbro Unit and the Mafic-Ultramafic, Contact Table Mountain, Bay of Islands Complex Newfoundland." Washington, Seattle, 1981.

5769
Moore, T. "Geology of the Baie d'Espoir Kalgudeck Region, Newfoundland." McGill, 1953.

5770
Nelson, Karl Douglas. "Geology of the Badger Bay-Seal Bay Area, North Central Newfoundland." SUNY, Albany, 1979.

5771
Peters, Ronald George. "Secondary Dispersion of Sulphur from Sulphide Deposits in the Notre Dame Bay Area, Newfoundland." London, 1974.

5772
Phair, George. "Geology of the Southwestern Part of the Long Range, Newfoundland." Princeton, 1949.

5773
Popper, George H.P. "Paleobasin Analysis and Structure of the Anguille Group, West-Central Newfoundland." Lehigh, 1970.

5774
Relly, Bruce Hamilton. "The Geology of Buchan's Mine, Newfoundland." McGill, 1960.

5775
Riccio, Luca. "Stratigraphy and Petrology of the Peridotite-Gabbro Component of the Western Newfoundland Ophiolites." Western Ontario, 1976.

5776
Rosencrantz, Eric John. "The Geology of the Northern Part of North Arm Massif, Bay of Islands Ophiolite Complex, Newfoundland: With Applications to Upper Oceanic Crust Lithology, Structure and Genesis." SUNY, Albany, 1980.

5777
Sampson, Edward. "The Ferrugenous Chert Formations of Notre Dame Bay, Newfoundland." Princeton, 1920.

5778
Smit, David Ernst. "Stratigraphy and Sedimentary Petrology of the Cambrian and Lower Ordovician Shelf Facies of Western Newfoundland." Iowa, 1971.

5779
Smith, Charles H. "The Bay of Islands Igneous Complex, Newfoundland - Northern Half." Yale, 1952.

5780
Smyth, Walter Ronald. "The Stratigraphy and Structure of the Southern Part of the Hare Bay Allochthon, Northwest Newfoundland." Memorial University of Newfoundland, 1973.

5781
Snelgrove, Alfred Kitchener. "Geology and Ore Deposits of Betts Cove-Tilt Cove Area, Notre Dame Bay, Newfoundland." Princeton, 1930.

5782
Stevens, Robert Keith. "Lower Paleozoic Evolution of West Newfoundland." Western Ontario, 1976.

5783
Stouge, Svend Sandbergh. "Conodonts of the Table Head Formation (Middle Ordovician), Western Newfoundland." Memorial University of Newfoundland, 1981.

5784
Sullivan, Kathryn Dwyer. "The Structure and Evolution of the Newfoundland Basin, Offshore Eastern Canada." Dalhousie, 1978.

5785
Talkington, Raymond Willis. "The Geology, Petrology and Petrogenesis of the White Hills Peridotite, St. Anthony Complex, Northwestern Newfoundland." Memorial University of Newfoundland, 1981.

5786
Thurlow, John Geoffrey. "Geology, Ore Deposits and Applied Rock Geochemistry of the Buchans Group, Newfoundland." Memorial University of Newfoundland, 1981.

5787
Troelsen, Johannes C. "Geology of the Bonne Bay-Trout Area, Newfoundland." Yale, 1947.

5788
Tuke, Michael Francis. "The Lower Paleozoic Rocks and Klippen of the Pistolet Bay Area, Northern Newfoundland." Ottawa, 1966.

5789
Upadhyay, Hansa Datt. "The Betts Cove Ophiolite and Related Rocks of the Snooks Arm Group, Newfoundland." Memorial University of Newfoundland, 1973.

5790
Van Alstine, Ralph Erskine. "Geology and Mineral Deposits of the St. Lawrence Area, Burin Peninsula, Newfoundland." Princeton, 1944.

5791
Walthier, Thomas N. "Geology and Mineral Deposits of the Area Between Corner Brook and Stephenville, Western Newfoundland." Columbia, 1950.

5792
Watson, Kenneth Depencier. "Geology and Mineral Deposits of the Baie Verte-Mings Bight Area." Princeton, 1940.

5793
Weitz, Joseph Leonard. "Geology of the Bay of Islands Area, Western Newfoundland." Yale, 1954.

5794
Werner, Harry Jay. "The Geology of Humber Valley, Newfoundland." Syracuse, 1956.

5795
Wessel, James M. "Sedimentary Petrology of the Springdale and Botwood Formations, Central Mobile Belt, Newfoundland, Canada." Massachusetts, 1975.

5796
White, Donald E. "Geology and Molybdenite Deposits of the Rencontre East Area, Fortune Bay, Newfoundland." Princeton, 1939.

5797
Widmer, Kemble. "The Geology of the Hermitage Bay Area, Newfoundland." Princeton, 1951.

5798
Younce, Gordon Baldwin. "Structural Geology and Stratigraphy of the Bonavista Bay Region, Newfoundland." Cornell, 1970.

5799
Zajac, Ihor Stephan. "The Stratigraphy and Mineralogy of the Sokoman Formation in the Knob Lake Area, Quebec and Newfoundland." Michigan, 1972.

Northwest Territories/Territoires du Nord-Ouest

Adams, William Peter. See No./Voir no 4654

5800
Adshead, John Douglas. "Mineralogical Studies of Bottom Sediments from Western Hudson and James Bays." Missouri, 1973.

5801
Aksu, Ali Engin. "Late Quaternary Stratigraphy, Paleoenvironmentology and Sedimentation History of Baffin Bay and Davis Strait." Dalhousie, 1981.

5802
Ali, Syed Afaq. "Chemical Composition of Pore Waters from Sediments of Subtropical and Arctic Environments: A Comparison." Rensselaer Polytechnic Institute, 1974. [Baffin Bay/Baie de Baffin]

5803
Badham, John Patrick Nicholas. "Volcanogenesis, Orogenesis and Metallogenesis, Camsell River Area, Northwest Territories." Alberta, 1973.

5804
Baker, Robert William. "The Influence of Ice-Crystal Size and Dispersed-Solid Inclusions on the Creep of Polycrystalline Ice." Minnesota, 1977. [Barnes Ice Cap, Baffin Island/Calotte glaciaire Barnes, Île de Baffin]

5805
Baker, Seymour R. "Sedimentation in an Arctic Marine Environment: Baffin Bay Between Greenland and the Canadian Arctic Archipelago." Rensselaer Polytechnic Institute, 1971.

5806
Barnes, Frederick Quilliam. "The Snowdrift and McLean Bay Map-Areas, Great Slave Lake, Northwest Territories." Toronto, 1953.

Bassett, Henry Gordon. See No./Voir no 5381

5807
Bernacsek, G.M. "New Devonian Jawed Fishes from Northern Canada." Bristol, 1976.

5808
Berry, Richard. "Geochemistry and Mineralogy of the Clay-Sized Fractions of Some North Atlantic and Arctic Ocean Bottom Sediments." Washington, St. Louis, 1963.

5809
Bihl, Gerhard. "Palynostratigraphic Investigation of Upper Maastrichtian and Paleocene Strata Near Tate Lake, N.W.T." British Columbia, 1973.

Blusson, Stewart L. See No./Voir no 5909

5810
Bonham-Carter, Graeme Francis. "The Geology of the Pennsylvanian Sequence of the Blue Mountains, Northern Ellesmere Island." Toronto, 1966.

5811
Boyle, Robert William. "The Mineralization of the Yellowknife Gold Belt with Special Reference to the Factors Which Controlled its Localization." Toronto, 1953.

5812
Braman, Dennis Richard. "Upper Devonian-Lower Carboniferous Miospore Biostratigraphy of the Imperial Formation, District of MacKenzie and Yukon." Calgary, 1981.

5813
Brand, Uwe. "Geochemistry of Paleozoic Corals Crinoids and Associated Carbonate Rocks from Arctic Canada, Iowa and Missouri." Ottawa, 1979.

5814
Broad, David Stephen. "Upper Silurian and Lower Devonian Heterostraci from Yukon and Northwest Territories, Canada." Bristol, 1972.

5815
Brook, George Albert. "Geomorphology of the North Karst, South Nahanni River Region, Northwest Territories, Canada." McMaster, 1977.

5816
Brown, Ira C. "Structure of the Yellowknife Gold Belt, Northwest Territories." Harvard, 1949.

5817
Bruner, Frank H. "Contributions to the Exact Age Determination of the Hottah Lake Uraninite." Missouri, 1936.

5818
Campbell, Douglas D. "Geology of the Pitchblende Deposits of Port Radium, Great Bear Lake, N.W.T." California Institute of Technology, 1955.

5819
Cecile, Michael Peter. "Stratigraphy and Depositional History of the Upper Goulburn Group, Kilohigok Basin, Bathurst Inlet, N.W.T." Carleton, 1976.

5820
Church, Michael Anthony. "Baffin Island Sandar: A Study of Arctic Fluvial Environments." British Columbia, 1975.

5821
Clark, David Barrie. "Tertiary Basalts of the Baffin Bay Area." Edinburgh, 1969.

5822
Coleman, Leslie Charles. "Mineralogy of the Giant Yellowknife Gold Mine, Yellowknife, Northwest Territories." Princeton, 1955.

5823
Crawford, William James Page. "Metamorphic Iron Formations of Eqe Bay and Adjacent Parts of Northern Baffin Island." Washington, Seattle, 1973.

5824
Darby, Dennis Arnold. "Carbonate Cycles and Clay Mineralogy of Arctic Ocean Sediment Cores." Wisconsin, 1971.

5825
Davidson, Anthony. "Metamorphism and Intrusion in the Benjamin Lake Map-Area, Northwest Territories." British Columbia, 1967.

5826
Davies, Edward Harold. "Jurassic and Lower Cretaceous Dinoflagellate Cysts of the Sverdrup Basin, Arctic Canada: Taxonomy, Biostratigraphy, Chronostratigraphy." Toronto, 1979.

5827
Davis, Philip Thompson. "Late Holocene Glacial, Vegetational and Climatic History of Pangnirtung and Kingnait Fiora Area, Baffin Island, N.W.T., Canada." Colorado, 1980.

5828
Eade, Kenneth E. "Petrology of the Gneiss Formation of the Clyde Area, Baffin Island." McGill, 1955.

5829
Easton, Robert Michael. "Tectonic Significance of the Akaitcho Group, Wopmay Orogen, Northwest Territories, Canada." Memorial University of Newfoundland, 1982.

5830
Embry, Ashton Fox. "The Middle-Upper Devonian Clastic Wedge of the Franklinian Geosyncline." Calgary, 1976.

5831
England, John Howard. "The Glacial Geology of the Archer Fiord/Lady Franklin Bay Area, Northeastern Ellesmere Island, N.W.T., Canada." Colorado, 1974.

5832
Feniak, Michael W. "The Geology of Dowdell Peninsula, Great Bear Lake, Northwest Territories." Minnesota, 1947.

5833
Fensome, Robert Allan. "Miospores from the Jurassic-Cretaceous Boundary Beds, Aklavik Range, Northwest Territories, Canada." Saskatchewan, 1983.

5834
Folinsbee, Robert Edward. "Zone-Facies of Metamorphism in Relation to the Ore Deposits of the Yellowknife Beaulieu Region, Northwest Territories." Minnesota, 1942.

5835
Frisch, Thomas Ottokar. "Metamorphism and Plutonism in Northernmost Ellesmere Island, Canadian Arctic Archipelago." California, Santa Barbara, 1968.

5836
Furnival, George M. "A Silver-Pitchblende Deposit at Contact Lake, Great Bear Lake Area, Northwest Territories, Canada." Massachusetts Institute of Technology, 1935.

5837
Garven, Grant. "The Role of Groundwater Flow in the Genesis of Stratabound Ore Deposits: A Quantitative Analysis." British Columbia, 1982.

5838
Gibling, Martin R. "Sedimentation of the Siluro-Devonian Clastic Wedge of Somerset Island, Arctic Canada." Ottawa, 1978.

5839
Gilchrist, Carol Mary. "The Glacial Geology of the Southeastern Area of the District of Keewatin, Northwest Territories, Canada." Massachusetts, 1982.

5840
Gill, James Wendell. "The Takiyuak Metavolcanic Belt: Geology, Geochemistry and Mineralization." Carleton, 1977.

5841
Green, David Christopher. "Precambrian Geology and Geochronology of the Yellowknife Area, N.W.T." Alberta, 1968.

Hanfield, Robert Charles. See No./Voir no 5104

5842
Henderson, John Bennett. "Petrology and Origin of the Sediments of the Yellowknife Group (Archean), Yellowknife, District of MacKenzie, Canada." Johns Hopkins, 1970.

5843
Hildebrand, Robert Shepard. "A Continental Volcanic Arc of Early Proterozoic Age at Great Bear Lake, N.W.T." Memorial University of Newfoundland, 1982.

5844
Hill, John David. "The Structural Development and Crystallization of the Kenoran Granitoid Plutons in the Nose Lake-Bach River Area, Northwest Territories." Western Ontario, 1980.

5845
Hoen, Ernst Leon. "The Anhydrite Diapirs and Structure of Central Western Axel Heiberg Island, Canadian Arctic Archipelago." McGill, 1963.

5846
Hoffman, Paul F. "Stratigraphy and Depositional History of a Proterozoic Geosyncline East Arm of Great Slave Lake, Northwest Territories, Canada." Johns Hopkins, 1970.

5847
Horn, David Russell. "Recent Marine Sediments and Sub-marine Topography, Sverdrup Islands, Canadian Arctic Archipelago." Texas, 1967.

5848
Isherwood, Dana Joan. "Soil Geochemistry and Rock Weathering in an Arctic Environment." Colorado, 1975.

5849
Jackson, Stewart Albert. "The Carbonate Compl and Lead Zinc Ore Bodies, Pine Point, Northwe Territories, Canada." Alberta, 1971.

5850
Jamieson, E.R. "The Alexander Reef-Compl (Frasnian), Hay River Area, N.W.T., Canada: Str tigraphy, Sedimentology and Paleoecology Reading, 1967.

5851
Jolliffe, Fred T. "Pitchblende in a Giant Quartz Ve Beaverlodge Lake, Northwest Territories." Princ ton, 1935.

5852
Jones, Brian C. "Facies and Faunal Aspects of t Silurian Read Bay Formation of Northern Somers Island, District of Franklin, Canada." Ottaw 1974.

5853
Jory, Lisle Thomas. "Mineralogical and Isotopic Rel tions in the Port Radium Pitchblende Depos Great Bear Lake, Canada." California Institute Technology, 1964.

5854
Kamineni, Dayananda Choudhari. "Petrology and Ge chemistry of Some Archean Metamorphic Roc near Yellowknife District of Mackenzie." Ottaw 1973.

5855
Kerans, Charles. "Sedimentology and Stratigraphy the Dismal Lakes Group." Carleton, 1982.

5856
Kitchell, Jennifer Ann. "Analysis and Paleoecolo Implications of Arctic and Antarctic Deep-S Biogenic Traces." Wisconsin, 1978. [Arctic Car dian Basin/Bassin de l'Arctique canadien]

5857
Klassen, Rodney Alan. "Quaternary Stratigraphy a Glacial History of Bylot Island, N.W.T., Canad Illinois, 1982.

5858
Koerner, R.M. "A Mass Balance Study: The Dev Island Ice Cap, Canada." London, 1966.

5859
Krause-Schroeder, Federico Fernando. "Sedimen logy and Stratigraphy of a Continental Terra Wedge: The Lower Cambrian Sekwi and June La Formations (Godlin River Group), Macken Mountains, Northwest Territories, Canad Calgary, 1979.

5860
Kravitz, Joseph Henry. "Sediments and Sedime Processes in a High Arctic Glacial Marine Basi George Washington, 1983. [Ellesmere Island/Île Ellesmere]

5861
Kuo, Say Lee. "Geology and Geochemistry of Stra bound Ore Deposits in South-Central Yukon Ter tory and Southwestern District of Mackenz Northwest Territories." Alberta, 1976.

5862
Kyle, James Richard. "Development of Sulfi Hosting Structures and Mineralization, Pine Poi Northwest Territories." Western Ontario, 1977.

5863

Lee, Sang Man. "Geology of the South Hopewell Sound Area, East of Hudson Bay, Province of Quebec and Northwest Territories." McGill, 1962.

5864

Lemon, Roy Richard Henry. "Proterozoic and Paleozoic Sediments of the Admiralty Inlet Region, Baffin Island." Toronto, 1957.

5865

Locke, William Willard, III. "The Quaternary Geology of the Cap Dyer Area, Southernmost Baffin Island, Canada." Colorado, 1980.

5866

Martin, Leonard John. "Stratigraphy and Depositional Tectonics of the North Yukon - Lower Mackenzie Area." Northwestern, 1957.

5867

Martineau, M.P. "The Petrology and Geochemistry of the Big Spruce Lake Syenite Complex, N.W.T., Canada." Oxford, 1970.

5868

McLaren, Patrick. "The Coasts of Eastern Melville and Western Byam Martin Islands: Coastal Processes and Belated Geology of a High Arctic Environment." South Carolina, 1977.

5869

Miall, Andrew D. "The Sedimentary History of the Peel Sound Formation, Prince of Wales Island, Northwest Territories." Ottawa, 1969.

5870

Michel, Frederick Alfred. "Isotope Investigations of Permafrost Waters in Northern Canada." Waterloo, 1982.

5871

Miller, Gifford Hubbs. "Glacial and Climatic History of Northern Cumberland Peninsula, Baffin Island, Canada, During the Last 10,000 Years." Colorado, 1975.

5872

Miller, R.G. "The Metallogeny of Uranium in the Great Bear Batholith Complex, Northwest Territories." Alberta, 1982.

5873

Mode, William Niles. "Quaternary Stratigraphy and Palynology of the Clyde Foreland, Baffin Island, N.W.T., Canada." Colorado, 1980.

5874

Moore, John C.G. "Geology of the Courageous - Matthews Lakes Gold Belt, Northwest Territories, Canada." Harvard, 1955.

Morganti, John Michael. See No./Voir no 5922

5875

Morrow, David Watts. "Stratigraphy and Sedimentology of Lower Paleozoic Formations near and on Grinnell Peninsula, Devon Island, N.W.T." Texas, 1973.

5876

Mossop, Grant Dilworth. "Anhydrite-Carbonate Cycles of the Ordovician Baumann Fiord Formation, Ellesmere Island, Arctic Canada: A Geological History." London, 1973.

5877

Mursky, Gregory. "Mineralogy, Petrology and Geochemistry of Hunter Bay Area, Great Bear Lake, N.W.T., Canada." Stanford, 1963.

5878

Nassichuk, Walter William. "Pennsylvanian Ammonoids from Ellesmere Island, Canadian Arctic Archipelago." Iowa, 1965.

5879

Nelson, Alan Robert. "Quaternary Glacial and Marine Stratigraphy of the Qivitu Peninsula, Northern Cumberland Peninsula, Baffin Island, Canada." Colorado, 1978.

5880

Nielsen, Peter A. "Metamorphic Petrology and Mineralogy of the Arseno Lake Area, N.W.T." Alberta, 1977.

5881

Olson, Reginald Arthur. "Geology and Genesis of Zinc-Lead Deposits within a Late Proterozoic Dolomite, Northern Baffin Island, N.W.T." British Columbia, 1977.

5882

Osterman, Lisa Ellen. "Late Quaternary History of Southern Baffin Island, Canada: A Study of Foraminifera and Sediments from Frobisher Bay." Colorado, 1982.

5883

Peterson, Robert Emil. "A Study of Suspended Particulate Matter: Arctic Ocean and Northern Oregon Continental Shelf." Oregon State, 1977.

5884

Pheasant, David Richard. "The Glacial Chronology and Glacio-isostasy of the Narpaing/Quajon Fiord Area, Cumberland Peninsula, Baffin Island." Colorado, 1971.

5885

Prusti, Bansi D. "Geology of the O'Connor Lake Area, N.W.T. with Special Reference to the Mineral Deposits." McGill, 1954.

5886

Quinn, Harold A. "Geology and Gold Deposits of the Gianque Lake Section, Yellowknife Area, Canada." Cornell, 1950.

5887

Ramsay, Colin Robert. "Metamorphism and Gold Mineralization of Archean Meta-Sediments Near Yellowknife, Northwest Territories, Canada." Alberta, 1973.

Richards, Barry Charles. See No./Voir no 5925

Richmond, William Oliver. See No./Voir no 5453

5888

Ricketts, Brian David. "Sedimentology and Stratigraphy of Eastern and Central Belcher Islands, Northwest Territories." Carleton, 1979.

5889

Ridland, George C. "Mineralogy of the Negus and Con Mines, Yellowknife, Northwest Territories." Princeton, 1939.

5890

Riley, George C. "The Geology of the Cumberland Sound Region, Baffin Island." McGill, 1957.

5891

Robinson, Brian William. "Studies on the Echo Bay Silver Deposit, Northwest Territories, Canada." Alberta, 1971.

Savigny, K. Wayne. See No./Voir no 4493

5892
Shawa, M.S. "Sedimentology, Stratigraphy and Diagenetic History of the Taglu Member and Equivalents, Mackenzie Delta Area, Canada." St.
Andrews, 1979.

5893
Smith, Edward Hanson. "Arctic Ice, With Reference
to Its Distribution into the North Atlantic Ocean."
Harvard, 1930.

5894
Smith, Peter Henderson. "The Structure and Petrology
of the Basler-Eau Claire Granite Complex, District
of Mackenzie, N.W.T., Canada." Northwestern,
1966.

5895
Snowdon, Lloyd R. "Organic Geochemistry of the
Upper Cretaceous Tertiary Delta Complexes of the
Beaufort-Mackenzie Sedimentary Basins, Northern
Canada." Rice, 1978.

5896
Squair, H. "Geology and Mineralization at the Tundra
Gold Mine, Northwest Territories, Canada."
London, 1965.

5897
Stanworth, C.W. "A Study of the Sosan Group and Its
Uranium Mineralization, East Arm, Great Slave
Lake, Canada." Southampton, 1980.

5898
St. Onge, Marc Robert. "Metamorphic Conditions of
the Low-Pressure Internal Zone of North-Central
Wopmay Orogen, Northwest Territories, Canada."
Queen's, 1981.

5899
Tan, Jee-Theng Tony. "Late Triassic-Jurassic Dino-
flagellate Biostratigraphy, Western Arctic,
Canada." Calgary, 1979.

5900
Temple, Peter G. "Geology of the Bathurst Island
Group, District of Franklin, Northwest Terri-
tories." Princeton, 1965.

5901
Thorsteinson, Raymond. "Geology of Cornwallis and
Little Cornwallis Islands, Arctic Archipelago,
Northwest Territories." Kansas, 1956.

5902
Tipnis, Ravindra S. "Biostratigraphy and Paleontology
of Late Cambrian to Late Middle Ordovician
Conodonts from Southwestern District of
Mackenzie, Northwest Territories." Alberta, 1978.

5903
Tippett, Clinton Raymond. "A Geological Cross-
Section Through the Southern Margin of the Fox
Folde Belt, Baffin Island, Arctic Canada, and Its
Relevance to the Tectonic Evolution of the North-
eastern Churchill Province." Queen's, 1980.

5904
Washburn, Albert Lincoln. "Reconnaissance Geology
of Portions of Victoria Island and Immediately
Adjacent Regions, Arctic Canada." Yale, 1942.

5905
Wright, Grant M. "Geology of the Ranji Lake and
Ghost Lake Areas, Northwest Territories, Canada."
Yale, 1950.

5906
Yardley, Donald H. "The Geology of the Northern
Part of the Chalco Lake Area, Northwest Terri-
tories, Canada." Minnesota, 1952.

Yukon

5907
Anderton, Peter Wightman. "Structural Glaciology of
a Glacier Confluence, Kaskawulsh Glacier, Yukon
Territory." Ohio State, 1967.

5908
Bell, Alfred H. "The Geology of Whitehorse District,
Yukon Territory." Chicago, 1926.

5909
Blusson, Stewart Lynn. "Geology and Tungsten
Deposits near the Headwaters of Flat River, Yukon
and Southwest District of Mackenzie, Canada."
California, Berkeley, 1965.

Braman, Dennis Richard. See No./Voir no 5812
Broad, David S. See No./Voir no 5814
Bryan, Merwyn Leonard. See No./Voir no 4682

5910
Cairnes, Delorme Donaldson. "The Wheaton River
District, Yukon Territory, Canada." Yale, 1910.

5911
Campbell, Richard Bradford. "The Texture, Origin and
Emplacement of the Granitic Rocks of Glenlyon
Range, Yukon Territory, Canada." California Insti-
tute of Technology, 1959.

5912
Campbell, Susan Wendy. "Geology and Genesis of
Copper Deposits and Associated Host Rocks in and
near the Quill Creek Area, Southwestern Yukon."
British Columbia, 1981.

Cavanaugh, Lorraine Marie Monnier. See No./Voir no
5184

5913
Cockfield, William Egbert. "Sixtymile and Ladue
Rivers Area, Yukon." Princeton, 1918.

Cwynar, Leslie Peter Chester. See No./Voir no 6541

5914
Denton, George Henry. "Late Pleistocene Glacial
Chronology, Northeastern St. Elias Mountains,
Canada." Yale, 1965.

5915
Driscoll, Fletcher Graves. "Formation and Wastage of
Neoglacial Surge Moraines of the Klutlan Glacier,
Yukon Territory, Canada." Minnesota, 1976.

5916
Erdmer, Philippe. "Nature and Significance of the
Metamorphic Minerals and Structures of Cataclas-
tic Allochthonous Rocks in the White Mountain,
Last Peak and Fire Lake Areas, Yukon Territory."
Queen's, 1982.

5917
Godwin, Colin Inglis. "Geology of Casino Porphyry
Copper-Molybdenum Deposit, Dawson Range,
Yukon Territory." British Columbia, 1975.

5918
Gordey, Steven P. "Stratigraphy, Structure and Tectonic Evolution of the Southern Pelly Mountains,
the Indigo Lake Area, Yukon Territory." Queen's,
1977.

919
Foster, Emlyn Howard. "Experimental Studies of Coarse-Grained Sedimentation." Ottawa, 1977.

Kuo, Say Lee. See No./Voir no 5861

Lambert, Maurice Bernard. See No./Voir no 5257

Le Couteur, Peter Clifford. See No./Voir no 5261

5920
Lees, Evert John. "Geology of the Labarge Area, Yukon." Toronto, 1931.

5921
Link, Peter Karl. "Stratigraphy of the Mount White-Eastern Little Atlin Area, Yukon Territory, Canada." Wisconsin, 1965.

Martin, Leonard John. See No./Voir no 5866

5922
Morganti, John Michael. "The Geology and Ore Deposits of the Howards Pass Area, Yukon and Northwest Territories: The Origin of Basinal Sedimentary Stratiform Sulphides Deposits." British Columbia, 1980.

5923
Morrison, Gregg William. "Setting and Origin of Skarn Deposits in the Whitehorse Copper Belt, Yukon." Western Ontario, 1981.

Nickling, William G. See No./Voir no 4687

Poole, William Hope. See No./Voir no 5309

5924
Rampton, Vernon Neil. "Pleistocene Geology of the Snag-Klutlan Area, Southwestern Yukon, Canada." Minnesota, 1969.

5925
Richards, Barry Charles. "Uppermost Devonian and Lower Carboniferous Stratigraphy Sedimentation, and Diagenesis, Southwestern District of Mackenzie and Southeastern Yukon." Kansas, 1983.

5926
Sticht, John H.H. "Geomorphology and Glacial Geology Along the Alaska Highway in Yukon Territory and Alaska." Harvard, 1952.

5927
Templeman-Klint, Dirk Jacob. "The Stratigraphy and Structure of the Keno Hill Quartzite in Tombstone Area, Central Yukon." McGill, 1966.

5928
Wheeler, John Oliver. "Evolution and History of the Whitehorse Trough as Illustrated by the Geology of Whitehorse Map-Area, Yukon." Columbia, 1956.

Ontario

5929
Allen, Charles Cameron. "Geology of Poohbah Lake, Ontario." Minnesota, 1940.

5930
Allen, John Murray. "Silicate-Carbonate Equilibria in Calcareous Metasediments of the Tudor Township Area, Ontario: A Test of the $P-T-XCO_2-XH_2O$ Model of Metamorphism." Queen's, 1976.

5931
Anderson, Thane Wesley. "Postglacial Vegetative Changes in the Lake Huron-Lake Simcoe District, Ontario, with Special Reference to Glacial Lake Algonquin." Waterloo, 1971.

5932
Anderson, Wells Foster. "Calcium Sulphate in Western New York and the Ontario Peninsula." Wisconsin, 1930.

5933
Appleyard, Edward C. "Nepheline Gneisses of the Wolfe Belt, Lyndoch Township, Ontario." Cambridge, 1963.

5934
Archbold, Norbert Lee. "Late Precambrian Diabase Dikes in Eastern Ontario and Western Quebec." Michigan, 1962.

5935
Armbrust, George Aimé. "Wall Rock Alteration and Paragenesis of the Tribag Mine, Batchawana Bay, Ontario." Colorado, 1967.

5936
Armstrong, Herbert Stoker. "The Gold Ores of Little Long Lac Area, Ontario." Chicago, 1942.

5937
Arndt, Nicholas Thomas. "Ultramafic Rocks of Munro Township and Their Volcanic Setting." Toronto, 1975.

5938
Arth, Joseph George, Jr. "Geochemistry of Early Precambrian Igneous Rocks, Minnesota-Ontario." SUNY, Stony-Brook, 1973.

5939
Ashwal, Lewis David. "Petrogenesis of Massif-Type Anorthosites: Crystallization History and Liquid Line of Descent of the Adirondack and Morin Complexes." Princeton, 1979.

5940
Ayres, Lorne Dale. "Early Precambrian Stratigraphy of Part of Lake Superior Provincial Park, Ontario, Canada, and its Implications for the Origin of the Superior Province." Princeton, 1969.

5941
Bain, George William. "Geology and Problems of the Webbwood Area, Canada." Columbia, 1927.

5942
Bain, Ian. "The Geology of the Grenville Belt through Actinolite, Ontario." Toronto, 1960.

5943
Bannerman, Harold M. The Nickel Lake Iron Range, Rainy River District, Ontario." Princeton, 1927.

5944
Barker, J.F. "Methane in Groundwaters - a Carbon Isotype Geochemical Study." Waterloo, 1979. [Greenbrook Field, Swift's Brook, Hillman Creek]

5945
Barnes, Christopher Richard. "Conodont Biofacies Analysis of Some Wilderness (Middle Ordovician) Limestone, Ottawa Valley, Ontario." Ottawa, 1964.

5946
Bartley, Melville William. "The Geology and Iron Deposits at Steeprock, Ontario." Toronto, 1940.

5947
Bass, Manuel Nathan. "An Interpretation of the Geologic History of Part of the Timiskaming Subprovince, Canada." Princeton, 1956.

5948
Bateman, John D. "Geology and Gold Deposits of Uchi-Slate Lake Area, Ontario." Yale, 1939.

5949
Bau, Andrew Fook-Shing. "History of Regional Deformation of Archean Rocks in the Kashabowie Lake-Lac Des Mille Lacs Area, Northwest Ontario." Toronto, 1979.

Beakhouse, Gary Philip. See No./Voir no 5489

5950
Beaty, David Wayne. "Part I. Comparative Petrology of the Apollo 11 Mare Basalts. Part II. The Oxygen Isotope Geochemistry of the Abitibi Greenstone Belt." California Institute of Technology, 1980.

5951
Bedell, Frank G. "The Sudbury Mining District." Kansas, 1906.

5952
Bell, Archibald M. "Major Structural Patterns in Parts of the Canadian Shield." Wisconsin, 1935.

5953
Bell, James Mackintosh. "Report on the Michipicoten Iron Range." Harvard, 1904.

5954
Bell, Leslie Victor. "Geology of the Boston-Skead Area with Special Reference to Rock Alteration, (Carbonation) in This and Related Canadian Precambrian Areas." Toronto, 1930.

5955
Best, Edward W. "Pre-Hamilton Devonian Stratigraphy, Southwestern Ontario, Canada." Wisconsin, 1953.

5956
Birk, Wolf Dieter. "The Nature and Timing of Granitoid Plutonism in the Wabigoon Volcanic-Plutonic Belt, Northwestern Ontario: Geochemistry, Rubidium/Strontium Geochronology, Petrography and Field Investigation." McMaster, 1978.

5957
Bishop, Eric G. "Geology of Portion of the Winnummin Lake Area." McGill, 1927.

5958
Blackadar, Robert Gordon. "Differentiation and Assimilation in the Logan Sills, Port Arthur, Ontario." Toronto, 1954.

5959
Blain, Christopher F. "Regional Geochemistry in the Superior Province of the Canadian Shield." Queen's, 1972.

5960
Blair, Alexander Marshall. "Surface Extraction of Non-Metallic Minerals in Ontario, Southwest of the Frontenac Axis." Illinois, 1965.

5961
Blecha, Matthew. "The Origin of the Breton Breccia Batchawana Area, Ontario." McGill, 1969.

5962
Bogle, Edward Warren. "Factors Affecting Lake Sediment Geochemistry in the Southern Grenville Province." Queen's, 1980.

5963
Bolton, Thomas Elwood. "Silurian Stratigraphy and Paleontology of the Niagara Escarpment in Ontario." Toronto, 1955.

5964
Bond, Ivor John. "Lithostratigraphy and Conodont Biostratigraphy of the Lower Ordovician of the Ottawa-St. Lawrence Lowlands, Ontario and New York." Queen's, 1974.

5965
Brigham, Robert John. "Structural Geology of Southwestern Ontario and Southeastern Michigan." Western Ontario, 1972.

5966
Brooks, Elwood Ralph. "Nature and Origin of the Grenville Front North of Georgian Bay, Ontario." Wisconsin, 1964.

5067
Brown, Jim McCaslin. "Structure and Origin of the Grenville Front South of Coniston, Ontario." Wisconsin, 1968.

5068
Brownell, George McLeod. "The Geology of the Lyndhurst Area, Ontario." Minnesota, 1928.

Burwash, Edward Moore Jackson. See No./Voir no 5172

5969
Byers, Alfred R. "The Geology and Mineral Deposits of the Night Hawk Lake Area, Ontario." McGill, 1936.

5970
Caley, John Fletcher. "The Ordovician of Manitoulin Island, Ontario." Toronto, 1934.

5971
Cameron, Barry Winston. "Stratigraphy and Sedimentary Environments of Lower Trentonian Series (Middle Ordovician) in Northwestern New York and Southeastern Ontario." Columbia, 1968.

5972
Cannon, William Francis. "Plutonic Evolution of the Cutter Area, Ontario." Syracuse, 1968.

5973
Card, Kenneth D.H. "Geology of the Agnew Lake Area, Ontario, a Study in Precambrian Stratigraphy, Structure and Metamorphism." Princeton, 1963.

5974
Carlson, H.D. "The Origin of the Corundum Deposits of Renfrew County, Ontario." Queen's, 1953.

5975
Carmichael, Dugald Macaulay. "Structure and Progressive Metamorphism in the Whetstone Lake Area, Ontario, with Emphasis on the Mechanism of Prograde Metamorphic Reactions." California, Berkeley, 1967.

5976
Casshyap, Satyendra Mohan. "Sedimentary Petrology of the Huronia Rocks, Española-Willisville Area, Ontario." Western Ontario, 1967.

5977
Cermignani, Claudio. "Metamorphic Reactions in the System Albite-Anorthite-Nepheline - $Na_2 CO_3$ $CaCO_3$ - H_2O, with Application to the Haliburton-Bancroft Alkaline Rocks." Toronto, 1979.

5978
Chandler, Frederick William. "Geology of the Huronian Rocks of Harrow Township and Surrounding Areas, North Shore of Lake Huron, Ontario." Western Ontario, 1969.

5979
Chapman, Diana Ferguson. "Petrology, Structure and Metamorphism of a Concordant Granodiorite Gneiss in the Grenville Province of Southeastern Ontario." Rutgers, 1968.
5980
Chappell, John Francis. "The Clare River Structure and Its Tectonic Setting." Carleton, 1979.
5981
Charlewood, Geoffrey Herbert. "The Nature of Carbonates in Altered Rocks and in Veins." Toronto, 1933.
5982
Chayes, Felix. "Alkaline and Carbonate Intrusives near Bancroft, Ontario." Columbia, 1942.
5983
Chesworth, Ward. "The Origin of Certain Granitic Rocks Occurring in Glamorgan Township, Southeastern Ontario." McMaster, 1967.
5984
Chew, K.J. "The Origin of Certain Base Metal Sulphide Deposits at Manitouwadge, Ontario." Aberdeen, 1977.
5985
Chute, Newton E. "The Upper Contact of the Sudbury Nickel Intrusive." Harvard, 1938.
5986
Chyi, Lindgren Liu. "Distribution of Some Noble-metals in Sulfide and Oxide Minerals in Strathcona Mine, Sudbury." McMaster, 1972.
5987
Clauson, Victor. "Geology of the Sudbury Basin Area, Ontario, Canada." Washington, Seattle, 1947.
5988
Coker, William Bernard. "Lake Sediment Geochemistry in the Superior Province of the Canadian Shield." Queen's, 1974.
5989
Colvine, Alexander Combe. "The Petrology, Geochemistry and Genesis of Sulphide-Related Alteration at the Temagami Mine, Ontario." Western Ontario, 1974.
5990
Colwell, John Allison. "Geochemistry and Petrology of the Nipissing Diabase in Ontario." Michigan State, 1967.
5991
Cook, Robert Bradley. "The Biochemistry of Sulfur in Two Small Lakes." Columbia, 1981. [Experimental Lakes area, northeastern Ontario/Région expérimentale des lacs du Nord-est de l'Ontario]
5992
Cooke, David Lawrence. "The Timiskaming Volcanics and Associated Sediments of the Kirkland Lake Area." Toronto, 1966.
5993
Cowan, William Richard. "Stratigraphy and Quantitative Analysis of Wisconsinian Tills, Brantford-Woodstock Area, Ontario, Canada." Colorado, 1975.
5994
Crombie, Gordon Peers. "A Study of the Insoluable Residues of the Paleozoic Rocks of Southwestern Ontario." Toronto, 1943.
5995
Cronin, Thomas Mark. "Late Wisconsin Foraminifera, Ostracoda and Environments of the St. Lawrence Lowlands." Harvard, 1977.
5996
Cunningham-Dunlop, Peter K. "Geology of Economic Uraniferous Pegmatites in the Bancroft Area, Ontario." Princeton, 1967.
5997
Currie, John Bickell. "The Occurrence and Relationships of Some Mica and Apatite Deposits in Southeastern Ontario." Toronto, 1950.
5998
Dadson, Alexander Stewart. "The Role of Electric Potential in Ore Deposition in the Timiskaming District, Ontario." Toronto, 1938.
5999
Dass, Ajay Sankar. "Wallrock Alteration Enclosing the Silver Deposits, Cobalt, Ontario." Carleton, 1970.
6000
Davenport, Peter H. "The Application of Geochemistry to Base-Metal Exploration in the Birch-Uchi Lakes Volcano Sedimentary Belt, Northwestern Ontario." Queen's, 1973.
6001
Davies, John Clifford. "The Petrology and Geochemistry of Basic Intrusive Rocks, Kakagi Lake-Wabigoon Lake Area, District of Kenora, Ontario." Manitoba, 1966.
6002
Derby, Andrew Whitelaw. "The Algoman Intrusives of the Matachewan-Kirkland Lake Area, Northern Ontario." Toronto, 1935.
6003
Dickson, Charles William. "Ore Deposits of Sudbury Ontario." Columbia, 1903.
6004
Divi, Sri R. R. "Structural Analysis of Grenville Rocks near Bancroft, Ontario, Canada." Ottawa, 1972.
6005
Donovan, John Francis. "Geology of the Woman River Iron Range, District of Sudbury, Ontario Canada." Cornell, 1963.
6006
Dostal, Jaroslav. "Geochemistry and Petrology of the Loon Lake Pluton, Ontario." McMaster, 1974.
6007
Dugas, Jean. "Geology of the Perth Map Area, Lanark and Leeds Counties of Ontario." McGill, 1952.
6008
Dutch, Steven Ian. "The Creighton Pluton, Ontario and Its Significance to the Geology History of the Sudbury Region." Columbia, 1976.
Dwibedi, Kamalakanta. See No./Voir no 5494
6009
Dyer, W.S. "Stratigraphy and Paleontology of the Credit River Section of the Upper Cincinnati Series of Ontario." Toronto, 1923.
6010
Egboka, Boniface C.E. "Bomb Tritium in Shallow Sand Aquifers." Waterloo, 1980. [Ottawa]
6011
Elias, Richard Jacob. "Late Ordovician Solitary Rugose Corals of Eastern North America." Cincinnati, 1979.

6012
Ellsworth, Hardy Vincent. "A Study of Certain Minerals from Cobalt, Ontario." Toronto, 1916.

6013
Emery, David James. "Genesis of Copper Deposits in Pre-Cambrian Iron Formation near the Round Lake Batholith, Boston Creek Area, Ontario." Harvard, 1959.

6014
Ermanovics, Ingomar Frank. "Evidence Bearing on the Origin of the Perth Road Pluton, Southern Ontario." Queen's, 1968.

6015
Evans, Anthony Meredith. "Geology of the Bancroft Uranium Mine, Ontario." Queen's, 1963.

6016
Evans, James E.L. "Porphyry of the Porcupine District, Ontario." Columbia, 1945.

6017
Ewert, Wayne D. "Metamorphism of Siliceous Carbonate Rocks in the Grenville Province of Southeastern Ontario." Carleton, 1977.

6018
Fagerstrom, John Alfred. "The Age, Stratigraphic Relations and Fauna of the Middle Devonian Formosa Reef Limestone of Southwestern Ontario." Michigan, 1960.

6019
Fay, Ignatius Charles. "Paleoecology of Lower Silurian Bioherms, Manitoulin Island, Ontario." Saskatchewan, 1983.

6020
Ferguson, Stewart Alexander. "Ore Deposits of the Kamiskotia Area, Ontario." Toronto, 1945.

6021
Fowler, Anthony David. "The Age, Origin, and Rare-Earth Element Distributions of Grenville Province Uraniferous Granites and Pegmatites." McGill, 1980.

6022
Franklin, James McWillie. "Metallogeny of the Proterozoic Rocks of Thunder Bay District, Ontario." Western Ontario, 1970.

6023
Fransham, Peter Bleadon. "Regional Geology and Groundwater Controls of Natural Slope Stability." McGill, 1980. [Ottawa Valley/Vallée de l'Outaouais]

6024
Freeman, Bruce Clark. "The Long Lake Diorite and Associated Rocks, Sudbury District, Ontario." Chicago, 1932.

6025
Fritz, Madeleine Alberta. "The Stratigraphy and Paleontology of the Workman's Creek Section of the Cincinnatian Series of Ontario." Toronto, 1926.

6026
Gibbins, Walter Arnold. "Rubidium-Strontium Mineral and Rock Ages at Sudbury, Ontario." McMaster, 1974.

6027
Giblin, Peter Edwin. "A Study of the Magnetite Deposits of Mayo Township, Ontario." Toronto, 1960.

6028
Giles, Peter Strachan. "Stratigraphy, Petrology and Diagenesis of Beekmantown Carbonate Rocks, Western Ontario." Western Ontario, 1976.

6029
Gill, James Edward. "Gunflint Iron-Bearing Formation, Ontario." Princeton, 1925.

6030
Gillett, Lawrence Britton. "Bedrock and Pleistocene Geology of the Vienne - Blaiklock Area, Quebec, with Observations on Magnetic Diabase Dikes, Northeast Ontario and Northwest Quebec." Princeton, 1962.

6031
Ginn, R. M. "The Relationship of the Bruce Series to the Granites in the Española Area." Toronto, 1960.

6032
Gittins, John. "Petrology of the Nepheline-Bearing Rocks of Glamorgan and Monmouth Townships, Ontario, Canada." Cambridge, 1959.

6033
Gledhill, Thomas Lloyd. "The Gold Quartz Veins and Igneous Rocks of the Sturgeon Lake Goldfield District of Thunder Bay, Ontario." Massachusetts Institute of Technology, 1926.

6034
Goodwin, Alan M. "The Stratigraphy of the Gunflint Iron-Bearing Formation of Ontario." Wisconsin, 1953.

6035
Gordon, Charles Henry. "Syenite-Gneiss from the Apatche Region of Ottawa County, Canada." Chicago, 1895.

6036
Gorman, William A. "The Geology of the Lower Seine River Area, Rainy River District, Ontario." Minnesota, 1933.

6037
Gower, Charles Frederick. "The Tectonic and Petrogenetic History of Archean Rocks from Kenora Area, English River Subprovince, Northwest Ontario." McMaster, 1979.

6038
Grant, James Alexander. "The Nature of the Grenville Front near Lake Timagami, Ontario." California Institute of Technology, 1964.

6039
Gravenor, Conrad P. "Pleistocene Geology of the Peterborough and Rice Lake Districts, Ontario." Indiana, 1953.

6040
Green, Anthony Heber. "Evolution of Fe-Ni Sulfide Ores Associated with Archean Ultramafic Komatites, Langmuir Township, Ontario." Toronto, 1978.

6041
Greenman, Lawrence. "The Petrology of the Footwall Breccias in the Vicinity of the Strathcona Mine, Levack, Ontario." Toronto, 1970.

6042
Griffis, Arthur T. "The Timiskaming Series and the Early Pre-Cambrian." Cornell, 1939.

6043
Groeneweld, Meyer W.O.J. "The Geochemistry of the Platinum Metals with Respect to their Occurrence in Nickeliferous Sulphide Deposits." Queen's, 1954.

6044
Gross, William Harvey. "An Investigation of the Control of Gold Mineralization in Northwestern Ontario." Toronto, 1950.

6045
Hadley, Donald Gene. "The Sedimentology of the Huronian Lorrain Formation, Ontario and Quebec." Johns Hopkins, 1969.

6046
Hall, Richard Drummond. "Metamorphism of Sulfide Schists, Limerick Township, Ontario." Western Ontario, 1980.

6047
Hanes, John Alexander. "AN^{40}Ar/^{39}Ar Geochronological Study of Precambrian Diabase Dykes." Toronto, 1979. [Munro Township/Municipalité de Munro]

6048
Hanson, George. "Some Canadian Occurrences of Pyritic Deposits in Metamorphic Rocks." Massachusettes Institute of Technology, 1920.

6049
Harding, William Duffield. "The Structure and Origin of the Porcupine Porphyries." Wisconsin, 1933.

6050
Harris, S.A. "Stratigraphy and Distribution of the Youngest Tills Near Waterloo, Ontario, and the Probable Bearing of These Tills and Parent Ice Sheets on the Evolution of the Present Landforms." London, 1968.

6051
Harrison, J.M. "Certain Anorthosites in Southeastern Ontario." Queen's, 1943.

6052
Harrison, John Edward. "Quaternary Geology of the North Bay-Mattawa Region." Syracuse, 1971.

6053
Harvie, Robert. "Ontario Gabbros and Associated Ores." Wisconsin, 1912.

Hawley, James P. See No./Voir no 2340

6054
Hay, Robert E. "The Geology of the Sault Ste. Marie Map Area." McGill, 1964.

6055
Heimlich, Richard Allen. "Structure and Petrology of Acid Plutons in the Deer Lake Area, Northern Ontario, Canada." Yale, 1959.

6056
Henderson, John Russell. "Structural and Petrologic Relations Across the Grenville Province-Southern Province Boundary, Sudbury District, Ontario." McMaster, 1967.

6057
Hesslein, Raymond Henry. "The Fluxes of methane, sigma (Carbon-Dioxide), and Ammonia-Nitrogen from Sediments and their Consequent Distribution in a Small Lake." Columbia, 1977.

6058
Hewins, Roger Herbert. "The Petrology of Some Marginal Mafic Rocks Along the North Range of the Sudbury Irruptive." Toronto, 1971.

6059
Hewitt, Donald F. "A Study of the Timiskaming Series of the Kirkland Lake-Larder Lake Belt, Ontario." Wisconsin, 1950.

6060
Hixon, Sumner Best. "Petography of the Middle Devonian Bois Blanc Formation of Michigan and Ontario." Michigan, 1964.

6061
Hodder, Robert William. "Alkaline Rocks and Niobium Deposits near Neniegos, Ontario." California, Berkeley, 1959.

6062
Hodges, Lance Thomas. "Megafossil Orientation of Selected Silurian, Devonian and Pleistocene Reefs of North America." Loma Linda, 1977. [Devonian site at Ridgemount/Emplacement dévonien à Ridgemount]

6063
Hoffman, Eric Lawrence. "The Platinum Group Element and Gold Content of Some Nickel Sulphide Ores." Toronto, 1978.

6064
Hoiles, Randolph Gerald. "Geology of the Bankfield Vicinity, Little Long Lac Area, Ontario." Arizona, 1943.

6065
Holmes, Terence C. "The Geology of Hart Township, Ontario and Adjacent Areas." Chicago, 1936.

6066
Holstein, A. "Heavy Minerals in Silurian Rocks of the Niagara Escarpment, Ontario." Toronto, 1936.

6067
Hood, Peter Jonathan. "Paleomagnetic Studies of Some Precambrian Rocks in Ontario." Toronto, 1958.

6068
Hriskevich, Michael Edward. "Petrology of the Nipissing Diabase Sheet of the Cobalt Area of Ontario." Princeton, 1952.

6069
Hsu, Mao-Yang. "Analysis of Strain, Shape and Orientation of the Deformed Pebbles in the Seine River Area, Ontario." McMaster, 1971.

6070
Hughes, Owen Lloyd. "Surficial Geology of Smooth Rock and Iroquois Falls Map-Areas, Cochrane District, Ontario." Kansas, 1959.

6071
Huhn, Frank Jones. "An Atmospheric Dispersion Model for the Sudbury, Ontario Area." McMaster, 1982.

6072
Hume, George Sherwood. "The Stratigraphy and Geologic Relations of the Paleozoic Outlier of Lake Timiskaming." Yale, 1920.

Hurst, Richard William. See No./Voir no 5706

6073
Hutchison, Murray Noel. "Refinement and Application of the Sphalerite Geobarometer." Toronto, 1978.

6074
Hyde, Richard Stuart. "Sedimentology, Volcanology, Stratigraphy, and Tectonic Setting of the Archean Timiskaming Group, Abitibi Greenstone Belt, Northeastern Ontario, Canada." McMaster, 1978.

6075
Ignatius, Heikki Gustaf. "Late Wisconsin Stratigraphy in North-Central Quebec and Ontario, Canada." Yale, 1956.

6076
Imbault, Joseph Paul E. "The Olga-Geoland Lake Area, Abitibi-East County." McGill, 1950.

6077
Ingham, Walter Norman. "Structure and Radioactivity of the Bourlameque and Elzevir Batholiths." Toronto, 1944.

6078
Jambor, John Leslie. "Sulfosalts from Madoc, Ontario." Carleton, 1966.

6079
James, William. "Geology of Dungannon and Mayo Townships in Southeastern Ontario." McGill, 1957.

6080
Jeffries, Dean Stuart. "Ontario Precipitation Chemistry and Heavy Metal Speciation." McMaster, 1976.

6081
Jennings, David Stevane. "Origin and Metamorphism of Part of the Hermon Group near Bancroft, Ontario." McMaster, 1970.

6082
Jensen, Larry Sigfred. "A Petrogenic Model for the Archaean Abitibi Belt in the Kirkland Lake Area, Ontario." Saskatchewan, 1981.

6083
Johnson, Helgi. "The Stratigraphy and Paleontology of the Cataract Formation in Ontario." Toronto, 1934.

6084
Johnston, Laura M. "Geolimnological Studies in the Kingston Basin-Upper St. Lawrence River Region." Queen's, 1978.

6085
Johnston, William G. "The Maxam Lake Cross Lake Section of the Timiskaming-Grenville Contact." Massachusetts Institute of Technology, 1950.

6086
Jones, William Alfred. "1) Petrography of the Rocks in the Vicinity of Killarney, Ontario and 2) Killarney Gneisses and Xenoliths at Sudbury." Toronto, 1930.

6087
Karvinen, William O. "Metamorphogenic Molybdenite Deposits in the Grenville Province." Ottawa, 1974.

6088
Keith, Mackenzie L. "Petrology of the Alkaline Intrusive at Blue Mountain, Ontario." Massachusettes Institute of Technology, 1939.

6089
Khan, Takir Raza. "Correlation of Geochemical Data on Organic Matter and Metal Ions in the Indian River." Carleton, 1979.

6090
Kindle, Edward Darwin. "An Analysis of the Structural Features of the Sudbury Basin and Their Bearings on Ore Deposition." Wisconsin, 1933.

6091
Kirwan, J.L. "Geological History of the Pre-Cambrian Rocks in Parts of the Porcupine Mining Area, Canada." London, 1968.

6092
Knight, Colin Joseph. "Rubidium-Strontium Isochr Ages of Volcanic Rocks in the North Shore of La Huron, Ontario, Canada." Toronto, 1967.

6093
Krause, Jerome B. "Chemical Petrology of Clinop roxene Gneisses from the Frontenac Axis, Gre ville Province, Ontario." Queen's, 1971.

6094
Krogh, Thomas Edward. "Strontium Isotopic Variati and Whole Rock Isochron Studies in the Grenvi Province of Ontario." Massachusetts Institute Technology, 1965.

6095
Kuo, Hsiao Yu. "Rare-Earth Elements in the Sudbu Nickel Irruptive." McMaster, 1975.

6096
Kurtz, Dennis Darl. "Stratigraphy and Genesis Early Proterozoic Diamictites: North America Rice, 1980. [Gowganda Formation/Formation Gowganda]

6097
Kwak, Teunis A.P. "Metamorphic Petrology a Geochemistry Across the Grenville Provinc Southern Province Boundary, Dill Townshi Sudbury, Ontario." McMaster, 1968.

La Berge, Gene Ludger. See No./Voir no 5133

6098
Laird, Harry Clarence. "Nature and Origin of Chert the Lockport and Onandaga Formations Ontario." Toronto, 1932.

6099
Lajtai, Emery Zoltan. "Pleistocene Sediments of t Bloor-Danforth Subway Section, Toronto, Canad Toronto, 1966.

6100
Lal, Ravindra Kumar. "The Petrology of t Cordierite-Gedrite Rocks and Associated Gneiss on Fishtail Lake, Harcourt Township, Ontari Toronto, 1966.

6101
Langford, F. F. "The Geology of Levack Townshi Princeton, 1960.

6102
Langford, George Burwash. "The Beardmore-Hez Gold Area, Ontario." Cornell, 1930.

Lasenby, David Charles. See No./Voir no 11085

6103
La Tour, Timothy Earle. "The Nature and Origin the Grenville Front near Coniston, Ontario: Reinterpretation." Western Ontario, 1979.

6104
Laurin, André. "The Problems of the Bounda Between Grenville and Keewatin-Timiskaming Pr vinces, Ontario." Laval, 1955.

6105
Lawson, Andrew Cowper. "Report on the Geology the Rainy Lake Region." Johns Hopkins, 1888.

6106
Lawton, Killip David. "The Round Lake Batholith a Its Satellitic Intrusions in the Kirkland Lake Are Toronto, 1955.

6107
Le Anderson, Paul James. "The Metamorphism of 'Impure' Marbles Calcareous Schists and Amphibolites in a Portion of Limerick Township, Ontario." Queen's, 1978.

6108
Legault, Jocelyne Andrée. "Chitinozoa and Acritarcha of the Hamilton Group (Middle Devonian) of Southern Ontario." Oklahoma, 1971.

6109
Lewis, Thomas Leonard. "A Paleocurrent Study of the Potsdam Sandstone of New York, Quebec and Ontario." Ohio State, 1963.

6110
Liberty, Bruce Arthur. "Stratigraphy and Paleontology of the Lake Simcoe District, Ontario." Toronto, 1954.

6111
Lindsey, David Allen. "The Sedimentology of the Huronian Gowganda Formation, Ontario, Canada (with Special Reference to the Whitefish Falls Area)." Johns Hopkins, 1967.

6112
Lippitt, Louis. "Statistical Analysis of Regional Facies Change in Ordovician Cobourg Limestone in Northwestern New York and Southern Ontario." Columbia, 1959.

6113
Long, Darrel G.F. "The Stratigraphy and Sedimentology of the Huronian (Lower Aphebian) Mississagi and Serpent Formations." Western Ontario, 1977.

6114
Longstaffe, Frederick John. "The Oxygen Isotope and Elemental Geochemistry of Archean Rocks from Northern Ontario." McMaster, 1978.

6115
Lonker, Steven Wayne. "Conditions of Metamorphism in High Grade Pelites from the Frontenac Axis, Ontario, Canada." Harvard, 1979.

6116
Low, John Hay. "Geology of the Star Gold Mine and Vicinity (Barrie Township)." Toronto, 1941.

6117
Lumbers, Sydney Blake. "Stratigraphy, Plutonism, and Metamorphism in the Ottawa River Remnant in the Bancraft-Madoc Area of the Grenville Province of Southeastern Ontario." Princeton, 1967.

6118
MacGregor, Ian Duncan. "A Study of the Contact Metamorphic Aureole Surrounding the Mount Albert Ultramafic Intrusion." Princeton, 1964.

6119
MacKenzie, Graham Stewart. "Some Mineral Deposits of Post Cambrian Age in the St. Lawrence Basin." Toronto, 1934.

6120
MacLachlan, Donald C. "Warren Shore Line in Ontario and in the Thumb of Michigan and Its Deformation." Michigan, 1939.

6121
MacPherson, Harry Gordon. "A Chemical and Petrographic Study of Pre-Cambrian Sediments." Toronto, 1955.

6122
MacRae, Neil D. "Petrology and Geochemistry of Ultramafic-Galbroic Intrusions in Abitibi Area, Ontario." McMaster, 1966.

Marchand, Michael. See No./Voir no 5714

6123
Martini, Ireneo Peter. "The Sedimentology of the Medium Formation Outcropping Along the Niagara Escarpment (Ontario and New York State)." McMaster, 1966.

6124
Massey, Nicholas William D. "The Geochemistry of Some Keweenawan Metabasites from Mamainse Point, Ontario." McMaster, 1980.

6125
Mather, William B. "The Geology and Pargenesis of the Gold Ores of the Howey Mine, Red Lake, Ontario, Canada." Chicago, 1936.

6126
Matheson, Archie Farquhar. "The Geology of Michipicoten River Area, District of Algoma, Ontario, Canada." Minnesota, 1932.

6127
May, Ronald William. "Copper, Nickel, Zinc, Chromium, Calcium Oxide, Magnesium Oxide Content of Wisconsin Tells in Southern Ontario." Western Ontario, 1971.

6128
Maynard, James Edward. "The Origin of the Precambrian Banded Iron Formations." Toronto, 1928.

6129
McDougall, David J. "The Geology of Southern Pascalis Township with Special Reference to the Luminescence of Certain Minerals of the Eruptive Rocks." McGill, 1952.

6130
Meddaugh, William Scott. "Age and Origin of Uraninite in the Elliot Lake, Ontario Uranium Ores." Harvard, 1983.

6131
Michener, Charles Edward. "Minerals Associated with Large Sulphide Bodies of the Sudbury Type." Toronto, 1940.

6132
Milne, Victor Gordon. "The Petrography and Alteration of Some Spodumene Pegmatites near Beardmore, Ontario." Toronto, 1962.

6133
Mirynech, Edward. "The Pleistocene Geology of the Trenton-Campbellford Map-Area, Ontario." Toronto, 1963.

6134
Misra, Kula Chandra. "Phase Relations in the Fe-Ni-S System." Western Ontario, 1972.

6135
Moore, Elwood S. "Geology of the Onaman Iron Range Area, District of Thunder Bay, Ontario." Chicago, 1909.

6136
Moore, Richard Lewis. "Metamorphic Petrology of the Area Between Mattawa North Bay and Temiscaming, Ontario." Carleton, 1976.

6137
Morin, James Arthur. "A Study of the Petrology of Granitic Rocks in the Tustin-Bridges Area, Northwestern Ontario." Saskatchewan, 1979.

6138
Morley, Lawrence Whitaker. "Correlation of the Susceptibility and Remanent Magnetism with the
Petrology of Rocks from Some Precambrian Areas
in Ontario." Toronto, 1952.

6139
Morrow, Harold F. "The Geology of the MacLeod-
Cockshutt Gold Mine, Little Long Lac, Geraldton,
Ontario." McGill, 1951.

6140
Morse, Robert H. "The Surficial Geochemistry of
Raduim, Radon and Uranium near Bancroft,
Ontario with Applications to Prospecting for Ura-
nium." Queen's, 1970.

6141
Morton, Penelope. "Archean Volcanic Stratigraphy
and Petrology and Chemistry of Mafic and Ultra-
mafic Rock, Chromite, and the Shebandowan Ni-
Cee Mine Shebandowan, Northwestern Ontario."
Carleton, 1982.

6142
Mukherjee, Kalyan Kumar. "Petrology of the Black
River Limestone in Southwestern Ontario."
Western Ontario, 1968.

6143
Mummery, Robert Craig. "Coronite Amphibolites
from the Whitestone Area, Parry Sound, Ontario."
McMaster, 1973.

6144
Munro, B.R. "Ordovician Conodont Biostratigraphy of
the Lake Timiskaming Paleozoic Outlier." Waterloo, 1976.

6145
Murray, Albert Nelson. "Limestone Oil Reservoirs of
the North-Eastern United States and Ontario,
Canada." Illinois, 1928.

6146
Norman, David Irwin. "Geology and Geochemistry of
the Tribag Mine, Batchawana Bay, Ontario." Minnesota, 1977.

6147
Nowlan, James Parker. "The Silurian Stratigraphy of
the Niagaran Escarpment in Ontario." Toronto,
1935.

6148
Papezik, Vladimir Stephen. "Trace Elements in Anorthosites." McGill, 1961.

6149
Park, Frederick Blair. "Genesis of the Marmoraton
Pyrometasomatic Iron Deposit, Marmora, Ontario."
Queen's, 1967.

6150
Parks, Thomas. "Reservoir Conditions in the Norfolk
(Big Lime) Formation of Southwestern Ontario."
Toronto, 1950.

6151
Parks, William Arthur. "The Huronian of the Basin of
the Moose River." Toronto, 1900.

6152
Parsons, Myles Lyle. "Groundwater Movement and
Subsurface Temperatures in a Glacial Complex,
Cochrane District, Ontario." Michigan, 1969.

6153
Patchett, Joseph Edmund. "A Study of the Radio-
active Minerals of the Uraniferous Conglomerates,
Blind River Area." Toronto, 1960.

6154
Patterson, George Cameron. "The Geology of th
Kapkichi Lake Ultramafic Mafic Bodies an
Related Cu-Ni Mineralization, Pickle Lak
Ontario." Carleton, 1980.

6155
Payne, J.G. "Geology and Geochemistry of Blu
Mountain Nepheline Syenite." McMaster, 1966.

6156
Peach, Peter Angus. "Some Pegmatites from Easter
Ontario and their Geological Environment.
Toronto, 1950.

6157
Pearson, George Raymond. "The Development of
Granitic Gneisses Around the Clare River Synclin
Hastings and Lennox and Addington Countie
Ontario." Queen's, 1958.

6158
Pearson, Walter John. "Origin of the Kyanite Occu
rences in the Wanapitei and Crocan Lake Areas of
Ontario." Queen's, 1959.

6159
Pearson, William Norman. "Copper Metallogen
North Shore Region of Lake Huron, Ontario
Queen's, 1980.

6160
Pegrum, Reginald H. "The Alkaline Syenites ar
Asssociated Rocks of the French River Regio
Ontario." Princeton, 1927.

6161
Pelletier, René A. "Geology of the Thurso Are
Quebec and Ontario." McGill, 1927.

6162
Pemberton, Stuart George. "Selected Studies in Low
Paleozoic Ichnology." McMaster, 1979.

6163
Percival, John Allan. "Geological Evolution of Part
the Central Superior Province Based on Relatio
ships Among the Abitibi and Wawa Sub-provinc
and the Kapuskasing Structural Zone." Queen
1981.

6164
Perdie, Henry S. "Coutchiching, Kashabowie Lak
Ontario." Chicago, 1938.

6165
Peredery, Walter Volodymyr. "The Origin of Rocks
the Base of the Onaping Formation, Sudbur
Ontario." Toronto, 1972.

6166
Pesonen, Lauri J. "Paleomagnetic, Paleointensity a
Paleosecular Variation Studies of Keweenaw
Igneous and Baked Contact Rocks." Toronto, 197

6167
Peterson, Nathan N. "Carbonite Petrology, Structu
and Stratigraphy of the Middle Ordovician Carb
nate Rocks in the Vicinity of Kingston, Ontar
Canada." Queen's, 1969.

6168
Peterson, Rex Marion. "Ostracods of the Fam
Quasillitidae from the Middle Devonian Strata
Michigan, Ohio, New York and Ontario." Michig
1961.

6169
Pettijohn, Francis John. "A Field and Laboratory Study of a Series of Precambrian Sedimentary Rocks near Sioux Lookout, Ontario: Their Petrography, Structure, and Geologic Significance." Minnesota, 1930.

6170
Pezzetta, John Mario. "The St. Clair River Delta." Michigan, 1968.

6171
Pfeffer, Helmut William. "Petrogenesis of the Doritic Rocks (Metadiabases) O'Sullivan Lake Area, Ontario." Toronto, 1951.

6172
Phemistes, Thomas C. "A) The Post-Huronian Basis Rocks of Ontario. B) The Role of Water in Basaltic Magma." Cambridge, 1933.

6173
Phipps, Charles V. G. "The Petrology and Environment of the Alkaline Rocks of the Blue Mountain Area of Ontario." Toronto, 1955.

6174
Pienaar, Petrus Johannes. "Stratigraphy, Petrography and Genesis of the Elliot Group, Including the Uraniferous Conglomerates, Quirke Lake Syncline, Blind River Area, Ontario." Queen's, 1959.

6175
Pollock, Donald W. "The Geology of the Addington-Preston Area." McGill, 1957.

6176
Pope, Fredrick John. "Investigations of Magnetic Iron-Ores from Eastern Ontario." Columbia, 1899.

6177
Potter, Ralph Richard. "The Geology of the Burnt Hill Area and Ore Controls of the Burnt Hill Tungsten Deposit." Carleton, 1969.

6178
Prest, Victor Kent. "The Precambrian Miminiska-Fort Hope Area." Toronto, 1941.

6179
Purdy, John Winston. "A Rubidium-Strontium and Potassium-Argon Isotopic Age Investigation Within the Superior Province of the Precambrian Canadian Shield." Toronto, 1967.

6180
Pye, Edgar George. "Petrographic Study of the Texture of Differentiated Basic Igneous Rocks, Ontario." Toronto, 1950.

6181
Quay, Paul Douglas. "An Experimental Study of Turbulent Diffusion in Lakes." Columbia, 1977. [Experimental Lakes area in Northwestern Ontario/Région expérimentale des lacs du Nord-ouest de l'Ontario]

6182
Quinn, Howard Edmond. "Some Structural and Genetic Details of Gold Occurrence at the Hollinger Mine, Porcupine, Ontario." Harvard, 1932.

6183
Quirke, Terence Thomas. "Geology of Española District, Ontario, Canada." Chicago, 1915.

6184
Ramaekers, Paul Peter J. "A Study of Dental Variability in Early Wasatchian Phenacolemur (Paramomyidae, Primates)." Toronto, 1975. [A study of materials in the Royal Ontario Museum and the National Museum of Canada/Étude de documents du Musée royal de l'Ontario et du Musée national du Canada]

6185
Rambaldi, Ermanno R. "The Distribution of Elements among Feldspars, Micas, and Epidote in Some Metamorphic Rocks near Bancroft, Ontario." Ottawa, 1971.

6186
Reeve, Edward John. "Geochemistry of the Golding-Keene Pegmatite and Adjacent Rocks." Toronto, 1972.

6187
Reinhardt, Edward Wade. "Phase Relations of Corderite, Garnet, Biotite and Hypersthene in High-Grade Pelitic Gneisses of the Gananoque Area, Ontario." Queen's, 1966.

Rice, William A. See No./Voir no 5127

6188
Ridler, Roland Hartley. "The Relationship of Mineralization to Volcanic Stratigraphy in the Kirkland Lake Area, Ontario." Wisconsin, 1969.

6189
Rittenhouse, Gordon. "Geology of a Portion of the Savant Lake Area, Ontario." Chicago, 1935.

6190
Rivers, Charles James Toby. "Structures and Textures of Metamorphic Rocks, Ompah Area, Grenville Province, Ontario." Ottawa, 1976.

6191
Robinson, Donald James. "Stratigraphic Relationships, Geochemistry and Genesis of the Redstone Volcanic-Hosted Nickel Deposit, Timmins, Ontario." Western Ontario, 1982.

6192
Robinson, Peter Campbell. "Geology and Evolution of the Manitouwadge Migmatite Belt, Ontario, Canada." Western Ontario, 1979.

6193
Robinson, S.C. "The Lead-Antimony-Sulphur System Mineralogy and Mineral Synthesis." Queen's, 1947.

6194
Rose, E.R. "Iron Deposits of Eastern Ontario and Their Origin." Queen's, 1954.

6195
Rowe, Robert B. "Petrology of the Richardson Deposit, Wilberforce, Ontario, Canada." Wisconsin, 1951.

6196
Saha, Ajit Kumar. "The Mode of Emplacement of Some Granitic Plutons in Southeastern Ontario." Toronto, 1957.

6197
Sampson, Geoffrey Alexander. "Petrology of Some Grenville Volcanic and Pelitic Rocks from near Madoc, Southeastern Ontario." Toronto, 1972.

6198
Sandefur, Bennett T. "The Geology and Paragenesis of the Nickel Ores of the Cuniptau Mine, Goward, Nipissing District, Ontario." Chicago, 1943.

6199
Sangster, Alan Lane. "Metallogeny of Base Metal, Gold and Iron Deposits of the Grenville Province of Southeastern Ontario." Queen's, 1970.

6200
Sawford, Edward Clayton. "Sedimentary Facies of the Black River Group (Ordovician), Ottawa Valley, Canada." Carleton, 1972.

6201
Schmus, William Randall. "The Geochronology of the Blind River-Bruce Mines Area, Ontario, Canada." California, Los Angeles, 1964.

6202
Schofield, Richard Edward. "Petrology of the Dundonald Komatites, Dundonald, Ontario." Rutgers, 1982.

Schopf, Thomas Joseph Morton. See No./Voir no 6577

6203
Schwartz, Franklin W. "Digital Simulation of Hydrochemical Patterns in Regional Groundwater Flow." Illinois, 1972. [The results of a simulation from the Upper Kettle Watershed, Ontario/Résultats d'une simulation à partir de Upper Kettle Watershed, Ontario]

6204
Scoates, Reginald Francis Jon. "Ultramafic Rocks and Associated Copper-Nickel Sulphide Ores, Gordon Lake, Ontario." Manitoba, 1972.

6205
Seccombe, Philip Kenneth. "Sulphur Isotope and Trace Element Geochemistry of Sulphide Mineralization in the Birch-Uchi Greenstone Belt, Northwestern Ontario." Manitoba, 1973.

6206
Sethuraman, Kasiviswanathan. "Petrology of Grenville Metavolcanic Rocks in the Bishop Corners-Donaldson Area, Ontario." Carleton, 1972.

6207
Shaw, Ernest William. "The Guelph and Eramosa Formations of the Ontario Peninsula." Toronto, 1937.

6208
Shegelski, Roy Jan. "Stratigraphy and Geochemistry of Archean Iron Formation in the Sturgeon Lake-Savant Lake Greenstone Terrain, Northwestern Ontario." Toronto, 1978.

6209
Skinner, Robert Gerald. "Quaternary Stratigraphy of Moose River Basin, Ontario, Canada." Washington, Seattle, 1971

6210
Smith, Bennett Lawrence. "The (Precambrian) Grenville Geology of Southeastern Ontario." Syracuse, 1954.

6211
Smith, Morland Ellis. "Element Distribution Between Coexisting Feldspars in High-Grade Metamorphic Rocks from the Frontenac Axis, Ontario." Queen's, 1966.

6212
Speers, Elmer Clarence. "The Age Relations and Origin of the Sudbury Breccia." Queen's, 1956.

6213
Spence, William Henry. "Relict Plagioclase Phenocrysts from Metavolcanic Rocks Mantling Granite Dome and the Petrology of the Associate Rocks in the Grenville Province of Southeaster Ontario." Rutgers, 1968.

6214
Sproule, John Campbell." A Study of the Cobour Formation." Toronto, 1935.

6215
Stewart, Robert Arthur. "Glacial and Glacic lacustrine Sedimentation in Lake Maumee nea Port Stanley, Southwestern Ontario." Wester Ontario, 1982.

Stockwell, Clifford Howard. See No./Voir no 5533

Stone, Denver Cedrill. See No./Voir no 5534

6216
Studemeister, Paul Alexander. "An Archean Felsi Stock with Peripheral Gold and Copper Occurren ces, Abotossaway Township, District of Algoma Ontario." Western Ontario, 1982.

6217
Tarzi, Joseph Gergy. "Weathering of Mica Minerals i Selected Ontario Soils." Guelph, 1977.

6218
Taylor, Frederick C. "The Petrology of the Serpentin Bodies in the Matheson District, Ontario." McGil 1955.

6219
Teal, Philip Rae. "Stratigraphy, Sedimentology, Vo canology and Development of the Archean Manito Group, Northwestern Ontario, Canada." McMaste 1979.

6220
Terasmae, Joan. "A Palynological Study Relating 1 the Toronto Formation (Ontario) and the Pleisto cene Deposits in the St. Lawrence Lowlar (Quebec)." McMaster, 1955.

6221
Theis, Nicholas J. "Uranium-Bearing and Associate Minerals in Their Geochemical and Sedimentolo gical Context, Elliot Lake, Ontario." Queen' 1976.

6222
Thompson, Peter Hamilton. "Stratigraphy, Structu and Metamorphism of the Flinton Group in th Bishop Corners-Madoc Area, Grenville Provinc Eastern Ontario." Carleton, 1972.

6223
Thomson, Ellis. "1. Quantitative Microscopic Analysi 2. A Qualitative and Quantitative Determination the Ores of Cobalt, Ontario." Howard, 1929.

6224
Thomson, James Edgar. "The Nature and Origin of th Nepheline Syenites and Related Alkali Syenites Coldwell, Ontario." Wisconsin, 1932.

6225
Thomson, Robert. "A Study of the Nickel Intrusiv Sudbury, Ontario." Chicago, 1935.

6226
Thurston, Phillips Cole. "The Volcanology and Trad Element Geochemistry of Cyclical Volcanism the Archean Confederation Lake Area, Nort western Ontario." Western Ontario, 1981.

6227
Tillman, John Robert. "Variation in Species of Micro-spirifer from Middle Devonian Rocks of Michigan, Ontario and Ohio." Michigan, 1962.

6228
Tolman, Carl. "The Geology of the Big Eddy Lake Area, Sudbury District, Ontario, Canada." Yale, 1927.

6229
Traill, R.J. "The Atomic Structure of High Temperature Albite." Queen's, 1956.

6230
Trzcienski, Walter Edward, Jr. "Staurolite and Garnet and Parageneses and Related Metamorphic Reactions in Metapelites from the Whetstone Lake Area, Southeastern Ontario." McGill, 1971.

6231
Tuck, Ralph. "The Geology and Origin of a Lead-Zinc Deposit at Geneva Lake, Ontario." Cornell, 1930.

6232
Twyman, James DeWitt. "The Generation, Crystallization, and Differentiation of Carbonatite Magmas: Evidence from the Argor and Cargill Complexes, Ontario." Toronto, 1983.

6233
Vagners, Uldis Janis. "Mineral Distribution in Tills in Central and Southern Ontario." Western Ontario, 1970.

6234
Venkitasubramanyan, Calicut S. "Large Scale Superimposed Folds in Precambrian of the Actinolite-Kaladar Area, Southeastern Ontario." Queen's, 1970.

6235
Votaw, Robert Barnett. "Conodont Biostratigraphy of the Black River Group (Middle Ordovician) and Equivalent Rocks of the Eastern Midcontinent, North America." Ohio State, 1972.

6236
Walker, John W. "Geology of the Jackfish-Middleton Area, District of Thunder Bay, Ontario, Canada." California, Los Angeles, 1961.

6237
Wallach, Joseph Leonard. "The Metamorphism and Structural Geology of the Hinchinbrooke Gneiss and Its Age Relationship to Meta-sedimentary and Metavolcanic Rocks of the Grenville Group." Queen's, 1973.

6238
Watson, Donald Whitman. "The Geology and Structural Evolution of the Geco Massive Sulfide Deposit at Manitouwadge, Northwestern Ontario." Michigan, 1970.

6239
Way, Harold G. "The Silurian of Manitoulin Island, Ontario." Toronto, 1936.

6240
Wells, Gary S. "A Morphological, Chemical and Petrological Examination of Archean Pillow Basalts from the Abitibi Greenstone Belt." Queen's, 1980.

6241
Westerman, Christopher John. "Tectonic Evolution of a Part of the English River Subprovince, Northwestern Ontario." McMaster, 1978.

6242
White, Joseph Clancy. "A Study of Deformation Within the Flinton Group Conglomerates of Southeastern Ontario." Western Ontario, 1980.

6243
White, Owen Lester. "Pleistocene, Geology of the Bolton Area, Ontario (30m/13)." Illinois, 1970.

6244
Whitman, Alfred Russell. "Genesis of the Ores of the Cobalt District, Ontario, Canada." California, Berkeley, 1921.

6245
Wilson, Alfred William Gunning. "Physical Geology of Central Ontario." Harvard, 1901.

6246
Wilson, Alice Evelyn. "A Geological Report on the Cornwall Map Area, Canada." Chicago, 1929.

6247
Winder, Charles G. "Paleoecology and Sedimentation of Mohawkian Limestones in South Central Ontario: A Revision of Mohawkian and Cincinnatian Stratigraphy." Columbia, 1953.

6248
Wright, Harold Douglas. "Mineralogical Study of Certain Colorado and Ontario Uraninite Deposits." Columbia, 1952.

6249
Wright, James Douglas. "The Age of Some Granite Batholiths North of Lake Huron and the Genetic Relation of the Arsenical Gold Ores to the Keweenawan Granites." Toronto, 1934.

6250
Wright, John Frank. "The Geology of the Brockville-Mallorytown Map Area (Ontario)." Chicago, 1923.

6251
Wynne-Edwards, Hugh Robert. "The Structure and Petrology of the Greenville-Type Rocks in the Westport Area, Ontario." Queen's, 1959.

6252
Yorath, Christopher J. "The Determination of Sediment Dispersal Patterns by Statistical and Factor Analyses, Northeastern Scotian Shelf." Queen's, 1968.

6253
Young, William L. "The Iron Bearing Formations of the Michipicoten Area, Ontario." McGill, 1953.

6254
Zimmermann, Robert Allen. "The Interpretation of Apatite Fission Track Ages with an Application to the Study of Uplift Since the Cretaceous in Eastern North America." Pennsylvania, 1977.

Quebec/Québec

6255
Aarden, Hendrikus Marinus. "Hiortdahlite from Kipawa River, Quebec - Its Chemistry and Mineralogy." Toronto, 1969.

6256
Allard, Gilles O. "The Geology of a Portion of McKenzie Township, Chibougamau District." Johns Hopkins, 1956.

6257
Allcock, John Brindley. "Gaspé Copper: A Devonian Porphyry Copper/Skarn Complex." Yale, 1978. [Gaspé Peninsula/Péninsule de Gaspé]

6258
Anderson, Alfred Titus, Jr. "A Contribution to the Mineralogy and Petrology of the Brûlé Lake Anorthosite Massif, Quebec." Princeton, 1963.

Archbold, Norbert Lee. See No./Voir no 5934

6259
Assad, Joseph Robert. "The Geology of the East Sullivan Deposit, Val d'Or, Quebec." McGill, 1958.

6260
Averill, E.L. "Area Geography of the Campbell Chibougamau Mine and Adjacent Areas, Quebec." McGill, 1955.

6261
Ayrton, William Grey. "A Structural Study of the Chandler-Port Daniel Area of Gaspé Peninsula, Quebec." Northwestern, 1964.

6262
Bachechi, Fiorella. "Crystal Structure of the Naturally Occuring Au Telluride-Montbrayite, $Au_2 Te_3$." Toronto, 1970.

6263
Backman, Olen L. "Makamik Area, Abitibi District, Quebec." Minnesota, 1933.

6264
Baker, Donald John. "The Metamorphic and Structural History of the Grenville Front near Chibougamau, Quebec." Georgia, 1980.

6265
Banfield, Armine F. "The Geology of Beattie Gold Mines (Quebec) Limited, Duparquet, Quebec, Canada." Northwestern, 1941.

6266
Barraud, Claude. "Évolution tectonique des granulites de la région de Pine Hill, sud-ouest du complexe anorthositique de Morin, province de Grenville, Québec, Canada." Montréal, 1977.

6267
Barton, Jackson M., Jr. "A Geochronologic and Stratigraphic Study of the Precambrian Rocks North of Montreal." McGill, 1971.

6268
Beaton, William Douglas. "Trace Element Partition in Sulphides, Noranda, Quebec." McGill, 1970.

6269
Béland, Jacques. "Geology of Shawinigan Map-Area, Champlain and St. Maurice Counties, Quebec." Princeton, 1953.

6270
Benoît, Fernand. "Geology of the St. Sylvestre and St. Joseph West Half Areas." Laval, 1958.

6271
Bérard, Jean. "Géologie de la région du lac aux Feuilles, Nouveau-Québec." Laval, 1959.

Bergeron, Robert. See No./Voir no 5690

6272
Berrangé, J.P. "The Plutonic Geology of Part of the Grenville Province North of Lake St. John, Quebec." London, 1962.

6273
Bertrand, Claude M.L. "Metamorphism at the Normetal Mine, Northwestern Quebec." Western Ontario, 1970.

6274
Birkett, Tyson C. "Metamorphism of a Cambro Ordovician Sequence in South Eastern Quebec." Montréal, 1982.

6275
Black, James M. "The Bell River Igneous Complex." McGill, 1942.

6276
Black, Philip T. "The Geology of Malartic Gold Field Mine." McGill, 1954.

6277
Blais, Roger Adelard. "A Petrologic and Decrepit metric Study of the Gold Mineralization at the O'Brien Mine, Northwestern Quebec." Toronto, 1954.

6278
Block, Fred. "A Multivariate Chemical Classification of Rocks from the Monteregian Petrographic Province, Quebec, Canada." Pennsylvania State, 197

6279
Bouchard, Michel A. "Late Quaternary Geology of the Témiscamingue Area, Central Québec." McGill, 1981.

6280
Bourne, James Hilary. "The Petrogenesis of the Humite Group Minerals in Regionally Metamorphosed Marbles of the Grenville Supergroup." Queen's, 1974.

6281
Bray, John V.G. "The Petrology of La Lièvre Area, Roberval County, Quebec." McGill, 1961.

6282
Brisebois, Daniel. "Stratigraphie du permocarbonifère des Îles-de-la-Madeleine." Montréal, 1981.

6283
Brown, Robert A. "The Geology of the North Shore Gaspé-Bay, Quebec." McGill, 1939.

6284
Brummer, Johannes J. "Geology of the Northwest Quarter of Holland Township, Gaspé-North, Quebec." McGill, 1955.

6285
Buckland, Francis C. "The Dolomitic Magnesite Deposits of Grenville Township, Argenteuil County, Quebec." McGill, 1937.

6286
Buffam, Basil Scott Whyte. "Destor Area, Abitibi County, Quebec." Princeton, 1927.

6287
Burk, Cornelius F., Jr. "A Regional Study of the Silurian Stratigraphy of Gaspé Peninsula, Québec." Northwestern, 1959.

6288
Burton, Frederick R. "Geology of the District About Lake Aylmer, Eastern Township, Quebec." McGill, 1933.

6289
Butler, Patrick, Jr. "Mineral Compositions and Equilibria in the Metamorphosed Iron Formation of the Gagnon Region, Quebec, Canada." Harvard, 1968.

6290
Byrne, Anthony William. "The Stratigraphy and Paleontology of the Beekman Town Group in the St. Lawrence Lowlands, Quebec." McGill, 1958.

6291
Campiglio, Carlo. "Étude géochimique et pétrologique du batholite de Bourlamaque, Abitibi, Québec." Montréal, 1974.

6292
Carbonneau, Côme. "Geology of the Big Berry Mountains Map-Area, Gaspé-Peninsula, Québec." McGill, 1953.

6293
Carignan, Jacques. "Géochimie et géostatique appliquées à l'exploration des gisements volcanogènes: le gisement de Millenback." Montréal, 1980.

6294
Carrara, Alberto. "Structural Geology of Lower Paleozoic Rocks, Mt. Albert Area, Gaspé Peninsula, Québec." Ottawa, 1972.

6295
Carter, George F. E. "Ordovician Ostracoda from the St. Lawrence Lowlands of Quebec." McGill, 1958.

6296
Chagnon, Jean-Yves. "The Geology of the Des Quinze Lake-Barrière Lake Area, Temiscamingue County, Quebec." McGill, 1965.

6297
Charbonneau, Jean-Marc. "Le front appalachien au nord immédiat de la frontière Québec-Vermont." Laval, 1981.

6298
Chown, Edward H.M. "Amphibolites of the Papachouesati River Area, Mistassini Territory, Quebec." Johns Hopkins, 1963.

6299
Clark, Thomas Henry. "Studies in the Beekmantown Series of Lévis, Québec." Harvard, 1923.

6300
Clarke, Peter Johnston. "Geology in the Vicinity of the Grenville Front, Mount Wright District, Quebec." Manitoba, 1964.

6301
Claveau, Jacques. "Geology of the Wakeham-Forget Lakes Region, North Shore, Gulf of St. Lawrence." Toronto, 1944.

6302
Clendening, John Albert. "Sporological Evidence of the Geological Age of the Dunkard Strata in the Appalachian Basin." West Virginia, 1970.

Collins, Jon A. See No./Voir no 5641

6303
Cooper, Gerald E. "Geology of the Johan Beetz Area, Saguenay County, Quebec." McGill, 1953.

6304
Corwall, Frederick W. "Rock Alteration and Primary Base Metal Dispersion at Barvue, Golden Manitou and New Calumet Mines, Quebec." McGill, 1956.

6305
Costa, Umberto Raimundo. "Hydrothermal Footwall Alteration and Ore Formation at Matagami Lake Mine, Matagami, Quebec." Western Ontario, 1980.

6306
Côté, Pierre E. "Geology and Petrology of the Anorthosite and Associated Rocks of the Chertsey Map Area." McGill, 1948.

6307
Crickmay, Geoffrey William. "The Geology of the Matapedia River Map-Area, Quebec." Yale, 1930.

Cronin, Thomas Mark. See No./Voir no 5995

6308
Crown, Edward H.M. "Amphibolites of the Papachowesati River Area, Mistassini Territory, Quebec." Johns Hopkins, 1963.

6309
Cumming, Leslie M. "Silurian and Lower Devonian Sedimentary Rocks of Eastern Gaspé, Quebec." Wisconsin, 1955.

6310
Davies, Raymond. "Geology of the Mutton Bay Intrusion and Surrounding Area, North Shore, Gulf of St. Lawrence, Quebec." McGill, 1968.

6311
De, Aniruddha. "Petrology of Dikes Emplaced in the Ultramafic Rocks of Southeastern Quebec." Princeton, 1961.

6312
Dean, Ronald Samuel. "A Study of St. Lawrence Lowland Shales." McGill, 1963.

6313
Deland, André N. "Geology of the Surprise Lake Area, Quebec." Yale, 1955.

6314
Denis, Bertrand. "Guillet Township Map Area (Quebec)." McGill, 1938.

6315
De Romer, Henry S. "Geology of the Eastman-Orford Lake Area, Eastern Townships, Province of Quebec." McGill, 1960.

6316
De Rosen-Spence, Andrée F. "Stratigraphy, Development and Petrogenesis of the Central Noranda Volcanic Pile, Noranda, Quebec." Toronto, 1976.

6317
Dilabio, Ronald N. W. "Glacial Dispersal of Rocks and Minerals in the Lac Mistassini-Lac Waconichi Area, Quebec, with Special Reference to the Icon Dispersal Train." Western Ontario, 1976.

Donaldson, John Allan. See No./Voir no 5696

Dredge, Lynda Ann. See No./Voir no 4755

6318
Duffield, Susan L. "Late Ordovician-Early Silurian Acritarch Taxonomy and Biostratigraphy, Anticosti Island, Quebec." Waterloo, 1982.

Dufresne, Cyrille. See No./Voir no 5697

6319
Duquette, Gilles. "Geology of the Weedon Lake Area and Its Vicinity, Wolfe and Compton Counties." Laval, 1961.

6320
Eakins, Peter R. "Geological Settings of Malartic Gold Deposits, Quebec." McGill, 1952.

6321
Eby, George Nelson. "Rare Earth Yttrium and Scandium Geochemistry of the Oka Carbonatite Complex, Oka, Quebec." Boston University, 1971.

Elias, Richard Jacob. See No./Voir no 6011

6322
Emo, Wallace Brooks. "The Geology of the Wacouno Region, Saguenay Co., P.Q." McGill, 1958.

6323
Enos, Paul Portenier. "Anatomy of a Flysch-Middle Ordovician Cloridorme Formation, Northern Gaspé Peninsula." Yale, 1965.

6324
Fairbairn, Harold W. "The Structure and Metamorphism of the Mountains of Brome County, Quebec." Harvard, 1932.

6325
Fitzpatrick, Michael Morson. "Gravity in the Eastern Townships of Quebec." Harvard, 1960.

6326
Floran, Robert John. "Mineralogy and Petrology of the Sedimentary and Contact Metamorphosed Gunflint Iron Formation, Ontario-Minnesota." SUNY, Stony Brook, 1975.

6327
Fortier, Yves O. "Geology of the Orford Map-Area in the Eastern Townships of the Province of Quebec, Canada." Stanford, 1946.

Frarey, Murray James. See No./Voir no 5701

6328
Freeman, Peter V. "Geology of the Béraud-Mazerac Area, Quebec." McGill, 1957.

6329
Frith, Ronald Anthony. "Rubidium-Strontium Isotopic Studies of the Grenville Structural Province in the Chibougamau and Lac St. Jean Area." McGill, 1971.

6330
Fuh, Tsu-Min. "Correlation of Rocks Across the Grenville Front near Val d'Or, Quebec." Queen's, 1971.

6331
Gadd, Nelson Raymond. "Pleistocene Geology of the Bécancour Map-Area, Quebec." Illinois, 1955.

6332
Gandhi, Sunil K. S. "The Igneous Petrology of Mount Yamaska, Quebec." McGill, 1967.

6333
Gaucher, Edwin H. S. "The Magnetic Anomaly of the Magnetite Serpentinite at the Montagne du Sorcier, Chibougamau, Province of Quebec." Harvard, 1960.

6334
Gauthier, Georges. "Recherches sur le hanneton commun du Québec." Laval, 1943.

6335
Gauthier, Michel. "Métallogénie du zinc dans la région de Maniwaki, Gracefield, Québec." Montréal, 1983.

6336
Gélinas, Léopold. "Géologie de la région de Fort Chimo et des lacs Gabriel et Thévenet, Nouveau-Québec." Laval, 1978.

6337
Gilbert, Joseph E.J. "The Geology of the Capsisit-Inconnu Lake Area, Abitibi-East, Quebec." McGill, 1949.

Gillett, Lawrence Britton. See No./Voir no 6030

6338
Gillies, Norman B. "The Geology of the Caniniti River Area, Pontiac County, Quebec." McGill, 1951.

6339
Girard, Paul. "The Madeleine Copper Mine, Gaspé Quebec: A Hydrothermal Deposit." McGill, 1971.

Glendinning, Robert Morton. See No./Voir no 4759

6340
Gold, David P. "The Relationship Between the Limestones and the Alkaline Igneous Rocks of Oka and St. Hilaire, Quebec." McGill, 1964.

6341
Goldie, Raymond J. "The Flavrian and Powell Pluton Noranda Area, Quebec." Queen's, 1976.

6342
Gorman, W. Alan. "The Geology of the Ste. Justin Map Area." McGill, 1956.

6343
Gosh-Dastidar, Priyabrata. "A Study of the Trace Elements in Selected Appalachian Sulphide Deposits." New Brunswick, 1969.

6344
Goulet, Normand. "Stratigraphy and Structural Relationships Across the Cadillac-Larder Lake Fault, Rouyn-Beauchastal Area, Quebec." Queen's 1978.

6345
Graham, Robert Bruce. "The Geology of the Duquesne and Lanaudière Map-Area, Destor and Duparque Townships, with Particular Reference to Porphyr tization." Toronto, 1948.

6346
Greig, Edmund Wendell. "The Geology of the Matamec Lake Map Area, Saguenay County Quebec." Princeton, 1941.

6347
Grenier, Florian. "Étude stratigraphique et chimique des sédiments du lac Lauzon." Montréal, 1952.

6348
Grenier, Paul. "Géologie et pétrologie de la région du lac Beetz, comté de Saguenay." Laval, 1952.

6349
Grimes-Graeme, Rhoderick C.H. "The Origin of the Intrusive Igneous Breccias in the Vicinity of Montréal, Québec." McGill, 1935.

6350
Gross, Gordon A. "The Metamorphic Rocks of the Mount Wright and Matonipi Lake Areas of Quebec Wisconsin, 1955.

6351
Güssow, William C. "Petrogeny of the Major Ac Intrusives of the Rouyn-Bell River Area, North western Quebec." Massachusetts Institute of Technology, 1938.

6352
Guy-Bray, John Victor. "The Petrology of La Lièvre Area, Roberval County, Quebec." McGill, 1961.

Hadley, Donald Gene. See No./Voir no 6045

6353
Halet, Robert A.F. "The Geology and Mineral Deposits of the Beattie-Galatea Area (Quebec) McGill, 1934.

6354
Hannah, Raymond G.J. "Petrology of the Macquerea Series (Gaspé-Peninsula, Quebec)." Laval, 1954.

6355
Hargraves, Robert Bero. "Petrology of the Allard Lake Anorthosite Suite, and Paleomagnetism of the Ilmenite Deposits." Princeton, 1959.

Hashimoto, Tsutomu. See No./Voir no 5703

6356
Hawkins, William Maxwell. "A Spectrochemical Study of Rocks Associated with the Sulphide Ore Deposits of Chibougamau District, Quebec." McGill, 1961.

6357
Hein, Frances Jessie. "Deep-Sea Valley-Fill Sediments: Cap Enrage Formation, Quebec." McMaster, 1979.

6358
Héroux, Yvon. "Stratigraphie de la formation de Sayabec (silurien) dans la vallée de Matapédia (Québec)." Montréal, 1976.

6359
Higgins, Michael Denis. "Age and Origin of the Sept-Iles Anorthosite Complex, Quebec." McGill, 1980.

6360
Hiscott, Richard Nicholas. "Sedimentology and Regional Implications of Deep-Water Sandstones of the Tourelle Formation, Ordovician, Quebec." McMaster, 1977.

6361
Hoag, Roland Boyden, Jr. "Hydrogeochemistry of Springs near the Eustis Mine, Quebec." McGill, 1975.

6362
Hocq, Michel. "Contribution à la connaissance pétro-tectonique et minéralogique des massifs anorthosiques et mangératiques de la région du réservoir Pipmuacau." Montréal, 1978.

6363
Hodgson, Christopher John. "Monteregian Dike Rocks." McGill, 1969.

Hoffmann, Hans. See No./Voir no 509

6364
Hogan, Howard R. "The Geology of the Nipissis River and Nipisso Lake Map-Areas." McGill, 1953.

6365
Holmes, Stanley W. "The Geology and Mineral Deposits of the Fancamp-Hauy Area, Abitibi County East, Quebec, Canada." Columbia, 1953.

6366
Horscroft, Frank D. "The Petrology of Gabbroic Sills in the Volcanic Series of Roy and McKenzie Townships, Chibougamau Region, Quebec." McGill, 1957.

6367
Hubert, Claude M. "Stratigraphy of the Quebec Complex in the L'Islet, Kamouraska Area." McGill, 1965.

6368
Husain, Bilal R. "Semi-Micro Fossils of the Black River and Trenton Groups of Quebec." McGill, 1955.

Ignatius, Heikki G. See No./Voir no 6075
Imbault, Joseph Paul E. See No./Voir no 6076
Ingham, Walter Norman. See No./Voir no 6077

6369
Jacoby, Russell Stephen. "Petrogenesis and Tectonic Evolution of a Perthitic Gneiss Complex in the Central Grenville Province: The Baskatong Reservoir Area, Quebec." Queen's, 1969.

6370
James, William Fleming. "Geology of Duparquet Map-Area, Quebec." Princeton, 1923.

6371
Jeffery, William Gordon. "The Geology of the Campbell-Chibougamau Mine, Quebec." McGill, 1959.

6372
Johnson, Hugh N. "Segment Occupance of the St. François Mining Region." Washington, St. Louis, 1950.

Johnston, William G. See No./Voir no 6085

6373
Jooste, René F. "Geology of the Bourget Map-Area, Chicoutimi County, Quebec." McGill, 1949.

6374
Kaçira, Niyazi. "Geology of Chromotite Occurrences and Ultramafic Rocks of the Thetford Mines-Disraeli Area, Quebec." Western Ontario, 1972.

6375
Karrow, Paul Frederick. "Pleistocene Geology of the Grondines Map-Area, Quebec." Illinois, 1957.

6376
Katz, Michael Barry. "The Nature and Origin of the Granulites of the Southern Part of Mont Tremblant Park, Quebec." Toronto, 1967.

6377
Kavanagh, Paul Michael. "Geology of the Hyland Lake Area, New Quebec, Canada." Princeton, 1954.

6378
Keating, Bernard J. "Geology of the Augmentation of Grenville Township, Province of Quebec." McGill, 1937.

6379
Kelly, James Michael. "Geology, Wall Rock Alteration and Contact Metamorphism Associated with Massive Sulfide Mineralization at the Amulet Mine, Noranda District, Quebec." Wisconsin, 1975.

6380
Kerr, Forrest Alexander. "Geology of the Memphremagog (Quebec) Map Area." Chicago, 1929.

6381
Kindle, Cecil Haldane. "The Geology of the Southeastern Part of Gaspé Peninsula, Quebec." Princeton, 1931.

6382
Kirkland, Robert W. "A Study of Part of the Kaniapiskau System Northwest of Attilamagen Lake, New Quebec." McGill, 1950.

6383
Kish, Laszlo. "The Geology of the Hart-Jaune River Area, Saguenay County." Laval, 1966.

6384
Klugman, Michael A. "The Geology of an Area Between the Pigou and Sheldrake Rivers, Saguenay County, Quebec, with a Detailed Study of the Anorthosites." McGill, 1956.

6385
Kluyver, Huybert M. "Lower Paleozoic Tectono-Stratigraphy of the Northern Appalachians and the Caledonides." Queen's, 1972.

6386
Knox, John K. "Geology of the Serpentine Belt Coloraine Sheet, Thetford-Black Lake Mining District, Quebec." Chicago, 1917.

6387
Kranck, Svante Hakan. "Chemical Petrology of Metamorphic Iron Formations and Associated Rocks in the Mount Reed Area, Quebec." Massachusetts Institute of Technology, 1959.

6388
Kretz, Ralph. "The Chemical Petrology of Garnet, Biotite, and Hornblende Gneisses from Southwestern Quebec." Chicago, 1959.

6389
Krishnan, Thekkey K. "Structural Studies of the Schefferville Mining District, Quebec-Labrador, Canada." California, Los Angeles, 1976.

6390
Laguitton, Daniel. "La microanalyse par sonde électronique: application à l'étude de la mise en valeur d'une magnétite titanifère de la région de Magpie (province de Québec)." Laval, 1974.

6391
Laird, Jo. "Phase Equilibria in Mafic Schist and the Polymetamorphic History of Vermont." California Technical, 1977.

6392
Lajoie, Jean. "The Siluro-Devonian Stratigraphy of the Matapedia-Temiscouata Area." McGill, 1964.

6393
Lamarche, Robert Y. "Géologie de la région de Sherbrooke, comté de Sherbrooke." Laval, 1966.

6394
Lao, Khedang. "Thermo-géochimie appliqué aux inclusions fluides reliées à Rouyn-Noranda, Québec." Montréal, 1983.

6395
Larochelle, André Joseph Edgar. "A Study of Paleomagnetism of Rocks from Yamaska and Brome Mountains, Quebec." McGill, 1959.

6396
Laurin, André F. "Geology of Ducharme-Mignault Map-Area, Roberval County Quebec." Laval, 1957.

Lee, Hurlbert A. See No./Voir no 5616

Lee, Sang Man. See No./Voir no 5863

6397
Lespérance, Pierre Jacques. "The Silurian and Devonian Rocks of the Temiscouata Region, Quebec." McGill, 1961.

6398
L'Espérance, Robert L. "The Geology of Duprat Township and Some Adjacent Areas, Northwest Quebec." McGill, 1952.

Lewis, Thomas Leonard. See No./Voir no 6109

6399
Lickus, Robert John. "Geology and Geochemistry of the Ore Deposits at the Vauze Mine, Noranda District, Quebec." McGill, 1965.

6400
Longley, William W. "The Geology of the Kamshigama Map Area, Abitibi District, Quebec." Minnesota, 1937.

6401
Lowther, George K. "Geology of an Area near Shawinigan Falls, Province of Quebec." McGill, 1935.

6402
Lunde, Magnus. "The Precambrian and Pleistocene Geology of the Grondines Map-Area, Quebec." McGill, 1953.

6403
Lyall, Harry Bruce. "Geology of the Hainau Champagne Area, Pontiac County, Quebec." Laval, 1959.

6404
MacGeehan, Patrick John. "The Petrology and Geochemistry of Volcanic Rocks at Matagami, Quebec and Their Relationship to Massive Sulphide Mineralization." McGill, 1979.

6405
MacKay, Bertram Reid. "Geology and Physiography of the Beauceville Map Area, Quebec, with Special Reference to Placer Gold Deposits." Chicago, 1920.

MacKenzie, Graham Stewart. See No./Voir no 6119

6406
MacLaren, Alexander S. "Peridotites of Northwestern Quebec." McGill, 1953.

6407
Malouf, Stanley E. "The Geology of the Francoeur Arntfield District, Beauchastel Township, Quebec." McGill, 1942.

6408
Marleau, Alban Raymond. "Geology of the Woburn East Megantic and Armstrong Areas, Frontenac and Beauce Counties, Quebec." Laval, 1959.

6409
Martens, James Hart Curry. "Some Pre-Cambrian Rocks in Northern Quebec." Cornell, 1926.

6410
Mason, George David. "A Stratigraphic and Paleoenvironmental Study of the Upper Gaspé Limestone of Eastern Gaspé Peninsula, Quebec." Carleton, 1972.

6411
Mattinson, Cyril Rodger. "The Geology of the Mount Logan Area, Gaspé, Quebec." McGill, 1958.

6412
Mawdsley, James Buckland. "St. Urbain Area, Charlevoix District, Quebec." Princeton, 1924.

6413
McDonald, Barrie Clifton. "Pleistocene Events and Chronology in the Appalachian Region of Southeastern Quebec, Canada." Yale, 1967.

6414
McGerrigle, Harold W. "The Geology of the Lacolle Quadrangle, Southern Quebec." Princeton, 1930.

6415
McMillan, Ronald Hugh. "Petrology, Geochemistry and Wallrock Alteration at Opemiska - A Vein Copper Deposit Crosscutting a Layered Archean Ultramafic-Mafic Sill." Western Ontario, 1973.

6416
McQuade, Bernard N. "Petro-Chemistry of the Bachelor Lake Volcanic Complex and Associated Ore Deposits, Abitibi East N.W. Quebec." Ottawa, 1981.

6417
Mehrtens, Charlotte Jean. "A Paleoenvironmental Reconstruction of a Shelf Margin: The Caradoc (Middle Ordovician) of Southern Quebec." Chicago, 1979.

6418
Melihercsik, Stephen J. "Petrology of the Charny Formation." Laval, 1952.

6419
Michone, James Gregory. "Lamprophyre Dikes of New England." North Carolina, 1978.

6420
Miller, Allan Ross. "Petrology and Geochemistry of the 2-3 Ultramafic Sill and Related Rocks, Cape Smith-Wakeham Bay Fold Belt, Quebec." Western Ontario, 1977.

6421
Miller, Murray Lloyd. "Geology of the St. Simeon-Tadoussac Map Area, Quebec." Minnesota, 1953.

Miller, Robert J. M. See No./Voir no 5519

6422
Mills, John Peter. "Petrological Studies in the Sakami-Lake Greenstone Belt of Northwestern Quebec." Kansas, 1974.

6423
Milner, Robert L. "Geology and Ore Deposits of Barry Lake Map-Area, Northern Quebec." McGill, 1940.

6424
Mitra, Rabindranath. "A Study of Metamorphic Facies at the New Calumet Mine, Quebec." Toronto, 1954.

6425
Moorhouse, Walter W. "Geology of the Zinc-Lead Deposit on Calumet Island, Quebec." Columbia, 1941.

6426
Morin, Marcel. "Geology of the Labrieville Map-Area, Saguenay County, Quebec." Laval, 1956.

6427
Moss, Albert E. "Geology of the Siscoe Gold Mine, Siscoe, P.Q." McGill, 1940.

6428
Moyer, Paul Tyson, Jr. "The Geology and Amphibolites of the Brock-St. Urcisse Area, Abitibi and Mistassini Territories, Quebec." Michigan, 1968.

6429
Murphy, Daniel Lawson. "Precambrian Geology of the Lake Carheil Area, Saguenay Electoral District, Quebec." Michigan, 1961.

6430
Murray, Louis G. "Wall Rock Alteration in the Vicinity of Base Metal Sulphide Deposits in the Eastern Townships of Quebec." McGill, 1955.

6431
Neale, Ernest R.W. "Geology of the Bethoulat Lake Area, Mistassini Territory, Quebec." Yale, 1953.

6432
Neilson, James M.H. "Geology of the Lake Mistassini Region, Northern Quebec." Minnesota, 1950.

6433
Northrop, Stuart Alvord. "Geology of the Port Daniel-Gascons Area, Quebec." Yale, 1929.

6434
Nunes, Arturo de F. "Geology of the Island of Orleans, Montmorency County, Quebec." Laval, 1958.

Occhietti, Serge. See No./Voir no 4765

6435
Ogunyomi, Olugbenga. "Diagenesis and Deep-Water Depositional Environments of Lower Paleozoic Continental Margin Sediments in the Quebec City Area, Canada." McGill, 1980.

6436
Okulitch, Vladimir J. "The Geology of the Black River Group in the Vicinity of Montreal." McGill, 1934.

6437
Ollerenshaw, Neil Campbell. "Stratigraphic Problems of the Western Shickshock Mountains in the Gaspé Peninsula." Toronto, 1963.

6438
O'Neill, John Johnston. "Geology and Petrography of the Beloeil and Rougemont Mountains, Quebec." Yale, 1912.

6439
Oshin, Igbekele. "The Abundances and Geochemistry of Some Noble Metals in Thetford Mines Ophiolites, P.Q." McMaster, 1981.

6440
Ouellet, Marcel. "Paleoecological Studies of Three Late-Quatenary Lacustrine Deposits from the Kingston Region and Some Geochemical Observations of Bottom Surface Sediments of Lakes from Southwestern Quebec." Ottawa, 1974.

6441
Owens, Edward Henry. "The Geodynamics of Two Beach Units in the Magdalen Islands, Quebec, Within the Framework of Coastal Environments of the Southern Gulf of St. Lawrence." North Carolina, 1975.

6442
Owens, Owen E. "The Geology of Part of the Labrador Trough South of Leaf Lake, New Quebec." McGill, 1955.

6443
Parkash, Barham. "Depositional Mechanism of Greywackes, Cloridorme Formation (Middle Ordovician) Gaspé-Quebec." McMaster, 1969.

6444
Peale, Rodgers. "Some Ore Deposits of the Rouyn District, Northwestern Quebec, Canada." Harvard, 1930.

Peattie, Roderick. See No./Voir no 4768
Pelletier, René A. See No./Voir no 6161
Perrault, Guy Gilles. See No./Voir no 5719

6445
Petruk, William. "The Clearwater Copper-Zinc Deposit and Its Setting, with a Special Study of Mineral Zoning Around Such Deposits." McGill, 1950.

6446
Philpotts, Anthony R. "Petrology of the Morin Series in Southern Quebec." Cambridge, 1963.

6447
Pirie, James. "Mobilization in a Migmatite from the Grenville Province, Quebec." Queen's, 1972.

6448
Pirie, Robert Gordon. "Petrology and Physical-Chemical Environment of Bottom Sediments of the Rivière Bonaventure-Chaleur Bay Area, Quebec, Canada." Indiana, 1963.

6449
Potevin, Eugène. "Étude des transformations minéralogiques d'origine profondes et externes qui se sont produites dans le Felon-Couche, Black Lake, Thetford Co., de Mégantic." Montréal, 1922.

6450
Pouliot, Gaston. "The Thermal History of the Monteregian Intrusives Based on a Study of the Feldspars." McGill, 1962.

6451
Prabhu, Mohan Keshav. "Geology, Geochemistry and Genesis of Montauban Lead-Zinc Deposits." McGill, 1982. [Grenville Province/Province de Grenville]

6452
Price, Peter. "The Geology and Ore Deposits of the Horne Mine, Noranda, Quebec." McGill, 1933.

6453
Pyke, Dale Randolph. "Precambrian Geology of the Montauban Area, Quebec." McGill, 1967.

6454
Quirke, Terence Thomas, Jr. "Mineralogy and Stratigraphy of the Temiscamie Iron-Formation, Lake Albanel Iron Range, Mistassini Territory, Quebec, Canada." Minnesota, 1958.

6455
Rajasekaran, Konnur C. "Mineralogy and Petrology of Nepheline Syenite in Mont St. Hilaire, Québec." McGill, 1968.

6456
Raychaudhuri, Sunil Kumar. "Trace Elements in the Sulfide Deposits of the Chibougamau District, Quebec." McGill, 1960.

6457
Retty, Joseph Arlington. "The Geology of the Townships of Gaboury and Blondeau, Timiskaming County, Quebec." Princeton, 1931.

6458
Riddell, John E. "Wall Rock Alteration Around Base Metal Sulphide Deposits of Northwestern Quebec." McGill, 1953.

6459
Riordan, Peter H. "Geology of the Thetford-Black Lake District of Quebec, with Special Reference to the Asbestos Deposits." McGill, 1952.

6460
Ritter, Charles John. "Trace Elements of Gold-Bearing Quartz Veins of the Lamaque Mine, Bourlamaque P.Q., Canada." Michigan, 1971.

6461
Riverin, Gerald. "Wall-Rock Alteration at the Millenbach Mine, Noranda, Quebec." Queen's, 1977.

6462
Robert, Jean Louis. "Géologie de la région du lac Kipawa, comté de Témiscamingue." Laval, 1967.

6463
Roberts, Robert Gwilym. "The Geology of the Mattagami Lake Mine, Galinee Township, Quebec." McGill, 1967.

6464
Robinson, Edwin George. "Environment and Genesis of Apatite and Mica Deposits of West Portland Township, Quebec." Toronto, 1951.

6465
Robinson, William G. "The Flavrian Lake Map Area and the Structural Geology of the Surrounding District (Quebec)." McGill, 1941.

6466
Rocheleau, Michel. "Stratigraphie et sédimentologie de l'archéen dans la région de Rouyn, Abitibi, Québec." Montréal, 1981.

6467
Roliff, W.A. "Stratigraphic and Environmental Studies of the Potsdam Group, St. Lawrence Lowland Eastern Canada." London, 1968.

Rose, E.R. See No./Voir no 6194

6468
Ross, Stewart H. "The Geology of the Lac Deschene Map Area, Quebec." Syracuse, 1952.

6469
Roth, Horst. "A Structural Study of the Sutton Mountains, Quebec." McGill, 1965.

6470
Sabourin, Robert J.E. "Geology of the Bristol-Masham Area, Pontiac and Gatineau Counties, Quebec." Laval, 1955.

6471
Sahakian, Armen Souren. "Paleocurrent Study of the Potsdam Sandstone of New York and Quebec." Harvard, 1964.

6472
Saint-Julien, Pierre. "Géologie de la région d'Oford Sherbrooke." Laval, 1966.

6473
Sakrison, Herbert Charles. "Chemical Studies of the Host Rocks of the Lake Dufault Mine, Quebec." McGill, 1967.

6474
Sauvé, Pierre. "The Geology of the East Half of the Gerido Lake Area, New Quebec, Canada." John Hopkins, 1957.

Sawford, Edward Clayton. See No./Voir no 6200

6475
Schimann, Karl. "Geology of the Wakeham Bay Area, Eastern End of the Cape Smith Belt, New Quebec." Alberta, 1978.

6476
Schindler, Norman R. "Igneous Rocks of Duprat Lake and Rouyn Lake Areas, Quebec." McGill, 1934.

Schopf, Thomas Joseph Morton. See No./Voir no 6577

6477
Schwellnus, Jurgen E.G. "Ore Controls in Deposits of the Knob Lake Area, Labrador Trough." Queen's, 1957.

6478
Shafiquillah, Muhammad. "The Diffusion Characteristics of Argon in Nepheline and the K-Ar Geochronology of the Oka Carbonatite Complex and Its Aureole." Carleton, 1972.

6479
Shalaby, Hany. "Microfacies algaires de la plate forme du Saint-Laurent." Montréal, 1982.

6480
Sharma, Kamal M. "Structural Analysis of the Piscatosin Synform Baskatong Reservoir (E) Map Area Quebec." Queen's, 1969.

6481
Sharpe, John L. "Precambrian Geology and Sulphide Deposits of Matagami Area, Quebec." McGill, 1964.

6482
Shelton, Kevin Louis. "Evolution of the Porphyry Copper and Skarn Deposits at Murdochville, Gaspé Peninsula, Quebec: A Geochemical, Stable Isotopic, and Fluid Inclusion Study." Yale, 1982.

6483
Shepherd, Norman. "The Petrography and Mineralogy of the Cross Lake Area, Ungava, New Quebec." Toronto, 1960.

6484
Sheridan, Robert Edmund. "Seaward Extension of the Canadian Appalachians." Columbia, 1968.

6485
Shilts, William Weimer. "Pleistocene Geology of the Lac Megantic Region, Southeastern Quebec, Canada." Syracuse, 1970.

6486
Sikander, Abdul Hakim. "Structural Analysis of the Lower Paleozoic Rocks of Western Gaspé, Quebec." Ottawa, 1968.

6487
Skidmore, Wilfred B. "The Geology of the Gastonguay-Mourier Area, Gaspé Peninsula." Princeton, 1959.

6488
Slipp, Robert M. "Base Metal Deposits in the Labrador Trough Between Lake Harveng and Lac Aulneau, New Quebec." McGill, 1957.

6489
Spence, Andrée F. "Stratigraphy, Development and Petrogenesis of the Central Noranda Volcanic Pile, Noranda, Quebec." Toronto, 1976.

6490
Stamatelopoulou-Seymour, Karen Catherine. "Volcanic Petrogenesis in the Lac Guyer Greenstone Belt, James Bay Area, Quebec." McGill, 1982.

6491
Stevenson, John S. "Mineralization of the Eustis Mine, Eustis, Quebec." Massachusetts Institute of Technology, 1934.

Terasmae, Joan. See No./Voir no 6220
Thiessen, Richard Leigh. See No./Voir no 5535

6492
Treiman, Allan Harvey. "The Oka Carbonatite Complex, Quebec: Aspects of Carbonatite Petrogenesis." Michigan, 1982.

6493
Tremblay, Leo-Paul. "Geology of the Lacorne-Barraute Area, Abitibi County, Quebec." Toronto, 1947.

6494
Trudel, Pierre. "Le volcanisme archéen et la géologie structurale de la région de Cléricy, Abitibi, Québec." Montréal, 1979.

6495
Twenhofel, William Henry. "Geology, Stratigraphy and Physiography of Anticosti Island." Yale, 1912.

6496
Umar, Pervez Akhtar. "Mineral Resource Potential: Rouyn-Noranda Region, Quebec." McGill, 1978.

6497
Valiquette, Guy. "Géologie des régions du lac des Montagnes et du lac Lemare, territoire de Mistassini." Laval, 1965.

6498
Valliant, Robert Irwin. "The Geology, Stratigraphic Relationships and Genesis of the Bousquet Gold Deposit, Northwest Quebec." Western Ontario, 1981.

6499
Wahl, William G. "The Canica-Cawatose Map Area." McGill, 1947.

6500
Walters, Martin. "Biostratigraphy of Middle and Upper Ordovician Graptolites from the St. Lawrence Lowlands." Montréal, 1980.

6501
Wang, Shin. "Sphalerite Pole Figure Analysis and Metamorphic Textures, Matagami Lake Mine, Quebec, Canada." Columbia, 1973.

6502
Williams-Jones Anthony Eric. "A Field and Theoretical Study of the Thermal Metamorphism of Trenton Limestone in the Aureole of Mount Royal, Quebec." Queen's, 1973.

6503
Williamson, John T. "The Origin and Occurrence of the Chromite Deposits of the Eastern Townships, Quebec." McGill, 1933.

6504
Wilson, Morley Evans. "Preliminary Memoir on the Abitibi District, Pontiac County, Quebec." Yale, 1912.

6505
Wilson, Norman L. "An Investigation of the Metamorphism of the Orijarvi Type with Special Reference to the Zinc-Lead Deposits of Montauban-les-Mines, P.Q." McGill, 1939.

6506
Wolfe, Stephen Howard. "Part I. Geology of the Manicouagan-Mushalagan Lakes Structure. Part II. Geochronology of the Manicouagan-Mushalagan Lakes Structure." California Institute of Technology, 1972.

6507
Woussen, Gerard. "Pétrologie du complexe Igue de Brome." Montréal, 1976.

6508
Young, George Albert. "Geology and Petrology of Mount Yamaska, Province of Quebec." Yale, 1904.

Zajac, Ihor Stephen. See No./Voir no 5799
Zimmermann, Robert Allen. See No./Voir no 6254

PALEONTOLOGY/ PALÉONTOLOGIE

GENERAL ITEMS/OUVRAGES GÉNÉRAUX

6509
Brooks, Harold Kelly. "The Paleozoic Eumalacostraca of North America." Harvard, 1962.

6510
Koch, Carl Fred. "Evolutionary and Ecological Patterns of Upper Cenomanian (Cretaceous) Mollusc Distribution in the Western Interior of North America." George Washington, 1977.

6511
Lee, Chunsun. "Lower Permian Ammonoid Faunal Provinciality." Iowa, 1975. [British Columbia, Northwest Territories, and Yukon/Colombie-Britannique, Territoires du Nord-Ouest et Yukon]

6512
Madden, Casey Thomas. "Mammoths of North America." Colorado, 1981.

6513
Rouse, Glenn Everett. "The Disclosure and Paleobotanical Evaluation of Plant Microfossils from Selected Cretaceous Coalbearing Strata of Canada." McMaster, 1956.

6514
Sweet, Arthur Richard. "The Taxonomy Evolution and Stratigraphic Value of Azolla and Azollopsis in the Upper Cretaceous and Early Tertiary." Calgary, 1972.

REGIONAL STUDIES/ÉTUDES RÉGIONALES

Eastern Canada/Est du Canada

6515
Globensky, Yvon Raoul. "Upper Mississipian Non-Carbonate Microfauna from the Windsor Group of the Atlantic Provinces." New Brunswick, 1965.

6516
Hooper, K. "Studies in Some Post-Wisconsin Foraminiferal Faunas and Sediments of Eastern Canada and the Atlantic Continental Shelf." London, 1969.

6517
Koch, William Frederick II. "Brachiopod Paleoecology, Paleobiogeography, and Biostratigraphy in the Upper Middle Devonian of Eastern North America: An Ecofacies Model on the Appalachian, Michigan and Illinois Basins." Oregon State, 1978.

Lucas, Margaret Jennifer. See No./Voir no 5660

6518
Poore, Richard Zell. "Late Cenozoic Planktonic Foraminiferal Biostratigraphy and Paleoclimatology of the North Atlantic Ocean: DSDP Leg 12." Brown, 1975. [Labrador Sea/Mer du Labrador]

6519
Schwert, D.P. "Paleoentomological Analyses of Two Postglacial Sites in Eastern North America." Waterloo, 1978.

After a marked increase in output in the 1970's, (23) from Canadian universities, the first four years of this decade have not continued the rapid growth observed in other disciplines. There seems to be a lull in American doctoral research in the eighties as well, with only three dissertations produced so far, compared to 15 in the 1970's and 1960's. Twenty-seven American universities have approved a total of 46 dissertations. The University of Michigan is the leader with six studies. The universities of Harvard, Iowa, Colorado, Princeton and Ohio State have produced three studies each, and Oregon State, Stanford University, the University of Kansas, and Columbia have produced two each. Of the twelve Canadian universities with students working at the doctorate level in this area, Toronto leads with 10 studies, followed by Waterloo, McGill, and British Columbia with four each. The universities of McMaster, Alberta and Saskatchewan have each approved three doctoral studies while the universities of New Brunswick, Ottawa and Western Ontario have approved two and Dalhousie and Queen's each have one approved graduate dissertation.

Four British universities produced three studies in the 1960's, and five in the 1970's; London and Bristol three each, and Cambridge and Wales, each produced one doctoral dissertation.

De 1970 à 1980, on a pu noter une nette augmentation du nombre de thèses dans les universités canadiennes, mais le mouvement ne s'est pas poursuivi dans les années 1980 et il n'y a pas eu d'augmentation de la production comme dans d'autres disciplines. La recherche américaine au niveau des études de doctorat semble diminuer dans les années 1980, si l'on en juge par les trois seules thèses qui ont été produites jusqu'à maintenant, alors que les années 1960 et 1970, on en comptaient quinze. Vingt-sept universités américaines ont approuvé un total de 46 thèses. L'Université du Michigan vient en tête, avec 6 thèses, suivie des universités Harvard, Iowa, Colorado, Princeton et Ohio State qui ont produit chacune trois études, et Oregon State, Stanford, Kansas et Columbia avec chacune deux thèses. Des 12 universités canadiennes qui ont travaillé au niveau du doctorat en ce domaine, l'Université de Toronto a produit 10 thèses, suivie par les universités Waterloo, McGill et de la Colombie-Britannique avec quatre chacune, les universités McMaster, de l'Alberta et de la Saskatchewan avec chacune trois, celle du Nouveau-Brunswick, d'Ottawa et Western Ontario avec deux et enfin, celles de Dalhousie et Queen n'en ont produit qu'une.

Quatre universités britanniques ont accordé trois doctorats dans les années 1960 et cinq dans les années 1970; les universités de Londres et Bristol en comptent chacune trois, celles de Cambridge et Wales chacune une.

Western Canada/Ouest du Canada

6520
Hall, Russell Lindsay. "Lower Bajocian Jurassic Ammonoid Faunas of the Western Americas." McMaster, 1976.

Harker, Peter. See No./Voir no 5411

6521
Norris, Arnold Willy. "Study of the Genius Atrypa of Western Canada." Toronto, 1956.

6522
Poulton, Terence P. "Jurassic Trigoniidae of Western Canada and United States and a Review of the Family." Queen's, 1975.

6523
Stelck, Charles R. "Cenomanian-Albian Foraminifera of Western Canada." Stanford, 1951.

British Columbia/Colombie-Britannique

Baxter, Sonny. See No./Voir no 6559

Blome, Charles David. See No./Voir no 5162

6524
Boneham, Roger Frederick. "Palynology of Three Tertiary Coal Basins in South-Central British Columbia." Michigan, 1968.

Crickmay, Colin H. See No./Voir no 5195

6525
Hebda, Richard Joseph. "The Paleoecology of a Raised Bog and Associated Deltaic Sediments of the Fraser River Delta." British Columbia, 1977.

Lee, Chunsun. See No./Voir no 6511

6526
Mathewes, Rolf W. "Paleoecology and Post-Glacial Sediments in the Fraser Lowland Region of British Columbia." British Columbia, 1973.

6527
Piel, Kenneth Martin. "Palynology of Middle and Late Tertiary Sediments from the Central Interior of British Columbia, Canada." British Columbia, 1969.

6528
Satterthwait, Donna F. "Paleobiology and Paleoecology of Middle Cambrian Algae from Western North America." California, Los Angeles, 1976.

6529
Smith-Evenden, Roberta. "Glacio-Marine Foraminifera of British Columbia and Southeast Alaska." British Columbia, 1967.

6530
Stanley, George D., Jr. "Triassic Coral Buildups of Western North America." Kansas, 1977.

Usher, John L. See No./Voir no 5362

6531
Wilson, Mark V.H. "Fossil Fishes of the Tertiary of British Columbia." Toronto, 1974.

New Brunswick/Nouveau-Brunswick

Globensky, Yvon Paul. See No./Voir no 6515

6532
Korpijaako, Maija-Leena. "On the Origin and Geo-Botanical Development of Muskeg in New Brunswick." New Brunswick, 1976.

Newfoundland and Labrador/Terre-Neuve et Labrador

6533
Davidheiser, Carolyn E. "Bryozoans and Bryozoan-Like Corals - Affinities and Variability of Diplotrypa, Monotrypa, Labyrinthites, and Cladopora (Trepostoniata and Tabulata) from Selected Ordovician-Silurian Reefs in Eastern North America (Newfoundland, Pennsylvania, Michigan)." Pennsylvania State, 1980.

Elias, Scott Armstrong. See No./Voir no 6543

6534
Fletcher, Terence P. "Geology and Lower to Middle Cambrian Trilobite Faunas of the Southwest Avalon, Newfoundland." Cambridge, 1972.

6535
Grayson, John Francis. "The Post-Glacial History of Vegetation and Climate in the Labrador-Quebec Region as Determined by Palynology." Michigan, 1957.

Howell, Benjamin Franklin. See No./Voir no 5754

Jordan, Richard Heath. See No./Voir no 721

6536
Short, Susan Kathleen. "Holocene Palynology in Labrador-Ungava: Climatic History and Culture Change on the Central Coast." Colorado, 1978.

Northwest Territories and the Yukon/ Territoires du Nord-Ouest et Yukon

6537
Campbell, John Duncan. "Paleobotany and Stratigraphic Sequence of the Pleistocene Klondike Muck Deposits." McGill, 1952.

6538
Chamney, T.P.A. "Biostratigraphy (Foraminifera) of the Canadian Arctic Mainland." London, 1975.

6539
Chi, Byung Il. "Devonian Megaspores and Their Stratigraphic Significance in the Canadian Arctic." Calgary, 1974.

6540
Collinson, Charles W. "The Ordovician Cephalopod Fauna of Baffin Island." Iowa, 1952.

6541
Cwynar, Leslie Peter C. "A Late Quaternary Vegetation History from Hanging Lake, Northern Yukon." Toronto, 1980.

6542
Dixon, James. "The Stratigraphy and Invertebrate Paleontology of Early Paleozoic Rocks, Somerset and Prince of Wales Islands, N.W.T." Ottawa, 1974.

6543
Elias, Scott Armstrong. "Paleoenvironmental Interpretations of Holocene Insect Fossil Assemblages from Three Sites in Arctic Canada." Colorado, 1980.

6544
Elliott, D.K. "New Pteraspididae from Arctic Canada." Bristol, 1979.

6545
Harington, C.R. "Pleistocene Mammals of the Yukon Territory." Alberta, 1977.

6546
Harper, Francis. "A Faunal Reconnaissance in the Athabaska and Great Slave Lake Region." Cornell, 1925.

6547
Lenz, Alfred C. "Devonian Stratigraphy and Paleontology of Lower Mackenzie Valley, Northwest Territories." Princeton, 1959.

6548
Leslie, Robert James. "Ecology and Paleoecology of Hudson Bay Foraminifera." Southern California, 1965.

6549
Loeffler, E.J. "The Ostracodern Faunas of the Delorme Formation and Associated Siluro-Devonian Strata in the District of Mackenzie, Northwest Territories, Canada." Bristol, 1975.

6550
Ludvigsen, Rolf. "Middle Ordovician Trilobites, South Nahanni River Area, District of Mackenzie." Western Ontario, 1975.

6551
Nowlan, Godfrey. "Late Cambrian to Late Ordovician Conodont Evolution and Biostratigraphy of the Franklinian Miogeosyncline, Eastern Canadian Arctic Islands." Waterloo, 1977.

6552
Ormiston, Allen Roger. "Lower and Middle Devonian Trilobites of the Canadian Arctic Islands." Harvard, 1964.

6553
Perry, David George. "Paleontology and Biostratigraphy of Delorme Formation (Siluro-Devonian), Northwest Territories." Western Ontario, 1975.

6554
Roy, Sharat Kumar. "The Upper Ordovician Fauna of Frobisher Bay, Baffin Land." Chicago, 1941.

6555
Smith, Roy Edward. "Lower Devonian (Lochkovian) Brachiopods, Paleoecology and Biostratigraphy of the Canadian Arctic Islands." Oregon State, 1976.

Nova Scotia/Nouvelle-Écosse

6556
Bambach, Richard Karl. "Bivalvia of the Siluro-Devonian Arisaig Group, Nova Scotia." Yale, 1969.

6557
Harper, Charles Woods, Jr. "The Brachiopod Fauna of the Arisaig Series (Silurian-Lower Devonian) of Nova Scotia." California Institute of Technology, 1964.

6558
Railton, John Bryan. "Vegetational and Climatic History of Southwestern Nova Scotia in Relation to a South Mountain Ice Cap." Dalhousie, 1973.

The Prairie Provinces/Provinces des Prairies

General Item/Ouvrage général

Wickenden, Robert Thomas Daubigny. See No./Voir no 5375

Alberta

6559
Baxter, Sonny K. "Conodont Biostratigraphy of th[e] Mississippian of Western Alberta and Adjacen[t] British Columbia, Canada." Ohio State, 1972.

6560
Brideaux, Wayne Wilfred. "Palynology of the Lowe[r] Colorado Group (Later Lower Cretaceous) and I[ts] Lithological Equivalents in Central and West Central Alberta, Canada." McMaster, 1968.

6561
Chandrasekharam, A. "An Analysis of the Megafoss[il] Flora from the Genesee Locality, Alberta." Albe[r]ta, 1972.

6562
Christophel, David Charles. "An Investigation of th[e] Fossil Floras of the Smoky Tower Localit[y,] Alberta." Alberta, 1973.

6563
Germundsen, Robert Kenneth. "Stratigraphy an[d] Micropaleontology of Some Late Cretaceous Paleo[o]cene Continental Formations, Western Interio[r] North America." Missouri, 1965.

Harker, Peter. See No./Voir no 5411

6564
Howe, Robert Crombie. "Paleontology of the Mississ[i]ppian, Sunwapta Pass, Alberta." Wisconsin, 1965.

Landes, Robert W. See No./Voir no 5425

6565
Lillegraven, Jason Arthur. "The Latest Cretaceo[us] Mammals of the Upper Part of the Edmont[on] Formation of Alberta, Canada, and a Review of th[e] Marsupial-Placental Dichotomy in Mammalian Ev[o]lution." Kansas, 1968.

6566
Loranger, D.M.L. "Micropaleontology of the Midd[le] and Upper Devonian of Northeastern Albert[a,] Canada." London, 1963.

Pollock, C.A. See No./Voir no 5448

6567
Tozer, Edward Timothy. "Uppermost Cretaceous an[d] Paleocene Non-Marine Molluscan Faunas of Sout[h]western Alberta." Toronto, 1952.

6568
Uyeno, Thomas Tadashi. "Conodonts of the Waterwa[y] Formation (Upper Devonian) of Northeastern an[d] Central Alberta." Iowa, 1966.

Manitoba

6569
Caramanica, Frank Phillip. "Ordovician Corals of th[e] Williston Basin Porphyry." North Dakota, 1973.

McCammon, Helen Mary. See No./Voir no 5514

McNeil, David Harvey. See No./Voir no 5517

Nelson, Samuel J. See No./Voir no 5524

Saskatchewan

Brooke, Margaret Martha. See No./Voir no 5543

6570
Delorme, Larry Denis. "Pleistocene and Post-Pleist[o]cene Ostracoda of Saskatchewan." Saska[t]chewan, 1966.

571
Storer, John Edgar, III. "The Wood Mountain Fauna: An Upper Miocene Mammalian Assemblage from Southern Saskatchewan." Toronto, 1971.

Ontario

5572
Bickel, Edwin David. "Pleistocene Non-Marine Mollusca of the Gatineau Valley and Ottawa Areas of Quebec and Ontario, Canada." Ohio State, 1970.

5573
Brett, Carlton Elliott. "Systematics and Paleoecology of Late Silurian (Wenlockian) Pelmatozoan Echinoderms from Western New York and Ontario." Michigan, 1978.

Cameron, Barry Winston. See No./Voir no 5971

5574
Diffendal, Robert Francis, Jr. "The Biostratigraphy of the Delaware Limestone (Middle Devonian) of Southwestern Ontario." Nebraska, 1971.

Dyer, W.S. See No./Voir no 6009

5575
Eldredge, Robert Niles. "Geographic Variation and Evolution in Phacops Rana (Green, 1832) and Phacops iowensis (Delo, 1935) in the Middle Devonian of North America." Columbia, 1969.

Fagerstrom, John Alfred. See No./Voir no 6018

Fritz, Madeleine Alberta. See No./Voir no 6025

Johnson, Helgi. See No./Voir no 6083

Liberty, Bruce Arthur. See No./Voir no 6110

6576
Melik, James Charles. "The Hingement and Contact Margin Structure of Palaeocopid Ostracodes from Some Middle Devonian Formations of Michigan, Southwestern Ontario, and Western New York." Michigan, 1963.

Ramaekers, Paul Peter J. See No./Voir no 6184

6577
Schopf, Thomas J. M. "Conodonts of the Trenton Group (Ordovician) in New York, Southern Ontario, and Quebec." Ohio State, 1964.

6578
Screenivasa, Bangalore Annalyappa. "Paleoecological Studies of Sunfish Lake and Its Environs." Waterloo, 1973.

6579
Thusu, Bindraban. "Stratigraphy, Sedimentation and Micropaleontology (Ostracodes and Acritarchs) of the Rochester Formation (Middle Silurian) in Southern Ontario, Canada." Bristol, 1972.

Quebec/Québec

6580
Ahern, Kevin E. "Ecology and Biogeography of Llandovery Beyrichiid Ostracodes." California, Berkeley, 1978. [Jupiter Formation, Anticosti Island/Formation de Jupiter, Île d'Anticosti]

Bickel, Edwin David. See No./Voir no 6572

Duffield, Susan Linda. See No./Voir no 6318

Grayson, John F. See No./Voir no 6535

6581
Guilbault, Jean Pierre. "A Stratigraphic Approach to the Study of the Late-Glacial Champlain Sea Deposits with the Use of Foraminifera." Aarhus Universitel (Denmark), 1980.

Husain, Bilal R. See No./Voir no 6368

Ouellet, Marcel. See No./Voir no 6440

Schopf, Thomas J.M. See No./Voir no 6577

Short, Susan Kathleen. See No./Voir no 6536

GEOPHYSICS/GÉOPHYSIQUE

The first five Canadian doctorates in geophysics were earned in the 1950's. This number increased to 12 in the 1960's, and quadrupled in the 1970's. The first American doctorate in geophysics was granted during the 1940's. The output increased each decade, paralleling the Canadian output, but at a much slower pace. Among the 15 Canadian universities engaged in advanced studies in geophysics. Toronto and British Columbia rank number one and two in output. Columbia University and the University of Washington (Seattle), rate number one and two among American universities, but with far fewer titles to their credit. Only one dissertation from Great Britain is listed; it was produced at Cambridge in 1969.

C'est dans les années 1950 que les cinq premiers doctorats canadiens en géophysique ont été décernés. Ce nombre s'est accru jusqu'à douze dans les années 1960 et a quadruplé dans les années 1970. Aux États-Unis, le premier doctorat en géophysique a été octroyé dans les années 1940. De décade en décade, la production a augmenté, parallèlement à la production canadienne, mais à rythme beaucoup plus lent. Parmi les 15 universités canadiennes qui se sont lancées dans les études avancées en géophysique, l'Université de Toronto et celle de la Colombie-Britannique se classent aux premiers rangs. Aux États-Unis, les universités Columbia et de Washington (Seattle) occupent ces rangs même si elles détiennent un plus petit nombre d'études. On ne relève qu'une seule thèse provenant de la Grande-Bretagne; elle a été présentée à Cambridge en 1969.

GENERAL ITEMS/OUVRAGES GÉNÉRAUX

6582
Atkinson, Gerald. "A Theory of Polar Substorms." British Columbia, 1967.

6583
Bannister, J.R. "A Magnetometer Array Study of Polar Magnetic Substorms." Alberta, 1977.

6584
Chandra, Nellutla Naveena. "Microseisms in Canada." Alberta, 1970.

6585
Cumming, George L. "Correlation of Age Determination with Accurate Discontinuities in the Structure of North America." Toronto, 1955.

6586
Gurbuz, Mehmet Behic. "Structure of the Earth's Crust and Upper Mantle Under a Portion of Canadian Shield Deduced from Travel-Times and Spectral Amplitudes of Body Waves Using Data from Project Early Rise." Manitoba, 1970.

6587
Hajnal, Zoltan. "A Continuous Deep-Crustal Seismic Refraction and Near-Vertical Reflection Profile in the Canadian Shield Interpreted by Digital Processing Techniques." Manitoba, 1970.

6588
Hodgson, John Humphrey. "A Seismic Survey in the Canadian Shield." Toronto, 1951.

6589
Innes, Morris J.S. "Some Structural Features of the Precambrian Shield as Revealed by Gravity Anomolies." Toronto, 1952.

6590
Lee, Sheng-Shyong. "Secular Variation of the Intensity of the Geomagnetic Field During the Past 3000 Years in North, Central, and South America." Oklahoma, 1975.

6591
Lodha, Ganpat Singh. "Time Domain and Multi-frequency Electromagnetic Responses in Mineral Prospecting." Toronto, 1977. ⌈Canadian Shield/Bouclier canadien⌉

Milne, William G. See No./Voir no 4480

6592
Murthy, Gummulueu S.. "Paleomagnetic Studies in the Canadian Shield." Alberta, 1970.

6593
Neave, Kendal Gerard. "Icequake Seismology." Toronto, 1971. ⌈Athabaska Glacier/Glacier Athabaska⌉

6594
Reid, Alan Barry. "A Paleomagnetic Study at 1800 Million Years in Canada." Alberta, 1972.

6595
Reiter, Leon. "Rayleigh Wave Alternation in the 15 to 50 Second Period Range and Regional Models of the Intrinsic Attenuation of Shear Waves in the Crust and Uppermost Mantle of North America." Michigan, 1971. ⌈Eastern Canada Shield/Est du Bouclier canadien⌉

6596
Reynolds, Peter Herbert. "A Lead Isotope Study of Ores and Adjacent Rocks." British Columbia, 1968. ⌈Some from British Columbia/De la Colombie-Britannique⌉

6597
Rossiter, James R. "Interpretation of Radio Interferometry Depth Sounding, with Emphasis on Random Scattering from Temperate Glaciers and the Lunar Surface." Toronto, 1977. ⌈Alberta, Ontario and Northwest Territories/Alberta, Ontario et Territoires du Nord-Ouest⌉

6598
Sternberg, Ben Kollock. "Electrical Resistivity Structure of the Crust in the Southern Extension of the Canadian Shield." Wisconsin, 1977. ⌈Most. Wisconsin/Surtout au Wisconsin⌉

6599
Teskey, Dennis James. "Design of a Semi-automated Three-Dimensional Interpretation System for Potential Field Data." McGill, 1978. ⌈Kirkland Lake, Ontario, Bathurst, New Brunswick and the Atlantic Nickel Area, New Brunswick/Kirkland Lake, Ontario, Bathurst, Nouveau-Brunswick et région de Atlantic Nickel, Nouveau-Brunswick⌉

6600
Waddington, Edwin Donald. "Accurate Modelling of Glacier Flow." British Columbia, 1982.

6601
White, Antony. "Magnetic Variations in Canada and Scotland." Cambridge, 1969.

REGIONAL STUDIES/ÉTUDES RÉGIONALES

Eastern Canada/Est du Canada

6602
Cochrane, Norman Alton. "Geomagnetic and Geoelectric Variations in Atlantic Canada." Dalhousie 1973.

6603
Kurtz, Ronald Douglas. "A Magnetotelluric Investigation of Eastern Canada." Toronto, 1973.

6604
Sbar, Marc Lewis. "Contemporary Compressive Stress and Seismicity in Eastern North America: An Example of Intra-Plate Tectonics. Columbia, 1972.

6605
York, James Earl. "Seismotectonics in Intraplate and Interplate Regions: Eastern North America, Eastern Taiwan, China and the New Hebrides. Cornell, 1977.

Western Canada/Ouest du Canada

6606
Camfield, Paul Adrian. "Studies with a Two Dimensional Magnetometer Array in Northwestern United States and Southwestern Canada." Alberta 1973.

6607
Caner, Bernard. "Electrical Conductivity Structure in the Lower Crust and Upper Mantle in Western Canada." British Columbia, 1969.

6608
Dey-Sarkar, Samir Kumar. "Upper Mantle P-Wave Velocity Distributions Beneath Western Canada." Toronto, 1974.

6609
Sanderman, Llewellyn Arthur. "Part I. Radium Content of Some Inshore Bottom Samples in the Pacific Northwest. Part II. Radium Content of Ocean Bottom Sediments from the Arctic Ocean, Bering Sea, Alaska Peninsula and the Coasts of Southern Alaska and Western Canada." Washington, Seattle 1943.

Alberta

6610
Clowes, Ronald Martin. "Seismic Reflection Investigations of Crustal Structure in Southern Alberta." Alberta, 1970.

6611
Hjortenberg, Erik. "Microseisms in Alberta." Alberta, 1964.

6612
Nourry, Gerard Robert. "Interplanetary Magnetic Field, Solar Wind and Geomagnetic Micropulsation." British Columbia, 1976. ⌈Station at Ralston, Alberta/Station à Ralston, Alberta⌉

6613
Roxburgh, Kenneth Reid. "A Theory for the Generation of Intervals of Pulsations of Diminishing Period." British Columbia, 1970. ⌈Ralston, Alberta⌉

British Columbia/Colombie-Britannique

6614
Ager, Charles Arthur. "The Three Dimensional Structure of Batholiths as Deduced from Gravity Data." British Columbia, 1975.

6615
Au, Chong Ying Daniel. "Crustal Structure from an Ocean Bottom Seisometer Survey of the Nootka Fault Zone." British Columbia, 1981.

6616
Buddemeier, Robert Worth. "A Radiocarbon of Saanich Inlet, British Columbia." Washington, Seattle, 1969.

6617
Couch, Richard William. "Gravity and Structures of the Crust and Subcrust in the Northeast Pacific Ocean West of Washington and British Columbia." Oregon State, 1970.

6618
Culbert, Richard Revis. "A Study of Tectonic Processes and Certain Geochemical Abnormalities in the Coast Mountains of British Columbia." British Columbia, 1971.

6619
Davis, Earl Edwin. "The Northern Juan de Fuca Ridge: A Geophysical Investigation of an Active Sea Floor Spreading Center." Washington, Seattle, 1975.

6620
Dragert, Herbert. "Broad-Band Geomagnetic Depth-Sounding Along an Anomalous Profile in the Canadian Cordillera." British Columbia, 1973.

6621
Johnson, Stephen Hans. "Crustal Structures and Tectonism in Southeastern Alaska and Western British Columbia from Seismic Refraction, Seismic Reflection, Gravity, Magnetic and Microearthquake Measurements." Oregon State, 1972.

6622
Kniže, Stanislaw. "Marine Deep Seismic Sounding off the Coast of British Columbia." British Columbia, 1976.

6623
Miller, Hugh Gordon. "An Analysis of Geomagnetic Variations in Western British Columbia." British Columbia, 1973.

6624
Nienber, Wilfred. "A Laboratory Analogue Model and Field Station Study of Electromagnetic Induction for an Island Situated near a Continent." Victoria, 1978. [Vancouver Island region/Région de l'Île de Vancouver]

6625
Pearson, William Chelsie. "A Gravity Study of the Juan de Fuca Ridge and Sovanco Fracture Zone in the Northeast Pacific Ocean." Washington, Seattle, 1975.

6626
Rogers, Garry Colin. "Seismotectonics of British Columbia." British Columbia, 1983.

6627
Tiffin, Donald Lloyd. "Continuous Seismic Reflection Profiling in the Strait of Georgia, British Columbia." British Columbia, 1970.

6628
White, William Robert Hugh. "The Structure of the Earth's Crust in the Vicinity of Vancouver Island as Ascertained by Seismic and Gravity Observations." British Columbia, 1963.

Manitoba

Hunter, James A.M. See No./Voir no 6654
Ozard, John Malcolm. See No./Voir no 6660

Maritime Provinces/Provinces maritimes

General Item/Ouvrage général

6629
Garland, George D. "The Relationship Between Gravity and Magnetic Anomalies, as Illustrated by Observations Made in the Maritime Provinces and Ontario, Canada." St. Louis University Institute of Technology, 1951.

New Brunswick/Nouveau-Brunswick

Gupta, Vinod Kumar. See No./Voir no 1750

Newfoundland and Labrador/Terre-Neuve et Labrador

Bottomley, Richard John. See No./Voir no 6649
6630
Kirschvink, Joseph Lynn. "I. A Paleomagnetic Approach to the Precambrian-Cambrian Boundary Problem. II. Biogenic Magnetite: Its Role in the Magnetization of Sediments and as the Basis of Magnetic Field Detection in Animals." Princeton, 1979.

6631
Kristofferson, Yngve. "Labrador Sea: A Geophysical Study." Columbia, 1977.

6632
Mayhew, Michael Allen. "Marine Geophysical Measurements in the Labrador Sea: Relations to Precambrian Geology and Sea-Floor Spreading." Columbia, 1969.

6633
Salisbury, Matthew Harold. "Investigation of Seismic Velocities in the Bay of Islands, Newfoundland Ophiolite Complex for Comparison with Oceanic Seismic Structure." Washington, Seattle, 1974.

Northwest Territories and Yukon/ Territoires du Nord-Ouest et Yukon

6634
Ahern, Timothy Keith. "The Development of a Completely Automated Oxygen Isotope Mass Spectrometer." British Columbia, 1980. ⌈Samples taken from the Steele Glacier, Yukon Territory/Échantillons pris du Glacier Steele, Territoire du Yukon⌉

6635
Argenal, Roger. "Covariance Structure of Aeromagnetic Data from Slave Lake and Churchill Structural Provinces, Canada." Texas, 1975.

6636
Berkhout, Aart W. J. "Gravity in the Prince of Wales, Somerset and Northern Baffin Islands Region, District of Franklin, Northwest Territories." Queen's, 1968.

6637
Chagarlamudi, Pakiraiah. "Mapping Rock Outcrops from Landsat Digital Data." Manitoba, 1980. ⌈Coppermine area/Région de Coppermine⌉

6638
Dewart, Gilbert. "Seismic Investigation of Ice Properties and Bedrock Topography at the Confluence of Two Glaciers, Kashawulsh Glacier, Yukon Territory, Canada." Ohio State, 1968.

6639
Jackson, Charles Ian. "The Meteorology of Lake Hazen, Ellesmere Island, N.W.T. Based on Observations Made During the International Geophysical Year 1957-58." McGill, 1961.

Koziar, Andrew. See No./Voir no 6656

6640
Kristjansson, Leo Geir. "A Magnetic Study of Tertiary Igneous Rocks from Greenland, Baffin Island and Iceland." Memorial University of Newfoundland, 1973.

6641
Landry, Burnelle S. "Numerical Simulation of Geophysical Heat Transfer in Permafrost Areas." Houston, 1973.

6642
Lougheed, Milford Seymour. "Radioactivity of the Rocks at Fort Radium, Great Bear Lake, Northwest Territories." Princeton, 1953.

6643
Narod, Brian Barry. "Ultrahigh Frequency Radio Echo Sounding of Yukon Glaciers." British Columbia, 1979.

6644
Olhoeft, Gary Roy. "The Electrical Properties of Permafrost." Toronto, 1975. ⌈Tuktoyaktuk, Northwest Territories/Tuktoyaktuk, Territoires du Nord-Ouest⌉

6645
Rabinowitz, Philip David. "The Continental Margin of the Northwest Atlantic Ocean: A Geophysical Study." Columbia, 1973.

6646
Ram, Avadh. "The Identification and Interpretation Upper Mantle Travel Time Branches from Slowne Measurements Made in Data Recorded at the Ga ribidanaur (India) and Yellowknife (Canada) Seism Arrays." Western Ontario, 1976.

6647
Tsong, Chin Fong. "Studies of Uranium-Lead System tics by Volatilization and the Evolution of t Yellowknife Area, Northwest Territories Alberta, 1974.

Waddington, Edwin Donald. See No./Voir no 6600

Ontario

6648
Allis, Richard George. "Constraints on Crustal Stru ture from Heat Flow Measurements in Lakes Northwest Ontario." Toronto, 1977.

6649
Bottomley, Richard John. "40Ar-39Ar Dating of Me Rock from Impact Craters." Toronto, 198 ⌈Wanapitei⌉

6650
Buchan, Kenneth Lorne. "Paleomagnetic and Ro Magnetic Studies of Multicomponent Remanenc in Metamorphosed Rocks of the Grenville Provin of the Canadian Precambrian Shield Toronto, 1977.

6651
Campbell, Bruce Samuel. "Geology and Electrical a Electromagnetic Modeling of Volcanogenic Sulfi Bodies near Savant Lake, Ontario." Pennsylvan State, 1980.

6652
Coles, Richard Leslie. "Relationships Betwe Measured Rock Magnetizations and Interpretatio of Longer Wavelength Anomalies in the Superi Province of the Canadian Shield." Manitoba, 1973

Garland, George D. See No./Voir no 6629

6653
Hamza, Valiya Mannathal. "Vertical Distribution Radioactive Heat Production in the Grenville Ge logical Province and the Sedimentary Sectio Overlying It." Western Ontario, 1973.

6654
Hunter, James Alexander M. "Crustal Seismic Studi in Northern Ontario and Manitoba from Proje Early Rise Data." Western Ontario, 1971.

6655
Judge, Alan Stephen. "Geothermal Measurements in Sedimentary Basin." Western Ontario, 197 ⌈Southern Ontario/Sud de l'Ontario⌉

6656
Koziar, Andrew. "Applications of Audio Frequen Magnetotellurics to Permafrost, Crustal Soundin and Mineral Exploration." Toronto, 1976. ⌈3 site Cavendish, the Geotraverse and Tuktoyuktuk/Tr emplacements: Cavendish, Geotraverse Tuktoyuktuk⌉

6657
Langley, Richard Brian. "Precision Geodesy a Astrometry with a Three Station Long Baseli Interferometer." York, 1979.

Morley, Lawrence Whitaker. See No./Voir no 6138

6658
Mwenifumbo, Campbell Jonathan. "Interpretation of Mise-à-la-masse Data for Vein Type Bodies." Western Ontario, 1980. ⌈Cavendish Geophysical Test Site/Site d'essai géophysique à Cavendish⌉

6659
Nozdryn-Plotnicki, Michael John. "On the Short-Term Forecasting of Spring Floods in Real Time." Queen's, 1980. ⌈Grand and Rideau Rivers/Rivières Grand et Rideau⌉

Oldham, Charles H. G. See No./Voir no 5298

6660
Ozard, John Malcolm. "Solid Source Lead Isotope Studies with Application to Rock Samples from the Superior Geological Province." British Columbia, 1970. ⌈Vogt-Hobbs area/Région de Vogt-Hobbs⌉

6661
Pearce, Andrew John. "Mass and Energy Flux in Physical Denudation, Defoliated Areas, Sudbury." McGill, 1973.

Pesonen, Lauri J. See No./Voir no 6166

Purdy, John Winston. See No./Voir no 6179

6662
Wright, Jeffrey. "Seismic Crustal Studies in North-Western Ontario." Toronto, 1977.

6663
Young, Roger Adams. "Seismic Crustal Structure Northwest of Thunder Bay, Ontario." Toronto, 1980.

Quebec/Québec

6664
Evernden, J.F. "Direction of Approach of Rayleigh Waves and Related Phenomena." California, Berkeley, 1951.

6665
Gentile, Francesco. "Nature et origine de la minéralisation cupro-zincifère de la formation des schistes de Weedon, Québec." Montréal, 1973.

6666
Haslam, Christopher R. S. "Magnetotellurics in the Eastern Townships of Quebec." McGill, 1974.

6667
Lewis, Trevor John. "A Geothermal Survey at Lake Dufault, Québec." Western Ontario, 1975.

6668
Linton, John Alexander. "Gravity Meter Development and Use in a Search for Core Made Oscillations." York, 1977.

6669
Richard, Pierre. "La méthode d'addition symbolique et la définition de la structure cristalline de l'ékinite de Saint-Hilaire, P.Q." Montréal, 1971.

Saskatchewan

6670
Dent, Brian Edward. "Studies of Large Impact Craters." Stanford, 1974. ⌈Deep Bay⌉

Dyck, John Henry. See No./Voir no 4582

Arctic/Arctique

6671
Hall, John Kendrick. "Arctic Ocean Geophysical Studies: The Alpha Ridge and Mendeleyev Ridge." Columbia, 1970.

6672
Hunkins, Kenneth Leland. "Elastic Wave Studies in the Arctic Ocean." Stanford, 1960.

6673
Ostenso, Ned Allen. "Geophysical Investigations of the Arctic Ocean Basin." Wisconsin, 1962.

Great Lakes/Grands Lacs

6674
Anzoleaga, Rodolfo. "Crustal Structure in Western Lake Superior from the Integration of Seismic and Gravity Data." Wisconsin, 1971.

6675
Baba, Nobuyoshi. "A Numerical Investigation of Lake Ontario: Dynamics and Thermodynamics." Princeton, 1974.

6676
Berry, Michael John. "Some Interpretation Techniques in Crustal Seismology with Application to the Lake Superior Experiment." Toronto, 1965.

6677
Chandler, Val William. "Correlation of Gravity and Magnetic Data Over the Great Lakes Region, North America." Purdue, 1977.

6678
Kite, Geoffrey W. "Crustal Movement Among the Great Lakes." Ottawa, 1973.

6679
Morgan, Nabil Assad. "Geophysical Studies in Lake Erie by Shallow Marine Seismic Methods." Toronto, 1964.

6680
O'Hara, Norbert W. "An Aeromagnetic Survey and Geophysical Interpretation of the Precambrian Framework and Tectonic Structure of the Eastern Lake Superior Region." Michigan State, 1967.

6681
Wall, Robert E. "Geophysical Investigation in the Central Basin of Lake Erie." Columbia, 1965.

See also Oceanography/Voir aussi Océanographie

HEALTH SCIENCES/ SCIENCES DE LA SANTÉ

The health sciences include, public health services and care, health science, health education, mental health, alcoholism, drugs, diet and nutrition, hospital administration, economics and services, doctors and medicine, medical education, medical science and research, veterinary science, dentists and dentistry, pharmacy and pharmacists, and nursing, nursing

education, the profession of nursing, and science of nursing. These subjects became popular as a field for advanced research in Canada in the 1970's and 1980's. The last four years have produced almost as many dissertations as the entire 1970's. Prior to 1970, only one study in 1934, three in the 1950's, and four in the 1960's, had been done in Canada. Compare those figures with over 100 in the 1970's. The University of Toronto has produced three times as many dissertations in this field as McGill University and the University of Alberta, which ranks second in output. The Universities of British Columbia, Montreal, and Ottawa are third, fourth, and fifth respectively. The American output is considerably less than the Canadian output. Almost half of this total appeared in the 1970's. Of the 35 universities producing dissertations in this area, Columbia University produced the most (14), with the remaining 34 universities ranging in output from four to one. Eight universities in Britain produced a total of 13 studies, five from the University of London.

————

Les sciences de la santé couvrent les services et les soins de santé publique, les sciences de la santé, l'enseignement portant sur le nursing (santé), la santé mentale, l'alcoolisme, les narcotiques, l'alimentation et la nutrition, les hôpitaux (administration, rentabilité et services), les médecins et la médecine, l'enseignement médical, la science et la recherche médicales, la science vétérinaire, les dentistes et l'art dentaire, la pharmacie et les pharmaciens, le nursing, la formation des infirmières, la profession infirmière et les sciences infirmières. Les sciences de la santé ont fait l'objet de recherche avancée au Canada dans les années 1970 et 1980. Au cours des quatre dernières années, on a compté presque autant de thèses que dans l'ensemble des années 1970. Avant cette date, on n'avait eu au Canada qu'une étude en 1934, trois dans les années 1950 et quatre entre 1960 et 1970. Il est intéressant de comparer ces chiffres avec les 100 thèses et plus des années 1970. L'Université de Toronto a produit trois fois autant de thèses en ce domaine que les universités McGill et de l'Alberta, qui viennent au second rang; les universités de la Colombie-Britannique, de Montréal et d'Ottawa sont respectivement au troisième, quatrième et cinquième rang. La production américaine est moins importante que celle du Canada; presque la moitié de ce total date des années 1970. Des 35 universités qui ont produit des thèses en ce domaine, c'est l'Université Columbia qui peut se prévaloir du plus grand nombre (14); les 34 autres ont des productions variant de quatre thèses à une seule. Huit universités de Grande-Bretagne ont produit un total de 13 études, dont cinq à l'Université de Londres.

PUBLIC HEALTH SERVICES AND CARE/ SERVICES OU SOINS DE SANTÉ PUBLIQUE

General Items/Ouvrages généraux

Blake, E.A. See No./Voir no 585
6682
Champagne, François. "L'évolution de la raison d'être d'un centre hospitalier." Montréal, 1983.
6683
Duxbury, Linda Elizabeth. "The Effects of Community Characteristics and Health Services on Indian Health and Use of Health Care Facilities." Waterloo, 1983.
Ross, Hazel Miriam. See No./Voir no 369

National/Niveau national

6684
Jackson, Suzanne Fraser. "Planning for Health in a Changing Society: A Study of the Relationship Between a Changing Social Paradigm, Turbulence, Non-Conventional Health Care Practices and Planning." Waterloo, 1981.
6685
King, Floris Ethia. "Historical Study of the Voluntary Tuberculosis Community Health Program in Canada with Projective Emphasis." North Carolina, 1967.
McGinnis, J.P.D. See No./Voir no 7149
6686
Owen, Thomas Howard. "Toward Post-Industrial Policy-Making and Administration: Transformation in Canadian Health Care." Syracuse, 1977.
6687
Sherman, Gregory John. "Canadian Cancer Incidence: Completeness, Correlation and Ecological Association in Selected Sites, 1969-1973." Toronto, 1981.
6688
Weiss, David Maurice. "Chronic Illness and Health Services Use: A Before-After Study of Canadian National Health Insurance." Pittsburgh, 1976.

Provincial/Niveau provincial

Loyer, Marie des Anges. See No./Voir no 6879
6689
Warner, M.M. "Community Participation in Primary Health Care Delivery in the United Kingdom and Canada." Wales, Swansea, 1978.

British Columbia/Colombie-Britannique

6690
Arlett, Christine. "A Comparative Evaluation of an Infant Stimulation Program for Public Health Utilization." British Columbia, 1977.

Northwest Territories/Territoires du Nord-Ouest

Wahn, Michael Brian. See No./Voir no 1194

Ontario

Bator, Paul Adolphus. See No./Voir no 7222

6691
Browne, Joseph A. "Health Professionals' Participation at Hospital Ward Meetings and the Effect of that Participation on Patient Care Plans." Toronto, 1977.

6692
Browne, Regina Maria. "Patient and Professional Interaction and Its Relationship to Patient's Health Status and Frequent Use of Health Services." Toronto, 1977.

6693
Hall, George Brent. "A Causal Model of Individual Responses to Community Health Care." McMaster, 1980.

6694
Lindsay-Reid, Elizabeth Ann. "Readiness and Modifying Factors in Exercise Adoption." Toronto, 1979. [124 firefighters/124 pompiers]

6695
MacDougall, Heather Anne. " 'Health is Wealth': The Development of Public Health Activity in Toronto, 1834-1890." Toronto, 1982.

6696
Rosenberg, Mark Warren. "The Location of Public Facilities with Special Reference to Community Health Centres in Metropolitan Toronto, 1951 to 1971." London, 1980.

6697
Sharma, Ram Karan. "Benefit Cost Analysis and Public Health: A Case Study of the Tuberculosis Control Program in Ontario, 1948-1966." Western Ontario, 1973.

6698
Smith, Richard David. "Social Class and Health Behaviour." Toronto, 1980.

6699
Weir, Robin Elizabeth. "Treatment and Outcome as a Function of Staff-Patient Interaction." Toronto, 1978. [Rheumatoid arthritis patients in a rehabilitation setting/Patients atteints de poly-arthrite chronique dans un cadre de réhabilitation]

Quebec/Québec

6700
Desaulniers, Gilles. "Application de la fluorescence X indentée par des protons au dépistage de l'amiante dans l'eau de rivière: étude de la rivière Bécancour." Montréal, 1983.

6701
Fortin, Fabienne. "Validation empirique d'une mesure de fonctionnement social." McGill, 1979.

6702
Renaud, Marc. "The Political Economy of the Quebec State Interventions in Health: Reform or Revolution." Wisconsin, 1976.

6703
Rochon, Jean A. "The Development of a Model for the Delivery of Health Services in the Province of Quebec." Harvard, 1973.

6704
Rodwin, Victor George. "Health Planning and Implementation: France, Quebec and England." California, Berkeley, 1980.

6705
Siemiatycki, Jack Aaron. "Evaluation of Strategies for Household Health Surveys." McGill, 1976. [Montreal/Montréal]

6706
Willems, Jane Sisk. "Institutional Methods of Delivering Health Care: Comparative Costs." McGill, 1976.

Saskatchewan

6707
Beck, Robert Glen. "An Analysis of the Demand for Health Care in Saskatchewan." Alberta, 1971.

Boudreau, Françoise. See No./Voir no 6758

Hardie, Nena Elizabeth. See No./Voir no 6777

Johnston, Elizabeth Macleod. See No./Voir no 6801

Kaplan, Faith Kindler. See No./Voir no 3095

Liberakis, Eustace Anastaseos. See No./Voir no 6803

Linn, Hilareon Dewell. See No./Voir no 4745

6708
Philippon, D.J. "Monetary Returns to Non-University Health Personnel Training in Saskatchewan." Alberta, 1979.

HEALTH SCIENCE/SCIENCES DE LA SANTÉ

6709
Aubry, Francine. "Prevalence Study of Respiratory Effects Associated with Long-Term Exposure to Community Air Pollution in Three Greater Montreal Populations." McGill, 1977.

6710
Aucoin, Peter C. "Health Scientists and the Making of Health Science Policy in Canada." Queen's, 1973.

Baldwin, John Stiles. See No./Voir no 6828

6711
Battista, Renaldo N. "Adult Cancer Prevention in Primary Care: The Quebec Study." Harvard, 1982.

6712
Baumgart, A.J. "Compliance with Drug Therapy Among Hypertensive Patients: A Test of the Health Belief Model." Toronto, 1983.

Dart, Richard James. See No./Voir no 6832

Evers, Susan Eleanor. See No./Voir no 459

6713
French, Susan Elizabeth. "Negotiations in Patient and Health Professional Interactions." Toronto, 1981.

6714
Gauthier, P.A. "Hemodynamic Effects of Exercise and Training in Angina Patients." Alberta, 1978.

6715
Gibson, Rosalind Susan. "Use of Hair as a Biopsy Material for the Assessment of Trace Metal Status in Canadian Low Birthweight Infants." London, 1979.

Hanley, James A. See No./Voir no 3311

Higgins, Christopher Alan. See No./Voir no 1152

6716
Hovanec, Margret. "The Experience of Rheumatoid Arthritis." Toronto, 1981.

6717

Kurland, Leonard T. "The Frequency and Geographic Distribution of Multiple Sclerosis as Indicated by Mortality Statistics and Morbidity Surveys in the United States and Canada." Johns Hopkins, 1951.

6718

MacKinnon, Joyce Roberta. "An Empirical Investigation of Dyadic Verbal Interaction in the Chronic Paediatric Health Case Delivery Systems." British Columbia, 1980.

6719

Mitchell, Donna Lianne Marie. "Learned Helplessness and Patient Education." Toronto, 1979.

6720

Niskala, Helena. "Learning Needs of Persons in Home Hemodialysis." British Columbia, 1976.

6721

Parkos, William George. "Productivity Studies of Lakes Superior, Michigan, Huron and Erie Utilizing the Carbon-IY Technique." Minnesota, 1969.

6722

Pederson, Linda Lue. "Compliance with Physician Advice to Quit Smoking Among Patients with Pulmonary Disease." Western Ontario, 1980. [London and/et Hamilton, Ontario]

6723

Phillipson-Price, Adrienne. "Expectancy and the Experience of Childbirth: The Effect of the Relationship on Postpartum Affect." McGill, 1982.

6724

Pye, Carol Jean. "Post Partum Depression: A Multivariate Prospective Study of Normal Primiparous Women." Queen's, 1981.

6725

Ramsay, Janice Ann. "Sample Selection Bias in Investigations of Medical Treatment Noncompliance." Manitoba, 1981.

6726

Ratner, Dennis P. "The Effects of Hemodialysis on the Cognitive and Sensory Motor Functioning of the Adult Hemodialysis Patient." Windsor, 1979.

6727

Sidney, Kenneth Harry. "Response of Elderly Subjects to a Program of Progressive Exercise Training." Toronto, 1975.

6728

Turner, Lorne Craig. "Effects of a Behavioral Self-Control Package on Drug Prescription Compliance Behavior of Chronic Arthritic Patients." Manitoba, 1981.

6729

West, Roy. "Juvenile-Onset Diabetes in Montreal." McGill, 1979.

HEALTH EDUCATION/ENSEIGNEMENT PORTANT SUR LE NURSING (SANTÉ)

Andrews, Michael Bruce Barrington. See No./Voir no 3720

6730

Cahoon, Margaret Cecilia. "The Development of Empirical Guiding Principles and Criteria for School Health Programs in Canada." Michigan, 1967.

6731

Cox, Michael Howard. "The Influence of an Employ Fitness Program upon Job Performance, Absente ism and Productivity." Toronto, 1982.

6732

Gerrard, Brian Alexander. "The Outcomes of Comprehensive Interpersonal Skills Training Pr gramme for Health Professionals." Toronto, 1982

6733

Goldring, Leslie Warren. "Effect of Tonsillar Defec upon the Attendance, Intelligence and Progress School Children." Toronto, 1939.

Pépin, Jean-Guy. See No./Voir no 3314

Peszat, Lucille Catharine. See No./Voir no 3721

Pickard, Lynette Elizabeth. See No./Voir no 1948

6734

Scott, Anne. "Implementing Performance Chang Among Health Care Professionals." Briti Columbia, 1980.

6735

Sullivan, P.L. "Primary Health Education Duri Pregnancy: A Programmed Approach." Albert 1976.

6736

Van Der Merwe, Marina Suzanne. "The Relationsh Between Physical Fitness and the Health Status Selected Canadian College Women." Ohio Stat 1981.

ALCOHOLISM/ALCOOLISME

Cormier, Roger Bernard. See No./Voir no 9252

6737

Ferrier, William K. "Programs for Alcohol Educati in the United States and Canada." Oregon Stat 1953.

6738

Goulet, Robert John. "State Dependent Learning: T Effects of Alcohol on Learning and Recall Information about Alcohol Abuse and Its Cons quences Among Light and Heavy Social Drinkers Manitoba, 1979.

McKittrick, Edith Patricia. See No./Voir no 3343

DRUGS/NARCOTIQUES

Bowman, Marilyn Laura. See No./Voir no 8966

Box, Colin Edward. See No./Voir no 3294

6739

Brown, William Cecil. "Psycho-Educational Evaluati of Drug Education Programming." Alberta, 1977.

6740

Keown, Lauriston Livingston. "Family Decisions a Drug Use." Alberta, 1977.

Lapp, Janet E. See No./Voir no 8923

6741

Mandelzys, Nathan. "Relapse to Narcotic Addictic The Role of Methadone in Modifying Condition Abstinence Symptoms in Humans." Ottawa, 1978.

6742

Paré, Eileen Mercedes. "Morphine Levels in Bra Tissue of Heroin Addicts." Windsor, 1982.

743
Reid, Normand. "Dépendance psychologique au regard de la dépendance aux drogues." Montréal, 1978.

Pevack, Michael G. See No./Voir no 3286

744
Sykes, Susan E. "Tolerance and Physical Dependence in Morphine Addiction." Waterloo, 1977.

VENEREAL DISEASE/MALADIE VÉNÉRIENNE

Anderson, Donald O. See No./Voir no 6922

DIET AND NUTRITION/ ALIMENTATION ET NUTRITION

745
Archibald, Juanita Helen. "A Nutrition Education Programme in Cape Sable Island." Columbia, 1952. [Off Nova Scotia/Au large de la Nouvelle-Écosse]

746
Atkinson, Stephanie Ann. "Human Milk Feeding of Premature Infants Less Than 1.3 Kg Birthweight: Milk Analysis and Clinical Studies During Early Postnatal Life." Toronto, 1980.

747
Bowring, James R. "Economic Problems of an Adequate Diet in Canada." Iowa State, 1946.

Caron, Liliane. See No./Voir no 4016

748
Feniak, Mary Elizabeth. "A Dietary Study of a Group of Rural Manitoba Families." Minnesota, 1966.

749
Gougeon, Réjeanne. "Effets métaboliques de diètes hypocaloriques chez l'obèse." Montréal, 1979.

Johnston, Elizabeth Macleod. See No./Voir no 6801

750
Johnston, Janice Louise. "The Effects of Tyrosine Supplements on Catecholamine Metabolism, Certain Endocrine Functions, Protein Metabolism, and Sodium Homeostasis in Normal Weight and Obese Women." Toronto, 1983.

751
Leprohon, Carol Elizabeth. "The Effect of Maternal Diet on Weanling Serotonin Metabolism and Protein Feeding Behavior." Toronto, 1981.

752
MacArthur, A. Isabel. "Factors Associated with the Satisfactions of Dieticians in Canada - What Implications for Recruitment?" Teachers College, Columbia, 1952.

Muller, Thomas Edward. See No./Voir no 2231

753
Reed, Debra J. "Weight Loss During Hypocaloric Carbohydrate Restriction and Refeeding in Obese Adults." Montréal, 1983.

754
Sullivan, Ann Dolores. "Diet and Cardiovascular Disease: Interrelationships Among Nutrition Attitudes, Knowledge, Practice and Biodemographic Characteristics of Adult Members of Community Centres." British Columbia, 1980.

6755
Woolcott, Donna Myles. "A Study of Nutrition Knowledge and Preventive Nutrition Behaviour and Their Psychosocial Correlates in a Group of Men." Guelph, 1979.

6756
Zlotkin, Stanley Howard. "Cysteine Metabolism in Premature Infants." Toronto, 1981.

MENTAL HEALTH/SANTÉ MENTALE

Bate Buerup, J.L.D. See No./Voir no 8952

6757
Bontrager-Lehman, Carol. "The Sex-Roles and Life Styles of Married Women in Relation to Mental Health Indices of the California Psychological Inventory (CPI)." Ottawa, 1980.

6758
Boudreau, Françoise. "Changes in the System for the Distribution of Psychiatric Care in Quebec, 1964-1974." Toronto, 1978.

6759
D'Arcy, Kenneth C.R. "Change and Consequence in a Mental Health System: Theoretical and Empirical Chapters in a Sociology of Mental Illness." Toronto, 1976. [Examines changing psychiatric care system of the Province of Saskatchewan for the last 75 years/Étude du système de soin psychiatrique en Saskatchewan pendant les 75 dernières années]

6760
Desroches, Frederick John. "Mental Illness in the Family: The Decision to Enter the Mental Hospital." Waterloo, 1980.

6761
Earle, Richard C.B. "The Professional Mental Patient." Toronto, 1973.

Hall, George Brent. See No./Voir no 6693

Hardie, Nena Elizabeth. See No./Voir no 6777

Jamal, Muhammad. See No./Voir no 2073

6762
Lavi-Levin, Hannah. "Individual Autonomy, Social Needs and Societal Processes: The Case of the Mentally Ill." Toronto, 1982.

Lowe, Graham Stanley. See No./Voir no 1278

6763
Needham, Merrill Arthur, Jr. "Social Integration and Mental Illness in New Brunswick." Tufts, 1975.

6764
Nelson, Ernest. "Intrinsic Religion and Mental Health: An Empirical Investigation." Ottawa, 1981.

Nichol, Diane Sue. See No./Voir no 8927

6765
Nogradi, George Steve. "An Analysis of Existing Relationships Between the Administrative Processes and Organizational Commitment, and Job Involvement of Recreational Staff Members Within Mental Health Centers Across Canada." Oregon, 1977.

6766
Pollock, Sheila Joy. "Social Policy for Mental Health in Ontario 1939-1967." Toronto, 1974.

6767
Ramsay, Richard Lyon. "A Proposed Guide for the Recreation Program for Mentally Ill Patients in the Mental Health Services of British Columbia." Teachers College, Columbia, 1962.

Riediger, Alfred J. See No./Voir no 2193

6768
Savaria, Richard. "L'influence du support social sur la santé mentale de la personne agée." Montréal, 1982.

Schultz, Lynda Kay. See No./Voir no 9470

Schwartz, Michael. See No./Voir no 9100

Stalwick, H.N. See No./Voir no 7102

HOSPITALS: ADMINISTRATION, ECONOMICS AND SERVICES/HÔPITAUX: ADMINISTRATION, RENTABILITÉ ET SERVICES

Albert, Edward Henry. See No./Voir no 6787

6769
Anderson, David L. "Public Sector Output Measurement in the Hospital Clinical Laboratory." Queen's, 1976.

6770
Barer, Morris Lionel. "A Methodology for Derivation of Marginal Costs of Hospital Cases, and Application to Estimation of Cost Savings from Community Health Centres." British Columbia, 1977.

Bloch, Maurice. See No./Voir no 9116

Bradley, Christine Felecia. See No./Voir no 8967

6771
Craig, Ronald George. "A Descriptive Model of the Emergency Care System as It Affects Use Choice." Waterloo, 1979. ⌈Kitchener-Waterloo area/Région de Kitchener-Waterloo⌉

Cudmore, James Sedley. See No./Voir no 1622

Davis, Teresa Mina Anne. See No./Voir no 9123

Desroches, Frederick John. See No./Voir no 6760

6772
Dixon, Charles Linus. "Problems in Role Negotiation and Decision Making in a Psychiatric Team." Toronto, 1981. ⌈Psychiatric hospital/Hôpital psychiatrique⌉

6773
Eakins-Hoffmann, Joan Margaret. "Democratization of the Boards of Directors of Anglophone Hospitals in Quebec." McGill, 1980.

Earle, Richard C.B. See No./Voir no 6761

6774
Evans, George Dewey. "The Hospital Administrator: Role Making, Organizational Structure and Administrative Processes." Alberta, 1974.

6775
Fuchs, Donald Michael. "Determinants of the Use of a Teenage Clinic in a Metropolitan Hospital." Toronto, 1980. [Toronto hospital/Hôpital à Toronto]

Gosselin, Roger. See No./Voir no 6798

6776
Grainger, Robert Neil. "Major Common Spatial Patterns of Diagnostic Specific Hospital Utilization in Ontario, 1970-72." Waterloo, 1980.

6777
Hardie, Nena E. "The Measurement and Meaning Patient Involvement in the Treatment Goals of Provincial Hospital: An Historical and Empiri Study." York, 1975.

6778
Hochstein, Alan Peter. "The Reallocation of Lc Stay Hospital Patients: The Impact on Hea Cost." McGill, 1979.

Horne, John MacGregor. See No./Voir no 1628

6779
Jenkins, Alexander William. "A Policy Orient Analysis of Hospital Costs." Western Ontar 1977.

6780
Kirudja, Charles Mugambi. "Planning and Resour Allocation with Goal Programming in a Structur Management Decision Environment: The Case an Ontario General Hospital." Western Ontar 1978.

6781
Kushner, Joseph. "Economics of Scale in the Gene Hospital Industry." Western Ontario, 1969.

Larkin, Jill. See No./Voir no 9026

Liberakis, Eustace Anastasios. See No./Voir no 6803

Lindenfield, Rita Graham. See No./Voir no 1629

6782
Lundman, Susan Brenda. "An Economic Investigati of the Quality of Hospital Care in British Colu bia." British Columbia, 1982.

Manga, Pranlal. See No./Voir no 1630

6783
McGill, Mary Elizabeth. "Observation of Communic tion Behavior: The Development of a Resear Method for Use in Health Care Organization British Columbia, 1976. ⌈Hospitals in southe Saskatchewan/Hôpitaux du sud de la Saska chewan⌉

Niskala, Helena. See No./Voir no 6720

6784
Peitchinis, Jacquelyn A. "A Study of the Effecti ness of Communication Between Hospital Staff a Patients." Calgary, 1972.

Pickard, Lynette Elizabeth. See No./Voir no 1948

Ponak, Allen M. See No./Voir no 6918

Sethi, A.S. See No./Voir no 2141

Shulof, Victoria. See No./Voir no 9185

Spekkens, André. See No./Voir no 1633

6785
Stanley, Thomas Brock. "A Cost-Benefit Model Evaluating Tradeoffs Between Centralization a Decentralization in the Decision to Expa Existing Hospital Facilities." Waterloo, 19 ⌈Ontario⌉

Strilaef, Florence. See No./Voir no 6920

Taylor, I.D.S. See No./Voir no 4566

Taylor, Malcolm G. See No./Voir no 1634

6786
Torrance, George Murray. "The Underside of Hospital: Recruitment and the Meaning of W Among Non-Professional Hospital Worker Toronto, 1978.

Whitaker, Roy Alexander. See No./Voir no 4627, 693

Willems, Jane Sisk. See No./Voir no 6706

6787
Albert, Edward Henry. "The Language of Discovery and Presentation of Illness and Injury by Emergency Room Clients." York, 1978. [Ontario]

6788
Andrews, Margaret R.W. "Medical Services in Vancouver, 1886-1920: A Study in the Interplay of Attitudes, Medical Knowledge, and Administrative Structures." British Columbia, 1979.

Baudry, Jeannine. See No./Voir no 6912

Boudreau, Françoise. See No./Voir no 6758

6789
Chambers, Larry William. "Evaluation of Family Practice Nurse Deployment in Urban Medical Practice in Newfoundland." Memorial University of Newfoundland, 1978.

6790
Cheung, Young-Mo. "An Economic Analysis of Physician's Earnings - A Case Study of Alberta." Case Western Reserve, 1976.

6791
Cheung, Yuet Wah. "The Social Organization of Missionary Medicine: A Study of Two Canadian Protestant Missions in China Before 1937." Toronto, 1982.

6792
Contandriopoulos, André-Pierre. "Un modèle de comportement des médecins en tant que producteurs de services." Montréal, 1977.

Cudmore, James Sedley. See No./Voir no 1622

6793
Daggett, Christopher Jarvis. "A Study to Determine the Role of Attending Physicians in the Clinical Training of Medical Students and Resident Physicians." Massachusetts, 1977. [Montreal Children's Hospital/Hôpital pour enfants de Montréal]

Dailey, Robert Clifton. See No./Voir no 726

6794
Eglin, Peter Anthony. "Terms for Canadian Doctors: Language and Sociology, Ethnosemantics and Ethnomethodology." British Columbia, 1975.

6795
Ford, James Ellsworth. "Doing Obstetrics: The Organization of Work Routines in a Maternity Service." British Columbia, 1974.

6796
Foster, Mary Kathleen. "Attitudes of Canadian Physicians in the United States: The Role of Selection in Socialization." Columbia, 1976.

6797
Gruen, Mary Ann. "Career Choice in Medicine." Minnesota, 1974. [University of Toronto Faculty of Medicine/Faculté de médecine de l'Université de Toronto]

Goldberg, Theodore Irving. See No./Voir no 1623

6798
Gosselin, Roger. "A Study of the Interdependence of Medical Specialists in Quebec Teaching Hospitals." McGill, 1978.

Hammond, Joseph Angus Bernard. See No./Voir no 1624

Hamovitch, Maurice B. See No./Voir no 1625

Hetherington, Robert William. See No./Voir no 1626

Higgins, Chris Alan. See No./Voir no 1152

6799
Hunt, Larry Ralph. "The Effects of Preoperative Counselling on Postoperative Recovery - Open Heart Surgery Patients." Toronto, 1978.

6800
James, Herman Delano. "The Use of Medical Services in a Canadian Metropolis: A Multi-Factor Analysis." Pittsburgh, 1972.

6801
Johnston, Elizabeth Macleod. "Maternal and Infant Nutrition Attitudes and Practices of Physicians in British Columbia." British Columbia, 1975.

Katz, Bruce Allen. See No./Voir no 361

6802
Kelly, David Francis. "The Emergence of Roman Catholic Medical Ethics in North America." University of St. Michael's College, 1978.

6803
Liberakis, Eustace A. "Some Factors Predisposing to Institutionalism in Chronic Psychiatric Patients." Memorial University of Newfoundland, 1978. [Examines patients in the wards of the only mental hospital in Newfoundland/Examen de patients dans les salles du seul hôpital psychiatrique de Terre-Neuve]

6804
Marsden, Lorna R. "Doctors Who Teach – An Influence on Health Delivery in Ontario." Princeton, 1972.

6805
Martens, Ethel G. "Utilization of Medical Care by Saskatchewan Indians, North Battleford Area: A Comparative Study." Saskatchewan, 1973.

McKay, William Angus. See No./Voir no 7158

6806
Meilicke, Carl Alexander. "The Saskatchewan Medical Care Dispute of 1962: An Analytic Social History." Minnesota, 1969.

6807
Minden, Karen Paula. "Missionaries, Medicine and Modernization: Canadian Medical Missionaries in Sichuan, 1925-1952." York, 1981.

6808
Nancarrow, Clarke J.E. "Medicalization in the Past Century in the Province of Ontario: The Physician as Moral Entrepreneur." Waterloo, 1980.

Naylor, C.D. See No./Voir no 1631

Ness, Robert Conrad. See No./Voir no 408

6809
Onuoha, A.R.A. "Job Satisfaction of Educators in Rehabilitation Medicine in Canada." Alberta, 1980.

Pederson, Linda Lue. See No./Voir no 6722

6810
Poston, William Roger. "Organizational Effectiveness in Biomedical Communications Systems." West Virginia, 1977. [Total health care centers/Total des centres de soins]

Pye, Carol Jean. See No./Voir no 6724

6811
Rhodes, Ernest Cornell. "Organizational Constraints and the Dispersal of Medical Treatment Across Clinical Loci in a Canadian Metropolis." Pittsburgh, 1977.

6812
Ross, Helen Elizabeth. "Social Factors in the Hospitalization of Psychogeriatric Patients." Toronto, 1978.
6813
Stewart, Moira Anne. "A Study of the Holistic Approach in Primary Care." Western Ontario, 1975.
6814
Stoddart, Gregory Lloyd. "An Episodic Approach to the Demand for Medical Care." British Columbia, 1975.
6815
Tuohy, Carolyn Joy. "The Political Attitudes of Ontario Physicians: A Skill Group Perspective." Yale, 1974.
6816
Warren, Sharon Ann. "Physicians and Health Regionalization: Patterns of Response to Government Policy." Western Ontario, 1974.
6817
Westbury, Robert Clifton. "Before and After Medicare: The Effect of the Introduction of a Compulsory State Sponsored Universal Health Care Program on Utilization and Servicing Patterns in an Albertan General Practice." Cambridge, 1979.
6818
Wier, Richard Anthony. "Patterns of Interaction Between Interest Groups and the Political System: The Case of the Canadian Medical Association." Georgetown, 1970.
Willems, Jane Sisk. See No./Voir no 6706
6819
Wolfson, Alan David. "The Supply of Physicians' Services in Ontario." Harvard, 1975.

Medical Education/Enseignement médical

6820
Cohen, Robert. "The Impact of Work-Setting on the Clinical Training of Medical Students." Toronto, 1977.
Daggett, Christopher Jarvis. See No./Voir no 6793
6821
Davis, John Campbell. "Factors Affecting the Admission of Applicants to a Medical School." McMaster, 1979.
6822
Harasym, Peter Humphrey. "The Analysis of Various Techniques Used for Scoring Patient Management Problems." Alberta, 1980.
Kahn, Joan Yess. See No./Voir no 4243
6823
Lodhia-Patel, Vimla. "The Effects of a Clinical Clerkship Program on the Clinical Competence of Senior Medical Students." McGill, 1981.
6824
McGrath, Gerard Michael. "Institutional Socialization: A Symbolic Interactionist Examination of a New Developmental Institution." Calgary, 1974. [Calgary Faculty of Medicine/Faculté de médecine, Calgary]
Onuoha, A.R.A. See No./Voir no 6809

6825
Tiberius, Richard Gordon. "An Interactive Approa to Education for Independence in Fourth Ye Medical Students." Toronto, 1975.

Medical Science and Research/ Science et recherche médicale

6826
Allen, Hugh A.J. "An Investigation of Water Hardne Calcium and Magnesium in Relation to Mortality Ontario." Waterloo, 1972.
Anderson, Donald O. See No./Voir no 6922
6827
Baker, G. Ross. "Collaboration and Conflict: Scie tific Change and the Social Structure of Biomec cal Research." Toronto, 1982.
6828
Baldwin, John Stiles. "Effects of Thermal Feedba Training and Pre-Headache Cue Identification Migraine Management." Manitoba, 1979.
6829
Balram, Bodhnarine C.M. "Coronary Heart Disea Risk Factors in Newfoundland Children." Memori University of Newfoundland, 1982.
Bradley, Christine Felecia. See No./Voir no 8967
6830
Buehler, Sharon Lyn Kelly. "The Epidemiology Hodgkin's Disease in Newfoundland." Memori University of Newfoundland, 1983.
6831
Christou, Nicolas Velos. "Alterations in Host Defen Mechanisms of Surgical and Trauma Patients wi Particular Reference to Polymorphonuclear Leuk cyte Function and Predisposition to Major Seps and Mortality." McGill, 1980. [1776 patient 1776 malades]
6832
Dart, Richard James. "Reducing Stress in You Children: Effects of Mother's Picture and Voi Recordings in Response to Hospitalization Waterloo, 1980.
6833
De Andrade-Lopes, José-Maria. "Respiratory Musc Function During Sleep." Toronto, 1982.
6834
Dempster, George. "Epidemic Influenza in Canada Edinburgh, 1953.
6835
Duckworth, Geoffrey Stafford. "Studies of Diagnos and Outcome in Geropsychiatric and Chronic Ps chiatric Patients." Toronto, 1980.
6836
Elwood, J.M. "An Epidemiological Study of Aneuc phalus in Canada." Queen's, Belfast, 1976.
6837
Eyssen, Gail Elizabeth. "Methods of Assessing Radi graphic Progression in the Pneumoconioses McGill, 1975. [Studies of 285 workers in th Quebec chrysolite industries/Études sur 285 o vriers des industries minières du Québec]
Field, Lanora Leigh. See No./Voir no 360

838
ournier-Massey, Gisèle. "Pulmonary Function in Quebec Asbestos Workers: Relationship to Clinical Symptoms, Pulmonary Radiology, Dust Exposure and Smoking." McGill, 1973.

839
rancoeur, Ann-Michèle. "Analysis of Virus - Cell Interactions with T1026, a Mutant of Vesicular Stomatitis Virus." Toronto, 1980. [Ten years of research in the laboratory of Dr. C.P. Stanners at the Ontario Cancer Institute/Dix ans de recherche au laboratoire de C.P. Stanners à l'Institut de cancer de l'Ontario]

840
Gadbois, Pierre. "I. La maladie de Morquio dans la province de Québec. II. Biochimie du kératan-sulfate cornéen. "Laval, 1978.

841
Gibbs, Graham William. "The Epidemiology of Pleural Calcification." McGill, 1973. [Quebec miners and millers/Mineurs et meuniers du Québec]

Gibson, Rosalind Susan. See No./Voir no 6715

842
Girt, J.L. "A Consideration of Some Relationships of Environment to Disease in Leeds and Newfoundland: Two Case Studies in the Ecology of Human Disease." Leeds, 1972.

Goldman, Janice Olivia Babcock. See No./Voir no 3888

843
Hanis, Nancy Marilyn. "A Study of Intestinal Cancer Mortality in a Population of Canadian Oil Workers." Western Ontario, 1977.

844
Haynes, Robert Brian. "A Randomized Clinical Trial of Three Strategies to Improve Patient Compliance with Antihypertensive Therapy." McMaster, 1976. [Steel plant]

845
Laskin, Richard. "Knowledge and Opinions Concerning Cancer with Respect to Language, Sex, and Age Difference in a Small Canadian Town." Pennsylvania State, 1959. [In Quebec/Au Québec]

6846
Latimer, Paul Ross. "A Comparative Psychophysiological Study of Normal Subjects, Psychoneurotic Patients and Patients with Irritable Bowel Syndrome." McMaster, 1980.

6847
Lawani, Stephen Majebi. "Quality Collaboration and Citations in Cancer Research: A Bibliometric Study." Florida State, 1980.

6848
Lima, Oriane A.S. "Factors Affecting Bronchial Healing Following Lung Transplantation: An Experimental Study." Toronto, 1981.

Lowry, R.B. See No./Voir no 475

6849
Martin, Sheilagh Marie. "Physiological Responses in Man During Cold Water Immersion." Calgary, 1977.

6850
Nommik, Salme. "Serological Tests in Canadian Hydatid Disease." McGill, 1958.

6851
O'Neil-Lowry, M.K. "Psychosocial Factors and Depressive Symptoms in University Students." Toronto, 1983.

6852
Paterson, Donald Hugh. "Alterations of Cardiovascular Function with Mild and Intense Physical Training of Post Myocardial Infraction of Subjects." Toronto, 1978.

Ramsay, Janice Ann. See No./Voir no 6725

6853
Rathgerber, Eva-Maria L. "The Movement of Paradigm of Medical Knowledge and Research Between Canada and Kenya: An Investigation into the Sociology of Knowledge Transfers." SUNY, Buffalo, 1982.

6854
Richler, Avrum. "A Study of Ocular Refraction in Western Newfoundland." Memorial University of Newfoundland, 1979.

6855
Ross, Ian D. "Medicolegal Categories of Death: Taxonomic Problems." Alberta, 1981.

6856
Ross, Mary Alexander. "A Survey of Mortality of Diphtheria, Scarlet Fever, Whooping Cough, Measles, Tuberculosis, Typhoid Fever, Influenza and Other Respiratory Diseases, and Diabetes for Fifty Years in Ontario, and an Analysis of the Results of the Use of Toxoid in the Prevention of Diphtheria in Toronto School Children." Toronto, 1934.

6857
Sadovnick, Adele Delia. "Genetic and Epidemiologic Aspects of Multiple Sclerosis in British Columbia." British Columbia, 1980.

6858
Smith, Nancy Johnson. "Evaluation of Both Outdoor and Indoor Exposure to Carbon Monoxide and Their Health Significance in Calgary, Alberta, Canada." Johns Hopkins, 1976.

6859
Sullivan, Elizabeth Michelle. "A Study of Impact of the Family Volunteer as a Social Support Intervention with Mothers of Newborns." Western Ontario, 1983.

6860
Vandenberghe, Hilde M. "Analysis and Pharmokinetics of Morphine: Studies in Children During Balanced Anaesthesia and the Postoperative Period." Toronto, 1982.

Wells, James Ralph. See No./Voir no 631

6861
Westlund, Knut B. "Studies on Multiple Sclerosis in Winnipeg, Manitoba and New Orleans, Louisiana." Johns Hopkins, 1953.

6862
Winsor, Elizabeth Joan T. "A Genetic Comparison of Two Nova Scotian Communities." Dalhousie, 1973.

6863
Wood-Dauphinee, Sharon Lee. "A Trial of Team Care in the Treatment of Acute Stroke." McGill, 1982.

VETERINARY SCIENCE/SCIENCE VÉTÉRINAIRE

6864
Hudson, Robert John. "Immunology of Lungworm (Protostrongylus) Infections of the Rocky Mountain Bighorn Sheep." British Columbia, 1971.

6865
Hudson, William Anderson. "A Descriptive Study of Selected Aspects of Curriculum and Instruction in Veterinary Medical Gross Anatomy." Tennessee, 1982.

6866
Wobeser, Gary Arthur. "Aquatic Mercury Pollution: Studies of the Occurrence and Pathologic Effects on Fish and Mink." Saskatchewan, 1973. [Saskatchewan River/Rivière Saskatchewan]

6867
Yuill, Thomas Mackay. "Viral and Parasitic Infections of Snowshoe Hares in Alberta." Wisconsin, 1964.

DENTISTS AND DENTISTRY/ DENTISTES ET ART DENTAIRE

6868
Fortin, Jean-Louis. "L'impact de la formation universitaire sur les modes de pratique dentaire." Montréal, 1983.

6869
Infante-Rivard, Claire. "Prévalence, incidence et facteurs de risque de la carie dentaire dans une cohorte d'âge scolaire élémentaire." McGill, 1982.

6870
Little, Robert Merl. "A Survey of the Attitudes and Professional Activities of Dental-Graduates from the Universities of British Columbia and Washington Presently Engaged in Dental Practice." Washington, Seattle, 1974.

6871
Lott, Frank Melville. "Proposed Dental Service for the Defense Forces of Canada." Toronto, 1940.

6872
Ramer, Donald Gordon. "The Premack Principle, Self-Monitoring, and the Maintenance of Preventive Dental Health Behaviour." British Columbia, 1979.

6873
Reid, Angus Edward. "Professional Socialization and the Effect of the Professional School: The Case of Dental Education in Canada." Carleton, 1974.

PHARMACY AND PHARMACISTS/ PHARMACIENS ET PHARMACIE

6874
Anderson, Arthur James. "A Pharmaceutical Investigation of Selected Alberta Bentonites." Washington, Seattle, 1960.

Chan, Mick Ying-Pui. See No./Voir no 3886

6875
DesRoches, Bernard Paul. "A Comparative Study of the Pharmacist as Perceptor in Wisconsin and Ontario." Wisconsin, 1970.

6876
Fielding, David Wilson. "Performance Evaluation of a Program in Pharmacy Continuing Education." British Columbia, 1977.

6877
Lang, Ronald William. "The Politics of Drugs: Comparative Pressure Group Study of the Pharmaceutical Manufacturers Association of Canada a the Association of the British Pharmaceutic Industry, 1930-1970." London, 1974.

6878
Tindall, William Norman. "Some Legal and Econom Implications of Utilizing Non-Professional Perso nel in Canadian Retail Pharmacy." Pittsburg 1969.

NURSING

General Item/Ouvrage général

6879
Loyer, Marie des Anges. "Leadership and the Effe tiveness of Community Health Nursing Services Ottawa, 1982.

Nursing Education/Enseignement du nursing

6880
Allemang, Margaret May. "Nursing Education in th United States and Canada, 1873-1950. Leadin Figures, Forces, Views on Education." Washingto Seattle, 1974.

6881
Barron, Sister Marion. "Possible Consequences Diploma Nursing Education in Ontario as a Su system of Colleges of Applied Arts and Techn logy." Catholic, 1972.

6882
Bonin, Marie A. "Trends in Integrated Basic Degr Nursing Programs in Canada, 1942-1972." Ottaw 1977.

6883
Brown, Isabel. "The Effects of a Death Educati Programme for Nurses Working in a Long-Te Care Hospital." Toronto, 1980.

6884
Campbell, Margaret Amelia. "The Selection of Nu sing Education Programs by Nursing Students British Columbia." Teachers College, Columbi 1970.

6885
Checkley, Kenneth Lloyd. "The Influence of a Hum Relations Laboratory in the Effectiveness of Thi Year Psychiatric Nurses." Alberta, 1971.

6886
Douglin, Janette J. "Nurse Educators Receptivity Educational Change: An Empirical Study Toronto, 1973. [Ontario]

Dyck, Merla Hélène. See No./Voir no 2839

Fleming, Stephen J. See No./Voir no 8991

6887
Forest, Soeur Jeanne. "Opinions de sept groupes personnes en contact avec l'étudiante infirmiè par rapport à des comportements généraleme désirables ou inacceptables." Ottawa, 1965.

6888
Fortier-Havelka, Colette. "Les attitudes d'étudiant infirmières à l'égard de leur fonction d'enseign ment et les activités de laboratoire clinique Montréal, 1981 or/ou 1982.

6889
Garner, Doris Derbyshire. "The Conduct, Use and Utility of Program Evaluation in Nursing Education in Canada." Calgary, 1983.

6890
Glass, Helen Preston. "Teaching Behavior in the Nursing Laboratory in Selected Baccalaureate Nursing Programs in Canada." Columbia, 1971.

6891
Good, Shirley Ruth. "Preparation of University Teachers of Nursing in Canada: Proposals for the Professional Education Component of a Master's Program." Teachers College, Columbia, 1967.

Griffin, Amy Elizabeth. See No./Voir no 4426

6892
Hannah, Kathryn J.N. "A Descriptive Study of the Administrative Behaviour of Nursing Deans in Canadian Universities." Alberta, 1981.

6893
Hart, Margaret Elder. "Needs and Resources for Graduate Education in Nursing in Canada." Teachers College, Columbia, 1962.

Hearn, Margaret Therese. See No./Voir no 4164

Kergin, Dorothy Jean. See No./Voir no 6915

6894
Kerr, Janet C.R.. "Financing University Nursing Education in Canada: 1919-1976." Michigan, 1978.

6895
Lazure, Hélène. "Les effets d'un programme créatif de problémation sur la capacité d'idéation d'infirmières psychiatriques." Laval, 1980.

6896
Lee, Margaret Naomi. "Preferences for University Teaching as the Career Goal of Baccalaureate Students of Nursing Graduates from Selected Universities in Canada." Teachers College, Columbia, 1966.

6897
Létourneau, Marguerite. "Trends in Basic Diploma Nursing Programs Within the Provincial Systems of Education in Canada, 1964 to 1974." Ottawa, 1975.

6898
Léveillé, Michèle. "Étude sur l'apprentissage du rôle professionnel de l'infirmière." Ottawa, 1982.

6899
MacLaggan, Katherine. "A Plan for the Education of Nurses in the Province of New Brunswick." Teachers College, Columbia, 1965.

6900
Monette, Marcelle. "Les conceptions des soins infirmiers des finissantes en techniques infirmières de cinq CÉGEPs de Montréal et des finissantes au baccalauréat en sciences infirmières à l'Université de Montréal." Montréal, 1982.

6901
Mousseau, Yolande. "La compréhension du concept du soin total et continu du malade chez les étudiants-infirmières et chez les institutrices-cliniques." Ottawa, 1965.

6902
Mussalem, Helen. "A Plan for the Development of Nursing Education Programs Within the General Education System of Canada." Teachers College, Columbia, 1963.

6903
Rainville, Thérèse. "La relation d'aide en nursing: effets d'un programme de formation systématique." McGill, 1979. [Training program for student nurses/Programmes de formation pour étudiants-infirmiers]

6904
Roessler, Grayce Maurine. "A Comparative Study of the Similarities and Differences of Opinions of Nurse Faculty in Selected Associate Degree and Diploma in Nursing Programs in the United States and Canada as Related to Specific Aspects of Community/Technical College Programs in Nursing." California, Los Angeles, 1976.

6905
Rovers, Maria Dina. "A Generalizability Theory Approach to Estimating the Reliability of Nursing Students' Clinical Performance Scores." Toronto, 1982.

6906
Roy, Sister Eugènie-De-Rome. "Projection of a Basic Nursing Program Leading to a Bachelor's Degree: Designed for the Province of Quebec." St. Louis, 1965.

6907
Samson, Pierrette. "A Comparative Study of the Problem-Solving Proficiency of Baccalaureate and CEGEP Nurses of the Province of Quebec." Catholic, 1978.

6908
Savoie, Mary Leona. "Continuing Education for Nurses: Predictors of Success in Courses Requiring a Degree of Learner Self-Direction." Toronto, 1979. [Toronto]

Schultz, Lynda Kay. See No./Voir no 9470

Wain, Olev Martin. See No./Voir no 6930

6909
Weaver, Wendy Clifton. "An Interpersonal Coping Skills Program for Student Nurses." Toronto, 1978.

Weinstein, Edwin Lawrence. See No./Voir no 3600

The Profession of Nursing/
Profession du nursing

6910
Abu-Saad, Huda. "Nursing: A World View." Florida, 1977.

6911
Batra, Carol Dawn. "Analysis of the Relationship Which Exists Between Diploma, Baccalaureate and Master Preparation in Canada for Leadership Positions in Nursing Administration." Wayne State, 1975.

6912
Baudry, Jeannine. "Étude comparative de la formation des fonctions et du statut professionnel de l'infirmière et de l'assistant médical, dans six régions." Montréal, 1975.

6913
Binger, Jane Louise. "A Portrait of the Journal Editor in Nursing in the United States and Canada." Stanford, 1982.

Chambers, Larry William. See No./Voir no 6789

Colquhoun, Dorothy Rebecca. See No./Voir no 4221

6914
Desjean, Georgette. "The Problem of Leadership in French Canadian Nursing." Wayne State, 1975.
Garry, Carl. See No./Voir no 4347
6915
Kergin, Dorothy Jean. "An Exploratory Study of the Professionalization of Registered Nurses in Ontario and the Implications for the Support of Change in Basic Nursing Educational Programs." Michigan, 1968.
6916
Leatt, Peggy. "Technology Size, Environment and Structure in Nursing Units." Alberta, 1980.
Léveillé, Michèle. See No./Voir no 6898
Loyer, Marie des Anges. See No./Voir no 6879
6917
Pepperdine, Barbara Joan. "The Occupation of Nursing and Careers: A Study of the Careers of Diploma and Degree Nurses." Toronto, 1974.
6918
Ponak, Allen M. "Registered Nurses and Collective Bargaining: An Analysis of Job-Related Goals." Wisconsin, 1977. ⌈Ottawa⌉
6919
Roon, Leonore M. "The History of Nursing Legislation in the British Commonwealth, 1891-1939." Radcliffe, 1952.
6920
Strilaeff, Florence. "Turnover of Nurses in Hospitals: A Study of a Service Organization." Toronto, 1974.
6921
Tenove, S.C. "Community Health Nurse Evaluation: The Stakeholder's Perspective." Alberta, 1982.

Science of Nursing/Sciences infirmières

6922
Anderson, Donald O. "The Sociological Analysis of the V.D. Repeater Patient." British Columbia, 1954.
Baudry, Jeannine. See No./Voir no 6912
6923
Du Gas, Beverly Witter. "An Analysis of Certain Factors in the Diffusion of Innovations in Nursing Practice in the Public General Hospitals of the Province of British Columbia." British Columbia, 1969.
6924
Field, Peggy Anne. "An Ethnography: Four Nurses' Perspectives of Nursing in a Community Setting." Alberta, 1980.
Fleming, Stephen J. See No./Voir no 8991
Gow, Kathleen Mavourneen. See No./Voir no 10081
6925
Martin, Thomas O. "Contact with Death, Professional Experience, and the Coping Responses of Nurses." Ottawa, 1979.
6926
Parker, Nora Inez. "The Effects of Error Modeling on the Learning of a Complex Procedure in Nursing." Toronto, 1972.
6927
Scollie, June R. "Perceptions of the Public Health Staff Nurse in Manitoba, Canada, as to the Decision-Making Authority in the Initiation of Physical Nursing Care." Columbia, 1972.

6928
Segall, Alexander. "Sociocultural Variation in Illnes Behaviour: A Comparative Study of Hospitalize Anglo-Saxon Protestant and Jewish Female Pa tients." Toronto, 1972.
6929
Shady, Gary Anthony. "Death Anxiety and AB Thera peutic Styles and Factors in Helping Patients Wit Different Coping Styles Accept Life-Threatenin Illness." Manitoba, 1977.
6930
Wain, Olev Martin. "The Validity of Patient-Manage ment-Problems for Assisting the Skills of Bacca laureate Nursing Students in Solving Nursing-Car Problems." Toronto, 1981.
6931
Whitaker, Roy A. "An Algorithm for Estimating th medians of a Weighted Graph Subject to Sid Constraints, and an Application to Rural Hospita Location in British Columbia." British Columbi 1971.

HISTORY/HISTOIRE

Prior to 1970, the American output in this classifica tion had exceeded that of Canadian universities but, a in all other areas, the rapid growth in output tha occured during the 1970's and 1980's brought th Canadian total up to the American level. An extra polation of the statistics demonstrates that th Canadian output will probably exceed the America output for the remainder of this decade. Included i this classification is the first doctoral dissertatio written on a Canadian topic, Thomas D. Rambaut's " Sketch of the Constitutional History of Canada accepted by Columbia University in 1884. Four mo studies appeared in the 1890's (two from Corne University and two from Johns Hopkins University followed by 17 more in the next two decades. It w in the 1920's that the first three Canadian dissert tions on Canadian history were approved. Of the 8 American universities producing studies in this are none of the universities has emerged as a significat centre for Canadiana, although the schools of Harvar Duke, Columbia, Chicago, Minnesota, Illinoi Michigan, and Yale, in that order, were major contr butors, with ten or more titles each. In Canada, th University of Toronto has emerged as the maj producer with the University of Ottawa second, b with only one-third of Toronto's output. The unive sities of Laval, Queen's, and Montreal vie for thi place and McGill University, the universities Western Ontario, Alberta, and York follow in th order. Eleven additional universities contributed t remainder, with one to seven dissertations each.

This classification placed number one in British studi of Canada, with the University of London producing of a total of 83 dissertations. Of the remaining t

British universities contributing to this number, Oxford is second with 18 studies, and Cambridge third with seven.

———

Avant 1970, la production américaine dans cette catégorie surpassait celle des universités canadiennes, mais, comme dans tous les autres domaines, une rapide augmentation de la production dans les années 1970 et 1980 ont fait grimper le total des productions canadiennes au niveau du total américain. Une extrapolation des statistiques indique que la production canadienne excèdera probablement la production américaine à la fin de l'actuelle décennie. Dans cette catégorie, on trouve la première thèse de doctorat écrite sur un sujet canadien, "A Sketch of the Constitutional History of Canada" de Thomas D. Rambaut, acceptée par l'Université Concordia en 1884. Quatre autres thèses sont apparues dans les années 1890 (deux de l'Université Cornell et deux de l'Université Johns Hopkins), suivies par 17 de plus dans les deux décennies suivantes. C'est dans les années 1920 que les trois premières thèses canadiennes sur l'histoire canadienne ont été approuvées. Sur les quelque 80 universités américaines qui ont produit des thèses en ce domaine, il n'en est pas une qui ait réussi à devenir un centre intéressant pour les ouvrages canadiens, bien que les universités de Harvard, Duke, Columbia, Chicago, Minnesota, Illinois, Michigan et Yale, citées ici dans l'ordre, aient été d'importants producteurs, avec dix titres ou plus par établissement. Au Canada, l'Université de Toronto vient en tête suivie de l'Université d'Ottawa avec seulement un tiers de la production de Toronto. Les universités Laval, Queen's et de Montréal se disputent la troisième place; viennent ensuite, dans l'ordre, McGill, Western Ontario, Alberta et York. Onze autre universités se partagent les autres thèses, comptant de une à sept études chacune.

Dans cette catégorie, les études britanniques sur le Canada viennent au premier rang; l'Université de Londres a produit 38 thèses sur un total de 83. Dix autres universités britanniques se partagent les thèses restantes; Oxford arrive au second rang avec 18 thèses et Cambridge troisième, avec sept.

GENERAL ITEMS/OUVRAGES GÉNÉRAUX

Blais, André-Marc. See No./Voir no 8750

6932
Brown, Michael Gary. "Jewish Foundations in Canada: the Jews, the French and the English to 1914." SUNY, Buffalo, 1976. [1759-1914]

6933
Charbonneau, Yvon. Desloges, Yvon Lafrance, Marc R. "Les fortifications de Québec du XVIIe au XIXe siècle." Laval, 1983.

6934
Fenwick, Rudy. "White America looks at School Desegregation, 1964-1968." McGill, 1974.

6935
Graham, Domenick Stuart. "British Intervention in Defense of the American Colonies, 1748-1956." London, 1965.

6936
MacKirdy, Kenneth Alexander. "Regionalism: Canada and Australia." Toronto, 1959.

6937
Martin, Paul-Louis. "La chasse au Québec, ethnographie d'une activité de loisir depuis les origines de la Nouvelle-France jusqu'à la Première Guerre mondiale." Laval, 1980.

6938
McLean, Kenneth Hugh. "The Treatment of History in Canadian Fiction." York, 1980. [1932 to present — ranging through Canadian history from 1638 to 1970/De 1932 à aujourd'hui — parcourant l'histoire canadienne de 1638 à 1970]

6939
Roussin, Marcel. "Le Canada, fils et héritier de la coutume." Ottawa, 1945.

6940
Shifferd, Patricia Allen. "Trade, Land Expropriation and Conquest: The Effects of European Contact on the Native Peoples of Africa and North America." Wisconsin, 1980.

Wilson, Harold Fisher. See No./Voir no 840

Woodsworth, Glen James. See No./Voir no 1218

HISTORIOGRAPHY/HISTORIOGRAPHIE

6941
Archer, John Hall. "A Study of Archival Institutions in Canada." Queen's, 1969.

6942
Bowden, Bruce William. "Adam Shortt." Toronto, 1979.

6943
Bush, Mary T. "Representative Nineteenth Century New England Historians View Manifest Destiny." Ottawa, 1963.

Cauthers, Janet Helen. See No./Voir no 450, 7447

6944
Eagan, William Edward. "Joseph Burr Tyrrell, 1858-1957." Western Ontario, 1971.

6945
Francis, Robert Douglas. "Frank H. Underhill: Canadian Intellectual." York, 1976.

6946
Gagnon, Serge. "Idéologue et savoir historique: historiographie de la Nouvelle-France de Garneau à Groulx (1845-1915)." Laval, 1975.

6947
Gorman, David J. "Frank Hayward Severance: Historian of the Niagara Frontier." Notre Dame, 1966.

Jain, Geneviève Laloux. See No./Voir no 2497

6948
Koester, Charles Beverly. "Nicholas Flood Davin: A Biography." Alberta, 1971. [1843-1901]

6949
Mawer, David Ronald. "The Return of the Catholic Past: The Debate between François-Xavier Garneau and His Critics, 1831-1945." McGill, 1977. [1809-1866]

Meikle, William Duncan. See No./Voir no 3722

6950

Neill, Robert Foliet. "The Work of Harold Adams Innis: Content and Context." Duke, 1967. ⌈1894-1952⌉

Persky, Joel. See No./Voir no 1058

6951

Reilly, Mary Purissima. "Francis Parkman and the Spiritual Factors at Work in New France." St. Louis, 1942.

6952

Sherrin, Phyllis Marilyn. "The World, the Flesh, and the Devil: The Crusade of Lionel Groulx, 1878-1967." York, 1976.

See also Agricultural History, Education History, Economic History, Finance History, Historical Geography, Labor History, Religious History/Voir aussi Histoire de l'agriculture, Histoire de l'enseignement, Histoire de l'économie, Histoire des finances, Géographie historique, Histoire du travail, Histoire des religions.

NATIONAL HISTORY/HISTOIRE NATIONALE

French Canada - 1763/Canada français - 1763

General Items/Ouvrages généraux

6953

Bilodeau, Rosario. "Liberté économique et politique des Canadiens sous le régime français." Montréal, 1956.

6954

Cahall, Raymond Dubois. "The Sovereign Council of New France: A Study in Canadian Constitutional History." Columbia, 1915.

Carmical, Oline, Jr. See No./Voir no 7023

Cell, Gillian M.T. See No./Voir no 7164

6955

Dawson, John M. W. "An Institutional and Sociological Study of the French Intendants 1652-1715." Toronto, 1978.

6956

Delande, Jean. "Le conseil souverain de la Nouvelle-France." Montréal, 1925.

6957

Dickason, Olive Patricia. "The Myth of the Savage and the Beginnings of French Colonialism in the Americas." Ottawa, 1976.

6958

Folmer, Henri. "Franco-Spanish Rivalry in North America, 1524-1763." Chicago, 1949.

6959

Foote, William Alfred. "The American Independent Companies of the British Army 1664-1764." California, Los Angeles, 1966.

6960

Gottesman, Daniel Harvey. "The Expense of Spirit: Indians, Ideology and the Origins of National Identity in British North America 1630-1776." Toronto, 1979.

6961

Hammelef, John Christensen. "British and American Attempts to Coordinate the Defences of the Continental Colonies to Meet French and Northern Indian Attacks, 1643-1754." Michigan, 1955.

6962

Idle, Dunning. "The Post of the St. Joseph Rive During the French Régime, 1679-1761." Illinois 1946.

Igartua, José Eduardo. See No./Voir no 1224

6963

Kennedy, John Hopkins. "New France and the Euro pean Conscience." Yale, 1942.

6964

Lamansney, Patrick J. "The Relations Betwee Church and State in New France." St. Louis, 1932.

6965

Lee, Frederic Edward. "The Influence of the Jesuit on the Social Organization of the North America Indians." Yale, 1916.

6966

McNeill, John Robert. "Theory and Practice in th Bourbon Empires of the Atlantic: The Roles o Louisbourg and Havana, 1713-1763." Duke, 1981.

6967

Milot, Victor J. "Le Richelieu, route militaire de l Nouvelle-France." Laval, 1949.

6968

Moody, Robert Earle. "The Maine Frontier, 1607 1763." Yale, 1933.

Moogh, Peter Nicholas. See No./Voir no 2089

6969

Morrison, Kenneth M. "The People of the Dawn: Th Abnaki and Their Relations with New England an New France, 1600-1727." Maine, 1975.

6970

Munro, William Bennett. "The Feudal System i Canada: A Study in the Institutional History of th Old Régime." Harvard, 1900.

6971

O'Neil, Emmett Francis. "English Fear of Frenc Encirclement in North America, 1680-1763. Michigan, 1941.

Peterson, Jacqueline Louise. See No./Voir no 496

6972

Séguin, Robert Lionel. "L'habitant aux dix-septièm et dix-huitième siècles." Laval, 1964.

Simpson, Geoffrey Sedgwick. See No./Voir no 4893

6973

Thomas, Hartley Munro. "The Intendancy in Ne France." Harvard, 1933.

Sixteenth Century/Seizième siècle

6974

Umstead, Kenneth H.H. "The French in the America During the Sixteenth Century." California Berkeley, 1940.

Seventeenth Century/Dix-septième siècle

6975

Gaston, Leroy Clifton, III. "Crucifix and Calume French Missionary Efforts in the Great Lake Region, 1615-1650." Tulane, 1978.

6976

Goldstein, Robert Arnold. "French-Iroquois Diplo matic and Military Relations, 1609-1701." Min nesota, 1959.

6977
Hardcastle, David Paul. "The Defense of Canada under Louis XIV, 1643-1701." Ohio State, 1970.
6978
Kolling, Harold. "The New England Confederation of 1643: Its Origins, Nature, and Foreign Relations, 1643-52." Chicago, 1957.
6979
Kupp, Theodorus Johannes. "Fur Trade Relations, New Netherland-New France: A Study of the Influence Exerted by the Fur Trade Interests of Holland and New Netherland in the Settlement of New France During the Years 1600 to 1664." Manitoba, 1968.
6980
Mulvey, Mary Doris. "French Catholic Missionaries in the Present United States (1604-1794)." Catholic, 1936.
6981
Paradis, Jean-Marc. "Le lieu de l'hivernement de l'expédition Dollier-Gallinée en 1669-1670." Laval, 1967.
6982
Reid, John Graham. "Acadia, Maine and New-Scotland: Marginal Colonies in the Seventeenth Century." New Brunswick, 1976.
6983
Rhéault, Michel. "La noblesse au Canada, 1636-1686." Ottawa, 1967.
6984
Rocher, Guy A.A. "The Relations Between Church and State in New France During the Seventeenth Century." Harvard, 1958.
6985
Steck, Francis Borgia. "The Jolliet-Marquette Expedition, 1673." Catholic, 1928.

1700 - 1763

Allaire, Gratien. See No./Voir no 1219
Arceneaux, Maureen G. See No./Voir no 820
6986
Beattie, Daniel John. "General Jeffrey Amherst and the Conquest of Canada, 1758-1760." Duke, 1976.
6987
Belting, Natalia M. "Kaskaskia Under the French Régime." Illinois, 1940.
6988
Brown, Ian William. "Early 18th Century French-Indian Culture Contact in the Yazoo Bluffs Region of the Lower Mississippi Valley." Brown, 1979.
6989
Caldwell, Norman W. "The French in the West, 1740-1750." Illinois, 1936.
Carr, Paul Omega. See No./Voir no 7024
6990
Chard, Donald F. "The Impact of Île Royale on New England 1713-1763." Ottawa, 1973.
6991
Clark, Charles Edwin. "The Eastern Parts: Northern New England, 1690-1760." Brown, 1960. [French and Indian War/Guerre entre Français et Indiens]
6992
Cooper, Johnson Gaylord. "Oswego in the French-English Struggle in North America, 1720-1760." Syracuse, 1961.

6993
Crowley, Terence A. "Government and Interests: French Colonial Administration at Louisbourg, 1713-1758." Duke, 1975.
6994
Devine, Joseph A., Jr. "The British North American Colonies in the War of 1739-1748." Virginia, 1968.
6995
Filion, Maurice. "La pensée et l'action coloniales de Maurepas vis-à-vis le Canada (1723-1749)." Montréal, 1970.
6996
Fraser, E.J.S. "The Pitt-Newcastle Convention and the Conduct of the Seven Years' War, 1757-1760." Oxford, 1976.
Gradish, Stephen F. See No./Voir no 7408
Graham, Domenick Stuart. See No./Voir no 6935
6997
Griffiths, Naomi E.A. "The Acadian Deportation: Causes and Development." London, 1969.
6998
Guzzardo, John Christopher." Sir William Johnson's Official Family: Patron and Clients in an Anglo-American Empire, 1742-1777." Syracuse, 1975. [Loyalists Fleeing to Canada/Loyalistes en fuite au Canada]
Henderson, Susan Wright. See No./Voir no 6683
Kennett, Lee Boone. See No./Voir no 7412
6999
Kraushopf, Frances. "The French in Indiana, 1700-1760: A Political History." Illinois, 1953.
7000
MacLeod, Malcolm. "French and British Strategy on Canada's Western Front." Ottawa, 1974.
7001
Masterson, James Raymond. "Records of Travel in North America: 1700-1776." Harvard, 1936.
7002
Menig, Paul Henri. "Public Opinion in Massachusettes Relative to Anglo-French Relations 1748-1756." Washington, Seattle, 1962.
7003
Merriam, George Henry. "Israel Williams, Monarch of Hampshire, 1709-1788." Clark, 1961.
7004
Morris, John Louis. "The French Régime in Illinois, 1689-1763." Illinois, 1926.
Mulvey, Mary Doris. See No./Voir no 6980
7005
Nichols, Franklin T. "The Braddock Expedition." Harvard, 1947.
7006
Nish, Cameron. "The Canadian Bourgeoisie, 1729-1748: Character, Composition and Functions." Laval, 1968.
O'Neil, Emmett Francis. See No./Voir no 6971
7007
Ott, Edward R. "The Influence of Church and Trade on French Colonial Policy as Seen in the History of Detroit, 1700-1752." Northwestern, 1936.
7008
Palm, Sister Mary Borgias. "The Jesuit Missions of the Illinois Country, 1673-1763." St. Louis, 1931.

7009
Parker, King Lawrence. "Anglo-American Wilderness Campaigning, 1754-1764: Logistical and Tactical Developments." Columbia, 1970.

Ray, Arthur Joseph Jr. See No./Voir no 4838

7010
Pemberton, Ian Cleghorn Blancahrd. "Justus Sherwood, Vermont Loyalist, 1747-1798." Western Ontario, 1973.

7011
Rawlyk, George A. "New England and Louisbourg, 1744-1745." Rochester, 1966.

7012
Swanson, Carl Eliot. "Predators and Prizes: Privateering in the British Colonies During the War of 1739-1748." Western Ontario, 1979.

7013
Thorpe, Frederick John. "The Politics of French Public Construction in the Islands of the Gulf of St. Laurent 1695-1758." Ottawa, 1974.

7014
Vanasse, Alfred Rowland. "A Social History of the Seignorial Régime in Canada, (1712-1739)." Montréal, 1959.

7015
Van Kirk, Sylvia M. "The Role of Women in the Fur Trade Society of the Canadian West, 1700-1850." London, 1975.

7016
Wetherell, Albert Anthony. "General James Murray and British Canada: The Transition from French to British Canada, 1759-1766." St. John's, 1979.

7017
Zaccano, Joseph Peter, Jr. "French Colonial Administration in Canada to 1760." Pittsburgh, 1961.

7018
Ziebarth, Robert E. "The Role of New York in King George's War, 1739-1748." New York, 1972.

1763-1812

7019
Arthur, Marion E. "The French Canadians Under British Rule, 1760-1800." McGill, 1949.

7020
Baker, N. "The Treasury Administration of Contracts for the Supply of the British Armies in North America and the West Indies, 1775-1783." London, 1967.

7021
Bell, David V.J. "Nation and Non-Nation: A New Analysis of the Loyalists and the American Revolution." Harvard, 1969.

7022
Bower, R.A. "The Influence of Logistical Problems in British Operations in North America, 1775-1782." London, 1971.

7023
Carmical, Oline, Jr. "Plans of Union, 1634-1783: A Study and Reappraisal of Prospects for Uniting the English Colonies in North America." Kentucky, 1975.

7024
Carr, Paul Omega. "Defense of the Frontier Line, 1760-1775." Iowa, 1932.

7025
Coffin, Victor E. "The Province of Quebec and th Early American Revolution: A Study in Englis American Colonial History." Cornell, 1893.

7026
Custer, John Sherman. "The Constitutional Act 1791: A Study in British Colonial Policy for th Period from 1774 to 1791." Wisconsin, 1917.

7027
Dunham, Douglas. "The French Element in th American Fur Trade, 1760-1816." Michigan, 1950.

7028
Elliott, George Reid. "Empire and Enterprise in th North Pacific, 1785-1825: A Survey and Interpre tation Emphasizing the Role and Character Russian Enterprise." Toronto, 1959. [Britis Columbia/Colombie-Britannique]

7029
Faibisy, John Dewar. "Privateering and Piracy: Th Effects of New England Raiding upon Nova Scot During the American Revolution, 1775-1783 Massachusetts, 1972.

7030
Goltz, Herbert C. W., Jr. "Tecumseh, the Prophet ar the Rise of the Northwest Indian Confederation Western Ontario, 1973.

7031
Graham, Gerald. "British Policy and Canada, 177 1791: A Study in Eighteenth Century Mercar tilism." Cambridge, 1929.

7032
Greenwood, Frank Murray. "The Development of Garrison Mentality Among the English in Low Canada, 1793-1811." British Columbia, 1970.

7033
Hare, John. "Lexicologie politique du Canada frança (1784-1812)." Laval, 1972.

7034
Hunt, Richard Irving, Jr. "The Loyalists of Maine Maine, 1980.

7035
Lester, Malcolm. "Anglo-American Diplomat Problems Arising from British Naval Operations American Waters, 1793-1802." Virginia, 1954.

7036
Manning, Helen Taft. "British Colonial Governmel After the American Revolution, 1782-1820." Yal 1924.

7037
Martin, T.R. "The Place Settlement of 1783: Angl American Phase." Yale, 1951.

McGuigan, Gerald Frederick. See No./Voir no 136

McLintock, A.H. See No./Voir no 7168

7038
Metzger, Charles Henry. "The Toleration Clauses the Quebec Act." Michigan, 1930.

7039
Neatby, Hilda M. "The Administration of Justic Under the Quebec Act." Minnesota, 1934.

7040
Pacheco, Josephine F. "French Secret Agents America, 1763-1778." Chicago, 1951.

7041
Pendergast, Russell Anthony. "The XY Company 1798-1804." Ottawa, 1957.
Peterson, Jacqueline Louise. See No./Voir no 496
Porter, John Robert. See No./Voir no 947
7042
Proctor, Donald John. "From Insurrection to Independence: The Continental Congress and the Military Launching of the American Revolution." Southern California, 1965.
7043
Rashid, Zenab Fsmat. "The Peace of Paris of 1763." Liverpool, 1951.
7044
Roberts, Stephen George. "Imperial Policy, Provincial Administration and Defence in Upper Canada, 1796-1812." Oxford, 1975.
7045
Ross, Beatrice Spence. "Adaptation in Exile: Loyalist Women in Nova Scotia After the American Revolution." Cornell, 1981.
7046
Schell, Ernest H. "Justice and Policy in a Candid World: Republican Ideology and American Foreign Policy, 1789-1816." Temple, 1981.
7047
Sirridge, Agnes T. "Spanish, British, and French Activities in the Sea-Otter Trade of the Far North Pacific, 1774-1790." St. Louis, 1954.
7048
Smith, L.A.H. "The Working of the 1791 Constitutional Experiment in Lower Canada, 1805-1811." Oxford, 1956.
7049
Stevens, Wayne Edson. "The Northwest Fur Trade, 1763-1800." Illinois, 1916.
7050
Stewart, Charles Lockwood. "Martinez and López de Haro on the Northwest Coast, 1788-1789." California, Berkeley, 1936. [British Columbia/ Colombie-Britannique]
7051
Tevis, Raymond Harry. "American Options and Attitudes Toward British Retention of the Western Posts and American Attempts to Obtain the Western Posts, 1783-1790." St. Louis, 1977.
7052
Toussignant, Pierre. "La genèse et l'avènement de la constitution de 1791." Montréal, 1971.
7053
Ubbelohde, Carl W., Jr. "The Vice-Admiralty Courts of British North America, 1763-1776." Wisconsin, 1954.
7054
Vernon, Howard A., Jr. "The Impact of the French Revolution on Lower Canada, 1789-1795." Chicago, 1952.
7055
Wallot, Jean Pierre. "Le Bas-Canada sous l'administration de Craig (1807-1811)." Montréal, 1965.
7056
Webster, Thomas Stewart. "Napoleon and Canada." Chicago, 1962.
Wetherell, Albert Anthony. See No./Voir no 7016

7057
White, Patrick C.T. "Anglo-American Relations 1803 to 1815." Minnesota, 1954.
7058
Wilson, Bruce Gordon. "Elites of the Niagara Peninsula, 1776-1820: The Enterprises of Robert Hamilton: A Study of Wealth and Influence in Early Upper Canada." Toronto, 1978.
7059
Wylie, William Newman Thomas. "Arbiters of Commerce, Instruments of Power: A Study of the Civil Courts in the Midland District, Upper Canada, 1789-1812." Queen's, 1980.

War of 1812-1815/Guerre de 1812-1815

7060
Brown, Roger Hamilton. "A Republic in Peril: The Crisis of 1812." Harvard, 1960.
7061
Clancy, Martin. "Rules of Warfare Observed by American Military Forces in the Revolutionary War and the War of 1812." Georgetown, 1952.
7062
Dietz, Anthony George. "The Prisoner of War in the United States During the War of 1812." American, 1964.
7063
Gates, Charles M. "The Peace Negotiations Between Great Britain and the United States, 1812-1814." Minnesota, 1935.
7064
Gilpin, Alec Richard. "General William Hull and the War on the Detroit in 1812." Michigan, 1950.
7065
Handren, B.E. "The Anglo-American Connection in Wartime, 1812-1815." Edinburgh, 1961.
7066
Hein, Edward Bernard. "Niagara Frontier and the War of 1812." Ottawa, 1949.
7067
Horsman, Reginald. "The Causes of the War of 1812." Indiana, 1958.
7068
Kimball, Jeffrey Philip. "Strategy on the Northern Frontier: 1814." Louisiana State, 1969.
7069
Makan, Howard F. "Joseph Gales, the National Intelligency, and the War of 1812." Columbia, 1958.
7070
Pratt, Julius William. "Expansionists of 1812." Chicago, 1924.
Schell, Ernest H. See No./Voir no 7046
7071
Strum, Harvey Joel. "New York and the War of 1812." Syracuse, 1978.

1815 - 1867

7072
Beers, Henry. "The Western Military Frontier, 1815-1846." Pennsylvania, 1935.

7073
Bernard, Jean-Paul. "La pensée et l'influence des Rouges (1848-1867)." Montréal, 1968.

Boulianne, Réal Gérard. See No./Voir no 2430

7074
Bradshaw, Frederick. "Self Government in Canada and How it Was Achieved: The Story of Lord Durham's Report." London, 1904.

Bridgman, Harry John. See No./Voir no 9784

Coelho, Anthony. See No./Voir no 823

7075
Cornell, Paul Grant. "The Alignment of Political Groups in the United Province of Canada, 1841-1867." Toronto, 1955.

7076
Courtemanche, R.A. "Vice-Admiral Sir Alexander Milne, K.C.B. and the North American and West Indian Station, 1860-1864." London, 1967.

Elliott, George Reid. See No./Voir no 7028

7077
Fallis, Laurence Sidney, Jr. "The Idea of Progress in the Province of Canada: 1841-1867." Michigan, 1961.

7078
Garner, John E. "The Franchise and Politics: The Development of the Franchise in the British North American Colonies from the Establishment of Their Representative Assemblies to Their Confederation as the Dominion of Canada." Toronto, 1958.

7079
Gilmore, C.G. "The Constitutional and Financial Aspects of the Administration of Lord Dalhousie in Canada." Durham, 1930.

7080
Goldring, P. "British Colonists and Imperial Interests in Lower Canada, 1820-1841." London, 1978.

7081
Gough, Barry Morton. "The Royal Navy on the North-West Coast of North America, 1810-1910." London, 1969. ⌈British Columbia/Colombie-Britannique⌉

7082
Guthrie Dorothy A. "The Imperial Federation Movement in Canada." Northwestern, 1940.

7083
Ingram, Earl Glynn. "The Age of Ambiguity: Responsible Government in Canada 1840-1846." Georgia, 1973.

Irwin, Leonard B. See No./Voir no 2308

7084
Johnson, Stephen Marshall. "Baron Wrangel and the Russian-American Company 1829-1849: Russian-British Conflict and Cooperation on the Northwest Coast." Manitoba, 1978.

7085
Jones, Elwood Hugh. "The Great Reform Convention of 1859." Queen's, 1972.

Karamanski, Theodore John. See No./Voir no 1245

7086
Kenny, Stephen. "Cultural Patterns in the Union of Canada: The First Decade." Ottawa, 1979.

7087
Kenyon, John P. B. "High Churchmen and Politics, 1845-1865." Toronto, 1967.

Kolish, Evelyn. See No./Voir no 7260

7088
Lawrence, Alan Harvey. "The Influence of British Ideas in the British North American Revolution." Minnesota, 1960.

7089
Lefort, André. "Les deux missions de Denis-Benjamin Viger en Angleterre, en 1828 et de 1831 à 1834." McGill, 1975.

Little, John Irvine. See No./Voir no 3163

McDougall, Elizabeth Anne. See No./Voir no 9885

7090
Martig, Ralph R. "The Hudson's Bay Company Claim 1846-1869." Illinois, 1934.

McCarthy, Mary Martha Cecilia. See No./Voir no 745

7091
McKillop, Alexander Brian. "A Disciplined Intelligence: Intellectual Enquiry and the Moral Imperative in Anglo-Canadian Thought, 1850-1890." Queen's, 1977.

7092
McLaughlin, Merlyn. "Imperial Aspects of the North West Company in Western Canada to 1870." Colorado, 1952.

7093
McNab, D.T. "Herman Merivale and the British Empire, 1806-1874, with Special Reference to British North America, Southern Africa and India." Lancaster, 1978.

Milloy, J.S. See No./Voir no 7453

7094
Mitchinson, Wendy Lynn. "Aspects of Reform: Four Women's Organizations in Nineteenth Century Canada." York, 1977.

7095
Monet, Jacques. "The Last Cannon Shot: A Study of French-Canadian Nationalism, 1837-1850." Toronto, 1969.

7096
Morrison, Hugh Mackenzie. "The Crown Land Policies of the Canadian Government, 1838-1872." Clark, 1933.

7097
Owram, Douglas Robb. "The Great Northwest: The Canadian Expansionist Movement and the Image of the West in the Nineteenth Century." Toronto, 1976.

Peterson, Jacqueline Louise. See No./Voir no 496

Porter, John R. See No./Voir no 947

7098
Rasporich, Anthony Walter. "Political Development of the Province of Canada (1848-1858): The Decline of Ideology and the Emergence of Social Thought." Manitoba, 1970.

7099
Raudzens, George Karl. "The British Ordnance Department in Canada, 1815-1855." Yale, 1970.

Senior, Elinor Kyte. See No./Voir no 7273

7100
Silverman, Jason Howard. " 'Unwelcome Guests': American Fugitive Slaves in Canada, 1830-1860." Kentucky, 1981.

7101
Smith, Jennifer Irene. "A Treatment of Political Institutions in the Confederation Debate." Dalhousie, 1981.

7102
Stalwick, H.N. "A History of Asylum Administration and Lunacy Legislation in Canada Before Confederation." London, 1969.

7103
Trotter, Reginald George. "A Study of the More Immediate Influences Leading to the Federation of the Dominion of Canada." Harvard, 1921.

7104
Waite, Peter Busby. "Ideas and Politics in British North America, 1864-1866: A Study of Opinion on the Subject of Federal Government." Toronto, 1953.

7105
Wearing, J. "Elections and Politics in Canada West Under Responsible Government 1847-1863." Oxford, 1965.

7106
Wright, Anna Margaret. "The Canadian Frontier, 1840-1867." Toronto, 1943.

1867 - 1918

7107
Agnew, Christopher M. "The Failure of the Imperial Idea in Canada." Delaware, 1980.

Andrews, Margaret Winters. See No./Voir no 6788

7108
Ayearst, Morley James. "The Parti Rouge: A Study in Canadian Radicalism." Princeton, 1932.

7109
Bacchi, Carol Lee. "Liberation Deferred: The Ideas of the English-Canadian Suffragists, 1877-1918." McGill, 1977.

Beaven, Brian Philip Newman. See No./Voir no 8651

7110
Berger, Carl Clinton. "The Vision of Grandeur: Studies in the Ideas of Canadian Imperialism, 1867-1914." Toronto, 1967.

Bliss, John William Michael. See No./Voir no 1260

7111
Boudreau, Joseph Amédée. "The Enemy Alien Problem in Canada, 1914-1921." California, Los Angeles, 1965.

7112
Bray, Robert Matthew. "The Canadian Patriotic Response to the Great War." York, 1977.

7113
Burke, Sister Teresa Avila. "Canadian Cabinets in the Making: A Study in the Problems of a Pluralistic Society: 1867-1896." Columbia, 1958.

7114
Calder, William Arnold. "The Federal Penitentiary System of Canada, 1867-1899: A Social and Institutional History." Toronto, 1979.

7115
Clark, Lovell Crosby. "A History of the Conservative Administrations, 1891-1896." Toronto, 1968.

Coelho, Anthony. See No./Voir no 823

7116
Cooper, John I. "French-Canadian Conservatism in Principle and in Practice 1873-1891." McGill, 1939.

7117
Crosslin, Michael Paul. "The Diplomacy of George Gray." Oklahoma State, 1980. [Anglo-American Joint High Commission meeting in Quebec, 1898-1899 and North Atlantic Fisheries Case in 1910/ Réunion de la haute-commission conjointe anglo-américaine au Québec 1898-1899 et le cas des pêches de l'Atlantique nord en 1910]

7118
Erickson, Lynn Ellyn. "A World of Larger Scope: The Liberal Party in Transition, 1874-1880." Toronto, 1977.

Ferguson, Barry Glen. See No./Voir no 1380

7119
Foster, Joan M.V. "Reciprocity in Canadian Politics from the Commercial Union Movement to 1910." Bryn Mawr, 1937.

7120
Friesen, Gerald Arnold. "Studies in the Development of Western Canadian Regional Consciousness, 1870-1925." Toronto, 1974.

7121
Gilbert, Angus Duncan. "The Political Influence of Imperialist Thought in Canada, 1899-1923." Toronto, 1974.

Gough, B.M. See No./Voir no 7081

7122
Green, Janet Jarmé. "Government and Wildlife Preservation, 1885-1922: The Emergence of a Protective Policy." York, 1975.

Haebler, Peter. See No./Voir no 834

7123
Hale, A.W.C. "The National Policies of Canada: Myth and Reality, 1867-1890." Wales, 1979.

Little, John Irvine. See No./Voir no 3163

MacDougall, Heather Anne. See No./Voir no 6695

7124
MacKinnon, Clarence Stuart. "The Imperial Fortresses in Canada: Halifax and Esquimault, 1871-1906." Toronto, 1965.

7125
MacLean, Guy Robertson. "The Imperial Federation Movement in Canada, 1884-1902." Duke, 1958.

7126
Macleod, Roderick Charles. "The North-West Mounted Police 1873-1905: Law Enforcement and the Social Order in the Canadian North-West." Duke, 1972.

7127
Maxwell, James Douglas. "Royal Commissions and Social Change in Canada, 1867-1966." Cornell, 1969.

7128
McClymont, Ian. "Canadian Expansionism, 1903-1914." Michigan State, 1970.

7129
McLaughlin, Kenneth Michael. "Race, Religion and Politics: The Election of 1896 in Canada." Toronto, 1974.

7130
Meen, Sharon Patricia. "The Battle for the Sabbath: The Sabbatarian Lobby in Canada, 1890-1912." British Columbia, 1979.

7131
Miller, James Rodger. "The Impact of the Jesuits' Estates Act on Canadian Politics, 1888-1891." Toronto, 1972.

Mitchinson, Wendy Lynn. See No./Voir no 7094

7132
Morrison, William Robert. "The Mounted Police on Canada's Northern Frontier, 1895-1940." Western Ontario, 1973.

7133
Nicholson, Janice E. "Conflicts of Authority: An Analysis of Relations Among Authority Structures in the Nineteenth Century Gold Rush Camps." York, 1973.

7134
Ostergaard, Karen. "Canadian Nationalism and Anti-Imperialism, 1896-1911." Dalhousie, 1976.

Owram, Douglas Robb. See No./Voir no 7097

Regehr, Theodore David. See No./Voir no 2315

7135
Rider, Peter Edward. "The Imperial Munitions Board and Its Relationship to Government, Business and Labour, 1914-1920." Toronto, 1974.

Robin, Martin. See No./Voir no 2103

7136
Rutherford, Paul F.W. "The New Nationality, 1864-1897: A Study of the National Aims and Ideas of English Canada in the Late Nineteenth Century." Toronto, 1973.

7137
Shortt, Samuel E.D. "Conviction in an Age of Transition: A Study of Selected Canadian Intellectuals, 1890-1930." Queen's, 1973.

7138
Socknat, Thomas Paul. "'Witness Against War': Pacifism in Canada, 1900-1945." McMaster, 1981.

7139
Spigelman, Martin Samuel. "The Acadian Renaissance and the Development of Acadian-Canadian Relations, 1864-1912." Dalhousie, 1976.

7140
Strong-Boag, Veronica Jane. "The Parliament of Women: The National Council of Women of Canada, 1893-1929." Toronto, 1975.

7141
Taylor, Robert John. "The Darwinian Revolution: The Responses of Four Canadian Scholars." McMaster, 1976.

7142
Tippett, Maria W. "The History of the Canadian War Memorial Scheme as a Study of Patronage and Visual Record of the Great War." London, 1982.

7143
Tway, Duane Converse. "The Influence of the Hudson's Bay Company upon Canada, 1870-1889." California, Los Angeles, 1963.

7144
Weise, Selene H.C. "Negotiating the Washington Treaty, 1871." Syracuse, 1974. ⌜United States, Canada, Great Britain/États-Unis, Canada, Grande-Bretagne ⌝

7145
Wetherell, Donald Grant. "Rehabilitation Programmes in Canadian Penitentiaries, 1867-1914: A Study of Official Opinion." Queen's, 1980.

Abella, Irwing Martin. See No./Voir no 2109

Beadle, Gordon Bruce. See No./Voir no 1078

7146
Behiels, Michael Derek. "Prelude to Quebec's 'Quiet Revolution': The Re-Emergence of Liberalism and the Rise of Neo-Nationalism, 1940-1960." York, 1978.

7147
Blauer, Marvin. "The Confederation Crisis and the 1965 Election." McGill, 1971.

Boldt, Menno. See No./Voir no 447

7148
Horn, Michael Steven Daniel. "The League for Social Reconstruction: Socialism and Nationalism in Canada, 1931-1945." Toronto, 1969.

Horowitz, Gad. See No./Voir no 2112

MacPherson, George R. I. See No./Voir no 7482

Maxwell, James Douglas. See No./Voir no 7127

7149
McGinnis, J.P.D. "From Health to Welfare: Federal Government Policies Regarding Standards of Public Health for Canadians, 1919-1945." Alberta, 1980.

7150
Meisel, J. "The Canadian General Election of 1957." London, 1959.

7151
Mills, Allen George. "The Canadian Forum, 1920-1934: A Study in the Development of English Canadian Socialist Thought." Western Ontario, 1976.

Opheim, Lee Alfred. See No./Voir no 2287

Shortt, Samuel Edward D. See No./Voir no 7137

Socknat, Thomas Paul. See No./Voir no 7138

7152
Vipond, Mary Jean. "National Consciousness in English-Speaking Canada in the 1920's: Seven Studies." Toronto, 1974.

7153
Vogel, Hal. "They Brought Their Own Storms: The MacGregor Arctic Expedition (1937-1938)." Union Graduate School, 1976.

Canada and World War II/
Canada et la Deuxième Guerre mondiale

7154
Bagley, John Francis. "The First Quebec Conference, August 14-24, 1943: Decisions at the Crossroads." Georgetown, 1973.

7155
Conacher, James B. "Canadian Participation in the Sicilian Campaign, 1943: The Role of the First Canadian Infantry Division." Harvard, 1949.

7156
Faulkner, Charles T. S. " 'For Christian Civilization': The Churches and Canada's War Effort, 1939-1942." Chicago, 1975.

7157
Lubin, Martin. "Conscription, the National Identity Enigma and the Politics of Ethno-Cultural Cleavage in Canada During World War II." Illinois, 1973.

7158
McKay, William Angus. "The Royal Canadian Army Medical Corps in Northwest Europe, 1944-1945." Toronto, 1951.

Young, William Robert. See No./Voir no 1073

PROVINCIAL AND URBAN HISTORY/ HISTOIRE PROVINCIALE ET URBAINE

General Items/Ouvrages généraux

Saywell, John Tupper. See No./Voir no 8682

British Columbia/Colombie-Britannique
7159
Christian, John Willis. "The Kootenay Gold Rush: The Placer Decade, 1863-1872." Washington State, 1967.
7160
Ormsby, Margaret A. "The Relations Between British Columbia and the Dominion of Canada, 1871-1885." Bryn Mawr, 1937.

Sage, Walter Noble. See No./Voir no 7313
7161
Wynne, Robert Edward. "Reaction to the Chinese in the Pacific Northwest and British Columbia, 1850-1910." Washington, Seattle, 1964.

The Maritime Provinces/Provinces maritimes

General Items/Ouvrages généraux

Brookes, Alan Alexander. See No./Voir no 7629
Forbes, Ernest R. See No./Voir no 2280
Johnson, Arthur L. See No./Voir no 2283
7162
Whitelaw, William M. "The Maritimes and Canada Before Confederation." Columbia, 1934.

New Brunswick/Nouveau-Brunswick

Boggs, Theodore Harding. See No./Voir no 7616
Conrad, Harold Everett. See No./Voir no 7618
7163
Mailhot, Raymond. "Prise de conscience collective acadienne au Nouveau-Brunswick (1860-1891) et comportement de la majorité anglophone." Montréal, 1973.

Moncton

Medjuck, Beth Sheva. See No./Voir no 395

Saint John/Saint-Jean

McGahan, Elizabeth Moore Walsh. See No./Voir no 1290

Newfoundland/Terre-Neuve
7164
Cell, Gilian M.T. "The English in Newfoundland, 1557-1660." Liverpool, 1964.

7165
Clark, Richard L. "Newfoundland 1934-1949: A Study of the Commission of Government and Confederation with Canada." California, Los Angeles, 1951.

Davies, G.J. See No./Voir no 1222
7166
Gunn, Gertrude E. "The Political History of Newfoundland, 1832-1864." London, 1958.
7167
Hiller, James Kelsey. "A History of Newfoundland, 1874-1901." Cambridge, 1971.
7168
McLintock, A.H. "The Establishment of Constitutional Government in Newfoundland, 1783-1832." London, 1938.
7168a
Robison, Houston T. "Newfoundland's Surrender of Dominion Status in the British Empire, 1918-1934." Chicago, 1950.
7169
Thompson, Frederic F. "The Background to the Newfoundland Clauses of the Anglo-French Agreement of 1904." Oxford, 1954.

St. John's/Saint-Jean
7170
Baker, Melvin. "The Government of St. John's, Newfoundland, 1800-1921." Western Ontario, 1981.

Nova Scotia/Nouvelle-Écosse
7171
Armstrong, Maurice Whitman. "The Great Awakening in Nova Scotia, 1776-1809." Harvard, 1945.
7172
Bernard, Frère Antoine. "Une nouvelle Acadie (1755-1933)." Montréal, 1934.

Boggs, Theodore Harding. See No./Voir no 7616
7173
Brebner, John Bartlet. "New England's Outpost: Acadia Before the Conquest of Canada." Columbia, 1927.

Faibisy, John Dewar. See No./Voir no 7029
Hamilton, William Baillie. See No./Voir no 2472
7174
Hutcheson, Austin E. "Pre-Loyalist Nova Scotia: Provincial Settlement Government, Economy, and Institutions under the Old British Empire." Pennsylvania, 1937.

MacLeod, Donald Eric. See No./Voir no 1280
7175
Martell, J.S. "Origins of Self-Government in Nova Scotia, 1815-1836." London, 1935.

Moody, Barry M. See No./Voir no 7290
7176
Morgan, Robert J. "Orphan Outpost: Cape Breton Colony, 1784-1820." Ottawa, 1973.
7177
Muise, Delphin Andrew. "Elections and Constituencies: Federal Politics in Nova Scotia, 1867-1878." Western Ontario, 1971.
7178
Pryke, Kenneth George. "Nova Scotia and Confederation, 1864-1874." Duke, 1962.

7179
Ray, Eldon Pringle. "Transition to Responsible Government in Nova Scotia, 1835-1864." Toronto, 1945.
Ross, Beatrice Spence. See No./Voir no 7045

Amherst

7180
Reilly, J. Nolan. "Emergence of Class Consciousness in Industrial Nova Scotia: Amherst 1891-1925." Dalhousie, 1983.

Halifax

7181
Sutherland, David Alexander. "The Merchants of Halifax, 1815-1850: A Commercial Class in Pursuit of Metropolitan Status." Toronto, 1975.

Louisburg

McNeill, John Robert. See No./Voir no 6966

Prince Edward Island/Île-du-Prince-Édouard

7182
Bolger, Francis W. P. "Prince Edward Island and Confederation, 1863-1873." Toronto, 1959.

Northwest Territories and Yukon/ Territoires du Nord-Ouest et Yukon

7183
Guest, Henry James. "City of Gold: Dawson, Yukon Territory, 1896-1918." Manitoba, 1982.
7184
Lalonde, André-N. "Settlement in the Northwest Territories by Colonization Companies, 1881-1891." Laval, 1971.
7185
Lingard, Charles Cecil. "Territorial Government in Canada: The Autonomy Question in the Old Northwest Territories." Chicago, 1940.
Looy, Anthony Jacobus. See No./Voir no 7451
7186
Taylor, John Leonard. "The Development of an Indian Policy for the Canadian Northwest 1869-1879." Queen's, 1976.
7187
Thomas, Lewis Herbert. "Responsible Government in the Canadian North-West Territories, 1870-1897." Minnesota, 1953.

Ontario

7188
Aitchison, James Hermiston. "The Development of Local Government in Upper Canada, 1783-1850." Toronto, 1953.
7189
Baldwin, Douglas Owen. "Political and Social Behaviour in Ontario, 1879-1891: A Quantitative Approach." York, 1973.
Ball, Norman Roger. See No./Voir no 91

7190
Barron, Frank Laurie. "The Genesis of Temperance i Ontario: 1828-1850." Guelph, 1976.
Beaven, Brian Philip Norman. See No./Voir no 8651
7191
Bowsfield, Hartwell Walter Lewis. "Upper Canada i the 1820's: The Development of Political Con sciousness." Toronto, 1977.
7192
Butt, William Davison. "The Donnellys: History Legend, Literature." Western Ontario, 1977.
7193
Choquette, J.E. Robert. "The Roman Catholic Churc and English-French Conflict in Ontario: 1897 1927." Chicago, 1972.
7194
Decarie, Malcolm G. "The Prohibition Movement i Ontario: 1894-1916." Queen's, 1972.
7195
Dembski, Peter E.P. "William Ralph Meredith Leader of the Conservative Opposition in Ontario 1878-1894." Guelph, 1977.
7196
Deshaies, Bruno. "Évolution des états du Québec et d l'Ontario entre 1867 et 1871." Montréal, 1973.
7197
Dunham, Aileen. "Political Unrest in Upper Canada 1815-1836." London, 1924.
7198
Fraser, Robert Lochiel, III. "Like Eden in Her Summe Dress: Gentry, Economy, and Society: Uppe Canada, 1812-1840." Toronto, 1979.
Gaffield, Charles Mitchell. See No./Voir no 2490
7199
Killan, Gerald. "Preserving Ontario's Heritage: History of the Ontario Historical Society. McMaster, 1973.
7200
Léger, Lauraine. "Les sanctions populaires en Acadi région du comté de Kent." Laval, 1976.
Macleod, Marion J. See No./Voir no 130
McGuigan, Gerald Frederick. See No./Voir no 136
7201
Morrison, Terrence Robert. "The Child and Urba Social Reform in Late Nineteenth Century Ontaric 1875-1900." Toronto, 1971.
7202
Nelles, Henry Vivian. "The Politics of Developmen Forests, Mines and Hydro-Electric Power i Ontario, 1890-1939." Toronto, 1970.
7203
Palmer, Bryan Douglas. "Most Uncommon Me Craft, Culture and Conflict in a Canadian Com munity, 1860-1914." SUNY, Binghamton, 1977.
7204
Patterson, Graeme Hazlewood. "Studies in Election and Public Opinion in Upper Canada." Toront 1969.
7205
Pendle, Frank Ernest, Jr. "Land Settlement an Development Problems in Southwestern Uppe Canada, 1791-1867." Kent State, 1980. ⌈Middl sex and Elgin Counties/Comtés de Middlesex et Elgin⌋

7206
Read, Colin Frederick. "The Rising in Western Upper Canada, 1837-1938: The Duncombe Revolt and After." Toronto, 1974.

Roberts, S.C. See No./Voir no 7044

7207
Rosser, Frederick Thomas. "The Welsh Settlement in Upper Canada." Ottawa, 1953.

7208
Simpson, Donald George. "Negroes in Ontario from Early Times to 1870." Western Ontario, 1971.

7209
Swainson, Donald Wayne. "The Personnel of Politics: A Study of the Ontario Members of the Second Federal Parliament." Toronto, 1969.

7210
Talman, James John. "Life in the Pioneer Districts of Upper Canada, 1815-1840." Toronto, 1930.

7211
Westfall, William Edward. "The Sacred and the Secular: Studies in the Cultural History of Protestant Ontario in the Victorian Period." Toronto, 1976.

Wilson, Bruce Gordon. See No./Voir no 7058

Wylie, William N.T. See No./Voir no 7059

Berlin/Kitchener/Waterloo

7212
Bloomfield, Elizabeth Phyllis. "City-Building Processes in Berlin, Kitchener, and Waterloo, 1870-1930." Guelph, 1981.

Buxton

7213
Walton, Jonathan William. "Blacks in Buxton and Chatham, Ontario, 1830-1890: Did the 49th Parallel make a Difference?" Princeton, 1979.

Chatham

7214
Farrell, John Kevin Anthony. "The History of the Negro Community in Chatham, Ontario, 1787-1865." Ottawa, 1955.

Hamilton

7215
Heron, W. Craig. "Working-Class Hamilton, 1895-1930." Dalhousie, 1981.

Kingston

7216
Bindon, Kathryn M. "Kingston: A Social History, 1785-1830." Queen's, 1979.

Harris, Simon Richard. See No./Voir no 2240

Ottawa

7217
Brault, Lucien. "Ottawa de ses débuts à nos jours." Ottawa, 1941.

Palmerston

7218
Smith, Mary Dolores. "A History of Palmerston, Ontario." Cincinnati, 1980. [1871-1980]

Peterborough

7219
Doyle, Kevin. "Stability and Change in Mid-Victorian Canada: The Case of Peterborough, 1851-1871." Dalhousie, 1981.

Sudbury

7220
Cuthbert-Brandt, Gail Patricia. " 'J'y suis, j'y reste': The French Canadians in Sudbury, 1883-1913." York, 1977.

Toronto

7221
Armstrong, Frederick Henry. "Toronto in Transition: The Emergence of a City 1829-1838." Toronto, 1965.

7222
Bator, Paul Adolphus. " 'Saving Lives on the Wholesale Plan': Public Health Reform in the City of Toronto, 1900-1930." Toronto, 1979.

7223
Brown, Thomas Edward. "Living with God's Afflicted: A History of the Provincial Lunatic Asylum at Toronto, 1820-1911." Queen's, 1981.

7224
Burns, Robert Joseph. "The First Elite of Toronto: An Examination of the Genesis, Consolidation and Duration of Power in an Emerging Colonial Society." Western Ontario, 1975.

Davison-Wood, Karen Margaret. See No./Voir no 942

7225
Dyster, Barrie Drummond. "Toronto, 1840-1860: Making it a British Protestant Town." Toronto, 1970.

7226
Jarvis, Eric James. "Mid-Victorian Toronto: Panic, Policy and Public Response, 1857-1873." Western Ontario, 1979.

Mays, Herbert Joseph. See No./Voir no 131

7227
McKee, Leila Gay Mitchell. "Voluntary Youth Organizations in Toronto, 1880-1930." York, 1983.

Morrison, Philip Scott. See No./Voir no 4951

Morrison, Terrence Robert. See No./Voir no 7201

7228
Nicolson, Murray William Wood. "The Catholic Church and the Irish in Victorian Toronto." Guelph, 1981.

7229
Pitsula, James Michael. "The Relief of Poverty in Toronto, 1880-1930." York, 1979.

7230
Stagg, Ronald John. "The Yonge Street Rebellion of 1837: An Examination of the Social Background and a Re-Assessment of the Events." Toronto, 1976.

White, William Alan. See No./Voir no 4833

The Prairie Provinces/Provinces des prairies

General Items/Ouvrages généraux

7231
Breen, David Henry. "The Canadian West and the Ranching Frontier, 1875-1922." Alberta, 1972.
7232
Thompson, John. "The Harvests of War: The Prairie West 1914-1918." Queen's, 1975.

Alberta

7233
Drouin, Eméric O. "La colonie Saint-Paul-des-Métis, Alberta, 1896-1909." Ottawa, 1962.
Foster, Franklin Lloyd. See No./Voir no 7340
7234
Harper, Irene M. "A History of the Real Old Times of Fort Edmonton (Canada) and Its Hinterland (1835-1905)." Cambridge, 1932.
7235
Malliah, Holavanahally L. "A Socio-Historical Study of the Legislators of Alberta, 1905-1967." Alberta, 1970.
7236
Palmer, Howard Delbert. "Nativism and Ethnic Tolerance in Alberta: 1920-1972." York, 1974.
Sheehan, Nancy Mary. See No./Voir no 2444
7237
Swann, Francis Richard. "Progressive Social Credit in Alberta, 1935-1940." Cincinnati, 1971.
7238
Thomas, Lewis G. "The Liberal Party in Alberta: A Political History of the Province of Alberta, 1905-1921." Harvard, 1954.
7239
Voisey, Paul Leonard. "Forging the Western Tradition: Pioneer Approaches to Settlement and Agriculture in Southern Alberta Communities." Toronto, 1983.

Calgary

7240
Foran, Maxwell Laurence. "The Civic Corporation and Urban Growth: Calgary 1884-1930." Calgary, 1981.

Edmonton

7241
Betke, C.F. "The Development of Urban Community in Prairie Canada: Edmonton 1898-1921." Alberta, 1981.
Harper, Irene M. See No./Voir no 7234

Manitoba

Crunican, Paul Eugene. See No./Voir no 2456
Foster, John Elgin. See No./Voir no 2740
7242
McCutcheon, Brian Robert. "The Economic and Social Structure of Political Agrarianism in Manitoba: 1870-1900." British Columbia, 1974.
Pritchett, John P. See No./Voir no 4740

Brandon

7243
Clark, Walter Leland R. "Politics in Brandon City, 1899-1949." Alberta, 1976.

Winnipeg

7244
Artibise, Alan Francis Joseph. "The Urban Development of Winnipeg, 1874-1914." British Columbia, 1971.
Bellan, Ruben C. See No./Voir no 4962
Grenke, Arthur. See No./Voir no 776

Saskatchewan

7245
Brennan, James Williams. "A Political History of Saskatchewan, 1905-1929." Alberta, 1976.
7246
Huel, Raymond J. A. "La Survivance in Saskatchewan Schools, Politics and the Nativist Crusade for Cultural Conformity." Alberta, 1975.
7247
Milnor, Andrew Johnson. "Agrarian Protest in Saskatchewan, 1929-1948: A Study in Ethnic Politics." Duke, 1962.
7248
White, Clinton Oliver. "Saskatchewan Builds an Electrical System." Saskatchewan, 1969.

Quebec/Québec

7249
Armstrong, Elizabeth H. "The Crisis of Quebec, 1914-1918." Columbia, 1937.
7250
Bernier, Gérald. "Développement politique, dépendance et analyse historique. Un champ d'application: la société québécoise de 1837 à 1867." Laval, 1978.
Coffin, Victor E. See No./Voir no 7025
7251
Corbeil, Pierre. "Les députés anglophones et le premier gouvernement du Québec de 1867 à 1871." Montréal, 1979.
Deshaies, Bruno. See No./Voir no 7196
7252
Dickinson, John Alexander. "Justice et justiciables La procédure civile à la prévôté de Québec, 1667-1759." Toronto, 1977.
7253
Fahmy-Eid, Nadia. "L'idéologie ultramontaine au Québec (1848-1871): composantes, manifestations et signification au niveau de l'histoire sociale de la période." Montréal, 1974.
7254
Garff, Dennis Royal. "Heirs of New France: An Ethnic Minority in Search of Security." Tufts, 1970.
7255
Gordon, Richard Irving. "The Nationalist Prism: A Study of Ethnicity, Social Class, and Nationalism in Quebec Province: 1919-1936." California, Irvine, 1982.

7256

Gravel, Jean-Yves. "Les Voltigeurs de Québec dans la milice canadienne (1862-1878)." Laval, 1971.

Greenwood, Frank Murray. See No./Voir no 7032

7257

Greer, Allan Robert. "Habitants of the Lower Richelieu: Rural Society in Three Quebec Parishes, 1740-1840." York, 1980.

Griffin, Elizabeth Anne. See No./Voir no 8573

7258

Hamelin, Marcel. "L'assemblée législative de la province de Québec: 1867-1878." Laval, 1972.

7259

Hardy, René. "Les Zouaves pontificaux et la diffusion de l'ultra-montanisme au Canada français, 1860-1870." Laval, 1979.

7260

Kolish, Evelyn. "Changement dans le droit privé au Québec et au Bas-Canada entre 1760 et 1840: attitudes et réactions des contemporains." Montréal, 1981.

7261

Lafleur, Normand. "La vie traditionnelle des coureurs de bois dans les régions de Charlevoix, Mauricie et Outaouais." Laval, 1968.

7262

Levitt, Joseph. "The Social Program of the Nationalists of Quebec (1900-1914)." Toronto, 1968.

McGuigan, Gerald Frederick. See No./Voir no 136

Ouellet, Fernand. See No./Voir no 1252

Reid, Allana G. See No./Voir no 7275

Rossignol, Leo. See No./Voir no 7268

Rouillard, Jacques. See No./Voir no 2131

7263

Silver, Arthur Isaac. "Quebec and the French-Speaking Minorities, 1864-1917." Toronto, 1973.

Smith, L.A.H. See No./Voir no 7048

7264

Swan, G.R. "The Economy and Politics in Quebec, 1774-1791." Oxford, 1978.

Têtu, Michel. See No./Voir no 2132

7265

Ullman, Walter. "The Quebec Bishops and Federal Politics, 1870-1896." Rochester, 1961.

Beauport

7266

Larouche, Georges. "La civilisation rurale à Beauport au XVIIe siècle." Laval, 1965.

Herbertville

7267

Séguin, Normand. "Notre-Dame d'Herbertville, 1850-1900, une paroisse de colonisation au XIXe siècle." Ottawa, 1976.

Hull

7268

Rossignol, Léo. "Histoire documentaire de Hull, 1792-1900." Ottawa, 1941.

Montreal/Montréal

7269

Bertley, Leo W. "The Universal Negro Improvement Association of Montreal, 1917-1979." Concordia, 1980.

7270

Germain, Anne. "Mouvements sociaux de réforme urbaine à Montréal de 1880 à 1920." Montréal, 1981.

7271

Linteau, Paul A. "Histoire de la ville de Maisonneuve, 1883-1918." Montréal, 1975.

7272

Richardson, Joan T. "Organized Instability: The Women's Movement in Montreal (1974-1977)." New School, 1983.

7273

Senior, Elinor Kyte. "An Imperial Garrison in Its Colonial Setting: British Regulars in Montreal, 1832-1854." McGill, 1976.

7274

Zeitz, Mordecai. "The History of the Federation of Jewish Philanthropies of Montreal." Yeshiva, 1974.

Quebec/Québec

7275

Reid, Allana G. "The Growth and Importance of the City of Quebec, 1608-1760." McGill, 1951.

7276

Ruddel, David-Thiery. "Quebec City, 1765-1831: The Evolution of a Colonial Town." Laval, 1981.

HISTORICAL PERSONALITIES/ PERSONNAGES HISTORIQUES

-1763

Beauharnois de la Boische, Charles, Marquis de (1670-1749)

7277

Standen, Sydney Dale. "Charles, Marquis de Beauharnois de la Boische, Governor General of New France, 1726-1747." Toronto, 1975.

Bigot, François (1703-1775)

7278

Porteous, H.A. "The Administration of François Bigot as Intendant of New France." Oxford, 1978.

Bradstreet, John (1714-1774)

7279

Godfrey, William G. "John Bradstreet: An Irregular Regular, 1714-1774." Queen's, 1974.

Cartier, Jacques (1491-1557)

7280

Sevenster Gelshe. "La vie et l'oeuvre de Jacques Cartier." Montréal, 1961.

Chartier de Lotbinière, Michel (1748-1822)

7281

Maschino, Sylvette. "Michel Chartier de Lotbinière: l'action et la pensée d'un Canadien du 18e siècle." Montréal, 1978.

Dablon, Claude (1619?-1697)

7282
Charette, S. "Claude Dobbon, S.J. et la Nouvelle-France, (1655-1697)." Montréal, 1954.

Denonville, Jacques René de Brisay, Marquis de (d.1710)

7283
Leclerc, Jean. "Denonville et l'alliance anglo-iroquoise." Ottawa, 1968.

7284
Prince-Falmagne, Thérèse. "Un gouverneur de la Nouvelle-France: Jacques René de Brisay, Marquis de Denonville." Montréal, 1959.

Frontenac, Louis de Buade, Comte de (1620-1698)

7285
Eccles, William J. "Frontenac and New France, 1672-1698." McGill, 1955.

Hamilton, Henry (1732-1796)

7286
Jaebker, Orville John. "Henry Hamilton: British Soldier and Colonial Governor." Indiana, 1954.

Hocquart, Gilles (1694-1783)

7287
Horton, Donald James. "Gilles Hocquart, Intendant of New France, 1729-1748." McGill, 1975.

Loudoun, John Campbell, 1st Earl of (1598-1663)

7288
Pargellis, Stanley McCrory. "Lord Loudoun and the Seven Years War." Yale, 1929.

Marie de l'Incarnation (1599-1672)

7289
Marie-Emmanuel, Soeur. "Marie de l'Incarnation d'après ses lettres." Ottawa, 1946.
Michel, Robert. See No./Voir no 8300

Mascarene, Paul (1684-1760)

7290
Moody, Barry M. "A Just and Disinterested Man: The Nova Scotia Career of Paul Mascarene, 1710-1752." Queen's, 1977.

Murray, General James (1721-1794)

Wetherell, Albert Anthony. See No./Voir no 7016

Ramezay, Claude de (1659-1724)

7291
Hardie, Thomas Neil. "Claude de Ramezay." Montréal, 1957.

Smith, William (1728-1793)

7292
Upton, Leslie F. S. "William Smith, Chief Justice of New York and Quebec, 1728-1793." Minnesota, 1957.

Talon, Jean-Baptiste (1625?-1694)

7293
La Montagne, Roland. "Jean Talon et la colonisation de la Nouvelle-France." Montréal, 1953.

Vaudreuil, Philippe de Rigaud de (1643-1725)

7294
Zoltvany, Yves-François. "Philippe de Rigaud de Vaudreuil, Governor of New France, (1703-1725)." Alberta, 1964.

1763-1812

Calvet, Pierre du (d.1786)

7295
Gascon, Adélard, "Pierre du Calvet, monographie." Ottawa, 1947.

Carleton, Sir Guy (1724-1808)

7296
Gorn, Michael Herman. "To Preserve Good Humor and Perfect Harmony: Guy Carleton and the Governing of Quebec, 1766-1774." Southern California, 1978.

7297
Jones, Eldon Lewis. "Sir Guy Carleton and the Close of the War of Independence, 1782-1783." Duke, 1968.

7298
Leroy, Perry Eugene. "Sir Guy Carleton as a Military Leader During the American Invasion and Repulse in Canada, 1775-1776." Ohio State, 1960.

Des Barres, Joseph Frederick Wallet (1721-1824)

7299
Evans, Geraint N.D. "North American Soldier, Hydrographer, Governor: The Public Career of J.F.W. Des Barres, 1721-1824." Yale, 1965.

Fothergill, Charles (1782-1840)

7300
Romney, Paul Martin. "A Man out of Place: The Life of Charles Fothergill: Naturalist, Businessman, Journalist, Politician, 1782-1840." Toronto, 1981.

Gratiot, Charles (?-.1817)

7301
Barnhart, Warren Lynn. "The Letterbooks of Charles Gratiot, Fur Trader: The Nomadic Years, 1767-1797, Edited with an Historical Introduction." St Louis, 1972.

Haldimand, Frederick (1718-1791)

7302
Dendy, John Oliver. "Frederick Haldimand and the Defence of Canada, 1778-1784." Duke, 1972.

Hamilton, Robert (1750-1809)

Wilson, Bruce Gordon. See No./Voir no 7058

Ingraham, Benjamin (1743-1810)

7303
Thomas, Earle Schwartz. "Benjamin Ingraham, Loyalist: A Case Study." Concordia, 1979.

Mountain, Jacob (1793-1825)

Millman, Thomas R. See No./Voir no 9899

Murray, General James

Wetherell, Albert Anthony. See No./Voir no 7016

Salaberry, Ignace Michel Louis Antoine d'Irumberry de (1752-1828)

7304
Gagné, Lucien. "Salaberry." Montréal, 1948.

Simcoe, John Graves (1752-1806)

7305
Danglade, James Kirby. "John Graves Simcoe and the United States, 1775-1796: A Study in Anglo-American Frontier Diplomacy." Ball State, 1972.

Vancouver, George (1757-1798)

7306
Anderson, Bern. "Captain George Vancouver, R.N., 1757-1798." Harvard, 1954.
7307
Boone, Lalla R. "Captain George Vancouver on the Northwest Coast." California, Berkeley, 1940.

1813-1867

Baldwin, Robert (1804-1858)

7308
Wilson, George Earl. "The Life of Robert Baldwin." Harvard, 1926.

Baillairge, Charles (1826-1906)

Cameron, Christina. See No./Voir no 930

Brown, George (1818-1880)

Careless, James M.S. See No./Voir no 1081

Buller, Charles (1808-1848)

7309
Sweetman, E. "Life and Times of the Right Honourable Charles Buller." London, 1952.

Cartier, Georges-Étienne (1814-1872)

7310
Best, Henry B.M. "Georges-Étienne Cartier." Laval, 1970.

Chambreau, Edward (1820-1902)

7311
Wehrkamp, Timothy Lee. "Edward Chambreau: His Autobiography. Edited with an Introduction." Oregon, 1976.

Dorion, Jean-Baptiste-Éric (1826-1866)

7312
Carrier, Maurice. "Le libéralisme de Jean-Baptiste-Éric Dorion." Laval, 1968.

Douglas, Sir James (1803-1877)

7313
Sage, Walter Noble. "Sir James Douglas and British Columbia." Toronto, 1925.

Ellice Edward (1781-1863)

7314
Colthart, James Myron. "Edward Ellice and North America." Princeton, 1971.
7315
Long, Dorothy Elizabeth. "Edward Ellice." Toronto, 1941.

Fabre, Édouard Raymond (1799-1854)

7316
Roy, Jean-Louis. "Édouard Raymond Fabre, bourgeois patriote du Bas-Canada, 1799-1854." McGill, 1972.

Fothergill, Charles (1782-1840)

Romney, Paul Martin. See No./Voir no 7300

Galt, John (1779-1839)

7317
Gordon, Robert Kay. "John Galt." Toronto, 1920.

Head, Sir Edmund (1795-1868)

7318
Kerr, D.G.G. "The Work of Sir Edmund Head in British North America, 1848-1861." London, 1937.

Head, Sir Francis Bond (1793-1875)

7319
Jackman, Sydney W. " 'Galloping Head': The Life of the Right Honourable Sir Francis Bond Head, Bart., P.D., etc., 1793-1875, Late Lieutenant Governor of Upper Canada." Harvard, 1953.

Hincks, Francis (1807-1885)

7320
Longley, Ronald S. "Francis Hincks, Canadian Politician and Statesman." Harvard, 1934.

Holton, Luther Hamilton (1817-1880)

7321
Klassen, Henry Cornelius. "L.H. Holton: Montreal Business Man and Politician, 1817-1867." Toronto, 1970.

Howe, Joseph (1804-1873)

7322
MacLean, Raymond Angus. "Joseph Howe and British-American Union." Toronto, 1966.

Langevin, Hector-Louis (1826-1906)

7323
Désilets, Andrée. "Un père de la Confédération canadienne, Hector-Louis Langevin (1826-1906)." Laval, 1968.

Lartigue, J.J. (1777-1840)

Chausse, Gilles. See No./Voir no 9892

Macdonald, John Sandfield (1820-1872)

7324
Hodgins, Bruce Willard. "The Political Career of John Sandfield Macdonald to the Fall of His Administration in March, 1864: A Study in Canadian Politics." Duke, 1965.

Macdonell, Alexander (1762-1840)

7325
Rea, James E. "Alexander Macdonell and the Politics of Upper Canada." Queen's, 1971.
Somers, Hugh Joseph. See No./Voir no 9905

Mackenzie, William Lyon (1795-1861)

7326
Kilbourn, William Morley. "The Firebrand: William Lyon Mackenzie and the Rebellion in Upper Canada." Harvard, 1957.

Maitland, Peregrine (1777-1854)

7327
Quealey, Francis Michael. "The Administration of Peregrine Maitland, Lieutenant Governor of Upper Canada." Toronto, 1968.

McGee, Thomas D'Arcy (1825-1868)

7328
Burns, Robin Bruce. "Thomas D'Arcy McGee: Biography." McGill, 1976.

Papineau, Louis-Joseph (1786-1871)

Balthazar, Louis Rémus. See No./Voir no 8467

Parent, Étienne (1801-1874)

Nourry, Louis. See No./Voir no 8468

Viger, Denis Benjamin (1777-1864)

Lefort, André. See No./Voir no 7089

1868-1932

Anglin, Timothy Warren (1822-1896)

7329
Baker, William Melville. "No Shillelagh: The Life Journalism and Politics of Timothy Warren Anglin. Western Ontario, 1972.

Benoit, Paul (1850-1915)

7330
Dupasquier, Maurice. "Paul Benoit et le nouvea monde, 1850-1915." Laval, 1971.

Blake, Edward (1833-1912)

7331
Banks, Margaret Amelia. "Edward Blake, Irish Nation alism, 1892-1907." Toronto, 1953.
7332
Livermore, John D. "Towards 'A Union of Hearts The Early Career of Edward Blake, 1867-1880. Queen's, 1975.

Borden, Sir Robert (1854-1939)

7333
Crowley, James A. "Sir Robert Borden: The Motiva tion Behind the Introduction of Conscription an the Formation of the Union Government, 1917. Ottawa, 1958.
7334
Eagle, John Andrew. "Sir Robert Borden and th Railway Problem in Canadian Politics, 1911-1920. Toronto, 1972.
7335
English, John Richard. "Sir Robert Borden, the Con servative Party and Political Change, 1901-1920. Harvard, 1974.
7336
Wilson, Harold Arnold. "The Imperial Policy of Si Robert Borden, 1911-1920: A Study in th Advancement of Dominion Status." Iowa State 1961.

Bourassa, Henri (1868-1952)

337
Bousquet, D. "Henri Bourassa and the Evolution of Anglo-Canadian Relations, 1899-1931." Cambridge, 1953.
MacMillan, Charles Michael. See No./Voir no 8463
338
O'Connell, Martin Patrick. "Henri Bourassa and Canadian Nationalism." Toronto, 1954.

Bourassa, Napoléon (1827-1916)

339
Lemoine, Roger. "Napoléon Bourassa: sa vie, son oeuvre." Laval, 1970.

Brownlee, John Edward (1884-1961)

340
Foster, Franklin Lloyd. "John Edward Brownlee: A Biography." Alberta, 1981.

Cartwright, Sir Richard John (1835-1912)

341
Graham, William Roger. "Sir Richard Cartwright and the Liberal Party, 1863-1896." Toronto, 1950.

Chapleau, Sir Joseph-Adolphe (1840-1898)

342
Munro, Kenneth. "The Political Career of Sir Joseph-Adolphe Chapleau." Ottawa, 1973.

Chown, Samuel Dwight (1853-1933)

Schwarz, Edward Richard. See No./Voir no 9904

Coaker, Sir William Ford (1871-1938)

McDonald, D.H.I. See No./Voir no 2140

Currie, Sir Arthur (1875-1933)

Hyatt, Albert Mark John. See No./Voir no 7411

Dafoe, John Wesley (1866-1944)

Cook, George Ramsey. See No./Voir no 8464

Davin, Nicholas Flood (1867-1914)

Koester, Charles Beverley. See No./Voir no 6948

Denison, George Taylor III (1839-1925)

343
Gagan, David Paul. "The Queen's Champion: The Life of George Taylor Denison III, Soldier, Author, Magistrate and Canadian Tory Patriot." Duke, 1969.

Dollar, Robert (1844-1932)

O'Brien, Gregory Charles. See No./Voir no 2028

Dufferin and Ava, Frederick Temple Blackwood, 1st Marquess of/(1826-1902)

7344
Irving, R.G. "A Study of Certain Powers of the Canadian Governor-Generalship Under Lord Dufferin, 1872-1878." Oxford, 1964.

Ewart, John Skirving (1849-1933)

7345
Cole, Douglas Lowell. "The Better Patriot: John S. Ewart and the Canadian Nation." Washington, Seattle, 1968.

Ferguson, Howard (1870-1946)

7346
Oliver, Peter Nesbitt. "The Making of a Provincial Premier, Howard Ferguson and Ontario Politics: 1870-1923." Toronto, 1969.

Feild, Bishop Edward (1801-1876)

Jones, Frederick. See No./Voir no 9896

Fleming, Sir Sandford (1827-1915)

7347
Richeson, David Randall. "Sandford Fleming and the Establishment of a Pacific Cable." Alberta, 1972.

Galt, Sir Alexander T. (1817-1893)

7348
Otter, Andy Albert Den. "Sir Alexander T. Galt and the Northwest: A Case Study of Entrepreneurialism on the Frontier." Alberta, 1975.

Godbout, Adélard (1892-1956)

7349
Genest, Jean-Guy. "Vie et oeuvre d'Adélard Godbout, 1892-1956." Laval, 1978.

Greenway, Thomas (1838-1908)

7350
Hilts, Joseph Alfred. "The Political Career of Thomas Greenway." Manitoba, 1974.

Grey, Albert Henry George, 4th Earl of (1851-1917)

7351
Hallett, Mary E. "The 4th Earl Grey as Governor-General of Canada, 1904-1911." London, 1970.

Hughes, Sir Sam (1853-1921)

7352
Haycock, Ronald Graham. "Sir Sam Hughes: His Public Career, 1892-1916." Western Ontario, 1976.

Langevin, Sir Hector-Louis (1826-1906)

Désilets, Andrée. See No./Voir no 7323

Lansdowne, Lord (1845-1927)

7353
Gordon, John Lee, Jr. "Lord Lansdowne in Canada, 1883-1888: The Office of Governor General in a Self-Governing Dominion." Vanderbilt, 1972.

Laurier, Sir Wilfrid (1841-1919)

7354
Baxter, Neil H. "The Influence of Sir Wilfrid Laurier on the Formation of the British Commonwealth of Nations." Iowa, 1937.
7355
Colvin, J.A. "Sir Wilfrid Laurier and the Imperial Problem, 1896-1906." London, 1955.
7356
McMinn, Kayron Campbell. "Laurier Versus Chamberlain: Anglo-Canadian Relations, 1896-1905." Oklahoma, 1977.
7357
Neatby, Herbert Blair. "Laurier and a Liberal Quebec: A Study in Political Management." Toronto, 1956.
7358
Stevens, Paul Douglas. "Laurier and the Liberal Party in Ontario, 1887-1911." Toronto, 1966.
7359
Strand, William Eugene. "The Canadianism of Sir Wilfrid Laurier: A Study of His Liberalism and Nationalism from 1871 to 1911." George Peabody, 1967.
7360
Walsh, Robert James Patrick. " 'Silver-Tongued' Laurier and the Imperialists, 1876-1906: A Character Study in Imperial History." South Carolina, 1979.

Le Sage, Siméon (1835-1909)

7361
Trépanier, Pierre. "Siméon Le Sage, haut fonctionnaire (1835-1909) — contribution à l'histoire administrative du Québec." Ottawa, 1976.

Macdonald, Sir John A. (1815-1891)

Heick, Welf Henry. See No./Voir no 7363
7362
Stewart, Alice R. "The Imperial Policy of Sir John A. Macdonald, Canada's First Prime Minister." Radcliffe, 1946.

Mackenzie, Alexander (1822-1892)

7363
Heick, Welf Henry. "Mackenzie and Macdonald Federal Politics and Politicians in Canada, 1873-1878." Duke, 1966.

John Macoun (1831-1920)

Waiser, William Andrew. See No./Voir no 5082

Macphail, Sir Andrew (1860-1938)

7364
Robertson, Ian Ross. "Sir Andrew Macphail as a Social Critic." Toronto, 1974.

McCarthy, D'Alton (1836-1898)

7365
Kulisek, Larry Lee. "D'Alton McCarthy and the True Nationalization of Canada." Wayne State, 1973.

Meredith, William Ralph (1840-1923)

Dembski, Peter Edward Paul. See No./Voir no 7195

Mills, David (1831-1903)

7366
McMurchy, Donald J. A. "David Mills: Nineteenth Century Canadian Liberal." Rochester, 1969.

Minto, Gilbert John Elliot-Murray-Kynynmound, 4th Earl of (1845-1914)

7367
Miller, C.C.I. "The Public Career of the 4th Earl of Minto in Canada." London, 1971. [1899-1904]

Mount Stephen, Sir George Stephen, Bart, 1st Baron (1829-1921)

7368
Donald, Heather M. "The Life of Lord Mount Stephen, 1829-1921." London, 1953.

Mowat, Sir Oliver (1820-1903)

7369
Evans, Anna Margaret. "Oliver Mowat and Ontario, 1872-1896: A Study in Political Success." Toronto, 1967.

Normanby, George Augustus Constantine Phipps, Earl of Mulgrave and Marquess of (1819-1890)

7370
Heatley, Alistair John. "Lord Normanby: A Study of the Governorship in the Self-Governing Colonies in the Late Nineteenth Century." McMaster, 1972.

Nowlan, George (1898-1965)

7371
Conrad, Margaret Rose S. "George Nowlan and the Conservative Party in the Annapolis Valley, Nova Scotia, 1925-1965." Toronto, 1979.

Olivier, W.P. (1912-   )

Thomson, Colin Argyle. See No./Voir no 2556

Parkin, Sir George (1846-1922)

7372
Cook, Terry Gordon. "Apostle of Empire: Sir George Parkin and Imperial Federation." Queen's, 1977.

Paull, Andrew (1892-1959)

Patterson, E. Palmer II. See No./Voir no 480

Pearce, William (1848-1930)

7373
Mitchner, Ernest Alyn. "William Pearce and Federal Government Activity in Western Canada, 1882-1904." Alberta, 1971.

Riel, Louis (1844-1885)

7374
Amiott, William Kenneth. "The Status of the Sanity of Louis Riel as Revealed by His Regina Prison Diary." North Dakota, 1968.

7375
Jonasson, Jonas A. "The Riel Rebellions." Stanford, 1934.

7376
Lamb, Robert E. "Friction Between Ontario and Quebec Caused by the Risings of Louis Riel." Ottawa, 1954.

7377
Stanley, C.F.G. "The Second Riel Rebellion, 1870-1886." Oxford, 1935.

Rowell, Newton Wesley (1867-1941)

7378
Prang, Margaret Evelyn. "The Political Career of Newton W. Rowell." Toronto, 1959.

Roy, Paul-Eugène (1859-1926)

See also History of French Canada/Voir aussi Histoire du Canada français

Seghers, Charles John (1839-1886)

Steckler, Gerard George. See No./Voir no 9906

Sellar, Robert (1841-1919)

7379
Hill, Robert Andrew. "Robert Sellar and the Huntingdon Gleaner: The Conscience of Rural Protestant Quebec, 1863-1919." Toronto, 1970.

Seton, Ernest Thompson (1860-1946)

Wadland, John Henry. See No./Voir no 951

Sévigny, Albert (1880-1961)

7380
Bélanger, Réal. "Albert Sévigny et le parti conservateur (1902-1918)." Laval, 1980.

Sifton, Sir Clifford (1861-1929)

7381
Hall, David John. "The Political Career of Clifford Sifton, 1896-1905." Toronto, 1973.

Smith, Goldwin (1823-1910)

7382
McEachern, Ronald Alexander. "Goldwin Smith." Toronto, 1934.

Tarte, Joseph Israël (1848-1907)

7383
LaPierre, Laurier J. L. "Politics, Race and Religion in French Canada: Joseph Israël Tarte." Toronto, 1962.

Taschereau, Elzéar Alexandre (1820-1898)

Gaudin, Jean R. See No./Voir no 9894

Taschereau, Louis-Alexandre (1867-1952)

7384
Vigod, Bernard L. "Responses to Economic and Social Change in Quebec: The Provincial Administration of Louis-Alexandre Taschereau, 1920-1929." Queen's, 1975.

Thompson, Sir John Sparrow David (1844-1894)

7385
Heisler, John Phalen. "Sir John Thompson, 1844-1894." Toronto, 1955.

Tilley, Sir Leonard (1818-1896)

7386
Wallace, Carl Murray. "Sir Leonard Tilley: A Political Biography." Alberta, 1972.

Tupper, Sir Charles (1821-1915)

7387
McIntosh, Alan Wallace. "The Career of Sir Charles Tupper in Canada, 1864-1900." Toronto, 1960.

Whitney, Sir James Pliny (1843-1914)

7388
Humphries, Charles Walter. "The Political Career of Sir James P. Whitney." Toronto, 1967.

Willison, Sir John Stephen (1856-1927)

7389
Clippingdale, Richard T. G. "J.S. Willison, Political Journalist from Liberalism to Independence, 1881-1905." Toronto, 1970.

Wood, Henry Wise (1860-1941)

7390
Rolph, William K. "Henry Wise Wood and the Agrarian Movement in Western Canada, 1915-1932." Brown, 1950.

Woodsworth, James Shaver (1874-1942)

7391
McNaughton, K.W.K. "James Shaver Woodsworth: From Social Gospel to Social Democracy, 1874-1921." Toronto, 1950.

1933-1982

Bourassa, Henri (1868-1957)

Bousquet, D. See No./Voir no 7337
O'Connell, Martin Patrick. See No./Voir no 7338

Brownlee, John Edward (1884-1961)

Foster, Franklin Lloyd. See No./Voir no 7340

Buchan, John (1875-1940)

7392
Turner, Arthur C. "John Buchan." California, Berkeley, 1952.

Couture, Joseph-Marie (1885-1949)

See also History of French Canada/Voir aussi Histoire du Canada français

Dafoe, John Wesley (1866-1944)

Cook, George Ramsey. See No./Voir no 8464

Diefenbaker, John George (1895-1979)

7393
Winn, William Edwin. "The Diefenbaker Achievement: Vision and Struggle." California, Berkeley, 1973.

Groulx, Lionel (1878-1967)

Sherrin, Phyllis Marilyn. See No./Voir no 6952

Irvine, William (1885-1962)

7394
Hart, John Edward. "William Irvine and Radical Politics in Canada." Guelph, 1972.

King, William Lyon Mackenzie (1874-1950)

7395
Esberey, Joy Elaine. "Personality and Politics: Study of William Lyon Mackenzie King." Toron 1974.

Paquet, Louis-Adolphe (1859-1942)

See also History of French Canada/Voir aussi Histo du Canada français

Plaunt, Alan (1904-1941)

Nolan, Michael Joseph. See No./Voir no 1136

Robichaud, Louis Joseph (1925-   )

7396
Stanley, Della M. M. "Louis Joseph Robichaud: Political Biography." New Brunswick, 1980.

Stefansson, Vilhjalmur (1879-1962)

Diubaldo, Richard J. See No./Voir no 4586

Stephens, George W. (1866-1942)

7397
Vallely, Lois Mary. "George W. Stephens and the Sa Basin Governing Commission." McGill, 1965.

Trudeau, Pierre Elliott (1919-   )

Lynch, Mary Agnes. See No./Voir no 8469
7398
Pammett, Jon Howard. "Personal Identity and Po tical Activity: The Action-Trudeau Campaign 1968." Michigan, 1971.

HISTORY OF THE ARMED SERVICES IN CANADA, HISTOIRE DES SERVICES ARMÉS AU CANADA

7399
Beahen, William. "A Citizen's Army: The Growth a Development of the Canadian Militia, 1904 1914." Ottawa, 1980.
7400
Burke, David Patrick. "The Unification of the Can dian Armed Forces: The Politics of Defense in t Pearson Administration." Harvard, 1975.
7401
Byers, Roddick Beaumont. "Reorganization of t Canadian Armed Forces: Parliamentary, Milita and Interest-Group Perceptions." Carleton, 1972.
7402
Cohen, Eliot Asher. "Systems of Military Servic The Dilemmas of a Liberal-Democratic Wor Power." Harvard, 1982. [History of conscripti since 1870 - includes Canada/Histoire de conscription depuis 1870 - incluant le Canada]
Conacher, James B. See No./Voir no 7155
7403
Conway, S.R. "Military-Civilian Crime and the Briti Army in North America, 1775-81." London, 1982.

7404
Cotton, Charles Alexander. "The Divided Army: Role Orientations among Canada's Peacetime Soldiers." Carleton, 1980.

7405
Day, Robert Douglas. "The British Army and Sport in Canada: Case Studies of the Garrisons at Halifax, Montreal and Kingston to 1871." Alberta, 1981.

7406
Douglas, William A.B. "Nova Scotia and the Royal Navy, 1713-1766." Queen's, 1973.

7407
Eyre, K.C. "'Custos borealis': The Military in the Canadian North." London, 1981.

Foote, William Alfred. See No./Voir no 6959

Gough, Barry Morton. See No./Voir no 7081

7408
Gradish, Stephen Francis. "The Manning of the British Navy During the Seven Years War, 1755-1762." Toronto, 1971.

7409
Gravel, Jean-Yves. "Le Royal 22e Régiment à Chypre." Ottawa, 1968.

Hammelef, John C. See No./Voir no 6961

7410
Harris, Stephen John. "Canadian Brass: The Growth of the Canadian Military Profession 1860-1919." Duke, 1979.

Henderson, Susan Wright. See No./Voir no 6683

7411
Hyatt, Albert M.J. "The Military Career of Sir Arthur Currie." Duke, 1965.

7412
Kennett, Lee Boone. "The French Armies in the Seven Years' War: A Study in Military Organization and Administration." Virginia, 1962.

7413
Lefroy, Donald Arthur. "Differences on Psychological Measures Related to Military Attrition." McGill, 1981. [Canadian volunteer military force faces a major manning problem/La force militaire volontaire du Canada confronte un problème grave de recrutement]

McFarland, John M. See No./Voir no 10345

McKay, William Angus. See No./Voir no 7158

7414
Milner, Joseph Marc. "No Higher Purpose: The Royal Canadian Navy's Mid-Atlantic War, 1939-1944." New Brunswick, 1983.

Milot, Victor. See No./Voir no 6967

7415
Mitchell, Donald W. "The History of the United States Navy." Southern California, 1939.

7416
Morton, D.D.P. "Authority and Policy in the Canadian Militia, 1874-1904." London, 1968.

7417
Mowbray, James Arthur. "Militiaman: A Comparative Study of the Evolution of Organization in the Canadian and British Voluntary Citizen Military Forces, 1896-1939." Duke, 1975.

Raudzens, George Karl. See No./Voir no 7099

7418
Roy, Reginald Herbert. "The British Columbia Dragoons and Its Predecessors." Washington, Seattle, 1965.

7419
Sarty, R.F. "Silent Sentry: A Military and Political History of Canadian Coast Defence 1860-1945." Toronto, 1983.

Shy, John Willard. See No./Voir no 7469

Singh, Raj Kumar. See No./Voir no 4033

7420
Stacey, Charles Perry. "Canada and the British Army, 1846-1871: A Study in the Practice of Responsible Government in the British Colonies." Princeton, 1933.

Tippett, Maria W. See No./Voir no 7142

CONSTITUTIONAL HISTORY/ HISTOIRE CONSTITUTIONNELLE

7421
Browne, G.P. "The Judicial Committee of the Privy Council and the Distribution of Legislative Powers in the British North America Act, 1867." Oxford, 1963.

Cahall, Raymond Dubois. See No./Voir no 6954

Delande, Jean. See No./Voir no 6956

McLintock, A.H. See No./Voir no 7168

7422
Rambaut, Thomas D. "A Sketch of the Constitutional History of Canada." Columbia, 1884.

7423
Renaud, P.E. "Le pouvoir constituant au Canada depuis les origines jusqu'à nos jours." London, 1927.

Roussin, Marcel. See No./Voir no 6939

Smith, L.A.H. See No./Voir no 7048

Toussignant, Pierre. See No./Voir no 7052

ECONOMIC HISTORY/ HISTOIRE ÉCONOMIQUE

See also Economics: Economic History/Voir aussi Économie: Histoire économique

HISTORY OF THE NATIVE PEOPLES OF CANADA/ HISTOIRE DES AUTOCHTONES DU CANADA

General Items/Ouvrages généraux

7424
Abler, Thomas Struthers. "Factional Dispute and Party Conflict in the Political System of the Seneca Nation (1845-1895): An Ethno-historical Analysis." Toronto, 1969.

Boldt, Menno. See No./Voir no 447

7425
Collins, June McCormick. "The Influence of White Contact on Class Distinction and Political Authority among the Indians on Northern Puget Sound." Chicago, 1949.

Graham, Elizabeth Jane. See No./Voir no 535

Shankel, George Edgar. See No./Voir no 717

Shifferd, Patricia Allen. See No./Voir no 6940

7426
Wyatt, David John. "The Indian History of the Nicola Valley, British Columbia." Brown, 1972.

Sixteenth and Seventeenth Centuries/ Seizième et dix-septième siècles

Bailey, Alfred Goldsworthy. See No./Voir no 498

7427
Cutcliffe, Stephen Hosmer. "Indians, Furs and Empire: The Changing Policies of New York and Pennsylvania, 1674-1768." Lehigh, 1976.

Dickason, Olive Patricia. See No./Voir no 6957

Goldstein, Robert Arnold. See No./Voir no 6976

Gottesman, Daniel Harvey. See No./Voir no 6960

7428
Hauser, Raymond E. "An Ethnohistory of the Illinois Indian Tribe, 1673-1832." Northern Illinois, 1973.

Herman, Mary W. See No./Voir no 466

7429
Hunt, George T. "The Inter-Tribal Relations of the Great Lakes Indian Tribes, 1609-1684." Wisconsin, 1936.

7430
Leger, Sister Mary Celeste. "The Catholic Indian Missions in Maine, 1611-1820." Catholic, 1929.

7431
MacFarland, Ronald Oliver. "Indian Relations in New England, 1620-1760: A Study of a Regulated Frontier." Harvard, 1933.

7432
Moore, James Talmadge. "The Amerind-Jesuit Encounter: A Study in Cultural Adaptation in Seventeenth Century French North America." Texas A&M, 1980.

Morrison, Kenneth M. See No./Voir no 6969

Mulvey, Mary Doris. See No./Voir no 6980

Reynolds, Wynn R. See No./Voir no 7441

Eighteenth Century/Dix-huitième siècle

7433
Aquila, Richard. "The Iroquois Restoration: A Study of Iroquois Power Politics and Relations with Indians and Whites, 1700-1744." Ohio State, 1977.

Calloway, C.G. See No./Voir no 7461

Cutcliffe, Stephen Hosmer. See No./Voir no 7427

7434
Fisher, Robin Anthony. "Indian-European Relations in British Columbia: 1774-1890." British Columbia, 1974.

7435
Gifford, Jack Jule. "The Northwest Indian War, 1784-1795." California, Los Angeles, 1964.

Goltz, Herbert C.W., Jr. See No./Voir no 7030

Gottesman, Daniel Harvey. See No./Voir no 6960

7436
Graymont, Barbara. "The Border War: The Iroquois in the American Revolution." Columbia, 1969.

7437
Haan, Richard L. "The Covenant Chain: Iroquois Diplomacy on the Niagara Frontier, 1697-1730." California, Santa Barbara, 1976.

7438
Hatheway, G.G. "The Neutral Indian Barrier State: Project in British North American Policy, 174[?] 1815." Minnesota, 1957.

Hauser, Raymond E. See No./Voir no 7428

Leclerc, Jean. See No./Voir no 7283

Leger, Sister Mary Celeste. See No./Voir no 7430

MacFarland, Ronald O. See No./Voir no 7431

7439
Mishoff, Willard O. "The Indian Policy of Sir Willia[m] Johnson." Iowa, 1934.

Morrison, Kenneth M. See No./Voir no 6969

Mulvey, Mary Doris. See No./Voir no 6980

7440
Ourada, Patricia K. "The Menominee Indians: History." Oklahoma, 1973.

7441
Reynolds, Wynn Robert. "Persuasive Speaking of t[he] Iroquois Indians at Treaty Councils: 1678-1776. Study of Techniques as Evidenced by Transcripts [of] the Interpreters' Translations." Columbia, 1957.

7442
Smith, Marc J. "Joseph Brant, Mohawk Statesman[?] Wisconsin, 1946.

7443
Tootle, James Roger. "Anglo-Indian Relations in t[he] Northern Theatre of the French and Indian Wa[r], 1748-1761." Ohio State, 1972.

Nineteenth Century/Dix-neuvième siècle

War of 1812/Guerre de 1812

7444
Chalou, George Clifford. "The Red Pawns Go to Wa[r]: British American Indian Relations, 1810-1815[.]" Indiana, 1971.

7445
Heath, Herschel. "The Indians as a Factor in the W[ar] of 1812." Clark, 1933.

General Items/Ouvrages généraux

7446
Boswell, Marion Joan. "Civilizing the Indian: Gover[n]ment Administration of Indians, 1876-1896[.]" Ottawa, 1978.

Calloway, C.G. See No./Voir no 7461

7447
Cauthers, Janet Helen. "The North American Indi[an] as Portrayed by American and Canadian Historia[ns], 1830-1930." Washington, Seattle, 1974.

Fisher, Robin Anthony. See No./Voir no 7434

Hauser, Raymond E. See No./Voir no 7428

7448
Jennings, John Nelson. "The Northwest Mounte[d] Police and Canadian Indian Policy, 1873-1896[.]" Toronto, 1979.

7449
Larner, John William, Jr. "The Kootenay Plai[ns] (Alberta) Land Question and Canadian Indian La[nd] Policy, 1799-1947." West Virginia, 1972.

Leger, Sister Mary Celeste. See No./Voir no 7430

7450
Leighton, James Douglas. "The Development of Federal Indian Policy in Canada, 1840-1890." Western Ontario, 1975.

7451
Looy, Anthony Jacobus. "The Indian Agent and His Role in the Administration of the North-West Superintendency, 1876-1893." Queen's, 1977.

7452
McCarthy, Mary Martha Cecilia. "The Missions of the Oblates of Mary Immaculate to the Athapaskans 1846-1870: Theory, Structure and Method." Manitoba, 1981.

7453
Milloy, J.S. "The Era of Civilization: British Policy for the Indians of the Canadas 1830-1860." Oxford, 1978.

Taylor, John Leonard. See No./Voir no 7186

Twentieth Century/Vingtième siècle

Cauthers, Janet Helen. See No./Voir no 450, 7447
Dosman, Edgar Joseph Edward. See No./Voir no 733
Patterson, E. Palmer, II. See No./Voir no 480
Rothman, Mark. See No./Voir no 4128
Ullman, Stephen Hayes. See No./Voir no 722

HISTORY OF CANADIAN ALIEN AND IMMIGRATION POLICY AND OF MIGRATION TO AND FROM CANADA/ HISTOIRE DES ÉTRANGERS AU CANADA ET DES POLITIQUES D'ÉMIGRATION ET D'IMMIGRATION CANADIENNES

See also Immigration and Migration/Voir aussi Immigration et Migration

PRESS AND PERIODICALS IN CANADIAN HISTORY/ LA PRESSE ET LES PÉRIODIQUES DANS L'HISTOIRE CANADIENNE FRENCH CANADA/CANADA FRANÇAIS

7454
Johnson, Warren Bertran. "The Content of American Colonial Newspapers Related to International Affairs, 1704-1763." Washington, Seattle, 1962. [French and Indian War/Guerre entre les Français et les Indiens]

Nineteenth Century/Dix-neuvième siècle

Angers, Gérard. See No./Voir no 1077
Baker, William Melville. See No./Voir no 7329
7455
Borzo, Henry. "The Times (London) and Anglo-Canadian Relations 1819-1849." Chicago, 1955.
Brunskill, Ronald. See No./Voir no 1080
Careless, James M.S. See No./Voir no 1081
Davison-Wood, Karen Margaret. See No./Voir no 942
Heintzman, Ralph Ripley. See No./Voir no 7458
Hill, Robert Andrew. See No./Voir no 7379
Lefebvre, André. See No./Voir no 1089

7456
Macdonald, Helen Grace. "Canadian Public Opinion on the American Civil War." Columbia, 1926.
MacLean, Raymond Angus. See No./Voir no 7322
Mary Julia, Sister. See No./Voir no 1105
Nish, Margaret Elizabeth. See No./Voir no 1091
Nourry, Louis. See No./Voir no 8463
Saint-Germain, Yves. See No./Voir no 1100

7457
Vaucamps, Françoise. "La France dans la presse canadienne-française de 1855 à 1880." Laval, 1978.

Twentieth Century/Vingtième siècle

Beadle, Gordon Bruce. See No./Voir no 1078
Epp, Frank Henry. See No./Voir no 1084
7458
Heintzman, Ralph Ripley. "The Struggle for Life: The French Daily Press of Montreal and the Problems of Economic Growth in the Age of Laurier, 1896-1911." York, 1977.
Mills, Allen George. See No./Voir no 7151
Pride, Cletis Graden. See No./Voir no 1096
Saint-George, Jean. See No./Voir no 1099
Siegel, Arthur. See No./Voir no 1103

CANADA, GREAT BRITAIN AND THE EMPIRE/ CANADA, GRANDE-BRETAGNE ET L'EMPIRE To 1763

Davies, G.J. See No./Voir no 1222

1763-1867

7459
Beaglehole, J.C. "The Royal Instructions to Colonial Governors, 1783-1854: A Study in British Colonial Policy." London, 1929.
Borzo, Henry. See No./Voir no 7455
7460
Buckner, Phillip Alfred. "Colonial Office Government in British North America, 1828-1847." London, 1969.
7461
Calloway, C.G. "British Relations with North American Indians from the End of the War of Independence to the End of the War of 1812." Leeds, 1978.
7462
Cell, John Whitson. "British Colonial Policy in the 1850's: A Study in the Decision Making Process." Duke, 1965.
Conway, S.R. See No./Voir no 7403
Handcock, W.G. See No./Voir no 7619
7463
Hendrickson, David Calvin. "British Imperial Policy 1760-1765: A Study in the Theory of Imperialism." Johns Hopkins, 1982.
7464
Hitsman, J. Mackay. "Defence of Canada, 1763-1871: A Study of British Strategy." Ottawa, 1964.
Jones, M.A. See No./Voir no 7631

7465

Kinchen, Oscar A. "Lord John Russell and Canadian Self-Government: A Study in British Imperial Policy." Iowa, 1935.

7466

Macdonald, N. "The Imperial Land Regulations as Applied to Canada, 1763-1841." Edinburgh, 1932.

7467

Martin, Gerald Warren. "Britain and the Future of British North America, 1837-1867." Cambridge, 1973.

McNab, D.T. See No./Voir no 7093

7468

Mitcham, Peter. "The Attitude of British Travellers to North America Between 1790 and 1850." Edinburgh, 1959.

Raudzens, George Karl. See No./Voir no 7099

Shepperson, Wilbur S. See No./Voir no 7635

7469

Shy, John Willard. "The British Army in North America, 1760-1775." Princeton, 1961.

Stacey, Charles Perry. See No./Voir no 7420

7470

Turner, Wesley Barry. "Colonial Self-Government and the Colonial Agency: Changing Concepts of Permanent Canadian Representation in London, 1848 to 1880." Duke, 1971.

7471

Tyler, W.P.N. "Sir Frederic Rogers, Permanent Undersecretary at the Colonial Office, 1860-1871." Duke, 1963.

7472

Wallace, H.N. "British Exploration in the Canadian Arctic, 1829-1860: A Study of Routes, Techniques and Personalities." London, 1975.

7473

Young, D.M. "The Working of the British Colonial Office, 1812-1830." London, 1955.

1867-1918

7474

Akhtar, Mushtaq Ahmad. "The Royal Titles Bill: Public Opinion in the Royal United Kingdom, India and Canada." McGill, 1969.

7475

Bousquet, Denis. "Les conférences impériales et la création du troisième empire britannique (1887-1931)." Montréal, 1954.

Browne, C.P. See No./Voir no 7421

7476

Cook, George Leslie. "Canada's Relations with Britain, 1911-1919: Problems of Imperial Defense and Foreign Policy." Oxford, 1968.

7477

Cross, J.A. "The Dominions Department of the Colonial Office: Origins and Early Years, 1905-1914." London, 1965.

7478

Farr, D.M.L. "The Colonial Office and Canada, 1867-1887." Oxford, 1952.

7479

Judd, D.C. "Balfour and the Evolution and Problems of the British Empire 1874-1906." London, 1967.

7480

Kendle, J.E. "The Colonial and Imperial Conference 1887-1911: A Study in Imperial Organization and Politics." London, 1965.

7481

Kirkpatrick, R.L. "British Imperial Policy, 187-1880." Oxford, 1953.

7482

MacPherson, George R.I. "The Search for the Commonwealth the Co-operative Union of Canada 1909-1939." Western Ontario, 1971.

7483

Page, R.J.D. "Canada and the Empire During Joseph Chamberlain's Tenure as Colonial Secretary." Oxford, 1971.

7484

Penlington, Norman. "Anglo-Canadian Relations and the Boer War." California, Berkeley, 1946.

7485

Porterfield, Richard Maurice. "The Influence of the Canadian Dominion Model upon British Imperial Policy 1887-1902." Temple, 1979.

7486

Schurman, D.M. "Imperial Defense, 1868-1887." Cambridge, 1955.

7487

Shields, Robert A. "The Quest for Empire Unity: The Imperial Federationists and Their Cause, 186-1893." Pennsylvania, 1961.

7488

Smith, Gaddis. "Nation and Empire: Canadian Diplomacy During the First World War." Yale, 1960.

7489

Troop, William Hamilton. "Canada and the Empire: Study of Canadian Attitudes to the Empire and Imperial Relationships since 1867." Toronto, 1934.

Turner, Wesley Barry. See No./Voir no 7470

7490

Watts, Floyd E. "The Imperial Conference of 1911." Wisconsin, 1959.

Weise, Selene Harding Curd. See No./Voir no 7144

Wertimer, S. See No./Voir no 7652

HISTORY OF CANADIAN - AMERICAN RELATIONS
HISTOIRE DES RELATIONS CANADO-AMÉRICAINES

General Items/Ouvrages généraux

7491

Aitken, William Benford. "The Dominion of Canada: A Study of Annexation." Columbia, 1980.

7492

Black, James William. "Maryland's Attitude in the Struggle for Canada." Johns Hopkins, 1891.

7493

Callahan, James M. "The Neutrality of the American Lakes and Anglo-American Relations." Johns Hopkins, 1897.

7494

Gell, Kenneth E. "What American High School Graduates Should Know about Canada." Harvard, 1950.

7495
Gibbins, Roger. "Nationalism: Community Studies of Political Belief." Stanford, 1974.
7496
Grow, Mary Marsh. "Boundaries and United States Diplomacy: Two Case Studies." Tufts, 1969.
7497
Keenleyside, Hugh Llewellyn. "Canada and the United States: Some Aspects of the History of the Republic and the Dominion. . .with an Introduction by W.P.M. Kennedy." Clark, 1923.
Ryan, Jerry Bill. See No./Voir no 4892

Early Relations/Relations précoces

7498
Manning, William R. "The Nootka Sound Controversy." Chicago, 1904.
7499
McDonald, Ronald H. "Nova Scotia Views the United States, 1784-1854." Queen's, 1974.
Setser, Vernon G. See No./Voir no 2348

Nineteenth Century/Dix-neuvième siècle

General Item/Ouvrage général

7500
Smith, Allan Charles Lethbridge. "The Imported Image: American Publications and American Ideas in the Evolution of the English Canadian Mind, 1820-1900." Toronto, 1972.

1800-1850

See also "War of 1812", Voir aussi "Guerre de 1812"

7501
Corey, Albert B. "Relations of Canada with the United States from 1830-1842." Clark, 1934.
7502
Doherty, Edward J. "The Oregon Boundary Settlement, 1840-1846." Loyola, 1956.
7503
Dykstra, David L. "The United States and Great Britain and the Shift in the Balance of Power in the North American Continent, 1837-1848." Virginia, 1973.
7504
Fay, Terence James. "Rush-Bagot Agreement: A Reflection of the Anglo-American Détente, 1815-1818." Georgetown, 1974.
7505
Leach, Hamish A. "A Politico-Military Study of the Detroit River Boundary Defense During the December 1837-March 1838 Emergency." Ottawa, 1963.
Leader, Herman Alexander. See No./Voir no 1246
7506
McCabe, J.O. "Great Britain and the Evolution of the Western Part of the International Boundary of Canada." Glasgow, 1941.
7507
Moore, David Richard. "Canada and the United States, 1815-1830." Chicago, 1910.

7508
Myers, Phillip Earl. "Mask of Indifference: Great Britain's North American Policy and the Path to the Treaty of Washington, 1815-1871." Iowa, 1978.
7509
Shafer, Joseph. "The Acquisition of Oregon by the United States." Wisconsin, 1906.
Silverman, Jason Howard. See No./Voir no 7100
7510
Stevens, Kenneth Ray. "The Caroline Affair: Anglo-American Relations and Domestic Politics, 1837-1842." Indiana, 1982.
7511
Tiffany, O. Edward. "The Relations of the United States to the Canadian Rebellion of 1837-1838." Michigan, 1905.
White, William Alan. See No./Voir no 4833

1850-1900

General Items/Ouvrages généraux

7512
Brown, Robert Craig. "Canadian-American Relations in the Latter Part of the Nineteenth Century." Toronto, 1962.
7513
Caswell, John E. "United States Scientific Expeditions to the Arctic, 1850-1909." Stanford, 1952.
Irwin, Leonard B. See No./Voir no 2308
7514
Morchain, Janet Kerr. "Anti-Americanism in Canada, 1871-1891." Rochester, 1967.
Myers, Phillip Earl. See No./Voir no 7608
Overman, William D. See No./Voir no 1996
Silverman, Jason Howard. See No./Voir no 7100
7515
Stanton, Stephen B. "The Bering Sea Dispute." Columbia, 1890.
7516
Warner, Donald F. "The Movement for the Annexation of Canada to the United States, 1849-1893." Yale, 1940.

1850 - 1860

Mary Julia, Sister. See No./Voir no 1105
Masters, D.C. See No./Voir no 1283
7517
Murray, Alexander Lowell. "Canada and the Anglo-American Anti-Slavery Movement: A Study in International Philanthropy." Pennsylvania, 1960.
7518
Robinson, Chalfant. "The Reciprocity Treaty with Canada in 1854." Yale, 1902.
7519
Tansill, Charles Callan. "The Canadian Reciprocity Treaty of 1854." Johns Hopkins, 1918.
7520
Van Alstyne, R.W. "British-American Diplomatic Relations, 1850-1860." Stanford, 1928.

1860 - 1872

7521
Craig, Gerald M. "The Influence of the American Background on the Struggle for Self-Government in Upper Canada." Minnesota, 1947.

7522
Gluek, Alvin C., Jr. "The Struggle for the British Northwest: A Study in Canadian-American Relations." Minnesota, 1953.

7523
Hill, David Fred. "Some Aspects of Canadian Nationalism, 1858-1865: A Study of Public Opinion with Special Reference to the Influence of the United States." Southern California, 1958.

7524
Kendall, John Charles. "Blueprint Defiance of Manifest Destiny: Anti-Americanism and Anti-Republicanism in Canada West, 1858-1867." McGill, 1969.

7525
Long, John W., Jr. "The San Juan Island Boundary Controversy: A Phase of 19th Century Anglo-American Relations." Duke, 1949.

7526
Smith, J.P. "Certain Aspects of the Movement for the Annexation of Canada, 1865-1872." Chicago, 1930.

7527
Snell, James G. "The Eagle and the Butterfly: Some American Attitudes Towards British North America, 1864-1867." Queen's, 1971.

7528
Stouffer, Allen Philip. "Canadian-American Relations, 1861-1871." Claremont, 1971.

7529
Tallman, Ronald Duea. "Warships and Mackerel: The North Atlantic Fisheries in Canadian-American Relations, 1867-1877." Maine, 1971.

Weise, Selene Harding. See No./Voir no 7144

The American Civil War/Guerre civile américaine

Macdonald, Helen Grace. See No./Voir no 7456
7530
Raney, William Francis. "The Diplomatic and Military Activities of Canada, 1861-1865, as Affected by the American Civil War." Wisconsin, 1919.

7531
Winks, Robin William. "Maple Leaf and Eagle: Canadian-American Relations During the American Civil War." Johns Hopkins, 1957.

The Fenian Movement/Le mouvement fenian

7532
Brusher, Joseph Stanislaus. "The Fenian Invasions of Canada." St. Louis, 1943.

7533
Cuddy, Henry. "The Influence of the Fenian Movement on Anglo-American Relations, 1860-1872." St. John's, 1953.

7534
D'Arcy, William. "The Fenian Movement in the United States, 1858-1886." Catholic, 1947.

7535
Pieper, Ezra Henry. "The Fenian Movement." Illinois, 1931.

7536
Walker, Mabel G. "The Fenian Movement, 1858-187: Ohio State, 1929.

Alaska

7537
Davidson, Donald C. "The Alaska Boundary: Historical Survey." California, Berkeley, 1938.

7538
Farrar, Victor John. "The Purchase of Alaska Wisconsin, 1927.

Olmstead, Marvin Lynn. See No./Voir no 7560
7539
Tarnovecky, Joseph. "The Purchase of Alaska: Bac ground and Reactions." McGill, 1968.

1867-1914

Bicha, Karel Denis. See No./Voir no 103
7540
Coder, George David. "The National Movement Preserve the American Buffalo in the Unit States and Canada Between 1880 and 1920." Oh State, 1975.

7541
Matthews, John Herbert. "John Sherman and Amer can Foreign Relations, 1883-1898." Emory, 1976.

Oberlander, Barbara J. See No./Voir no 7644
7542
Pennanen, Gary Alvin. "The Foreign Policy of Willia Maxwell Evarts." Wisconsin, 1969.

7543
Poland, Eleanor. "Diplomatic Negotiations Concerni Canadian-American Reciprocity, 1867-191 Radcliffe, 1932.

Twentieth Century/Vingtième siècle

General Items/Ouvrages généraux

7544
Barghothi, Jawad I. "The Political Status of Inte national Waterways: Four Case Studies." Southe Illinois, 1968. [St. Lawrence River/Fleuve Sair Laurent]

7545
Cohen, Martin Bernard. "The First Legation: Can dian Diplomacy and the Opening of Relations wi the United States." George Washington, 1975.

7546
Cuneo, Carl John. "Social Class, Language and t National Question in Canada: An Analysis of t Social Support for the Integration of Canada wi the United States." Waterloo, 1973.

7547
Galbraith, John S. "The United States and the Briti Commonwealth, 1917-1930." Iowa, 1944.

7548
Gay, James Thomas. "American Fur Seal Diplomacy Georgia, 1971.

Gold, Norman Leon. See No./Voir no 7642
7549
Johannson, Peter R. "British Columbia's Intergove mental Relations with the United States." Joh Hopkins, 1975.

550
Sharp, Paul F. "The Agrarian Revolt in Western Canada: A Comparative Study Showing American Parallels." Minnesota, 1947.

551
Willoughby, William Reid. "The Impact of the United States upon Canada's Foreign Policy." Wisconsin, 1943.

552
Winter, Carl G. "American Impetus to Canadian Nationhood: Canadian-American Relations, 1905-1927." Stanford, 1951.

1900 - 1922

7553
Bayard, Ross Hawthorne. "Anti-Americanism in Canada and the Abortive Reciprocity Agreement of 1911." South Carolina, 1971.

7554
Chacko, Chirakaikaran J. "The International Joint Commission Between the United States of America and the Dominion of Canada." Columbia, 1932.

Coder, George David. See No./Voir no 7540

7555
Dreisziger, Nandor A.F. "The International Joint Commission of the United States and Canada, 1895-1920: A Study of Canadian-American Relations." Toronto, 1974.

7556
Fry, M.G. "Anglo-American-Canadian Relations with Special Reference to Far Eastern and Naval Issues, 1918-1922." London, 1964.

7557
Hannigan, Robert E., Jr. "Dollars and Diplomacy: United States Foreign Policy, 1909-1913." Princeton, 1978.

Herwig, Aletha Marguerite. See No./Voir no 109

7558
Hussey, Lyman Andrew, Jr. "Anglo-Canadian Relations During the Roosevelt Era, 1901-1908." Georgia, 1969.

7559
Meaney, Neville Kingsley. "The American Attitude Towards the British Empire from 1919 to 1922: A Study in the Diplomatic Relations of the English-Speaking Nations." Duke, 1959.

7560
Olmstead, Marvin Lynn. "An Analysis of the Argumentation of the Alaskan Boundary Tribunal." Washington, Seattle, 1969.

Troper, Harold Martin. See No./Voir no 7585

7561
Weaver, John Charles. "Imperilled Dreams: Canadian Opposition to the American Empire, 1918-1930." Duke, 1973.

7562
Whitney, Harriet Eleanor. "Sir George C. Gibbons and the Boundary Waters Treaty of 1909." Michigan State, 1968.

7563
Bragdon, Chandler. "Canadian Attitudes to the Foreign Policy of the United States in the Period 1938-1939." Rochester, 1961.

7564
Brown, Robert James. "Emergence from Isolation: United States-Canadian Diplomatic Relations, 1937-1941." Syracuse, 1968.

7565
Howell, Colin Desmond. "The Eclipse of Canadian Nationalism: Economic Nationalism, Continental Integration, Provincial Allegiances, and the Federal Idea in Canada, 1919-1939." Cincinnati, 1976.

7566
Joynt, Carey B. "Canadian Foreign Policy: 1919-1939." Clark, 1951.

7567
Kasurak, Peter Charles. "The United States Legation at Ottawa, 1927-1941: An Institutional Study." Duke, 1976.

7568
Kottman, Richard Norman. "The Diplomatic Relations of the United States and Canada, 1927-1941." Vanderbilt, 1958.

7569
Matson, William Lawrence. "William Lyon MacKenzie King and Franklin Delano Roosevelt: Their Effect on Canadian-American Relations, 1935-1939." Maine, 1973.

7570
McAndrew, William James. "Canada, Roosevelt and the New Deal: Canadian Attitudes to Reform in Relation to the American Reform Experiments of the 1930's." British Columbia, 1973.

7571
Ovendale, R. "The Influence of United States and Dominion Opinion on the Formation of British Policy, 1937-1939." Oxford, 1972.

7572
Rowland, Benjamin Moore. "Commercial Conflict and Foreign Policy: A Study in Anglo-American Relations, 1932-1938." Johns Hopkins, 1975.

Weaver, John Charles. See No./Voir no 7561

World War II/Deuxième Guerre mondiale

7573
Beatty, David Pierce. "The Canada-United States Permanent Joint Board on Defense." Michigan State, 1969.

7574
Cressy, A. Cheever. "Canadian-American Cooperation in World War II." Tufts, 1952.

7575
Dziuban, Stanley W. "United States Military Collaboration with Canada in World War II." Columbia, 1955.

7576
Little, John Michael. "Canada Discovered: Continentalist Perceptions of the Roosevelt Administration, 1939-1945." Toronto, 1975.

IMMIGRATION AND MIGRATION/
IMMIGRATION ET MIGRATION

The general heading of "Immigration" enables the compiler to piece together an interesting mosaic of theses dealing with 25 nationalities or specific groups in Canada, ranging from Americans to Yugoslavs. Also included are theses dealing with domestic migration, the history of Canadian alien and immigration policy, migration to and from Canada, and immigration, migration, and the economy.

While the first theses dealing with the subject appeared in Canada in the 1920's, in the United States, Yale University approved one as early as 1904, and several others appeared in the first decade of this century. Few others were approved on either side of the border over the next fifty years until the 1970's. Canada has approved as many as 36 theses in the last 14 years, twice as many as the 18 which appeared in the United States, making a total of 53 for Canada and 47 for the United States. Again, the University of Toronto is the major contributor with 28 theses and McGill University is second with seven. Of the remaining thirteen Canadian universities producing dissertations in this area, Montreal and Queen's approved five theses each. Of the 26 American universities, Harvard produced six, Yale six, Columbia five, California (Berkeley) three, Duke three, and Minnesota three. Twenty other American universities produced one thesis each. Of the ten British universities which produced 17 studies, London is the leader, with seven to its credit.

Le titre général d'"Immigration" permet au compilateur de réunir une intéressante mosal'que de thèses touchant 25 nationalités et groupes spécifiques au Canada, allant des Américains aux Yougoslaves. Il y a aussi des thèses sur les migrations internes, sur l'histoire de la politique canadienne en matière d'immigration et de sujets étrangers, sur les migrations vers le Canada ou à partir du Canada ainsi que sur les questions d'immigration et de migration liées à l'économie.

Les premières thèses dans ce domaine sont apparues au Canada dans les années 1920, alors que l'Université Yale, aux États-Unis, en avait déjà approuvé une dès 1904, et plusieurs autres avaient été écrites entre 1900 et 1910. Que ce soit d'un côté ou de l'autre de la frontière, il n'y a eu que très peu de thèses au cours des 50 années qui ont suivi, jusqu'en 1970. Dans les 14 dernières années, le Canada en a approuvé 36, deux fois autant que la production des États-Unis pendant cette période. Au total, on compte 53 thèses pour le Canada et 47 pour les États-Unis. De nouveau, l'Université de Toronto se trouve au premier rang (28) et McGill au second (7). Parmi les 13 universités canadiennes qui s'intéressent à ce domaine, Montréal et Queen's ont approuvé cinq thèses chacune. Des 26 universités américaines, les universités Harvard et

Yale ont approuvé 6 thèses chacune, Columbia California (Berkeley) Duke et Minnesota, trois chacune. Les 20 universités restantes n'ont à leur actif qu'une thèse chacune. Dix universités britanniques ont également produit 17 thèses sur ce sujet; pour sa part, l'Université de Londres est en tête avec sept thèses.

General Items/Ouvrages généraux

Comay, Peter Y. See No./Voir no 2380
7577
Disman, Milada. "Stranger's Homecoming: A Study the Experience of Immigration." Toronto, 1981.
7578
Draper, P.J. "The Accidental Immigrants: Canad and the Interned Refugees." Toronto, 1983.
Langley, Paul C. See No./Voir no 2382
7579
Nair, Murali Dharan. "New Immigrants' Use of For Social Service Agencies in a Canadian Metropolis Columbia, 1978. [Toronto]
7580
Ossenberg, Richard J. "Ideology in a Plural Societ Canadian Dualism and the Issue of Immigration SUNY, Buffalo, 1966.
7581
Parai, Louis. "Canadian International Immigratio 1953-1965: An Empirical Study." Yale, 1969.
Polyzoi, Eleoussa. See No./Voir no 780
7582
Poteet, Maurice. "The Image of Quebec in Franc American Fiction of Immigration and Assimil tion." Montreal, 1981.
7583
Richmond, A.H. "The Absorption of Post-War Imm grants in Canada." London, 1965.
Seldon, James Ralph. See No./Voir no 1356

NATIONALITIES IN CANADA/
NATIONALITÉS AU CANADA

Americans/Américains

Blandy, Richard John. See No./Voir no 2379
Salsedo, André Joseph. See No./Voir no 742
7584
Surrey, David Sterling. "The Assimilation of Vietnam Era Draft Dodgers and Deserters into Canada: Matter of Class." New School for Social Researc 1980.
7585
Troper, Harold Martin. "Official Canadian Goverr ment Encouragement of American Immigration 1896-1911." Toronto, 1971.

Africans/Africains

7586
McClain, Paula Denice. "The Political Behavior Afro-Canadians." Howard, 1977. [Toronto Montreal and Halifax/Toronto, Montréal Halifax]
Moeno, Sylvia Ntlantla. See No./Voir no 740

British/Britanniques

587
Needham, William R. "Immigration to Canada from the British Isles 1951-1964: A Regional Analysis of Sending Areas." Queen's, 1968.

588
Reynolds, Lloyd G. "The British Immigrant: His Social and Economic Adjustment in Canada." Harvard, 1936.

589
Wilson, James Albert. "The Depletion of National Resources of Human Talent in the United Kingdom: A Special Aspect of Migration to North America, 1952-64." Queen's, Belfast, 1964.

Caribbean and West Indians/Antillais

Akoodie, M.A. See No./Voir no 745
Frechette, Errol James. See No./Voir no 746
Lewis, G.K. See No./Voir no 747

590
Poole, Gail Richard. "Development in the West Indies and Migration to Canada." McGill, 1979.

Chinese/Chinois

Andrachi, Stanislaw. See No./Voir no 7597
Chow, Wing-Sam. See No./Voir no 750
Fisher, Stephen Frederick. See No./Voir no 751
Lam, Laurence. See No./Voir no 7604
Mandel, Dorothy E. See No./Voir no 753
Mann, Robert Ernest. See No./Voir no 9263
Smye, Marti Diane. See No./Voir no 754
Yeh, Ming-che. See No./Voir no 756

Croatians/Croates

Godler, Zlata. See No./Voir no 7649

Czechs and Slovacs/Tchèques et Slovaques

7591
Adolf, Jacek. See No./Voir no 7557

7591
Hruby, Jiri G. "Immigration de Tchèques et de Slovaques au Canada." Montréal, 1954.

Dutch/Hollandais

7592
Francis, Robert J. "The Significance of American and Dutch Agricultural Settlement in Central British Columbia." Minnesota, 1966.

7593
Petersen, William. "Planned Migration: The Social Determinants of the Dutch-Canadian Movement." California, Berkeley, 1955.

7594
Sas, Anthony. "Dutch Migration to and Settlement in Canada: 1945-1955." Clark, 1957.

East Indians/Indiens

Akoodie, M.A. See No./Voir no 745
Buchignani, N.L. See No./Voir no 760
Subramandeam, I.A. See No./Voir no 761

French/Français

Grossmaire, Jean-Louis. See No./Voir no 4760

Germans/Allemands

Crooks, W.R. See No./Voir no 775
Currie, A.W. See No./Voir no 2297
Grenke, A. See No./Voir no 776

Greeks/Grecs

Bredimas-Assimopoulas, C. See No./Voir no 777
Gavaki, E. See No./Voir no 778
Orlowski, D.E. See No./Voir no 779
Polyzoi, E. See No./Voir no 780

Indians (Asiatic)/Indiens (Asiatiques)

Joy, Annamma. See No./Voir no 788
Nasser-Bush, M.H. See No./Voir no 789

Irish/Irlandais

Adams, W.F. See No./Voir no 7627
Nolte, W.M. See No./Voir no 7634
Wilson, E.C. See No./Voir no 7615

Italians/Italiens

7595
Sidlofsky, Samuel. "Post War Immigrants in the Changing Metropolis, with Special Reference to Toronto's Italian Population." Toronto, 1969.
Castelli, G. See No./Voir no 791
Colalillo, G. See No./Voir no 792
Duce, G. See No./Voir no 793
Ribordy, F. See No./Voir no 794

Jews/Juifs

7596
Kage, Joseph. "Jewish Immigration and Immigrant Aid Effort in Canada (1760-1957)." Montréal, 1959.
Evans, R.C. See No./Voir no 5587
Mastai, J.A.F. See No./Voir no 800

Muslims/Musulmans

Razaul, Haque M. See No./Voir no 811

Orientals/Orientaux

7597
Andracki, Stanislaw. "Immigration of Orientals into Canada, with Special Reference to Chinese." McGill, 1958.

7598
Cheng, Tien-fang. "Oriental Immigration in Canada." Toronto, 1926.

7599
King, William L.M. "Oriental Immigration to Canada." Harvard, 1909.

7600
Ujimoto, Koji Victor. "Post-War Japanese Immigrants in Canada: Job Transferability, Work, and Social Participation." British Columbia, 1973.
Ward, W.P. <u>See No./Voir no</u> 7636
Wong, A.T. <u>See No./Voir no</u> 4084
Wynne, RE. <u>See No./Voir no</u> 7161

Poles/Polonais

Adolf, Jacek Z. <u>See No./Voir no</u> 757
7601
Helenowski, Vincent. "L'émigration polonaise au Canada." Montréal, 1929.

Portuguese/Portugais

Anderson, G.M. <u>See No./Voir no</u> 7653
7602
Pereira-Da-Rosa, Victor Manuel. "Émigration portugaise et développement inégal: les Açoréens au Québec." McGill, 1980.

Slavs/Slaves

Herman, Harry V. <u>See No./Voir no</u> 817

Ugandan Asians/Asiatiques ougandais

7603
Pereira, Cecil Patrick. "A Study of the Effects of the Ethnic and Non-Ethnic Factors on the Resettlement of the Ugandan Asian Refugees in Canada." Wisconsin, 1981.

Ukrainians/Ukrainiens

Currie, A.W. <u>See No./Voir no</u> 2297

Vietnamese/Vietnamiens

7604
Lam, Laurence. "Vietnamese-Chinese Refugees in Montreal." York, 1983.

Yugoslaws/Yougoslaves

Herman, H.V. <u>See No./Voir no</u> 817

DOMESTIC MIGRATION/ MIGRATION INTERNE

Denton, Trevor D. <u>See No./Voir no</u> 453
7605
Gerber, Linda Maria. "Minority Survival: Community Characteristics and Out-Migration from Indian Communities Across Canada." Toronto, 1976.
7606
Kelly, John Joseph. "Composite Interprovincial Migration Estimates: An Exploratory Study Using Administrative Data Sources." York, 1978.
7607
Matthews, David Ralph Lee." Communities in Transition: An Examination of Government Initiated Community Migration in Rural Newfoundland." Minnesota, 1970.

7608
Ralston, Margaret H. J. "Career Aspirations and t Migration Process: A Longitudinal Study Amc Young Adults of Nova Scotia." Carleton, 1973.
7609
Sharma, Raghubar D. "Migration and Fertility ir Western Canadian Metropolis." Alberta, 19: [Edmonton]
Stewart, Donald Alexander. <u>See No./Voir no</u> 445
7610
Wegner, Robert Edward Chesley. "Analysis of Gr Migration for Metropolitan Areas in Cana Between 1966 and 1971." New York, 1979.

HISTORY OF CANADIAN ALIEN AND IMMIGRATION POLICY AND OF MIGRATION TO AND FROM CANADA/ HISTOIRE DES ÉTRANGERS AU CANADA ET DES POLITIQUES D'ÉMIGRATION ET D'IMMIGRATION CANADIENNES

General Items/Ouvrages généraux
7611
Allyn, Nathaniel Constantine. "European Immigrati into Canada, 1846-1951." Stanford, 1953.
Cheng, Tien-fang. <u>See No./Voir no</u> 7598
7612
Dixon, J.T. "Aspects of Yorkshire Emigration North America, 1960-1880." Leeds, 1982.
7613
Johnson, Stanley C. "A History of Emigration fro the United Kingdom to North America, 1763-191: London, 1914.
Kage, Joseph. <u>See No./Voir no</u> 7596
Macleod, Betty Belle Robinson. <u>See No./Voir no</u> 121
7614
Nord, Douglas Charles. "Immigration as an Inte national Problem: Canada, the United States a East Asia." Duke, 1979.
Thompson, Richard Henry. <u>See No./Voir no</u> 755
Thornton, Patricia. <u>See No./Voir no</u> 4859
7615
Wilson, Edna C. "The Impact of a Century of Iri Catholic Immigration in Nova Scotia (1750-1850 Ottawa, 1961.
<u>See also</u> Cultural and Urban Anthropology/<u>Voir au</u> Anthropologie culturelle et urbaine.

1750-1815
7616
Boggs, Theodore Harding. "The Influence Exerted the United Empire Loyalists in the Life and Po tics of Nova Scotia and New Brunswick." Ya 1908.
7617
Condon, Ann Gorman. "The Envy of the Americ States: The Settlement of the Loyalists in Ne Brunswick, Goals and Achievements." Harvar 1975.
7618
Conrad, Harold E. "The Loyalist Experiment in Ne Brunswick." Toronto, 1935.

7619
Handcock, W.G. "Migration from S.W. England to Newfoundland During the Late 18th and Early 19th Centuries." Birmingham, 1979.

MacKinnon, Neil Joseph. See No./Voir no 4030

7620
McLean, Marianne L. " 'In the New Land a New Glengarry': Migration from the Scottish Highlands to Upper Canada, 1750-1820." Edinburgh, 1982.

7621
Page, N. M. G. "A Study of Emigration from Great Britain, 1801-1860." London, 1931.

7622
Smith, Paul Hubert. "American Loyalists in British Military Policy, 1775-1781." Michigan, 1962.

7623
Textor, Lucy Elizabeth. "A Colony of Émigrés in Canada, 1798-1816." Yale, 1904.

7624
Troxler, Carole Watterson. "The Migration of Carolina and Georgia Loyalists to Nova Scotia and New Brunswick." North Carolina, 1974.

7625
Walker, James William. "The Black Loyalist in Nova Scotia and Sierra Leone." Dalhousie, 1973.

7626
Winzerling, Oscar W. "The Removal of Acadian Exiles from New France to Louisiana, 1763-1785." California, Berkeley, 1949.

1816-1867

7627
Adams, William Forbes. "Ireland and Irish Emigrations to the New World from 1815 to the Famine." Yale, 1929.

7628
Bickerton, B.C. "Scottish Emigration to British North America, 1837-1852." Cambridge, n.d.

7629
Brookes, Alan Alexander. "The Exodus: Migration from the Maritime Provinces to Boston During the Second Half of the Nineteenth Century." New Brunswick, 1979.

7630
Carrothers, W.A. "Emigration from the British Isles, 1815-1921." Edinburgh, 1921.

7631
Jones, M.A. "The Role of the United Kingdom in the Trans-Atlantic Emigrant Trade, 1815-1875." Oxford, 1956.

7632
Keep, George Rex Crowley. "The Irish Migration to North America in the Second Half of the Nineteenth Century." Dublin, 1951.

7633
Morehouse, F.M.I. "Migration from the United Kingdom to North America, 1840-1850." Manchester, 1926.

7634
Nolte, William Michael. "The Irish in Canada, 1815-1867." Maryland, 1975.

7635
Shepperson, Wilbur S. "British Views of Emigration to North America, 1837-1860." Case Western Reserve, 1952.

7636
Ward, William P. "White Canada Forever: Some Aspects of the Canadian Response to Orientals, 1853-1914." Queen's, 1973.

Wynne, Robert Edward. See No./Voir no 7161

1868-1918

7637
Avery, Donald Howard. "Canadian Immigration Policy and the Alien Question, 1896-1919: The Anglo-Canadian Perspective." Western Ontario, 1973.

7638
Barber, Marilyn J. "The Assimilation of Immigrants in the Canadian Prairie Provinces, 1896-1918: Canadian Perception and Canadian Policies." London, 1975.

7639
Bhatti, F.M. "East Indian Immigration into Canada, 1905-1973." Surrey, 1975.

Bicha, Karel Denis. See No./Voir no 103

7640
Boudreau, Joseph Amédée. "The Enemy Alien Problem in Canada, 1914-1921." California, Los Angeles, 1965.

Brookes, Alan Alexander. See No./Voir no 7629

Early, Frances Horn. See No./Voir no 827

7641
Ganzevoort, Herman. "Dutch Immigration to Canada 1892-1940." Toronto, 1975.

7642
Gold, Norman Leon. "American Immigration to the Prairie Provinces of Canada, 1890-1933." California, Berkeley, 1933.

Haebler, Peter. See No./Voir no 834

7643
Kanzler, Eileen McAuliffe. "Processes of Immigration: The Franco Americans of Manchester, New Hampshire, 1875-1925." Illinois State, 1982.

Keep, George Rex Crowley. See No./Voir no 7632

King, William L. M. See No./Voir no 7599

7644
Oberlander, Barbara J. "American Immigration Restriction as a Problem in American Foreign Relations, 1882-1906." Brandeis, 1974.

7645
Parr, Gwynth, Joy. "The Home Children: British Juvenile Immigrants to Canada, 1868-1924." Yale, 1977.

7646
Roberts, Barbara A. "Purely Administrative Proceedings: The Management of Canadian Deportation, Montreal, 1900-1935." Ottawa, 1980.

7647
Sturino, Franc. "Inside the Chain: A Case Study in Southern Italian Migration to North America, 1850-1930." Toronto, 1981.

7648
Switzer, Kennee B. "Baron de Hirsch, the Jewish Colonization Association and Canada, 1891-1914." London, 1982.

Troper, Harold Martin. See No./Voir no 7585

Ward, William P. See No./Voir no 7636

Wynne, Robert Edward. See No./Voir no 7161

Bhatti, F.M. See No./Voir no 7639
Ganzevoort, Herman. See No./Voir no 7641
7649
Godler, Zlata. "Croatia to Canada: Migration Between the Wars." Toronto, 1982.
Gold, Norman Leon. See No./Voir no 7642
7650
Hawkins, Frieda Elizabeth. "Canadian Immigration: A Study in Public Policy, 1946-1969." Toronto, 1968.
7651
Lines, Kenneth. "British and Canadian Immigration to the United States Since 1920." Hawaii, 1977.
Parr, Gwynth Joy. See No./Voir no 7645
Richmond, A.H. See No./Voir no 7583
Roberts, Barbara A. See No./Voir no 7646
7652
Wertimer, S. "Migration from the United Kingdom to the Dominions in the Interwar Period, with Special Reference to the Empire Settlement Act of 1922." London, 1952.

IMMIGRATION AND MIGRATION
AND THE ECONOMY/
IMMIGRATION, ÉMIGRATION ET L'ÉCONOMIE

7653
Anderson, Grace Merle. "The Channel Facilitators Model of Migration: A Model Tested Using Portuguese Blue-Collar Immigrants in Metropolitan Toronto." Toronto, 1971.
Bicha, Karel Denis. See No./Voir no 103
Blandy, Richard John. See No./Voir no 2379
Cheng, Tien-fang. See No./Voir no 7598
7654
Christiansen-Ruffman, Linda. "Newcomer Careers: An Exploratory Study of Migrants in Halifax." Columbia, 1976.
Comay, Peter Yochanan. See No./Voir no 2380
Corbett, David C. See No./Voir no 1201
Davies, Gordon Wilson. See No./Voir no 1345
7655
Farrar, Floyd Alvin. "Migration and Economic Opportunity in Canada, 1921-1951." Pennsylvania, 1962.
7656
Hussain, Matlub. "Interregional Return Migration in Canada, 1950-1975." McGill, 1978.
7657
Johnson, Caswell Lewington. "The Structure of Immigration and the Labour Force: An Enquiry into the Economic Characteristics of Canada's Postwar Immigration, 1946-1962." Columbia, 1967.
7658
Kim, J.G. "To God's Country: Canadian Missionaries in Korea and the Beginning of Korean Migration to Canada." Toronto, 1983.
King, William L.M. See No./Voir no 7599
Langley, Paul Christopher. See No./Voir no 2382
Lithwick, Irwin. See No./Voir no 1209
Macleod, Betty Belle Robinson. See No./Voir no 1211
7659
Marr, William Lewis. "The Economic Impact of Canadian Inward and Outward Migration and Their Determinants, 1950-1967." Western Ontario, 1973.

7660
Moldofsky, Naomi. "The Economic Adjustment North African Immigrants in Montreal McGill, 1969.
7661
Ovedovitz, Albert C. "A Comparative Study of Internal Migration." CUNY, 1974.
Parai, Louis. See No./Voir no 7581
7662
Percy, Michael B. "Migration Flows during the Deca of the Wheat Boom in Canada, 1900-1910: Neoclassical Analysis." Queen's, 1977.
Petersen, William. See No./Voir no 7593
Ralston, Helen. See No./Voir no 2192
Reynolds, Lloyd G. See No./Voir no 7588
Rothenberg, Stuart. See No./Voir no 8853
Seldon, James Ralph. See No./Voir no 1356
Sidlofsky, Samuel. See No./Voir no 7595
Sturino, Franc. See No./Voir no 7647
Ujimoto, Koji Victor. See No./Voir no 7600
Young, James Walton. See No./Voir no 2126
7663
Wong, W.H.C. "Migration Patterns in West-Centr Alberta." Alberta, 1979.

IMMIGRATION AND ALIEN LAW/
IMMIGRATION ET DROIT ÉTRANGER

See also Law: Immigration and Alien Law/Voir aus Émigration et droit étranger

LANGUAGE/LANGUE

Included under this heading is a sizeable sectio dealing with bilingualism, and the learning ar teaching of a second language. Studies on Canadia English, French in Canada, German, Ukrainian, and th numerous Native languages are also included.

The first studies approved, date back to 1892 at Joh Hopkins University, Clark University (1894) ar Harvard and Columbia (1904). The first Canadia dissertation in this category was produced at th University of Toronto in 1913. Only another Canadian dissertations followed in the next hal century. However, the 1970's and 1980's have adde substantially to this number.

The same observation can be made for the America universities which, in the last fourteen years double their output from all previous years. Over the sam period of time three titles were produced in Grea Britain, two at the University of London and one the University of Edinburgh.

Sous ce titre, on trouve une section importante to chant au bilinguisme ainsi qu'à l'apprentissage et l'enseignement d'une langue seconde; la sectio

comprend aussi des thèses sur l'anglais canadien, le français du Canada, l'allemand, l'ukrainien et de nombreuses langues autochtones.

Les premiers travaux américains datent de 1892 à l'Université Johns Hopkins; les universités Clark (1894), Harvard et Columbia (1904) en ont produit à leur tour. La première thèse canadienne a été rédigée à l'Université de Toronto en 1913. Au cours du demi-siècle suivant, il n'y a eu que 15 thèses canadiennes. Les années 1970 et 1980 ont largement augmenté le nombre.

On peut faire la même observation pour les universités américaines qui, dans les 14 dernières années, ont doublé leur production de toutes les années précédentes. Au cours de cette période, il y a eu trois ouvrages en Grande-Bretagne dont deux à l'Université de Londres et un à Édimbourg.

GENERAL ITEMS/OUVRAGES GÉNÉRAUX

7664
Andrew, Christine McCleave. "An Experimental Approach to Grammatical Focus." Alberta, 1974.

Gante, M. See No./Voir no 3861

7665
Glicksman, Louis. "Improving the Prediction of Behaviours Associated with Second Language Acquisition." Western Ontario, 1981.

7666
Heller, Monica Sara. "Language, Ethnicity and Politics in Quebec." California, Berkeley, 1982.

7667
Inman, Marianne Elizabeth Pizak. "An Investigation of the Foreign Language Needs of U.S. Corporations Doing Business Abroad." Texas, 1978.

7668
Picard, Diane. "L'influence d'un entraînement aux techniques de créativité sur l'acquisition d'une compétence de communication en langue étrangère." Laval, 1983.

7669
Preston, Donald Wesley. "Survey of Canadian English Slang." Victoria, 1973.

Sabourin, Conrad. See No./Voir no 1187

BILINGUALISM/BILINGUISME

General Items/Ouvrages généraux

Algardy, Françoise. See No./Voir no 7722

Arana, Milton Eulogio. See No./Voir no 4109

Ardanaz, Nicolas. See No./Voir no 7712

7670
Black, Norman Fergus. "English for the Non-English." Toronto, 1913.

7671
DeVries, John. "Structural Determinants of Bilingualism." Wisconsin, 1975.

Favreau, Micheline. See No./Voir no 9520

7672
Gatbonton-Segalowitz, Elizabeth. "Systematic Variations in Second Language Speech: A Socio-Linguistic Study." McGill, 1976.

7673
Gryz, Zbigniew. "Socio-Demographic Determinants of Language Shift in Canada." Carleton, 1980. [English and French/Français et anglais]

7674
Mougeon, Raymond. "Malbay: A Sociolinguistic Community Study." McGill, 1973. [Gaspé, Québec]

7675
Paribakht, Tahereh. "The Relationship Between the Use of Communication Strategies and Aspects of Target Language Proficiency: A Study of Persian ESL Students." Toronto, 1982.

7676
Patrice, Frère. "Le bilinguisme chez les franco-américains." Montréal, 1950.

7677
Schneiderman, Eta Isabel. "Attitudinal Determinants of the Linguistic Behaviour of French-English Bilinguals in Welland, Ontario." SUNY, Buffalo, 1975.

Schweda, Nancy Lee. See No./Voir no 837

Wilson, Harry Rex. See No./Voir no 7720

7678
Wilton, Murray Thomas. "Bilingual Lexicography: Theoretical Foundations and Practical Methodology with Special Reference to Canadian French and English." Simon Fraser, 1979.

7679
Ycas, Martynas Albert. "Divergent Thinking and Bilingualism." McGill, 1975.

BILINGUALISM AND EDUCATION/ BILINGUISME ET ENSEIGNEMENT

7680
Adiv, Ellen. "An Analysis of Second Language Performance in Two Types of Immersion Programs." Toronto, 1980.

7681
Benhacoun-Troise, Simy. "Immersion précoce ou immersion différée comme voile d'apprentissage du français langue seconde." Montréal, 1982.

7682
Birch, T.A. "The Teaching of English to French Speaking Students in Professional Schools." Montréal, 1934.

Booth, Mary Joyce. See No./Voir no 3403

7683
Bourque, Lorraine. "An Application of the Theory of Achievement Motivation to Achievement in Second Language Learning." Ottawa, 1980.

Bradford, Florence Emily. See no./Voir no 7724

Burnaby, Barbara Jane. See No./Voir no 4110

7684
Carlton, Richard Austin Michael. "Differential Educational Achievement in a Bilingual Community." Toronto, 1969.

7685
Chaudron, Craig Johnson. "Simplicity and Salience in Instruction in English as a Second Language Classes: Variations in Topic Reinstatement and Their Effect on Comprehension." Toronto, 1982.

7686
Chiasson, R.J. "Bilingualism in the Schools of Eastern Nova Scotia." London, 1959.

Cleghorn, Ailie. See No./Voir no 3005

7687
Clément, Joseph Jacques Richard. "Motivational Cha-
racteristics of Francophones Learning English:
Predictive and Descriptive Aspects." Western
Ontario, 1976. [Montréal high school students/
Étudiants du secondaire à Montréal]

7688
Colletta, Salvatore. "Community and Parental
Influence: Effects on Student Motivation and
French Second Language Proficiency." Ottawa,
1983.

Colman, Rosalie Marson. See No./Voir no 824

Cummings, Jim Patrick. See No./Voir no 9432

De Bagheera, Georgette. See No./Voir no 4305

7689
De Bagheera, Ivan J. "L'attitude des élèves canadiens
francophones du niveau secondaire à l'égard de leur
langue seconde." Montréal, 1975.

Desjarlais, Lionel. See No./Voir no 3117

7690
Duhamel, Ronald Joseph. "Various Forms of Support
and Non-Support of Bilingual Immersion Programs
in Schools." Toronto, 1973. [Carleton, Ottawa,
Toronto and Metropolitan Toronto/Conseils scolaires de Carleton, d'Ottawa, de Toronto et du
Toronto métropolitain]

Edwards, John Robert. See No./Voir no 828

7691
Gayle, Grace Marguerite Hope. "An Examination of
the Interaction Between Personality and Cognitive
Factors as They Relate to Attitudes Towards
Second Language Learning." Ottawa, 1976.

7692
Genesee, Fred Henry. "Bilingual Education: Social
Psychological Consequences." McGill, 1974.

Gliksman, Louis. See No./Voir no 7665

7693
Hartmann, Sister Mary Andrew. "Three Techniques
for Measuring Bilingualism." Ottawa, 1961.
[Grades six, seven, eight/Sixième, septième et
huitième années]

Hody, Maud. See No./Voir no 2465

Hottel-Burkhart, Nancy Greene. See No./Voir no 7715

Kistler, Ruth B. See No./Voir no 2412

Klassen, Bernard Roduly. See No./Voir no 3395

7694
Krichev, Alan. "The Comparative MMPI Performance
of Compound Coordinate French-English Bilingual
Students." Windsor, 1972.

Lamarre, Joseph Léo Paul André. See No./Voir no
3965

7695
Lee, Hon-Wing; Donald Hill. "Student Integrative
Motive in Second-Language Learning and Student-
Teacher Match-Mismatch in Field-Dependence-
Independence." Ottawa, 1979.

7696
Lemire, Gilles. "La présentation de la situation, étude
empirique de la situation, production de discours en
classe." Laval, 1981.

7697
Lepicq, Dominique Louise Marie. "Aspects théorique
et empiriques de l'acceptabilité linguistique: le ca
du français des élèves des classes d'immersion.
Toronto, 1980 [From grade six on in Ontari
English schools/De la sixième année dans les écol
anglaises d'Ontario]

MacDonald, Robert James. See No./Voir no 8297

7698
Maneckjee, Marie-Claire. "Apprentissage de l'anglai
comme seconde langue, étude de l'acquisition d'un
série de morphèmes grammaticaux." Ottawa
1979.

7699
Marrin-McConnell, Mary Irene. "Norm and Variatio
in Language: Implications for Second Languag
Teaching with Reference to the Teaching c
French in Ontario." Toronto, 1978.

7700
Masson, Louis I. "The Influence of Developmenta
Level Upon the Learning of a Second Languag
Among Children of Anglo-Saxon Birth." Ottawa
1963.

7701
Maurice, Louis J. "An Analysis of Semiotic Factors i
Cartoon Visuals and Their Effect of Conveyin
Meaning in Second Language Teaching." Alberta
1970.

7702
Naiman, Neil. "Imitation, Comprehension and Produc
tion of Certain Syntactic Forms by Young Childre
Acquiring a Second Language." Toronto, 1974.

7703
Nelson, John E. "Language Systems in Adult Informa
Second Language Learners." McGill, 1980.

7704
Orlowski, Duane Edmund. "Unstable Urban Bilir
gualism: The Mother Tongue Socialization of th
Children of Greek Immigrants in Toronto, Canada
Illinois, 1977.

7705
Painchaud-Leblanc, Gisèle. "Étude comparative d
fautes commises par deux groupes d'adultes angl
phones apprenant le français langue seconde
Montréal, 1978.

7706
Retfalvi, Terez. "L'influence de la motivati
intégrative sur les schèmes de comportemen
proxemiques dans le contexte de l'apprentissag
d'une langue seconde." Ottawa, 1983.

Richards, Merle Saundra Kazdan. See No./Voir no 311

7707
Rizzuto, Malcolm F. "An Experimental Comparison c
Inductive and Deductive Methods of Teaching Cor
cepts of Language Structure." Ottawa, 1968.

Schloss, Brigitte. See No./Voir no 2624

Seah, Hong Ghee. See No./Voir no 4051

7708
Terroux, Georges. "Intensiveness as a Factor
Second Language Learning." Montreal, 1970.

7709
Toohey, Kelleen Ann. "Northern Native Canadi
Second Language Education: A Case Study of Fo
Albany, Ontario." Toronto, 1982. [Swampy Cree
Cri]

7710
Tryphonopoulos, Jeannie Hager. "The Representation of Information: The Effect of Context on Bilingual Recognition Memory." York, 1982.

7711
Vaid, Jyotsna. "Hemisphere Differences in Bilingual Language Processing: A Task Analysis." McGill, 1982.

Zielinski, Wasyl Gregory. See No./Voir no 4133

STUDIES OF LANGUAGES SPOKEN IN CANADA/ ÉTUDES DES LANGUES PARLÉES AU CANADA

English/Anglais

7712
Ardanaz, Nicolas. "A Measurement of English Vocabulary – Acquisition and Lexical Borrowing and Related Non-Formal Pedagogical Variables of 200 Francophone Children Living in the West Island Area of Montreal Prior to Formal Instruction in English as a Second Language." Laval, 1976.

7713
Assam, Ann Padmore. "A Comparison of Written English of Non-West Indian Canadian-Born and Immigrant West-Indian Students in Canada." SUNY, Buffalo, 1981.

7714
Harris, Barbara Pritchard. "Selected Political, Cultural and Socio-Economic Areas of Canadian History as Contributions to the Vocabulary of Canadian English." Victoria, 1975.

7715
Hottel-Burkhart, Nancy Greene. "Cohesion in the English Essays of Canadian Speakers of French." Texas, 1981.

7716
Ireland, Robert John. "Canadian Spelling: An Empirical and Historical Survey of Selected Words." York, 1979.

7717
Séguinot, Candace Lee Carsen. "Some Aspects of the Intonations of the Yes-No Questions in Canadian English." Toronto, 1976.

7718
Tilly, George Anthony. "Canadian English in the Novels of the 1970's." York, 1980.

7719
Wanamaker, Murray. "The Language of King's County, Nova Scotia." Michigan, 1965.

Widdowson, John David Allison. See No./Voir no 8335

7720
Wilson, Harry Rex. "The Dialect of Lunenburg County, Nova Scotia: A Study of the English of the County, with Reference to Its Sources, Preservation of Relics, and Vestiges of Bilingualism." Michigan, 1959.

Wilton, Murray Thomas. See No./Voir no 7678

7721
Woods, Howard Bruce. "A Socio-Dialecticology Survey of the English Spoken in Ottawa: A Study of Sociological and Stylistic Variation in Canadian English." British Columbia, 1979.

7722
Algardy, Françoise. "Contenu socio-culturel de quelques méthodes contemporaines de français langue seconde ou étrangère: image de la famille dans les méthodes audio-visuelles de français langue seconde produites entre 1965 et 1975." Laval, 1982.

7723
Bougaieff, André. "Étude de morphologie et de phonétique: l'article défini et le pronom personnel de troisième personne dans le parler populaire du Québec." Laval, 1976.

7724
Bradford, Florence Emily. "A Pioneer Project in Teaching French: Ottawa Public School Oral French Programme (1957-1963)." Middlebury College, 1979.

7725
Brent, Edmund. "Canadian French: A Synthesis." Cornell, 1971.

7726
Cagnon, Maurice Arthur. "The Dialectical Origins of the Canadian-French Lexicon: An Analysis of the Glossaire du parler français au Canada." Pennsylvania, 1967.

7727
Carrière, Laurier. "Le vocabulaire français des écoliers franco-ontariens." Montréal, 1952.

7728
Charles, Arthur Howard, Jr.. "A Comparative Study of the Grammar of Acadian and Cajun Narratives." Georgetown, 1975.

Colletta, Salvatore. See No./Voir no 7688

7729
Connors, Kathleen Frances. "Calquing in Canadian French." California, Berkeley, 1972.

7730
Dagenais, Louise. "Système de diphtongaison, dans des dialectes de l'ouest de la France et du Québec: un problème de filiation linguistique." Montréal, 1982.

7731
Dallard, Albert. "Le parler rural à Saint-Laurent (Île d'Orléans)." Laval, 1981.

7732
Daoust-Blais, Denise. "L'influence de la négation sur certains indéfinis en français québécois." Montréal, 1975.

7733
Demharter, Cheryl Ann Marie. "Une étude phonologique du français parlé à Sainte-Flore, province de Québec." Tulane, 1981.

Deshaies-Lafontaine, D. See No./Voir no 436

7734
Dumas, Denis. "Phonologie des réductions vocaliques en français québécois." Montréal, 1978.

7735
Fischer, Robert Allen. "A Generative Phonological Description of Selected Ideolects of Canadian French in Lewiston, Maine." Pennsylvania State, 1975.

7736
Geddes, James, Jr. "Study of an Acadian Dialect (Spoken on the North Shore of the Baie-des-Chaleurs)." Harvard, 1894.

7737
Ginsberg, Raymond Emmanuel. "Study of the Syntax and Intonation of the Lexical Interrogative Sentence in the French Speech of Welland, Ontario (1969)." Toronto, 1976.

7738
Godin, Louise. "Error Analysis of the Errors of Francophone Students of Junior College Level in Québec City." Laval, 1981.

7739
Guillette, Claude. "Effets de structures ludiques dans des programmes d'enseignement assisté du micro-ordinateur pour l'apprentissage de l'orthographe d'homophones du français." Montréal, 1983.

7740
Hamayan, Else. "Acquisition of French Syntactic Structures: Production Strategies and Awareness of Errors by Native and Non-Native Speakers." McGill, 1978.

7741
Harley, Mary Birgitta. "Age-Related Differences in the Acquisition of the French Verb System by Anglophone Students in French Immersion Programs." Toronto, 1982.

7742
Hayward, Annette Marie. "Le conflit entre les régionalistes et les 'exotiques' au Québec (1900-1920)." McGill, 1981.

7743
House, Anthony B. "Study of a French-Canadian Dialect in an Ontario Town (Lafontaine)." Toronto, 1966.

7744
Hull, Alexander, Jr. "The Franco-Canadian Dialect of Windsor, Ontario: A Preliminary Study." Washington, Seattle, 1955.

7745
Kelley, Henry Edward. "Phonological Variables in a New England French-Speaking Community." Cornell, 1980. [Maine and/et New Hampshire]

7746
King, Ruth Elizabeth. "Variation and Change in Newfoundland French: A Sociolinguistic Study of Clitic Pronouns." Memorial University of Newfoundland, 1983.

Kistler, Ruth Barthold. See No./Voir no 2412
Laberge, Suzanne. See No./Voir no 766

7747
La Follette, James E. "Étude linguistique de quatre contes folkloriques du Canada français." Laval, 1953.

7748
Lanclos, Teresa Gloria. "A Linguistic Profile of Acadian-French Kindergarten Children of Landry Parish, Louisiana." Louisiana State, 1972.

7749
Landry, Joseph Allyn. "The Franco-Canadian Dialect of Papineauville, Québec, Canada." Chicago, 1943.

7750
Lapkin, Sharon Judith. "A Syntactic Analysis of Functional Elements in Canadian and Continental French." Toronto, 1974.

Lemire, Gilles. See No./Voir no 7696
Marrin-McConnell, Mary Irene. See No./Voir no 7699

7751
McArthur, James Franklin. "A Phonological Study of the Franco-Canadian Dialect of Saint-Jérome-de-Terrebonne, Québec, Canada." Georgetown, 1969.

Mougeon, Raymond. See No./Voir no 7674

7752
Nemni, Esther Monique. "Vers une définition syntaxique et phonologique de l'incise en franco canadien et en français standard." Toronto, 1973.

7753
Oukada, Larbi. "Louisiana French: A Linguistic Study with a Descriptive Analysis of Lafourche Dialect." Louisiana State, 1977.

7754
Painchaud, Louis. "Les marques du pluriel du français parlé dans la région de Sherbrooke." Montréal, 1975.

7755
Paret, Marie-Christine. "La maturation syntaxique du français écrit au secondaire." Montréal, 1983.

Patrice, Frère. See No./Voir no 7676
Robertson, Barbara Mae. See No./Voir no 771

7756
Rosoff, Gary H. "A Study of Liaison in the Extemporaneous Speech of Montreal French Speakers." Columbia, 1970.

7757
Saint-Pierre, Madeleine. "Aspects pragmatiques des interrogatives globales en français de Montréal." Montréal, 1977.

7758
Sales, M. "Language Contact: Synonymy and the Analysis of Semantic Differentiation in Franco Québécois." Edinburgh, 1980.

Schweda, Nancy Lee. See No./Voir no 837

7759
Soltesz, Joseph Attila. "Le parler des îles de Berthier-Sorel (Province de Québec, Canada): étude linguistique – aperçus ethnographiques." Laval, 1972.

7760
Stein, Dominique Shuly. "The French-Canadian Dialect of County Charlevoix, Québec." Michigan, 1974.

7761
Szmidt, Yvette. "L'interrogation totale dans le parler franco-canadien de la Fontaine, Ontario – ses formes et ses modalités intonatives." Toronto, 1976.

7762
Tassie, James Stewart. "The Noun, Adjective, Pronoun and Verb of Popular Speech in French Canada: An Examination of the Morphology and Syntax of the Spoken Word in the French-Canadian Novel." Toronto, 1957.

7763
Tessier, Jules Jacques. "Les particularités de vocabulaire de Félix-Antoine Savard." Toronto, 1981.

7764
Thomas, Alain Maurice Georges. "Variations sociophonétiques du français parlé à Sudbury (Ont.)." Toronto, 1982.
7765
Verreault, Claude. "Étude sur la suffixation en -ble et en -ant en français québécois actuel." Laval, 1981.
7766
Wightman, John Roaf. "The French Language in Canada." Johns Hopkins, 1888.
Wilton, Murray Thomas. See No./Voir no 7678
7767
Wrenn, Phyllis Margaret. "Declarative Melodic Structures in Canadian French as Spoken at Lafontaine, Ontario." Toronto, 1974.
7768
Yaeger, Malcah. "Context Determined Variation in Montreal French Vowels." Pennsylvania, 1979.

German/Allemand

7769
Dyck, Henry Dietrich. "Language Differentiation in Two Low German Groups in Canada." Pennsylvania, 1964.
7770
Eberhardt, Elvire. "The Bessarabian German Dialect in Medicine Hat, Alberta." Alberta, 1973.
7771
Gɮerzen, Jakob Warkentin. "Low German in Canada: A Study of 'Ploutdîts' as Spoken by Mennonite Immigrants from Russia." Toronto, 1952.
7772
Lehn, Walter Isaak. "Rosental Low German, Synchronic and Diachronic Phonology." Cornell, 1957.
7773
Mierau, Eric. "A Descriptive Grammar of Ukrainian Low German." Indiana, 1965.
7774
Palmer, Philip Motley. "Der Finfluss der Neuen Welt auf den Deutschen Wortschatz, 1492-1700." Harvard, 1931.
7775
Richter, Manfred Martin. "The Phonemic System of the Pennsylvania German Dialect in Waterloo County, Ontario." Toronto, 1969.
7776
Rossberg-Leipnitz, Elizabeth. "American Council Alpha German Test, Prepared for the Modern Foreign Language Study Under the Auspices of the American Council on Education and the Conference of Canadian Universities." Wisconsin, 1926.
7777
Thiessen, Jack. "Studies in the German Vocabulary of the Canadian Mennonites." University of Marburg, Germany, 1961. [In German/En allemand]

Greek/Grec

Orlowski, Duane Edmund. See No./Voir no 779

Languages from the Soviet Union/ Langues d'Union Soviétique

Doukhobor

7778
Harshenin, Alex Peter. "A Generative Phonology of Doukhobor Conjugation." Washington, Seattle, 1974.

Low German/Bas allemand

See also German/Voir aussi Allemand

Ukrainian/Ukrainien

7779
Bilash, Boryslav. "Canadianisms and Their Stylistic Functions in the Language of the Ukrainian-Canadian Writers." Ukrainian Free University, Munich, Germany, 1965. [In Ukrainian/En ukrainien]
7780
Lewyckyj, Jurij Myroslaw. "Les canadianismes lexicaux dans la langue des Ukrainiens de Montréal." Montréal, 1961.
Mierau, Eric. See No./Voir no 7773
7781
Pelège, Michael Nicholas. "A Comparative Study of the Teaching of Russian in the United States of America and Ukrainian in Canada." Ukrainian Free University, Munich, Germany, 1972.

LANGUAGES OF THE CANADIAN ABORIGINAL PEOPLE/ LANGUES DES PEUPLES AUTOCHTONES AU CANADA

General Items/Ouvrages généraux

Arana, Milton Eulogio. See No./Voir no 4109
Burnaby, Barbara Jane. See No./Voir no 4110
7782
Dundes, Alan. "The Morphology of North American Indian Folktales." Indiana, 1962.
7783
MacKenzie, Marguerite Ellen. "Towards a Dialectology of Cree-Montagnais-Naskapi." Toronto, 1982.
7784
Martin, Jeanette Helen Price. "A Survey of the Current Study and Teaching of North American Indian Languages in the United States and Canada." Utah, 1974.
7785
Sherzer, Joel F. "An Areal - Typological Study of the American Indian Languages North of Mexico." Pennsylvania, 1968.
Toohey, Kelleen Ann. See No./Voir no 7709
Weitz, Jacqueline Marie. See No./Voir no 491

Algonquian/Algonquin

7786
Hanzeli, Victor Egon. "Early Descriptions by French Missionaries of Algonquin and Iroquoian Languages: A Study of Seventeenth and Eighteenth Century Practice in Linguistics." Indiana, 1961.

7787
Jones, William. "Some Principles of Algonquian Word Formation." Columbia, 1904.

7788
Pentland, David Harry. "Algonquian Historical Phonology." Toronto, 1979.

Blackfoot/Pied-Noir

7789
Frantz, Donald Gene. "Toward a Generative Grammar of Blackfoot, with Particular Attention to Selected Stem Formation Processes." Alberta, 1970.

7790
Taylor, Allan Ross. "A Grammar of Blackfoot." California, Berkeley, 1969.

Cree/Cri

7791
Béland, Jean-Pierre. "Atikamekiv Morphology and Lexicon." California, Berkeley, 1978. [A Cree dialect spoken in southwestern Quebec/Dialecte cri parlé dans le sud-ouest du Québec]

MacKenzie, Marguerite Ellen. See No./Voir no 7783
Tookey, Kelleen Ann. See No./Voir no 7709
Urion, Carl Armand. See No./Voir no 517

7792
Wolfart, Hans Cristoph. "An Outline of Plains Cree Morphology." Yale, 1969.

Zielinski, Wasyl Gregory. See No./Voir no 4133

Micmac

Fidelholtz, James Lawrence. See No./Voir no 521

7793
Proulx, Paul Martin. "Micmac Inflection." Cornell, 1978.

Van Horn, Lawrence Franklin. See No./Voir no 526

Mississauga

7794
Chamberlain, Alexander F. "The Language of the Mississauga Indians of Skúgog. A Contribution to the Linguistics of the Algonkian Tribes of Canada." Clark, 1892.

Montagnais

MacKenzie M.E. See No./Voir no 7783

Naskapi

MacKenzie, M.E. See No./Voir no 7783

Ojibwa

Echlin, Kimberly Ann. See No./Voir no 534

7795
Nichols, John David. "Ojibwa Morphology." Harvard 1980.

7796
Piggott, Glyne Leroy. "Aspects of Odawa Morpho phonemics." Toronto, 1974. [Dialect o Ojibwa/Dialecte Ojibwa]

7797
Rhodes, Richard Alan. "The Morphosyntax of th Central Ojibwa Verb." Michigan, 1976.

7798
Rogers, Jean Hayes. "Participant Identification an Role Allocation in Ojibwa." Toronto, 1973. [Parr Island Reserve, Ontario/Réserve de l'Île Parry e Ontario]

7799
Shrofel, Salina Margaret. "Island Lake Ojibwa Mor phophonemics." Toronto, 1981.

7800
Todd, Evelyn Mary. "A Grammar of the Ojibwa Language: The Severn Dialect." North Carolina 1970.

Athapaskan

General Item/Ouvrage général

7801
Lawson, Virginia Kathryn. "Object Categorization an Nominal Classification in Some Athapaskan Lan guages: A Generative-Semantic Analysis." Iowa 1972.

Carrier

Munro, John B. See No./Voir no 560

Chipewyan

7802
Carter, Robin Michael. "Chipewyan Semantics: Form and Meaning in the Language and Culture of a Athapaskan-Speaking People of Canada." Duke 1974.

Dogrib

7803
Coleman, Phyllis Young. "Dogrib Phonology." Iowa 1976. [An Athapaskan Indian Language Spoken i the Northwest Territories of Canada/Dialect athapaskan parlé dans les Territoires du Nord Ouest du Canada]

Haida

7804
Anker, Daniel Ezra. "Haida Kinship Semantics, 1900 1974." Duke, 1975.

7805
Edwards, Elizabeth A. "The Importance of Pragmatic Factors in Haida Syntax." Washington, Seattle, 1982.

7806
Enrico, John James. "Masset Haida Phonology." California, Berkeley, 1980.

7807
Levine, Robert Daigon. "The Skidegate Dialect of Haida." Columbia, 1977. [Queen Charlotte Islands, British Columbia/Îles Reine-Charlotte, Colombie-Britannique]

Hare

7808
Rice, Keren Dichter. "Hare Phonology." Toronto, 1976. [Northwest Territories/Territoires du Nord-Ouest]

Iroquoian/Iroquois

Hanzeli, Victor Egon. See No./Voir no 7786

7809
Lounsbury, Floyd G. "Comparative Iroquoian Morphology." Yale, 1949.

7810
Michelson, Karin Eva. "A Comparative Study of Accent in the Five Nations Iroquoian Languages." Harvard, 1983.

Mohawk

7811
Beatty, John Joseph. "Mohawk Morphology." CUNY, 1972. [Montreal/Montréal]

7812
Bonvillain, Nancy Lee. "A Grammar of Akwesasne Mohawk." Columbia, 1972. [Quebec/Québec]

7813
Feurer, Hanny Marie. "Questions and Answers in Mohawk Conversation." McGill, 1976.

7814
Postal, Paul M. "Some Syntactic Rules in Mohawk (Caughnawaga Dialect)." Yale, 1963.

Tuscarora

7815
Rudes, Blair Arnold. "Historical Phonology and the Development of the Tuscarora Sound System." SUNY, Buffalo, 1976.

Kootenayan

7816
Garvin, Paul L. "Kutenai Grammar." Indiana, 1947.

Salishan

7817
Werker, Janet Feldman. "The Development of Cross Language Speech Perception: The Influence of Age, Experience and Content on Perceptual Organization." British Columbia, 1982.

Clallam

7818
Fleisher, Mark Stewart. "Clallam: A Study in Coast Salish Ethnolinguistics." Washington State, 1976.

Comox

7819
Harris, Herbert Raymond. "A Grammatical Sketch of Comox." Kansas, 1981. [Spoken in British Columbia/Parlé en Colombie-Britannique]

Halkomelem

7820
Galloway, Brent Douglas. "A Grammar of Chilliwack Halkomelem." California, Berkeley, 1977.

7821
Gerats, Donna Blanche. "Objective and Absolutive in Halkomelem Salish." California, San Diego, 1982.

7822
Leslie, Adrian Roy. "A Grammar of the Cowichan Dialect of the Halkomelem Salish." Victoria, 1979.

Okanagan

7823
Herbert, Yvonne Marie. "Transivity in (Nicola Lake) Okanagan." British Columbia, 1982.

7824
Watkins, Donald. "A Description of the Phonemes and Position Classes in the Morphology of Head of the Lake Okanagan (Salish)." Alberta, 1972.

Shuswap

7825
Gibson, James Albert. "Shuswap Grammatical Structure." Hawaii, 1973.

Songish

7826
Raffo, Yolanda Adela. "A Phonology and Morphology of Songish, a Dialect of Straits Salish." Kansas, 1972.

Sooke

7827
Efrat, Barbara Silverman. "A Grammar of Non-Particles in Sooke, a Dialect of Straits Coast Salish." Pennsylvania, 1969.

Siouan
Dakota

7828
Shaw, Patricia Alice. "Dakota Phonology and Morphology." Toronto, 1976. [Waxpetuwa Santee Dialect of Sioux Valley, Manitoba and Stoney Dialect of Morley, Alberta/Dialecte Waxpetuwa Santee de la vallée Sioux, Manitoba et dialecte Stoney de Morley, Alberta]

Tsimshian

7829
Dunn, John Asher. "Coast Tsimshian Phonology." New Mexico, 1971.

Wakashan
Kyuquot

7830
Rose, Suzanne Maria. "Kyuquot Grammar." Victoria, 1981. [Kyuquot Nootka]

Nootka

7831
Swadesh, Morris. "The Internal Economy of the Nootka Word." Yale, 1933.

Eskimo/Inuit

Inuktitutk

7832
Kalmar, Ivan. "Case and Context in Inuktituta (Eskimo)." Toronto, 1976.

Tagagmiut

7833
Graburn, Nelson H. "Tagagmiut Eskimo Kinship Terminology." Chicago, 1964.
7834
Massenet, Jean-Marie. "Quelques aspects de la quantité vocalique et consonantique en Eskimo." Toronto, 1978.

Ungalaklingmiut

7835
Correll, Thomas Clifton. "Ungalaklingmiut: A Study in Language and Society." Minnesota, 1972.

Yupik and/et Inupik

7836
St. Clair, Robert Neal. "Theoretical Aspects of Eskimo Phonology." Kansas, 1974.

LAW/DROIT

The legal classifications in the Table of Contents contain a wide range of topics, including an historical section on early Canadian law, provincial law, and the courts.

The first dissertation in law was approved at McGill University in 1918. During the 1970's Canada produced a total of 86 dissertations, the United States produced 24 and Great Britain produced 33. The universities generating the largest number of disser[ta]tions were: Montreal (18), Ottawa (17), Laval (1[4], Alberta (7), McGill (13), and York (12) Toronto [6], British Columbia (2), and Queen's (2). The Univers[ity] of British Columbia produced the first doctorate [in] legal study in 1926.

Among the British universities only four produc[ed] studies in this area: London (20), Oxford [(]Cambridge (2), and Edinburgh (2).

––––––––––

Les classifications juridiques de la table des matiè[res] contiennent une grande variété de sujets, dont u[ne] section historique sur les premières lois canadiennes [et] provinciales et sur les premiers tribunaux.

En 1918, McGill a approuvé la première thèse en dro[it]. Au cours des années 1970, le Canada a produit un to[tal] de 86 thèses, les États-Unis (24) et la Grande-Bretag[ne] (33). Les universités qui viennent en tête so[nt] Montréal (18), Ottawa (17), Laval (14), Alberta ([7], McGill (13) et York (12), Toronto (6), Colomb[ie] Britannique (2) enfin Queen's (2). L'Université de [la] Colombie-Britannique a produit le premier doctorat [en] droit en 1926.

Seulement quatre universités britanniques ont présen[té] des études sur ce sujet: Londres (20), Oxford [(]Cambridge (2) et Édimbourg (2).

GENERAL ITEMS/OUVRAGES GÉNÉRAUX

Baum, Ruth Elizabeth. See No./Voir no 781
Krivy, Gary Joseph. See No./Voir no 2807
Marchant, Cosmo Kenningham. See No./Voir no 739
7837
Slattery, B. "The Land, Rights of Indigenous Canadi[an] Peoples, as Affected by the Crown's Acquisition [of] Their Territories." Oxford, 1979.

EARLY CANADIAN LAW/
PREMIÈRE LOI CANADIENNE

Bounadère, René. See No./Voir no 2516
7838
Cairns, J.W. "The 1808 Digest of Orleans and 18[66] Civil Code of Lower Canada: An Historical Stu[dy] of Legal Change." Edinburgh, 1981.
Cameron, John Duncan. See No./Voir no 7924
Lachance, André. See No./Voir no 7905
7839
Lester, Geoffrey Standish. "The Territorial Rights [of] the Inuit of the Canadian Northwest Territories: [A] Legal Argument." York, 1982.
Mackenzie, J.A. See No./Voir no 7922
Macleod, Roderick Charles. See No./Voir no 7126
Matthiasson, John Stephen. See No./Voir no 612
7840
Morrisey, Francis G. "The Juridical Status of t[he] Catholic Church in Canada (1534-1840)." Ottaw[a,] 1972.
Neatby, Hilda M. See No./Voir no 7039

7841
Orkin, Mark M. "Professional Autonomy and the Public Interest: A Study of the Law Society of Upper Canada." York, 1972.
7842
Scott, Seaman Morley. "Chapters in the History of the Law of Quebec, 1764-1775." Michigan, 1933.
Stewart, Bryce Morrison. See No./Voir no 2174

ADMINISTRATIVE LAW/DROIT ADMINISTRATIF

7843
Shumiatcher, Morris Cyril. "A Study in Canadian Administrative Law: The Farmers Creditors Arrangement Acts." Toronto, 1945.

AIR AND SPACE LAW/ LOI AÉRIENNE ET LOI DE L'ESPACE

Haanappel, Peter P.C. See No./Voir no 2271
Lioy, Michel L. See No./Voir no 10089
Magdelenot, Jean-Louis. See No./Voir no 7908
Reukema, Barbara Ann. See No./Voir no 2274

CANON LAW/DROIT CANON

7844
Bélanger, Louis-Eugène." Le statut canonique des ukrainiens catholiques du rite-grec-ruthène au Canada." Laval, 1945.
Bounadère, René. See No./Voir no 2516
7845
Desrochers, Bruno. "Le premier concile plénier de Québec et le code de droit canonique." Catholic, 1942.
7846
Duffie, Donald C. "Comparative Marriage Law in the Catholic Church and the Province of Canada (Quebec Excepted)." Laval, 1948.
7847
Granville, James. "Moral Personality in Canon Law and in the Law of Canada." Laval, 1948.
7848
Hinz, Leo G. "The Celebration of Marriage in Canada: A Comparative Study of Civil and Canon Law Outside of the Province of Quebec." Ottawa, 1953.
7849
Moncion, Jean. "L'incorporation civile des instituts religieux au Canada." Ottawa, 1978.
7850
Sanson, Robert J. "A Preliminary Investigation in Marriage Nullity Trials." Ottawa, 1977.
7851
Sylvestre, Abbé Lucien. "La cathédratique: histoire, commentaire cannonique et législation canadienne." Laval, 1946.
7852
Walsh, John J. "The Jurisdiction of the Interritual Confessor in the United States and Canada." Catholic, 1951.

CIVIL LAW/DROIT CIVIL

7853
Bergeron, Viateur. "L'attribution d'une protection légale aux malades mentaux." Ottawa, 1980.
7854
De Mestier du Bourg, Hubert Jean Marie. "Étude comparative des causes et des effets du divorce: droit canadien." McGill, 1974.
7855
Fréchette, Jean-Guy. "Détermination d'une règle de conflits de lois en matière de biens successoraux et de régimes matrimoniaux." Montréal, 1971.
7856
Frénette, François. "L'institution d'Emphytéose." Ottawa, 1976.
7857
Frénette, Orville. "L'incidence du décès de la victime d'un délit ou d'un quasi-délit sur l'action en indemnité." Ottawa, 1960.
Groves, Patricia Heffron. See No./Voir no 7921
Hinz, Leo George. See No./Voir no 7848
7858
Marquis, Paul-Yvan. "La nature juridique et les causes principales de la responsabilité civile du notaire officier public." McGill, 1973.
7859
Prior, Richard Byrvell Leathers. "A Historical Study of Pleadings, Discovery and Delay in Civil Actions in England and Canada." London, 1976.
Roussin, Marcel. See No./Voir no 6939
Sanson, Robert J. See No./Voir no 7850
7860
Senay, Alphonse. "La séparation des patrimoines en matière de succession." Montréal, 1943.
7861
Sinclair, Pierrette. "La victime face à l'assureur dans le régime d'assurance automobile du Québec." McGill, 1977.
7862
Smith, J. "Duties and Powers of Corporate Executives and Promoters in Quebec, with Particular Reference to the Interaction of Civil Law and Common Law." London, 1972.
Welt, F. See No./Voir no 7888

COMMERCIAL LAW/ DROIT COMMERCIAL

Bohemier, Albert. See No./Voir no 7894
7863
Demers, Robert. "The Reception of English Law in Quebec: Peculiarities of Quebec Company Law." Cambridge, 1976.
7864
Ducharme, Léo. "De l'acte de commerce en droit québécois." Montréal, 1976.
7865
Duncan, Gaylen Arthur. "Canadian Business and Economic Implications of Protecting Computer Programmes." Texas, 1975.
7866
Fox, Harold George. "The Canadian Law of Trade Marks and Industrial Designs (Including the Law of Trade Marks and Unfair Competition." Toronto, 1940.

7867

Gosse, R.F. "Legal Aspects of Governmental Control of Monopoly and Restrictive Practices in Canada." Oxford, 1960.

Hébert, Gérard J. See No./Voir no 2139

Johnston, Derek Samuel. See No./Voir no 7876

7868

McEwen, A.C. "Newfoundland Law of Real Property: The Origin and Development of Local Ownership." London, 1979.

7869

Mitchell, Victor E. "Canadian Commercial Corporations." McGill, 1918.

Slutsky, B.V. See No./Voir no 1954

COMMON LAW/DROIT COMMUN

Magwood, John M. See No./Voir no 7879

Martin, William Stewart Arnold. See No./Voir no 2173

Sanson, Robert J. See No./Voir no 7850

Smith, J. See No./Voir no 7862

Ziegel, J.S. See No./Voir no 7890

COMPARATIVE LAW/ DROIT COMPARATIF

7870

Adell, B.L. "The Legal Status of Collective Agreements in Canada, United States and England." Oxford, 1967.

7871

Aschinger, Richard Franz. "Industrial Urbanization, the Road to Serfdom. A Comparative Analysis of the Freedom Functionability of Liberal Democratic Institutions in Canada and Switzerland in the Context of the Urban Problem-Solving Process." York, 1975.

Caparros, Ernest. See No./Voir no 7940

7872

Carr, M.C. "Employees Inventions — Comparisons of all English-Speaking Countries Emphasizing United Kingdom, United States, and Canada." London, 1964.

Dean, Ronald Edward. See No./Voir no 7895

7873

Dickerson, R.W.V. "The Use of the Trust and the Company for Tax Avoidance in U.S., Great Britain, and Canada." London, 1964.

Duffie, Donald C. See No./Voir no 7846

7874

Enemeri, S.S.G. "A Comparative Study of the Powers and Duties of Directors and Controlling Share-Holders Under English, French and Canadian Law." London, 1964.

Granville, James. See No./Voir no 7847

Hinz, Leo G. See No./Voir no 7848

7875

Issalys, P.F. "Ethnic Pluralism and Public Law in Selected Commonwealth Countries." London, 1972.

Johnson, Daniel. See No./Voir no 1714

7876

Johnston, Derek Samuel. "Parallel Importation. Toronto, 1982. [With respect to copyright law patents, property rights, trade mark, etc/Tenan compte du droit de reproduction, des brevêts, de droits de propriété, des marques de fabrique, etc.]

7877

Laperrière, René. "Les systèmes juridiques de déter mination des salaires: expériences québécoise canadiennes et étrangères." Montréal, 1972.

7878

MacKinnon, Victor Stuart. "Comparative Federalis and Judicial Interpretation, A Jurisprudential Stud with Particular Reference to Interstate Commerc in the United States, Canada, and Australia Harvard, 1963.

7879

Magwood, John McLean. "The Common Law Back ground for and the Development of Competitio Law in Canada: Some Comparisons with America Jurisprudence." Toronto, 1981.

7880

Misra, B. "Legal Positions of Aliens in the Commor wealth." London, 1966.

7881

Morissette, Y.-M.J.R. "Improperly Obtained Evidenc Other than Confessions: A Comparative Stud Canada, England, Scotland, Northern Ireland, Eir Australia, New Zealand, and the United States Oxford, 1977.

7882

Murphy, E.E. "A Comparative Legal Study of the W Power in the Constitutions of Australia, Canad and the United States of America." Oxford, 1951.

7883

O'Connor, D. "The Power of the Criminal Appe Courts to Order New Trials: An Historical ar Comparative Study of the Law of Australi Canada, and England." London, 1969.

7884

Ohene-Djan, I.L. "The Fugitive Offender and the La of Extradition in the Commonwealth." Londo 1965.

Peterson, James Scott. See No./Voir no 1721

7885

Ponnuswami, Krishnaswami. "The Raising and Maint nance of Capital — A Comparative Study of Son Problems in the Law of Corporate Finance McGill, 1969.

7886

Sivaramayya, Bhamidipati. "Women's Rights of Inher tance: A Comparative Study of the Hindu, Muslir New York and Quebec Laws." McGill, 1971.

Slutsky, B.V. See No./Voir no 1954

Smith, Alexander. See No./Voir no 2335

7887

Thompson, Andrew Royden. "Basic Contrasts Betwe Petroleum Land Policies of Canada and the Unite States. Sovereignty and Natural Resources — Study of Canadian Legislation." Columbia, 1968.

7888
Welt, F. "Comparison Between the Divorce Law of the British Commonwealth, U.S.A., and Certain Continental Systems of Law with Particular Regard to the Execution of Foreign Judgments." Edinburgh, 1941.

Williams, John. See No./Voir no 1774

7889
Williams, Sharon Anne Clare. "The International and National Protection of Cultural Property: A Comparative Study." York, 1976.

7890
Ziegel, J.S. "The Canadian Law of Conditional Sales and Hire Purchase, Being a Study of the Jurisprudence and Legislation of the Common Law Provinces and Territories of the Dominion with Comparative References to the Law of England and Other Commonwealth Countries, and the United States of America." London, 1962.

CONSTITUTIONAL LAW/
DROIT CONSTITUTIONNEL

7891
Alheritière, Dominique. "Les aspects constitutionnels de la gestion des eaux au Canada." Laval, 1974.

7892
Bernard, J. "Federalism and Public Administration in Canada. A Study in Constitutional Law and Practice." London, 1964.

7893
Blache, Pierre. "Aspects constitutionnels du statut de l'acte règlementaire." Montréal, 1975.

7894
Bohemier, Albert. "La compétence législative en matière de faillite en droit constitutionnel canadien." Montréal, 1971.

7895
Dean, Ronald Edward. "Obscenity Standards in Canada and the United States: A Comparative Study in Constitutional Law." Tennessee, 1974.

Dussault, R. See No./Voir no 7944

Elliott, D.W. See No./Voir no 8551

7896
Gilbert, Christopher David. "Judicial Interpretation of the Australian and Canadian Constitutions, 1867-1982." York, 1983.

7897
Grunis, Asher Dan. "Freedom of Assembly in Canada." York, 1977.

La Forest, Gerard V. See No./Voir no 1717

7898
Hudon, Edward Gerard. "The Canadian Constitutional Tradition from the Point of View of an American." Laval, 1976.

Murphy, E.E. See No./Voir no 7882

7899
Ouellette, Yves. "La responsabilité extra-contractuelle de l'état fédéral au Canada; étude critique du système de responsabilité délictuelle et quasi-délictuelle de la couronne du chef du Canada." Montréal, 1965.

7900
Plischke, Elmer O.A.. "Jurisdiction in the Polar Regions: Study of the Juridical Principles Governing the Original Acquisition of Polar Territory in the Arctic with Special Reference to the Sector Principle." Clark, 1943.

CRIMINAL LAW, CRIMINAL PROCEDURE,
PENAL CODE AND JUSTICE/
DROIT CRIMINEL, PROCÉDURE CRIMINELLE,
CODE PÉNAL ET JUSTICE

7901
Cheang, Molly. "Sentencing: A Study in the Proper Allocation of Responsibility." York, 1974.

7902
Ennis, Pamela Ann Koza. "The Scales of Justice: The Influence of Equity Norms and Role Expectations on the Sentencing Practices of Provincial Court Judges." York, 1976.

7903
Fortin, Jacques André. "Le mens rea en droit pénal canadien." Montréal, 1971.

Green, Bernard. See No./Voir no 7920

Groves, Patricia Heffron. See No./Voir no 7921

7904
Hagan, John Lee. "Criminal Justice in a Canadian Province: A Study of the Sentencing Process." Alberta, 1974.

7905
Lachance, André. "La justice criminelle du roi en Canada, 1712-1748." Ottawa, 1975.

7906
Lagarde, Irénée. "Une méthode d'interprétation et de synthèse du droit pénal et de la procédure criminelle au Canada." Montréal, 1960.

7907
Létourneau, Gilles. "The Prerogative Writs in Canadian Criminal Law and Procedure." London, 1975.

7908
Magdelenat, Jean-Louis. "Les droits et obligations des états d'assurer la sécurité de l'aviation internationale contre le terrorisme." McGill, 1981.

7909
Manganas, Antoine. "La défense d'erreur de droit et son application en droit pénal canadien." Laval, 1983.

7910
Miers, David Robert. "Responses to Victimization: A Study of Compensation to Victims of Crime in Ontario and Great Britain." York, 1976.

Morissette, Y.-M. J.R. See No./Voir no 7881

7911
Nadin-Davis, Paul. "Quantum of Sentence in Canadian Federal Law." Ottawa, 1982.

O'Connor, D. See No./Voir no 7883

Ohene-Djan, I.L. See No./Voir no 7884

7912
Schiffer, Marc Evan. "Legal Aspects of the Relationship Between Psychiatrists and Offenders in the Canadian Criminal Justice System." Cambridge, 1981.

7913
Snider, D. Laureen. "Does the Legal System Reflect the Power Structure: A Test of Conflict Theory." Toronto, 1978.

7914
Stace, Michael Vincent. "Legal Form and Moral Phenomena: A Study of Two Events." York 1980. [Clean up Yonge Street campaign in Toronto 1973-1978/Campagne de nettoyage de la rue Yonge à Toronto 1973-1978]

7915
Tardif, Guy. "La police et la politique: une étude de leurs rapports vus à travers le métier et la carrière de chefs de police municipaux du Québec." Montréal, 1974.

7916
Tollefson, E.A. "The Privilege Against Self-Incrimination in England and Canada." Oxford, 1976.

COURTS/COURS

See also Politics: The Judiciary/Voir aussi Politique judiciaire

7917
Canagarayar, Jegadishwara Kalingarayar. "Diversion of Traffic Offenders." York, 1977.

Cheang, Molly. See No./Voir no 7901

7918
Darrough, William D. "Another Chance: Some Sociological Conditions of Juvenile Probation in a Family Court." British Columbia, 1975.

Ennis, Pamela Ann Koza. See No./Voir no 7902

7919
Gérin, Alexandre. "Du domicile et de la juridiction des tribunaux." Montréal, 1922.

7920
Green, Bernard. "The Determination of Delinquency in the Juvenile Court of Metropolitan Toronto." Harvard, 1969.

7921
Groves, Patricia Heffron. "Lawyer-Client Interviews and the Social Organization of Preparation for Court in Criminal and Divorce Cases." British Columbia, 1973.

Hans, Valerie Patricia. See No./Voir no 9686
Jobson, Keith Bertram. See No./Voir no 2432

7922
Mackenzie, J.A. "The Courts and Canadian Federalism: An Historical, Analytical, Evaluative Study of the Interpretation of the British North American Act." London, 1970.

O'Connor, D. See No./Voir no 7883
Wylie, William Newman Thomas. See No./Voir no 7059

IMMIGRATION AND ALIEN LAW/ DROIT ÉTRANGER ET IMMIGRATION

7923
Atkinson, W.J. "Administrative Discretion and the Implementation of Policy in Canadian and English Public Law with Special Reference to Immigration Law." London, 1975.

7924
Cameron, John Duncan. "The Law Relating to Immigration in Canada." Toronto, 1945.

7925
Cockram, G. "The Legal Aspects of Intra-Commonwealth Migration." London, 1963.

Misra, B. See No./Voir no 7880
Ribordy, F.X. See No./Voir no 794

INTERNATIONAL LAW/ DROIT INTERNATIONAL

7926
Castro-Rial, Juan. "La personnalité internationale du Canada." Montréal, 1951.

Donnelly, Brian Eugene. See No./Voir no 2236

7927
Glos, George Ernest. "International Rivers: A Policy-Oriented Perspective." Yale Law, 1960.

7928
Groffier, Ethel. "L'obligation alimentaire en droit international privé québécois et comparé." McGill 1972.

Koh, Kwang-Lim. See No./Voir no 1858

7929
Maduro, Morris F., Jr. "The Law of International Straits and Interoceanic Canals." Alberta, 1978.

7930
Mayrand, Léon. "Le Canada et la mer territoriale." Montréal, 1933.

7931
Piper, Don Courtney. "The International Law of the Great Lakes." Duke, 1961.

Plischke, Elmer. See No./Voir no 7900

7932
Talpis, Jeffrey Alan. "La loi qui doit régler le domaine du statut Riel dans les contrats pour le transfert entre vifs de la propriété mobilière u Senguli en droit international privé québécois." Montréal, 1970.

LABOR LAW/DROIT DU TRAVAIL

Adell, B.L. See No./Voir no 7870
Carrothers, Alfred William Rooke. See No./Voir no 2155

7933
Cutler, Philip. "The Quebec Labor Code and Court Review." Montréal, 1968.

Stewart, Bryce Morrison. See No./Voir no 2174

7934
Stewart, Ian Hampton. "Labour Parties, Labour Unions, and Labour Laws: A Comparative Analysis of British Columbia, and Manitoba." Queen's, 1983

7935
Verge, Pierre. "Le statut d'association accréditée selon le code du travail du Québec." Laval, 1971.

MARITIME LAW/DROIT MARITIME

7936
Cantin, Serge A. "Juridiction d'amirauté canadienne et compétence de la cour fédérale en matière maritime." Ottawa, 1979.

Laing, Lionel H. See No./Voir no 2284

7937
Payne, Richard J. "The Influence of Transnational Corporations on the Development of Transnational Law: Sea Law." Howard, 1975. [Chapter VI - Canada/Chapitre VI - Canada]

PROVINCIAL LAW/DROIT PROVINCIAL

Labrador

7938
Patenaude, Luce. "Le Labrador à l'heure de la contestation." Ottawa, 1971.

Ontario

Green, Bernard. See No./Voir no 7920
Léger, Lauraine. See No./Voir no 7200
Miers, David Robert. See No./Voir no 7910

Quebec/Québec

7939
Boucher, André. "La loi des fabriques du Québec." Ottawa, 1968.
Bounadère, René. See No./Voir no 2516
7940
Caparros, Ernest. "Les ligues de force de l'évolution des régimes matrimoniaux en droit comparé et québécois." Laval, 1973.
7941
Ciotola, Pierre. "Le Don Manuel en droit-privé-québécois et des effets du divorce en droit." Montréal, 1973.
7942
Colas, Émile. "Les caractéristiques originales de la coopération en droit québécois." Ottawa, 1980.
Cutler, Philip. See No./Voir no 7933
7943
Damé-Castelli, Mireille. "Patrimoine et conjoint. L'évolution comparée de la place du conjoint dans la famille en France et au Québec à travers le droit des successions et des libéralités." Laval, 1974.
Dickinson, John Alexander. See No./Voir no 7252
7944
Dussault, R. "Judicial Review of Administrative Action in Quebec." London, 1962.
7945
Ferland, Philippe. "Étude critique d'institutions de la procédure civile dans la province de Québec." Montréal, 1954.
7946
Giroux, Lorne. "Aspects juridiques du règlement de zonage au Québec." Laval, 1976.
Groffier, Ethel. See No./Voir no 7928
Hagan, John Lee. See No./Voir no 7904
Hébert, Gérard. See No./Voir no 2139
7947
Heleine, François. "Les pouvoirs ménagers de la femme mariée en droit québécois." Montréal, 1972.
7948
Keniff, Patrick John. "The Public Control of Land and the Use of Land Resources in the Law of the Province of Quebec." London, 1973.

7949
Lacasse, Jean-Paul. "Le claim en droit québécois." Ottawa, 1975.
Laperrière, René. See No./Voir no 7877
7950
Lemelin, Abbé Roméo. "Les registres paroissiaux de la province civile de Québec." Laval, 1944.
7951
Parent, Simon G. "Le nom patronymique dans le droit québécois." Laval, 1951.
7952
Payette, L. "The Floating Charge in the Law of Quebec." Oxford, 1972.
7953
Rivard, M. Eugène. "Les droits sur les successions dans la province de Québec." Laval, 1956.
Scott, Seaman Morley. See No./Voir no 7842
Senay, Alphonse. See No./Voir no 7860
Sivaramayya, Bhamidipati. See No./Voir no 7886
Talpis, Jeffrey Alan. See No./Voir no 7932
Tardif, Guy. See No./Voir no 7915
Verge, Pierre. See No./Voir no 7935

TAX LAW/LOI SUR L'IMPÔT

Johnson, Daniel. See No./Voir no 1714
La Forest, Gerard Vincent. See No./Voir no 1717
Peterson, James Scott. See No./Voir no 1721

LIBRARIES AND LIBRARY SCIENCE/BIBLIOTHÈQUES ET BIBLIOTHÉCONOMIE

Four Canadian universities have granted a total of 15 doctorates in library studies. The University of Toronto, has produced the largest number (10), followed by the University of Western Ontario (2), Queen's University (2), and the University of Ottawa (1). The University of Toronto has the honour of being the first university to approve the first study in this area in 1912, and another in 1917. It was not until the 1960's that another doctorate was granted, followed by two in the 1970's and ten in the first four years of the 1980's. Sixteen American universities have produced 28 titles: Chicago (5), Columbia (4), Michigan (3), Rutgers (2), Florida State (2), Illinois (2), and the remaning ten universities, one each. In Great Britain, the University of London produced one thesis in 1980.

After a listing of general items, the national, provincial, and municipal systems are studied, in addition to lower school, university libraries and library schools.

Perhaps an explanation for the comparatively small number of doctorates in this profession lies in the fact that a master's degree in library studies is generally sufficient for employment.

Seulement quatre universités canadiennes ont accordé un total de 15 doctorats en bibliothéconomie. L'Université de Toronto a eu la plus forte production (10), suivie par Western Ontario (2), Queen's (2) et Ottawa (1). L'Université de Toronto a été la première université canadienne à approuver des thèses en cette discipline en 1912 puis en 1917. Ce n'est ensuite qu'au cours des années 1960 qu'un autre doctorat a été accordé, suivi par deux autres dans les années 1970 et dix entre 1980 et 1984. Seize universités américaines ont produit 28 ouvrages: Chicago (5), Columbia (4), Michigan (3), Rutgers (2), Florida State (2), Illinois (2) et les dix universités restantes, une chacune. En Grande-Bretagne, l'Université de Londres a produit une thèse en 1980.

Après une liste d'études portant sur des sujets généraux, on trouve des thèses sur les organismes nationaux, provinciaux et municipaux qui s'ajoutent aux thèses sur les bibliothèques universitaires, sur celles des établissements d'enseignement de moindre importance et enfin sur les écoles de bibliothéconomie.

L'explication du nombre relativement modeste de doctorats en cette discipline réside peut-être dans le fait qu'une maîtrise en bibliothéconomie suffit généralement pour trouver un emploi.

GENERAL ITEMS/OUVRAGES GÉNÉRAUX

Antczak, Janice. See No./Voir no 8091
Archer, John Hall. See No./Voir no 6941
7954
Cook, Charles Donald. "The Effectiveness of the Anglo-American Cataloguing Rules in Achieving Standardization of Choice and Form of Heading for Certain Library Materials Cataloged in Canada, Great Britain and the United States from 1968 Through 1972." Columbia, 1977.
7955
Crouch, Richard Keith Chamberlain. "Interpersonal Communication in the Reference Interview." Toronto, 1981.
7956
Denis, Laurent-Germain. "Academic and Public Librarians in Canada: A Study of the Factors Which Influence Graduates of Canadian Library Schools in Making Their First Career Decision in Favor of Academic or Public Libraries." Rutgers, 1970.
7957
Deschatelets, Gilles. "Towards an Optimal Level of Participation of the Intermediary in the User-System Interface of Bibliographic Online Search Services." Western Ontario, 1983.
7958
Emery, John Whitehall. "The Library, the School and the Child." Toronto, 1917.
7959
England, Claire St. Clere. "The Climate of Censorship in Ontario: An Investigation into Attitudes Toward Intellectual Freedom and the Perceptual Factors Affecting the Practice of Censorship in Public Libraries Serving Medium-Sized Populations." Toronto, 1974.

7960
Hardy, Edwin Austin. "The Public Library: Its Place in our Educational System." Toronto, 1912.
7961
Kwei, John Chi Ber. "Bibliographic and Administrative Problems Arising from the Incorporation of Chinese Books in American Libraries." Chicago, 1931 [United States and Canada/États-Unis et Canada]
Miller, Judith Helen. See No./Voir no 8019
Packer, Katherine Helen. See No./Voir no 3736
Phillips, Delores Joan Lavoie. See No./Voir no 7979
7962
Rogers, Amos Robert. "American Recognition of Canadian Authors Writing in English, 1890-1960." Michigan, 1964.
7963
Saye, Jerry Dale. "Continuing Education for Library Educators: An Inquiry into the Current Practices, Perceptions, Preferences and Opinions of Selected Library Educators." Pittsburgh, 1979.
7964
Smith, Alice Margaret Gullen. "Significant Encounters: A Critical and Historical Evaluation of Landmarks in the Development of Imaginative Literature Printed in English for Children and Youth, 1658-1865; and Their Availability in Fifteen Selected Great Lakes Area Collections." Wayne State, 1966.
7965
Whitlock, G.L. "My Kingdom Still: A Comparative Study of Periodical Literature in Canada, Australia and the West Indies." Queen's, 1983.
Young, William Curtis. See No./Voir no 1043

National/Niveau national

7966
Bishop, Olga Bernice. "Publications of the Government of the Province of Canada, 1841-1867." Michigan, 1962.
7967
Donnelly, Sister Francis Dolores. "The National Library of Canada: Forces in Its Emergence and in the Identification of Its Role and Responsibilities." Illinois, 1971.
7968
Morton, Elizabeth. "Libraries in the Life of the Canadian Nation 1931-1967." Chicago, 1969.
Phillips, Delores Joan Lavoie. See No./Voir no 7979

Provincial/Niveau provincial

7969
Beard, John Robert. "Canadian Provincial Libraries." Columbia, 1965.
7970
Coughlin, Violet Louise. "Factors in the Development of Larger Units of Public Library Service in Canada, with Particular Reference to the Provinces of Prince Edward Island, Nova Scotia, and New Brunswick." Columbia, 1966.

7971
Foster, Helen Marie. "Philosophies, Practices and Policies of Book Selection in Medium-Sized and Large Public Libraries in Two Canadian Provinces, Alberta and Ontario." Toronto, 1982.
7972
Hagler, Ronald Albert. "The Selection and Acquisition of Books in Six Ontario Public Libraries in Relation to the Canadian Publishing System." Michigan, 1961.
7973
Jain, Nirmal. "Effectiveness of Users' Information Services in Academic Libraries in the Province of Nova Scotia." Simmons College, 1977.
Killan, Gerald. See No./Voir no 7199
7974
Nauratil, Marcia Jeanne. "An Investigation into the Congruence/Incongruence Between Espoused Theory and Theory-in-Use Relating to Public Library Service to Older Adults in Ontario and New York." Toronto, 1982.
7975
Reeves, William Joseph. "Occupational Institutions and Organizational Work Arrangements: An Analysis of the Relationship Between Standards of Librarianship and Work Arrangements in Libraries." Stanford, 1978. [Alberta]

Municipal/Niveau municipal

7976
Amey, Lorne James. "Information Seeking Activities of Adolescents of Different Socio-Economic Classes in a Canadian Urban Center." Toronto, 1982. [Halifax, Nova Scotia/Nouvelle-Écosse]
7977
Carter, Mary Duncan. "A Survey of Montreal Library Facilities and a Proposed Plan for a Library System." Chicago, 1942.
Crouch, Richard K.C. See No./Voir no 7955
Fleming, Erin Patricia Lockhart. See No./Voir no 1074
7978
Lajeunesse, Marcel. "Associations littéraires et bibliothèques à Montréal au XIXe siècle et au début du XXe siècle: l'apport sulpicien." Ottawa, 1978.
7979
Phillips, Delores Joan Lavoie. "Factors in the Accessibility of Government Publications: A Study Based on Land Use Planning Publications for the City of Toronto." Toronto, 1980.

School Libraries/Bibliothèques scolaires

Brackstone, Demaris Darlene. See No./Voir no 4261
Hambleton, Alixe Lyons. See No./Voir no 3008
Henslowe, Shirley Anne. See No./Voir no 3958
7980
Wiedrick, Laurence George. "Student Use of School Libraries in Edmonton Open Area Elementary Schools." Oregon, 1973.

University Libraries/Bibliothèques universitaires

7981
Howard, Helen Arlene. "The Relationship Between Certain Organizational Variables and the Rate of Innovation in Selected University Libraries." Rutgers, 1977.
Jain, Nirmal. See No./Voir no 7973
Murray, Virginia Elizabeth. See No./Voir no 3634
Packer, Katherine Helen. See No./Voir no 3736
7982
Pannu, Gurdial Singh. "Cataloguing Efficiency and Its Relation to Individual Work Group Discussion and Selected Student Characteristics." Indiana, 1971. [University of Alberta/Université d'Alberta]
7983
Person, Roland Conrad. "The Role of the Undergraduate Library in United States and Canadian Universities." Southern Illinois, 1982.
7984
Rao, Inna Kedage, Ravichandra. "Document and User Distribution in Transaction Records of Canadian University Libraries." Western Ontario, 1981.
7985
Sharp, Patricia Tipton. "Children's Literature Collections in Fifty-four Colleges and Universities: What They Are and What They Might Be." Iowa, 1980.
7986
Tauber, Maurice Falcolm. "Reclassification and Cataloging in College and University Libraries." Chicago, 1941.
7987
Wilkinson, John Provost. "A History of the Dalhousie University Main Library, 1867-1931." Chicago, 1966.

Library Schools/Écoles de bibliothéconomie

7988
Cairns, Sister Marie Laurine. "Factors Affecting Selected Admission and Retention of Students in Graduate Library Programs." Florida State, 1972.
7989
Collins, Audrey White. "Serials Education in Masters' Degree Programs in Accredited Library Schools in the United States and Canada." Florida State, 1980.
7990
Sayer, John Leslie, Jr. "Utilization of Individualized Instruction (Non-Computerized) in Accredited Graduate Library Schools in the United States and Canada." Texas, 1973.

LITERATURE/LITTÉRATURE

Canadian literature has always been popular as a subject for doctoral research in Canadian graduate schools. There has been a tremendous growth of interest during the 1970's and 1980's, however American research in Canadian literature was minimal

until the 1970's. It is interesting to note that of the American total of 69, 20 of the more recent studies were on Malcolm Lowry, an adopted son.

Twenty Canadian universities have engaged in doctoral research in this area with widely varying output. The leaders are the universities of Laval, Ottawa, Montreal, Toronto, York, New Brunswick, Queen's, McGill, British Columbia, Alberta, Western Ontario, Sherbrooke, Dalhousie, Memorial University of Newfoundland, McMaster, Calgary, Manitoba, Saskatchewan, Simon Fraser, and Saint Paul, in that order. There is wide disparity between the numbers produced by the first few universities and the last ten. It should be noted that eight universities of major stature did not produce dissertations in this area. The number of theses completed in the 1980's, thus far, indicated that this decade will surpass the 1970's in output.

Among the 35 American universities represented, 20 produced one dissertation. Columbia University produced nine, the University of Indiana six, the University of Harvard and the University of Pennsylvania each produced five doctoral dissertations on this subject.

British universities produced 16 items, three of which are studies of Malcolm Lowry and most were completed during the 1970's and 1980's. The earliest studies were accepted at the University of Glasgow in 1927, followed by one at the University of London in 1930, and one at the University of Aberdeen in 1934. The remainder were produced much later.

La littérature canadienne a toujours été un sujet de thèse très recherché dans les établissements d'enseignement supérieur du Canada. Une recrudescence extraordinaire de l'intérêt est observée dans les années 1970 et 1980. Jusqu'en 1970, la recherche américaine en littérature canadienne a été minime. Il est intéressant de constater que sur un total de 69 thèses en Amérique, 20 des plus récentes étaient sur Malcolm Lowry, que les Canadiens ont adopté pour l'un des leurs.

Vingt universités canadiennes ont approuvé des thèses en ce domaine et la production est extrêmement variée. Les universités Laval, d'Ottawa, de Montréal et de Toronto sont en tête, puis viennent dans l'ordre, les universités York, du Nouveau-Brunswick, Queen's, McGill, de la Colombie-Britannique, de l'Alberta, Western Ontario, de Sherbrooke, Dalhousie, Memorial, McMaster, celle de Calgary, du Manitoba, Simon Fraser et Saint Paul. Il existe une grande différence entre le nombre de thèses produites par les premières universités citées et les dix dernières. Il faut noter que huit universités très importantes n'ont pas produit une seule thèse en littérature. Le nombre des thèses rédigées dans les années 1980, jusqu'à présent, indique que la production de cette décennie surpassera celle des années 1970.

Parmi les 35 universités américaines représentées, 2⁰ n'ont produit qu'une seule thèse. Les université Columbia (9 thèses), Indiana (6), Harvard (5) e Pennsylvania (5) sont en tête.

Les universités britanniques ont produit 16 thèses dont trois sur Malcolm Lowry; la plupart ont ét rédigées dans les années 1970 et 1980. Les plu anciennes thèses ont été acceptées à Glasgow en 1927 suivies par une thèse à Londres en 1930 et une autre Aberdeen en 1934. Les autres ont été produites plu tard.

GENERAL ITEMS/OUVRAGES GÉNÉRAUX

7991
Altfest, Karen Caplan. "Canadian Literary National ism, 1836-1914." CUNY, 1979

7992
Batts, John Stuart. "Unpublished Diaries of the Nine teenth Century: An Annotated List." Ottawa 1972.

7993
Carpenter, David Cameron. "Alberta in Fiction. Alberta, 1973.

7994
Chawla, Saroj. "Canadian Fiction: Literature as Rol Exploration – An Analysis of Novels Written b Women, 1920-1974." York, 1981.

7995
Cohn-Sfetcu, Ofelia. "To Live in Abundance of Life A Study of Time in Five Canadian Authors. McMaster, 1982.

7996
Culham, T.A. "The Royal Canadian Mounted Police i Literature." Ottawa, 1947.

7997
Dagg, Melvin Harold. "Beyond the Garrison: A Stud of the Image of the Indian in Canadian Literature. New Brunswick, 1983.

7998
Daugherty, George Henry. "North American India Literature." Chicago, 1925.
Davies, Gwendolyn. See No./Voir no 1083

7999
Davis, Richard Clarke. "Voyages of Discovery: 20t Century Evolution of the Narratives of Wildernes Travel in the Canadian North." New Brunswick 1979.
Davison-Wood, Karen Margaret. See No./Voir no 942

8000
Downey, Deane Ernest David. "National Identity an Recent Canadian Fiction." Alberta, 1974.

8001
Drolet, Gilbert. "The National Identities in Canada' English and French War Novels, 1935-65." Mon tréal, 1970.
Durand, Marielle. See No./Voir no 3207

8002
Fairbanks, Carol Louise. "Garmented with Space American and Canadian Prairie Women's Fiction. Minnesota, 1982.

8003
Gagnon, Claude-Marie. "Une psycholecture des aventures étranges de l'agent IXE-13, l'as des espions canadiens: contribution à une socio-psychocritique du roman d'espionnage populaire." Laval, 1981.

8004
Giltrow, Janet Lesley. "North American Travel Writing." Simon Fraser, 1980. [Anna Jameson, Susanna Moodie, Thomas Haliburton, John Richardson, Catharine Parr Traill, Frances Brooke, St. Jean de Crevecoeur, F.P. Grove, etc.]

8005
Harrison, Richard Terrence. "The Unhoused Imagination: The Struggle for Imaginative Survival in Canadian Prairie Fiction." Western Ontario, 1975.

8006
Harvey, Roderick Wilson. "The New Sensibility and Recent Canadian Writing." Alberta, 1975.

8007
Heidenreich, R.E. "Strategies of Narrative Communication in the Canadian and Quebec Novel Since 1945." Toronto, 1983.

Hodgson, J.M.D. See No./Voir no 4648

8008
Itwaru, Arnold Harrichand. "The Invention of Canada: The Literary Production of Consciousness in Ten Immigrant Writers." York, 1983.

8009
Jackel, Susan Elizabeth. "Images of the Canadian West, 1872-1911." Alberta, 1977.

8010
Jones, A.K. "The Female Athlete, Her Image in Fact and Fiction: A Study in Sociology Through Literature." Alberta, 1981.

8011
Kroller, Eva-Marie. "The Function of Place in the Canadian Literature." Alberta, 1978.

8012
Lamont, Daniel R. "The Novels and Society: A Discussion of the Novels of Christopher Isherwood and Rex Warner, 1928-1941." Queen's, 1973.

8013
Lecker, Robert Allan. "Time and Form in the Contemporary Canadian Novel." York, 1980.

Leechman, Douglas. See No./Voir no 474

8014
Lemieux, Gérard. "Le soldat dans la littérature canadienne d'expression anglaise et française du XXe siècle." Laval, 1963.

8015
MacLulich, Thomas Donald. "The Emergence of the Exploration Narrative in Canada." York, 1976.

8016
Macri, Francis Maria. "The Garden, the Cage, the Universal Solution: A Typology in Canadian Fiction." Alberta, 1981.

8017
Martinello, Margaret Pappert. "Self-Portraits: Autobiographical Writing in Canada." York, 1981. [19th and 20th centuries/XIXe et XXe siècle]

McDougall, Robert Law. See No./Voir no 1090

McLean, Kenneth Hugh. See No./Voir no 6938

8018
McLeod, Gordon Duncan. "A Descriptive Bibliography of the Canadian Prairie Novel, 1871-1970." Manitoba, 1974.

8019
Miller, Judith Helen. "The Canadian Short Story Database: Checklists and Searches." York, 1981.

8020
Mitcham, Elizabeth Allison. "The Influence of the Canadian Environment on Themes of Isolation in the French and English Canadian Novel During the Period 1940 to 1971." New Brunswick, 1972.

8021
Northey, Margot Elizabeth. "Gothic and Grotesque Elements in Canadian Fiction." York, 1974.

8022
Oates, Thomas Raymond. "The Fur Trade: Northern Border/Rivers South: A Study in the Persistent Vision of the European Explorers of the American Heartland." Saint Louis, 1979.

8023
O'Connell, Mary Sheila. "Images of Canadians in Children's Realistic Fiction." Columbia, 1966.

8024
O'Connor, John Joseph William. "The Last Three Steppes: The Canadian West as 'Frontier' in Prairie Literature." Toronto, 1977.

8025
Osachoff, Margaret Gall. "Pastoralism and Technology in Recent Canadian Fiction." Alberta, 1978.

Oster, John Edward. See No./Voir no 4268

Palmer, Denise. See No./Voir no 10435

Parker, George Lawrence. See No./Voir no 1075

8026
Paustian, Shirley Irene. "The Literature about the Depression 1929-1939 in the Prairie Provinces of Canada." Alberta, 1975.

8027
Perley, Linda. "The Impact of the Holocaust on Canadian Jewish Writing." Montreal, 1981.

Plant, Richard Lester. See No./Voir no 1030

8028
Poupeney, Catherine. "L'image de l'espace dans les journaux de voyage de l'expédition Malespine (côte nord-ouest de l'Amérique du Nord, 1791)." Montréal, 1982.

8029
Rackowski, Cheryl Stokes. "Women by Women: Five Contemporary English and French Canadian Novelists." Connecticut, 1978.

8030
Reimer, Howard James. "Darwinism in Canadian Literature." McMaster, 1975.

8031
Reiter, David Philip. "Magic Trout and Other Stories." Denver, 1982.

8032
Ricou, Laurence Rodger. "Canadian Prairie Fiction: The Significance of the Landscape." Toronto, 1971.

8033
Robertson, Robert T. "The Not Unsimilar Face — Developments and Problems in the Study of Commonwealth Literature." Queen's, 1970.

8034
Saint-Pierre, Yvonne. "Resources stylistiques du français et de l'anglais d'après le roman canadien contemporain." Laval, 1966.

8035
Sarkar, Eileen. "The Concept of Freedom in English Canadian and French Canadian Novels of the 1950's." Ottawa, 1978.

8036
Seidner Kedar, E.H. "Ghosts in the Air of America: Transformation as Themes and Technique in North American Dark Romance." Toronto, 1983.

8037
Shouldice, Larry Mason. "Contemporary Quebec Criticism." Montréal, 1978.

8038
Stich, Klaus Peter. "Immigration and the Canadian West from Propaganda to Fiction." York, 1974.

8039
Stockdale, John. "The Development of the Canadian Novel in French and English from 1920 to 1950: A Study in the Comparative Development of Themes." Laval, 1978.

8040
Taube, Eva. "Exiles and Survivors: Images of the Immigrant and the Impact of the Holocaust in the Contemporary Canadian Novel." Wisconsin, 1976.

8041
Thacker, Robert William. "Landscape and Technique: The Background and Development of the North American Prairie Novel." Manitoba, 1981.

8042
Thompson, Eric Callum. "The Prairie Novel in Canada: A Study in Changing Form and Perception." New Brunswick, 1974.

8043
Thompson, Joyce Lesley. "Emphatically Middling: A Critical Examination of Canadian Literature in the 1930's." Queen's, 1975.

8044
Turner, Gordon Philip. "The Protagonists' Initiatory Experiences in the Canadian Bildungsroman: 1908-1971." British Columbia, 1979.

8045
Wainwright, John Andrew. "Motives for Metaphor: Art and the Artist in Seven Canadian Novels." Dalhousie, 1978.

Whitlock, G.L. See No./Voir no 7965

8046
Wood, Susan Joan. "The Land in Canadian Prose 1840-1945." Toronto, 1975.

Zanes, John Page. See No./Voir no 3551

ENGLISH-CANADIAN LITERATURE/ LITTÉRATURE CANADIENNE-ANGLAISE

8047
Arnason, David Ellis. "The Development of Prairie Realism: J.C. Stead, Douglas Durkin, Martha Ostenso and Frederick Philip Grove." New Brunswick, 1980.

8048
Baker, Ray Palmer. "A History of English-Canadian Literature to the Confederation: Its Relation to the Literature of Great Britain and the United States." Harvard, 1916.

8049
Birbalsingh, Frank Mahabal. "National Identity and the Canadian Novel in English, 1917-1967." London, 1972.

Butt, William Davison. See No./Voir no 7192

8050
Craig, Terrence L. "Attitudes Towards Race in Canadian Prose Fiction in English, 1905-1980." Toronto, 1982.

8051
Engel, Mary Frances. "Bankrupt Dreams: The Isolated and the Insulated – Selected Works of Canadian and American Prairie Literature." Kent State, 1978.

8052
Fee, Margery Elizabeth. "English-Canadian Literary Criticism, 1890-1950: Defining and Establishing a National Literature." Toronto, 1981.

8053
Fredericks, Carrie MacMillan. "Patterns of the Artist in English-Canadian Fiction." McMaster, 1977.

8054
Gerson, Carole Fainstat. "Shaping the English Canadian Novel, 1820-1900." British Columbia, 1977.

8055
Gnarowski, Michael. "A Reference and Bibliographical Guide to the Study of English Canadian Literature." Ottawa, 1967.

8056
Goldie, Terence William. "Canadian Dramatic Literature in English 1919-1939." Queen's, 1978.

8057
Hoy, Helen Elizabeth. "The Portrayal of Women in Recent English-Canadian Fiction." Toronto, 1977.

8058
Irvine, Lorna Marie. "Hostility and Reconciliation: The Mother in English Canadian Fiction." American, 1977.

8059
Johnson, C.G. "After the Last Frontiers: Themes from the Old and the New Wilderness in English Canadian and Australian Drama." Leeds, 1976.

8060
Jolly, Nora Patricia. "Address: Buffalo Coulee." Utah, 1972. [A novel based on the author's childhood in the Canadian prairies during the Depression/Roman basé sur l'enfance de l'auteur dans les prairies canadiennes durant la dépression.

8061
Lindquist, Vernon Rolfe. "The Soil and the Seed, the Birth of the Canadian Short Story in English: Haliburton, Moodie, and Others, 1830-1867." New Brunswick, 1979.

8062
Magee, William Henry. "Trends in the English Canadian Novel in the Twentieth Century." Toronto, 1950.

8063
McCaffrey, Helen Katherine. "Le Canadien français dans le roman canadien-anglais." Montréal, 1971.

8064
Monkman, Leslie Gordon. "White on Red: Perspectives of the Indian in English-Canadian Literature." York, 1975.

8065
Moss, John George. "Patterns of Isolation in English Canadian Fiction." New Brunswick, 1973.

8066
Retzleff, Marjorie Anne Gilbert. "The Primitive Mystique: Romance and Realism in the Depiction of the Native Indian in English-Canadian Fiction." Saskatchewan, 1981.

8067
Sharman, Vincent Douglas. "The Satiric Tradition in the Works of Seven English-Canadian Satirists." Alberta, 1969.

8068
Smiley, Calvin Lindsay. "Picturesque Past and Problematical Present: English-Canadian Fiction in Transition 1880-1920." Toronto, 1979.

8069
Sorfleet, John Robert. "French Canada in Nineteenth Century English-Canadian Historical Fiction." New Brunswick, 1975.

8070
Spettigue, Douglas Odell. "The English-Canadian Novel: Some Attitudes and Themes in Relation to Form." Toronto, 1966.

8071
Struthers, John Russell Tim. "Interesting Orbits: A Study of Selected Story Cycles by Hugh Hood, Jack Hodgins, Clark Blaise, and Alice Munro, in their Literary Contexts." Western Ontario, 1982.

8072
Tanaszi, M.J. "Feminine Consciousness in Contemporary Canadian Fiction with Special Reference to Margaret Atwood, Margaret Lawrence, and Alice Munro." Leeds, 1977.

Tilly, George Anthony. See No./Voir no 7718
Verduyn, Christl. See No./Voir no 8247

8073
Walden, Keith. "The Symbol and Myth of the Royal Canadian Mounted Police in Some British, American and English Canadian Popular Literature 1873-1973." Queen's, 1980.

8074
Watt, Frank William. "Radicalism in English: Canadian Literature Since Confederation." Toronto, 1958.

STUDIES OF ENGLISH-CANADIAN WRITERS/ ÉTUDE DES ÉCRIVAINS CANADIENS-ANGLAIS

Atwood, Margaret (1939-   )

8075
Baer, Elizabeth Roberts. "The Pilgrimage Inward: The Quest Motif in the Fiction of Margaret Atwood, Doris Lessing, and Jean Rhys." Indiana, 1981.

Packer, Miriane. See No./Voir no 8118
Rackowski, Cheryl Stokes. See No./Voir no 8029
Tanaszi, M.J. See No./Voir no 8072

Blaise, Clark (1940-   )

Struthers, John. See No./Voir no 8071

Bucke, Richard Maurice (1837-1902)

8076
Jaffe, Harold. "Richard Maurice Bucke's 'Walt Whitman': Edited with an Introduction and Variant Readings." New York, 1968.

8077
Lozynsky, Artem. "The Letters of Dr. Richard Maurice Bucke to Walt Whitman, Edited with a Critical Introduction and Historical Annotations." Wayne State, 1974.

Callaghan, Morley (1903-   )

8078
Darte, Marie Madeleine Cecilia. "Moral Vision and Naturalistic Technique: The Conflict in the Novels of Morley Callaghan." Toronto, 1976.

8079
Heaton, Cherrill Paul. "The Great Sin: A Critical Study of Morley Callaghan's Novels." Florida State, 1966.

8080
Martineau, François. "Morley Callaghan as a Novelist." Montréal, 1961.

8081
McDonald, Lawrence T.R. "Beginnings and Endings: A Study of Morley Callaghan's Fiction." Queen's, 1978.

8082
Ozbalt, Marija Ana. Irma. "Social Misfits in Morley Callaghan's and Ivan Cankar's Fiction." McGill, 1978.

Pell, Barbara Helen. See No./Voir no 8154

Carrel, Armand (1800-1836)

8083
McLaren, Angus Gordon. "The 'National' Under the Editorship of Armand Carrel." Harvard, 1971.

Cohen, Leonard (1934-   )

8084
Malus, Avrum. "The Face of Holiness in the Writing of Leonard Cohen." Montreal, 1975.

Cohen, Nathan (1921-   )

8085
Gould, Allan Mendel. "A Critical Assessment of the Theatre Criticism of Nathan Cohen with a Bibliography and Selected Anthology." York, 1977.

Davies, Robertson (1913-   )

8086
Monk, Patricia. "The Smaller Infinity: The Jungian Self in the Novels of Robertson Davies." Queen's, 1974.

Plant, Richard Lester. See No./Voir no 1030

8087
White, Douglas-Perry. "The Savour of Salterton and the Deptford Lives: Narrative Strategies in the Novels of Robertson Davies." Queen's, 1979.

De la Roche, Mazo (1885-1961)

8088
Daymond, Douglas M. "Tradition and Individual Freedom: The Life and Work of Mazo de la Roche." Queen's, 1972.

Duncan, Sara Jeannette (1861-1922)

Fortier, Darlene Nelita. See No./Voir no 8107
8089
McKenna, Isobel Kerwin. "Sara Jeannette Duncan: The New Woman. A Critical Biography." Queen's, 1981.

Dunlop, William (1792-1848)

8090
Draper, Douglas Gary. " 'Tiger': A Study of the Legend of William Dunlop." Western Ontario, 1978.

Durkin, Douglas (1884-1968)

Arnason, David Ellis. See No./Voir no 8047

Frye, Northrop (1912-   )

8091
Antczak, Janice. "The Mythos of a New-Romance: A Critical Analysis of Science Fiction for Children as Informed by the Literary Theory of Northrop Frye." Columbia, 1979.
8092
Bogdan, Deanne Gail Eleanor. "Instruction and Delight: Northrop Frye and the Educational Value of Literature." Toronto, 1980.
8093
Saluzinszky, I.L. "The Neo-Romantic Imagination in North American Criticism and Poetry Since 1945, with Particular Reference to the Criticism of Northrop Frye, Its Influence and Its Relation to the Work and Influence of Wallace Stevens." Oxford, 1983."

Galt, John (1779-1839)

8094
Aberdlin, J.W. "The Life and Work of John Galt." Aberdeen, 1934.
8095
Bowman, James Martin. "The Romance of Reality: Aspects of the Gothic and Sentimental Modes in the Fiction of John Galt." Montréal, 1982.
8096
Reilly, P.M.A. "The Regional Novels of Marie Edgeworth and John Galt." Edinburgh, 1980.

Gallant, Mavis (1922-   )

8097
Besner, Neil Kalman. "Mavis Gallant's Short Fiction: History and Memory in the Light of Imagination." British Columbia, 1983.

Gorman, Larry (1846-1917)

Ives, Edward Dawson. See No./Voir no 981

Graham, Gwethalyn (1913-1965)

8098
Opala, Barbara. "Gwethalyn Graham: A Critic Biography." Montreal, 1981.

Grove, Frederick Philip (1872-1942)

Arnason, Douglas Ellis. See No./Voir no 8047
8099
Broad, Margaret. "Rhetorical Control in Relation Meaning in the Novels of Frederick Philip Grove Ottawa, 1982.
Cohn-Sfetcu, Obelia. See No./Voir no 7995
8100
Hjartarson, Paul Ivar. "Frederick Philip Grove Work: The Drafts of the Master of the Mil Queen's, 1981.
8101
Larbalestier, Paul D.B. "F.P. Grove: An Interpret tion." Queen's, 1977.
8102
Makow, Henry. "An Edition of Selected Unpublish Essays and Lectures by Frederick Philip Gro Bearing on his Theory of Art." Toronto, 1982.
8103
Raudsepp, Enn. "Frederick Philip Grove and t 'Great Tradition'." McGill, 1977.
8104
Rubio, Mary Henley. "F.P. Grove's Children's Nov Its Text and Larger Context." McMaster, 1982.

Gustafson, Ralph (1909-   )

8105
Keitner, Wendy J.R. "Ralph Gustafson: Heir Centuries in a Country Without Myths." Queen 1973.

Haliburton, Thomas Chandler (1796-1865)

8106
Chitteck, Victor Lovitt Oakes. "Thomas Chandl Haliburton (Sam Slick): A Study in Provinci Toryism." Columbia, 1924.
8107
Fortier, Darlene Nelita. "The European Connectio A Study of Thomas Haliburton, Gilbert Parker, a Sara Jeannette Duncan." Toronto, 1981.
Giltrow, Janet Lesley. See No./Voir no 8004
8108
Harding, L.A.A. "The Humour of Haliburton Montréal, 1964.
Lindquist, Vernon Rolfe. See No./Voir no 8061

Henry, Alexander (1739-1824)

8109
Waldon, Freda F. "Alexander Henry, Esq. of Montrea Fur Trader, Adventurer and Man of Letters London, 1930.

Hodgins, Jack (1938-)

Struthers, John R. See No./Voir no 8071

Hood, Hugh (1928-)

Pell, Barbara Helen. See No./Voir no 8154
Struthers, John Russell Tim. See No./Voir no 8071

Howe, Joseph (1804-1873)

8110
Beaton, Margaret. "Joseph Howe, a Literary Figure."
Montréal, 1958.

Jameson, Anna Brownell (1794-1860)

Giltrow, Janet Leslie. See No./Voir no 8004
8111
Thomas, Clara Eileen. "Anna Jameson: The Making of
a Reputation, 1794-1840." Toronto, 1962.

Lampman, Archibald (1861-1899)

8112
Whitridge, Margaret E. "Annotated Checklists of
Lampman Manuscripts in Known Repositories in
Canada." Ottawa, 1970.

Laurence, Margaret (1926-)

8113
Curry, Gwen Cranfill. "Journeys Toward Freedom: A
Study of Margaret Laurence's Fictional Women."
Indiana, 1980.
8114
Githae-Mugo, Micere M. "Visions of Africa in the
Fiction of Chinua Achebe, Margaret Laurence,
Elspeth Huxley and Ngugi Wa Thiong'o." New
Brunswick, 1973.
8115
Hughes, Terrance Ryan. "Gabrielle Roy et Margaret
Laurence: deux chemins, une recherche." McGill,
1980.
8116
Long, Tanya C. "The Heroine in the Novels of
Margaret Laurence." Toronto, 1973.
8117
Maeser, Angelika Maria. "Myth and Reality: The
Religious Dimension in the Novels of Margaret
Laurence." McGill, 1978.
8118
Packer, Miriam. "Beyond the Garrison: Approaching
the Wilderness in Margaret Laurence, Alice Munro
and Margaret Atwood." Montréal, 1978.
Rackowski, Cheryl Stokes. See No./Voir no 8029
Tanaszi, M.J. See No./Voir no 8072
8119
Warwick, Susan Jane. "Telling Tales: Voice, Time and
Image in the Fiction of Margaret Laurence and
Willa Cather." York, 1983.

Leacock, Stephen (1869-1944)

8120
Chopra, Vishnu R.K. "Stephen Leacock: An Edition of
Selected Letters." McGill, 1976.
8121
Curry, Ralph Leighton. "Stephen Leacock: Humorist
and Humanist." Pennsylvania, 1956.
8122
Rasporich, Beverly Jean Matson. "Stephen Leacock:
Canada's Gentleman Humorist." Calgary, 1979.

Livesay, Dorothy (1909-)

8123
O'Donnell, Kathleen. "Dorothy Livesay." Montréal,
1959.

Lowry, Malcolm (1909-1957)

8124
Albaum, Elvin. "La Mordida: Myth and Madness in the
Novels of Malcolm Lowry." SUNY, Stony Brook,
1971.
8125
Barnes, Jimmy Weaver. "Fiction of Malcolm Lowry
and Thomas Mann: Structural Tradition."
Arkansas, 1972.
8126
Baxter, C. "Pessimism and Religious Experience in
the Fiction of Malcolm Lowry." London, 1975.
8127
Baxter, Charles Morley. "Black Holes in Space: The
Figure of the Artist in Nathaniel West's Miss
Lonelyhearts, Djuna Barne's Nightwood and Mal-
colm Lowry's Under the Volcano." SUNY, Buffalo,
1974.
8128
Binns, R.G. "Self-Consciousness and Form in the
Fiction of Malcolm Lowry." East Anglia, 1976.
8129
Casari, Laura Elizabeth Rhodes. "Malcolm Lowry's
Drunken Divine Comedy: Under the Volcano and
Shorter Fiction." Nebraska, 1967.
8130
Considine, Raymond Howard. "Malcolm Lowry's Major
Prose Fiction." Tennessee, 1972.
8131
Costa, Richard Hauer. "A Quest for Eridanus: The
Evolving Art of Malcolm Lowry's Under the
Volcano." Purdue, 1969.
8132
Cowan, David Timothy. "Malcolm Lowry's Aggregate
Daemon: A Study on the Psychology of Influence."
Michigan, 1981.
8133
Doyle, Linda Sheidler. "A Study of Time in Three
Novels: Under the Volcano, One Hundred Years of
Solitude, and Gravity's Rainbow." Notre Dame,
1978.
8134
Edmonds, Dale Harlan, II. "Malcolm Lowry: A Study
of His Life and Work." Texas, 1965.
8135
Epstein, Perle Sherry. "Cabbalistic Elements in Mal-
colm Lowry's Under the Volcano." Columbia, 1967.

8136
Finnegan, James Joseph. "Malcolm Lowry, George Orwell and Graham Greene: Three Views of Fascism." American, 1981.

8137
Grace, Sherrill Elizabeth. "The Voyage That Never Ends: Time and Space in the Fiction of Malcolm Lowry." McGill, 1974.

8138
Hagen, William Morice. "Realism and Creative Fable in Nostromo and Under the Volcano: An Approach to Technique and Structure." Iowa, 1974.

8139
Harrison, John Keith. "Under the Volcano and October Ferry to Gabriola: The Weight of the Past." McGill, 1972.

8140
Howard, Benjamin Willis. "Malcolm Lowry: The Ordeal of Bourgeois Humanism." Syracuse, 1971.

8141
Knoll, John Francis. "Malcolm Lowry and the Cinema." Saint Louis, 1972.

8142
Koerber, Betty Turner. "Humor in the Work of Malcolm Lowry." California, Los Angeles, 1975.

8143
Lemmon, Kathleen Sutton. "Malcolm Lowry: The Evolution of His Craft." Chicago, 1978.

8144
Nyland, Agnes Cecilia. "The Luminous Wheel: The Evolution of Malcolm Lowry's Style." Ottawa, 1967.

8145
O'Kill, Brian Laurence. "A Stylistic Study of the Fiction of Malcolm Lowry." Cambridge, 1975.

8146
Pottinger, Andrew John. "The Revising of Under the Volcano: A Study in Literary Creation." British Columbia, 1978.

8147
Rankin, Elizabeth Deane. "The Artist Metaphor in the Fiction of Malcolm Lowry." SUNY, Binghamton, 1980.

8148
Silverman, Carl M. "A Reader's Guide to Under the Volcano." SUNY, Buffalo, 1972.

8149
Sturgess, Philip John Moore. "Subjectivity in the Fiction of Malcolm Lowry." London, 1976.

8150
Tibbetts, Bruce Hamilton. "Malcolm Lowry's Long Night's Journey Into Day: The Quest for Home." Tulsa, 1975.

8151
Veitch, Douglas W. "The Fictional Landscape of Mexico: Readings in D.H. Lawrence, Graham Greene and Malcolm Lowry." Montréal, 1974.

8152
York, Thomas Lee. "Under the Volcano: The Novel as Psychodrama." Tulane, 1982.

MacLennan, Hugh (1907-   )

8153
Hyman, Roger Leslie. "The Prose of Hugh MacLennan: A Re-Evaluation." Toronto, 1972.

8154
Pell, Barbara Helen. "Faith and Fiction: Religious Vision and Form in the Novels of Hugh MacLennan, Morley Callaghan and Hugh Hood." Toronto, 1981.

8155
Zezulka, Joseph Martin. "Historical, Philosophical and Scientific Perspectives in the Works of Hugh MacLennan." Queen's, 1972.

MacMechan, Archibald (1862-1933)

8156
Baker, Janet E. "Archibald MacMechan: Canadian Man of Letters." Dalhousie, 1977.

McCulloch, Thomas (1776-1843)

McMullin, Stanley G. See No./Voir no 3549

McLuhan, Marshall (1911-1982)

See also/Voir aussi Communications

Moir, Charles (1838-1927)

8157
Shrive, Frank Norman. "Charles Moir: A Study in Canadian Literary Nationalism." Queen's, 1961.

Moodie, Susanna (1803-1885)

Lindquist, Vernon Rolfe. See No./Voir no 8061

Moore, Brian (1921-   )

8158
Dahlie, Hallvard. "The Novels of Brian Moore." Washington, Seattle, 1967.

8159
Foster, John Wilson. "Separation and Return in the Fiction of Brian Moore, Michael McLaverty, and Benedict Kiely." Oregon, 1970.

8160
Scanlan, John Allen, Jr. "States of Exile: Alienation and Art in the Novels of Brian Moore and Edna O'Brien." Iowa, 1975.

Munro, Alice (1931-   )

Packer, Miriam. See No./Voir no 8118

8161
Powell, Barbara Pezalla. "Narrative Voices of Alice Munro." York, 1981.

Struthers, John Russell Tim. See No./Voir no 8071
Tanaszi, M.J. See No./Voir no 8072

Ostenso, Martha (1900-1963)

Arnason, David Ellis. See No./Voir no 8047

8162
Buckley, Joan Naglestad. "Martha Ostenso: A Critical Study of Her Novels." Iowa, 1976.

Parker, Horatio Gilbert (1860-1932)

Fortier, Darlene Nelita. See No./Voir no 8107

Pratt, Edwin John (1882-1964)

8163
Beckmann, Susan Alison. "Pratt on Pratt: The Prose Commentaries of E.J. Pratt." Toronto, 1977.

8164
Jewinski, Edwin. "Methods of Telling: The Narrative Art of E.J. Pratt." Toronto, 1981.

McAuliffe, Angela T.S. See No./Voir no 8416

See also Poetry/Voir aussi Poésie

Richler, Mordecai (1931-   )

Cohn-Sfetcu, Obelia. See No./Voir no 7995

8165
Miller, David Edwin. "Complex Business: Realism and the Study of Businessmen in Four Contemporary Novels." Duke, 1982. [The Apprenticeship of Duddy Kravitz is one of the four studied/L'Apprentissage de Duddy Kravitz est l'un des quatre romans étudiés]

8166
Ramraj, Victor Jammona. "The Ambivalent Vision: Richler and the Satirical Tradition in the Canadian Novel." New Brunswick, 1976.

8167
Ryan, Diane Elizabeth. "Time and Geography in the Novels of Mordecai Richler." Oklahoma, 1978.

Roberts, Charles G.D. (1860-1943)

Conway, Charles Donald. See No./Voir no 8418

Ryerson, Egerton (1803-1882)

8168
McDonald, F.J. "Egerton Ryerson: A Pedagogical and Historical Essay." Ottawa, 1937.

Seton, Ernest Thompson (1860-1946)

Wadland, John Henry. See No./Voir no 951

Stead, Robert (1880-1959)

Arnason, David Ellis. See No./Voir no 8047

8169
Varma, Premlata. "The Life and Works of Robert Stead." Ottawa, 1981.

Strickland, Samuel (1804-1867)

See also Literature: General Items/Voir aussi Littérature. Ouvrages généraux

Stringer, Arthur (1874-1950)

8170
Meadowcroft, Barbara Wales. "Arthur Stringer as Man of Letters: A Selection of His Correspondence with a Critical Introduction." McGill, 1983.

Traill, Catharine Parr (1802-1899)

8171
Ballestadt, Carl P.A. "The Literary History of the Strickland Family." London, 1965.

Wiebe, Rudy (1934-   )

8172
Dill, Vicky Schreiber. "The Idea of Wilderness in the Mennonite Novels of Rudy Wiebe." Notre Dame, 1983.

Wilson, Ethel (1890-1980)

8173
Mitchell, Beverley Joan. "The Interested Traveller: Major Themes in the Fiction of Ethel Wilson." New Brunswick, 1976.

CANADIAN LITERATURE IN FRENCH AND/OR ABOUT FRENCH CANADA/ LITTÉRATURE CANADIENNE EN FRANÇAIS OU AU SUJET DU CANADA FRANÇAIS

8174
Arguin, Maurice. "Symptômes du colonialisme et signes de libération dans le roman québécois (1944-1954)." Laval, 1981.

8175
Bachert, Gerhard. "L'élément religieux dans le roman canadien-français; étude de son évolution dans les romans de 1900 à 1950." Laval, 1954.

8176
Barrois de Sarigny, Jacqueline. "L'image du roman québécois en France, de 1945 à 1975." Montréal, 1982.

8177
Beaudoin, Réjean. "Messianisme littéraire au Canada français (1850-1890)." McGill, 1982.

8178
Bégin, Denis. "Témoin de son milieu et modèle pédagogique." Sherbrooke, 1979.

8179
Belleau, André. "Le personnage de l'écrivain dans le roman québécois (1940-1960)." Montréal, 1979.

8180
Bénéteau, Amédée. "Le paysan dans la littérature française et dans la littérature canadienne-française." Ottawa, 1942.

8181
Bernier, Hélène. "Le conte-type 706 dans la tradition orale de langue française en Amérique du Nord." Laval, 1968.

8182
Biolik, Anna. "Deux romans de la terre québécois et polonais: Trente Arpents de Rinquet et Les Paysans de Ladislas Reymont." Montréal, 1982.

8183
Black, George Alexander. "The Treatment of Love in the French-Canadian Novel." Western Ontario, 1971.

8184
Blondin, Félix. "L'influence américaine dans la littérature de nos premiers journaux canadiens-français, 1775-1840." Ottawa, 1942.

8185
Bosco, Monique. "L'isolement dans le roman canadien-français." Montréal, 1953.

8186
Bourassa, André G. "Surréalisme et littérature québécoise." Montréal, 1975.

8187
Bourgeois, Mariette. "L'évaluation sociale dans le roman canadien-français de 1930 à 1950." Laval, 1967.

8188
Boynard-Frot, Janine. "Espace de l'homme, espace de la femme dans le roman du terroir canadien-français de 1860-1960." Sherbrooke, 1978.

8189
Bronner, Frédéric Y.-L. "L'influence du romantisme dans le Canada français de 1855 à 1914." Ottawa, 1944.

8190
Carmel, Marie. "La littérature française dans la Nouvelle-Angleterre." Laval, 1945.

8191
Collet, Paulette F.J. "L'hiver dans le roman canadien-français." Laval, 1963.

8192
Corbett, Edward M. "Les contes du terroir depuis 1900." Laval, 1948.

8193
Crausaz, Robert Martin. "The Race Consciousness in the French Canadian Novel." Pittsburgh, 1933.

8194
Dorsinville, Max. "Caliban Without Prospero: The Novels of Black America and French Canada." CUNY, 1972.

8195
Edwards, Mary Jane. "Fiction and Montreal, 1769 to 1885." Toronto, 1969.

8196
Egan, Marie-Jogues. "Le Canada français et les écrivains français depuis 1850 jusqu'à nos jours." Laval, 1944.

8197
Fraser, Ian F. "The Spirit of French Canada." Columbia, 1939.

8198
Graham, Robert Somerville. "Bilingualism and the Creative Writer of French Canada." Colorado, 1955.

8199
Grenier-Francoeur, Marie. "L'élocution littéraire grotesque: un modèle de sémiotique comparée." Laval, 1981.

8200
Gross, Raphael Henry. "The Idea of a Catholic Novel." Montréal, 1952.

Guillet, Ernest Bernard. See No./Voir no 833

8201
Haeck, Philippe. "Naissances de l'écriture québécoise." Sherbrooke, 1979.

8202
Harger, Virginia Ann. "Alienation and the Search for Self in the Nouveau Roman of France and of Quebec." British Columbia, 1973.

8203
Hathorn, Ramon. "Le monde anglo-saxon dans le roman canadien-français." Ottawa, 1975.

8204
Hayne, David M. "The Historical Novel and Fren[c] Canada." Ottawa, 1945.

Hayward, Annette Marie. See No./Voir no 7742

8205
Hébert, Pierre. "Figures temporalité et forme [] discours narratif: essai de modèle et lectures [] quelques oeuvres québécoises." Laval, 1977.

8206
Hesse, Marta Gudrun. "The Theme of Death in t[] French Canadian Novel from 1945 to 196[] Toronto, 1969.

8207
Hogan, Sister Mary Ignatia. "Les Canadiens frança[] d'après les romans canadiens-français de 1840 [] 1900." Laval, 1946.

8208
Howe, Ruth J. "Évolution du roman au Canada fra[] çais." Montréal, 1939.

8209
Jobin, Anthony J.. "The Regional Literature of Fren[] Canada." Michigan, 1936.

8210
Keffer, Lowell William. "Frustration, conflit et r[] volte: une étude socio-psychologique de vingt-tr[] romans québécois des années 1938 à 1961." Lava[] 1980.

8211
Ladouceur-Lacasse, Madeleine. "La société québé[] coise de la révolution tranquille et ses appare[] d'état, textes journalistiques." Sherbrooke, 1978.

8212
Laforest, Marie-Thérèse. "La mère dans le rom[] canadien-français contemporain, 1930-196[] Montréal, 1961.

8213
Lafrance, Jeanne. "Les personnages dans le rom[] canadien-français (1837-1862)." Laval, 1970.

Lajeunesse, Marcel. See No./Voir no 7978

8214
Lamy, Jean-Paul. "La fidélité dans les récits [] terroir canadien-français." Ottawa, 1972.

8215
Leblanc, Arthur Joseph. "The Quest for Perso[] Values in the French-Canadian Novel (1940-196[] Western Ontario, 1977.

8216
Lemieux, G. "Le soldat dans la littérature canadien[] d'expression anglaise et française du XXe siècl[] Laval, 1963.

8217
Lemieux, Germain. "Sources et parallèles du cont[] type 938 Placide Eustache." Laval, 1961.

8218
Lemieux-Michaud, Denise. "L'enfance dans la socié[] et le roman québécois." Laval, 1979.

8219
Lemire, Maurice Roland. "Les grands thèmes nation[] listes du roman historique canadien-françai[] Laval, 1967.

8220
Lennox, John Watt. "The Castle's Art: Elements [] the Gothic in Selected Fiction of French Cana[] and the American South." New Brunswick, 1976.

8221
Maheu-Latouche, Louise. "Le diable dans les contes québécois du XIXe siècle." Montréal, 1971.

8222
Maillet, Marguerite. "Développement de la littérature écrite en Acadie (1604-1957)." Ottawa, 1982.

8223
Major, Robert. "Parti Pris: idéologies et littérature." Ottawa, 1977.

8224
Marie-Diomède, Soeur. "Essai sur la littérature française au Manitoba." Ottawa, 1947.

8225
Marion, Séraphin. "Classicisme et romantisme au Canada français (1829-1894)." Montréal, 1934.

8226
Mary Ignatia, Soeur. "Les Canadiens français d'après les romans canadiens-français de 1840 à 1900." Laval, 1946.

8227
Mayes, Hubert G. "Rythmes et structures dans le roman québécois de 1950 à 1965." Laval, 1975.

8228
Michel, Éléanor Louise. "Les Canadiens français d'après le roman canadien-français contemporain." Laval, 1942.

Mitcham, Elizabeth Allison. See No./Voir no 8020

8229
Montigny, Louvigny de. "La revanche de Maria Chapdelaine." Montréal, 1938.

8230
Nardocchio, Elaine. "Les idéologies nationalistes chez trois dramaturges québécois: Marcel Dubé, Jacques Ferron, Michel Tremblay." Laval, 1979.

8231
Plante, Jean-René. "L'échec de la littérature québécoise au XIXe siècle." McGill, 1983.

Poteet, Maurice. See No./Voir no 7582

8232
Roy, Paul-Émile. "L'évolution religieuse du Québec d'après le roman de 1940 à 1960." Montréal, 1981.

8233
Saheb, Arlette. "Ironie, dire et vouloir-dire chez Roch Carrier, Marie-Claire Blais, Réjean Ducharme." Montréal, 1979.

8234
Sallenave, Pierre. "Essai de théorie littéraire: le roman canadien-français du dix-neuvième siècle." Sherbrooke, 1978.

8235
Santerre, Richard. "Le roman franco-américain en Nouvelle-Angleterre, 1878-1943." Boston College, 1974.

8236
Schmitz, Nancy. "Le conte-type 710 dans la tradition orale du Canada français et de l'Irlande." Laval, 1968.

8237
Schoderboeck, Anna. "The Element of Frustration in the French Canadian Novel, 1940-1954." Western Ontario, 1958.

8238
Sénécal, André-Joseph. "Les débuts d'une tradition romanesque au Canada français, 1837-1852." Massachusetts, 1976.

8239
Shek, Ben-Zion. "Aspects of Social Realism in the French-Canadian Novel, 1944-1964." Toronto, 1968.

Shouldice, Larry Mason. See No./Voir no 8037

8240
Steiger, A. "The Québécois Novel: A Collective Voice." Sussex, 1977.

8241
Stewart, Brinsley Elford Alister. "The Search for Objectivity and Impartiality in French Canadian Literary Criticism." British Columbia, 1976.

8242
Thériault, Alma. "La littérature française de Nouvelle-Angleterre." Laval, 1945.

8243
Trudel, Marcel. "L'influence de Voltaire sur les écrivains français du Canada, de 1760 à 1900." Laval, 1945.

8244
Tuchmaier, Henri Samuel. "L'évolution de la technique du roman canadien-français." Laval, 1959.

8245
Urbas, Jeannette. "Le personnage féminin dans le roman canadien-français de 1940 à 1967." Toronto, 1971.

8246
Van Roey-Roux, Françoise. "La littérature intime au Québec, de 1960 à 1979." Montréal, 1982.

8247
Verduyn, Christl. "L'idée de la découverte de soi dans le roman féminin canadien depuis 1960: études d'oeuvres québécoises et canadiennes-anglaises." Ottawa, 1979.

8248
Warwick, Jack. "The Journey in French Canadian Literature." Western Ontario, 1963.

8249
Whitfield, Agnes. "La problématique de la narration dans le roman québécois à la première personne depuis 1960." Laval, 1981.

STUDIES OF FRENCH-CANADIAN WRITERS/ ÉTUDES DES ÉCRIVAINS CANADIENS-FRANÇAIS

Aquin, Hubert (1929-)

8250
Ferland, Léon Gérald. "Hubert Aquin ou l'écriture éclatée." Montréal, 1982.

8251
Iqbal, Françoise. "L'oeuvre romanesque de Hubert Aquin." British Columbia, 1972.

8252
Lapierre, René. "L'imaginaire captif, une lecture d'Hubert Aquin." Montréal, 1981.

8253
Malcuzynski, M. Pierrette. "La fiction néobaroque aux Amériques, 1960-1970, littérature carnavalisée et aliénation narrative chez Hubert Aquin, Guillermo Cabrera Infante et Thomas Pynchon." McGill, 1982.

8254
Smart, Patricia Purcell. "L'ironie et ses techniques dans les romans de Jacques Godbout, d'Hubert Aquin et de Réjean Ducharme." Queen's, 1977.

Aubin, Napoléon (1812-1890)

8255
Tremblay, Jean Paul. "Aimé-Nicolas dit Napoléon Aubin: sa vie et son oeuvre." Laval, 1966.

Baillargeon, Pierre (1916-1967)

8256
Gaulin, André. "Pierre Baillargeon, l'homme et l'oeuvre." Sherbrooke, 1975.

Baron, Jacques (1905-)

8257
Ahearn, Catherine. "Cahiers de Jacques Baron: texte et commentaires." Ottawa, 1979.

Barthe, Joseph Guillaume (1816-1893)

8258
Dessureault, Fernande. "Joseph Guillaume Barthe; biographie." Laval, 1966.

Beauchemin, Nérée (1850-1931)

8259
Guilmette, Armand. "Édition critique des oeuvres complètes de Nérée Beauchemin." Laval, 1969.

Beaugrand, Honoré (1849-1906)

8260
Bance, Pierre. "Beaugrand et son temps." Ottawa, 1964.

Bégon, Elisabeth (1696-1755)

8261
Landels, Isabel. "La correspondance de Madame Bégon." Laval, 1947.

Bessette, Gérard (1920-)

8262
Piette, Alain. "Rhétorique et narration chez Gérard Bessette." Montréal, 1981.

Blais, Marie-Claire (1939-)

8263
Morin, Yvon. "Une saison dans la vie d'Emmanuel. Les structures de l'oeuvre et le style de Marie-Claire Blais." Montréal, 1972.
Rackowski, Cheryl Stokes. See No./Voir no 8029
Saheb, Arlette. See No./Voir no 8233

Bugnet, Georges (1879-1981)

8264
Papen, Jean. "Georges Bugnet, homme de lettres canadien." Laval, 1970.

Buies, Arthur (1840-1901)

8265
Lamontagne, Léopold. "Arthur Buies, 'chroniqueur voyageur spasmodique... et bohème incurable'." Ottawa, 1945.

Bussières, Arthur de (1877-1913)

8266
Paquin, Frère, Léon Victor. "Arthur de Bussières, sa vie et son oeuvre." Ottawa, 1958.

Carrier, Roch (1937-)

Saheb, Arlette. See No./Voir no 8233

Casgrain, Henri-Raymond (1834-1904)

8267
Hudon, Jean-Paul. "L'abbé Henri-Raymond Casgrain: l'homme et l'oeuvre." Ottawa, 1978.

Choquette, Robert (1905-)

8268
Legris, Renée. "Le monde romanesque et dramatique de Robert Choquette." Sherbrooke, 1972.

Conan, Laure (Angers, Félicité) (1845-1924)

8269
Roden, Lethem Sutcliffe. "Laure Conan: The First French Canadian Woman Novelist (1845-1924)." Toronto, 1956.

Constantin-Weyer, Maurice (1881-1964)

8270
Motut, Roger G. "La fortune littéraire de Maurice Constantin-Weyer." Washington, Seattle, 1969.

Dantin, Louis (Seers, Eugène) (1865-1945)

8271
Gaboury, Placide. "Louis Dantin et la critique d'identification." Montréal, 1970.
8272
Garon, Yves. "Louis Dantin: sa vie et son oeuvre. Laval, 1960.
Hayward, Annette Marie. See No./Voir no 7742

Dubé, Marcel (1931-)

Nardocchio, Elaine. See No./Voir no 8230

Ducharme, Réjean (1942-)

Saheb, Arlette. See No./Voir no 8233
Smart, Patricia P. See No./Voir no 8254

Dugas, Marcel-Henri (1883-1947)

273
Brouilette, Léonce. "Marcel Dugas: sa vie et son oeuvre." Laval, 1974.

Dunn, Oscar (1844-1885)

8274
Provost, Guy. "Oscar Dunn, son vie et son oeuvre." Laval, 1974.

Ferland, Albert (1872-1943)

8275
Branchaud, Irène. "Albert Ferland; l'homme et l'oeuvre." Ottawa, 1965.

Ferron, Jacques (1921-   )

8276
Cantin, Pierre. "Jacques Ferron polygraphe." Ottawa, 1981.
8277
L'Hérault, Pierre. "Le pays et l'imaginaire dans l'oeuvre de Jacques Ferron." McGill, 1977.
Nardocchio, Elaine. See No./Voir no 8230
8278
Smith, Donald. "Les idées sociales dans l'oeuvre de Jacques Ferron." Ottawa, 1979.

Fournier, Jules (1884-1918)

8279
Thériault, Adrien. "Jules Fournier, journaliste de combat." Laval, 1953.

Fréchette, Louis-Honoré (1839-1908)

8280
Klinck, George A. "Louis Fréchette, prosateur, une réestimation de son oeuvre." Laval, 1953.
8281
Skinner, Daniel T. "The Poetic Influence of Victor Hugo on Louis Fréchette." Harvard, 1953.

Garneau, François-Xavier (1809-1866)

8282
Smith, Harry Douglas. "L'influence d'Augustin Thierry sur François-Xavier Garneau." Laval, 1947.

Garneau, Hector de Saint-Denys (1912-1943)

8283
Bourneuf, Roland Henri. "Saint-Denys Garneau et ses lectures européennes." Laval, 1966.
8284
Dobbs, Bryan Griffith. "A Critical Edition of Hector de Saint-Denys Garneau's Regards et jeux dans l'espace." Wisconsin, 1970.
8285
Gagnon, Jean. "Saint-Denys Garneau: l'autour, le centre." Montréal, 1982.
Riser, Georges. See No./Voir no 8371

Gaspé, Philippe-Joseph Aubert de (1786-1871)

8286
Curran, Verna Isabel. "Philippe-Joseph Aubert de Gaspé: His Life and Works." Toronto, 1957.

Gérin-Lajoie, Antoine (1824-1882)

8287
Dionne, René. "Antoine Gérin-Lajoie, homme de lettres (1824-1882)." Sherbrooke, 1975.

Giguère, Roland (1929-   )

Malenfant, Chanel. See No./Voir no 8304

Godbout, Jacques (1933-   )

8288
Bellemare, Yvon. "La technique romanesque de Jacques Godbout." Laval, 1981.
Smart, Patricia P. See No./Voir no 8254

Harvey, Jean-Charles (1891-1967)

8289
Teboul, Albert Victor. "Idéologie, culture et littérature dans Le jour de Jean-Charles Harvey de 1937 à 1940." Montréal, 1981.

Hébert, Anne (1916-   )

8290
Chiasson, Arthur Paul. "The Tragic Mood in the Works of Anne Hébert." Tufts, 1974.
8291
Edmond, Maurice. "Le monde imaginaire d'Anne Hébert dans Les chambres de bois, Kamouraska et Les enfants du Sabbat." Laval, 1981.
8292
Juéry, René. "Oeuvres en prose d'Anne Hébert — Essai sémiotique narratif et discursif de La robe corail et de Kamouraska." Ottawa, 1976.
8293
Lemieux, Pierre Hervé. "Entre songe et parole: lecture du Tombeau des rois d'Anne Hébert." Ottawa, 1974.
8294
Paterson, Janet Mary. "L'architexture de Chambres de bois: modalité de la représentation chez Anne Hébert." Toronto, 1981.
Rackowski, Cheryl Stokes. See No./Voir no 8029
8295
Thériault, Serge A. "La quête d'équilibre dans l'oeuvre romanesque d'Anne Hébert — Étude psycho-structurale." Ottawa, 1978.

Hémon, Louis (1880-1913)

8296
Héroux, Raymonde. "La fortune littéraire de Maria Chapdelaine en France." Montréal, 1974.

Legendre, Napoléon (1841-1907)

8297
MacDonald, Robert J. "Napoléon Legendre, l'homme
et l'oeuvre." Laval, 1967.

Lozeau, Albert (1878-1924)

8298
Séguin, Jeanne d'Arc. "Le sentiment de la nature chez
Lozeau." Ottawa, 1963.

Major, André (1942-   )

See also Literature: General Items/Voir aussi: Litté-
rature.Ouvrages généraux

Marie de l'Incarnation (1599-1672)

8299
Labelle, Suzanne (Soeur Sainte-Marie). "L'esprit apos-
tolique d'après Marie de l'Incarnation." Ottawa,
1966.
Marie-Emmanuel, Soeur. See No./Voir no 7289
8300
Michel, Robert. "La voie de l'esprit chez Marie de
l'Incarnation." Saint Paul, 1971.

Martin, Claire (1914-   )

Rackowski, Cheryl Stokes. See No./Voir no 8029

Mère Duplessis de Sainte-Hélène (1687-1760)

8301
Gies, Mary L. "Mère Duplessis de Sainte-Hélène;
annaliste et épistolière." Laval, 1949.

Montreuil, Gaétane de (1867-1951)

8302
Hamel, Réginald. "Gaétane de Montreuil, sa vie, son
oeuvre, 1867-1951." Montréal, 1971.

Nevers, Edmond de (1862-1906)

8303
Galarneau, Claude. "Edmond de Nevers et l'avenir du
peuple canadien-français." Laval, 1957.

Ouellette, Fernand (1930-   )

8304
Malenfant, Chanel. "La partie et le tout: parcours de
lecture chez Fernand Ouellette et Roland
Giguère." Laval, 1980.

Panneton, Philippe (Ringuet) (1895-1960)

8305
Labonté, René. "Le style de Ringuet." Montréal,
1973.

Petitclair, Pierre (1813-1860)

8306
Noël, Jean-Claude." Pierre Petitclair, sa vie, s
oeuvre et le théâtre de son époque." Ottawa, 197

Rivard, Adjutor (1868-1945)

8307
Léo, Frère Antonio. "Adjutor Rivard: régionalist
philologue et critique." Ottawa, 1950.

Roquebrune, Robert de (1889-1978)

8308
Hudon, Jean-Guy. "Robert de Roquebrune: entre
fiction et l'autobiographie." Laval, 1981.

Roy, Camille (1870-1943)

Hayward, Annette Marie. See No./Voir no 7742
8309
Ross, Allan Charles Moffat. "Camille Roy, Litera
Critic." Toronto, 1953.

Roy, Gabrielle (1909-1983)

8310
Babby, Ellen Reisman. "The Language of Spectac
and the Spectacle of Language in Selected Texts
Gabrielle Roy." Yale, 1980.
8311
Gagné, Marc. "L'homme et le monde dans l'oeuvre
Gabrielle Roy." Laval, 1972.
Hughes, Terrance Ryan. See No./Voir no 8115
8312
Merzisen, Yves. "L'inspiration romanesque
Gabrielle Roy." British Columbia, 1974.
8313
Socken, Paul-Gerald. "The Influence of Physical a
Social Environment of Character in the Novels
Gabrielle Roy." Toronto, 1974.

Roy, Paul-Eugène (1859-1926)

8314
Welton, Mary Amedeus. "Un orateur apôtre au Can-
da, Sa Grandeur Monseigneur Paul-Eugène Ro
archevêque du Québec (1859-1926)." Laval, 1940.

Savard, Félix-Antoine (1896-1982)

8315
Belgrave, Robert-Oliver. "L'imaginaire de Féli
Antoine Savard." Montréal, 1979.
Tessier, Jules Jacques. See No./Voir no 7763

Simard, Jean (1916-   )

8316
Candelon, Danielle. "L'auteur implicite dans le di
cours du récit narratif: une analyse de l'oeuvre
Jean Simard." Laval, 1977.

Taché, Joseph Charles (1820-1894)

8317
Bosse, Eveline. "Joseph Charles Taché, son temps, son oeuvre." Montréal, 1969.

Tardivel, Jules-Paul (1851-1905)

8318
Savard, Pierre. "La France et les États-Unis dans l'oeuvre de Jules-Paul Tardivel (1851-1905)." Laval, 1965.

Thériault, Yves (1915-1984)

8319
Charbonneau, Gérald. "Le regard dans l'oeuvre romanesque d'Yves Thériault." Ottawa, 1979.

FOLKLORE, FOLKSONGS AND POPULAR TRADITIONS/FOLKLORE, CHANSONS FOLKLORIQUES ET TRADITIONS POPULAIRES

8320
Ballad, Charles Guthrie. "The Unpromising Hero: A Structural Analysis of One Naskapi Myth from Little Whale River." Oklahoma State, 1979. [Algonguian/Algonquin]

Cauchon, Michel. See No./Voir no 941

Charron, Claude-Yves. See No./Voir no 591

8321
Coldwell, Joyce-Ione Harrington. "Treasure Stories and Beliefs in Atlantic Canada." Memorial University of Newfoundland, 1977.

Dundes, Alan. See No./Voir no 7782

Echlin, Kimberly Ann. See No./Voir no 534

Haywood, Charles. See No./Voir no 464

8322
Henderson, Margaret Carole. "Many Voices: A Study of Folklore Activities in Canada and Their Role in Canadian Culture." Pennsylvania, 1975.

8323
Jolicoeur, Catherine. "Le vaisseau fantôme; légende étiologique." Laval, 1963.

8324
Kirshenblatt-Gimblett, Barbara. "Traditional Story-telling in the Toronto Jewish Community: A Study in Performance and Creativity in an Immigrant Culture." Indiana, 1972.

8325
Klymasz, Robert Bogdan. "Ukrainian Folklore in Canada: An Immigrant Complex in Transition." Indiana, 1971.

Kodish, Debora Gail. See No./Voir no 404

La Follette, James E. See No./Voir no 7747

8326
Low, Margaret. "L'oiseau mystérieux du château volant: monographie internationale du conte-type 708A (462)." Laval, 1978.

Macmillan, Cyrus John. See No./Voir no 962

8327
McCarl, Robert Smith. "Occupational Folklife: An Examination of the Expressive Aspects of Work Culture with Particular Reference to Fire Fighters." Memorial University of Newfoundland, 1980.

8328
Mealing, Francis Mark. "Our People's Way: A Study in Doukhobor Hymnody and Folklife." Pennsylvania, 1972.

8329
Perry, Marie-Alphonse. "Le folklore des enfants à Waterville, Maine." Laval, 1950.

Pocius, Gerald Lewis. See No./Voir no 409

8330
Sanchagrin, Marie U. (Soeur Marie Ursule). "Le folklore des Lavalois." Laval, 1947.

8331
Shaw, John William. "A Cape Breton Gallic Story-Teller." Harvard, 1982.

Small, Lawrence George. See No./Voir no 411

Suarez, Frère. See No./Voir no 3139

8332
Tallman, Richard Sensor. "The Tall Tale Tradition and the Teller: A Biographical-Contextual Study of a Story-Teller, Robert Coffil of Blomidon, Nova Scotia." Memorial University of Newfoundland, 1974.

8333
Thomas, Gerald Rowland. "Stories, Storytelling and Storytellers in Newfoundland's French Tradition: A Study of the Narrative Art of Four French Newfoundlanders." Memorial University of Newfoundland, 1977.

8334
Tsuchiyama, Tamie. "A Comparison of the Folklore of the Northern, Southern, and Pacific Athabaskans: A Study in Stability of Folklore Within a Linguistic Stock." California, Berkeley, 1947.

Wenker, Jerome Richard. See No./Voir no 963

8335
Widdowson, John David Allison. "Aspects of Traditional Verbal Control: Threats and Threatening Figures in Newfoundland Folklore." Memorial University of Newfoundland, 1973.

Wiget, Andrew O. See No./Voir no 634

8336
Wilson, Mary Louise Lewis. "Traditional Louisiana — French Folk Music: An Argument for Its Preservation and Utilization as a State Cultural Heritage." Pittsburgh, 1977. [Includes folksongs of a province of Canada/Contient des chansons folkloriques de la province du Canada]

8337
Wycoco, Remedios Santiago. "The Types of North American Indian Tales." Indiana, 1951.

POETRY IN CANADA/POÉSIE AU CANADA

General Items/Ouvrages généraux

8338
Bayard, Caroline Anne. "Concrete Poetry in Canada and Quebec, 1963-1975." Toronto, 1977.

8339
Glover, Thomas. "Nature in Early Canadian Poetry." Montréal, 1959.

8340
Hornsey, Richard Fraser. "The Function of Poetry and the Role of the Poet in Canadian Literary Magazines from New Frontier Through Delta." Alberta, 1975.

8341
Johnson, James Francis. "The Narrative Tradition in Canadian Poetry: William Kirby to James Reamey." York, 1981.

8342
King, Joanne. "Canadian Women Poets." Montréal, 1950.

Macodrum, M.M. See No./Voir no 8428

8343
MacRae, Christopher Frederick. "The Victorian Age in Canadian Poetry." Toronto, 1953.

8344
Mallinson, Anna Jean. "Versions and Subversions: Formal Strategies in the Poetry of Contemporary Canadian Women." Simon Fraser, 1981.

8345
Matthews, John Pengwerne. "A Comparative Study of the Development of Australian and Canadian Poetry in the Nineteenth Century." Toronto, 1957.

8346
McLaren, Lydia Bernice. "Application of Criteria for Poetry to the Selection of 70 Canadian Poems from Early Childhood." Columbia, 1967.

8347
McLeod, Leslie Thomas. "Cold Stars: The Movement Selfward in Late Nineteenth Century Canadian Poetry." Calgary, 1981.

8348
Mezei, Kathy. "A Magic Space Wherein the Mind can Dwell: Place and Space in the Poetry of Archibald Lampman, Émile Nelligan, and Duncan Campbell Scott." Queen's, 1977.

8349
Munton, Margaret Ann. "The Paradox of Silence in Modern Canadian Poetry: Creativity or Sterility." Dalhousie, 1981.

8350
Ricketts, Alan Stuart. "Idealism, Theosophy and Social Passion in Canadian Poetry: 1920-1940." Alberta, 1979.

8351
Stevens, Peter S. "The Development of Canadian Poetry Between the Wars and Its Reflection of Social Awareness." Saskatchewan, 1968.

8352
Zmurkevych, Stephanie. "Ukrainian Canadian Poetry: An Attempt to Define the General Idea." Ottawa, 1951. [In Ukrainian/En ukrainien]

FRENCH-CANADIAN POETRY/ POÉSIE CANADIENNE-FRANÇAISE

8353
Bélanger, Jeannine. "La poésie au Canada sous le régime français." Ottawa, 1939.

8354
Bessette, Gérard. "Les images en poésie canadienne-française." Montréal, 1950.

8355
Blais, Jacques. "La poésie au Québec de 1934 à 1944: dialectique et métamorphoses des valeurs." Laval, 1974.

8356
Chasse, Paul P. "Les poètes franco-américains de la Nouvelle-Angleterre, 1875-1925." Laval, 1969.

8357
Chowaniec, C.T. "By Precept and Example: A Critical Study of Five Montreal Poets (1925-1975)." Leeds, 1976.

8358
Damé-Dallard, Sylvie. "Trois poètes québécois exemplaires (1940-1970)." Laval, 1978.

8359
Ennemond, Frère. "L'école poétique de Québec et ses paysages littéraires." Ottawa, 1951.

8360
Fadin, Max. "Les dimensions du corps chez Crémazie, Nelligan, Saint-Denys Garneau et Grandbois." Montréal, 1981.

8361
Giguère, Richard. "Une poésie de dissidence: étude comparative de l'évolution des poésies québécoise et canadienne modernes à Montréal, 1925-1955." British Columbia, 1979.

8362
Lortie, Jeanne d'Arc. "La poésie nationaliste au Canada français (1606-1867)." Laval, 1973.

8363
MacIntosh, Roderick James. "A Comparative Study of French-Canadian and Mexican-American Contemporary Poetry." Texas Tech, 1981.

8364
Marcotte, Gilles. "Description critique de la poésie nouvelle au Canada français." Laval, 1969.

8365
Nepveu, Pierre. "Poésie et silence, lecture de Fernand Ouellette, Gaston Miron et Paul-Marie Lapointe." Montréal, 1977.

8366
Pelosse, Cécile. "La recherche du pays dans la poésie québécoise de 1945 à 1970." Montréal, 1974.

8367
Proulx, Ovide. "Un siècle de mythologie dans la poésie canadienne-française." Ottawa, 1941.

Tisdall, Douglas Michael. See No./Voir no 8390

8368
Turnbull, Jane M. "Essential Traits of French Canadian Poetry." Chicago, 1936.

STUDIES OF INDIVIDUAL FRENCH CANADIAN POETS/ ÉTUDES DES POÈTES CANADIENS-FRANÇAIS

Aubin, Napoléon (1812-1890)

Tremblay, Jean Paul. See No./Voir no 8255

Crémazie, Octave (1827-1879)

8369
Condemine, Odette. "Édition critique des poésies d'Octave Crémazie." Ottawa, 1970.

Fadin, Max. See No./Voir no 8360

Garneau, Alfred (1836-1904)

8370
Prince, Suzanne. "Alfred Garneau: édition critique de son oeuvre poétique." Ottawa, 1974.

Garneau, Hector de Saint-Denys (1912-1943)

Fadin, Max. See No./Voir no 8360

8371
Riser, Georges. "Conjonctions et disjonction – étude théorique de leur fonctionnement en poésie et application à l'oeuvre de Saint-Denys Garneau." Ottawa, 1981.

Grandbois, Alain (1900-1975)

8372
Bolduc, Yves. "Lecture de Rivages de l'homme d'Alain Grandbois." Ottawa, 1981.

Fadin, Max. See No./Voir no 8360

8373
Fournier, Claude. "Alain Grandbois: poésie et structures mythiques." Ottawa, 1978.

8374
Gallays, François. "Les mots et les images dans la poésie d'Alain Grandbois." Ottawa, 1971.

Lapointe, Paul-Marie (1929-   )

Nepveu, Pierre. See No./Voir no 8365

Loranger, Jean-Aubert (1896-1942)

8375
Guilmette, Bernadette. "Jean-Aubert Loranger – Oeuvre poétique: édition établie, annotée et présentée." Ottawa, 1982.

Miron, Gaston (1929-   )

8376
Larocque, Hubert. "L'imaginaire dans L'Homme rapaille et Courtepointes de Gaston Miron." Ottawa, 1982.

Nepveu, Pierre. See No./Voir no 8365

Montreuil, Gaétane de (1867-1951)

Hamel, Réginald. See No./Voir no 8302

Morin, Paul (1889-1963)

8377
Morel de la Durantaye, Jean-Paul. "Paul Morin, l'homme et l'oeuvre." Ottawa, 1978.

Nelligan, Émile (1879-1941)

Fadin, Max. See No./Voir no 8360

8378
Fortier, Roger (Frère Lévis). "Le Vaisseau d'Or d'Émile Nelligan." Ottawa, 1950.

Hayward, Annette Marie. See No./Voir no 7742

Mezei, Kathy. See No./Voir no 8348

Ouellette, Fernand (1930-   )

Nepveu, Pierre. See No./Voir no 8365

Panneton, Philippe (1895-1960)

8379
Panneton, Jean. "Philippe Panneton, poète, homme de théâtre, moraliste et romancier." Laval, 1973.

Poisson, Adolphe (1849-1922)

8380
Bouchard, Lionel. "Adolphe Poisson, le barde d'Athabaska, 1849-1922." Ottawa, 1950.

Rainier, Lucien (1877-1956)

8381
Timmins, Marie A.-L. (Durocher, Olivier). "Lucien Rainier (Abbé Joseph-Marie Mélançon): l'homme et l'oeuvre." Laval, 1965.

ENGLISH-CANADIAN POETRY/ POÉSIE CANADIENNE-ANGLAISE

8382
Beattie, Alexander Munro. "The Advent of Modernism in Canadian Poetry in English 1912-1940." Columbia, 1957.

8383
Bhojwani, Maia. "Pan's Green Flower, the Earth: Vegetative Myths in Nineteenth Century Canadian Poetry." Toronto, 1979.

8384
Djwa, Sandra Ann. "Metaphor, World View and the Continuity of Canadian Poets with a Computer Concordance to Metaphor." British Columbia, 1968.

8385
Knowles, L.C. "In Search of a National Voice: Similarities Between Scottish and Canadian Poetry, 1860-1930." St. Andrews, 1981.

8386
Norris, Kenneth Wayne. "The Role of the Little Magazine in the Development of Modernism and Post-Modernism in Canadian Poetry." McGill, 1980.

8387
Precosky, Donald Alexander. "Canadian Poetry 1910 to 1925: The Beginnings of Modernism." New Brunswick, 1979.

8388
Roy, George Ross. "Symbolism in English-Canadian Poetry (1880-1939)." Montréal, 1959.

8389
Steele, Charles Reginald. "Canadian Poetry in English: The Beginnings." Western Ontario, 1974.

8390
Tisdall, Douglas Michael. "The Not Unsimilar Face: A Comparative Study of the Influence of Culture, Religion and Locale on French-Canadian and English-Canadian Poetry." Toronto, 1971.

8391
Ware, Martin Peter. "Canadian Romanticism in Transition: Divergent Perspectives in an Era of Upheaval." Dalhousie, 1980.

8392
Watkin, Janis Kathryn. "Extended Forms: The Use of Myth in Modern and Contemporary English Canadian Poetry." Alberta, 1981.

STUDIES OF ENGLISH-CANADIAN POETS/ ÉTUDES DES POÈTES CANADIENS-ANGLAIS

Avison, Margaret (1918-   )

Cohn-Sfetcu, Obelia. See No./Voir no 7995
8393
Mansbridge, Francis. "The Poetry of Raymond Souster and Margaret Avison." Ottawa, 1975.

Campbell, Wilfred (1861?-1918)

Bhojwani, Maia. See No./Voir no 8383
8394
Boone, Laurel Blenkinsop. "The Collected Poems of William Wilfred Campbell." New Brunswick, 1981.
8395
Klinck, Carl F. "Wilfred Campbell: A Study in Late Provincial Victorianism." Columbia, 1943.

Carman, Bliss (1861-1929)

Bhojwani, Maia. See No./Voir no 8383

Crawford, Isabella Valancy (1850-1887)

8396
Burns, Robert Alan. "The Intellectual and Artistic Development of Isabella Valancy Crawford." New Brunswick, 1982.
8397
Petrone, Serafina Penny. "The Imaginative Achievement of Isabella Valancy Crawford." Alberta, 1977.
8398
Ross, Catherine Louise. "Dark Matrix: A Study of Isabella Valancy Crawford." Western Ontario, 1976.

Heavysege, Charles (1816-1876)

8399
Dale, Thomas R. "The Life and Works of Charles Heavysege, 1817-1876." Chicago, 1951.

Jones, David G. (1929-   )

8400
Dilworth, Thomas Robert. "The Technique of Allusion in the Major Poems of David Jones." Toronto, 1977.

Kirby, William (1817-1906)

Johnson, James Francis. See No./Voir no 8341

Klein, Abraham Moses (1909-1972)

8401
Caplan, Usher. "A. M. Klein: An Introduction." SUNY, Stony Brook, 1976.

8402
Fischer, Gretl Kraus. "A. M. Klein: Religious Philoso phy and Ethics in His Writings." McGill, 1972.
8403
Spiro, Solomon Joseph. "A Study and Interpretation the Judaic Allusions in 'The Second Scroll' and 'T Collected Poems of A. M. Klein': Annotations a Commentary." McGill, 1980.
8404
Wieland, James M. "The Ensphering Mind: A Comp rative Study of Six Commonwealth Poets: Klei Curnow, Hope, Ezekiel, Walcott, Okigbo." Queen 1978.

Lampman, Archibald (1861-1899)

Bhojwani, Maia. See No./Voir no 8383
8405
Connor, Carl Yoder. "Archibald Lampman, Canadi Poet of Nature." Columbia, 1927.
8406
Davies, Edward Barrie. "The Alien Mind: A Study the Poetry of Archibald Lampman." New Brun wick, 1970.
8407
Early, Leonard Roy. "Lampman and Romant Poetry." York, 1980.
Mezei, Kathy. See No./Voir no 8348
Whitridge, Margaret E. See No./Voir no 8112

Layton, Irving (1912-   )

8408
Adams, Richard Gordon. "Irving Layton: The Ear Poetry 1931-1945." New Brunswick, 1983.
8409
Mayne, Seymour. "A Study of the Poetry of Irvi Layton." British Columbia, 1972.

Livesay, Dorothy (1909-   )

O'Donnell, Kathleen. See No./Voir no 8123

Mandel, Eli (1922-   )

8410
Downton, Dawn Rae. "Postmodern Elements in t Poems of Eli Mandel, Michael Ondaatje, a Robert Kroetsch." Dalhousie, 1983.

Nichol, bp (1944-   )

8411
Henderson, Robert Brian. "Radical Poetics: Dada, Nichol, and the Horsemen." York, 1982.

Odell, Jonathan (1737-1818)

8412
Cafferty, Pastora Sanjuan. "Loyalist Rhapsodies: T Poetry of Stansbury and Odell." George Washin ton, 1971.

Pratt, Edwin John (1882-1964)

8413
Gibbs, Robert John. "Aspects of Irony in the Poetry of E.J. Pratt." New Brunswick, 1970.

8414
Keyworth, Vida. "Irony in the Poetry of E.J. Pratt." Montréal, 1962.

8415
Maggs, William Randall. "Tradition and Technology in the Poetry of E.J. Pratt." New Brunswick, 1977.

8416
McAuliffe, Angela T.C. " 'Between the Temple and the Cave': An Exploration of the Religious Dimensions of the Poetry of E.J. Pratt." Dalhousie, 1979.

8417
Saint Dorothy Marie, Sister. "The Poetic Imagery of Edwin John Pratt." Ottawa, 1958.

Purdy, Alfred W. (1918-)

Cohn-Sfetcu, Ofeba. See No./Voir no 7995

Reaney, James (1926-)

Johnson, James Francis. See No./Voir no 8341

Roberts, Charles G.D. (1860-1943)

Bhajwani, Maia. See No./Voir no 8383

8418
Conway, Charles Donald. "Sufficient Vision: A Reading of the Poetry and Prose Fiction of Charles G.D. Roberts." New Brunswick, 1982.
Ware, Martin Peter. See No./Voir no 8391

Roberts, Theodore Goodridge (1877-1953)

Ware, Martin Peter. See No./Voir no 8391

Scott, Duncan Campbell (1862-1947)

8419
Dragland, Stanley L. "Poetics and Related Themes in the Poetry of Duncan Campbell Scott." Queen's, 1971.

8420
Kelly, Catherine Elizabeth. "The Foreappointed Quest: A Study of Transcendence in the Poetry of Duncan Campbell Scott." New Brunswick, 1978.
Mezei, Kathy. See No./Voir no 8348

8421
Slonim, Leon. "A Critical Edition of the Poems of Duncan Campbell Scott." Toronto, 1978.
Ware, Martin Peter. See No./Voir no 8391

Smith, A.J.M. (1902-1980)

8422
Darling, Michael Edward. "A Variorum Edition of the Poems of A.J.M. Smith with a Descriptive Bibliography and Reference Guide." York, 1979.

Souster, Raymond (1921-)

Mansbridge, Francis. See No./Voir no 8393

UNITED STATES, BRITAIN, FRANCE AND GERMANY AND CANADIAN LITERATURE/ LITTÉRATURE AMÉRICAINE, BRITANNIQUE, FRANÇAISE, ALLEMANDE ET CANADIENNE

General Items/Ouvrages généraux

Baker, Ray Palmer. See No./Voir no 8048
8423
Massey, Lucy Alice. "Folkways of Pre-Expulsion Acadians in Selected French, British, and American Writers: A Comparative Analysis of Similarities and Differences in Expressed Thought." New York, 1960.

United States and Canadian Literature/ Littérature américaine et canadienne

Blondin, Félix. See No./Voir no 8184
8424
Doyle, James. "The Image of Canada in Literature of the United States." British Columbia, 1975.
8425
Gauthier, Joseph D. "Le Canada français et le roman américain." Laval, 1949.
Guillet, Ernest Bernard. See No./Voir no 833
Rogers, Amos Robert. See No./Voir no 7962
8426
Rousseau, Guildo. "L'image des États-Unis dans la littérature canadienne-française de 1775 à 1935." Sherbrooke, 1974.

Britain and Canadian Literature/ Littérature britannique et canadienne

Aberdlin, J.W. See No./Voir no 8094
8427
Blanar, Michael. "Early British Travellers in French Canada." Montréal, 1960.
8428
Macodrum, M.M. "Survivals of the English and Scottish Popular Ballads in Canada: A Study of the Ways of Tradition with Verse." Glasgow, 1927.
Mitcham, Peter. See No./Voir no 7468
Reimer, Howard James. See No./Voir no 8030

France and Canadian Literature/ Littérature française et canadienne

8429
Dorion, Gilles. "Paul Bourget et le Canada." Laval, 1974.
8430
Fitzpatrick, Marjorie Ann. "The Fortunes of Molière in French Canada." Toronto, 1968.
8431
Maillet, Antonine. "Rabelais et les traditions populaires en Acadie." Laval, 1970.
8432
Marie-Médéric, Frère. "Un siècle de voltairianisme au Canada français (1760-1875)." Ottawa, 1939.
Trudel, Marcel. See No./Voir no 8243

8433
Weyl, Shalom. "North America (Canada and the United States) in German Literature (1918-1945)." Toronto, 1952.

POLITICS/POLITIQUE

It is interesting to observe that Canadian politics is one of the areas in which American output in doctoral research exceeds the Canadian. However, it appears that in the 1980's, the Canadian total will surpass that of the United States. Of the 19 Canadian universities with political doctorates to their credit, the University of Toronto has produced more than three times the output of Carleton University, which holds second place. Queen's University, and the University of Alberta, McGill, York, Laval, Ottawa, and McMaster follow with ten or more doctorates each. Among the numerous American universities, Duke has been the most productive, with Columbia second, and Harvard a close third. The universities of Michigan, Chicago, Illinois, and Johns Hopkins follow with ten or more doctorates to their credit.

Twelve British universities have produced 46 titles, with London (23) and Oxford (17) dominating, and Cambridge (3), Exeter (1), Essex (1), and Manchester (1) completing the list.

———

Il est intéressant d'observer que la politique canadienne est l'un des secteurs où la production américaine de thèses de doctorat dépasse celle du Canada. Cependant, il semble que dans les années 1980, le total canadien surpassera celui des États-Unis. Des 19 universités canadiennes qui ont à leur crédit des thèses de doctorat sur la politique, l'Université de Toronto a produit trois fois plus d'études que l'Université Carleton, qui vient au second rang. Les universités Queen's, de l'Alberta, McGill, York, Laval, d'Ottawa et McMaster suivent avec dix doctorats ou plus chacune. Parmi les nombreuses universités américaines, Duke a été la plus productive, suivie de Columbia, puis de Harvard. Les universités du Michigan, de Chicago, de l'Illinois et Johns Hopkins suivent avec dix doctorats ou plus à leur crédit.

Douze universités britanniques ont produit 46 thèses, avec Londres (23) et Oxford (17) en tête; Cambridge (3), Exeter (1), Essex (1) et Manchester (1) complètent la liste.

8434
Arnold, Phil Warren. "Political Integration in Culturally Plural States: A Comparison of Political Preferences in Canada, Belgium and Argentina." Wisconsin, 1974.

8435
Bashevkin, Sylvia Beth. "Women and Change: Comparative Study of Political Attitudes France, Canada and the United States." York, 1981.

8436
Bellavance, M. "Public Policy and Canadian Politics." Wisconsin, 1970.
Boldt, Menno. See No./Voir no 447

8437
Brodie, M. Janine. "Pathways to Public Office: Canadian Women in the Postwar Years." Carleton, 1981.
Canning, Patricia M. See No./Voir no 3004

8438
Cannon, Gordon E. "Canada and Consociational Democracy: A Case Study." Connecticut, 1978.
Charlebois, Carol Ann. See No./Voir no 1082

8439
Cloutier, Cartier Édouard. "Two General Types Equalitarian Division Behavior: A Game Theoretical Experiment with American, English Canadian and French Canadian Players." Rochester, 1975.
Ezekiel, J.W. See No./Voir no 1109
Goulson, Carolyn Floyd. See No./Voir no 2423

8440
Grondin, Conde Rosaire. "The Development of Political Cynicism Among a Selected Sample of Adolescents in Alberta." Alberta, 1975.

8441
Hurwitz, Leon Henry. "An Empirical Study of Political Stability in Twenty Selected Democratic Countries." Syracuse, 1971.

8442
Jackson, Michael Wesley. "Science Policy in Canada: A Conjunction of Philosophy, Science and Politics." Alberta, 1976.
Lavi-Levin, Hannah. See No./Voir no 6762

8443
Levy, Gary. "Canadian Participation in Parliamentary Associations." Laval, 1974.

8444
Livada, Valentin Radu. "The Legal, Political, Strategic, Technical and Environmental Implications Arctic Basin Resources." Tufts, 1977.
McClain, Paula Denice. See No./Voir no 7536

8445
Mechikoff, Robert Alan. "The Politicalization of the XXI Olympiad." Ohio State, 1977.

8446
Mercier, Jean Charles. "Cultural and Organizational Determinants of the Crozier Model of Bureaucratic Behavior in English and French Canada." Syracuse, 1982.

8447
Mishler, William Thomas Earle, II. "Political Participation and the Process of Political Socialization Canada: A Computer Simulation." Duke, 1973.

8448
Munro, Gary Wayne. "Generations and Life Cycles in Canadian Politics." Carleton, 1979.

8449
Ogmundson, Richard Lewis. "Social Class and Canadian Politics: A Reinterpretation." Michigan, 1972.

8450
Olsen, Dennis. "The State Elite in Canadian Society." Carleton, 1978. [Includes people in the federal and provincial governments, the courts, cabinet ministers, judges, lawyers, etc./Y compris des gens des gouvernements fédéral et provinciaux, de la cour, des cabinets de ministres, de juges, d'avocats, etc.]

8451
Pyrcz, Gregory Emanuel. "Voluntary Social Cooperation in the Liberal Regime." Alberta, 1979.

8452
Rice, J.J. "The Effect of Particular Variables on the Development of Canadian Public Policy." Exeter, 1977.

Robin, Martin. See No./Voir no 2103

8453
Scicluna, Edward John. "The Measurement of Output and Productivity in the Public Sector: Police Services." Toronto, 1982.

Spector, Norman. See No./Voir no 1142

8454
Tupper, Allan James. "Canadian Concepts of Public Enterprise." Queen's, 1977.

8455
Uhlaner, Carole Jean. "Political Participation in a Segmented Society: The Canadian Case." Harvard, 1978.

Ullman, Stephen Hayes. See No./Voir no 722

Van Loon, Richard J. See No./Voir no 8482

POLITICAL ECONOMY/ÉCONOMIE POLITIQUE

See also Economics: Political Economy/Voir aussi Économie: Politique

POLITICAL SOCIOLOGY/SOCIOLOGIE POLITIQUE

See also Sociology: Political Sociology/Voir aussi Sociologie: Politique

POLITICAL THEORY AND THEORISTS/THÉORIE POLITIQUE ET THÉORICIENS

General Items/Ouvrages généraux

Clarke, Phyllis Esphere. See No./Voir no 1376

Cloutier, Cartier Édouard. See No./Voir no 8439

Ferguson, Barry Glen. See No./Voir no 1380

Hanna, Allan Alexander. See No./Voir no 1787

8456
Hogan, James Bennett. "Mobilization and Political Consequences: An Application of Comparative Politics Theory to the States and Provinces of Mexico, Canada and the United States." Cornell, 1970.

Hornosty, Jennie Mary. See No./Voir no 9771

8457
Janzen, Eileen Rose. "The Development of Democratic Socialist Ideas in English Canada within the Context of an Emerging Canadian Political Consciousness: F.A. Underhill; Frank R. Scott; J. King Gordon." Indiana, 1980.

Johnston, William Atchison. See No./Voir no 10026

8458
Knopff, Rainer. "In Defence of Liberal Democracy: An Inquiry into the Philosophical Premises Underlying Canadian Liberalism's Battle with Theocracy and Nationalism." Toronto, 1981.

8459
Landry, Réjean. "Aspects régionaux de la croissance des systèmes scientifiques et techniques canadiens, ontariens et québécois: 1960-2025: une perspective de simulation basée sur la dynamique de système à niveaux et à buts multiples de Mesarovic." York, 1975.

Mills, Allan George. See No./Voir no 7151

8460
Penner, Norman. "The Socialist Idea in Canadian Political Thought." Toronto, 1975.

8461
Schneck, Rodney Edward. "The Susceptibility of Small Businessmen to the Ideology of Right-Wing Extremism: An Empirical Test of a Hypothesis Through a Case Study of a Small Western Canadian City." Washington, Seattle, 1965. [Alberta]

Shiry, John. See No./Voir no 8740

Siegel, Sanford Benjamin. See No./Voir no 2083

Smith, Jennifer Irene. See No./Voir no 7101

Sutherland, S.L. See No./Voir no 3704

Aberhart, William (1878-1943)

8462
Schultz, Harold John. "William Aberhart and the Social Credit Party: A Political Biography." Duke, 1959.

Bourassa, Henri (1868-1952)

8463
MacMillan, Charles Michael. "Majorities and Minorities: Henri Bourassa and Language Rights in Canada." Minnesota, 1980.

Dafoe, John Wesley (1866-1944)

8464
Cook, George Ramsay. "The Political Ideas of J.W. Dafoe, 1866-1944." Toronto, 1960.

Durham, John Lambton (1792-1840)

8465
Ajzenstat, Janet. "The Political Thought of Lord Durham." Toronto, 1979.

Grant, George (1835-1902)

8466

O'Donovan, Joan Elizabeth. "The Problem of History in the Political Thought of George Grant." University of St. Michael's College, 1980.

Papineau, Louis-Joseph (1786-1871)

8467

Balthazar, Louis Rémus. "The Political Ideas of Louis Joseph Papineau: A Comparative Study." Harvard, 1971.

Parent, Étienne (1801-1874)

8468

Nourry, Louis. "La pensée politique d'Étienne Parent, 1831-1852." Montréal, 1952.

Trudeau, Pierre Elliott (1921-)

Foote, John Allan. See No./Voir no 8520
8469

Lynch, Mary Agnes. "The Rhetorical Style of Pierre Elliott Trudeau during the Canadian Liberal Leadership Campaign, 1968." Michigan, 1975.
Pammett, Jon Howard. See No./Voir no 7398

CONSTITUTION

8470

Cowell, David Arthur. "Devising an Amendment Formula for Canada. The Development of the Fulton-Favreau Formula." Georgetown, 1968.

8471

Gérin-Lajoie, P. "Process of Constitutional Amendment in Canada." Oxford, 1948.
Hudson, Edward Gerard. See No./Voir no 7898

8472

Maxwell, William Anthony. "The Canadian Constitutional Conference (1968-1971): A Study of Conflicting Perceptions of Federalism." Georgetown, 1975.
Murphy, E.E. See No./Voir no 7882
Rambaut, Thomas D. See No./Voir no 7422

8473

Sheldon, Charles Harvey. "Constitutionalism and Subversion: A Comparative Study of Communist Parties and High Courts." Oregon, 1965. [Canada, Australia, West Germany and the United States/-Canada, Australie, Allemagne de l'Ouest et États-Unis]

See also Constitutional History and Constitutional Law/Voir aussi Histoire constitutionnelle et Droit constitutionnel

FEDERAL GOVERNMENT/GOUVERNEMENT FÉDÉRAL

General Items/Ouvrages généraux

8474

Dingwall, John Scott. "Rhetoric, Logic and Politics: Parliamentary Debate in Canada." Yale, 1978.

8475

Fitzgerald, Gerald. "Canada's Final Steps to the Fullness of Sovereign Power." Ottawa, 1943.
Friedman, Kenneth Michael. See No./Voir no 8605
Hanna, Allan Alexander. See No./Voir no 1787
8476

Kubiski, Walter S. "Management System in Transition: Crisis and Succession in a Branch of the Canadian Federal Government." York, 1977.
Massami, Bryan Hazlewood. See No./Voir no 179
McIntyre, Geoffrey R. See No./Voir no 2287
8477

McLellan, David Ross. "Canadian Government Procurement." Ottawa, 1952.
8478

Neuendorf, Gwendoline. "Studies in the Evolution of Dominion Status; (I) The Governor-Generalship of Canada: (II) The Development of Canadian Nationalism." London, 1941.
8479

Potter, Alexander Oberlander. "Canada as a Political Entity." Columbia, 1922.
8480

Smith, David Edward. "Emergency Government in Canada and Australia: 1914-1919: A Comparison." Duke, 1964.
8481

Szablowski, George Jerzy. "Decisional Technology and Political Process in Canada." McGill, 1979.
Thompson, Richard Henry. See No./Voir no 755
8482

Van Loon, Richard Jerome. "Canadian Electoral Participation: The Canadian Public in the 1965 Federal Election." Queen's, 1968.
8483

Vaughan, Ronald Frederick. "Reflections on the Canadian Founding." Chicago, 1968.
Waite, Peter Busby. See No./Voir no 7104
Waterhouse, Michael Francis. See No./Voir no 10475
Yang, C.N. See No./Voir no 8833

Federalism and Federal-Provincial Relations/ Fédéralisme et relations fédérales-provinciales

8484

Bernard, L. "Federalism and Public Administration in Canada: A Study in Constitutional Law and Practice." London, 1964.
8485

Black, Edwin Robert. "Canadian Concepts of Federalism." Duke, 1962.
Brunskill, Ronald. See No./Voir no 1080
8486

Cahill, Elizabeth Mary. "A Study of Political Attitudes in Pontiac County." McGill, 1971.
Careless, A.G.S. See No./Voir no 4782
8487

Cody, Howard Hugh. "Towards a Perspective on the Perpetuation of the Canadian Federal System, the Federal-Ontario Relations in University Education 1945-1970." McMaster, 1977.
Cox, Joseph Christopher. See No./Voir no 1377

8488
Dacks, Gurston. "Integration, Federalism and Authority: The Canadian Case." Princeton, 1975.

De Wilde, James Frederick. See No./Voir no 1743
Dyck, Perry Rand. See No./Voir no 8507
8489
Gillis, D.H. "The Determinants of Canadian Federalism." London, 1948.
8490
Gow, Donald J.S. "Canadian Federal Administrative and Political Institutions: A Role Analysis." Queen's, 1968.

Grey, R.Y. See No./Voir no 1319
8491
Haight, David Ernest. "Sharing of Functions in Canadian Federalism." Chicago, 1963.
8492
Hunt, Wayne Austin. "The Federal-Provincial Conference of First Ministers, 1960-1976." Toronto, 1982.
8493
Levy, Thomas Allen. "Some Aspects of the Role of the Canadian Provinces in External Affairs: A Study in Canadian Federalism." Duke, 1974.

Lindenfield, Rita Graham. See No./Voir no 1629
MacKirdy, Kenneth Alexander. See No./Voir no 6936
Maxwell, William Anthony. See No./Voir no 8472
Mayer, Lawrence Clark. See No./Voir no 8535
McCready, Douglas Jackson. See No./Voir no 1325
8494
Oberlander, Henry Peter. "Community Planning and Housing: An Aspect of Canadian Federalism." Harvard, 1957.
8495
Sabourin, Louis. "Canadian Federalism and International Organizations: A Focus on Quebec." Columbia, 1971.
8496
Savoie, D.J. "Collaboration in Federal-Provincial Relations in Canada: A Case Study of the Canada-New Brunswick General Development Agreement." Oxford, 1979.

Schultz, Richard John. See No./Voir no 2264
8497
Sheeran, Francis Burke. "Federalism in the United States, Canada and Australia, with Particular Reference to Selected Institutional and Functional Aspects." Southern California, 1958.
8498
Simeon, Richard Edmund Barrington. "Federalism and Policy-Making: Federal-Provincial Negotiation in Canada." Yale, 1968.
8499
Stark, Frank. "Federalism as a Symbol of Political Integration: Canada and Cameroon." Northwestern, 1972.

Thatcher, Max B. See No./Voir no 8764
8500
Todres, Elaine Meller. "Canadian Federal-Provincial Relations: The Case of the Ontario Tax Credit System." Pittsburgh, 1977.

Waite, Peter Busby. See No./Voir no 7104
Walsh, David Francis. See No./Voir no 8765
Westmacott, Martin William. See No./Voir no 2267

Federal Policies and Programs/ Politiques et programmes fédérales

8501
Axworthy, N. Lloyd. "The Task Force on Housing and Urban Development - A Study of Democratic Decision-Making in Canada." Princeton, 1972.
8502
Brereton, Thomas Francis. "Planning in the National Capital: A Study of Organizations and Problems in Three Federal Capital Cities." Syracuse, 1973. [Ottawa, Canberra and/et Washington, D.C.]
8503
Dandurand, Louise. "The Nature of the Politicization of Basic Science in Canada: NRC's Role, 1945-1976." Toronto, 1982.
8504
Dirks, Gerald Edward. "Canadian Policies and Programmes Toward Political Refugees." Toronto, 1972.
8505
Doerr, Audrey Diane. "The Role of White Papers in the Policy-Making Process: The Experience of the Government of Canada." Carleton, 1973.
8506
Donnelly, Warren H. "Government Operations for Nuclear Energy in the United States, the United Kingdom and Canada." New York, 1962.
8507
Dyck, Perry Rand. "Poverty and Policy-Making in the 1960's: The Canada Assistance Plan." Queen's, 1973.

Farrell, John Terrence. See No./Voir no 2178
8508
Fuller, John David. "A Long Term Energy Policy Model for Canada." British Columbia, 1980.

Good, David Allen. See No./Voir no 1712
8509
Hamel, Marie. "Le contexte politico-social de l'assistance au Canada." Ottawa, 1963.
8510
Ingraham, Patricia Wallace. "Patterns of Social Welfare Policies in Western Societies." SUNY, Buffalo, 1979.

Johnson, Andrew Frank. See No./Voir no 1646
Knuttila, Kenneth Murray. See No./Voir no 117
8511
Leman, Christopher Kent. "Welfare Reform and the Working Poor: The Setting of Poverty Policy in Canada and the United States." Harvard, 1977.
8512
Lyon, Kenneth Redman Vaughan. "Democracy and the Canadian Political System: An Analysis of the Responsiveness of the Political System to Pressures to Increase Citizen Participation in Policy-Making." British Columbia, 1975.
8513
MacNaughton, Bruce Douglas. "Public Finance for Political Profit: The Politics of Social Security in Canada, 1941-1977." Carleton, 1980.
8514
McInnes, Simon M.C.. "Federal-Provincial Negotiation: Family Allowances 1970-1976." Carleton, 1978.

8515
McLernon, Sylvia G. "Government Provision for the Aged in Great Britain, Canada and New Zeland." Radcliffe, 1949.

8516
Schneider, Saundra Kay. "The Evolution of the Modern Welfare State: A Comparative Analysis of the Development of Social Welfare Programs in the United States, Canada, and Western Europe." SUNY, Binghamton, 1980.

Trevithick, Morris Henry. See No./Voir no 1589

Weaver, Robert Kent. See No./Voir no 2320

8517
Woodrow, Robert Brian. "The Development and Implementation of Federal Pollution Control Policy and Programs in Canada, 1966-1974." Toronto, 1977.

EXECUTIVE/POUVOIR EXÉCUTIF

Burke, Sister Teresa Avila. See No./Voir no 7113

8518
Courtney, John Childs. "Canadian Royal Commissions of Inquiry, 1946 to 1962: An Investigation of an Executive Instrument of Inquiry." Duke, 1964.

8519
Dodd, Larry Cloyd. "Party Coalitions and Cabinet Government: A Game-Theoretic Analysis of Cabinet Formation and Maintenance in Seventeen Western Parliaments, 1918-1972." Minnesota, 1972.

8520
Foote, John Allen. "Prime Minister Pierre Elliott Trudeau, the Prime Minister's Office and the Canadian Political Communication System, 1968-1972." Johns Hopkins, 1979.

Hull, William H.N. See No./Voir no 1131

8521
Johnson, A.T.W. "The Structure of the Canadian Cabinet, 1948-1963." Oxford, 1980.

Langford, John W. See No./Voir no 2258

8522
Matheson, William Alexander. "The Canadian Cabinet and the Prime Minister: A Structural Study." Carleton, 1973.

8523
Mueller, Steven. "The Canadian Prime Ministers, 1867-1948: An Essay on Democratic Leadership." Cornell, 1958.

Ouellette, Yves. See No./Voir no 7899

Pammett, Jon Howard. See No./Voir no 7398

8524
Stewart, John Benjamin. "Parliament and Executive in Wartime Canada, 1939-1945." Columbia, 1953.

8525
Tennant, Paul Richard. "French Canadian Representation in the Canadian Cabinet: An Overview." Chicago, 1971.

8526
White, Walter Leroy. "The Treasury Board in Canada." Michigan, 1965.

LEGISLATURE AND LEGISLATION/ LÉGISLATURE ET LÉGISLATION

General Items/Ouvrages généraux

8527
Abrams, Matthew John. "The Canada-United States Interparliamentary Group: 1959-1969." Columbia, 1971.

Browne, C.P. See No./Voir no 7421

8528
Falcone, David J. "Legislature Change and Output Change: A Time-Series Analysis of the Canadian System." Duke, 1974.

8529
Forsey, E.A. "The Royal Power of Dissolution of Parliament in the British Commonwealth." McGill, 1941.

8530
Heeren, Harry Ewald. "Judicial Control Over Legislation in Australia and Canada." Wisconsin, 1914.

8531
Hockin, Thomas Alexander. "The Loyal Opposition in Canada." Harvard, 1966.

Johnson, James Donald. See No./Voir no 8606

8532
Kornberg, Allan. "Some Differences in Role Perceptions Among Canadian Legislators." Michigan, 1964.

Laing, Lionel H. See No./Voir no 2284

8533
Mahler, Gregory Steven. "The Political Socialization and Recruitment of Legislators in Israel and Canada: A Comparative Analysis." Duke, 1976.

8534
March, Roman Robert. "An Empirical Test of M.C. Ostrogorski's Theory of Political Evolution in British Parliamentary System." Indiana, 1968.

Martin, William Steward Arnold. See No./Voir no 217

8535
Mayer, Lawrence Clark. "Federalism and Party Cohesion in Canada and Australia: Legislative Roll-Call Analysis." Texas, 1969.

Nish, Margaret Elizabeth. See No./Voir no 1091

8536
Osborne, Richard John. "Equal Pay for Equal Work: Study of Legislation in the United States, the United Kingdom, Canada and New Zealand." Cornell, 1976.

8537
Reesor, Bayard William. "Parliamentary Control of Subordinate Legislature in Canada." Alberta, 197

8538
Sohn, Herbert Alvin. "Human Rights Legislation in Canada: A Study of Social Action." Toronto, 1976.

Stewart, John B. See No./Voir no 8524

8539
Strayer, Barry Lee. "Judicial Review of Legislation in Canada." Harvard, 1966.

Swainson, Donald Wayne. See No./Voir no 7209

8540
Wallace, Mary Elisabeth. "The Changing Canadian State: A Study of the Changing Conception of the State as Revealed in Canadian Social Legislation 1867-1947." Columbia, 1950.

Whitaker, W. R. See No./Voir no 10884

Senate/Sénat

8541
Campbell, Edwin Colin. "Appointees to Public Office: The Case of Canadian Senators." Duke, 1974.

8542
Kunz, Frank Andrew Ferenc. "The Senate and Contemporary Politics: A Reappraisal, 1925-1961." McGill, 1963.

8543
MacKay, Robert Alexander. "The Unreformed Senate of Canada." Princeton, 1924.

House of Commons/Chambre des communes

8544
Dawson, W.F. "The Development of Procedure in the House of Commons of Canada." Oxford, 1958.

8545
Geller-Schwartz, Linda Fay. "The Multi-Party System and Parliament: A Study of the Interrelationship in the Canadian House of Commons." Toronto, 1977.

8546
Jones, John Alfred. "An Analysis of Arguments in the Canadian House of Commons on the Issue of Nuclear Weapons for Canada." Illinois, 1970.

8547
Smiley, Donald Victor. "A Comparative Study of Party Discipline in the House of Commons of the United Kingdom and Canada and in the Congress of the United States." Northwestern, 1954.

8548
Thomas, Paul Griffith. "The Role of Committees in the Canadian House of Commons, 1960-1972." Toronto, 1976.

8549
Ward, Norman McQueen. "The Canadian House of Commons: Representation." Toronto, 1949.

JUDICIARY/POUVOIR JUDICIAIRE

Browne, G.P. See No./Voir no 7426
Debicki, Marek. See No./Voir no 10282

8550
Dussault, R. "Judicial Review of Administrative Action in Québec." London, 1962.

8551
Elliott, D.W. "Some Principles of Judicial Review of Administrative Action in Canada." Oxford, 1976.

8552
Fouts, Donald Emil. "The Canadian Supreme Court, 1950-60: A Study of Judicial Policy-Making." Minnesota, 1967.

Hans, Valerie Patricia. See No./Voir no 9686
Heeren, Harry Ewald. See No./Voir no 8530

8553
Johnston, Richard Edward. "The Effect of Judicial Review on Federal-State Relations in Australia, Canada and the United States." Texas, 1967.

8554
Klein, William John. "Judicial Recruitment in Manitoba, Ontario and Quebec, 1905-1970." Toronto, 1975.

Laing, Lionel H. See No./Voir no 2284
Lioy, Michelle Louisette. See No./Voir no 10089

8555
Sharman, George Campbell. "The Courts and the Governmental Process in Canada." Queen's, 1973.
Sheldon, Charles H. See No./Voir no 8473
Strayer, Barry Lee. See No./Voir no 8539
Ubbelohde, Carl W. See No./Voir no 7053

8556
Wright, Claudia Francis Ayres. "Legitimation by the Supreme Courts of Canada and the United States: A Case Study of Japanese Exclusion." Claremont, 1973.

FEDERAL CIVIL SERVICE/FONCTION PUBLIQUE FÉDÉRALE

Caiden, G.E. See No./Voir no 2134

8557
Kuruvilla, P.K. "A Comparative Study of Recruitment and Training of Higher Federal Civil Servants in Canada and India." Carleton, 1972.

Prives, Moshe Zalman. See No./Voir no 2138

8558
Wilson, Vincent Seymour. "Staffing in the Canadian Federal Bureaucracy." Queen's, 1971.

GOVERNMENT AGENCIES, BOARDS, COMMISSIONS, CORPORATIONS/AGENCES GOUVERNEMENTALES, CONSEILS, COMMISSIONS ET CORPORATIONS

Bachand, Raymond C. See No./Voir no 1927
Courtney, John Childs. See No./Voir no 8518

8559
Dalton, William J. "Advisory Boards and Responsible Government in Canada." Ottawa, 1960.

Farrell, John Terrence. See No./Voir no 2178

8560
Jewett, Pauline M. "The Wartime Prices and Trade Board: A Case Study in Canadian Public Administration." Radcliffe, 1950.

8561
McDougall, John Norman. "The National Energy Board and Multi-National Corporations." Alberta, 1975.

Rider, Peter Edward. See No./Voir no 7135
Robinson, John Bridger. See No./Voir no 4790
Trevithick, Morris Henry. See No./Voir no 1589
White, Walter Leroy. See No./Voir no 8526

NATIONALISM AND SEPARATISM/ NATIONALISME ET SÉPARATISME

8562
Amyot, Pierre Raymond. "Factors of Integrative Attitudes in French Canada." Northwestern, 1971.
Arnold, Phil Warren. See No./Voir no 8434
Arthur, Marion E. See No./Voir no 7019
Aunger, Edmund Alexander. See No./Voir no 8701
Behiels, Michael Derek. See No./Voir no 7146
Boldt, Menno. See No./Voir no 447

8563
Burman, Patrick Walsh. "The Dialectical Contexts of English-Canadian Nationalism." Notre Dame, 1979.

8564
Butler, Pamela Jean. "Ottawa and Quebec: The Politics of Confrontation, 1967." McGill, 1980.

8565
Calhoun, John H., Jr. "The National Identity of Newfoundlanders." Pittsburgh, 1970.

8566
Carruthers, Gerald Steven. "Neo-nationalism in Quebec: Adaptation of a Traditional Culture and the Role of the Middle Class." Tufts, 1973.

8567
Cimino, Louis Francisco. "Ethnic Nationalism Among the Acadians of New Brunswick: An Analysis of Ethnic Political Development." Duke, 1977.

8568
Coleman, William Donald. "A Structural Approach to the Study of Political Change with a Case Study of the Movement Towards Independence in Quebec Since 1949." Chicago, 1979.

Cuneo, Carl John. See No./Voir no 7546

8569
Fenwick, Rudy. "Communal Politics in Quebec: Ethnic Segmentation and Support for Political Independence Among French Québecois." Duke, 1978.

8570
Flowers, Mary Kathryn. "Authority Relations and Legitimacy: A Conflict Analysis of Quebec Nationalism." New York, 1980.

8571
Forbes, Hugh Donald. "Nationalism, Ethnocentrism, and Personality: A Canadian Study." Yale, 1976.

Fortin, Gérald-Adelard. See No./Voir no 1085
Gaffield, Charles Mitchell. See No./Voir no 2490
Garff, Dennis Royal. See No./Voir no 7254
Gibbins, Roger. See No./Voir no 7495

8572
Goell, Yosef Israel. "Bi-nationalism and Bilingualism in Three Modernized States: A Comparative Study of Canada, Belgium, and White South Africa." Columbia, 1971.

Gordon, Richard Irving. See No./Voir no 7255
Gordon, Robert Arthur. See No./Voir no 3542

8573
Griffin, Elizabeth Anne. "Six Functions of Separatism in Quebec." New York, 1975.

8574
Hagy, James William. "The Quebec Separatists: An American Viewpoint." Georgia, 1969.

8575
Halary, Charles. "Étude de la question nationale dans les formations sociales industrialisées: le cas du mouvement ouvrier québecois." Montréal, 1977.

Handler, Richard. See No./Voir no 439
Hill, David Fred. See No./Voir no 7528
Horn, Michael Steven Daniel. See No./Voir no 7148

8576
Irvine, William Peter. "Cultural Conflict in Canada: The Erosion of Consociational Politics." Yale, 1971.

Irwin, Leonard B. See No./Voir no 2308
Jain, Genevieve Laloux. See No./Voir no 2497
Janzen, Eileen Rose. See No./Voir no 8457
Kistler, Ruth Barthold. See No./Voir no 2412
Knopff, Rainer. See No./Voir no 8458
Laczko, Leslie Stephen. See No./Voir no 10179

8577
Lapid, Yosef. "Ethnic Puzzles in World Politics: Tw North American Examples." Columbia, 1981.

Latham, A.B. See No./Voir no 1177

8578
Lee, Danielle Marie Juteau. "The Impact of Modern zation and Environmental Impingements Up Nationalism and Separatism: The Quebec Case Toronto, 1974.

Lefebvre, André. See No./Voir no 1089
Lefebvre, Jean-Marie. See No./Voir no 1986
Lubin, Martin. See No./Voir no 7157
MacMillan, Charles Michael. See No./Voir no 8463
Marchant, Cosmo Kenningham. See No./Voir no 739

8579
McKinsey, Lauren Stuart. "Political Integration ar Disintegration: The Canadian Dilemma." Cas Western Reserve, 1973.

8580
McRoberts, Kenneth Harvey. "Mass Acquisition of Nationalist Ideology: Quebec Prior to the 'Quie Revolution'." Chicago, 1976.

Monet, Jacques. See No./Voir no 7095

8581
Montcalm, Mary Beth. "Class in Ethnic Nationalisr Quebec Nationalism in Comparative Perspective Carleton, 1983.

Neuendorff, Gwendoline. See No./Voir no 8478

8582
Nevitte, Neil Hugh. "Religion and the 'New Nationa ism': The Case of Quebec." Duke, 1978.

8583
Novek, Joel Leonard. "Cooperation and Conflict Dual Societies: A Comparison of French-Canadi and Afrikaner Nationalism." Alberta, 1974.

8584
Oberle, James Peter. "Consociational Democracy ar the Canadian Political System." Maryland, 197 [Socio-economic impact of the division betwee French and English Canadians/Impact soci économique de la division des Canadiens anglais français]

O'Connell, M.P. See No./Voir no 7338

8585
Oliver, Michael K. "The Social and Political Ideas French-Canadian Nationalists, 1920-1945." McGil 1957.

Olzak, Susan Maria Grumick. See No./Voir no 770
Ostergaard, Karen. See No./Voir no 7134
Paul, Alix-Herald. See No./Voir no 8873

8586
Peterson, Erick James. "Nationalism in Canada ar Mexico: An Empirical Study." Northwester 1976.

8587
Pool, Jonathan Robert. "Language and Political Int gration: Canada as a Text of Some Hypotheses Chicago, 1972.

8588
Quenneville, Jean-Guy R. "The Emergence of Fren Canada in Domestic and External Politics." Not Dame, 1974.

Quinn, Herbert Furlong. See No./Voir no 8670

8589
Redlick, Amy Sands. "The Impact of Transnational Interactions on Terrorism: A Case Study of the Quebec Terrorist Movement." Tufts, 1977.

8590
Reilly, Wayne Gerard. "Political Attitudes Among French and English Speaking Law Students in Quebec: An Investigation of Canadian Political Integration." Pittsburgh, 1969.

Resnick, Philip. See No./Voir no 1393

8591
Richert, Jean-Pierre. "Children and Politics in Quebec: A Comparative Study of Political Cultures." Brown, 1972.

8592
Ripple, Joe Edward. "Prognosis for a Bicultural Federal State, Canada: 'A Case Study'." Colorado, 1971.

8593
Robertson, Nancy Susan. "L'action française: l'appel à la race." Laval, 1971.

Rutherford, Paul Frederic William. See No./Voir no 7136

Sancton, A.B. See No./Voir no 8762

Schwartz, Mildred Anne. See No./Voir no 1072

See, Katherine O'Sullivan. See No./Voir no 790

8594
Singer, Howard Lewis. "Institutionalization of Protest: The Quebec Separatist Movement." New York, 1976.

8595
Spina, Joseph M. "Adolescent Attachment to Canada and Commitment to a National Community." Chicago, 1975.

Stahl, William Austin. See No./Voir no 9990

Thatcher, Max B. See No./Voir no 8764

8596
Torrance, Judy Margaret Curtis. "Cultural Factors and the Response of Governments to Violence: The Case of Canada." York, 1975.

8597
Tremblay, J.J. "Patriotisme et nationalisme." Ottawa, 1938.

Trenton, Thomas Norman. See No./Voir no 3707

Uhlaner, Carole Jean. See No./Voir no 8455

Vipond, Mary Jean. See No./Voir no 7152

CIVIL LIBERTIES/LIBERTÉS CIVILES

Grunis, Asher Dan. See No./Voir no 7897

Horn, Michael S.D. See No./Voir no 7148

8598
Janzen, William. "The Limits of Liberty in Canada: The Experience of the Mennonites, the Hutterites, and the Doukhobors." Carleton, 1981.

8599
Kernaghan, William David Kenneth. "Freedom of Religion in the Province of Quebec with Particular Reference to the Jews, Jehovah's Witnesses and Church-State Relations 1930-1960." Duke, 1966.

8600
Krauter, Joseph Francis. "Civil Liberties and the Canadian Minorities." Illinois, 1968.

8601
Phillips, Lester Henry. "The Impact of the Defense of Canada Regulations Upon Civil Liberties." Michigan, 1945.

Sheldon, Charles Harvey. See No./Voir no 8473

8602
Straus, Melvin Potter. "The Control of Subversive Activities in Canada." Illinois, 1959.

LOBBYISTS AND PUBLIC SPECIAL INTEREST AND PRESSURE GROUPS/REPRÉSENTANTS DE GROUPES D'INTÉRÊTS PUBLICS SPÉCIAUX ET DE GROUPES DE PRESSION

8603
Beattie, Margaret Eileen. "Pressure Group Politics: The Case of the Student Christian Movement of Canada." Alberta, 1972.

8604
Bennett, Scott. "Some Relationships Between Changes in the Number of Interest Group Organizations and Changes in Other Political System Organizations." York, 1982.

Clark, Samuel Delbert. See No./Voir no 1200

8605
Friedman, Kenneth Michael. "Cigarette Smoking and Public Policy: A Comparative Study of Government and Interest Group Response." Michigan State, 1973. [United States, Great Britain and Canada/États-Unis, Grande-Bretagne et Canada]

Gutzke, David William. See No./Voir no 1273

Himes, Mel. See No./Voir no 8895

8606
Johnson, James Donald. "Interest Groups and the Legislative Process in Canada: A Case Study in Anti-Combines Legislation." Michigan, 1973.

Kwavnick, David. See No./Voir no 8672

Lawrie, Neil John. See No./Voir no 1385

Meen, Sharon Patricia. See No./Voir no 7130

Ross, Arthur Larry. See No./Voir no 141

8607
Sinclair, John Earl. "Legislations and Lobbyists in Canada and the United States." SUNY, Buffalo, 1973.

Strong-Boag, Veronica Jane. See No./Voir no 7140

Wier, Richard Anthony. See No./Voir no 6818

Wilkinson, Paul Frank. See No./Voir no 4718

Williams, W. Blair. See No./Voir no 5

VOTING/VOTE

Bacchi, Carol Lee. See No./Voir no 7109

8608
Black, Jerome Harold. "Second Choice Voting in Canadian Federal Elections: A Test of the Multi-candidate Calculus of Voting." Rochester, 1976.

8609
Blake, Donald Edward. "Regionalism in Canadian Voting Behaviour, 1908-1968." Yale, 1972.

8610
Cleverdon, Catherine L. "The Woman Suffrage Movement in Canada." Columbia, 1950.

8611
Denham, William Alfred, III. "Systematic Patterns, Contextual Variables and Radical Voting: The U.S. Midwest and the Province of Ontario, 1968 and 1972." Northern Illinois, 1980. [Voting turnout and analysis/Décompte et analyse du scrutin]

8612
Gagné, Wallace Donald George. "Class Voting in Canada." Rochester, 1970.

Garner, John. See No./Voir no 7079

Grayson, John Paul. See No./Voir no 8768

Pammett, Jon Howard. See No./Voir no 7398

8613
Phillips, Harry John Charles. "Challenge to the Voting System in Canada, 1874-1974." Western Ontario, 1976.

Van Loon, Richard J. See No./Voir no 8482

8614
Woolstencroft, Robert Peter. "National, Regional, Provincial and Constituency Effects in Canadian Voting Behaviour, 1953-1965." Alberta, 1977.

8615
Zipp, John Francis. "Social Class and Canadian Federal Electoral Behavior: A Reconsideration and Elaboration." Duke, 1978.

POLITICAL PARTIES: NATIONAL AND PROVINCIAL/PARTIS POLITIQUES FÉDÉRAUX ET PROVINCIAUX

General Items/Ouvrages généraux

Arnold, Phil Warren. See No./Voir no 8434

8616
Chu, George Pei-Chang. "A Study of the Causes and Conditions of the Two- and Multi-Party Systems in Twenty Western Democracies." Southern Illinois, 1974.

8617
Costain, Wilfred Douglas. "Party Competition and the Development of the Canadian Party System: 1908-1972." Johns Hopkins, 1979.

8618
Drummond, Robert Johnston. "Party Choice in a Canadian Province: The Case of Ontario." Northwestern, 1975.

Gagné, Wallace Donald George. See No./Voir no 8612

Geller-Schwartz, Linda Fay. See No./Voir no 8545

8619
Harrill, Ernest Eugene. "The Structure of Organization and Power in Canadian Political Parties: A Study in Party Financing." North Carolina, 1958.

Horn, Michael Steven Daniel. See No./Voir no 7148

Horowitz, Gad. See No./Voir no 2112

8620
Hougham, George Millard. "Minor Parties in Canadian National Politics, 1867-1940." Pennsylvania, 1954.

8621
Jenson, Jane. "Party Identification in Canada: A Rationally Limited Allegiance." Rochester, 1974.

8622
Johnston, Richard Gregory Chalmers. "Party Alignment and Realignment in Canada, 1911-1965." Stanford, 1976.

8623
LeDuc, Lawrence William, Jr. "The Leadership Selection Process in Canadian Political Parties: A Case Study." Michigan, 1970.

8624
Leslie, Peter Malcolm. "The Role of Constituency Party Organizations in Representing the Interests of Ethnic Minorities and Other Groups." Queen's, 1968.

8625
Lovink, Johannes Anton Alexander. "The Politics of Quebec: Provincial Political Parties, 1897-1936." Duke, 1967.

8626
Schuetz, Charles. "The Party System - The Fundamental Institution of Canadian Democracy." Ottawa, 1961.

8627
Serfaty, Meir. "Structure and Organization of Political Parties in Alberta, 1935-1971." Carleton, 1976.

8628
Skogstad, Grace Darlene. "Farmers' Political Belief Systems." British Columbia, 1977.

8629
Smith, Patrick Joseph. "The Sociology of Urban Party Organizations and Political Behaviour: Contemporary Party Membership with Special Reference to England and Canada." London, 1977.

Sutherland, S.L. See No./Voir no 3704

Terry, John Charles. See No./Voir no 8683

8630
Torrence, Lois Evelyn. "The National Party System in Canada, 1945-1960." American, 1961.

8631
Vox, Vicki Elaine. "The Development of Quantitative Models to Account for the Longitudinal Variation in the Electoral Support of American and Canadian Political Parties." Washington, St. Louis, 1977.

8632
Watson, George Lee. "The Origins of a Political Party Identification Among Party Activists in Canada and the United States: A Four City Survey." Duke, 1972.

8633
Winn, Conrad Leslie James. "Spatial Models of Party Systems: An Examination of the Canadian Case." Pennsylvania, 1972.

Cooperative Commonwealth Federation/ Fédération coopérative du Commonwealth

Conway, John Frederick. See No./Voir no 10024

8634
Engelmann, Frederick Charles. "The Cooperative Commonwealth Federation of Canada: A Study of Membership Participation in Party Policy-Making." Yale, 1954.

Horn, Michael Steven Daniel. See No./Voir no 7148

Johnson, Albert Welsey. See No./Voir no 8779

8635
Lipset, Seymour M. "Agrarian Socialism: The Cooperative Commonwealth Federation in Saskatchewan." Columbia, 1953.

8636
Olssen, Andrée Lévesque. "The Canadian Left in Quebec During the Great Depression: The Communist Party of Canada and the Cooperative Commonwealth Federation in Quebec, 1929-39." Duke, 1973.

8637
Sanford, Thomas Michael. "The Politics of Protest: The Cooperative Commonwealth Federation and Social Credit League in British Columbia." California, Berkeley, 1961.

8638
Silverstein, Sanford. "The Rise, Ascendancy and Decline of the Cooperative Commonwealth Federation of Saskatchewan, Canada." Washington, St. Louis, 1968.

8639
Sinclair, Peter Rayment. "Populism in Alberta and Saskatchewan: A Comparative Analysis of Social Credit and the Cooperative Commonwealth Federation." Edinburgh, 1972.

8640
Waggoner, Marion Arthur. "The Cooperative Commonwealth Federation in Saskatchewan: A Social Movement." Missouri, 1946.

8641
Wiseman, Nelson. "A Political History of the Manitoba CCF-NDP." Toronto, 1975.

8642
Young, Walter Douglas. "The National Cooperative Commonwealth Federation: Political Party and Political Movement." Toronto, 1965.

8643
Zakuta, Leo. "A Protest Movement Becalmed: A Study of Change in the C.C.F." Chicago, 1962.

Communist Party of Canada/ Parti communiste du Canada

Abella, Irving Martin. See No./Voir no 2109
Horn, Michael S.D. See No./Voir no 7148
Olssen, Andrée Levesque. See No./Voir no 8636
Robin, Martin. See No./Voir no 2103

8644
Rodney, W. "A History of the Communist Party of Canada, 1919-1929." London, 1961.
Sheldon, Charles Harvey. See No./Voir no 8473
Straus, Melvin Potter. See No./Voir no 8602

Conservative Party/Parti conservateur

8645
Alper, Donald Keith. "From Rule to Ruin: The Conservative Party of British Columbia, 1928-1954." British Columbia, 1976.
Bélanger, Réal. See No./Voir no 7380
Conrad, Margaret Rose Slavenwhite. See No./Voir no 7371

8646
Granatstein, Jack Lawrence. "The Conservative Party of Canada, 1939-1945." Duke, 1966.
Grayson, John Paul. See No./Voir no 8768

8647
Lederle, John William. "The National Organization of the Liberal and Conservative Parties in Canada." Michigan, 1942.

8648
Perlin, George Crosbie. "The Problem of Intra-Party Conflict in the Leadership Succession of John Diefenbaker in the Progressive Conservative Party of Canada." London, 1977.

8649
Surplis, David William. "A Study of Leadership Problems in the Progressive Conservative Party, 1963-1967." Toronto, 1976.

8650
Williams, John R. "The Conservative Party of Canada: 1920-1949." Duke, 1951.

Liberal Party/Parti libéral

8651
Beaven, Brian Philip Norman. "A Last Hurrah: Studies in Liberal Party Development and Ideology in Ontario, 1878-1893." Toronto, 1982.

8652
Caya, Marcel. "La formation du parti libéral au Québec, 1867-1887." York, 1981.
Erickson, Lynn Ellyn. See No./Voir no 7118

8653
Heppe, Paul Harry. "The Liberal Party of Canada." Wisconsin, 1957.
Lederle, John W. See No./Voir no 8647
Lynch, Mary Agnes. See No./Voir no 8469
Pammett, Jon Howard. See No./Voir no 7398

8654
Rayside, David Martin. "Linguistic Divisions in the Social Christian Party of Belgium and the Liberal Parties of Canada and Quebec." Michigan, 1976.

8655
Regenstreif, Samuel Peter. "The Liberal Party of Canada: A Political Analysis." Cornell, 1963.

8656
Whitaker, Reginald Alan. "The Government Party: Organizing and Financing the Liberal Party of Canada, 1930-1958." Toronto, 1976.

New Democratic Party/ Nouveau parti démocratique

8657
Barnett, John Ross. "Politics, Territory and Social Class: The New Democratic Party and Changing Cleavages in Canadian Politics." Iowa, 1975.

8658
Lyons, William Elmer. "The New Democratic Party in the Canadian Political System." Pennsylvania State, 1965.
McAllister, James Alexander. See No./Voir no 8700
Morley, John T. See No./Voir no 8731

8659
Wilson, Bruce Hamilton. "The New Democratic Party of Canada: An Example of Third Party Movement." New School for Social Research, 1976.
Wiseman, Nelson. See No./Voir no 8641

Parti québécois

8660
Beaud, Jean-Pierre. "Structures et élites: analyse diachronique du parti québécois." Laval, 1980.

Progressive Party/Parti progressiste

Conway, John Frederick. See No./Voir no 10024

Social Credit Party/Crédit social

8661
Anderson, Owen Arthur James. "The Alberta Social Credit Party: An Empirical Analysis of Membership, Characteristics, Participation, and Opinions." Alberta, 1972.
Conway, John Frederick. See No./Voir no 10024
8662
Finley, John Lawrence. "The Origins of the Social Credit Movement." Manitoba, 1968.
8663
Hiller, Harry Herbert. "A Critical Analysis of the Role of Religion in a Canadian Populist Movement: The Emergence and Dominance of the Social Credit Party in Alberta." McMaster, 1972.
8664
Pinard, Maurice J.L.M.. "The Rise of a Third Party: The Social Credit Party in Quebec in the 1962 Federal Election." Johns Hopkins, 1967.
Sanford, Thomas Michael. See No./Voir no 8637
Schultz, Harold John. See No./Voir no 8462
Sinclair, Peter Rayment. See No./Voir no 8639
8665
Stein, Michael Bernard. "Social Credit in Quebec: Political Attitudes and Party Dynamics." Princeton, 1967.

Socialist Party/Parti socialiste

8666
Johnson, Ross Alfred. "No Compromise — No Political Trading: The Marxian Socialist Tradition in British Columbia." British Columbia, 1975.
8667
Schwantes, Carlos Arnaldo. "Left-Wing Unionism in the Pacific Northwest: A Comparative History of Organized Labor and Socialist Politics in Washington and British Columbia, 1885-1917." Michigan, 1976.
8668
Smith, Matthew Eliot. "The Development of a Socialistic Opposition: The Case of British Columbia." North Carolina, 1978.

Union Nationale Party/Union nationale

8669
Dirks, Patricia Grace. "The Origins of the Union Nationale." Toronto, 1974.
8670
Quinn, Herbert Furlong. "The Union Nationale Party: A Study of Nationalism and Industrialism in Quebec." Columbia, 1959.

LABOR AND POLITICS/TRAVAIL ET POLITIQUE

Abella, Irving Martin. See No./Voir no 2109
Barnes, Samuel Henry. See No./Voir no 2047

8671
Coates, Daniel. "Organized Labor and Politics in Canada: The Development of a National Labor Code." Cornell, 1973.
Drennon, Herbert N. See No./Voir no 1746
Freeman, William Bradford. See No./Voir no 2143
Harris, Simon Richard. See No./Voir no 2240
Horowitz, Gad. See No./Voir no 2112
8672
Kwavnick, David. "Organized Labour and Government: The Canadian Labour Congress as a Political Interest Group During the Diefenbaker and Pearson Administrations." Carleton, 1972.
McBride, Stephen Kenneth. See No./Voir no 2061
Miller, Fern Audrey Rae. See No./Voir no 2062
Robin, Martin. See No./Voir no 2103
Schultz, Richard John. See No./Voir no 2264
Schwantes, Carlos Arnaldo. See No./Voir no 8667
Stewart, Bryce Morrison. See No./Voir no 2174
Stewart, Ian Hampton. See No./Voir no 7934
Underhill, Harold F. See No./Voir no 2175

PROVINCIAL AND MUNICIPAL POLITICS AND GOVERNMENT/POLITIQUES ET GOUVERNEMENTS PROVINCIAUX ET MUNICIPAUX

General Items/Ouvrages généraux

Baka, Richard Stevens Paul. See No./Voir no 10337
Boswell, David M. See No./Voir no 2652
8673
Conley, M.W. "Political Recruitment: The Selection of Candidates for Provincial Office in Canada." Exeter, 1980.
Cornell, Paul Grant. See No./Voir no 7075
Cox, Joseph Christopher. See No./Voir no 1377
8674
Cunningham, Walter Melvin. "Coalescence of Municipal Police and Fire Services: A Comparison of Experience in the United States, Canada and Great Britain." Claremont, 1968.
8675
Holm, Ernest Harold Sandstedt. "The Council of Maritime Premiers: The Process of Political Integration in the Canadian Maritimes." Tufts, 1977.
8676
Klass, Gary Martin. "The Dynamics of Politics and Policy in American States and Canadian Provinces." SUNY, Binghamton, 1980.
Levy, Thomas Allen. See No./Voir no 8493
8677
Loebel, Peter Bernard. "The Municipal Planning Process, Implications for Social Welfare." Toronto, 1976.
MacKirdy, Kenneth Alexander. See No./Voir no 6936
8678
MacNiven, Hugh Gordon. "The Legislative Assemblies of the Canadian Provinces." Minnesota, 1960.
8679
McCready, J. "Political Ideology and Social Policy Expenditure and Revenue in Three Canadian Provinces, 1947-60." Toronto, 1983.
8680
McLeod, Stuart Cameron. "The Government of Canadian Cities." Harvard, 1914.

8681
Poel, Dale Heeres. "The Correlates of Policy in the Canadian Provinces." Iowa, 1972.

Riley, Richard Brinton. See No./Voir no 1795

8682
Saywell, John Tupper. "The Office of the Lieutenant-Governor: A Study in Canadian Government and Politics." Harvard, 1956.

Smith, Patrick Joseph. See No./Voir no 8629

8683
Terry, John Charles Joseph. "Parties and Provinces: The Territorial Cleavage in Canadian Politics." York, 1977.

8684
Wallace, Elizabeth. "The Changing Canadian States: A Study of the Changing Convention of the State as Revealed in Canadian Social Legislation: 1867-1948." Columbia, 1950.

Alberta

8685
Bella, Leslie F. "The Politics of the Right Wing 'Welfare State'." Alberta, 1981.

Conway, John Frederick. See No./Voir no 10024

Dale, Edmund Herbert. See No./Voir no 4878

8686
Elton, David Kitchener Leslie. "Electoral Perception of Federalism: A Descriptive Analysis of the Alberta Electorate." Alberta, 1973.

Grondin, Conde Rosaire. See No./Voir no 8440

8687
Hulmes, Frederick George. "The Senior Executive and the Fifteenth Alberta Legislature: A Study in the Social and Political Background of Membership." Alberta, 1971.

Malliah, Holavanahally Lingappa. See No./Voir no 7235

8688
Oliver, Thelma Isabel. "Aspects of Alienation in Alberta." York, 1974.

8689
Schmidt, Erick. "The Morphology of Bureaucratic Knowledge." Alberta, 1975. [Bureaucracy in the Alberta government/Bureaucratie au sein du gouvernement de l'Alberta]

Serfaty, Meir. See No./Voir no 8627

British Columbia/Colombie-Britannique

8690
Brown, Lorne Alvin. "The Bennett Government: The Single Unemployed and Political Stability." Queen's, 1980.

Gibbins, Roger. See No./Voir no 7495

8691
Goddard, Arthur Morris. "Legislative Behavior in the British Columbia Legislative Assembly." Washington, Seattle, 1973.

8692
Hardenbergh, William Spencer. "British Government in British Columbia." Illinois, 1954.

8693
McConnell, William Howard. "The Judicial Review of Prime Minister Bennett's 'New Deal' Legislative Programme." Toronto, 1968.

Rumley, Dennis. See No./Voir no 4891

Stewart, Ian Hampton. See No./Voir no 7934

Underhill, Harold F. See No./Voir no 2175

8694
Wilson, Robert Jeremy. "The Impact of Modernization on British Columbia Electoral Patterns: Communications Development and the Uniformity of Swing, 1903-1975." British Columbia, 1978.

Manitoba

8695
Baden, John A. "The Management of Social Stability: A Political Ethnography of the Hutterites of North America." Indiana, 1967.

8696
Donnelly, Murray Samuel. "The Government of Manitoba." Toronto, 1957.

8697
Fisk, Larry John. "Controversy on the Prairies: Issues in the General Provincial Elections of Manitoba 1870-1969." Alberta, 1975.

8698
Kent, Robert Howard. "The Process of Urban Government Decision-Making: The Winnipeg Experiment." British Columbia, 1975.

8699
Lightbody, James William. "Adapting Urban Institutions: The Reform of Winnipeg, 1971." Queen's, 1977.

8700
McAllister, James Alexander. "Social Democracy: The New Democratic Party Government of Manitoba, 1969-1977." Carleton, 1979.

Stewart, Ian Hampton. See No./Voir no 7934

Maritime Provinces/Provinces maritimes

General Item/Ouvrage général

Holm, Ernest Harold Sandstedt. See No./Voir no 8675

New Brunswick/Nouveau-Brunswick

8701
Aunger, Edmund Alexander. "Social Fragmentation and Political Stability: A Comparative Study of New Brunswick and Northern Ireland." California, Irvine, 1978.

Brown, Matthew Paul. See No./Voir no 1373

Hardy, Helen Margaret. See No./Voir no 8724

8702
Llambias, Henry J. "The New Brunswick Ombudsman." Carleton, 1979.

8703
Ruff, Norman John. "Administrative Reform and Development: A Study of Administrative Adaptation to Provincial Development Goals and the Reorganization of Provincial and Local Government in New Brunswick, 1963-1967." McGill, 1973.

8704
Thorburn, Hugh Garnet. "The Politics of New Brunswick: A Study of the Political Influence of the Acadians." Columbia, 1958.

Newfoundland and Labrador/Terre-Neuve et Labrador

8705
Boswell, Peter Gordon. "Representational Role Style Perceptions of Municipal Councillors in Newfoundland and Labrador." Carleton, 1983.

Calhoun, John H., Jr. See No./Voir no 8565

Clark, Richard L. See No./Voir no 7165

Ibele, Oscar H., Jr. See No./Voir no 4887

8706
Mayo, H.B. "Newfoundland, the Tenth Province of Canada: The Case for Union Examined." Oxford, 1948.

8707
McCorquodale, Susan. "Public Administration in Newfoundland During the Period of the Commission of Government: A Question of Political Development." Queen's, 1974.

McLintock, A.H. See No./Voir no 7168

8708
Noel, S.J.R. "Government and Politics in Newfoundland 1904-1934: Prelude to the Surrender of Dominion Status." Oxford, 1965.

Nova Scotia/Nouvelle-Écosse

Atkinson, Michael Meredith. See No./Voir no 8717

8709
Beck, James Murray. "The Government of Nova Scotia." Toronto, 1954.

Brown, Matthew Paul. See No./Voir no 1373

8710
Livingston, Walter Ross. "The Evolution of Responsible Government in Nova Scotia (or the First Responsible Party Government in British North America)." Wisconsin, 1927.

Martell, J.S. See No./Voir no 7175

8711
Rowat, Donald C. "The Reorganization of Provincial-Municipal Relations in Nova Scotia." Columbia, 1951.

8712
Warren, Edward Gillingham, III. "Executive Leadership in Rhode Island and Nova Scotia: A Comparative Case Study." Brown, 1978.

Prince Edward Island/Île-du-Prince-Édouard

8713
MacKinnon, Francis Perley Taylor. "The Government of Prince Edward Island, a Study of Colonial and Provincial Government." Toronto, 1950.

Northwest Territories and the Yukon/ Territoires du Nord-Ouest et Yukon

8714
Bériault, Yvon. "Les problèmes politiques du nord canadien." Ottawa, 1941.

Lesage, Germain. See No./Voir no 4816

8715
Judy, Robert Dale. "Territorial Government: Th Canadian Northwest Territories and the Yukon California, Berkeley, 1960.

Ontario

8716
Armstrong, Christopher. "The Politics of Federalism Ontario's Relations with the Federal Governmen 1896-1941." Toronto, 1972.

8717
Atkinson, Michael Meredith. "Backbench Participatio in Legislative Policymaking: A Test of the Amb tion Hypothesis." Carleton, 1978.

Beaven, Brian Philip Norman. See No./Voir no 8651

Brice, Max O. See No./Voir no 1371

8718
Burt-Pintar, Sandra Dawn. "The Political Participa tion of Women in Ontario." York, 1981.

Davidson, Gary. See No./Voir no 61

8719
Drabek, Stanley. "The Ontario Department of Lanc and Forests, 1941-1967: A Study of Headquarters Field Relationships." Toronto, 1972.

Drummond, Robert Johnston. See No./Voir no 8618

8720
Dwivedi, Onkar Prasad. "Administration of the Publi Personnel Functions in the Province of Ontario. Queen's, 1968.

8721
Foster, Richard Henry, Jr. "Canadian Intergovern mental Relations and the Reform of Local Govern ment: Regional Local Governments in Ontario. Oklahoma, 1974.

8722
Gardner, Donald Hambidge. "The Field Services o Ontario Government Departments: A Study i Dispersal and Administrative Decentralization. Toronto, 1973.

8723
Hannigan, John Andrew. "Municipal Reorganizatio and Crisis Management Agencies: The Impact o Regional Government in Ontario on Emergency an Protective Services." Ohio State, 1976.

8724
Hardy, Helen Margaret. "The Effect of Federa Grants on Provincial Expenditure and Revenu Decisions: Ontario and New Brunswick Compared. McMaster, 1973.

8725
Higgins, Donald J.H. "Community and Local Govern ment: Boundary Determination." Carleton, 1973.

8726
Kay, Barry James. "Decision-Making Patterns in a Urban Legislature: An Issue, Time and Systen Level Study of Toronto City Council. Rochester, 1977.

8727
Kosny, Mitchell Ernest. "A Tale of Two Cities: A Evaluation of Local Government Organizatio Theory and Its Implications for Municipal Re organization in Thunder Bay, Ontario." Waterloo 1978.

8728
Martin, Terry Homer. "A Framework for Evaluating Public Policy Outcome in Ontario, Canada, for the Environmental Assessment Act, 1975." SUNY, Buffalo, 1979.

8729
McDougall, Allen Kerr. "Policing in Ontario: The Occupational Dimension to Provincial-Municipal Relations." Toronto, 1971.

8730
McGilly, Francis James. "The Functions of Conflict in the Council of the Municipality of Metropolitan Toronto, 1953-1966." Pittsburgh, 1972.

8731
Morley, John T. "NDP Success and Working Class Culture in Ontario." Queen's, 1978.

Nelles, Henry Vivian. See No./Voir no 7202

Patrick, Glenda M. See No./Voir no 3558

Patterson, Graeme Hazlewood. See No./Voir no 7204

8732
Plehwe, Rudolf. "Administrative Responsibility and Autonomous Commissions: A Study of Selected Regulatory Commissions in Ontario and Quebec." Duke, 1969.

8733
Price, Trevor. "City-Manager Government in Windsor: A Study of Its Evolution and Mode of Operation." Queen's, 1975.

8734
Pross, August Paul. "The Development of a Forest Policy: A Study of the Ontario Department of Lands and Forests." Toronto, 1967.

8735
Proudfoot, Stuart Bradley. "High-Rise and Neighbourhood Change: The Politics of Development in Toronto." Michigan, 1977.

8736
Rich, Harvey. "Higher Civil Servants in Ontario: A Case Study of an Administrative Elite." California, Berkeley, 1973.

8737
Schindeler, Frederick Fernand. "Legislative-Executive Relations in Ontario." Toronto, 1965.

8738
Sesay, Chernoh M. "The Role of Private Land Developers in the Decision-Making Process in the Regional Municipality of Ottawa-Carleton: A Test of Lorimer's Hypothesis - That Private Land Developers Run City Hall." Carleton, 1978.

8739
Sharratt, Kenneth Orrin. "Major Policy-Making Variables for High-Density Residential Development in Toronto, 1961-1970." Western Ontario, 1974.

8740
Shiry, John David. "Political Patterns in Selected Policy Areas in Ontario: A Test of Lowi's Arenas of Power Scheme." Queen's, 1977.

8741
Slack, Naomi Enid. "The Budgetary Response of Municipal Governments to Provincial Transfers: The Case of Ontario." Toronto, 1977.

Swainson, Donald Wayne. See No./Voir no 7209

8742
Walker, David Charles. "Public Policy and Community: The Impact of Regional Government on Pelham, Ontario." McMaster, 1976.

Whebell, C.F.J. See No./Voir no 4895

8743
White, Graham George. "Social Change and Political Stability in Ontario: Electoral Forces 1867-1977." McMaster, 1979.

8744
White, Randall Craig. "Citizen Politics in Riverdale." Toronto, 1977.

8745
Williams, Robert James. "Political Recruitment in Ontario: A Study of the Twenty-Eighth Parliament." Toronto, 1973.

Quebec/Québec

8746
Archibald, Clinton. "Corporatisme et néo-corporatisme au Québec, une constante négligée: 1930 à nos jours (du passage d'une idéologie corporatiste "sociale" à un idéologie corporatiste "politique"). Carleton, 1982.

8747
Ba, Tran Quang. "Le comportement électoral dans une circonscription du Québec." Montréal, 1975.

8748
Bélanger, André-Jacques. "L'apolitisme des idéologies québécoises: le grand tournant de 1934-1936." Laval, 1973.

8749
Bernard, André. "Les inégalités structurelles de représentation. La carte électorale du Québec, 1867-1967." Montréal, 1969.

8750
Blais, André-Marc. "Politique agricole et résultats électoraux en milieu agricole au Québec." York, 1978.

Butler, Pamela Jean. See No./Voir no 8564

Cahill, Elizabeth Mary. See No./Voir no 8486

Cannon, Gordon E. See No./Voir no 8438

Carruthers, Gerald Steven. See No./Voir no 8566

Caya, Marcel. See No./Voir no 8652

8751
Close, David W. "Representative Democracy and Parliamentary Institutions: A Study Focusing on the Committee System of the Quebec National Assembly." McGill, 1978.

8752
Crête, J. "The Determinants of Public Policies Among Local Authorities in Quebec — a Micro Analysis." Oxford, 1979.

Fenwick, Rudy. See No./Voir no 8569

8753
Fournier, Pierre. "A Study of Business in Quebec Politics." Toronto, 1975.

8754
Gagnon, Alain Gustave. "Le développement régional, l'état et le rôle des groupes populaires: le cas de l'est du Québec." Carleton, 1983.

8755
Giner, Marcel. "Structures et processus de planification au Ministère des affaires sociales au Québec de 1972 à 1976: problèmes et réformes." Laval, 1980.

8756
Glenday, Daniel. "Dependency and Class Relations and Politics in Rouyn, Noranda, Quebec." Carleton, 1981.

Gordon, Robert Arthur. See No./Voir no 3542

Gow, James Iain. See No./Voir no 1069

Griffin, Elizabeth Anne. See No./Voir no 8573

Hamelin, Marcel. See No./Voir no 7258

Heller, Monica Sara. See No./Voir no 7666

Hornosty, Jennie Mary. See No./Voir no 9769

Kernaghan, William David K. See No./Voir no 8599

8757
Laliberté, G.-Raymond. "L'Ordre de Jacques Cartier ou l'utopie d'un césarisme laurentien." Laval, 1981.

Larin, Gilles Normand. See No./Voir no 1500

8758
Léveillée, Jacques. "Développement urbain et politiques gouvernementales urbaines dans l'agglomération montréalaise, 1943-1975." Montréal, 1977.

Lovink, J.A.A. See No./Voir no 8625

8759
Marceau, Richard. "Une théorie cybernétique de la sélection de l'agenda gouvernemental." Laval, 1981.

Olssen, Andrée. See No./Voir no 8636

Plehwe, Rudolf. See No./Voir no 8732

8760
Posgate, Wilfred Dale. "Social Mobilization and Political Change in Quebec." SUNY, Buffalo, 1972.

Reilly, Wayne Gerard. See No./Voir no 8590

Richert, Jean-Pierre. See No./Voir no 8591

Rivard, M. Eugène. See No./Voir no 7953

Robertson, Nancy Susan. See No./Voir no 8593

Sabourin, Louis. See No./Voir no 8495

8761
Sait, Edward McChesney. "Clerical Control in Quebec." Columbia, 1911.

8762
Sancton, A.B. "Governing Montreal: The Impact of French-English Differences in Metropolitan Politics." Oxford, 1978.

8763
Séguin, Claude-André. "Reorganizing the Provision of Urban Public Services: The Case of the Montreal Urban Community Police Department." Syracuse, 1978.

8764
Thatcher, Max B. "The Political Island of Quebec: A Study in Federalism." Northwestern, 1953.

8765
Walsh, David Francis. "The External Relations of Quebec, 1960-1970: An Aspect of the Jurisdictional Crisis Within the Canadian Federal System." Connecticut, 1975.

Saskatchewan

Conway, John Frederick. See No./Voir no 10024

8766
Corman, J.S. "The Impact of State Ownership on State Proprietary Corporation: The Pota Corporation of Saskatchewan." Toronto, 1983.

Dosman, Edgar J.E. See No./Voir no 733

8767
Eager, Evelyn Lucille. "The Government of Saska chewan." Toronto, 1958.

8768
Grayson, John Paul. "Neighborhood and Voting: T Social Basis of Conservative Support in Broa view." Toronto, 1972.

8769
Johnson, Albert Wesley. "Biography of a Governmen Policy Formulation in Saskatchewan, 1944-196. Harvard, 1963.

Lipset, Seymour M. See No./Voir no 8635

McCrorie, James Napier. See No./Voir no 140

8770
McLeod, Thomas Hector Macdonald. "Public Ente prise in Saskatchewan: The Development of Pub Policy and Administrative Controls Harvard, 1960.

Ross, Arthur Larry. See No./Voir no 141

Taylor, Malcolm G. See No./Voir no 1634

Waggoner, Marion Arthur. See No./Voir no 8640

ARMED SERVICES/SERVICES ARMÉS

Brazeau, Ernest Jacques. See No./Voir no 4105

Cohen, Eliot Asher. See No./Voir no 7402

Cotton, Charles Alexander. See No./Voir no 7404

8771
Freney, Michael Aloysius. "The Political Element Military Expertise." Rice, 1976. [The Roy Military College, Kingston, Ontario/Collège mil taire royal, Kingston, Ontario]

8772
Hatch, Fred J. "The British Commonwealth A Training Plan, 1939 to 1945." Ottawa, 1969.

8773
Jones, Frank Edward. "The Infantry Recruit: Sociological Analysis of Socialization in the Can dian Army." Harvard, 1954.

Lefroy, Donald Arthur. See No./Voir no 7413

Lightman, Ernie Stanley. See No./Voir no 2187

8774
Melville, Thomas Richard. "Canada and Sea Powe Canadian Naval Thought and Policy 1860-1910 Duke, 1981.

8775
Rousseau, Marcel. "Les traits de personnalité, besoin de réalisation et l'adaptation au changeme chez un groupe de jeunes militaires canadien français." Montréal, 1983.

8776
Simpson, Susanne P. "The Performance Evaluation Women in the Canadian Forces in Relation Supervisors' Attitudes toward Women and th Theory of Self-Fulfilling Prophecy." Ottawa, 198.

CANADIAN DIPLOMACY, POLICY, FOREIGN RELATIONS AND MILITARY POWER/DIPLOMATIE, POLITIQUES, RELATIONS EXTÉRIEURES ET POUVOIR MILITAIRE CANADIENS

General Items/Ouvrages généraux

8777
Ambrose, Paul Benjamin. "Canada Becomes a Potential Nth Country: 1943-1951." Pennsylvania, 1966.

8778
Anglin, D.C. "Canadian Policy Towards International Institutions, 1939-50." Oxford, 1956.

8779
Axworthy, Thomas Sidney. "Soldiers without Enemies: A Political Analysis of Canadian Defence Policy, 1945-1975." Queen's, 1979.

8780
Barry, Donald Joseph. "Continuity and Change in Canadian Foreign Policy: From the Pre-War to the Post-War Experience, 1935-1957." Johns Hopkins, 1978.

Berry, Glynn R. See No./Voir no 1370

8781
Bertrand, Denis. "La politique extérieure et militaire du Canada et la réaction canadienne-française à la veille de la deuxième grande guerre (1935-1939)." Montréal, 1965.

Caragata, Patrick James. See No./Voir no 1375

8782
Cuthbertson, Brian Craig Uniache. "The Continental Imbalance and Canadian Defence Options." London, 1975.

Daggett, Athern Park. See No./Voir no 1871

8783
Davy, Grant Robert. "Canada's Role in the Disarmament Negotiations: 1946-1957." Tufts, Fletcher School of Law and Diplomacy, 1962.

8784
Farrell, Robert B. "Planning and Control of Canadian Foreign Policy." Harvard, 1953.

8785
Forbes, A.J. De B. "The Attitude of the Dominions to Organization for International Security Welfare, 1939-1945." Oxford, 1954.

8786
Horan, James Francis. "Patterns of Canadian Foreign Policy: A Study in the Shaping of Canada's External Relations from Confederation to Suez." Connecticut, 1972.

Jones, John Alfred. See No./Voir no 8546
Joynt, Carey B. See No./Voir no 7566
Koh, Kwang-Lim. See No./Voir no 1858
Levy, Thomas Allen. See No./Voir no 8493
McLean, Elizabeth M.M. See No./Voir no 1091

8787
McLin, Jon B. "Canada's Changing Alliance Policy, 1957-1964." Johns Hopkins, 1966.

Melville, Thomas Richard. See No./Voir no 8774

8788
Milstein, Donald Ellis. "Canadian Peacekeeping Policy: A Meaningful Role for a Middle Power." Michigan, 1968.

8789
Moore, George Bissland. "The Effect on Canada of Norad, the North American Defence Command." Ottawa, 1967.

8790
Munton, Donald James. "External Influences on Canadian Foreign Policy Behavior: Developing and Testing Three Theoretical Models." Ohio State, 1973.

8791
Ossman, Albert John, Jr. "The Development of Canadian Foreign Policy with Particular Emphasis on the Period 1943-1953." Syracuse, 1963.

8792
Sherman, Michael Eric. "Nuclear Sharing: The Canadian Experience, 1942-1967." Harvard, 1968.

8793
Spicer, James Keith. "External Aid in Canadian Foreign Policy: A Political and Administrative Study of Canada's Assistance Under the Colombo Plan." Toronto, 1962.

Swygard, Kline Ruthwen. See No./Voir no 1855

8794
Thakur, Ramesh Chandra. "Canada, India and the Vietnam War: Peacekeeping Foreign Policy and International Politics." Queen's, 1978.

8795
Thibault, Claude F. "Canada's External Relations, 1600-1969: A Bibliography." Rochester, 1973.

8796
Tucker, Michael John. "Canada's Roles in the Disarmament Negotiations: 1957-1971." Toronto, 1977.

Walsh, David Francis. See No./Voir no 8765

8797
Warnock, John William, Jr. "The Defence Policy of a Middle Power: Canada as a Case Study." American, 1971.

8798
Wiseman, Henry. "Theoretical Approaches and Policy Examination of Canada's Role in Peace Keeping." Queen's, 1971.

The League of Nations and Canada/ La Société des Nations et le Canada

Carter, Gwendolen Margaret. See No./Voir no 8817

8799
Després, Jean-Pierre. "Le Canada et l'organisation internationale du travail." Laval, 1946.

8800
Page, Donald Murray. "Canadians and the League of Nations Before the Manchurian Crisis." Toronto, 1972.

8801
Story, Donald Clarke. "The Bennett Government: The League of Nations and Collective Security, 1930-1935." Toronto, 1977.

8802
Veatch, Richard. "Canadian Foreign Policy and the League of Nations, 1919-1939." Université de Genève, 1973.

The United Nations and Canada/
Les Nations Unis et le Canada

Aikman, C.C. See No./Voir no 8816

8803
Armstrong-Reid, Susan Edwina. "Canada's Role in the United Nations Relief and Rehabilitation Administration, 1942-1947." Toronto, 1982.

8804
Bishop, Peter Victor. "Canada and the Controversy Over the Financing of U.N. Peace-Keeping Operations." Toronto, 1969.

8805
Collins, Edward Jr. "The Commonwealth, Communism and Colonialism: A Comparative Study of Commonwealth Foreign Policy in the United Nations." Emory, 1960.

8806
Miller, Anthony John. "Functionalism and Foreign Policy: An Analysis of Canadian Voting Behaviour in the General Assembly of the United Nations, 1946-1966." McGill, 1971.

OECD, NATO and Canada/
L'OCDE, l'OTAN et le Canada

8807
Cronin, Maureen Patricia. "Canada and NATO." Stanford, 1958.

8808
Davis, Jerome D. "To the NATO Review: Constancy and Change in Canadian NATO Policy, 1949-1969." Johns Hopkins, 1973.

8809
Gerst-Kohn, Walter S. "The North Atlantic Treaty." New School for Social Research, 1954.

8810
Marshall, Richard Eugene. "Canada in the Role of a Middle Power: A Study of Canadian Non-Military Collaboration Vis-à-vis the Organization for Economic Cooperation and Development and the North Atlantic Treaty Organization, 1960-1967." Pennsylvania, 1971.

Great Britain and Canada/Grande-Bretagne et Canada

8811
Henderson, Michael Dennis. "The Dominions and British Foreign Policy 1919-1923: A Case Study in Inter-governmental Co-operation." London, 1970.

8812
Hillmer, George Norman. "Anglo-Canadian Relations, 1926-1937: A Study of Canada's Role in the Shaping of Commonwealth Policies." Cambridge, 1975.

8813
Ilori, Joseph Abiodun. "From Colony to Dominion Within the British Empire, 1914-1931." North Texas State, 1975.

8814
Kronenberg, Vernon Joshua. "Patterns of Defense Organization: Britain, Canada and the United States." John Hopkins, 1974.

8815
Wigley, Philip George Edward. "The End of Imperial Unity: British Canadian Relations 1917-1926." Cambridge, 1972.

The British Dominions, the Commonwealth and Canada Since World War I/Les dominions britanniques, le Commonwealth et le Canada depuis la Première Guerre mondiale

8816
Aikman, C.C. "The British Commonwealth and the United Nations." London, 1948.

Burke, Mavis E. See No./Voir no 2403

8817
Carter, Gwendolen Margaret. "The British Dominions and Collective Security Through the League of Nations, with Particular Reference to the Sino-Japanese Dispute and the Italo-Ethiopian Conflict." Radcliffe, 1938.

Collins, Edward See No./Voir no 8805

Cook, George Leslie. See No./Voir no 7476

8818
Cross, Hartley W. "The Status of the British Dominions." Clark, 1929.

8819
Dewey, Alexander Gordon. "The Dominions and Diplomacy: The Canadian Contribution." Columbia, 1935.

Forbes, A.J. De B. See No./Voir no 8785

Galbraith, John S. See No./Voir no 7547

8820
Gey van Pittius, E.F.W. "Nationality Within the British Commonwealth of Nations." London, 1928.

Hastedt, Glenn Peter. See No./Voir no 8839

8821
Hayes, Frank Randall. "The Evolution of Canadian Commonwealth Relations: 1945-1968." Toronto, 1979.

Hillmer, George Norman. See No./Voir no 8813

8822
Holland, R.E. "The Commonwealth in the British Official Mind: A Study in Anglo-Dominion Relations 1925-1937." Oxford, 1977.

8823
Ilsley, Lucretia Little. "The Administration of Mandates by the British Dominions." Illinois, 1932.

8824
Johnston, Victor Kenneth. "The International Status of the British Dominions." Chicago, 1926.

8825
Madge, S.J. "The Domesday of Crown Lands: A Study of the Parliamentary Confiscations, Surveys and Sales During the Commonwealth." London, 1938.

Neuendorff, Gwendoline. See No./Voir no 8478

8826
Ollivier, Maurice. "Le Statut de Westminster." Montréal, 1933.

8827
O'Neill, M.P. "The Changing Concept of the Commonwealth, with Special Reference to the Policies of the Labour Government." Manchester, 1977.

8828
Ramsey, Julia H. "The Foreign Policy of the British Dominions, 1931-1936." Georgetown, 1949.

8829
Schultz, John Alfred. "Canadian Attitudes Toward the Empire, 1917-1939." Dalhousie, 1975.

8830
Shinn, Ridgway Foulks, Jr. "The Right of Secession in the Development of the British Commonwealth of Nations." British Columbia, 1958.

8831
Toxey, Walter William, Jr. "Immigration and Citizenship in the Commonwealth of Nations." Texas, 1964.

Wertiner, S. See No./Voir no 7652

8832
Wilmot, L.H. "The Functions and Activities of the British High Commission, 1928-39, with Particular Emphasis on the British High Commission at Ottawa." London, 1978.

8833
Yang, C.N. "The Distribution of Functions Among Central Government Departments in the United Kingdom, with Some Comparison of the United States of America and British Dominions." Oxford, 1948.

The United States and Canada
Since World War II/Les États-Unis et le Canada
depuis la Deuxième Guerre mondiale

8834
Abrams, Matthew John. "The Canada-United States Interparliamentary Group, 1959-1969." Columbia, 1971.

8835
Bartholomew, Mark Alan. "The Effect of International Interdependence on Foreign Policy Making: Canadian and United States Nuclear Technology Export." Miami, 1980.

Burman, Patrick Walsh. See No./Voir no 8563

8836
Clark, Melissa Helen. "The Canadian State and Staples: An Ear to Washington." McMaster, 1980.

Clement, Wallace. See No./Voir no 2328

8837
Friesen, Brock Frederick James. "International Management of Niagara River Flow." Waterloo, 1981.

8838
Ghent, Jocelyn Maynard. "Canadian-American Relations and the Nuclear Weapons Controversy, 1958-1963." Illinois, 1976.

Hagy, James William. See No./Voir no 8574

8839
Hastedt, Glenn Peter. "The Impact of the Policy Making Process on Policy Outcomes: Military Unification in the United States, Canada, and Great Britain." Indiana, 1979.

Hauck, Arthur Andrew. See No./Voir no 2405

8840
Jockel, Joseph Thomas. "The United States and Canadian Efforts at Continental Air Defense, 1945-1957." Johns Hopkins, 1978.

8841
Kasensky, Renee Goldsmith. "Refugees from Militarism: Draft Age Americans in Canada." California, Berkeley, 1972.

8842
Keating, Thomas. "Nongovernmental Participation in Foreign Policy Decisions, Affecting Canada's Fisheries Relations with the United States." Dalhousie, 1982.

8843
Kirton, John James. "The Conduct and Coordination of Canadian Decision-Making Towards the United States." Johns Hopkins, 1977.

8844
Koehler, Wallace Conrad, Jr. "Government Dominance and World Politics: Changing Canadian-American Relations in Energy Trade and Foreign Ownership Policies." Cornell, 1977.

8845
Kohler, Larry R. "Canadian/American Oil Diplomacy: The Adjustment of Conflicting National Oil Policies, 1955-1973." Johns Hopkins, 1983.

8846
Kronenberg, Vernon Joshua. "Patterns of Defense Organization: Britain, Canada and the United States." Johns Hopkins, 1974.

Lattin, Richard Thomas. See No./Voir no 3182

8847
Mattson, Lawrence Garfield. "The Historic Continentalist-Nationalist Debate and the American Corporation in Canada: Their Relationship in Current Canadian Controversy over the American Corporations." Claremont, 1976.

McIntyre, Geoffrey R. See No./Voir no 2287

8848
McMenemy, John Murray. "The Columbia River Treaty, 1961-1964: A Study of Opposition and Representation in the Canadian Political System." Toronto, 1969.

8849
Middlemiss, Danford William. "A Pattern of Co-ordination: The Case of the Canadian-American Defence Production and Development Sharing Arrangements, 1958-1963." Toronto, 1976.

8850
Moseley, Frederick Eugene, Jr. "The United States-Canadian Great Lakes Pollution Agreement: A Study in International Pollution Control." Kent State, 1978.

8851
Murray, Douglas Joseph. "The Relation Between International Politics and Domestic Politics: The Politics of North American Defense." Texas, 1979.

8852
Redding, Forest William, Jr. "Sharing the Living Resources of the Sea: An Analysis of Contemporary American-Canadian Fisheries Relations." Oklahoma, 1979.

8853
Rothenberg, Stuart. "United States-Canadian Relations 1950-1973: The Limits of Community." Connecticut, 1977.

8854
Schuster, Leslie. "The Impulse of Independence: Canada's Political Relations with Its Superpower Ally, The United States." SUNY, 1979.

8855
Searle, R. Newell, Jr. "A Land Set Apart." Minnesota, 1975. [Quetico-Superior-Minnesota-Ontario Boundary/Frontières de Quetico-Supérieur-Minnesota - Ontario]

8856
Singh, Indu B. "A Study of Canada-US Cooperation in Space Communication Programs with Special Reference to the Communications Technology Satellite Project." Ohio University, 1977.

8857
Souto-Maior, Joel. "The Analysis of Complex Decision-Making Negotiations of the Saint-John River Basin Agreement (Canada-U.S.A.)." British Columbia, 1981.

8858
Stephens, William Eldon. "Critical Attitudes Toward the American Policy: A Comparison of Canadian and U.S. University Students." Kent State, 1976.

8859
Swainson, Neil Alexander. "The Evolution of the Canadian Position on the International Development of the Columbia River: A Study in Political and Administrative Behaviour." Stanford, 1974.

8860
Swanson, Roger Frank. "An Analytical Study of the United States/Canada Defense Relationship as a Structure, Response and Process: Problems and Potentialities." American, 1969.

8861
Tynan, Thomas Martin. "Canadian-American Relations: The Arctic in Light of the Voyage of the Manhattan." Catholic, 1976.

8862
Wagner, James Richard. "Partnership: American Foreign Policy Toward Canada, 1953-1957." Denver, 1966.

8863
Wandesforde-Smith, Geoffrey Albert. "A Comparative Analysis of American and Canadian Governmental Arrangements for the Development of Regional Water Policy in the Columbia River Basin." Washington, Seattle, 1970.

8864
Wilson, William Edgar. "Environment as a Cross-National Policy Problem: The Great Lakes 1950-1970." Tufts, 1974.

St. Lawrence Seaway/ Voie maritime du Saint-Laurent

8865
Beck, Sister M. Celeste. "An Historical Evaluation of the St. Lawrence Seaway Controversy, 1950-1953." St. Johns, 1954.

8866
Comstock, Rudolph Swayne. "The St. Lawrence Seaway and Power Project: A Case Study in Presidential Leadership." Ohio State, 1956.

8867
Thompson, Dwayne Thomas. "The St. Lawrence Project: A Case Study in American Politics." George Peabody, 1957.

8868
Walles, M.J.S. "The St. Lawrence Seaway Development: A Study in American Politics and Pressure Groups." London, 1958.

Caribbean and Canada/Caraïbes et Canada

8869
Burke, Mavis E. "An Analysis of Canadian Education Assistance to the Commonwealth Caribbean, Leeward and Windward Islands, 1960-1970." Ottawa, 1975.
Paragg, Ralph Ramsarup. See No./Voir no 1391

Cuba and/et Canada

8870
Boyer, Harold. "Canada and Cuba: A Study International Relations." Simon Fraser, 1973.

Latin America and Canada/Amérique latine et Canada

8871
Bell, George Gray. "Canadian Foreign Policy Toward Latin America, 1960-1963: A Study of Selected Foreign Policy Decisions." McGill, 1972.

8872
Guy, James John. "Canada's External Relations with Latin America Environment Process, and Prospects." St. Louis, 1975.

8873
Paul, Alix-Herald. "Canada's Relations with Latin America: The Dynamics of Two Brands of Present Day Nationalism Stemming from Dependency the United States." American, 1976.

Europe and/et Canada

8874
Strempel, U. "Towards Complex Interdependence Canada and the European Community, 1958-1980." Alberta, 1982.

France and/et Canada

Butler, Pamela Jean. See No./Voir no 8564
8875
Couture, Paul Morgan. "The Politics of Diplomacy: The Crisis of Canada-France Relations, 1940-1942." York, 1981.

USSR and Canada/URSS et Canada

8876
Balawyder, Aloysius. "Canada-Soviet Relations, 1920-1935." McGill, 1936.

8877
Barnes, Samuel Henry. "The Ideologies and Policies of Canadian Labor Organizations." Duke, 1957.
Lalande, Jean-Guy. See No./Voir no 1088
Pride, Cletis Graden. See No./Voir no 1096
Straus, Melvin Potter. See No./Voir no 8602

Africa and Canada/Afrique et Canada

8878
Freeman, Linda Alison Isobel. "The Nature of Canadian Interests in Black Southern Africa." Toronto, 1978.

8879
Houndjahoué, Michel. "Une étude de la coopération bilatérale entre le Canada et les pays francophones de l'Afrique de l'ouest: 1960-1975." Laval, 1982.

Rathgerber, Eva-Maria L. See No./Voir no 6853

8880
Redekop, Clarence George. "Canada and Southern Africa, 1946-1975: The Political Economy of Foreign Policy." Toronto, 1977.

8881
Schlegel, J.P.R. "The Influence of Federalism and Biculturalism on the Emergence of a Canadian Presence in Black Africa: 1957-1971." Oxford, 1976.

8882
Tennyson, B.D. "Canada's Policy Towards South Africa, 1899-1961." London, 1978.

8883
Wagenberg, R.H. "Commonwealth Reactions to South Africa's Racial Policy, 1948-1961." London, 1966.

Middle East and Canada/Moyen-Orient et Canada

8884
Pompa, Edward Michael. "Canadian Foreign Policy During the Suez Crisis of 1956." St. John's, 1969.

8885
Stanislawski, Howard Jerry. "Elites Domestic Interest Groups, and International Interests in the Canadian Foreign Policy Decision-Making Process: The Arab Boycott of Canadians and Canadian Companies Doing Business with Israel." Brandeis, 1981.

Far East and Canada/Extrême-Orient et Canada

General Items/Ouvrages généraux

8886
Bangsberg, Harry Frederick. "The Colombo Plan, 1950-1956." Iowa, 1957.

China and Canada/Chine et Canada

8887
Foster, John William. "The Imperialism of Righteousness: Canadian Protestant Missions and the Chinese Revolution, 1925-1928." Toronto, 1977.

8888
Langlais, Jacques. "Les jésuites canadiens-français en Chine (1918-1956), leur perception des traditions chinoises." McMaster, 1977.

Minden, Karen Paula. See No./Voir no 6807

8889
Nossal, Kim Richard. "Strange Bedfellows: Canada and China in War and Revolution, 1942-1947." Toronto, 1977.

8890
Raabe, Francis Conrad. "The China Issue in Canada: Politics and Foreign Policy." Pennsylvania State, 1970.

Japan and Canada/Japon et Canada

8891
Bennett, Neville R. "The Anglo-Japanese Alliance and the Dominions, 1902-1911." London, 1966.

8892
Gowen, Robert Joseph. "Canada's Relations with Japan, 1895-1922: Problems of Immigration and Trade." Chicago, 1966.

Korea and Canada/Corée et Canada

8893
Galan, Meroslav. "Canada-Korea Relations 1947-1955: The Continentalization of Canadian Foreign Policy." McGill, 1981.

8894
Stairs, Denis Winfield. "The Role of Canada in the Korean War." Toronto, 1969.

Bangladesh and/et Canada

8895
Himes, Mel. "Interest Groups and Canadian Foreign Policy: The Case of Bangladesh." McGill, 1978.

Vietnam and/et Canada

8896
Levant, Avrom Victor. "The Political Economy of Canadian Foreign Policy in Vietnam." McGill, 1981.

8897
Ross, Douglas Alan. "In the Interests of Place: Canadian Foreign Policy and the Vietnam Truce Supervisory Commission." Toronto, 1979.

PSYCHOLOGY/PSYCHOLOGIE

Canadian psychology, the fifth largest classification, is unique in that almost all of the approximately 1000 dissertations have been completed in Canadian universities, while only 15 were produced in the United States. None came from Great Britain. This field has greatly expanded during the last 15 years. Three dissertations were produced by the University of Toronto in the 1920's, four by Toronto and McGill in the 1940's, eleven in the 1950's (ten by the University of Ottawa), and 41 in the 1960's. The 1970's saw a huge increase in the number of dissertations produced, and the first four years of the 1980's are continuing this trend. Of the 23 Canadian universities producing dissertations in psychology, Toronto is the leader in output, with York a close second, and Ottawa and Montreal close behind.

The major sub-classifications include general psychology, clinical psychology (with numerous sub-classifications), developmental, counseling, educational, experimental, military, industrial, and social, psychology.

Les études de psychologie, qui forment la cinquième plus vaste classification, représentent une collection unique du fait que presque toutes ces 1000 thèses (approximativement) ont été rédigées dans des universités canadiennes; on en compte une quinzaine aux États-Unis et aucune ne vient de Grande-Bretagne. C'est seulement dans les 15 dernières années que cette discipline s'est véritablement affirmée. L'Université de Toronto a produit trois thèses dans les années 1920; les universités de Toronto et McGill, ensemble, quatre thèses dans les années 1940; onze thèses ont paru dans les années 1950 (dont 10 à l'Université d'Ottawa) et 41 dans les années 1960. Le barrage a sauté dans les années 1970 et, de 1980 à 1984, plus de thèses ont été produites que dans les années 1970. Des 23 universités canadiennes qui ont produit des thèses de psychologie, celle de Toronto vient au premier rang suivie de près par York, Ottawa et Montréal.

Parmi les principales sous-classifications, se trouvent des thèses portant sur la psychologie en général, la psychologie clinique (subdivisée en de nombreuses sections), la psychologie du développement, la psychologie éducative, expérimentale, militaire, industrielle et sociale.

General Items/Ouvrages généraux

Bass, Marian Helen. See No./Voir no 1119
8898
Bell, Ronald Gordon. "Rod and Frame Test Data in Field Dependence/Independence Cognitive Style." York, 1977.
Boness, Daryl John. See No./Voir no 10601
Bontrager-Lehman, Carol. See No./Voir no 6757
8899
Bowd, Joy Carolyn. "Field Independence as Related to Intelligence and Spatial Ability: An Investigation into Individual, Age and Sex Differences." Manitoba, 1978.
8900
Bradley, Michael Timothy. "Accuracy Demonstrations, Threat and the Detection of Deception: Cardiovascular, Electrodermal, and Pupillary Measures." Manitoba, 1980.
Busby, Keith. See No./Voir no 3897
8901
Butchard, Neil Joseph. "Developmental Changes in the Perception of Emotion in Adult Speech, Age Differences in Perception of and Reaction to Vocal-Verbal Emotional Messages." Manitoba, 1983.
8902
Cavoukian, Ann J. "The Influence of Eyewitness Identi fication Evidence." Toronto, 1980.
8903
Chrisjohn, Roland David. "Substantive Approach to the State-Trait Distinction in Anxiety." Western Ontario, 1981. [Subjects were 136 male and 38 female students/136 étudiants et 38 étudiantes en étaient les sujets]
8904
Corfield, Vera Catherine. "The Role of Arousal and Cognitive Complexity in Susceptability to Social Influences." Alberta, 1967.

8905
Corlett, Susan Gail. "Power in the Workplace and th Professionalization of Psychology." Toronto, 1982
8906
Danial, Antoinette. "The Relationship Between Couple's Pattern of Financial Management and th Dominant 'Orientation Other' of Each Spouse Montréal, 1979.
8907
Dell, Gary Santmyers. "Phonological and Lexica Encoding in Speech Production: An Analysis c Naturally Occurring and Experimentally Elicite Speech Errors." Toronto, 1980.
8908
Delli Colli, Pascal Joseph. "Mental Deterioration an the Ottawa Wechsler." Ottawa, 1964.
8909
Doan, Brian David. "Belief Among Academics in Fre Will and in the Veracity of Scientific Judgement McGill, 1981.
8910
Fabi, Bruno. "Exploration de variables psychologiqu et socio-économiques relatives au choix et a transfert de secteur organisationnel: une étud longitudinale comparative chez des M.B.A. québe cois." Montréal, 1981.
8911
Farley, Jean-Claude. "Évaluation d'un programme c formation: étude de la relation entre la probabilit subjective du transfert et le changement au nivea du comportement." Montréal, 1983.
8912
Fedoravicius, Algirdas Stasys. "Self-Instructional an Relaxation Variables in the Systematic Densensit zation Treatment of Speech Anxiety." Waterlo 1971.
8913
Galloway, William Robert. "An Investigation of Som Effects of Congener Substances of Alcoholi Beverages on the Sleep Cycle in Man." Queen' 1979.
Gifford, Robert Durrell. See No./Voir no 934
8914
Gilmor, Timothy McLeod; Corey, David T. "Th Relationship Between Locus of Control and th Four Causal Factors of Weiner's Attributic Model." York, 1979 [University students/Étudian universitaires]
Griffith, Gwyneth Proctor. See No./Voir no 4026
Gruson, Linda Margaret. See No./Voir no 955
8915
Guse, Linda Lydia. "Vulnerability to External Influence: Gender, Sex-Role Identity, and Mod Gender as Variables." Manitoba, 1981.
Hanel, Frank Joseph. See No./Voir no 1938
8916
Houle, Jocelyne. "L'intimité du jeune adulte d'après concept eriksonnien." Montréal, 1982.
8917
Hourany, Lawrence Joseph. "Differences in Verb Abilities in Relation to Age." Western Ontari 1976.

8918
Humphreys, Carolyn Ann. "Single Mothers: An Investigation of Their Experience as Single Parents." Toronto, 1980.

8919
Kehoe, Dalton Anthony. "The Interpersonal Basis of Consensus on Emergent Leadership in Small Discussion Groups." York, 1973.

8920
Kern, Alan Steven. "The Perception of Community Environments: The Use of a Phenomenological Community Mapping Technique in a Rural and Suburban Area." York, 1973.

8921
Kyle, Neil John. "Groupthink in Decision Making: Testing for Its Existence, Effects and Prevention." British Columbia, 1980.

8922
Labreche, Thomas Michael. "The Victoria Revision of the Halstead Category Test." Victoria, 1983.

8923
Lapp, Janet E. "Contributors to Female Use of Psychopharmacological Agents: A Multifactorial Cognitive and Social Analysis." McGill, 1980.

8924
Levin, Deborah Marcias. "Psychological Adjustment Among the Physically Disabled: The Role of Social Support and Coping Strategies." Western Ontario, 1982.

Marshall, John Charles. See No./Voir no 10373

8925
Miller, Marilyn Sue. "Executive Schemes vs. Mental Capacity in Predicting Intellectual Underperformance Among Lower Socioeconomic Status Groups." York, 1980.

8926
Moore, Joseph A.L. "Loneliness: Personality, Self-Discrepancy, and Demographic Variables." York, 1972.

Mosley, James Lawrence. See No./Voir no 3834

8927
Nichol, Diane Sue. "Factors Affecting the Negativity of Attitudes Toward Suicide." York, 1973.

8928
Pallota-Cornick, Maria Angela Carvalho. "Evaluation of a Behaviour Modification Manual for Aiding Staff in the Supervision of Work Performance of Retarded Clients in Sheltered Workshops." Manitoba, 1980.

8929
Papatola, Kathleen Joan. "The Effects of Ontogenic Microsystem and Mesosystem Variables in the Outcome of Child Abuse." British Columbia, 1982.

8930
Pezer, Vera Rose. "Some Determinants of Curling Performance." Saskatchewan, 1977.

Pieroni, Rita Maria. See No./Voir no 2191

8931
Pugh, George MacLaggan. "The Use of Psychological Tests for the Selection of Policemen." Alberta, 1978.

8932
Ralph, Diana Sharon. "Work and Madness: The Rise of Community Psychiatry." Regina, 1980.

8933
Rappeport, Martin Steven. "Putting Your Best Face Forward: Facial Symmetry in the Expression of Emotion." York, 1980.

8934
Rivard, Reynald. "L'instabilité émotive dans les grands orphelinats de la province de Québec." Ottawa, 1955.

8935
Rivers, Stephen Martin. "Suggested Amnesia in the Context of Directed Forgetting." Carleton, 1980.

8936
Roth, John D.T. "Applying the Weighted-Averaging Model to Perceived Overt-Covert Relationships." York, 1981.

8937
Roth, Marvin Carson. "The Effects of Verbal Non-Immediacy and Cognitive Incompatibility on the Reciprocity of Self-Disclosure." Alberta, 1973.

8938
Rubino, Carl Angelo. "Rapid Visual Identification and Unilateral Temporal Lobe Damage." York, 1969.

8939
Schultz, Katherine Joyce. "Bilateral Cerebral Activation in Relation to Verbal and Spatial Task Performance, Sex and Handedness." Manitoba, 1983.

8940
Shedletsky, Ralph. "Trait Versus State Anxiety and Authoritarianism-Rebelliousness." York, 1972.

8941
Smith, June Margaret M. "Interpretation of the Field-Independence Dimension: The Effect of Variations in Stimulus Input on the Performance of Field-Dependent Subjects." British Columbia, 1970.

8942
Smith, Martin Sherer. "Kin Investment in Grandchildren." York, 1981. [587 grandparents completed the questionnaire/587 grands-parents ont rempli le questionnaire]

8943
Smith, Trevor Vincent Goldhawk. "Cognitive Correlates of Response to a Behavioral Weight Control Program." Queen's, 1979. [30 women/30 femmes]

8944
Solomon, Elizabeth Theresa Echlin. "Learned Helplessness and Immunization: The Effect of Prior Success Experience on Responses to Uncontrollable Failure." Queen's, 1980.

Strasburger, Erick Leopold. See No./Voir no 3703

8945
Toner, Brenda Bernadette. "Self-Report Psychophysiological and Behavioural Indices of Test Anxiety During Anticipation and Test Periods." Toronto, 1983.

Tudiver, Judith Gail. See No./Voir no 9230

CLINICAL PSYCHOLOGY/PSYCHOLOGIE CLINIQUE

General Items/Ouvrages généraux

8946
Amell Semkow, Verna Jean. "Locus of Control and Outcome Expectancy: A Complementary Model of Women's Attributions to Failure." Ottawa, 1980.

8947
Anderson, Allen. "A Study of Cerebral Dominance in Children at 3 Age and Intelligence Levels." Ottawa, 1978.

8948
Annis, Helen Marie. "Vicarious Learning and Verbal Reinforcement in the Modification of Expressed Attitudes Toward Self and Others." York, 1970. [A study of 130 male undergraduates/Une enquête sur 130 étudiants]

8949
Arnold, Larry Sherwood. "An Examination of the 'Warm-Cold' E Variable in Verbal Conditioning." York, 1971. [144 female teachers college students/144 étudiantes en pédagogie]

8950
Austin, Gary Wayne. "Marital-Shared Problem-Solving Conceptualization and Assessment." Western Ontario, 1983.

Baldwin, John Stiles. See No./Voir no 6828

8951
Barker, Stephen David. "The Parental Couple and the Child's Development: An Exploratory Study." Toronto, 1980.

8952
Bate Boerup, John Leonard Daniel. "Employment and Unemployment Impact on MMPI Profiles." York, 1982.

8953
Beharry, Edward A. "The Effect of Interviewing Style upon Self-Disclosure in a Dyadic Interaction." Windsor, 1975.

8954
Beirness, Douglas James. "Reinforcement Contingencies Control the Development of Behavioural Tolerance in Social Drinkers." Waterloo, 1983.

8955
Belfrage, Linda Catherine Pearson. "The Prognostic Utility of Selected Variables in Three Hospitalized Groups." York, 1975.

8956
Benner, David Gordon. "Instructed Neutral Image Visualization as an Anxiety Neutralizing Response in Systematic Desensitization." York, 1972.

8957
Berek, John J. "A Factor Reliability Study of a Picture-Preference Test." Windsor, 1975.

8958
Blain, Deborah. "Avoidance-Learning Deficits in Criminal Offenders." McGill, 1973.

8959
Blakely, Karen B. "Chronic Renal Failure: A Study of Death Anxiety in Dialysis and Kidney Transplant Patients." Manitoba, 1977.

8960
Blewett, June Caryll Cosbey. "Practices and Attitudes in Counter-Culture Communes in British Columbia." Regina, 1975.

8961
Blodgett, Christopher Jay. "The Process of Adjustment in Chronic Renal Failure and Hemodialysis." Manitoba, 1983.

8962
Boisvert, Jean-Marie. "Le renforcement matériel la motivation intrinsèque chez des patients ps chiatriques." Montréal, 1978.

8963
Bolle, Arthur. "The Personality Structure of Thyro Patients on the Rorschach Test." Ottawa, 1959.

8964
Bond, Catherine Ruth. "The Relationships Betwe Marital Distress and Child Behaviour Problem Maternal Personal Adjustment, Maternal Persona ty and Maternal Parenting Behaviour." Briti Columbia, 1983.

8965
Bourque, Paul. "An Investigation of Various Perfc mance Based Treatments with Acrophobic. Laval, 1979.

8966
Bowman, Marilyn Laura. "Chronic Heavy Use Cannabis sativa: Psychological Effects." McGi 1972.

8967
Bradley, Christine Felecia. "The Effects of Hospi Experience on Postpartum Feelings and Attitud of Women." British Columbia, 1976.

8968
Brasfield, Charles Randolph. "Intimacy of Se Disclosure, Availability of Reaction to Disclosu and Formation of Interpersonal Relationship British Columbia, 1971.

8969
Burger, Michael P. "The Effects of Dream Work o: Manifestly Innocent But Latently Meaningful Pr Sleep Stimulus." Windsor, 1979. [800 psycholc students/800 étudiants en psychologie]

8970
Burtt, Brian Irvine. "Schedule-Induced Drinking a Escape-Avoidance Behaviour as a Function Fixed-Time Schedule, Chamber Size and Chamb Wall Stimulie." Window, 1983.

Butchard, Neil Joseph. See No./Voir no 8901

8971
Buttrum, Stephen Michael. "The Use of Behaviou Rehearsal, Modelling Projected Consequences a Cognitive Modification in Assertive Trainin, Western Ontario, 1974.

Byrd, Mark Dodds. See No./Voir no 9506

8972
Campagna, Jean-Louis. "Implementation and Evalu tion of a Suicide Prevention Program in Quebe California School of Professional Psychology, L Angeles, 1976.

8973
Campbell, John Alexander. "A Behavioural Approa to the Maintenance and Rehabilitation of Indepe dent Functioning with the Institutionaliz Elderly." British Columbia, 1978.

8974
Carruthers, Benjamin Carl. "Conditioned Inhibition Mentally Retarded and Retarded Person Western Ontario, 1972.

8975
Clyne-Jackson, Sheila Anne. "Defensiveness in Dream Recall in Response to a Provocative Day Residue." Windsor, 1982.

Cochrane, Nancy J.H. See No./Voir no 4060

Cole, James Randy. See No./Voir no 4017

Colletta, Salvatore. See No./Voir no 7688

8976
Crausman, Burt. "Temporal Perception of Good and Poor Readers." Ottawa, 1958.

8977
Crouse, Dorothy Jean. "Internal-External Control in Thought Samples, Defensive Styles and Observed Interpersonal Behaviors in a Psychiatric Population." Alberta, 1974.

8978
Cupchik, William. "Clinical Imaginative Imagery." Toronto, 1979.

8979
Dacey, Christine. "The Effects of a Modelling Treatment Program Upon Sex-Role Stereotypes and Achievement Behavior of Women." Ottawa, 1980.

8980
Daniels, Ultimus Phillip. "The Effect of Perceived Locus of Control and Psychological Stress on Intuitive Problem Solving." York, 1973.

8981
David, Hélène. "La relation entre les manifestations psychologiques de crise chez la femme enceinte primipare et son niveau d'androgynie." Montréal, 1980.

8982
Devins, Gerald Michael. "Helplessness, Depression and Mood in End Stage Renal Disease." McGill, 1981.

8983
De Vries, Robert Eric. "An Application of Multivariate Analytical Techniques to Psychiatric Classification." Toronto, 1978. [437 patients from the psychiatric ward of Toronto General Hospital/437 patients de l'hopital général psychiatrique de Toronto]

8984
Doering, Robert William. "Parental Reinforcement of Gender-Typed Behaviours in Boys with Atypical Gender Identity." Toronto, 1981.

8985
Donoghue, Eileen. "Social Influence in Humor: The Effects of Canned Laughter and a Companion on Field-Dependent and Field-Independent Females." Ottawa, 1982.

Duckworth, Geoffrey Stafford. See No./Voir no 6835

8986
Duguay, Monique. "Réactions somatiques et psychologiques de femmes lors de l'hospitalisation et de la convalescence de leur jeune enfant ou de leur conjoint." Montréal, 1979.

8987
Dushenko, Terrance William. "Differential Effects on the Two Cerebral Hemispheres that Result from Loss of REM Sleep: Deprivation and Epileptic vs. Nonepileptic Subjects." Manitoba, 1982

8988
Elkin, Lorne. "Sociology of Stupidity." Saskatchewan, Regina, 1972. [720 grade eight students/720 étudiants de huitième année]

8989
Ferrari, John Remo. "The Impact of Selected Verbal Communications on Mood." Western Ontario, 1981.

8990
Finlayson, Gregor James. "Effects of Exposure to and Re-appraisal of Facial Expressions Depicting Affect." Toronto, 1972.

8991
Fleming, Stephen J. "Nurses' Death Anxiety and Clinical Geriatric Training." York, 1974. [Student nurses' attitudes towards death/Attitude des étudiants infirmiers face à la mort]

8992
Fogle, Dale Onward. "Effects of a Paradoxical 'Giving-Up' Treatment for Chronic Self-Defined Insomnia." Waterloo, 1980.

8993
Foucault, Pierre. "Conséquences psychologiques d'un inceste." Montréal, 1981.

8994
Francoeur, Mary Ellen. "The Relationship of Degree of Intimacy to Life Satisfaction in Persons 65 Years of Age and Over." Ottawa, 1976. [Senior citizens in Ottawa/Personnes âgées à Ottawa]

8995
Fuller, Jerry B. "Factors Influencing Rotation on the Bender-Gestalt Performance of Children." Ottawa, 1960.

8996
Gagnon, Joanne. "Étude de l'anxiété situationnelle de quinze couples observés avant et après une vasectomie." Montréal, 1982.

8997
Gagnon, Pierre. "Le cycle du sommeil dans des conditions de sommeil prolongé chez le jeune adulte." Ottawa, 1982.

Gante, M. See No./Voir no 3861

8998
Garke, Mary Elaine. "Response, Speed and Eysenckian Extraversion: Predictors of Intellectual Functioning in the Older Adult." Ottawa, 1976. [Senior citizens in Ottawa/Personnes âgées à Ottawa]

8999
Gattuso, Mathieu. "Effets d'une suggestion verbale associée à l'imagerie mentale sur la fréquence cardiaque." Montréal, 1982.

9000
Genest, Myles. "Cognition, Hypnotic Susceptibility and Laboratory Induced Pain." Waterloo, 1982.

Gerrard, Brian Alexander. See No./Voir no 6732

9001
Gerson, Ann Charlotte. "The Relationship of Chronic and Situational Loneliness to Social Skills and Social Sensitivity." Manitoba, 1978.

Gliksman, Louis. See No./Voir no 7665

9002
Gordon, Arthur. "The Treatment of Social Phobias by Flooding." Queen's, 1981.

9003
Greenberg, Corin Merle. "Parameters of Dyadic Interaction Between Children of Different Sociometric Status." York, 1977.

9004
Gyra, John Charles. "The Relationship of Maternal Personality Factors to Early Maternal Attachment Behaviour to the Infant." Toronto, 1982.

9005

Hafen, Gregor A. "Agression Management: A Comparison of Cognitive Restructuring Versus Social Learning Techniques." Ottawa, 1982.

9006

Halloran, Gerard. "The Differential Effect of Moral Judgment and Internal and External Incentives on Cheating Behavior." Ottawa, 1981.

9007

Harris, Georgina Bernice. "Pain and the Individual." Western Ontario, 1981.

9008

Harris, Nancy Jane Adams. "The Effects of Two Sets of Relaxation Instructions on Autonomic and Self-Report Measures of Relaxation." York, 1980.

9009

Hartman, Lorne Michael. "The Preventive Reduction of Psychological Risk in Asymptomatic Adolescents: A Behavioral Approach." McGill, 1977. [120 high school students/120 étudiants du secondaire]

Hayes, Bonnie Jean. See No./Voir no 1046

9010

Henshaw, David Charles. "A Cognitive Analysis of Creative Problem Solving." Waterloo, 1978.

9011

Herscovitch, Joel. "The Effects of Short-Term Cumulative Partial Sleep Deprivation and Recovery Oversleeping Performance, Efficiency, Cognitive Processing, and Subjective Feeling Status." Ottawa, 1981.

9012

Horvath, Peter. "The Effects of Demand Characteristics Referring to the Self in Covert Treatments." Ottawa, 1979.

9013

Hover, Gerald Robert. "The Development and Evaluation of the Goal Attainment Scaling Process." British Columbia, 1980.

9014

Isaacs, Paul. "Hypnotic Responsiveness and the Dimensions of Imagery and Thinking Style." Waterloo, 1982.

9015

Jessup, Barton Allen. "Autogenic Relaxation and Hand Temperature Biofeedback for Migraine." Western Ontario, 1978.

9016

Kendrick, Margaret Joan. "Reduction of Musical Performance Anxiety by Attentional Training and Behaviour Rehearsal: An Exploration of Cognitive Mediational Processes." British Columbia, 1979.

9017

Kennett, Keith Franklin. "Serum Uric Acid, Intellect and Personality." Saskatchewan, 1972. [54 freshmen of the University of Saskatchewan/54 étudiants de première année de l'Université de la Saskatchewan]

9018

Kindelan, Kevin M. "Value System Similarity, Sex and Value Type Effects on Attributed Marital Adjustment." Ottawa, 1978. [University of Ottawa students/Étudiants de l'Université d'Ottawa]

9019

King, Michael Christopher. "The Prevention of Maladaptive Avoidance Responses Through Observational Learning: An Analogue Study." McGill, 1975 [Grade one children/Enfants de première année]

9020

Kobayaski, Nobako. "Effects of Sex-Role Identification, Sex-Role Orientation of Tasks and Competitive Conditions on Women's Performance Achievement Oriented Situations." Ottawa, 1976.

9021

Kord, Dennis. "La concordance inter-juges (parent professeurs, thérapeutes) quant aux changement subis par des enfants traités en clinique externe Montréal, 1978.

9022

Krahn, Gloria Louise. "The Complementarity of Continuous and Discrete State Analysis of Family Interaction." Manitoba, 1980.

9023

Kramer, Edwin Arthur. "The Relative Effects Selected Cognitive Personality and Incentive Variables in Self-Control." Manitoba, 1980.

9024

Krank, Marvin Douglas. "Motivational Interaction The Role of Inhibition in Pavlovian Aversive Appetitive Transfer." McMaster, 1982.

Labreche, Thomas Michael. See No./Voir no 8922

9025

Lamont, Donald John. "The Effectance Motive York, 1980.

Lange, James Dubois. See No./Voir no 9221

9026

Larkin, Jill. "A Problem Ability Classification (PAC Diagnosis and Outcome with Psychiatric Hospit Patients." York, 1978.

9027

Ledwidge, Michael Barry. "Differences among Obsessive-Compulsive Agoraphobic and Other Phob Patients with Respect to Symptomatology, Natur History and Personality." Simon Fraser, 1983.

9028

Lewandowski, Arthur Joseph. "An Investigation Cognitive and Attitudinal Correlates of the Cor nary-Prone Behavior Pattern." Waterloo, 1979.

9029

Linden, Wolfgang. "Social Competence as a Mediatin Variable in Essential Hypertension." McGill, 1981

9030

Mack, Judith Elaine. "Cognitive Functioning Mothers of Autistic Children." York, 1980.

9031

Manley, Ronald Stuart. "Maintenance Strategies ar Self-Efficiency in the Behavioural Treatment Cigarette Smoking." Queen's, 1983.

9032

McDermott, M. Elizabeth. "Children's Perceptions the Elderly: An Attributional Analysis." Windso 1983.

McFadden, Scot Robert. See No./Voir no 10374

9033

McLaughlin, Judith B. "Relationship of Sibling Con tellation Factors and Figural Creativity Scores Grade Five Boys and Girls." Ottawa, 1978.

9034
Medling, James. "Marital Adjustment over Segments of the Family Life Cycle: The Issue of Value Similarity." Ottawa, 1979.

9035
Meek, Frederick Ivan. "A Study of the Effect of Death Confrontation on Death Concern Variables." Windsor, 1982.

Mercier, Jocelyn. See No./Voir no 3830

9036
Merrill, Lesly. "Identity Status, Resolution of Previous Psychosocial Stages and Social Support in College Women." Ottawa, 1980.

9037
Michaud-Achorn, Aurelda. "The Effects of Extraversion and Attention on Short-Term Habituation of Auditory Evoked Potential Responses." Ottawa, 1982.

9038
Miller, Rickey Shelley. "An Investigation of the Behavioural Correlates and Function of Interpersonal Intimacy." Waterloo, 1980.

9039
Mills, Laura Jane. "Visual Field and Sex-Related Differences in a Mental Rotations Task." Manitoba, 1982.

9040
Mohr, Erich. "Does the Concept of Lateralization Sufficiently Explain Dichotic Listening Performance." Victoria, 1982.

Molino, Joseph. See No./Voir no 3831

Moore, Robert John. See No./Voir no 1071

9041
Munn, John Duncan. "Perception of Maternal Behaviour and Body Image in Adult Males." Toronto, 1979. [Male college students/Jeunes collégiens]

9042
Munns, Evangeline F. "The Development of a Teacher's Observation Scale for the Identification of Children with Learning Disabilities." York, 1971. [From six to thirteen years old/De 6 à 13 ans]

9043
Murray, Charles B. "Cooperative Behavior in Internal-External Locus-of-Control Adolescents Under Affect-Laden Information." Ottawa, 1978.

9044
Mustello, Anthony J. "Psychosocial Adjustment, Context and Adolescent Ego Identity." Ottawa, 1981.

Nelson, Ernest. See No./Voir no 6764

9045
Newton, James Harry. "Attitudes of the Seriously Ill Elderly: An Application of a Clinical-Quantitative Research Strategy for Attitude Assessment Among a Clinical Population." Regina, 1977.

9046
Palumbo, Richard V. "Internal-External Locus of Control and Performance with Children." Ottawa, 1981.

9047
Papazian, Jack H. "Locus of Control, Age, Sex and Interpersonal Bargaining in Children." Ottawa, 1978.

9048
Peer, Miri. "A Clinical Typology of Assaultive Adolescent Males." York, 1980.

9049
Pellerin, André R. "L'ordre de difficulté croissante des items dans un test de puissante à temps limité, L'examen intermédiaire Otis-Ottawa d'habilité mentale: sa constance et ses effets sur la valeur discriminants des items." Ottawa, 1978.

9050
Platt, John Gordon. "An Investigation of the Differential Efficacy of Animated and Imaginal Hierarchy Presentation in the Systematic Desensitization of Test Anxiety." York, 1971.

9051
Porter, Carol Anne. "Blame Depression and Coping in Battered Women." British Columbia, 1983.

Potvin, Robert John Michael. See No./Voir no 4418

Raphael, Irwin Allan. See No./Voir no 9465

9052
Reker, Gary Theodore. "Interpersonal Conceptual Structures of Emotionally Disturbed and Normal Boys." Waterloo, 1973.

Richardson, Wayne Ronald. See No./Voir no 3919

9053
Rozario, Wilson Robert. "The Management of Ability Attributions Via Defensive and Counterdefensive Attributional Strategies." Ottawa, 1981.

9054
Rose, Malcolm. "The Effect of Anxiety Management Training on the Course and Control of Juvenile Diabetes Mellitus." Ottawa, 1981.

9055
Rubenstein, Arnold Hugh. "A Longitudinal Study of Psychological Changes Occuring During Pregnancy." Toronto, 1976.

9056
Ruckman, Maribeth Ruth. "Sex Differences in Hemispheric Specialization for Cognitive and Memory Functions." Queen's, 1981.

9057
Safran, Jeremy David. "Cognitive Processes Mediating the Effect of Expectations on the Perception of Interpersonal Behavior." British Columbia, 1982.

9058
Sauder-Trueman, Cynthia. "Generalization of Verbally Conditioned Self-Acceptance and Acceptance of Others." York, 1974.

9059
Schoen, Virginia E. "The Effect of Some Stimulus Variations on the Rotation of Bender-Gestalt Configurations in Non-Patient Young Adult Females." Ottawa, 1964.

9060
Sexton, David Lorne. "Attributional Cues Employed by Observers in Assessing Maladjustment." Manitoba, 1980.

9061
Shapiro, Paul L. "The Availability and Use of Self-Mediated Feedback in Impulsive, Moderate and Reflective Children." Ottawa, 1977.

9062
Shershen, Eugene D. "Shading in the H-T-P: Its Relationship to Situationally Specific Anxiety and Other Variables in a Male and Female Canadian University Sample." Ottawa, 1976.

9063
Sinclair, Carole Mary Jane. "Differential Processing of Neutral and Sexual Stimuli: A Study of the Effect of Anxiety on Intellectiual Functioning." York, 1973. [20 male volunteers/20 hommes volontaires]

9064
Sirois-Berliss, Michelle. "L'effet du stress ressenti pendant les phases prémenstruelle et menstruelle sur le contenu des rêves." Ottawa, 1981.

9065
Slatterie, Elinor Faith. "A Comparative Study of Selected Effects of Alcohol and Marijuana on Verbal and Non-Verbal Behavior." York, 1972.

9066
Smith, Douglas Lane. "The Effects of Directive Parental Counseling on Parental Acceptance and Perception of Personality Changes." Windsor, 1980.

9067
Smith, Gerald P. "Psychological Androgyny and Attitudes Toward Feminism in Relation to the Perception of Dominance and Sexuality." Windsor, 1981.

9068
Solyom, Carol Anne Elizabeth. "Specificity of Biofeedback in the Treatment of Headaches." Concordia, 1981.

9069
Sordoni, Carl Richard. "Experiments in Humor: Creativity, Locus of Control and Their Relationship to Two Dimensions of Humor." Waterloo, 1979.

9070
Spence, Graeme. "A Descriptive Study of the Adjustment and Social Competency of Adolescents of Borderline Mentality Living in Foster Homes." Ottawa, 1958.

9071
Steibe, Susan. "Level of Fairness-Reasoning and Human Values as Predictors of Social Justice-Related Behavior." Ottawa, 1980.

9072
Stein, Barry Michael. "The Influence of Trait Anxiety and Feedback Message on Client Self-Disclosing Behavior, Self-Reported and Behavioral Anxiety in Videotape Self-Confrontation (Video Feedback)." Western Ontario, 1978.

9073
Stevens, Carey. "Moral Recognition Versus Spontaneous Production of Moral Reasoning: A Cross-Sectional Investigation of 15-72 Year Olds." Ottawa, 1978.

9074
Stirling, Paul Hunter. "Some Issues in Adjustment to a Chronic Physical Disability." Western Ontario, 1980.

9075
Swaine, John Ronald. "The Effects of Locus of Control and Incentives on Binary-Choice Probability Learning Task Performance." Ottawa, 1980.

9076
Szalai, John Paul. "The Role of Deployment Attention in Concept Learning with Aggressive a Non-Aggressive Stimuli." York, 1982.

9077
Tan, Siang-Yang. "Acute Pain in a Clinical Settin Effects of Cognitive-Behavioral Skills Trainin McGill, 1980.

9078
Tilby, Penelope Jean. "Sex Roles and the Percepti of Psychopathology." Queen's, 1975.

9079
Tookey, Herbert Barton. "Non-Specific Effects in t Behavioural Treatment of Insomnia." York, 1980.

9080
Travis, Keith Ian. "The Effects of Modifying Interru tions of Organized Behavioral and Cogniti Sequences." Toronto, 1970.

9081
Tuokko, Holly Anna. "Cognitive Correlates of Arit metic Performance in Clinic-Referred Childre Victoria, 1983.

9082
Usher, Sarah. "Self-Esteem in the Mature Marri Woman as a Function of Working Status and Fem nist Attitudes." York, 1977.

9083
Vallis, Terrance Michael. "The Role of Individu Difference Factors in the Efficacy of Cove Modeling and Self-Instructional Training for Fe Reduction." Western Ontario, 1983.

9084
Vanier, Guy. "Influence de l'auto-observation et l'auto-génération des objectifs sur le contrôle tabagisme." Montréal, 1982.

9085
Von Baeyer, Carl Lucius. "Listening in Dyadic Inte action: Verbal and Non-Verbal Cues of Inte personal Acceptance." Waterloo, 1978. [college students/58 étudiants de collège]

9086
Waxer, Peter Harold. "Group Risk Taking in Grou Versus Gatherings." York, 1969.

9087
Wiener, Melvin H. "Personal and Social Character tics of Blood Donors and Non-Donors." Ottaw 1978.

Wilchesky, Marc H. See No./Voir no 3793

9088
Wolff, Anthony Bernard. "Recognition and Reprodu tion of Rhythmic Patterns by the Dea McGill, 1979.

Woodward, James Brian. See No./Voir no 9483

9089
York, Mary Neris. "Investigation of Operant Behavi in Elderly Psychiatric Patients with Memory D order." York, 1970.

9090
Zucy, James B. "Psychic Immaturity and Marria Nullity." Ottawa, 1981.

Psychoanalysis and Psychosis/Psychanalyse et psychose

9091
Blacha, Michael Dietrich. "The Inventory of Defenses: A New Instrument for the Measurement of Psychoanalytic Defense Mechanisms." York, 1981.

9092
Davis, Ralph E. "A Study of Differences in Body Image of Normal and Psychotic Aged Men." Ottawa, 1960.

9093
Paton, Richard T. "The Influence of Three Reinforcement Modifications on Perseveration in Psychotic Children." Queen's, 1969.

Mental Health/Santé mentale

Delli Colli, Pascal Joseph. See No./Voir no 8908

9094
Lazerson, Judith Schoenholtz. "Psychological Androgyny, Sex Stereotyping and Mental Health." British Columbia, 1981.

Psychopathology/Psychopathologie

9095
Bauberger, Glenn Joseph. "A Multidimensional Model of Psychopathy." York, 1979.

9096
Benaroya, Sygmund. "A Cognitive Approach for Assessment and Evaluation of Some Aspects of Severe Psycho-Pathology of Childhood." Montréal, 1971.

9097
Holden, Ronald Robert. "Item Subtlety, Face Validity and the Structure Assessment of Psychopathology." Western Ontario, 1982.

9098
Keleher, Gary Raymond. "Object Representation and the Rorschach: Investigation of a Continuum of Object Relations Impairment Across a Broad Spectrum of Psychopathology." Windsor, 1982.

9099
Moore, Debra Lynn. "Effects of the Interaction of Sex Role Stereotypes, Sex, and Source of Stress on Perceptions of Psychopathology." Toronto, 1983.

9100
Schwartz, Michael. "The Relationship Between Conceptual Tempo and Psychopathology in Children." Toronto, 1979. [Mental health clinic - from six to fourteen years old/Clinique de santé mentale de 6 à 14 ans]

Tilby, Penelope Jean. See No./Voir no 9078

9101
Vinet, Alain. "Un asile psychiatrique au Québec: institution et signification de la maladie mentale." Laval, 1975.

Stress

Carrier, Maurice A. See No./Voir no 9430
Daniels, Ultimus Phillip. See No./Voir no 8980
Dart, Richard James. See No./Voir no 6832

9102
DeKoninck, Joseph-M. "Dreams and the Mastery of Stress." Manitoba, 1973.

9103
Horsley, Frederick Richard. "The Effect of Stress on the Cognitive Behavior of Impulsive Adolescents: A Study to Compare the Relationship Between Impulsivity and Performance in Cognitive Control Tests Among Institutionalized Juvenile Delinquents Under Conditions of Stress and Non-Stress." Queen's, 1974.

9104
Long, Bonita Clarice. "A Comparison of Aerobic Conditioning and Stress Inoculation and Stress-Management Interventions." British Columbia, 1982.

9105
Matheson, George Clifford R. "The Differential Relationship of Stress to the Eye Movement Behaviour of Repressors and Sensitizers." York, 1973. [210 female undergraduates/210 étudiantes]

9106
Nielson, Warren Robert. "Coronary-Prone Behavior and Cardiovascular Response to Uncontrollable Stress: A Multidimensional Approach." Western Ontario, 1982.

Sirois-Berliss, Michelle. See No./Voir no 9064

9107
Sommer, Daniel. "Influence de la personnalité sur les réactions pathologiques à des événements stressants liés au chômage." Montréal, 1982.

9108
Théroux, Charles Paul-Émile. "The Adaptive Function of Dreams in Dealing with Stress." Manitoba, 1980. [24 obese females/24 femmes obèses]

Psychomotor and Psychometrics/ Psychomoteur et psychométrie

9109
Angers, William P. "A Psychometric Study of Institutionalized Epileptics on the Webster-Bellevue." Ottawa, 1955.

9110
Donnelly, Peter George. "An Instrument and Methodology for the Detection, Assessment and Bio-Feedback Training of Covert Motor Responses." York, 1972.

9111
Jones, Anne Marie. "The Effects of Vestibular Stimulation on Eye Movements in Psychiatric Patients." Ottawa, 1981.

9112
Lotto, David Joshua. "EEG-Alpha Enhancement with Auditory Feedback." York, 1974.

9113
Mandel, Allan Rudolf. "Effects of Biofeedback and Reinforcement upon the Acquisition of Motor Responses in Children." York, 1982.

Psychotherapy/Psychothérapie

9114
Appelle, Morry. "The Effect of Group Marital Therapy on Self-Disclosure, Social Distance and Self-Spouse Perception." Toronto, 1974.

9115
Bailey, Carole. "Effects of Therapist Contact and a Self-Help Manual in the Treatment of Sleep-Onset Insomnia." Concordia, 1982.

9116
Bloch, Maurice. "An Evaluation of Inpatients Treated by Different Kinds of Primary Therapists in a Psychiatric Hospital." British Columbia, 1980.

9117
Breitman, Kenneth E. "Relationships of Field Dependence and Selected Personality Characteristics to Successes and Dropouts in a Short-Term Psychotherapeutic Intervention." Ottawa, 1976.

9118
Caillier, Paul Melvin. "Effects of Session Frequency and Session Duration on Process and Outcome in Short Term Time-Limited Psychotherapy." Manitoba, 1980.

9119
Caspary, Arthur Courtney. "Outcomes of Intensive Psychotherapy Changes Consequent to the Intensive Period in Primal Therapy." Waterloo, 1978.

9120
Chiappone, David. "Therapist-Client Relationship and Group Discussion as Enhancer of Assertion Training." Ottawa, 1979.

9121
Church, Michael Seymour. "Sequential Analysis of Momentary-Moment Psychotherapy Interactions." York, 1981. [53 clients/53 clients]

9122
Cox, Beverlee Ann. "Communication Systems in Psychotherapy - An Empirical Investigation into Treatment Ideologies Held by Patients and Therapists." Simon Fraser, 1977.

9123
Davis, Teresa Mina Anne. "Videotape Self-Confrontation in Group Psychotherapy." Alberta, 1976.

9124
Fatis, Michael. "Relative Preference for Two Cognitively-Oriented Therapeutic Approaches to Problems of Shyness as a Function of Locus-of-Control." Ottawa, 1979.

9125
Gentile, Andrew-Salvatore. "The Effects of Symbolic, Modelling and Behaviour Rehearsal in an Assertive Training Programme with Prison Inmates." British Columbia, 1977.

9126
Gilmour-Barrett, Karen C. "Managerial Systems and Interpersonal Treatment Processes in Residential Centers for Disturbed Youth." Waterloo, 1974.

9127
Grégoire, Pierre A. "Divers modes de participation à l'expérience vécue: variations de la conductance électrodermale dans les situations favorisant des attitudes rencontrées en psychothérapie." Montréal, 1969.

9128
Grimes, Catherine. "The Therapeutic Efficacy of Verbal Conditioning: Its Effects in the Real World." York, 1974.

9129
Hanson, Robert George. "Reciprocal Verbal Interaction Personality Correlates of Participation a Leader Feedback in Sensitivity Training Groups York, 1973. [University students a staff/Étudiants et personnel d'université]

9130
Holmes, Christopher Patrick. "Self Observation, Se Consciousness and the Prompting of Client with Therapy Activity." Waterloo, 1978.

9131
Houde, Denis Bernard. "Effets d'une méthode thér peutique corporelle sur l'actualisation et l'image moi, l'anxiété et la tension musculaire Montréal, 1979.

9132
Howes, Richard John. "Satisfaction with Thera Early Termination, Missed Sessions and Patien Views of their Therapists as a Function of Patien Therapist Personality Similarity." Manitoba, 198

9133
Jaffe, Peter George. "Modeling and Instruction Treatments with Asocial Chronic Psychiat Patients." Western Ontario, 1974.

9134
Juneman, Georgina. "Valeur d'un traitement psych thérapeutique pour un groupe d'enfants para tiques cérébraux." Montréal, 1954.

9135
King, Marlene Dolores. "Between Two Worlds: T Story of a Boy — A Case Study in Experienti Psychotherapy." Alberta, 1975.

Kord, Dennis. See No./Voir no 9021

9136
Kotkov, Benjamin. "The Presence and Role of Iden fication in Group Psychotherapy." Ottawa, 1954.

9137
Lalonde, Gilles. "Le groupe de rencontre: effe différentiels d'approches verbale et non-verbale Montréal, 1982.

9138
Loughner-Gillin, Cheryl. "Sex of the Therapist: Exploration of Competence Attributions as a Fun tion of Therapist's Gender." Windsor, 1981.

9139
Maidstone, Peter. "Making Sense of a Diagnost Category: A Study of the Relationship Betwe Theory and Practice." British Columbia, 198 [The theory and methods of the work of psych therapists in a psychiatric hospital are examine Théorie et méthodes du travail des psychothér peutes dans un hôpital psychiatrique]

9140
Martini, Janie Lilia. "Patient-Therapist Value Co gruence and Rating of Client Improvement Western Ontario, 1978. [London, Ontario]

9141
McLachlan, John Francis Clifford. "Patient and The apist Correlates of Change During Group Psych therapy." Toronto, 1971.

9142
McMullen, Linda Mae. "Degree of Choice in Clien and Therapist's Language During Psychotherapy Saskatchewan, 1981.

9143
Nashef, Ahmad Adam. "The Effects of Group Therapy on the Affective States, Social Distance, Interpersonal Locus of Control, Life Satisfaction, and Ward Behaviour Among the Institutionalized Aged." Toronto, 1980. [Metropolitan Toronto area/Région métropolitaine de Toronto]

9144
Nixon, Deborah Susan. "The Relationship of Primal Therapy Outcome with Experiencing Voice Quality and Transference." York, 1980.

9145
Pezzot-Pearce, Terry Diane. "Effectiveness and Cost-Effectiveness of Behavioral Self-Help Manuals for the Treatment of Obesity: A Study of Degree of Therapist Contact and Group Versus Individual Format." Manitoba, 1980.

9146
Pierson, Donald Fredrick. "Self-Injurious Behavior: Sensory Awareness Training as Group Treatment and an Etiological Analysis." Toronto, 1979.

9147
Richard, Marc-André. "Comparaison des résultats d'une thérapie de groupe, d'une thérapie individuelle et d'une biothérapie dans le traitement behavioral de l'obésité." Montréal, 1981.

9148
Roback, Howard Byron. "An Experimental Comparison of Outcomes in Insight and Non-Insight Oriented Therapy Groups." York, 1970. [Male hospitalized psychiatric patients/Patients psychiatriques mâles hospitalisés]

9149
Robinson, Mary Jane. "Attributional Processes in Therapeutic Relationships Attributions of Causality, Stability and Maladjustment of Clients' Problems as Affected by Sex of Client and Therapist Sex Role Ideology." Manitoba, 1981.

9150
Syer, David Dirk. "Videotape Feedback Variables in Psychotherapy." York, 1972.

9151
Werth, Elizabeth Marie. "A Comparison of Pretraining Methods for Encounter Group Therapy." Queen's, 1979.

9152
Williams, Sharon Mona. "A Comparison of Effectiveness of Psychotherapy and Behaviour Therapy for Incarcerated Sex Offenders." Queen's, 1980.

Neurology, Neurotics and Neuropsychology/ Neurologie, neurasthémie et neuropsychologie

Baribeau-Braun, Jacinthe. See No./Voir no 9163
9153
Bornstein, Robert A. "Neuropsychological Assessment of Changes Following Carotid Endarterectomy." Ottawa, 1981.

9154
Carberry, Hugh H. "A Comparison of Three Methods of Need Assessment with Normal and Neurotic Subjects." Ottawa, 1964.

9155
Clark, Campbell McGillivrary. "The Reliability of Ear Advantage and Attentional Capacity in Dichotic Listening." Victoria, 1982.

9156
Dorosh, Marshall E. "The Effects of Age, Depression, Sex Differences and Educational Level on the Halstead-Retan Neuropsychological Test Battery." York, 1978.

9157
Dupont, Gilles. "Dessins du H-T-P: concept de soi et niveaux de conscience chez des sujets névrosés dans une situation de diagnostic." Ottawa, 1971.

Gates, Robert D. See No./Voir no 3782
Johnson, Olive Skene. See No./Voir no 9192
9158
Maxwell, James Kirk. "A Neuropsychological Assessment of Cerebral Interhemispheric Relations During Early Childhood." Carleton, 1981.

Meier, Augustine. See No./Voir no 9176
Perrault, Yvonne. See No./voir no 3510
9159
Plate, David R. "A Hypnotic Investigation of Neurotic Adaptations and Connotative Meaning." Windsor, 1976.

9160
Regard, Marianne. "Cognitive Rigidity and Flexibility: A Neuropsychological Study." Victoria, 1982. [Brain damage/Dommage au cerveau]

Schizophrenia/Schizophrénie

9161
Ally, Gilles. "Personalité et réponse au placebo chez le schizophrène chronique." Montréal, 1974.

9162
Apanasiewicz, Nina. "A Validation Study of a Picture-Preference Test of Thought Disorder." Windsor, 1982.

9163
Baribeau-Braun, Jacinthe. "Corrélats neurophysiologiques d'attention focalisée et divisée chez des patients schizophrènes." Ottawa, 1981.

9164
Beckett, Susan Jane. "The Assessment and Training of Conversational Skills in Schizophrenics." Queen's, 1982.

9165
Bernstein, S.M. "Drift and Crossover Effects in the Reaction Time Performance of Schizophrenics and Non-Schizophrenics." Waterloo, 1976.

9166
Broga, Mary Irena. "An Information Processing Approach to the Study of Schizophrenic Memory and Thought." Western Ontario, 1980.

9167
Carroll, Rita Carmen. "The Use of Personal Construct and Balance Theory in the Examination of Thought Disordered and Non-Thought Disordered Schizophrenics." Toronto, 1980.

9168
Chaikelson, June Steinberg. "Change in Cognitive Capacity with Aging in Normal and Schizophrenic Adults." McGill, 1971.

9169
Cousineau, Pierre. "Effects of Regular and Irregular Stimulation on the Electrodermal and Cardiac Auditory Response in Normal and Schizophrenic Subjects." Waterloo, 1980.

9170
Finkelstein, Richard Joseph. "The Relationship Between Distractibility and Language Behavior in Paranoid and Non-paranoid Schizophrenics." McGill, 1979.

9171
Graftieaux, Pierre-Ivan Charles. "Le concept de finiture et la perception de l'espace et du temps dans la schizophrénie." Montréal, 1981.

9172
Hellkamp, David T. "Extent of Psychological Differentiation Among Hospitalized Male Schizophrenics Classified Along the Process-Reactive and Delusional-Hallucinatory Dimensions." Ottawa, 1967.

9173
Jackson-Whaley, Iris Patricia. "Stimulus Structure and Schizophrenia." Waterloo, 1980.

9174
Klinka, Jan Antonin. "Hospitalized and Released Schizophrenic and Non-Psychiatric Subjects' Performance on Measures of Thought Disorder." British Columbia, 1981.

9175
McDowell, Gloria M. "The Reality of Psychological Distance in Chronic Schizophrenics." Ottawa, 1957.

9176
Meier, Augustine. "Ego Function Patterns Among Families of Schizophrenic and Neurotic Patients." Ottawa, 1982.

9177
Mook, Bertha. "Causal Thought in Schizophrenic Children." Ottawa, 1967.

9178
Nivoli, Gian Carlo. "Le schizophrène meurtrier." Montréal, 1975. [Philippe Pinel Institute in Montreal/Institut Philippe Pinel de Montréal]

9179
Oczkowski, Gene. "The Effects of the A-B Tolerance of Ambiguity, and Attachment Therapist Variables Upon Reactions to the Schizophrenic Patient." Manitoba, 1982.

9180
Palchanis, A.-Eugène. "Overinclusion and Divergent Thinking in Schizophrenics." Ottawa, 1966.

9181
Proud, Donald W. "A Comparison of Conceptual Ability in Reactive and Process Schizophrenics." Ottawa, 1964.

9182
Putterman, Allan Howard. "Referential Speaker Processes in Process-Reactive Schizophrenia." York, 1973.

9183
Robertson, Roberta Gail. "Memory Attributes in Schizophrenia." Manitoba, 1978.

9184
Schneider, Richard Delmont. "Reaction Time in Schizophrenics and Normals." Calgary, 1979.

9185
Shulof, Victoria. "Étude comparative de la sexualité chez les déprimés, les schizophrènes et les employés hospitaliers." Montréal, 1980.

9186
Sperrazzo, Gerald. "Convergent Thinking in Schizophrenic Patients." Ottawa, 1966.

Depression/Dépression

9187
Colby, Catherine Ann. "Memory Deficit in Moderately Depressed University Students." Western Ontario, 1982.

9188
Cole, Ester. "Role-Playing as a Modality for Alleviating Depressive Symptoms in 10-12 Year Old Children." Toronto, 1979.

9189
Derry, Paul Allan. "The Self as a Content-Specific Schema for the Processing of Personal Information in Clinical Depression." Western Ontario, 1981.

Devins, Gerald Michael. See No./Voir no 8982

9190
Giles, Donna Elaine. "A Test of the Cognitive Triad in Beck's Cognitive Theory of Depression." Western Ontario, 1982.

9191
Gotlieb, Ian Henry. "Self Monitoring, Self-Evaluation, and Self-Reinforcement in Depressed and Non-Depressed Psychiatric Patients: An Investigation of a Self-Control Model of Depression." Waterloo, 1981.

9192
Johnson, Olive Skene. "An Investigation of Some Neuropsychological Cognitive and Behavioral Aspects of Depression." British Columbia, 1980.

9193
Miller, Barbara. "The Effects of Bilateral and Unilateral Electroconvulsive Therapy (ECT) on Non-Verbal Memory for Depressed Psychiatric Patients." McGill, 1973.

9194
Moreau, Margaret Ellen. "The Effectiveness of Jogging as a Treatment for Depression." Simon Fraser, 1981. [48 housewives/48 ménagères]

9195
Morris, Norman Edward. "A Group Self-Instruction Method for the Treatment of Depressed Outpatients." Toronto, 1975.

9196
Mothersill, Kerry James. "Probability Learning and Coping in Depression and Obsessive Compulsiveness." Western Ontario, 1980.

9197
Moyal, Barbara Ruth Roback. "The Identification of Depressive Children." Toronto, 1980.

9198
Pellegrini, Wayne L. "Critical Life Events, Irrational Beliefs and Locus of Control as Components of Steady State Depression." Ottawa, 1979.

Porter, Carol Anne. See No./Voir no 9051

Pye, Carol Jean. See No./Voir no 6724

9199
Shenker, Leonard J. "Selective Attention to Dysphoric Stimuli by Depressed and Nondepressed Individuals." McGill, 1981.

Shulof, Victoria. See No./Voir no 9185

9200
Southmayd, Stephen Eric. "Sleep Deprivation in the Treatment of Depressive Illness: Outcome of Controlled Single Case Studies." Queen's, 1982.

9201
Sugrue, Dennis Patrick. "The State of the Bereaved Ego: An Examination of Conjugual Bereavement in Light of Bibring's Hypothesized Mechanism of Depression." Windsor, 1981.

9202
Tam, Chung-Ngoh Isaac. "Learned Helplessness and Reactive Depression." Alberta, 1980. [Depressed college students/Collégiens déprimés]

9203
Watson, Graham Martin Wallett. "Depressive Attributional Style in Psychiatric Inpatients and Undergraduates: Effects of Reinforcement Level and Assessment Procedure." Manitoba, 1983.

Homosexuality: Lesbianism, Transsexualism/ Homosexualité: lesbianisme et transsexualité

9204
Clark, Thomas R. "Homosexuality as a Criterion Predictor of Psychopathology and Emotional Adjustment in Non-Patient Males Expressing Varying Degrees of Homosexual Behavior and Preference as Compared to Exclusively Heterosexual Males." Windsor, 1972.

9205
Elliot, Phyllis E. "Lesbian Identity and Self-Disclosure." Windsor, 1981.

9206
Schneider, Margaret Shari. "An Investigation of the Coming Out Process Lifestyle, and Sex-Role Orientation of Lesbians." York, 1983.

9207
Tuthill, Robert Joseph. "A Clinical Study of the Psychology of Male Transsexualism." Toronto, 1978.

Weight: Loss of, Obesity and Anorexia nervosa/ Perte de poids, obésité et anorexie

Ansley, Sylvia. See No./Voir no 4056
Arlette, Christine. See No./Voir no 6690
Asarnow, Joan. See No./Voir no 3050

9208
Aves, Penelope Jill. "Effects of Response Habits on the Performance of Obese, Average and Fluctuator Subjects." British Columbia, 1976.

9209
Baron, Pierre. "Self-Monitoring Efficacy for Weight Loss as a Function of Goal-Setting and Monitoring Unit." Ottawa, 1979.
Belton, Gerald. See No./Voir no 9502

9210
Bernier, Michel. "Validation du construit des attentes d'efficacité dans le cadre d'un traitement behavioral de l'obésité." Montréal, 1982.
Berry, Richard. See No./Voir no 9327
Borrie, Roderick Allen. See No./Voir no 9647
Breitman, Kenneth E. See No./Voir no 9117
Burke, Harley. See No./Voir no 3802
Buser, Mary M. See No./Voir no 9652
Christopher, Doris. See No./Voir no 9431
Cieply, Alfred. See No./Voir no 1123
Dixon, Charles. See No./Voir no 6772
Doherty, Gillian. See No./Voir no 3810
Elias, John. See No./Voir no 3812

9211
Elterman, Michael Frank. "The Effects of Assertion Training and Husband Involvement in the Behavioral Treatment of Obesity." Queen's, 1981.
Finlayson, Gregor. See No./Voir no 8990
Fryatt, Maurice. See No./Voir no 9438

9212
Garner, David Marshall. "Perceptual/Conceptual Disturbances in Anorexia nervosa and Obesity." York, 1975.
Hansen, Christine. See No./Voir no 9687
Hardie, Nena. See No./Voir no 6777
Howard, Louis. See No./Voir no 10260
Hunt, Larry. See No./Voir no 6799
Janzen, Henry. See No./Voir no 3683
Kaplan, Faith. See No./Voir no 3095

9213
Katz-Mendelson, Beverley. "The Development of Self-Body Image in Overweight Youngsters." Concordia, 1982.
Klemplatz, Morrie. See No./Voir no 9624
Krichev, Alan. See No./Voir no 9450
Lescheld, Alan. See No./Voir no 10265
Mark, Devon Joy. See No./Voir no 9309
Martin, Thomas. See No./Voir no 6925
McRae, Bradley. See No./Voir no 9312
Mendelson, Beverley K. See No./Voir no 9560
Nicholl, George. See No./Voir no 3253
Oxman, Joel. See No./Voir no 3925

9214
Pearce, John Walter. "The Role of Spouse Involvement in the Behavioral Treatment of Overweight Women." Manitoba, 1980.
Pezzot-Pearce, Terry Diane. See No./Voir no 9145
Picard-Gerber, Marilen. See No./Voir no 3939
Porter, James. See No./Voir no 3790
Rabie-Azoory, Vera. See No./Voir no 9631
Ralph, Diana. See No./Voir no 8932
Ramer, Donald. See No./Voir no 6872
Ramsay, Richard. See No./Voir no 6767
Ratner, Dennis. See No./Voir no 6726
Rendle, Gary. See No./Voir no 9317
Richard, Marc-André. See No./Voir no 9147
Sanchez-Craig, B. See No./Voir no 3514
Sarwar, Kaiserrudlin. See No./Voir no 9572
Shady, Gary. See No./Voir no 6930
Smiley, Wesley. See No./Voir no 10274
Smith, Trevor V.G. See No./Voir no 8943
Smyth, Frances. See No./Voir no 3702

9215
Stuckler-Gropper, Anna Sophia. "External Cues and Eating Behaviour in Anorexia nervosa." York, 1982.

Sweeney, James. See No./Voir no 3140

Théroux, Charles Paul-Émile. See No./Voir no 9108

Thomas, Paul. See No./Voir no 4077

Thompson, Lynda. See No./Voir no 3893

Trigg, Linda. See No./Voir no 3270

Verniero, Sharon. See No./Voir no 3713

Walker, John R. See No./Voir no 4203

Weinberger, Alex. See No./Voir no 3277

White, Ronald. See No./Voir no 9409

Wood, H. Diane. See No./Voir no 3078

Yates, Elizabeth. See No./Voir no 9232

Zarb, Janet. See No./Voir no 10277

SEX IN PSYCHOLOGY/SEXE EN PSYCHOLOGIE

9216
Ain, Marilyn. "The Effects of Stimulus Novelty on Viewing Time and Processing Efficiency of Hyperactive Children." McGill, 1981.

Aitchison, Douglas Wayne. See No./Voir no 9636

Amin, Shukri. See No./Voir no 9638

Bontrager-Lehman, Carol. See No./Voir no 6757

9217
Brickman, Julian Ruth Rogers. "Erotica: Sex Differences in Stimulus Preferences and Fantasy Content." Manitoba, 1978. [272 male and 272 female undergraduate psychology students/272 étudiants et 272 étudiantes de premier cycle en psychologie]

9218
Cardillo, Ralph Michael. "Evaluation of Sexual Morality Regarding Responsible Engaged Couples." Ottawa, 1969.

Clark, Thomas R. See No./Voir no 9204

9219
Courey, Linda Susan. "The Role of Genital Vasocongestive Changes in the Labelling of Sexual Arousal in Women." Concordia, 1981.

Desjardins, Jean-Yves. See No./Voir no 9662

Earls, Christopher Michael. See No./Voir no 9517

Harris, Ronald George. See No./Voir no 9237

9220
Henderson, Jule Ann. "The Content of Women's Reported Sexual Fantasies as a Function of Personality and Sex Guilt." Manitoba, 1982.

Lafortune, Mireille. See No./Voir no 9704

LaMothe, D.M. See No./Voir no 9708

9221
Lange, James Dubois. "Impotence: An Analogue Experimnt of its Causes and Treatment." Dalhousie, 1979.

Lazerson, Judith S. See No./Voir no 9094

Loughner-Gillin, Cheryl. See No./Voir no 9138

9222
Mainemer, Nathan. "Sex-Role Expectations in Intimate Relationships: A Multi-Staged Empirical Investigation." Regina, 1982.

9223
Miles, J.J. "The Effect of Behavioral Self-Management Treatments on Nonorgasmic Women without Partners." Calgary, 1981.

9224
Nemetz, Georgia Helen. "Time-Limited Sex Therapy for Couples: A Controlled Evaluation of Group and Individual Couple Intervention." British Columbia, 1981.

9225
Pencer, Irwin. "Personal Space: The Effects of Sex Role, Sex, and Status on Distancing Behaviour." Ottawa, 1981.

Perrault, Yvonne L. See No./Voir no 3510

9226
Piccolo, Ornella. "Menstrual-Cycle Distress: A Study of Its Relation to Feminine Identity and Sexual Inhibitions." Windsor, 1981.

9227
Record, Stephen A. "Personality, Sexual Attitudes and Behaviour of Sex Offenders." Queen's, 1977.

9228
Ridley, Clifford Keith. "Inhibitory Aspects of Sex Guilt, Social Censure and Need for Approval." Manitoba, 1976. [University students/Étudiants universitaires]

Sinclair, Carole Mary Jane. See No./Voir no 9063

9229
Stermac, Lana Elizabeth. "The Social Competence of Incarcerated Sex Assaulters." Toronto, 1982.

9230
Tudiver, Judith Gail. "Parents and the Sex Role Development of the Child." Western Ontario, 1980. [Boys and girls of nursery school age/Garçons et filles d'âge pré-scolaire]

Tuthill, Robert J. See No./Voir no 9207

Williams, Sharon M. See No./Voir no 7889

Woodward, James. See No./Voir no 9483

9231
Wydra, Alina E. "Control of Sexual Arousal and Discrimination Between Cues of Rapists and Non Rapists." Queen's, 1981.

9232
Yates, Elizabeth Prewitt. "'Anger' Evoked by Insult and Disinhibition of Sexual Arousal to Rape Cues." Queen's, 1980.

PHYSIOLOGICAL PSYCHOLOGY/ PSYCHOLOGIE PHYSIOLOGIQUE

Bradley, Michael Timothy. See No./Voir no 8900

9233
Brodsky, Patricia Aline. "A Construct Validation Study of Piaget's Equilibration Process." Manitoba, 1981. [57 nursery and kindergarten children/57 enfants de garderie et de maternelle]

9234
Brown, Juele Marie. "Imaginal Coping Strategies in the Treatment of Migraine." Carleton, 1982. [75 university students/75 étudiants universitaires]

Courey, Linda Susan. See No./Voir no 9219

9235
Finegan, Jo-Anne Kathryn. "The Influence of Genetic Amniocentesis on Obstetric Outcome and Neonatal Behaviour." York, 1983.

9236
Gendron, Carole. "Différences individuelles et rétroaction dans le contrôle volontaire de l'accélération du rythme cardiaque." Montréal, 1983.

9237
Harris, Ronald George. "Relationships Among Human Vaginal Blood Volume, Pulse Pressure, and Self-Report of Arousal As a Function of Erotic Stimulation." McGill, 1981.

9238
Heslegrave, Ronald James. "A Psychophysiological Analysis of the Detection of Deception: The Role of Information, Retrieval, Novelty and Conflict Mechanisms." Toronto, 1982.

9239
Hewchuk, Eugene William. "Semantic and Phonetic Generalization of the Orienting Response to Aurally Presented Word Stimuli." Regina, 1981.

9240
Hiatt, Gina Jaccarino. "Impairment of Cognitive Organization in Patients with Temporal-Lobe Lesions." McGill, 1978.

Latimer, Paul Ross. See No./Voir no 6846

9241
Provost, Marc-André. "Les fluctuations de la fréquence cardiaque des enfants de 9-12 mois en fonction des émotions spécifiques manifestées lors de situations naturelles." Montréal, 1975.

Schultz, Katherine Joyce. See No./Voir no 8939

9242
Sherwin, Barbara B. "Effects of Estrogen and Androgen on Somatic, Affective, Sexual and Cognitive Functioning in Hysterectomized and Oophorectomized Women." Concorda, 1983.

9243
Slingsby, Judith Marion. "Factors Affecting Urinary Excretion of Arylalhylamines in a Randomly Selected Psychiatric Population." Saskatchewan, 1975.

9244
Snow, William Garfield. "The Physiological and Subjective Effects of Several Brief Relaxation Training Procedures." York, 1977. [Female college students/Étudiantes de collège]

9245
Stam, Henderikus Johannes. "Hypnotic Analgesia and the Placebo Effect: Controlling Ischemic Pain." Carleton, 1982.

9246
Taenzer, Paul. "Self-Control of Post-Operative Pain: Effects of Hypnosis and Waking Suggestion." McGill, 1983.

9247
Valley, Victoria. "Performance Impairment in Relation to Concomitant Physiological Vigilance Levels and Subjective States in Patients with Narcolepsy Compared to Matched Controls." Ottawa, 1981.

ALCOHOLISM AND ALCOHOLICS/ ALCOOLISME ET ALCOOLIQUES

9248
Barnes, Gordon E. "The Clinical Alcoholic Personality." York, 1977.

9249
Brochu, Serge. "Lieu du contrôle et niveau d'anxiété des alcooliques en cours de traitement." Montréal, 1982.

9250
Brown, Melvin Douglas. "The Effectiveness of Personality Dimensions of Dependency, Power and Internal-External Locus of Control in Differentiating Among Unremitted and Remitted Alcoholics and Non-Alcoholic Controls." Windsor, 1975.

Burtt, Brian Irvine. See No./Voir no 8970

9251
Condra, Michael St. John. "The Effectiveness of Training in Relapse-Prevention Skills in the Treatment of Alcohol Problems." Queen's, 1982.

9252
Cormier, Roger Bernard. "Effects of Training on Alcoholic Clients' Self Disclosure in Group Counselling." Alberta, 1978.

9253
DiTecco, Donald Anthony. "A Social-Psychological Investigation of Alcohol Use Among Young Adult Males." Waterloo, 1981.

Ferrier, William K. See No./Voir no 6737

9254
Fleiger, David Lorenzo. "Covert Sensitization Treatment with Alcoholics." Alberta, 1972.

Galloway, William Robert. See No./Voir no 8913

9255
Gibbins, Robert John. "Parental Attitudes Toward Drinking and the Prevalence and Character of Filial Alcoholism." Toronto, 1962.

9256
Giesbrecht, Norman Abe. "Changes in the Drinking Patterns of Skid Row Alcoholics: A Study in the Sociology of the Normalization of the Deviants." Toronto, 1980.

9257
Goldenthal, Lyn M. "Personality Characteristics of Alcoholics in a Religious Treatment." Windsor, 1981.

Goulet, Robert John. See No./Voir no 6738

9258
Greenwood, Donald Eric. "Aversive Conditioning with Alcoholics: A Comparison of Instrumental and Classical Paradigms and a Validational Study." York, 1974.

9259
Grey, Pauline Margaret. "An Evaluation of Industrial Programming for Alcohol Problems." York, 1981.

9260
Larkin, Edward James. "Voluntary Termination of Out-Patient Treatment by Alcoholics." York, 1972.

9261
Lightfoot, Lynn O. "Behavioural Tolerance to Low Doses of Alcohol in Social Drinkers." Waterloo, 1980.

9262
Macdonald, Grant. "The Role of Personal Networks in the Recovery from Alcoholism." Toronto, 1982.

9263
Mann, Robert Ernest. "Studies of Behavioural Tolerance to Alcohol in Male Social Drinkers." Waterloo, 1981.

Martini, Janie Lilia. See No./Voir no 9140

9264
McKirnan, David James. "A Community Approach to the Primary Identification of Alcohol Abuse." McGill, 1978.

9265

McLatchie, Brian Hugh. "Expectancy Manipulation and Pseudoconditioning in Aversive Conditioning Therapy with Alcoholics." York, 1975.

9266

Mottin, James Leon. "Drug-Induced Attenuation of Alcohol Consumption: Effects of Trihexyphenidyl Hydrochloride on Schedule-Induced Alcohol Polydipsia." York, 1972.

9267

Newman, Albert F. "Alcoholism in Frontenac County: A Survey of the Characteristics of an Alcoholic Population in Its Native Habitat." Queen's, 1966.

9268

Poizner, Sonja. "Some Effects of Cannabis and Alcohol Intoxication on Moral Judgements." York, 1973.

Poudrier, Lucien Mark. See No./Voir no 4074

Riediger, Alfred J. See No./Voir no 2193

9269

Rossi, Jean J. "A Process Analysis of Three Types of Group Psychotherapy with Hospitalized Alcoholics." Ottawa, 1957.

Slatterie, Elinor Faith. See No./Voir no 9065

Smith, Archibald Ian. See No./Voir no 1957

9270

Staples, Edward A. "Blood Alcohol Concentration Discrimination in Male Alcoholics." Waterloo, 1977. [Rosewood Sanatorium, Guelph/Sanatorium Rosewood, Guelph]

9271

Teare, Jane Lake. "An Evaluation of Changes in Alcoholic Patients Following Three Different Treatments." Toronto, 1976.

9272

Viguie, Francis. "Niveau de différenciation psychologique d'une population alcoolique classée selon le continuum essentiel-réactionnel." Ottawa, 1971.

Wahn, Michael Brian. See No./Voir no 1194

9273

Walker, Keith Donald. "Covert Sensitization and Problem-Solving Therapies in the Modification of Drinking Tendencies." Toronto, 1979. [Toronto halfway house/Maison à Toronto]

9274

West, Peter Templar. "Three Modes of Training Alcoholics in Interpersonal Communication Skills: A Comparative Study." Western Ontario, 1979.

9275

Young, James Albert. "Alcohol Consumption and Response: Effects of the Cognitive Context." McGill, 1981.

9276

Zeichner, Amos. "Alcohol and Aggression: The Role of Behavior Contingencies and Instigator Intent." McGill, 1978.

See also Psychology Guidance and Counselling/Voir aussi Psychologie: conduite et counselling

9277

Adam-Carrière, Dyane. "Efficacité d'un nouveau programme d'enrichissement conjugual à rencontre ses objectifs à intermédiaire, à court et à long terme." Ottawa, 1980.

Adsett, Nancy Leigh. See No./Voir no 9635

9278

Booth, John Alexander Gordon. "Client/Counselor Similarity, Mutual Dogmatism and Client Perceptions of Prison Counseling." Alberta, 1978.

9279

Bourbonnais, Yvon. "An Innovative Approach for Training Beginning Counselors and a Definition of Good Interviewer Behaviour." Regina, 1981.

9280

Brewster, Linda Joan. "Counsellor-Trainee Attribute and Acquisition of Counselor Skills." York, 1978.

9281

Brown, Douglas D. "Directive Parental Counselling: An Appraisal of Its Effects on Extra-Conditioning Variables." Windsor, 1975.

9282

Capelle, Ronald Gordon. "The Effects of Systematic Counsellor Training Versus Counselling Instruction on Counsellor-Focused and Client-Focused Criteria." York, 1976.

9283

Chislett, Lise Perrier. "Congruence, Consistency and Differentiation of Career Interest: A Study of Construct Validity and Relationships with Achievement, Satisfaction and Personality Adjustment." Ottawa, 1978.

Chiu, Clifton Ya-Lam. See No./Voir no 4178

9284

Cooper, Christopher Michael. "Effects and Noneffects of Self-Instructional Therapy and Skills Training in the Treatment of Public Speaking Anxiety." Queen's, 1978.

Cormier, Roger Bernard. See No./Voir no 9252

9285

Coupal, Michel. "Étude des facteurs qui influencent les rôles d'expert et de facilitateur du consultant externe." Montréal, 1975.

9286

Davis, Gerald Albert. "Anger Arousal in Child Abuse Counselling: An Experimental Evaluation of Systematic Desensitization and Cognitive Self-Control Training." McGill, 1982.

9287

Davis, Melvin Peter. "Psychology of Power and Its Relationship to Counselling." Alberta, 1979.

9288

Farquhar, Marcia Fay. "Applicant Expectations About Homes for the Aged and the Need for Preadmission Counseling." York, 1974. [Female applicants to three homes for the aged/Candidates de 3 foyers pour les gens agés]

9289

Fellbaum, George Anthony. "Directive Parental Counseling: Setting, Sibling, Behavioural, Reinforcing Agent, and Temporal Generality." Windsor, 1978.

9290
Ferguson, Tamara Jocelyn. "Actor-Observer Differences in Causal Attribution and Sanctioning Evaluation." Alberta, 1980.

9291
Feigehen, Sandra Louise. "First Impressions: Their Formation and Implications for Interpersonal Processes in Counseling." Toronto, 1980.

9292
Ford, Gary R. "Immediacy, the 'Core Conditions' and Communications Training: An Exploration of Interrelationships." Alberta, 1978.

Franklin, Donald Robert. See No./Voir no 9599

Franzoni, Edward Matthew. See No./Voir no 4434

9293
Fulgenzi, Janet Marie. "Stimulus and Response Generalization Effects of the Directive Parental Counseling Program." Windsor, 1978.

9294
Gingras, Marie. "Enrichissement conjugal: la contribution de variables de processus à un nouveau programme." Ottawa, 1980.

Glaze, Avis Elane. See No./Voir no 4182

9295
Hamel, Claude. "Vers une définition opérationnelle du concept de valeur du travail: synthèse théorique et application pratique en milieu québécois." Montréal, 1974.

Hearn, Margaret Therese. See No./Voir no 4164

9296
Hindmarch, Brian. "Differential Client Perceptions of Lay vs. Professional Counsellors." Alberta, 1977.

9297
Hlasny, Robert G. "The Effects of Simulated Client-Psychotherapist Value Similarity and Therapist Nonpossessive Warmth in Client Trust and Attribution of Therapeutic Effectiveness." Ottawa, 1979.

9298
Horvath, Adam O. "An Exploratory Study of the Working Alliance: Its Measurement and Relationship to Therapy Outcome." British Columbia, 1981.

Howard, Louis Wayne. See No./Voir no 10260

Hum, Andrew. See No./Voir no 4165

Hundleby, Sigrid Anne. See No./Voir no 3227

Hunt, Larry Ralph. See No./Voir no 6799

9299
Hyde, Naida Denise Dyer. "Directive Parental Counselling: An Empirical Study." Windsor, 1975.

Kennedy, William J. See No./Voir no 9487

9300
Kimmis, Richard Clark. "The Effects of Evaluation on Required Counselling Interviews." Alberta, 1976. [University of Alberta students/Étudiants de l'Université de l'Alberta]

9301
Klassen, Daniel. "An Empirical Investigation of the Rogerian Counselling Conditions and Locus of Control." Ottawa, 1979.

Klug, Leo F. See No./Voir no 4148

Koziev, Roberta Louise. See No./Voir no 9448

9302
Kovitz, Karen Elizabeth. "A Multidimensional Approach to the Analysis of Marital Functioning: Multimethod Assessment, Production and Description." Calgary, 1980.

9303
Leckett, Walter. "A Comparison of Three Training Approaches, Audio-Training, Role-Playing, and Micro-Training, in the Administration of Empathic Understanding, on Self-Exploration and Perceived Empathy." Ottawa, 1976.

9304
Lefroy, Donald A.L. "Differences on Psychological Measures Related to Military Attrition." McGill, 1981.

9305
Liburd, Rosemary. "Facing Change: Relationships Between Styles of Living and Styles of Dying." Alberta, 1980.

Loughner-Gillin, Cheryl. See No./Voir no 9138

9306
Luedecke, Barbara Mary. "Some Aspects of Interpersonal Influence on Candidate Assessment in an Applied Setting." York, 1978.

9307
Malik, Hargulshan Singh. "The Relationship of Career Decision Making Ability to Personality, Socio-Economic Status and Vocational Maturity." Alberta, 1971.

9308
Mann, Brenda Lynn. "Assertiveness Training as a Facilitation to Client Self-Disclosure." Alberta, 1980. [40 women in Edmonton/40 femmes d'Edmonton]

9309
Mark, Devon Joy. "Change and the Overweight Game." Alberta, 1979.

Marshall, Elizabeth Anne. See No./Voir no 4150

McAndrew, Joan Kathleen. See No./Voir no 4151

9310
McLean, Mona Marie. "The Differential Effects of Three Training Programs on Attained Levels of Facilitative Conditions: Empathy, Warmth and Genuineness." Toronto, 1979.

9311
McMahon, James H. "Some General and Specific Counseling Observations Obtained from Surveys and Studies of Selected Groups of Hearing Impaired Persons." Montréal, 1978.

9312
McRae, Bradley Collins. "A Comparison for a Behavioral and a Lecture-Discussion Approach to Pre-Marital Counselling." British Columbia, 1975. [Pastoral Institute of British Columbia and Burnaby Family Life Institute/L'institut pastoral de la Colombie-Britannique et l'institut de vie familiale de Burnaby]

9313
Mendonca, James Dominic. "Effectiveness of Problem-Solving and Anxiety Management Training in Modifying Vocational Indecision." Western Ontario, 1974.

9314
Meuser, Peter Eric. "Personal, Vocational and Non-Counselees Compared in Terms of Holland's Person ality Typology and Related Pattern Characteristics of Consistence and Differentiation." Ottawa, 1978.

Minor, N. Kathleen Mary. See No./Voir no 4167

9315
Moses, Barbara Beryl. "How Type A and Type B Men Experience Evaluation in the Work Place." Toronto, 1982. [72 male professionals working for a major corporation/72 professionnels travaillant dans de grandes corporations]

9316
Napier, Robert E. "Counselor Development: Longitudinal Study of the Association Between Trainee Effectiveness and Supervisory Relationship." Ottawa, 1979.

9317
Noonan, Barrie Albert. "Toward an Existential Approach to Therapy with Women." Alberta, 1980.

Piché, Louise. See No./Voir no 2078

9318
Pitsel, Patricia Lynne. "Career Decision-Making for Adults." Calgary, 1980. [Development and evaluation of a career decision-making program for adults/Mise sur pied et évaluation d'un programme de prise de décision de carrière pour adultes]

Potvin, Robert John Michael. See No./Voir no 4418

Pugh, George MacLaggan. See No./voir no 8931

9319
Rendle, Gary Alan. "The Proxemic Behaviour of Clients in Relation to Their Perception of the Therapeutic Relationship and Introversion-Extraversion." Ottawa, 1976.

9320
Richardson, Barbara Joan. "The Role of Cognition in Micro-counselling." Western Ontario, 1979. [45 female undergraduate psychology majors/45 étudiantes de premier cycle en psychologie]

9321
Russell, Mary. "Microteaching Feminist Counselling Skills: An Evaluation." Simon Fraser, 1982.

Ryant, Joseph Charles. See No./Voir no 2080

9322
Schner, Joseph George. "An Investigation of Effective Modes of Preparation for an Inter-Personal Coping Skills Program." Toronto, 1978.

Skarsten, Steinar Stan. See No./Voir no 10200

Smith, Douglas Lane. See No./Voir no 9066

Spricer, Rosa. See No./Voir no 9476

Stein, Marsha L. See No./Voir no 9578

9323
Telka, Eugene. "The Effects of Client Concern Intensity and Counselor Experience Level on Perceived Counselor Credibility." Ottawa, 1980.

9324
Teta, Diana C. "The Effect of the Counselor's Intolerance on the Expressed Level of Empathy Under Varying Conditions of Ethnicity." Ottawa, 1976.

9325
Tucker, David Harold. "Attributions for Success and Failure in the Employment Interview." Waterloo, 1979.

Usher, Bryan Robert. See No./Voir no 4170

Van der Kraben, Jacobus Johannes Maria. See No./Voir no 10107

Werth, Elizabeth Marie. See No./Voir no 9151

DEVELOPMENTAL PSYCHOLOGY/ PSYCHOLOGIE DU DÉVELOPPEMENT

Infancy/Enfance

9326
Barrera, Maria Eugenia Caraza. "Face Perception and Memory in the Three-Month-Old Infant." McMaster, 1979.

9327
Berry, Richard Edwin. "The Relationship Between Infant Temperament and the Organizational Pattern of Infant-Mother Attachment Behavior." York, 1980.

9328
Bull, Dale Harold. "Infants' Visual Tracking of Sights and Sounds." Toronto, 1982.

9329
Chang, Hsing-Wu. "Infants' Processing of Auditory Patterns." Toronto, 1978.

9330
Cook, Donald Baird. "An Exploratory Study of the Effects of Maternal Personality and Language Style Upon Mother-Infant Interaction." Toronto, 1980.

9331
Creighton, Dianne E. "An Investigation of Three Measures of Infant Cognitive Development and Their Relationships to Early Home Environmental and Material Stimulation Variables." Queen's, 1980.

9332
Darquenne-Brossard, Martine. "Les effets de trois programmes de stimulation socio-affectives et perceptives sur le développement d'enfants de deux à six mois placés en institution." Montréal, 1979.

Duchesne, Hermann. See No./Voir no 3020

9333
Goldman, Barbara Davis. "Transfer of Contingency Awareness in Six-Month-Old Infants." Waterloo, 1980.

Gyra, John C. See No./Voir no 9004

9334
Harris, Leonard Stephen. "Object Search and the Object Concept in Eight Month Old Infants." Queen's, 1980.

9335
Humphrey, Gary Keith. "Auditory-Visual Integration of Temporal Relations in Infants." British Columbia, 1980.

9336
Hunter, Michael Arthur. "The Effect of Stimulus Complexity and Amount of Familiarization on Infants' Preference for Novel and Familiar Stimuli." Simon Fraser, 1981.

9337
José, Teresito Adolfo. "Mother Infant Interaction: A Functional Analysis of Communicative Behavior." Alberta, 1980.

9338
Kasman, Entus Anne. "Hemispheric Asymmetry in Infants." McGill, 1978.

9339
Keith, Eileen Patrick. "Imitation in Infancy." Toronto, 1980.

9340
Landy, Sarah Edith. "An Investigation of Teenage Mothers, Their Infants and the Resulting Mother-Infant Dyads." Regina, 1982.

9341
Lewis, Terri Lorraine. "The Development of Nasal Field Detection in Young Infants." McMaster, 1980.

9342
Long, Beverly Jean. "Early Thought and Language." Toronto, 1979. [From three to 30 months old/De 3 à 30 mois]

9343
Magidson, Ethel. "The Differential Effects of Varied Stimulation on Three Aspects of Motor Development in Institutionalized Infants." Montréal, 1978.

9344
Oviatt, Sharon Lynn. "The Development of Language Comprehension in Infancy." Toronto, 1979.

9345
Pain, Kerrie Susan. "The Effects of Temperament on Mother-Infant Interactions." Alberta, 1980.

9346
Pinkus, Joan. "A Prospective Study of Relationships Between Prenatal Maternal Parameters and Early Infant Development." Toronto, 1977.

9347
Raeburn, John Maxwell. "Infant Sleep, a Methodological and Descriptive Study." Queen's, 1969.

9348
Sinclair, Mark Lanham. "Antecedents of Imitation in Infancy: Facilitation and Inhibition of Motor Behavior." Queen's, 1980.

9349
Young, Gerald. "The Expression of Distress and Anger in Nine-Month-Old and Twelve-Month-Old Infants." Montréal, 1974.

9350
Zucker, Kenneth Jay. "The Development of Search for Mother During Brief Separation." Toronto, 1982. [From seven to ten months old/De 7 à 10 mois]

Child Psychology/Psychologie de l'enfance

9351
Anderson, Allen. "A Study of Cerebral Dominance in Children at 3 Age Intelligence Levels." Ottawa, 1978.

9352
Amend, Dexter Roland. "Propositional Logic, Conservation and Transitivity in Six to Nine Year Olds." Alberta, 1975.

9353
Arena, Francesco. "Aspects du développement de l'interaction dyadique non-verbale chez des enfants de trois à six ans." Montréal, 1980.

Asarnow, Joan. See No./Voir no 3050

Baker, Lois Josephine. See No./Voir no 3016

Bigelow, Ann. See No./Voir no 9620

9354
Birnbaum, Dana Wolfe. "Preschooler's Stereotypes About Sex Differences in Emotionality: An Investigation of Possible Etiologies." Carleton, 1979.

Bolus, Charles. See No./Voir no 3913

Bonta, James L. See No./Voir no 3921

Burstein, Samuel. See No./Voir no 3071

9355
Burtis, Paul Judson. "A Study of the Development of Short-Term Memory in Children." York, 1977.

Canning, Patricia M. See No./Voir no 3004

9356
Coady, Henry. "Behavioral Correlates of Moral Judgement." Ottawa, 1971.

9357
Coron, David. "Influence of Sex of Experimenter on Assessment of Gender Identity in Preadolescent Children." Ottawa, 1979.

9358
Cyr, Francine. "Vulnérabilité de l'enfant d'âge scolaire à la séparation de ses parents." Montréal, 1982.

Dart, Richard James. See No./Voir no 6832

9359
Derry, Suzanne M. "An Empirical Investigation of the Concept of Death in Children." Ottawa, 1980.

9360
Dubic, Benoit. "Processus de mise en forme d'un dessin chez les enfants de maternelle, de quatrième et de sixième années." Montréal, 1982.

9361
Dubois, René. "Évolution d'idée de mort chez des enfants de maternelle, de deuxième et de cinquième année scolaire." Montréal, 1974.

9362
Durbach, Edna. "The Role of the Mother in Promoting Toddler Friendship." Toronto, 1982.

9363
Durocher, Louise. "Observation du comportement socio-affectif de l'enfant de maternelle en milieu défavorisé." Montréal, 1976.

9364
Emmott, Shelagh Deirdre. "The Influence of Parenting Style on Sex Differences in Perceptual-Cognitive Abilities (Field-Dependence/Independence) Among 10-Year-Old Children." York, 1983.

9365
Esses, Lillian Marlene. "The Young Child's Perception of Duration." McGill, 1978.

9366
Evans, Mary Ann. "Children's Explanations of Childhood Games: A Study in Communicative Development." Waterloo, 1980.

Fish, James. See No./Voir no 2972

Forrest, Donna. See No./Voir no 3953

9367
Fortin, Raymond. "La génèse de la conscience de soi et les réactions à l'image spéculaire chez l'enfant de 14 à 32 mois." Montréal, 1983.

Fradkin, Barbara. See No./Voir no 3093

9368
Gadoua, Gilles. "La relation du fonctionnement analytique avec l'intelligence, l'expression de l'image corporelle, la pensée opératoire concrète et la personnalité chez des enfants de 6 à 9 ans." Montréal, 1976.

Gignac, Leonard Joseph. See No./Voir no 3214

9369
Girard, Ghislain. "L'influence des attitudes parentales et d'autres variables intermédiaires sur la performance scolaire de l'enfant de 1ère et 4ième année." Montréal, 1980.

9370
Glasberg, Rhoda Elizabeth. "Children's Understanding of Sadness: A Developmental Approach." McGill, 1978.

Goldberg, Gerald. See No./Voir no 9681

Goodman, Doba. See No./Voir no 3215

Goodman, Sherryl Hope. See No./Voir no 3023

9371
Gorman, Maureen Catherine. "Children's Concepts of Death and Animistic Thinking." York, 1983.

Greckol, Sonja. See No./Voir no 3218

9372
Gutman, Gloria Margaret. "Balance and Agreement in Children's Social Perception." British Columbia, 1970.

Johnston, Nancy. See No./Voir no 3027

Kinkaide, Alexandra. See No./Voir no 3235

9373
Kobrick, Judi B. "Early Language Development as Related to Maternal Interaction and Communication Style." Toronto, 1977.

9374
Koch, W.J. "Maternal Command Role and Child Compliance." Alberta, 1981.

Krasnor, Linda Doreen Rose. See No./Voir no 3028

Kuchar, Eva. See No./Voir no 9547

9375
Kuzynski, Leon. "Reasoning with Children: Motivational Determinants of Children's Self-Control." Toronto, 1979.

9376
L'Allier-Sturgess, Louise. "Influence de medium et de la couleur sur les dessins d'enfants entre 8 et 11 ans d'âge chronique." Montréal, 1969.

9377
Levin, E.A. "Understanding Messages: The Production and Comprehension of Requests and Questions by Children." Waterloo, 1978.

Long, Beverly. See No./Voir no 9342

Mandel, Allan R. See No./Voir no 9113

9378
Maioni, T.L. "The Emergence of Symbolic Play in Young Children." Waterloo, 1978.

9379
Mamen, Margaret. "Cerebral Organization and Conceptual Development in Early Fluent Readers and Older Dyslexics." Carleton, 1981.

9380
Marcovitch, Sharon Fenton. "Maternal Stress and Mother-Child Interaction with the Developmentally Delayed Preschool Child." York, 1983.

Mason, Patricia. See No./Voir no 3971

9381
McDonald, Mary K. "The Development of Speech for Self and Role-Taking Ability in Aggressive and Non-aggressive Boys." Windsor, 1979. [Grades two/four and six/Deuxième, quatrième et sixième année]

McIlwraith, Robert D. See No./Voir no 1048

9382
Mendelson, R. "The Development of Children's Conceptions of Parent-Child and Friend-Friend Relationships." Queen's, 1983.

9383
Messier, Denise. "L'évolution de la motivation scolaire chez des enfants, de la maternelle à la troisième année." Montréal, 1982.

9384
Mongeon, Madeleine. "Vers une plus grande participation des mères à l'hospitalisation de leur enfant d'âge pré-scolaire: évaluation d'une intervention simple." Montréal, 1975.

9385
Morin, Lise. "Les interactions sociales de dominance chez les jumeaux identiques entre 18 et 24 mois." Montréal, 1979.

Moyal, Barbara. See No./Voir no 9197

9386
Nelson, Janice Edith. "Friendships in Childhood and Their Contribution to the Development of Social Knowledge." McGill, 1982.

O'Sullivan, Julia Therese. See No./Voir no 9565

9387
Painter, Susan Lee. "Maternal Adaptation in Parenthood in the Second Year." British Columbia, 1980.

9388
Pelland, Flore. "Viens vers le Père en regard des besoins psychologiques et des capacités de l'enfant de six ans." Ottawa, 1966.

9389
Pepler, Debra June. "The Effects of Play on Convergent and Divergent Problem Solving." Waterloo, 1979. [Three and four years old/3 et 4 ans]

9390
Perner, Josef. "The Development of Children's Understanding of Principles Governing Decisions under Risk or Uncertainty." Toronto, 1978.

9391
Pilon, Robert. "The Transition from Egocentric to Decentered Thought in the Coordination of Perspectives Task." Queen's, 1982. [From four to six and a half years olds/De 4 à 6 1/2 ans]

9392
Power, Marianita. "A Developmental Study of One Aspect of Moral Development and Its Relation to Psychosocial Development in Children." Alberta, 1974.

9393
Poznansky, Ellen. "The Effect of Parental Cognitive Styles and Locus of Control of the Moral Development of Children." Montréal, 1979.

Preston, Charles F. See No./Voir no 3015

9394
Priddle, Ruth E. "Psycho-Motor Development in Children." Waterloo, 1981.

9395
Reich, Lee Campbell. "Equivalence Concepts in Cross-Cultural Perspective: A Developmental Comparison of Eskimo and White Children." Harvard, 1969.

9396
Rigal, Robert A. "Le développement psychomoteur de l'enfant et ses relations avec les apprentissages scolaires." Montréal, 1976.

9397
Rotenberg, Kenneth Jesse. "The Development of Moral Judgment of Self and Other in Children." Western Ontario, 1979. [Kindergarten, grades two to grade four/Maternelle, deuxième et quatrième année]

9398
Russell, Cristine Louise. "The Development of Symbolic Play from Ages One to Three: A Longitudinal Study of Mother-Child Play Interaction." Simon Fraser, 1982.

9399
Saxby, Lorie Nelson. "Hemispheric Specialization for Emotion in Children." Waterloo, 1983.

Schneider, Barry Howard. See No./Voir no 3100

Segal, Melvyn. See No./Voir no 3033

9400
Sheehan, Teresa Danula. "Children's Originality and Dependence and Their Relation to Parental Control and Affect." Waterloo, 1982.

9401
Sreenivasan, Uma. "A Study of Effeminate Behaviour in Boys." Memorial University of Newfoundland, 1982.

9402
Surkes, Jean Kathleen. "Patterns of Generalization Between Imitative Affection and Aggression in Young Children." Victoria, 1980. [Four groups of seven year-old boys and girls/4 groupes de garçons et de filles de 7 ans]

9403
Tanguay, Yolande. "Les réactions de jeunes enfants à la perte du milieu familier." Montréal, 1969.

9404
Tierney, Mary C. "Developmental Changes in Children's Knowledge of Effective Helping Strategies." Windsor, 1977.

9405
Tomlinson, Peter. "An Investigation into the Development of Short-Term Retention Capacity in Children as a Function of Age and Item Familiarity." Toronto, 1971.

9406
Tupper, David Edward. "Behavioral Correlates of the Development of Inter-Hemispheric Interaction in Young Children." Victoria, 1982.

9407
Verreault, René. "La créativité au T.T.C.T. (Torrance Tests of Creative Thinking) et la régression au service du moi en fonction du sexe et du milieu socio-économique chez des enfants de 5ième et de 6ième année." Montréal, 1978.

9408
Villeneuve, Richard. "Exploration et étude comparative des interactions typiques des familles ordinaires et des familles de garçons adoptés." Montréal, 1970.

9409
White, Ronald George. "Children's Cognitive Spatial Development and Facilitative Environmental Design." York, 1975.

Wintre, Maxine. See No./Voir no 3039

Wright, Kathleen. See No./Voir no 3040

Abrahamson, David. See No./Voir no 3317

9410
Baker, Carolyn Diane. "An Interpretive Approach to the Study of Adolescent Socialization and Identity." Toronto, 1980.

9411
Bechard, Monique. "Le chef adolescent (d'après une recherche faite dans le mouvement scout." Montréal, 1947.

Ben-Dor, Tsilia. See No./Voir no 4175

9412
Dimitri, Robert H. "The Effectiveness of Family Climate on Adolescent Self-Esteem." Ottawa, 1983.

9413
Dolenz, John Joseph. "Reading and Its Relationship to Self-Descriptions and Measures of Parental Identification of Freshmen for Catholic High Schools." Ottawa, 1970.

Doyle, Mother Hortense. See No./Voir no 3492

9414
Eisenberg, Mildred. "The Relationship Between Personality Development and Role Emphasis for Male and Female Adolescents." Montréal, 1977.

Gfellner, Barbara. See No./Voir no 9679

9415
Kelly, Margaret. "The Self Concept of Adolescent Females: A Test of Roger's Concept of Congruence." Ottawa, 1982.

9416
Lefebvre, Yvon. "Idéologie de la mort, adolescence et classe sociale." Montréal, 1977.

9417
Marceau, Denis. "Effets d'une activité structurée de reconnaissance de soi par autrui sur l'identité des adolescents qui ont une confusion d'identité." Laval, 1978.

Murray, Charles B. See No./Voir no 9043

Mustello, Anthony. See No./Voir no 9044

9418
Njaa, Lloyd Johan. "Validation of the Hoffer-Osmond Diagnostic Test on an Adolescent Sample." Alberta, 1972.

9419
Polovy, Patricia. "A Study of Moral Development and Personality Relationships in Adolescents and Young Adult Catholic Students." Ottawa, 1979.

Salame, Ramzi F. See No./Voir no 3513

Sas, L.D. See No./Voir no 10273

Schneider, Barry. See No./Voir no 3100

9420
Séguin, Guylaine. "Le développement de la conscience interpersonnelle chez les adolescentes en rééducation." Montréal, 1982.

9421
Shymko, Dolores Lillian. "An Exploratory Investigation of Some Aspects of Psychosexual Development in Adolescents." Toronto, 1974.

Smye, Marti Diane. See No./Voir no 754

9422
Spence, C.G. "A Descriptive Study of the Adjustment and Social Competency of Adolescents of Borderline Mentality Living in Foster Homes." Ottawa, 1958.

9423
Wellington, Norman David. "The Influence of Therapeutic Intervention upon the Experience of Personal Causation in Adolescent Boys." Calgary, 1978.

9424
West, Lloyd Wilbert. "Patterns of Self-Disclosure for a Sample of Adolescents and the Relationship of Disclosure Style to Anxiety and Psychological Differentiation." Alberta, 1968.

Zarb, Janet. See No./Voir no 10277

EDUCATIONAL PSYCHOLOGY/ PSYCHOLOGIE DE L'ÉDUCATION

General Items/Ouvrages généraux

9425
Atkinson, Mary Helen Elizabeth. "Power Management in a Team Organization." Alberta, 1980.

Baker, Carolyn Diane. See No./Voir no 9410

9426
Baum, Nehama Tchia. "A Multi-Focal Approach in the Assessment and Treatment of Multi-Handicapped Adolescents: An Individual Case Study." Toronto, 1980.

9427
Branch, Edward Beverly. "A Formative and Experimental Evaluation of a Simulation Game of Marital Communication." Alberta, 1976.

9428
Braun, Peter Hans. "A Cross-Sectional Study of Attitudinal Function Fluctuation." Alberta, 1972.

Byrd, Mark Dodds. See No./Voir no 9506

9429
Colistro, Frank Peter Salvatore. "Empathy Client Depth of Experiencing and Goal Attainment Scaling: A Within-Session Examination of the Client-Centered Therapy Process." British Columbia, 1978.

9430
Carrier, Maurice Aurèle. "Étude de la relation entre le niveau de localisme et des cosmopolitisme d'un cadre scolaire et l'incidence des tensions manifestées en situations de stress au travail." Ottawa, 1979.

Chin, John Carlton. See No./Voir no 10246

9431
Christopher, Doris Marianne. "Cognitive Versus Social Rigidity in Old Age: Implications for Therapy." Calgary, 1981.

Clark, Linda Esther. See No./Voir no 9508

9432
Cohen, Mikal Rae. "A Study of Educational Priorities in a Middle-Sized Urban Area." York, 1976.

9433
Cummins, Jim Patrick. "Bilingualism and Cognitive Representation." Alberta, 1974.

Davis, Teresa Mina Anne. See No./Voir no 9123

Davison, James H. See No./Voir no 3732

9434
De March, Joseph Paul. "A Study of Adults' Perceptions of Neonates." Calgary, 1982.

9435
Dub, Pavel. "Processes of Learning in Becoming Men and Women." Toronto, 1982.

9436
Eaves, Linda Crawford. "Some Predictive Antecedents of Poor School Achievement." Simon Fraser 1983.

England, Gordon Douglas. See No./Voir no 3853

9437
Frazer, Henry Mason. "Agoraphobia: Parental Influence and Cognitive Structures." Toronto 1980.

9438
Fryatt, Maurice John. "Comparative Effects of Small Group Social Competence Training for Psychiatric Patients." Toronto, 1981.

Greckol, Sonja Ruth. See No./Voir no 3218

Gruson, Linda Margaret. See No./Voir no 955

Hallschmid, Claus A. See No./Voir no 3220

Harasym, Peter Humphrey. See No./Voir no 6822

9439
Hayduck, Allen Walter. "Teaching Voluntary Hand warming for the Promotion of Hand Efficiency a Cold Temperatures." Alberta, 1979.

9440
Heemsberger, Donald Bastiaan. "Planning as a Cognitive Process: An Empirical Investigation. Alberta, 1980.

9441
Heisel, Brian E. "Children's Use and Transfer of Retrieval Strategy." Western Ontario, 1982.

9442
Henninger, Polly Johnson. "Problem Solving Strategie of Musically Trained and Untrained Subjects an Hemisphere Activation." Toronto, 1982.

9443
Hoestlandt-Noël, Christine. "Étude exploratoire de processus cognitifs d'adultes résolvant un problème complexe dans un cadre peu structuré." Montréal 1981.

Hurst, Paul Eugene. See No./Voir no 3916

9444
Josefowitz, Nina. "Placing Assertion Within a Situation: How Others' Emotional Expressions Influence Assertive Behavior." Toronto, 1981. [96 under graduate students/96 étudiants de premier cycle]

9445
Kalmoni-Baassiri, Faika. "A Study of the Relationshi Between Locus of Control of Reinforcement and Performance on Deductive Conditional Reasonin Tasks." Ottawa, 1982.

9446
Kanchier, Carole Joyce. "Occupational Change: Psy chosocial Variables Which Differentiate Manageria Changers from Non-Changers." Calgary, 1981.

Koe, George Gerald. See No./Voir no 4006

9447
Koewn, L.L. "Family Decisions and Drug Use." Alberta, 1977.

9448
Koziev, Roberta Louise. "The Construction and Validation of the Remote Possibilities Test." Alberta 1976.

9449
Krausher, Randall John Robert. "Interrelationship Among Propositional Logic, Social Perspective Taking, Moral Stage and Delinquent I-Leve Classification." Alberta, 1980.

9450
Krichev, Alan. "The Comparative MMPI Performance of Compound and Coordinate French-English Bilingual Students." Windsor, 1972.

9451
Lessard, Francine. "Inventaire des caractéristiques de l'élève, à l'usage du professeur, tel qu'appliqué à la classe d'adaptation." Montréal, 1979.

9452
Lorrain, Jean. "Syndicalisation des cadres: élaboration d'un modèle théorique et vérification empirique." Montréal, 1983.

9453
Martin, Jack F. "A Functional Analysis of Communication Behavior in Small Learning Groups." Alberta, 1973.

McAndrew, Joan Kathleen. See No./Voir no 4151

McCluskey, Kenneth Wilfred. See No./Voir no 3918

9454
Meuser, Dorothy M. "Basic Interest Scale Patterns on the Strong-Campbell Interest Inventory as Predictors of Academic Success and Satisfaction." Ottawa, 1978.

Miles, J.J. See No./Voir no 9223

9455
Mischey, Eugene John. "Faith, Development and Its Relationship to Moral Reasoning and Identity Status in Young Adults." Toronto, 1976.

9456
Moore, Joyce Elaine. "Facilitating Children's Social Understanding Through Cognitive Conflict and Role Playing." Toronto, 1980.

9457
Morris, George Barry. "Irrational Beliefs, Life Orientation and Temporal Perspective of Prison Inmates." Alberta, 1974.

Moyal, Barbara Ruth Roback. See No./Voir no 9197

9458
Muir, William Russell. "Measurement of Similarity of Verbal Material by a Paired Comparison Procedure." Alberta, 1968.

9459
Murray, Yves. "L'abandon scolaire chez des étudiants favorisés de niveau collégial." Montréal, 1982.

9460
Palardy, Yvette. "Réactions initiales au placement en famille d'accueil à l'âge scolaire." Montréal, 1982.

9461
Parent, Richard. "Effets de la contrainte du temps sur la résolution de problèmes dans un groupe en coopération." Montréal, 1979.

Perkins, Marjorie Joyce Morrison. See No./Voir no 4463

9462
Pigeon, Richard. "Relation entre la différenciation psychologique et l'évaluation de cours par des étudiants dans une perspective de commerce cognitive." Ottawa, 1982.

9463
Pollock, Nathan Lionel. "The Relationship Between Criminal Behaviour and Constricted Role-Taking Activity." Toronto, 1980.

Polyzoi, Eleoussa. See No./Voir no 780

9464
Proulx, Guy B. "The Effects of Anxiety on Event-Related Potentials During a Learning Task." Ottawa, 1981.

9465
Raphael, Irwin Allan. "The Effects of Imagery Cognitive Modification and Cognitive Style, in Dealing with Pain." Alberta, 1981.

9466
Rodberg, Gloria John. "Self Concept as a Learner." Calgary, 1982.

9467
Rungsinan, Winai. "Scoring of Originality of Creative Thinking Across Cultures." Georgia, 1976.

9468
Scher, Anat. "Spatial Cognition: Processes and Development." Calgary, 1980. [School youngsters and adults in Calgary/Jeunes étudiants et adultes à Calgary]

9469
Schmidt, Lanalee Carol. "Sex Role Attitudes and Changing Lifestyles of Professional Women." Alberta, 1973.

9470
Schultz, Lynda Kay. "The Influence of Pre-Training Selection Factors on the Acquisition of Helping Skills in Non-Professionals." Manitoba, 1980.

9471
Seaman, Lorne Douglas. "Predicting the Performance of Volunteers: Multiple Regression Approach." Alberta, 1981. [Uncles at Large Program in Edmonton/Programme à Edmonton]

9472
Shore, Bruce Malcolm. "Outward Location Bias in Selective Perception." Calgary, 1971.

9473
Silver, Judith A. "Therapeutic Aspects of Folk Dance: Self-Concept, Body Concept, Ethnic Distancing and Social Distancing." Toronto, 1981.

9474
Simmons, Joyce Nesker. "Behavioural Disturbance in the School: A Study of the Interactional Nature of Deviance." Toronto, 1981.

9475
Souch, Stanley Grant. "A Cross-Sectional Study of Reflection-Impulsivity with Special Reference to Sex, Social Class and Maternal Conceptual Systems." Alberta, 1970.

9476
Spricer, Rosa. "Adulthood: Developmental Tasks of Adult Women." Alberta, 1981.

9477
Stacey, Rosalind. "A Comparison of Adults' and Children's Understanding of and Memory for Potential Inference Sentences." Western Ontario, 1977.

St-Onge, Louise. See No./Voir no 3700

9478
St-Pierre-Desrosiers, Pauline. "Étude de facteurs associés à la fréquence et à la durée d'intervention des enseignants titulaires en activité physique." Laval, 1981. [Primary school/École primaire]

Summers, Randal William. See No./Voir no 1959

9479
Thompson, J. Wayne. "Empathy Training via Cognitive and Affective-Cognitive Modes." Alberta, 1978.

9480

Vitaro, Frank. "Apprentissage de la notion de conservation par observation: rôle de la compétence initiale et du processus d'imitation." Montréal, 1983.

Warner, Ronald Earl. See No./Voir no 9495

9481

Wasescha, Blaine Eugene. "Comparison of American Indian, Eskimo, Spanish-American, and Anglo Youthful Offenders on the Minnesota Counseling Inventory." Utah, 1971.

9482

Wasson, Avtar Singh. "Relationships Between the Stimulus-Seeking Motive, School Climate and Self-Reported School Deviant Behavior." Ottawa, 1982.

9483

Woodward, James Brian. "Interpersonal Needs as a Basis for Triangulation in Groups." Calgary, 1978.

9484

Yackulic, Richard Alan. "Multidimensional Scaling Evaluation of Aptitude Treatment Interactions." Alberta, 1981. [University students studying a unit of statistics/Universitaires étudiant une unité de statistique]

9485

Yee, Paul Him-Ngar. "Sex Stereotypes: Their Effects on Impression Formation and Evaluations." Toronto, 1981.

Yu, Agnes Yinling. See No./Voir no 3282

Parental Behaviour/Comportement des parents

9486

Denton, Leonard Robert. "Perception of Parents as Related to Levels of Perceptual Differentiation." Alberta, 1967.

Duguay, Monique. See No./Voir no 8986

Kaplan, Faith K. See No./Voir no 3095

Kendall, Mary Ellen. See No./Voir no 3096

9487

Kennedy, William J. "Perceived Parental Behaviors and Belief Systems of Prostitutes." Alberta, 1978.

Kovitz, Karen E. See No./Voir no 9302

9488

Leduc, Lucien. "A Comparative Study of Training Programs for the Establishment and Maintenance of Appropriate Parental Behaviors in Mothers Using Programmed Instruction Techniques with Videotapes." Montréal, 1976.

MacLean, Marvin E. See No./Voir no 10114

9489

Patsula, Philip James. "Felt Powerlessness as Related to Perceived Parental Behavior." Alberta, 1969.

Poznansky, Ellen. See No./Voir no 9393

Schneider, Barry Howard. See No./Voir no 3100

Intelligence

Ellis, Edward Norman. See No./Voir no 4223

9490

Jamieson, Elmer. "The Mental Capacity of Southern Ontario Indians." Toronto, 1928.

9491

Munro, Peter Fraser. "An Experimental Investigation of the Mentality of the Jew in Ryerson Public School, Toronto." Toronto, 1926.

9492

Tanser, Harry Ambrose. "The Settlement of Negroes in Kent County, Ontario and a Study of Mental Capacity of Their Descendants." Toronto, 1939.

9493

Williams, Trevor Hugh. "Cultural Deprivation and Intelligence: Extensions of the Basic Model." Toronto, 1973.

9494

Wingfield, Alexander Hamilton. "Twins and Orphans, the Inheritance of Intelligence." Toronto, 1927.

Educational Psychology in the Elementary Schools/ Psychologie de l'enseignement dans les écoles primaires

See also Education: Elementary Education/Voir aussi Éducation. Enseignement primaire

Educational Psychology in the Secondary Schools/ Psychologie de l'enseignement dans les écoles secondaires

See also Education: Secondary Education/Voir aussi Éducation. Enseignement secondaire

Educational Psychology in Post-Secondary Schools/ Psychologie de l'enseignement dans les écoles post-secondaires

9495

Warner, Ronald Earl. "The Effect of Homogeneous Grouping of Coping Styles on Measures of Process and Outcome in an Interpersonal Coping Skills Program." Toronto, 1978.

EXPERIMENTAL PSYCHOLOGY/ PSYCHOLOGIE EXPÉRIMENTALE

9496

Aboud, Francis E. "Evaluational and Information Seeking Consequences of Social Discrepancy as Applied to Ethnic Behaviour." McGill, 1973.

9497

Alcock, James Edward. "A Cross-Cultural Study of Bargaining Behaviour." McMaster, 1972.

Avigan, Helen Ruth. See No./Voir no 9641

9498

Baker, Patricia Anne. "Spatial and Temporal Determinants of the Increment Threshold Edge Effect." Concordia, 1982.

9499

Baron, Judith E. "Effects of the Menstrual Cycle on Manifest Content and Affect in Dream Report." York, 1974.

9500

Beal, Audrey Lynne. "Musical Judgements and Musical Skill: Overtones in Auditory Memory." Waterloo, 1980.

Bebko, James Mark. See No./Voir no 3865

9501
Bégin, Guy. "The Effects of Success and Failure on Helping Behaviour." McMaster, 1976.

9502
Belton, Gerald Paul. "The Effects of Psychiatric Labelling on Nonverbal Interpersonal Behaviours." Calgary, 1976.

Benezra, Esther. See No./Voir no 3885

Bernfeld, Gary Alan. See No./Voir no 3190

9503
Biersdorff, Kathleen Karol. "The Role of Association Retrieval in Recognition and Recall of Episodic Material." Alberta, 1981. [University of Alberta students/Étudiants de l'Université de l'Alberta]

9504
Black, Edward Lyal. "Multiple Baseline, Multiple Component Analysis of Public Speaking Behaviors Across Subjects and Behavioral Categories." Manitoba, 1979.

9505
Bryson, Susan Elizabeth. "The Identification of Letters and Their Left-Right Mirror Images: Development of Hemispheric Asymmetry." McGill, 1981. [Grades five, seven and nine/ Cinquième, septième et neuvième année]

Bull, Dale Harold. See No./Voir no 9328

Burtt, Brian Irvine. See No./Voir no 8970

9506
Byrd, Mark Dodds. "Age Difference in Memory for Prose Passages." Toronto, 1982.

9507
Campbell, Donna Marie. "The Role of Temporal Factors and Dimensional Salience in Concept Attainment by Young Children." Carleton, 1977.

Carmone, Frank. See No./Voir no 2779

Chattaway, Erma. See No./Voir no 3199

9508
Clark, Linda Esther. "Changes in Learning Capacity with Age, as Indicated by Performance on the Dichotic Listening Task." Queen's, 1973. [Aging adults/Gens du troisième âge]

Clément, Joseph. See No./Voir no 7687

Connolly, Jennifer. See No./Voir no 3019

Cook, Donald. See No./Voir no 9330

9509
Corlett, John Thomas. "Developmental Aspects of Motor Short Term Memory." Simon Fraser, 1980. [90 school children/90 élèves]

9510
Coulombe, Daniel. "Improvement of Memory for Classically Conditioned Associations by Post-Training Self-Stimulation." McGill, 1982.

Courey, Linda Susan. See No./Voir no 9219

9511
Curie-Jedermann, Janice Lynn. "The Role of Function in Conceptual Development." Waterloo, 1981. [Three years old to adult/De 3 ans à l'âge adulte]

9512
Cziko, Gary Andrew. "An Analysis and Comparison of First and Second-Language Reading." McGill, 1978.

9513
D'Anglejan-Chatillon, Alison. "Dynamics of Second Language Development: A Search for Linguistic Regularity." McGill, 1975. [Adult learners of English/Adultes apprenant l'anglais]

9514
De Bosch Kemper, William Peter. "Age Differences in the Effects of Informative Feedback on Continuous Recognition Learning." Victoria, 1979.

DeKoninck, Joseph-M. See No./Voir no 9102

Di Pasquale, Glenn. See No./Voir no 3951

Dubois, René. See No./Voir no 9361

9515
Dumoff, Myron G. "Discriminating Emotion and Mental Effort with Autonomic Measures: Pupil Size and Heart Rate as Differential Measures of Cognition and Anxiety." Manitoba, 1979.

9516
Duncan, David T. "The Effect of a Stressor (Aperiodic Noise) on an Individual's Level of Aggression." Windsor, 1978.

9517
Earls, Christopher Michael. "Erectile Responding Below 10% in the Human Male." Queen's, 1981.

9518
Ecclestone, Charles Edward J.B.. "Anagram Problem Solving: An Examination of the Effects of Providing Additional Retrieval Cues." Queen's, 1981.

9519
Ellis, Robert James. "Arousal and Causal Attribution." Waterloo, 1981.

Esses, Lillian. See No./Voir no 9365

9520
Favreau, Micheline. "Automatic and Conscious Attentional Processes in the First and the Second Languages of Fluent Bilinguals: Implications for Reading." Concordia, 1981.

9521
Ferencz, Joseph. "Physiological and Subjective Concomitants of Human Information Processing Under Conditions of Distraction." Waterloo, 1982.

Ferguson, Tamara Jocelyn. See No./Voir no 9290

9522
Fernandez, Donald Anthony. "Dimensional Dominance and Stimulus Discriminability." Victoria, 1974.

Forget, Jacques. See No./Voir no 3158

9523
Forsberg, Lois Anne. "The Role of Field Dependence-Field Independence in the Conservation of Mass, Weight, and Volume." Manitoba, 1973.

9524
Franklin, Patricia E. "Memory Scanning: The Importance of Experimental Procedure." York, 1981.

9525
Gallivan, Joanne Patricia. "The Acquisition of English Motion Verbs." Waterloo, 1981. [From two and a half to five years old/Enfants de 2 1/2 à 5 ans]

9526
Gazam, Carroll Dianne. "The Encounter Group as an Alternative to Day Hospitalization." Alberta, 1974.

Gareau, André. See No./Voir no 9676

9527
Gauzas, Lawrence. "Exploratory Behaviour as a Function of Arousal, Perceptual Deprivation and Personality Differences." Windsor, 1980.

Gerry, James. See No./Voir no 9678

9528
Giroux, Luc. "L'économie cognitive en mémoire sémantique." Montréal, 1982.

Glasberg, Rhoda. See No./Voir no 9370

Goldman, Barbara. See No./Voir no 9333

Goodman, Sherryl. See No./Voir no 3023

Goodz, Naomi. See No./Voir no 3024

Grant, Marion Elder. See No./Voir no 3217

9529
Greenberg, Allen Morley. "Giving Credit Where Credit is Due: Attributions by Actors and Observers in a Teaching Situation." Carleton, 1974.

9530
Greenberg, Norman Arthur. "Young Children's Perceptional Judgements of Nonredundant Cardinal Numbers Equivalence." Western Ontario, 1981.

9531
Griffin, Harvey Richard. "Brief Progressive Relaxation as a Function of Locus of Control and Experimenter-Cued Feedback with Pregnant Women." Manitoba, 1981.

9532
Guirguis, Talaat F. "Extraversion-introversion, stimulus chromatiques et mémoire immédiate." Ottawa, 1981.

9533
Haller, Otto. "An Investigation of Reference Systems of Individual Subjects." Calgary, 1979.

9534
Hallman, David William. "The Effects of Binaural Click Integration as Represented in the Auditory Brainstem Evoked Response (Ber)." Simon Fraser, 1980.

Hamayan, Else. See No./Voir no 7740

9535
Hambley, Walter Douglas. "Word Concreteness and Visual Imaging Ability as a Function of Recall and Recognition Short-Term Memory." York, 1971. [82 female college students/82 étudiantes collégiales]

9536
Hamers, Josiane Frieda-Aline. "Interdependent and Independent States of the Bilingual's Two Languages." McGill, 1973.

Hammond, Leslie. See No./Voir no 4310

Hardwick, Claudia. See No./Voir no 3816

9537
Hardy, Larry Michael. "Observational and Vicarious Influences on the Motor Performance of Severely Retarded Males." Manitoba, 1975.

Harris, Georgina Bernice. See No./Voir no 9007

Harvey, Michael Dobbs. See No./Voir no 9689

Heisel, Brian E. See No./Voir no 9441

Henninger, Polly Johnson. See No./Voir no 9442

Heslegrave, Ronald James. See No./Voir no 9238

9538
Hochester, Marilyn Goulden. "Ear Asymmetry and Restricted Frequency Speech and Non-Speech Sounds." Victoria, 1983.

9539
Hodkin, Barbara. "Language Effects in Assessment of Class Inclusion Ability." McMaster, 1981.

9540
Howe, Mark LeBas. "The Structure of Associative Memory Traces: A Mathematical Analysis of Learning Associative Clusters." Western Ontario, 1982.

Humphrey, Gary. See No./Voir no 9335

9541
Jansen, Lyn Ellen. "Towards a Developmental Model for Same Different Judgments." Ottawa, 1980.

9542
Johnson, Janice Marie. "The Development of Metaphor Comprehension: Its Mental-Demand Measurement and Its Process Analytical Models." York, 1982.

Johnston, Nancy. See No./Voir no 3027

9543
Katzko, Michael William. "Aspects of Cognitive Representation: Examination of the 'Mental Rotation' Paradigm." Alberta, 1980.

Keith, Eileen. See No./Voir no 9339

Keller, Martha Perry Freese. See No./Voir no 3824

Keller, Sandra M. See No./Voir no 10401

9544
Klein, Danny. "Perceptual Asymmetrics and Attentional Mechanisms in Tachistoscopic Recognition of Words and Faces." York, 1975.

9545
Kontos, Donna June Krochman. "The Effects of Mother-Infant Separation in the Early Post Partum Hours and Days in Later Maternal Attachment Behaviour." Toronto, 1977.

9546
Koop, Sandra Jean. "A Behavioral Coaching Strategy to Reduce Swimming Stroke Errors with Beginning Age-Group Swimmers." Manitoba, 1982.

9547
Kuchar, Eva. "Children's Understanding and Mother's Use of Information Presented in the Verbal and Nonverbal Modes: Implications for Language Development." Toronto, 1980. [Three to five years old/Enfants de 3 à 5 ans]

9548
Kuiper, Nicholas A. "The Self as an Agent in the Processing of Personal Information about Others." Calgary, 1979.

Kyle, Jack Leslie. See No./Voir no 1070

Lake, Deborah. See No./Voir no 3874

9549
Laurence, Jean Roch. "Memory Creation in Hypnosis." Concordia, 1983.

9550
Lawson, Glen Allen. "Number, Language and Cognitive Development." McMaster, 1978.

9551
Leigh, Gillian Mary. "Alcohol and Cigarette Smoking Effects on Critical Flicker Frequency." Waterloo, 1980. [35 university males/35 étudiants universitaires]

Leonhart, William Boyd. See No./Voir no 3826

Lewis, Terri. See No./Voir no 9341

9552
Libman, Mark Norman. "Proximity and Density Effects in Helping Behaviour." York, 1974.

Lightfoot, Lynn. See No./Voir no 9261

Lowther, Rachel. See No./Voir no 3828

9553
Lustig, Stephen David. "Modeling Influences on Senior Citizens." Victoria, 1978.

9554
Luther, Michael Gerard. "A Developmental Study of the Blocking of Incidental Learning: Its Extent, the Influence Therein of Integral and Separable Compound Cues, and the Relationship Between Hypotheses and Their Choice Responses." York, 1981.

9555
Lyons, Helen Ida. "The Perception and Resolution of Tonal Ambiguity in Short Melodic Sequences." Ottawa, 1981.

9556
Maher, Timothy Francis. "A Cross-Cultural Comparison of Verbal and Exploratory Responses to Harmonic Musical Intervals." Toronto, 1980.

9557
Mann, Barbara Elizabeth. "An Examination of the Strength and Locus of Interior Activities During Periods of Non-Reinforcement on Various Simple and Multiple Schedules of Food Reinforcement." Western Ontario, 1982.

9558
Mann, John Fraser. "Cognitive, Behavioral and Situational Determinants of Ethnic Perception." McGill, 1976.

Mann, Robert. See No./Voir no 9263

9559
Marton, John Peter. "Film Provoked Aggression in Children: Effects of Prior Affection Training." Victoria, 1980. [Four and five years old attending a day care center in Victoria/Enfants de 4 et 5 ans d'une garderie à Victoria]

9560
Mendelson, Beverley Katz. "The Development of Self-Body-Image in Overweight Youngsters." Concordia, 1982.

9561
Metcalfe, Janet Ann. "A Composite Holographic Associative Recall Model." Toronto, 1982.

9562
Minden, Harold Allen. "The Effects of Perceptual-Motor Training on Intellectual and Academic Functionning." York, 1969. [84 grade two boys and girls of North York, Ontario/84 garçons et filles de deuxième année à North York, Ontario]

Neufeld, Gordon. See No./Voir no 3252

9563
Newman, Jean Ellen. "Explorations of the Function of Emphasis in Connected Speech." Toronto, 1981.

9564
O'Hara, Thomas John. "A Comparison of the Biofeedback and Cognitive Stress Reduction Methods in Competitive Motor Performance Using Personality Variables as Moderators." Ottawa, 1980.

Olenick, Debra. See No./Voir no 3836

9565
O'Sullivan, Julia Therese. "The Effectiveness of Metamemory Instruction in Promoting Generalisation of the Keyword Mnemonic Strategy: A Developmental Study." Western Ontario, 1983.

9566
Pawlicki, Robert Edward. "The Influence of Contingent and Non-Contingent Social Reinforcement upon Internal and External Controlling Children in a Simple Operant Task." York, 1970. [170 grade three children in York/170 enfants de troisième année à York]

9567
Penner, Ronald Steven. "An Investigation of Age Differences in Divided Attention and Intrahemispheric Competition." Victoria, 1982.

Perner, Josef. See No./Voir no 9390

9568
Perry, Raymond Paul. "An Experimental Examination of Impression Communication as an Interpersonal Behavioural Pattern." Calgary, 1971.

9569
Pirot, Michael Alphonse. "Some Determinants of Affectionate Behavior in Young Children." Victoria, 1976.

Pulos, Steven. See No./Voir no 3260

Pulton, Thomas William. See No./Voir no 3858

9570
Rasmussen, Per Gorm. "Complex Color Stimuli and Emotional Responses." British Columbia, 1979.

9571
Rice, Marnie Elizabeth. "The Development of Vicarious Reinforcement Effects." York, 1975. [From two and a half to five years old/De 2 1/2 à 5 ans]

9572
Sarwar, Kaiserruddin. "Some Effects of Fear and Cue-Prominence on the Eating Behavior of Obese and Normal Subjects." Laval, 1976.

9573
Schacter, Daniel Lawrence. "Feeling of Knowing and the Expression of Knowledge from Episodic Memory." Toronto, 1981.

9574
Schlotterer, George Richard. "Changes in Visual Information Processing with Normal Aging and Progressive Dementia of the Alzheimer Type." Toronto, 1977.

9575
Schmidtgoessling, Nancy. "Effects of Forseeability, Ambiguity of Casuality, and Severity of Outcome on Attribution of Responsibility for an Accident." Ottawa, 1978. [200 female students from the University of Ottawa/200 étudiantes de l'Université d'Ottawa]

9576
Shapson, Stanley Mark. "Hypothesis Testing and Cognitive Style in Children." York, 1973.

Solomon, Elizabeth Theresa Echlin. See No./Voir no 8944

9577
Spinaris, Caterina Georgia. "Automatic Activation in Memory as a Function of Age in Adulthood." Calgary, 1982.

9578
Stein, Marsha L. "Matching Counselee Conceptual Level to Counselor-Offered Degree of Structure in an Initial Interview." Western Ontario, 1976.

9579
Stewart, Dermot Michael. "Short-Term Memory in Dichotic Listening." York, 1975.

9580
Stober, Stephen Robert. "An Investigation of Sustained and Transient Mechanisms in the Human Visual System Using the Reaction Time and Metacontrast Paradigms." Concordia, 1982.

9581
Strauss, Esther Helen. "Facial Expressions and Hemispheric Asymmetries." Toronto, 1980.

9582
Sugar, Judith Ann. "Sentence Similarity: A Developmental Study." York, 1981. [Four groups of children, eight, nine, ten and eleven years old/4 groupes d'enfants de 8, 9, 10 et 11 ans]

Surkes, Jean. See No./Voir no 9402

9583
Syrotnik, John M. "The Relative Efficiency of Several Parole Prediction Strategies." Windsor, 1973.

9584
Taylor, Margo Jane. "Intramodal and Intermodal Matching of Auditory and Visual Temporary Patterns." McGill, 1981.

9585
Taylor, Nancy Douglas. "Children's Responses to Rearrangement Lenses." McGill, 1969.

9586
Te Linde, Derek John. "Picture-Word Differences in Decision Latency: A Test of Common Coding Assumptions." Western Ontario, 1981.

Theis, John. See No./Voir no 10308

9587
Trehub, Sandra E. "Auditory-Linguistic Sensitivity Infants." McGill, 1973.

Turner, Lorne Craig. See No./Voir no 6728

Vaid, Jayotsna. See No./Voir no 7711

9588
Wann, Phillip Daley. "Differential Effects of Hippocampal Epileptic Foci and Lesions on Learning and Memory." Carleton, 1980.

9589
Waters, Gloria Sydna. "Interference Effects on Reading: Implications for Phonological Recoding." Concordia, 1981.

Werker, Janet Feldman. See No./Voir no 7817

Williams, Wilfred. See No./Voir no 3849

Willows, Dale. See No./Voir no 3987

9590
Willson, Sheila Catharine. "Development of the Language Comprehension Process Required to Identify Meaning Similarities Across Different Contexts." Toronto, 1977. [From grades five to nine/Étudiants de la cinquième à la neuvième année]

9591
Wrighton, Patricia Ann. "Comparative Effects of Demerit Tokens, Response Cost and Time-Out to Decrease Self-Stimulating Behavior During Positive Training with Severely and Profoundly Retarded Women." Manitoba, 1978.

Ycas, Martynas. See No./Voir no 7679

Young, Gerald C. See No./Voir no 9349

9592
Znaniecki, Barbara A.R. "Effects of Fenestration and Room Size on Mood and Mood Change." Ottawa, 1979.

Zucker, Kenneth Jay. See No./Voir no 9350

9593
Zussman, David R. "The Convergent-Divergent Abilities of Students and Their Teachers." McGill, 1975.

MILITARY, PERSONNEL AND INDUSTRIAL PSYCHOLOGY/PSYCHOLOGIE MILITAIRE, PERSONNELLE ET INDUSTRIELLE

Bate Boerop, J.L.D.B. See No./Voir no 2176

9594
Blair, William R.N. "The Prediction of Military Delinquency." Ottawa, 1956.

9595
Bordeleau, Yvon. "Les motivations au travail, conception des objectifs des entreprises et la relation entre ces deux variables chez un groupe d'étudiants canadiens-français en commerce." Montréal, 1974.

9596
Cram, John Murray. "Perceived Need Satisfactions of Workers in Isolated Environments." British Columbia, 1969. [Northwest Territories and the Yukon/Territoires du Nord-Ouest et Yukon]

9597
El-Gazzar, Mohamed E. "The Adequacy of Different Decision-Making Models: A New Approach for Considering Individual and Situational Determinants of Decision-Making." Waterloo, 1973.

9598
Fournier, Bruce Anthony. "The Relationship of Job Satisfaction Measures to Self-Report and Objective Criteria Measures and the Effect of Moderator Variables for Canadian Military Personnel." York, 1976.

9599
Franklin, Donald Robert. "Personality Inferences the Personnel Selection Interview." Calgary, 1979.

9600
Garwood, John Bates. "The Effects of Intrinsic and Extrinsic Job Characteristics, Demographic and Personality Variables on Organizational Choice at Different Academic Levels." Waterloo, 1973.

Gingras, Marie. See No./Voir no 9294

9601
Hosek, James Charles. "The Prediction of Ego Involvement and Its Relation to Job Performance." Waterloo, 1971.

9602
Kronenberger, Earl J. "An Investigation of Interpersonal Aspects of Industrial Accident and Non Accident Men." Ottawa, 1959.

9603
Laroche, Jean-Pierre. "Le conflit individuel et conflit familial en industrie: leur relation avec satisfaction au travail." Montréal, 1969.

9604
Lesage, Pierre Bernard. "Measuring Leadership Attitudes: A Construct Validation Study." Michigan, 1973. [566 English Canadian managers from six large industrial organizations/566 directeurs canadiens anglophones de six grands organismes industriels]

9605
Mallette, Rolland Roger. "A Study of Organizational Attachment in Terms of the Work Exchange." York, 1974. [Canadian armed forces officers/Officiers des forces armées canadiennes]

9606
Mathieu, Robert. "Étude du stress professionnel et des répercussions psychologiques du travail de chauffeur d'autobus." Montréal, 1981.

9607
Morton, Nelson W. "The Industrial Quality of the Unemployed, with Particular Reference to Occupational Classification." McGill, 1933.

Noël, Guy. See No./Voir no 2737

Norris, Kenneth Everett. See No./Voir no 2400

9608
Otke, Paul Gerald. "The Relationship Between Job Satisfaction and Job Requirements." York, 1970. [Canadian armed services officers/Officiers des services armés canadiens]

9609
Peacock, Andrew Charles. "Dynamics of Inferential Judgment in the Employment Interview." Western Ontario, 1981.

Piché, Louise. See No./Voir no 2078

9610
Piedalue, Marc. "Les valeurs de travail en relation avec l'âge et le niveau de spécialisation chez divers groupes d'employés canadiens-français d'une grande entreprise." Montréal, 1976.

Pugh, G. M. See No./Voir no 8931

9611
Rivard, Carole. "Étude transversale de valeurs de travail chez des étudiants en psychologie et chez des psychologues." Montréal, 1974.

9612
Robins, Patrick James. "The Nature and Effect on Bargaining of Occupational Stereotyping in a Labour Relations Context." Manitoba, 1983.

9613
Rondeau, Alain. "Les caractéristiques individuelles des accidents en fonction de leur responsabilité dans l'accident et le concept de prédisposition aux accidents." Montréal, 1974.

Rousseau, Marcel. See No./Voir no 8775

9614
Signori, Edro Italo. "The Arnprior Experiment! An Appraisal of Pilot Selection Procedures in the RCAF and RAF." Toronto, 1947.

9615
Simas, Kathleen A. "Authoritarianism and Sex-Role Stereotypes: Influence on the Assessment and Selection of Job Applicants in an Employment Interview - Analogue." Ottawa, 1976.

Smith, Bryan James. See No./Voir no 1958

9616
Solberg, Patricia A. "Some Value Attitudes of Returned Canadian Volunteers." Chicago, 1949.

9617
Spearman, Donald. "The Adaptation Development and Evaluation of an Industrial Merit Rating Plan." Montréal, 1947.

9618
Stephenson, Peter John. "Planning and Implementing Change in a Complex Organization: A Case Study." Toronto, 1982.

Tucker, David Harold. See No./Voir no 9325

9619
Waldie, Valerie Lynn. "An Investigation of the Processes of Impression Formation and Behaviour Prediction Through the Use of Introspective Report." York, 1972.

Yeh, Ming-che. See No./Voir no 756

PERSONALITY/PERSONALITÉ

Ally, Gilles. See No./Voir no 9161

9620
Bigelow, Ann Eileen. "The Development of Self-Recognition in Young Children." Simon Fraser, 1976.

9621
Cavalier, Robert Peter. "Personality and Adjustment to Arctic Isolation." Columbia, 1961.

Doyle, Mother Hortense. See No./Voir no 3492

Goldenthal, Lyn M. See No./Voir no 9257

9622
Hare, William Francis. "A Sense of Responsibility and Its Development." Toronto, 1971.

9623
Honorez, Jean-Marie. "Le devenir d'enfants maltraités." Montréal, 1981.

Janzen, Henry Laurence. See No./Voir no 3683

9624
Klemplatz, Morrie M. "The Effects of Cultural and Individual Supports on Personality Variables Among Children of Holocaust Survivors in Israel and North America." Windsor, 1980.

Krichev, Alan. See No./Voir no 9450

9625
Lang, William Arthur. "A Factor Analytic Study of Selected Group-Relevant Personality Traits." Calgary, 1982.

9626
LeBlanc, Eugène A. "Effects of Order of Presentation of Consonant and Dissonant Personality Interpretations and Level of Discrepancy on Changes in Self-Perception." Windsor, 1975. %University of Windsor undergraduates/Étudiants de premier cycle de l'Université de Windsor]

9627
Lefevre, Esther. "Personality Correlates and Situational Determinants of Self-Report and Role-Playing Assertion." Concordia, 1983.

MacLean, Marvin E. See No./Voir no 10114

9628
Marcoux, Yves. "L'influence de la perte d'un parent durant l'enfance et l'adolescence sur la personalité adulte." Montréal, 1981.

McFerran, John Ronald. See No./Voir no 10299

9629
Mendonca, Augustine, Rev. "Antisocial Personality and Nullity of Marriage." Ottawa, 1982.

9630
Meyer, James Alan. "An Analysis of the Dispositional, Situational, and Interactional Models of Personality in Relation to Two Cognitive Styles of Personality Functioning." Regina, 1981.

Perrault, Yvonne. See No./Voir no 3510
Porter, James E. See No./Voir no 3790
9631
Rabie-Azoory, Vera. "Creativity in the Obsessive-Compulsive Personality." Montréal, 1977.
Record, Stephen A. See No./Voir no 9227
Richard, Bruno. See No./Voir no 4330
Rousseau, Marcel. See No./Voir no 8775
9632
Ryks, Dolf. "Leader Legitimacy and Influences in Hierarchical Groups." Alberta, 1974.
9633
Salameh, Waleed Anthony. "La personalité du comédien: théorie de la conciliation tragi-comique." Montréal, 1981.
Smith, Douglas Lane. See No./Voir no 9066
Strang, John Douglas. See No./Voir no 3791
Thomas, Paul French. See No./Voir no 4077
9634
Violato, C. "A Behavioral Study of Personality: The Transsituational Consistency of Behavioral Persistence." Alberta, 1982.

SOCIAL PSYCHOLOGY/PSYCHOLOGIE SOCIALE

Aboud, Francis E. See No./Voir no 9496
9635
Adsett, Nancy Leigh. "Locus of Control, Self-Concept and Attitudes of Parents Anonymous Volunteers." Toronto, 1976.
9636
Aitchison, Douglas Wayne. "Sexism and Sexual Discrimination." Waterloo, 1978.
9637
Alain, Michel. "Empathy, Expectation, and Vicarious Learned Helplessness." Waterloo, 1981.
9638
Amin, Shukri. "Picture-Preference Test to Measure the Trait of Avoidance of Sexual Intimacy in Females." Windsor, 1975.
9639
Aubé, Nicole. "Le fontionnement du couple d'après leur niveau socio-économique." Montréal, 1982.
9640
Austrom, Douglas Richard. "The Consequences of Being Single." York, 1982.
9641
Avigan, Helen Ruth. "An Experimental Study of Informal Advice Strategies: Benefits, Intentions and Responsibility." Windsor, 1983.
9642
Avison, William R. "Affect, Cognitive Styles and Causal Attributions for Success and Failure." Alberta, 1977.
9643
Barilko, M. Olga. "Perceptions of Self and Others, Human Relations, Values and Satisfaction Among Three Groups of Roman Catholic Women: Lay, Religious and Ex-Religious." Windsor, 1973.
Beer, Anne Maria. See No./Voir no 4057
Bégin, Guy. See No./Voir no 9501
Belton, Gerald Paul. See No./Voir no 9502

9644
Benabou, Charles. "L'identification de l'individu l'organisation qui l'emploie, son sentiment de com pétence et ses conflits de rôle." Montréal, 1980 [Federal employees in Ottawa/Employés fédérau à Ottawa]
Berens, Anne Elizabeth. See No./Voir no 3053
9645
Berger, Charlene. "Psychological Characteristics c Anglophone and Francophone Initial and Repea Aborters and Contraceptors." Concordia, 1978.
9646
Blall, Madiha. "Les messages chez les familles e situation de crise." Montréal, 1982.
9647
Borrie, Roderick Allen. "The Use of Sensory Depriva tion in a Programme of Weight Control." Britis Columbia, 1978.
9648
Bouchard, Jacqueline. "Facteurs de sortie des commu nautés religieuses féminines du Québec Montréal, 1970.
9649
Bresver, Barbara. "A Psychological Comparison c Two-Generation and Three-Generation Families Toronto, 1975.
9650
Brown, Bruce Leonard. "The Social Psychology c Variations in French Canadians' Speech Styles McGill, 1969.
9651
Burgher, Peter L. "Social Network Characteristic Social Support, and Compliance to a Chroni Hemodialysis Regimen." Windsor, 1982.
9652
Buser, Mary M. "A Reanalysis of Schachter's Exter nality Theory: The Relationship Between Exter nality and Obesity." Manitoba, 1980.
Cavalier, Robert Peter. See No./Voir no 9621
9653
Charlesworth, Maxine Anne. "Interpersonal Trus The Role of Risk in Trust Behaviour." Britis Columbia, 1980.
9654
Chelladurai, Packianathan. "A Contingency Model Leadership in Athletics." Waterloo, 1979.
9655
Chris, Stephen Alexander. "The Effects of the Lev of Self-Monitoring and Level of Anonymity c Attitude Change in the Forced Compliance Situa tion: A Test of Cognitive Dissonance and Impre sion Management Theories." Toronto, 1979.
9656
Cohen, Constance Rose. "The Perception of Voc Emotion by Canadian Anglophones and Franc phones of White- and Blue-Collar Status Manitoba, 1983.
9657
Côté, Pauline. "Éléments pour une théorie de l'idé logie urbaine: l'idéologie technocratique du Burea de l'Aménagement de l'Est du Québec (BAEQ) les relocalisés de l'Est du Québec." Montréa 1980.

9658
Coutts, Larry M. "Affiliative Conflict Theory: Exploration of the Notions of Intimacy Equilibrium and Behavioral Compensation." Windsor, 1975. [Female undergraduates/Étudiantes de premier cycle]

9659
Cumming, David Boyd. "Maladjustment Among the Physically Disabled: A Test of the Social-Rejection and Role-Conflict Hypotheses." Manitoba, 1977.

9660
Delisle, Paule. "Étude du fonctionnement psychique de conjoints en situation de crise maritale." Montréal, 1983.

Deosaran, Ramesh Anthony. See No./Voir no 3491

9661
Desbiens, Danielle. "Étude intraculturelle des valeurs connotatives de cadres francophones du Québec." Montréal, 1979.

9662
Desjardins, Jean-Yves. "Les parents et les pairs dans l'apprentissage sexuel." Montréal, 1978.

DiTecco, Donald Anthony. See No./Voir no 9253

Donoghue, Eileen. See No./Voir no 8985

9663
Dosey, Michael A. "Status Comparison Processes: An Exploratory Study." York, 1973.

9664
Dotzenroth, Susan E. "Perceiving the Causes of Social Successes and Failures: A Study in Self-Esteem and Heterosexual Relations." Ottawa, 1978.

Dubé, Clémence. See No./Voir no 9769

9665
Dutton, Donald George. "Role Performance and Social Perception." Toronto, 1969.

9666
Earn, Brian Mark. "Experimental Compensation Task Interest and the Cooperation with Demand Characteristics of Volunteer and Sign-Up Subjects." Toronto, 1977.

9667
Echols, Christina Sligh. "A Conceptual and Empirical Approach Towards Disentangling the Traditional Confounding of Predictability and Controllability." Manitoba, 1983.

9668
Edwards, Jack Leonard. "Problem-Solving Language and Semantic Memory in the Game of Twenty Questions." York, 1980.

Edwards, John Robert. See No./Voir no 828

9669
Elder, Joy Louise Davey. "The Relationship Between Role-Taking, Prosocial Reasoning and Prosocial Behaviour." Western Ontario, 1982. [Young children/Jeunes enfants]

9670
Elnecave-Steinberg, Mireille. "Relation entre l'androgynie psychologique et l'adaptation post-divorce dans des familles d'enfants de quatre à sept ans." Montréal, 1983.

9671
Evans, Laurence Kenneth. "The Utilization of Space in an Isotopic Environment: A Predictive Model of Beach User Behaviour." British Columbia, 1977.

9672
Fischer, Donald George. "Anti-Semitism, Stress, and Aggressive Cue Value of the Stimulus Target." Alberta, 1968. [University students/Étudiants universitaires]

9673
Forest, Elizabeth. "Élaboration d'une nouvelle façon de concevoir et de mesurer la comptabilité chez les jeunes couples." Montréal, 1977.

Fréchette, Errol James. See No./Voir no 746

9674
Fullerton, John Timothy. "An Investigation of Christian Orthodoxy and Right-Wing Authoritarianism in a Collegiate Population." Manitoba, 1980.

9675
Gagnebin, Pierre-André. "Étude structurale des aspects socio-cognitifs liant individu, groupe et tâche dans le cas de créativité groupale à expression conceptuelle et à expression imaginaire." Montréal, 1969.

9676
Gareau, André Normand. "Victims' Responses to Inequity: An Equity Theory Approach." Alberta, 1980.

9677
Geller, Sheldon Herbert. "Subject Roles and Conforming Behaviour." York, 1972.

Gemme, Robert. See No./Voir no 10196

Genesee, Fred Henry. See No./Voir no 7692

9678
Gerry, James. "Social Reinforcement: An Experimental Study of the Opportunity for Aggression and the Opportunity for Courtship as Operant Reinforcers." Dalhousie, 1975.

9679
Gfellner, Barbara Mary. "Moral Development, Ego Development and Sex Differences in Adolescence." Manitoba, 1981. [Over 500 rural junior and senior high school students and 1st year university students/Plus de 500 étudiants d'école secondaire de campagne et de première année d'université]

Gliksman, Louis. See No./Voir no 7665

9680
Goebel, Allan Ronald. "Self-Anchoring Scaling to Determine Perception of Self and Perception of Others: Canadian Indians and White Canadians." York, 1975.

9681
Goldberg, Gerald Elliott. "Behavior: Relationship of Authenticity and Adult Approval of Viewed Behavior to Children's Aggression." Windsor, 1980.

9682
Grant, Peter Russell. "Descriptive and Affective Distancing of an Outgroup: The Formation and Use of Group Images under Threat." Waterloo, 1980.

9683
Green, Anne Jacqueline. "The Effects of Success/ Failure Feedback on Selective Memory for Self-Relevant Personality Information." Toronto, 1980.

9684
Greenglass, Esther Ruth. "The Effects of Prior Help and Hindrance on Willingness to Help Another: Reciprocity or Social Responsibility." Toronto, 1967.

9685
Guppy, L. Neil. "Occupational Prestige and Collective Conscience: The Consensus Debate Reassessed." Waterloo, 1981.

9686
Hans, Valerie Patricia. "The Effects of the Unanimity Requirement on Group Decision Procedures in Simulated Juries." Toronto, 1978.

9687
Hansen, Christine Marion. "Sensitivity to External Negative Social Stimuli in Overweight Women." Toronto, 1979.

9688
Hansvick, Christine Louise. "Comparing Urban Images: A Multivariate Approach." Windsor, 1977.

9689
Harvey, Michael Dobbs. "Observing Social Transgressions and Subsequent Helping Behavior: A Cognitive Social Norm Interpretation." Alberta, 1980. [University students/Étudiants universitaires]

9690
Heilbronn, Marybeth. "A Longitudinal Study of the Development and Dissolution of Friendship." Windsor, 1975.

Himes, Mavis Carole. See No./Voir no 3094

9691
Holtzblatt, Karen Asher. "A Study of Women's Friendship Relationships: Involvement and the Psychological Sense of Continuity." Toronto, 1982.

9692
Howitt, Rhoderick P.E. "A Self-Other Attributional Model of Friendship Formation." Windsor, 1976.

Huard, Michel. See No./Voir no 958

9693
Hunt, Valerye Agnes. "Third Party Preferences Among Resolutions of Inequity in the Criminal-Victim Dyad." British Columbia, 1976.

9694
Iida-Miranda, Maria Lia. "La relation entre les changements récents et les maladies chez les immigrants portugais à Montréal." Montréal, 1975.

9695
Jonah, Brian Austin. "Authoritarianism and Punishment: A Personality by Situation Approach." Western Ontario, 1980.

9696
Joscelyn, Lela Ames. "The Effects of the Transcendental Technique on a Measure of Self-Actualization." Windsor, 1978.

Josephson, Wendy Louise. See No./Voir no 1133

9697
Kee, Herbert William. "The Development and the Effects upon Bargaining of Trust and Suspicion." British Columbia, 1969.

Kennedy, William J. See No./Voir no 9487

Kern, Alan Steven. See No./Voir no 8920

9698
Kiely, Margaret C. "Ego Identity and Creativity in Religious Women." Montréal, 1970.

9699
Kilpatrick, Doreen Leila. "The Effect of Sex of Rater in Adult Ratings of Child Behaviour." Victoria, 1976.

9700
Kirsh, Sharon Louise. "Emotional Support Systems of Working-Class Women." Toronto, 1981.

9701
Klaiman, Stephen. "Selected Perceptual, Cognitive, Personality, and Socialization Variables as Predictors of Non-Verbal Sensitivity." Ottawa, 1979. [Students at University of Ottawa/Étudiants d l'Université d'Ottawa]

Klug, Leo F. See No./Voir no 4148

9702
Koke, Conrad J. "Turn-Taking and Sex of Interactants." York, 1979.

Krasnor, Linda Rose. See No./Voir no 3028

Kuczynski, Leon. See No./Voir no 9370

9703
Lacome, Bernard. "A Reductionist Approach to Coalition Formation Research: A Simulated Political Convention Game." York, 1970.

9704
Lafortune, Mireille. "Le sentiment de culpabilité et l choix d'une méthode contraceptive chez le femmes." Montréal, 1973.

9705
Laing, Gordon Wayne. "Contact and Attractio Between English Canadians and French Canadians. Michigan, 1976.

9706
Lake, Robert Arlington. "The Social Consequences o Validation Seeking." Toronto, 1969.

9707
LaMarche, Luc. "Une mesure de l'estime de nou comme indicateur du changement des valeurs a sein d'une élite nationaliste." Montréal, 1973.

9708
LaMothe, Dennis Michael. "Female Heterosexua Prostitution and Love Deficit." Alberta, 1979.

9709
Leiper, Robert Neil. "The Relationship of Cognitiv Developmental Structures to the Formation of Eg Identity in Young Men." Simon Fraser, 1981. [4 male college students, from 18 to 24 years old/4 étudiants de collège entre 18 et 24 ans]

9710
Lendenman, Karl Werner. "The Effects of Grou Formation and Intergroup Conflict on Member Decisions Regarding the Allocation of Join Earnings: Equality Versus Equity." Toronto, 1980.

9711
Lesko, Wayne A. "Aversive Environments: Effects o Noise and Density on Physical Aggression and Tas Performance." Windsor, 1978.

9712
Loh, Wallace Ozu. "A Social Psychological Study o Political Commitment in Quebec and Belgium. Michigan, 1971.

Luce, Sally R. See No./Voir no 3690

Luedecke, Barbara Mary. See No./Voir no 9306

9713
MacKinnon, Kenneth Robert. "Child Adjustmen Following Marital Separation or Divorce Relevance of Current Family Functioning." York 1983.

9714
Marques de Sa, Leticia Lucena. "Adaptation de coopérants canadiens en Amérique latine. Montréal, 1982.

9715
Marshall, Peter Graham. "Assertiveness in a Prison Population: Its Measurement, Modification and Correlates." Queen's, 1976. [Ontario]

9716
McCann, Charles Douglas. "Preserving Sequential Order: Goal-Directed Processing and Social-Cognitive Consequences." Western Ontario, 1982.

9717
McCormack, James. "The Influence of Emotional Cues on the Subsequent Aggression of Prejudiced Persons." Alberta, 1972.

9718
McGill, Ann Carley. "An Assessment of the Instrumental, Emotional and Social Needs of Widowed People in the City of Calgary." Calgary, 1982.

9719
McGinnis, James Harold. "The Effects of Altruistic Social Models on the Behaviour and Perceptions of Observers." Waterloo, 1979.

McGinnis, Paul St. Clair. See No./Voir no 4032

McRae, Bradley Collins. See No./Voir no 9312

9720
McTiernan, Timothy Patrick John. "Some Referential and Causal Attributions Underlying Stereotype Content." British Columbia, 1982.

9721
Mercer, George William. "A Model of Adolescent Drug Use." York, 1975.

9722
Meunier, Jean-Marc. "Conditions influençant l'engagement du père envers son premier-né: participation à la naissance et sexe de l'enfant." Montréal, 1979.

9723
Miller, Catherine M.L. "Classicism vs. Romanticism as an Aspect of Introversion-Extroversion." Windsor, 1982. [388 subjects/388 sujets]

9724
Monette, Marcel. "Comparaison entre jeunes couples fiancés et leurs parents: degré d'accord sur certaines variables." Montréal, 1978.

Mongeau, Jean-Claude. See No./Voir no 3879

9725
Moonay, Sheldon Murray. "Social Figure Responses of Social Inadequates and Normals." Ottawa, 1963.

Morin, Lise. See No./Voir no 9385

Moses, Barbara Beryl. See No./Voir no 9315

9726
Murray, Michael Allan. "Satisfaction with Leisure as a Function of Perceived Constraints to Leisure, Life Situation, and Changes in Life Situation." York, 1983.

9727
Myers, Anita Margaret. "The Psychological Measurement of Masculinity-Femininity: Cultural Definitions and Self-Ratings." York, 1980.

9728
Navarre, Kathleen. "Attitude Change of the Non-disabled Toward Disability as a Function of Exposure to Disabled Individuals Engaging in Athletic Competition." Windsor, 1980. [The Ontario Games/Les jeux de l'Ontario]

Neehall, J. See No./Voir no 4071

9729
Nelson, Geoffrey Brian. "Families Coping with the Loss of Father by Death or Divorce." Manitoba, 1979. [Winnipeg]

9730
Norris, Joan Elizabeth A. "Social Disengagement in Adults: Controversial But Measurable." Waterloo, 1979.

9731
Olson, James Murray. "Selective Recall: Attitudes, Schematic, and Memory." Waterloo, 1980. [Issue of abortion/Conséquence de l'avortement]

9732
Oostendorp, Anke. "The Identification and Interpretation of Dimensions Underlying Aesthetic Behaviour in the Daily Urban Environment." Toronto, 1978.

9733
Ouellet, Gaetan. "Relations entre les valeurs de travail et de loisir d'étudiants de niveaux collégial et universitaire." Montréal, 1974.

9734
Paunonen, Sampo Vilho. "Behavioral Consistency and Individual Differences in Predictive Structure." Western Ontario, 1982.

Pettem, Marie O.L. See No./Voir no 3694

9735
Phillips, Dorothy Anne. "Self-Esteem and Interpersonal Attractions Toward Competent and Friendly Persons." Alberta, 1974. [Male undergraduates of the University of Alberta/Étudiants mâles de premier cycle de l'Université de l'Alberta]

9736
Pierce, William David. "Altering a Status-Order: Contingencies of Reinforcement Controlling Group Structure." York, 1975.

9737
Pisterman, Susan Jane. "Differential Judgements of Male and Female Juvenile Offenders." Queen's, 1983.

9738
Poitras, Lorraine Rolande. "A Study of Aggression in Crowded Families." Montréal, 1979.

9739
Posner, Judith Susan. "Perceptions of Physical and Mental Incompetence in a Home for the Aged." Toronto, 1975.

Quarter, Jack Joel. See No./Voir no 3697

Rabie-Azoory, Vera. See No./Voir no 9631

9740
Rayko, Donald Stephen. "Metavalidity of Impression Formation Primacy Effects." Queen's, 1981.

Reich, Lee Campbell. See No./Voir no 9395

9741
Rice, Judith Anne. "Trust-Mistrust and Internality-Externality as Determinants of Organization Assessment by White-Collar Francophones in Quebec." Michigan, 1978.

9742
Ricks, Frances Arlene Souvenir. "A Study of Voluntary Social Organizations." York, 1972.

9743
Rondeau, Roger. "Éléments de diagnostic sur les groupes restreints dans la psychosociologie d'expression française." Montréal, 1979.

9744
Rubin-Porret, Josianne. "Impact de la maladie d'un enfant atteint d'arthrite rhumatoïde sur le vécu familial." Montréal, 1983.

9745
Sahoo, Fakir Mohan. "Affective Sensitivity and Cognitive Style: The Relationship Between the Interpersonal Competence and the Restructuring Components of Field Dependence-Field Independence." Queen's, 1981.

Savoie, André. See No./Voir no 2891

Schlesinger, R.C. See No./Voir no 2064

9746
Schmidt, Allan D. "Application of the Social Ecological Approach to Compliance with Hemodyalysis Treatment." Windsor, 1982. [180 patients]

Schneider, Margaret Shari. See No./Voir no 9206

9747
Scott, Wilfred George. "Certain Factors Connected wih the Successful Placement of Children in Adoptive Foster Homes." Toronto, 1944.

9748
Sexton, Christine Sophie. "Career Orientation, Sex Role Orientation and Perceived Equity as Factors Affecting Marital Power." Manitoba, 1979.

9749
Shelton, Georjia Anne. "The Generalization of Understanding to Behaviour: The Role of Perspective in Enlightenment." British Columbia, 1982.

9750
Short, Judith Ann C. "The Effect of Affiliation Motives and Incentives on Achievement-Related Performance." Western Ontario, 1980.

Sikand, Jagpal Singh. See No./Voir no 515

9751
Simard, Lise Monique. "Cross-Cultural Interaction: The Potential for Informal Social Contact." McGill, 1975. [Two studies with French and English Canadians along ethnolinguistic boundaries/ Deux enquêtes avec des canadiens français et anglais le long de frontières ethnolinguistiques]

Simic, Joan Elaine. See No./Voir no 3843

9752
Skinner-Gardner, Eleanor Jo-Anne. "Induced Abortion: A Psychological Perspective." York, 1975.

Smetanka, John Andrew. See No./Voir no 1956

9753
Smyth, Michael. "Self-Disclosure in Homogeneous and Heterogeneous Dominant Dyads." York, 1975.

9754
Sokoloff, Elliott. "A Study of Scapegoating in Normal or Maladjusted Families." Montréal, 1973.

9755
Solomon, Susan Linda Zener. "The Effects of Previous Powerlessness and Present Costs on the Uses of Power." Toronto, 1970.

9756
Spinner, Barry. "Subject Behaviour in the Laboratory: Objective Self-Awareness or Evaluation Apprehension." Manitoba, 1979.

Spricer, Rosa. See No./Voir no 9476

Steibe, Susan. See No./Voir no 9071

9757
Stein, Steven J. "Effects of Communication Training and Contracting on Disturbed Marital Relationships." Ottawa, 1978.

Stermac, Lana Elizabeth. See No./Voir no 9229

Summers, Randal William. See No./Voir no 1959

Taylor, Donald Maclean. See No./Voir no 365

Thomas, Alan Miller. See No./Voir no 1059

9758
Turnbull, Allen A. "Privacy, Community and Activity Space: An Exploratory Investigation." Carleton, 1977.

Usher, Sarah. See No./Voir no 9082

9759
Villeneuve, Richard. "Exploration et étude comparative des interactions typiques des familles ordinaires et des familles de garçons adoptés. Montréal, 1970.

9760
Visscher, Adrian. "Instrumental and Social-Emotional Dimension in the Interaction of Engaged Couples While Discussing Their Prospective Domicile and Family." Montréal, 1974.

9761
Volge, M.P. "An Exploratory Study of Attitudes and Behaviours During Retirement." Toronto, 1983.

9762
Wade, Gwendolyn Gibbs. "Psychological Needs, Black Consciousness, and Socialization Practices Among Black Adolescents in Nova Scotia, Canada and Michigan, U.S.A." Michigan State, 1972.

Walker, Keith Donald. See No./Voir no 9273

Walters, Jean Elizabeth Maddox. See No./Voir no 327

9763
Williams, Dana Adrienne. "Sex Differences in Causal Attributions after Competition." York, 1980. [11 males and 178 females visiting the Ontario Science Centre/114 hommes et 178 femmes qui ont visité le Centre des sciences de l'Ontario]

9764
Willis, Kathleen Diane. "Marriage and Marital Interaction from an Equity Theory Perspective." Victoria, 1982.

Wilson, Franklin. See No./Voir no 3280

9765
Wong-Rieger, Durhane. "Matching Self-Concept, Behavior, and Cultural Norms in the Process of Adaptation Across Cultures." McGill, 1982.

9766
Wood, Linda Adele. "Loneliness and Social Structure. York, 1976.

9767
Younger, Jonathan Cole. "The Lucky Streak: Studies of Observer Belief in the Stability of Chance Determined Outcomes." Toronto, 1978.

RELIGION/RELIGION

Examining the almost 300 titles in this classification, we find that Canadian universities had a five-fold increase in the 1970's over the amount produced in the 1960's. In addition to a number of general items, Canadian religious history is examined in some depth, along with numerous other religious denominations in Canada. A fairly large number of dissertations are listed, examining Canadian religious personalities; the church and state in Canada; the psychology and sociology of religion; and finally, religion and education in elementary and secondary schools, colleges and universities. On the American side, Columbia University produced the first dissertation on religion in 1911, whereas it was not until the 1920's that the University of Toronto provided its first study.

Eleven dissertations were produced by six British universities, with Edinburgh (3) and Oxford (3) the leaders.

En examinant les 300 ouvrages de cette section, il appert que, dans les années 1970, les universités canadiennes ont eu une production cinq fois plus élevée que dans les années 1960. Outre un certain nombre d'ouvrages généraux, d'autres thèses étudient en profondeur l'histoire religieuse du Canada, en même temps que les nombreuses confessions religieuses ayant des représentants au Canada. Il existe un assez grand nombre de thèses sur des personnalités religieuses du Canada; certaines traitent de l'Église et de l'État au Canada, de la psychologie et de la sociologie du point de vue religieux et, finalement de la religion et de l'enseignement dans les écoles élémentaires et secondaires, les collèges et les universités. Du côté américain, l'Université Columbia a accordé le premier doctorat en religion en 1911 et ce n'est que dans les années 1920 que l'Université de Toronto a approuvé sa première thèse en cette discipline.

Onze thèses proviennent d'universités britanniques avec Édimbourg et Oxford avec trois thèses chacune.

GENERAL ITEMS/OUVRAGES GÉNÉRAUX

9768
Doyle, Denise Joan. "Religious Freedom in Canada." Ottawa, 1982.

9769
Dubé, Clémence. "Vie religieuse et vie laïque: étude comparée de l'actualisation de soi, du dogmatisme et de l'anxiété." Montréal, 1978.

9770
Gesner, Lloyd Roscoe. "The Practice of Ministry in Congregations: A Descriptive Study." Toronto, 1982.

9771
Hornosty, Jennie Mary. "The Contemporary Marxist-Christian Dialogue: A Study in the Political Economy of Religion with Special Reference to Quebec." York, 1979.

9772
Keast, Ronald Gordon. "The Effects of the Technique and the Technology of Communication upon Religious Thought and Religious Organization in the West as Elucidated and Suggested by the Works of Harold Innis." McMaster, 1974.

9773
Kerbrat, Dominique Joseph. "Identification of Designated Talents Among a Group of Sisters from the Province of Manitoba Using the TSCS and the POI." Kansas, 1975.

Kistler, Ruth Barthold. See No./Voir no 2412
Klug, Leo F. See No./Voir no 4148
Knopff, Rainer. See No./Voir no 8458
Knutson, Franklin Albert. See No./Voir no 1157

9774
Langer, Hans Dieter. "Vom Wort der Oekumene Zur Oekumene des wortes. (Theologisch Hermeneutische Erwaegungen zu Einer Interkonfessionellen Ekklesiologie Dargestellt Anhand der Ekklesiolagischen Ausgangs-Positionen des Zweiten Vatikanischen Konzils und der Vierten Faith and Order Conference von Montréal." Graduate Theological Union, 1970.

Lowry, Douglas Bradley. See No./Voir no 1179
MacInnes, Daniel William. See No./Voir no 2115
Marchant, Cosmo K. See No./Voir no 739
Miner, Horace Mitchell. See No./Voir no 769

9775
Morris, John Francis. "The Planning Behaviour and Conceptual Complexity of Selected Clergymen in Self-Directed Learning Projects Related to Their Continuing Professional Education." Toronto, 1977.

Nelson, Ernest. See No./Voir no 6764

9776
Nield, John Everson. "Developing a More Meaningful Program for Infant Baptism at Cedar Park Church in Pointe Claire, Quebec." Drew, 1982.

9777
Paterson, George Morton. "Radical Kenosis: A Study of the Referential Base of Religious Language." Toronto, 1971.

Roy, Paul-Émile. See No./Voir no 8232
Schroeder, Harold John. See No./Voir no 1189
Séguin, Pierre. See No./Voir no 1066
Stahl, William Austin. See No./Voir no 9990
Wolf, Morris. See No./Voir no 661

RELIGIOUS HISTORY/HISTOIRE DES RELIGIONS

General Items/Ouvrages généraux

9778
Diffendal, Anne Elizabeth Polk. "The Society for the Propagation of the Gospel in Foreign Parts and the Assimilation of Foreign Protestants in British North America." Nebraska, 1974. [Nova Scotia/ Nouvelle-Écosse]

9779
Eichhorn, David M. "A History of Christian Attempts to Convert the Jews in the United States and Canada." Hebrew Union, 1949.

Harrison, Deborah Ann. See No./Voir no 9988

9780
Ion, A.H. "British and Canadian Missionaries in the Japanese Empire, 1905-1925." Sheffield, 1978.

9781
Jean, Marguerite. "Évolution des communautés religieuses de femmes au Canada, 1639-1973." Ottawa, 1974.

9782
Keirstead, Charles W. "Church History of the Canadian Northwest." Yale, 1936.

Kim, J.G. See No./Voir no 7658

9783
Lebedoff, Victor Richard. "The Development of Religious Liberty in Canada Since the British Conquest." Maryland, 1965.

O'Donovan, Joan Elizabeth. See No./Voir no 8466

Stephenson, Peter Hayford. See No./Voir no 786

Vecsey, Christopher Thomas. See No./Voir no 544

Villiers-Westfall, William Edward II. See No./Voir no 9791

-1867

Armstrong, Maurice Whitman. See No./Voir no 7171

9784
Bridgman, Harry John. "Three Scots Presbyterians in Upper Canada: A Study in Emigration, Nationalism and Religion." Queen's, 1978.

9785
Carrington, George Williams. "Foreigners in Formosa, 1841-1874." Oxford, 1973 [Presbyterian missionaries/Missionnaires presbytériens]

Danylewycz, Marta Helen. See No./Voir no 9795

Dyster, Barry D. See No./Voir no 7225

Fahmy-Eid, Nadia. See No./Voir no 7253

9786
Gorvans, Alan Wilbert. "A History of Church Architecture in New France." Princeton, 1950.

Kenyon, John Peter Blythe. See No./Voir no 7087

9787
Kewley, Arthur E. "Mass Evangelism in Upper Canada Before 1830." Victoria, 1960.

9788
MacKinnon, I.F. "The Origin of Protestant Churches in Relation to Settlement from the Founding of Halifax to the American Revolution." Edinburgh, 1930.

9789
MacVean, William Campbell. "The Clergy Reserves: An Attempted Establishment." Bishop's, 1965.

Millman, Thomas R. See No./Voir no 9899

Moore, James Talmadge. See No./Voir no 7432

Mulvey, Mary Doris. See No./Voir no 6980

Ott, Edward R. See No./Voir no 7007

Palm, Sister Mary B. See No./Voir no 7008

9790
Pannekoek, Frits. "The Churches and the Social Structure in the Red River Area, 1818-1870." Queen's, 1973.

9791
Villiers-Westfall, William Edward de. "The Sacred and the Secular: Studies in the Cultural History of Protestant Ontario in the Victorian Period." Toronto, 1976.

9792
Vogel, Claude L. "Capuchins in French Louisia (1722-1766)." Catholic, 1928.

9793
Wilson, George Alan. "The Political and Admin trative History of the Upper Canada Clergy Res ves, 1790-1885." Toronto, 1959.

1867-1983

9794
Allen, Alexander Richard. "The Crest and Crisis the Social Gospel in Canada, 1916-1927." Du 1967.

Cheung, Yuet Wah. See No./Voir no 6791

9795
Danylewycz, Marta Helen. "Taking the Veil Montreal, 1840-1920: An Alternative to Marria Motherhood and Spinsterhood." Toronto, 1982.

Faulkner, Charles Thompson Sinclair. See No./Voir 7156

Foster, John William. See No./Voir no 8887

Hiller, Harry Herbert. See No./Voir no 8663

9796
Hodges, Jerry Whitfield. "The Religious Aspect of Agrarian Movement." Ottawa, 1959.

9797
Howell, David Francis. "The Social Gospel in Ca dian Protestantism, 1895-1925: Implications Sport." Alberta, 1980.

9798
Levine, Gregory James. "In God's Service: The R of the Anglican, Methodist, Presbyterian, Roman Catholic Churches in the Cultural G graphy of Late Nineteenth Century Kingst Queen's, 1980.

MacInnes, Daniel William. See No./Voir no 2115

9799
Markell, H. Keith. "Canadian Protestantism agai the Background of Urbanization and Industri zation in the Period from 1885 to 1914." Chica 1972.

McLaughlin, Kenneth Michael. See No./Voir no 712

Meen, Sharon Patricia. See No./Voir no 7130

Miller, James Rodger. See No./Voir no 7131

Nicolson, Murray William Wood. See No./Voir no 72

Ryan, William Francis. See No./Voir no 1300

9800
Sharum, Elizabeth Louise. "A Strange Fire Burning: History of the Friendship House Movement." Te Tech, 1977. [1930-   ]

9801
Strevig, Jennie May. "History of the Missionary E cation Movement in the United States Canada." New York, 1930.

RELIGIOUS DENOMINATIONS, DOCTRINES AND HISTORY/PROFESSIONS, DOCTRINE ET HISTOIR RELIGIEUSES

General Items/Ouvrages généraux

Diffendal, Anne E.P. See No./Voir no 9778

Hornosty, Jennie Mary. See No./Voir no 9771

Young, Mary McPherson. See No./Voir no 371

Baptist/Baptiste

302
oombs, Douglas V. "Kingsway Baptist Church, Toronto: A Strategy for Growth 1980-1985." Fuller Theological Seminary, 1980.

303
ill, Mary Bulmer Reid. "From Sect to Denomination in the Baptist Church in Canada." SUNY, Buffalo, 1971.

304
asiciel, Ernest Kurt. "The Interrelationship Between Sociocultural Factors and Denominationalism: A Comparison of the Early and Modern Sociocultural Profiles of the North American Baptist General Conference, 1874-1974." Baylor, 1974.

305
ierce, William Lloyd. "Implementing a Program of Visitation Evangelism in Blythwood Road Baptist Church in Toronto, Ontario." Southern Baptist Theological Seminary, 1975.

enfree, Henry Alexander. See No./Voir no 9924
obertson, Elizabeth Irene. See No./Voir no 9925

306
ichman, Gustaf T. "History of the Swedish Baptists in the United States and Canada." Southwestern, 1912.

Brethren in Christ/Frères dans le Christ

Climenhaga, Asa W. See No./Voir no 9925

Roman Catholic/Catholiques romains

ee also Religion and Education/Voir aussi Religion et Éducation

807
aeszler, Sister St. Alfred of Rome. "The Congregation of Notre Dame in Ontario and the United States: The History of Holy Angels' Province." Fordham, 1944.

Beck, Jeanne Ruth Merifield. See No./Voir no 9889

808
lain, Jean. "L'église de la Nouvelle-France 1632-1675: la mise en place des structures." Ottawa, 1967.

Boucher, Réal. See No./Voir no 9890

809
ounadère, René. "Justification historique des petits séminaires de la province de Québec." Laval, 1945.

Cadieux, Lorenzo, Rev. See No./Voir no 9890
Castelli, Giuseppe. See No./Voir no 791
Chausse, Gilles. See No./Voir no 9892
Choquette, J.E. Robert. See No./Voir no 7193

810
Cloutier, Nicole. "L'iconographie de Sainte-Anne au Québec." Montréal, 1983.

811
alton, Roy Clinton. "The History of the Jesuits' Estates, 1760-1888." Minnesota, 1957.

9812
Darcy, Françoise. "Concepts et attitudes concernant la mort et l'au-delà: une recherche théorique, exploratoire et expérimentale chez un groupe d'enfants canadiens catholiques." Ottawa, 1970.

Desrochers, Bruno. See No./Voir no 7845

9813
Dickson, Elinor J. "Core Religious Experience and the Process of Self-Actualization Within the Context of a Religious Congregation." Ottawa, 1978.

Dubé, Clémence. See No./Voir no 9769

9814
Dumais, Monique. "L'église de Rimouski et un plan de développement (1963-1972)." Union Theological Seminary in the City of New York, 1977.

Dupont, Antonin. See No./Voir no 9893

9815
Flynn, Brian John. "A Study of Religious Beliefs and Moral Commitments of Roman Catholics in Calgary: Implications for Religious Socialization." Calgary, 1981.

Gaudin, Jean Roch. See No./Voir no 9894

9816
Giguère, Georges Émile. "La restauration de la Compagnie de Jésus au Canada, 1839-1857." Montréal, 1965.

9817
Gillen, Marie A. "Women Religious in Transition: A Qualitative Study of Personal Growth and Organizational Change." Toronto, 1980. [Halifax Sisters of Charity/Les Soeurs de la Charité d'Halifax]

Gowans, Alan Wilbert. See No./Voir no 935
Héroux, Simon. See No./Voir no 9895
Hornosty, Jennie Mary. See No./Voir no 9771
Jaenen, Cornelius John. See No./Voir no 9915

9818
Jones, Richard Alan. "L'idéologie de l'Action Catholique, 1917-1939." Laval, 1972.

Kelly, David Francis. See No./Voir no 6802
Kerbrat, Dominique Joseph. See No./Voir no 9773
Kernaghan, William. D.K. See No./Voir no 8599
Lamansney, Patrick J. See No./Voir no 6964

9819
Landry, Pauline. "The Financial Management of Roman Catholic Religious Congregations in Canada." Indiana, 1982.

Langlais, Jacques. See No./Voir no 8888
Lee, Frederic Edward. See No./Voir no 6965
Leger, Sister Mary Celeste. See No./Voir no 7430
Lemelin, Abbé Roméo. See No./Voir no 7950
Levine, Gregory James. See No./Voir no 9798
Lupul, Manoly Robert. See No./Voir no 9917
Lyons, Sister Letitia Mary Francis. See No./Voir no 9898
Mawer, David Ronald. See No./Voir no 6949
McCarthy, Mary Martha Cecilia. See No./Voir no 7452
Millman, Thomas R. See No./Voir no 9899
Miner, Horace M. See No./Voir no 769
Morrisey, Francis G. See No./Voir no 7840
Mulhall, David B. See No./Voir no 9900
Nevitte, Neil. See No./Voir no 8582
Nicolson, Murray William Wood. See No./Voir no 7228

9820
Northover, Wallace E. "Religious Disaffection and Perceived Value Discrepancy Among Roman Catholics." York, 1972.

9821
Painchaud, Robert Paul. "The Catholic Church and the Movement of Francophones to the Canadian Prairies, 1870-1915." Ottawa, 1976.

9822
Parenton, Vernon J. "The Rural French-Speaking People of Quebec and South Louisiana: A Comparative Study of Social Structure and Organization with Emphasis on the Role of the Catholic Church." Harvard, 1948.

Perin, Robert. See No./Voir no 9901

9823
Porter, Fernand. "L'institution catéchistique au Canada français, 1633-1833." Catholic, 1945.

9824
Proulx, Jean-Pierre. "Information religieuse au Québec, de 1965 à 1974: la praxis de quatre bureaux de presse diocésains." Montréal, 1979.

9825
Riddell, Walter Alexander. "The Rise of Ecclesiastical Control in Quebec." Columbia, 1916.

Robillard, Denise. See No./Voir no 9902
Rocher, Guy A. See No./Voir no 6984
Rodrique, Denise. See No./Voir no 948
Sait, Edward McChesney. See No./Voir no 8761
Sargent, Robert John. See No./Voir no 9903

9826
Schmeiser, James A. "General Principles of Sacred Liturgy in Canadian Catechisms, Councils and Rituals, Laval to First Plenary Council of Quebec." Ottawa, 1971.

9827
Scorsone, Suzanne Rozell. "Authority, Conflict and Integration: The Catholic Charismatic Renewal Movement and The Roman Catholic Church." Toronto, 1979. [Archdiocese of Toronto/Archevêché de Toronto]

Stortz, Thomas G. See No./Voir no 9907
Sylvestre, Abbé Lucien. See No./Voir no 7851
Ullman, Walter. See No./Voir no 7265
Voisine, Nive. See No./Voir no 9909
Walsh, John J. See No./Voir no 7852
Welton, Mary Amedeus. See No./Voir no 8314

Orthodox Eastern/Orthodoxe de l'est

Bélanger, Louis-Eugène. See No./Voir no 7844

9828
Kazymera, Bohdan. "The Beginnings of the Ukrainian Catholic Hierarchy in Canada." University of Vienna, Austria, 1954.

9829
Marbach, Joseph F. "Marriage Legislation for the Catholics of Oriental Rites in the United States and Canada." Catholic, 1946.

9830
Yuzyk, Paul. "The Ukrainian Greek Orthodox Church of Canada, 1918-1951." Minnesota, 1958.

Church of England (Anglican, Episcopalian)/ Église d'Angleterre (anglicane, épiscopalienne)

9831
Fahey, Curtis James Clifton. "A Troubled Zion: The Anglican Experience in Upper Canada, 1791-1854." Carleton, 1981.

9832
Fingard, Judith J. "The Church of England in Brit North America, 1787-1825." London, 1970.

9833
Headon, Christopher Fergus. "The Influence of Oxford Movement upon the Church of England Eastern and Central Canada, 1840-1900." McC 1940.

9834
Kater, John L., Jr. "The Episcopal Society for C tural and Racial Unity and Its Role in the Episco Church, 1959-1970." McGill, 1973

9835
Knickle, Harry James. "The Anglican Church Colonial Nova Scotia." Temple, 1960.

Levine, Gregory James. See No./Voir no 9798

9836
Pinnington, J.E. "Anglican Reactions to the Challe of a Multi-Congressional Society, with Spec Reference to British North America, 1763-185 Oxford, 1971.

9837
Thompson, Arthur N. "The Expansion of the Church England in Rupert's Land from 1820 to 1839 Un the Hudson's Bay Company and the Church M sionary Society." Cambridge, 1962.

9838
Wilson, Thomas H. "An Historical Study of the Re tionship of the Anglican Church of Canada Kingston Penitentiary 1815-1913." Ottawa, 1980

Church of Christ/Église de Jésus-Christ

Allen, Alexander Richard. See No./Voir no 9794
Lansdell, Clyde Edison. See No./Voir no 3503

9839
Smith, Robert Frederick. "Criteria for the Evaluat of 'Episcope' in the Proposed Church of Christ Canada." Boston University, 1973.

Congregational/Congrégationaliste

See United Church of Canada/Voir Église Unie Canada

Doukhobors

9840
Fry, Gary Dean. "The Doukhobors, 1801-1855: Origins of a Successful Dissident Sect." Americ 1976.

Janzen, William. See No./Voir no 8598

Evangelical United Brethren/ Église évangélique des Frères-Unis

9841
Bloede, Louis William. "Development of New C gregations in the United States and Canada by Evangelical United Brethren Church." Boston U versity, 1960.

Hutterite

Heiken, Diane Ellen Bray. See No./Voir no 782
Janzen, William. See No./Voir no 8598

842
eters, Victor. "A History of the Hutterian Brethren, 1528-1958." University of Göttingen, Germany, 1960.

Lyan, John. See No./Voir no 88

tephenson, Peter Hayford. See No./Voir no 786

Iroquois

t. John, Donald Patrick. See No./Voir no 652

Islam

843
Chi, Tony Poon-Chiang. "A Case Study of the Missionary Stance of the Ahmadiyya Movement in North America." Northwestern, 1973.

Jehovah's Witnesses/Témoins de Jéhovah

Kernaghan, William David K. See No./Voir no 8599

Judaism/Judaïsme

Eichhorn, David M. See No./Voir no 9279
Glickman, Jacob. See No./Voir no 10147
Kernagham, William David K. See No./Voir no 8599
Latowsky, Evelyn Kallen. See No./Voir no 799
haffir, William B.Z. See No./Voir no 802
iemens, Gerhard J. See No./Voir no 803
peisman, Stephen Alan. See No./Voir no 804
844
zuk, Yogev. "A Jewish Communal Welfare Institution in a Changing Society: Montreal; 1920-1980." Concordia, 1981.
Zeitz, Mordecai E. See No./Voir no 7274

Lutheran/Luthérien

845
cola, Leander J. "The Reintroduction of the Eucharistic Prayer in the Lutheran Churches of North America." Ottawa, 1981.

Mennonite

Appavoo, Muthiah David. See No./Voir no 806
Ens, Adolf. See No./Voir no 9914
846
Hamm, Peter Martin. "Continuity and Change Among Canadian Mennonite Brethren, 1925-1975: A Study of Socialization and Secularization in Sectarianism." McMaster, 1978.
Janzen, William. See No./Voir no 8598
847
Krahn, John Jacob. "A History of the Mennonites in British Columbia." British Columbia, 1955.
Thielman, George G. See No./Voir no 810
Van Dyke, Edward William. See No./Voir no 366
Young, Mary McPherson. See No./Voir no 371

Methodism/Méthodisme

See also United Church of Canada/Voir aussi Église Unie du Canada

Mormon (Church of Jesus Christ of Latter Day Saints)/ Mormon (Église de Jésus-Christ des Saints des derniers jours)

9848
Ellsworth, Samuel G. "A History of Mormon Missions in the United States and Canada, 1830-60." California, Berkeley, 1951.
Hyde, William Paul. See No./Voir no 2662
9849
Tagg, Melvin Salway. "A History of the Church of Jesus Christ of Latter Day Saints in Canada, 1830-1963." Brigham Young, 1963.

Presbyterian/Presbytérien

See also United Church of Canada/Voir aussi Église Unie du Canada

Seventh Day Adventist/Adventiste du septième jour

9850
Devnich, Donald Douglas. "An Assessment of the Organizational Climate for Creativity in the Canadian Union Conference of Seventh-Day Adventists — Recommendations for Change Based on the Perceptions of Leading Church Members." Andrews, 1978.
9851
Evans, Larry Robert. "Toward the Development of a Church Planing Strategy for the Local Seventh Day Adventist Church in North America." Andrews, 1981.
9852
Olson, Boyd Edward. "A Follow-up Study of the Children of American and Canadian Seventh Day Adventist Missionaries Serving in Countries of the Far East and Latin America." Nebraska, 1967.

Society of Friends (Quaker)/ Société des Amis (Quaker)

9853
Dorland, Arthur Garratt. "A History of the Society of Friends (Quakers) in Canada." Toronto, 1927.

United Church of Canada/Église Unie du Canada

General Items/Ouvrages généraux

9854
Allman, James Gordon. "Developing Mission Support Criteria for Toronto Conference, the United Church of Canada." Drew, 1982.
9855
Bacon, Douglas Arthur. "The Impact of a Study of Christian Worship (with Special Reference to the Sacrament of the Lord's Supper) on a Congregation of the United Church of Canada." Drew, 1982.

9856
Barker, Ralph Whitehead. "The United Church of Canada and the Social Question." Victoria, 1961.

9857
Bradford, Magnus Andrew. "Consummation of Church Union in Canada in 1925." Temple, 1938.

9858
Clarke, William F. "The Volunteer Lay Leadership of the United Church of Canada in Rural Saskatchewan." Teachers College, Columbia, 1949.

File, Edgar Francis. See No./Voir no 9966

9859
Gundrum, Waldemar. "Transitions as a Potential for Growth in the Life of an Elderly Congregation in Lachine, Quebec." Drew, 1983.

9860
Gunn-Walberg, Kenneth Wayne. "The Church Union Movement in Manitoba, 1902-1925: A Cultural Study of the Decline of Denominationism Within the Protestant Ascendency." Guelph, 1971.

9861
Hughes, Norah L. "A History of the Development of Ministerial Education in Canada from Its Inception Until 1925 in Those Churches Which Were Tributary to the United Church of Canada in Ontario, Quebec, and the Maritime Provinces of Canada." Chicago, 1945.

9862
Kiesekamp, Burkhard. "Community and Faith: The Intellectual and Ideological Bases of the Church Union Movement in Victorian Canada." Toronto, 1975.

9863
MacLeod, Henry Gordon. "The Transformation of the United Church of Canada, 1946-1977: A Study in the Sociology of the Denomination." Toronto, 1980.

9864
MacRury, Ian MacDonald. "A Sharing of the Varied Communion Rites Inherent in the United Church of Canada in an Attempt to Foster Koinonia." Drew, 1982.

9865
Mandich, Michael M. "A Companion to the 'Service Book' of the United Church of Canada." San Francisco Theological Seminary, 1981.

9866
Morrow, Ernest Lloyd. "Doctrinal Significance of the Church Union Movement in Canada." Chicago, 1923.

Nield, John Everson. See No./Voir no 9776

9867
Plato, William Russell. "Eucharistic Worship and the United Church of Canada." Institute of Christian Thought, University of St. Michael's College, 1974.

9868
Price, William Joseph. "Go Forth with God: The History of the Bay of Quinte Conference of the United Church of Canada, 1925-1975." Ottawa, 1981.

9869
Ross, Douglas Harry. "A Theological Analysis of the Socio-Critical Role of the United Church of Canada Between 1925 and 1939." Ottawa, 1982.

Schwarz, Edward Richard. See No./Voir no 9904

Smith, Robert Bell. See No./Voir no 9951

Congregational/Congrégationaliste

9870
Eddy, Earl Bronson. "The Beginnings of Congregationalism in the Early Canadas." Toronto, 1957.

9871
Smith, L.E. "Nineteenth Century Canadian Preaching in Methodist, Presbyterian and Congregational Churches." Victoria, 1953.

Methodism/Méthodisme

9872
Brooks, William Howard. "Methodism in the Canadian West in the Nineteenth Century." Manitoba, 1972.

9873
Burnside, Albert. "The Bible Christians in Canada 1832-1884: A Study in the Indigenization of Methodist Sect, Its Transplantation, Survival, and Limited Growth, Its Absorption and Continuing Legacy." Victoria, 1969.

9874
Emery, George Neil. "Methodism in the Canadian Prairies, 1896 to 1914: The Dynamics of an Institution in a New Environment." British Columbia, 1970.

9875
French, Goldwin Sylvester. "Wesleyan Methodism in Upper Canada and the Maritime Provinces: The Heroic Age, 1780-1855." Toronto, 1958.

Levine, Gregory James. See No./Voir no 9798

9876
Maine, Star Floyd. "Early Methodism in Upper Canada." Chicago, 1932.

9877
McNairn, Norman Alexander. "The American Contribution to Early Methodism in Canada 1790-1840." Iliff School of Theology, 1969.

9878
Semple, Neil Austin Everett. "The Impact of Urbanization on the Methodist Church in Central Canada 1854-1884." Toronto, 1979.

Smith, L.E. See No./Voir no 9871

Presbyterian/Presbytérien

9879
Archibald, F.E. "The Contribution of the Scottish Church to New Brunswick Presbyterianism." Edinburgh, 1932-33.

9880
Binnington, Alfred Fernes. "The Glasgow Colonial Society and its Work in the Development of the Presbyterian Church in British North America 1825-1840." Victoria, 1960.

Bridgman, Harry John. See No./Voir no 9784

9881
Fraser, Brian John. "The Christianization of Our Civilization: Presbyterian Reformers and The Defence of a Protestant Canada, 1875-1914." York, 1983.

9882
Johnston, John A. "The Factors Leading to the Formation of the Presbyterian Church in Canada 1875." McGill, 1956.

Levine, Gregory James. See No./Voir no 9798

83
acDermid, Gordon Edward. "The Religious and Ecclesiastical Life of the Northwest Highlands 1750-1843: The Background of the Presbyterian Emigrants to Cape Breton, Nova Scotia." Aberdeen, 1967.

84
atheson, James Evan. "The Constructive Utilization of Part-Time Ministry Within the Presbytery of Montreal." Fuller Theological Seminary, 1979.

85
cDougall, Elizabeth Ann. "The Presbyterian Church in Eastern Lower Canada, 1815-1842." McGill, 1969.

86
oss, John Arthur. "Regionalism, Nationalism and Social Gospel Support in the Ecumenical Movement of Canadian Presbyterianism." McMaster, 1974.

87
im, Edward Rajamony. "Congregational Renewal and Community Outreach in Morven United Church." Drew, 1982. [Kingston Presbytery/Presbytère de Kingston]

mith, L.E. See No./Voir no 9871

88
alker, J.C. "The Early History of the Presbyterian Church in Western Canada from the Earliest Times to the Year 1881." Edinburgh, 1928.

CANADIAN HISTORICAL RELIGIOUS PERSONALITIES/PERSONNAGES RELIGIEUX HISTORIQUES CANADIENS

89
eck, Jeanne Ruth Merifield. "Henry Somerville and the Development of Catholic Social Thought in Canada: Somerville's Role in the Archdiocese of Toronto, 1915-1943." McMaster, 1977.

90
oucher, Réal. "Monseigneur Charles La Rocque, Évêque de Saint-Hyacinthe (1809-1875)." Ottawa, 1979.

91
adieux, Lorenzo, Rév. "Le père Joseph-Marie Couture, S.J., missionnaire de l'Ontario-nord et premier prêtre aviateur canadien (1885-1949)." Laval, 1958.

92
hausse, Gilles. "J.J. Lartigue, prêtre canadien et premier évêque de Montréal (1777-1840)." Montréal, 1973.

upasquier, Maurice. See No./Voir no 7330

93
upont, Antonin. "The Relations Between the Church and the State Under Louis-Alexandre Taschereau, 1920-1936." McGill, 1971.

94
audin, Jean Roch. "Les rapports entre l'église et l'état d'après le Cardinal Elzéar-Alexandre Taschereau (1820-1898)." Ottawa, 1972.

95
éroux, Simon. "Le Cardinal L.N. Bégin et les relations entre l'église et l'état." Ottawa, 1973.

9896
Jones, Frederick. "Bishop Field, a Study in Politics and Religion in Nineteenth Century Newfoundland." Cambridge, 1972.

Labelle, Suzanne (Soeur Sainte-Marie). See No./Voir no 8299

9897
Lambert, James. "Joseph-Octave Plessis, Church, State and Society in Lower Canada." Laval, 1981.

Lesage, Germain. See No./Voir no 4816

9898
Lyons, Sister Letitia Mary Francis. "Norbert Blanchet and the Founding of the Oregon Missions (1838-1848)." Catholic, 1940.

Mawer, David Ronald. See No./Voir no 6949
McMullin, Stanley G. See No./Voir no 3549

9899
Millman, Thomas R. "Jacob Mountain, First Lord Bishop of Quebec, 1793-1825: A Study in Church and State." McGill, 1944.

9900
Mulhall, David Bernard. "The Missionary Career of A.G. Morice, O.M.I.." McGill, 1979.

9901
Perin, Robert. "Bourget and the Dream of a Free Church in Quebec." Ottawa, 1975.

9902
Robillard, Denise. "Le Cardinal Paul-Émile Léger, archêveque de Montréal, 1950-1967: son évolution idéologique à partir de ses interventions publiques." Ottawa, 1979.

9903
Sargent, Robert John. "The Thought of Monseigneur Louis-Adolphe Paquet as a Spokesman for French-Canadian Ultramontanism." Union Theological Seminary, 1968.

9904
Schwarz, Edward Richard. "Samuel Dwight Chown: An Architect of Canadian Church Union." Boston University, 1961.

9905
Sommers, Hugh Joseph. "The Life and Times of the Hon. and Rt. Rev. Alexander Macdonnell, D.D., First Bishop of Upper Canada, 1762-1840." Catholic, 1931.

9906
Steckler, Gerard George. "Charles John Seghers: Missionary Bishop in the American Northwest, 1839-1886." Washington, Seattle, 1963.

9907
Stortz, Thomas Gerald John. "John Joseph Lynch, Archbishop of Toronto: A Biographical Study of Religious, Political and Social Commitment." Guelph, 1980.

9908
Usher, Jean Edwards. "William Duncan of Metlakatla: A Victorian Missionary in British Columbia." British Columbia, 1969.

9909
Voisine, Nive. "Louis-François Laflèche, deuxième évêque de Trois-Rivières: dans le sillage de Pie IX et de Mgr Bourget (1818-1878)." Laval, 1979.

9910

Weale, David Emrys. "The Ministry of the Reverend Donald McDonald on P.E.I., 1826-1867." Queen's 1976.

Welton, Mary Amedeus. See No./Voir no 8314

Church and State/Église et État

Adams, Howard Joseph. See No./Voir no 2429

9911

Barkwell, Gordon. "The Clergy Reserves in Upper Canada - A Study in the Separation of Church and State, 1791-1854." Chicago, 1953.

9912

Carney, Robert James. "Relations in Education Between Federal and Territorial Governments and the Roman Catholic Church in the Mackenzie District, Northwest Territories, 1867-1961." Alberta, 1971.

Dupont, Antonin. See No./Voir no 9893

9913

Eastman, Mack. "Church and State in Early Canada." Columbia, 1915.

9914

Ens, Adolf. "Mennonite Relations with Governments: Western Canada (1870-1925)." Ottawa, 1979.

Gaudin, Jean R. See No./Voir no 9894

Héroux, Simon. See No./Voir no 9895

9915

Jaenen, Cornelius John. "The Relations Between Church and State in Canada 1647-1685." Ottawa, 1962.

Kernaghan, William David Kenneth. See No./Voir no 8599

Lambert, James. See No./Voir no 9887

9916

Lomasney, Patrick John. "The Relations Between Church and State in New France." St. Louis, 1932.

9917

Lupul, Manoly Robert. "Relations in Education Between the Roman Catholic Church and the State in the Canadian Northwest with Special Reference to the Provisional District of Alberta from 1880 to 1905." Harvard, 1963.

Millman, Thomas R. See No./Voir no 9899

9918

Moir, John Sargent. "The Relations of Church and State in Canada West, 1840-1867." Toronto, 1954.

Morrisey, Francis G. See No./Voir no 7840

Rocher, Guy A.A. See No./Voir no 6984

9919

Thomas, Theodore Elia. "The Protestant Churches and the Religious Issue in Ontario Public Schools: A Study in Church and State." Columbia, 1972.

Ullman, Walter. See No./Voir no 7265

Religion and Education/Religion et enseignement

General Items/Ouvrages généraux

Adams, Howard Joseph. See No./Voir no 2429

9920

Coppin, Norman Roderick. "Religion in Secular Education." Calgary, 1982.

9921

Feder, Herbert Abraham. "Literature and Moral Ed cation: An Examination of the Moral Aspects Literature, Their Significance for Aesthetic Va and Their Influence on Moral Developmen Toronto, 1978. [Moral and religious instruction Ontario public education/Enseignement moral religieux dans le système d'éducation public Ontario]

Morris, John Francis. See No./Voir no 9775

Strevig, Jennie May. See No./Voir no 9801

9922

Webster, Clara Margaret. "Towards a Cognit Developmental Approach in Religious Educatio Toronto, 1975.

Denominational Education/Enseignement confessionn

General Items/Ouvrages généraux

9923

Cooper, George Albert. "Some Differential Effects Denominational Schooling in Newfoundland on Beliefs and Behavior of Students." Toronto, 1972

Baptist/Baptiste

9924

Renfree, Henry Alexander. "The Development of Integrated Educational Design for the Bap Union of Western Canada." Southern Baptist The logical Seminary, 1976.

9925

Robertson, Elizabeth Irene. "Person-Cente Teacher Training for Canadian Baptist Sund Schools." Southwestern Baptist Theological Se nary, 1958.

Brethren in Christ Church/ Église des Frères dans le Christ

9926

Climenhaga, Asa W. "Administrative Practices of Educational Program of the Brethren in Ch Church of the United States and Canad Syracuse, 1945.

Catholic (Roman and Eastern Orthodox)/ Catholique (Romaine et Orient Orthodoxe)

9927

Anctil, Raymond. "Catéchèse québécoise au niv secondaire: analyse critique de sa concept anthropologique." Ottawa, 1981.

9928

Baillargeon, Noël. "Le séminaire de Québec s l'épiscopat de Mgr de Laval, 1663-168 Laval, 1970.

9929

Bizier, Jeanne. "L'éducation chrétienne à l'éc perspective du Rapport Parent et perspective l'église." Ottawa, 1968.

Boland, Francis J. See No./Voir no 3553

Digout, Stanislaus Lawrence. See No./Voir no 3327

9930

Hamilton, Lorne Daniel. "The Issue of Public Aid to Catholic Parochial Schools in the United States with Reference to Education in Quebec." Harvard, 1953.

Hunsberger, Bruce E. See No./Voir no 9959

Kerbrat, Dominique Joseph. See No./Voir no 9773

Klos, Frank William, Jr. See No./Voir no 1156

9931

Kowalski, Alvin Edwin. "A Study of the Role of the Priest in Education in a Selected School System in Alberta." Calgary, 1972.

Langley, Gerald James. See No./Voir no 2544

9932

Lefebvre, Bernard. "Le comité catholique du conseil de l'instruction publique et son oeuvre." Montréal, 1973.

9933

Lehane, Aidan Patrick. "The Idealization of Religious Values in a Catholic School." Toronto, 1977.

Lyons, Peter Andrew. See No./Voir no 9960

MacLean, Rev. Donald Alexander. See No./Voir no 2809

9934

McCarthy, Thomas Noble. "Personality Trait Consistency During the Training Period for a Roman Catholic Congregation of Teaching Brothers." Ottawa, 1956.

Nacke, Margaret D'Arc. See No./Voir no 4070

O'Toole, Padraig. See No./Voir no 2873

Pajonas, Patricia Joan. See No./Voir no 3508

9935

Penney, Mary Paula. "A Study of the Contributions of Three Religious Congregations to the Growth of Education in the Province of Newfoundland." Boston College, 1980. [Sisters of the Presentation, Sisters of Mercy, and the Christian Brothers/Soeurs de la Présentation, Soeurs de la Grâce et Frères Chrétiens]

Plante, Lucienne. See No./Voir no 2537

Ryan, Frances Sheila Ann. See No./Voir no 9962

Ryan, Sister Marie Margaret. See No./Voir no 4200

9936

Timko, Paul Joseph. "Parent, Student, and Teacher Perceptions of the Tasks of Catholic Education in a Selected Alberta Catholic School District." Oregon, 1975.

Church of England (Anglican, Episcopalian)/ Église Anglicane (Anglicane et Épiscopalienne)

9937

Lancaster, Charles F. "Religious Education Under the Church of England in Canada, with Special Application to the Secondary School." Harvard, 1973.

Netten, John Wilfred. See No./Voir no 2462

Porter, Eric Ronald. See No./Voir no 4127

Judaism/Judaïsme

9938

Fialkoff, Steven Alan. "Two [North] American Yeshivot Gedolot: A Character Study of Their Organizations and Functions." Teachers College, Columbia, 1977. [Yeshivah Gedolah Merkaz Hatorah, Montréal, Québec]

Glickman, Jacob. See No./Voir no 10147

9939

Kronitz, Leo. "The Education of Jewish Children in the Province of Quebec." Jewish Theological Seminary, 1969.

9940

Prystowsky, Seymour. "The Purpose and Direction of Contemporary Reform Religious Schools in the United States and Canada: A Study of Concepts and Their Implementation." Dropsie, 1974.

Lutheran/Luthérien

Klos, Frank William, Jr. See No./Voir no 1156

Mennonite

Hunsberger, Bruce Elgin. See No./Voir no 9959

9941

Klassen, Peter George. "A History of Mennonite Education in Canada 1786-1960." Toronto, 1970.

9942

Miller, Ira Ebersole. "The Development and the Present Status of Mennonite Secondary and Higher Education in the United States and Canada." Temple, 1953.

Methodist/Méthodiste

9943

Lawrie, Bruce Raymond. "Educational Missionaries in China: A Case Study of the Educational Enterprise of the Canadian Methodist Mission in Szechwan, West China, 1891-1925." Toronto, 1979.

Mormons

Hyde, William Paul. See No./Voir no 2662

Protestant

9944

Cochrane, Everett George. "The Development of the Curriculum of the Protestant Elementary Schools of Montreal." Toronto, 1968.

9945

Mobley, Jack Arthur. "Protestant Support of Religious Instruction in Ontario Public Schools." Michigan, 1962.

9946

Patterson, Laurence P. "A Plan for the Reorganization of the Administrative Structure of Protestant Education in Greater Montreal." Teachers College, Columbia, 1947.

9947
Teale, Arthur Ernest. "Religious Education Among Protestants in Quebec." The Hartford Seminary Foundation, 1930.

Thomas, Theodore E. See No./Voir no 9919

Seventh Day Adventist/ Adventiste du septième jour

9948
Hillier, Robert Melville. "A Comparative Study of Provincial and Seventh Day Adventist Secondary and Higher Education in Ontario and Alberta." Nebraska, 1971.

9949
Kim, Jung-Gun. "To God's Country: Canadian Missionaries in Korea and the Beginning of Korean Migration to Canada." Toronto, 1983.

9950
Kuhn, Leroy Raymond. "Factors Affecting Mobility Rates of Principals and Teachers in Canadian Seventh Day Adventist Schools." Andrews, 1978.

Du Preez, Ingram Frank. See No./Voir no 3238

United Church of Canada/Église Unie du Canada

Hughes, Norah L. See No./Voir no 9861

Hunsberger, Bruce Elgin. See No./Voir no 9959

9951
Smith, Robert Bell. "The Theory and Practice of Moral Education: A Manual for Use in the United Church." Toronto, 1975.

Elementary and Secondary Schools/ Écoles primaires et secondaires

Cochrane, Everett George. See No./Voir no 9944

9952
Creamer, David Gordon. "Moral Education: A Critical Evaluation of a Jesuit High School Values Program." Toronto, 1982.

Digout, S.L. See No./Voir no 3327

Feder, Herbert Abraham. See No./Voir no 9921

Finley, Eric Gault. See No./Voir no 2525

Fullerton, John Timothy. See No./Voir no 9674

Hamilton, Lorne Daniel. See No./Voir no 9930

Hillier, Robert Melville. See No./Voir no 9948

Lancaster, Charles F. See No./Voir no 9937

Langley, Gerald James. See No./Voir no 2544

Lansdell, Clyde Edison. See No./Voir no 3503

Lorincz, Louis Michael. See No./Voir no 2690

Matthews, William David Edison. See No./Voir no 2503

Miller, Ira Ebersole. See No./Voir no 9942

Mobley, Jack Arthur. See No./Voir no 9945

Pajonas, Patricia Joan. See No./Voir no 3508

Ryan, Sister Marie Margaret. See No./Voir no 4200

Woolard, Louis Clyde. See No./Voir no 4246

Colleges and Universities/Collèges et universités

Beattie, Margaret Eileen. See No./Voir no 8603

Bellagamba, Anthony D. See No./Voir no 3540

Boland, Francis J. See No./Voir no 3553

9953
Boon, Harold Watson. "The Development of the Bible College or Institute in the United States and Canada Since 1880 and Its Relationship to the Field of Theological Education in America." New York, 1950.

9954
Bruins, Elton John. "The New Brunswick Theological Seminary, 1884-1959." New York, 1962.

Budd, Henry Harold. See No./Voir no 3609

9955
Campbell, Douglas F. "Religion and Values Among Nova Scotia College Students." Catholic, 1954.

9956
Cooper, Alvin John. "The Development of a Department of Practical Theology at St. Stephens College, Edmonton, Canada." Teachers College, Columbia, 1950.

Ferguson, Marianne. See No./Voir no 3677

9957
Gazard, Peter Robin. "A Needs Assessment of Transfer Credit Procedures in Canadian Bible Colleges." Calgary, 1980.

9958
Glazier, Kenneth MacLean. "The Place of Religion in the History of Non-Catholic Universities in Canada." Yale, 1944.

Hillier, Robert Melville. See No./Voir no 9948

9959
Hunsberger, Bruce Elgin. "Religious Denominational Education and University Students' Reported Agreement with Parents' Religious Beliefs." Manitoba, 1973.

Lessard, Claude. See No./Voir no 9978

9960
Lyons, Peter A. "Theological Foundations of Catholic Higher Education: A Study of the Relationship Between Ecclesiology and the Self-Understanding of Catholic Colleges and Universities in North America from 1940 to the Present." Institute of Religious Thought, University of St. Michael's College, 1974.

9961
Rose, Robert Arthur. "The Evolution of the Role of the Board of Trustees in the Governance of Canadian Bible College." Alberta, 1981. [Regina, Saskatchewan]

9962
Ryan, Frances Sheila Ann. "A Small Group Approach to Professional Socialization." York, 1977. [Seminary students' training for the Roman Catholic priesthood/Formation de séminaristes pour devenir prêtres catholiques romains]

Weinhauer, Carlin Eugene. See No./Voir no 3528

9963
Wilson, Lon Ervin. "The Status of Speech and Homiletics in Bible Schools in the United States and Canada." Northern Baptist Theological Seminary, 1958.

PSYCHOLOGY OF RELIGION/PSYCHOLOGIE DE LA RELIGION

Ellis, Robert Sydney. See No./Voir no 598

SOCIOLOGY OF RELIGION/SOCIOLOGIE DE LA RELIGION

Anderson, Alan Betts. See No./Voir no 418
Barilko, M. Olga. See No./Voir no 9643
Cardillo, Ralph Michael. See No./Voir no 9218
Castelli, Giuseppe. See No./Voir no 791

9964
Currie, Raymond Francis. "Religion and Images of Man Among Calgary Youth." Fordham, 1973.

9965
Denys, Jozef G. "A Comparative Study of the Effects of Roman Catholic High Schools and Public High Schools on the Roman Catholic Commitment of Roman Catholic Students in Southern Ontario." Waterloo, 1972.

9966
File, Edgar Francis. "A Sociological Analysis of Church Union in Canada." Boston University, 1961.

Flynn, Brian John. See No./Voir no 9815
Kerbrat, Dominique Joseph. See No./Voir no 9773
Kiely, Margaret C. See No./Voir no 9698
Latowsky, Evelyn Kallan. See No./Voir no 799
MacLeod, Henry Gordon. See No./Voir no 9863

9967
Mann, William Edward. "Social Conditions Underlying the Growth of Religious Sects in Calgary, Alberta." Toronto, 1953.

9968
O'Hearn, M.J. "The Political Transformation of a Religious Order." Toronto, 1983.

Parenton, Vernon J. See No./Voir no 9822
Schroeder, Harold John. See No./Voir no 1189
Segall, Alexander. See No./Voir no 6928

9969
Small, Helen Francis. "Changes in Traditional Norms of Enclosure: A Study of the Secularization of Religious Women." McMaster, 1973.

9970
Westley, Frances R. "The Complex Forms of the Religious Life: A Durkheimian View of New Religious Movements." McGill, 1978. [Montreal area/Région de Montréal]

Zeitz, Mordecai Eliezer. See No./Voir no 7274

SOCIOLOGY/SOCIOLOGIE

Research in the numerous sub-classifications of sociology has come of age in Canadian society. There was very little doctoral research done in this area between 1920 and 1970. One dissertation was produced in the 1930's, two in the 1940's, four in the 1950's, 22 in the 1960's, and ten times that number in the 1970's. The eighties give evidence of surpassing that total.

Of the twenty Canadian universities producing dissertations in this area, the University of Toronto, has contributed forty percent of the Canadian total. The University of Montreal is second, and the universities of Alberta, York, and British Columbia are third, fourth, and fifth, respectively. Of the 43 American universities, Columbia is first with 13 dissertations. Great Britain has produced a total of only five studies from four universities, the University of London accounting for two.

————

Dans les nombreuses sous-classifications de la sociologie, la recherche s'est intensifiée au fur et à mesure que la société canadienne prenait de l'importance. On trouve très peu de recherche en vue d'un doctorat entre 1920 et 1970. On a compté une thèse dans les années 1930, deux dans les années 1940, quatre dans les années 1950, 22 dans les années 1960, et enfin dix fois ce nombre dans les années 1970; les années 1980 semblent devoir surpasser ce total.

Parmi les 20 établissements canadiens qui produisent des thèses en ce domaine, l'Université de Toronto a fourni à elle seule 40% du total canadien. L'Université de Montréal arrive en seconde position, suivie des universités de l'Alberta, York et de la Colombie-Britannique, respectivement au troisième, quatrième et cinquième rang. Parmi les 43 universités américaines, Columbia vient en premier avec 13 thèses. La Grande-Bretagne apporte en tout cinq thèses, provenant de quatre universités; l'Université de Londres, pour sa part, en a fourni deux.

GENERAL ITEMS/OUVRAGES GÉNÉRAUX

Baker, G. Ross. See No./Voir no 6827
Beer, Anne Maria. See No./Voir no 4057
Boldt, Menno. See No./Voir no 447

9971
Campbell, Brian Lewis. "Disputes Among Experts: A Sociological Case Study of the Debate over Biology in the Mackenzie Valley Pipeline Inquiry." McMaster, 1983.

Carrington, Peter John. See No./Voir no 1739
Chawla, Saroj. See No./Voir no 7994
Clark, Melissa Helen. See No./Voir no 8836
Cliche, Pierre. See No./Voir no 4754

9972
Coughlin, Richard Maurice. "Ideology and Social Policy: A Comparative Study of the Structure of Public Opinion in Eight Rich Nations." California, Berkeley, 1977.

9973
Covello, Vincent T. "The Process of Status Attainment in Contemporary Societies: A Cross-National Comparison." Columbia, 1976. [Canada is one of the eight countries studied/Le Canada est parmi les huits pays étudiés]

Dalto, Guy Calvin. See No./Voir no 1742

9974
Edginton, Barry Eugene. "The Formation of the Asylum in Upper Canada." Toronto, 1981.

Eglin, Peter Anthony. See No./Voir no 6794

9975
Fisher, Helen Elizabeth. "Professional Associations in Canada." Toronto, 1925.

Fox, Bonnie J. See No./Voir no 2058

Ghorayski, F.P. See No./Voir no 66

Gibbons, Jacqueline Anne. See No./Voir no 944

9976
Goldenberg, Sheldon. "Composition or Character-Structural Alternatives to Cultural Explanations of Canadian-American Institutional Differences." Northwestern, 1974.

Gordon, Richard Irving. See No./Voir no 7255

Goulding, James Wray. See No./Voir no 1169

Guppy, L. Neil. See No./Voir no 9685

Hart, Douglas John. See No./Voir no 1320

Itwaru, Arnold H. See No./Voir no 8008

Klein, William J. See No./Voir no 8554

9977
Kopinak, Kathryn Mary. "Sex Differences in Ontario Political Culture." York, 1978.

Lautard, E. Hugh. See No./Voir no 1276

Leatt, P. See No./Voir no 6916

9978
Lessard, Claude Robert Théophile. "Modernization and the Institutionalization of Differentiation: The Quebec Case." Toronto, 1975.

9979
Lockhart, R.A. "Future Failure: A Systematic Analysis of Changing Middle Class Opportunities in Canada." Essex, 1978.

McCrorie, James Napier. See No./Voir no 140

Mifflen, Frances James. See No./Voir no 1292

Moffett, Samuel Erasmus. See No./Voir no 2333

9980
Moore, Dorothy Emma. "Multiculturalism – Ideology or Social Reality." Boston University, 1980.

9981
Morrison, Kenneth Leslie. "Readers' Work: Devices for Achieving Pedagogic Events in Textual Materials for Readers as Novices to Sociology." York, 1976.

Olsen, Dennis. See No./Voir no 8450

9982
Pardo, Luis Enrique. "Stigma and Sociological Justice: The Effects of Physical Disability vis à vis Moral Turpitude." York, 1974.

Poupart, Jean. See No./Voir no 10375

9983
Regehr, Henry John. "Expectation, Trust and the Management of Complaints: The Case of Auto Repair Work." Waterloo, 1983.

9984
Renaud, Jean. "Langues, ethnies et revenus." Montréal, 1979.

9985
Robichaud, Jean-Bernard. "Indicators of Development in Canada." Chicago, 1974.

Ross, Ian D. See No./Voir no 6855

9986
Rousseau, Jacques. "Analyse de la représentatio professionnelle." Laval, 1979.

Ryant, Joseph Charles. See No./Voir no 2080

Schlesinger, R.C. See No./Voir no 2064

Schmidt, Eric. See No./Voir no 8689

Schneider, Saundra Kay. See No./Voir no 8516

Smith, Richard David. See No./Voir no 6698

Spina, Joseph M. See No./Voir no 8595

Tomovic, Vladislav A. See No./Voir no 3746

Ward, James Stanley. See No./Voir no 4914

CULTURAL AND URBAN ANTHROPOLOGY/ ANTHROPOLOGIE CULTURELLE ET URBAINE

See also Anthropology/Voir aussi Anthropologie

Canadian Social Thought/Pensée sociale canadienne

9987
Gaudreau, Sister Marie Agnes of Rome. "The Socia Thought of French Canada as Reflected in th Semaines Sociales." Catholic, 1945.

Goulding, James Wray. See No./Voir no 1169

9988
Harrison, Deborah Ann. "Canada and the Limits o Liberalism: A Study of S.D. Clark." York, 1979.

Maidstone, Peter. See No./Voir no 9139

9989
Moore, Mary Candace. "The Theory, Practice an Rhetoric of Loyalty." York, 1983.

9990
Stahl, William Austin. "Symbols of Canada: Civi Religion, Nationality, and the Search for Meaning Graduate Theological Seminary, 1981.

9991
Tax, Joel Perry. "Information and Exclusion." York 1982.

9992
Thornton, David Andrew "The Theory of Populatio Instability and Mortality: A Sociological Investiga tion of Stress Related Mortality in Ontario. Waterloo, 1976.

EDUCATIONAL SOCIOLOGY/ SOCIOLOGIE DE L'ÉDUCATION

Akhtar, Muhammad Mumtaz. See No./Voir no 4290

Akoodie, Mohammed. See No./Voir no 745

Baker, Robert Andrew. See No./Voir no 3318

Barakett-Brand, Joyce. See No./Voir no 4294

Barrados, Maria. See No./Voir no 3319

Bryans, David Garth. See No./Voir no 3305

Cooke, Geoffrey James. See No./Voir no 4271

Corlett, Susan Gail. See No./Voir no 8905

Curtis, Bruce Malcolm. See No./Voir no 2485

Darville, Richard Tulloss. See No./Voir no 1379

Denys, Jozef G. See No./Voir no 9965

Elkin, Lorne. See No./Voir no 8988

Farley, John Edward. See No./Voir no 10010

9993
Foster, Lois Elaine. "A Sociological Analysis of th Royal Commission on Education in Alberta, 1957 1959." Alberta, 1975.

Gorlick, Carolyne Ann. See No./Voir no 4115

9994
Grabb, Edward George. "Language Group Differences in Career Orientation: An Analysis of 'Career Dissociation' Among French and English Canadian Secondary School Students." Waterloo, 1976.

9995
Herberg, Edward Norman. "Education Through the Ethnic Looking-Glass: Ethnicity and Education in Five Canadian Cities." Toronto, 1980. [Halifax, Montréal, Toronto, Winnipeg and/et Vancouver]

Hitchman, Gladys Simon. See No./Voir no 3682

9996
Horwich, Herbert R. "Social and Cultural Factors Affecting Student Retentions or Attritions at the Secondary and Post-Secondary Levels." Montréal, 1979.

Lamontagne, Jacques. See No./Voir no 3654
Legault, Gisèle. See No./Voir no 10088
MacDonald, Peter Ian. See No./Voir no 2500
MacFarland, Gertrude Cecile. See No./Voir no 3656

9997
MacNab, Grace Lowe. "The Relationship Between an Ambivalent School Climate and the Socialization of Second Language (French) Learning." Carleton, 1977.

9998
Martin, Wilfred Benjamin Weldon. "Interactions in the School: A Study in Negotiation." York, 1972.

9999
Mason, Graham Archdale. "Deprived Children: An Ethnographic Study of Identity Through the Schooling Process." British Columbia, 1973.

Massot, Alain. See No./Voir no 2983

10000
Maxwell, Mary Percival. "Social Structure Socialization and Social Class in a Canadian Private School for Girls." Cornell, 1970.

Murphy, Raymond J.J. See No./Voir no 4267
Oakes, Jocelyn Diane. See No./Voir no 4154

10001
Ollivier, Emile. "Analyse sociologique d'un programme d'éducation populaire: l'expérience multimédia au Québec." Montréal, 1981.

Pajonas, Patricia Joan. See No./Voir no 3508
Parducci, Ronald Edmond. See No./Voir no 2582

10002
Parks-Trusz, Sandra Lynn. "A Sociological Study of Knowledge Production and Control: Comparative Education in North America, 1945-1975." SUNY, Buffalo, 1979.

Ping, Benjamin Leung Kai. See No./Voir no 3695
Podmore, Christopher John. See No./Voir no 2415

10003
Pomfret, Dennis Alan. "The Politization of a New Setting: Perspectives, Networks and Planned Organizational Change." Toronto, 1981.

Randall, Frances S. See No./Voir no 845
Rauf, Abdur. See No./Voir no 2587
Richer, Stephen Irwin. See No./Voir no 3351
Robinson, Barrie W. See No./Voir no 3698
Runge, Janis Margaret. See No./Voir no 2589
Russell, Susan Jessie. See No./Voir no 3352

10004
Singh, Amarjit. "Self-Concept of Ability and School Achievement of Seventh Grade Students in New-foundland: A Symbolic Interactionist Approach." Michigan State, 1972.

10005
Smith, D.L. "Consistency and Congruency in Levels of Occupational Aspiration and Expectation of Students in Selected Single Enterprise Communities." Alberta, 1980.

10006
Sopp, Trudy Jane. "A New Model of Teambuilding That Accounts for the Power and Politics Operating in Organizational Settings." Toronto, 1982.

Sparham, Donald Cauthers. See No./Voir no 2401
Taylor, Gerald Dale. See No./Voir no 4157
Taylor, Gilbert Frederick. See No./Voir no 2976
Trottier, Claude René. See No./Voir no 2800

10007
Weary, Bettina. "Occupational Differentials in the Perceptions and Opinions of Foreign Students." American, 1960.

Weeks, Peter Alan Donald. See No./Voir no 1009

10008
Weinzweig, Paul Alan. "Socialization and Sub-Culture in Elite Education: A Study of a Canadian Boys' Private School." Toronto, 1970.

RURAL SOCIOLOGY/SOCIOLOGIE RURALE

10009
Hale, Sylvia Marion. "Decision Processes in Rural Development." British Columbia, 1976.

Pilon, Lise. See No./Voir no 138
Wahn, Michael Brian. See No./Voir no 1194

URBAN SOCIOLOGY/SOCIOLOGIE URBAINE

Amey, Lorne James. See No./Voir no 7976
Beaman, Jay Gillmore. See No./Voir no 4897

10010
Farley, John Edward. "Effects of Residential Setting, Parental Lifestyle, and Demographic Characteristics of Childrens' Activity Patterns." Michigan, 1977.

Germain, Anne. See No./Voir no 7270
Gill, Warren George. See No./Voir no 4921

10011
Gillis, Allison Ronald. "Density and Crowding." Alberta, 1975. [Calgary and/et Edmonton]

Grayson, John Paul. See No./Voir no 8768
Harris, Simon Richard. See No./Voir no 2240
Lipman, Marvin Harold. See No./Voir no 10033
Lowe, Graham Stanley. See No./Voir no 1278
McCaskill, Donald Neil. See No./Voir no 476
Parakulam, George G. See No./Voir no 10069

10012
Reed, Paul Bramwell. "Life Style as an Element of Social Logic: Patterns of Activity, Social Characteristics, and Residential Choice." Toronto, 1976. [Toronto]

10013
Rhyne, Darla Lindop. "Organizational Life in River City: A Case Study of Class, Ethnicity, Geographical Mobility and Status." Toronto, 1979. [Northern Manitoba/Nord du Manitoba]

10014
Stafford, James Dale. "Explaining Urban Development in Canada." Alberta, 1975.

10015
Van Vliet, Willem. "Use, Evaluation, and Knowledge of City and Suburban Environments by Children of Employed and Non-Employed Mothers." Toronto, 1980.

10016
Wayne, Jack. "Networks of Informal Participation in a Suburban Context." Toronto, 1971. [York]

INDUSTRIAL SOCIOLOGY/
SOCIOLOGIE INDUSTRIELLE

10017
Atack, W.A. "The Structure of Group Cohesion: An Analysis of Retail Selling." Carleton, 1978.

10018
Calzavera, L.M. "Social Networks and Access to Job Opportunities." Toronto, 1983.

Carrington, Peter John. See No./Voir no 1739

10019
Carroll, William Kingsley. "Capital Accumulation and Corporate Interlocking in Post-War Canada." York, 1981.

10020
Dasko, Donna Anne. "Incomes, Income Attainment and Income Inequality Among Race-Sex Groups: A Test of the Dual Industry Theory." Toronto, 1982.

Garry, Carl. See No./Voir no 4347

10021
Hardy-Roch, Marcel. "La sélection sociale dans l'entreprise, étude monographique." Carleton, 1980.

James, Hugh Mackenzie. See No./Voir no 1205

Laxer, Gordon David. See No./Voir no 1277

10022
MacKinnon, Malcolm Hector. "The Industrialized Operative in the Liberal Democratic State: Instrumentalized or Radicalized." York, 1978.

Mayer, Janet Judith. See No./Voir no 2060

McAllister, Barbara H. See No./Voir no 2117

10023
McDermott, Patricia Catherine. "From Franchising to Microelectronics: An Analysis of Corporate Strategy." Toronto, 1982.

Parent, Robert. See No./Voir no 1884

Schenk, Christopher Robert. See No./Voir no 2215

POLITICAL SOCIOLOGY/SOCIOLOGIE POLITIQUE

Bashevkin, Sylvia Beth. See No./Voir no 8435

Carroll, William Kingsley. See No./Voir no 10019

10024
Conway, John Frederick. "To Seek a Goodly Heritage: The Prairie Populist Resistance to the National Policy in Canada." Simon Fraser, 1979.

10025
Divay, Gérard. "Réforme institutionnelle locale et fourniture des biens collectifs locaux: une approche sociopolitique." Laval, 1977.

Glenday, Daniel. See No./Voir no 8756

Hannigan, John Andrew. See No./Voir no 8723

10026
Johnston, William Atchison. "Social Class and Political Ideology in Canada." York, 1982.

Kelly, Lawrence Alexander. See No./Voir no 1647

Knuttila, Kenneth Murray. See No./Voir no 117

SOCIOLOGY OF RELIGION/
SOCIOLOGIE DE LA RELIGION

See also Religion/Voir aussi Religion

FAMILY LIFE AND RELATIONS/
VIE FAMILIALE ET RELATIONS FAMILIALES

General Items/Ouvrages généraux

10027
Anderson, Joan Madge. "Making Sense of Normality An Interpretive Perspective on 'Normal' and 'Disturbed' Family." British Columbia, 1981.

10028
Blair, Mansell John. "Familism and Style of Participation in the Christian Family Movement in Canada." Notre Dame, 1968.

Bresver, Barbara. See No./Voir no 9649

10029
Butler, Peter Marshall. "Involvement in Work and Family Worlds: A Study of Work-Family Linkages in Single-Earner and Dual-Earner Families." Toronto, 1974.

10030
Chebat, Jean-Charles. "Famille et classe sociale: une approche systémique à la communication intra-familiale." Montréal, 1976.

10031
Farina, Margaret Radcliffe. "The Relationship of the State to the Family in Ontario: State Intervention in the Family on Behalf of Children." Toronto, 1982.

Gray-Snelgrove, Rosemary. See No./Voir no 10198

Guest, Henry Hewson. See No./Voir no 3408

10032
Hagarty, Linda Margaret Mary. "The Family at Home A Comparison of the Time-Budgets of Families in Highrise Apartments and Detached Houses in Suburban Metropolitan Toronto." Toronto, 1975.

Kitchen, Brigitte. See No./Voir no 1323

10033
Lipman, Marvin Harold. "Relocation and Family Life a Study of the Social and Psychological Consequences of Urban Renewal." Toronto, 1968.

10034
Maidman, Frank Victor. "Family Openness and Adolescent Social Engagement." Toronto, 1972.

Papatola, Kathleen Joan. See No./Voir no 8929

10035
Rosenthal, Carolyn Judith. "Generational Relations and Succession: A Study of Authority and Responsibility in Families." McMaster, 1982.

10036
Siddique, Muhammad. "Work and Family in a Contemporary Urban-Industrial Society: An Analysis of Canadian Data." Toronto, 1980.

10037
Smith, Doreen Lucille. "Consistency and Congruency in Levels of Occupational Aspiration and Expectation of Students in Selected Simple Enterprise Communities." Alberta, 1980.

10038
Turk, James Leonard. "The Measurement of Intra-Familial Power." Toronto, 1970.

Van Vliet, Willem. See No./Voir no 10015

Marital Relations/Relations conjugales

Appelle, Morry. See No./Voir no 9114

10039
Boivin, Micheline. "Communication conjugale en milieu défavorisé urbain québécois." Ottawa, 1973.

10040
Brillinger, M.E. "Individuals' Intentional Changes Related to Marriage." Toronto, 1983.

10041
Brintnell, Eldonna S.G. "The Spinal Cord Injured and Spouse: A Case Study of Role Change and Dyadic Adjustment." Alberta, 1981.

10042
Chan, Kwok Bun. "Husband-Wife Violence in Toronto." York, 1978.

10043
Chimbos, Peter D. "Marital Violence: A Study of Inter-Spouse Homicide." York, 1976.

10044
Da Costa, Derek Mendes. "Divorce in Canada." Harvard, 1972.

10045
Davies, T.G. "A Marriage Encounter Episode as Witnessed Through Dialogue." Toronto, 1983.

10046
Demmler-Kane, Jean. "Multiple Migration and the Social Participation of Married Women." McMaster, 1980. [Recent migrants to the Hamilton-Burlington area of Ontario/Émigrants nouveaux dans la région de Hamilton-Burlington en Ontario]

10047
Gee, Ellen Margaret Thomas. "Fertility and Marriage Patterns in Canada, 1851-1971." British Columbia, 1978.

10048
Heffner, Charles Watson. "A Comparative Study of Two Approaches to Marital Counseling." Toronto, 1982.

Humphreys, Carolyn Ann. See No./Voir no 8918

10049
Irving, Howard Harris. "A Study of the Patterns of Relationships Between Married Clients and their Parents and Parents-in-Law." Toronto, 1975.

Kincaid, Patricia Jean. See No./Voir no 4147

Kovitz, Karen Elizabeth. See No./Voir no 9302

10050
Martin-Matthews, Anne Elizabeth. "Wives Experiences of Relocation: Status Passage and the Moving Career." McMaster, 1980. [Ontario]

McRae, Bradley Collins. See No./Voir no 9312

Meade, Edward Simon. See No./Voir no 4153

Medling, James. See No./Voir no 9034

Mendonca, Augustine, Rev. See No./Voir no 9629

10051
Pearlman, Sheldon. "Convergence of Therapist and Client Goals in the Initial Stage of Marital Counseling and Its Relationship to Continuance in Treatment." Toronto, 1977.

10052
Redekop, Paul Isaac. "Morals in Marriage: A Developmental Analysis of Marital Expectations." York, 1978.

10053
Sheppard, Deborah Lee. "Awareness and Decision-making in Dual-Career Couples." York, 1981.

10054
Stanton, John Ormond. "A Social Work Model for Developing and Empirically Testing Practice Principles in Marital Counseling." Toronto, 1972.

10055
Vachon, Mary L. Suslak. "Identity Change over the First Two Years of Bereavement: Social Relationships and Social Support in Widowhood." York, 1979.

10056
Veevers, Jean Eleanor. "Voluntarily Childless Wives: An Exploratory Study." Toronto, 1973.

Births, Birth Control and Planning and Fertility/ Naissances, contrôle et planification des naissances et fertilité

Adsett, Nancy Leigh. See No./Voir no 9635

10057
Beaudet-Carisse, Colette. "Une étude de la planification des naissances en milieu canadien-français." Montréal, 1964.

10058
Blais, Hervé. "Les tendances engénistes au Canada." Montréal, 1942.

Barker, Stephen David. See No./Voir no 8951

Branch, Edward B. See No./Voir no 9427

10059
Chao, John Chin-Tsai. "A Cohort Approach to the Study of Fertility Trends in Quebec, Canada." Catholic, 1971.

10060
Cloutier-Cournoyer, Renée. "Interaction conjugale et planification des naissances en milieu défavorisé urbain québécois." Laval, 1979.

10061
Condon, Thomas Francis. "Bi-Culturalism and Adolescent Aspirations: A Comparison of English and French-Speaking Canadians' Family Size Expectations." Minnesota, 1971.

Derow, Ellan Odiorne. See No./Voir no 2177

10062
Desmarteaux, Denise. "Influence des valeurs et des rôles conjugaux sur le choix de méthodes naturelles et artificielles de régulation des naissances chez des couples québécois." Montréal, 1982.

Gee, Ellen Margaret Thomas. See No./Voir no 10047

10063
Guyatt, Doris Elsie. "Adolescent Pregnancy: A Study
of Pregnant Teenagers in a Suburban Community in
Ontario." Toronto, 1976.
Hyde, Naida. See No./Voir no 9299
Kennedy, William J. See No./Voir no 9487
Keown, Lauriston Livingston. See No./Voir no 6740
Kindelan, Kevin M. See No./Voir no 9018
10064
Kyriazis, Natalie. "A Socioeconomic Framework for
the Analysis of Marital Fertility: Canada, 1971."
Indiana, 1977.
Lemieux-Michaud, Denise. See No./Voir no 8218
Lloyd, Cynthia Brown. See No./Voir no 1178
Looker, Ellen Dianne. See No./Voir no 10210
Madduri, V.B.N.S. See No./Voir no 10313
10065
Mazany, Robin Leigh. "A Model of the Joint Determi-
nation of Labour Force Participation and Fertility
Decisions of Married Women." British Columbia,
1982.
10066
McCurley, Donna Anne. "The Effect of Ethnic Diver-
sity within Catholicism on Differential Catholic
Fertility in Canada, 1971." Tulane, 1983.
10067
McDaniel, Susan Anderson. "Family Size Expectations
in Edmonton: A Cohort Approach." Alberta, 1978.
McInnes, Simon. See No./Voir no 8514
10068
Morah, Benson Chukwuma "Timing of Births in
Edmonton: Patterns and Consequences." Alberta,
1977.
Painter, Susan Lee. See No./Voir no 9387
10069
Parakulam, George G. "Physical Density, Perceived
Crowding and Reproductive Orientation: An
Exploratory Survey of Urban Middle Class
Husbands from Transitional and Modern Contexts."
Toronto, 1978.
Piché, Louise. See No./Voir no 2078
Preston, Valerie Ann. See No./Voir no 1580
Proulx, Monique Cécile. See No./Voir no 3696
10070
Rao, Namperumal Baskara. "Fertility and Income in
Canada: A Time Series and Cross Section
Analysis." Alberta, 1973.
Razaul, Haque M. See No./Voir no 811
10071
Sangadasa, A. "Married Female Labour Force Partici-
pation and Fertility in Canada." Alberta, 1981.
Sexton, Christine Sophie. See No./Voir no 9748
Sharma, Raghubar D. See No./Voir no 7609
Simmons, Joyce N. See No./Voir no 9474
Skarsten, Steinar Stan. See No./Voir no 10101
Thomlison, Raymond John. See No./Voir no 10102
Veevers, Jean Eleanor. See No./Voir no 10056
Wahn, M.B. See No./Voir no 1194
Wisniewski, Lawrence John. See No./Voir no 2086
Woolcott, Donna Myles. See No./Voir no 6755

SOCIAL WORK AND SOCIAL WELFARE/ TRAVAIL SOCIAL ET BIEN-ÊTRE SOCIAL

General Item/Ouvrage général

10072
Irving, A. "The Life and Work of Harry Cassidy."
Toronto, 1983.

Social Work/Travail social

10073
Beaudoin, André. "The Value Orientations of Social
Work Practitioners in the Province of Quebec."
Pittsburgh, 1976.
10074
Bennett, Victor George. "An Analysis of Predictors of
Job Satisfaction Among Social Caseworkers in
Newfoundland." Northern Colorado, 1977.
10075
Berlinguet, Marie. "La pratique des travailleurs
sociaux du Québec dans les requêtes de stérilisa-
tion volontaire." Toronto, 1975.
10076
Bohm, Peter Emblidge. "Client Variables Associated
with Outcomes of Conciliation Counseling."
Toronto, 1981.
Côté, Serge. See No./Voir no 1814
10077
Curtis, Hugh Jefferson. "School Social Work Roles and
Services in Canada." Utah, 1978.
10078
Darrach-Pearse, Shirley Anne. "The Continuing
Practice-Related Learning of Professional Social
Workers — An Exploratory Study." Toronto, 1982.
10079
Egli, André. "Idéologies et travailleurs sociaux:
Québec, 1980." Toronto, 1981.
10080
Gendron, Jean-Louis. "La structuration du pouvoir
dans l'implantation des CLSC en Estrie." Laval,
1979.
10081
Gow, Kathleen Mavourneen. "A Comparison of Judg-
ments of Social Workers and Public Health Nurses
Concerning Orientation to the Social Education
Ideology: A Case Study of Professionals as Moral
Entrepreneurs." York, 1973.
10082
Hagarty, Stephen Leo Francis. "A Study of the
Primary Relationships of the Psychiatric Patient."
Toronto, 1975.
10083
Johnson, Dennis Brian. "Client Perception of Social
Workers." Alberta, 1972.
10084
Keirn, William Clair. "Social Service in Genetic Units
in the United States and Canada: A Descriptive
Survey." Southern California, 1976.
10085
Kimberley, Mark Harry Dennis. "Organization Devel-
opment Practice Theory for Social Work Within
Management Context: A Demonstration Study."
Toronto, 1978.

10086
Kufeldt, Kathleen Sylvaria. "Temporary Foster Care: Theoretical Perspectives and Participants' Perceptions." Calgary, 1981.

10087
Latimer, Elspeth Anne. "An Analysis of the Social Action Behaviour of the Canadian Association of Social Workers from its Organizational Beginning to the Modern Period." Toronto, 1972.

10088
Legault, Gisèle. "Community Education and Citizen Participation." Columbia, 1976. [Montréal]

10089
Lioy, Michele L. "The Social Organization of Case Processing by Administrative Tribunals." British Columbia, 1975.

Macdonald, J. Grant. See No./Voir no 9262

10090
MacFadden, Robert James. "Worker Burnout in Child Protection." Toronto, 1982. [Children's Aid Societies/Sociétés d'aide à l'enfance]

10091
Marino, Robert Vincent. "A Study of the Helping Mechanisms in a Peer Therapy Self-Help Group." Toronto, 1981.

10092
McIntyre, Eilene L. Goldberg. "The Provision of Day Care in Ontario: Responsiveness of Provincial Policy to Children at Risk Because their Mothers Work." Toronto, 1979.

10093
McMahon, Peter Casey. "A Study of Social Service Graduates in Ontario." Toronto, 1977.

10094
Mullaly, R.P. "Access to Social Services by Families with a Mentally Retarded Child." Toronto, 1983.

10095
Paley, David Thomas. "Person Perceptive Skills and the Helping Relationship: A Study of Alberta Social Service Aides." Alberta, 1972.

10096
Palmer, S.E. "The Effects of Training in C.A.S. Workers' Handling of Separation." Toronto, 1983.

10097
Polgar, Alexander T. "A Structural-Development Analysis of Levels of Social Reasoning in Correctional Volunteers." Toronto, 1982.

10098
Rondeau, Gilles. "Evaluative Research with Clients on the Services Received in the Family Agencies of Metropolitan Montreal." Pittsburgh, 1976.

10099
Rothery, M.A. "Structure and Responsivity: An Exploratory Study of Interviewing Behaviors." Toronto, 1983.

10100
Simard-Trottier, Marie. "La sélection d'un centre de services sociaux comme ressource d'aide." Toronto, 1981.

10101
Skarsten, Steinar Stan. "An Examination of the Potential Effectiveness of Social Work Intervention into Marital Sexual Dysfunctions." Toronto, 1977.

Smith, Richard David. See No./Voir no 6698

10102
Thomlison, Raymond John. "A Behavioral Model for Social Work Intervention with the Marital Dyad." Toronto, 1973.

10103
Trute, Barry. "Social Indicators as Predictors of Social Integration in Saskatchewan and California." California, Berkeley, 1975.

10104
Tucker, David John. "Interorganizational Relations and the Delivery of Social Services." Toronto, 1978.

10105
Vachon, Jacques. "Foster Care in Montreal: A Replication Study of Filial Deprivation." Columbia, 1978.

10106
Van derKrabben, Jacobus Johannes Maria. "A Test of R.J. House's Path-Goal Theory of Leader Effectiveness in a Human Service Organization." Toronto, 1977. [A hospital for the mentally retarded/Un hôpital pour retardés mentaux]

10107
Villeneuve, Abbé Rudolph. "Catholic Social Work." Montréal, 1937.

10108
Watt, Mary Susan. "Therapeutic Facilitator: The Role of the Social Worker in Acute Treatment Hospitals in Ontario." California, Los Angeles, 1977.

10109
Westwood, Marvin James. "An Examination of Social Worker-Client Relationship Effectiveness." Alberta, 1972.

Social Welfare/Bien-être social

10110
Atkinson, Donald Robert. "Understanding Poverty." Toronto, 1980. [Toronto Regent Park Community/Communauté du Parc Régent à Toronto]

Baker, Walter. See No./Voir no 10141

Campfens, Hubert Leo. See No./Voir no 10131

10111
Chacko, James Kunju Mundakaparampil. "Executive Role-Set: A Study of Executive Role in Organizational Changes." Toronto, 1971. [Welfare agencies/Agences du bien-être]

Coughlin, Richard M. See No./Voir no 9972

Cummings, Joan E. See No./Voir no 3739

Dyck, Perry R. See No./Voir no 8507

Garry, Carl. See No./Voir no 4347

Gripton, James M. See No./Voir no 10200

Hutton, Miriam F. See No./Voir no 3740

10112
Ingraham, Patricia Wallace. "Patterns of Social Welfare Policies in Western Societies." SUNY, Binghamton, 1979.

Jennings, Daniel E. See No./Voir no 3653

Leman, Christopher Kent. See No./Voir no 8511

10113
Levy, Steven Stanley. "Leisure and Poverty." Toronto, 1977.

Loebel, Peter Bernard. See No./Voir no 8677

Lundy, Lawrence A. See No./Voir no 3741

10114
MacLean, Marvin E. "An Experimental Analysis of Personality Factors Associated with Chronic Welfare Dependency: Implications for Treatment and Future Research." Alberta, 1973.

Marshall, Chirstine M. See No./Voir no 3742

McInnes, Simon. See No./Voir no 8514

McCready, J. See No./Voir no 8679

10115
Morgan, Catherine E. Therapeutic Solutions to Deviance: The Social Organization of Treating Disturbed Young People." Toronto, 1982.

Munns, Violet B. See No./Voir no 3743

Murase, Kenneth. See No./Voir no 3744

Nair, Murali D. See No./Voir no 7579

Nancarrow, Clarke Joanne E. See No./Voir no 6808

Roncari, Jean I.D. See No./Voir no 2729

Rousseau, Jacques. See No./Voir no 9986

10116
Rowlatt, John Donald Foss. "Welfare and the Incentive to Work: The Alberta Case." Princeton, 1971.

Singer, Charles. See No./Voir no 568

10117
Soper, Nancy E. "The Stigma of Public Assistance Programs." Carleton, 1980. [Manitoba]

10118
Splane, Richard Beverley. "The Development of Social Welfare in Ontario, 1791-1983: The Role of the Province." Toronto, 1961.

Stanton, John O. See No./Voir no 10054

10119
Staranczak, Genio Alexander. "Welfare Implications of Ontario's Public Housing Program." Queens', 1979.

10120
Strong, Kirkpatrick Margaret. "Public Welfare Administration in Canada." Chicago, 1928.

Tracy, Martin Booth. See No./Voir no 2066

Tzuk, Yogev. See No./Voir no 9844

Vine, William G. See No./Voir no 10139

Social Security, Pensions and Assistance for the Aged and others/ Assurances sociales, pensions et assistance aux personnes âgées

Ascah, Louis Gordon. See No./Voir no 1640

10121
Bellamy, Donald Frederick. "A Study in Accommodation: The Development of Income Security for the Aged in Canada." Columbia, 1970.

10122
Breul, Frank R. "Family Allowances in Canada." McGill, 1951.

10123
Bryden, Walter Kenneth. "Old Age Pensions and Policy Making in Canada." Toronto, 1971.

10124
Campbell, Wesley Glenn. "Impact of Social Security Expenditures on Canadian Government Finance." Harvard, 1948.

10125
Deutsch, Antal. "Income Redistribution Throug Canadian Federal Allowances and Old Age Bene fits." McGill, 1967.

Farquhar, Marcia Fay. See No./Voir no 9288

Hamel, Marie. See No./Voir no 8509

10126
Konzak, Burt. "Retirement and Aging in Canadia Society." Toronto, 1977.

10127
Laycock, Joseph E. "The Canadian System of Old Ag Pensions." Chicago, 1952.

Lindenfield, Rita Graham. See No./Voir no 1629

Lustig, Stephen David. See No./Voir no 9553

MacNaughton, Bruce Douglas. See No./Voir no 8513

McLernon, Sylvia G. See No./Voir no 8515

10128
Melichercik, John. "Old Age Pensions in Canada: Th Development of Implementation, and Revisions c the Old Age Security and Old Age Assistance Act of 1951." Chicago, 1969.

Posner, Judith Susan. See No./Voir no 9739

Soper, Nancy E. See No./Voir no 10117

10129
Willard, Joseph William. "Some Aspects of Socia Security in Canada: An Analysis of the Growth c Social Security Expenditures and the Developmen of Family Allowances and Old Aged Income Secur ty Programs in Canada." Harvard, 1954.

Housing/Logement

10130
Breslauer, Helen Joyce. "Residential Satisfaction in Cooperative Housing Project: A Case Study. Rutgers, 1978.

10131
Campfens, Hubert Leo. "Landlord and Tenant Rela tions in Apartment Developments; Examination c Interests and Behaviour." Toronto, 1971.

10132
Gauthier-Larouche, Georges. "Le conditionemen physique de la maison rurale traditionnelle dans k région de Québec." Laval, 1972.

10133
Gillies, James M. "Canadian Housing Legislation; Case Study of Housing Problems and Policies. Indiana, 1952.

10134
Hoffman, Arlene Rochelle. "Factors Associated wit Morale Among Residents in Senior Citizen Housing A Sociological Analysis." Toronto, 1981.

10135
House, John Douglas. "The Social Organization c Residential Real Estate." McGill, 197 [Montréal]

10136
Kennedy, Leslie W. "Residential Mobility as a Cycli cal Process: The Evaluation of the Home Environ ment Both Before and After the Move." Toronto 1975. [Regent Park/Parc Régent]

Kurtz, Larry Robert. See No./Voir no 1384

Lipman, Marvin Harold. See No./Voir no 10033

10137

Long, Larry Howard. "Residential Mobility: International Comparisons." Texas, 1969. [A Comparison of Japan, United States, Canada, and Great Britain/Une comparaison entre le Japon, les États-Unis, le Canada et la Grande-Bretagne]

Mason, Gregory Creswell. See No./Voir no 1389

Pilette, Danielle. See No./Voir no 1949

Preston, Valerie Ann. See No./Voir no 1580

10138

Scheu, William John. "The Effects of Residential Opportunity Structures on Participation Patterns in Voluntary Organizations." British Columbia, 1975.

Staranczak, Genio Alexander. See No./Voir no 10119

10139

Vine, William George. "A Case Study of the Relationship Between a Community and the Province of Ontario in Developing Policies for Residential Care." Toronto, 1980.

SOCIAL COMMUNITY AND PROFESSIONAL ORGANIZATIONS/ORGANISATIONS SOCIALES, COMMUNAUTAIRES ET PROFESSIONNELLES

10140

Abugov, Albert. "An Analysis of Accountability in Community Organization." Toronto, 1975.

10141

Baker, Walter J. "The Place of the Private Agency in the Administration of Government Policies: A Case Study: The Ontario Children's Aid System, 1893-1965." Queen's, 1966.

10142

Bélanguer, Marc, "L'association volontaire: le cas des chambres de commerce." Laval, 1969.

10143

Bertrand, Marie Jeannette. "Nouveau genre d'institution pour enfance abandonnée." Ottawa, 1946.

Boudreau, Françoise. See No./Voir no 6758

10144

Brundage, Donald Hazen. "YMCA Work with the Family in Canada." Teachers College, Columbia, 1968.

Cheung, Yuet Wah. See No./Voir no 6791

10145

Delaney, Joseph Roger Claude. "A Study of the Influence of Professionalization and Bureaucratization of the Organizational Climate of Children's Aid Societies of Northern Ontario." Toronto, 1979.

Devnich, Donald Douglas. See No./Voir no 9850

Divay, Gérard. See No./Voir no 10025

10146

Doucet, Laval J. "L'évaluation de l'efficacité organisationnelle dans les organismes de services volontaires: une étude des conseils régionaux de loisirs au Québec." Toronto, 1978.

Fisher, Helen Elizabeth. See No./Voir no 9975

10147

Glickman, Jacob. "Organizational Indicators and Social Correlates of Collective Jewish Identity." Toronto, 1976. [Metropolitan Toronto/Toronto métropolitain]

Hannigan, John Andrew. See No./Voir no 8723

10148

Hannin, Daniel. "Selected Factors Associated with the Participation of Adult Ojibway Indians in Formal Voluntary Organizations." Wisconsin, 1967.

Hyde, William Paul. See No./Voir no 2662

10149

Khalidi, Musa S. "Correlates of Participation in Cooperatives in Carman, Manitoba." Alberta, 1973.

10150

Knapen, Joseph Mathijs Peter. "Participation in Voluntary Organizations as Status Inconsistency." British Columbia, 1982.

Lioy Michele L. See No./Voir no 10089

MacInnes, Daniel William. See No./Voir no 2115

10151

Markus, Nathan. "A Study of the Participation of Staff Members in Social Service Organizations in Activities Aimed at Influencing Changes in the Services and Functions of the Employing Agencies." Toronto, 1969.

10152

Moore, Edith Elizabeth. "Matching in Helping Relationships." Toronto, 1977. [Family Services Department of the Metropolitan Toronto Children's Aid Society/Département des services familiaux de la Société d'aide à l'enfance de Toronto métropolitain]

Nair, Murali Dharan. See No./Voir no 7579

10153

Offenbach, Lilly. "The Anatomy of an Ethnic Organization." Brandeis, 1970.

Posner, Judith Susan. See No./Voir no 9739

10154

Pullman, Douglas Robert. "A Study of Social Organizations in Relation to Economic Change." Toronto, 1960. [Fredericton, Nova Scotia/Frédéricton Nouvelle-Écosse]

10155

Rahn, Sheldon Lloyd. "Organizational Control and Participation." Toronto, 1975. [Ontario]

10156

Rancier, Gordon J. "The Dynamics of Alberta Newstart: An Analysis of a Complex Social Organization." Ottawa, 1972.

Ricks, Frances Arlene. See No./Voir no 9742

Roberts, Hayden Wayne. See No./Voir no 10171

Rondeau, Gilles. See No./Voir no 10098

10157

Ross, Bonnie Fay. "Eclectic Analysis of an Inter-Organizational Network: A Case Study of Six Canadian Cooperative Organizations." York, 1981.

10158

Sacouman, Robert James. "Social Origins of Antigonish Movement Co-operative Associations in Eastern Nova Scotia." Toronto, 1976.

Seaman, Lorne Douglas. See No./Voir no 9471

Simard-Trottier, Marie. See No./Voir no 10100

Tzuk, Yogev. See No./Voir no 9844

Van der Krabben, Jacobus J.M. See No./Voir no 10106

10159

Wasteneys, Hortense Catherine Fordell. "A History of the University Settlement of Toronto, 1910-1958." Toronto, 1975.

Whetten, N.L. See No./Voir no 1308

Zeitz, Mordecai Eliezer. See No./Voir no 7274

COMMUNITY STUDIES/ÉTUDES COMMUNAUTAIRES

10160
Burnet, Jean R. "The Problem of Community Instabil-
ity in East Central Alberta." Chicago, 1948.
10161
Chance, Normand Alec. "Portsmouth (Nova Scotia):
The Study of a Bi-Cultural Community Under
Stress." Cornell, 1957.

Crysdale, Robert Cecil Stewart. See No./Voir no 2053
10162
Donovan, Patrick. "Étude ethno-géographique de la
représentation de l'espace proche et lointain à
Saint-Côme de Beauce." Montréal, 1979.
10163
Doyle, Robert Urban. "Perceived Effectiveness of
Community Development Organizations in Three
Canadian Communities." Toronto, 1972.
10164
Foote, Raymond Leslie. "A Case Study: The Social
Consequences of Rapid Industrialization." Toronto,
1974. [Port Hawkesbury, Nova Scotia/Nouvelle-
Écosse]

Goulding, James W. See No./Voir no 1169

Grayson, John Paul. See No./Voir no 8768
10165
Guindon, Jean-Charles. "La participation des citoyens
à l'action collective." Toronto, 1972. [Saguenay/
Lac Saint-Jean/Lake St.John]

Iutcovich, Mark. See No./Voir no 762

Jansen, Janni Margaretha. See No./Voir no 1867

Legault, Gisèle. See No./Voir no 10088
10166
Lindop, Darla Rhyne. "Organizational Life in River
City: A Case Study of Class, Ethnicity, Geographical Mobility and Status." Toronto, 1979.
10167
Michaud, Marguerite M. "La reconstruction française
au Nouveau-Brunswick - Bouctouche, paroisse
type." Montréal, 1949.

Miner, Horace Mitchell. See No./Voir no 769

Mougeon, Raymond. See No./Voir no 7674

Mozersky, Kenneth Avrum. See No./Voir no 4909
10168
Paré, Simone. "Social Participants in Beauport, Province of Quebec." Columbia, 1961.

Philbrook, Thomas Vere. See No./Voir no 4909
10169
Powell, Alan Thomas Rees. "Participation in Issues as
a Measure of Integration into a Small Town."
Toronto, 1973. [Georgetown, Ontario]
10170
Richards, Leonard. "Community Development in
Alberta." Toronto, 1974.
10171
Roberts, Hayden Wayne. "Concept and Action: The
Use of Conceptual Models in Community Develop-
ment." Union Graduate School-West, 1976.
10172
Roberts, Lance William. "Wage Employment and Its
Consequences in Two Eastern Arctic Communi-
ties." Alberta, 1977.

10173
Self, George Doyle. "A Policy Relevant Macro-
Structural Theory of Development: A Path
Analytic Social Indicator Study of Twelve Rural
Communities in Kent County, New Brunswick,
1969-1973." Cornell, 1975.

Siegel, Sanford Benjamin. See No./Voir no 2083
10174
Tremblay, Marc-Adélard. "The Acadians of Portsmouth: A Study in Culture Change." Cornell,
1954.
10175
Van der Merwe, Hendrik Willem. "Leadership in a
Saskatchewan Community: The Impact of Industrialization." California, Los Angeles, 1963.
10176
Verdet, Paula. "Interethnic Problems of a Roman
Catholic Parish: A French-Canadian Institution
and Its Bilingual Membership." Chicago, 1959.

Wahn, Michael Brian. See No./Voir no 1194

SOCIAL CHANGE AND PLANNING/
CHANGEMENT SOCIAL ET PLANIFICATION

Alexander, Malcolm Lawrence. See No./Voir no 1367
10177
Christy, Richard David. "Social Change and Post-
Modernity: An Analysis of Social Space and Social
Time in Canada and the United States." Toronto,
1977.
10178
Decore, Anne Marie June. "Women and Work in
Canada, 1961 and 1971." Alberta, 1976.

Foote, Raymond Leslie. See No./Voir no 10164
10179
Laczko, Leslie Stephen. "The Two Solitudes Reex-
amined: Pluralism and Inequality in Quebec."
McGill, 1982.
10180
Le Cavalier, Patricia Fitzsimmons. "Resourceful
Movements: The Mobilization of Citizens for
Neighbourhood Planning Control." McGill, 1983.

Legendre, Camille George. See No./Voir no 1819
10181
MacKay, Harry Earle. "Inequality of Opportunity for
Youth in Transition from School to Work." York,
1978.

Matthews, David Ralph Lee. See No./Voir no 7607
10182
McNiven, Christiane Rachel Marie. "Social Planning
in Vancouver: A Case Study." Columbia, 1973.
10183
Morris, Cerise Darlene. "No More Than Simple
Justice: The Royal Commission on the Status of
Women and Social Change in Canada." McGill,
1982.

Pomfret, Denis Alan. See No./Voir no 10003
10184
Prince, Samuel Henry. "Catastrophe and Social
Change Based upon a Sociological Study of the
Halifax Disaster." Columbia, 1920.

Sohn, Herbert Alvin. See No./Voir no 8538
10185
Stephenson, Marylee Grace. "Being in Women's Liberation: A Case Study in Social Change." British
Columbia, 1975. [Vancouver]

10186
Westhues, Anne. "A Comparative Analysis of Social Planning in Quebec and Ontario, 1966-1981." Columbia, 1983.

HUMAN DEVELOPMENT AND SOCIAL RELATIONS/ DÉVELOPPEMENT HUMAIN ET RELATIONS SOCIALES

10187
Abu-Laban, Sharon McIrvin. "Social Bonds in the Urban Industrial Setting: A Metasociological Analysis." Alberta, 1974.
Albert, Edward Henry. See No./Voir no 6787
Anderson, Donald O. See No./Voir no 6922
Avison, William R. See No./Voir no 9642
10188
Baker, Maureen. "Women as a Minority Group in the Academic Profession." Alberta, 1975.
10189
Baureiss, Gunter A. "The Theory of Evaluative Orientation and the Socio-Technical System: A Study of Workers' Responses in an Industrial Training Program." Alberta, 1976.
10190
Berg, Dale Herbert. "Sexual Subcultures and Interaction: A Study in Discrepant Meanings." Alberta, 1973.
Blewett, June Caryll Cosbey. See No./Voir no 8960
10191
Cape, Elizabeth Ann. " 'Going Downhill': Responses to Terminality in a Population of Institutionalized Aged Ill." Toronto, 1979.
10192
Chappell, Neena Lane. "Work, Commitment to Work, and Self-Identity Among Women." McMaster, 1978.
10193
Coburn, David. "Work and Society: The Social Correlates of Job Control and Job Complexity." Toronto, 1973. [Study of 1000 workers in Victoria, British Columbia/Étude de 1000 ouvriers à Victoria, Colombie-Britannique]
Cotton, Charles Alexander. See No./Voir no 7404
Davis, John Campbell. See No./Voir no 6821
DeVries, John. See No./Voir no 7671
10194
Farquharson, William Andrew Fletcher. "Peers as Helpers: Personal Change in Members of Self-Help Groups in Metropolitan Toronto." Toronto, 1975.
10195
Fetterly, Robert Gordon. "Owners and Trainers: Patterns of Establishing and Maintaining Autonomy in a Worker-Client Relationship." Toronto, 1976. [Harness racing trainers/Entraîneurs de course aux harnais]
Filson, Glen Charles. See No./Voir no 4023
Fullan, Michael. See No./Voir no 2070
Fullerton, John Timothy. See No./Voir no 9674
10196
Gemme, Robert. "Les relations prémaritales dans la société post-industrielle." Montréal, 1978.
Giesbrecht, Norman Abe. See No./Voir no 9256
Gonnsen, August. See No./Voir no 2148

10197
Gorwaney, Naintara. "Quality of Life Experience: A Multi-Dimensional Model of Life Satisfaction-Effects of Demography Characteristics, Self-Esteem, Social Comparison Processes, and Social Participation." Toronto, 1982.
10198
Goyder, John C. "Subjective Social Class Identification and Objective Socio-Economic Status." McMaster, 1972.
10199
Gray-Snelgrove, Rosemary Hilda. "The Human Experience of Giving Care to a Parent Dying of Cancer: Meanings Identified Through the Process of Shared Reflection." Toronto, 1980.
10200
Gripton, James MacPherson. "A Study of the Relationship of Job Attitudes and Work Organization of Public Assistance Field Staff." Toronto, 1967.
10201
Gurdin, Joseph Barry. "Amitié/Friendship. The Socio-Cultural Construction of Friendship in Contemporary Montreal." Montréal, 1978.
Hansen, Christine Marion. See No./Voir no 9687
10202
Himelfarb, Alexander. "Fat Man, Thin World: A Participant Observation Study of Weight Watchers." Toronto, 1975.
10203
Home, Alice Marian. "Change in Womens' Consciousness-Raising Groups: A Study of Four Types of Change and of Some Factors Associated with Them." Toronto, 1978.
10204
Hornick, J.P. "Premarital Sexual Attitudes and Behaviour: A Reference Group Contingent-Factor Theory." Waterloo, 1975.
10205
Johns, David Paul. "The Physical Educator and the Structuring of His Professional World: An Ethnographic Account." Alberta, 1979.
10206
Kepkay, Paul E. "Seism and Sexual Discrimination." Waterloo, 1978. [Women/Femmes]
Knapen, Joseph Mathijs Peter. See No./Voir no 10150
10207
Knight, Graham. "Embourgeoisement and Class Stratification." Carleton, 1978.
10208
Laforest, Lucien. "La théorie de l'anomie et la déviance alcoolique: une application au contexte rural québécois." Laval, 1975.
LaMothe, Dennis Michael. See No./Voir no 9708
Lautard, Emile Hugh. See No./Voir no 1276
10209
Lindquist, Neil Eric. "Adaptation to Marginal Status: The Case of Gay Males." Alberta, 1976.
10210
Looker, Ellen Dianne. "The Role of Value Elements in the Intergenerational Transmission of Social Status." McMaster, 1977. [Hamilton area, 400 teenagers and parents/Région de Hamilton, 400 adolescents et parents]

10211
Lucas, Rex Archibald. "Social Behavior Under Conditions of Extreme Stress: A Study of Miners Entrapped by a Coal Mine Disaster." Columbia, 1967.

10212
Lundy, Katherina Lillian Pauline. "The Effect of Organizational Setting on Secretary-Executive Interaction." Toronto, 1978.

10213
MacDonald, Mairi Teresa St. John. "Informal Helping Relationships Among Adults - A Study of the Reasons for Choosing a Helper and of the Ways in Which He Helps." Toronto, 1968.

10214
MacKeracher, Dorothy Margaret. "A Study of the Experience of Aging from the Perspective of Older Women." Toronto, 1982.

McGinnis, Paul St. Clair. See No./Voir no 4032

10215
McKee, Janet Doris. "The Housewife, Class and Class-Related Attitudes." York, 1982.

McKie, Donald C. See No./Voir no 1942

10216
McRoberts, Hugh Arthur. "Social Stratification in Canada: A Preliminary Analysis." Carleton, 1976.

10217
Miralles-Nobel, Teresa. "Attitude sexuelle de la population dans le Montréal métropolitain." Montréal, 1971.

Needham, Merrill Arthur. See No./Voir no 6763
Parducci, Ronald E. See No./Voir no 2582
Park, James. See No./Voir no 4417

10218
Petrunik, Michael G. "The Quest for Fluency: A Study of the Identity Problems and Management Strategies of Adult Stutterers and Some Suggestions for an Approach to the Management of Deviance." Toronto, 1977.

Price, Kenneth Arthur. See No./Voir no 763
Robinson, Barrie W. See No./Voir no 3698
Ryan, Frances Sheila Ann. See No./Voir no 9962

10219
Shulman, Norman. "Urban Social Networks: An Investigation of Personal Networks in an Urban Setting." Toronto, 1972.

10220
Stein, Leonard Milton. "The Treatment of Sex Guilt: A Comparative Study." Western Ontario, 1977.

Stephenson, Marylee Grace. See No./Voir no 10185

10221
Stuebing, William Kenneth. "Adjustment to Anomie: A Study of Young Males in Red Deer." Alberta, 1977.

10222
Tardif, Marie Marthe. "La prostitution féminine: analyse et interprétation interactioniste d'un phénomène de déviance." Montréal, 1981.

Thibault, André. See No./Voir no 4094
Tindale, Joseph Arthur. See No./Voir no 4285
Vachon, Mary L. Suslak. See No./Voir no 10055

10223
Warren, C.E. "Perceptions of Achievement: A Study of Women in Two Occupations in England and in Canada." London, 1979.

10224
Wexler, Mark N. "The Service Society and the Organization of Human Services for Profit Studies in the Micro-Organization of Yoga, the Martial Arts and Mind Development." York, 1978. [Toronto Vancouver]

10225
Wilmot, Marilyn Susan. "Ideology, Leadership and Following: A Study in the Sociology of Group Psychotherapy." York, 1973.

Wisniewski, Lawrence John. See No./Voir no 2086
Zipp, John Francis. See No./Voir no 8615

Human Relations/Relations humaines
General Items/Ouvrages généraux

Aboud, Francis E. See No./Voir no 9496

10226
Beattie, Christopher Fraser. "Minority Men in a Majority Setting: Middle-Level Francophones at Mid-Career in the Anglophone Public Service of Canada." California, Berkeley, 1970.

Boldt, Menno. See No./Voir no 447

10227
Currie, Albert Wayne. "Interethnic Marriage and Identification Among German and Ukrainian Ethnic Groups in Canada: A Study of the Effect of Socioeconomic Status on Structural Ethnic Identification." Toronto, 1980.

10228
Deutschmann, Linda Harriet Bell. "Decline of the Wasp: Dominant Group Identity in a Multi-Ethnic Society." Toronto, 1979.

10229
Douey, John Donald. "Skills Training, Contracts and Outcomes in Human Relations Laboratories." Toronto, 1982.

10230
Ford, Blake George. "The Differential Effectiveness of an Integrated Didactic-Experiential Human Relations Training Program for Parents of Personality Disordered Preadolescent Boys." Calgary, 1974.

Fullerton, John Timothy. See No./Voir no 9674
Hatt, Fred Kenneth. See No./Voir no 495

10231
Jubas, Harry Leib. "The Adjustment Process of Americans and Canadians in Israel and Their Integration into Israeli Society." Michigan State, 1974.

10232
Keddie, Vincent Gordon. "A Study of Manual Workers Attitude Toward Social Class in Four Ontario Communities." McMaster, 1974.

10233
Mann, George Adolf. "Functional Autonomy Among English School Teachers in the Hutterite Colonies of Southern Alberta: A Study of Social Control." Colorado, 1974.

10234
Martin, Roger Duane. "Videotape Self-Confrontation in Human Relations Training." Alberta, 1969.

10235
Metzger, Leonard Paul. "A Factorial Study of Attitudes Toward Jews." Wisconsin, 1962.

Ramcharan, Subhas. See No./Voir no 748

10236
Scott, Nolvert Preston, Jr. "The Perception of Racial Discrimination by Negroes in Metropolitan Winnipeg, Manitoba, Canada." Pennsylvania State, 1971.

Simon, Pierre. See No./Voir no 2739

CONFLICT/CONFLIT

Huxley, Christopher Victor. See No./Voir no 2113
10237
Jackson, John David. "Toward a Theory of Social Conflict: A Study of French-English Relations in an Ontario Community." Michigan State, 1967.

Kinsley, Brian Leslie. See No./Voir no 2162

Moore, Dorothy Emma. See No./Voir no 9980
10238
Novek, Joel Leonard. "Cooperation and Conflict in Dual Societies: A Comparison of French Canadian and Afrikaner Nationalism." Alberta, 1974.

Pannu, Rajinder Singh. See No./Voir no 3637

Park, James. See No./Voir no 4417

Price, Kenneth Arthur. See No./Voir no 763

Roncari, Jean Isobel Dawson. See No./Voir no 2729
10239
Smith, Courtney David Campbell. "Invasion, Succession and Conflict: The Case of St. Leonard, Quebec." Pennsylvania State, 1974.

Snider, Dawn Laureen. See No./Voir no 7913

DELINQUENCY AND ADOLESCENT OFFENDERS/ DÉLINQUANCE ET LES JEUNES DÉLINQUANTS

10240
Bastien, Pierre. "Réhabilitation du délinquant: perspective communautaire." Montréal, 1983.
10241
Beaupré, Henri. "La délinquance juvénile à Québec." Laval, 1953.
10242
Beausoleil, Julien. "Comment prévenir la délinquance." Montréal, 1950.
10243
Biron, Louise. "Engagement, risque et délinquance." Montréal, 1978.
10244
Blum, Frank J. "Further Investigation of Extraversion-Intraversion and Subsequent Recidivism for a Selected Group of Young Adult Offenders." Ottawa, 1965.
10245
Brill, Ronald Woodrow Jr. "Effects of Residential Program Structure and Conceptual Level in Treatment of Delinquent Boys." Toronto, 1977.
10246
Chin, John Carlton. "An Investigation of Information Processing Complexity in Juvenile Delinquents, Non-Juvenile Delinquents and Their Parents." Calgary, 1980.
10247
Crespo, Manuel. "Deviance and Aspirations in Adolescence: The Influence of School Absenteeism, Drug Use, and Mental Disorder on Educational and Occupational Aspirations." McGill, 1978.

10248
Cusson, Maurice. "La resocialisation du jeune délinquant en institution." Montréal, 1972.

Darrough, William D. See No./Voir no 7918
10249
Deslauriers, Lise. "Perception et relations interpersonnelles chez les adolescents délinquants et non-délinquants." Montréal, 1974.
10250
Elie, Daniel. "Agressivité et délinquance." Montréal, 1974.
10251
Gagné, Denis. "Caractère social et déviance chez les adolescents de milieu ouvrier et aise." Montréal, 1970.
10252
Gandy, John Manuel. "The Exercise of Discretion by the Police in the Handling of Juveniles." Toronto, 1967.
10253
Geller, Gloria Rhea. "Streaming of Males and Females in the Juvenile Justice System." Toronto, 1981.
10254
Gérin-Lajoie, Marie. "Un T.A.T. pour délinquants: comparaison entre les réponses d'adolescents délinquants et non-délinquants." Montréal, 1969.
10255
Gomme, I.M. "A Multivariate Analysis of Juvenile Delinquency Among Ontario Public and Separate School Districts." Toronto, 1983.
10256
Goyer-Michaud, Francine. "Les valeurs motivantes engendrées par l'anxiété chez les délinquants." Montréal, 1971.

Green, Bernard. See No./Voir no 7920
10257
Griffin, Douglas Keith. "An Analysis of Staff Perspectives in Five Ontario Correctional Centres." Toronto, 1976.
10258
Gubern Garriga-Nogués, Santiago. "La Delincuencia Juvenile in Canada." Barcelona (Spain), 1967.
10259
Guindon, Jeannine. "Les processus de rééducation du jeune délinquant par l'actualisation des forces du moi." Montréal, 1969.

Horsley, Frederick Richard. See No./Voir no 9103
10260
Howard, Louis Wayne. "WESTFIELD: The Design and Production of a Videotaped Film Based on Residential Milieu Treatment of Disturbed and Delinquent Juveniles and the Assessment of Film Impact on Viewer Attitudes." Alberta, 1974.

Klarreich, Samuel Henry. See No./Voir no 4166

Krausher, Randall J.R. See No./Voir no 9449
10261
Kupfer, George. "Middle Class Delinquency in a Canadian City." Washington, Seattle, 1966. [Edmonton, Alberta]
10262
Lachapelle, Pierre-Paul. "Structures des groupes de rééducation pour jeunes délinquants." Montréal, 1975.
10263
Leahey, Jean. "Le concept de soi des jeunes filles délinquantes." Montréal, 1975.

10264

Leblanc, Marc. "Délinquance juvénile: perspectives épidémiologiques et stigmatiques." Montréal, 1970.

10265

Leschied, Alan David Winfield. "Effects of Detention Home Structure on Juvenile Offenders as a Function of Conceptual Level." Western Ontario, 1980.

10266

Limages, Thérèse. "Délinquance juvénile et milieux urbains." Montréal, 1971.

10267

Masse, Martin. "Développement, maturité interpersonnelle et délinquance." Montréal, 1982.

10268

Maxim, Paul Stefan. "Some Trends in Juvenile Delinquency in Canada: 1958-1973." Pennsylvania, 1980.

10269

Melebamane-Mia-Musunda, Berthollet. "Contribution du père à l'interaction familiale en tant que cause de la délinquance et de la criminalité." Montréal, 1973.

10270

Morin, Pierre. "Étude phénoménologique des modes de fonctionnement du moi chez le jeune délinquant." Montréal, 1965.

10271

Mourant, François. "La typologie des niveaux de maturité interpersonnelle validation de construit." Montréal, 1976.

Peer, Miri. See No./Voir no 9048

Pisterman, Susan Jane. See No./Voir no 9737

10272

Richard, Hélène. "Comparaison entre le système de valeurs de la délinquante juvénile et celui de sa mère." Montréal, 1968.

10273

Sas, Louise Dezwirek. "The Manipulation of Moral Judgment and Behavior of Juvenile Probationers Using Three Forms of Behavior Contracts." Western Ontario, 1980.

10274

Smiley, Wesley Carson. "Multivariate Classification of Male and Female Delinquent Personality Types." Western Ontario, 1977.

10275

Tellier, Yvan. "Les perceptions du soi chez des parents d'adolescents délinquants et chez des parents d'adolescents ordinaires." Montréal, 1961.

10276

Warescha, Blaine Eugene. "Comparison of American Indian, Eskimo, Spanish-American, and Anglo Youthful Offenders on the Minnesota Counseling Inventory." Utah, 1971.

10277

Zarb, Janet Mary. "Correlates of Recidivism and Social Adjustment Among Training School Graduates." Toronto, 1977. [30 delinquent boys, ages 14 and 15/30 délinquants de 14 et 15 ans]

CRIME, CRIMINALS, CRIMINAL JUSTICE, PENAL INSTITUTIONS AND POLICE/CRIME, CRIMINELS, JUSTICE CRIMINELLE, INSTITUTIONS PÉNALES ET FORCE POLICIÈRE

10278

Basu, Sreemay. "Models of Escape Behavior of Minimum Security Inmates in Ontario: The Use of Positive Administrative Data for Risk Assessments." Cornell, 1983.

Blain, Deborah. See No./Voir no 8958

Booth, J.A.G. See No./Voir no 9278

Calder, William Arnold. See No./Voir no 7114

10279

Carlson, Kenneth Allen. "A Multivariate Classification of Reformatory Inmates." Western Ontario, 1971.

Cavoukian, Ann J. See No./Voir no 8902

10280

Chandler, David Ballantine. "Capital Punishment and the Canadian Parliament: A Test of Durkkeims Hypothesis on Repressive Law." Cornell, 1970.

10281

Connidis, Ingrid A. "A Theoretical Development of Social Systems Analysis and an Examination of Its Applicability to the Criminal Justice System." Toronto, 1978.

10282

Debicki, Marek. "A Structure Under Stress: A Study of the Sentencing Process and Decisions in a Lower Criminal Court." Carleton, 1979. [Winnipeg Magistrates Court/Cours de magistrats à Winnipeg]

10283

Demers, Donald Joseph. "Discretion, Disparity and the Parole Process." Alberta, 1978.

10284

Diamond, Frederic Lionel. "Murder in Toronto: A Ten Year Study: 1966-1976." York, 1979.

10285

Dubois, Pierre. "Facteurs psychologiques associés à certains aspects du rendement des policiers." Montréal, 1971.

10286

Fréchette, Marcel. "Le processus d'identification chez les criminels récidivistes." Montréal, 1967.

10287

Gardner, Patricia. "A Participant-Observation Study of a Therapeutic Prison." Toronto, 1979.

Geller, Gloria Rhea. See No./Voir no 10253

Gemme, Robert. See No./Voir no 10196

Gentile, Andrew-Salvatore. See No./Voir no 9125

Griffin, Douglas Keith. See No./Voir no 10257

Grove, P.H. See No./Voir no 7921

Hagan, John Lee. See No./Voir no 7904

Hans, Valerie Patricia. See No./Voir no 9686

10288

Hasenpusch, Burkhard. "Future Trends in Crime and Crime Control in Canada." Montréal, 1982.

10289

Houston, Susan Elizabeth. "The Impetus to Reform: Urban Crime, Poverty and Ignorance in Ontario 1850-1875." Toronto, 1974.

10290
Ingalls, Glen Ralph. "The Relationship Between Educational Programs and the Rate of Recidivism Among Medium Security Prison Parolees and Mandatory Supervision Cases from Drumheller Institution in the Province of Alberta." Washington State, 1978.

Jobson, Keith Bertran. See No./Voir no 2432

10291
Karlinsky, Sidney. "Job Satisfaction Among Living Unit and Non-Living Unit Correctional Staff in a Canadian Penitentiary." York, 1979.

10292
Kell, John Thompson. "Three Approaches to the Influencing of Self-Disclosure and Trust Among Prison Inmates." Western Ontario, 1977.

10293
Klein, John Frederick. "Official Morality and Offender Perceptions of the Bargaining Process." Alberta, 1974.

10294
Lagier, Pierre Marie. "L'enracinement criminel." Montréal, 1979.

Lambert, Leah Rae. See No./Voir no 3644

10295
La Plante, Jacques. "Le petit criminel d'habitude et le dépendant chronique: étude évaluative." Montréal, 1970.

10296
Lefrançois, Richard. "Classes sociales et criminalité adulte." Laval, 1979. [Québec]

10297
Ligondée, Paultre. "Le syndrome carcéral: implications cliniques de l'emprisonnement dans un milieu de privation externe." Montréal, 1970.

10298
Maillet, Léandre. "Modèles d'analyse et de prévision de la satisfaction et du rendement chez des agents de services correctionnels." Montréal, 1981.

Marshall, Peter Graham. See No./Voir no 9715

10299
McFerran, John Ronald. "Effects of Division and District Assignment on Police Work Attitudes and Personality Traits." Manitoba, 1980.

Morissette, Y.-M. J.R. See No./Voir no 7881

10300
Nelson, Susan Hess. "Jurors' Verdicts in a Mock Rape Trial Experiment: A Social Learning Approach." Carleton, 1980. [Ottawa area/Région d'Ottawa]

Nivoli, Gian Carlo. See No./Voir no 9178

10301
Parlett, Thomas Arthur Anthony. "The Development of Attitudes and Morality in Adult Offenders." Victoria, 1974.

10302
Perrier, David Conrad. "The Tailoring of Pre-Sentence Reports by a Probation Officer of the Courts." York, 1976.

10303
Pires, Alvaro A. Penna de Oliveira. "Stigmate pénal et trajectoire sociale." Montréal, 1983.

Pollock, Nathan Lionel. See No./Voir no 9463

Pugh, G.M. See No./Voir no 8931

Record, Stephen A. See No./Voir no 9227

10304
Rizkalla, Samir. "Un modèle d'évaluation de la police; coût, temps et pertinence de l'action policière concernant les vols d'auto." Montréal, 1975.

10305
Sacco, Vincent Frank. "Public Perceptions of Crime: A Theoretical and Empirical Examination." Alberta, 1981. [Alberta]

Schiffer, Marc Evan. See No./Voir no 7912

10306
Schuh-Kuhlmann, Jeorg. "Les aspects victimologiques dans les délits d'extorsion et de chantage." Montréal, 1971.

10307
Shearing, Clifford Denning. "Real Men, Good Men, Wise Men and Cautious Men: A Study of Culture, Role Models and Inter-Action Within a Police Communications Centre." Toronto, 1977.

Snider, Dawn Laureen. See No./Voir no 7913

Syrotiuk, John M. See No./Voir no 9583

Tardif, Guy. See No./Voir no 7915

10308
Theis, John Peter. "The Development of Measures of Impulsiveness Useful for Studies of Rehabilitation of Prisoners." Windsor, 1980.

10309
Topping, Coral Wesley. "Canadian Penal Institutions." Columbia, 1929.

10310
Watson, Catherine Margaret. "Women Prisoners and Modern Methods of Prison Control: A Comparative Study of Two Canadian Women's Prisons." McGill, 1981.

Wetherell, Donald Grant. See No./Voir no 7145

10311
Whittingham, Michael David. "Criminality and Correctional Reformism in Ontario, 1931 to 1954." York, 1981.

Wilson, Thomas H. See No./Voir no 9838

Zarb, Janet Mary. See No./Voir no 10277

POPULATION: GEOGRAPHY AND DEMOGRAPHY/ POPULATION: GÉOGRAPHIE ET DÉMOGRAPHIE

This is a classification of limited studies in all three countries, with a total of 21 dissertations. Fourteen were completed at six Canadian universities, with Alberta in the lead (4), followed by McGill and Montreal (3), Laval (2) and Carleton and Western Ontario (1). American universities produced five dissertations, three of which were completed in the

1970's. Great Britain, produced two, from the University of Aberdeen in 1980 and Manchester University in 1938.

Dans cette section, le nombre de thèses est limitée à 21 ouvrages dans les trois pays. Quatorze thèses proviennent de six universités canadiennes; l'Alberta vient en tête (4), suivie par McGill (3), Montréal (3), Laval (2), enfin Carleton (1) et Western Ontario (1). Les universités américaines en comptent cinq, dont trois ont été rédigées dans les années 1970. La Grande-Bretagne en a produit deux, respectivement aux universités d'Aberdeen (1980) et de Manchester (1938).

GENERAL ITEMS/OUVRAGES GÉNÉRAUX

Anderson, Karen. See No./Voir no 640
Corbett, David C. See No./Voir no 1201
10312
Coulibaly, Sidiki Philippe. "Les migrations voltaïques: les origines, les motifs et les perceptions des politiques." Montréal, 1979.
Davies, Gordon Wilson. See No./Voir no 1345
De Vries, John. See No./Voir no 7671
Gryz, Zbigniew Jan. See No./Voir no 7673
Kliewer, Erich Victor. See No./Voir no 737
Lithwick, Irwin. See No./Voir no 1209
10313
Madduri, Venkata B.N.S. "Economic Analysis of Fertility Behaviour in Canada: An Examination of 1971 Census Data." Alberta, 1979.
Minore, James Bruce. See No./Voir no 364
Nicks, Gertrude Cecilia. See No./Voir no 479
Parakulam, George G. See No./Voir no 10069
10314
Sinclair, Alasdair MacLean. "Internal Migration in Canada, 1871-1951." Harvard, 1966.
Sorg, Marcella Harnish. See No./Voir no 839
10315
Zodgekar, Arvind V. "Interrelation in Time Series of Demographic and Economic Variables: Australia and Canada." Pennsylvania, 1972.

REGIONAL STUDIES/ÉTUDES RÉGIONALES

Alberta

Jones, Stephen B. See No./Voir no 4727
Wong, William Ho-Ching. See No./Voir no 7663

British Columbia/Colombie Britannique

Miller, Philip Carl. See No./Voir no 387

Newfoundland and Labrador/
Terre-Neuve et Labrador

10316
Adams, James Gordon. "Newfoundland Population Movements with Particular Reference to the Post-War Period." McGill, 1971.

10317
Staveley, Michael. "Migration and Mobility in Newfoundland and Labrador: A Study in Population Geography." Alberta, 1973.
10318
Summers, William F. "A Geographical Analysis of Population Trends in Newfoundland." McGill, 1957.
Thornton, David Andrew. See No./Voir no 9992
Thornton, Patricia. See No./Voir no 4859

Northwest Territories/Territoires
du Nord-ouest

Krech, Shepard, III. See No./Voir no 416

Quebec/Québec

10319
Bourbeau, Robert. "Étude démographique et épidémiologique des accidents de la route au Québec depuis 1926." Montréal, 1982.
10320
Dugas, Clermont. "La dispersion de la population dans l'est du Québec." Laval, 1977.
10321
Jetté, René. "Reconstitution de recensements à partir de registres paroissiaux: analyse méthodologique sur échantillon." Montréal, 1980.
10322
Marois, Claude. "Étude méthadologique et critique de deux modèles de projections de population à micro-échelle." Laval, 1980.

Saskatchewan

10323
Alty, Stella W. "The Historical Demography of Saskatchewan." Manchester, 1938.

SPORTS, PHYSICAL EDUCATION AND RECREATION/ SPORTS, ÉDUCATION PHYSIQUE ET LOISIRS

Since physical education and recreation are usually associated with sports, the three areas have been combined for purposes of this study.

The greatest increase in all three areas is found during the 1970's and 1980's. Of the 16 Canadian universities involved in research in this classification, Alberta's 5 titles are more than the combined total of the other 15 universities. The universities of Toronto, Waterloo, Montreal, and British Columbia follow in that order. Among the American universities, Ohio State is the leader in sports, with Oregon the leader in physical education and recreation.

Du fait que l'éducation physique et les loisirs sont habituellement associés aux sports, les trois disciplines sont réunies en une seule section.

Dans les trois disciplines, le point culminant de l'augmentation de la production se situe dans les années 1970 et 1980. Des 16 universités canadiennes où des recherches ont été faites en ce domaine, celle de l'Alberta (51 thèses) dépasse l'ensemble du total des thèses des 15 autres universités. Les universités de Toronto, de Waterloo, de Montréal et de la Colombie-Britannique suivent. Quant aux universités américaines, celle d'Ohio State occupe le premier rang pour les sports; l'Université d'Oregon domine en éducation physique et en loisirs.

GENERAL ITEMS/OUVRAGES GÉNÉRAUX

10324
Chelladurai, Packianathan. "A Contingency Model of Leadership in Athletics." Waterloo, 1979.

Holman, Roy Paul. See No./Voir no 10407

10325
Huberman, John. "A Psychological Study of Participants in High Risk Sports." British Columbia, 1968.

10326
Jackson, John James. "Diffusion of an Innovation: An Exploratory Study of the Consequences of Sport Participation: Canada's Campaign at Saskatoon, 1971-1974." Alberta, 1975.

Jones, A.K. See No./Voir no 8010

10327
Klavora, Peter. "State Anxiety and Athletic Competition." Alberta, 1974.

10328
Korchinsky, Nestor Nicky. "The Equality of Men and Women in Sport as Portrayed Through the History, Development, and the Analysis of Performance in Age Class Competition of Selected Canadian Sports." Oregon, 1978.

Leith, Larry McKenzie. See No./Voir no 10410

Navarre, Kathleeen. See No./Voir no 9728

10329
Orlick, Terrance Douglas. "A Socio-Psychological Analysis of Early Sports Participation." Alberta, 1972. [Eight and nine year olds in Edmonton/8 et 9 ans à Edmonton]

10330
Proteau, Luc. "Étude des contraintes relatives à la prise de décision rapide en contexte sportif." Montréal, 1980.

Ruckenstein, Michael. See No./Voir no 10465

Salter, Michael Albert. See No./Voir no 485

Scott, Harvey Alexander. See No./Voir no 10369

10331
Smith, Garry John. "An Analysis of Sport as a Vehicle of Social Integration." Alberta, 1974. [Edmonton]

10332
Yerles, Magdaleine. "Similarities and Differences in Modes of Integration and Strategies Among French and Quebec Sports Executives." Illinois, 1980.

NATIONAL GOVERNMENT AND SPORTS/ GOUVERNEMENT FÉDÉRAL ET LES SPORTS

10333
Anderson, David Frederick. "A Synthesis of the Canadian Federal Government Policies in Amateur Sports, Fitness and Recreation Since 1961." Northern Colorado, 1974.

10334
Bedecki, Thomas George. "Modern Sport as an Instrument of National Policy with Reference to Canada and Selected Countries." Ohio State, 1971.

10335
Corran, Robert. "A Comparison of the Involvement of the Federal Governments of Canada and the United States in Sport and Physical Education Since 1960." Ohio State, 1979.

10336
Semotiuk, Darwin Michael. "The Development of a Theoretical Framework for Analyzing the Role of National Government Involvement in Sport and Physical Education and Its Application to Canada." Ohio State, 1970.

PROVINCES AND SPORTS/ PROVINCES ET SPORTS

10337
Baka, Richard Stevens Paul. "A History of Provincial Government Involvement in Sport in Western Canada." Alberta, 1978.

Chambers, David Lee. See No./Voir no 10360

Davidson, Stewart A. See No./Voir no 10340

McFarland, John M. See No./Voir no 10345

Mott, Morris Kenneth. See No./Voir no 10346

10338
Vienneau, Jean-Guy. "A Study of Leadership Behavior of Volunteer Administrators in Amateur Sports Organizations in the Province of New Brunswick, Canada." Florida State, 1982.

HISTORY OF SPORTS IN CANADA/ HISTOIRE DES SPORTS AU CANADA

10339
Cox, Allan Elton. "A History of Sports in Canada: 1868-1900." Alberta, 1969.

10340
Davidson, Stewart A. "A History of Sports and Games in Eastern Canada Prior to World War I." Teachers College, Columbia, 1952.

Day, Robert Douglas. See No./Voir no 7405

Howell, D.F. See No./Voir no 9799

10341
Jobling, Ian Frank. "Sport in Nineteenth Century Canada: The Effects of Technological Changes on Its Development." Alberta, 1971.

10342
Jones, Kevin George. "Sport in Canada, 1900-1920." Alberta, 1970.

Keyes, Mary Eleanor. See No./Voir no 10351

10343
Lappage, Ronald Sidney. "Selected Sports and Canadian Society 1921-1939." Alberta, 1974.

10344
Lindsay, Peter Leslie. "A History of Sport in Canada: 1807-1867." Alberta, 1969.

10345
McFarland, John M. "A History of the Role Played by the Military in the Development of Competitive Sport in Nova Scotia, 1930-1969." Springfield College, 1978.

Moriarty, Richard James. See No./Voir no 10354

10346
Mott, Morris Kenneth. "Manly Sports and Manitobans, Settlement Days to World War One." Queen's, 1980.

10347
Redmond, Gerald. "The Scots and Sport in Nineteenth Century Canada." Alberta, 1972.

SPORTS ASSOCIATIONS/ASSOCIATIONS SPORTIVES

10348
Bratton, Robert Dickson. "Consensus on the Relative Importance of Association Goals and Personal Motives Among Executive Members of Two Canadian Sports Associations." Illinois, 1970.

10349
Broom, Eric Frederick. "A Comparative Analysis of the Central Administrative Agencies of Amateur Sport and Physical Recreation in England and Canada." Illinois, 1971.

10350
Burelle, Jacques Vincent. "Qualifications of Athletic Directors of Member Institutions of the Canadian Intercollegiate Athletic Union." Indiana, 1975.

10351
Keyes, Mary Eleanor. "The History of the Women's Athletics Committee of the Canadian Association for Health, Physical Education and Recreation, 1940-1973." Ohio State, 1980.

10352
Kurtzman, Joseph Balfour. "A Critical Analysis of the Canadian Intercollegiate Athletic Union." Iowa, 1969.

10353
Lansley, Keith Leonard. "The Amateur Athletic Union of Canada and Changing Concepts of Amateurism." Alberta, 1971.

10354
Moriarty, Richard James. "The Organization History of the Canadian Intercollegiate Athletic Union Central (CIAUC) 1906-1955." Ohio State, 1971.

WORLD OLYMPICS AND CANADA/ JEUX OLYMPIQUES ET CANADA

10355
Colwell, Beverly Jane. "Socio-Cultural Determinants of International Sporting Success: The 1976 Summer Olympic Games." Waterloo, 1982.

10356
Mashiach, Asher. "A Study to Determine the Factors Which Influenced American Spectators To Go To See the Summer Olympic Games in Montreal, 1976." Ohio State, 1977.

Mechikoff, Robert Alan. See No./Voir no 8445

10357
Stauble, Vernon Ronald. "The Impact of Changin Organizational and Practical Perspectives: Th Olympic Games Movement, 1976-1984." Clare mont, 1981. [Montréal, 1976]

AMATEUR AND PROFESSIONAL SPORTS/ SPORTS AMATEURS ET PROFESSIONNELS

Anderson, David Frederick. See No./Voir no 10333
Broom, Eric Frederick. See No./Voir no 10349

10358
Cosentino, Frank. "A History of the Concept of Pro fessionalism in Canadian Sport." Alberta, 1973.

Lansley, Keith Leonard. See No./Voir no 10353
Poupart, Jean. See No./Voir no 10375

10359
Watkins, Glenn Gregory. "Professional Team Spor and Competition Policy: A Case Study of th Canadian Football League." Alberta, 1972.

COACHING IN SPORT/ ENTRAÎNEMENT DANS LES SPORTS

10360
Chambers, David Lee. "An Analysis of the Pro fessional Preparation and Attitudes of Male Secon dary School Coaches in Selected Sports in th Province of Ontario." Ohio State, 1972.

10361
Danielson, Richard Raymond. "Leadership in Coach ing: Description and Evaluation." Alberta, 197 [Hockey coaching/Entraînement au hockey]

10362
Gravelle, Lucien H. "Master Coach and Swim Team An Ethnographic Account." Alberta, 1977.

10363
Kennedy, John Robinson. "A History of the Develop ment of the Coaching Certification Programme i Canada." Ohio State, 1981.

Koop, Sandra Jean. See No./Voir no 9546
Scott, Harvey Alexander. See No./Voir no 10369

SPORTS SPECIFIC/SPORTS SPÉCIFIQUES

Basketball/Ballon panier

10364
Blais, Marc. "Perspectives cognitives de la motivatio d'accomplissement de joueurs de basketball franco phones de la province de Québec." Montréal, 1982

10365
Dewar, John Duncan. "The Life and Professiona Contributions of James Naismith." Florid State, 1965.

10366
Griffiths, Glynis. "Focus of Attention and Free-Thro Shooting Performance." Alberta, 1982.

Catching/Lutte

10367
Starkes, Janet Lynn. "Components of Skill in Catch ing." Waterloo, 1980. [From age eight t adulthood/De 8 ans à l'âge adulte]

Curling

ezer, Vera Rose. See No./Voir no 8930

Football

0368
Manz, Raymond Leonard. "Histochemical, Bio-
chemical and Performance Profiles of Canadian
Intercollegiate Football Players." Alberta, 1978.

0369
cott, Harvey Alexander. "Self Coach and Team: A
Theoretical and Empirical Application of the Social
Interactionist Perspective to Teenage Sports Can-
didacy and Participation." Alberta, 1973.

Watkins, Glenn Gregory. See No./Voir no 10359

Gymnastics/Gymnastique

0370
Gauthier, Roger Regent. "The Reliability of Gymnastic Ratings and Gymnastic Judges." Alberta, 1974.

Harness Racing/Course de chevaux

Fetterly, Robert Gordon. See No./Voir no 10195

Ice Hockey/Hockey sur glace

0371
Kingston, George Edward. "The Organization and
Development of Ice Hockey during Childhood in the
Soviet Union, Czechoslovakia, Sweden and
Canada." Alberta, 1977.

0372
Kurtz, Morris. "A History of the 1972 Canada -USSR
Ice Hockey Series." Pennsylvania State, 1981.

10373
Marshall, John Charles. "The Competitive Environment: Effects and Influences on the Young
Athlete." York, 1980. [Hockey players from ages
nine to sixteen years old/Joueurs de hockey de
9 ans à 16 ans]

10374
McFadden, Scot Robert. "An Investigation of the
Relative Effectiveness of Two Types of Imagery
Rehearsal Applied to Enhance Skilled, Athletic
Performance." Toronto, 1982. [Goal tending/
Garder les buts]

10375
Poupart, Jean. "Le hockey junior et l'engagement à la
carrière professionnelle." McGill, 1978.

10376
Thiffault, Charles. "Tachistoscopic Training and Its
Effect upon Visual Perceptual Speed of Ice Hockey
Players." Southern California, 1974. [A study of
youngsters from Quebec/Étude sur les jeunes du
Québec]

Thom, Douglas John. See No./Voir no 2733

Pole Vault/Saut à la perche

10377
Gros, H.J. "Computerized Analysis of the Pole Vault
Utilizing Biomechanics Cinematography and Direct
Force Measurements." Alberta, 1982.

Running/Course

10378
Jacobs, Larry Wallace. "Running as an Addiction
Process." Alberta, 1980.

Skiing/Ski

10379
Bedingfield, Wendy Andrews. "Kinematic and Descrip-
tive Comparison of Skijumping Techniques."
Indiana, 1978. [Mount Norway, Thunder Bay,
Ontario]

10380
Wells, Ward M. "An Evaluation of the Methods Either
in Use or Proposed for Use to Determine Winners
in Interscholastic and Intercollegiate Ski Competition Held in the United States and Canada."
Indiana, 1955.

Swimming/Natation

Gravelle, Lucien H. See No./Voir no 10362
Koop, Sandra Jean. See No./Voir no 9546

SPORT IN EDUCATION/SPORT EN ÉDUCATION

10381
Brawn, Christopher Alan. "An Instrument for Evaluating the Intramural Sports Programs for Men at
Degree-Granting Institutions in Canada." Indiana,
1970.

10382
Grambeau, Rodney James. "A Survey of the Adminis-
tration of Intramural Sports Programs for Men in
Selected Colleges and Universities in North and
South America." Michigan, 1959.

Kurtzman, Joseph Balfour. See No./Voir no 10352
Manz, R.L. See No./Voir no 10368
Moriarty, Richard James. See No./Voir no 10354
Scott, Harvey Alexander. See No./Voir no 10369
Wells, Ward M. See No./Voir no 10380

PHYSICAL EDUCATION, RECREATION AND LEISURE TIME ACTIVITIES/ÉDUCATION PHYSIQUE, RÉCRÉATION ET LOISIRS

General Items/Ouvrages généraux

10383
Barton, James Wesley. "The Effects of EMG Biofeedback and Autogenic Training on Anxiety Control
and Performance of Aviation Pilots." Alberta,
1981.

Boswell, David M. See No./Voir no 2652

10384
Burgess, Arthur Charles. "The Development of a
Model for a Community Fitness Campaign."
Alberta, 1981. [Western Canada: Alberta, British
Columbia, Manitoba/L'Ouest du Canada: Alberta,
Colombie-Britannique et Manitoba]

Corran, Robert. See No./Voir no 10335

10385

Eaton, John Douglas. "The Life and Professional Contributions of Arthur Stanley Lamb, M.D. to Physical Education in Canada." Ohio State, 1964.

Gauthier, P.A. See No./Voir no 6714

Jacobs, Larry Wallace. See No./Voir no 10378

Johns, David P. See No./Voir no 10205

10386

Jones, Brian Cyril. "The Effect of Isokinetic Training on the Force-Velocity Relationship and Maximal Power in Female Forearm Flexor Muscles." Alberta, 1977. [Female volunteers, from 18 to 21 years old/Femmes volontaires de 18 à 21 ans]

Kennedy, John Robinson. See No./Voir no 10363

10387

Lenskyj, H. "The Role of Physical Education in the Socialization of Girls in Ontario, 1890-1930." Toronto, 1983.

10388

Magee, David J. "The Effect of Isokinetic Exercise on Human Heart Rate and Blood Pressure." Alberta, 1980.

10389

Markon, P.J. "The Effect of Fitness and Diet Information on Serum Lipids in Sedentary Adults." Alberta, 1982.

10390

Quinney, Henry Arthur. "The Relationship of Influences of Three Selected Variables in the Aerobic Capacity of Citizens of an Urban Canadian Community." Alberta, 1974.

Sarrasen, Joanne. See No./Voir no 4092

10391

Sawula, Lorne William. "The Natural Physical Fitness Act of Canada, 1943-1954." Alberta, 1977.

Semotiuk, Darwin Michael. See No./Voir no 10336

10392

Smith, D.J. "Physiological and Performance Components of Endurance." Alberta, 1981.

10393

Smith, William Donald. "A Study of the Development of the Physical Education Branch, Department of Education, Province of Ontario, Canada." SUNY, Buffalo, 1957.

10394

Turner, A.A. "Effects of Different Training Methods on Flexibility." Alberta, 1982.

10395

Turner, Douglas Jack. "Evaluation of a Prescriptive Physical Fitness Program Used by the Police Department, City of Calgary." Oregon, 1982.

10396

Wanzel, Robert Stewart. "Determination of Attitudes of Employees and Management of Canadian Corporations Toward Company Sponsored Physical Activity Facilities and Programs." Alberta, 1974.

SCHOOLS/ÉCOLES

General Items/Ouvrages généraux

Gibson, B.J. See No./Voir no 3814

10397

Kennedy, William F.R. "A History of Professional P paration in Health, Physical Education, a Recreation in Canada." Teachers Colleg Columbia, 1956.

Morrow, Leslie Donald. See No./Voir no 2635

10398

Plewes, Doris H. "A Course of Study in Healt Physical Education, and Recreation, Londo Ontario (Kindergarten – Grade XIII)." Teache College, Columbia, 1943.

10399

Van Vliet, Maurice L. "A Guide to Administrati Policies for Physical Education in Canadian Pub Schools, Grades One Through Nine." Californi Berkeley, 1951.

Valiquette, John Edmund. See No./Voir no 3847

10400

Zechetmayr, Monika. "Government Involvement Public School Physical Education in Canada and t German Democratic Republic, 1945 to 1979 – Sociological Comparison." Alberta, 1980.

Elementary Schools/Écoles primaires

Jensen, P.K. See No./Voir no 3045

10401

Keller, Sandra M. "Endurance Fitness Training and t Elementary School Child: Effects on Physical a Psychological Well-Being." Concordia, 1981.

10402

Martens, Fred Lewis. "The Relative Effectiveness Physical Education Programs in Selected Priva and Public Elementary Schools in Victoria, Briti Columbia." Oregon, 1968.

Robbins, Stuart G. See No./Voir no 4331

Intermediate and Secondary Schools/ Écoles intermédiaires et secondaires

10403

Andrews, Barry Craig. "Physical Fitness Levels Canadian and South African School Boys." Uta 1975.

10404

Botterill, Calvin Bruce. "Goal Setting and Perfo mance on an Endurance Task." Alberta, 1977.

10405

Butcher, Janice Elsie. "Physical Activity Particip tion of Adolescent Girls." Alberta, 1980.

10406

Grenier, Jacques. "The Status of Physical Educati in the French 'Régionales' Secondary Schools Quebec, Canada." Oregon, 1973.

10407

Holman, Roy Paul. "The Perceived Status of Fema Athletes by Male and Female Athletes and No Athletes in Canada and the United States." Nor Carolina, Greensboro, 1978. [Thunder Ba Ontario]

10408
Hunt, Edmund Arthur. "Teacher, Parent and Student Differences Concerning Curriculum Objectives: The Physical Education Case." British Columbia, 1976.

10409
Hunt, Stanley Jack. "The Relationship Between Height, Weight, Age and the Ability to Perform Manitoba's Physical and Motor Performance Test for Junior High School Students." Northern Colorado, 1974.

Johns, David P. See No./Voir no 10205

10410
Leith, Larry McKenzie. "An Experimental Analysis of the Effect of Direct and Vicarious Participation in Physical Activity on Subject Aggressiveness." Alberta, 1977. [Wallaceburg, Alberta]

10411
Nixon, Howard R. "A Score Card for Evaluating Canadian High School Health and Physical Education Programs." Indiana, 1959.

10412
Rasmussen, Roy Leonard. "Longitudinal Investigation of Selected Variables in Physically Active and Inactive Boys: Studies During Their Circumpubertal Years." Saskatchewan, 1978.

Shields, Gerald Bruce. See No./Voir no 2968

Thom, Douglas John. See No./Voir no 2733

10413
Wood, Nancy L. "Incentive Motivation in Sport: A Theoretical Analysis and the Development of a Measuring Instrument." Alberta, 1980.

Colleges and Universities/Collèges et universités

10414
Bowie, Garald William. "A Survey to Obtain Relevant Information from Selected Colleges in the Province of Alberta to Develop and Apply an Evaluation Instrument for Men's Physical Education Programs." Utah, 1970.

Burelle, Jacques Vincent. See No./Voir no 10350

10415
Chouinard, Normand Paul. "An Analysis of the Physical Education Programs in the Community Colleges of Ontario." Illinois State, 1979.

10416
Daniel, Juri Vrzesnevski. "Differential Roles and Faculty Job Satisfaction in Departments of Physical Education and Athletics in Ontario Universities." Illinois, 1971.

10417
Errington, Joseph. "An Evaluation of Undergraduate Professional Preparation in Physical Education for Men in Canada." Indiana, 1958.

10418
Fairbanks, Bert Lamarr. "A Study to Determine the Academic Status of Physical Education in Canadian Universities." Brigham Young, 1970.

10419
Frey, Richard D. "Selective Attention and the Judgement of Temporal Order." Alberta, 1978.

10420
Gibson, William Garret. "Self, Leader and Group in Outdoor Education Value Change Through Management of Curricula by Objectives." Alberta, 1977.

10421
Goodwin, Luther. "An Evaluation of Teacher Education in the Physical Education Degree Program at the University of Alberta." Washington, Seattle, 1962.

Gravelle, Lucien H. See No./Voir no 10362

10422
Kadatz, Dennis Melvin. "An Analysis of Indoor Physical Education Space at Selected Universities in Canada." Oregon, 1980.

10423
Kramer, John Frank. "Electromyographical and Cinematographical Analysis of Walking Backwards." Alberta, 1979.

Kurtzman, Joseph Balfour. See No./Voir no 10352

10424
Leblanc, Hugues. "Études théoriques et appliquées de micro-enseignement dans la formation d'éducateurs physiques à l'aide de la théorie de l'apprentissage social de Bandura." Ottawa, 1981.

Maloney, Timothy Lawrence. See No./Voir no 3657

Manz, R.L. See No./Voir no 10368

10425
Marshall, Joseph Melville. "Evaluation of Undergraduate Professional Preparation in Physical Education in Canada." Minnesota, 1970.

10426
Meagher, John William. "Projected Plan for Reorganization of Physical Education Teacher Training Programs in Canada." Pennsylvania State, 1958.

Moriarty, Richard James. See No./Voir no 10354

10427
Newton, Donald McKay. "An Evaluation of Undergraduate Professional Preparation Programs in Physical Education for Men in Canadian Universities." Northern Colorado, 1969.

10428
O'Bryan, Maureen Hazel. "Physical Education: A Study of Professional Education in Ontario Universities." Toronto, 1973.

Padfield, Clive A.F. See No./Voir no 3636

10429
Palmer, Guy Mathew. "A Study of the Relationships of Leadership Behavior, Organizational Climate and Demographic Data in Physical Education Departments at Selected Colleges and Universities in Canada and the United States." Oregon, 1982.

Proteau, Luc. See No./Voir no 10330

10430
Proulx, J. Roger. "L'analyse de la cathexis corporelle chez des étudiants inscrits à un programme de formation universitaire de premier cycle en sciences de l'activité physique." Montréal, 1982.

10431
Soucie, Daniel G. "An Analysis of the Perceived Actual Ideal Profile of Organizational Characteristics of Physical Education Departments in the Colleges of Quebec." Oregon, 1975.

Tufuor, Joseph Kwame. See No./Voir no 3730

10432
Waldenberger, Robert Wesley. "An Analysis of Leader Behavior Group Interaction and Organizational Climate in Physical Education Departments of Selected Canadian Universities." Oregon, 1975.

10433
Williams, Carole C. "The Changing Physical Education Major Curriculum in American and Canadian Institutions of Higher Learning." North Carolina, Greensboro, 1971.

RECREATION, PLAY AND LEISURE TIME ACTIVITIES/ RÉCRÉATIONS, JEUX ET MOMENTS DE LOISIRS

General Items/Ouvrages généraux

10434
Isaacman, Daniel. "Jewish Summer Camps in the United States and Canada, 1900-1969." Dropsie, 1970.
10435
Palmer, D. "Attitudes Toward the Pursuit of Games and Pastimes in Childhood as Portrayed by the Authors of Children's Literature 1780-1855." Alberta, 1977.
10436
Thomson, L.A. "Recreation Leadership: Historical Analytical Review and an Empirical Study." Alberta, 1982.

Recreation in the Schools/Récréation dans les écoles

10437
Aloia, Alex Dominic. "The Organization of Student Recreation in Selected Large Institutions of Higher Learning." Southern California, 1951.
10438
Arnold, Donald John. "Attitudes of Public School and Municipal Recreation Authorities in Southeast Ontario Toward Politics for the Joint Acquisition, Development, and Utilization of School Facilities for School and Recreational Use." Indiana, 1970.
10439
Kelsey, John Marvin. "Study of Programs of Recreation in Selected Institutions of Higher Learning in North, Central, and South America." Iowa State, 1956.
Plewes, Doris H. See No./Voir no 10398
White, William Hart. See No./Voir no 10458

PUBLIC RECREATION AND LEISURE TIME ACTIVITIES/RÉCRÉATION PUBLIQUE ET MOMENTS DE LOISIRS

General Items/Ouvrages généraux

Anderson, David Frederick. See No./Voir no 10333
Broom, Eric Frederick. See No./Voir no 10349
Johnson, Ronald Clifford Arthur. See No./Voir no 4846
10440
Laub, Michael Elwood. "The Economic Evaluation of Non-Marketed Recreational Resources." British Columbia, 1972.
10441
Lazarowich, Nicholas Michael B. "Urbanization and Outdoor Recreation in Canada." Cincinnati, 1977.

10442
Leicester, John Beauchamp. "Environmental and Recreational Aspects in Open Space Planning." Waterloo, 1980.
10443
Lyons, Renée Felice. "Analysis of Services to Special Populations by Municipal Recreation Departments in Canada." Oregon, 1981.
10444
McFarland, Elsie Marie. "A Historical Analysis of the Development of Public Recreation in Canadian Communities." Illinois, 1969.
10445
Morey, Edward Rockendorf. "The Demand for Site Specific Recreational Activities: A Characteristic Approach." British Columbia, 1978.
Nogradi, George Steve. See No./Voir no 6765
10446
Prosser, Laurence Edwin Keith. "A Model for Planning and Managing National Parks." Oregon, 1977.
10447
Reid, D.G. "Urban and Rural Municipal Councilors Attitudes Toward Recreation, Willingness to Co operate, and Need for Control." Waterloo, 1978.

Alberta

10448
Beres, Larry Ralph. "Principles of Public Recreation Practice in Alberta, Canada." Texas A & M, 1981.
10449
Cheng, Jacqueline Ruth. "Images of Banff and Canmore and the Use of Banff National Park by Motel Visitors." Calgary, 1978.
10450
Smith, Emmett Hughes. "A Perspective of Snowmobile Owners in the Province of Alberta." Texas A & M, 1976.

British Columbia/Colombie-Britannique

10451
Larsen, John Knud. "The Characteristics and Duties of Municipal Parks and Recreation Employees in British Columbia." Oregon, 1976.
Marsh, John Stuart. See No./Voir no 4614
Ramsay, Richard Lyon. See No./Voir no 6767
10452
Schrodt, Phyllis Barbara. "A History of Pro-Rec: The British Columbia Provincial Recreation Programme 1934 to 1953." Alberta, 1979.
10453
Thorsell, James Westvick. "Wilderness Recreation Users – Their Characteristics, Motivations and Opinions: A Study of Three British Columbia Provincial Parks." British Columbia, 1971.

Manitoba

10454
Brown, William Alan Nicholas. "The Role of Outdoor Recreation in Regional Development: A Study of Hecla Provincial Park." Manitoba, 1977.

10455
Pandey, Rama Kant. "Estimation of Demand for Wildlife Recreation in Southwestern Manitoba." Manitoba, 1972.
10456
Ross, Carlyle Bonston Albert. "Estimation of Demand for and Benefits Derived from Recreation Areas at Proposed Sites in the Souris River Basin, Manitoba." Manitoba, 1974.

New Brunswick/Nouveau-Brunswick

10457
Fahs, Lois S. "The Social Situation in Seven Rural Communities in New Brunswick Studied as the Basis for Planning a Program of General Recreation with Special Emphasis on Dancing." Teachers College, Columbia, 1941.

Nova Scotia/Nouvelle-Écosse

10458
White, William Hart. "The Development and Evaluation of Guidelines for the Use of Public School Facilities for Community Recreation in Nova Scotia." Boston University, 1980.

Ontario

Arnold, Donald John. See No./Voir no 10438
10459
Bowles, Jane Margaret. "Effects of Human Disturbance on the Sand Dunes at Pinery Provincial Park." Western Ontario, 1980.
Griffith, Charles Arthur. See No./Voir no 4065
Hallman, Donald Emerson. See No./Voir no 4691
10460
Heit, Michael Joseph James. "A Procedure for Evaluating the Feasibility of Tourist Accommodation Development as Applied to Southern Ontario." Texas A & M, 1975.
Helleiner, Frederick Maria. See No./Voir no 4693
10461
Jaakson, Reiner. "The Influence of Water-Level Fluctuation in Cottage-Based Recreation Including the Development of a Draw-Down Tolerance Model on the Trent Canal Reservoir Lakes." Waterloo, 1973.
Joseph, Jacob R. See No./Voir no 4548
Leicester, John B. See No./Voir no 10442
Levy, Steven Stanley. See No./Voir no 10113
Lucas, Robert Charles. See No./Voir no 4701
Paul, Alexander Humphrey. See No./Voir no 4707
10462
Plumb, Jon Michael. "Public Policy for Enjoyment and Enrichment: The Case of the Leisure Industries in Ontario." Toronto, 1979.
10463
Rugg, Robert D. "The Use and Non-Use of Urban Parks: Accessibility and Social Characteristics in Relation to Public Outdoor Recreation in Selected Neighborhoods of Ottawa-Hull." Ottawa, 1974.
Taylor, James Addison. See No./Voir no 4715
Wolfe, Roy Israel. See No./Voir no 4719

Quebec/Québec

10464
Auger, Jacques Arthur. "A Visitation Model for Selected Campgrounds in the Province of Quebec." Michigan State, 1974.
Brière, Roger. See No./Voir no 4751
Doucet, Laval J. See No./Voir no 10146
Rajotte, Freda. See No./Voir no 4772
10465
Ruckenstein, Michael. "Leisure Pursuits of the English and French-Canadians in an Urban Population." Boston University, 1980. [Montreal/Montréal]
10466
Soubrier, Robert. "Méthode pour évaluer la demande d'équipement de loisir en milieu urbain." Montréal, 1982.
10467
Thibault, André. "La situation professionnelle des travailleurs en loisirs du Québec comme un déterminant de la faisabilité différentielle de l'éducation au loisir." Laval, 1980.

Saskatchewan

Scace, Robert Chaston. See No./Voir no 4802

URBAN AND REGIONAL PLANNING/ PLANIFICATION URBAINE ET RÉGIONALE

Doctoral research on urban and regional planning is comparatively new. The first study appeared at McGill University in 1953, the second at Harvard University in 1957, and the third at Cornell University in 1958. During the 1960's, two studies appeared, one at the University of Ottawa in 1962, and one at the University of Toronto in 1968. Eleven studies were completed in the United States in the following 15 years, while 41 were completed in Canada during that same period. The University of Waterloo, accounts for half that number (21) while the University of British Columbia is second with eight. Two studies were completed in Great Britain at the University of London in 1976 and 1977. On the basis of the Canadian total for the first four years of the 1980's, the output of this decade will exceed the last. Of the ten American universities contributing dissertations in this area, Cornell produced three, the University of California (Berkeley) produced two and the remaining eight produced one each.

———

La recherche en vue d'une thèse de doctorat sur la planification urbaine et régionale est une nouveauté; c'est à l'Université McGill, en 1953, qu'une thèse en ce

domaine a été présentée pour la première fois. Ensuite, Harvard, en 1957, a suivi, puis Cornell, en 1958. Dans les années 1960, deux thèses ont paru, une à Ottawa en 1962 et une à Toronto en 1968. Au cours des 15 années suivantes, onze études ont été faites aux États-Unis et 41 au Canada au cours de la même période, dont la moitié (21) à l'Université de Waterloo; celle de Colombie-Britannique vient en second lieu avec 8 thèses. Deux thèses ont paru en Grande-Bretagne, à l'Université de Londres, l'une en 1976, l'autre en 1977. De 1980 à 1984, si l'on se base sur le nombre total des thèses canadiennes, les années 1980 seront plus productives que les années 1970. Des dix universités américaines auxquelles on doit des thèses en ce domaine, seulement Cornell (3) et California (Berkeley) (2), ont fourni plus d'une étude.

REGIONAL STUDIES/ÉTUDES RÉGIONALES

10468
Aasen, Clarence Theodor. "Ethnicity, Politics and Urban Planning: Political Uses of French and Italian Ethnicity in Two Local Area Planning Processes." Waterloo, 1979. [Ottawa-Hull]
10469
Akkerman, Abraham. "Structural Foundations for a Single-Region Analysis of Household Population Growth: Reflections on Demographic Input to Regional Planning." Waterloo, 1983.
Aschinger, Richard Franz. See No./Voir no 7871
Cross, Kevin James. See No./Voir no 932
10470
Delgaauw, Mieke Keisk. "The Integration of Manpower and Regional Economic Development Policies: A Comparative Analysis." Waterloo, 1982.
10471
Gunton, Thomas Ian. "Evolution of Urban and Regional Planning in Canada: 1900-1960." British Columbia, 1981.
10472
Lardinois, Christian. "Problèmes d'optimisation combinatoire de grande taille et inférence statistique: application à la planification urbaine et régionale." Montréal, 1980.
Leicester, John Beauchamp. See No./Voir no 10442
Migneron, Jean-Gabriel. See No./Voir no 1943
Oberlander, Henry Peter. See No./Voir no 8494
Pierce, John T. See No./Voir no 4911
Ricklefs, John Edward. See No./Voir no 2292
10473
Rizvi, Amjad Ali Bahadur. "City and Regional Planning Education: Response of Selected North American Institutions to the Needs of Underdeveloped Countries." British Columbia, 1971.
Shimizu, Kaien Masaru. See No./Voir no 939
Shkelnyk, Anastasia Maria. See No./Voir no 486
Stanley, Thomas Brock. See No./Voir no 6785
Trevithick, Morris Henry. See No./Voir no 1589
10474
Van Nus, Walter. "The Plan-Makers and the City: Architects, Engineers, Surveyors and Urban Planning in Canada, 1890-1939." Toronto, 1975.

10475
Waterhouse, Michael Francis. "Canadian Energy Planning and Policy Making in a Turbulent Environment." Waterloo, 1980. [Oil and gas/Huile et essence]
Wegner, Robert Edward Chesley. See No./Voir no 7610
10476
Winters, Tobey Lee. "Deep Water Ports: Economics and the Environment." Syracuse, 1975.

REGIONS/RÉGIONS

Alberta

10477
Carvalho, Emanuel. "Economic Planning for Balanced Development in a Diversified Resource Region: The Alberta Peace." Waterloo, 1982.
10478
Trnavskis, Boris. "Passenger Demand for a 1976 QSTOL Aircraft System in the Calgary-Edmonton Corridor." Calgary, 1974.
10479
Webster, Douglas Richard. "The Incidence Impact of a Regional Development Program Based on Employment Creation: The Lesser Slave Lake, Alberta Case." California, Berkeley, 1977.
Wright, John Ross. See No./Voir no 10503

British Columbia/Colombie-Britannique

10480
Bottomley, John. "Ideology Planning and the Landscape: The Business Community Urban Reform and the Establishment of Town Planning in Vancouver, British Columbia, 1900-40." British Columbia, 1977.
Evans, Lawrence Kenneth. See No./Voir no 9671
10481
Gerecke, John Kent. "Toward a New Model of Urban Planning." British Columbia, 1974. [Greater Vancouver/Vancouver métropolitain]
10482
McAfee, Rosemary Ann. "Interactive Evaluation: A User Oriented Process to Assist Housing Program Reformulation." British Columbia, 1975. [Vancouver]
Miller, Philip Carl. See No./Voir no 387
10483
Nann, Richard C. "Urban Renewal and Relocation of Chinese Community Families." California, Berkeley, 1970. [Vancouver]
Thorsell, James Westvick. See No./Voir no 10453

Manitoba

Sharma, Satish Chandra. See No./Voir no 4528

Newfoundland/Terre-Neuve

Goulding, James W. See No./Voir no 1169

Northwest Territories and the Yukon/ Territoires du Nord-Ouest et Yukon

10484
Fenge, Terence Alfred Edward. "Environmental Policy in Northwest Territories: The Case of Environmentally Significant Areas." Waterloo, 1982.

10485
Naysmith, John Kennedy. "Land Use and Public Policy in Northern Canada." British Columbia, 1975.

Ridge, Frank G. See No./Voir no 4651

Ontario

Aasen, Clarence Theodor. See No./Voir no 10468

Basu, Sreemay. See No./Voir no 10278

Brown, Si. See No./Voir no 1908

10486
Campbell, Neil MacDougall. "An Evaluation and Policy Proposal: Ontario Farm Enlargement and Consolidation Program." Waterloo, 1972.

10487
Coleman, Derek Jardine. "An Ecological Input to Regional Planning." Waterloo, 1974. [Waterloo]

10488
Eagles, Paul Franklin John. "The Institutional Arrangements for Environmentally Sensitive Area Planning and Management in Ontario." Waterloo, 1980.

Foster, Richard Henry, Jr. See No./Voir no 8721

Friesen, Brock Frederick James. See No./Voir no 8837

10489
Giesbrecht, Herbert. "Environmental Planning for New Communities." Waterloo, 1979.

Gillen, David William. See No./Voir no 4928

10490
Goldschmidt, Carl. "Supervision of Local Land Use Control: The Ontario Municipal Board." Pittsburgh, 1970.

Grima, Angelo Paul. See No./Voir no 4929

Hall, George Brent. See No./Voir no 6693

10491
Hossé, Hans August. "Projected Development Trends and Conceptual Structure of the Ottawa Region: A Treatise on Regional Planning." Ottawa, 1962.

10492
Hulchanski, John David. "The Origins of Urban Land Use Planning in Ontario, 1900-1916." Toronto, 1981.

Jaakson, Reiner. See No./Voir no 10461

Jackson, Suzanne F. See No./Voir no 6684

Kosny, Mitchell Ernest. See No./Voir no 8727

Leicester, John Beauchamp. See No./Voir no 10442

Lipman, Marvin Harold. See No./Voir no 10033

McCabe, Robert Wylie. See No./Voir no 4905

McComb, Lloyd A. See No./Voir no 2259

Olagbaiye, Joseph Ajiboye. See No./Voir no 4953

10493
Onibokun, Adepoju Gabriel. "A Comparative Analysis of the Relative Habitability of Public Housing Projects in Southwestern Ontario." Waterloo, 1971.

Oostendorp, Anke. See No./Voir no 9732

Proudfoot, Stuart Bradley. See No./Voir no 8735

10494
Rigby, Douglas W. "Citizen Participation in Urban Renewal Planning: A Case Study of an Inner City Residents' Association." Waterloo, 1975. [Kensington, Toronto]

Saccomanno, Fedel Frank Mario. See No./Voir no 2262

Smith, L. Graham. See No./Voir no 1797

10495
Unsoy, Jeelee. "Managing Land Inventories for Residential Development in Kitchener (Ontario) 1967-1977." Waterloo, 1982.

Van Zyle, François David Wallace. See No./Voir no 1041

Waterhouse, Michael Francis. See No./Voir no 10475

Prince Edward Island/Île-du-Prince-Édouard

10496
Connor, Thomas R. "Evaluation of a Community Development Project in Two Towns of Prince Edward Island, Canada." Cornell, 1970.

Quebec/Québec

Aasen, Clarence Theodor. See No./Voir no 10468

Auger, Jacques Arthur. See No./Voir no 10464

10497
Frost, Robert. "Système urbain et planification urbaine." Montréal, 1972.

10498
Guay, L. "The Ecological Differentiation of Urban Social Space: Montreal, 1951-1971." London, 1977.

10499
Hamel, Pierre. "Analyse des pratiques urbaines revendicatives à Montréal, de 1963 à 1976." Montréal, 1980.

10500
Mayer, Robert. "L'idéologie du réaménagement urbain à Québec (quartier Saint-Roch) et à Montréal (quartier Petite Bourgogne)." Laval, 1977.

10501
Ploegaerts, Léon. "Le zonage dans l'aménagement de l'espace urbain au Québec." Montréal, 1974.

10502
Prost, Robert. "Système urbain et planification urbaine." Montréal, 1972.

Rodwin, Victor George. See No./Voir no 6704

10503
Wright, John Ross. "Democratization of the Regional Planning Process." Waterloo, 1973.

SCIENTIFIC STUDIES/
ÉTUDES SCIENTIFIQUES

The number of dissertations concerned with scientific studies that have been classified under this general heading, constitutes the third largest section. Almost all the 27 major Canadian universities have produced at least one scientific study dealing with Canada. The University of British Columbia has the largest number due to its work in botany and forestry. The University of Toronto is second, and McGill University is close behind. McGill's major specialization in scientific studies is entomology. The sub-classifications are listed below.

Le nombre total des thèses portant sur des études scientifiques classées sous ce titre constitue la troisième plus vaste section. Presque toutes les 27 plus importantes universités canadiennes ont produit au moins une étude scientifique se rapportant au Canada. L'Université de la Colombie-Britannique, en raison de ses travaux en botanique et foresterie, se classe au premier rang, Toronto vient en second, McGill suit de très près. La principale spécialisation de McGill en ce domaine est l'entomologie. Voici la liste des sous-classifications.

GENERAL ITEMS/OUVRAGES GÉNÉRAUX

Bartell, Marvin. See No./Voir no 2
10504
Bergeron, Yves. "Étude écologique intégré des moitiés ouest de cantons d'Hébécourt et de Roquemaure en Abitibi, Québec." Montréal, 1983.
Boyd, Archibald D. See No./Voir no 2048
Dandurand, Louise. See No./Voir no 8503
10505
Doern, George Bruce. "Scientists and the Making of Science Policies in Canada." Queen's, 1970.
Jackson, Michael Wesley. See No./Voir no 8442
10506
Pelton, Terrance Ronald. "Canadian Scientists: Their Research Department Structure and Research Output in Four Types of Organizations." British Columbia, 1970.

HISTORY OF SCIENCE IN CANADA/
HISTOIRE DES SCIENCES AU CANADA

These are few in number. Of the eleven items listed, nine were produced at Canadian universities and two at American universities; almost all during the 1970's and 1980's.

Il y a peu de travaux en ce domaine. Des 11 sujets généraux énumérés, neuf ont fait l'objet de thèses dans des universités canadiennes et deux dans des universités américaines; presque toutes ces thèses datent des années 1970 et 1980.

Belfield, Robert Blake. See No./Voir no 1782
10507
De Vecchi, Vittorio Maria Guiseppe. "Science and Government in Nineteenth Century Canada." Toronto, 1978.
10508
Newell, Dianne Charlotte Elizabeth. "Technological Change in a New and Developing Country: A Study of Mining Technology in Canada West — Ontario, 1841-1891." Western Ontario, 1981.
Wadland, John Henry. See No./Voir no 951

BACTERIOLOGY AND MICROBIOLOGY/
BACTÉRIOLOGIE ET MICROBIOLOGIE

Of the twenty-five dissertations listed, 17 are from Canadian universities and eight from American universities.

Des vingt-cinq thèses de cette section, 17 viennent de universités canadiennes et 8 des université américaines.

10509
Alarie, Albert M. "A Systematic Study of Amylolyti Bacteria, That Decompose Cellulose, Isolated from Quebec Soils." McGill, 1945.
Chan, Yin Kwok. See No./Voir no 11831
10510
Desrochers, Raymond. "Étude écophysiologique d'une population de bactéries réductrices de soufre dan la rivière Ottawa." Montréal, 1962.
10511
Dular, Ram. "The Microbiology of Cryopedogeni Soils of the Subarctic with Particular Reference t the Churchill Region." Manitoba, 1968.
10512
Frantsi, Christopher. "Epidemiology of Infectiou Pancreatic Necrosis (IPN) Virus in Fishes i Ontario Waters." Guelph, 1972.
10513
Gossen, Randall Garth. "Microbial Degradation c Crude Oil in Arctic Soils." Calgary, 1973.
10514
Hayles, Launcellott Barrington. "Transmission c Western Equine Encephalitis Virus by Saskatchewa Mosquitoes and Behavior of the Virus in Selecte Laboratory Vertebrates in Relation to Epidemiolo gical Studies." Saskatchewan, 1971.
10515
Howard, David Lee. "Methane Oxidation in situ and k Isolated Cultures of Bacteria as Important Facto in Carbon Cycling and Sources of Carbon Dioxic in Lake Erie." Ohio State, 1974.

0516
shaque, Muhammad. "Physiological Activity of Bacteria Indigenous to a Lagoon Stabilizing Domestic Wastes." Manitoba, 1968. [Charleswood Lagoon, Manitoba/Lagune Charleswood, Manitoba]

0517
Kennedy, Robert Stephen. "Cytological and Physiological Effects of Chlorinated Hydrocarbon Pesticides and Dissolved Oxygen Concentrations on a Pseudomonas SP Isolated from Lake Erie." Ohio State, 1970.

10518
Lee, Sai Keung. "The Survival of Bacteria in Different Types of Canadian Arctic Soil and Mechanism of Death after Freezing and Thawing." McGill, 1977.

10519
Long, D.V.M. "Studies in Necrotic Enteritis in Broiler Chickens with Emphasis on the Role of Clostridium perfruigens." Guelph, 1974.

10520
Lucyszyn, Elizabeth Lupien. "The Isolation and Physiological Characterization of Autochthonous Bacteria from Lake Ontario." Saint Bonaventure, 1978.

10521
Martin, Jayne Frances Carney. "Suspended Particles from Lake Erie: Amino Acid Composition and the Effect of Detergents on Their Interactions with Bacteria." Ohio State, 1971.

10522
McClary, Dan O. "Factors Affecting the Morphology of Canadian Albicans." Washington, St. Louis, 1951.

McDonald, William C. See No./Voir no 11516

10523
Neish, Gordon Arthur. "Observations on the Pathology of Saprolegniasis of Pacific Salmon and on the Identity of the Fungi Associated with the Disease." British Columbia, 1977.

10524
Nelson, Louise Mary. "Influence of Temperature, Nutrient Limitation and Growth Rate on the Growth and Survival of Bacteria Isolated from an Arctic Soil." Calgary, 1976.

10525
Obiekwe, Christian Okechukwu. "Microbial Corrosion of Crude Oil Pipeline." Alberta, 1980. [North Central Alberta/Centre nord de l'Alberta]

10526
Olchowecki, Oleksa Alexander. "Taxonomy of the Genus Ceratocystis in Manitoba." Manitoba, 1972.

Schmidt, Jerome Paul. See No./Voir no 10703

10527
Simard, Ronald E. "Yeasts from the St. Lawrence River." McGill, 1970.

10528
Smallbone, Barry William. "Chemical and Physical Studies of Polar Lipids in Extremely Halophilic Bacteria." Ottawa, 1982.

Spieker, John Oscar. See No./Voir no 10816

10529
Stace-Smith, Richard. "Rubus Viruses in British Columbia and Their Relationship with the Aphid Vector Amphorophora Rubi. Kaltenbach." Oregon State, 1954.

10530
Tennant, Alan D. "Bacterial Indices of Pollution in Oyster Producing Areas in Prince Edward Island." McGill, 1955.

10531
Warnes, Carl Edward. "The Microbiology of Chitin Decomposition in Lake Erie Sediments." Ohio State, 1974.

10532
Wyndham, Robert Campbell. "Adaptations of Aquatic Microorganisms to the Biodegradation of Oil Sands Hydrocarbons of the Athabaska." Calgary, 1982.

10533
Zarnke, Randall Lee. "Occurrence of Selected Microbial Pathogens in Alberta Wild Mammals." Wisconsin, 1978.

PARASITOLOGY/PARASITOLOGIE

Of the 29 studies recorded 23 came from Canadian universities and six came from American universities.

––––––––––

Des 29 études mentionnées, 23 viennent des universités canadiennes et 6 des universités américaines.

See also Entomology/Voir aussi Entomologie

10534
Addison, Edward M. "Life Cycle of Dipetalonema sprenti Anderson (Nematoda: Filarioidea) of Beaver (Castor canadenses)." Guelph, 1972.

10535
Anteson, Reginald Kwaku. "Biological Studies of Monanema marmotae (Webster 1967), a Filarioid Parasite of the Woodchuck, Marmota monax Canadenses." Connecticut, 1968.

10536
Appy, Ralph Grant. "Parasites of Cod, Gadus morhua L. in the Northwestern Atlantic Ocean." New Brunswick, 1979. [Gulf of St. Lawrence, Nova Scotian Shelf and Bay of Fundy/Golfe Saint-Laurent, plate-forme de la Nouvelle-Écosse et de la baie de Fundy]

10537
Arthur, Alfred Pibus. "The Indigenous Parasites of the European Pine Shoot Moth Rhyacionia buoliana (Schiffermueller), (Lepidoptera olethrentidae) in Ontario." Ohio State, 1956.

10538
Arthur, James Richard. "Studies on the Parasites of Pacific Herring (Clupea harengus pallasi) in North American Waters." Calgary, 1978.

10539
Baker, Michael Robert. "Taxonomy and Biology of Monoxenous Nematode Parasites of Reptiles and Amphibians in Southern Ontario." Guelph, 1978.

Bower, Susan Mae. See No./Voir no 10648

10540
Bursey, Carl Cedric. "The Biology and Experimental Systematics of Cestodes in the Genus Taenia L., 1958. S. Stra." New Brunswick, 1979. [Tapeworms in bobcats in New Brunswick/Vers solitaires chez les lynx du Nouveau-Brunswick]

10541
Chan, Guat-Lian. "A Study of Some Parasites of the White Sucker Catostomus commersoni (Lacepede), and the Fathead Minnow, Pimephales promelas Rafenesque, in a Reservoir and Its Contiguous Streams." Waterloo, 1981.

10542
Choquette, Laurent P.E. "Studies on Some Helminths Parasitic in the Trout Salvelinus fontinalis (Mitchell) in Quebec." McGill, 1953.

10543
Cone, David Knight. "The Biology of Urocleidus adspectus (Monogeriea) Parasitizing Perca flavescens." New Brunswick, 1980. [Little Maguadavic Lake, New Brunswick/Petit lac Maguadavic, Nouveau-Brunswick]

10544
Coppel, Harry C. "The Role of Parasitoids and Predators in the Control of the Spruce Budworm (Archips fumiferana Clem.) in British Columbia." New York State University College of Forestry, 1955.

10545
Drouin, Theodore Emile. "Parasites and Parasitism of The Whitefish of Lake McGregor and Travers' Reservoir." Calgary, 1983.

10546
Fallis, Albert Murray. "A Study of the Helminth Parasites of Lambs in Ontario." Toronto, 1937.

Frantsi, Christopher. See No./Voir no 10512

10547
Hanek, George. "Micro-Ecology and Spatial Distribution Patterns of the Gill Parasites Infesting Lepomis gibbosus (L.) and Ambloplites rupestris (Raf.) in the Bay of Quinte Area, Ontario." Waterloo, 1973.

Hare, Gerard Murdock. See No./Voir no 10983

Hart, John Lawson. See No./Voir no 11016

10548
Kakonge, Sam Atwoki K. "The Ecology of Some Metazoan Parasites of and Their Effect on Small Stream Fishes and Fry." Waterloo, 1972.

Khan, Muhammad M.R. See No./Voir no 10949

10549
Kingscote, Barbara F. "The Ecology of Leptospires in Ontario." Guelph, 1971.

10550
Ko, Ronald Chun Chung. "The Transmission of Achertia marmotae Webster, 1967 of Groundhogs (Marmota monax) by Ixodes Cookei." Guelph, 1971.

10551
Leong, Raymond Tak Seng. "Metazoan Parasites of Fishes of Cold Lake, Alberta: A Community Analysis." Alberta, 1975.

10552
Margolis, Leo. "Studies on Parasites and Diseases of Marine and Anadromous Fish from the Canadian Pacific Coast." McGill, 1953.

Mavor, James Watt. See No./Voir no 10888

10553
McGugan, Blair M. "Insect Parasites of the Spru Budworm in the Lake Nipigon Area of Ontario Wisconsin, 1951.

McFarlane, Samuel H. See No./Voir no 10958

10554
Mullen, Gary Richard. "The Taxonomy and Bionomi of Aquatic Mites (Acarina: Hydrachnellae) Paras tic on Mosquitoes in North America." Corne 1974. [Eastern Canada/Est du Canada]

10555
Pawaputanon, Kamonporn. "Effects of Parasit Copepod Salmincola californiensis (Dana, 1852) Juvenile Sockeye Salmon Oncorhynchus ner (Walbaum)." British Columbia, 1980.

10556
Platt, Thomas Reid. "The Life Cycle and Systemati of Parelaphostrongylus odocoilei (Nematoc Metastrongyloidea), a Parasite of Mule De (Odocoileus hemionus), with Special Reference the Molluscan Intermediate Host." Alberta, 1978.

10557
Rao, N.S. Krishna. "a. Taxonomic Studies of t Parasites of the Sea Gull, Larus argentatus Tak from the Ottawa River near Ste. Anne de Bellevu Québec, b. The Intermediate Host of Monoiez Expanza (rud. 1819) on Macdonald College Campu Québec." McGill, 1950.

10558
Riedel, Dieter Gunter. "A Description of Tr panosoma herpetosoma Tamiasi N. Sp. (Protozc Sciuridae) with Observations on Its Morphology a Biology in Rodent and Insect Hosts and in vitro Toronto, 1973.

Schmidt, Jerome Paul. See No./Voir no 10703

Sippell, William Lloyd. See No./Voir no 11289

Stromberg, Paul Charles. See No./Voir no 10918

10559
Tedla, Shibru. "The Ecology of Some Metazo Parasites of the Yellow Perch, Perca fluviatilis L Waterloo, 1969. [Ontario]

10560
Weinstein, Martin Sunny. "Studies on the Relationsh Between Sagitta elegans (Verrill) and Endoparasites in the Southwestern Gulf of S Lawrence." McGill, 1973.

Wolfgang, Robert W. See No./Voir no 11350

10561
Woo, Patrick Tung Kee. "A Study of t Trypanosomes of Amphibians and Reptiles Southern Ontario." Guelph, 1968.

Yuill, Thomas Mackay. See No./Voir no 6867

ANIMALS, WILDLIFE/ANIMAUX, VIE SAUVAGE

This section deals with animals peculiar to Canad Seventeen Canadian universities approved 127 disse tations. The University of British Columbia (25 Alberta (21), Guelph (13), Toronto (12), and McGill (1 are the ranking five. Ninety-five of these titles we produced during the 1970's and 1980's.

Twenty-seven American universities produced 50 di sertations. The majority were approved during th last 15 years. Wisconsin is the leader.

Les études de cette section ont été groupées sur les animaux spécifiques du Canada; on y trouve 127 thèses approuvées par 17 universités canadiennes. Parmi ces dernières, les cinq plus productives ont été l'Université de la Colombie-Britannique (29), celle de l'Alberta (21), de Guelph (13), de Toronto (12) et enfin McGill (10). Quatre-vingt-quinze thèses ont paru dans les années 1970 et 1980.

Vingt-sept universités américaines ont fourni 50 thèses. Le plus grand nombre a été approuvé de 1970 à 1985. L'Université du Wisconsin est en tête de production.

General Items/Ouvrages généraux

10562
Cameron, Austin W. "The Mammals of the Islands in the Gulf of St. Lawrence." McGill, 1956.

10563
Chabwela Weza, Harry Nixon. "Effects of Aggregate Mining Operations on Wildlife in Southern Ontario." Guelph, 1982.

10564
Cringan, Alexander Thom. "Some Factors in Selecting Units for Managing Wildlife in Ontario." Michigan, 1965.

10565
Doucet, G. Jean. "Effect of Habitat Manipulation on the Activity of an Animal Community." McGill, 1975. [Laurentians/Laurentides]

10566
Fimreite, Norvald. "Mercury Contamination in Canada and Its Effects on Wildlife." Western Ontario, 1971.

10567
Foster, John Bristol. "The Evolution of the Native Land Mammals of the Queen Charlotte Islands and the Problem of Insularity." British Columbia, 1964.

Green, Janet Jarmé. See No./Voir no 7122

Middleton, John David. See No./Voir no 11645

10568
Morris, Douglas William. "The Pattern and Structure of Habitat Utilization in Temperate School Mammals." Calgary, 1980. [Ontario]

10569
Osborne, Dale James. "The Systematics of Certain Small Mammals of the Quebec Peninsula." McGill, 1958.

10570
Quick, Horace Floyd. "The Fur Resource of a Wilderness Region in Northern British Columbia." Michigan, 1956.

10571
Wilson, John W., III. "Analytical Zoogeography of North American Mammals." Chicago, 1972.

Zarnke, Randall Lee. See No./Voir no 10533

Carniverous Mammals/Mammifères carnivores
Burrowing Coyote, Polar Bear/Coyote fouisseur, Ours polaire

10572
Taylor, Mitchel Kerry. "The Distribution and Abundance of Polar Bears Ursis Maritimus) in the Beaufort and Chukchi Seas." Minnesota, 1982.

10573
Bowen, William Donald. "Social Organization of the Coyote in Relation to Prey Size." British Columbia, 1979. [Jasper National Park/Parc national de Jasper]

10574
Mottus, Leonard Waldemar. "Differential Responses of Captive Coyotes to Various Canid Scents." Alberta, 1972. [Edmonton]

Nellis, Carl Hansen. See No./Voir no 10585

10575
Todd, Arlen Wesley. "Population Dynamics of Coyotes in Alberta." Wisconsin, 1982.

Fox/Renard

10576
Ellenton, Jennifer Anne. "Microchromosomes of the Ontario Red Fox (Vulpes vulpes Linnaeus)." Guelph, 1979.

10577
Henry, John David. "Adaptive Strategies in the Behaviour of the Red Fox (Vulpes vulpes)." Calgary, 1976

10578
Johnson, Wendel John. "Food Habits of the Isle Royal Red Fox and Population Aspects of Three of Its Principal Prey Species." Purdue, 1969.

10579
MacPherson, Andrew Hall. "A Study of Canadian Fox Populations." McGill, 1967.

10580
Speller, Stanley Wayne. "Food Ecology and Hunting Behaviour of Denning Arctic Foxes at Aberdeen Lakes, Northwest Territories." Saskatchewan, 1972.

10581
Underwood, Lawrence Stratton." The Bioenergetics of the Arctic Fox (Alopex lagopus L.)." Pennsylvania State, 1971.

Cat Family/Famille du chat

Domestic Cat/Chat domestique

10582
Lloyd, Andrew Thomas. "Population Genetics of Domestic Cats (Felis catus L) in New England and the Canadian Maritime Provinces: An Investigation of the Historical Migration Hypothesis." Boston University, 1983.

Lynx

10583
Brand, Christopher James. "Lynx Demography during a Snowshoe Hare Decline in Alberta." Wisconsin, 1978.

Bursey, Carl Cedric. See No./Voir no 10540

10584
Mehrer, Clifford Francis. "Some Aspects of Reproduction in Captive Mountain Lions Felio concolor, Bobcats Lynx rufus and Lynx Lynx canadensis." North Dakota, 1975.

10585
Nellis, Carl Hansen. "Ecology of Coyotes and Lynxes in Central Alberta." Wisconsin, 1975.

10586
Saunders, Jack Kenneth, Jr. "The Biology of the Newfoundland Lynx (Lynx canadensis subsolanus Bangs), Cornell, 1961.

Marten/Martre

10587
De Vos, Antoon. "The Ecology and Management of Fisher and Marten in Ontario." Wisconsin, 1952.

10588
Hagmeier, Edwin Moyer. "The Genus Martes (Mustelidae) in North America: Its Distribution, Variations, Classification Phylogeny and Relationship to Old World Forms." British Columbia, 1956.

Mink/Vison

10589
Friend, Douglas Walter. "Studies on the Suitability of Some Newfoundland Marine Products in Mink Nutrition." McGill, 1961.

10590
Gilbert, Frederick Franklin. "The Effects of Social Deprivation on the Social Behavior and Reproduction Potential of the Ranch Mink." Guelph, 1968.

10591
Hatler, David Francis. "The Coastal Mink on Vancouver Island, British Columbia." British Columbia, 1976.

Raccoon/Raton laveur

10592
Cowan, Wayne Fraser. "Ecology and Life History of the Raccoon (Procyon lotor hirtus Nelson and Goldman) in the Northern Part of Its Range." North Dakota, 1973. [Southwestern Manitoba/ Sud-ouest du Manitoba]

Weasel/Belette

10593
Simms, David Arthur. "The Ecology of the Short-Tailed Weasel (Mustela erminea) in Southern Ontario and Its Relationship to Other North American Weasels." York, 1979.

Wolf/Loup

10594
Carbyn, Ludwig Norbert. "Wolf Predation and Behavioural Interactions with Elk and Other Ungulat in an Area of High Prey Diversity." Toronto, 197

10595
Clark, Kim Robert Ferris. "Food Habits and Behavio of the Tundra Wolf on Central Baffin Island Toronto, 1971.

Domestic Mammal or Herbiverous Quadruped/ Mammifère domestique ou quadrupède herbivore

10596
Welsh, David Albert. "Population, Behavioural ar Grazing Ecology of the Horses of Sable Islan Nova Scotia." Dalhousie, 1975.

Marine Animals (Echinoids)/ Animaux marins (Échinoïdes)

Guerinot, Mary Lou. See No./Voir no 11952

10597
Smith, Annette Louise. "The Role of the Pacific Sar Dollar Dendraster excentricus, in Intertid. Benthic Community Structure." Alberta, 198 [Hornby Island in the Puget Sound to Strait (Georgia/Île Hornby dans Puget Sound au détroit (Georgie]

Marine Carnivores/Carnivores marins

Otter/Loutre

10598
Tarasoff, Frederick John. "Anatomical Observation on the River Otter, Sea Otter and Harp Seal wit Reference to Thermal Regulation and Diving McGill, 1973.

10599
Van Zull de Jong, Constantinus Gerhard. "A Systema tic Study of the Nearctic and Neotropical Rive Otters (Order: Carnivora; Family: Mustelidae) Toronto, 1968.

Seal/Phoque

10600
Bigg, Michael Andrew. "Control of Annual Reproduc tion in the Female Harbour Seal, Phoca vitulina. British Columbia, 1972.

10601
Boness, Daryl John. "The Social System of the Gre Seal, Halichoerus grypus (Fab.) on Sable Island Nova Scotia." Dalhousie, 1979.

10602
Boulva, Jean. "The Harbour Seal, Phoca vitulin Concolor, in Eastern Canada." Dalhousie, 1973.

10603
Peterson, Richard Spencer. "Behavior of the Norther Fur Seal." Johns Hopkins, 1965.

10604
Renouf, Deane. "The Sensitivity and Function of the Vibrissae of Harbour Seals (Phoca vitulina)." Dalhousie, 1978. [Nova Scotia/Nouvelle-Écosse]

10605
Smith, Thomas G. "Population Dynamics of the Ringed Seal in the Canadian Eastern Arctic." Toronto, 1971.

Tarasoff, Frederick John. See No./Voir no 10598

Walrus/Morse

10606
Mansfield, Arthur Walter. "The Biology of the Walrus Odobenus rosmarus rosmarus (Linnaeus), Eastern Canadian Arctic." McGill, 1958

Whale/Baleine

10607
Brodie, Paul Frederick. "Life History of the White Whale, Delphinapterus leucas (Pallas) in the Waters of Baffin Island, Canada." Dalhousie, 1970.

Ruminants/Ruminants

Antelope/Antilope

10608
Barrett, Morley William. "Ranges, Habitat, and Mortality of Pronghorns of the Northern Limits of their Range." Alberta, 1982.

10609
Bromley, Peter Tyson. "Aspects of the Behavioural Ecology and Sociobiology of the Pronghorn (Antilocapra americana)." Calgary, 1977.

10610
Bullock, Robert Earl. "A Functional Analysis of Locomotion in the Pronghorn Antelope." Alberta, 1972.

10611
Mitchell, George Joseph. "Natality, Mortality and Related Phenomena in Two Populations of Pronghorn Antelope in Alberta, Canada." Washington State, 1965.

Bison

10612
Hawley, Alexander Wilson Lewis. "Comparison of Forage Utilization and Blood Composition of Bison and Hereford Cattle." Saskatchewan, 1979. [Slave River Lowlands/Basses terres de la rivière Slave]

10613
McDonald, Jerry Nealon. "The North American Bison: A Revised Classification and Interpretation of Their Evolution." California, Los Angeles, 1978.

Caribou

10614
Banfield, Alexander William Francis. "The Status, Ecology, and Utilization of the Continental Barren-Ground Caribou (Rangifer arcticus Arcticus)." Michigan, 1951.

10615
Bergerud, Arthur Thomas. "The Population Dynamics of Newfoundland Caribou." British Columbia, 1969.

10616
Lent, Peter Charles. "Calving and Related Social Behaviour in the Barren-Ground Caribou." Alberta, 1964.

10617
McEwen, Eoin Hall. "Reproduction of Barren-Ground Caribou Rangifer tarandus Groenlandicus (Linnaeus) with Relation to Migration." McGill, 1963.

10618
Miller, Donald Ray. "Wildfire and Caribou on the Taiga Ecosystem of Northcentral Canada." Idaho, 1976.

10619
Scotter, George Wilby. "Effects of Forest Fires on the Lichen Winter Ranges of Barren-Ground Caribou in Northern Canada." Utah State, 1968.

10620
Shoesmith, Merlin Wendell. "Social Organization of Wapiti and Woodland Caribou." Manitoba, 1978. [Reed Lake/Lac Reed]

Spiess, Arthur Eliot. See No./Voir no 846

Deer/Cerf

10621
Harestad, Alton Sidney. "Seasonal Movements of Black-Tailed Deer on Northern Vancouver Island." British Columbia, 1979.

10622
Mueller, Claus Curt. "An Investigation of the Occurrence of Sexual Precocity in Female Black-Tailed Deer (Odocoileus hemionus columbianus)." Simon Fraser, 1978. [Vancouver Island/Île de Vancouver]

10623
Raddi, Arvind Govind. "The Pelage of Columbia Black Tailed Deer Odiocoileus hemionus columbianus (Richardson)." British Columbia, 1968.

10624
Rochelle, James Arthur. "Mature Forests, Litterfall and Patterns of Forage Quality as Factors in the Nutrition of Black-Tailed Deer on Northern Vancouver Island." British Columbia, 1980.

10625
Thomas, Donald Charles. "The Ovary, Reproduction, and Productivity of Columbian Black-Tailed Deer." British Columbia, 1970. [Vancouver Island/Île de Vancouver]

10626
Townsend, Thomas William. "Factors Affecting Individual Rank in the Social Hierarchy of Penned White-Tailed Deer (Odocoileus virginianus borealis)." Guelph, 1973.

10627
West, Nels Oscar. "Hormonal Regulation of Reproduction and the Antler Cycle in the Male Columbian Black-Tailed Deer (Odocoileus hemionus columbianus)." British Columbia, 1975.

10628
Willms, Walter David. "The Effects of Fall Burning or Grazing on Agropyron spicatum (Pursh) Scribner and Smith and Its Selection by Deer and Cattle." Alberta, 1979. [Kamloops, British Columbia/Colombie-Britannique]

Elk/Orignal

Carbyn, Ludwig Norbert. See No./Voir no 10594
10629
Gates, Charles Cormack. "Patterns of Behaviour and Performance of Wapiti (Cervus elaphus nelsoni) in the Boreal Mixed Wood Forest." Alberta, 1980.
Shoesmith, Merlin Wendell. See No./Voir no 10620
10630
Weber, Yvonne B. "Aspects of the Physiology and Diseases of the North American Elk." Portland State, 1973.
10631
Westra, Robert. "The Effect of Temperature and Season on Digestion and Area Kinetics in Growing Wapiti." Alberta, 1978. [Alberta]

Moose/Élan

Aronoff, Stanley. See No./Voir no 1924
10632
Crete, Michel. "Population Dynamics of Moose (Alces alces americana) in Southwestern Quebec." Minnesota, 1981. [Impact of hunting on the population dynamics of moose/Impact de la chasse face à la population dynamique de l'élan]
10633
Eastman, Donald Sidney. "Habitat Selection and Use in Winter by Moose in Sub-Boreal Forests of North-Central British Columbia and Relationships to Forestry." British Columbia, 1978.
10634
Hatter, James. "The Moose of Central British Columbia." Washington State, 1953.
10635
Peterson, Randolph Lee. "A Study of North American Moose with Special Reference to Ontario." Toronto, 1950.
10636
Pimlott, Douglas Humphreys. "Reproduction Productivity and Harvests of Newfoundland Moose." Wisconsin, 1959.

Muskox/Boeuf musqué

10637
Gray, David Robert. "Social Organization and Behaviour of Muskoxen (Ovibos moschatus) on Bathurst Island, N.W.T.." Alberta, 1973.
10638
Tener, John Simpson. "A Study of the Muskox (Ovibos moschatus) in Relation to Its Environment." British Columbia, 1960.

Cattle/Bétail

Acres, Stephen Douglas. See No./Voir no 183
10639
Benjamin, Bontha Rathnakumar. "Bioclimatologic Studies on Domestic Cattle with Special Reference to Skin and Hair Structures." Saskatchewan, 1971.
Hawley, Alexander Wilson Lewis. See No./Voir no 10612
Willms, Walter David. See No./Voir no 10628

Sheep/Mouton

10640
Heitman, James Herbert. "Physiological and Metabolic Responses of Sheep to Acute and Chronic Cold Exposure." Alberta, 1973.
10641
Herbert, Daryll Marvin. "Altitudinal Migration as a Factor in the Nutrition of Bighorn Sheep." British Columbia, 1973.
10642
Hoefs, Manfred Ernest Gustav. "Ecological Investigation of Dall Sheep (Ovis dalli dalli Nelson) and Their Habitat on Sheep Mountain, Kluane National Park, Yukon Territory, Canada." British Columbia, 1976.
10643
Horejsi, Brian Louis. "Suckling and Feeding Behaviour in Relation to Lamb Survival in Bighorn Sheep (Ovis canadensis canadensis Shaw)." Calgary, 1976
10644
MacNaughton, William Norman. "Repeatability and Heritability of Birth, Weaning and Sheering Weights Among Range Sheep in Canada." Iowa State, 1956.
10645
Shackleton, David Maxwell. "Population Quality and Bighorn Sheep (Ovis canadensis canadensis Shaw). Calgary, 1973.
10646
Shank, Christopher Cassel. "Sexual Dimorphism in the Ecological Niche of Rocky Mountain Bighorn Sheep." Calgary, 1979.
10647
Stelfox, John Glyde. "Range Ecology of Rocky Mountain Big Horn Sheep in Canadian National Parks." Montana, 1975.

Flying Mammals/Mammifères volants
Bats/Chauve-souris

10648
Bower, Susan Mae. "Trypanosomes of the Subgenus Schizotrypanum in Bats from Southern Ontario. Guelph, 1980.
10649
Fenton, Melville Brockett. "Ecological Studies of Bats in Ontario and Adjacent Regions." Toronto, 1969.
10650
Trevor-Deutsch, Burleigh. "The Role of Hibernating Bats in the Winter Diet of Peromyscus Spp (Rodentia: Cricetidae) in Ontario." Carleton, 1973.

Rodents/Rongeurs

General Items/Ouvrage général

10651
Stebbins, Lucius Lebaron. "Seasonal and Latitudinal Variations in the Circadian Rhythms of Three Species of Small Rodents in Northern Canada." Alberta, 1969.

Beaver/Castor

Addison, Edward M. See No./Voir no 10534
10652
Alcoze, Thomas Moore. "Pre-Settlement Beaver Population Density in the Upper Great Lakes Region." Michigan State, 1981.
10653
Aleksiuk, Michael. "The Metabolic Adaptation of the Beaver (Castor canadensis Kuhl) to the Arctic Energy Regime." British Columbia, 1968.
10654
Novakowski, Nicholas Stephen. "Population Dynamics of a Beaver Population in Northern Latitudes." Saskatchewan, 1965.
10655
Payne, Neil Forrest. "Trapline Management and Population Biology of Newfoundland Beaver." Utah State, 1975.

Groundhog - Woodchuck/Marmotte d'Amérique

Anteson, Reginald Kwaku. See No./Voir no 10535
Ko, Ronald Chun Chung. See No./Voir no 10550
10656
Nuckle, Jacques R. "Étude bio-écologique de la marmotte commune (Marmota monax L.) dans un agro-système." Sherbrooke, 1983.

Hares and Rabbits/Lièvres et lapins

10657
Boutin, Stanley Albert. "An Experimental Analysis of Juvenile Survival and Dispersal in Snowshoe Hares." British Columbia, 1983.
Brand, Christopher James. See No./Voir no 10583
10658
Diersing, Victor Eugene. "A Systematic Revision of Several Species of Cottontails (Sylvilagus) from North and South America." Illinois, 1978. [British Columbia/Colombie-Britannique]
10659
Dodds, Donald Gilbert. "The Economics, Biology and Management of the Snowshoe Hare in Newfoundland." Cornell, 1962.
10660
MacLulich, Duncan Alexander. "Fluctuations in the Numbers of the Varying Hare, Lepus americanus." Toronto, 1937.
10661
Meslow, Edwin Charles. "Snowshoe Hare Population Studies at Rochester, Alberta." Wisconsin, 1970.

10662
Millar, John Steven. "Breeding of the Pika in Relation to the Environment." Alberta, 1971.
10663
Reynolds, John Keith. "The Biology of the European Hare (Lepus europaeus Pallas) in Southwestern Ontario." Western Ontario, 1952.
10664
Smith, Murray Cameron. "Studies of Seasonal Availability of Electrolytes on Adrenal Physiology of a Wild Population of Snowshoe Hares." Guelph, 1977. [Stokes Bay of the Bruce Peninsula/Baie Stokes de la péninsule de Bruce]
Yuill, Thomas Mackay. See No./Voir no 6867
Zarnke, Randall Lee. See No./Voir no 10533

Lemming

10665
Berberich, Joel John. "Cold Acclimation and Cold Diuresis in Arctic Lemmings." Iowa, 1975.
10666
Bunnell, Frederick Lindsley. "Computer Simulation of Nutrient and Lemming Cycles in an Arctic Tundra Wet Meadow Ecosystem." California, Berkeley, 1973.
10667
Krebs, Charles Joseph. "The Lemming Cycle at Baker Lake, N.W.T., during 1959-61." British Columbia, 1962.
10668
Mallory, Frank Pensom. "Reproductive Strategies and Population Dynamics of Small Mammals: The Collared Lemming, Dicrostonyx groenlandicus and Laboratory Mouse, Mus musculus." Guelph, 1979. [Eskimo Point, Northwest Territories/Territoires du Nord-Ouest]

Mice/Souris

Boshes, Michael. See No./Voir no 10690
10669
Didow, Larry Alvin. "Seasonal and Geographic Differences in Cold Resistance and Heat Production Capabilities of Two Species of Peromyscus." Carleton, 1972.
10670
Eedy, John Wilson. "Seasonal and Geographic Variations in the Thermoregulatory Behaviors of Two Species of Peromyscus." Carleton, 1973.
10671
Fairbairn, Daphne Janice. "Population Processes in Peromyscus: An Experimental Approach." British Columbia, 1976.
10672
Falls, James Bruce. "Activity and Local Distribution of Deer Mice in Relation to Certain Environmental Factors." Toronto, 1953.
10673
Harling, John. "Energy Consumption Relative to Energy Requirements in Wild Deermice (Peromyscus maniculatus." Simon Fraser, 1973.

10674
Herman, Thomas Bruce. "Population Ecology of Insular Peromyscus maniculatus." Alberta, 1979. [Vancouver Island and 24 islands of adjacent Barkley Sound/Île de Vancouver et 24 îles près de Barkley Sound]

10675
Hoffmeister, Donald Frederick. "Phylogeny of the Nearctic Cricetine Rodents with Especial Attention to Variation in Peromyscus truei." California, Berkeley, 1944.

10676
Koh, Hung-Sun. "A Phenetic Study of Deer Mice, Peromyscus maniculatus Wagner (Cricetidae Rodentia) from Continental North America, with Chromosomal Analysis from Four Canadian Populations." Toronto, 1980.

10677
Kott, Edward. "Factors Affecting Estimates of Meadow Mouse Populations." Toronto, 1965.

10678
Sullivan, Thomas Priestley. "Conifer Seed Predation by the Deer Mouse: A Problem in Reforestation." British Columbia, 1979. [Maple Ridge, British Columbia/Colombie-Britannique]

10679
Taitt, Mary Joan. "Population Dynamics of Peromyscus maniculatus austerus and Microtus townsendii with Supplementary Food." British Columbia, 1978.

10680
Thomas, Barry. "Evolutionary Relationships among Peromyscus from the Georgia Strait, Gordon Goletas and Scott Islands of British Columbia, Canada." British Columbia, 1971.

10681
Thomas, Howard H. "The Systematics and Zoogeography of Blarina brevicauda, Peromyscus maniculatus, Elethrionomys gapperi, and Microtus pennsylvanicus on the Island and Adjacent Mainland Areas of the Canadian Maritimes." Northeastern, 1982.

Trevor-Deutsch, Burleigh. See No./Voir no 10650

10682
Vickery, William Lloyd. "Activity and Food Consumption of Three Sympatric Species of Forest Mice." McGill, 1976. [Lac Carré, Québec]

10683
Wrigley, Robert Ernest. "Biology and Systematics of the Woodland Jumping Mouse, Napaeozapus insignis." Illinois, 1970.

Muskrat/Rat Musqué

10684
MacArthur, Robert Allan. "Behavioral and Physiological Aspect of Temperature Regulation in the Muskrat (Ondatra zibethicus)." Manitoba, 1977. [Delta Marsh]

10685
Proulx, Gilbert. "Relationship Between Muskrat Populations, Vegetation and Water Level Fluctuations and Management Considerations at Luther Marsh, Ontario." Guelph, 1982.

10686
Stevens, Ward Earl. "Adjustments of the North western Muskrat (Ondatra zibethicus spatulatus) t a Northern Environment." British Columbia, 1956.

Porcupine/Porc-épic

10687
Perrotta, Carmine Ann. "Fetal Membranes of th Canadian Porcupine, Erethizon dorsatu Linnaeus." Wisconsin, 1956.

10688
Struthers, Park H. "The Prenatal Skull of the Cana dian Porcupine (Erethizon dorsatum)." Syracuse 1927.

Squirrels, Chipmunks/Écureuils et tamias rayés

10689
Aniskowicz, Boguslawa Theresa. "Social and Spatia Organization of Tamias striatus Wildlife Saskat chewan Communities and Related Aspects o Behavior." Ottawa, 1978.

10690
Boshes, Michael. "An Analysis of Feeding Behaviou and Feeding Patterns in the Species of Hibernatin Rodents, the Golden-Mantled Ground Squirre Spermophilus lateralis and the Edible Dormouse Glis glis." Toronto, 1978.

10691
Davis, Donald Wayne. "The Behavior and Populatio Dynamics of the Red Squirrel Tamiasciuru hudsonicus) in Saskatchewan." Arkansas, 1969.

10692
Ferron, Jean. "Étude ethologique de l'écureuil rou d'Amérique (Tamiasciurus hudsonicus)." Montréa 1975.

10693
Goulet, Louise Anna. "Aspects of Population Dyna mics and Social Behavior in the Richardson' Ground Squirrel as Modified by a Chemosterilan (Mestranol)." Simon Fraser, 1980. [Alberta]

10694
Hampson, Cyril Gladstone. "Locomotion and Som Associated Morphology in the Northern Flyin Squirrels." Alberta, 1966.

10695
Kivett, Vaden Keith. "Variations in Integumentar Gland Activity and Scent Marking in Columbia Ground Squirrels (Spermophilus c. Columbianus). Alberta, 1975. [Alberta]

10696
Lindsay, Stephen Leslie. "Morphologic Variation an Its Systematic Significance in Tree Squirrel Specie (Tamiasciurus) in Western North America." Mem phis State, 1982. [British Columbia, Washingto and Oregon/Colombie-Britannique, Washington e Oregon]

10697
McLean, Ian Gordon. "Social Ecology of the Arcti Ground Squirrel Spermophilus Parrajii." Alberta 1981.

10698
Meredith, Don Howard. "Habitat Selection and Inter-
specific Agonism in Two Parapatric Species of
Chipmunks (Eutamias)." Alberta, 1975. [Alberta]
10699
Michener, Daniel Ralph. "Population Dynamics of
Richardson's Ground Squirrels." Saskatchewan,
Regina, 1972.
10700
Mitchell, Ormond Glenn. "The Gross Anatomy and
Histology of the Male Reproductive Tract of the
Arctic Ground Squirrel Spermophilus undulatus,
with Observations on the Sexual Cycle." Southern
California, 1957.
10701
Pauls, Ronald Walter. "Daily Energy Expenditure of
the Red Squirrel (Tamiasciurus hudsonicus):
Effects of Seasonal Temperature Change." Mani-
toba, 1979.
10702
Radvanyi, Andrew. "Inherent Rhythms of Activity of
the Northern Flying Squirrel in Relation to Illumi-
nation and to Lunar and Solar Photoperiodism."
British Columbia, 1959.
Riedel, Dieter Gunter. See No./Voir no 10558
10703
Schmidt, Jerome Paul. "The Effect of Hibernation on
the Host-Parasite Relations in the Arctic Ground
Squirrel." New Hampshire, 1963.
10704
Sheppard, David Henry. "Ecology of the Chipmunk
Eutamias amoenus luteiventrus (Allen) and E.
Minimus oreocetes Merriam." Saskatchewan, 1965.
[Alberta]
10705
Smith, Roger Francis C. "Demography of the Little
Northern Chipmunk (Eutamias minimus Borealis
(Allen) Near Heart Lake, Northwest Territories."
Alberta, 1973.
10706
Zammuto, Richard Michael. "Effects of a Climatic
Gradient on Columbian Ground Squirrel (Spermo-
philus columbianus) Life History." Western
Ontario, 1983. [Southwestern Alberta/Sud-ouest
de l'Alberta]

Vole/Campagnol

10707
Beacham, Terry Dale. "Dispersal Survival and Popula-
tion Regulation of the Vole Microtus Townsendii."
British Columbia, 1979. [Vancouver]
10708
Boonstra, Rudy. "Experimental Studies of the Popula-
tion Processes in the Vole Microtus Townsendii."
British Columbia, 1977.
10709
Elliott, Peter Wayne. "Dynamics and Regulation of a
Clethrionomys Population in Central Alberta."
Alberta, 1969.
10710
Hawes, David Bruce. "Experimental Studies of
Competition Among Four Species of Voles."
British Columbia, 1976.

10711
Hilborn, Ray William. "Fates of Disappearing Indivi-
duals in Fluctuating Populations of Microtus Town-
sendii." British Columbia, 1974.
10712
Ludwig, Daniel Robert. "The Population Biology and
Life History of the Water Vole, Microtus richard-
soni." Calgary, 1981.
10713
Martell, Arthur Melvin. "Demography of Tundra and
Taiga Populations of Clethrionomys rutilus."
Alberta, 1978. [Northwest Territories/Territoires
du Nord-Ouest]
10714
Mihok, Steven. "Demography, Behavior and Protein
Polymorphism in Subarctic Clethrionomys gapperi."
Alberta, 1979. [Heart Lake Biological Station,
Northwest Territories/Station biologique du lac
Heart, Territoires du Nord-Ouest]
10715
Riewe, Roderick Ralph. "Ecology of the Meadow Vole,
Microtus pennsylvanicus terraenovae on the Islands
of Notre Dame Bay, Newfoundland, Canada."
Manitoba, 1971.
Taitt, Mary Joan. See No./Voir no 10679

Insectivorus Mammals/Mammifères insectivores

Shrews/Musaraigne

10716
Buckner, Charles H. "Studies on Feeding Habits and
Population of Shrews in Southeastern Manitoba."
Western Ontario, 1959.
10717
Hawes, Myrnal Leong. "Ecological Adaptations in Two
Species of Shrews." British Columbia, 1975.
10718
Randolph, James Collier. "The Ecological Energetics
of a Homeothermic Predator." Carleton, 1972.
[Ontario]

Moles/Taupes

10719
Schaefer, Valentin Henry. "Aspects of Habitat Selec-
tion in the Coast Mole (Scapanus orarius) in British
Columbia." Simon Fraser, 1979.

Amphibians and Reptiles/Amphibies et reptiles

General Items/Ouvrages généraux

Baker, Michael Robert. See No./Voir no 10539
10720
Bleakney, John S. "A Zoogeographical Study of the
Amphibians and Reptiles of Eastern Canada."
McGill, 1957.
Woo, Patrick Tung Kee. See No./Voir no 10561

Amphibians/Amphibies

10721
Adamson, Martin Leif. "Life History of Gyrinicola batrachiensis (Oxyuroidea: Nematoda) in Tadpoles and a Revision of the Rhigonematida and the Oxyurida in Arthropods." Guelph, 1981. [Tadpoles in Guelph/Têtards à Guelph]

10722
Cook, Francis Russell. "An Analysis of Toads of the Bufo americanus Group in a Contact Zone in Central Northern America." Manitoba, 1978. [Manitoba]

10723
Green, David Martin. "Theoretical Analysis of Hybrid Zones Derived from an Examination of Two Dissimilar Zones of Hybridization in Toads (Genus bufo)." Guelph, 1982. [Manitoba, Ontario]

10724
Grobman, Arnold Brams. "The Distribution of the Salamanders of the Genus Plethodon in Eastern United States and Canada." Rochester, 1944.

10725
Neish, Iain Charles. "A Comparative Analysis of the Feeding Behaviour of Two Salamander Populations in Marion Lake, B.C." British Columbia, 1970.

10726
Schueler, Frederick William. "Geographic Variation in Skin Pigmentation and Dermal Glands in the Northern Leopard Frog, Rana pipiens." Toronto, 1979. [Long Point, Ontario]

Reptiles

10727
Gibson, Andrew Ralph. "The Ecological Significance of a Colour Polymorphism in the Common Garter Snake (Thamnophis sirtalis (L.)." Toronto, 1979. [Ontario]

10728
Gregory, Patrick Thomas. "Life History Parameters of a Population of Red-Sided Garter Snakes (Thamnophis sirtalis parietalis) Adapted to a Rigorous and Fluctuating Environment." Manitoba, 1974. [Manitoba]

10729
Murray, Leo T. "A Comparative Study of the Dermal Skeletons of the Inland Cryptodiran Turtles of the United States and Canada." Cornell, 1935.

BIRDS/OISEAUX

A comparative study of output shows the United States and Canada statistically even with many of the American studies being done on the Canada goose. Seventeen Canadian universities approved studies in this field, most within the last 15 years. The universities of Toronto and British Columbia ranked first and second in output, with five other universities producing only one study. Twenty-eight American universities were involved in this area. Cornell University and the University of Wisconsin ranked first and second, with 14 universities producing only one dissertation each.

————

Une étude comparative de la production montre que les États-Unis et le Canada sont statistiquement à égalité en raison du grand nombre d'études américaines sur l'oie canadienne. Dix-sept universités canadiennes ont approuvé des études sur les oiseaux, la plupart de 1970 à 1985; les universités de Toronto et de la Colombie-Britannique viennent en premier et cinq universités ont produit une seule étude. Vingt-huit universités américaines ont fait des recherches dans ce domaine; aux premiers rangs se trouvent les universités Cornell et du Wisconsin, quatorze ont produit une seule thèse.

General Items/Ouvrages généraux

10730
Austin, Oliver Luther, Jr. "The Avifauna of Newfoundland Labrador: Its Distribution and Origin." Harvard, 1931.

10731
Burt, Jonathan Robert. "The Estimation of Avian Nesting Success with Special Reference to the North American Nest Record Card Program." Cornell, 1979.

10732
Flack, J.A. Douglas. "Bird Populations of Aspen Forests in Western North America." Wisconsin, 1970. [Alberta to Manitoba/De l'Alberta au Manitoba]

10733
Gillespie, Walter Lee. "Breeding Bird and Small Mammal Populations in Relation to the Forest Vegetation of the Subarctic Region of Northern Manitoba." Illinois, 1960.

10734
Martin, Norman Duncan. "An Analysis of Bird Populations in Relation to Plant Succession at Algonquin Park, Ontario." Illinois, 1956.

10735
Musacckia, Xavier J. "A Study of Lipid Metabolism in Liver and Kidney of Arctic Migratory Birds." Fordham, 1949.

10736
Parmelee, David Freeland. "The Annual Avian Breeding Cycle at High Latitudes in the Canadian Arctic." Oklahoma, 1957.

10737
Richardson, William John. "Bird Migration over Southeastern Canada, the Western Atlantic, and Puerto Rico: A Radar Study." Cornell, 1976.

10738
Sutton, George Miksch. "The Birds of Southampton island, Hudson Bay." Cornell, 1932.

Single Studies of Birds/Études sur les oiseaux

10739
Burton, Jean. "La migration des oiseaux de rivage (charadriidae et scolopacidae) dans l'est de l'Amérique du Nord." Montréal, 1975.

10740
Cawthorn, Richard Joseph. "The Biology of Diplotriaena triscupis (Fedtschenko, 1874) (Nematoda: Diplotriaenoidea) of Corvidae." Guelph, 1979. [Crows, Essex County, Ontario]

10741
Clark, Richard James. "A Field Study of the Short-Eared Owl (Asio flammens) Pontoppidan in North America." Cornell, 1970.

10742
Guzman, Juan Ramón. "The Wintering of Sooty and Short-Tailed Shearwaters (Genus Puffinus) in the North Pacific." Calgary, 1981.

10743
Haugh, John Richard. "A Study of Hawk Migration and Weather in Eastern North America." Cornell, 1970. [Lake Erie, Lake Ontario, Lake Manitoba/Lac Érié, lac Ontario, lac Manitoba]

10744
Hussell, David John Trevis. "Factors Affecting Clutch Size in Arctic Passerines." Michigan, 1970.

10745
James, Ross David. "Ethological and Ecological Relationships of the Yellow-Throated and Solitary Vireos (Aves: Vireonidae) in Ontario." Toronto, 1973.

10746
Johnson, Stephen Robert. "Thermal Adaptation in North American Sturnidae." British Columbia, 1972.

10747
McLaren, Peter Lorimer. "Habitat Selection and Resource Utilization in Four Species of Wood Warblers (Aves: Parulidae)." Toronto, 1975. [Algonquin Park/Parc Algonquin]

10748
Nettleship, David N. "Breeding Success of the Common Puffin (Fratercula arctica L.) on Different Habitats at Great Island, Newfoundland." McGill, 1970.

10749
O'Donald, Peter. "Ecology and Evolution in the Arctic Skua." Cambridge, 1962.

10750
Ouellet, Henri Roger. "Biosystematics and Ecology of Picoides villosus (L.) and P. Pubescens (L.), (Aves: Picidae)." McGill, 1977. [Eastern Canada/Est du Canada]

Picman, Jaroslaw D. See No./Voir no 10753

10751
Szijj, Laszlo Josef. "A Comparative Study of the Sympatric Species of Meadowlarks (Genus Sturnella) in Ontario." Toronto, 1963.

10752
Zach, Reto. "Foraging Behaviour of the Overbird (Aves: Parulidae) in a Patchy Environment." Toronto, 1977.

Blackbirds/Carouges

10753
Picman, Jaroslaw D. "Behavioral Interactions Between Red-Winged Blackbirds and Long-Billed Marsh Wrens and their Role in the Evolution of the Redwing Polygynous Mating System." British Columbia, 1980.

10754
Richard, David Irving. "The Movement Patterns of Populations of Red-Winged Blackbirds, Agelaius phoniceus, in the Western Lake Erie Basin." Ohio State, 1968. [Lake Alco, Ontario/Lac Alco, Ontario]

10755
Saad, Randa-Pierre. "Influence des oiseaux noirs sur la fauna des coléoptères de trois champs de maïs fourager de la station de recherche de Lennoxville (Québec, Canada)." Sherbrooke, 1981.

10756
Stepney, Philip Harold Robert. "Competitive and Ecological Overlap Between Brewer's Blackbird and the Common Grackle, with Consideration of Associated Foraging Species." Toronto, 1979. [Ontario]

Ducks, Mallards and Waterfowl/ Canards, malards et sauvagerie

10757
Alison, Robert Michael. "The Breeding Biology of the Oldsquaw (Clangula hyemalis Linnaeus) at Churchill, Manitoba." Toronto, 1972.

10758
Alliston, William George. "The Population Ecology of an Isolated Nesting Population of Redheads (Aythya americana)." Cornell, 1979. [Hens, ducklings and mallards/Canes, canardeaux et malards]

10759
Bailey, Robert Owen. "The Postbreeding Ecology of the Redhead Duck (Aytha americana) on Long Island Bay, Lake Winnipegosis, Manitoba." McGill, 1982.

10760
Bartonek, James Cloyd. "Summer Foods and Feeding Habits of Diving Ducks in Manitoba." Wisconsin, 1968.

10761
Blohm, Robert James. "The Breeding Ecology of the Gadwall in Southern Manitoba." Wisconsin, 1979.

10762
Bowers, Emory Frank. "Population Dynamics and Distribution of the Wood Duck (Aix sponsa) in Eastern North America." Louisiana State, 1977.

10763
Diem, Kenneth L. "A Study of the Factors Influencing Waterfowl Censuses in the Parklands, Alberta, Canada." Utah State, 1958.

10764
Featherstone, John David. "Aspects of Nest Site Selection in Three Species of Ducks." Toronto, 1975. [Delta Marsh, Manitoba]

10765
Foster, John Arnold. "Nutritional Requirements of Captive Breeding Mallards." Guelph, 1976.

10766
Gollop, James Bernard. "Dispersal and Animal Survival of the Mallard (Anosplaty rhynchos)." Saskatchewan, 1965.

10767
Hochbaum, George Sutton. "Components of Hunting Mortality in Ducks: A Management Analysis." British Columbia, 1980. [Manitoba]

10768
Kaminski, Richard Marvin. "Dabbling Duck and Aquatic Invertebrate Responses to Manipulated Wetland Habitat." Michigan State, 1979. [South Central Manitoba/Centre-sud du Manitoba]

10769
Keith, Lloyd Burrows. "A Study of Water-Fowl Ecology on Small Impoundments in Southeastern Alberta." Wisconsin, 1959.

10770
Lemieux, Louis. "Histoire naturelle et aménagement de la Grande Oie Blanche Chen Hyperborea Atlantica, le naturaliste canadien, 1959." Laval, 1959.

10771
McHenry, Merril Gene. "Breeding and Post-Breeding Movements of Blue-Winged Teal (Anas discors) in Southwestern Manitoba." Oklahoma, 1971.

10772
Moisan, Gaston. "The Green-Winged Teal: Its Distribution, Migration and Population Dynamics." Laval, 1966.

10773
Nudds, Thomas David. "Resource Variability, Competition and the Structure of Waterfowl Communities." Western Ontario, 1980. [Prairie region of Western Canada/Prairies à l'ouest du Canada]

10774
Patterson, James Howard. "The Role of Wetland Heterogeneity in the Regulation of Duck Populations in Eastern Ontario." Carleton, 1972.

10775
Reed, Austin F. "The Breeding Ecology of the Black Duck in the St. Lawrence Estuary." Laval, 1971.

10776
Schmutz, Josef Konrad. "Coloniality of the Hudson Bay Eider Duck." Queen's, 1981. [500 Hudson Bay eider ducks studied at La Perouse Bay near Churchill, Manitoba, 1979-1980/500 canards eider de la Baie d'Hudson étudiés à la baie La Perouse près de Churchill, Manitoba, 1979-1980]

10777
Seymour, Norman Reginald. "Social Aspects of Reproductive Behaviour in the Black Duck (Anas rubripes) in Eastern Nova Scotia." McGill, 1977.

10778
Stewart, Robert Earl, Jr. "Forests, Wetlands and Waterfowl Populations in the Turtle Mountains of North Dakota and Manitoba." North Dakota, 1972.

10779
Sugden, Lawson Gordon. "Foods, Food Selection, and Energy Requirements of Wild Ducklings in Southern Alberta." Utah State, 1969.

10780
Titman, Roger Donaldson. "The Role of the Pursuit Flight in the Breeding Biology of the Mallard." New Brunswick, 1973.

10781
Trauger, David Lee. "Population Ecology of Lesser Scaop (Aythya affinis/affinis) in Subarctic Taiga." Iowa State, 1971.

Geese/Oies

10782
Abraham, Kenneth Floyd. "Breeding Site Selection o Lesser Snow Geese." Queen's, 1980. [La Perouse Bay, Manitoba/Baie La Perouse, Manitoba]

10783
Akesson, Thomas Ryan. "Endocrine Correlates o Social Behavior of Canada Geese." California Davis, 1980.

10784
Ankney, Claude Davison. "The Importance of Nutrien Reserves to Breeding Blue Geese." Western Ontario, 1974. [McConnell River/Rivière McConnell]

10785
Balham, Ronald Walter. "The Behavior of the Canada Goose (Branta canadensis) in Manitoba." Wisconsin, 1968.

10786
Barry, Thomas Woodams. "Geese of the Anderson River Delta, Northwest Territories." Alberta 1967.

10787
Campbell, Robert Ronald. "Ecophysiological Studie in Lesser Snow Geese (Anser caerulescens) of the La Perouse Bay Colony." Guelph, 1980.

10788
Cooper, James Alfred. "The History and Nesting Biology of the Canada Geese of Marshy Point Manitoba." Massachusetts, 1974.

10789
Cowan, Peter John. "Individual Parental Calls and Auditory Discrimination Learning by Young Gallus gallus and Branta canadensis." Manitoba, 1974.

10790
Craven, Scott Robert. "Distribution and Migration of Canada Geese Associated with Horicon Marsh, Wisconsin." Wisconsin, 1979. [Manitoba, Ontario]

10791
Dimmick, Ralph W. "A Population Study of Canada Geese in Jackson Hole, Wyoming." Wyoming, 1965.

10792
Hanson, Harold Carsten. "Studies in the Physiology of Wintering and of Molting Canada Geese (Branta canadensis interior)." Illinois, 1958.

10793
Harwood, John. "The Grazing Strategies of Blue Geese, Anser caerulescens." Western Ontario, 1975.

10794
Hubbard, James Alan. "Social Organization, Dispersion and Population Dynamics in a Flock of Pen-reared Wild Canada Geese." Tennessee, 1976.

10795
Jarvis, Robert Leo. "Ecological and Physiological Aspects of Soybean Impaction in Canada Geese." Southern Illinois, 1969.

10796
Khalili, Abdolamir. "Optimal Economic Management of Wildlife, over Time with Special Reference to Canada Geese of the Swan Lake National Wildlife Refuge." Missouri, 1970.

10797
Klapman, Robert B. "Certain Aspects of the Social Behaviour of the Canada Goose (Branta canadensis canadensis)." Cambridge, 1960.

10798
Krohn, William Barry. "The Rocky Mountain Population of the Western Canada Goose: Its Distribution, Habitats, and Management." Idaho, 1977.

10799
Lesselles, C.M. "Some Causes and Consequences of Family Size in the Canada Goose, Branta canadensis." Oxford, 1982.

10800
Lieff, Bernard Charles. "The Summer Feeding Ecology of Blue and Canada Geese at the McConnell River, N.W.T." Western Ontario, 1973.

10801
Limpert, Roland John C. "Subspeciation and Wintering Ecology of Canada Geese on the Western Shore, Chesapeake Bay." Johns Hopkins, 1981.

10802
MacInnes, Charles Donald. "Interaction of Local Units Within the Eastern Arctic Population of Small Canada Geese." Cornell, 1963.

10803
Macken, Catherine Anne. "Towards a Stochastic Model for the Growth of a Migratory Bird Population." Cornell, 1977.

10804
Malecki, Richard Allen. "The Breeding Biology of the Eastern Prairie Population of Canada Geese." Missouri, 1976.

10805
Marquardt, Richard Earl. "Ecology of the Migrating and Wintering Flocks of the Small White-Cheeked (Canada) Geese Within the South Central United States." Oklahoma State, 1962.

10806
Martin, Fant W. "Behavior and Survival of Canada Geese in Utah." Utah State, 1963.

10807
Michelson, Peter Glenn. "Breeding Biology of Cackling Geese (Branta canadensis Minima, Ridgway) and Associated Species on the Yukon-Kuskokwim Delta, Alaska." Michigan, 1973.

10808
Mori, John Giovanni. "Certain Ecophysiological Aspects in the Animal Life Cycle of the Canada Goose (Branta canadensis interior)." Guelph, 1977.

10809
Munro, David Aird. "A Study of Some Factors Affecting Reproduction of the Canada Goose, Branta canadensis." Toronto, 1956.

10810
Ortego, James Brent. "Nest Survival of the Canada Goose (Branta canadensis L.) at Eufaula National Wild Life Refuge, Alabama – Georgia 1977-1979." Auburn, 1980.

10811
Prevett, John Paul. "Family Behavior and Age-Dependent Breeding Biology of the Blue Goose Anser caerulescens." Western Ontario, 1973.

10812
Raveling, Dennis Graff. "Sociobiology and Ecology of Canada Geese in Winter." Southern Illinois, 1967.

10813
Rudersdorf, Ward James. "Canada Goose Investigations in the Vicinity of the W.K. Kellogg Bird Sanctuary, Kalamazoo County, Michigan." Michigan State, 1962.

10814
Ryder, John Pemberton. "Timing and Spacing of Nests and Breeding Biology of Ross' Goose." Saskatchewan, 1970. [Karrah Lake/Lac Karrah]

10815
Sherwood, Glen Alan. "Canada Geese of the Seney National Wildlife Refuge." Utah State, 1966.

10816
Spieker, John Oscar. "Virulence Assay and Other Studies of Six North American Strains of Duck Plague Virus Tested in Wild and Domestic Waterfowl." Wisconsin, 1978.

10817
Stier, Jeffrey Charles. "The Economics of a Dual Externality: Agriculture and Canada Geese in Wisconsin." Wisconsin, 1978.

10818
Tuggle, Benjamin Noel. "A Study of Gizzard Nematodes and Renal Coicidiosis in Canada Geese (Branta canadensis interior) of the Mississippi Valley Population." Ohio State, 1982.

10819
Wang, Ying Thomason. "Factors Affecting Hatching Success in Gosling Survival in Giant Canada Geese." Ohio State, 1982.

10820
Wege, Michael Lane. "Migration Behavior of Giant Canada Geese." California, Davis, 1979. [Manitoba to Rochester, Minnesota/Du Manitoba à Rochester, Minnesota]

10821
Williams, John Edwin. "Energy Requirements of the Canada Goose in Relation to Distribution and Migration." Illinois, 1965.

10822
Wood, Jack Sheehan. "Reproductive Development and Factors Affecting Reproduction in Semi-Domesticated Canada Geese." Michigan State, 1963.

10823
Zicus, Michael Chester. "Fall Sociology and Flock Behavior of a Flock of Canada Geese Resident at Crex Meadows, Wisconsin." Minnesota, 1976.

Grebes and Loons/Grèbes et huarts

10824
Barr, Jack Francis. "The Feeding Biology of the Common Loon (Gavia immer) in Oligotrophic Lakes of the Canadian Shield." Guelph, 1973. [Algonquin Park/Parc Algonquin]

10825
Davis, Rolph Aubrey. "A Comparative Study of the Use of Habitat by Arctic Loons and Red-Throated Loons." Western Ontario, 1972.

10826
Nuechterlein, Gary Lee. "Courtship Behavior of the Western Grebe." Minnesota, 1980. [Marshy Point and the Delta Marsh of Lake Manitoba/Marshy Point et Delta Marsh du lac Manitoba]
10827
Riske, Morley Edward. "Environmental and Human Impacts upon Grebes Breeding in Central Alberta." Calgary, 1976.

Gulls and Terns/Goélands et sternes

10828
Fetterolf, Peter Marcus. "Agonistic Behavior of Ring-Billed Gulls during the Post-Hatching Period." Toronto, 1981.
10829
Hawksley, Oscar. "A Study of the Behavior and Ecology of the Arctic Tern Sterna paradisaea Brunnich." Cornell, 1950.
10830
Lock, Anthony. "A Study of the Breeding Biology of Two Species of Gulls Nesting on Sable Island, Nova Scotia." Dalhousie, 1973.
10831
Ludwig, James P. "Dynamics of Ring-Billed Gull and Caspian Tern Populations of the Great Lakes." Michigan, 1968.
Rao, N.S. Krishna. See No./Voir no 10557
10832
Smith, Neal Griffith. "Evolution of Some Arctic Gulls (Larus): A Study of Isolating Mechanisms." Cornell, 1963.
10833
Vermeer, Rees. "A Study of Two Species of Gulls (Larus californicus and L. Delawarensis Breeding in an Island Habitat." Alberta, 1968.
10834
Ward, John Gordon. "Reproductive Success, Food Supply and the Evolution of Clutch-Size in the Gloucous-winged Gull." British Columbia, 1973.
10835
Weseloh, Datlaf Vaughn. "Local Distribution Patterns of Gulls in Relation to their Seasonal Centers of Activity and to Urban Garbage Dumps at Calgary, Alberta." Calgary, 1976.

Grouse, Partridges, Pheasants, Ptarmigan and Turkeys/ Tétras, perdrix, faisans, lagopèdes et dindes

10836
Ash, Andrew N. "The Effect of Urea Fertilizer on the Habitat Population Dynamics and Local Distribution of Blue Grouse." Toronto, 1979. [Vancouver Island/Île de Vancouver]
10837
Boag, David Archibald. "A Population Study of the Blue Grouse in Southwest Alberta." Washington State, 1964.
10838
Brendell, James Francis S. "A Study of the Life History and Population Dynamics of the Sooty Grouse Dendragapus obscurus fuliginosus (Ridgway)." British Columbia, 1954. [Vancouver Island/Île de Vancouver]

10839
Caldwell, Patrick John. "Energetic and Populatio Considerations of Short-Tailed Grouse in the Aspe Parkland of Canada." Kansas State, 1976.
10840
Clarke, Charles Henry Douglas. "Fluctuations i Numbers of Ruffed Grouse, Bonasa umbellus (Linn with Special Reference to Ontario." Toronto 1935.
10841
Doerr, Phillip David. "Ruffed Grouse Ecology i Central Alberta-Demography, Winter-Feedin Activities, and the Impact of Fire." Wisconsin 1973.
10842
Fetherston, Kathleen E. "A Study of the Ring-Necke Pheasant on Pelee Island, Ontario." Cornell, 1950.
10843
Fowle, Charles D. "An Analysis of the Territoria Behaviour of the Ruffed Grouse (Bonasa umbellu (L.))." Toronto, 1953.
10844
Garbutt, Allen Stuart. "Effects of Various Factors o the Reproductive Biology of Ruffed Grouse. Guelph, 1980. [Parry Sound, Ontario]
10845
Gibson, George Gordon. "The Taxonomy and Biolog of Splendidofilariine Nematodes of the Tetraonida of British Columbia." British Columbia, 1965.
10846
Hannon, Susan Jean. "Female Aggressivenes Breeding Density and Monogamy in Willo Ptarmigan." British Columbia, 1982.
10847
Keppie, Daniel MacKenzie. "Dispersal, Overwinte Mortality and Population Size of Spruce Grouse (Canochites canadensis Franklini)." Alberta, 1975.
10848
McNicholl, Martin Kell. "Behaviour and Social Organi zation in a Population of Blue Grouse on Vancouve Island." Alberta, 1978.
10849
Peters, Stuart Sanford. "Population Dynamics of th Newfoundland Willow Ptarmigan on the Avalo Peninsula." Cornell, 1963.
10850
Redfield, James Allen. "Demography and Genetics i Colonizing Populations of Blue Grouse Dendragapus obscurus." Alberta, 1972 [Vancouver Island/Île de Vancouver]
10851
Rusch, Donald Harold. "Ecology of Predation an Ruffed Grouse Populations in Central Alberta. Wisconsin, 1971.
10852
Stokes, Allen W. "Population Studies of the Ring Necked Pheasant on Pelee Island, Ontario. Wisconsin, 1952.
10853
Weeden, Robert B. "The Ecology and Distribution o Ptarmigan in Western North America." Britis Columbia, 1960.
10854
Zwickel, Fred Charles. "Early Mortality and th Numbers of the Blue Grouse." British Columbia 1965. [Vancouver Island/Île du Vancouver]

Pigeons

10855

March, Gordon Lorne. "The Biology of the Band-Tailed Pigeon (Columba fasciata) in British Columbia." Simon Fraser, 1971.

10856

Young, Duane Eugene. "Ecological Considerations in the Extinction of the Passenger Pigeon (Ectopistes migratorius), Heath Hen (Tympanuchus cupido cupido) and the Eskimo Curlew (Numenius borealis)." Michigan, 1953.

Sparrows/Pinsons

10857

Dixon, Clara Louise. "A Population Study of Savannah Sparrows of Kent Island in the Bay of Fundy." Michigan, 1972.

10858

Knapton, Richard W. "Behavioural Ecology of the Clay-Colored Sparrow, Spizella pallida." Manitoba, 1978. [Manitoba]

10859

Rees, William Ernest. "Comparative Ecology of Three Sympatric Sparrows of the Genus Zonotrichia." Toronto, 1973.

10860

Tompa, Frank Stephen. "Factors Determining the Numbers of Song Sparrows on Mandarte Island, British Columbia." British Columbia, 1964.

10861

Weatherhead, Patrick James. "The Ecology and Behavior of Reproduction in a Tundra Population of Savannah Sparrows." Queen's, 1978.

Falcons/Faucons

10862

Nelson, Robert Wayne. "Behavioral Ecology of Coastal Peregrines (Falco peregrinus paelei)." Calgary, 1977.

10863

Platt, Joseph Belnap. "The Breeding Behavior of Wild and Captive Gyrfalcons in Relation to their Environment and Human Disturbance." Cornell, 1977.

Oystercatchers/Huîtriers

10864

Groves, Sarah. "Aspects of Foraging in Black Oystercatchers (Aves: Haematopodidae)." British Columbia, 1982.

10865

Hartwick, Earl Brian. "Foraging Strategy of the Black Oystercatcher." British Columbia, 1973.

Cranes/Grues

10866

Melvin, Scott Merrill. "Migration Ecology and Wintering Grounds of Sandhill Cranes from the Interlake Region of Manitoba." Wisconsin, 1982.

10867

Niemeier, Myra Ann Louise. "Structural and Functional Aspects of Vocal Ontogeny in Grus canadensis (Gruidae: Aves)." Nebraska, 1980.

Sandpipers/Maubèches

10868

Miller, Edward Henry. "Breeding Biology of the Least Sandpiper, Calidris minutilla (Vieill), on Sable Island, Nova Scotia." Dalhousie, 1977.

10869

Tallman, Erika Jansic. "An Analysis of the Trematode Fauna of Two Intercontinental Migrants: Tringa solitaria and Calidris melantos (Aves: Charadriiformes)." Louisiana State, 1983.

FISH FROM CANADIAN WATERS/ POISSONS DES EAUX CANADIENNES

While almost the same number of Canadian and American universities were involved in research on fish in Canada, the former produced approximately 100 more studies than the latter. It is only during the 1970's and 1980's that there was a substantial increase in the number of dissertations produced by Canadian universities. The schools of Toronto, British Columbia, McGill, and Alberta are the leaders in that order. In the United States, the universities of Michigan, Ohio State, and Washington (Seattle) are equal leaders. One dissertation was approved in Great Britain at the University of Liverpool in 1980.

———

Alors que le même nombre d'universités canadiennes et américaines poursuivent des recherches sur les poissons au Canada, les premières ont produit environ une centaine de thèses de plus que les autres. De plus, ce n'est qu'au Canada que s'est produit une augmentation appréciable de thèses dans les années 1970 et 1980. Les universités de Toronto, de la Colombie-Britannique, McGill et de l'Alberta sont en tête de liste. Aux États-Unis, les universités du Michigan, d'Ohio State et de Washington (Seattle) sont également parmi les plus productives.

Une thèse a été aprouvée en Grande-Bretagne à l'Université de Liverpool, en 1980.

General Items/Ouvrages généraux

10870

Beamish, Richard James. "Factors Affecting the Age and Size of the White Sucker Catostomus commersoni, at Maturity." Toronto, 1970.

10871

Brown, Joseph A. "A Comparative Study of Behavioural Ontogeny in Four Species of Centrarchid Fish." Queen's, 1983.

10872
Coad, Brian W. "On the Intergeneric Relationship of North American and Certain Eurasian Cyprinid Fishes (Cypriniformes cyprinidae)." Ottawa, 1976.

10873
Dill, Peter Arnott. "On the Development of Diel Activity Rhythms in Atlantic Salmon and the Rainbow Trout." Western Ontario, 1971. [New Brunswick, Nova Scotia and Ontario/Nouveau-Brunswick, Nouvelle-Écosse et Ontario]

10874
Fitzgerald, Gerard John. "The Effects of Density of Adult Fish on Reproduction and Parental Behavior in Convict Cichlid Fish (Cichlasoma nigrofasciatum (Günther)." Western Ontario, 1976.

10875
Garside, Edward Thomas. "Some Aspects of the Developmental Rate and Meristic Numbers in Salmonids." Toronto, 1961.

10876
Gibson, Robert John. "The Interrelationships of Brook Trout, Salvelinus fontinalis (Mitchill) and Juvenile Atlantic Salmon, Salmo salar (L.)." Waterloo, 1973.

10877
Hallam, Jack Charles. "The Modification of Vertebral Number in Salmonidae." Toronto, 1974.

10878
Henderson, Nancy Elizabeth. "Study of the Reproductive Cycles of the Guppy Lebistes reticulatus (Peters) and the Brook Trout, Salvelinus fontinalis (Mitchill)." Toronto, 1960.

10879
Johnson, Walter Henry. "The Food and Feeding of the Herring (Clupea harengus Linn.)" Toronto, 1937.

Kakonge, Sam Atwoki K. See No./Voir no 10548

10880
McCrimmon, Hugh Ross. "Survival of Planted Salmon (Salmo salar) in Streams." Toronto, 1949.

10881
McMurrick, James Playfair. "The Osteology and Myology of Amiurus catus (L.) Gill." Johns Hopkins, 1885.

10882
Muir, Barry Sinclair. "Estimates of Mortalities and Population Size for the Nogies Creek Maskinonge (Esox masquinongy Mitchill)." Toronto, 1961.

10883
Narita, Tetsuya. "Psysiological, Ecological and Morphological Differences Between Two Forms of Ninespine Stickleback Pungitius pungitius, in North America." Manitoba, 1970.

Wang, Der-Hsiung. See No./Voir no 1860

10884
Whitaker, W.R. "Age-Determination of the North American Pilchard (Sardinia sagax) by the Otolith Method." Toronto, 1936.

10885
Wiggs, Alfred James. "Acclimation of the Thyroid Proteinase of the Burbot Lota lota Linneaeus to Seasonal Temperature Change." Alberta, 1968.

Eastern Canada/Est du Canada

Appy, Ralph Grant. See No./Voir no 10536

10886
Buerkle, Udo. "Detection of Trawling Noise by Atlantic Cod, Gadus morhua L." McGill, 1973.

10887
Di Capua, Richard Anthony. "A Study of the Similarities and Differences of Antigens Found in the Serum of Atlantic Sea Herring." Rutgers, 1964.

10888
Mavor, James Watt. "Studies on Myxosporidia Found in the Gall Bladder of Fishes from the Eastern Coast of Canada." Harvard, 1913.

10889
McCracken, Francis Derwood. "Seasonal Movement of the Winter Flounder Pseudopleuronectes americanus (Walbaum) on the Atlantic Coast." Toronto, 1954.

10890
Needler, Alfred Walker Hollinshead. "The Migration of Haddock and the Interrelationships of Haddock Populations in North American Waters." Toronto, 1930.

10891
Wells, Alan W. "Systematics, Variation and Zoogeography of Two North American Cyprinid Fishes." Alberta, 1978.

Gulf of St. Lawrence/Golfe Saint-Laurent

10892
Able, Kenneth William. "Life History, Ecology and Behavior of Two New Liparis (pisces cyclopteridae) from the Western North Atlantic." William and Mary, 1974. [From the Gulf of St. Lawrence southward/Du Golfe Saint-Laurent vers le sud]

10893
Brunel, Pierre. "The Vertical Migrations of Cod in the Southwestern Gulf of St. Lawrence with Special Reference to Feeding Habits and Prey Distribution." McGill, 1968.

10894
MacKay, Kenneth Tod. "Population Biology and Aspects of Energy Use of the Northern Population of Atlantic Mackerel, Scomber scombus." Dalhousie, 1976.

10895
Messieh, Shoukry N. "Biological Characteristics of Spring and Autumn Herring Populations in the Gulf of St. Lawrence and Their Interrelations." McGill, 1973.

10896
Powles, Percival M. "Some Factors Affecting Stocks and Landings of American Plaice (Hippoglossoides platessoides F.) in the Southwestern Gulf of St. Lawrence." McGill, 1964.

10897
Schiefer, Karl. "Ecology of Atlantic Salmon with Special Reference to Occurrence and Abundance of Grilse in North Shore Gulf of St. Lawrence Rivers." Waterloo, 1972.

10898
Winters, George Henry. "Population Dynamics of the Southern Gulf of St. Lawrence Herring Stock Complex and Implications Concerning Its Future Management." Dalhousie, 1975.

Central Canada/Centre du Canada

10899
Clarke, Redmond McVitty. "The Systematics of Ciscoes (Coregonidae) in Central Canada." Manitoba, 1973.

Western Canada/Ouest du Canada

10900
Franzin, William Gilbert. "Genetic Studies of Protein Variants and Their Use in a Zoogeographic Study of Lake Whitefish Coregonus clupeaformis (Mitchill) in Western Canada." Manitoba, 1974.
10901
Smith, Gerald Ray. "Distribution and Evolution of the North American Fishes of the Subgenus Pantosteus." Michigan, 1965.

Great Lakes/Grands Lacs

General Items/Ouvrages généraux

10902
Booke, Henry Edward. "Cytotaxonomic Studies of the Coregonine Fishes of the Great Lakes, U.S.A.: DNA and Karotype Analysis." Michigan, 1968.
10903
Coble, Daniel Wiggin. "On the Growth of Some Great Lakes Fishes with Special Reference to Temperature." Toronto, 1965.
10904
Koelz, Walter. "Coregonid Fishes of the Great Lakes." Michigan, 1920.
Wells, Alan W. See No./Voir no 10891
10905
Youson, John Harold. "The Morphology of the Opisthonephric Kidney of the Great Lakes Lamprey, Petromyzon marinus L." Western Ontario, 1969.

Lake Erie/Lac Érié

10906
Adams, William James. "The Toxicity and Residue Dynamics of Selenium in Fish and Aquatic Invertebrates." Michigan State, 1976.
10907
Barans, Charles Anthony. "Seasonal Temperature Selections of White Bass, Yellow Perch, Emerald Shiners and Smallmouth Bass from Western Lake Erie." Ohio State, 1972.
10908
Bodola, Anthony. "The Life History of the Gizzard Shad, Dorosoma cepedianum (Lesueur) in Western Lake Erie." Ohio State, 1955.
10909
Daiber, Franklin Carl. "The Life History and Ecology of the Sheepshead Aplodinotus grunniens, Rafinesque, in Western Lake Erie." Ohio State, 1951.

10910
Deason, Hilary J. "Morphometric and Life History Studies of the Pike Perches, Stizostedion of Lake Erie." Michigan, 1936.
10911
Doan, Kenneth Henry. "Some Meteorological and Limnological Conditions as Factors in the Abundance of Certain Fishes in Lake Erie." Ohio State, 1941.
10912
Jobes, Frank Watkins. "Age and Growth of the Yellow Perch, Perca flavescens (Mitchill), in Lake Erie." Michigan, 1940.
10913
Kinney, Edward Coyle, Jr. "A Life History Study of the Silver Chub, Hybopsis storeriana (Kirtland) in Western Lake Erie with Notes on Associated Species." Ohio State, 1954.
10914
Lawler, George Herbert. "Fluctuations in the Success of Year-Classes Among Whitefish (Coregonus clupeaformis Mitchill) Populations with Special Reference to Lake Erie." Toronto, 1959.
10915
Metcalf, Isaac S.H. "The Influence of a Shore Community on the Distribution of Certain Fishes in Lake Erie with Especial Reference to the White Bass." Case Western Reserve, 1940.
10916
Scott, William Beverley. "The Lake Erie Cisco (Leucichthys artedi) Population." Toronto, 1950.
10917
Stone, Frederick L. "A Study of the Taxonomy of the Blue and Yellow Pikeperches (Stizostedion) of Lake Erie and Lake Ontario." Rochester, 1949.
10918
Stromberg, Paul Charles. "The Life History and Population Ecology of Camallanus oxycephalus Ward and Magath, 1916 (Nematoda: Camallanidae) in Fishes of Western Lake Erie." Ohio State, 1973.

Lake Huron/Lac Huron

10919
Dodge, Douglas P. "Comparative Bio-Ecology of Rainbow Trout (Salmo gairdneri Richardson), of Their Tributaries to the Owen Sound, Lake Huron." Guelph, 1973.
10920
Spangler, George Russell. "Mortality Factors and Dynamics of a Lake Huron Lake Whitefish Population." Toronto, 1974.
10921
Van Oosten, John. "Life History of the Lake Herring (Leucichthys artedi), LeSueur) of Lake Huron as Revealed by Its Scales with a Critique of the Scale Method." Michigan, 1926.

Lake Ontario/Lac Ontario

10922

Pritchard, Andrew Lyle. "Descriptions of the Spawning Habits and Fry of the Lake Herring (Leucichthys artedi) in Lake Ontario. Spawning Habits and Fry of the Cisco (Leucichthys artedi) in Lake Ontario: Taxonomic and Life History Studies of the Ciscoes of Lake Ontario." Toronto, 1930.

Sheri, Ahmad Nadeem. See No./Voir no 11025

Stone, Frederick L. See No./Voir no 10917

Lake Superior/Lac Supérieur

10923

Griswold, Bernard Lee. "The Ecology of the Ninespine Stickleback Pungitius pungitius (Linnaeus) in Western Lake Superior." Minnesota, 1970.

10924

Schaefer, Wayne Ford. "Population Dynamics of Rainbow Smelt in Lake Superior." Brigham Young, 1979.

Alberta

10925

Bidgood, Bryant Frederick. "Divergent Growth in Lake Whitefish Populations from Two Eutrophic Alberta Lakes." Alberta, 1972.

10926

Diana, James Stephen. "An Energy Budget for Northern Pike (Esox lucius) in Lac Ste. Anne, Alberta." Alberta, 1979.

Drouin, Theodore Emile. See No./Voir no 10545

10927

Kavaliers, Martin Imants. "The Role of Photoperiod and Twilight in the Control of Locomotory Rhythms in the Lake Chub Couesius plumbeus (Agassiz)." Alberta, 1978.

Leong, Raymond Tak Seng. See No./Voir no 10551

10928

Paetz, Martin Joseph. "A Study of Hybridization Between Two Species of Coregonine Fishes, Coregonus clupeaformis (Mitchill) and C. Artedii Lesueur in Alberta." Alberta, 1972.

Wells, Alan W. See No./Voir no 10891

British Columbia/Colombie-Britannique

10929

Alverson, Dayton Lee. "A Study of Demersal Fishes and Fisheries of the Northeastern Pacific Ocean." Washington, Seattle, 1967.

10930

Biette, Raymond Millo. "The Effect of Temperature and Ration on Growth Rates, Food Conversion Efficiencies and the Fate of Carbon-14 Labelled Food by Underyearling Sockeye Salmon, Oncorhynchus nerka." Simon Fraser, 1978.

10931

Brannon, Ernest Leroy. "Mechanisms Controlling Migration of Sockeye Salmon Fry." Washington, Seattle, 1972. [Fraser River/FLeuve Fraser]

10932

Brett, John Roland. "Temperature Tolerance in Young Pacific Salmon Genus Oncorhynchus." Toronto, 1951.

10933

Bryan, James Ernest. "Prey Specialization by Individual Trout Living in a Stream and Ponds; Some Effects of Feeding History and Parental Stock on Food Choice." British Columbia, 1972.

10934

Chapman, Wilbert M. "Oceanic Fishes from the Northeastern Pacific Ocean Collected by the International Fisheries Commission." Washington, Seattle, 1937.

10935

Craik, Gwenneth Jean Steele. "A Further Investigation of the Homing Behaviour of the Intertidal Cottid Oligocottus maculosus Girard." British Columbia, 1978. [Vancouver Island/Île de Vancouver]

10936

Crossman, Edwin John. "Factors Involved in the Predator-Prey Relationship of Rainbow Trout (Salmo gairdneri Richardson) and Redside Shiners (Richardsonius balteatus Richardson) in Paul Lake, British Columbia." British Columbia, 1958.

10937

Daxboeck, Charles. "A Study of the Cardiovascular System of the Rainbow Trout (Salmo gairdneri) at Rest and During Swimming Exercise." British Columbia, 1981.

10938

Donaldson, Sven. "Developmental Adaptations in the Commensal Hydroid, Proboscidactyla flavicinota." Victoria, 1977.

10939

Glova, Gordon John. "Pattern and Mechanism of Resource Partitioning Between Stream Populations of Juvenile Coho Salmon (Oncorhynchus kisutch) and Coastal Cutthroat Trout (Salmo clarki clarki)." British Columbia, 1978.

10940

Godin, Jean-Guy Joseph. "Diel Rhythms of Behavior in Juvenile Pink Salmon (Oncorhynchus gorbuscha Walbaum)." British Columbia, 1979.

10941

Green, John Marshall. "A Field Study of the Distribution and Behavior of Oligocottus maculosus Girard, a Tidepool Cottid of the Northeast Pacific Ocean." British Columbia, 1968. [Vancouver Island/Île de Vancouver]

10942

Grossman, Gary David. "Ecological Adaptation in the Bay Goby (Lepidogobius lepidus) Behavior, Demography, and Feeding." California, Davis, 1979.

10943

Gunderson, Donald Raymond. "Population Biology of Pacific Ocean Perch (Sebastes alutus) Stocks in the Washington-Queen Charlotte Sound Region and Their Response to Fishing." Washington, Seattle, 1976.

10944

Henderson, Michael Andrew. "An Analysis of Prey Detection in Cutthroat Trout (Salmo clarki Clarki) and Dolly Varden Charr (Salvelinus malma)." British Columbia, 1982.

10945
Henry, Kenneth Albin. "Racial Identification of Fraser River Sockeye Salmon (Oncorhynchus nerka Walbaum) by Means of Scales and Its Applications to Salmon Management." Washington, Seattle, 1961.

10946
Hourston, Alan Steward. "Population Dynamics of Juvenile Herring in Barkley Sound, British Columbia as an Integral Part of the Life History." California, Los Angeles, 1956.

10947
Hyatt, Kim Dennis. "Mechanisms of Food Resource Partitioning and the Foraging Strategies of Rainbow Trout (Salmo gairdneri) and Kokanee (Oncorhynchus nerka) in Marion Lake, British Columbia." British Columbia, 1980.

Jones, Barry Cyril. See No./Voir no 10386

10948
Ketchen, Keith Stuart. "Factors Influencing the Survival of the Lemon Sole (Parophrys vetulus Girard) in Hecate Strait, British Columbia." Toronto, 1953.

10949
Khan, Muhammad M.R. "Studies on the Lipoxidase in the Flesh of British Columbia Herring." British Columbia, 1952.

10950
Khoo, Hong Woo. "The Homing Behaviour of an Inter-Tidal Fish Oligocottus maculosus Girard." British Columbia, 1971.

10951
Kruzynski, George Maria. "Some Effects of Dehydroabietic Acid (DHA) on Hydromineral Balance and Other Physiological Parameters in Juvenile Sockeye Salmon Oncorhynchus nerka." British Columbia, 1979.

10952
Kutty, Madasseri Krishnan. "An Ecological Study and Theoretical Considerations of Butter Sole (Isopsetta isolepis) Population in Hecate Strait." British Columbia, 1964.

10953
Larson, Gary Lee. "Social Behavior and Feeding Ability of Two Phenotypes of Gasterosteus aculeatus in Relation to Their Spatial and Trophic Segregation in a Temperate Lake." British Columbia, 1972.

10954
Low, Robert Alan, Jr. "Variability in Ocean Fishing Success for Salmon (Oncorhynchus Spp.) off Washington and Vancouver Island and Its Relationship with Inside Run Strength." Washington, Seattle, 1979.

10955
Mace, Pamela Margaret. "Predator-Prey Functional Responses and Predation by Staghorn Sculpins (Leptocottus armatus) in Chum Salmon Fry (Oncorhynchus keta)." British Columbia, 1983.

Margolis, Leo. See No./Voir no 10552

10956
Marliave, Jeffrey Burton. "The Behavioral Transformation from the Planktonic Larval Stage of Some Marine Fishes Reared in the Laboratory." British Columbia, 1976.

10957
McCart, Peter James. "A Polymorphic Population of Oncorhynchus nerka at Babine Lake, B.C., Involving Anadromous (Sockeye) and Non-Anadromous (Kokanee) Forms." British Columbia, 1971.

10958
McFarlane, Samuel H. "A Study of Trematodes from Marine Fishes of Departure Bay, British Columbia." Illinois, 1934.

10959
Miura, Taizo. "Early Life History and Possible Interaction of Fine Inshore Species of Fish in Nicola Lake, British Columbia." British Columbia, 1963.

10960
Moodie, Gordon Eric Edmund. "Predation as a Mechanism in the Evolution of an Unusual Population of Sticklebacks in the Queen Charlotte Islands, Canada (Pisces: Gasterosteidae)." Alberta, 1970.

10961
Mottley, Charles McCammon. "Biometrical and Experimental Studies in the Taxonomy of Kamloops Trout, Salmo kamloops, Jordan." Toronto, 1934.

10962
Nakamura, Royden. "The Comparative Ecology of Two Sympatric Tidepool Fishes, Oligocottus maculosus (Girard) and Oligocottus snyderi (Greeley)." British Columbia, 1970. [Vancouver Island/Île de Vancouver]

10963
Neave, Ferris. "Principles Affecting the Size of Pink and Chum Salmon Populations in British Columbia." British Columbia, 1952.

10964
Nelson, Joseph Scheiser. "Hybridization and Isolating Mechanisms in Catostomus commersonii and Catostomus machrocheilus (Pisces: Catostomidale)." British Columbia, 1966.

10965
Northcote, Thomas Gordon. "Migratory Behavior of Juvenile Rainbow Trout, Salmo gairdneri, in Outlet and Inlet Streams of Loon Lake, British Columbia." British Columbia, 1960.

10966
Pace, Danny Roy. "Environmental Control of Red Sea Urchin (Strongylocentratus franciscamus) Vertical Distribution in Barkley Sound, British Columbia." Simon Fraser, 1976.

10967
Parker, Robert Ray. "Growth and Mortality in Relation to Maximum Yield in Pounds of Chinook Salmon (Oncorhynchus tshawytscha)." British Columbia, 1959.

Pawaputanan, Kamonporn. See No./Voir no 10555

10968
Ricker, William Edwin. "Studies of the Limnological Factors Affecting the Propagation and Survival of the Sock-Eye Salmon Oncorhyncus nerka, at Cultus Park, British Columbia." Toronto, 1936.

10969
Sandercock, Frederick Keith. "Bioenergetics of the Rainbow Trout (Salmo gairdneri) and the Kokanee (Oncorhynchus nerka) Populations of Marion Lake, British Columbia." British Columbia, 1970.

10970
Scott, David Paul. "Effect of Food Quantity on Fecundity of Kamloops Trout, Salmo gairdneri kamloops Jordan." British Columbia, 1956.
Smith, Annette Louise. See No./Voir no 10597
10971
Smith, Stuart Boland. "Racial Characteristics in Stocks of Anadromous Rainbow Trout Salmo gairdneri Richardson." Alberta, 1968.
10972
Stevenson, James Cameron. "Distribution and Survival of Herring Larvae (Clupea pallasi Valenciennes) in British Columbia Waters." Toronto, 1955.
10973
Tautz, Arthur Frederick. "Effects of Variability in Space and Time on the Production Dynamics of Salmonid Fishes." British Columbia, 1977.
10974
Tester, Albert Louis. "The Extent of Intermingling of the Runs of Herring (Clupea pallasi) in British Columbia Coastal Waters; and a Consideration of Year Class Variation and Fishing Activity as Potential Causes of Fluctuation in Abundance." Toronto, 1936.
10975
Ward, Frederick James. "Regular Fluctuations in the Annual Abundance of Adams River Race Sockeye Salmon and the Operation of Possible Causal Agents." Cornell, 1962.
10976
Weisbart, Melvin. "Osmotic and Ionic Regulations in Embryos Alevens and Fry of the Five Species of Pacific Salmon." British Columbia, 1967.
Wells, Alan W. See No./Voir no 10891
10977
Wilson, Nadine. "Isolation and Amino-Acid Sequence of Neuropypo-Physical Hormones of Pacific Chinook Salmon (Oncorhynchus tschawytscha)." British Columbia, 1968.

Manitoba

10978
Kelso, John Richard Murray. "Population Parameters and Bioenergetic Demands of Walleye Stizostedion vitreum vitreum (Mitchill), in Relation to Their Trophic Dynamic Ecology, West Blue Lake, Manitoba." Manitoba, 1972.
10979
Newsome, George Edwin. "A Study of Prey Preference and Selection by Creek Chub, Semotilus atromoculatus in the Mink River, Manitoba." Manitoba, 1975.

Maritime Provinces/Provinces Maritimes

General Item/Ouvrage général

Wolfgang, Robert W. See No./Voir no 11350

New Brunswick/Nouveau-Brunswick

10980
Carscadden, James Eric. "Studies on American Sha (Alosa sapidissima, Wilson) in the St. John Rive and Miramichi River, New Brunswick with Specia Reference to Homing and R-K Selection." McGill 1975.
10981
Clarke, Linda Ann. "Migration and Orientation of Tw Stocks of Atlantic Salmon (Salmo salar L.) Smolts. New Brunswick, 1981. [North American Salmo Research Center, St. Andrews, and Chamcock Harbour, and Passamaquoddy Bay/Centre de recherche sur le saumon de l'Amérique du Nord, St-Andrew Chamcock Harbour et Baie Passamaguaddy]
Cone, David Knight. See No./Voir no 10543
10982
Hamor, Tamas. "Environmental Regulation of Developmental Metabolism of Embryos of Atlantic Salmon." Dalhousie, 1975.
10983
Hare, Gerard Murdock. "Atlantic Salmon (Salmo salar) Parasites as Biological Tags in the Miramichi River System, New Brunswick." New Brunswick, 1974.
10984
Johnston, Charles Edward. "A Study of Purines in the Integument of Juvenile Atlantic Salmon (Salmo salar L.) During Parrsmolt Transformation." New Brunswick, 1968.
10985
Komourdjian, Martin Paul. "Photoperiod and the Anterior Pituitary Hormones in Growth and Development of the Atlantic Salmon, Salmo salar L. with Hormone and Prolactin." Ottawa, 1976.
10986
Lacroix, Gilles Lucien. "The Reproductive Environment of Landlocked Atlantic Salmon (Salmo salar L.)." New Brunswick, 1980 [Palfrey Lake/Lac Palfrey]
10987
Leggett, William Claude. "Studies on the Reproduction Biology of the American Shad (Alosa s apidissima, Wilson). A Comparison of Populations from Four Rivers of the Atlantic Seaboard. McGill, 1969.
10988
MacDonald, John Stevenson. "Food Resource Utilization by Five Species of Benthic Feeding Fish in Passamaquoddy Bay, N.B." Western Ontario, 1983.
10989
Peterson, Richard Harry. "The Effects of Temperature Change on Metabolism and Spontaneous Activity of Atlantic Salmon (Salmo salar L.) and on Metabolism of Salmon Brain Tissue." Carleton 1968.
10990
Randall, Robert George. "Production Rate of Juvenile Atlantic Salmon (Salmo salar Linnaeus) in Relation to Available Food in Two Miramichi River N.B. Nursery Streams." New Brunswick, 1981.

10991
Riddell, Brian Everett. "Environmental and Genetic Sources of Geographic Variation in Populations of Atlantic Salmon, Salmo salar Linnaeus." McGill, 1979.

10992
Rimmer, David Michael. "On the Autumnal Habitat Change of Juvenile Atlantic Salmon (Salmo salar L.)." New Brunswick, 1980.

10993
Tyler, Albert Vincent. "Food Resource Division in a Community of Marine Fishes." Toronto, 1968. [Passamaquoddy Bay/Baie Passamaquoddy]

Newfoundland/Terre-Neuve

10994
Backus, Richard H. "The Marine and Freshwater Fishes of Labrador." Cornell, 1953.

10995
Chadwick, Edward Michael Pakenham. "Dynamics of an Atlantic Salmon Stock (Salmo salar) in a Small Newfoundland River." Memorial University of Newfoundland, 1982.

10996
Kao, Ming-Hsuing. "Some Aspects of the Biology of Sea Stars Asterias vulgaris Verrill and Leptasterias polaris (Muller and Troschel) in Newfoundland Waters." Memorial University of Newfoundland, 1980.

10997
May, Arthur William. "Biology and Fishery of Atlantic Cod (Gadus morhua morhua L.) from Labrador." McGill, 1966.

10998
O'Connell, Michael Francis. "The Biology of Anadromous Salvelinus fontinalis (Mitchill, 1815) and Salmo trutta Linnaeus, 1758, in River Systems Flowing into Placenta Bay and St. Mary's Bay, Newfoundland." Memorial University of Newfoundland, 1983.

10999
Pierotti, Raymond John. "The Reproductive Behaviour and Ecology of the Herring Gull in Newfoundland." Dalhousie, 1979.

11000
Pippy, John Herbert Charles. "Larval Anisakis simplex in Atlantic Salmon (Salmo salar) and Their Values as Biological Indicators." Guelph, 1975.

11001
Pitt, Thomas Kenton. "The Biology and Fishery of American Plaice (Hippoglossoides platessoides Fabricius) with Special Reference to the Grand Banks." Memorial University of Newfoundland, 1976.

Nova Scotia/Nouvelle-Écosse

11002
Dahlberg, Michael Daniel. "A Systematic Review of the North American Species of Menhaden, Genus Brevoortia." Tulane, 1966.

11003
Das, Naresh. "Spawning, Distribution, Survival and Growth of Larval Herring (Clupea harengus L.) in Relation to Hydrographic Conditions in the Bay of Fundy." McGill, 1968.

Di Capua, Richard Anthony. See No./Voir no 10887

11004
Elson, Paul Frederick. "Effects of Current Temperature and Light on Movements of Speckled Trout." Toronto, 1939. [Cape Breton, Nova Scotia/Cap Breton, Nouvelle-Écosse]

Komourdjian, Martin Paul. See No./Voir no 10985

11005
McEachran, John Douglas. "Aspects of the Distribution and Biology of Seven Species of Skates (Pisces: Rajidae) Which Occur on the Continental Shelf of the East Coast of North America (Cape Hatteras, North Carolina to Nova Scotia)." William and Mary, 1973.

11006
Raymond, James Anthony. "Absorption Inhibition as a Mechanism of Freezing Resistance in Polar Fishes." California, San Diego, 1976. [Nova Scotia flounder/Flets de la Nouvelle-Écosse]

11007
Steiner, William Wayne, II. "A Comparative Study of the Pure Tonal Whistle Vocalisations from Five Western North Atlantic Dolphin Species." Rhode Island, 1980. [From Nova Scotia to the Caribbean/De la Nouvelle-Écosse aux Caraïbes]

Ontario

11008
Ayles, George Burton. "The Inheritance of Early Survival in Salvelinus namaycush X. S. Fontinalis Hybrids (Splake Trout)." Toronto, 1973.

11009
Casselman, John Malcolm. "Calcified Tissue and Body Growth of Northern Pike, Esox lucius Linnaeus)." Toronto, 1978.

Chan, Guat Lian. See No./Voir no 10541

11010
Craigie, David Edward. "The Geographical Distribution and Spatial Associations of Fishes in Georgian Bay, Ontario, 1958-1963." Toronto, 1971.

11011
Foster, John Robert. "Factors Influencing the Predator-Prey Relations of a Small Esocid, the Grass Pickerel (Esox americanus vermiculatus." Toronto, 1980. [Long Point, Lake Erie]

Frantsi, Christopher. See No./Voir no 10512

11012
Fry, Frederick Ernest Joseph. "The Summer Migration of the Cisco Leucichthys artedi (Le Sueur) in Lake Nipissing, Ontario." Toronto, 1936.

11013
Goddard, Christopher Ian. "The Effect of Photoperiod on the Seasonal Fluctuations of the Brook Trout." York, 1979.

11014
Gunn, William Walker Hamilton. "Reverse Migration in the Pelee Region in Relation to the Weather." Toronto, 1951.

11015
Hackney, Peter Albert. "Ecology of the Burbot (Lota lota) with Special Reference to Its Role in the Lake Opeongo Fish Community." Toronto, 1973.

11016
Hart, John Lawson. "The Spawning and Early Life History of the Whitefish, Coregonus clupeaformis (Mitchill) in the Bay of Quinte, Ontario. The Growth of the Whitefish. The Food of the Whitefish... in Ontario Waters, with a Note on the Parasites." Toronto, 1930.

11017
Kennedy, William Alexander. "The Whitefish, Coregonus clupeaformis (Mitchill) of Lake Opeongo, Algonquin Park, Ontario." Toronto, 1941.

11018
Lalancette, Louis-Marie. "Studies in the Growth, Reproduction and Diet of the White Sucker, Catostomus commersoni commersoni (Lacépède) of Gamelin Lake, Chicoutimi, Quebec." Waterloo, 1975.

11019
Mahon, Robin Campbell. "Patterns in the Fish Taxocenes of Small Streams in Poland and Ontario: A Tale of Two River Basins, with a Test for Accuracy of Quantitative Sampling." Guelph, 1981.

11020
McGlade, Jacqueline Myriam. "Genotypic and Phenotypic Variations in the Brook Trout, Salvelinus fontinalis (Mitchill)." Guelph, 1982. [From Ungava Bay, Quebec, down to Appalachian Georgia/De la Baie d'Ungava au Québec vers la Géorgie Apalache]

11021
Mills, Kenneth Harold. "The Responses of a Lake Whitefish (Coregonus clupeaformis) Population to Whole-Lake Fertilization." Manitoba, 1981. [Experimental lakes area, northwestern Ontario/ Région expérimentale des lacs, nord-ouest de l'Ontario]

11022
Neville, Christine Mary. "The Effects of Environmental Acidification on Rainbow Trout." Toronto, 1980. [Toronto]

11023
Osterberg, Donald. "Food Consumption Feeding Habits and Growth of Walleye (Stizostedion vitreum) and Sauger (Stizostedion canadence) in the Ottawa River near Ottawa-Hull." Ottawa, 1978.

Pritchard, Andrew Lyle. See No./Voir no 10922
11024
Robbins, William Harvey. "Population Dynamics of Potamodromous Small-Mouth Bass (Micropterus dolomieni Lacépède) and Responses to Environmental Stimuli." Guelph, 1975. [Lake Simcoe and Pefferlaw River/Lac Simcoe et rivière Pefferlaw]

11025
Sheri, Ahmad Nadeem. "Growth Dynamics of White Perch, Roccus americanus, During Colonization of Bay of Quinte, Lake Ontario." Waterloo, 1969.

11026
Steele, Robert Gordon. "Species Recognition and Reproductive Isolation in Two Species of Sunfish (Antrarchidae)." Western Ontario, 1974.

11027
Tedla, Shibru. "The Ecology of Some Metazoan Parasites of the Yellow Perch, Perca fluviatilis L. Waterloo, 1969.

Quebec/Québec

11028
Coleman, John Reed. "The Ecology and Life History of Salvelinus fontinalis in Ungava. Waterloo, 1970. [Brook Trout/Truites]

11029
Delisle, Claude E. "Écologie, croissance et comportement de l'éperlan du lac Heney, comté de Gatineau, ainsi que la répartition en eau douce au Québec." Ottawa, 1970.

11030
Fortin, Réjean. "Dynamique de la population de Perca flavescens (Mitchill) de la grande anse de l'Île Perrot au lac Saint-Louis." Montréal, 1971.

11031
Jean, Yves. "A Study of Spring and Fall Spawning Herring (Clupea harengus L.) at Grand River, Bay of Chaleur, Québec." Toronto, 1955.

11032
Marcotte, Alexandre. "Notes sur la biologie de l'éperlan de la province de Québec." Laval, 1947.

McGlade, Jacqueline Myriam. See No./Voir no 11020
11033
Mongeau, Frère Jean René. "Croissance du brochet commun Esox lucius L. dans deux lacs du parc du Mont Tremblant, province de Québec." Montréal, 1960.

11034
O'Connor, Joseph Francis. "On the Brook Trout (Salvelinus fontinalis) Production and Trophic Dynamics of Four Streams in the Matamek River System, Quebec." Waterloo, 1975.

11035
Pageau, Gérard. "Comportement, alimentation et croissance de l'achigan à petite bouche (Micropterus dolomieni Lacépède dans la plaine de Montréal et dans les Laurentides." Montréal, 1967.

11036
Richardson, Laurence R. "The Freshwater Fishes of South-Eastern Quebec." McGill, 1935.

11037
Saunders, Lloyd Harrell. "Ecology of Brook Trout American Smelt and Arctic Char of Matamek Lake, Quebec." Waterloo, 1969.

11038
Simard, André. "Contribution à l'étude de la biologie du Touladi, Salvelinus mamaycush, du lac l'Assomption et du lac Tremblant, Québec." Montréal, 1970.

Arctic, Northwest Territories and the Yukon/ Arctique, Territoires du Nord-Ouest et Yukon

11039
Bodaly, Richard Andrew. "Evolutionary Divergence Between Currently Sympatric Lake Whitefish Coregonus clupeaformis in the Yukon Territory. Manitoba, 1977.

11040
Dutil, Jean-Denis. "Periodic Changes in the Condition of the Arctic Charr (<u>Salvelinnus alpinus</u>) of the Nauyuk Lake System." Manitoba, 1982.

11041
Freeman, Milton Malcolm Roland. "Reproduction and Distribution in Arctic <u>Gasterosteus aculeatus</u> L. (Teleostei: Gasterosteidae)." McGill, 1965.

11042
Grainger, Edward H. "Of the Age, Growth, Migratory Habits and Reproductive Potential of the Arctic Char (<u>Salvelinus alpinus</u>) of Frobisher Bay, Baffin Island." McGill, 1954.

11043
Hanzely, Joseph B. "The Respiratory Metabolism of Excised Tissues of the Arctic Blackfish (<u>Dallia pectoralis</u> Bean) at Various Temperatures." Catholic, 1959.

11044
Hunter, John Gerald. "Production of Arctic Char (<u>Salvelinus alpinus</u> Linnaeus) in a Small Arctic Lake." McGill, 1968.

11045
McPhail, John Donald. "The Postglacial Dispersal of Freshwater Fishes in Northern North America." McGill, 1963.

11046
Power, Geoffrey. "Studies on the Atlantic Salmon (<u>Salmo salar</u> Linn.) of Subarctic Canada." McGill, 1959.

11047
Walters, Vladimir. "Fishes of Western Arctic America and Eastern Arctic Siberia: Taxonomy and Zoogeography." New York, 1954.

Saskatchewan

Kavaliers, Martin Imants. See No./Voir no 10927

CRUSTACEANS AND MOLLUSKS/ CRUSTACÉS ET MOLLUSQUES

This classification reflects the fact that very little research was carried out in the United States or Canada until the 1970's, when the Canadian output increased significantly. Fifteen Canadian universities produced more than 60 studies; British Columbia and Toronto are the leading contributors with 12 titles each. the universities of McGill (8), Dalhousie (7), Alberta (5), and Laval (5) are the other important contributors. Eight American universities have produced a total of 12 dissertations. Ohio State and George Washington University are the leaders with three titles each.

———

Cette classification reflète le fait que très peu de recherches ont été faites aux États-Unis ou au Canada jusqu'en 1970, date où la production canadienne s'est accrue de façon importante. Quinze universités canadiennes ont produit plus de 60 études; avec 12 titres chacune, les universités de la Colombie-Britannique et de Toronto ont été en tête de la production. Viennent ensuite les universités McGill (8), Dalhousie (7), de l'Alberta (5) et Laval (5) dont la contribution est également importante. Huit universités américaines ont produit un total de 12 thèses. Ohio State et George Washington mènent le jeu avec trois thèses chacune.

General Items/Ouvrages généraux

Briggs, Derek Ernest Gilmour. See No./Voir no 11131
11048
Couture, Richard. "Écologie d'<u>Argis dentata</u> (Crustacea decapoda)." Laval, 1971.

11049
Daborn, Graham Richard. "Community Stricture and Energetics in an Argillotrophic Lake, with Special References to the Giant Fairy Shrimp <u>Branchinecta gigas</u> Lynch." Alberta, 1973.
Fleming, Lesley Carolyn. See No./Voir no 11337
11050
McLay, Colin Lindsay. "Competitive Exclusion of Ostracod Species in a Temporary Environment." British Columbia, 1970.

11051
Pohle, Gerhard Werner. "Setal Morphology and Post-Embryonic Development of Two Pinnotherid Crabs, <u>Dissodactylus crinitchelis</u> moreira, 1901 and D. <u>Primitivus</u> Bouvier, 1917 (Brachyura: Pinnotheridae), Symbiotic with Echinoids." Toronto, 1982.

Eastern Canada/Est du Canada

11052
Dadswell, Michael John. "Distribution, Ecology and Post-Glacial Dispersal of Certain Crustaceans and Fishes in Eastern North America." Carleton, 1973.

11053
MacIntyre, Robert John. "<u>Gammarus</u>: Some Aspects of the Genus with Particular Reference to <u>Gammarus oceanicus</u> from Eastern Canada." McGill, 1960.

11054
Steele, Donald Harold. "Studies in the Marine Amphipoda of Eastern and Northeastern Canada (Marine Amphipoda of Eastern Canada)." McGill, 1961.

Western Canada/Ouest du Canada

11055
Castillo, Jorge Gonzalo. "Analysis of the Benthic <u>Cumacea</u> and Gammaridean Amphipoda from the Western Beaufort Sea." Oregon State, 1976.

Gulf of St. Lawrence/Golfe Saint-Laurent

11056
Berkes, Fikret. "Production and Comparative Ecology of Euphausiids in the Gulf of St. Lawrence." McGill, 1973.

11057
Pennell, William. "Studies on a Member of the Pleuston, <u>Anomalocera opalus</u> N.S. (Crustacea copepoda) in the Gulf of St. Lawrence." McGill, 1973.

Lake Erie/Lac Érié

11058
Andrews, Theodore F. "The Life History, Distribution, Growth, and Abundance of Leptodora kindtii (Focke) in Western Lake Erie." Ohio State, 1948.

11059
Jahoda, William J. "Seasonal Differences in Distribution of Diaptomus (Copepoda) in Western Lake Erie." Ohio State, 1949.

Alberta

11060
Aiken, David Edwin. "Environmental Regulation of Molting and Reproduction in the Crayfish Orconectes viriles (Hagen) in Alberta." Alberta, 1967.

11061
Lim, Richard Peter. See No./Voir no 11086
Menon, Poimplasseri Sivaramakrishna. "Population Ecology of Gammarus lacustris Sars in Big Island Lake." Alberta, 1967.

British Columbia/Colombie-Britannique

11062
Berkeley, Alfreda Alice. "The Post-Embryonic Development of the Common Pandalids of British Columbia." Toronto, 1930.

11063
Carl, George Clifford. "The Distribution of Cladocera and Free-Living Copepods in British Columbia, with Special Reference to the Centropagidae." Toronto, 1937.

11064
Evans, Marlene Sandra. "The Distributional Ecology of the Calanoid Copepod Pareuchaeta elongata Esterly." British Columbia, 1973. [Vancouver]

11065
Gilfillan, Edward Smith, III. "The Effects of Changes in Temperature, Salinity in Undefined Properties of Sea Water on the Respiration of Euphausia pacifica Hansen (Crustacea) in Relation to the Species' Ecology." British Columbia, 1970. [British Columbia coastal waters/Eaux territoriales de la Colombie-Britannique]

11066
Hargrave, Barry Thomas. "Inter-Relationships Between a Deposit-Feeding Amphipod and Metabolism of Sediment Microflora." British Columbia, 1969.

11067
Harrison, Brenda Jane. "The Biological Determinants of the Structure of Harpacticoid Copepod Communities in an Estuarine Intertidal Flat (Fraser River Delta, B.C.)." British Columbia, 1981.

11068
Hart, Josephine Frances Lavinia. "The Larval and Adult Phases of Certain Hermit Crabs (Anomura) of British Columbia, with Special Reference to Characters Significant in a Study of Their Interrelationships." Toronto, 1937.

11069
Harvey, Brian John. "Bioluminescence and Color Change in Euphausia pacifica." Victoria, 1979.

11070
McLaughlin, Patsy Ann. "The Hermit Crabs of the Genus Pagirus (Crustacea: Decapoda Paguridae) from Northwestern North America, with a Partial Revision of the Genus." George Washington, 1972.

11071
Regan, Lance. "Euphausia pacifica and Other Euphausiids in the Coastal Waters of British Columbia: Relationships to Temperature Salinity and Other Properties in the Field and Laboratory." British Columbia, 1968.

11072
Stone, David Philip. "Copepod Distributional Ecology in a Glacial Run-Off Fjord." British Columbia, 1978. [Knight Inlet]

11073
Woodhouse, Charles Douglas, Jr. "A Study of the Ecological Relationships and Taxonomy Status of Two Species of the Genus Calanus (Crustacea Copepoda)." British Columbia, 1971.

11074
Zittin, David. "Factors Influencing the Vertical Distribution of Two Intertidal Porcelain Crab Populations." British Columbia, 1979. [Barkley Sound]

Manitoba

11075
Arnason, Ingolfur Gilbert. "A Survey of the Entomostraca of Manitoba and a Study of Feeding of Lake Winnipeg Ciscoes." Manitoba, 1951.

Maritime Provinces/Provinces Maritimes

General Items/Ouvrages généraux

11076
Dewey, Christopher Paul. "The Taxonomy and Palaeoecology of Lower Carboniferous Ostracodes and Peracarids (Crustacea) from Southwestern Newfoundland and Central Nova Scotia." Memorial University of Newfoundland, 1983.

11077
Templeman, Wilfred. "Local Differences in the Life History of the Lobster (Homarus americanus) on the Coast of the Maritime Provinces of Canada." Toronto, 1933.

Newfoundland/Terre-Neuve

Dewey, Christopher Paul. See No./Voir no 11076

Nova Scotia/Nouvelle-Écosse

11078
Anderson, Edward Philip. "Tropic Interactions Among Ctenophores and Copepods in St. Margaret's Bay Nova Scotia." Dalhousie, 1974.
Bartlett, Grant Aulden. See No./Voir no 11842
11079
Black, William B. "The Mysidacea of the Bras d'Or Lakes." McGill, 1956.

11080
Breen, Paul Allan. "Relations Among Lobsters, Sea Urchins and Kelp in Nova Scotia." Dalhousie, 1975.
11081
Cooley, John Morgan. "The Life History, Population Dynamics and Production of Leptodiaptomis minutus Lillj. (Copeposa: Calanoida) in Bluff Lake, Nova Scotia." Dalhousie, 1974.
Dewey, Christopher Paul. See No./Voir no 11076
11082
Marcotte, Brian Michael. "The Ecology of Meiobenthic Harpacticords (Crustacea: Copepoda) in West Lawrencetown, Nova Scotia." Dalhousie, 1978.
11083
McCain, John Charles. "The Caprellidae (Crustacea: Amphipoda) of the Western North Atlantic." George Washington, 1968.

Ontario

11084
Langford, Raymond Robert. "The Distribution and Utilization of the Limnetic Crustacea of Lake Nipissing, Ontario." Toronto, 1936.
11085
Lasenby, David Charles. "The Ecology of Mysis relicta in an Arctic and a Temperate Lake." Toronto, 1971. [Stony Lake/Lac Stony]
11086
Lim, Richard Peter. "Community Description, Population Dynamics and Production of Cladocera with Special Reference to the Littoral Region of Pinehurst Lake, Ontario." Waterloo, 1976.

Quebec/Québec

11087
Bernard, Jean-Guy. "Spectre planétonique (Cladoceres et Copepodes) du lac Bédard, forêt Montmorency, Québec." Laval, 1972.
11088
Corrivault, George Wilfrid. "Contribution à l'étude de la biologie du homard des eaux de la province de Québec." Laval, 1948.
11089
Filteau, Gabriel. "Étude écologique des copépodes pélagiques de la baie des Chaleurs." Laval, 1951.

Saskatchewan

11090
Moore, James Edward. "The Entomostraca of Southern Saskatchewan." Toronto, 1950.

Arctic and Northwest Territories/ Arctique et Territoires du Nord Ouest

11091
Cairns, Alan Andrew. "Seasonal Cycles, Population Dynamics, and Production of Copepods in the Arctic." McGill, 1969. [Ellesmere Island, Northwest Territories/Île d'Ellesmere, Territoires du Nord-Ouest]

11092
Damkaer, David Martin. "Calanoid Copepods of the Genera Spinocalanus and Mimocalanus from the Central Arctic Ocean, with a Review of the Spinocalanidae." George Washington, 1973. [Fletcher's Ice Island/Glacier de Fletcher]
Lasenby, David Charles. See No./Voir no 11085
11093
Reed, Edward Brandt. "The Ecology of Freshwater Entomostraca in the Western Arctic and Sub-Arctic North America." Saskatchewan, 1959.

Mollusks/Mollusques

General Items/Ouvrages généraux

11094
Bradbury, Helen Elizabeth. "Observations of the Functional Anatomy of the Ommastrephid illex illecebrosus (Lesueur, 1821) (Coleoidea: Cephalapoda), with Emphasis on Musculature and the Blood Vascular System." Memorial University of Newfoundland, 1970.
11095
Kerswill, Charles James. "Some Environmental Factors Limiting Growth and Distribution of the Quahaug, Venus mercenaria L." Toronto, 1941.
11096
Medcof, John C. "Studies on the Larva of the Canadian Oyster." Illinois, 1938.

Eastern Canada/Est du Canada

11097
Chichester, Lyle Franklin. "The Zoogeography, Ecology and Taxonomy of Arionid and Linacid Slugs Introduced into Northeastern North America." Connecticut, 1968. [Nova Scotia and Quebec/ Nouvelle-Écosse et Québec]
11098
Logie, Robert Reed. Epidemic Disease in Canadian Atlantic Oysters (Crassostrea virginica)." Rutgers, 1958.
11099
Mallet, André L. "Quantitative Genetics of the Atlantic Canadian Oyster, Crassostrea virginica (Gmelin)." Dalhousie, 1982.
11100
Robert, Ginette. "The Sublittoral Mollusca of the St. Lawrence Estuary, East Coast of Canada." Dalhousie, 1974.

Alberta

11101
Morris, James Robert. "An Ecological Study of the Basommataphoran Snail Helisoma trivolvis in Central Alberta." Alberta, 1970.
11102
Sankuwrathri, Chandra Sekhar. "The Effects of Thermal Effluent on the Population Dynamics of Physa gyrina Say (Mollusca: Gastropoda) and its Helminth Parasites at Wabamun Lake, Alberta." Alberta, 1974.

British Columbia/Colombie-Britannique

11103

Behrens, Sylvia. "Ecological Interaction of Three Littorina (Gastropoda, Prosobranchia) Along the West Coast of North America." Oregon, 1974.

11104

Denny, Mark William. "The Role of Mucus in the Locomotion and Adhesion of the Pulmonate Slug, Ariolimax columbianus." British Columbia, 1979.

11105

Fankboner, Peter Vaughn. "Behaviour, Digestion, and the Role of the Zooxanthellae in Giant Clams (Eulamelli branchia, Tridacmidae)." Victoria, 1972.

11106

Himmelman, John Henry. "Factors Regulating the Reproductive Cycles of Some West Coast Invertebrates." British Columbia, 1976. [Vancouver Island, Strait of Georgia - chitons, etc./Île de Vancouver, détroit de Georgie – chitine, etc.]

11107

Rollo, Christopher David. "The Behavioral Ecology of Terrestrial Slugs." British Columbia, 1978.

Maritime Provinces/Provinces maritimes

11108

Bacon, George Beverley. "Marine Algal Settlement and Fouling of Collectors in an Oyster Culture Area of Prince Edward Island." New Brunswick, 1972.

11109

Barnes, David Hugh. "An Ecological Study of Epibionts Associated with the Shell of the Sea Scallop, Placopecten magellanicus (Gmelin, 1791) (Mollusca: Pelecypoda)." Memorial University of Newfoundland, 1974. [St. Mary's Bay/Baie St-Mary]

11110

Béland, Pierre. "The Effect of Environmental Stress on the Demography of Two Intertidal Gastropods." Dalhousie, 1975. [Off the Coast of Nova Scotia/ Hors des côtes de la Nouvelles-Écosse]

11111

Dickie, Lloyd Merlin. "Fluctuations in Abundance of the Giant Scallop, Placopecten magellanicus (Gmelin), in the Digby Area of the Bay of Fundy." Toronto, 1953.

11112

Hum, Jennifer Roslyn. "Oxygen Consumption and Growth of Mytilus edulis on the Atlantic Coast of North America South of Newfoundland." McGill, 1976.

11113

Newcombe, Curtis Lakeman. "Factors Influencing the Growth of the Soft Shelled Clam Mya arenaria L. in the Bay of Fundy." Toronto, 1933.

Manitoba

11114

Pip, Eva. "A Study of Aquatic Plant-Snail Associations." Manitoba, 1977. [Delta Marsh, southern part of Lake Manitoba/Delta Marsh, partie sud du lac Manitoba]

Ontario

11115

Bhajan, William Rudolph. "Studies on the Ecology of Bosmina longirostris in Sunfish Lake." Waterloo, 1970.

Bickel, Edwin David. See No./Voir no 6572

11116

Mackie, Gerald L. "Biology of Musculium securis (Pelecypoda: Sphaeriidae) in Two Temporary Forest Ponds, a River and a Permanent Pond near Ottawa, Canada." Ottawa, 1974.

Quebec/Québec

11117

Bensink, Angela Helen Arthington. "Observations on the Biology and Population Dynamics of Land Snails in a Quebec Apple Orchard." McGill, 1969.

Bickel, Edwin. See No./Voir no 6572

11118

Corbeil, Henri Étienne. "Étude écologique sur les mollusques dans la Baie des Chaleurs: bioécologie de Mya arenaria L. et essai d'acclimation d'Ostrea virginica Gmelin." Laval, 1952.

11119

Pinel-Alloul, Bernadette. "Étude écologique des Lymnaeidae (mollusques, gastéropodes, pulmones) du lac Saint-Louis près de Montréal, Québec." Montréal, 1975.

Saskatchewan

11120

Murray, Alan Roderick. "The Ecology of Saskatchewan Sphaeriidae (Mollusca Bivalvia): An Evaluation of Some Components of Their Environment." Saskatchewan, 1975.

Gulf of St. Lawrence/Golfe Saint-Laurent

11121

Davis, John Dunning. "A Study of the Arctic Wedge Clams, Mesodesma deauratum (Turton) and Mesodesma arctatum (Conrad) of the Northwestern Atlantic." New Hampshire, 1963. [Gulf of St. Lawrence/Golfe Saint-Laurent]

ENTOMOLOGY/ENTOMOLOGIE

This is one of the larger sections of the scientific studies. Nineteen Canadian universities produced more than 160 dissertations, McGill is the specialist in the area, with over 40 titles to its credit. The universities of Alberta, British Columbia, Toronto, Manitoba, and Simon Fraser follow in that order. Three quarters of the studies were approved during the 1970's and 1980's. Of the 25 American universities with theses in this area, 14 produced one title each. The University of Cornell produced 14 titles and the schools of Harvard and Minnesota produced four each.

C'est l'une des plus vastes sections de la classification des études scientifiques. Dix-neuf universités canadiennes ont produit plus de 160 thèses; McGill, l'université spécialisée en ce domaine, a 40 thèses à son crédit. Les universités de l'Alberta, de la Colombie-Britannique, de Toronto, du Manitoba et Simon Fraser, suivent dans l'ordre. Les trois quarts des thèses ont été approuvées dans les années 1970 et 1980. Sur 25 universités américaines qui ont également produit des thèses en cette discipline, 14 n'en comptent qu'une seule chacune; Cornell a produit 14 titres, et Harvard et Minnesota quatre chacune.

General Items/Ouvrages généraux

11122
Ahmadi, Ali Asghar. "A Revision and Review of the North American Species of Agrotis and Felitia Known to Occur North of the Mexican Border (Lepidoptera Noctuidae)." Cornell, 1977.

11123
Anderson, John Murray. "Some Responses of the White Pine Weevil Pissodes strobi Peck to Airborne Chemical Stimuli Produced by Certain Coniferous Trees." Toronto, 1958.

11124
Angerilli, Nello Pasquale Doro. "Some Influence of Aquatic Plants on the Development and Survival of Mosquito Populations." Simon Fraser, 1978. [Canadian ponds/Étangs canadiens]

11125
Arntfield, Peter William. "Systematics and Biology of the Genus Chasmatonotus Loew (Diptera: Chironomidae: Orthocladinae) from North America." McGill, 1977.

11126
Barron, John Robert. "A Revision of the Trogositidae of America, North of Mexico (Coleoptera, Cleroidea)." Alberta, 1969.

11127
Bennett, Gordon Fraser. "Studies in the Genus Protocalliphora (Diptera: Calliphoridae). I. Taxonomic Studies on the Third-Instar Larvae and the Puparia of the North American Species. II. Occurrence and Distribution of Protocalliphora Spp. in Nests of Various Birds in Different Habitats. III. Studies in the Life History of Species of Protocalliphora." Toronto, 1957.

11128
Borkent, Art. "The Systematics and Phylogeny of Xestochironomus harrisius and Holarctic and Neotropical Stenochironomus (Diptera: Chironomidae)." Carleton, 1982.

11129
Bradley, George Arthur. "A Study of the Systematics and Biology of Aphids of the Genus Cinara curtis in Canada." McGill, 1961.

11130
Brady, Allen Roy. "Lynx Spiders of North America, North of Mexico (Araneae: Oxyopidae)." Harvard, 1964.

11131
Briggs, Derek Ernest Gilmor. "Arthropods from the Burgess Shale, Middle Cambrian, Canada." Cambridge, 1976.

11132
Brown, Richard Lee. "A Revision of the Genus Epinotia (Hubner) (Tortricidae: Eucosmini). Part I. The North American Species of the Stoemiana Lineage." Cornell, 1980.

11133
Bush, Guy Louis, Jr. "A Revision of the Genus Rhagoletis in North America (Tephritidae, Diptera)." Harvard, 1964.

11134
Curran, C.N. "Keys to the Families and Genera of North American Diptera." Montréal, 1933.

11135
Dondale, Charles Denton. "Revision of the Genus Philodromus (Araneae: Thomisidae) in North America." McGill, 1959.

11136
Edwards, Donald K. "A Study of Acclimatization and Other Factors Affecting Respiration and Survival in Tribolium confusum Duval." McGill, 1957.

11137
Edwards, Robert J. "A Taxonomic Revision of the Spider Subfamily Clubioninae of the United States, Canada, and Alaska." Rochester, 1951.

11138
Eidt, Douglas Conrad. "The Anatomy and Histology of the Mature Larva of the Prairie Grain Wireworm, Ctenicera aeripensis destructor (Brown) (Coleoptera, Elateridae)." Saskatchewan, 1955.

11139
Erwin, Terry Lee. "A Reclassification of Bombardier Beetles and a Taxonomic Revision of the North and Middle American Species (Caribidae: Brachinida)." Alberta, 1969.

11140
Ferguson, Douglas Campbell. "A Revision of the Moths of the Subfamily Geometrinae Occurring in America, North of Mexico." Cornell, 1967.

11141
Foster, David Edward. "The Taxonomy and Biology of the Genus Trichodes Herbst of North America (Coleoptera: Cleridiae)." Idaho, 1973.

11142
Freeman, Thomas Nesbitt. "A Revision of the North American Species of the Sub-family Archipinae (Lepidoptera, Tortricidae)." Toronto, 1946.

11143
Freitag, Richard. "A Revision of the Species of the Genus Evarthrus Le Conte (Coleoptera: Caribidae)." Alberta, 1968.

11144
Garland, John Allan. "The Taxonomy of the Chrysopidae of Canada and Alaska (Insecta: Neuroptera)." McGill, 1982.

11145
Garnett, William Brighton. "Biology and Immature Stages of Suillia (Diptera: Heleomyzidae) in Boreal North America." Washington State, 1974.

Gauthier, Georges. See No./Voir no 6334

11146
Ghouri, Ahmad Said Khan. "The Effect of Temperature and Nutrition on the Development of the House Cricket, Acheta domesticae (L.) Gryllidae, Orthoptera, and Two Related Species of Cricket." McGill, 1956.

11147
Golini, Victor Italo. "Cytology, Taxonomy and Ecology of Species in the Genus Hellichiella (Diptera: Simuliidae)." McMaster, 1982.

11148
Goulet, Henri. "The Genera of the Holarctic Elaphrini and Species of the Elaphrus fabricius (Coleoptera: Caribidae): Classification Phylogeny and Zoogeography." Alberta, 1978.

11149
Haddock, James Devere. "The Biosystematics of the Caddis Fly Genus Leptocella in North America with Emphasis on the Aquatic Stages." California, Berkeley, 1970.

11150
Hansen, Dean Cyrus. "Systematics and Morphology of the Nearctic Species of Diamera (Meigen, 1835) (Diptera Chironomidae)." Minnesota, 1973.

11151
Hellman, John Leroy. "A Taxonomic Revision of the Genus Hydrochus of North America, Central America and West Indies." Maryland, 1975.

11152
Hogue, Steve Monroe. "Biosystematic of the Genus Trirhabda leconte of America North of Mexico (Chrysomelidae Coleoptera)." Idaho, 1970.

11153
Hung, Akey Chang-Fu. "A Systematic Study of the Formica obscuriventris Subgroup, with Notes on Colony-Founding in the Formica rufa Group (Hymenoptera: Formicidae)." North Dakota, 1973. [New Brunswick, Ontario, Quebec/Nouveau-Brunswick, Ontario, Québec]

11154
Jacques, Richard Leo, Jr. "Taxonomic Revision of the Genus Leptinotarsa (Coleoptera: Chrysomelidae) of North America." Purdue, 1972.

11155
Johnson, Victor. "A Review of the Coniopterygidae of North and Central America." Kentucky, 1977.

11156
Kane, Michael Matthew. "Systematics, Morphology, and Natural History of Polyxenus lagurus (Linné, 1758) (Diplopoda: Polyxenidae) in North America." Michigan State, 1981. [British Columbia and Nova Scotia/Colombie-Britannique et Nouvelle-Écosse]

11157
Khattat, Abdul-Razzak. "The Relation Between Population Density and Population Movement of Lygus lineolaris (Palisot de Beauvois), (Hemiptera: Miridae), and Crop Damage." McGill, 1978.

11158
Lattin, John Daniel. "The Scutellerinae of America North of Mexico (Hemiptera: Heteroptera Pentatomidae)." California, Berkeley, 1964.

11159
Lemonde, André. "Contribution à l'étude de la nutrition des larves de trois espèces d'insectes." Laval, 1952.

11160
Leonard, Mortimer Demarest. "A Revision of the Dipterous Family Rhagionidae (Leptidae) in the United States and Canada." Cornell, 1921.

11161
MacGown, Matthew W. "The Platygastridae (Hymenoptera: Proctotrupoidea) Parasitic on Midges (Cecidomyiidae) Found on Conifers in Canada and the United States." Mississippi State, 1978.

11162
Madge, Ronald Bradley. "A Revision of the Genus Lebia latreille in America North of Mexico (Coleoptera: Carabidae)." Alberta, 1963.

11163
Marshall, Stephen Archer. "A Review of the Nearctic Limosininae (Diptera: Sphaeroceridae), with Revisions of Selected Genera." Guelph, 1982.

11164
McCabe, Timothy Lee. "A Reclassification of the Polia Complex for North America (Lepidoptera Noctuidae)." Cornell, 1978.

11165
McCauley, Victor John Edmund. "Life Tables for Some Natural Populations of Chironomidae (Diptera) in a Typha Marsh." Alberta, 1975.

11166
McCorkle, David Vernon. "A Revision of the Species of Elophorus fabricius in America, North of Mexico." Washington, Seattle, 1967.

11167
McDonald, Frederick James Dougald. "The Male and Female Genitalia of North American Pentatomoidea (Hemoptera: Heteroptera): Morphology and Bearing on Classification." Alberta, 1965.

11168
McFadden, Max Wulfsohn. "A Taxonomic Study of the Soldier Fly Larvae Occurring in America North of Mexico (Diptera: Stratiomyidae)." Alberta, 1963.

11169
Mead, Frank Waldreth. "A Revision of the Genus Oliarus in North America, North of Mexico (Homoptera: Cixiidae)." North Carolina State 1968.

11170
Menke, Arnold Stephan Ernst. "A Revision of the North American Ammophila (Hymenoptera Sphecidae)." California, Davis, 1965.

Mutch, Robert Alexander. See No./Voir no 11187

11171
Parry, Richard Howell. "The Systematics and Biology of the Flea Beetle Genus Crepidodera chevrolat in America, North of Mexico Including Electrophoretic Studies on a Few Local Populations (Coleoptera: Chrysomelidae)." Carleton, 1977.

11172
Roby, Dominique. "Structures génétiques de populations de lépidotères en fonction de leur stratégie d'alimentation et de leur dispersion géographique." Montréal, 1982.

11173
Saffer, Barbara. "A Systematic Revision of the Genus Cenocoelius (Hymenoptera, Braconidae) in North America, Including Mexico." Fordham, 1977.

11174
Sanborne, Paul Michael. "Classification, Zoogeography, and Phylogeny of the Genus Sinophorus foerster (Hymenoptera: Ichneumonidae)." McMaster, 1982.

11175
Sawchyn, William Walter. "Environmental Controls in the Seasonal Succession and Synchronization of Development in Some Pond Species of Damselflies (Ordonata Zygoptera)." Saskatchewan, 1972.

11176
Skolko, Arthur John. "A Cultural and Cytological Investigation of a Two-Spored Basidiomycete Aleurodiscus canadensis, N. Sp." Toronto, 1943.

11177
Stainer, John Evelyn Randall. "A Study of the Genus Conocephalus in Northern North America (Orthoptera: Tettigonioidae)." McGill, 1978.

11178
Swaine, James Malcolm. "Canadian Bark Beetles, a Preliminary Classification with an Account of the Habits and Means of Control." Cornell, 1919.

11179
Vickery, Vernon R. "The Genus Chorthippus (Orthoptera: Acrididae) in North America." McGill, 1964.

11180
White, Noel David George. "Interrelations in Stored-Wheat Ecosystems Infested with Multiple Species of Insects: A Descriptive and Multivariate Analysis." Manitoba, 1979.

11181
Williamson, David Lee. "Carbon Dioxide Sensitivity in Drosophila affinis and Drosophila athabasca." Nebraska, 1959.

Eastern Canada/Est du Canada

11182
Clark, William Cummin. "Spatial Structure and Population Dynamics in an Insect Epidemic Ecosystem." British Columbia, 1979. [Spruce Budworms/ Tordeuses d'épinette]

11183
Duarte de Oliveira, Domingos. "Recherches sur la biologie et la dynamique des populations naturelles de Diprion frutelorum F. (Hymenoptera: Diprionidae) dans les Cantons de l'Est." Sherbrooke, 1974.

11184
Palaniswamy, Pachagounder. "Perception of the Female Sex Pheromone and Male Odors by the Eastern Spruce Budworm, Choristoneura fumiferana (Clem) (Lepidoptera: Tortricidae): A Behavioral and Electrophysiological Study." New Brunswick, 1980.

11185
Thomas, James B. "The Identification of Larvae of Some Species of Bark Beetles Breeding on Coniferous Trees in Eastern Canada." McGill, 1955.

Western Canada/Ouest du Canada

11186
Kavanaugh, David Henry. "The Nearctic Species of Nebria Latreille (Coleoptera: Carabidae: Nebrium): Classification, Phylogeny, Zoogeography and Natural History." Alberta, 1978.

11187
Mutch, Robert Alexander. "Life Histories of Two Insect Shredders and Their Role in Detritus Degadation in Rocky Mountain Streams." Calgary, 1981.

11188
Shorthouse, Joseph David. "The Roles of Insect Inhabitants in Six Diplolepis (Cynipidae, Hymenoptera) Rose Leaf Gulls of Western Canada." Saskatchewan, 1975.

11189
Stark, Ronald William. "Population Dynamics of the Lodgepole Needle Miner Recurvaria starki Free (Lepidoptera: Gelechiidae) in Canadian Rocky Mountain Parks." British Columbia, 1957.

Great Lakes/Grands lacs

11190
Britt, Noah W. "The Life History and Ecology of the White May Fly, Ephoron album Say, in Lake Erie." Ohio State, 1950.

11191
Marshall, Anna C. "A Qualitative and Quantitative Study of the Trichoptera of Western Lake Erie, (as Indicated by Light Trap Material." Ohio State, 1939.

Alberta

11192
Abdelnur, Osman Mohamed. "The Biology of Some Black Flies (Diptera: Simuliidae) of Alberta." Alberta, 1967.

11193
Berte, Stephen Bernard. "Life Histories of Four Species of Limnephilid Caddisflies in a Pond in Southern Alberta." Calgary, 1982.

11194
Boerger, Hans J. "Life History and Microhabitat Distribution of Midges (Diptera: Chironomidae) Inhabiting a Brown-Water Stream of Central Alberta, Canada." Alberta, 1978.

11195
Carter, Alan Richard. "Aspects of the Population Biology of Agonum retractum Leconte (Coleoptera: Carabidae) and Its Role and That of Some Other Soil Arthropods in the Cycling of Chemical Elements in an Aspen Woodland Ecosystem." Calgary, 1975.

11196
Cerezke, Herbert Frederick. "The Distribution and Abundance of the Root Weevil, Hylobius warreni Wood in Relation to Lodgepole Pine Stand Conditions in Alberta." British Columbia, 1969.

11197
Graham, Peter. "A Comparison of Methods for Sampling Adult Mosquito Populations with Observations on the Biology of the Adult Female in Central Alberta, Canada." Alberta, 1968.

11198
Happold, David Christopher Dawber. "Studies in the Ecology of Mosquitoes in the Boreal Forest of Alberta." Alberta, 1963.

11199

Harper, Alexander Maitland. "The Sugar Beet Root Aphid Pemphigus betae (Donne) with Notes on Closely Related Aphids of Southern Alberta." Washington State, 1957.

11200

Hudson, James Edward. "Seasonal Biology of Anopheles culex and Culiseta in Central Alberta (Diptera: Culicidae)." Alberta, 1977.

11201

Larson, David John. "The Predaceous Water Beetles (Coleoptera, Dytiscidae) of Alberta: Taxonomy, Biology and Distribution." Calgary, 1974.

McCauley, Victor John Edmund. See No./Voir no 11165

11202

Mitchell, Myron James. "Ecology of Oribatid Mites (Acari: Cryptosigmata) in an Aspen Woodland Soil." Calgary, 1974.

Nimmo, Andrew Peebles. See No./Voir no 11222

11203

Richards, Kenneth W. "Population Ecology of Bumblebees in Southern Alberta." Kansas, 1975.

11204

Rosenberg, David Michael. "Effects of Dieldrin on Diversity of Macroinvertebrates in a Slough in Central Alberta." Alberta, 1973.

11205

Sehgal, Vinod Kumar. "A Taxonomic Survey of Agromyzid Flies of Alberta and a Study of Host-Plant Relationships of an Oligophagous Species Phytomyza matricariae Hendel (Diptera: Agromyzidae)." Alberta, 1970.

11206

Thomas, Anthony William. "Autogeny and Anautogeny in Some Species of Tabinids (Diptera: Tabanidae) in Alberta, Canada." Alberta, 1972.

British Columbia/Colombie-Britannique

Ahmadi, Ali Asghar. See No./Voir no 11122

11207

Alfaro, Rene Ivan. "Host Selection by Pissodes strobi Peck: Chemical Interaction with the Host Plant." Simon Fraser, 1980. [Pine weevils/Charançons du pin]

11208

Burnett, John Allen. "Biosystematics of the New Oak-Gallwasp Genus, Weldia of Western North America (Hymenoptera: Cynipidae)." California, Riverside, 1977.

11209

Campbell, Alan. "Seasonal Changes in Abundance of the Pea Aphid and Its Associated Parasites in the Southern Interior of British Columbia." Simon Fraser, 1974.

11210

Conroy, John Charles. "The Taxonomy and Ecology of the Water Mites in Marion Lake, British Columbia, with a Description of a New Species, Pionopsis nov sp. (Acari: Pionidae)." Manitoba, 1974.

Coppel, Harry C. See No./Voir no 10544

11211

Gillespie, David Roy. "Introduced and Natural Leaprollers (Lepidoptera: Tortricidae) on Berry Crops in the Lower Fraser Valley, B.C." Simon Fraser, 1982.

11212

Green, Wren Quinton. "An Antagonistic Insect/Host Plant System: The Problem of Persistence." British Columbia, 1974. [Nanaimo, British Columbia/Colombie-Britannique]

11213

Hardman, John Michael. "The Hunting Tactics of a Unspecialized Predator, Pardosa vancouver (Araneae: Lycosidae) with Reference to Spatial Heterogeneity and the Components of the Functional Response." Simon Fraser, 1973.

11214

Holmberg, Robert George. "Selective Predation in Polyphagous Invertebrate Predator, Pardosa vancouveri (Arachnida, Araneae)." Simon Fraser, 1979. [Spiders/Araignées]

11215

Jamieson, Glen Stewart. "Coexistence in the Gerridae." British Columbia, 1973.

11216

Kamp, Joseph William. "Biosystems of the Grylloblattodea." British Columbia, 1973.

11217

Leffler, Sanford Ross. "Tiger Beetles of the Pacific Northwest (Coleoptera: Cicindelidae)." Washington, Seattle, 1979.

11218

Lindgren, Bo Staffan. "Pheromone-Based Management of Ambrosia Beetles in Timber Processing Areas of Vancouver Island." Simon Fraser, 1982.

11219

Macqueen, Angus. "Horn Fly Breeding, Nitrogen Loss and Nutrient Immobilization Associated with Cattle Dung in the Southern Interior of British Columbia." Simon Fraser, 1973.

McCorkle, David Vernon. See No./Voir no 11166

11220

McLean, John Alexander. "Primary and Secondary Attraction in Gnathotrichus sulcatus (Leconte) (Coleoptera: Scolytidae) and Their Application in Pest Management." Simon Fraser, 1976.

11221

Miller, Gordon Edward. "Biology, Sampling and Control of the Douglas-Fir Cone Gall Midge Contarnia oregonensis Foote (Diptera: Cecidomyiidae) in Douglas-Fir Seed Orchards in British Columbia." Simon Fraser, 1983.

11222

Nimmo, Andrew Peebles. "The Adult Rhyacophilidae and Limnephilidae (Trichoptera) of Alberta and Eastern British Columbia with an Examination of the Post-Glacial Origins of the Fauna." Alberta, 1970.

11223

Peterman, Randall Martin. "Some Aspects of the Population Dynamics of the Mountain Pine Beetle Dendroctonus ponderosae in Lodgepole Pine Forests of British Columbia." British Columbia, 1974.

1224
Raworth, David Arnold. "Population Dynamics of the Cabbage Aphid Brevicoryne brassicae (L.) (Homoptera: Aphididae) in Vancouver, British Columbia: A Quantitative Study and Synthesis of Ecological Relationships." British Columbia, 1982.

1225
Reynolds, Julian Douglas. "Aspects of the Ecology of Two Species of Cenocorixa (Corixidae: Hemiptera) in Allopatry and Sympatry." British Columbia, 1974.

1226
Richards, Laura Jean. "Foraging Behaviour of the Intertidal Beetle Thinopinus Pictus (Staphylinidae). British Columbia, 1982.

1227
Richerson, Jim Vernon. "Host Finding Mechanisms of Coeloides brunneri Viereck (Hymenoptera: Braconidae)." Simon Fraser, 1972.

1228
Roze, Liga Dace. "The Biological Control of Centaurea diffusa Lam, and C. Maculosa Lam by Urophora affinis Frauenfeld and U. Quadrifasciata meigen (Diptera: Tephritidae)." British Columbia, 1981.

1229
Safranyik, Laszlo. "Development of a Technique by Sampling Mountain Pine Beetle Populations in a Lodgepole Pine." British Columbia, 1969.

11230
Shore, Terence Leckie. "A Pheromone Mediated Mass-Trapping Program for Three Species of Ambrosia Beetle in a Commercial Sawmill." British Columbia, 1982.

11231
Spence, John Richard. "Microhabitat Selection and Regional Coexistence in Water-Striders (Heteroptera: Gerridae)." British Columbia, 1979. [Fraser Plateau/Plateau du Fraser]

11232
Thong, Cyril How Sik. "Bark Beetle Nematodes in British Columbia with Emphasis on the Biology and Host-Parasite Relationship of Contortylenchus reversus." Simon Fraser, 1974.

11233
Topping, Milton Stanlee. "Giant Chromosomes, Ecology, and Adaptation in Chironomus tentans." British Columbia, 1969.

11234
Zanuncio, José Cola. "Biology of Gnathotrichus sulcatus (Leconte 1868) (Col: Scolytidae) with Special Emphasis on Host Colonization and Brood Production." British Columbia, 1981. [Trees of the University of British Columbia's research forest at Maple Ridge/Arbres de la réserve forestière de l'Université de la Colombie-Britannique à Maple Ridge]

Manitoba

11235
Bracken, Garth Kyles. "Some Aspects of Host Orientation and Species Distribution of Tabanidae (Diptera) in Manitoba." Manitoba, 1962.

11236
Galloway, Terry Don. "Application of the Mermithid Nematode, Romanomermis culicivorax Ross and Smith, 1976, for Mosquito Control in Manitoba and Taxonomic Investigations in the Genus Romanomermis Coman, 1961." Manitoba, 1977.

11237
Handford, Richard H. "The Identification of Nymphal Melanopli in Manitoba and Adjacent Areas." Minnesota, 1939.

11238
Joia, Balbir Singh. "Insecticidal Efficacy and Residues of Cypermethrin and Fenvalerate in Stored Wheat." Manitoba, 1983.

11239
Kalpage, Kingsley Samuel Perera. "The Effect of Daylength and Temperature on the Induction and Termination of Diapause in Aedes atropalpus (Coquillett), and Field and Laboratory Studies of Autogeny and Hibernation in Some Mosquitoes from Manitoba." Manitoba, 1970.

11240
Neill, Garnet Bruce. "Bionomics of the Sunflower Beetle, Zygogramma exclamationis (F.) (Coleoptera: Chrysomelidae) and Its Parasites in Manitoba." Manitoba, 1982.

11241
Richardson, Howard Percival. "Some Vector Virus, Host-Plant Relationships of the Six-Spotted Leafhopper Macrosteles fascifrons (Stal) and Aster Yellows in Manitoba." Manitoba, 1966.

11242
Subasinghe, S.M. Chandrasiri. "Variation in the Effects of Host Plant on the Pea Aphid, Acyrthosiphon risum (Harris) (Homoptera: Aphididae)." Manitoba, 1983.

11243
Tauthong, Pensook. "The Biology and Systematics of Aedes campestris Dyar and Knab (Diptera: Culicidae) and Related Species in Manitoba and Saskatchewan." Manitoba, 1975.

11244
Taylor, Bruce Wayne. "The Effect of Photoperiod and Temperature on the Induction, Maintenance, and Termination of Embryonic Diapause in Aedes vexans (Meigen) (Diptera: Culicidae)." Manitoba, 1981.

11245
Ure, George Brian. "Systemic Insecticidal Control of the Aster Leafhopper (Macrosteles fascifrons Stal) and Aster Yellows in Carrots and Celery in Manitoba." Manitoba, 1981.

New Brunswick/Nouveau-Brunswick

Lewis, David James. See No./Voir no 11263

11246
Schaeffer, Paul William. "Population Ecology of the Browntail Moth (Euproctis chrysorrhola L.) (Lepidoptera: Lymantriidae) in North America." Maine, 1974.

Newfoundland/Terre-Neuve

Hudak, Janos. See No./Voir no 11734

11247
Milne, Louis Johnson. "Trichoptera of Continental America, North of Mexico." Harvard, 1936.

Arctic, Northwest Territories/ Arctique, Territoires du Nord–Ouest

11248
Addison, Janet Anne. "Ecology of Collembola at the High Arctic Site, Devon Island, Northwest Territories." Calgary, 1976.

11249
Behan, Valerie Mary. "Diversity, Distribution and Feeding Habits of North American Soil Acari." McGill, 1978.

11250
Brennan, James Marks. "The Pangoniinae (Tabinidae, Diptera) of Nearctic America." Kansas, 1933.

11251
Fisher, Elizabeth G. "A Comparative Study of the Male Terminalia of the Mycetophilidae of Nearctic America." Cornell, 1937.

11252
Kevan, Peter Graham. "High Arctic Insect-Flower Relations: The Interrelationships of Arthropods and Flowers at Lake Hazen, Ellesmere Island, N.W.T., Canada." Alberta, 1971.

11253
Mason, William R.M. "A Preliminary Revision of the Nearctic Cteniscini (Ichneumonidae)." Cornell, 1953.

11254
Oliver, Donald Raymond. "Arctic and Subarctic lakes, with Special Reference to the Chironomidae." McGill, 1961.

11255
Parsons, Carl Taylor. "A Revision of Nearctic Nitidulidae (Coleoptera)." Harvard, 1941.

11256
Proctor, Dennis Lester Coor. "Energy Flow Through Free-Living Soil Nematodes in High Arctic Terrestrial Communities." Alberta, 1979.

11257
Ryan, James Kenneth. "Energy Flow Through Arctic Invertebrates at Truelove Lowland, Devon Island, N.W.T., 75 Degrees 40'N 84 Degrees 40'W." Alberta, 1977.

11258
Schauff, Michael Eugene. "Revision of the Genera of the Holarctic Mymaridae (Hymenoptera: Chalcidoidea)." Maryland, 1982.

11259
Smith, Stephen Murray. "The Biting Flies of the Baker Lake Region, Northwest Territories (Diptera: Culicidae and Simuliidae)." Manitoba, 1970.

11260
Townes, Henry K., Jr. "The Nearctic Species of Paniscus (Hymenoptera, Ichneumonidae)." Cornell, 1937.

Nova Scotia/Nouvelle-Écosse

11261
Archibald, Kalman Dale. "Forest Aphidae (Aphididae of Nova Scotia." Ohio State, 1954.

11262
Embree, Douglas Gordon. "Studies on the Population Dynamics of the Winter Moth Operophtera brumata (L.) (Lepidoptera: Geometridae) in Nova Scotia. Ohio State, 1961.

Fisher, Elizabeth G. See No./Voir no 11251

11263
Lewis, David James. "The Biting Flies of the Nova Scotia-New Brunswick Border Region." Memorial University of Newfoundland, 1976.

11264
Neil, Kenneth. "Life History, Taxonomy and Host Plant Specificity of Some Nova Scotian Cutworm (Lepidoptera: Noctuidae) with Descriptions of the Larvae and Redescriptions of Some Adults. Dalhousie, 1981.

11265
Neilson, Murray Morris. "Pathogenicity and Host Relationships of a Cytoplasmic Polyhedrosis Virus Introduced Against the Winter Moth Operophtera brumata (L.) (Geometridae, Lepidoptera) in Nova Scotia." Minnesota, 1962.

Schaeffer, Paul William. See No./Voir no 11246

Ontario

11266
Abu, John Frank. "Integrated Control of the Alfalfa Weevil, Hypera postica (Glyllenhal) (Coleoptera Curculionidae) in Ontario." Guelph, 1976.

11267
Agha, Ikram Mohyuddia. "The Insect Complexes of Calystegia and Convolvulus: The Biology, Phenology Host Spectrum and Its Chemical Basis in Four Oligophagous Species Feeding on These in the Belleville, Ontario, Area." Queen's, 1977.

11268
Bailey, Clyde Gregory. "Population Dynamics, Bioenergetics and Feeding Biology of Melanophus bivittatus (Say) and Menoplus femurrubrum (Degeer) (Orthoptera Acrididae)." McGill, 1974.

Broadbent, Arnot Bruce. See No./Voir no 11355

11269
Cannon, Lester Robert Glen. "Studies on the Life Cycles and Ecology of Bunodera sacculata and B. Luciopercae (Trematoda: Allocreadiidae) from Algonquin Park." Toronto, 1970.

11270
Corkum, Lynda Dale. "A Comparative Study of Behaviour Relating to Differential Drift of Two Species of Mayflies." Toronto, 1976. [Life history studies at Forks of the Credit River, Peel County Études d'histoire biologique aux bifurcations de la rivière Credit, comté de Peel]

11271
Davies, Douglas Mackenzie. "The Ecology and Life History of Blackflies (Simuliidae, Diptera) in Ontario, with a Description of a New Species. Toronto, 1949.

11272
Fettes, James Joseph Francis Patrick. "Investigations of Sampling Techniques for Population Studies of the Spruce Budworm on Balsam Fir in Ontario." Toronto, 1951.

11273
Finnegan, Raymond Rene. "Ecological Studies of Hylobius radicis, Buch., Hylobius pales (Hbst.) and Pissodes approximatus, Hopk. (Coleoptera: Curculionidae) in Southern Ontario." British Columbia, 1959.

11274
Folsom, Todd Christopher. "Predation Ecology and Food Limitation of the Larval Dragonfly Anax junius (Aeshnidae)." Toronto, 1981. [Four sites near Mississauga/4 endroits près de Mississauga]

11275
Fuller, Randall Lynn. "Contributions to the Ecology of Some Species of Hydropsyche (Trichoptera: Hydropsychidae) in the Humber River, Ontario." Toronto, 1980.

11276
Gardiner, Lorne M. "Deterioration of Fire-Killed Pine by Wood-Boring Beetles (Coleoptera: Cerambycidae) in the Mississagi Region of Ontario." McGill, 1955.

11277
Harcourt, Douglas George. "The Biology and Ecology of the Diamondback Moth, Plutella maculipennis Curtis in Eastern Ontario." Cornell, 1954.

11278
Harper, Peter Paul. "Taxonomical and Ecological Studies on the Plecoptera of Ontario." Waterloo, 1971.

11279
Kinoshita, Garry Bing. "Biology and Control of Phyllotreta cruciferae (Goeze) (Coleoptera: Chrysomelidae) in Southwestern Ontario." Guelph, 1976.

11280
Latheef, Mohamed Abdul. "Population Dynamics of the Colorado Potato Beetle, Leptinotarsa decemlineata (Say) on Tomato in Eastern Ontario." Carleton, 1972.

11281
Lesage, Laurent. "Taxonomy and Ecology of Cricotopus Species from Salem Creek, Ontario (Diptera: Chironomidae)." Waterloo, 1979.

11282
Liu, Helen Jadwiga. "Biology and Some Aspects of Control of Blissus Leucopterus hirtus Montandon (Hemiptera: Lygaeidae) in Southern Ontario." Guelph, 1978.

11283
MacFarland, Roderick Peter. "Ecology of Bombinae (Hymenoptera: Apidae) of Southern Ontario, with Emphasis on Their Natural Enemies and Relationships with Flowers." Guelph, 1974.

11284
Madder, Douglas James. "Biological Studies on Culex pipiens L. and Culex restuans Theo. (Diptera: Culicidae) in in Southern Ontario." Guelph, 1981.

11285
Pengelly, David Harvey. "The Biology of Bees of the Genus Megachile with Special Reference to Their Importance in Alfalfa Seed Production in Southern Ontario." Cornell, 1955.

11286
Phillips, John Henry H. "A Study of the Life History and Ecology of Pulvinariavitis (L.) (Hemiptera: Coccoidea), the Cottony Scale Attacking Peach in Ontario." McGill, 1960.

11287
Rossignol, Philippe Albert. "Studies on the Bionomics Behaviour, Sensory Apparatus and Larval Head Capsule of Eucorethra underwood Underwood (Diptera: Chaoboridae)." Toronto, 1978. [Algonquin Provincial Park/Parc provincial Algonquin]

11288
Shehata, Shehata Mohamed. "Some Anatomical and Physiological Responses in Queen Honeybees (Apis mellifera L.) to Season and to Long-Term Solitary Confinement." Guelph, 1979.

11289
Sippell, William Lloyd. "A Study of the Forest Tent Caterpillar, Malacasoma disstria H.B.N., and Its Parasite Complex in Ontario." Michigan, 1957.

11290
Smereka, Edward Peter. "The Life History and Ecology of Energia decolor Walker (Lepidoptera: Noctuidae) in Northwestern Ontario." Minnesota, 1970.

11291
Smith, Ian Michael. "A Study of the Systematics of the Water Mite Family Pionidae (Acari: Parasitengona)." Toronto, 1974.

11292
Spence, John Andrew. "The Life Cycles, Larval Behaviour and Ecology of Some Chironomidae." Waterloo, 1971.

11293
Sprules, William Memberg. "Factors Affecting the Distribution of Aquatic Insects in the Madawaska River System, Ontario." Toronto, 1942.

11294
Steenburgh, William Elgin. "Laboratory and Field Observations on Trichogramma minutum Riley with Special Reference to the Oriental Fruit Moth, (Laspeyresia molesta Busch) in Ontario." Toronto, 1931.

11295
Taylor, Robert Gordon. "Population Dynamics of the Asparagus Beetle, Crioceris asparagi L. (Coleoptera: Chrysomelidae)." Carleton, 1979.

11296
Teskey, Herbert Joseph. "The Larvae and Pupae of Some Eastern North American Tabinidae (Diptera)." Cornell, 1968.

11297
Trottier, Robert. "Effect of Temperature and Humidity on the Emergence and Ecdysis of Anax junius Drury (Odonata: Aeshnidae)." Toronto, 1970.

11298
Tyler, Barrington Michael John. "The Northern Corn Rootworm, Diabrotica longicornis (Say) (Coleoptera: Chrysomelidae), and Other Selected Arthropods in Their Tillage Systems in Ontario." Guelph, 1979.

11299

Urquhart, Frederick Albert. "I. An Ecological Study of the Orthoptera of Point Pelee, Ontario. II. The Orthoptera of Essex County, Ontario." Toronto, 1941.

11300

Wyphema, Ronald Conrad Peter. "The Role of Avian Predators in the Control of Spruce Budworm at Endemic Levels." Queen's, 1982.

Quebec/Québec

11301

Alleyne, Eslie Herman. "Biology, Importance and Control of Pemphigus bursarius (L.) Gall Forming Species." McGill, 1975.

11302

Ba-Angood, Saeed Abdulla Saeed. "Experimental Studies on Occurrence of Cereal Aphids and Resulting Damage to Small Grain Crops in Southwestern Quebec." McGill, 1980.

Bensink, Angela Helen Arthington. See No./Voir no 11117

11303

Boivin, Guy. "Bionomics of Five Species of Phytophagous mirids (Hemiptera: Miridae) in an Apple Orchard in Southwestern Quebec." McGill, 1981.

11304

Bousquet, Yves. "Morphologie et cycle vital des espèces du genre Pterostichus (Coleoptera Carabidae: Pterostichini) du Québec." Montréal, 1982.

Cameron, Peter James. See No./Voir no 346

11305

Chan, Kai-Lok. "Systematics of the Forcipomyiinal (Diptera: Ceratopoginidae) with Ecology of Certain Quebec Forms." McGill, 1965.

11306

Cheng, Hsien-Hua. "Population Dynamics of the Birch Leaf Miner, Fenusa pusilla (Lepeletier) on the Blue Birch, Betula caerulea grandis Blanchard, in Quebec." McGill, 1969.

11307

Dominique, Cyril Ray Michael. "Bionomics of the Northern Corn Rootworm Diabrotica longicornis (Say) (Coleoptera: Chrysomelidae) in Southern Quebec." McGill, 1983.

11308

Duranthon-Gautheron, Françoise. "Notes écologiques sur les trichoptères de la station de biologie de Saint-Hippolyte (Comté de Terrebonne, Québec)." Montréal, 1971.

11309

Dyck, Victor Arnold. "The Microclimate in Relation to the Development and Behavior of a Population of Melanoplus femurrubrum (Degeer) (Orthoptera: Acrididae)." McGill, 1970.

11310

Earnshaw, Alice Petronilla Russell. "The Ecology Distribution and Dispersion of Agelenopsis utahana (Chamberlin and Ivie), 1933, and Agelenopsis potteri (Blackwall) 1846, in the Morgan Arboretum of Macdonald College, Province of Quebec." McGill, 1973.

11311

Emberson, Rowan Mark. "The Mesostigmata o Certain Coniferous Forest Soils in Western Quebec with a Preliminary Account of the North America Rhodacaridae (Acarina)." McGill, 1968.

11312

Gibbs, K. Elizabeth. "Observations on the Biology an Seasonal Distribution of Some Ephemeroptera in Stream System at Rigaud, Quebec." McGill, 1971.

11313

Guèvremont, Hélène. "Recherche sur la biologie et l dynamique des populations naturelles de Coleo phora fuscedinella Zell. (Lepidoptera: Coloeo phonidae) dans la région de Sherbrooke, Québec. Sherbrooke, 1975.

11314

Hill, John Richard. "Studies to Evaluate the Influenc of Forest Cover Type and Other Factors on th Presence and Populations of Oribatid Mites. McGill, 1976. [Morgan Arboretum, Macdonal College/Arboretum Morgan, Collège Macdonald]

11315

Journet, Alan R.P. "Systematic Study of the Genu Craspedolepta Enderlein, 1921 (Homoptera: Psyl lidae) in North America." McGill, 1974.

11316

Kwan, Wan Hing. "Culicoides Spp. (Diptera: Cerato pogonidae) at Lac Serpent, Quebec, with Emphasi on the Larval Habitats and Numbers of C. Sangui suga (Coquillett) and C. Obsoletus (Meigen). McGill, 1972.

11317

LeBlanc, Jean-Pierre R. "Trapping and Monitoring Techniques for Plum Curculio, Conotrachelus nenu phar (Herbst) (Coleoptera: Curculionidae) in Southwestern Quebec Apple Orchard." McGill, 1982.

11318

Lim, Kiok-Puan. "Bionomics of the Common June Beetle Phyllophaga anxia (Leconte) (Coleoptera Scarabaeidae), with Particular Reference to Distribution, Life History and Natural Enemies in Southern Quebec." McGill, 1979.

11319

Lyons, Leslie Allan. "Population Studies on Neodiprion swainei Middleton (Hymenoptera: Diprionidae) in Quebec." Minnesota, 1960.

11320

MacKay, Rosemary Joan. "The Life Cycle and Ecology of Pycnopsyche gentilis (McLachlan), Pycnopsyche Luculenta (Betten) and Pycnopsyche Scabripennis (Rambur) (Trichoptera: Limnephilidae) in West Creek, Mont St. Hilaire, Quebec." McGill, 1972.

11321

Madrid, Francisco Javier. "Laboratory and Field Studies of Lymantria dispar L. (Lepidoptera: Lymantridae) in Quebec." McGill, 1979.

11322

Manuel, Raymond Lewis. "A Study of the Chrysopids (Neuroptera: Chrysopidae) in Two Old Fields in Quebec." McGill, 1982.

11323

Marshall, Valin George K. "Studies on the Micro-Arthropod Fauna of Two Quebec Woodland Humus Forms." McGill, 1965.

1324
Matin, Abdul Mohammad. "Development and Application of Population Sampling Methods for the Stages of Northern Corn Rootworm, Diabrotica longicornis (Say) (Coleoptera: Chrysomedidae) in Quebec Corn Fields." McGill, 1983.

1325
McLeod, John Malcolm. "The Bionomics of the Spruce Needleminer in Quebec, Evagora pecealla (KFT) (Lepidoptera: Gelechiidae)." Syracuse, 1961.

1326
Mukerji, Mukul Kumar. "A Laboratory Study of the Biology and Energetics of a Quebec Strain of the Predator Podisus maculiventris (Say) (Hemiptera: Pentatomidae)." McGill, 1965.

1327
Pottinger, Robert Peter. "The Biology and Dynamics of Lithocolletis blancardella Fabr. on Apple in Quebec." McGill, 1965.

1328
Pucat, Amalia Margaret. "Bionomics of Some Ceratopogonidae at Lac Serpent, Quebec." McGill, 1974.

1329
Ritchot, Claude. "Biologie et répression des larves des racines, Hylemyia spp. infestant les cultures de crucifères." McGill, 1968.

Saad, Randa-Pierre. See No./Voir no 10755

1330
Samarasinghe, Srimathie. "The Biology and Dynamics of the Oystershell Scale, Lepidosaphes ulmi (Lepeltier) (Homoptera: Coccidae) on Apple in Quebec." McGill, 1965.

1331
Smith, Thomas Donald." The Effects of Six Insecticides on Non-Target Soil Mesoarthropods from Pasture on Ste. Rosalie Clay Loam, St. Clet, Quebec." McGill, 1979.

1332
Wallace, Ronald Richard. "The Effects of Methoxychlor (1, 1, 1-Trichloro-2, 2-Bis (P.-Methoxy - phenyl Ethane) on, and the Accumulation of Methoxychlor in, Some Insects of Running Waters." Waterloo, 1974.

Saskatchewan

11333
Arnason, Arni P. "Arthropod Populations of the Vegetation of Wheatland and Native Grassland at Saskatoon, Saskatchewan." Illinois, 1942.

Olfert, Owen Orton. See No./Voir no 170

11334
Paul, Lorne C. "Appraisal of Grasshopper Control Methods in Saskatchewan." Iowa State, 1940.

11335
Singh, Noreen. "Energy Dynamics and Feeding Ecology of Two Grasshopper Populations in a Grassland Ecosystem." Regina, 1972.

11336
Swanson, Stella Marie. "Ecology and Production of Macrobenthos of Waldsea Lake, Saskatchewan, with Emphasis on Cricotopus ornatus (Diptera: Chironomidae)." Saskatchewan, 1978.

Tauthong, Pensook. See No./Voir no 11243

This is an extremely small section with a total of 27 titles. Twenty-five studies came from ten Canadian universities. McGill University is the leading contributor with seven titles, followed by Guelph and Toronto with four each. The ten remaining titles are divided among seven universities. Only one thesis was accepted by an American university, Ohio State in 1947, and one by a British University, Cambridge in 1976.

––––––––––

C'est une section très modeste avec un total de 27 thèses. Vingt-cinq études viennent de 10 universités canadiennes; l'Université McGill est en tête de production avec sept titres, suivie par celles de Guelph et de Toronto avec chacune quatre titres. Sept autres universités se partagent les dix autres thèses. L'Université d'Ohio State est la seule université américaine à avoir accepté une thèse à ce sujet, en 1947. L'Université de Cambridge, en Grande-Bretagne, a accepté une thèse en 1976.

General Items/Ouvrages généraux

Addison, Edward M. See No./Voir no 10534

11337
Fleming, Lesley Carolyn. "On the Biology of Turbellaria Associated with the Queen Crab, Chionoecetes opilio (O. Fabricius)." New Brunswick, 1979.

11338
Gibbs, Harold Cuthbert. "Studies on Dochmoides stenocephala (Railliet, 1884), the Northern Carnivore Hookworm." McGill, 1958.

11339
Kennedy, Murray James. "Geographic and Host-Induced Variations of Haematoloechus buttensis and a Re-Evaluation of Representatives of the Genus in Canada and the United States." British Columbia, 1978.

11340
Mace, Thomas Francis Andrew. "Studies on the Biology of the Giant Kidney Worm, Dioctophyma renale (Goeze, 1782) (Nematoda: Dioctophymoidea)." Guelph, 1975.

11341
McDonald, Howard. "The Biology and Control of Heliothis onomis, Schiff, an Important New Pest of Flax in Western Canada." Ohio State, 1947.

11342
Mommik, Salme. "Seriological Tests in Canadian Hydatid Disease." McGill, 1958.

11343
Morris, Simon Conway. "Worms of the Burgess Shale, Middle Cambrian, Canada." Cambridge, 1976.

11344
Scott, David M. "The Life History and Ecology of the Cod-Worms Porrocaecum decipiens (Krabbe, 1878), in Canadian Atlantic Waters." McGill, 1950.

11345
Swales, William E. "The Life Cycle of Fascioloides magna (Bassi, 1875) Ward, 1917, in Canada, with Observations upon the Histopathology of Fascioloidiasis magna and Its Bearing on the Occurrence of the Disease in North America." McGill, 1935.

Alberta

11346
Anthony, Desmond Darrington. "Taxonomy and Ecology of Diphyllobothrium in Alberta and British Columbia." Alberta, 1967.
11347
Dash, Madhab Chandra. "Ecology of Enchytraeidae (Oligochaeta) in Rocky Mountain Forest Soil (Kananaskis Region, Alberta, Canada)." Calgary, 1970.
11348
Denny, Michael. "Taxonomy and Seasonal Dynamics of Helminths in Gammarus lacustris in Cooking Lake, Alberta." Alberta, 1967.
11349
Wrona, Frederick John. "The Influence of Biotic and Abiotic Parameters on the Distribution and Abundance of Two Sympatric Species of Hirudinoidea." Calgary, 1982.

Arctic/Arctique

Bilyard, Gordon Richard. See No./Voir no 11835

British Columbia/Colombie-Britannique

Anthony, Desmond Darrington. See No./Voir no 11346
Gibson, George Gordon. See No./Voir no 10845
McFarland, Samuel H. See No./Voir no 10958

Maritimes Provinces/Provinces maritimes

11350
Wolfgang, Robert W. "Stephanostomum histrix (Dug. 1845) Taxonomy, Morphology and Biology of the Adult and Metacercaria with Notes on Distribution." McGill, 1952.

New Brunswick/Nouveau-Brunswick

11351
McLaughlin, John Daniel. "Helminth Studies on New Brunswick Waterfowl." New Brunswick, 1970.

Nova Scotia/Nouvelle-Écosse

11352
Davis, Derek Sidney. "Effects of Infection by Digenetic Trematodes on the Gastropod Littorena saxatiles (Olive) in Nova Scotia." Dalhousie, 1972.

Northwest Territories/Territoires du Nord-Ouest

11353
Newbury, Thomas K. "Adaptations of Chaetognaths to Subarctic Conditions." McGill, 1971.

Ontario

11354
Boddington, Martin John. "Dugesia polychroa (Turbellaria: Tricladida): A Contribution to Its Comparative Ecology." Toronto, 1974.
11355
Broadbent, Arnot Bruce. "Assessment of a Litterbag Technique for Studying the Decomposition of Leaf Litter and the Effects of Carbofuran on Non Target Soil Invertebrates." Guelph, 1980.
Cannon, Lester Robert Glen. See No./Voir no 11269
11356
Crichton, Vincent Frederick Joseph. "The Biology of Dracunculus spp. (Dracunculoidea: Dracunculidae) in Wildlife from Ontario." Guelph, 1972.
11357
Fischer, Hartwig. "Studies on the Life Cycles and Ecology of Proteocephalus ambloplitis, P. fluviatilis and P. pearsei (Cestoda) from Lake Opeongo Algonquin Park." Toronto, 1972.
11358
Miller, Richard Birnie. "The Ecology of the Chironomidae of Costello Lake, Ontario, with a Note on Corethra (Chaoborus) punctipennis." Toronto 1939.
11359
Stockdale, Peter Howard Gough. "Migration Pattern and Development of Metastrongyloids in Carnivores." Guelph, 1969.
11360
Wu, Liang-Yu. "Life History Studies on Three Genera of Trematodes Found in the Ottawa River." McGill, 1952.

Prairie Provinces/Provinces des Prairies

General Item/Ouvrage général

Eidt, Douglas Conrad. See No./Voir no 11138

Manitoba

Olchowecki, Oleksa Alexander. See No./Voir no 10526

BOTANY/BOTANIQUE

Botany is another sizeable section with over 200 titles from Canadian universities, and almost 100 from American universities. The Canadian list follows the pattern of large growth during the 1970's. The American list, also grew during the 1970's. Harvard University has the distinction of producing the first dissertation on Canadian botany in 1917. Of the 2 Canadian universities contributing to this field, British Columbia is first with over 50 titles. Toronto is second with half that number and the universities of Saskatchewan, Alberta, Manitoba, and Western Ontario follow in descending order. Examination of the output from American universities does not reveal an outstanding contributor. The schools of Harvard Michigan, Ohio State, and Wisconsin are equal leaders.

La botanique est une autre section importante avec plus de 200 thèses produites dans les universités canadiennes et presque 100 dans les universités américaines. La production canadienne a suivi la courbe ascensionnelle des années 1970. La courbe américaine s'est également améliorée dans les années 1970. L'Université Harvard s'est distinguée en produisant la première thèse en botanique canadienne en 1917. Des 22 universités canadiennes qui ont travaillé en ce domaine, la Colombie-Britannique arrive première avec plus de 50 thèses. Toronto est seconde avec la moitié de ce nombre puis, les universités de la Saskatchewan, de l'Alberta, du Manitoba et Western Ontario suivent dans l'ordre. Quant aux universités américaines, aucune ne se distingue particulièrement; Harvard, Michigan, Ohio State et Wisconsin, toutes sur le même plan, se classent en tête des autres universités.

General Items/Ouvrages généraux

11361
Arekal, Govindappa Dasappa. "Embryology of Canadian Scrophulariaceae." Toronto, 1962.

11362
Atherton, Lorraine G. "Studies of the Fungal Spore Population of a Permanent Pasture and the Adjacent Air." Dalhousie, 1979.

11363
Balbach, Harold Edward. "Variation and Speciation in Populations of Apocynum in North America." Illinois, 1965.

11364
Barnes, William J. "The Autecology of the Lonicera X bella Complex." Wisconsin, 1972.

11365
Bell, Katherine Lapsley. "Autecology of Kobresia bellardii: Why Winter Snow Accumulation Patterns Affect Local Distribution." Alberta, 1974.

11366
Bellis, Vincent Jerome. "An Ecological Study of Cladophora glamerata." Western Ontario, 1966.

11367
Best, Charles Alexander. "Studies in the Eastern North America Native Lilium Species." Toronto, 1962.

11368
Bhatti, Waqar Hamid. "Histological Studies with Histological Key of the Species of the Genus Salvia of Northeastern United States and Adjacent Canada." Philadelphia College of Pharmacy and Science, 1965.

11369
Britt, Robert Franklin. "A Revision of the Genus Hypoxis in the United States and Canada." North Carolina, 1967.

11370
Carr, Robert Leroy. "A Taxonomic Study in the Genus Hackelia in Western North America." Oregon State, 1974.

11371
Castle, Hempstead. "A Revision of the Species of Radula of the United States and Canada." Yale, 1926.

11372
Coupland, Robert T. "Ecology of Mixed Prairie in Canada." Nebraska, 1949.

11373
Dale, Hugh Munro. "Experimental Studies on the Morphological Development of Elodea canadensis Michx." Toronto, 1956.

11374
Dawson, John Ernest. "A Biosystematic Study of Section Rumex in Canada and the United States." Carleton, 1979.

11375
Dibben, Martyn James. "The Chemasystematics of the Lichen Genus Pertusaria in North America, North of Mexico." Duke, 1975.

11376
Fulford, Margaret Hannah. "The Genus Bazazania in the United States and Canada." Yale, 1935.

11377
Gale, Shirley. "Rhynchospora Section Eurhynchospora in Canada, United States and the West Indies." Radcliffe, 1941.

11378
Gill, Lachman Singh. "A Biosystematic Survey of the Canadian Labiatae." Waterloo, 1971.

11379
Gilliam, Martina Dickson Smith. "Taxonomy and Biology of Marasmius (Tricholomataceae, Agaricales, Basidiomycetes) in the Northeastern United States and the Adjacent Part of Canada." Michigan, 1973.

11380
Glennie, Charles William. "A Comparative Phytochemical Study of the Caprifoliaceae." British Columbia, 1970.

11381
Hoch, Peter Coonan. "Systematics and Evolution of the Epilobium ciliatum Complex in North America (Onagraceae)." Washington, St. Louis, 1978.

11382
Hume, Lawrence Pierson Wilson. "Variation Among Populations of the Widespread Perennial Weed, Rumex crispus L." Western Ontario, 1979. [Ontario to Nova Scotia/De l'Ontario à la Nouvelle-Écosse]

11383
Imshaug, Henry Andrew. "The Lichen-Forming Species of the Genus Buellia Occurring in the United States and Canada." Michigan, 1951.

11384
Kam, Yee Kiew. "Comparative Developmental Studies of the Floret and Embryo Sac in Five Species of Oryzopsis (Gramineae)." British Columbia, 1973.

11385
LeClerc-Chevalier, Denise. "Contribution à l'étude biologique comparative des alcaloïdes et des formes galéniques de l'Hydrastis canadensis L." Montréal, 1966.

11386
Luck-Allen, Etta Robena. "Taxonomic and Cultural Studies of the Genus Sebacina." Toronto, 1958. [British Columbia, Ontario and Quebec/Colombie-Britannique, Ontario et Québec]

11387
MacDonald, Marilyn Anne. "Effects of Environmental Heterogeneity on the Abundance of Barbarea vulgaris R.Bh." Western Ontario, 1977.
11388
Meyer, Hans K. "Inheritance of Lipoxidase Activity and Stem Solidness in Stewart Golden Bull Durham Wheat." Manitoba, 1963.
Middleton, John David. See No./Voir no 11645
11389
Milstead, Wayne Lavine. "A Revision of the North American Species of Prenanthes." Purdue, 1964.
11390
Parmelee, John Aubrey. "Life History of Studies in the Uredinales." Toronto, 1961.
11391
Peterson, Wilbur. "A Revision of the Genera Dicranum and Orthodicranum (Musci) in North America North of Mexico." Alberta, 1979.
11392
Redhead, Scott Alan. "A Study of the Sphagnicolous Fleshy Basidiomycetes in the Eastern Sections of the Canadian Boreal Forest." Toronto, 1979.
11393
Reznicek, Anton Albert. "The Taxonomy of the Stellulatae Group of Carex in North America." Toronto, 1978.
11394
Robitaille, Gilles. "The Effect of Copper Smelter Effluents on Vegetation." Ottawa, 1978.
11395
Routledge, Richard Donovan. "The Zonation of Vascular Plants in Salt Marshes." Dalhousie, 1975.
11396
Scott, Peter John. "A Taxonomic Study of Some Species of Ranunculus L." Memorial University of Newfoundland, 1973.
11397
Southall, Russell Melvin. "A Taxonomic Revision of Kalmia (Ericaceae)." North Carolina State, 1973.
11398
Stocking, Kenneth M. "Some Taxonomic and Ecological Considerations of Marah, Echinopepon and Echinocystis in Canada, the United States and Northern Mexico." Southern California, 1950.
11399
Stuckey, Ronald Lewis. "The Taxonomy and Distribution of the Genus Rorippa (Cruciferae) in North America." Michigan, 1965.
11400
Taylor, Andrew Ronald Argo. "A Developmental Study of Zostera marina L." Toronto, 1955.
11401
Vander Kloet, Samuel P. "The North American Blueberries Revisited: A Taxonomic Study of Vaccinium Section Cyanococcus Gray." Queen's, 1972.
11402
Vitt, Dale Hadley. "The Family Orthotrichaceae (Musci) in North America, North of Mexico." Michigan, 1970.
11403
Warrington, Patrick Douglas. "The Natural History and Parasitism of Geocanlon lividium (Santalaceae)." British Columbia, 1970.

11404
Webster, Terry Richard. "Morphology and Development of the Root in Several Species of Selaginel Spring." Saskatchewan, 1965.
Willms, Walter David. See No./Voir no 10628
11405
Wilson, Doreen Edith. "A Study of Eight Nort American Species of Coryne." Toronto, 1962.
11406
Wilton, Arthur C. "Cytologic, Morphological ar Agronomic Aspects of the Boreal North America Bromopsis and Closely Related Taxa." Manitob 1965.
11407
Wood, Benjamin William. "Response of Canada Mil vetch [Astragaius canadensis var. Morton (Nutt.wats)] to Range and Forest Improvemer Practices in Northwestern Oregon." Oregon Stat 1971.
11408
Zales, William Milton. "A Taxomic Revision of th Genus Philonotis for North America, North Mexico." British Columbia, 1973.

Central Canada/Centre du Canada

11409
Bird, Ralph Durham. "Biotic Communities of th Aspen Parkland of Central Canada." Illinois, 1929

Eastern Canada/Est du Canada

11410
Doré, William G. "Pasture Associations of Easter Canada." Ohio State, 1948.
11411
Ellis, William Haynes. "Revision of Section Rubia Acer in Eastern North America Excluding Ace saccharinum L." Tennessee, 1963.
11412
Greene, Craig William. "The Systematics of Calam gostis (Gramineae) in Eastern North America Harvard, 1980.
11413
Haber, Erich. "A Biosystemic Study of the Easter North American Species of the Genus Pyrola Toronto, 1972.
Herrick, James William. See No./Voir no 647
11414
Kott, Laima S. "The Taxonomy and Biology of th Genus Isoetes L. in Northeastern North America Guelph, 1980.
11415
Madore, M. Rose Bernadette. "An Ecological Study the Genus Carex in Eastern Sub-Arctic Canada Catholic, 1951.
11416
Marcks, Brian Gene. "Population Studies in Nor American Cyperus Section Laxiglumi (Cyper ceae)." Wisconsin, 1972.
11417
Muhle, Herman. "Bryophyte and Lichen Succession Decaying Logs in Eastern Canada." Ottawa, 1973.

11418
Punugu, Adilakshmamma. "Coprophilous ascomycetes from Eastern Canada." Toronto, 1972.

11419
Roberts, Marvin Lee. "Systematic Studies of North American Bidens Section Bidens (Compositae)." Ohio State, 1982. [St. Lawrence River Estuary/Estuaire du fleuve Saint-Laurent]

11420
Taylor, Ronald Maxwell. "Studies of the Littoral Lichens of Northeastern North America." Michigan State, 1974.

11421
Whittick, Alan. "The Taxonomy, Life History and Ecology of Some Species of the Ceramiceae (Rhodophyta) in the North-West Atlantic." Memorial University of Newfoundland, 1973.

Southern Canada/Sud du Canada

11422
Marsh, Vernon L. "A Taxonomic Revision of the Genus Poa of United States and Southern Canada." Washington, Seattle, 1951.

Western Canada/Ouest du Canada

11423
Bagnell, Charles Robert. "Pollen Morphology of Abies Picea and Pinus Species of the U.S. Pacific Northwest Using Scanning Electron Microscopy." Washington State, 1974. [Western Canada/Ouest du Canada]

11424
Dugle, Janet Mary Rogge. "A Taxonomic Study of Western Canadian Species in the Genus Betula." Alberta, 1965.

McDonald, Howard. See No./Voir no 11341

Norris, Arnold Willy. See No./Voir no 6521

Packer, J.G. See No./Voir no 11550

11425
Rhoades, Frederick M. "Growth, Production, Litterfall and Structure in Populations of the Lichen Lobaria oregana (Tuck.) Mull. Arg. in Canopies of Old-Growth Douglas Fir." Oregon, 1978.

Great Lakes/Grands Lacs

11426
Ovrebo, Clark Ledin. "A Taxonomic Study of the Genus Tricholoma (Agaricales) in the Great Lakes Region." Toronto, 1981.

11427
Parker, Robert Davis Richard. "Observations on the Ecology of the Ulothrix zonata Community in Western Lake Superior." Minnesota, 1975.

Gulf of St. Lawrence/Golfe Saint-Laurent

Chen, Lawrence Chien-Ming. See No./Voir no 11524

Alberta

11428
Akhlaq, Sheikh Mohammad. "Microbial Activity in Aspen Soil of the Kananaskis Woodland Area (Alberta, Canada), with Particular Reference to Cellulose Decomposition." Calgary, 1973.

11429
Baig, Mirza Naeem. "Ecology of the Timberline Vegetation in the Rocky Mountains of Alberta." Calgary, 1972.

11430
Bissett, John Douglas. "Ecology of Fungi Occurring in Soils Along an Alpine Ridge." Calgary, 1975. [Mount Allen/Mont Allen]

11431
Busby, John Robert. "Energy and Water Relations of Some Boreal Forest Mosses." Alberta, 1976.

11432
Case, James William. "Epiphytic Lichens as Biological Monitors of Air Pollution in West-Central Alberta." Calgary, 1978.

11433
Chinnappa, Chendanda Chengappa. "A Biosystematic Study of the Stellaria longipes Complex (Caryophyllaceae)." Waterloo, 1973. [Lake Athabaska/Lac Athabaska]

11434
Cormack, Melville Wallace. "The Relation of Cylindrocarpon and Fusarium to Rootrot and Winter-Killing of Alfalfa and Sweet Clover in Alberta." Minnesota, 1936.

11435
Hettinger, Loren Robert. "The Vegetation of the Vine Creek Drainage Basin, Jasper National Park." Alberta, 1975.

11436
Hoffs, Gordon A. "The Role of Bees in Pollinating Alfalfa in Southern Alberta." Oregon State, 1952.

11437
Kalgutkar, Ramakant Mukundrao. "Ecological Studies of Corticolous Lichens in Southwestern Alberta." Calgary, 1973.

11438
Kuchar, Peter. "Alpine Tundra Communities and Dryas octopetala S.S.P. Hookeriana in the Bald Hills, Jasper National Park." Alberta, 1975.

11439
Legge, Allan Herbert. "The Gene-Ecology of Crepis nana (Richardson) and Crepis elegans (Hooker) in Arctic and Alpine, North America." Oregon State, 1971.

Lieffers, Victor James. See No./Voir no 11513

11440
Raup, Hugh Miller. "A Survey of the Vegetation of Shelter Point, Athabasca Lake." Pittsburgh, 1928.

Scott, Peter John. See No./Voir no 11396

11441
Shaw, Robert Keith. "A Taxonomic and Ecologic Study of the River-Bottom Forest on St. Mary River, Lee Creek and Belly River in Southwest Alberta, Canada." Brigham Young, 1974.

11442
Stringer, Paul William. "An Ecological Study of Grasslands at Low Elevations in Banff, Jasper and Waterton Lakes National Parks." Alberta, 1970.

11443
Swailes, George Edward. "Ecology of the Cabbage Root Maggot Hylemya brassicae (Bouche) in Southern Alberta." Iowa State, 1956.
11444
Tan, Wai Koon Lau. "Genotype-Environment Interaction, Stability and Combining Ability in Smooth Bromegrass." Alberta, 1978.
11445
Walker, David G. "The Genetic Potential of Native Alberta Grasses." Alberta, 1979.
11446
Wildman, Howard Geoffrey. "The Mycoflora of Living Populus tremuloides Michx. Leaves." Calgary, 1979. [Kananaskis Valley/Vallée Kananaskis]
11447
Winner, William Eugene. "The Ecological and Physiological Impact of Sulfur-Dioxide Pollution on Plants, Particularly Mosses." Calgary, 1978. [West-Central Alberta/Centre-ouest de l'Alberta]
11448
Wylie, Mary Eileen. "The Lichen Genus Ramalina (Ramalinaceae) in Alberta, Saskatchewan and Manitoba." Calgary, 1977.

British Columbia/Colombie-Britannique

11449
Anderson, James Hugh. "A Geobotanical Study in the Atlin Region in Northwestern British Columbia and South Central Yukon Territory." Alaska, 1970.
11450
Annas, Richard Morris. "Boreal Ecosystems of the Fort Nelson Area of Northeastern British Columbia." British Columbia, 1977.
11451
Beil, Charles Edward. "The Plant Associations of the Cariboo-Aspen-Lodgepole Pine-Douglas Fir Parkland Zone." British Columbia, 1970.
11452
Booth, James Thomas. "Taxonomic and Ecologic Aspects of Zoosporic Fungi in Coastal and Steppe Soils." British Columbia, 1971.
11453
Bourne, Victor Laurence. "Fine Structural Studies on Some Marine Algae from the Pacific Coast of British Columbia and Washington." British Columbia, 1971.
11454
Brooke, Robert Charles. "Vegetation Environment Relationships of Sub-Alpine Mountain Hemlock Zone Ecosystems." British Columbia, 1966.
11455
Buchanan, Ronald James. "A Study of the Species Composition and Ecology of the Protoplankton of a British Columbia Inlet." British Columbia, 1966.
11456
Buttrick, Steven Colby. "The Alpine Vegetation Ecology and Remote Sensing of Teresa Island, British Columbia." British Columbia, 1978.
11457
Céska, Adolf. "Vegetation Classification: I. A Computer Method for Handling Vegetation Data. II. Wetland Plant Communities in the Wet Douglas Fir Subzone of Vancouver Island." Victoria, 1978.

11458
Chang, Yola Chiou-Yueh. "Hyphomycetes from Sediments of Marion Lake, British Columbia." British Columbia, 1975.
Darker, Grant Dooks. See No./Voir no 11568
11459
Druehl, Louis Dix. "On the Taxonomy, Distribution and Ecology of the Brown Algal Genus Laminaria in the Northeast Pacific." British Columbia, 1965.
11460
Drumke, John S. "A Systematic Survey of Corylus in North America." Tennessee, 1964.
11461
Dunn, Michael Thomas. "Hyphomycetes Decaying the Litter of Thuja plicata Donn." British Columbia, 1981.
11462
Eady, Karen. "Ecology of the Alpine and Timberline Vegetation of Big White Mountain, British Columbia." British Columbia, 1971.
11463
Eis, Slavoj. "Statistical Analysis of Tree Growth and Some Environmental Factors of Plant Communities in a Selected Area of the Coastal Western Hemlock Zone." British Columbia, 1962.
11464
Errington, John Charles. "Natural Revegetation of Disturbed Sites in British Columbia." British Columbia, 1975.
11465
Fraser, Bruce Erland Clyde. "Vegetation Development on Recent Alpine Glacier Forelands in Garibaldi Park, British Columbia." British Columbia, 1970.
11466
Funk, Alvin. "Studies in the Genus Caliciopsis." Toronto, 1962.
11467
Gilmartin, Malvern. "The Primary Production of British Columbia Fjord." British Columbia, 1960.
11468
Godfrey, Judith Louise Dean. "The Hepaticae and Anthocertae of Southwestern British Columbia." British Columbia, 1977.
11469
Gornall, Richard John. "Generic Limits and Systematics of Boykinia and Allies (Saxifragaceae)." British Columbia, 1981.
11470
Hanic, Louis Anthony. "Life History Studies of Urospora and Codiolum from Southern British Columbia." British Columbia, 1965.
11471
Hsiao, Stephen I-Chao. "Nutritional Requirements for Gametogenesis in Laminaria saccharina (L.) Lamouroux." Simon Fraser, 1972.
Keller, Rodney Alan. See No./Voir no 11691
11472
Kojima, Satoru. "Phytogeocoenoses of the Coastal Western Hemlock Zone in Strathcona National Park, British Columbia, Canada." British Columbia, 1972.

11473

Krueger, Kenneth William. "Comparative Photosynthesis and Respiration Rates of Douglas Fir Seedlings from Vancouver Island and Montana Under Various Conditions of Light and Temperature." Oregon State, 1963.

11474

Lang, Frank Alexander. "A Cytotaxonomic Study of the Polypodium vulgare Complex in Northwestern North America." British Columbia, 1965.

11475

Lee, Robert Kui-Sung. "Development of Marine Benthic Algal Communities on Juan de Fuca Strait, British Columbia." British Columbia, 1966.

Leggett, Mary Elizabeth. See No./Voir no 321

11476

Lister, Geoffrey Richard. "Observations on the Growth and Physiology of Pinus strobus L. Seedlings Grown Under Various Conditions of Soil Moisture and Nitrogen and Phosphorus Nutrition." Simon Fraser, 1968.

11477

Markham, James Wilbur. "An Ecological Study of Lamanaria sinclairii and L. Longipes." British Columbia, 1969.

Mathewes, Rolf Winter. See No./Voir no 6526

11478

Mathieson, Arthur Curtis. "Contributions to the Life History and Ecology of the Marine Brown Alga Phaeostrophion irregulare (S. et G.) on the Pacific Coast of North America." British Columbia, 1965. [Glacier Point, British Columbia/Colombie-Britannique]

11479

McAvoy, Blanche. "Ecological Survey of the Bella Coola Region." Chicago, 1930.

11480

McBride, Douglas Leonard. "Studies on Some British Columbian Representatives of the Erythropeltidacea (Rhodophyceae, Bangiophycidae)." British Columbia, 1972.

11481

McLean, Alastair. "Plant Communities of the Similkameen Valley, British Columbia, and their Relationships to Soils." Washington State, 1969.

11482

McMinn, Robert Gordon. "Water Relations in the Douglas Fir Region of Vancouver Island." British Columbia, 1957.

11483

Medlyn, David Arthur. "A Review of Selected Genera of Middle Jurassic to Middle Cretaceous Conifers from North America." Brigham Young, 1976.

11484

Mumford, Thomas Freuzel, Jr. "Observations on the Taxonomy of Some Species of Porphyra from Washington and Vancouver Island, British Columbia." Washington, Seattle, 1973.

11485

Nelson, Wendy Alison. "Analipus japonicus (Harv.) Wynne (Phaeophyta): Studies of Its Biology and Taxonomy." British Columbia, 1981.

11486

Noble, Willa Jane. "The Lichens of the Coastal Douglas-Fir Dry Subzone of British Columbia." British Columbia, 1983.

11487

Nordin, Richard Nels. "The Biology of Nodularia (Cyanophyceae)." British Columbia, 1974. [British Columbia pond/Étang de la Colombie-Britannique]

11488

Ogwang, Bob Humphrey. "Some Plant-Mediated Processes in the Maritime Wetlands of South-Western British Columbia." British Columbia, 1979.

11489

Ohlsson, Karl E. "A Revision of the Lichen Genus (Sphaerophorus)." Michigan State, 1973.

11490

Orloci, Laszlo. "Vegetational and Environmental Variations in the Coastal Western Hemlock Zone." British Columbia, 1964.

11491

Perkins, Walter Ethen. "Systematics of Saxifraga rufidula and Related Species from the Columbia River Gorge to Southwestern British Columbia." British Columbia, 1978.

11492

Peterson, Everett Bruce. "Plant Associations in the Sub-Alpine Mountain Hemlock Zone in Southern British Columbia." British Columbia, 1964.

11493

Pojar, James Joseph. "The Relation of the Reproductive Biology of Plants to the Structure and Function of Four Plant Communities." British Columbia, 1974.

11494

Pomeroy, William Martin. "Benthic Algae Ecology and Primary Pathways of Energy Flow on the Squamish River Delta, British Columbia." British Columbia, 1977.

11495

Quenet, Robin Vincent. "Growth Simulation of Trees, Shrubs, Grasses and Forbs in a Big-Game Winter Range." British Columbia, 1973.

11496

Randhawa, Ajit Singh. "Variability in Saxifraga ferruginea Graham (Saxifragaceae)." British Columbia, 1969.

11497

Revel, Richard David. "Phytogeocoenoses of the Sub-Boreal Spruce Biogeoclimatic Zone in North Central British Columbia." British Columbia, 1973.

11498

Robinson, Gordon George Christopher. "Cytological Investigations of the Genus Alaria Greville as It Occurs on the West Coast of North America." British Columbia, 1968.

11499

Roelofs, Adrienne Kehde. "The Distribution of Diatoms in the Surface Sediments of British Columbia Inlets." British Columbia, 1983.

11500

Roemer, Hans Ludwig. "Forest Vegetation and Environments on the Saanich Peninsula, Vancouver Island." Victoria, 1973.

11501

Szczawinski, Adam F. "Corticolous and Lignicolous Plant Communities in the Forest Associations of the Douglas Fir Forest on Vancouver Island." British Columbia, 1954.

11502
Tan, Benito Ching. "A Moss Flora of Selkirk and Purcell Mountain Ranges, Southeastern British Columbia." British Columbia, 1981.

11503
Tanner, Christopher Jean Eugene. "The Taxonomy and Morphological Variation of Distromatic Ulvaceous Algae (Chlorophyta) from the Northeast Pacific." British Columbia, 1979. [Vancouver and Vancouver Island/Vancouver et Île de Vancouver]

11504
Tisdale, Edwin W. "An Ecological Study of Montane Forest Vegetation in Southern Interior British Columbia." Minnesota, 1949.

11505
Turner, Nancy Jean. "Plant Taxonomic Systems and Ethnobotany of Three Contemporary Indian Groups of the Pacific Northwest (Haida, Bella Coola, and Lillooet)." British Columbia, 1973.

11506
Ulke, Titus. "The Flora of Yoho Park, British Columbia." Catholic, 1934.

11507
Wagner, David Henry. "Taxonomic Investigations of the Genus Polystichum in Western North America." Washington State, 1976.

11508
Wali, Mohan Kishen. "Vegetation-Environment Relationships of Sub-Boreal Spruce Zone Ecosystems in British Columbia." British Columbia, 1970.

11509
Yarie, John Anthony. "The Role of Understory Vegetation in the Nutrient Cycle of Forested Ecosystems in the Mountain Hemlock Biogeoclimatic Zone." British Columbia, 1978.

11510
Ziemkiewicz, Paul Frank. "Effects of Fertilization on the Nutrient and Organic Matter Dynamics of Reclaimed Coal-Mined Areas and Native Grasslands in Southeastern British Columbia." British Columbia, 1979.

Manitoba

Anderson, Jonathan Robert. See No./Voir no 247
11511
Bird, Charles Durham. "Vegetational Changes as Related to Waterfowl Habitat in Agricultural Water Bodies of Manitoba and Saskatchewan, Canada." Oklahoma State, 1960.

11512
Brouillet, Luc. "A Biosystematic Study of Aster ciliolatus Lindley and Aster laevis Linnaeus (Asteraceae: Astereae) with a Survey of Other Heterophylli." Waterloo, 1981. [Canadian Prairies eastward to Ontario/Prairies canadiennes à l'est de l'Ontario]

11513
Lieffers, Victor James. "Environment and Ecology of Scirpus maritimus L. var. Paludosus (Nels.) Kuk in Saline Wetlands of the Canadian Prairies." Manitoba, 1981.

11514
Macaulay, Alexander James. "Taxonomic and Ecological Relationships of Scirpus acutus Muhl. and S. Validus Vahl. (Cyperaceae) in Southern Manitoba." Manitoba, 1974.

11515
Masters, Margaret Jean. "Chytrid Parasitism of Phytoplankton in the Delta Marsh Manitoba." Western Ontario, 1970.

11516
McDonald, William C. "The Distribution and Pathogenicity of the Fungi Associated with the Crown and Root Rotting of Alfalfa in Manitoba." Wisconsin, 1954.

Olchowecki, Oleksa Alexander. See No./Voir no 10526
11517
Phillips, Samuel Floyd. "The Relationship Between Evapotranspiration by Phragmites communis Trin and Water Fluctuations in the Delta Marsh Manitoba." Manitoba, 1976.

11518
Pip, Eva. See No./Voir no 11114
11519
Ralston, Robert Dean. "The Grasslands of the Red River Valley." Saskatchewan, 1968.

Routledge, Richard Donovan. See No./Voir no 11395
11520
Rowe, John Stanley. "Vegetation of the Southern Boreal Forest in Saskatchewan and Manitoba." Manitoba, 1956.

Smeiris, Fred Eldon. See No./Voir no 328
11521
Waddington, John. "The Influence of Management Practices on the Growth Cycle of Bromus inermus Leyss in Southern Manitoba." Manitoba, 1969.

11522
Walker, Jennifer Mary. "Vegetation Changes with Falling Water Levels in the Delta Marsh Manitoba." Manitoba, 1966.

Wylie, Mary Eileen. See No./Voir no 11448

Maritime Provinces/Provinces maritimes

11523
Catling, Paul Miles. "Systematics of Spiranthes L.C. Richard in Northeastern North America." Toronto, 1981. [New Brunswick/Nouveau-Brunswick]

11524
Chen, Lawrence Chien-Ming. "Morphological and Culture Studies of Two Strains of Chondrus crispus Stackhouse." New Brunswick, 1977. [Cap d'Or Bay of Fundy/Cap d'Or, Baie de Fundy]

11525
Damman, Antoni William Hermannus. "The Forest Vegetation of Western Newfoundland and Site Degradation Associated with Vegetation Changes." Michigan, 1967.

Grayson, John Francis. See No./Voir no 6535
Hoch, Peter Coonan. See No./Voir no 11381

1526
Keddy, Paul Anthony. "The Population Ecology of Cakile edentula (Brassicaceae) in Heterogeneous Environments." Dalhousie, 1978. [Nova Scotia/ Nouvelle-Écosse]

Korpijakko, Maija Liena. See No./Voir no 6532

Lenk, Cecilia. See No./Voir no 11607

Magasi, Laszlo Paul. See No./Voir no 11580

11527
Miller, John David. "Fungi from the Bay of Fundy and Their Role in Biodegradation." New Brunswick, 1981.

11528
Roland, Albert Edward. "The Flora of Nova Scotia." Wisconsin, 1944.

Shetler, Stanwyn Gerald. See No./Voir no 11553

Short, Susan Kathleen. See No./Voir no 6536

11529
Silver, George Thomas. "Studies on the Arborvitae Leaf-Miners in New Brunswick." SUNY, College of Forestry, Syracuse, 1956.

11530
Starling, Robert Neale. "Modern Pollen in the Salmon River Basin." Queen's, 1978.

Taylor, Ronald Maxwell. See No./Voir no 11420

Wilce, Robert Thayer. See No./Voir no 11617

Arctic, Northwest Territories and Yukon/ Arctique, Territoires du Nord–Ouest et Yukon

11531
Addison, Paul Andrew. "Autecological Studies of Luzula confusa: A Plant's Response to the High Arctic Environment on King Christian Island, N.W.T." Alberta, 1977.

Anderson, James Hugh. See No./Voir no 11449

11532
Ashmed, Moin V. "The Occurrence of Raffinose oligosaccharides in Plants and Their Metabolism in the Watermelon (Citrullis vulgaris Schrad var. Early Klondike)." Western Ontario, 1963.

11533
Barrett, Paul Edward. "Phytogeocoenoses of a Coastal Lowland Ecosystem, Devon Island, N.W.T." British Columbia, 1972.

11534
Brassard, Guy R. "The Mosses of Northern Ellesmere Island: Floristics and Bryogeography." Ottawa, 1970.

11535
Clebsch, Edward Ernst Cooper. "Comparative Morphological and Physiological Variation in Arctic and Alpine Populations of Trisetum spicatum." Duke, 1961.

Cwynar, Leslie Peter C. See No./Voir no 6541

11536
Duman, Miximilian G. "The Genus Carex in Eastern Arctic Canada." Catholic, 1941.

11537
Foreman, Elvie Maxine Ford. "Growth, Flowering, and Vivipary in Arctic and Alpine Populations of Deschampsia caespitosa (L.) Beauv. Poa Alpina L. and Trisetum spicatum (L.) Richt." Colorado, 1971.

11538
Geale, Dorothy Wilhelmina. "Definition and Ecology of Plant Communities Polar Bear Pass, Bathurst Island, N.W.T." Saskatchewan, 1981.

11539
Grace, Barry Wayne. "A Study of Threshold Sulfur-Dioxide Concentrations for the Lichen Cladina Ranjiferina (L.) Harm." Guelph, 1980. [Mackenzie Valley/Vallée du Mackenzie]

11540
Johnson, Edward Arnold. "Vegetation Change and Fire Frequency in the Western Subarctic." Saskatchewan, 1977.

11541
Kerby, Norma Joann. "The Relationships Between Microclimactic, Soil and Vegetation Patterns within Semi-Permanent Snowbeds of the Richardson Mountains, Northwest Territories." Carleton, 1979.

Kevan, Peter Graham. See No./Voir no 11252

11542
Korpijaakko, Erkki Olavi. "Aerial Interpretation of Muskeg: A Critical Analysis of Form Features in the Canadian Muskeg Complex." McMaster, 1970.

11543
Lambert, John David Hamilton. "The Ecology and Successional Trends of Tundra Plant Communities in the Low Arctic Subalpine Zone of the Richardson and British Mountains of the Canadian Western Arctic." British Columbia, 1968.

11544
Larsen, James Arthur. "The Vegetation of the Ennadai Lake Area, N.W.T.: Studies in Subarctic and Arctic Bioclimatology." Wisconsin, 1968.

11545
Laursen, Gary A. "Higher Fungi in Soils of Coastal Arctic Tundra Plant Communities." Virginia Polytechnic Institute and State University, 1975.

11546
MacInnes, Kaye Lucile. "Reproductive Ecology of Four Arctic Species of Pedicularis (Scrophularisceae)." Western Ontario, 1973.

11547
Maguire, Bassett. "A Monograph of the Genus Arnica. The Subgenera Arctica and Austromontana." Cornell, 1938.

McCartney, Nancy Glover. See No./Voir no 895

11548
Mooney, Harold Alfred. "Comparative Physiological Ecology of Arctic and Alpine Populations of Oxygyna digyna." Duke, 1960.

11549
Muc, Michael. "Ecology and Primary Production of High Arctic Sedge-Moss Meadows, Devon Island, N.W.T., Canada." Alberta, 1976.

11550
Packer, J.G. "Cytotaxonomic Studies in Some Flowering Plants of Western and Arctic Canada and the Distribution of Polyploid Species in the Arctic Archipelago." London, 1969.

11551
Polunin, N.V. "Contributions to Arctic Botany." Oxford, 1935.

Rencz, Andrew Nicholas. See No./Voir no 295

11552
Schulten, Ronald Brendan. "Ecology and Nitrogen Nutrition of Two Polar Desert Populations of Cerastium alpinum, Devon Island, N.W.T., Canada." Massachussetts, 1981.

Scott, Peter John. See No./Voir no 11396

Scotter, George Wilby. See No./Voir no 10619

11553
Shetler, Stanwyn Gerald. "Variation and Evolution of the Neartic Harebells (Campanula subsect: Heterophylla)." Michigan, 1979. [Arctic Archipelago/ Archipel de l'Arctique]

11554
Spongberg, Stephen A. "Systematic and Evolutionary Study of North American Arctic and Alpine Monocephalus Species of Erigeron (Compositae)." North Carolina, 1971.

11555
Stutz, Reuben Craig. "Nitrogen Fixation in a High Arctic Ecosystem." Alberta, 1973.

11556
Svoboda, Josef. "Primary Production Processes within Polar Semi-Desert Vegetation, Truelove Lowland, Devon Island, Northwest Territories, Canada." Alberta, 1974.

11557
Webber, Patrick John. "Gradient Analysis of the Vegetation Around the Lewis Valley, North-Central Baffin Island, Northwest Territories, Canada." Queen's, 1972.

11558
Younkin, Walter Erwin. "Ecological Studies of Arctagrostis latifolia (R.Br.) Griseb, and Calamagrostis canadensis (Michx) Beauv. in Relation to Their Colonization Potential in Disturbed Areas, Tuktoyaktuk Region, Northwest Territories." Alberta, 1974.

Ontario

Anderson, Jonathan Robert. See No./Voir no 247

11559
Bayly, Isabel Law. "The Ecology of Genus Typha in Wetland Communities of the Eastern Ontario-Western Quebec Region of Canada." British Columbia, 1974.

11560
Bowes, Garry George. "Effect of Density on Ion Cycling in a Crataegus punctata Jacq. Ecosystem." Guelph, 1974.

11561
Bradbury, Ian Keith. "The Strategy and Tactics of Solidago canadensis L. in Abandoned Pastures." Guelph, 1974.

11562
Brisson, Jean Denis. "A Comparative Anatomical Survey of Fruits and Seeds of Selected Species of Vaccinium L. (Ericaceae Juss.)." Guelph, 1978.

11563
Caisi, Roy Franklin. "Coprophilous sphaeriales of Ontario." Toronto, 1933.

Catling, Paul Miles. See No./Voir no 11523

11564
Clough, Katherine Sarah. "Biotic Factors Affectin the Survival of Thielaviopsis basicola (Berk and Br Ferraris in Soil." Toronto, 1975. [Durhan County/Comté de Durham]

11565
Comeau, Gilberte. "Influence de la pollution de l'ai sur les bryophytes et les lichens." Ottawa, 197? [Sudbury]

11566
Costescu, Leslie Whitby. "The Ecological Conse quences of Airborne Metallic Contaminants fror the Sudbury Smelters." Toronto, 1975.

11567
Cruise, James E. "A Floristic Study of Norfol County, Southwestern Ontario." Cornell, 1954.

11568
Darker, Grant Dooks. "The Hypodermataceae of Coni fers." Harvard, 1931. [Timagami Fores Reserve/Réserve de la forêt Timagami]

11569
De Catanzaro, Jennifer Barbara. "Effects of Nicke Contamination on Nitrogen Cycling in Borea Forests in Northern Ontario." Toronto, 1983.

Desrochers, Raymond. See No./Voir no 10510

11570
Devine, Malcolm David. "Glyphosate Uptake, Trans location and Distribution in Quackgrass (Agropyro repens (L.) Beauv.) and Canada Thistle (Cirsiu arvense (L.) Scop.)." Guelph, 1981.

11571
Drexler, Robert V. "Community and Geographic Rela tions of Bryophytes in Southwestern Ontario Illinois, 1940.

11572
Fitchko, Yaroslaw. "The Distribution, Mobility an Accumulation of Nickel, Copper and Zinc in River System Draining the Eastern Part of th Metal-Polluted Sudbury Smeltering Area Toronto, 1978.

Freedman, William. See No./Voir no 260

11573
Frost, Roger Anthony. "Aspects of the Comparativ Biology of Three Weedy Species of Amaranthus i Southwestern Ontario." Western Ontario, 1973.

11574
Griffin, Howard Dennis. "The Genus Ceratocystis i Ontario." Toronto, 1965.

11575
Hawthorn, Wayne Rothan. "Population Dynamics o Two Weedy Perennials, Plantago major L. an Rugelii Decne." Western Ontario, 1973.

11576
Hildebrand, Alexander Anderson. "Investigations o Two Diseases of the Root of Ginseng in Ontario Toronto, 1933.

11577
Husain, Syed Shahid. "A Study of Rhizoctonia fra gariae Sp. Nov. in Relation to Strawberry Degene ration in Southwestern Ontario." Wester Ontario, 1963.

11578
Larson, Douglas William. "Aspects of the Ecology o Coastal Tundra Raised Beach Ridges in North western Ontario." McMaster, 1975.

11579
Lee, Peter Ferguson. "Biological, Chemical and Physical Relationships of Wild Rice, Zizania aquatica L. in Northwestern Ontario and Northeastern Minnesota." Manitoba, 1979.

11580
Magasi, Laszlo Paul. "A Comparative Study of Polyporus abietinus in Ontario and New Brunswick." Syracuse, 1972.

11581
Moir, David Ross. "A Floristic Survey of the Severn River Drainage Basin of Northwestern Ontario." Minnesota, 1958.

11582
Morrison, Robert George. "Primary Succession on Sand Dunes at Grand Bend, Ontario." Toronto, 1973.

11583
Shafi, Muhammad Iqbal. "Secondary (Postfire) Succession in the Cochrane District of Northern Ontario." Toronto, 1972.

11584
Soper, James Herbert. "A Study of the Flora of the Lake Erie Region of Southern Ontario." Harvard, 1943.

11585
Sreenivasa, Mannada Rani. "Recent and Extant Diatom Assemblages in Southern Ontario." Waterloo, 1970.

11586
Staniforth, Richard John. "The Comparative Ecology of Three Riverbank Annuals, Polygonum lapathifolium L., P. Pensylvanicum L. and P. Persicaria L." Western Ontario, 1975.

11587
Thaler, Gary Ross. "The Study of the Tension Zone Between the Boreal and Carolinian Floras in Ontario." Toronto, 1970.

11588
Thomas, Amos Gordon. "Autecological Studies on Hieracium in Wellington County, Ontario." Guelph, 1972.

11589
Ward, Daniel Bertram. "Relationships Among Certain Species of Sisyrinchium in Northeastern North America." Cornell, 1959.

11590
Weaver, Susan Emerson. "The Role of Disturbance in the Population Dynamics of Rumex crispus L. and Rumex obtusifolius L." Western Ontario, 1978.

Middleton, John David. See No./Voir no 11645

Quebec/Québec

Bayly, Isabel Law. See No./Voir no 11559

11591
Blanchet, Bertrand. "Les cédrières du Québec." Laval, 1976.

11592
Bowman, Paul William. "Study of a Peat Bog near The Matamek River, Quebec, Canada, by a Method of Pollen Analysis." Virginia, 1930.

Catling, Paul Miles. See No./Voir no 11523

11593
Cléonique-Joseph, Frère. "Étude d'évolution floristique dans la région d'Ottawa, Montréal, Trois-Rivières." Montréal, 1937.

11594
Cogbill, Charles Van Horn. "Analysis of Vegetation, Environment, and Dynamics in the Boreal Forests of the Laurentian Highlands, Quebec." Toronto, 1982.

11595
Comtois, Paul. "Structure et dynamisme des populations clonales de Populus balsamifera L. au Golfe de Richmond (Nouveau-Québec.)" Laval, 1983.

11596
Dai, Tze-Sen. "Studies on the Ecological Importance of Waterflow in Wetlands." Toronto, 1971. [Kennedy Bog]

11597
Doyon, Dominique. "Étude éco-dynamique de la végétation du comté de Lévis." Laval, 1974.

11598
Forest, Philippe. "La végétation de Poste-de-la-Baleine, Nouveau Québec." Sherbrooke, 1976.

Frankton, Clarence. See No./Voir no 135

11599
Gagnon, Réjean. "Fluctuations holocènes de la limite des forêts, Rivière-aux-Feuilles, Québec nordique: une analyse macrofossile." Laval, 1983.

11600
Gauthier, Robert. "Les sphaignes et la végétation des tourbières du parc des Laurentides, Québec." Laval, 1980.

Grayson, John Francis. See No./Voir no 6535

11601
Hall, Gustav Wesley. "A Biosystematic Study of the North American Complex of the Genus Bidens (Compositae)." Indiana, 1967.

11602
Irénée-Marie, Frère. "La flore desmidiale de la région de Montréal et plus spécialement de la tourbière de Saint-Hubert." Montréal, 1938.

11603
Joyal, Robert. "Description de la tourbière Mer Bleue." Ottawa, 1970.

11604
Kowal, Robert Raymond. "Senecio auereus and Allied Species on the Gaspé Peninsula of Quebec." Cornell, 1968.

11605
LeBlanc, Lucien Fabuis. "Écologie et phytosociologie des Epiphytes corticoles du sud du Québec." Montréal, 1961.

11606
Leduc, Albert. "Contribution à l'étude de la composition minérale de quelques herbes de certains pâturages de la région de Montréal." Montréal, 1947.

11607
Lenk, Cecilia. "The Post-Glacial Population Dynamics of Fagus grandifolia Ehrh. in the Region of the Northern Limit." Harvard, 1982.

11608
Marr, John Winton. "The Forest-Tundra Ecotone on the East Coast of Hudson Bay." Minnesota, 1942.

11609

Posluszny, Usher. "Floral Development in the Najadales." McGill, 1975. [Macdonald Herbarium, Sainte-Anne-de-Bellevue/Herbier Macdonald, Sainte-Anne-de-Bellevue]

11610

Potter, David. "Botanical Evidence of a Post-Pleistocene Marine Connection Between Hudson Bay and the St. Lawrence Basin." Harvard, 1931.

11611

Rousseau, Camille. "Recherches sur la distribution des principales espèces de la flore vasculaire de la péninsule du Québec-Labrador." Laval, 1972.

11612

Rousseau, Jacques. "Les astragalus du Québec." Montréal, 1934.

11613

St. John, Harold. "A Report on a Botanical Expedition of the South Shore of the Labrador Peninsula, Saguenay County, Quebec, Including an Annotated List of the Species of Vascular Plants." Harvard, 1917.

11614

Scoggan, Homer J. "Ecological Studies of the Arctic-Alpine Flora of the Gaspé Peninsula and of Bic." McGill, 1942.

Short, Susan Cathleen. See No./Voir no 6536

11615

Sylvestre, R.F. "Le cuivre dans les végétaux du Québec." Montréal, 1942.

11616

Vowinchel, Thomas. "The Effect of Climate on the Photosynthesis of Picea mariana at the Subarctic Tree Line." McGill, 1975.

11617

Wilce, Robert Thayer. "Studies of the Marine Algae of the Labrador Peninsula and Northwest Newfoundland: Ecology and Distribution." Michigan, 1957.

Saskatchewan

Bird, Charles Durham. See No./Voir no 11511

Chinnappa, Chendanda Chengapa. See No./Voir no 11433

11618

Dirschl, Herman John. "Ecology of the Vegetation of the Saskatchewan River Delta." Saskatchewan, 1970.

Halm, Benjamin Jackson. See No./Voir no 285

11619

Hammer, Ulrich Theodore. "An Ecological Study of Certain Blue-Green Algae (Cyanophyta) in Saskatchewan Lakes." Saskatchewan, 1963.

11620

Ionescu, Margaret Evelyn (Ching). "Natural Vegetation and Environmental Aspects of Strip Mined Land in Lignite Fields of Southeastern Saskatchewan." Saskatchewan, 1974.

11621

Jeglum, John Karl. "Lowland Vegetation at Candle Lake, Southern Boreal Forest, Saskatchewan." Saskatchewan, 1968.

Lieffers, Victor James. See No./Voir no 11513

11622

Maini, Jagmohon S. "Invasion of Grasslands by Polulus tremuloides in the Northern Great Plains." Saskatchewan, 1960.

11623

Misra, Kailash Chandra. "Geography, Morphology and Environmental Relationships of Certain Stipa Species in the Northern Great Plains." Saskatchewan, 1962.

11624

Newsome, Richard Duane. "A Phytosociological Study of the Forests of the Cypress Hills." Saskatchewan, 1965.

Rowe, John Stanley. See No./Voir no 11520

11625

Swan, John Marcus Allan. "The Phytosociology of Upland Vegetation at Candle Lake, Saskatchewan." Saskatchewan, 1967.

11626

Walker, Brian Harrison. "Ecology of Herbaceous Wetland Vegetation in the Aspen Grove and Grassland Regions of Saskatchewan." Saskatchewan, 1968.

11627

Wilson, Malcolm Alan. "The Climatic and Vegetational History of the Postglacial in Central Saskatchewan." Saskatchewan, 1981. [La Ronge area/ Région de la Ronge]

Wylie, Mary Eileen. See No./Voir no 11448

Canada Thistle/Chardon du Canada

11628

Aslander, J. Alfred O. "Experiments on the Eradication of Canada Thistle (Cirsium arvense), with Chlorates and Other Herbicides." Cornell, 1928.

11629

Bondarenko, Donald David. "3-Amino-1, 2, 4-Triazole as an Herbicide on Canada Thistle (Cirsium arvense (L.) Scop.) and Its Effect on Soil Microorganisms." Ohio State, 1957.

11630

Carson, Alex Gyandoh. "Studies on Competitive Ability, Seedling Development, Chemical Control, and Translocation of Dicamba and 2, 4-D in Canada Thistle." Guelph, 1974.

Devine, Malcolm David. See No./Voir no 11570

11631

Friesen, George. "The Herbicidal Action of CMU (3-(P. Chlorophenyl) -1, 1- Dinethyl-Area) on Canada Thistle (Cirsium arvense)." Washington State, 1956.

11632

Gale, Alvin Frank. "Evaluation of Tillage Plus Herbicides for Control of Canada Thistle and Their Effect upon Subsequent Crops." Wyoming, 1972.

11633

Hill, Gideon Dee, Jr. "Herbicide Studies: 1. Herbicides and Adjuvants on Canada Thistle (Cirsium arvense, Town.). II. The Relation of 2, 4- Dichlorophenoxyacetic Acid to Certain Soils and Soil-Like Materials." Ohio State, 1953.

11634

Hodgson, Jesse Moroni. "Differences in Lipids on Canada Thistle Leaves as Influenced by Ecotype and Site." Montana State, 1970.

11635
Hoefer, Raymond Henry. "Canada Thistle (Cirsium arvense) Root Bud Initiation, Biology, and Translocation of 14C-Glyphosate as Influenced by Nitrogen, Temperature, Photoperiod, and Growth Stage." Nebraska, 1981.

11636
Hunter, James Hopkins. "Persistence of Picloram and Its Effectiveness for the Control of Canada Thistle in Cereals." Manitoba, 1971.

11637
Lee, Gary Albert. "The Influence of Selected Herbicides and Temperatures on the Carbohydrate and Protein Levels of Canada Thistle Ecotypes." Wyoming, 1971.

11638
Martin, Alexander Robert. "Bud Dormancy in Canada Thistle as Influenced by Shoot Excision and Plant Hormones." Ohio State, 1970.

11639
McAllister, Ray Scott. "Influence of Environmental Factors on Root Bud Growth and Development, and on Assimilate and Glyphosate Translocation in Canada Thistle (Cirsium arvense)." Nebraska, Lincoln, 1982.

11640
Zilke, Samuel. "Effect of Environment on Seed Germination and Early Seedling Development of Cirsium arvense (L.) Scop." South Dakota State, 1967. [Saskatchewan]

FORESTRY AND FORESTS/ SYLVICULTURE ET FORÊTS

There is a vast difference in output from Canadian and American universities. Canada produced over 100 titles, and the United States approximately 40. Over two thirds of the Canadian theses were produced during the last 15 years. The University of British Columbia is the outstanding leader with over 60 titles to its credit. The University of Toronto is second and Laval University ranks third. Of the 18 American universities, Yale stands out with five titles, followed by Minnesota and Syracuse with an equal number. The bulk of the American output was produced during the 1960's and 1970's.

———

Dans ce domaine, il existe une grande différence entre la production des universités canadiennes et celle des universités américaines. Le Canada a produit plus de 100 titres et les États-Unis environ 40. Plus des deux tiers des thèses canadiennes ont été rédigées entre 1970 et 1985. La Colombie-Britannique est de loin l'université qui a le plus de thèses en ce domaine à son actif avec 60 titres; Toronto vient avec seulement un quart de la production de la Colombie-Britannique, et Laval, troisième. Des 18 universités américaines, Yale (5) tient la tête, suivie par les universités du Minnesota et de Syracuse, avec un nombre égal de thèses. La plus grande partie de la production américaine date des années 1960 et 1970.

11641
Barnes, Carleton P. "Geographic Influences in the Present Distribution of the Forests in Nearctic North America." Clark, 1929.

11642
Eggens, Jack L. "Physiological Considerations of the Vegetative Propagation of Populus alba pyramidalis Bunge." Guelph, 1970.

Flack, J.A. Douglas. See No./Voir no 10732

11643
Foster, Neil William. "The Importance of Chemical Reactions and Microbial Activity in Immobilizing Urea Nitrogen in Jack Pine Humus." Guelph, 1979.

11644
La Roi, George Henri, III. "An Ecological Study of the Boreal Spruce-Fir Forests of the North American Taiga." Duke, 1964.

Martell, David Leigh. See No./Voir no 11747

11645
Middleton, John David. "On Certain Spatial Characteristics of the Distribution of Woodland Species in Farmland." Carleton, 1983.

11646
Mossison, Ian Kenneth. "The Absorption of Nutrients by Roots of Coniferous Seedlings in Relation to Root Characteristics and Soil Conditions." Toronto, 1969.

11647
Paul, Peter Montgomery. "A National Fire Weather Forecasting System for the Forests of Canada." Cornell, 1974.

11648
Rouleau, Ernest. "Les peupliers de la section Tacamahaca en Amérique du Nord." Montréal, 1948.

Rouse, Wayne R. See No./Voir no 4983

11649
Shain, William Arthur. "A Survey of Continuous Forest Inventory in the United States and Canada." Michigan State, 1963.

11650
Widden, Paul Rodney. "The Ecology of Pine Forest Soil Fungi and Their Reaction Following a Forest Fire." Calgary, 1971.

Wood, Benjamin William. See No./Voir no 11407

Northern Canada/Nord du Canada

11651
Elliott, Deborah Louise. "The Stability of the Northern Canadian Tree Limit: Current Regenerative Capacity." Colorado, 1979.

Eastern Canada/Est du Canada

Clark, William Cummin. See No./Voir no 11182

11652
Greenidge, Kenneth N.H. "Die-Back: A Disease of Yellow-Birch (Betula lutea Michx) in Eastern Canada." Harvard, 1951.

11653
Linzon, Samuel Nathan. "Studies on the Nature and Etiology of Semimature Tissue Needle Blight of Eastern White Pine." Toronto, 1964.

Western Canada/Ouest du Canada

Johnson, Edward Arnold. See No./Voir no 11540
Rhoades, Frederick M. See No./Voir no 11425

11654
Richards, James Harlan. "Ecophysiology of a Deciduous Timberline Tree, Larix lyallii Parl." Alberta, 1981. [Rocky Mountains/Montagnes Rocheuses]

11655
Wang, I-Chen. "Black Liquor Extraction of Lodgepole Pine (Pinus contorta var. Latifolia Engelm.) Tree Residues." British Columbia, 1981.

Alberta

11656
Corns, Ian George William. "Tree Growth Prediction and Plant Community Distribution in Relation to Environmental Factors in Lodgepole Pine, White Spruce, Black Spruce and Aspen Forests of Western Alberta Foothills." Alberta, 1978.

11657
Duffy, Patrick James Barry. "Relationships Between Site Factors and Growth of Lodgepole Pine (Pinus contorta var (Dougl.). Latifolia Engelm.) in the Foothills Section of Alberta." Minnesota, 1962.

11658
Jeffrey, Walter William. "Hydrologic Significance of Stand Density Variations in Alberta Lodgepole Pine (Pinus contorta, Dougl. (Moench) Voss. Var. Latifolia, Engelm.) Forests." Colorado State, 1968.

11659
Johnstone, Wayne David. "Dry-Matter Production and Complete-Tree Utilization of Lodgepole Pine in Alberta." British Columbia, 1973.

11660
Kearney, Michael Sean. "Late Quaternary Vegetational and Environmental History of Jasper National Park, Alberta." Western Ontario, 1981.

11661
Ogilvie, Robert Townley. "Ecology of Spruce Forests in the East Slope of the Rocky Mountains in Alberta." Washington State, 1962.

11662
Porter, William Barry. "Aspects of the Biology and Dynamics of Phyllocnistis populiella Chambers on Trembling Aspen in the Rocky Mountain Foothills of Southern Alberta." Calgary, 1976.

Richards, James Harlan. See No./Voir no 11654
Shaw, Robert Keith. See No./Voir no 11441

11663
Van Zinderen Bakker, Eduard Meine. "An Ecophysiological Study of Black Spruce in Central Alberta." Alberta, 1974.

British Columbia/Colombie-Britannique

Alfaro, René Ivan. See No./Voir no 11207

11664
Bailey, Gordon Raymond. "Log Allocation by Dynamic Programming." British Columbia, 1970.

11665
Barr, Percy Munson. "The Effect of Soil Moisture on the Establishment of Spruce Reproduction in British Columbia." Yale, 1929.

Beil, Charles Edward. See No./Voir no 11451

11666
Bell, Marcus Arthur Money. "Phytocenoses in the Dry Subzone of the Interior Western Hemlock Zone of British Columbia." British Columbia, 1964.

11667
Bellefleur, Pierre. "Analysis and Modelling of Interspecies Competition During Forest Secondary Succession." British Columbia, 1978.

11668
Bloomberg, William Joseph. "A Critical Study of the Cankering of Certain Poplars by Cytospora chrysosperma (Pers.) Fr. with Special Reference to Water Relations of the Host." British Columbia, 1960.

11669
Bonita, Manuel Libres. "A Simulation Model for Planning and Control of Forest Harvesting Operations." British Columbia, 1972.

11670
Brayshaw, Thomas Christopher. "An Ecological Classification of the Ponderosa Pine Stands in the Southwestern Interior of British Columbia." British Columbia, 1956.

11671
Brière, Denis. "The Stratification of Forested Landscapes for Intensive Management: Development and Application." British Columbia, 1979.

11672
Buckland, Donald Channing. "Investigation of Decay in Western Red Cedar in British Columbia." Yale, 1945.

11673
Byron, Ronald Neil. "Community Stability and Regional Economic Development: The Role of Forest Policy in the North Central Interior of British Columbia." British Columbia, 1976.

11674
Cordes, Lawrence David. "An Ecological Study of the Sitka Spruce Forest on the West Coast of Vancouver Island." British Columbia, 1973.

11675
Cown, David John. "Densitometric Studies on the Wood of Young Coastal Douglas-Fir (Pseudotsuga menziesii (Mirb.) Franco)." British Columbia, 1976.

11676
DeHayes, Donald Henry. "Genetic Variation in Cold/Hardiness and Its Effects on the Performance of Ponderosa Pine (Pinus ponderosa) in Michigan." Michigan State, 1977.

Eastman, Donald Sidney. See No./Voir no 10633
Eis, Slavoj. See No./Voir no 11463

11677
El-Kassaby, Yousry Aly. "Isozyme Patterns of a Selected Pseudotsuga menziesii (Mirb.) Franco Population." British Columbia, 1980. [University of British Columbia Research Forest/Réserve forestière de l'Université de la Colombie-Britannique]

11678
El-Lakasay, Mohamed Hosny Hassan. "Studies on the Effects of Ionizing Radiation on Some Western Coniferous Species." British Columbia, 1969.

11679
Emmingham, William H. "Physiological Responses of Four Douglas-Fir Populations in Three Contrasting Field Environments." Oregon State, 1974. [Vancouver Island/Île de Vancouver]

11680
Falkenhagen, Emil Richard. "A Study of the Phenotypic and Genotypic Variation of 545 Single Tree Progenies of 38 Provenances of the 1970 I.U.F.R.O. Sitka Spruce (Picea sitchensis (Bong.) Carr) Collection." British Columbia, 1974.

11681
Feller, Michael Charles. "Initial Effects of Clear-Cutting on the Flow of Chemicals Through a Forest-Watershed Ecosystem in Southwestern British Columbia." British Columbia, 1975.

11682
Forsythe, Warren Louis. "Site Influence on the Post-Fire Composition of a Rocky Mountain Forest." Montana, 1975.

11683
Foster, Raymond Edwin. "The Decays and Decay Relationships of Western Hemlock (Tsuga heterophylla (Raf.) Sarg) on the Queen Charlotte Islands, B.C." Toronto, 1949.

11684
Gokhale, Atulchandra Anant. "Wetwood in Black Cottonwood (Populus trichocarpa Torrey and Gray): The Effects of Microaerobic Conditions on the Development of Decay." British Columbia, 1976.

11685
Golding, Douglas Lawrence. "Regulation of Water Yield and Quality in British Columbia Through Forest Management." British Columbia, 1968.

11686
Goulding, Christopher John. "Simulation Techniques for a Stochastic Model of the Growth of Douglas-Fir." British Columbia, 1972.

11687
Haley, David. "An Economic Appraisal of Sustained Yield Forest Management for British Columbia." British Columbia, 1966.

Hardwick, Walter Gordon. See No./Voir no 1809

11688
Heger, Ladislav. "Morphogenesis of Stems of Douglas Fir (Pseudotsuga menziesii (Mirb.) Franco)." British Columbia, 1965.

11689
Hetherington, Eugene Douglas. "Investigation of Orographic Rainfall in South Coastal Mountains of British Columbia." British Columbia, 1976.

11690
Hull, Dale Lester. "A Programming Evaluation of Spatial and Inter-Temporal Allocation Policies with Respect to Interior Provincial Crown Forest Land in British Columbia." McGill, 1976.

11691
Keller, Rodney Alan. "Tolerance in Western Hemlock." British Columbia, 1973.

11692
Ker, John William. "Volume, Growth, and Yield of the Important Timber Species in the Arrow Lakes District of British Columbia." Yale, 1957.

Keser, Nurettin. See No./Voir no 236

11693
Klinka, Karel. "Ecosystem Units, Their Classification, Interpretation and Mapping in the University of British Columbia Research Forest." British Columbia, 1976.

Krueger, Kenneth William. See No./Voir no 11473

11694
Krumlik, George Jiri. "Comparative Study of Nutrient Cycling in the Subalpine Mountain Hemlock Zone of British Columbia." British Columbia, 1979.

11695
Leadem, Carole Louise Scheuplein. "Effects of Carbon Dioxide and Daylength on Growth Development and Hardiness of Douglas-Fir (Pseudotsuga menziesii)." British Columbia, 1979.

McMinn, Robert Gordon. See No./Voir no 11482

11696
McNaughton, Keith Graham. "A Study of the Energy Balance of a Douglas-Fir Forest." British Columbia, 1974.

11697
Meagher, Michael Desmond. "Studies of Variation in Hemlock (Tsuga) Populations and Individuals from Southern British Columbia." British Columbia, 1976.

11698
Mellor, Gary Edward. "Nitrogen and Conifer Studies." British Columbia, 1972.

11699
Moss, Alan. "A Comparative Study of Forest Policy and Management Practices in Scotland and British Columbia, with Particular Reference to the Use of Pinus contorta in Scottish Forestry." Edinburgh, 1969.

11700
Mueller-Dombois, Dieter. "The Douglas Fir Forest Association on Vancouver Island in Their Initial Stages of Secondary Succession." British Columbia, 1960.

11701
Munro, Donald Deane. "Methods for Describing Distribution of Soundwood in Mature Western Hemlock Trees." British Columbia, 1968.

11702
Murison, William F. "Macronutrient Deficiency and Its Effects on Coniferous Growth." British Columbia, 1960.

11703
Nagle, George Shorten. "Economics and Public Policy in the Forestry Sector of British Columbia." Yale, 1970.

11704
Newnham, Robert Montague. "The Development of a Stand Model for Douglas Fir." British Columbia, 1964.

Nnyamah, Joseph Ugbogu. See No./Voir no 239

11705
Nokoe, Tertius Sagary. "Minimum-Variance Sampling Schemes for the Scaling of Logs by Weight." British Columbia, 1976.

11706
Offosu-Asiedu, Albert. "The Distribution of Thermophilic and Thermotolevant Fungi in a Spruce-Pine Chip Pile and Their Effects on Some Coniferous Woods." British Columbia, 1970. [Prince George]

11707
O'Loughlin, Colin Lockhart. "An Investigation of the Stability of the Steepland Forest Soils in the Coast Mountains, Southwest British Columbia." British Columbia, 1973.

11708
Orr-Ewing, Alan Lindsay. "An Investigation into the Effects of Self-Pollination on Pseudotsuga menziesii (Mirb.) Franco." British Columbia, 1956.

11709
Osborn, John Edward. "Influence of Stocking and Density Upon Growth and Yield of Trees and Stands of Coastal Western Hemlock." British Columbia, 1968.

Otchere-Boateng, Jacob K. See No./Voir no 241

11710
Paillé, Gilbert. "Description and Prediction of Mortality in Some Coastal Douglas Fir Stands." British Columbia, 1970.

11711
Parker, Arthur Kneeland. "Studies in Europhium trinacriforme, the Perfect Stage of Leptographinum Isolated from Lesions on Western White Pine Affected with Pole Blight." British Columbia, 1956.

11712
Plamondon, André Paul. "Hydrologic Properties and Water Balance of the Forest Floor of a Canadian West Coast Watershed." British Columbia, 1973.

11713
Roche, Laurence. "Geographic Variation in Picea glauca in British Columbia." British Columbia, 1968.

Rochelle, James Arthur. See No./Voir no 10624

Safranyik, Laszlo. See No./Voir no 11229

11714
Sastry, Cherla Bhaskara Rama. "Weight-Length Relationships of Coniferous Wood Tracheid Skeletons." British Columbia, 1972.

11715
Smith, Richard Barrie. "Edaphic Aspects of an Ecological Classification of the Interior Western Hemlock Dry Subzone Forests of British Columbia." British Columbia, 1963.

11716
Stanek, Walter Karl Leopold. "Occurrence, Growth, and Relative Value of Lodgepole Pine and Engelmann Spruce in the Interior of British Columbia." British Columbia, 1966.

11717
Stevens, Roderick R. "Variation in the Foliar Nutrient Status of Several Douglas-Fir Provenances." Oregon State, 1978. [Vancouver Island/Île de Vancouver]

Sullivan, Thomas Priestley. See No./Voir no 10678

11718
Sziklai, Oscar. "Variation and Inheritance of Some Physiological and Morphological Traits in Pseudotsuga menziesii (Mirb.) Franco Var. Menziesii." British Columbia, 1964.

Tan, Chin-Sheng. See No./Voir no 244

11719
Teller, Hans Leo. "An Evaluation of Multiple-Use Practices on Forested Municipal Catchments of the Douglas Fir Region." Washington, Seattle, 1963.

11720
Thomas, Charles Eugene. "Use of Competition, Indices in the Selection of Western Hemlock Plus Trees." British Columbia, 1980.

11721
Thomas, George Philip. "A Contribution to a Further Understanding of the Occurence of the Indian Paint Fungus, Echinodontium tinctorum E. and E., in British Columbia Forests." British Columbia, 1956.

11722
Timmis, Roger. "Cold Acclimation and Freezing in Douglas-Fir Seedlings." British Columbia, 1973.

11723
Tusko, Frank Ferenc. "A Study of Variability in Certain Douglas Fir Populations in British Columbia." British Columbia, 1963.

11724
Williams, Douglas Harold. "Integrating Stand and Forest Models for Decision Analysis." British Columbia, 1977. British Columbia Forest Service/Service forestier de la Colombie-Britannique]

11725
Yang, Richard Chun-Hsiung. "A Least Squares Analysis of Inventory Data in British Columbia Forest Zones." British Columbia, 1978.

Yarie, John Anthony. See No./Voir no 11509

Ziller, Wolf Gunther. See No./Voir no 324

Manitoba

11726
Sims, Herbert Percival. "Some Ecological Effects of Prescribed Burning on Cut-Over Jack Pine (Pinus banksiana Lamb.) Sites, Southeastern Manitoba." Duke, 1973.

11727
Steneker, Gustav Adolf. "Size and Suckering of Trembling Aspen (Populus tremuloides Michaux) Clones in Manitoba." Michigan, 1972.

Maritime Provinces/Provinces Maritimes

General Item/Ouvrage général

11728
Blenis, Henry Wallace, Jr. "The Forest Technician in the Atlantic Provinces of Canada." Pennsylvania State, 1969.

11729
Davidson, Alexander Grant. "Decay of Balsam Fir Abies balsamea (L. Mill.) in the Maritime Provinces of Canada." Toronto, 1955.

Labrador

11730
Foster, David Russell. "Phytosociology, Fire History, and Vegetation Dynamics of the Boreal Forest of Southeastern Labrador." Minnesota, 1983.

New Brunswick/Nouveau-Brunswick

11731
Flinn, Marguerite Adele. "Heat Penetration and Early Postfire Regeneration of Some University Species in the Acadian Forest." New Brunswick, 1980. [Acadia Forest Experiment Station, New Brunswick/Station expérimentale forestière de l'Acadie, Nouveau-Brunswick]

11732
MacLean, David Andrew. "Fire and the Nutrient Cycle of New Brunswick Pine and Hardwood Stands: Field Studies and Computer Simulation Studies." New Brunswick, 1978.

Wynn, Graeme Clifford. See No./Voir no 4853

Newfoundland/Terre-Neuve

11733
Carroll, William Joseph. "Some Aspects of the Neodiprion abietics (Harr.) Complex in Newfoundland." Syracuse, 1962.

11734
Hudak, Janos. "Microbial Deterioration of Balsam Fir Damaged by the Balsam Wooly Aphid in Western Newfoundland." SUNY, College of Environmental Science and Forestry, Syracuse, 1975.

11735
Munro, John Alexander. "Public Timber Allocation Policy in Newfoundland." British Columbia, 1978.

Nova Scotia/Nouvelle-Écosse

11736
Green, David Geoffrey. "Nova Scotian Forest History: Evidence from a Statistical Analysis of Pollen Data." Dalhousie, 1976.

11737
Piene, Harald. "Changes in Carbon and Nitrogen Mineralization in Spaced Stands of Young Balsam Fir, Cape Breton Highlands, Nova Scotia." New Brunswick, 1976.

11738
Rogers, Robert Spencer. "A Community Study of Forests Dominated by Eastern Hemlock (Tsuga canadensis) at the Northern Edge of Hemlock's Range." Minnesota, 1976.

11739
Runyon, Kenneth Lee. "Cost Effective Timber Management Planning: A Problem Analysis for the Province of Nova Scotia." Michigan State, 1983.

11740
Timmer, Victor Robert. "Foliar Diagnosis of Nutrient Status and Growth Response in Forest Trees." Cornell, 1979.

Northwest Territories/ Territoires du Nord-Ouest

11741
Sims, Richard Allan. "Ground-Truth and Large-Scale 70mm Aerial Photographs in the Study of Reindeer Winter Rangeland, Tuktoyaktuk Peninsula Area, N.W.T." British Columbia, 1983.

Ontario

11742
Carleton, Terence John. "A Phytosociological Analysis of Boreal Forests South of James Bay." Toronto, 1978.

11743
Chen, Chien-pin. "The Quality and Quantity of Protein Derived from Hybrid Poplar Tissues." Toronto, 1979.

De Catanzaro, Jennifer Barbara. See No./Voir no 11569

11744
Dwyer, Lianne Marie. "Forest Floor Heterogeneity as a Functional Component in Litter Decomposition." Carleton, 1978.

Freedman, William. See No./Voir no 260

11745
Glerum, Christiaan. "Formation and Distribution of Food Reserves During Autumn and Their Subsequent Utilization in Jack Pine." Toronto, 1977.

11746
Hett, Joan Margaret. "Age Structural Dynamics of Abies balsamea and Tsuga canadensis." Wisconsin, 1969.

11747
Martell, David Leigh. "Contributions to Decision-Making in Forest Fire Management." Toronto, 1975.

Middleton, John David. See No./Voir no 11645

11748
Nordin, Vidar John. "Decay in Sugar Maple (Acer saccharum Marsh) in the Ottawa-Huron and Algoma Extension Forest Region of Ontario." Toronto, 1951.

Pross, August Paul. See No./Voir no 8734

11749
Sadig, Riyaz Ahmed. "Evaluation of Forest Stand Growth and Yield Models." Toronto, 1981. [Drury Forest in Southern Ontario/Forêt Drury dans le sud de l'Ontario]

11750
Shea, Sidney Ronald. "Growth and Development of Jack Pine (Pinus banksiana, Lamb.) in Relation to Edaphic Factors in Northeastern Ontario." Toronto, 1973.

11751
Shields, Walter Joseph. "Deterioration of Trembling Aspen Clones in the Great Lakes Region." Wisconsin, 1979.

11752
Suffling, Roger Charles. "Selected Ecological Factors Influencing British Control Using Tordon 101 Herbicide." Guelph, 1976. [Sudbury]

11753
Weary, Gregory Charles. "Litter Decomposition and Nutrient Release in a Red Maple Woodlet Under Natural Conditions and Under Insecticide and Herbicide Treatments." Carleton, 1974. [Ottawa]

11754
White, Lewis Theodore. "Decays of White Pine in Ontario." Toronto, 1950.

Quebec/Québec

Blanchet, Bertrand. See No./Voir no 11591

11755
Blouin, Jean-Louis. "Étude écologique et cartographique de la végétation du comté de Rivière-du-Loup." Laval, 1970.

11756
Bolghari, Hassanali. "Étude de la croissance et de la distribution de fréquence des tiges et de la surface terrière des peuplements de sapin baumier et d'épinette noire du Québec." Laval, 1975.

Booth, John Derek. See No./Voir no 4750

11757
Boudoux, Michel. "Modèle de simulation des forêts résineuses." Laval, 1979.

11758
Brazeau, Marcel. "Incidence de la fertilisation sur la nutrition et la croissance du sapin baumier (Abies balsamea (L.) Mill.) en forêt naturelle." Laval, 1979. [Montmorency Forest, 65 km northwest of Quebec/La forêt Montmorency à 65 km au nord-ouest de Québec]

11759
Camiré, Claude. "Fertilisation azotée en forêt de pin gris (Pinus banksiana Lamb)." Laval, 1979.

11760
Cauboue, Madeleine. "Modèle statistique pour l'étude écologique d'une serre physiographique à la forêt Beauséjour, comté de Lévis." Laval, 1980.

Carleton, Terence John. See No./Voir no 11742

11761
Ceck, Marian. "The Effect of Dynamic Transverse Compression Treatment on Drying Behaviour of Yellow Birch Lumber." Laval, 1970.

11762
Delorme, Gérard. "Le fer et le manganèse dans les principaux arbres à feuilles caduques du Québec." Montréal, 1939.

11763
Djolanic, Bahman. "Phénomènes d'hystérèse et effets de second ordre de l'absorption d'humidité dans le bois aux températures de 5°, 21°, 35° et 50°C." Laval, 1970.

11764
Doucet, René A. "Dry Matter Production in a Forty-year old Jack Pine Stand in Quebec." SUNY, College of Environmental Science and Forestry, Syracuse, 1974.

11765
Hormisdas, Frère. "Le manganèse et le fer dans les conifères de la province de Québec." Montréal, 1937.

11766
Ladouceur, Gilles. "Phytosociologie, pédalogie et nutrition de l'érable rouge (Acer rubrum L.), Province de Québec." Laval, 1968.

11767
Lemieux, Guy Joseph. "Ecology and Productivity of the Northern Hardwood Forests of Quebec." Michigan, 1964.

11768
Majcen, Zoran. "Relations entre la végétation, les caractères d'habitat et le rendement dans la station forestière d'Argenteuil, Québec." Laval, 1979.

Marr, John Winton. See No./Voir no 11608

11769
Richard, Joseph Robert Yvon. "A Study of Forest Stratification Used in the Quebec Boreal Forest Region." Syracuse, 1969.

11770
Thibault, J. Robert. "Contribution à l'étude des phytosubstances du sapin baumier et du peuplier baumier." Laval, 1977. [Region of St. Romuald/Région de Saint-Romuald]

11771
Villeneuve, Georges O. "Climatic Conditions of the Province of Quebec and Their Relationship to the Forests." Yale, 1964.

11772
Zarnovican, Richard. "Production stationnelle des sapinières dans le massif boisé du Lac Joffre en Gaspésie, Québec." Laval, 1983.

Saskatchewan

11773
Anderson, Howard George. "The Future Forests of Saskatchewan." Saskatchewan, 1976.

11774
Bella, Inire E. "Simulation of Growth, Yield and Management of Aspen." British Columbia, 1970.

Newsome, Richard Duane. See No./Voir no 11624

Scotter, George Wilby. See No./Voir no 10619

LIMNOLOGY AND FLORA AND FAUNA OF CANADIAN BODIES OF WATER/LIMNOLOGIE, FLORE ET FAUNE DES EAUX CANADIENNES

The major output for this area emerged during the last 15 years. Of the fewer than 100 titles approved in Canadian universities, more than three quarters of the work was produced during this period. The universities of Toronto, Waterloo, British Columbia, Dalhousie, and McGill were the leading producers. Fourteen American universities produced a total of 24 studies, with Ohio State accounting for one-third of the total. Eleven universities produced only one title each. Seventeen of the 24 titles were produced during the 1970's.

———

La plus grande partie des études en ce domaine a été faite entre 1970 et 1985. Parmi la centaine de thèses approuvées dans les universités canadiennes, plus des trois quarts datent de cette période. Les universités les plus productives sont Toronto, Waterloo, la Colombie-Britannique, Dalhousie et McGill. Aux États-Unis, l'Université Ohio State a produit un tiers des 24 thèses approuvées par 14 universités. Onze d'entre elles n'ont qu'un seul titre à leur actif et 17 des 24 thèses datent des années 1970.

General Items/Ouvrages généraux

11775
Cushing, Colbert Ellis. "Ecology of a Lake-Stream System." Saskatchewan, 1961.

11776
Dwernychuk, Leonard Wayne. "The Macro-Invertebrate Community Within the Littoral Zones of Six Freshwater Ponds: A Study in Succession." Regina, 1975.

11777
Fitzpatrick, Gordon James. "Coexistence of Species in a Fluctuating Environment." British Columbia, 1977.

11778
Flett, Robert John. "Nitrogen Fixation in Canadian Precambrian Shield Lakes." Manitoba, 1977.

11779
McCauley, Edward. "The Impact of Zooplankton on the Dynamics of Natural Phytoplankton Communities." McGill, 1983.

11780
Reckshow, Kenneth Howland. "Phosphorus Models for Lake Management." Harvard, 1977.

11781
Vascotto, Gian L. "The Zoobenthic Assemblages of Four Central Canadian Lakes and Their Potential Use as Environmental Indicators." Manitoba, 1977.

Great Lakes/Grands Lacs

General Items/Ouvrages généraux

11782
Barton, David Remle. "A Study of the Wave-Zone Macrobenthos Along the Canadian Shores of the St. Lawrence Great Lakes." Waterloo, 1976.

11783
Krezoski, John Roman. "The Influence of Zoobenthos on Fine-Grained Particle Reworking and Benthic Solute Transport in Great Lakes Sediments." Michigan, 1981.

11784
Swain, Wayland Roger. "The Ecology of the Second Trophic Level in Lakes Superior, Michigan and Huron." Minnesota, 1969.

11785
Wehr, Nancy Reed. "Phytoplankton Metabolism in the Laurentian Aquatic Ecosystem." Southern Illinois, 1979.

Lake Erie/Lac Érié

Adams, William James. See No./Voir no 10906
Andrews, Theodore F. See No./Voir no 11058
11786
Burkett, Robert Dale. "The Use of Cladophora to Monitor Mercury Occurrence in Western Lake Erie Waters." Ohio State, 1973.

11787
Carrick, Louis Burrell. "A Study of Hydras in Lake Erie: Contribution Toward a Natural History of the Great Lakes Hydridae." Ohio State, 1956.

11788
Cody, Terence Edward. "Primary Productivity in the Western Basin of Lake Erie." Ohio State, 1972.
Doan, Kenneth Henry. See No./Voir no 10911

11789
Gladish, David William. "The Phytoplankton Biomass, Primary Productivity and Physical Chemical Parameters at Two Stations in Western Lake Erie, 1975-76." Windsor, 1978.

11790
Herendorf, Charles Edward, III. "Limnological Investigations of the Spawning Reefs and Adjacent Areas of Western Lake Erie with Special Attention to Their Physical Characteristics." Ohio State, 1970.

11791
Lu, Julian D. "The Dynamics of Zooplankton Populations in Western Lake Erie Including the Effect of Thermal Effluent." Michigan State, 1977.

11792
Petersen, Richard Randolph. "A Paleolimnological Study of the Eutrophication of Lake Erie." Duke, 1971.

11793
Pliodzinskas, Algimantas Jonas. "Aquatic Oligochaetes in the Open Water Sediments of Lake Erie's Western and Central Basins." Ohio State, 1978.

11794
Rathke, David Edwin. "Plankton and Nutrient Distributions and Relationships in the Central Basin of Lake Erie During 1975." Ohio State, 1979.

11795
Rogick, Mary Dora. "The Freshwater Bryozoa of Lake Erie." Ohio State, 1934.

11796
Wood, Kenneth George. "Distribution and Ecology of Certain Bottom Living Invertebrates of the Western Basin of Lake Erie." Ohio State, 1953.

Lake Ontario/Lac Ontario

11797
Johnson, Murray Gordon. "Production, Energy Flow and Structure in Benthic Macroinvertebrate Communities of Lake Ontario." Toronto, 1970. [Bay of Quinte and Prince Edward Bay/Baies de Quinte et du Prince-Édouard]

11798
Landsberg, Dennis Robert. "On the Resultant Cyclonic Transport in Lake Ontario." SUNY, Albany, 1975.

11799
Pickett, Eric Elliott. "Modelling Limnological Systems: With Special Reference to Lake Ontario." Toronto, 1975.

11800
Rosemarin, Arno S. "Analysis of the Role Played by Growth and Nutrient Dynamics in the Competitive Success of Cladophora glomerata (L.) Kutz in Lake Ontario, with Reference to Potential Competitor Stigeoclonium tenue (Agardh) Kutz." Queen's, 1983.

11801
Warwick, William Frank. "Man and the Bay of Quinte, Lake Ontario: 2800 Years of Cultural Influence, with Special Reference to the Chironomidae (Diptera), Sedimentation and Eutrophication." Manitoba, 1978.

St. Lawrence/Saint-Laurent

11802
Demers, Serge. "Contrôle hydrodynamique et physiologie du phytoplancton de l'estuaire du Saint-Laurent." Laval, 1981.

11803
Fortier, Jacques Louis. "Environmental and Behavioural Control of Large-Scale Distribution and Local Abundance of Ichthyoplankton in the St. Lawrence Estuary." McGill, 1983.

11804
Gauthier, Benoît. "Recherches des limites hydrobiologiques du Saint-Laurent (Phytogéographie de l'hydrolittoral laurentien." Laval, 1978.

11805
Hudon, Christianne. "La communauté microépibenthique colonisant les substrats solides dans l'estuaire du Saint-Laurent." Laval, 1983.

11806
Lacroix, Guy. "Les fluctuations quantitatives du zooplankton de la Baie-des-Chaleurs (Golfe Saint-Laurent)." Laval, 1970.

11807
Legendre, Louis. "Phytoplankton Structures in Baie des Chaleurs." Dalhousie, 1972.

Wehr, Nancy Reed. See No./Voir no 11785

Alberta

11808
Anderson, Robert Stewart. "The Limnology of Snowflakes Lake and Other High Altitude Lakes in Banff National Park, Alberta." Calgary, 1968.

11809
Crowther, Roy Anderson. "Ecological Investigations of Hartley Creek, Alberta." Calgary, 1980.

11810
Haney, James Filmore. "Seasonal and Spatial Changes in the Grazing Rate of Limnetic Zooplankton." Toronto, 1970. [Heart Lake/Lac Heart]

Lim, Richard Peter. See No./Voir no 11086
11811
Osborne, Lewis Leroy. "The Effects of Chlorine on the Benthic Communities of the Sheep River, Alberta." Calgary, 1981.

British Columbia/Colombie-Britannique

Bhoojedhur, Seewant. See No./Voir no 233
11812
Brown, Sharon-Dale. "Environmental Characteristics and Sediment Diatoms of 51 Lakes on Southern Vancouver Island and Saltspring Island." Victoria, 1980.

11813
Buckingham, Sandra Lynn. "Functional Responses and Feeding Strategies of Freshwater Filter-Feeding Zooplankton." British Columbia, 1979.

11814
Carlton, James Theodore. "History, Biogeography and Ecology of the Introduced Marine and Estuarine Invertebrates of the Pacific Coast of North America." California, Davis, 1979. [Straits of Georgia/Détroit de Georgie]

11815
Chapman, Peter Michael. "Seasonal Movements of Subtidal Benthic Communities in a Salt Wedge Estuary as Related to Interstitial Salinities." Victoria, 1979. [Lower Fraser River/Bas du fleuve Fraser]

11816
Cloern, James Earl. "Population Dynamics of Cryptomonas ovata: A Laboratory Field, and Computer Simulation Study." Washington State, 197 [Phytoplankton in Kootenay Lake/Phytoplankton dans le lac Kootenay]

11817
Culp, Joseph Marion. "Ecological Effects of Logging on the Macroinvertebrates of a Salmon Stream British Columbia." Calgary, 1983.

11818
Duncan, Mary Jo. "Aspects of the Pigment Biology and Ecology of Nereocystis luetkeana." Simon Fraser, 1971. [Departure Bay, Burrard Inlet]

11819
Duval, Wayne Stuart. "Diel Rhythms in the Respiration and Feeding Rates of Zooplankton." Simon Fraser, 1974. [Eunice Lake/Lac Eunice]

Fitzpatrick, Gordon James. See No./Voir no 11777
11820
Fleming, William Norris. "A Model of the Phosphorus Cycle and Phytoplankton Growth in Skaha Lake British Columbia." British Columbia, 1974.

11821
Gardner, Grant Allan. "The Analysis of Zooplankton Population Fluctuations in the Strait of Georgia with Emphasis on the Relationship Between Calanus plumchrus Marukawa and Calanus marshallae Frost." British Columbia, 1976.

Himmelman, John Henry. See No./Voir no 11106
11822
Hoebel, Michael Francis. "The Role of Meiofauna the Benthic Community of a Small-Oligotrophic Lake." British Columbia, 1979. [Marion Lake/Lac Marion]

11823
Kleiber, Pierre Maxwell. "The Dynamics of Extracellular Dissolved Organic Material in the Sediments of Marion Lake, British Columbia." California, Davis, 1972.

11824
McKone, Warren Douglas. "Quantitative Studies of Stream Drift with Particular Reference to the McLay Model." British Columbia, 1975.

11825
Peacock, Adrienne Hazel. "Responses of Two Coexisting Cyclopoid Copepods to Experimental Manipulations of Food and Predators." British Columbia, 1981. [Zooplankton communities in two mountain lakes, University of British Columbia Research Forest/Groupes de zooplankton dans deux lacs des montagnes, réserve forestière de l'Université de la Colombie-Britannique]

Pieper, Richard Edward. See No./Voir no 11934
Stone, David Philip. See No./Voir no 11072
11826
Swift, Michael Crane. "Energetics of Vertical Migration in Chaoborus trivittatus Larvae." British Columbia, 1974. [Eunice Lake/Lac Eunice]

11827
Taylor, Kenneth Gordon. "Limnological Studies on Kootenay Lake, British Columbia, Canada." Washington State, 1972.

11828
Wallen, Donald George. "The Effect of Light Quality on Growth Rates, Photosynthetic Rates and Metabolism in Plankton Algae." Simon Fraser, 1970.

Labrador

11829
Carter, John Charteris Haig. "The Hydrography and Plankton of Tessiarsuk, a Coastal Meromictic Lake of Northern Labrador." McGill, 1963.

11830
Ostrofsky, Milton Lewis. "An Approach to the Modelling of Productivity in Reservoirs." Waterloo, 1977. [Smallwood and Ossokmannan Reservoirs/ Réservoirs Smallwood et Ossokmannan]

Tolderlund, Douglas Stanley. See No./Voir no 5095

Manitoba

11831
Chan, Yin Kwok. "Denitrification and Phytoplankton Assimilation of Nitrite in Lake 227 During Summer Stratification." Manitoba, 1977.

11832
Rudd, John William McCullagh. "Methane Cycling in Lake 227 and Its Effects on Whole Lake Metabolism." Manitoba, 1976.

New Brunswick/Nouveau-Brunswick

11833
Davidson, Viola May. "Fluctuations in the Abundance of Planktonic Diatoms in the Passamaquoddy Region, New Brunswick from 1924 to 1931 (with Notes on the Dinoflagellates and the Silicoflagellates)." Toronto, 1933.

Lacroix, Guy. See No./Voir no 11806
Legendre, Louis. See No./Voir no 11807

Newfoundland/Terre-Neuve

11834
Kerekes, Joseph Jeno. "A Comparative Limnological Study of Five Lakes in Terra Nova National Park, Newfoundland." Dalhousie, 1972.

The Arctic and Northwest Territories/ Arctique et Territoires du Nord-Ouest

11835
Bilyard, Gordon Richard. "Zoogeography and Ecology of Western Beaufort Sea Polychaeta." Oregon State, 1979.

11836
Buchanan, Claire L. "Arctic Investigations of Some Factors that Control the Vertical Distributions and Swimming Activities of Zooplankton." New Hampshire, 1978.

11837
Dunbar, Maxwell J. "Studies in the Arctic Plankton Comprising a Faunistic Survey of Certain of the Marine Planktonic Groups Collected in the Canadian Eastern Arctic and an Investigation of the Breeding Cycles of Five of the Most Important Species in the Eastern Arctic and in West Greenland." McGill, 1942.

11838
Ellis, Derek Victor. "Marine Infaunal Benthos in Arctic North America." McGill, 1957. [Baffin Island/Île de Baffin]

11839
Havas, Magda. "A Study of the Chemistry and Biota of Acid and Alkaline Ponds at the Smoking Hills, N.W.T." Toronto, 1981.

11840
McLaren, Ian Alexander. "The Hydrography and Zooplankton Biology of Ogac Lake, a Landlocked Fiord on Baffin Island." Yale, 1961.

11841
Paulin, Michel. "L'étude taxonomique et écologique d'une communauté époutique (Détroit de Manitounuk, Baie d'Hudson)." Laval, 1983.

Nova Scotia/Nouvelle-Écosse

11842
Bartlett, Grant Aulden. "Benthonic Foraminiferal Ecology in St. Margaret's Bay and Mahone Bay, Southeast Nova Scotia." New York, 1964.

11843
Case, James Michael. "Variations in Trace Metals and Major Ion Concentrations at Gays River, Nova Scotia." Dalhousie, 1980.

11844
Dale, Mark Randall Thomas. "The Analysis of Patterns of Zonation and Phytosociological Structure of Seaweed Communities." Dalhousie, 1980.

11845
Duerden, Floyd Colin. "Aspects of Phytoplankton Production and Phosphate Exchange in Bedford Basin." Dalhousie, 1973.

11846
Geen, Glen Howard. "Primary Production in Bras D'Or Lake and Other Inland Waters of Cape Breton Island, Nova Scotia." Dalhousie, 1965.

11847
Gregory, Murray Richard. "Distribution of Benthonic Foraminifera in Halifax Harbour, Nova Scotia, Canada." Dalhousie, 1971.

11848
Hamdan, Abdul Rahima Ahmad. "Ecology and Distribution of Recent Foraminifera on the Scotian Shelf." Queen's, 1972.

11849
Hollibaugh, James T. "Nitrogen Regeneration During Amino Acid Degradation and the Activity of Bacteria in Plankton Communities of Halifax Harbor, Nova Scotia, Canada." Dalhousie, 1977.

11850
Mackas, David Lloyd. "Horizontal Spatial Variability and Covariability of Marine Phytoplankton and Zooplankton." Dalhousie, 1975. [Scotian Shelf/ Plate-forme de Nouvelle-Écosse]

11851
Saifullah, Syed Mohammed. "The Relation Between Production and Standing Crop of Phytoplankton: A Study in St. Margaret's Bay, N.S." McGill, 1969.

11852
Schwinghamer, Peter. "Size Distribution of Benthic Organisms in the Bay of Fundy, Canada." Dalhousie, 1981.

11853
Therriault, Jean-Claude. "Studies of the Spatial Heterogeneity in the Phytoplankton of St. Margaret's Bay, Nova Scotia." Dalhousie, 1977.

Ontario

11854
Adamstone, Frank Bolton. "The Distribution and Economic Importance of the Bottom Fauna of Lake Nipigon." Toronto, 1924.

11855
Ang, Kok-Jee. "Seasonality and Dynamics of Littoral Zooplankton of Some Small Lakes and the Production of One of Them Simocephalus serrulatus (Koch)." Waterloo, 1972.

11856
Bird, Glen Alvin. "The Processing of Leaf Litter by Invertebrates in Three Reaches of Stream and in the Laboratory." Guelph, 1983. [Canagagigue Creek/Ruisseau Canagagigue]

11857
Chamberlain, William Maynard. "A Preliminary Investigation of the Nature and Importance of Soluble Organic Phosphorus in the Phosphorus Cycle of Lakes." Toronto, 1968. [Upper Bass Lake/Haut du lac Bass]

11858
Chatarpaul, Lakeram. "Laboratory Studies on Nitrogen Transformations in Stream Sediments." Guelph, 1978. [Canagagigue Creek/Ruisseau Canagagigue]

11859
Chua, Kian Eng. "A Qualitative Investigation of Interaction Between Three Tubificid Species and the Sediment." Toronto, 1969. [Toronto Harbour/Port de Toronto]

11860
Dillon, Peter James. "The Prediction of Phosphorus and the Chlorophyll Concentrations in Lakes." Toronto, 1974.

Evans, Robert Douglas. See No./Voir no 5587

11861
Holtby, Leslie Blair. "Determinants of Zooplankton Community Structure in Freshwaters." Toronto, 1981. [St. George Lake/Lac St-George]

11862
Iyengar, V.K. Sundararaja. "The Relationships Between Chironomidae and Their Substrate in Ten Freshwater Lakes of Southern Ontario." McMaster, 1959.

Johnston, Laura Margaret. See No./Voir no 6084

11863
Kaushik, Narinder Kumar. "Autumn-Shed Leaves in Relation to Stream Ecology." Waterloo, 1969.

11864
Knoechel, Roy. "A Study of the Seasonal Phytoplankton Species Dynamics in a North-Temperate Zone Lake, Utilizing 14C Track Autoradiography." McGill, 1976.

11865
Lee, Kenneth. "The Effects of Vanadium on Phytoplankton: Field and Laboratory Studies." Toronto, 1982.

11866
Liaw, Wen Kuang. "Standing Biomass and Selected Chemical Features of Particulata Dissolved and Periphytic Organic Matter in River Water." Guelph, 1975. [Grand River]

Lim, Richard Peter. See No./Voir no 11086

11867
Lush, Donald Lawrence. "Organic Detrital Cycles in Small Forested Watersheds." Waterloo, 1974. [Laurel Creek/Ruisseau Laurel]

11868
Mackay, Hector Hugh. "The Net Plankton of Lake Nipigon." Toronto, 1951.

11869
McNeely, Roger N. "Limnological Investigations of a Small Meromictic Lake, Little Round Lake, Ontario, 1968-1970." Queen's, 1973.

11870
Paterson, Colin G. "Reservoir Macro-Invertebrate Colonization with a Consideration of Selected Problems of Sampling Shallow Water Bodies." Waterloo, 1969. [Laurel Creek Reservoir/Réservoir du ruisseau Laurel]

11871
Pick, Frances Renata. "Vertical Stratification of Phytoplankton in Lake Water." Toronto, 198. [Jacks Lake, Brooks Bay, William Bay/Lac Jack, baies Brooks et William]

Pope, Gregory Frederick. See No./Voir no 11883

11872
Prepas, Ellie Edith. "An Approach to Predicting Short-Term Changes in the Phosphorus Concentration in Lake Water." Toronto, 1980. [Bob and Hulls Lakes, Algonquin Park/Lacs Bob et Hull, parc Algonquin]

11873
Rawson, Donald Strathern. "The Bottom Fauna of Lake Simcoe and Its Role in the Ecology of the Lake." Toronto, 1929.

11874
Smol, John Paul. "Postglacial Changes in Fossil Algal Assemblages from Three Canadian Lakes." Queen's, 1982.

11875
Taylor, William David. "Laboratory and Field Studies on the Bactivorus Ciliates of a Small Pond." Toronto, 1978.

11876
Waite, Don T. "Some Relationships Between Primary and Secondary Production in Sunfish Lake, Ontario." Waterloo, 1973.

11877
Williams, David Dudley. "Recolonization Mechanism of Stream Benthos as Derived from a Study of Some Temporary Streams in Southern Ontario." Waterloo, 1975.

11878
Zarull, Michael Anthony. "Spatial and Temporal Heterogeniety in Phytoplankton Communities." McMaster, 1979. [Hamilton Harbour/Port de Hamilton]

Quebec/Québec

11879
Adams, James Russell. "The Biotic Cycles in Northern Pond Communities." McGill, 1940.

11880
Côté, Raynald. "Aspects dynamiques de la production primaire dans le Saguenay, fjord subarctique du Québec." Laval, 1978.

11881
Cutten, Felicity Esme Arthington. "Ecological Investigations on the Macroinvertebrate Fauna in Loon Bay Creek, Province of Quebec, Canada." McGill, 1969.

Lacroix, Guy. See No./Voir no 11806

Legendre, Louis. See No./Voir no 11807

11882
Nakashima, Brian Shyozo. "The Contribution of Fishes to Phosphorus Cycling in Lakes." McGill, 1980. [Lake Memphremagog/Lac Memphremagog]

11883
Pope, Gregory Fredrick. "Variations in the Zooplankton Communities of Lakes of the Matamek River System Related to Fish." Waterloo, 1974.

11884
Ross, Philippe Edward. "The Role of the Ultraplankton in the Ecology of a Pre-Cambrian Shield Lake." Waterloo, 1980. [Lake Matamec/Lac Matamec]

11885
Smith, Ralph Elliott Henry. "Phosphorus Limitation and Competiton in the Phytoplankton." McGill, 1981. [Lake Memphremagog/Lac Memphremagog]

11886
Trucco, Ramiro. "Some Interactions of Lake Plankton with Heavy Metals." Ottawa, 1982. [Heney Lake/Lac Heney]

Saskatchewan

11887
Tones, Patricia Isabel. "Factors Influencing Littoral Fauna in Saline Lakes in Saskatchewan." Saskatchewan, 1977.

HYDROGRAPHY, HYDROLOGY AND OCEANOGRAPHY/HYDROGRAPHIE, HYDROLOGIE ET OCÉANOGRAPHIE

It is not surprising to learn that of the 12 Canadian universities working in these areas, British Columbia and Dalhousie produced more than half of the studies, with McGill a distant third. The entire Canadian output was completed during the 1970's and 1980's. Of the 17 American universities listed here, Washington (Seattle) was number one with ten titles, and Oregon State, second with five. Ten universities produced only one study each. Two theses were approved in Great Britain, both at the University of Liverpool.

* For the sake of convenience, these three subclassifications are combined.

———

Il n'est pas surprenant d'apprendre que des 12 universités canadiennes qui ont produit des thèses en ce domaine, la Colombie-Britannique et Dalhousie ont fourni plus de la moitié des études, McGill venant au troisième rang, loin derrière. Presque toutes les thèses canadiennes ont été faites au cours des années 1970 et 1980. Dix-sept universités américaines ont produit des thèses; Washington (Seattle) se classe première avec dix titres et Oregon State, seconde, avec cinq; dix autres universités n'ont produit qu'une étude chacune. Deux thèses ont été approuvées en Grande-Bretagne, toutes deux à l'Université de Liverpool.

Pour des raisons de commodité, ces trois sous-classifications ont été regroupées.

General Items/Ouvrages généraux

11888
Fulton, James F. "Secondary Currents in Straight Open Channels." Queen's, 1961.

11889
Gupta, Santosh Kumar. "A Distributed Digital Model for Estimation of Flows and Sediment Load from Large Ungauged Watersheds." Waterloo, 1974.

11890
Lambert, Anthony. "A Tiltmeter Study of the Response of the Earth to Ocean Tide Loading." Dalhousie, 1970.

11891
Newton, John Lebaron. "The Canada Basin: Mean Circulation and Intermediate Scale Flow Features." Washington, Seattle, 1973.

11892
Pocklington, Roger. "Dissolved Free Amino Acids of North Atlantic Ocean Waters." Dalhousie, 1970.

Sanderman, Llewellyn Arthur. See No./Voir no 6609

11893
Sklash, Michael Gregory. "The Role of Groundwater in Storm and Snowmelt Runoff Generation." Waterloo, 1978.

11894
Sullivan, Barbara Koster. "Vertical Distribution and Feeding of Two Species of Chaetognaths at Weather Station P. (Canadian)." Oregon State, 1977.

Pacific Coast/Côte du Pacifique

11895
Bathen, Karl Hans. "Heat Storage and Advection in the North Pacific Ocean." Hawaii, 1970. [Off British Columbia/Au large de la Colombie-Britannique]

11896
Chelton, Dudley Boyd, Jr. "Low Frequency Sea Level Variability Along the West Coast of North America." California, San Diego, 1980. [Alaska to Mexico/De l'Alaska au Mexique]
Goodman, Joseph Robert. See No./Voir no 11967

Great Lakes/Grands Lacs

General Item/Ouvrage général

11897
Pettis, Charles A. "Hydrology of the Great Lakes." Michigan, 1938.

Lake Erie/Lac Érié

Haq, Aminul. See No./Voir no 5005
11898
Olson, Franklyn C.W. "The Currents of Western Lake Erie." Ohio State, 1950.
11899
Yu, Kwang-Hwa Andrew. "Model Studies of Lake Erie." SUNY, Buffalo, 1978.

Lake Ontario/Lac Ontario

11900
Bennett, John Richard. "On the Dynamics of Wind Driven Lake Currents." Wisconsin, 1972.
11901
Elliott, Gillian Hope. "A Laboratory and Mathematical Study of the 'Thermal Bar'." British Columbia, 1970.
Landsberg, Dennis Robert. See No./Voir no 11798
11902
Liu, Paul Chi. "Temporal Spectral Growth and Non-Linear Characteristics of Wind Waves in Lake Ontario." Michigan, 1977.
11903
Sciremammano, Frank, Jr. "A New Method for a Long Range Forecast of the Lake Ontario Water Levels." Rochester, 1977.
11904
Tucker, William Allen. "Thermal Structure of Lakes." Michigan, 1976.
11905
Witten, Alan Joel. "Wind-Driven Circulation in Large Lakes with Spatially-Variable Eddy Viscosity." Rochester, 1975.

Lake Superior/Lac Supérieur

11906
Niebauer, Henry Joseph. "Wind Driven Coastal Upwelling in Lake Superior." Wisconsin, 1976.
11907
Smith, Ned Philip. "Summertime Temperature and Circulation Patterns in Lake Superior." Wisconsin, 1972.

Labrador Sea/Mer du Labrador

11908
Godin, J.J.Gabriel G. "The Tides in the Labrador Sea, Davis Strait and Baffin Bay." Liverpool, 1965.
11909
Huntley, Mark Edward. "Developing and Testing a New Method for Estimating the Production of Marine Zooplankton." Dalhousie, 1981.
11910
Ivers, William Dargan. "The Deep Circulation in the Northern North Atlantic with Special Reference to the Labrador Sea." California, San Diego, 1975.

St. Lawrence/Saint-Laurent

Beltagy, Ali Ibrahim Ali Mohammed. See No./Voir no 5085
11911
El-Sabh, Mohammed Ibrahim. "Transport and Currents in the Gulf of St. Lawrence." McGill, 1974.
11912
Forrester, Warren David. "Currents and Geostrophic Currents in the St. Lawrence Estuary." Johns Hopkins, 1967.
Rodrigues, Cyril Gerard. See No./Voir no 5139
11913
Sinclair, Michael Mackay. "Phytoplankton Distributions in the Lower St. Lawrence Estuary." California, San Diego, 1977.

British Columbia/Colombie-Britannique

11914
Brown, Penelope Stevenson. "The Production of Planktonic Herbiverous Food Chains in Large-Scale Continuous Cultures." British Columbia, 1979.
11915
Buckley, Joseph Roy. "The Currents, Winds and Tides of Northern Howe Sound." British Columbia, 1977.
11916
Cattell, Sidney Allen. "Dinaflagellates and Vitamin B12 in the Strait of Georgia, British Columbia." British Columbia, 1969.
11917
Chanasyk, David Steve. "A Model to Evaluate the Hydrologic Response to Land Use Changes." Alberta, 1980. [Jameson Creek Watershed near Vancouver/Ligne de partage des eaux du ruisseau Jameson près de Vancouver]
11918
Cheng, Jie-Dar. "A Study of the Stormflow Hydrology of Small Forested Watersheds in the Coast Mountains of Southwestern British Columbia." British Columbia, 1976.
11919
Clark, Robert Charles. "The Biochemistry of Aromatic and Saturated Hydrocarbons in a Rocky Intertidal Marine Community in the Strait of Juan de Fuca." Washington, Seattle, 1983.
11920
Crean, P.B. "Numerical Model Studies of the Tides Between Vancouver Island and the Mainland Pacific Coast." Liverpool, 1972.

1921
DeMora, Stephen John. "Manganese Chemistry in the Fraser Estuary." British Columbia, 1981.

Drake, Julian John. See No./Voir no 5101

1922
Falkowski, Paul Gordon. "The Mechanisms and Energetics of Nitrate Uptake by Marine Phytoplankton." British Columbia, 1975. [Knight Inlet]

1923
Farmer, David Malcolm. "The Influence of Wind on the Surface Waters of Alberni Inlet." British Columbia, 1972.

Gargett, Ann Elizabeth. See No./Voir no 4998

1924
Hay, Alexander Edward. "Submarine Channel Formation and Acoustic Remote Sensing of Suspended Sediments and Turbidity Currents in Rupert Inlet, B.C." British Columbia, 1981.

1925
Helbig, James Alfred. "On the Inertial Stability of Coastal Flows." British Columbia, 1979. [Strait of Georgia/Détroit de Georgie]

11926
Hodgins, Donald Ormond. "Salinity Intrusion in the Fraser River, British Columbia." British Columbia, 1974.

11927
Ingraham, Diane Verna. "Rainfall Estimation from Satellite Images." British Columbia, 1980.

11928
Jamart, Bruno M. "Finite Element Computation of Barotropic Tidal Motions in Deep Estuaries." Washington, Seattle, 1980. [Knight Inlet]

11929
Luternauer, John Leland. "Patterns of Sedimentation in Queen Charlotte Sound, British Columbia." British Columbia, 1972.

11930
McBean, Gordon Almon. "The Turbulent Transfer Mechanisms in the Atmosphere Surface Layer." British Columbia, 1970. [Ladner, British Columbia/Colombie-Britannique]

11931
Mills, Claudia Eileen. "Patterns and Mechanisms of Vertical Distribution of Medusae and Ctenophores." Victoria, 1983. [Saanich Inlet]

11932
Nasmyth, Patrick Walden. "Oceanic Turbulence." British Columbia, 1970. [Off west coast of British Columbia/Au large de la Colombie-Britannique]

Nienber, Wilfred. See No./Voir no 6624

11933
Phipps, James Benjamin. "Sediments and Tectonics of the Gorda-Juan de Fuca Plate." Oregon State, 1974.

11934
Pieper, Richard Edward. "A Study of the Relationship Between Zooplankton and High Frequency Scattering of Underwater Sound." British Columbia, 1971. [Saanich Inlet]

Plamondon, André Paul. See No./Voir no 11712

11935
Shim, Jae Hyung. "Distribution and Taxonomy of Planktonic Marine Diatoms in the Strait of Georgia, B.C." British Columbia, 1976.

11936
Spittlehouse, David Leslie. "Measuring and Modelling Evapotranspiration from Douglas-Fir Stands." British Columbia, 1981. [Courtenay, British Columbia/Colombie-Britannique]

11937
Stronach, James Alexander. "Observational and Modelling Studies of the Fraser River Plume." British Columbia, 1978.

11938
Trick, Charles Gordon. "Production of Unique Metabolites by the Marine Dinoflagellate Prorocentrum mincmum." British Columbia, 1982.

11939
Trites, Ronald Wilmot. "A Study of the Oceanographic Structure in British Columbia Inlets and Some of the Determining Factors." British Columbia, 1956.

11940
Tully, John P. "Oceanography of Alberni Inlet and Prediction of Pulp Mill Pollution in Alberni Inlet." Washington, Seattle, 1948.

11941
Waldichuk, Michael. "Physical Oceanography of the Strait of Georgia, British Columbia." Washington, Seattle, 1956.

11942
Woo, Ming-Ko. "Numerical Simulation of Snow Hydrology for Management Purposes." British Columbia, 1972.

11943
Zeman, Lubomir John. "Chemistry of Tropospheric Fallout and Streamflow in a Small Mountainous Watershed Near Vancouver, British Columbia." British Columbia, 1973.

Maritime Provinces/Provinces Maritimes

General Item/Ouvrage général

11944
Quinlan, Garry Michael. "Numerical Models of Postglacial Relative Sea Level Change in Atlantic Canada and the Eastern Canadian Arctic." Dalhousie, 1981.

Newfoundland and Labrador/Terre-Neuve et Labrador

Carter, John Charteris Haig. See No./Voir no 11829

11945
Kollmeyer, Ronald Charles. "Labrador Current Predictive Model." Connecticut, 1975.

Scotian Shelf/Plate-forme de la Nouvelle-Écosse

11946
Andrews, Daniel. "The Prediction and Measurement of Dissolved Silicate Flux Across Marine Sediments." Dalhousie, 1980.

11947
Cok, Anthony Edward. "Morphology and Surficial Sediments of the Eastern Half of the Nova Scotia Shelf." Dalhousie, 1971.

11948
Côté, Brenda. "Short Term Temporal Variability in the Photosynthetic Capacity of Natural Assemblages of Coastal Marine Phytoplankton." Dalhousie, 1980.

11949
Drapeau, Georges. "Sedimentology of the Surficial Sediments of the Western Portion of the Scotian Shelf." Dalhousie, 1971.

11950
Gagnon, Michael J. "The Fate of Anthropogenic Surfactants in the Marine System." Dalhousie, 1980. [Halifax Harbour/Port de Halifax]

11951
Gershey, Robert Michael. "The Isolation and Partial Chemical Characterization of Bubble Transportable Organic Matter in Seawater." Dalhousie, 1981. [Halifax Harbour/Port de Halifax]

11952
Guerinot, Mary Lou. "The Association of N_2-Fixing Bacteria with Sea Urchins." Dalhousie, 1977.

11953
Harrison, Paul Garth. "Growth and Detritus Formation in a Temperate Seagrass, Zostera Marina." Dalhousie, 1974.

11954
Holman, Robert Alan. "Infragravity Waves on Beaches." Dalhousie, 1979.

11955
Horne, Edward P.W. "The Dynamics of the Subsurface Front in the Slope Waters off Nova Scotia." Dalhousie, 1979.

Keddy, Paul Anthony. See No./Voir no 11526
Kepkay, Paul E. See No./Voir no 10206

11956
Ku, Lang-fa. "The Computation of Tides from GEOS-3 Altimeter Data." Dalhousie, 1983.

11957
Lee, Allan Hinglun. "The T-S Structure, Circulation and Mixing in the Slope Water Region East of the Scotian Shelf." Dalhousie, 1972.

11958
Petrie, Brian D. "Subsurface and Internal Tides on the Scotian Shelf and Slope." Dalhousie, 1974.

Scott, David Bruce. See No./Voir no 5677

11959
Sellner, Kevin G. "Primary Production and the Flux of Dissolved Organic Matter in Several Marine Environments." Dalhousie, 1978.

11960
Warner, James Lawrence. "Water Movement on the Scotian Shelf." Dalhousie, 1975.

Prince Edward Island/Île-du-Prince-Édouard

11961
Thomas, Martin Lewis Hall. "Studies on the Benthos of Bideford River, Prince Edward Island." Dalhousie, 1970.

Arctic/Arctique

11962
Andreas, Edgar L. "Observations of Velocity and Temperature and Estimates of Momentum and Heat Fluxes in the Internal Boundary Layer Over Arctic Leads." Oregon State, 1977.

11963
Beal, Miah Allan. "Bathymetry and Structure of the Arctic Ocean." Oregon State, 1969.

11964
Bernstein, Robert L. "Observations of Currents in the Arctic Ocean." Columbia, 1971.

11965
Coachman, Lawrence Keyes. "On the Water Masses of the Arctic Ocean." Washington, Seattle, 1962.

11966
Dixit, Bharat. "Some Mesoscale Flow Features in the Beaufort Sea During Aidjex 75-76." McGill, 1978.

11967
Goodman, Joseph Robert. "The Waters of the Northeast Pacific Ocean, Bering Sea and Arctic Ocean." Washington, Seattle, 1941.

Jenness, John L. See No./Voir no 4649

11968
Leblond, Paul Henri. "Planetary Waves in a Polar Ocean." British Columbia, 1964.

11969
Manley, Thomas Owen. "Eddies of the Western Arctic Ocean: Their Characteristics and Importance to the Energy, Heat, and Salt Balance." Columbia, 1981. [Beaufort Sea/Mer de Beaufort]

11970
Morison, James Howe. "Forced Internal Waves in the Arctic Ocean." Washington, Seattle, 1980.

11971
Newbury, Thomas K. "Adaptations of Chaetognaths to Subarctic Conditions." McGill, 1971.

11972
Paul, Allen Zachary. "Benthic Ecology of the High Arctic Deep-Sea." Florida State, 1973.

11973
Pautzke, Clarence Greer. "Phytoplankton Primary Production Below Arctic Ocean Pack Ice: A Ecosystems Approach." Washington, Seattle, 1979.

11974
Semtner, Albert J., Jr. "A Numerical Investigation of Arctic Ocean Circulation." Princeton, 1973.

11975
Shreffler, Jack Henry. "A Numerical Model of Heat Transfer to the Atmosphere From an Arctic Lead." Oregon State, 1975.

11976
Vilks, Gustavs. "A Study of Globorotalia pachyderma (Ehrenberg) — Globigerina pachyderma (Ehrenberg) in the Canadian Arctic." Dalhousie, 1974.

Northwest Territories and Yukon/ Territoires du Nord-Ouest et Yukon

11977
Arnold, Keith Charles. "Ice Ablation Measured by Stakes and by Terrestrial Photogrammetry: Comparison on the Lower Part of the White Glacier, Axel Heiberg Island, Canada." McGill, 1978.

11978
Collin, Arthur Edwin. "The Oceanography of Lancaster Sound." McGill, 1962.

11979
Forbes, Donald Lawrence. "Babbage River Delta and Lagoon: Hydrology and Sedimentology of an Arctic Estuarine System." British Columbia, 1981.

Godin, J.J.Gabriel G. See No./Voir no 11908

11980
Keys, John Erskine. "Water Regime of Ice-Covered Fiords and Lakes." McGill, 1977.

McLaren, Ian Alexander. See No./Voir no 11840

11981
Muench, Robin Davie. "The Physical Oceanography of the Northern Baffin Bay Region." Washington, Seattle, 1970.

Quinlan, Garry Michael. See No./Voir no 11944

11982
Sadler, Herbert Eric. "Flow of Water and Heat Through Nares Strait, Northwest Territories." Dalhousie, 1975.

Ontario

11983
Frape, Shaun Keith. "Interstitial Waters and Bottom Sediment Geochemistry Indicators of Ground Water Seepage." Queen's, 1979. [Perch Lake near Chalk River, Cataraqui River near Kingston, Indian Lake, North of Kingston/Lac Perch près de la rivière Chalk, rivière Cataraqui près de Kingston et lac Indian au nord de Kingston]

11984
Jackson, Richard Ervin. "Hydrogeochemical Processes Affecting the Migration of Radionuclides in a Shallow Ground Water Flow System at the Chalk River Nuclear Laboratories." Waterloo, 1979.

11985
Rannie, William Fraser. "An Approach to the Prediction of Suspended Sediment Rating Curves." Toronto, 1976.

Sharma, Tribeni Chandra. See No./Voir no 4563
Wallis, Peter Malcolm. See No./Voir no 11987
Whiteley, Hugh Russell. See No./Voir no 4569

Prairie Provinces/Provinces des Prairies

General Items/Ouvrages généraux

11986
O'Neill, Archibald Desmond Joseph. "The Energetics of Shallow Prairie Snowpacks." Saskatchewan, 1973.

Alberta

Beke, Gerard Johannes. See No./Voir no 219
Brown, Michael Joseph. See No./Voir no 4726
Rosenberg, David Michael. See No./Voir no 11204

11987
Wallis, Peter Malcolm. "Sources, Transportation, and Utilization of Dissolved Organic Matter in Groundwater and Streams." Waterloo, 1978. [Marmot Basin/Bassin de Marmot]

Manitoba

Al-Taweel, Bashir Hashim. See No./Voir no 246

11988
Lissey, Allan. "Surficial Mapping of Ground-Water Flow Systems with Application to the Oak River Basin, Manitoba." Saskatchewan, 1968.

Quebec/Québec

11989
Fitzgibbon, John E. "Generation of the Snowmelt Flood in the Subarctic, Schefferville, Québec." McGill, 1977.

11990
Wright, Richard Kyle. "The Water Balance of a Lichen Tundra Underlain by Permafrost." McGill,1980. [Near Schefferville, Quebec/Près de Schefferville, Québec]

PHYSICS/PHYSIQUE

Included under this heading are general topics such as astrophysics, astronautics, astronomy, atmospheric science, and geodesy. Thirty of the 45 dissertations were approved in the last 15 years. McGill University is the leader, followed by the University of British Columbia and Toronto. The American output is extremely small, with a total of six titles, five of which were produced during the 1970's by five universities, the University of Colorado presenting two. One dissertation was produced in Great Britain at the University of Edinburgh.

Il y a sous ce titre, des études sur des sujets généraux, sur l'astrophysique, l'astronautique, l'astronomie, la science atmosphérique et la géodésie. Trente des 45 thèses ont été approuvées entre 1970 et 1985. L'Université McGill vient en tête, suivie par celle de la Colombie-Britannique et de Toronto. La production américaine est extrêmement réduite avec un total de six titres, dont cinq produits dans les années 1970 par cinq universités; l'Université du Colorado en a présenté deux. La Grande-Bretagne a présenté une thèse soumise à l'Université d'Édimbourg.

Astrophysics, Astronautics, Astronomy, Atmospheric Science, and Geodesy/ Astrophysique, astronautique, astronomie, science atmosphérique et géodésie

11991
Alabi, Adeniyi Oluremi. "A Study of the North American Central Plains Conductivity Anomaly." Alberta, 1974.

Allis, Richard George. See No./Voir no 6648
Bannister, John Richard. See No./Voir no 6583

11992
Bennett, Richard Curtis. "Acoustic Radar Studies of Planetary Boundary Layer Structures Associated with Gravity Waves, Fronts and Lake Breezes." Toronto, 1975. [Toronto and Lake Ontario/Toronto et lac Ontario]

11993
Boudra, Douglas Bryant. "A Numerical Study Describing Modification of the Atmosphere by the Great Lakes." Michigan, 1977.

11994
Bradford, Henry Martin. "Analysis of the Spectra of Type III Solar Radio Bursts Detected by the Alouette I Satellite." Queen's, 1972.

Buchan, Kenneth Lorne. See No./Voir no 6650

11995
Bunn, Frank Edward. "6300 A Auroras: An Isis-II Spacecraft Experiment." York, 1974.

Davis, Donald Wayne. See No./Voir no 10691

11996
Delikaraoglou, Demitris. "An Investigation on the Short Wavelength Orbit Improvement and Sea Surface Computations from Local Satellite Tracking and Satellite Altimetry." New Brunswick, 1980. [Experiment in the Hudson Bay area/Essais dans la région de la baie d'Hudson]

11997
Fletcher, Ian Robert. "A Lead Isotopic Study of Lead-Zinc Mineralization Associated with the Central Metasedimentary Belt of the Grenville Province." Toronto, 1979.

Fuggle, Richard Francis. See No./Voir no 5050

Giovando, Lawrence Frank. See No./Voir no 4508

11998
Gómez-Treviño, Enrique. "Geoelectrical Soundings in the Sedimentary Basin of Southern Ontario. Using a Pseudo-Noise Source Electromagnetic System." Toronto, 1981.

Grenda, Robert Norman. See No./Voir no 5042

11999
Gross, James Matthew. "Lake Effect Storms of Lake Ontario." University of Miami, 1978.

12000
Halliday, Ian. "A Study of Stellar Luminosities from Stellar Spectra Taken at the David Dunlap Observatory." Toronto, 1954.

Helbig, James Alfred. See No./Voir no 11925

12001
Henry, William H. "Study and Improvement of the McGill Cyclotron." McGill, 1952.

12002
Herring, Robert William. "A Study of Meteor Trail Structure Using a Wide Aperture Antenna Array at High Radio Frequencies." Western Ontario, 1977. [Québec]

12003
Hone, David W. "The Deflection System of the McGill Cyclotron." McGill, 1951.

12004
Hunt, John W. "Studies of the External Beam of the McGill Synchro-Cyclotron." McGill, 1956.

12005
Jackson, Ray W. "The Synchronizing and Monitoring System of the McGill Synchro-Cyclotron." McGill, 1950.

12006
Keen, Richard Allan. "Temperature and Circulation Anomalies in the Eastern Canadian Arctic, Summer 1946-1976." Colorado, 1979. [Baffin Island and eastern Arctic/Île de Baffin et est de l'Arctique]

12007
Lambert, Steven J. "A Study of Planetary Wave Errors in a Spectral Numerical Weather Prediction Model." McGill, 1977.

12008
Larochelle, Normand. "Étude de la structure de quelques composés chimiques par diffraction des électrons et description de modifications apportées au diffractographe de l'Université de Montréal." Montréal, 1964.

12009
Leblond, André Joseph René. "Étude de modèles pour la prédiction de l'énergie interne du lac Clair." McGill, 1979.

LeDrew, Ellsworth Frank. See No./Voir no 5026

12010
Litva, John. "Observations of Travelling Ionospheric Disturbances at London, Canada, Using Phase Interferometry of Solar Radio Emissions." Western Ontario, 1974.

12011
Lommen, Paul Warren. "Integral Fluxes of Primary Cosmic Rays at Palestine, Texas, and Fort Churchill, Canada, Near Solar Minimum." Rochester, 1968.

12012
Maddukuri, C. Subbarao. "Air Flow Over an Urban Area: Some Numerical Experiments with a Two-Dimensional Time Dependent Boundary Layer Model." York, 1977. [Model simulating the lake breeze of Lake Ontario/Modèle simulant la brise sur le lac Ontario]

12013
Mahoney, Michael Joseph. "The Preparation of a Telescope for Operation at Millimeter Wavelengths and Observations of Carbon Monoxide in the Galactic Dust Cloud, Lynds 134." British Columbia, 1976.

12014
McKeown, Joseph. "Design and Performance of a Two-Arm Wire Chamber Spectrometer for Use at the Manitoba 50 Me V Cyclotron." Manitoba, 1970.

12015
Moore, Robert Bruce. "Magnetic Extraction of the Proton Beam from the McGill Synchro-Cyclotron." McGill, 1962.

12016
Moshupi, Matthew Coffat. "Isis-2 Observations of Aurora in the Ionospheric Trough Region." Calgary, 1977.

12017
Normandin, Martine Hazel Simard. "Rotation Measures and the Galactic Magnetic Field." Toronto, 1979. [Algonquin Radio Observatory and National Radio Astronomy Observatory in Greenbank/Observatoire de radio d'Algonquin et observatoire national de radio-astronomie à Greenbank]

12018
Nuñez, Manuel. "Energy Balance of an Urban Canyon." British Columbia, 1975. [Vancouver]

12019
Prochazka, Antonin. "The Design of the RF System for the Triumf Cyclotron." British Columbia, 1972.

12020
Reddy, Indupuru Kota. "Magnetotelluric Sounding in Central Alberta." Alberta, 1971.

12021
Root, Laurence Wilbur. "Experimental and Theoretical Studies of the Behaviour of a Negative Atomic Hydrogen Ion Beam During Injection and Acceleration in the Triumf Central Region Model Cyclotron." British Columbia, 1974.

12022
Ross, William Bruce. "Investigations of the Kennelly-Heaviside and Appleton Layers." McGill, 1934.

12023
Sheu, Yi-Tsuei Pai. "The Kinetic Energy Climatology of Tropospheric and Lower Stratospheric Flow Regimes Associated with 500MB Intermediate and Short Waves over North America." Purdue, 1979. [Southern Canada/Sud du Canada]

12024
Southon, Frank Charles Gray. "Measurement of Wide and Narrow Mass Differences on the Manitoba II Mass Spectrometer." Manitoba, 1973.

12025
Stagg, James M. "Papers in Terrestrial Magnetism, with Special Reference to the Magnetic and Non-Photographic Auroral Data Brought Back from Fort Rae, North West Canada." Edinburgh, 1936.

12026
Steeves, Robin Roy. "Estimation of Gravity Tilt Response to Tiltmetric Station Using a Least Squares Response Method." New Brunswick, 1981.

Stronach, James Alexander. See No./Voir no 11937

12027
Summers, Peter. "An Urban Ventilation Model Applied to Montreal." McGill, 1964.

12028
Telford, William M. "The Radio Frequency System of the McGill Synchro-Cyclotron." McGill, 1949.

12029
Ulrych, Tadeusz Jan. "Gas Source Mass Spectrometry of Trace Leads from Sudbury, Ontario." British Columbia, 1962.

12030
Venugopal, Virinchipuram R. "A Study of the 21-Cm Line in the Solar Neighbourhood." British Columbia, 1969. [Penticton, British Columbia/-Colombie-Britannique]

12031
Vij, Kewal Kishore. "Investigations of Bremsstrahlung X-Rays at Cold Lake, Alberta and Fort Churchill, Manitoba by Rocket and Balloon Borne Scintillation Detectors." Calgary, 1973.

12032
Woods, Stuart B. "A Search for the Photo-Disintegration of Neon with the University of British Columbia Van de Graaff Generator." British Columbia, 1952.

HOW TO USE THE INDEX OF NAMES

The theses included in this bibliography are listed in alphabetic order according to **authors' names.** Each name is followed by the **entry number** under which the thesis is found. Theses that have been put into microform by the National Library of Canada are identified by the **microform number,** which appears within parentheses after the entry number.

COMMENT UTILISER L'INDEX DES NOMS?

Dans cette bibliographie, les **noms des auteurs** des thèses sont répertoriés par ordre alphabétique. Chaque nom est suivi d'un **numéro** sous lequel la thèse peut être trouvée. Les thèses microfilmées par la Bibliothèque nationale du Canada sont identifiées par un **numéro de microforme** qui se trouve, entre parenthèses, après le nom et le numéro.

Anderson, Amos McIntyre 2463
Anderson, Arthur James 6874
Anderson, Barbara Marlene 3750
  (MIC.TC-58386)
Anderson, Barry Douglas 2559
  (MIC.TC-8785)
Anderson, Barry Lowell 1311
  (MIC.F.T-971)
Anderson, Bern 7306 (G246 V3 A7)
Anderson, Charles Dennis 2223
  (MIC.F.TC-31550)
Anderson, Darrell Vail 4044
  (MIC.F.TC-25094)
Anderson, Darwin Wayne 282
Anderson, David Frederic K. 10333
Anderson, David L. 6769
  (MIC.F.TC-30090)
Anderson, Dianne Evelyn 3187
  (MIC.F.TC-27600)
Anderson, Donald O. 6922
Anderson, Douglas Edward 3863
  (MIC.F.TC-56842)
Anderson, Edward Charles 3444
Anderson, Edward Philip 11078
  (MIC.F.TC-22801)
Anderson, Francis D. 5592
Anderson, Franz Elmer 5144
Anderson, Grace Merle 7653
  (MIC.F.TC-31153)
Anderson, Henrietta Alexandrina
  Ramage 2881
Anderson, Howard George 11773
  (MIC.F.TC-27525)
Anderson, James Hugh 11449
Anderson, James Thomas Milton 2434
Anderson, Joan Madge 10027
  (MIC.F.TC-54957)
Anderson, John Murray 11123
Anderson, Jonathan Robert 247
  (MIC.TC-9044)
Anderson, Karen Lee 640
  (MIC.F.TC-58311)
Anderson, Owen Arthur James 8661
  (MIC.TC-11110)
Anderson, Patricia Marie 848
  (MIC.F.T-1330)
Anderson, Richard Svend 2326
Anderson, Robert Newton 2789
  (MIC.T-142)
Anderson, Robert Stewart 11808
  (MIC.TC-2734)
Anderson, Terry Ross 329
  (MIC.F.TC-42155)
Anderson, Thane Wesley 5931
  (MIC.TC-7956)
Anderson, Thomas Dole 4778
Anderson, Walton J. 7
Anderson, Wells Foster 5932
Anderton, Peter Wightman 5907
Andracki, Stanislaw 7597
  (JV7285 C5 A64)
Andrade, James Edward 580
Andrade, Teresa Manalad 3927
  (LB1573 A54 fol.)
Andreas, Edgar L. 11962
Andress, Donald Douglas 4938
  (MIC.F.TC-36239)
Andrew, Caroline Parkin 1368
  (MIC.F.TC-31154)
Andrew, Christine McCleave 7664
  (MIC.F.TC-21745)
Andrews, Barry Craig 10403
Andrews, Bruce Alfred 2435
  (MIC.F.TC-40550)
Andrews, Daniel 11946
  (MIC.F.TC-48154)
Andrews, Helen Katherine 4429
Andrews, J.T. 4655
Andrews, Margaret R.W. 6788
  (MIC.F.TC-46062)
Andrews, Michael Bruce
  Barrington 3720 (MIC.F.TC-36344)
Andrews, Samuel Dalton 4385
  (MIC.T-356)
Andrews, Theodore F. 11058
Andrews, William Robinson 4172
  (MIC.TC-4914)
Andrichuk, John M. 5378
Ang, Kok-Jee 11855 (MIC.TC-10360)
Angerilli, Nello Pasquale Doro 11124
  (MIC.F.TC-38420)

Angers, Gérard 1077
Angers, William P. 9109
Angevine, Gerald Edwin 1961
  (MIC.T-632)
Anglin, Douglas C. 8778
Angrave, James 2417
Anim-Appiah, John 163
  (MIC.TC-10952)
Aniskowicz, Boguslawa Theresa 10689
Anker, Daniel Ezra 7804
Ankney, Claude Davison 10784
  (MIC.F.TC-23248)
Annas, Richard Morris 11450
Annett, Douglas R. 1990 (HF1479 A5)
Annis, Charles A. 1991 (MIC.TC-2794)
Annis, Helen Marie 8948
  (MIC.TC-5522)
Ansari, Salmuddin 4779
Ansley, Sylvia Lorraine 4056
  (MIC.TC-8952)
Antczak, Janice 8091 (MIC.F.T-1134)
Anteson, Reginald Kwaku 10535
Anthony, Desmond Darrington 11346
Antler, Ellen Pildes 397
  (MIC.F.T-1205)
Antler, Steven David 1234 (MIC.T-791)
Anton, Frank Robert 2153
Anwar, Muhammad 2988
  (MIC.F.TC-36582)
Anzoleaga, Rodolfo 6674
Apanasiewicz, Nina 9162
  (MIC.TC-57272)
Appana, Mohan 1839 (MIC.F.TC-48453)
Appavoo, Muthiah David 806
  (MIC.F.TC-40986)
Appell, Julian 4173 (MIC.F.TC-34014)
Appelle, Morry 9114 (MIC.F.TC-27780)
Appiah, Michael Roy 204
  (MIC.F.TC-41691)
Appleyard, Edward C. 5933
Appy, Ralph Grant 10536
  (MIC.F.TC-43875)
Aquila, Richard 7433
Arana, Milton Eulogio 4109
  (MIC.F.TC-1050)
Arango, Sebastian 1542
Arbess, Saul E. 429 (MIC.TC-2599)
Arceneaux, Maureen G. 820
Archbold, Norbert Lee 5934
Archer, John Hall 6941 (MIC.TC-3423)
Archibald, Clinton 8746
  (MIC.TC-55589)
Archibald, Douglas Arthur 5145
  (MIC.F.TC-61575)
Archibald, F.E. 9879
Archibald, Juanita Helen 6745
Archibald, Kalman Dale 11261
Archibald, Robert William 1369
  (MIC.F.TC-28165)
Archibold, Oliver William 4605
  (MIC.F.TC-25622)
Ardanaz, Nicolas 7712
Arekal, Govindappa Dasappa 1134
Arend, Sylvie Marie Jacqueline 2480
  (MIC.F.TC-53489)
Arena, Francesco 9353
  (MIC.F-2M11.525.7)
Argenal, Roger 6635
Arguin, Maurice 8174
  (MIC.F.TC-47887)
Arikado, Marjorie Sadako 4291
  (MIC.TC-16614)
Arima, Eugene Yuji 581
  (MIC.TC-16092)
Arinze, Edwin A. 4581
Arlett, Christine 6690
  (MIC.F.TC-34752)
Armbrust, George Aimé 5935
Armon, John William 4639
  (MIC.F.TC-26095)
Armstrong, Calvert William 5056
  (MIC.TC-5019)
Armstrong, Christopher 8716
  (MIC.TC-14833)
Armstrong, David Patrick 4013
  (MIC.TC-11532)
Armstrong, Elizabeth H. 7249
  (F5029.2 A742)
Armstrong, Frederick Henry 7221
  (MIC.TC-7490)

Armstrong, Henry Graham 2768
  (MIC.TC-13190)
Armstrong, Herbert Stoker 5936
Armstrong, John Edward 5146
Armstrong, Maurice Whitman 7171
Armstrong, Paul Frederic 5487
Armstrong, Robert 1258
Armstrong, Robert Clarke 5096
  (MIC.F.TC-30092)
Armstrong-Reid, Susan Edwina 8803
Arnason, Arni P. 11333
Arnason, David Ellis 8047
  (MIC.F.TC-47698)
Arnason, Ingolfur Gilbert 11075
Arndt, Nicholas Thomas 5937
  (MIC.F.TC-32730)
Arndt, Sven William 1974 (MIC.T-6)
Arnold, Charles Duncan 885
  (MIC.F.TC-39214)
Arnold, Donald John 10438
Arnold, Keith Charles 11977
  (MIC.F.TC-39592)
Arnold, Larry Sherwood 8949
  (MIC.TC-8954)
Arnold, Phil Warren 8434 (MIC.T-662)
Arnott, R.J. 5727
Arntfield, Pete William 11125
  (MIC.F.TC-35675)
Aronoff, Stanley 1924 (MIC.F.T-1349)
Aronsen, Lawrence Robert 2385
Arth, Joseph George, Jr. 5938
Arthur, Alfred Pibus 10537
Arthur, George William 921
  (MIC.F.TC-19748)
Arthur, James Richard 10538
  (MIC.F.TC-37244)
Arthur, Marion E. 7019
Artibise, Alan Francis Joseph 7244
  (MIC.TC-11201)
Arundale, Wendy Hanford 886
Arzola, Sergio 3299
Asamoa, Godfried Kofi 257
  (QE191 A83 fol.)
Asarnow, Joan Rosenbaum 3050
  (MIC.F.TC-45963)
Ascah, Louis Gordon 1640
  (MIC.F.TC-42877)
Asch, Michael Ira 579 (MIC.T-510)
Aschinger, Richard Franz 7871
  (MIC.F.TC-25688)
Ash, Andrew N. 10836
  (MIC.F.TC-40876)
Ashley, Gail Mowry 5147
  (MIC.F.TC-34754)
Ashmed, Moin V. 11532
Ashwal, Lewis David 5939
Asihene, Kwanie Anane Buahin 5148
Askari-Rankouhi, Mostafa 1584
  (MIC.F.TC-52866)
Aslander, J. Alfred O. 11628
Asper, Linda Barker 3661
  (MIC.F.TC-26333)
Assad, Joseph Robert 6259
Assal, Georges 2734
Assagba, Yao Ayékotan 3382
Assam, Ann Padmore 7713
  (MIC.F.T-1169)
Astling, Elford George 4967
Atack, W.A. 10017
Atherton, Lorraine G. 11362
  (MIC.F.TC-41208)
Atherton, Peter John 2756
  (MIC.TC-3351)
Atkinson, Donald Robert 10110
  (MIC.F.TC-47001)
Atkinson, Gerald 6582 (MIC.TC-1137)
Atkinson, Mary Helen Elizabeth 1925,
  9425
Atkinson, Michael Meredith 8717
  (MIC.F.TC-39023)
Atkinson, Stephanie Ann 6746
  (MIC.F.TC-47002)
Atkinson, W.J. 7923
Attridge, Carolyn Bernice 4292
  (MIC.F.TC-32732)
Au, Chong Ying Daniel 6615
  (MIC.F.TC-56583)
Aubé, Nicole 9639
Aubin-LaPointe, Monique 3410
Aubry, Francine 6709
  (MIC.F.TC-35677)

Aucoin, Peter C. 6710 (MIC.TC-13690)
Audet, Louis Philippe 2515
Audy, Jacques 3188
Auger, Jacques Arthur 10464
Auger, Jean 3417 (MIC.F-2M11.584.5)
Ault, Orvill E. 4386 (MIC.T-882)
Aumont, Marcel 3601 (MIC.T-797)
Aunger, Edmund Alexander 8701
    (MIC.F.T-972)
Auster, Ethel W. 2719
    (MIC.F.TC-36585)
Austin, Bobby William 743
Austin, Gary Wayne 8950
    (MIC.F.TC-56157)
Austin, Oliver Luther, Jr. 10730
Austrom, Douglas Richard 9640
    (MIC.F.TC-53490)
Averill, E.L. 6260
Avery, Donald Howard 7637
    (MIC.F.TC-20475)
Aves, Penelope Jill 9208
    (MIC.F.TC-27794)
Avigan, Helen Ruth 9641
    (MIC.F.TC-61954)
Avison, William R. 9642
    (MIC.F.TC-34283)
Avore, Joseph B., Jr. 3479
    (MIC.F.TC-23856)
Awender, Michael A.B.J. 2720
    (MIC.T-740)
Awomolo, Amos Ademola 4293
    (MIC.TC-16093)
Axelrod, Paul Douglas 3552
    (MIC.F.TC-44486)
Axworthy, N. Lloyd 8501 (MIC.T-466)
Axworthy, Thomas Sidney 8779
    (MIC.F.TC-42398)
Aycock, Daniel Alan 690
    (MIC.F.TC-27467)
Ayearst, Morley James 7109
Ayers, John Douglas L. 4104
Ayles, George Burton 11008
    (MIC.TC-16094)
Ayre, David John 2790
    (MIC.F.TC-53004)
Ayres, Lorne Dale 5940
Ayrton, William Grey 6261
Ayyad, Mohamed A.G. 349
Aziz, Rashid 1162 (MIC.F.TC-52200)
Azu, John Nene-Osom 330
    (MIC.F.TC-38884)

B

Ba, Tran Quang 8747
Ba-Angood, Saeed Abdulla Saeed 11302
    (MIC.F.TC-50383)
Baass, Karsten Goetz 2246
    (MIC.F.TC-42352)
Baba, Nobuyoshi 6675
Baba, Vishwanath Venkataraman 1926
    (MIC.F.TC-49892)
Baban, R.C.N. 1568
Babe, Robert Elwood 1118 (MIC.T-437)
Babby, Ellen Reisman 8310
Babcock, Gail Reichenbach 3418
    (MIC.F.TC-36346)
Babcock, Robert Harper 2091
    (MIC.T-622)
Babin, Patrick 4373
Bacchi, Carol Lee 7109
    (MIC.F.TC-35678)
Bachand, Raymond C. 1927
    (MIC.F.T-1117)
Bachechi, Fiorella 6262
    (MIC.F.TC-25537)
Bachert, Gerhard 8175
Bachor, Daniel Gustave 3772
    (MIC.F.TC-30331)
Bachor, Patricia Angelica Cranton 2560
    (MIC.F.TC-30332)
Backman, Joan Elizabeth 3928
Backman, Olen L. 6263
Backus, Richard H. 10994

Bacon, Douglas Arthur 9855
    (MIC.F.T-1316)
Bacon, George Beverley 11108
Bacon, John Alan 3617
    (AL.P67 A17 R4.17)
Bacon, William Russell 5149
Baden, John A. 8695
Badgley, Peter C. 5379 (MIC.F-663)
Badham, John Patrick Nicholas 5803
    (MIC.F.TC-17443)
Baer, Elizabeth Roberts 8075
    (MIC.F.T-1151)
Baerg, William John 983
Baergen, William Peter 3288
    (MIC.F.T-1323)
Baetz, Mark Conrad 1734
Baezler, Sister St. Alfred of
    Rome 9807
Bagley, John Francis 7154 (MIC.T-640)
Bagnell, Charles Robert 11423
Baguley, Robert Wayne 1464
Baig, Kamal 3795 (MIC.F.TC-36586)
Baig, Mirza Naeem 11429
    (MIC.TC-13822)
Bail, Pierre 4748 (MIC.F.TC-64430)
Bailes, Alan Harvey 5488
    (MIC.F.TC-43066)
Bailey, Alan Westlake 4404
    (MIC.T-173)
Bailey, Alfred Goldsworthy 498
    (E99 A35 B3 fol.)
Bailey, C.L. 2649
Bailey, Carole 9115 (MIC.F.TC-61896)
Bailey, Clyde Gregory 11268
    (MIC.F.TC-20656)
Bailey, David G. 5150
    (MIC.F.TC-39431)
Bailey, Gordon Archibald 3176
Bailey, Gordon Raymond 11664
    (MIC.TC-6963)
Bailey, Loraine Dolar 258
    (MIC.TC-9026)
Bailey, Michael Roy 4430
    (MIC.F.TC-17442)
Bailey, Robert Owen 10759
    (MIC.F.TC-60910)
Bailey, Warren Stevenson 4343
    (MIC.T-79)
Baillargeon, Madeleine 3080
    (MIC.F.TC-39096)
Baillargeon, Noël 9928 (LE3 O22 B33)
Bain, Colin M. 1235 (MIC.TC-16316)
Bain, David Alexander 3796
    (MIC.F.TC-25790)
Bain, George William 5941
Bain, Ian 5942
Baird, Andrew Falconer 60, 1929
Baird, David M. 5728
Baird, Norman Barnes 2775
    (LB2891 O6 B35)
Bajic, Vladimir P. 1576, 2324
    (MIC.F.TC-53005)
Baka, Richard Stevens Paul 10337
    (MIC.F.TC-40078)
Baker, Carolyn Diane 9410
    (MIC.F.TC-43610)
Baker, Donald John 6264
Baker, Elaine Meredith 3940
    (MIC.F.TC-48888)
Baker, G. Ross 6827 (MIC.F.TC-58315)
Baker, Harold Reid 1
Baker, Janet E. 8156
    (MIC.F.TC-36035)
Baker, Janice Elizabeth 3941
    (MIC.F.TC-47003)
Baker, John Garry 3797
    (MIC.F.TC-33624)
Baker, Laura Doris 3752
Baker, Lois Josephine 3016
    (MIC.F.TC-50969)
Baker, Maureen 10188
    (MIC.F.TC-23982)
Baker, Melvin 7170 (MIC.F.TC-54088)
Baker, Michael Robert 10539
    (MIC.F.TC-38885)
Baker, N. 7020
Baker, Patricia Anne 9498
    (MIC.F.TC-58491)
Baker, Richard C. 2354
Baker, Ray Palmer 8048

Baker, Robert Andrew 3318
    (MIC.F.TC-50224)
Baker, Robert Osborne 2150
Baker, Robert William 5804
Baker, Seymour R. 5805
Baker, Ted Edgar 232
    (MIC.F.TC-22023)
Baker, Walter J. 10141 (MIC.TC-268)
Baker, William Melville 7329
    (MIC.TC-10755)
Bakony, Leo Irwin 1339
Balawyder, Aloysius 8876
    (MIC.TC-430)
Balbach, Harold Edward 11363
Baldwin, Douglas Owen 7189
    (MIC.TC-15679)
Baldwin, John Russell 2268
Baldwin, John Stiles 6828
    (MIC.F.TC-43067)
Baldwin, Martha A. 3884
    (MIC.F.TC-32096)
Balham, Ronald Walter 10785
Balikci, Asen 582
Balkwill, Hugh Robert 5151
Ball, Norman Roger 91
    (MIC.F.TC-42161)
Ballabon, Maurice B. 4780
Ballad, Charles Guthrie 8320
Ballestadt Carl P.A. 8171
Balram, Bodhnarine C.M. 6829
    (MIC.F.TC-57250)
Balthazar, Louis Rémus 8467
Bambach, Richard Karl 6556
Bambrick, James R. 3895
    (MIC.F.TC-41929)
Bamber, Edward Wayne 5152
Bamwoya, James Jasper 5593
    (MIC.F.TC-38048)
Bana, John Peter 3149
    (MIC.F.TC-34286)
Banaga, Abdul Raouf Sulaiman 1591
    (MIC.F.T-1148)
Bance, Pierre 8260
Bancroft, Donald Asa 1698
    (MIC.T-320)
Bancroft, George Winston 2561
Bancroft, Joseph A. 5153
Banda, Meinrad R. 3177
    (MIC.F.TC-51431)
Banerjee, Ajit Kumar 259
    (MIC.TC-5574)
Banerjee, Nipa 3662 (MIC.F.TC-36587)
Banfield, Alexander William
    Francis 10614
Banfield, Armine F. 6265
Bangsberg, Harry F. 8886
Banks, Margaret Amelia 7331
    (DA958 B54 B3)
Banmen, John 4174
Bannerman, Harold M. 5943
Bannister, Geoffrey 1163
    (MIC.F.TC-27468)
Bannister, John Arthur 2481
Bannister, John Richard 6583
    (MIC.F.TC-34287)
Banting, Douglas Ralph 4656
    (MIC.F.TC-54089)
Banwell, Gregory T. 3899
Baragar, William R.A. 5688
Barakett-Brand, Joyce 4294
    (MIC.F-2M11.476.2)
Barans, Charles Anthony 10907
Barber, Clarence Lyle 1340
    (HB3755 B3)
Barber, Lloyd Ingram 1699 (MIC.T-8)
Barber, Marilyn J. 7638
Bardecki, Michael James 2235
    (MIC.F.TC-51358)
Bardock, Edison Frederick 2997
    (MIC.T-827)
Bardon, Michael Fredric Richard 4496
    (MIC.F.TC-37249)
Barendregt, René William 5380
    (MIC.F.TC-34581)
Barer, Morris Lionel 6770
    (MIC.F.TC-32409)
Barg, Benjamin 2386
Bargen, Peter Frank 2802 (LB2534 B3)
Barger, Walter Kenneth 583
Barghothi, Jawad I. 7544

Baribeau-Bratin, Jacinthe 9163
(MIC.F.TC-48458)
Barichello, Richard Ralph 2402
(LC5148 C3 B3)
Barilko, M. Olga 9643
(MIC.F.TC-19855)
Bariteau, Claude 430
(MIC.F.TC-42885)
Barka, Norman Forthun 882
Barker, James Franklin 5944
(MIC.F.TC-39847)
Barker, Mary Lynn 4588
(MIC.TC-14835)
Barker, Ralph Whitehead 9856
Barker, Stephen David 8951
Barkow, Ben 3519 (MIC.F.TC-25690)
Barkwell, Gordon 9911
(FC2922.1 L34 V64 fol.)
Barlow, Ivor Maxton 4963
(MIC.F.TC-39599)
Barman, Jean 2448 (MIC.F.TC-59157)
Barnabe, Clermont 2895 (MIC.T-798)
Barnes, Arthur 2466
Barnes, Carleton P. 11641
Barnes, Christopher Richard 5945
(MIC.TC-1763)
Barnes, David Benton 4208
Barnes, David Hugh 11109
(MIC.F.TC-20051)
Barnes, Frederick Quilliam 5806
(MIC.F.TC-22739)
Barnes, Gordon E. 9248
(MIC.F.TC-36973)
Barnes, James Gordon 1962
(MIC.F.TC-33081)
Barnes, Jimmy Weaver 8125
Barnes, Samuel 8877
Barnes, Samuel Henry 2047
Barnes, William J. 11364
Barnett, David Martin 4657
(MIC.F.TC-32192)
Barnett, Donald Frederick 1889
(MIC.TC-2794)
Barnett, Homer Garner 377
Barnett, John Ross 8657 (MIC.T-864)
Barnett, Le Roy Gene 4874
(MIC.F.T-1071)
Barnett, Robert Claude 4405
Barnhart, Warren Lynn 7301
Baron, Judith E. 9499
(MIC.F.TC-19995)
Baron, Lois 3942 (MIC.F.TC-38675)
Baron, Pierre 9209
Baron, Vernon Samuel 298
(MIC.F.TC-63326)
Barone, Anthony John 2957
(MIC.F.TC-36589)
Barr, Jack Francis 10824
(MIC.TC-16317)
Barr, Percy Munson 11665
Barr, Sandra Marie 5154
(MIC.TC-15095)
Barrados, Maria 3319
(MIC.F.TC-37336)
Barraud, Claude 6266 (MIC.F-035202)
Barrera, Maria Eugenia Caraza 9326
(MIC.F.TC-42797)
Barrett, Charles Raymond 2713
Barrett, Francis D. 2127
Barrett, Frank Alexander 4942
(MIC.T-610)
Barrett, Morley William 10608
(MIC.F.TC-56822)
Barrett, Paul Edward 11533
(MIC.TC-11202)
Barrington, Gail Vallance 3568
(MIC.F.TC-51433)
Barriault, Yvette 528 (E99 M87 B3)
Barrois de Sarigny, Jacqueline 8176
(MIC.F.TC-58021)
Barron, Frank Laurie 7190
Barron, John Robert 11126
(MIC.TC-4918)
Barron, Sister Marion 6881
(MIC.T-359)
Barron, Robert Frederick John 2989
(MIC.F.TC-40368)
Barry, Donald Joseph 8780
(MIC.F.T-1104)
Barry, J.K. 2418
Barry, Thomas Woodams 10786

Bart, John Telesphore 1673
(MIC.F.TC-23251)
Bartell, Marvin 2 (MIC.T-423)
Bartholomeus, Bonnie Noreen 3864
(MIC.TC-4574)
Bartholomew, Mark Alan 8835
(MIC.F.T-1105)
Bartlein, Patrick John 4992
Bartlett, Grant Aulden 11842
Bartley, Melville William 5946
Bartoletti, Mario Dante 3462
(MIC.F.TC-43612)
Barton, David Remle 11782
(MIC.F.TC-28589)
Barton, Jackson M., Jr. 6267
(MIC.TC-9200)
Barton, James Wesley 10383
(MIC.F.TC-53851)
Bartonek, James Cloyd 10760
Bartram, Peter Edward Raven 3586
(MIC.F.TC-47005)
Basham, Richard Dalton 431
(MIC.T-517)
Bashevkin, Sylvia Beth 8435
(MIC.F.TC-64855)
Basinger, James French 5155
(MIC.F.TC-43339)
Baskerville, Peter A. 2295
(MIC.TC-16473)
Bass, Manuel Nathan 5947
Bass, Marian Helen 1119
(MIC.F.TC-47827)
Bassett, Henry Gordon 5381
Bassyouni, Abdelrahman Ali
Mohamed 3607 (MIC.F.TC-41982)
Bastien, Pierre 10240 (MIC.T-3585)
Basu, Sreemay 10278 (MIC.F.T-1298)
Batchelor, Bruce Edward 4877
(MIC.F.TC-38424)
Batcher, Elaine 3070
(MIC.F.TC-50227)
Batchler, Mervyn William 2916
(MIC.F.TC-31936)
Bate Boerop, John Leonard Daniel
2176, 8952 (MIC.F.TC-53491)
Bateman, Alan Mara 5156
Bateman, John D. 5948
Bates, Duane Adair 993 (MIC.T-527)
Bates, Heather MacLean 4014
(MIC.F.TC-40879)
Bates, Howard Francis 5013
Bateson, David John 4295
(MIC.F.TC-54965)
Bathen, Karl Hans 11895
Bator, Paul Adolphus 7222
(MIC.F.TC-42162)
Batra, Carol Dawn 6911 (MIC.T-805)
Batstone, David Wilton 3122
(MIC.F.TC-54090)
Battista, Renaldo N. 6711
Battle, James 3051 (MIC.TC-11616)
Batts, John Stuart 7992
Bau, Andrew Fook-Shing 5949
(MIC.F.TC-42163)
Bauberger, Glenn Joseph 9095
(MIC.F.TC-40987)
Baudry, Jeannine 6912
Bauer, Milton F. 1526
Baugh, Elspeth Harcus Wallace 3189
Baulu, Mireille 3480
Baum, Nehama Tchia 9426
Baum, Ruth Elizabeth 781
Baumal, Ruth 3052 (MIC.F.TC-43614)
Baumann, Harold G. 1890
(MIC.TC-10855)
Baumgart, A.J. 6712
Baureiss, Gunter A. 10189
(MIC.F.TC-30612)
Baxter, C. 8126
Baxter, Charles Morley 8127
(MIC.T.-778)
Baxter, Neil H. 7354
Baxter, Sonny K. 6559
Bayard, Caroline Anne 8338
(MIC.F.TC-35172)
Bayard, Ross Hawthorne 7553
(MIC.T-378)
Bayly, Isabel Law 11559
(MIC.F.TC-19493)
Bayrock, Luboslaw Antin 5382
Beach, Hugh H. ,5383

Beacham, Terry Dale 10707
(MIC.F.TC-42583)
Beadle, Gordon Bruce 1078
Beaglehole, J.C. 7459
Beahen, William 7399
(MIC.F.TC-48461)
Beakhouse, Gary Philip 5489
(MIC.F.TC-61178)
Beal, Audrey Lynne 9500
(MIC.F.TC-45967)
Beal, Miah Allan 11963
Beales, Francis William 5384
Beaman, Jay Gillmore 4897
(MIC.T-431)
Beamish, Richard James 10870
(MIC.TC-9118)
Beard, John Robert 7969
(Z673 C187 fol.)
Beare, J.B. 1341
Beaton, Margaret 8110
Beaton, Mary Anne 3419 (LC3984 B4)
Beaton, William Douglas 6268
(MIC.TC-5988)
Beattie, Alexander Munro 8382
(MIC.T-9)
Beattie, Christopher Fraser 10226
(MIC.T-323)
Beattie, Daniel John 6986
Beattie, David 1735
Beattie, Margaret Eileen 8603
(MIC.TC-13294)
Beattie, Owen Beverly 861
(MIC.F.TC-50970)
Beatty, David Pierce 7573 (MIC.T-858)
Beatty, John Joseph 7811
Beaty, David Wayne 5950
Beaucage, André 1164 (MIC.T-3896)
Beauchamp, Hélène 1012
Beaud, Jean-Pierre 8660
(MIC.F.TC-56283)
Beaudet, Joseph Edward 2398
Beaudet-Carisse, Colette 10057
Beaudoin, André 10073
Beaudoin, Réjean 8177
Beaujot, Roderic Paul 374
(MIC.F.TC-26707)
Beaupré, Henri 10241
Beauregard, Ludger 4749
Beausoleil, Julien 10242 (HV9071 B4)
Beavan, Arthur Paul 5540
Beaven, Brian Philip Norman 8651
(MIC.F.TC-58357)
Bebko, James Mark 3865
(MIC.F.TC-51359)
Bechard, Monique 9411
Beck, James Murray 8709 (JL225 B4)
Beck, Jeanne Ruth Merifield 9889
(MIC.F.TC-36505)
Beck, Leslie S. 5541
Beck, Robert Glen 6707 (MIC.TC-8056)
Beck, Sister M. Celeste 8865
Beckett, Susan Jane 9164
(MIC.F.TC-59057)
Beckmann, Susan Alison 8163
(MIC.F.TC-42164)
Beddoe-Stephens, B. 5157
Bedecki, Thomas George 10334
(MIC.T-334)
Bedell, Frank G. 5951
Bedingfield, Wendy Andrews 10379
(MIC.F.T-1009)
Beebe, Mona Jane 3929
(MIC.F.TC-53854)
Beer, Anne Maria 4057
Beers, Henry 7072
Beggs, Donald William 3320
(MIC.F.TC-50229)
Bégin, Carmelle 975 (M41 B417 M98)
Bégin, Denis 8178
Bégin, Guy 9501 (MIC.F.TC-29525)
Behan, Valerie Mary 11249
(MIC.F.TC-38171)
Beharry, Edward A. 8953
(MIC.F.TC-29110)
Behiels, Michael Derek 7146
(MIC.F.TC-36974)
Behl, Dennis Lorman 1013
Behrens, Lot Ted 3321
(MIC.F.TC-34017)
Behrens, Sylvia 11103

Beil, Charles Edward 11451
(MIC.TC-5794)
Beirness, Douglas James 8954
(MIC.F.TC-61372)
Beke, Gerard Johannes 219
(MIC.TC-3829)
Béland, Jacques 6269
Béland, Jean-Pierre 7791
Béland, Pierre 11110
(MIC.F.TC-24907)
Bélanger, André-Jacques 8748
(F5429 B44)
Bélanger, Gérard 1811
(MIC.F.TC-46017)
Bélanger, Jeannine 8353
Bélanger, Laurent 1928
Bélanger, Louis-Eugène 7844
Bélanger, Réal 7380 (MIC.F.TC-41834)
Bélanguer, Marc 10142
Belfield, Robert Blake 1782
(MIC.F.T-1118)
Belfrage, Linda Catherine Pearson
8955 (MIC.F.TC-25692)
Belgrave, Robert Oliver 8315
(MIC.F-042401)
Bell, Alfred H. 5908
Bell, Archibald M. 5952
Bell, David V.J. 7021
Bell, George Gray 8871
(MIC.TC-11747)
Bell, Herbert Clifford 1236
Bell, James Mackintosh 5953
Bell, Joy Florence 672 (MIC.F.T-1334)
Bell, Katherine Lapsley 11365
(MIC.F.TC-20969)
Bell, Leslie Victor 5954
Bell, Marcus Arthur Money 11666
Bell, Richard Thomas 5158
Bell, Ronald Gordon 8898
(MIC.F.TC-26612)
Bell, Walter Andrew 5635
Bell, Walter Nehemiah 2482
(LA410 O6 B4)
Bella, Inire E. 11774 (MIC.TC-6875)
Bella, Leslie F. 8685 (MIC.F.TC-53859)
Bellagamba, Anthony D. 3540
Bellamy, Donald Frederick 10121
Bellan, Ruben C. 4962 (MIC.T-78)
Bellavance, M. 8436
Belleau, André 8179 (MIC.F-042402)
Bellefleur, Pierre 11667
(MIC.F.TC-40564)
Bellemare, Diane 1199
(MIC.F.TC-54742)
Bellemare, Marcel J. 821
Bellemare, Yvon 8288
(MIC.F.TC-56299)
Bellicha, Yoram 1736
(MIC.F.TC-42887)
Bellis, Vincent Jerome 11366
Bello, Richard Lawrence 69
(MIC.F.TC-5701)
Bellon, Aldo 4968
Belmont, Arthur David 5014
(QC994.8 M34 fol.)
Belt, Edward Scudder 5636
Beltagy, Ali Ibrahim Ali
Mohammed 5085 (MIC.F.TC-20661)
Belting, Natalia Maree 6987
(F549 K3 B4 fol.)
Belton, Gerald Paul 9502
(MIC.F.TC-34146)
Belyea, Helen Reynolds 5594
Benabou, Charles 9644
(MIC.F-2M11.576.5)
Benaroya, Sygmund 9096
Ben-Dor, Shmuel 584
Ben-Dor, Tsilia Romm 4175
(MIC.F.TC-42165)
Benedict, Winfred Gerald 331
Benezra, Esther 3885
(MIC.F.TC-51873)
Bénéteau, Amédée 8180
Benhacoun-Troise, Simy 7681
Beniskos, Jean-Marie 3930
Benjamin, Bontha Rathnakumar 10639
Benjey, William Grant 5015
Benmouyal, Joseph 928
(MIC.F.TC-53427)
Benner, David Gordon 8956
(MIC.TC-12575)

Bennett, Carol-Anne 3481
(MIC.F.TC-38677)
Bennett, Gordon Fraser 11127
Bennett, John Richard 11960
Bennett, Neville R. 8891
Bennett, Richard Curtis 11992
(MIC.F.TC-31163)
Bennett, Scott Edward 8604
(MIC.F.TC-53492)
Bennett, Victor George 10074
Benoît, Fernand 6270
Bensink, Angela Helen
Arthington 11117 (MIC.TC-4575)
Benson, David Gwyn 5595
Benson, John N. 1421
(MIC.F.TC-20228)
Benson, Ralph 2776 (MIC.F.TC-32736)
Benson, Raymond Philip 4533
Bentley, Charles F. 283
Benvenuto, Gary Louis 5159
(MIC.F.TC-39435)
Beraneck, Michel 4296
(MIC.F.TC-43964)
Bérard, Jean 6271
Berberich, Joel John 10665
Bercuson, David Jay 2092
(MIC.F.TC-18485)
Berek, John J. 8957 (MIC.F.TC-29112)
Berengaut, Julian 2327 (MIC.F.T-1032)
Berens, Anne Elizabeth 3053
(MIC.TC-15681)
Beres, Larry Ralph 10448
(MIC.F.T-1149)
Berg, Dale Herbert 10190
(MIC.F.TC-17451)
Berg, Jonathan Henry 5689
Berg, Wesley Peter 807
Bergen, John Jacob 2708
Berger, Carl Clinton 7110
(MIC.TC-5576)
Berger, Charlene 9645
(MIC.F.TC-38528)
Bergeron, Jacques C. 3150
(MIC.F-028908)
Bergeron, Robert 5690
Bergeron, Viateur 7853
Bergeron, Yves 10504
Bergerud, Arthur Thomas 10615
(MIC.TC-5071)
Berghofer, Desmond Edward 2650
(MIC.TC-13297)
Bériault, Yvon 8714 (F5045 B47)
Berkeley, Alfreda Alice 11062
Berkes, Fikret 11056 (MIC.TC-15790)
Berkhout, Aart W.J. 6636
(MIC.TC-1972)
Berlinguet, Marie 10075
(MIC.F.TC-31164)
Bernacsek, G.M. 5807
Bernard, André 8749
(JL259 A15 B47 fol.)
Bernard, Frère Antoine 7172
Bernard, J. 7892
Bernard, Jean-Guy 11087
(MIC.TC-12851)
Bernard, Jean-Louis 4086 (MIC.T-438)
Bernard, Jean-Paul 7073
Bernard, L. 8484
Bernardinucci, Don A. 1700
(MIC.F.TC-23023)
Berney, Robert Edward 1569
(MIC.T-10)
Bernfeld, Gary Alan 3190
(MIC.F.TC-58999)
Bernier, Gérald 7250
Bernier, Hélène 8181
Bernier, Michel 9210 (MIC.T-3672)
Bernstein, Deborah Ann 3943
(MIC.F.TC-56839)
Bernstein, Robert L. 11964
Bernstein, Stephen Mark 9165
(MIC.F.TC-28591)
Berrangé, J.P. 6272
Berry, Gerald Lloyd 3463 (MIC.T-11)
Berry, Glyn R. 1370 (MIC.F.TC-53628)
Berry, Michael John 6676
(MIC.TC-221)
Berry, Richard 5808
Berry, Richard Edwin 9327
(MIC.F.TC-51360)

Berte, Stephen Bernard 11193
(MIC.F.TC-57127)
Berti, Albert Anthony 5116
Bertley, Leo W. 7269
(MIC.F.TC-53488)
Bertrand, Claude M.L. 6273
(MIC.TC-5020)
Bertrand, Denis 8781
Bertrand, Frère 3123
Bertrand, Marie Jeannette 10143
Bérubé, Louise 3860
(MIC.F-2M11.606.5)
Beserve, Christopher Abilogun 3191
(MIC.F.TC-30333)
Besner, Neil Kalman 8097
Bessette, Gérard 8354 (PS8147 T7 B4)
Bessom, Richard Moody 1831
(MIC.T-148)
Best, Charles Alexander 11367
Best, Edward W. 5955
Best, Ernest Maurice 2419
Best, Henry B.M. 7310
Betke, C.F. 7241 (MIC.F.TC-53865)
Betasalel-Paesser, Raquel 3017
Bettamy, Jeffrey Roger 284
Betz, Frederick 5729
Beukes, Theodorus Ernst 1905
(MIC.F.T-994)
Bevan, George Henry 3303
(MIC.TC-6689)
Bevier, Mary Lou 5160
(MIC.F.TC-1295)
Bezeau, Lawrence Manning 2785
Bhajan, William Rudolph 11115
Bharath, Ramachandran 3608
(MIC.F.TC-30252)
Bhattacharya, Ashim Kumar 4572
(MIC.F.TC-35684)
Bhatti, F.M. 7639
Bhatti, Waqar Hamid 11368
Bhatty, Rajbir 3192 (MIC.F.TC-31677)
Bhojwani, Maia 8383 (MIC.F.TC-42166)
Bhoojedhur, Seewant 233
(MIC.F.TC-25798)
Biberdorf, John Robert 3798
(MIC.F.TC-22528)
Bicha, Karel Denis 103 (MIC.T-12)
Bickel, Edwin David 6572
(MIC.F.TC-40374)
Bickersteth, Patrick 3193
(MIC.F.TC-40374)
Bickerton, B.C. 7628
Bidgood, Bryant F. 10925
(MIC.TC-13300)
Biegen, Mary Sharon 3194
Bielawski, Ellen Eileen 887
(MIC.F.TC-52352)
Bielenstein, Hans 5385 (MIC.TC-5214)
Biersdorff, Kathleen Karol 9503
Biette, Raymond Millo 10930
(MIC.F.TC-38427)
Bigelow, Ann Eileen 9620
(MIC.F.TC-25625)
Bigg, Michael Andrew 10600
(MIC.TC-11204)
Bihl, Gerhard 5809 (MIC.F.TC-17158)
Bilash, Boryslav 7779
Bilodeau, Rosario 6953
Bilyard, Gordon Richard 11835
Binda, Pier Luigi 5386 (MIC.TC-6190)
Bindon, Kathryn M. 7216
(MIC.F.TC-42402)
Binger, Jane Louise 6913
Binhammer, Helmut Herbert 1779
Binnette, André 3663 (MIC.F-021403)
Binnington, Alfred Fernes 9880
Binns, R.G. 8128
Biolik, Anna 8182
Birbalsingh, Frank Mahabal 8049
Birch, A.H. 1496 (MIC.F.TC-42808)
Birch, John Worth 1812
Birch, T.A. 7682
Bird, David Charles 2651
(MIC.F.TC-56837)
Bird, Charles Durham 11511
Bird, Glen Alvin 11856
(MIC.F.TC-63329)
Bird, Marlene Isabelle 3991
(MIC.F.TC-43616)
Bird, Ralph Durham 11409)
Birk, Wolf Dieter 5956
(MIC.F.TC-37933)

Birkenstock, David 3618 (MIC.F.T-875)
Birkett, Tyson Clifford 6274
  (MIC.F.TC-22440)
Birnbaum, Dana Wolfe 9354
  (MIC.F.TC-44392)
Birnie, Howard Harry 2979
Biron, Louise 10243
  (MIC.F-2M11.375.4)
Birrell, J.H. 2001
Bishop, Charles Aldrich 505
Bishop, Donald Thomas 5161
Bishop, Eric G. 5957
Bishop, George Archibald 1570
Bishop, Olga Bernice 7966 (Z1373 B5)
Bishop, Peter Victor 8804
  (MIC.TC-3891)
Bishop, Robert Frederick 269
Bissett, John Douglas 11430
  (MIC.F.TC-24972)
Bisson, Margaret Mary 1014
Bizier, Jeanne 2420, 9929 (LA418 Q8
  B59)
Bjarnason, Carl 2709
Bjarnason, Emil Grover 2144
  (MIC.F.TC-30253)
Bjarnason, Harold Frederick 8
Blacha, Michael Dietrich 9091
  (MIC.F.TC-47830)
Blache, Pierre 7893 (MIC.F-023403)
Black, Edward Lyal 9504
  (MIC.F.TC-40004)
Black, Edwin Robert 8485 (MIC.T-13)
Black, George Alexander 8183
  (MIC.TC-8921)
Black, Hawley Lisle 1079
  (MIC.F.TC-50394)
Black, James M. 6275
Black, James William 7492
  (MIC.F.CC-4 No.05670)
Black, Jerome Harold 8608
  (MIC.F.T-925)
Black, Meredith Jean 499 (MIC.T-817)
Black, Norman Fergus 7670 (PE1068
  U5 B6)
Black, Philip T. 6276
Black, William B. 11079
Black, William Griffiths 4387
Blackadar, Robert Gordon 5958
Blackbourn, Anthony 4820
  (MIC.TC-3892)
Blackman, Margaret Berlin 636
  (MIC.T-593)
Blackmer, Hugh Allison 59 (MIC.T-735)
Blackmore, David E. 3054
  (MIC.F.TC-48892)
Blackwell, David McClaughry 4058
  (MIC.F.TC-50230)
Blackwood, George E. 3482
Blahey, Peter John 4297
  (MIC.F.TC-27472)
Blain, Christopher F. 5959
  (MIC.TC-11692)
Blain, Deborah 8958 (MIC.F.TC-18152)
Blain, Jean 9808
Blain, Lawrence Alexander 1259
  (MIC.F.TC-32412)
Blain, Robert 3304
Blair, Alexander Marshall 5960
Blair, Mansell John 10028 (MIC.T-258)
Blair, William R.N. 7587, 9594
Blais, André-Marc 8750
  (MIC.F.TC-38482)
Blais, Gilles 4344 (MIC.T-497)
Blais, Hervé 10058 (HQ751 B43)
Blais, Jacques 8355 (PS8153 B58)
Blais, Jeffrey Peter 2395 (MIC.T-813)
Blais, Marc 10364
Blais, Roger Adelard 6277
Blake, Donald A.W. 5542
Blake, Donald Edward 8609
  (MIC.T-434)
Blake, Elizabeth Anarye 585
  (MIC.F.TC-36357)
Blake, George Gordon 1992
Blake, Rick Nelson 3483
  (MIC.F.TC-28645)
Blakeley, Karen B. 8959
  (MIC.F.TC-35825)
Blakeslee, Donald John 419
Blakey, Janis Marie 3041

Blakley, Stewart William 1120
  (MIC.F.TC-1038)
Blall, Madiha 9646
Blanar, Michael 8427
Blanchet, Bertrand 11591
  (SD397 C4 B53)
Blanchette, Jean-François 850
Bland, Warren Roger 4863
Blandy, Richard John 2379 (MIC.T-360)
Blankstein, Kirk Robert 3484
  (MIC.TC-10907)
Blasing, Terence Jack 4969
Blauer, Marvin 7147 (MIC.TC-9210)
Blauer, Rosalind 1312 (MIC.TC-9211)
Bleakney, John S. 10720
Blecha, Matthew 5961 (MIC.F.TC-3939)
Bledsoe, James Barry 2562
  (MIC.F.TC-42168)
Blenis, Henry Willard, Jr. 3719, 11728
Blenkinsop, Padraig John 4096
  (MIC.F.TC-40881)
Blewett, June Caryll Cosbey 8960
  (MIC.F.TC-23635)
Bliss, John William Michael 1260
  (MIC.TC-12926)
Bliss, Neil W. 5490 (MIC.TC-15792)
Bloch, Maurice 9116 (MIC.F.TC-51628)
Block, Fred 6278
Blodgett, Christopher Jay 8961
  (MIC.F.TC-54475)
Bloede, Louis William 9841
Blohm, Robert James 10761
Blome, Charles David 5162
  (MIC.F.T-1119)
Blondin, Félix 8184
Bloomberg, William Joseph 11668
Bloomfield, Elizabeth Phyllis 7212
  (MIC.F.TC-55516)
Blouin, Jean-Louis 11755
Blowers, Elizabeth Anne 3753
  (MIC.F.TC-26710)
Blowers, Thomas Anthony 3001
  (MIC.TC-13303)
Blum, Frank J. 10244
Blum, William D. 2408
Blumell, Richard Emerson 2917
  (LB2822 B4 1964)
Blunt, Adrian 2423
Blusson, Stewart Lynn 5909
Boag, David Archibald 10837
Boag, Noël Harvey 3109
  (MIC.F.TC-44702)
Boak, Ronald Terrance Robert 3322
  (MIC.F.TC-19754)
Board, Peter Emile 3944
  (MIC.F.TC-58257)
Bock, Philip Karl 520
Bodaly, Richard Andrew 11039
  (MIC.F.TC-35827)
Boddington, Martin John 11354
  (MIC.F.TC-27794)
Bodola, Anthony 10908
Boeckh, John Anthony 1674
  (MIC.T-215)
Boerger, Hans J. 11194
  (MIC.F.TC-40091)
Bogdan, Deanne Gail Eleanor 8092
  (MIC.F.TC-43617)
Bogdanowicz, M.S. 1044
Boggs, Stephen Taylor 532
Boggs, Theodore Harding 7616
Bogle, Edward Warren 5962
  (MIC.F.TC-50105)
Bognar, Carl Joseph 3102
  (MIC.F.TC-67012)
Bohemier, Albert 7894
Bohm, Peter Emblidge 10076
  (MIC.F.TC-50231)
Boisvert, Jean-Marie 8962
  (MIC.F-2M11.380.4)
Boivin, Guy 11303 (MIC.F.TC-54746)
Boivin, Jean 2154 (MIC.F.TC-672)
Boivin, Micheline 10039
  (MIC.F.TC-26410)
Boland, Francis J. 3553
Boldt, Menno 447 (MIC.T-590)
Bolduc, Yves 8372 (MIC.F.TC-48471)
Bolger, Francis W.P. 7182 (F5327 B6)
Bolghari, Hassanali 11756
  (MIC.F.TC-26413)
Bolle, Arthur 8963

Bollman, Raymond Douglas 9
  (MIC.F.TC-38678)
Bolm, John Gary 5163
Bolton, Thomas Edward 5963
Bolus, Charles Robert 3913
Bond, Catherine Ruth 8964
  (MIC.F.TC-65031)
Bond, Ivor John 5964
  (MIC.F.TC-21149)
Bondarenko, Donald David 11629
Bone, Georgina Mary 3386
  (MIC.F.TC-48894)
Bone, Robert Martin 4813
Boneham, Roger Frederick 6524
Boness, Daryl John 10601
  (MIC.F.TC-44194)
Bonham-Carter, Graeme Francis 5810
  (MIC.TC-1057)
Boniferro, Thomas Joseph 4140
  (MIC.F.TC-26712)
Bonin, Marie A. 6882
Bonita, Manuel Libres 11669
  (MIC.TC-13199)
Bonneau, Gilles 3650
  (MIC.F.TC-47905)
Bonnichsen, Robson 356
  (MIC.F.TC-20971)
Bonta, James Louis 3921
  (MIC.F.TC-43972)
Bontrager-Lehman, Carol 6757
  (MIC.F.TC-48572)
Bonvillain, Nancy Lee 7812
  (MIC.T-511)
Booke, Henry Edward 10902
Boon, Harold Watson 9953
Boone, Lalla Rookh 7307 (G246 V3 B6)
Boone, Laurel Blenkinsop 8389
Boonstra, Rudy 10708
  (MIC.F.TC-32414)
Boonyawiroj, Somsak 3664
  (MIC.F.TC-59753)
Boorman, Joyce Lillian 3014
  (MIC.F.TC-44703)
Boos, Robert W. 3931
Boote, Maurice John 1701
Booth, James Thomas 11452
Booth, John Alexander Gordon 9278
  (MIC.F.TC-36358)
Booth, John Derek 4750
  (MIC.TC-11760)
Booth, Mary Joyce 3403
  (MIC.F.TC-40093)
Boothe, Paul Michael 1596
  (MIC.F.TC-56628)
Bordeleau, Yvan 9595
Boreham, Gordon Francis 1508
  (MIC.T-14)
Borgen, William Alfred 3195
  (MIC.F.TC-30623)
Borins, Sandford Frederick 2269
Borkent, Art 11128 (MIC.F.TC-65768)
Bornstein, Robert A. 9153
  (MIC.F.TC-48473)
Borrie, Roderick Allen 9647
  (MIC.F.TC-37577)
Borthwick, Burton Lloyd 2641
Borzo, Henry 7455
Bosco, Monique 8185
Bosetti, Rino Angelo 3569
  (MIC.F.TC-26714)
Boshes, Michael 10690
  (MIC.F.TC-36591)
Bosse, Eveline 8317
Bostock, Hugh Samuel 5164
Boston, Ralph Emerson 1737
Boswell, David M. 2652 (MIC.T-325)
Boswell, Marion Joan 7447
Boswell, Peter Gordon 8705
  (MIC.F.TC-59921)
Botterill, Calvin Bruce 10404
  (MIC.F.TC-34297)
Bottomley, John 10480
  (MIC.F.TC-34764)
Bottomley, Richard John 6649
  (MIC.F.TC-58356)
Bouchard, André 1145
  (MIC.F-2M11.388.9)
Bouchard, André Bernard 4808
Bouchard, André-Joseph 4097
  (MIC.T-174)

Bouchard, Claude 432 (MIC.F.T-937)
Bouchard, Jacqueline 9648
Bouchard, Jean-Marie 3799
Bouchard, Lionel 8380
Bouchard, Michel A. 6279
  (MIC.F.TC-51885)
Bouchard, Serge 433 (MIC.F.TC-51886)
Boucher, André 7939
Boucher, Michel 1702
Boucher, Paul 2128
Boucher, Réal 9890 (MIC.F.TC-43973)
Boudoux, Michel 11757
  (MIC.F.TC-41842)
Boudra, Douglas Bryant 11993
Boudreau, Berthe 4406
Boudreau, Françoise 6758
Boudreau, Joseph Amédée 7111, 7640
  (MIC.T-121)
Boudreau, Léonie 3908
Bougaieff, André 7723
  (MIC.F.TC-35348)
Boughton, Douglas Gordon 3114
  (MIC.F.TC-30625)
Boulet, François-Xavier 2918
  (MIC.F.TC-56904)
Boulianne, Réal Gérard 2430
  (MIC.TC-5990)
Boulva, Jean 10602 (MIC.F.TC-18567)
Bounadère, René 2516, 9809
  (BX910 C2 B6)
Bourassa, André G. 8186 (PS8073 B65)
Bourassa-Trépanier, Juliette 982
  (MIC.F.TC-18924)
Bourbeau, Robert 10319 (MIC.T-3339)
Bourbeau-Poirier, Louise 3375
  (MIC.F.T-988)
Bourbonnais, Yvon 9279
  (MIC.F.TC-50637)
Bourbonnière, Richard Arthur 5121
Bourdeau de Fontenay, Alain
  Jean-Marie Daniel 1165
Bourgeois, Jacques Charlemagne 1963
Bourgeois, Mariette 8187
Bourgeois, Roger Daniel 3151
  (MIC.F.TC-30624)
Bourne, James Hilary 6280
  (MIC.F.TC-22443)
Bourne, Larry Stuart 4943
  (NA9130 T6 B6)
Bourne, Victor Laurence 11453
  (MIC.TC-7995)
Bourneuf, Roland Henri 8283
  (PS8513 A75 Z57)
Bourque, Lorraine 7683
  (MIC.F.TC-48478)
Bourque, Paul 8965 (MIC.F.TC-41397)
Bourque, Paul-André 1121
  (MIC.F.TC-56027)
Bourque, Pierre 5637
Bousquet, D. 7337
Bousquet, Denis 7475
Bousquet, Marie-Elizabeth 2517
Bousquet, Yves 11304
Boutilier, Robert Gordon 3196
  (MIC.F.TC-56636)
Boutin, Stanley Albert 10657
  (MIC.F.TC-65055)
Boville, Byron Walter 4970
  (QC994.8 M343 fol.)
Bowd, Alan Douglas 4134
  (MIC.TC-10043)
Bowd, Joy Carolyn 8899
  (MIC.F.TC-37781)
Bowden, Bruce William 6942
  (MIC.F.TC-47013)
Bowen, William Donald 10573
  (MIC.F.TC-42591)
Bower, R.A. 7022
Bower, Susan Mae 10648
  (MIC.F.TC-43774)
Bowers, Emory Frank 10762
Bowers, Henry 3445 (O181 B6)
Bowes, Garry George 11560
  (MIC.F.TC-20896)
Bowie, Gérald William 10414
Bowker, Alan Franklin 3554
  (MIC.F.TC-32745)
Bowles, Jane Margaret 10459
  (MIC.F.TC-48299)
Bowman, Donald Fox 2002 (MIC.T-435)
Bowman, James Martin 8095

Bowman, Marilyn Laura 8966
  (MIC.TC-11763)
Bowman, Paul William 11592
Bowring, James R. 6747
Bowsfield, Hartwell Walter Lewis 7191
Box, Colin Edward 3294 (MIC.T-487)
Boyce, Eleanor 4242
Boyce, Raymond William 1450
  (MIC.F.TC-59920)
Boychuk, Halia Katherine 3420
  (MIC.F.TC-21770)
Boyd, Archibald D. 2048
Boyd, Evelyn Marie 4160
  (MIC.F.TC-53014)
Boydell, Anthony Nigel 4725
  (MIC.TC-13830)
Boyer, Harold 8870 (MIC.TC-12125)
Boyle, Lawrence James 1783
  (MIC.T-559)
Boyle, Robert William 5811
Boynard-Frot, Janine 8188
Boynton, Arthur John 2743
Bozinoff, Lorne 1964
  (MIC.F.TC-47014)
Bozzini, Luciano 2142 (MIC.F-022906)
Brabec, Dragan 5165 (MIC.TC-7996)
Bracken, Garth Kyles 11235
Brackhaus, Karl Heinz 4506
  (MIC.F.TC-25805)
Brackstone, Demaris Darlene 4261
  (MIC.F.TC-53015)
Brackstone, Ross Daniel 3945
  (MIC.F.TC-53016)
Bradbury, Helen Elizabeth 11094
  (MIC.TC-14285)
Bradbury, Ian Keith 11561
  (MIC.F.TC-17967)
Bradbury, John Henry 4915
  (MIC.F.TC-35884)
Bradbury, Ola Hinton 3197
  (MIC.TC-13310)
Bradfield, Frederick Michael 2201
  (MIC.T-344)
Bradford, Florence Emily 7724
  (MIC.F.T-1160)
Bradford, Henry Martin 11994
  (MIC.TC-8642)
Bradford, Magnus Andrew 9857
Bradley, Christine Felecia 8967
  (MIC.F.TC-34766)
Bradley, Daniel Albert 5730
Bradley, George Arthur 11129
Bradley, James Wesley 643
  (MIC.F.T-1048)
Bradley, Michael Timothy 8900
  (MIC.TC-43069)
Bradshaw, Bennie Albert 5128
Bradshaw, Frederick 7074 (JL51 B8)
Bradwell, David 4742 (MIC.T-15)
Bradwin, Edmund William 2093
  (HD7290 B7)
Brady, Allen Roy 11130
Bragdon, Chandler 7563
Braid, Andrew Falconor 1929
Brailsford, Eugene D. 3800
Braithwaite, Fitzwarren Carlton 1649
  (MIC.TC-8657)
Braithwaite, Roger James 5016
  (MIC.F.TC-39621)
Brakel, Pieter 1808 (MIC.F.TC-35177)
Braman, Dennis Richard 5812
  (MIC.F.TC-52353)
Brammer, Dennis Leslie 3198
  (MIC.F.TC-34300)
Branch, Edward Beverly 9427
  (MIC.F.TC-30628)
Branchaud, Irène 8275
Brand, Christopher James 10583
Brand, Stephen Richard 5691
Brand, Uwe 5813 (MIC.F.TC-43975)
Brandes, Hans-Gunther 2355
Brandon, Elizabeth 822
Brannon, Ernest Leroy 10931
Branscombe, Frederic Ray 4215
Braroe, Niels Winther 710
Brasfield, Charles Randolph 8968
  (MIC.T-10221)
Brassard, Guy R. 11534
  (MIC.TC-10644)
Brassard, Jean 3002
Bratton, Robert Dickson 10348

Brault, Diana Victoria 994
Brault, Florent 1465
Brault, Lucien 7271
Braun, Peter Hans 9428
  (MIC.TC-13311)
Brawn, Christopher Alan 10381
Bray, Dale Irving 4497 (MIC.TC-11118)
Bray, John V.G. 6281
Bray, Robert Matthew 7112
  (MIC.F.TC-30888)
Brayne, Robin Charles 2860
  (MIC.F.TC-42593)
Brayshaw, Thomas Christopher 11670
Brazeau, Ernest Jacques 4105
Brazeau, Marcel 11758
  (MIC.F.TC-43117)
Brazer, Harvey Elliot 1466
Brebner, John Bartlet 7173 (F5060 B7)
Brecher, Irving 1467
Breckenridge, Rocliff Morton 1422
Bredidas-Assimopoulos,
  Constantina 777 (MIC.F-023504)
Breen, David Henry 7231
  (MIC.TC-13312)
Breen, Paul Allan 11080
  (MIC.F.TC-24912)
Brehaut, Willard 3645
Breitman, Kenneth E. 9117
Brendell, James Francis S. 10838
Brennan, James Marks 11250
Brennan, James William 7245
  (MIC.F.TC-30629)
Brent, Edmund 7725
Brereton, Thomas Francis 8502
  (MIC.T-607)
Breslauer, Helen Joyce 10130
Bresver, Barbara 9649
  (MIC.F.TC-31170)
Breton, Albert Antoine 1543
Brett, Carlton Elliot 6573
Brett, John Roland 10932
Breul, Frank R. 10122
Brewer, Keith John 1865
  (MIC.F.TC-20668)
Brewer, Robert Franklin Ross 299
Brewster, Gordon Ross 220
  (MIC.F.TC-48302)
Brewster, Linda Joan 9280
  (MIC.F.TC-36977)
Briaud, Jean-Louis Charles 2270
Brice, Max O. 1371 (MIC.F.TC-43977)
Brickman, Julia Ruth Rogers 9217
  (MIC.F.TC-37782)
Bride, Kenneth Wilbert 4298
  (MIC.F.TC-17463)
Brideaux, Wayne Wilfred 6560
Bridgman, Harry John 9784
  (MIC.F.TC-42404)
Bridgewater, William R. 1237
Brien-Dandurand, Renée 735
  (MIC.T-3604)
Brière, Denis 11671 (MIC.F.TC-42595)
Brière, Roger 4751
Briggs, Derek Ernest Gilmour 11131
Briggs, Elizabeth Joanne 3946
  (MIC.F.TC-19682)
Briggs, Jean Louise 586
Brigham, Robert John 5965
  (MIC.TC-10852)
Brill, Ronald Woodrow, Jr. 10245
  (MIC.F.TC-35179)
Brillinger, Margaret Eleanor 10040
  (MIC.F.TC-59866)
Brindley, Selwyn Robert William 3421
  (MIC.F.TC-51237)
Bring, Gordon 2224
Brintnell, Eldonna S.G. 10041
Brisebois, Daniel 6282
  (MIC.F-2M11.551.8)
Briskey, Joseph A., Jr. 5166
  (MIC.F.T-1073)
Brisson, Jean Denis 11562
  (MIC.F.TC-38895)
Britan, Gerald Mark 398 (MIC.T-723)
Britnell, George Edwin 139
Britt, Noah W. 11190
Britt, Robert Franklin 11369
Broad, David Stephen 5814
Broad, James Charles 3896
Broad, Margaret 8099
  (MIC.F.TC-56468)

Broadbent, Arnot Bruce 11355
 (MIC.F.TC-48684)
Broadfoot, William Craig 314
Brochu, Serge 9249 (MIC.T-3341)
Brock, Byron B. 5167
Brodie, Henry 1313
Brodie, M. Janine 8437
 (MIC.F.TC-55593)
Brodie, Paul Frederick 10607
Brodsky, Patricia Aline 9233
 (MIC.F.TC-50913)
Brodt, Abraham Isaac 1423
Brody, Bernard 2202 (MIC.F.TC-42893)
Broga, Mary Irena 9166
 (MIC.F.TC-4835)
Bromley, Peter Tyson 10609
 (MIC.F.TC-34020)
Bronner, Frédéric-Y.-L. 8189
Bronson, Harold Emory 1800
 (MIC.T-151)
Brook, George Albert 5815
 (MIC.F.TC-37937)
Brook, Roger Charles 4539
Brookbank, Carman Roy 1930
 (MIC.F.TC-32748)
Brooke, Margaret Martha 5543
Brooke, Robert Charles 11454
 (MIC.TC-453)
Brooke, Wilfrid Michael 4059
 (MIC.TC-16620)
Brooker, Barry H. 3777
Brookes, Alan Alexander 7629
Brookes, Ian Alfred 4641
 (MIC.TC-7006)
Brooks, Elwood Ralph 5966
Brooks, Harold Kelly 6509
Brooks, Joel Elliott 1372
 (MIC.F.TC-52757)
Brooks, William Howard 9872
 (MIC.TC-12651)
Brooks-Hill, Frederick James 1650
 (MIC.T-612)
Broom, Eric Frederick 10349
 (MIC.T-351)
Broomes, Desmond Rodwell 3422
 (MIC.TC-11543)
Brophy, Beverly Isabel 2563
 (MIC.F.TC-31171)
Brosseau, John Francis 2861
 (MIC.F.TC-17467)
Broster, Bruce Elwood 5122
 (MIC.F.TC-50953)
Brother, Charles 4220
Broughton, Paul Leonard 5097
Broughton, Robert Stephen 270
 (MIC.TC-15801)
Brouillet, Luc 11512
Brouillette, Léonce 8273
 (MIC.F.TC-26423)
Brouillette, Normand 4882
 (MIC.F.TC-64445)
Brown, Alfred Malcolm 995
Brown, Anton 4658 (MIC.TC-8721)
Brown, Bruce Leonard 9650
Brown, Chesley Kenneth 3323
Brown, Corbin Alexander 2882
 (MIC.F.TC-31172)
Brown, Donald Dawson 5596
 (MIC.TC-10758)
Brown, Donald Murray 332
Brown, Douglas D. 9281
 (MIC.F.TC-29118)
Brown, George Williams 1238
Brown, Ian William 6988
Brown, Ira C. 5816
Brown, Isabel A. 6883
 (MIC.F.TC-47015)
Brown, Joseph A. 10871
 (MIC.F.TC-61727)
Brown, James Anthony 3003
 (MIC.F.TC-26718)
Brown, Jennifer 368
Brown, Jim McCaslin 5967
Brown, John Douglas 2862
 (MIC.F.TC-55709)
Brown, Juele Marie 9234
Brown, Lloyd Raymond 3124
 (MIC.TC-9906)
Brown, Lorne Alvin 8690
Brown, Malcolm Clarence 1544

Brown, Matthew Paul 1373
 (MIC.F.TC-55763)
Brown, Melvin Douglas 9250
Brown, Michael Charles 5387
 (GB601.8 B78)
Brown, Michael Gary 6932 (MIC.T-725)
Brown, Michael Joseph 4726
Brown, Penelope Stevenson 11914
 (MIC.F.TC-46082)
Brown, Peter Alan 5731
 (MIC.F.TC-26675)
Brown, Richard Arthur Cornelius 5388
Brown, Richard Lee 11132
Brown, Robert A. 6283
Brown, Robert Craig 7512 (MIC.TC-6)
Brown, Robert James 7564
Brown, Roger Hamilton 7060
 (F5073.2 B88)
Brown, Roger James Evan 4659
 (GB648.15 B7)
Brown, Ronald Duncan 1675
 (MIC.F.T-991)
Brown, Sheila Ann 4781
 (MIC.F.TC-21773)
Brown, Sharon-Dale 11812
 (MIC.F.TC-49390)
Brown, Si 1908 (MIC.F.TC-37844)
Brown, Thomas Edward 7223
 (MIC.F.TC-50109)
Brown, Thomas Harry Joshua 4141
 (MIC.F.TC-26720)
Brown, Wilfred John 2744
 (MIC.F.TC-26041)
Brown, William Alan Nicholas 10454
 (MIC.F.TC-30030)
Brown, William Cecil 6739
 (MIC.F.TC-31942)
Browne, Gerald Peter 7421 (JL65 B7)
Browne, Joseph A. 6691
Browne, Margaret Patricia Jane 3947
 (MIC.TC-9577)
Browne, Regina Maria 6692
Brownell, George McLeod 5968
Brownstone, Meyer 10
Brozowski, Roman Steve 4898
 (MIC.F.TC-31559)
Bruce, Everend Lester 5168
Bruce, Mary Jane (Sister Mary
 Teresina) 2467
Bruck, Margaret Ellen 3042
 (MIC.TC-11769)
Bruin, Gerardus Cornelis Anna 333
 (MIC.F.TC-48686)
Bruins, Elton John 9954
Bruinsma, Robert Walter 3948
 (MIC.F.TC-59225)
Brummell, Arden Craig 4899
 (MIC.F.TC-36512)
Brummer, Johannes J. 6284
Brundage, Donald Hazen 10144
Brunel, Pierre 10893 (MIC.TC-3098)
Bruner, Frank H. 5817
Brunet, Luc 3619 (MIC.F-2M11.585.2)
Brunger, Alan George 4864
 (MIC.F.TC-20481)
Brunskill, Ronald 1080
 (MIC.F.TC-26591)
Brunton, Bill Biozz 670
Brusher, Joseph Stanislaus 7532
Bryan, Ingrid Arvidsdotter 2247
 (MIC.TC-11120)
Bryan, James Ernest 10933
 (MIC.TC-11207)
Bryan, Merwyn Leonard 4682
 (MIC.T-548)
Bryans, David Garth 3305
 (MIC.TC-9578)
Bryce, Robert Curry 2639
Bryden, Walter Kenneth 10123
 (HD7106 C6 B7)
Bryson, Susan Elizabeth 9505
 (MIC.F.TC-54750)
Buchan, Kenneth Lorne 6650
 (MIC.F.TC-36597)
Buchanan, Claire L. 11836
Buchanan, Ronald James 11455
 (MIC.TC-455)
Buchignani, Norman Leroy 760
 (MIC.F.TC-35887)
Buchler, Ira Richard 587

Buchner, Anthony Paul 841
 (MIC.F.TC-49277)
Buchwald, Caryl Edward 5389
Buck, Geoffrey J. 4262
Buckingham, Sandra Lynn 11813
 (MIC.F.TC-42599)
Buckland, Donald Channing 11672
Buckland, Francis C. 6285
Buckley, Joan Naglestad 8162
Buckley, Joseph Roy 11915
 (MIC.F.TC-32423)
Buckley, K.A.H. 1651
Buckley, Suzann Caroline 1261
 (MIC.T-485)
Bucknam, Roland Franklin 128
Buckner, Charles H. 10716
Buckner, Phillip Alfred 7460
 (MIC.T-893)
Buckridan, Rakib 3801
Bucovetsky, Meyer Wilfred 1703
 (MIC.TC-10564)
Budd, Henry Harold 3609
 (MIC.F.T-1074)
Buddemeier, Robert Worth 6617
Buddington, Arthur Francis 5732
Buehler, Sharon Lyn Kelly 6830
 (MIC.F.TC-63582)
Buerkle, Udo 10886 (MIC.F.TC-18164)
Buettner, Edwin George John 4299
 (MIC.F.TC-54634)
Buffam, Basil Scott White 6286
Buffett, Frederick 2883
Bugaieff, André 7716
Bujea, Eleanor 4388
Bujold, Charles Eugene 3485
 (MIC.T-488)
Bull, Dale Harold 9328
 (MIC.F.TC-53019)
Bullen, Edward Lester 2837
 (MIC.F.TC-47019)
Bullock, Robert Earl 10610
 (MIC.TC-9579)
Bultman, Thomas Robert 5169
Bunch, Gary Owen 3866
 (MIC.F.TC-25108)
Bunn, Frank Edward 11995
 (MIC.F.TC-23558)
Bunn, Helen Hoque 2564
Bunnell, Frederick Lindsley 10666
Bunting, Trudi Elizabeth 4937
 (MIC.F.TC-32751)
Burbridge, Kenneth J. 104
Burch, Ernest S., Jr. 588
Burden, Elliott Thomas 5390
 (MIC.F.TC-60852)
Bureau, Luc 98 (MIC.T-569)
Burelle, Jacques Vincent 10350
Burge, Sister Irene 3723 (MIC.T-806)
Burger, Michael P. 8969
 (MIC.F.TC-441)
Burgess, Arthur Charles 10384
 (MIC.F.TC-51445)
Burgess, Donald Arthur 2518
Burgher, Peter L. 9651
 (MIC.F.TC-57313)
Burk, Cornelius F., Jr. 6287
Burke, David Patrick 7400
Burke, Gloria Victoria 4441
 (MIC.F.TC-48900)
Burke, Harley Lorne 3802
 (MIC.F.TC-40989)
Burke, Mavis E. 2403, 8869
Burke, Sharon Ogden 3090
 (MIC.F.TC-36599)
Burke, Sister Teresa Avila 7113
 (MIC.T-17)
Burke, Vincent P. 2468
Burkett, Robert Dale 11786
Burley, David Vincent 862
 (MIC.F.TC-41130)
Burman, Patrick Walsh 8563
 (MIC.F.T-1031)
Burman, Savitri G. 4632
Burnaby, Barbara Jane 4110
 (MIC.F.TC-38684)
Burnet, Jean R. 10160
Burnett, Edward 4209
Burnett, John Allen 11208
Burnie, Stephen Wilbur 5391
 (MIC.F.TC-44361)
Burns, George Emmett 4176

Burns, Robert Alan 8396
Burns, Robert Earle 5170
Burns, Robert Joseph 7224
 (MIC.F.TC-24501)
Burns, Robin Bruce 7328
 (MIC.F.TC-31721)
Burnside, Albert 9873
Burrill, Meredith F. 4834
Burrus, Robert Carlton 5171
Bursey, Card Cedric 10540
 (MIC.F.TC-47706)
Bursnall, John Treharne 5733
Burstein, Samuel Benjamin 3071
 (MIC.F.TC-45970)
Burt, Jonathan Robert 10731
Burt-Pintar, Sandra Dawn 8718
 (MIC.F.TC-51364)
Burtis, Paul Judson 9355
 (MIC.F.TC-30890)
Burton, A.M. 1262
Burton, David Anthony Travis 1342
 (MIC.F.TC-48308)
Burton, Frederick R. 6288
Burton, Gordon L. 11
Burton, Jean 10739
 (MIC.F-2M11.187.3)
Burtt, Brian Irvine 8970
 (MIC.F.TC-61958)
Burwash, Edward Moore Jackson 5172
Burwash, Ronald Allan McLean 5392
Busby, John Robert 11431
 (MIC.F.TC-30633)
Busby, Keith 3897 (MIC.F.TC-48483)
Buser, Mary M. 9652 (MIC.F.TC-47190)
Bush, Guy Louis, Jr. 11133
Bush, Mary T. 6943
Bushe, Cornelius 1146
 (MIC.F.TC-50238)
Bussières, Paul 4752
Bustin, Robert Marc 5173
Butchard, Neil Joseph 8901
 (MIC.F.TC-54423)
Butcher, Janice Elsie 10405
 (MIC.F.TC-44707)
Butkowsky, Irwin Sam 3778
 (MIC.F.TC-55300)
Butler, Edward Gregory 984
 (MIC.T-799)
Butler, Lenora Frances 3665
 (MIC.F.TC-30330)
Butler, Pamela Jean 8564
 (MIC.F.TC-50405)
Butler, Patrick, Jr. 6289
Butler, Peter Marshall 10029
 (MIC.F.TC-26043)
Butt, Khurshid Alam 5597
 (MIC.F.TC-30375)
Butt, William Davison 7192
 (MIC.F.TC-31563)
Buttrick, Steven Colby 11456
 (MIC.F.TC-40583)
Buttrum, Stephen Michael 8971
 (MIC.F.TC-23265)
Buyce, Milton Raymond 5086
Byers, Alfred R. 5969
Byers, Roddick Beaumont 7401
 (MIC.TC-8380)
Byles, Robert Hal 448
Byrd, Mark Dodds 9506
 (MIC.F.TC-53020)
Byrne, Anthony William 6290
Byrne, Timothy Clarke 2439
Byrne, William John 854 (MIC.T-515)
Byron, Ronald Neil 11673

C

Cadden, Patrick Guthrie 4794
 (MIC.F.TC-49278)
Cadieux, Lorenzo, Rév. 9890
Cadotte, Robert 4300 (MIC.T-3714)
Cafferty, Pastora Sanjuan 8412
Cagnon, Maurice Arthur 7726
Cage, William Edwin 1617 (MIC.T-168)
Cahall, Raymond Dubois 6954 (H31 C7)

Cahill, Elizabeth Mary 8486
 (MIC.TC-10395)
Cahoon, Allan Ray 1931 (MIC.T-676)
Cahoon, Margaret Cecilia 6730
Caiden, G.E. 2134
Caillier, Paul Melvin 9118
 (MIC.F.TC-47191)
Cairnes, Clive Elmore 5174
Cairnes, Delorme Donaldson 5910
Cairns, Alan Andrew 11091
 (MIC.TC-59903)
Cairns, J.W. 7838
Cairns, Sister Marie Laurine 7988
Cairns, Robert Douglas 1901
Cairns, Robert Ross 315
Caisi, Roy Franklin 11563
Calder, William Arnold 7114
 (MIC.F.TC-50239)
Calder, William Berry 3587
 (MIC.F.TC-56947)
Caldwell, Brian John 2757
 (MIC.F.TC-34306)
Caldwell, Norman W. 6989
Caldwell, Patrick John 10839
Caley, John Fletcher 5970
Calhoun, John H., Jr. 8565
Callahan, James M. 7493
 (MIC.F.CC-4)
Callahan, John Edward 5692
 (MIC.TC-16475)
Callaway, Donald Goodwin 449
Callender, Charles 500
Callier, Philippe 1597
 (MIC.F.TC-41132)
Calliste, Agnes Miranda 3306
 (MIC.F.TC-47020)
Calloway, C.G. 7461
Calvert, Sheila Gay Cunningham 863
 (MIC.F.TC-51633)
Calzavera, Liviana M. 10018
 (MIC.F.TC-59891)
Cameron, Alexander Rankin 5638
Cameron, Austin W. 10562
Cameron, Barry Winston 5971
Cameron, Christina 930
Cameron, David Murray 2777
 (MIC.TC-5221)
Cameron, Donald Alan 3588
 (MIC.F.TC-31178)
Cameron, Ian Julian 2863
 (MIC.F.TC-54976)
Cameron, John Duncan 7924
Cameron, Maxwell A. 2778
 (LB2890 C33)
Cameron, Peter James 346
 (MIC.F.TC-18169)
Cameron-Schumann, Monique 5057
 (MIC.F.TC-40103)
Camfield, Paul Adrian 6606
 (MIC.TC-15194)
Camiré, Claude 11759
 (MIC.F.TC-45913)
Cammarat, Salvatore 2980
Campagna, Jean-Louis 8972
Campbell, Alan 11209
 (MIC.F.TC-19239)
Campbell, Brian Lewis 9971
 (MIC.F.TC-57072)
Campbell, Bruce Samuel 6651
Campbell, Charles D. 5175
Campbell, Donna Marie 9507
 (MIC.F.TC-32152)
Campbell, Douglas D. 5818
Campbell, Douglas F. 9955 (MIC.T-18)
Campbell, Duncan Darroch 3620
 (MIC.F.TC-17756)
Campbell, Duncan Robert 1909
Campbell, Edwin Colin 8541
 (MIC.T-667)
Campbell, Elizabeth Jane 2049
 (MIC.F.TC-52208)
Campbell, Frank Gerard 4301
Campbell, Frederick H.A. 5491
 (MIC.TC-10316)
Campbell, Gordon 3570
 (MIC.TC-13837)
Campbell, Gordon Donald 4469
Campbell, Harry F. 1451
 (MIC.TC-14186)
Campbell, James Alfred 205
 (MIC.F.TC-42806)

Campbell, John Alexander 8973
 (MIC.F.TC-40584)
Campbell, John Duncan 3152, 6537
Campbell, Kenneth Vincent 5176
Campbell, Margaret Amelia 6884
Campbell, Neil MacDougall 10486
 (MIC.TC-12902)
Campbell, Nora Rene 1015
 (MIC.F.T-1308)
Campbell, Pearl Read 3748
Campbell, Richard Bradford 5922
Campbell, Robert Malcolm 1374
Campbell, Robert Ronald 10787
 (MIC.F.TC-48689)
Campbell, Susan Wendy 5912
 (MIC.F.TC-56643)
Campbell, Wesley Glenn 10124
Campbell-Yuhl, Joylin 988
Campfens, Hubert Leo 10131
 (MIC.TC-12211)
Campiglio, Carlo 6291
Campisi, Jack 667 (MIC.T-201)
Camu, Pierre 4835
Canagarayar, Jegadishwara
 Kalingarayar 7917
 (MIC.F.TC-36978)
Candelon, Danielle 8316
Caner, Bernard 6607 (MIC.TC-5075)
Cann, Marjorie Mitchell 4389
 (MIC.T-123)
Canning, Patricia M. 3004
 (MIC.F.TC-44443)
Cannon, Gordon E. 8438 (MIC.F.T-983)
Cannon, James Bernard 1738
Cannon, Lester Robert Glen 11269
 (MIC.TC-9123)
Cannon, William Francis 5972
Cant, Douglas James 5544
 (MIC.F.TC-32975)
Cantarella, Claudette 3324
 (MIC.T-3110)
Cantin, Gabrielle 4087 (MIC.F-014908)
Cantin, Pierre 8276 (Z8293.333 C36)
Cantin, Serge A. 7936
 (MIC.F.TC-43983)
Canzoneri, Matthew Buford 1343
 (MIC.T-686)
Capalbo, Susan Marie 1856
Caparros, Ernest 7940 (KA993.8 C37)
Cape, Elizabeth Ann 10191
 (MIC.F.TC-38686)
Capelle, Ronald Gordon 9282
 (MIC.F.TC-25699)
Caplan, Usher 8401
Caragata, Patrick James 1375
 (MIC.F.TC-58351)
Caramanica, Frank Phillip 6569
Carberry, Hugh H. 9154
Carbno, William Clifford 3486
 (MIC.F.TC-30336)
Carbonneau, Côme 6292
Carbyn, Ludwig Norbert 10594
Card, Kenneth D.H. 5973
Cardillo, Ralph Michael 9218
Careless, A.G.S. 4782
Careless, James M.S. 1081
Carey, Robert Gene 3803
 (MIC.F.TC-52955)
Cargill, Donald George 5177
 (MIC.F.TC-25111)
Caria, Antonio 3385 (MIC.F.T-1266)
Carignan, Jacques 6293
Carl, George Clifford 11063
Carleton, Terence John 11742
 (MIC.F.TC-36609)
Carlisle, Arthur Elliott 2372
 (HD70 C3 C37)
Carlos, Ann Martina 1239
 (MIC.F.TC-48310)
Carlsen, Alfred Edgar 1523
 (MIC.F.TC-31179)
Carlson, H.D. 5974
Carlson, Kenneth Allen 10279
 (MIC.TC-7598)
Carlson, Paul Erik 4971
 (QC941 M3 fol.)
Carlson, Thomas Warren 5129
Carlton, James Theodore 11814
Carlton, Richard Austin Michael 7684
 (MIC.TC-12930)
Carlton, Sylvia 2547

Carman, John Stanley 4470
Carmel, Marie 8190
Carmical, Oline, Jr. 7023
Carmichael, Dugald Macaulay 5975
Carmone, Frank Joseph, Jr. 2779
  (MIC.TC-8615)
Carney, Philip Francis 3804
  (MIC.F.TC-20233)
Carney, Robert James 9912
  (MIC.TC-8062)
Caron, André-H. 589
Caron, Liliane 4016
Caron, Margaret Ann Bjornson 1122
  (MIC.F.TC-39060)
Caron, Y. 1682
Carpenter, David Cameron 7993
  (MIC.F.TC-17471)
Carpenter, Edmund Snow 644
  (MIC.T-19)
Carr, Edwin R. 4854
Carr, M.C. 7872
Carr, Paul Omega 7024
Carr, Peter Alexander 5598
Carr, Robert Leroy 11370
Carrara, Alberto 6294
Carrick, Louis Burrell 11787
Carrier, Maurice 7312
Carrier, Maurice Aurèle 9430
  (MIC.F.TC-43985)
Carrière, Laurier 7727
Carrington, George Williams 9785
Carrington, Peter John 1739
  (MIC.F.TC-47023)
Carroll, Rita Carmen 9167
  (MIC.F.TC-47024)
Carroll, William Joseph 11733
Carroll, William Kingsley 10019
  (MIC.F.TC-53493)
Carrothers, Alfred William Rooke 2155
  (HD5508 A3 C3)
Carrothers, W.A. 7630
Carruth, Thomas Paige 1932
Carruthers, Benjamin Carl 8974
  (MIC.TC-10760)
Carruthers, Gerald Steven 8566
Carscadden, James Eric 10980
  (MIC.F.TC-24285)
Carsola, Alfred J. 5098
Carson, Alex Gyandoh 11630
  (MIC.F.TC-20106)
Carson, Bobb 5188
Carson, David John Temple 5179
  (MIC.TC-3070)
Carswell, Henry Thomas 5180
Carter, Alan Richard 11195
  (MIC.F.TC-24985)
Carter, Bruce Northleigh 2548
  (MIC.F.TC-17757)
Carter, George Edward 1468
Carter, George F.E. 6295
  (MIC.TC-12962)
Carter, Gwendolen Margaret 8817
  (DA18 C37 fol.)
Carter, John Charteris Haig 11829
Carter, Lionel 5181
Carter, Mary Duncan 7977 (MIC.T-561)
Carter, Nicholas Charles 5182
  (MIC.F.TC-23371)
Carter, Robin Michael 7802
  (MIC.T-741)
Carter, Thomas S. 4960
  (MIC.F.TC-40107)
Carter, William Harrison, Jr. 2387
Cartwright, Donald Gordon 4865
  (MIC.TC-16400)
Carvalho, Emanuel 10477
  (MIC.F.TC-58856)
Carvalho, Ilson Guimaraes 5183
  (MIC.F.TC-48311)
Casaday, Lauren Wilde 2110
Casari, Laura Elizabeth Rhodes 8129
Case, James Michael 11843
  (MIC.F.TC-48168)
Case, James William 11432
  (MIC.F.TC-39227)
Case, Robert Thomas 2565
  (MIC.TC-10201)
Casey, John Francis 5734
  (MIC.F.T-1075)
Caspary, Arthur Courtney 9119
  (MIC.F.TC-45973)

Casselman, John Malcolm 11009
  (MIC.F.TC-38688)
Casshyap, Satyendra Mohan 5976
Cassie, James Robert Bruce 4177
Castelli, Guiseppe 791
  (MIC.F.2M11.562.2)
Castillo, Jorge Gonzalo 11055
Castle, Hempstead 11371
Castro-Rial, Juan M. 7926
Caswell, John E. 7513
Catellier, M. Hubert 4990
Cathcart, William George 3153
  (MIC.TC-4923)
Catling, Paul Miles 11523
  (MIC.F.TC-55738)
Cattell, Sidney Allen 11916
  (MIC.F.TC-3702)
Cauboue, Madeleine 11760
  (MIC.F.TC-47926)
Cauchon, Michel 941
  (MIC.F.TC-41400)
Cauthers, Janet Helen 450, 7447
  (MIC.T-748)
Cauvin, Dennis Mederic 1832
  (MIC.T-532)
Cavalier, Robert Peter 9621
Cavanagh, Beverley Anne 590
  (MIC.F.TC-40885)
Cavanaugh, Kenneth Lankford 1545
Cavanaugh, Lorraine Marie
  Monnier 5184
Caverzan, Raymond Cornelius 3914
  (MIC.F.TC-17758)
Cavoukian, Ann J. 8902
  (MIC.F.TC-47026)
Cawker, Kenneth B. 4606
  (MIC.F.TC-41133)
Cawley, Richard William V. 4061
Cawthorn, Richard Joseph 10740
  (MIC.F.TC-38903)
Caya, Marcel 8652 (MIC.F.TC-51365)
Cayley, Charles E. 1866
Cecile, Michael Peter 5819
Ceck, Marian 11761
Cell, Gillian M.T. 7164
Cell, John Whitson 7462
Cerezke, Herbert Frederick 11196
  (MIC.TC-3703)
Cermignani, Claudio 5977
  (MIC.F.TC-38689)
Cèska, Adolf 11457 (MIC.F.TC-37194)
Chabassol, D.J. 3325
Chabwela Weza, Harry Nixon 10563
  (MIC.F.TC-59546)
Chacko, Chirakaikaran J. 7554
Chacko, James Kunju
  Mundakaparampil 10111
  (MIC.F.TC-27806)
Chadney, James Gaylord 787
  (MIC.F.T-876)
Chadwick, Edward Michael Pakenhan
  10995 (MIC.F.TC-57242)
Chae, Yeh Moon 234 (MIC.F.TC-46090)
Chagarlamudi, Pakiraiah 6637
Chagnon, Jean-Yves 6296
Chaikelson, June Steinberg 9168
  (MIC.TC-9232)
Chakandua, Jimmy G. 3169
  (MIC.F.TC-59237)
Chalmers, John West 4302
Chalou, George Clifford 7445
Chamberlain, Alexander Francis 7794
  (MIC.F.TC-02955)
Chamberlain, Joseph Annandale 5545
Chamberlain, William Maynard 11857
  (MIC.TC-3337)
Chambers, Alan David 4916
  (MIC.TC-8283)
Chambers, David Lee 10360
  (MIC.T-486)
Chambers, Fergus James 1314
Chambers, Larry William 6789
  (MIC.F.TC-36887)
Chamney, T.P.A. 6537
Champagne, François 6682
  (MIC.T-3442)
Chan, Guat-Lian 10541
  (MIC.F.TC-49738)
Chan, Kai-Lok 11305
Chan, Kwok Bun 10042
  (MIC.F.TC-36980)

Chan, Man-Wah Luke 1801
  (MIC.F.TC-37944)
Chan, Mick Ying-Piu 3886
Chan, Randolph Maurice 3487
  (MIC.F.TC-32760)
Chan, Yin Kwok 11831
  (MIC.F.TC-35829)
Chanasyk, David Steve 11917
  (MIC.F.TC-44711)
Chance, Norman Allee 10161
Chandler, David Ballantine 10280
  (MIC.T-274)
Chandler, Frederick William 5978
  (MIC.TC-4266)
Chandler, Val William 6677
Chandra, Nellutla Naveena 6584
  (MIC.TC-6193)
Chandrasekharam, Ashtakala 6561
  (MIC.TC-14018)
Chang, Hsing-Wu 9329
  (MIC.F.TC-38692)
Chang, Yola Chiou-Yueh 11458
  (MIC.F.TC-25115)
Chao, John Chin-Tsai 10059
  (MIC.T-316)
Chapman, Diana Ferguson 5979
Chapman, James William 3055
  (MIC.F.TC-43370)
Chapman, John Doneric 4607
Chapman, Norman Belfield 969
  (MIC.T-633)
Chapman, Peter Michael 11815
  (MIC.F.TC-42115)
Chapman, Robin James 2653
Chapman, Wilbert M. 10934
Chappell, John Francis 5980
  (MIC.F.TC-41662)
Chappell, Neena Lane 10192
Chaput, Jeanne S. 2627
Charbonneau, Gérald 8319
  (MIC.F.TC-43992)
Charbonneau, Jean-Marc 6297
  (MIC.F.TC-47928)
Charbonneau, Yvon 6933
Chard, Chester Steven 451
Chard, Donald F. 6990
Charette, S. 7282
Chari, Tuppal Ramanuja 4471
  (MIC.F.TC-25546)
Charland, Jean-Pierre 2519
  (MIC.F.TC-56921)
Charlebois, Carol Ann 1082
  (MIC.F.TC-36981)
Charles, Anthony Trevor 1851
  (MIC.F.TC-63070)
Charles, Arthur Howard, Jr. 7728
  (MIC.T-737)
Charles, Lawrence Moses 4345
  (MIC.F.TC-62209)
Charlesworth, Maxine Anne 9653
  (MIC.F.TC-49918)
Charlewood, Geoffrey Herbert 5981
Charron, Claude-Yves 591
  (MIC.F-034102)
Chasse, Paul P. 8356
Chatarpaul, Lakeram 11858
  (MIC.F.TC-38906)
Chattaway, Erma Jean 3199
  (MIC.F.TC-50916)
Chatterjee, Aumlaya Kumar 5639
  (MIC.F.TC-48169)
Chatwin, Arthur Edgar 4218
Chaudron, Craig Johnson 7685
  (MIC.F.TC-55770)
Chausse, Gilles 9892 (MIC.F-005003)
Chawla, Saroj 7994 (MIC.F.TC-51366)
Chayes, Felix 5982
Cheal, John Ernest 2409
Cheang, Molly 7901
Cheatley, Alice Mary Elizabeth 4450
  (MIC.F.TC-953)
Chebat, Jean-Charles 10030
  (MIC.F-029001)
Checkley, Kenneth Lloyd 6885
  (MIC.TC-8064)
Chelladurai, Packianathan 9654, 10324
  (MIC.F.TC-39851)
Chelton, Dudley Boyd, Jr. 11896
Chen, Chien-pin 11743
  (MIC.F.TC-42179)

Chen, Lawrence Chien-Ming 11524
(MIC.F.TC-38058)
Chen, Mervin Yaotsu 2050
(MIC.F.TC-29550)
Cheng, Chung-Sing 4390
Cheng, Hsien-Hua 11306
(MIC.TC-1288)
Cheng, Jacqueline Ruth 10449
(MIC.F.TC-37260)
Cheng, Jie-Dar 11918
(MIC.F.TC-28656)
Chêng, Tien-fang 7598 (MIC.M-2)
Cherneff, Robert V. 1546
Chernick, Sidney Earl 2203
Cherry, John Anthony 5546
Cherry, Michael Edward 5599
(MIC.F.TC-30379)
Cherwinski, Walter Joseph 2094
(MIC.TC-11125)
Chesworth, Ward 5983
Cheung, Young-Mo 6790 (MIC.F.T-877)
Cheung, Yuet Wah 6791
(MIC.F.TC-55769)
Chew, K.J. 5984
Chew, Poon Sian 334
(MIC.F.TC-38907)
Chi, Byung Il 6539 (MIC.F.TC-21251)
Chi, Tony Poon-Chiang 9843
Chiappone, David I. 9120
(MIC.F.TC-43993)
Chiasson, Arthur Paul 8290
(MIC.T-660)
Chiasson, Rémi Joseph 7686
(LA418 N6 C5)
Chichester, Lyle Franklin 11097
Chidekel, Beatrice Vivian 3116
Chidekel, Samuel J. 2745
Chieh, Shih-Huang 4515
Chiel, Arthur A. 797 (F5033 J3 C44)
Chien, Calvin Chi-Ching 4516
Chikombah, Cowden E.M. 4374
(MIC.F.TC-40385)
Child, Alan Herbert 2700
(MIC.TC-9583)
Chimbos, Peter D. 10043
(MIC.F.TC-26616)
Chin, John Carlton 10246
(MIC.F.TC-51243)
Chinnappa, Chendanda
Chengappa 11433 (MIC.TC-15721)
Chinta, Nagireddy P. 2204
(MIC.F.TC-57953)
Chisholm, Alexander James 5037
(MIC.F.TC-7016)
Chisholm, Derek 1509 (MIC.T-958)
Chislett, Lise Perrier 9283
Chitteck, Victor Lovitt Oakes 8106
(PS8515 A38 Z62)
Chiu, Clifton Ya-Lam 4178
(MIC.F.TC-32435)
Choksi, Shehirnaz 1875
(MIC.F.TC-50415)
Chopra, Vishnu R.K. 8120
Choquette, J.E. Robert 7193
Choquette, Laurent P.E. 10542
Choquette, Raymond 105
Chork, Chin Yoon 5600
(MIC.F.TC-38060)
Chorny, Mirron 3387
Chough, Sung Kwun 5693
(MIC.F.TC-38194)
Chouinard, Clément B. 4972
(MIC.F.TC-39636)
Chouinard, Normand Paul 10415
Chow, Wing-Sam 750 (MIC.F.T-1156)
Chowaniec, C.T. 8357
Chown, Edward H.M. 6298
Chris, Stephen Alexander 9655
(MIC.F.TC-40888)
Chrisjohn, Roland David 8903
(MIC.F.TC-50602)
Christensen, Carole Cecile Pigler 4161
(MIC.F.TC-51909)
Christensen, Douglas Harold 3364
Christian, John Willis 7159
Christiansen, Earl Alfred 5547
Christiansen-Ruffman, Linda 7654
Christianson, Carlyle Bruce 248
Christie, Archibald M. 5548
Christie, James Stanley 5185
(MIC.TC-15104)

Christie, Robert Loring 5186
Christie, Thomas Laird 506
Christofides, Loizos Nicolaou 1571
(MIC.F.TC-17164)
Christophel, David Charles 6562
(MIC.TC-17477)
Christopher, Doris Marianne 9431
(MIC.F.TC-55328)
Christopher, Peter Allen 5187
(MIC.TC-15105)
Christou, Nicolas Velos 6831
(MIC.F.TC-50417)
Christy, Richard David 10177
(MIC.F.TC-36616)
Chu, George Pei-Chang 8616
Chua, Anthony Q. 1592 (MIC.F.T-1135)
Chua, Kian Eng 11859 (MIC.TC-4490)
Chugh, Ram Lal 1975 (MIC.T-306)
Chung, Joseph Hee-Soo 1585
(MIC.TC-1080)
Church, Barry Neil 5188
(MIC.TC-1807)
Church, Edward John Maxwell 3018
Church, John Halcot 1825
(MIC.F.TC-36253)
Church, Michael Anthony 5820
(MIC.TC-14102)
Church, Michael Seymour 9121
(MIC.F.TC-53494)
Churchill, Anthony Aylward 1263
Churchley, Franklin Eugene 996
Chute, Newton E. 5985
Chyi, Lindgren Liu 5986
(MIC.F.TC-22588)
Chyurlia, Jerome Paul 5048
(MIC.F.TC-33414)
Cieply, Alfred 1123 (MIC.F.TC-42183)
Cimino, Louis Francisco 8567
Ciotola, Pierre 7941
Clabeaux-Streigel, Marie Kathryn 906
(MIC.T-983)
Clague, John Joseph 5189
(MIC.F.TC-17165)
Clancy, Martin 7061
Clandinin, Dorothy Jean 4303
(MIC.F.TC-59879)
Clark, Anthony M.S. 5694
(MIC.F.TC-20053)
Clark, Campbell McGillivrary 9155
Clark, Carolyn 1547
Clark, Charles Edwin 6991
Clark, David Barrie 5821 (MIC.T-877)
Clark, Isabelle Marie Forcier 3754
(MIC.F.TC-60513)
Clark, Kim Robert Ferris 10595
(MIC.TC-11554)
Clark, Linda Esther 9508
(MIC.TC-16477)
Clark, Lovell Crosby 7115
(MIC.TC-15389)
Clark, Melissa Helen 8836
Clark, Richard James 10741
Clark, Richard L. 7165
Clark, Robert Charles 11919
Clark, Robert M. 1704
Clark, Samuel Delbert 1200
(MIC.F.TC-21641)
Clark, Thomas 5190 (MIC.F.TC-24811)
Clark, Thomas Henry 6310
Clark, Thomas R. 9204
(MIC.TC-14733)
Clark, Walter Leland Rutheford 7243
(MIC.F.TC-30646)
Clark, William Cummin 11182
(MIC.F.TC-46094)
Clarke, Charles Henry Douglas 10840
(QH1 T68 fol.)
Clarke, Claude Reginald 3537
(MIC.F.TC-26729)
Clarke, David Edmond 3666
(MIC.TC-7612)
Clarke, John 4866 (MIC.TC-16817)
Clarke, Linda Ann 10981
(MIC.F.TC-55461)
Clarke, Neil William James 3571
Clarke, Peter Johnston 6300
Clarke, Phyllis Esphere 1376
(MIC.F.TC-35002)
Clarke, Redmond McVitty 10899
(MIC.F.TC-16889)

Clarke, Roger Mervyn 4633
(MIC.TC-15815)
Clarke, Stephen Glenn 1798
(MIC.TC-11697)
Clarke, William F. 9858
Clauson, Victor 5987
Claveau, Jacques 6301
Claxton, John David 1965
(MIC.TC-8546)
Clayton, Francis Alfred 1705
(MIC.TC-1097)
Clebsch, Edward E.C. 11535
Cleghorn, Ailie 3005 (MIC.F.TC-54763)
Cleland, Charles Edward 875
Cleland, Patricia Anna 3936
(MIC.F.TC-53024)
Clemens, Jerome McClain 5002
Clement, Joseph Jacques Richard 7687
(MIC.F.TC-28188)
Clement, Wallace 2328
(MIC.F.TC-29079)
Clemente, Ricardo Ama 1813
(MIC.T-276)
Clendening, John Albert 6302
Cléonique-Joseph, Frère 11593
Cleveland, Courtney E. 5191
Cleverdon, Catherine L. 8610
(JL192 C6)
Clibbon, Peter 4753
Cliche, Pierre 4754
Clifton, H. Edward 5640
Clifton, Rodney Alfred 3667
(MIC.F.TC-32764)
Climenhaga, Asa W. 9926
Clinton, Alfred 2970 (MIC.TC-13779)
Clinton, Kevin James 1694
(MIC.TC-16404)
Clippingdale, Richard Thomas George
7389 (MIC.F.TC-25465)
Cloern, James Earl 11816
Close, David W. 8751
(MIC.F.TC-39641)
Close, Nicholas 1687 (MIC.TC-14937)
Closs, Lloyd Graham 5735
(MIC.TC-16478)
Clough, Katherine Sarah 11564
(MIC.F.TC-31186)
Cloutier, Cartier Édouard 8439
(MIC.T-828)
Cloutier, Nicole 9810 (MIC.T-3531)
Cloutier-Cournoyer, Renée 10060
Clowes, Ronald Martin 6610
(MIC.TC-4926)
Clubine, Gordon Laverne 3376
Clubine, Ivan Ward 4270
Clubine, Mary Helen 3377
Clyne-Jackson, Sheila Anne 8975
(MIC.F.TC-57315)
Coachman, Lawrence Keyes 11965
Coad, Brian W. 10872
(MIC.F.TC-29434)
Coady, Henry 9356
Coates, Daniel 8671 (MIC.T-598)
Coates, Norman 1840
Coats, Colin J.A. 5492 (MIC.TC-496)
Coble, Daniel Wiggin 10903
(MIC.TC-79)
Coburn, David 10193
(MIC.F.TC-17258)
Cochrane, Everett George 9944
Cochrane, Nancy Joan Hutchison 4060
(MIC.F.TC-53026)
Cochrane, Norman Alton 6602
(MIC.TC-18584)
Cockerline, Jon Phillip 1548
(MIC.F.TC-51913)
Cockfield, William Egbert 5913
Cockram, G. 7925
Code, William Robert 4783
(MIC.T-832)
Coder, George David 7540 (MIC.T-656)
Codere, Helen Frances 691
(F99 K9 C6)
Cody, Howard Hugh 8487
(MIC.F.TC-36515)
Cody, Terence Edward 11788
Coe, Karen Jamie Fraser 3200
(MIC.F.TC-41993)
Coehlo, Anthony 823
Coesman, Norbert 3300
Coffey, Brian Lee 931 (MIC.F.T-1279)

Coffin, James Larry 452
Coffin, Victor E. 7025
(MIC.F.CC.4)
Cogbill, Charles Van Horn 11594
(MIC.F.TC-58371)
Cogley, John Graham 5017
(MIC.F.TC-26111)
Cohen, Constance Rose 9656
(MIC.F.TC-54442)
Cohen, Eliot Asher 7402
Cohen, Martin Bernard 7545
(MIC.T-850)
Cohen, Mikal Rae 9432
(MIC.F.TC-25703)
Cohen, Mitchell Evans 1124
Cohen, Robert 6820 (MIC.F.TC-36619)
Cohen, S.W. 4391
Cohn, Barry Phillip 5117
Cohn-Sfetcu, Ofelia 7995
(MIC.F.TC-56984)
Coish, Raymond Alpheaus 5736
(MIC.F.TC-33537)
Cok, Anthony Edward 11947
Coker, William Bernard 5988
(MIC.F.TC-22448)
Colalillo, Giuliana Giovanna 792
(MIC.F.TC-55739)
Colas, Émile 7942 (MIC.F.TC-48497)
Colby, Catherine Ann 9187
(MIC.F.TC-52956)
Coldwell, Joyce Ione Harrington 8321
(MIC.F.TC-38621)
Cole, Douglas Lowell 7345 (MIC.T-259)
Cole, Ester 9188 (MIC.F.TC-42186)
Cole, James Randy 4017
(MIC.F.TC-40889)
Cole, Peter George 3755
Colella, Francis J. 2337
Coleman, Derek Jardine 10487
(MIC.F.TC-19308)
Coleman, Herbert Thomas John 2483
(LA418 06 C6)
Coleman, John Reed 11028
Coleman, Leslie Charles 5822
Coleman, Peter Edward Fowler 2812
(MIC.F.TC-19513)
Coleman, Phyllis Young 7803
(MIC.F.T-878)
Coleman, William Donald 8568
Coles, Richard Leslie 6652
(MIC.F.TC-18068)
Colistro, Frank Peter Salvatore 9429
(MIC.F.TC-37592)
Collet, Paulette F.J. 8191
Collett, David Jonathon 2822
(MIC.F.TC-53885)
Colletta, Salvatore 7688
(MIC.F.TC-64047)
Collette, Jean-Paul 2594
Collin, Arthur Edwin 11978
Collin, Wilbur John 3572
(MIC.F.TC-34315)
Collins, Audrey White 7989
(MIC.F.T-1110)
Collins, Cecil Patrick 2896
Collins, Edward, Jr. 8805
Collins, Gary Walter 3621
Collins, Jon A. 5641 (MIC.F.TC-22449)
Collins, June McCormick 7425
Collins, Keith James 12
Collins, Lyndhurst 4821 (MIC.TC-9128)
Collinson, Charles W. 6539
Colman, Rosalie Marson 824
Colman-Sadd, Stephen Peter 5737
(MIC.F.TC-21474)
Colquhoun, Donald John 5099
Colquhoun, Dorothy Rebecca 4221
Colthart, James Myron 7314
(MIC.T-335)
Colvin, Alfred Cephus 2654
(MIC.F.TC-26736)
Colvin, J.A. 7355
Colvine, Alexander Combe 5989
(MIC.F.TC-23270)
Colwell, Beverly Jane 10355
(MIC.F.TC-53527)
Colwell, John Allison 5990
Comay, Peter Yochanan 2380
Comeau, Gilberte 11565
(MIC.TC-10793)
Comeau, Joseph Edward 2625

Comeau, Judith 3081 (MIC.F-026403)
Comeau, Robert Lyons 1469
(HJ793 C6)
Comeau, Roger 1220
Common, Sarah 1264
Comstock, Rudolph Swayne 8866
(MIC.T-124)
Comtois, Paul 11595
Con, Ronald Jonathan 4018
(MIC.T-838)
Conacher, James B. 7155
Condemine, Odette 8369
Condra, Michael St. John 9251
(MIC.F.TC-59135)
Cone, David Knight 10543
(MIC.F.TC-47720)
Condon, Ann Gorman 7617
(MIC.F.T-1157)
Condon, Richard Guy 592
Condon, Thomas Francis 10061
Conerly, William Booth 1652
Conklin, Elizabeth Nancy 434
(MIC.T-518)
Conley, M.W. 8673
Conlon, Robert Maxwell 2003
Connell, Robert Bruce 4179
(MIC.F.TC-36620)
Connelly, Dennis Eugene 1529
Connelly, Desmond J. 3373
Connelly, Mary Patricia 2051
(MIC.F.TC-30337)
Connidis, Ingrid Ariet 10281
(MIC.F.TC-36621)
Connidis, Ingegjerd Lilla Arnet 1841
(MIC.F.TC-39454)
Connolly, Jennifer Anne 3019
(MIC.F.TC-49593)
Connor, Carl Yoder 8405
(PS8473 A44 Z64)
Connor, Thomas R. 10496
Connors, Kathleen Frances 7729
Conrad, Harold Everett 7618
(MIC.TC-16622)
Conrad, Margaret Rose
Slavenwhite 7371
Conrad, Sister Greta 3668 (MIC.T-814)
Conroy, John Charles 11210
(MIC.F.TC-18069)
Considine, Raymond Howard 8130
(MIC.T-490)
Constant, Raymond Albert
Fernand 2897
Contandriopoulos, André-Pierre 6792
(MIC.F-2M11.385.5)
Conte, Richard A. 3887
(MIC.F.TC-59876)
Conway, Charles Donald 8418
Conway, Clifford-Bruce 3867
(LB3453.C6)
Conway, Geoffrey Robert 1688
Conway, John Frederick 10024
(MIC.F.TC-41135)
Conway, S.R. 7403
Conybeare, Charles E.B. 5549
Cook, Charles Donald 7954
(MIC.F.T-913)
Cook, Donald Baird 9330
(MIC.F.TC-43627)
Cook, Donald George 5192
(MIC.TC-1666)
Cook, Francis Russell 10722
(MIC.F.TC-37789)
Cook, Gail Carol Annabel 2780
(MIC.T-217)
Cook, George Ramsey 8464
Cook, George Leslie 7476 (MIC.T-894)
Cook, Harold Sterling 2520
(MIC.T-376)
Cook, John Thomas 4392
Cook, Norman Alan 4795
(MIC.TC-13334)
Cook, Robert Bradley 5991
Cook, Terry Gordon 7372
(MIC.F.TC-34604)
Cook, Thelma Lillian Sharp 4111
(MIC.T-989)
Cooke, David Lawrence 5992
(MIC.TC-633)
Cooke, Frank Albert 3464
Cooke, Geoffrey James 4271
(MIC.TC-11555)

Cooley, John Morgan 11081
(MIC.F.TC-18586)
Coombs, David Grosvenor 2095
(MIC.F.TC-36983)
Coombs, Douglas V. 9802
Coombs, H.C. 1424
Cooper, Alvin J. 9956
Cooper, Christopher Michael 9284
(MIC.F.TC-39456)
Cooper, Deborah Chesnie L. 2566
(MIC.F.TC-30338)
Cooper, George Albert 9923
Cooper, Gerald E. 6303
Cooper, Helen Elaine Sossin 3646
(MIC.F.TC-55768)
Cooper, James Alfred 10788
Cooper, John I. 7116
Cooper, John R. 5738
Cooper, Johnson Gaylord 6992
(MIC.T-125)
Cooper, Norma Colleen 3154
(MIC.F.TC-40389)
Cooper, Robert Gravlin 1740
(MIC.TC-14941)
Cooper, Thomas William 1055
(MIC.F.TC-53028)
Copeland, Murray John 5586
Coperthwaite, William Sherman 593
Coppel, Harry C. 10544
Coppin, Norman Roderick 9920
(MIC.F.TC-57158)
Corbeil, Henri Étienne 11118
Corbeil, Pierre 7251 (MIC.F-41404)
Corbett, Barbara Elizabeth 2484
Corbett, David C. 1201
Corbett, Edward M. 8192
Corbett, Frederick Charles 3295
Corbin, James E. 888
Corcoran, William Thomas 3388
(MIC.F.TC-40116)
Cordes, Lawrence David 11674
(MIC.TC-15108)
Corey, Albert B. 7501
Corey, David T. 8914
(MIC.F.TC-38487)
Corfield, Vera Catherine 8904
Cork, Elizabeth Fredericka 3125
(MIC.F.TC-43998)
Corkum, Lynda Dale 11270
(MIC.F.TC-35004)
Corlett, John Thomas 9509
(MIC.F.TC-44877)
Corlett, Susan Gail 8905
(MIC.F.TC-58316)
Corlis, Carol Anne 3201
(MIC.F.TC-33086)
Cormack, Melville Wallace 11434
Corman, June Shirley 8766
(MIC.F.TC-59880)
Cormier, Roger Armand 2898
(MIC.TC-6696)
Cormier, Roger Bernard 9252
(MIC.F.TC-36365)
Cormier, Rosilda Ghislaine 3724
Cornell, Paul Grant 7075
Cornell, Peter McCaul 1598
Cornish, Daniel J. 3622
(MIC.F.TC-31954)
Corns, Ian George William 11656
(MIC.F.TC-40117)
Coron, Cynthia Rose 5739
(MIC.F.TC-55767)
Coron, David 9357 (MIC.F.TC-43999)
Coron, Michel 3155
Corran, Robert 10335 (MIC.F.T-1057)
Correll, Thomas Clifton 7835
(MIC.T-800)
Corrigan, Anthony Francis 5393
(MIC.F.TC-24994)
Corrigan, Samuel Walter 684
Corrivault, Georges Wilfrid 11088
Corwall, Frederick W. 6304
Cosentino, Frank 10358
(MIC.F.TC-17483)
Cosgrove, Gregory Tracey 3091
(MIC.F.TC-62122)
Cosgrove, Ronald Michael 2678
(MIC.TC-13841)
Costa, Richard Hauer 8131
Costa, Umberto Raimundo 6305
(MIC.F.TC-48322)

Costain, Wilfred Douglas 8617
(MIC.F.TC-1051)
Costescu, Leslie Whitby 11566
(MIC.F.TC-36623)
Côté, Benoît 3423 (MIC.F.TC-54767)
Côté, Brenda 11948 (MIC.F.TC-48175)
Côté, Pauline 9657
(MIC.F-2M11.570.8)
Côté, Philip Richard 5740
(MIC.TC-4344)
Côté, Pierre E. 6306
Côté, Raynald 11880
Côté, Serge 1814 (MIC.F-2M11.476.3)
Cottell, Philip Leroy 2052
Cotton, Charles Alexander 7404
(MIC.F.TC-49485)
Couch, Richard William 5193, 6617
Coughlin, Richard Maurice 9972
Coughlin, Violet Louise 7970
Coulibaly, Sidihi Philippe 10312
Coulombe, Daniel 9510
(MIC.F.TC-54769)
Coupal, Michel 9285 (MIC.F-022210)
Couper, Walter J. 2111
Coupland, Robert T. 11372
Courchene, Thomas Joseph 1741
Courey, Linda Susan 9219
(MIC.F.TC-49595)
Courtemanche, R.A. 7076
Courtney, John Childs 8518 (MIC.T-20)
Courval, Jean 3488 (MIC.F-024809)
Courville, Serge 106
(MIC.F-2M11.482.1)
Cousineau, Pierre 9169
(MIC.F.TC-45976)
Cousineau, Rosario 1202
Coutts, Herbert Thomas 3992
Coutts, Larry M. 9658
(MIC.F.TC-29134)
Couture, Gaétan Yves 1425
(MIC.T-361)
Couture, Joseph Ernest 4135
(MIC.TC-11127)
Couture, Michel 271
Couture, Paul Morgan 8875
(MIC.F.TC-51367)
Couture, Richard 11048
(MIC.TC-10889)
Couturier, Thérèse Jacinthe 3773
Cove, John James 378 (MIC.TC-8286)
Covello, Vincent T. 9973
Cowan, David Timothy 8132
Cowan, Peter John 10789
(MIC.F.TC-18070)
Cowan, Ralph Keith 2356 (MIC.T-463)
Cowan, Wayne Fraser 10592
Cowan, William Richard 5993
Coward, Teresa R. 3202
(MIC.F.TC-25706)
Cowell, David Arthur 8470
(MIC.T-266)
Cowley, Richard William V. 4061
(MIC.F.TC-42177)
Cown, David John 11675
(MIC.F.TC-29812)
Cox, Allan Elton 10339 (MIC.TC-4929)
Cox, Beverlee Ann 9122
(MIC.F.TC-35897)
Cox, Joseph Christopher 1377
(MIC.F.TC-42808)
Cox, Marlene Joan 4112
(MIC.F.T-1022)
Cox, Michael Howard 6731
(MIC.F.TC-58372)
Cox, Richard Edmund 4634
Cox, Steven L. 399
Coyte, Peter Christopher 1621
(MIC.F.TC-52957)
Crabb, P. 58
Craddock, Sonia May 3949
Cragg, Edith Marion Catherine 3389
Craig, Alton Westwood 2156
Craig, Bruce Gordon 5394
Craig, Douglas B. 5194
Craig, Gerald M. 7521
Craig, Ronald George 6771
(MIC.F.TC-42356)
Craig, Terrence L. 8050
(MIC.F.TC-55757)
Craigie, David Edward 11010
(MIC.TC-11557)

Craik, Gwenneth Jean Steele 10935
(MIC.F.TC-37595)
Crainic, Teodor Gabriel 2296
(MIC.T-3782)
Cram, John Murray 9596
(MIC.TC-5081)
Cram, Ruby Victoria 3489
(MIC.F.TC-51645)
Cramm, Frank 2469
Crane, Robert George 4660
Cranstone, Donald Alfred 1876
(MIC.F.T-1271)
Crausaz, Robert Martin 8193
Crausman, Burt 8976
Craven, Jack Wolfe 2248
(MIC.F.TC-43071)
Craven, Paul 1265 (HD3616 C32 C72)
Craven, Scott Robert 10790
(MIC.F.T-1039)
Crawford, Douglas Gordon 3490
(MIC.TC-5223)
Crawford, William James Page 5823
Crealock, Carol Marie 3993
(MIC.F.TC-16623)
Creamer, David Gordon 9952
Crean, J.F.M. 2746
Crean, P.B. 11920
Creed, Philip John 2679
Creighton, Dianne Elizabeth 9331
(MIC.F.TC-46332)
Crespo, Manuel 10247
(MIC.F.TC-38201)
Cressman, Clare B. 4304
(MIC.F.TC-44010)
Cressy, A. Cheever 7574
Crête, J. 8752
Crete, Michel 10632
Crichton, Vincent Frederick
Joseph 11356 (MIC.TC-12630)
Crickmay, Colin H. 5195
Crickmay, Geoffrey William 6307
Cringan, Alexander Thom 10564
(MIC.T-247)
Crispo, John Herbert Gillespie 2135
Croal, Albert George 2636
Crocker, Oswald Kitchener 3994
Crombie, Gordon Peers 5994
Crommelin, Brian Michael L. 1378
(MIC.F.TC-25124)
Cronin, Maureen Patricia 8807
Cronin, Thomas Mark 5995
Crookell, Harold 2357 (HF5415 C76)
Crooks, William R. 775
Crosby, Donald G., Jr. 5642
Crosby, Percy 5196
Cross, Hartley W. 8818
Cross, J.A. 7477
Cross, Kevin James 932
Cross, Michael Sean 1240
(MIC.TC-8506)
Crossley, Thane Robert 3669
(MIC.F.TC-43629)
Crosslin, Michael Paul 7117
Crossman, Edwin John 10936
Croteau, Georges 2521
Crouch, Richard Keith
Chamberlain 7955
(MIC.F.TC-50242)
Crouse, Dorothy Jean 8977
(MIC.F.TC-20989)
Crowder, Thomas H. 4180
Crowe, Herman Albert 4106
Crowley, James A. 7333
Crowley, Terence Allan 6993
(MIC.T-793)
Crown, Edward H.M. 6308
Crown, Elizabeth Marie 3725
(MIC.F.TC-40118)
Crown, Peter Herbert 221
(MIC.F.TC-31958)
Crowther, Roy Anderson 11809
Crozier, Marilyn Elizabeth 3203
(MIC.TC-13340)
Cruise, James E. 11567
Crunican, Paul Eugene 2456
(MIC.F.TC-19691)
Crysdale, Robert Cecil Stewart 2053
(MIC.TC-15390)
Cuddy, Henry 7533
Cuddy, J.D.A. 1166

Cudmore, James Sedley 1622
Cuff, Harry Alfred 4431 (MIC.F-471)
Culbert, Richard Revis 6618
(MIC.TC-8418)
Culham, T.A. 7996
Cullen, Joy Lauren 3056
(MIC.F.TC-43379)
Culp, Joseph Marion 11817
(MIC.F.TC-63187)
Cumming, Charles Linnaeus 5601
Cumming, David Boyd 9659
(MIC.F.TC-35830)
Cumming, George 6585
Cumming, Leslie M. 6309
Cummings, Joan Elizabeth 3739
(MIC.F.TC-25467)
Cummins, Jim Patrick 9433
(MIC.F.TC-24004)
Cummins, John Gaylord 1815
Cuneo, Carl John 7546 (MIC.TC-16570)
Cunningham, Walter Melvin 8674
Cunningham, William Bannerman 2157
(HD5509 N4 C8)
Cunningham-Dunlop, Peter K. 5996
Cupchik, William 8978
(MIC.F.TC-38699)
Curie-Jedermann, Janice Lynn 9511
(MIC.F.TC-49752)
Curran, C.N. 11134
Curran, Verna Isabel 8286
Currie, Albert Wayne 10227
(MIC.F.TC-43630)
Currie, Allister Blaine 2421
(MIC.F.TC-40892)
Currie, Archibald William 2297
Currie, John Bickell 5997
Currie, L.B. 1510
Currie, Raymond Francis 9964
Curry, Gwen Cranfill 8113
Curry, Ralph Leighton 8121
Curtis, Bruce Malcolm 2485
Curtis, Clifford Austin 1426
Curtis, Douglas C.A. 1919
(MIC.TC-11790)
Curtis, Hugh Jefferson 10077
(MIC.F.T-984)
Curtis, John Margeson 2381
Curtis, Lawrence Wilson 5695
(MIC.F.TC-35193)
Cushing, Colbert Ellis 11775
Cusson, Maurice 10248 (MIC.F-003001)
Cust, Marlene A. 3670
(MIC.F.TC-40119)
Custer, John Sherman 7026
Cutcliffe, Stephen Hosmer 7427
Cuthbert-Brandt, Gail Patricia 7220
(MIC.F.TC-30887)
Cuthbertson, Brian Craig U. 8782
Cutler, Garnet Homer 13
Cutler, Philip 7933
Cutten, Felicity Esme
Arthington 11881 (MIC.TC-4083)
Cwynar, Leslie Peter Chester 6541
(MIC.F.TC-43631)
Cybulski, Jerome Stanley 712
(MIC.F.TC-21382)
Cyr, Francine 9358 (MIC.T-3571)
Cyr, Gérard J. 3446
Cziko, Gary Andrew 9512
(MIC.F.TC-39646)
Czitrom, Daniel Joseph 1056

D

Daborn, Graham Richard 11049
(MIC.F.TC-17487)
Dacey, Christine M. 8979
(MIC.F.TC-53212)
Dacks, Gurston 8488 (MIC.T-775)
Da Costa, Derek Mendes 10044
Dadson, Alexander Stewart 5998
Dadswell, Michael John 11052
(MIC.TC-16522)
Dagenais, Louise 7730
Dagenais, Marcel Gilles 1826

Dagg, Melvin Harold 7997
(MIC.F.TC-64200)
Dagger, G.W. 5602
Daggett, Athern Park 1871
Daggett, Christopher Jarvis 6793
Dagher, Joseph H. 1910 (MIC.TC-2643)
Dahlberg, Michael Daniel 11002
Dahlie, Hallvard 8158
(PS8526 O62 Z63)
Dai, Tze-Sen 11596 (MIC.F.TC-27816)
Daiber, Franklin Carl 10909
Daigle, Benoit Ludovic 2004
(HF2338 L3 D3 fol.)
Daigle, Jean 1221 (MIC.T-712)
Daignault, Jacques 2655
Dailey, Robert Clifton 726
Daily, Gavin Thomas 311
Dainty, Anton Michael 5087
Dalby, John Thomas 4010
(MIC.F.TC-49285)
Dale, Edmund Herbert 4878
Dale, Hugh Munro 11373
Dale, Mark Randall Thomas 11844
(MIC.F.TC-44213)
Dale, Nelson Clark 5741
Dale, Thomas R. 8399 (MIC.T-265)
Dales, John Harkness 1784 (HD9685)
Dallaire, Hélène 4088
Dallard, Albert 7731
Dalrymple, Robert Walker 5643
(MIC.F.TC-32982)
Dalto, Guy Calvin 1742
Dalton, Roy Clinton 9811
Dalton, William J. 8559
Daly, Donald 1706
Daly, Michael Joseph 1641
(MIC.F.TC-59096)
Damas, David 594
D'Amboise, Gérald Robert 1933
(MIC.T-715)
Damé-Castelli, Mireille 7943
Damé-Dallard, Sylvie 8358
Damkaer, David Martin 11092
Damman, Antoni William Hermannus
11525
D'Andrea, John Joseph 1586
(MIC.F.T-973)
Dandurand, Louise 8503
(MIC.F.TC-58374)
Danglade, James Kirby 7305
(MIC.T-427)
D'Anglejan-Chatillon, Allison 9513
(MIC.F.TC-24290)
Danial, Antoinette 8906
Daniels, Edwin Robert 2803
(MIC.F.TC-17488)
Daniel, Juri Vrzesnevski 10416
(MIC.T-352)
Daniels, Ultimus Phillip 8980
(MIC.TC-15685)
Danielson, Richard Raymond 10361
Danis, Claudia 2410
Danley, Raymond Roger 3057
(MIC.F.TC-55754)
Dansereau, Stéphanie 1147
(MIC.F-2M11.397.1)
Danylewycz, Marta Helen 9795
(MIC.F.TC-58271)
Danyluk, Joseph John 2919
(MIC.F.TC-51459)
Danziger, Flora 3092
(MIC.F.TC-35195)
Daoust-Blais, Denise 7732
Darby, Dennis Arnold 5824
Darcy, Françoise 9812
D'Arcy, Kenneth C.R. 6759
(MIC.F.TC-35005)
D'Arcy, William 7534 (E184 I6 D3)
Darker, Grant Dooks 11568
Darling, Michael Edward 8422
(MIC.F.TC-42137)
Darquenne-Brossard, Martine 9332
(MIC.F-043703)
Darrach-Pearse, Shirley Anne 10078
(MIC.F.TC-55755)
Darrough, William D. 7918
(MIC.F.TC-25836)
Dart, Richard James 6832
(MIC.F.TC-45977)
Darte, Marie Madeleine Cecilia 8078
(MIC.F.TC-35006)

Dartnell, Albert Lloyd 2005
Darville, Richard Tulloss 1379
(MIC.F.TC-40602)
Das, Naresh 11003 (MIC.TC-2647)
Das Gupta, Udayan 5395
(MIC.F.TC-43632)
Dash, Madhab Chandra 11347
(MIC.TC-6091)
Dasko, Donna Anne 10020
(MIC.F.TC-43383)
Dass, Ajay Sankar 5999 (MIC.TC-7185)
Datey, Blaise 2971 (MIC.F.TC-31192)
Daub, Mervin Austin 1344
Daugherty, George Henry 7998
Davenport, Peter Henry 6000
(MIC.TC-12987)
Davey, Ian Elliott 2486
(MIC.F.TC-31193)
David, Hélène 8981
David, Peter Pascal 5550
Davidheiser, Carolyn E. 6533
Davidowitz, Moshe 1057
Davidson, Anthony 5825
Davidson, Donald C. 7537
Davidson, Gary 61 (MIC.F.TC-5422)
Davidson, Gordon Charles 1241
(F5576 N8 D26)
Davidson, Iain Francis William
Knowles 3900 (MIC.F.TC-53030)
Davidson, Stewart A. 10340
Davidson, Viola May 11833
Davidson-Arnott, Robin George
Denison 4629 (MIC.F.TC-32771)
Davies, Douglas Mackenzie 11271
Davies, Edward Barrie 8406
(MIC.TC-8160)
Davies, Edward Harold 5826
(MIC.F.TC-40893)
Davies, Edward Julian Llewellyn 5197
Davies, G.J. 1222
Davies, Gordon Wilson 1345
(MIC.T-455)
Davies, Gwendolyn 1083
(MIC.F.TC-44491)
Davies, Ivor Garth 2225 (MIC.T-878)
Davies, James B. 1549 (MIC.T-926)
Davies, James Frederick 5493
Davies, Joan Anne Moreland 425
Davies, John Clifford 6001
(MIC.TC-498)
Davies, John Leslie 5603
(MIC.TC-10934)
Davies, Leland John 4019
(MIC.F.TC-43634)
Davies, Raymond 6310 (MIC.TC-2648)
Davies, Thomas Gerald 10045
(MIC.F.TC-59823)
Davis, David Gray 2471
Davis, Derek Sidney 11352
(MIC.TC-12282)
Davis, Dona Lee 400
Davis, Donald Wayne 10691
Davis, Earl Edwin 6619
Davis, George Herbert 5604
Davis, Gerald Albert 9286
(MIC.F.TC-58164)
Davis, Harold John 4222
(MIC.F.T-1322)
Davis, Jerome D. 8808 (MIC.T-456)
Davis, John Campbell 6821
(MIC.F.TC-42809)
Davis, John Dunning 11121
Davis, John Earl 3006 (MIC.TC-14844)
Davis, Leslie Beryl 922
(MIC.TC-15557)
Davis, Melvin Peter 9287
(MIC.F.TC-43383)
Davis, Newton Fraser Gordon 5198
Davis, Philip Thompson 5827
(MIC.F.T-1076)
Davis, Rolph Aubrey 10825
(MIC.TC-11035)
Davis, Ralph E. 9092
Davis, Richard Clarke 7999
(MIC.F.TC-41044)
Davis, Roger Allen 3671
(MIC.F.TC-27636)
Davis, Teresa Mina Anne 9123
(MIC.F.TC-36368)
Davis, Thomas Edward 1346
(MIC.T-152)

Davison, Alexander Grant 11729
Davison, Catherine Val 4045
(MIC.TC-13209)
Davison, James H. 3732
(MIC.F.TC-19310)
Davison-Wood, Karen Margaret 942
(MIC.F.TC-55657)
Davy, Grant Robert 8783
Dawson, Donald Allan 2781
(MIC.TC-5311)
Dawson, Graham Elliott 4507
(MIC.TC-5803)
Dawson, Ian N. 4803 (MIC.F.TC-19517)
Dawson, John Ernest 11374
(MIC.F.TC-49487)
Dawson, John Michael William 6955
(MIC.F.TC-36628)
Dawson, Kenneth Murray 5199
(MIC.TC-13210)
Dawson, Kenneth Ralph 5551
Dawson, Nora 435
Dawson, Oliver Glenn 185
(MIC.F-T-1293)
Dawson, W.F. 8544 (JL164 1962 D3)
Daxboeck, Charles 10937
Day, Arthur R. 1016 (MIC.F.T-1332)
Day, Robert Douglas 7405
(MIC.F.TC-51460)
Day, Thomas Charles 3623
(AL P67 A17 R4.16)
Day, Victor Hugh 3156
(MIC.F.TC-42425)
Daymond, Douglas M. 8088
(MIC.TC-12988)
Daywalt, William E. 713
De, Aniruddha 6311
Dean, James Michael 1707
Dean, James Woodburn 1470
Dean, Ronald Edward 7895
(MIC.T-684)
Dean, Ronald Samuel 6312
Dean, Veva K. 4886
Dean, William George 4689
De Andrade Lopes, José-Maria 6833
(MIC.F.TC-58264)
De Angelo, Rosalind Frances 2567
Dearden, Philip 4608
(MIC.F.TC-39393)
Deason, Hilary J. 10910
De Avila, Edward Allan 3204
(MIC.F.TC-21535)
De Bagheera, Georgette 4305
(MIC.T-3076)
De Bagheera, Ivan J. 7689
(MIC.F-2M11.196.2)
Debanné, Joseph Gabriel 1911
(MIC.F.TC-28595)
Debicki, Marek 10282
(MIC.F.TC-41664)
De Bosch Kemper, William Peter 9514
(MIC.F.TC-44519)
De Brentani, Ulrike 1934
(MIC.F.TC-40894)
De Camprieu, Renaud Marc 2226
(MIC.F.TC-40894)
Decarie, Malcolm G. 7194
(MIC.TC-12706)
De Catanzaro, Jennifer Barbara 11569
(MIC.F.TC-59822)
De Cea Chicano, Joaquin 2252
Dechow, Ernest William Chatham 5605
Decore, Anne Marie June 10178
(MIC.F.TC-30657)
DeCotiis, Constant J. 3178
Degen, Robert Arthur 1266
DeHayes, Donald Henry 11676
De-Heer-Amissah, Adrian
Nicholas 5044 (QC809 E6 D3 fol.)
Deiseach, Donal Fiontain 2758
(MIC.F.TC-20994)
De Jong, Reinder 206
(MIC.F.TC-37792)
De Jonge, Coen K. 4630
Dekin, Albert Arch, Jr. 889
(MIC.T-829)
DeKonninck, Joseph-M. 9102
(MIC.F.TC-16894)
DeLaguna, Frédérica Annis 952
Deland, André N. 6313
Delande, Jean 6956
Delaney, Joseph Roger Claude 10145
(MIC.F.TC-42197)

Del Bene, Terry Alan 842
Del Dotto, Jerel E. 3779
Delgaauw, Mieke Kiesk 10470
    (MIC.F.TC-58887)
Delikaraoglou, Demetrios 11996
Delisle, Claude E. 11029
    (MIC.TC-12351)
De Lisle, David De Garis 87
    (MIC.F.TC-27112)
De Lisle, Paule 9660
Dell, Carol Irene Green 5130
Dell, Gary Santmyers 8907
    (MIC.F.TC-47036)
Delli Colli, Pascal Joseph 8908
Delmas, Paul Julian George 1267
    (MIC.T-786)
Delorme, Gérard 11762
Delorme, Larry Denis 6570
De Lury, Justin Sarsfield 5552
De Medeiros, Luciano V. 4498
    (MIC.F.TC-43488)
De March, Joseph Paul 9434
    (MIC.F.TC-57106)
De Martinecourt, Jean-Pierre 4540
Dembski, Peter Edward Paul 7195
    (MIC.F.TC-33885)
De Melto, Dennis P. 1891
    (MIC.TC-7264)
Demers, Donald Joseph 10283
    (MIC.F.TC-40123)
Demers, Robert 7863
Demers, Serge 11802
    (MIC.F.TC-47943)
De Mestier du Bourg, Hubert Jean
    Marie 7854 (MIC.F.TC-20773)
Demharter, Cheryl Ann Marie 7733
    (MIC.F.T-1116)
Demmler-Kane, Jean 10046
    (MIC.F.TC-50807)
DeMora, Stephen John 11921
    (MIC.F.TC-54996)
Dempster, George 6834
Denburg, Susan Myra 3950
    (MIC.F.TC-48328)
Dendy, John Oliver 7302 (MIC.T-462)
Denham, William Alfred, III 8611
Denholm, James Johnstone 2864
Denis, Bertrand 6314
Denis, Laurent-Germain 7956
    (Z682 D45)
Denis, Margaret Mary 4020
    (MIC.F.TC-40896)
Dennis, Herbert Knight 825
Dennis-Escoffier, Shirley 1923
    (MIC.F.T-1170)
Denny, James Davidson 2541
Denny, Mark William 11104
    (MIC.F.TC-46113)
Denny, Michael 11348
Den Otter, Andy Albert 7348
Denson, Norman MacLaren 5396
Dent, Brian Edward 6670
Denton, George Henry 5914
Denton, Leonard Robert 9486
Denton, Trevor Davies 453
    (MIC.TC-9532)
Denys, Jozef G. 9965 (MIC.TC-10838)
Deosaran, Ramesh Anthony 3491
    (MIC.F.TC-35197)
De Pencier, Marni Frazer
    Lithgow 3544 (MIC.F.TC-36630)
Derby, Andrew Whitelaw 6002
Derevensky, Jeffrey L. 3805
    (MIC.F.TC-31748)
De Ridder, Jerome J. 1401
    (MIC.F.T-1098)
De Roche, Constance Pennacchio 394
De Romer, Henry S. 6315
De Rosen-Spence, Andrée F. 6316
    (MIC.F.TC-35137)
Derow, Ellan Odiorne 2177
    (MIC.F.TC-36631)
Derry, Paul Allan 9189
    (MIC.F.TC-50606)
Derry, Suzanne M. 9359
    (MIC.F.TC-48513)
Desaulniers, Gilles 6700 (MIC.T-3880)
Desbiens, Danielle 9661
    (MIC.F-043802)
Deschatelets, Gilles H. 7957
    (MIC.F.TC-56155)

Deschenes, Jean Hughes 4541
Deshaies, Bruno 7196 (MIC.F-005606)
Deshaies, Laurent 4589
Deshaies-Lafontaine, D. 436
Désilets, Andrée 7323
    (F5081.9 L28 D47)
Désilets, Germaine-Nicolas 4407
Désilets, Jean-Paul (Frère
    Donatien-Marie) 2522
Desjardins, Jean-Yves 9662
    (MIC.F-2M11.358.2)
Desjarlais, Lionel 3117
Desjean, Georgette 6914
Deslauriers, Lise 10241
Des Lierres, Thérèse 3326
    (MIC.F-2M11.501.6)
Desloges, Yvon 6607
Desmarais, Gilles 3205
Desmarteau, Denise 10062
Després, Jean-Pierre 8799
    (HD7801 D44)
Desrochers, Bruno 7845
    (BX837 C2 19092)
Desrochers, Raymond 10510
    (MIC.F.TC-27003)
DesRoches, Bernard Paul 6875
Desroches, Frederick John 6760
    (MIC.F.TC-45978)
Desroches, Jocelyn Jean-Yves 3589
    (MIC.F.TC-35009)
Dessureault, Fernande 8258
Detomasi, Don Dunford 2358
Detwiller, Frederick Emrey Jr. 454
Deutsch, Antal 10125 (MIC.TC-1305)
Deutschmann, Linda Harriet Bell 10228
    (MIC.F.TC-42201)
De Vecchi, Vittorio Maria
    Guiseppe 10507 (MIC.F.TC-38705)
Deverell, Alfred F. 2680
Devinante, S. 4181
Devine, Joseph A., Jr. 6994
Devine, Malcolm David 11570
    (MIC.F.TC-48705)
Devins, Gerald Michael 8982
    (MIC.F.TC-54777)
Devnich, Donald Douglas 9850
De Vos, Antoon 10587
De Vries, John 7671
De Vries, Robert Eric 8983
    (MIC.F.TC-36633)
Dewar, John Duncar 10365
    (MIC.T-153)
Dewar, Kenneth Cameron 1785
    (MIC.F.TC-32776)
Dewart, Gilbert 6638 (OE576 D34)
Dewey, Alexander Gordon 8819
    (F5046 D4)
Dewey, Christopher Paul 11076
    (MIC.F.TC-63556)
Dewey, Kenneth Frederic 4973
    (MIC.F.TC-19692)
Dewhirst, John Frederick 1471
    (MIC.T-262)
Dewson, Michael Richard James 3806
    (MIC.F.TC-50924)
De Wilde, James Frederick 1743
    (MIC.F.TC-42915)
De Wit, Maarten Johan 5742
De Witt, Kilby A. 2884
Dexter, Robert Cloutman 826
Dey, Balaram 5034
De Young, John H., Jr. 4472
Dey-Sarkar, Samir Kumar 6608
    (MIC.F.TC-27824)
Dhand, Hargopal 3179
Dhanvantari, Bobberjung N. 300
Dhillon, Pritam Singh 2549
Diamond, Frederic Lionel 10284
    (MIC.F.TC-53495)
Diana, James Stephen 10926
    (MIC.F.TC-43387)
Dibben, Martyn James 11375
Dibski, Dennis John 4375
    (MIC.TC-6701)
Di Capua, Richard Anthony 10887
Dick, Lawrence Allan 5100
    (MIC.F.TC-5122)
Dick, William W. 3672
Dickason, Olive Patricia 6957
Dickerson, R.W.V. 7873

Dickie, Geoffrey James 5397
    (MIC.TC-11129)
Dickie, Lloyd Merlin 11111
Dickinson, James Gary 4046
Dickinson, John Alexander 7252
    (MIC.F.TC-36634)
Dickson, Charles William 6003
Dickson, Elinor J. 9813
Dickson, Vaughan Andrew 1744
    (MIC.F.TC-33541)
Dickson, William Rushworth 2791
    (MIC.F.TC-978)
Didow, Larry Alvin 10669
    (MIC.TC-16523)
Didyk, John 2920 (MIC.F.TC-50925)
Diem, Kenneth L. 10763
Dienes, Zoltan Bertalan 4247
    (MIC.TC-14678)
Diersing, Victor Eugene 10658
Dietz, Anthony George 7062
Diffendal, Anne Elizabeth Polk 9778
    (MIC.T-754)
Diffendal, Robert Francis, Jr. 6574
Digout, Stanislaus Lawrence 3327
    (MIC.F.TC-40396)
Dilabio, Ronald Norman Wells 6317
    (MIC.F.TC-28206)
Dill, Peter Arnott 10873
    (MIC.TC-6674)
Dill, Vicky Schreiber 8172
Dilley, Marcia Grace 3206
    (MIC.F.TC-24523)
Dilling, Harold John 4113
    (MIC.F.TC-17261)
Dillon, Peter James 11860
    (MIC.F.TC-27826)
Dilworth, Thomas Robert 8400
Dimitri, Robert H. 9412
    (MIC.F.TC-60140)
Dimma, William Andrew 1745
    (MIC.T-568)
Dimmick, Ralph W. 10791
Dingle, James Frederic 1472
Dingwall, John Scott 8474
    (MIC.F.T-1002)
Dino, Richard Nicholas 1347
    (MIC.T-922)
Dion, Pierre 3807
Dionne, Georges E. 2227
    (MIC.F-2M11.512.1)
Dionne, Michel 3808
    (MIC.F-2M11.370.7)
Dionne, René 2250 (MIC.F-022206)
Dionne René 8287 (PS8413 E7 Z62)
Di Pasquale, Glenn William 3951
Dipchand, Cecil Ramnarine 1683
Dirks, Gerald Edward 8504
    (MIC.F.TC-35198)
Dirks, Patricia Grace 8669
    (MIC.F.TC-31198)
Dirschl, Herman John 11618
Dischel, Robert S. 4517
Disman, Milada 7577
    (MIC.F.TC-53034)
Disney, David Michael 2813
    (MIC.F.TC-31199)
DiTecco, Donald Anthony 9253
    (MIC.F.TC-49757)
Ditzel, Thomas Mervyn 1148
Diubaldo, Richard Julio 4586
    (MIC.TC-14610)
Divav, Gérard 10025
Divi, Sri Ramachandra Rao 6004
    (MIC.TC-12355)
Dixit, Bharat 11966 (MIC.F.TC-39652)
Dixon, Beverly Ruth 3414
Dixon, Charles Linus 6772
    (MIC.F.TC-50247)
Dixon, Clara Louise 10857
Dixon, Frederick Thomas 2006
    (MIC.T-697)
Dixon, J.T. 7612
Dixon, James 6542 (MIC.F.TC-19062)
Dixon, Robert Thomas 2481
Djamgouz, Okay Tewfik 4573
Djolanic, Bahman 11763
    (TS837 D56 fol.)
Djwa, Sandra Ann 8384 (MIC.TC-5979)
Doak, Ervin John 1473 (MIC.TC-9134)
Doake, David Brown 3937
    (MIC.F.TC-53895)

Doan, Arthur Wallace Ross 2958
Doan, Brian David 8909
  (MIC.F.TC-54779)
Doan, Kenneth Henry 10911
Dobbs, Bryan Griffith 8284
Dobie, James 49 (MIC.T-336)
Dobson, Lois Ann 3809
  (MIC.F.TC-53379)
Dodd, James Dale 350
Dodd, Larry Cloyd 8519
Dodds, Donald Gilbert 10659
Dodds, Robert Brian 4542
Dodds, Ronald Garrett 3868
  (MIC.F.TC-55791)
Dodge, David Allison 1653 (MIC.T-514)
Dodge, Douglas P. 10919
  (MIC.TC-14005)
Doering, Robert William 8984
Doerksen, Gerard Benjamin 3307
Doern, George Bruce 10505
  (MIC.TC-5498)
Doerr, Audrey Diane 8505
  (MIC.TC-16524)
Doerr, Phillip David 10841
Doherty, Edward J. 7163
Doherty, Gillian 3810 (MIC.TC-9089)
Doherty, Maryanne 2823
  (MIC.F.TC-53896)
Dolenz, John Joseph 9413
Dolmage, Victor 5200
Dominique, Cyril Ray Michael 11307
  (MIC.F.TC-64598)
Dominique, Frère 3869
Donaghy, David Ian 324
  (MIC.F.TC-17303)
Donahue, Paul Francis 864
Donald, Heather M. 7368
Donald, William John Alexander 1268
Donaldson, John Allan 5696
Donaldson, Sven 10938
  (MIC.F.TC-34107)
Dondale, Charles Denton 11135
Donnelly, Bert J. 2852
  (MIC.F.TC-53215)
Donnelly, Brian Eugene 2236
  (MIC.F.T-965)
Donnelly, Sister Francis Dolores 7967
  (MIC.T-353)
Donnelly, Murray Samuel 8696
  (JL290 D6)
Donnelly, Peter George 9110
  (MIC.TC-12581)
Donnelly, Warren H. 8506
Donner, Jeffrey Robert 3903
  (MIC.F.TC-60139)
Donoghue, Eileen E. 8985
  (MIC.F.TC-56528)
Donohoe, Howard Vane, Jr. 5606
  (MIC.F.TC-38067)
Donovan, Donal John 1550
  (MIC.F.TC-32449)
Donovan, John Francis 6005
Donovan, Patrick 10162
  (MIC.F-042005)
Doran, Jeffrey Bernard 5607
  (MIC.F.TC-43389)
Doré, Robert 3811 (MIC.T-3085)
Doré, William G. 11410
Dorion, Gilles 8429 (MIC.F.TC-26455)
Dorland, Arthur Garratt 9853
  (BX7650 D6)
Dorling, Michael John 162
Dorner, John Nicholas 4432
  (MIC.F.TC-37198)
Dorosh, Marshall Eugene 9156
  (MIC.F.TC-36986)
Dorothy Marie, Sister 8417
Dorsinville, Max 8194 (MIC.T-507)
Dosey, Michael Alan 9663
  (MIC.TC-15687)
Dosman, Edgar Joseph Edward 733
Dostal, Jaroslav 6006
Dotzenroth, Susan E. 9664
Doucet, Alfred 3673
Doucet, G. Jean 10565
  (MIC.F.TC-27119)
Doucet, Laval J. 10146
  (MIC.F.TC-36636)
Doucet, Michael John 4867
  (MIC.F.TC-36637)
Doucet, René A. 11764

Doucette, Andrew Leo 3447
Douey, John Donald 10229
Dougall, Herbert Edward 2298
Douglas, Bruce James 5201
  (MIC.F.T-1352)
Douglas, George Wayne 318
  (MIC.F.TC-17496)
Douglas, Robert J.W. 5398
Douglas, William A.B. 7406
  (MIC.F.TC-17911)
Douglin, Janette J. 6886
  (MIC.TC-16626)
Dow, Alexander Carmichael 1269
  (MIC.F.TC-47198)
Dow, Ian 2921
Down, Mary Margaret 357
Downes, Walter 2488
Downey, Deane Ernest David 8000
  (MIC.F.TC-21802)
Downey, Terrence James 1906
  (MIC.F.TC-33543)
Downie, David Alexander 3390
  (MIC.TC-6198)
Downie, Felix Philip 2782
Downing, George Leonard 4021
  (MIC.T-362)
Downton, Dawn Rae 8410
  (MIC.F.TC-63784)
Doxey, Isabel Marion 4408
  (MIC.F.TC-35200)
Doyle, Denise Joan 9768
  (MIC.F.TC-60142)
Doyle, Mother Hortense 3492
Doyle, James 8424 (MIC.F.TC-25130)
Doyle, Kevin Anthony 7219
  (MIC.F.TC-53666)
Doyle, Linda Sheidler 8133
Doyle, Patrick Joseph 5114
  (MIC.F.TC-34799)
Doyle, Robert Urban 10163
  (MIC.TC-14679)
Doyle, William John 595
Doyon, Dominique 11597
Doyon, Raymonde 3360
Drabek, Stanley 8719
  (MIC.F.TC-17262)
Dragert, Herbert 6620 (MIC.TC-15113)
Dragland, Stanley L. 8419
Drake, Julian John 5101
  (MIC.F.TC-20296)
Drapeau, Georges 11949
Draper, Dianne Louise 4804
  (MIC.F.TC-32103)
Draper, Douglas Gary 8090
Draper, Paula Jean 7578
  (MIC.F.TC-59824)
Dredge, Lynda Ann 4755
  (MIC.F.TC-33481)
Dreisziger, Nandor A.F. 7555
  (MIC.F.TC-27831)
Drennon, Herbert Neal 1746
Drewe, Fred Harold 2642
  (MIC.F.T-879)
Drexler, Robert V. 11571
Driben, Paul 494 (MIC.T-807)
Drinkwater, David Alan 2007
  (MIC.TC-8018)
Driscoll, Alma 4089
Driscoll, Fletcher Graves 5915
Driver, Jonathan Campbell 855
  (MIC.F.TC-39239)
Drolet, Gilbert 8001
Drolet, Jean-Yves 2523
Drost, Dale R. 3424 (MIC.F.TC-34327)
Drouin, Eméric O. 7233
Drouin, Theodore Emile 10545
  (MIC.F.TC-63232)
Drucker, Philip 455
Druehl, Louis Dix 11459 (MIC.TC-166)
Drumke, John S. 11460
Drummond, Arthur Darryl 5202
Drummond, Ian MacDonald 1270
Drummond, Robert Johnston 8618
  (MIC.T-859)
Drummond, Robert Norman 4644
Drummond, William M. 126
Drury, Donald Hazen 1402
  (MIC.F.T-880)
Dryden, Louis James 2824
  (MIC.F.TC-30509)
Drysdale, Charles Wales 5203

Duarte de Oliveira, Domingos 11183
Dub, Pavel 9435 (MIC.F.TC-53038)
Dubé, Clairette 2524 (MIC.F-042406)
Dubé, Clémence 9769
  (MIC.F-2M11.375.7)
Dubic, Benoit 9360
DuBois, Jean-Marie 4756
  (MIC.F.TC-48515)
Du Bois, Philip M. 5058
Du Bois, Pierre 10285
Dubois, René 9361 (MIC.F-014406)
Duce, Graciela E. 793
Ducharme, David Joseph 3296
  (MIC.F.TC-53039)
Ducharme, Léo 7864 (MIC.F-029706)
Duchesne, Hermann 3020 (MIC.T-3403)
Duckworth, Geoffrey Stafford 6835
Duckworth, Peter Battersby 4690
  (MIC.F.TC-32783)
Dudar, John Steve 5553
Dudley, Carlton Lewis, Jr. 1654
  (MIC.T-677)
Due, Jean Margaret Lucinda
  Mann 2329
Duerden, Floyd Colin 11845
  (MIC.F.TC-19301)
Duffie, Donald C. 7846
Duffield, Susan Linda 6318
  (MIC.F.TC-58855)
Duffy, Patrick James Barry 11657
Dufour, Albert 3493 (MIC.TC-14211)
Dufresne, Cyrille 5697
Dufresne, Donald Joseph 2922
  (MIC.F.TC-53040)
Dufresne, Raymond 3404
  (MIC.F-2M11.453.1)
Du Gas, Beverly Witter 6923
  (MIC.TC-5086)
Dugas, Clermont 10320
Dugas, Jean 6007
Dugle, Janet Mary Rogge 11424
Duguay, Monique 8986
  (MIC.F-2M11.463.4)
Duhamel, Ronald Joseph 7690
  (MIC.F.TC-20554)
Duignan, Patrick Augustine 2899
  (MIC.F.TC-43390)
Dukacz, A.S. 2600
Duke, Philip George 856
  (MIC.F.TC-57091)
Duke, William Richard 2759
  (MIC.TC-6703)
Dular, Ram 10511 (MIC.TC-2528)
Dumais, Louise 3674 (MIC.T-522)
Dumais, Monique 9814 (MIC.F.T-931)
Duman, Miximilian G. 11536
Dumanski, Julian 207 (MIC.TC-6199)
Dumas, Denis 7734
  (MIC.F-2M11.375.1)
Dumoff, Myron G. 9515
  (MIC.F.TC-40011)
Dunbar, Maxwell J. 11837
Duncan, Carson Michael 1403
  (MIC.F.TC-46026)
Duncan, Craig 4743
Duncan, David T. 9516
  (MIC.F.TC-39345)
Duncan, Deirdre Jean 2838
  (MIC.F.TC-30033)
Duncan, Gaylen Arthur 7865
  (MIC.T-851)
Duncan, Ian James 5204
  (MIC.F.TC-59247)
Duncan, Kate Corbin 548
Duncan, Mary Jo 11818
  (MIC.TC-10521)
Duncan, Michael A. 4535
Dundas, Kenneth Ninian Melville 2373
Dundes, Alan 7782 (E98 F6 D8)
Dunford, Fraser Edwin Frank 2299
  (MIC.F.T-26242)
Dungan, Douglas Peter 1167
Dunham, Aileen 7197 (F5072.2 D88)
Dunham, Douglas 7027
Dunlop, Edward Alexander 3555
  (MIC.F.TC-53042)
Dunlop, Florence S. 4142
Dunn, Darrel Eugene 5399
Dunn, John Asher 7829
Dunn, Michael James 2251

Dunn, Michael Thomas 11461
(MIC.F.TC-54999)
Dunn, Robert Martin, Jr. 2008
Dunne, William 164 (MIC.TC-14899)
Dunning, Robert William 533
(E78 O5 D8)
Duong, Ba Tien 1599 (MIC.F.TC-33544)
Dupasquier, Maurice 7330
(MIC.TC-10890)
Dupont, Antonin 9893
Dupont, Gilles 9157
Dupont, Robert 3675
Dupré, Joseph Stefan 1497
Du Preez, Ingram Frank 3328
Dupuis, Jean-Claude 2054
(MIC.F-034706)
Duquette, Gilles 6319
Durand, Marielle 3207
Duranthon-Gautheron, Françoise 11308
Durbach, Edna 9362 (MIC.F.TC-53043)
Durgin, Edward Charles 570
(MIC.T-758)
Durlach, Theresa Mayer 686
(E99 T6 D87)
Durocher, Louise 9363 (MIC.F-027802)
Durocher, Olivier 8382
(PS8526 E38 Z79)
Dushenko, Terrance William 8987
(MIC.F.TC-54420)
Dussault, R. 7944, 8550
Dusseault, Maurice Bernard 4499
(MIC.F.TC-31966)
Dutch, Steven Ian 6008
Dutil, Jean-Denis 11040
(MIC.F.TC-54411)
Dutton, Donald George 9665
(MIC.TC-8510)
Duval, Wayne Stuart 11819
(MIC.F.TC-19247)
Duxbury, Linda Elizabeth 6683
(MIC.F.TC-61277)
Dwernychuk, Leonard Wayne 11776
(MIC.F.TC-23640)
Dwibedi, Kamalakanta 5494
(MIC.TC-976)
Dwivedi, Onkar Prasad 8720
(MIC.TC-1866)
Dwyer, Lianne Marie 11744
(MIC.F.TC-37342)
Dyck, Henry Dietrich 7769 (MIC.T-3)
Dyck, Ian George 420
(MIC.F.TC-30670)
Dyck, John Henry 4582
Dyck, Merla Hélène 2839
(MIC.F.TC-40133)
Dyck, N.E. 456
Dyck, Perry Rand 8507
(MIC.TC-16482)
Dyck, Victor Arnold 11309
(MIC.TC-7268)
Dyde, Walters Farrell 2422
Dyer, Aldrich James 596
(MIC.F.TC-48934)
Dyer, W.S. 6009
Dyke, Arthur Silas 4661
Dykstra, David L. 7503
Dy Reyes, Felix Robles, Jr. 1551
(MIC.T-915)
Dyster, Barrie Drummond 7225
(MIC.TC-9135)
Dziuban, Stanley W. 7575

E

Eade, Kenneth E. 5828
Eady, Karen 11462 (MIC.TC-8294)
Eagan, William Edward 6944
(MIC.TC-8549)
Eagan, William Frank 4784
Eager, Evelyn Lucille 8767
(MIC.F.TC-21643)
Eagle, John Andrew 7334
(MIC.F.TC-31203)
Eagles, Paul Franklin John 10488
(MIC.F.TC-45980)

Eakins, Peter R. 6320
Eakins-Hoffmann, Joan Margaret 6773
Eapen, Arakkal Thomas 1474
(MIC.T-77)
Earl, Samuel Aubrey 4433
Earle, John Alfred 2900 (MIC.TC-3374)
Earle, Richard C.B. 6761
(MIC.F.TC-20558)
Earls, Christopher Michael 9517
(MIC.F.TC-52881)
Early, Frances Horn 827
(MIC.F.TC-46643)
Early, Leonard Roy 8407
(MIC.F.TC-44492)
Earmme, Seung Young 4796
(MIC.F.TC-43393)
Earn, Brian Mark 9666
(MIC.F.TC-36601)
Earnshaw, Alice Petronilla
Russell 11310 (MIC.F.TC-18199)
Easson, McGregor 2489 (LA416 E15)
Eastabrook, James Henry Glenn 3355
(MIC.F.TC-38709)
Eastcott, Leslie Raymond 2961
(MIC.F.TC-26750)
Easterbrook, William Thomas James 14
(HG2051 C38 E3)
Eastler, Thomas Edward 5743
Eastman, Donald Sidney 10633
(MIC.F.TC-37602)
Eastman, Harry C.M. 1475
Eastman, Mack 9905
Eastman, Sheila Baldwin
MacQueen 2158
Easton, Robert Michael 5829
(MIC.F.TC-57204)
Eastwood, George E.P. 5554
Eaton, Albert Kenneth 1271
Eaton, John Douglas 10385 (MIC.T-24)
Eaton, Philip 3021 (MIC.F.TC-25000)
Eaves, Linda Crawford 9436
(MIC.F.TC-58782)
Ebel, Bernd 1747 (MIC.F.TC-17500)
Eberhardt, Elvire 7770
(MIC.F.TC-17501)
Eby, George Nelson 6321
Eccles, John Kerby 5205
Eccles, William J. 7285
Ecclestone, Charles Edward John
Bennett 9518 (MIC.F.TC-52882)
Echlin, Kimberly Ann 534
(MIC.F.TC-56551)
Echols, Christina Sligh 9667
(MIC.F.TC-54401)
Ecola, Leander John 9845
(MIC.F.TC-53243)
Eddy, Earl Bronson 9862
Eddy, Wesley Percy 2840
Edginton, Barry Eugene 9974
(MIC.F.TC-50249)
Edie, Ralph W. 5555
Edmond, Maurice 8291
Edmonds, Dale Harlan, II 8134
Edmunds, Frederick Robin 5206
Edward, Wesley Grafton 3380
Edwardh, Melvin Oscar 2404
Edwards, Adrian Charles 1642
(MIC.T-248)
Edwards, Donald K. 11136
Edwards, Elizabeth A. 7805
Edwards, Jack Leonard 9668
(MIC.F.TC-94493)
Edwards, John Robert 828
(MIC.F.TC-20697)
Edwards, Linwell M. 186
(MIC.F.TC-24311)
Edwards, Mary Jane 8195
(MIC.F.TC-21387)
Edwards, Murray Dallas 1017
(MIC.T-25)
Edwards, Peter 3374 (MIC.F.TC-22071)
Edwards, Robert J. 11137
Eedy, John Wilson 10670
Efrat, Barbara Silverman 7827
Egan, Marie-Jogues 8196
Egboka, Boniface Chukwuka
Ezeanyaoha 6010 (MIC.F.TC-49762)
Eger, Albert Frederic 1587
(MIC.F.TC-32457)
Eggens, Jack L. 11642 (MIC.TC-6548)

Eggert, Wallace Victor 3103
(MIC.F.TC-34331)
Egli, André 10079 (MIC.F.TC-53046)
Eglin, Peter Anthony 6794
(MIC.F.TC-25845)
Eglington, Peter Cheston 1912
(MIC.F.TC-25846)
Egnatoff, John George 2923
Ehrlich, Walter Arnold 249
Eichhorn, David M. 9779
Eidt, Douglas Conrad 11138
Eis, Slavoj 11463
Eisbacher, Gerhard Heinz 5644
Eisenberg, Mildred 9414
(MIC.F-033507)
Ejeckam, Winifred C. 3329
(MIC.F.TC-5337)
Ekblaw, Walter Elmer 597
(MIC.F.M-24)
Elbaz, Freema Luwiesh 4306
(MIC.F.TC-47038)
Elchibegoff, Ivan M. 2359
Elder, Joy Louise Davey 9669
(MIC.F.TC-52962)
Eldon, Walter D.R. 1892
Eldredge, Robert Niles 6575
Eley, David Roche 1108
(MIC.F.TC-47332)
Eley, Malcolm Gordon 3082
(MIC.F.TC-17504)
Elias, Demetrius 4473
(MIC.F.TC-39658)
Elias, John Walter 3812
(MIC.F.TC-30898)
Elias, Peter Douglas 421
(MIC.F.TC-29477)
Elias, Richard Jacob 6011
Elias, Scott Armstrong 6543
Elie, Daniel 10250 (MIC.F-2M11.161.3)
El-Gazzar, Mohamed Elwy 9597
(MIC.TC-15723)
El-Kassaby, Yousry Aly 11677
(MIC.F.TC-51715)
Elkhoraribi, Mohamed Cherif
Eilman 4489 (MIC.F.TC-26688)
Elkin, Lorne 8988 (MIC.TC-12765)
El-Lakasay, Mohamed Hosny
Hassan 11678
Ellenton, Jennifer Anne 10576
(MIC.F.TC-38917)
Elliot, Phyllis E. 9205
(MIC.F.TC-53381)
Elliott, Charles Martyn 2901
Elliott, Craig Clifford 1018
Elliott, Deborah Louise 11651
Elliott, D.K. 6543
Elliott, D.W. 8551
Elliott, George Reid 7028
Elliott, Gillian Hope 11901
(MIC.TC-6888)
Elliott, Hilary Mary 1019
(MIC.F.TC-62112)
Elliott, Kim Andrew 1125
Elliott, Peter Wayne 10709
Ellis, David William Henry 4530
(MIC.F.TC-38711)
Ellis, Derek Victor 11838
(G601 A77 fol.)
Ellis, Edward Norman 4223
Ellis, Maxyne Evelyn Dormer 3590
Ellis, Robert James 9519
(MIC.F.TC-53539)
Ellis, Robert Sydney 598
Ellis, William Haynes 11421
Ellsworth, Hardy Vincent 6012
Ellsworth, Samuel G. 9848
Ellwood, Robert Brian 5400
El-Masri, Waguih 4272
El-Nahhas, Fathalla Mohamed 4500
(MIC.F.TC-51469)
Elnecave-Steinberg, Mireille 9670
(MIC.T-3881)
Elphick, Stephen Conrad 5495
El-Sabh, Mohammed Ibrahim 11911
(MIC.F.TC-20698)
El Senoussi, Veronica 3676
Elson, John Albert 5496
Elson, Paul Frederick 11004
Elterman, Michael Frank 9211
(MIC.F.TC-55934)

Elton, David Kitchener Leslie 8686
(MIC.TC-15217)
Elver, Robert Bruce 1893
Elwood, J.M. 6836
Emberson, Rowan Mark 11311
(MIC.TC-3119)
Embree, Douglas Gordon 11262
Embry, Ashton Fox 5830
(MIC.F.TC-28504)
Emerson, John N. 907
Emery, David James 6013
Emery, George Neil 9874
(MIC.TC-6890)
Emery, John Whitehall 7958
Emmingham, William H. 11679
Emmott, Shelagh Deirdre 9364
(MIC.F.TC-58752)
Emo, Wallace Brooks 6322
Emond, Maurice 8286
Empey, William Franklin 1655
(MIC.F.T-960)
Emslie, Ronald Frank 5497
Enemeri, S.S.G. 7874
Engel, Barney Mordecai 2637
Engel, Mary Frances 8051
(MIC.F.T-974)
Engelmann, Frederick Charles 8634
(MIC.T-207)
England, Claire St. Clere 7959
(MIC.F.TC-26084)
England, Gordon Douglas 3853
(MIC.F.TC-49292)
England, John Howard 5831
England, Raymond Edward 457
(MIC.TC-7865)
England, Wilburne Stanley 3291
Engle, Ronald Crim 358
English, Harry Edward 2009
English, John Frederick Kerr 2701
English, John Richard 7335
English, Marianne 5049
(MIC.TC-11807)
Engmann, Jeremias Edwin Oko 4501
(MIC.F.TC-21808)
Ennals, Peter Morley 4868
(MIC.F.TC-36606)
Ennemond, Frère 8359
Ennis, Pamela Ann Koza 7902
Enns, Frederick 2804 (LB2831 E5)
Enns, Leonard Jacob 985
(MIC.F.T-1278)
Enos, Paul Portenier 6323 (QE471 E54)
Enrico, John James 7806
Ens, Adolf 9914 (MIC.F.TC-44011)
Ephraty, N. 4248
Epp, Abram Ernest 1203 (MIC.T-602)
Epp, Ernest John 2865
(MIC.F.TC-50253)
Epp, Frank Henry 1084 (MIC.T-250)
Epstein, Maurry Hart 3563 (MIC.T-687)
Epstein, Perle Sherry 8135
Erdman, Oscar A. 5401
Erdmer, Philippe 5916
(MIC.F.TC-59132)
Erickson, Edwin Erich 458
Erickson, Lynn Ellyn 7118
(MIC.F.TC-35016)
Ermanovics, Ingomar Frank 6014
(MIC.T-1465)
Errington, John Charles 11464
(MIC.F.TC-25853)
Errington, Joseph 10417
Erwin, Terry Lee 11139 (MIC.TC-3840)
Esan, Benjamin Olatunji 143
(MIC.TC-11808)
Esberey, Joy Elaine 7395
(MIC.F.TC-31207)
Essene, Frank J., Jr. 599
Esses, Lillian Marlene 9365
(MIC.F.TC-39659)
Etienne, Eisenhower Celse 1913
(MIC.F.TC-52963)
Evans, Anna Margaret 7369
(MIC.TC-1857)
Evans, Anthony Meredith 6015
Evans, Charles Sparling 5207
Evans, Daniel Frederick 5698
(MIC.F.TC-46341)
Evans, George Dewey 6774
(MIC.F.TC-23361)
Evans, Geraint N.D. 7299 (MIC.T-263)

Evans, Ian Sylvester 4609
Evans, James Eric Lloyd 6016
(QE446 P6 E9 fol.)
Evans, John Charles 2055
Evans, Kenneth Charles 798
Evans, Larry Robert 9851
Evans, Laurence Kenneth 9671
(MIC.F.TC-34807)
Evans, Marlene Sandra 11064
(MIC.TC-15114)
Evans, Mary Ann 9366
(MIC.F.TC-49766)
Evans, Robert Douglas 5587
Evans, Simon Malin 4875
(MIC.F.TC-30513)
Even, Alexander 3330 (MIC.TC-3895)
Evernden, J.F. 6664
Evers, Susan Eleanor 459
(MIC.F.TC-48334)
Evoy, Ernest Franklin 5556
Ewert, Wayne David 6017
(MIC.F.TC-32157)
Ewing, Gordon Orr 4597
Ewing, John Morton 3763
Ewing, R.G. 4822 (MIC.T-867)
Ewing, Thomas Edward 5208
(MIC.F.TC-55007)
Eyford, Glen Allenby 943
(MIC.F.TC-32790)
Eyre, Kenneth Charles 7407 (UA601 Y8 E8)
Eyssen, Gail Elizabeth 6837
(MIC.F.TC-24315)
Ezekiel, Jeremiah William 1109
(MIC.F.TC-40139)
Ezrin, Sharyn A. 4422
(MIC.F.TC-35511)

F

Fabbri, Andrea Gabrielle 5498
Fabi, Bruno 8910 (MIC.T-3363)
Fadin, Max 8360 (MIC.F-2M11.576.3)
Fagan, Michael John 3208
(MIC.F.TC-38714)
Fagbamiye, Olukayode Emmanuel 2825
(MIC.TC-11570)
Fagerstrom, John Alfred 6018
Fahey, Curtis James Clifton 9831
Fahmy-Eid, Nadia 7253
Fahrig, Walter F. 5699
Fahs, Lois S. 10457
Faibisy, John Dewar 7029
Fair, James William 4451
(MIC.F.TC-21639)
Fairbairn, Daphne Janice 10671
(MIC.F.TC-28680)
Fairbairn, Harold W. 6324
Fairbanks, Bert Lamarr 10418
(MIC.T-615)
Fairbanks, Carol Louise 8002
Falaise, Noël 4757
Falcone, David J. 8528 (MIC.T-729)
Falkenberg, Eugene Edward 3573
(ALP67 A17 R4.8)
Falkenhagen, Emil Richard 11680
(MIC.F.TC-22073)
Falkowski, Paul Gordon 11922
(MIC.F.TC-25854)
Fallis, Albert Murray 10546
Fallis, Laurence Sidney, Jr. 7077
(MIC.T-176)
Falls, James Bruce 10672
Falusi, Arnold Joseph 2866
(MIC.TC-13782)
Famure, Oluwole Dada 187
(MIC.F.TC-40141)
Fankboner, Peter Vaughn 11105
(MIC.TC-11628)
Faribault, Marcel 1527
Farina, Margaret Radcliffe 10031
(MIC.F.TC-58318)
Faris, James Chester 401
(HN110 C3 F3)
Faris, Ronald Lyle 4022
(MIC.F.TC-18495)

Farley, Albert Leonard 4856
Farley, Jean-Claude 8911
Farley, John Edward 10010
(MIC.F.T-1010)
Farmer, David Malcolm 11923
(MIC.TC-11215)
Farquhar, Hugh Ernest 3529
Farquhar, Marcia Fay 9288
(MIC.F.TC-21537)
Farquharson, William Andrew Fletcher
10194 (MIC.F.TC-27841)
Farr, David M.L. 7478 (F5046 F3)
Farrand, William Richard 5131
Farrar, Floyd Alvin 7655 (MIC.T-26)
Farrar, Mary Patricia Thomas 3126
(MIC.F.TC-53047)
Farrar, Victor John 7538
Farrell, John Kevin Anthony 7214
Farrell, John Terrence 2178
(MIC.F.TC-54145)
Farrell, Marvin William 107
Farrell, Mona 3952
Farrell, Robert B. 8784
Fasano, James H. 3104
(MIC.F.TC-34339)
Fasola, Armando 5499
(MIC.F.TC-55801)
Fast, Raymond Garry 2902
Fatis, Michael 9124 (MIC.F.TC-44013)
Faulkner, Charles Thompson
Sinclair 7156
Faulkner, Edward Leslie 5557
Faulkner, Raymond T. 2855
(MIC.F.TC-48522)
Favreau, Micheline 9520
(MIC.F.TC-52653)
Fawley, Allan P. 5700
Fay, Ignatius Charles 6019
(MIC.F.TC-60528)
Fay, Terence James 7504
Featherstone, John David 10764
(MIC.F.TC-32793)
Feavyour, Herman Eldon 3157
Feder, Herbert Abraham 9921
(MIC.F.TC-36644)
Fedirchuk, Gloria Joyce 728
(MIC.T-763)
Fedoravicius, Algirdas Stasys 8912
(MIC.TC-9303)
Fee, Margery Elizabeth 8052
(MIC.F.TC-50256)
Feighen, Sandra Louise 9291
Feit, Harvey Allan 508
(MIC.F.TC-51947)
Feldman, Uri 4662 (MIC.F.TC-39924)
Fellbaum, George Anthony 9289
(MIC.F.TC-37137)
Feller, Michael Charles 11681
(MIC.F.TC-25146)
Felt, Paula Chegwidden 437
(MIC.T-730)
Fenge, Terence Alfred Edward 10484
(MIC.F.TC-55202)
Feniak, Mary Elizabeth 6748
Feniak, Michael W. 5832
Fenske, Milton Reinhold 2805
(MIC.TC-3379)
Fensome, Robert Allen 5833
(MIC.F.TC-60529)
Fenton, Mark MacDonald 5500
(MIC.F.TC-23279)
Fenton, Melville Brockett 10649
(MIC.TC-4494)
Fenwick, Rudy 6934
Fenwick, Rudy 8569 (MIC.F.T-979)
Ferencz, Joseph 9521
Ferguson, Barry Glen 1380
(MIC.F.TC-56554)
Ferguson, Douglas Campbell 11140
Ferguson, Marianne 3677
Ferguson, Robert Carlisle 4307
(MIC.F.TC-30339)
Ferguson, Stewart Alexander 6020
Ferguson, Tamara Jocelyn 9290
(MIC.F.TC-48939)
Ferland, Léon Gérald 8250
(MIC.T-3124)
Ferland, Madeleine 359
Ferland, Philippe 7945
Fernandez, Donald Anthony 9522
(MIC.F.TC-19230)

Fernandez, Marco Antonio 2056
  (MIC.F.TC-35834)
Fernandez, Ronald Louis 814
  (MIC.F.TC-38220)
Fernandez-Suarez, Antonio 1168
  (MIC.F-2M11.544.7)
Ferrari, John Remo 8989
  (MIC.F.TC-50609)
Ferrier, William K. 6737
Ferron, Jean 10692
  (MIC.F-2M11.187.4)
Fetherston, Kathleen E. 10842
Fetterly, Robert Gordon 10195
  (MIC.F.TC-35020)
Fettes, James Joseph Francis
  Patrick 11272
Fetterolf, Peter Marcus 10828
  (MIC.F.TC-53049)
Feurer, Hanny Marie 7813
  (MIC.F.TC-31769)
Fialkoff, Steven Alan 9938
Fidelholtz, James Lawrence 521
  (MIC.T-604)
Field, Lanora Leigh 360
  (MIC.F.TC-43643)
Field, Peggy Anne 6924
Field, Richard Harold George 1935
  (MIC.F.TC-53050)
Field, Tony Richard Osgood 312
  (MIC.F.TC-20907)
Fielder, John William 4062
  (MIC.F.TC-38716)
Fielding, David Wilson 6876
  (MIC.F.TC-34812)
Fiesinger, Donald William 5209
  (MIC.F.TC-25005)
Figur, Berthold 2814
File, Edgar Francis 9966 (MIC.T-27)
Filiatrault, Pierre 2228
  (MIC.F.TC-41416)
Filion, Maurice 6995
  (F5063.1 M38 F54)
Filson, Glen Charles 4023
  (MIC.F.TC-31212)
Filteau, Gabriel 11089
Fimreite, Norvald 10566
  (MIC.TC-7846)
Findlay, David Christopher 5210
Findlay, Marjorie Craven 600
Finegan, Jo-Anne Kathryn 9235
  (MIC.F.TC-58736)
Finegold, Menahem 3448
  (MIC.F.TC-27843)
Fingard, Judith J. 9832
Finkel, Alvin 1315 (MIC.F.TC-35021)
Finkelstein, Richard Joseph 9170
  (MIC.F.TC-47337)
Finkle, Peter Zach Ross 1381
  (MIC.F.TC-31213)
Finlay, John Robert 1316
  (MIC.F.TC-22461)
Finlayson, Gregor James 8990
  (MIC.TC-16100)
Finlayson, William David 908
  (MIC.F.TC-32797)
Finley, Eric Gault 2525
Finley, John Lawrence 8662
Finn, Basil J. 347
Finn, Theophilus George 3465
Finnegan, James Joseph 8136
Finnegan, Michael John 714
Finnegan, Raymond Rene 11273
Finnestad, Harvey L. 3756
  (MIC.F.T-1206)
Finnigan, Bryan 3678
Fiorino, Albert Francis 2550
  (MIC.F.TC-32798)
Firestone, Melvin M. 402
Fischbuch, Norman Robert 5402
Fischer, Donald George 9672
Fischer, Gretl Kraus 8402
Fischer, Hartwig 11357
  (MIC.TC-14686)
Fischer, Robert Allen 7735
  (MIC.T-738)
Fish, James 2972
Fisher, Anthony Dwight 502
  (MIC.T-986)
Fisher, Charles Wilfred 2959
  (MIC.F.TC-17263)

Fisher, Edward George 2172
  (MIC.F.TC-42627)
Fisher, Elizabeth G. 11251
Fisher, Harold Melvin 3574
Fisher, Harry King 2826
  (MIC.F.TC-35205)
Fisher, Helen Elizabeth 9975
Fisher, Reginald G. 843
Fisher, Robin Anthony 7434
  (MIC.F.TC-19530)
Fisher, Stephen Frederick 751
  (MIC.F.TC-44399)
Fishman, Laura Schrager 460
  (MIC.F.T-1053)
Fisk, John L. 3780 (MIC.F.TC-49240)
Fisk, Larry John 8697
  (MIC.F.TC-24027)
Fitch, James Harold 2464
  (MIC.F.CC-4)
Fitchko, Yaroslaw (Jerry) 11572
  (MIC.F.TC-38717)
Fitzgerald, Denis Patrick 4881
Fitzgerald, Gerald F. 8474
Fitzgerald, Gerard John 10874
  (MIC.F.TC-28218)
Fitzgerald, Vincent William John 1511
Fitzgibbon, John E. 11989
  (MIC.F.TC-39665)
Fitzharris, Brian Blair 4610
  (MIC.F.TC-25149)
Fitzhugh, William Wyvill, IV 883
  (E78 L3 F58 fol.)
Fitzpatrick, Gordon James 11777
  (MIC.F.TC-34813)
Fitzpatrick, Marjorie Ann 8430
  (MIC.F.TC-17264)
Fitzpatrick, Michael Morson 6325
Fitzsimmons, George William 3494
  (MIC.F.TC-20561)
Flack, J.A. Douglas 10732
Fladmark, Knut Reidar 865
  (MIC.F.TC-21272)
Flaherty, Gerard Francis 5608
Flaherty, Mary Josephine 4063
  (MIC.TC-3554)
Flannery, Regina 501
Flannigan, Terrance Roden 2924
Flather, Donald McIntosh 3449
Fleck, James Douglas 1636
Fleiger, David Lorenzo 9254
  (MIC.TC-9591)
Fleisher, Mark Stewart 7818
Fleming, Daryl Stanley 2252
  (MIC.F.TC-64226)
Fleming, David Russell 3127
  (MIC.F.TC-42208)
Fleming, Erin Patricia Lockhart 1074
Fleming, Howard A. 2300
  (HE2810 H8 F5)
Fleming, Lesley Carolyn 11337
  (MIC.F.TC-43896)
Fleming, Stephen J. 8991
  (MIC.F.TC-21539)
Fleming, William Gerald 3495
Fleming, William Morris 11820
  (MIC.F.TC-22079)
Fletcher, Christopher John N. 5211
  (MIC.TC-13216)
Fletcher, Daniel O. 2279
Fletcher, Ian Robert 11997
  (MIC.F.TC-40904)
Fletcher, Janet Florence 3901
  (MIC.F.TC-50257)
Fletcher, Ronald Austin 301
Fletcher, Terence P. 6534
Flett, Robert John 11778
  (MIC.F.TC-40014)
Fleurent, Maurice 2526
Flewelling, Robert William 3209
  (MIC.F.TC-29072)
Flinn, Marguerite Adele 11731
  (MIC.F.TC-47733)
Floran, Robert John 6326
Flores, Miguela Bustos 3496
  (BF431 F5 fol.)
Flowers, Edward Brown 2396
Flowers, John Franklin 3308
Flowers, Mary Kathryn 8570
  (MIC.F.T-1077)
Floyd, John Earl 15

Flynn, Brian John 9815
  (MIC.F.TC-55340)
Flynn, David Michael 1842
  (MIC.F.T-1058)
Flynn, John David 3591 (MIC.T-724)
Flynn, John Joseph 2925
  (MIC.F.TC-32799)
Fogel, Ira Lee 876
Foggin, Peter Michael 4964
Foght, Harold Waldstein 2542
Fogle, Dale Onward 8992
  (MIC.F.TC-49770)
Folan, William J. 379
Foley, Denis 645
Folinsbee, Robert Edward 5834
Folmer, Henri 6958 (E131 F6)
Folsom, Todd Christopher 11274
  (MIC.F.TC-47046)
Fookey, D.E. 1572
Foor, Thomas Allyn 923
Foord, Esme Noreen 3757
Foote, John Allen 8520
Foote, Raymond Leslie 10164
  (MIC.F.TC-26055)
Foote, William Alfred 6959
  (MIC.T-170)
Foran, Maxwell Laurence 7240
  (MIC.F.TC-55341)
Forbes, A.J. De B. 8785
Forbes, Donald Lawrence 11979
  (MIC.F.TC-56800)
Forbes, Ernest R. 2280
  (MIC.F.TC-32647)
Forbes, Hugh Donald 8571
  (MIC.F.T-881)
Ford, Barbara Cecile 4044
  (MIC.F.TC-14687)
Ford, Blake George 10230
  (MIC.F.TC-21274)
Ford, Gary R. 9292 (MIC.F.TC-40149)
Ford, James Ellsworth 6795
  (MIC.F.TC-22080)
Forde, Penelope Allison 1748
  (MIC.F.TC-54793)
Foreman, Elvie Maxine Ford 11537
Forest, Elizabeth 9673
Forest, Soeur Jeanne 6887
Forest, Philippe 11598
  (MIC.F.TC-32223)
Forget, Jacques 3158 (MIC.T-3074)
Foroud, Nader 4574 (MIC.F.TC-38225)
Forrest, Donna Lynn 3953
  (MIC.F.TC-45983)
Forrester, Warren David 11912
Forsberg, Lois Anne 9523
  (MIC.F.TC-17309)
Forsey, Eugene A. 8529 (JN577 F6)
Forster, John Jakob Benjamin 1242
  (MIC.F.TC-62285)
Forsyth, George Robert 2133
  (MIC.F.TC-28222)
Forsythe, Warren Louis 11682
Fortier-Havelka, Colette 6858
  (MIC.T-3121)
Fortier, Darlene Nelita 8107
  (MIC.F.TC-50259)
Fortier, Jacques Louis 11803
  (MIC.F.TC-64562)
Fortier, Roger, Frère Lévis 8378
Fortier, Yvan 933
Fortier, Yves O. 6327
Fortin, Bernard Fernand 2057
  (MIC.F.T-1059)
Fortin, Donald 2656 (MIC.F-04810)
Fortin, Fabienne 6701
  (MIC.F.TC-47341)
Fortin, Gérald-Adélard 1085
  (MIC.T-28)
Fortin, Jacques André 7903
Fortin, Jean-Louis 6868 (RK76 F67)
Fortin, Paul Arthur 2657
Fortin, Pierre 1427 (MIC.T-664)
Fortin, Raymond 9367
Fortin, Réjean 11030
Fortner, Robert Steven 1045
  (MIC.F.T-975)
Fortune, John Neill 1993
Forward, Charles Nelson 2010
Foster, David Edward 11141

Foster, David Russell 11730
(MIC.F.T-1356)
Foster, Franklin Lloyd 7340
(MIC.F.TC-59063)
Foster, Helen Marie 7971
Foster, Joan M.V. 7119
Foster, John Arnold 10765
(MIC.F.TC-28068)
Foster, John Bristol 10567
Foster, John Elgin 2740
Foster, John Robert 11011
(MIC.F.TC-47048)
Foster, John William 8887
Foster, John Wilson 8159
Foster, Lois Elaine 9993
(MIC.F.TC-24029)
Foster, Mary Kathleen 6796
(MIC.F.T-882)
Foster, Michael Kirk 646 (MIC.T-779)
Foster, Neil William 11643
(MIC.F.TC-41717)
Foster, Raymond Edwin 11683
Foster, Richard Henry, Jr. 8721
(MIC.T-802)
Foucault, Pierre 8993 (MIC.T-3882)
Fournier, Bruce Arthur 9598
(MIC.F.TC-25711)
Fournier, Claude 8373
Fournier, Jean-Pierre 4308
(MIC.T-3365)
Fournier, Leslie Thomas 2301
Fournier, Pierre 8753
(MIC.F.TC-31218)
Fournier-Massey, Gisèle 6838
(MIC.TC-15845)
Fouts, Donald Emil 8552 (MIC.T-251)
Fowke, Vernon Clifford 108
Fowle, Charles D. 10843
Fowler, Anthony David 6021
(MIC.F.TC-50442)
Fowler, David John 2375
(MIC.F.TC-32802)
Fox, Bonnie J. 2058 (MIC.F.TC-48944)
Fox, Catherine Anne 293
(MIC.F.TC-41718)
Fox, Frederick G. 5403
Fox, Harold George 7866 (T226 V2 F6)
Fox, James Harold 2721
Fox, Peter Edward 5212
Fradsham, Boyce Tennyson 2926
Fradkin, Barbara Fraser 3093
(MIC.F.TC-60150)
Francis, Jonathan Hervey 1994
(MIC.T-787)
Francis, Mary Ethel Annexstad 2399
(MIC.F.TC-47079)
Francis, Robert Douglas 6945
(MIC.F.TC-26624)
Francis, Robert J. 7615
Francoeur, Ann-Michèle 6839
(MIC.F.TC-47050)
Francoeur, Mary Ellen 8994
Frank, James Godfrey 2179
(MIC.F.TC-39473)
Frankcombe, Brian James 3180
Frankel, Allen Barry 1530 (MIC.T-503)
Frankel, Barbara Gail 3870
(MIC.F.TC-53823)
Frankel, Saul Jacob 2136
(HD8013 C23 F68)
Franklin, Donald Robert 9599
(MIC.F.TC-42008)
Franklin, James McWillie 6022
(MIC.TC-6158)
Franklin, Patricia E. 9524
(MIC.F.TC-47834)
Franklyn, Gaston J. 3331
Franks, Stephen Guest 5744
Frankton, Clarence 135
Fransham, Peter Bleadon 6023
Franstead, Dennis Lee 461
Frantsi, Christopher 10512
(MIC.TC-11077)
Frantz, Charles Eugene 758
Frantz, Donald Gene 7789 (PH2342 F7)
Franzin, William Gilbert 10900
(MIC.F.TC-21432)
Franzoni, Edward Matthew 4434
(MIC.F.TC-40153)
Frape, Shaun Keith 11983
(MIC.F.TC-42445)

Frarey, Murray James 5701
Fraser, Arthur McNutt 997
Fraser, Brian John 9881
(MIC.F.TC-58756)
Fraser, Bruce Erland Clyde 11465
(MIC.TC-5808)
Fraser, E.J.S. 6996
Fraser, Ian F. 8197 (PS8073 F7)
Fraser, John Keith 4663
Fraser, Robert Lochiel, III 7198
(MIC.F.TC-50261)
Frazer, Henry Mason 9437
(MIC.F.TC-43644)
Fréchette, André B. 4758
(TA523 Q42 F7 fol.)
Fréchette, Errol James 746
Fréchette, Jean-Guy 7855
Frechette, Marcel 10286
Fredeen, Howard T. 201
Frederick, James R. 1600
Frederick, Nicholas Octave 3624
(MIC.F.TC-43645)
Fredericks, Carrie MacMillan 8053
(MIC.F.TC-32990)
Freedman, Bruce Clark 6024
Freedman, Charles 2338
Freedman, William 260
(MIC.F.TC-38718)
Freeman, Linda Alison Isobel 8878
(MIC.F.TC-38719)
Freeman, Milton Malcolm
Roland 11041
Freeman, Nelson Graham Stephen 4537
(MIC.F.TC-55231)
Freeman, Peter V. 6328
Freeman, Richard J. 3898
(MIC.F.TC-37852)
Freeman, Thomas Nesbitt 11142
Freeman, William Bradford 2143
(MIC.F.TC-46857)
Freeze, Arthur Charles 5213
Freitag, Richard 11143
French, Goldwin Sylvester 9875
French, Robert W. 2388
French, Susan Elizabeth 6713
(MIC.F.TC-50262)
Frénette, François 7856
Frénette, Orville 7857
Freney, Michael Aloysius 8771
Frey, Kenneth David 4024
(MIC.F.TC-43646)
Frey, Richard D. 10419
(MIC.F.TC-36378)
Freyman, Andrew Jack 1885
Fric, Lawrence 2180 (MIC.F.TC-20562)
Friedl, Ernestine 507
Friedman, Kenneth Michael 8605
(MIC.T-594)
Friedmann-Winsberg, Suzanne 3734
Friend, Douglas Walter 10589
Friesen, Brock Frederick James 8837
(MIC.F.TC-53546)
Friesen, David 3309
Friesen, George 11631
Friesen, Gerald Arnold 7120
(MIC.F.TC-27847)
Fris, Joe 4346 (MIC.F.TC-32805)
Frisch, Jack Aaron 663
Frisch, Thomas Ottokar 5843
Friss, Edward 2927 (MIC.F.T-1078)
Frith, Ronald Anthony 6329
Fritz, Madeleine Alberta 6025
Froese, Edgar 5558
Frost, Robert 10497
Frost, Roger Anthony 11573
(MIC.TC-7988)
Frost, Ruth 3781 (MIC.F.TC-60859)
Fruen, Mary Ann 6797
Fry, Frederick Ernest Joseph 11012
(QH1 T68 fol.)
Fry, Gary Dean 9840 (MIC.T-688)
Fry, M.G. 7556 (MIC.T-24)
Fryatt, Maurice John 9438
(MIC.F.TC-53070)
Fryer, Brian Jackson 5059
Fu, Lewis Lean Wei 3210
Fuchs, Donald Michael 6775
(MIC.F.TC-47051)
Fuggle, Richard Francis 5050
(MIC.TC-9285)
Fuh, Tsu-Min 6330 (MIC.TC-7806)

Fulford, Margaret Hannah 11376
Fulgenzi, Janet Marie 9293
(MIC.F.TC-37139)
Fullan, Michael 2070 (MIC.TC-6306)
Fuller, George Newman 1223
Fuller, James O. 5745
Fuller, Jerry B. 8995
Fuller, John David 8508
(MIC.F.TC-51671)
Fuller, Randall Lynn 11275
(MIC.F.TC-47052)
Fullerton, John Timothy 9674
Fulton, James F. 11888
Fulton, Patricia 1708
(MIC.F.TC-48342)
Fulton, Robert John 5214
Fumerton, Stewart Lloyd 5559
(MIC.F.TC-44381)
Funk, Alvin 11466
Furniss, Elaine Rosemary 3954
(MIC.F.TC-40406)
Furnival, George M. 5836
Fyles, James T. 5215
Fyles, John Gladstone 5216

G

Gaboury, Placide 8271 (PS8537 E4 Z67)
Gabrielse, Hubert 5217
Gad, Gunter Helmut Karl 4944
(MIC.F.TC-35025)
Gadbois, Pierre 6840
Gadd, Nelson Raymond 6331
Gadoua, Gilles 9368 (MIC.F-028305)
Gadzella, Bernadette M. 2543
Gaffield, Charles Mitchell 2490
(MIC.F.TC-38721)
Gaffney, Michael Edward 403
Gagan, David Paul 7343 (MIC.T-220)
Gagné, Denis 10251
Gagné, Fernand 3651
(MIC.F-2M11.491.3)
Gagné, Jacques Réal 3007 (MIC.T-453)
Gagné, Lucien 7304
Gagné, Marc 8311 (MIC.TC-12859)
Gagné, Wallace Donald George 8612
Gagnebin, Pierre André 9675
Gagnon, Alain Gustave 8754
(MIC.F.TC-59910)
Gagnon, Claude-Marie 8003
Gagnon, Jean 8285 (MIC.T-3592)
Gagnon, Joanne 8996 (MIC.T-3080)
Gagnon, Michael J. 11950
(MIC.F.TC-48189)
Gagnon, Pierre 4590 (MIC.F.TC-30402)
Gagnon, Pierre 8997 (MIC.F.TC-60149)
Gagnon, Réjean 11599
(MIC.F.TC-64269)
Gagnon, Serge 6946
Gailey, Richard Willard 1149
Gainer, Walter Dunham 1452
Gaitskell, Charles Dudley 3378
(N130 S3)
Galan, Meroslav 8893
(MIC.F.TC-54796)
Galarneau, Claude 8303
(F5009.9 N4 G3 fol.)
Galbraith, John Alexander 1428
Galbraith, John S. 7547
Gale, Alvin Frank 11632
Gale, G.H. 5746
Gale, Shirley 11377
Gallacher, Daniel Thomas 1272
(MIC.F.TC-42633)
Gallagher, Maureen Theresa 5218
Gallays, François 8374
Gallivan, Joanne Patricia 9525
Galloway, Brent Douglas 7820
Galloway, Priscilla Anne 3391
(MIC.F.TC-36653)
Galloway, Terry Don 11236
(MIC.F.TC-35837)
Galloway, William Robert 8913
(MIC.F.TC-50135)
Galois, Robert Michael 4918
(MIC.F.TC-44895)

Gamache, Sister Margaret Theresa 4376
Gambell, Trevor John 3128 (MIC.F.TC-40155)
Gandhi, Prem Parkash 2360 (MIC.T-685)
Gandhi, Subbaraja Mohandas 5609 (MIC.F.TC-38073)
Gandhi, Sunil K. Sunderlal 6332 (MIC.TC-1317)
Gandy, John Manuel 10252
Gandz, Jeffrey 2071
Gannon, Neil Cecil 2903 (MIC.T-631)
Ganong, Carey Kierstead 2361
Gante, M. 3861
Ganzevoort, Herman 7641 (MIC.F.TC-32806)
Garant, Jean Pierre 1684 (MIC.T-313)
Garbutt, Allen Stuart 10844
Garcia de Siles, José Luis 188
Gardiner, Lorne M. 11276
Gardner, David Emmett 1020 (MIC.F.TC-59789)
Gardner, Donald Hambidge 8722 (MIC.F.TC-25476)
Gardner, Douglas A.C. 5219 (MIC.F.TC-34611)
Gardner, Eldon J. 1936 (MIC.F.TC-59791)
Gardner, Grant Allan 11821 (MIC.F.TC-29839)
Gardner, Patricia 10287 (MIC.F.TC-42211)
Gardner, Peter Nigel 1861 (MIC.F.TC-49943)
Gardner, Robert 3716 (MIC.F.TC-59788)
Gardner, Robert John Logie 1709 (MIC.F.TC-61179)
Gardner, William Ray, Jr. 1601
Gareau, André Normand 9676 (MIC.F.TC-44734)
Garff, Dennis Royal 7254
Garfield, Viola Edmundson 687 (MIC.F.MC-166)
Gargett, Ann Elizabeth 4998 (MIC.TC-6891)
Garke, Mary Elaine 8998
Garland, George D. 6629
Garland, John Allan 11144 (MIC.F.TC-58112)
Garland, Parnell 3283
Garneau, Jean 3813
Garner, Clyde Alan 1476
Garner, David Marshall 9212 (MIC.F.TC-25712)
Garner, Doris Derbyshire Melling 6889 (MIC.F.TC-63211)
Garner, John E. 7079
Garner, Stephen Warren 966
Garnett, John Arthur 5610 (MIC.F.TC-18785)
Garnett, William Brighton 11145
Garnier, Bernard 3625 (MIC.F.TC-50611)
Garon, Yves 8272
Garrett, William A. 3497 (MIC.F.TC-29152)
Garrow, Patrick 43
Garry, Carl 4347
Garside, Edward Thomas 10874
Garson, Chrystelle 3211 (MIC.F.TC-33417)
Garven, Grant 5837 (MIC.F.TC-63033)
Garvin, Paul Lucien 7816
Garvin, Wilfred James 144
Garwood, John Bates 9600 (MIC.TC-15728)
Gascon, Adélard 7295
Gascoyne, Melvyn 5060 (MIC.F.TC-46861)
Gaskarth, Joseph William 5560
Gaskill, Daniel Wills 5003
Gaskill, James Leslie 3159 (MIC.F.TC-42634)
Gasser, William John 1602 (MIC.T-717)
Gaston, Leroy Clifton, III 6975 (MIC.F.T-1198)
Gatbonton-Segalowitz, Elizabeth 7672 (MIC.F.TC-29357)

Gates, Charles Cormack 10629 (MIC.F.TC-48948)
Gates, Charles M. 7063
Gates, Lillian F. 129 (F-5072.2)
Gates, Robert D. 3782 (MIC.F.TC-57298)
Gates, Todd Michael 5061
Gathercole, Frederick James 2904
Gattuso, Mathieu 8999 (MIC.T-3671)
Gaucher, Edwin H.S. 6333
Gaudin, Jean Roch 9894
Gaudreau, Sister Marie Agnes of Rome 9987
Gaudry, Marc 2253 (MIC.T-556)
Gaulin, André 8256
Gauthier, Benoît 11804
Gauthier, Gaston 3472
Gauthier, Georges 6334
Gauthier, Joseph D. 8425
Gauthier, Michel 6335
Gauthier, Pierre A. 6714 (MIC.F.TC-43405)
Gauthier, Robert 11600 (QK203 Q8 G28)
Gauthier, Roger Regent 10370 (MIC.F.TC-21820)
Gauthier-Larouche, Georges 10132
Gauvreau, Jean-M. 2087
Gauzas, Lawrence 9527 (MIC.F.TC-49210)
Gavaki, Efrosini 778 (MIC.T-658)
Gay, Gary Robert 3450 (MIC.F.TC-30684)
Gay, James Thomas 7548
Gaydos, Andrew 4409
Gayle, Grace Marguerite Hope 7691
Gayler, Hugh James 4919 (MIC.F.TC-19536)
Gazam, Carroll Dianne 9526 (MIC.F.TC-21160)
Gazan, Sonja Chava 3022 (MIC.F.TC-30340)
Gazard, Peter Robin 9957 (MIC.F.TC-51262)
Geale, Dorothy Wilhelmina 11538 (MIC.F.TC-49161)
Gebeyehou, Getinet 351 (MIC.F.TC-49162)
Geddes, James, Jr. 7736
Gedney, Richard T. 4518
Gee, Ellen Margaret Thomas 10047 (MIC.F.TC-37608)
Geen, Glen Howard 11846
Gehlbach, Roger Dale 2568 (MIC.F.TC-27484)
Geiger, Kenneth Warren 5702
Gelcer, Esther 3915 (MIC.F.TC-35209)
Geldsetzer, Helmut 5088 (MIC.TC-7807)
Gélinas, Arthur 2658 (MIC.F.TC-40160)
Gélinas, Jean-Paul 2411 (MIC.F.TC-41871)
Gélinas, Léopold 6336
Gélinas, Pierre J. 4519 (MIC.F.TC-20496)
Gell, William Alan 4664 (MIC.F.TC-28687)
Gell, Kenneth E. 7494
Geller, Gloria Rhea 10253 (MIC.F.TC-50264)
Geller, Sheldon Herbert 9677 (MIC.TC-12585)
Geller-Schwartz, Linda Fay 8545 (MIC.F.TC-35210)
Gelman, Robert M. 1877
Gelowitz, Arnold Charles 4162 (MIC.F.T-1061)
Gemme, Robert 10196 (MIC.F-2M11.369.7)
Gendron, Carole 9236 (MIC.T-3601)
Gendron, Jean-Louis 10080 (MIC.F.TC-45922)
Gendzwill, Don John 5561
Genesee, Fred Henry 7692 (MIC.F.TC-24325)
Genest, Jean-Guy 7349
Genest, Myles 9000 (MIC.F.TC-58852)
Gentilcore, R. Louis 127
Gentile, Andrew-Salvatore 9125 (MIC.F.TC-29841)

Gentile, Francesco 6665
George, Peter James 2302 (MIC.TC-1834)
George, Ronald Edison 1317 (MIC.F.TC-49777)
Gephart, Robert Paul 1937 (MIC.F.TC-46137)
Gerats, Donna Blanche 7821
Gerber, Linda Maria 7605 (MIC.F.TC-35029)
Gerecke, John Kent 10481 (MIC.F.TC-19539)
Gérin, Alexandre 7919
Gérin-Lajoie, Jean 1656
Gérin-Lajoie, Marie 10254
Gérin-Lajoie, P. 8466
Gerland, Daniel Raymond 1552
Germain, Anne 7270
Germundsen, Robert Kenneth 6563
Gernant, Paul Leonard 2362 (MIC.F.T-933)
Gerrard, Brian Alexander 6732 (MIC.F.TC-55832)
Gerry, James 9678 (MIC.F.TC-28886)
Gershey, Robert Michael 11951 (MIC.F.TC-53683)
Gerson, Ann Charlotte 9001 (MIC.F.TC-37795)
Gerson, Carole Fainstat 8054
Gerst-Kohn, Walter S. 8809
Gerstle, Gary Lloyd 829
Gervais, Gaétan S. 2303 (MIC.F.TC-4403)
Gervais-Ranger, Flore 3129 (MIC.F-2M11.169.2)
Gesner, Lloyd Roscoe 9770 (MIC.F.TC-55790)
Gestrin, Bengt Victor 1593 (MIC.TC-638)
Getty, Gerald Ronald 3212 (MIC.F.TC-24540)
Geva, Esther 4005
Gey van Pittius, Ernest Frederick Wilhelm 8820 (JN901 G4)
Gfellner, Barbara Mary 9679 (MIC.F.TC-50928)
Ghaeli, Reza 1710 (MIC.F.TC-56986)
Ghent, Jocelyn Maynard 8838 (MIC.T-959)
Ghoneim, Nadia Sobhi Abdel-Nour Mohamed 2304 (MIC.F.TC-60876)
Ghorayshi, Fatemeh Parvin 66
Ghosh, Ranjit 5018
Ghouri, Ahmad Said Khan 11146
Giasson-Lachance, Jocelyne 3213
Gibbins, Robert John 9255 (MIC.TC-4)
Gibbins, Roger 7495
Gibbins, Walter Arnold 6026 (MIC.F.TC-20302)
Gibbons, Jacqueline Anne 944 (MIC.F.TC-42212)
Gibbs, Graham William 6841 (MIC.F.TC-18223)
Gibbs, Harold Cuthbert 11338
Gibbs, K. Elizabeth 11312 (MIC.TC-9724)
Gibbs, Robert John 8413 (MIC.TC-8177)
Gibling, Martin R. 5838
Giblin, Peter Edwin 6027
Gibson, Andrew Ralph 10727
Gibson, Barry John 3814 (MIC.F.TC-48950)
Gibson, David Whiteoak 5404 (MIC.TC-639)
Gibson, Edward Mark Walter 4920 (MIC.TC-11218)
Gibson, George D. 4114
Gibson, George Gordon 10845 (MIC.TC-172)
Gibson, James Albert 7825
Gibson, Robert John 10876 (MIC.TC-16577)
Gibson, Rosalind Susan 6715
Gibson, Sarah Duane 4945 (MIC.F.TC-50265)
Gibson, William Garrett 10420 (MIC.F.TC-34345)
Gies, Mary L. 8301
Giesbrecht, Edwin Cornelius 3425 (MIC.F.TC-36920)

Giesbrecht, Herbert 10489
(MIC.F.TC-39863)
Giesbrecht, Norman Abe 9256
(MIC.F.TC-43649)
Gifford, Jack Jule 7435
Gifford, Robert Durrell 934
(MIC.F.TC-30268)
Gignac, Janine 3815
Gignac, Léonard Joseph 3214
(MIC.F.TC-49213)
Giguère, Georges Émile 9816
Giguère, Richard 8361
(MIC.F.TC-42635)
Gilbert, Angus Duncan 7121
(MIC.F.TC-27854)
Gilbert, Christopher David 7896
(MIC.F.TC-58745)
Gilbert, Frederick Franklin 10590
(MIC.TC-6551)
Gilbert, Joseph E.J. 6337
Gilbert, Robert 5220
(MIC.F.TC-19541)
Gilbert, Sidney Norman 3310
(MIC.F.TC-20093)
Gilbertson, Albert Nicolay 601
(MIC.F.T-135)
Gilchrist, Carol Mary
Cunningham 5839 (MIC.F.T-1218)
Giles, Donna Elaine 9190
(MIC.F.TC-49783)
Giles, Peter Strachan 6028
(MIC.F.TC-29080)
Giles, Thomas Edward 2956
(MIC.F-144)
Gilfillan, Edward Smith, III 11065
(MIC.TC-6893)
Gill, Ajit Singh 4543 (MIC.TC-2476)
Gill, Allison Margaret 4737
(MIC.F.TC-54430)
Gill, Donald Allen 4665 (MIC.TC-8300)
Gill, James Edward 6029
Gill, James Wendell 5840
(MIC.F.TC-32158)
Gill, Lachman Singh 11378
(MIC.TC-9062)
Gill, Mohindra Pall 3332
Gill, Robert Monroe 3541 (MIC.T-794)
Gill, Warren George 4921
(MIC.F.TC-56768)
Gillen, David William 4928
(MIC.F.TC-53061)
Gillen, Marie A. 9817
(MIC.F.TC-47059)
Gillespie, David Roy 11211
(MIC.F.TC-53439)
Gillespie, Edgar Dean 2741
Gillespie, Gilbert Abraham 1126
(MIC.T-562)
Gillespie, Walter Lee 10733
Gillett, Lawrence Britton 6030
Gilliam, Martina Dickson Smith 11379
Gillies, E.L. 462 (MIC.T-884)
Gillies, Howard Earl 3626
(MIC.F.TC-50266)
Gillies, James M. 10133
Gillies, Norman B. 6338
Gillis, Allison Ronald 10011
(MIC.F.TC-26761)
Gillis, D.H. 8489
Gillis, John Hugh 2760 (MIC.TC-13384)
Gillis, John William 5645
(QE190 G5 fol.)
Gillis, Lynette Marie 1150
(MIC.F.TC-58285)
Gilmartin, Malvern 11467
Gilmor, Timothy McLeod 8914
(MIC.F.TC-38487)
Gilmore, C.G. 6750
Gilmour, James Muckle 4823
(MIC.TC-9137)
Gilmour-Barrett, Karen C. 9126
(MIC.F.TC-19315)
Gilpin, Alec Richard 7064
Giltrow, Janet Lesley 8004
(MIC.F.TC-44897)
Giner, Marcel M. 8755
(MIC.F.TC-41873)
Gingras, Marie 9294
Ginman, Peter John 1603 (MIC.T-221)
Ginn, R.M. 6031

Ginsberg, Raymond Emmanuel 7737
(MIC.F.TC-36659)
Giovando, Lawrence Frank 4508
Girard, André 3627
Girard, Donald Archie 2928
Girard, Ghislain 9369
Girard, Hermann C. 3602 (MIC.T-457)
Girard, Paul 6339 (MIC.TC-9293)
Giroux, Aline 2558
Giroux, Lorne 7946
Giroux, Luc 9528
Girt, J.L. 6842
Githae-Mugo, Micere M. 8114
(MIC.F.TC-18789)
Gittins, John 6032
Gladish, David William 11789
(MIC.F.TC-37143)
Gladwin, Thomas Neil 1749
Glaister, Rowland Perry 5405
Glasberg, Rhoda Elizabeth 9370
(MIC.F.TC-39676)
Glass, Helen Preston 6890 (MIC.T-326)
Glassford, Robert Gerald 602
Glauber, Robin Roth 830
Glaze, Avis Elane 4182
(MIC.F.TC-50267)
Glazier, Kenneth MacLean 9958
Gledhill, Thomas Lloyd 6033
Glenday, Daniel 8756
(MIC.F.TC-52774)
Glenday, Graham 2011 (MIC.F.T-1359)
Glendenning, Donald Ernest
Malcolm 2747
Glendinning, Robert Morton 4759
Glennie, Charles William 11380
(MIC.TC-5811)
Glerum, Christiaan 11745
(MIC.F.TC-36660)
Glick, Harvey Leonard 145
(MIC.F.TC-54465)
Glickman, Jacob 10147
(MIC.F.TC-38726)
Glicksman, Louis 7665
(MIC.F.TC-53824)
Glinz, Leslie Albert 2457
Globensky, Yvon Raoul 6515
Glos, George Ernest 7927
Glova, Gordon John 10939
(MIC.F.TC-40627)
Glover, David James 16
(MIC.F.TC-59882)
Glover, Joseph K. 5221
(MIC.F.TC-39480)
Glover, Thomas 8339
Gluek, Alvin C., Jr. 7522
Glynn, Edward Lewis 3498
(MIC.TC-4497)
Gnarowski, Michael 8055
Goble, Ronald James 5406
(MIC.F.TC-34612)
Godbout, Arthur J.E. 2491
Goddard, Arthur Morris 8691
(MIC.T-636)
Goddard, Christopher Ian 11013
(MIC.F.TC-40993)
Godfrey, Judith Louise Dean 11468
(MIC.F.TC-34820)
Godfrey, William G. 7279
(MIC.F.TC-18540)
Godin, J.J. Gabriel G. 11908
(CA2.1985-2362)
Godin, Jean-Guy Joseph 10940
(MIC.F.TC-46139)
Godin, Louise 7738
Godler, Zlata 7649 (MIC.F.TC-53062)
Godwin, Colin Inglis 5917
(MIC.F.TC-25162)
Godwin, Lois Ruth 3392
Goebel, Allan Ronald 9680
(MIC.F.TC-25714)
Goel, Madan Kumar 4531
(MIC.F.TC-27377)
Goell, Yosef Israel 8572 (MIC.T-780)
Goelman, Hillel 3955
(MIC.F.TC-42214)
Goerzen, Jakob Warkentin 7771
(PF5939 G6)
Goetz, Peter Andrew 5501
(MIC.F.TC-49496)
Goffman, Irving Jay 1711

Goh, Swee Chua 3647
(MIC.F.TC-47060)
Goheen, Peter G. 4869 (HC118 T6 G6)
Gokhale, Atulchandra Anant 11684
(MIC.F.TC-28689)
Golant, Stephen Myles 4900
(HQ1064 C2 Q6)
Gold, Christopher Malcolm 5407
(MIC.F.TC-36387)
Gold, David P. 6340
Gold, Gerald Louis 438 (MIC.T-363)
Gold, Marc Hilary 2363 (MIC.T-699)
Gold, Norman Leon 7642
Goldberg, Gerald Elliot 9681
Goldberg, Jack S. 3956 (MIC.F-023501)
Goldberg, Simon Abraham 1637
Goldberg, Theodore Irving 1623
Goldberg, Toby 1061 (MIC.T-337)
Goldenberg, Sheldon 9976
Goldenthal, Lyn M. 9257
(MIC.F.TC-51191)
Goldie, Raymond J. 6341
(MIC.F.TC-32653)
Goldie, Terence William 8056
(MIC.F.TC-37511)
Golding, Douglas Lawrence 11685
(MIC.TC-2364)
Goldman, Barbara Davis 9333
(MIC.F.TC-49782)
Goldman, Irving 557
Goldman, Janice Olivia Babcock 3888
(MIC.F.TC-29155)
Goldring, Cecil Charles 4224
(LB1131 G6)
Goldring, Leslie Warren 6733
Goldring, P. 7080
Goldschmidt, Carl 10490 (MIC.T-338)
Goldstein, Robert Arnold 6976
(F5064 G6)
Goldstick, Isidore 2633
Golick, Margaret 3909
(MIC.F.TC-33292)
Golini, Victor Italo 11147
(MIC.F.TC-61180)
Gollop, James Bernard 10766
Goltz, Herbert Charles Walter,
Jr. 7030 (MIC.TC-16413)
Gómez-Bueno, Cebers O. 4502
(MIC.F.TC-42361)
Gómez-Treviño, Eurique 11998
(MIC.F.TC-47063)
Gomme, Ian Modermid 10255
(MIC.F.TC-59886)
Gonick, Cyril Wolfe 2181 (MIC.T-148)
Gonnsen, August 2148 (HF6659 P4 G65)
Gonzalez, Ellice Becker 522
Gonzalez-Bonorino, Gustavo 5747
Good, David Allen 1712
Good, Leonard McRae 1127
(MIC.F.TC-23284)
Good, Shirley Ruth 6891
Goodale, Denis 1657 (MIC.T-544)
Goodchild, Michael Frank 4591
Goodfellow, Wayne David 5611
(MIC.F.TC-43900)
Goodison, Barry Edward 5045
(MIC.F.TC-36668)
Goodman, A.J. 5102
Goodman, Isaac B. 1318
Goodman, Doba Rebecca 3215
(MIC.F.TC-40995)
Goodman, Joseph Robert 11967
Goodman, Sherryl Hope 3023
(MIC.F.TC-37853)
Goodwin, Alan M. 6034
Goodwin, Craufurd David
Wycliffe 1204 (HB121 A2 G6)
Goodwin, John Robert 3628
Goodwin, Luther 10421
Goodz, Naomi Susan Sugarman 3024
(MIC.F.TC-35721)
Goonewardene, Laksiri Amura 189
(MIC.F.TC-36388)
Goranson, Edwin Alexander 5646
Gorbet, Frederick William 1348
(MIC.T-459)
Gordey, Steven P. 5918 (C.M42-318)
Gordon, Arthur 9002 (MIC.F.TC-52889)
Gordon, Bryan Herbert Copp 890
(MIC.F.TC-19780)

Gordon, Charles Henry 6035
(QE475 G55 G67)
Gordon, Irene Malinda 1676
(MIC.F.TC-51001)
Gordon, John Lee, Jr. 7353
(MIC.T-500)
Gordon, Richard Irving 7255
(MIC.F.T-1309)
Gordon, Robert Arthur 3542
(MIC.T-339)
Gordon, Robert Kay 7317
Gorlick, Carolyne Ann 4115
Gorman, David J. 6947
Gorman, Linda Grace 1604
(MIC.F.T-1282)
Gorman, Maureen Catherine 9371
(MIC.F.TC-58741)
Gorman, W. Alan 6342
Gorman, William A. 6036
Gorn, Michael Herman 7296
(MIC.T-937)
Gornall, Richard John 11469
(MIC.F.TC-51678)
Gorvans, Alan Wilbert 9786
Gorwaney, Naintara 10197
Gosh-Dastidar, Priyabrata 6343
Goss, Anthony John 3592 (MIC.T-460)
Gosse, R.F. 7867
Gosselin, Roger 6798
(MIC.F.TC-38238)
Gossen, Randall Garth 10513
(MIC.F.TC-16983)
Gotlieb, Ian Henry 9191
(MIC.F.TC-49783)
Gottesman, Daniel Harvey 6960
(MIC.F.TC-42216)
Gougeon, Réjeanne 6749
Gough, Barry Morton 7081 (MIC.T-909)
Gough, Ruby Louise 2638 (MIC.T-616)
Gould, Allan Mendel 8085
(MIC.F.TC-33632)
Gould, Edgar Nathan 2929 (MIC.T-430)
Gould, Lawrence Irwin 1453
(MIC.F.TC-32814)
Goulding, Christopher James 11686
(MIC.TC-13221)
Goulding, James Wray 1169
(HD3616 C34 N48)
Goulet, Georges 2601
Goulet, Henri 11148 (MIC.F.TC-36389)
Goulet, Louise Anna 10693
(MIC.F.TC-44899)
Goulet, Normand 6344
(MIC.F.TC-39482)
Goulet, Robert John 6738
(MIC.F.TC-43074)
Goulson, Carolyn Floyd 2423
(MIC.F.TC-27487)
Goupil, Georgette 3902 (HU1626 G68)
Goveia, John Charles 1553 (MIC.T-516)
Gow, Donald J.S. 8490 (MIC.TC-1209)
Gow, James Iain 1069
Gow, Kathleen Mavourneen 10081
(MIC.F.TC-17113)
Gowans, Alan Wilbert 935 (MIC.T-71)
Gowen, Robert Joseph 8892
Gower, Charles Frederick 6037
(MIC.F.TC-42820)
Goyder, John C. 10198 (MIC.TC-14643)
Goyecke, John R.M. 3216
Goyer-Michaud, Francine 10256
Goyette, Gabriel 2527
Grabb, Edward George 9994
(MIC.F.TC-28597)
Grabert, Garland Frederick 380
(MIC.T-970)
Graburn, Nelson H. 7833
Grace, Barry Wayne 11539
(MIC.F.TC-48730)
Grace, Sherrill Elizabeth 8137
(MIC.F.TC-23080)
Gracie, Bruce Alan 122
(MIC.F.TC-29607)
Graddy, Duane B. 1512 (MIC.T-808)
Gradish, Stephen Francis 7408
(MIC.F.TC-27861)
Grady, Patrick Michael 2339
(MIC.TC-16630)
Grady, William Ellis 3679 (MIC.T-617)
Graf, Joseph Lucas, Jr. 5612

Graff, Harvey Jay 2492
(MIC.F.TC-26056)
Graftieaux, Pierre-Ivan Charles 9171
(MIC.F-2M11.615.4)
Graham, Domenick Stuart 6935
(MIC.T-895)
Graham, Dorothy Marguerite 4116
(MIC.F.T-618)
Graham, Elizabeth Jane 535
(MIC.F.TC-20565)
Graham, Evelyn Elizabeth 3297
Graham, George Arthur 4393
Graham, Gerald 7031 (HF1533 G7)
Graham, James Benjamin 44
(MIC.F.TC-36268)
Graham, John Finlayson 1498
Graham, John Ronald 2827
(MIC.F.TC-42217)
Graham, Peter 11197
Graham, Robert Bruce 6345
Graham, Robert Edward 1638
(MIC.F.TC-33089)
Graham, Robert Somerville 8198
(MIC.T-31)
Graham, Thomas Francis 3083
Graham, William Roger 7341
(MIC.TC-87)
Grainger, Edward H. 11042
Grainger, Robert Neil 6776
(MIC.F.TC-49784)
Gram, Harold Albert 1691
Grambeau, Rodney James 10382
Granatstein, Jack Lawrence 8646
(MIC.T-177)
Granger, Isabelle Alix 1454
Granger, Orman Eloi 5004
(MIC.F.TC-27862)
Granger, Raymond Laurent 319
(MIC.F.TC-42931)
Grant, Alan Carson 5687
Grant, Douglas Roderick 5588
Grant, Harold Embree 4183
Grant, James Alexander 6038
Grant, Marion Elder 3217
Grant, Peter Russell 9682
(MIC.F.TC-45984)
Grantham, Herbert Harris 3451
Granville, Howard 4184
(MIC.F.TC-36670)
Granville, James 7847
Graub, Sup Mei 4163 (MIC.F.TC-23081)
Gravel, Jean-Yves 7256
(MIC.TC-10369)
Gravel, Jean-Yves 7409
Gravelle, Lucien H. 10362
(MIC.F.TC-34354)
Gravenor, Conrad P. 6039
Gray, Andrew Ross 4474
Gray, David Robert 10637
(MIC.TC-15241)
Gray, Gerald Eldon 3120 (MIC.F.T-884)
Gray, James Telfer 4683
(MIC.TC-9297)
Gray, John Andrew 1833 (MIC.T-328)
Gray, Richard H. 5647
Gray, Robert William 3581
(MIC.F.TC-25167)
Gray, William Barrisdale 2630
Graymont, Barbara 7436 (E99 I7 G67)
Gray-Snelgrove, Rosemary Hilda 10199
Grayson, John Francis 6535
Grayson, John Paul 8768
(MIC.TC-14851)
Greckol, Sonja Ruth 3218
(MIC.F.TC-44740)
Green, Alan George 4785 (HC115 G68)
Green, Anne Jacqueline 9683
Green, Anthony Heber 6040
(MIC.F.TC-38732)
Green, Bernard 7920
Green, David Christopher 5841
Green, David Geoffrey 11736
(MIC.F.TC-36088)
Green, David Martin 10723
(MIC.F.TC-52491)
Green, Edgar D., Jr. 2597
Green, George Henry Ebenezer 2618
(MIC.F.TC-25478)
Green, James Paul 998 (MIC.T-517)
Green, Janet Jarmé 7122
(MIC.F.TC-40996)

Green, Jerry Edward 4666
(MIC.F.T-914)
Green, John Marshall 10941
(MIC.TC-2365)
Green, Lewis H. 5222
Green, Nathan Louis 5223
(MIC.F.TC-37616)
Green, Stanton William 909
Green, Walter Henry H. 3473
Green, Wren Quinton 11212
(MIC.F.TC-19545)
Greenberg, Adolph Morris 536
(MIC.F.T-967)
Greenberg, Allen Morley 9529
(MIC.F.TC-20094)
Greenberg, Corin Merle 9003
(MIC.F.TC-33634)
Greenberg, Norman Arthur 9530
(MIC.F.TC-50612)
Greene, Craig William 11412
Greene, Gordon Mather 4994
(MIC.F.T-1171)
Greene, Ralph Irving 4025
Greenfield, Thomas Barr 3058
Greenglass, David Irwin 4064
(MIC.F.TC-42218)
Greenglass, Esther Ruth 9684
(MIC.TC-1858)
Greenhill, Craig James 3652
(MIC.F.TC-55020)
Greenidge, Kenneth N.H. 11652
Greenman, Lawrence 6041
(MIC.TC-9139)
Greenwood, Donald Eric 9258
(MIC.F.TC-20006)
Greenwood, Frank Murray 7032
(MIC.TC-6895)
Greenwood, Hans P. 1976 (MIC.T-152)
Greer, Allan Robert 7257
(MIC.F.TC-44495)
Greer, Ruth Nancy Elizabeth 3499
(MIC.F.TC-34825)
Greggs, Robert George 5408
Grégoire, Pierre A. 9127
Gregor, Alexander Douglas 3548
(MIC.T-818)
Gregory, Alan 4435 (MIC.F.TC-30270)
Gregory, Allan Walter 1349
(MIC.F.TC-55941)
Gregory, G.P. 5062
Gregory, Murray Richard 11847
Gregory, Patrick Thomas 10728
(MIC.F.TC-18075)
Greig, Edmund Wendell 6346
Grenda, Robert Norman 5042
(MIC.TC-1016)
Grenier, Florian 6347
Grenier, Jacques 10406 (MIC.T-647)
Grenier-Francoeur, Marie 8199
(MIC.F.TC-47987)
Grenier, Paul-Émile 6348
Grenke, Arthur 776 (MIC.F.TC-37797)
Grey, Charles E. 5409
Grey, Pauline Margaret 9259
(MIC.F.TC-51369)
Grey, R.Y. 1319
Grice, Reginald Hugh 5502
Griffin, Amy Elizabeth 4426
(MIC.T-32)
Griffin, Douglas Keith 10257
Griffin, Elizabeth Anne 8573
(MIC.T-839)
Griffin, Harvey Richard 9531
(MIC.F.TC-50929)
Griffin, Howard Dennis 11574
(MIC.TC-233)
Griffin, Peter J. 1907
(MIC.F.TC-53928)
Griffis, Arthur T. 6042
Griffith, Charles Arthur 4065
Griffith, Garry Richard 17
(MIC.F.TC-43800)
Griffith, Gwyneth Proctor 4026
(MIC.F.TC-58320)
Griffiths, Alan Keith 3452
(MIC.F.TC-40414)
Griffiths, Glynis 10366
(MIC.F.TC-56977)
Griffiths, Naomi E.A. 6997

Grigsby, Jefferson Eugene, Jr. 953
(MIC.T-33)
Grim, John Allen 537
Grima, Angelo Paul 4929
(TD226 A1 G7)
Grimes, Catherine 9128
(MIC.F.TC-17115)
Grimes-Graeme, Rhoderick C.H. 6349
Grindley, Thomas William 165
Gripton, James MacPherson 10200
Grisé, Jacques 2072 (MIC.TC-16416)
Griswold, Bernard Lee 10923
Griswold, Thomas Baldwin 5648
Grobman, Arnold Brams 10724
Groeneweg, Gerrit 3219
(MIC.F.TC-59742)
Groeneweld, Meyer W.O.J. 6043
Groffier, Ethel 7928 (MIC.TC-11833)
Grondin, Conde Rosaire 8440
(MIC.F.TC-24040)
Gros, Hans J. 10377
Grosmaire, Jean-Louis 4760
(MIC.T-3098)
Gross, Andrew Charles 2182
Gross, Carl Henry 2449
Gross, Gordon A. 6350
Gross, James Matthew 11999
Gross, Raphael Henry 8200
Gross, William Harvey 6044
Grossman, Gary David 10942
Groulx, Abbé Lionel 2528
Grouse, Nellis Maynard 4883
(FC315 C7)
Grove, Edward Willis 5224
(MIC.TC-15864)
Groves, Patricia Heffron 7921
(MIC.TC-15119)
Groves, Sarah 10864 (MIC.F.TC-59207)
Grow, Mary Marsh 7496
Grunau, Ruth Veronica Elizabeth 3043
(MIC.F.TC-25172)
Grunis, Asher Dan 7897
(MIC.F.TC-36989)
Gruson, Linda Margaret 955
(MIC.F.TC-49787)
Grywalski, Stanley 2640 (MIC.T-523)
Gryz, Zbigniew Jan 7673
Guay, L. 10499
Gubern, Garriga-Nogués,
Santiago 10258 (MIC.T-381)
Gue, Leslie Robb 711
Guemple, Donald Lee 603
Guérin, Gilles 3680 (MIC.F-002011)
Guerinot, Mary Lou 11952
(MIC.F.TC-44243)
Guernsey, Tarrant D. 5649
Guest, D.T. 1554
Guest, Gerald Richard 3361
(MIC.F.TC-29011)
Guest, Henry Hewson 3408
Guest, Henry James 7183
(MIC.F.TC-54541)
Guèvremont, Hélène 11313
Guignard, Michael James 831
Guilbault, Jean-Pierre 6581
Guillemin, Jeanne E. 832
Guillet, Ernest Bernard 833
(MIC.F.T-961)
Guillet, Raymond D. 2722
(MIC.F.T-1207)
Guillette, Claude 7739 (MIC.T-3456)
Guilmette, Armand 8259
Guilmette, Bernadette 8375
(MIC.F.TC-48536)
Guindon, Jean-Charles 10165
(MIC.F.TC-17266)
Guindon, Jeannine 10259 (LC4801 G8)
Guirguis, Fayeh Shoukyr 3426
(MIC.F-2M11.607.3)
Guirguis, Talaat F. 9532
(MIC.F.TC-53232)
Guité, Jean Charles Michel 1128
Gunderson, Donald Raymond 10943
Gundrum, Waldemar 9859
(MIC.F.T-1346)
Gunn, Gertrude E. 7166 (JL205 A1 G8)
Gunn, William Walker Hamilton 11014
Gunn-Walberg, Kenneth Wayne 9860
(MIC.TC-7884)
Gunning, H.C. 5225
Gunton, John E. 5103

Gunton, Thomas Ian 10471
(MIC.F.TC-55024)
Guppy, L. Neil 9685 (MIC.F.TC-49788)
Gupta, Santosh Kumar 11889
(MIC.F.TC-19318)
Gupta, Satyadeo 1886
(MIC.F.TC-46872)
Gupta, Vinod Kumar 1750
(MIC.F.TC-36677)
Gurbuz, Mehmet Behic 6586
(MIC.TC-4881)
Gurdin, Joseph Barry 10201
(MIC.F-2M11.389.1)
Guse, Linda Lydia 8915
(MIC.F.TC-50930)
Gusen, Peter 2330 (MIC.T-689)
Gushire, William Joseph 3292
Güssow, William C. 6351
Gustafson, David Axel 1021
(MIC.T-329)
Gutek, Larry Henry 325
(MIC.F.TC-26354)
Guthrie, Dorothy A. 7082
Gutman, Gloria Margaret 9372
Gutzke, David William 1273
(MIC.F.TC-62252)
Guy, Alexander John Young 2787
(MIC.TC-9594)
Guy, Allan Roy 2714 (MIC.F.TC-36678)
Guy, James John 8872 (MIC.T-822)
Guy-Bray, John Victor 6352
Guyatt, Doris Elsie 10063
(MIC.F.TC-35036)
Guzman, Juan Ramon P. 10742
(MIC.F.TC-55351)
Guzzardo, John Christopher 6998
Gwyn, Quintin Hugh 5118
(MIC.TC-8995)
Gyra, John Charles 9004
(MIC.F.TC-58290)

H

Haan, Richard 7437
Haanappel, Peter P.C. 2271
(MIC.F.TC-32951)
Haber, Erich 11413 (MIC.TC-12944)
Haberer, John Frederick 1404
Haché, Jean-Baptiste 2792
Hackett, Gerald Thomas 2493
Hackett, Robert Anthony 1129
Hackney, Peter Albert 11015
(MIC.F.TC-19708)
Hackshaw, Eugenia 3520
Haddad, Parviz 4544 (MIC.F.TC-35220)
Haddock, James Devere 11149
Hadleigh-West, Frederick 575
Hadley, Donald Gene 6045
Haebler, Peter 834 (MIC.T-690)
Haeck, Philippe 8201
Hafen, Gregor A. 9005
Hafez, Bahjat Mohammad 1170
(MIC.F.TC-42821)
Hagan, John Lee 7904
(MIC.F.TC-21022)
Hagarty, Linda Margaret Mary 10032
(MIC.F.TC-32835)
Hagarty, Stephen Leo Francis 10082
(MIC.F.TC-32836)
Hage, Keith Donald 4995
Hagen, William Morice 8138
(MIC.T-716)
Haggarty, James Colton 866
(MIC.F.T-1325)
Hagler, Ronald Albert 7972 (Z481 H3)
Hagmeier, Edwin Moyer 10588
Hagy, James William 8574 (MIC.T-538)
Haight, David Ernest 8491
Haimila, Norman Edward 5226
Haines, Leonard Paul 3957
(MIC.F.TC-5599)
Hajnal, Zoltan 6587 (MIC.TC-5539)
Halary, Charles 8575 (MIC.F-031109)
Hale, Alan MacDougall 4520
Hale, A.W.C. 7123

Hale, Sylvia Marion 10009
(MIC.F.TC-28697)
Hale, W.E. 5562
Halet, Robert A.F. 6353
Haley, David 11687 (MIC.TC-466)
Haliburton, Roy Edward 2930
(MIC.TC-9917)
Hall, Carl Ansel St. Clair 1786
(MIC.F.TC-15394)
Hall, David John 7381
(MIC.F.TC-18500)
Hall, Francine Marian 2841
(MIC.F.TC-31232)
Hall, George Brent 6693
(MIC.F.TC-50826)
Hall, Gustav Wesley 11601
Hall, Hubert H. 5410
Hall, James Larry 1130 (MIC.T-575)
Hall, John Kendrick 6671
Hall, John Laurence 381
(MIC.TC-50270)
Hall, John Raymond 4309
(MIC.F.TC-51266)
Hall, L.G. 2205
Hall, Richard Drummond 6046
(MIC.F.TC-48347)
Hall, Robert Burnett, Jr. 178
Hall, Roger Dennis 1243 (MIC.T-910)
Hall, Russell Lindsay 6520
(MIC.F.TC-32996)
Hallam, Jack Charles 10877
(MIC.F.TC-27867)
Haller, Otto 9533 (MIC.F.TC-52016)
Hallett, Mary E. 7351
Halliday, Ian 12000
Halliwell, Stanley Thomas 4225
(MIC.F.TC-35221)
Hallman, David William 9534
(MIC.F.TC-44907)
Hallman, Donald Emerson 4691
(MIC.T-768)
Halloran, Gerard 9006
Hallowell, Alfred I. 463
Halls, Henry Campbell 5132
(MIC.TC-15395)
Hallschmid, Claus A. 3220
(MIC.F.TC-34357)
Halm, Benjamin Jackson 285
Halnon, William 4394
Halpern, Honey Gael 3932
(MIC.F.TC-59240)
Halpin, Marjorie Myers 688
(MIC.TC-15122)
Halstead, Donald Paul 2364
(MIC.T-698)
Ham, Leonard Charles 673
Hamada, Koichi 1531
Hamayan, Else 7740 (MIC.F.TC-38242)
Hambleton, Alixe Lyons 3008
(MIC.F.TC-43667)
Hamblett, Edwin Clifford 1022
Hambley, Janice Marie 3130
(MIC.F.TC-36681)
Hambley, Walter Douglas 9535
(MIC.TC-8370)
Hambly, John Robert Stanley 2681
Hamdan, Abdul Rahima Ahmad 11848
(MIC.TC-10669)
Hamel, Claude 9295 (MIC.F-013706)
Hamel, Marie 8509 (HV105 H26 fol.)
Hamel, Pierre 10493
(MIC.F-2M11.491.2)
Hamel, Réginald 8302
(PN4913 M65 H3)
Hamelin, Marcel 7258
Hamers, Josianne Frieda-Aline 9536
(MIC.TC-15868)
Hames, Patricia Jane 3415
Hamilton, John McLean Parsons 4273
(MIC.F.TC-58381)
Hamilton, Lorne Daniel 9930
Hamilton, Tark Scott 5227
(MIC.F.TC-53932)
Hamilton, William Baillie 2472
(MIC.TC-6160)
Hamilton, William George 4611
Hamm, Peter Martin 9846
(MIC.F.TC-37965)
Hammelef, John Christensen 6961
Hammer, Ulrich Theodore 11619

Hammond, Allan Robert 3453
(MIC.F.TC-27656)
Hammond, Joseph Angus Bernard 1624
(MIC.F.TC-25718)
Hammond, Leslie Leigh Gardner 4310
(MIC.F.TC-25719)
Hamor, Tamas 10982
(MIC.F.TC-31500)
Hamori-Torok, Charles 664
(MIC.TC-1059)
Hamovitch, Maurice B. 1625
Hampson, Cyril Gladstone 10694
Hampson, Fen Osler 1382
(MIC.F.T-1310)
Hampton, Peter 1658
Hamwood, John Alban 2828
(MIC.F.TC-35222)
Hamza, Valiya Mannathal 6653
(MIC.TC-14951)
Hamzawi, Salah Gouda 4475
(MIC.F.TC-32159)
Handcock, W.G. 7619
Handford, Richard H. 11237
Handler, Richard 439
Handren, B.E. 7065
Handrick, Philip James 440
(MIC.F.T-1158)
Hanek, George 10547 (MIC.TC-15731)
Hanel, Frank Joseph 1938
(MIC.F.TC-50931)
Hanes, John Alexander 6047
(MIC.F.TC-42221)
Haney, James Filmore 11810
(MIC.TC-9144)
Hanfield, Robert Charles 5104
Hanic, Louis Anthony 11470
Hanis, Nancy Marilyn 6843
(MIC.F.TC-31589)
Hanley, James A. 3311
(MIC.TC-15732)
Hanna, Allan Alexander 1787
(MIC.F.TC-48350)
Hanna, Carolyn Linda 2815
Hanna, Gila 3427 (MIC.F.TC-55736)
Hannah, Kathryn J.N. 6892
Hannah, Raymond G.J. 6354
Hannibal, Emmett Ronald 945
Hannigan, John Andrew 8723
Hannigan, Robert E., Jr. 7557
Hannin, Daniel 10148
Hannon, Susan Jean 10846
(MIC.F.TC-63084)
Hans, Valerie Patricia 9686
(MIC.F.TC-38738)
Hansen, Christine Marion 9687
(MIC.F.TC-42222)
Hansen, Dean Cyrus 11150
Hansen, Forrest Carl 4249
(MIC.F.TC-53067)
Hansen, J.A.G. 4855
Hanson, Eric J. 1522
Hanson, Frank K. 970
Hanson, George 6048
Hanson, Harold Carsten 10792
Hanson, Raymond Lee 3362
(MIC.F.TC-26772)
Hanson, Robert George 9129
(MIC.F.TC-17116)
Hanson, William Bruce 5228
Hansvick, Christine Louise 9688
(MIC.F.TC-34543)
Hanvelt, Robin Alden 1645
(MIC.F.TC-51688)
Hanzeli, Victor Egon 7786
Hanzely, Joseph B. 11043
Happold, David Christopher
Dawber 11198
Haq, Aminul 5005
Harasym, Peter Humphrey 6822
(MIC.F.TC-44744)
Hararine, Harold 1514
Harasymiw, Elaine L. Verchomin 3466
(MIC.F.TC-55357)
Harcourt, Douglas George 11277
Hardcastle, David Paul 6977
Hardenbergh, William Spencer 8692
(MIC.T-34)
Hardie, Nena E. 6777
(MIC.F.TC-25720)
Hardie, Thomas Neil 7291
Harding, L.A.A. 8108

Harding, William Duffield 6049
Hardman, John Michael 11213
(MIC.TC-15477)
Hardwick, Claudia Shaw 3816
(MIC.F.TC-48351)
Hardwick, Walter Gordon 1809
(MIC.T-35)
Hardy, Edwin Austin 7960 (Z718 H29)
Hardy, Helen Margaret 8724
(MIC.F.TC-19406)
Hardy, James Roger 4185
(MIC.F.TC-44031)
Hardy, John Howard 2494
Hardy, John Stewart 2495
(MIC.F.TC-53069)
Hardy, Larry Michael 9537
(MIC.F.TC-26355)
Hardy, Léon H. 4761 (MIC.F.TC-31791)
Hardy, Madeline Isobel 4011
Hardy, René 7259 (MIC.F.TC-39148)
Hardy, Timothy Ashley 2569
(MIC.F.TC-27490)
Hardy-Roch, Marcel 10021
Hare, Frederick Kennett 5019
(MIC.MC-17)
Hare, Gerard Murdock 10983
(MIC.F.TC-41058)
Hare, John 7033 (MIC.TC-14214)
Hare, William Francis 9622
(MIC.TC-11579)
Harel Giasson, Francine 1171
(MIC.T-3100)
Harestad, Alton Sidney 10621
(MIC.F.TC-61145)
Harger, Virginia Ann 8202
(MIC.TC-15123)
Hargrave, Barry Thomas 11066
(MIC.TC-5093)
Hargraves, Robert Bero 6355
Harington, C.R. 6545
(MIC.F.TC-34359)
Haritos, Zissis 1455 (MIC.TC-14852)
Harker, Peter 5411
Harker, Stuart David 5374
(MIC.F.TC-36923)
Harland, Rex 5412 (MIC.TC-6712)
Harley, Mary Birgitta 7741
(MIC.F.TC-58344)
Harling, John 10673 (MIC.TC-15478)
Harling, Kenneth Foster 18
(MIC.F.T-1257)
Harman, Francis James 1659
Harman, William Gowans 4274
(MIC.TC-11580)
Harmon, Russell Scott 5063
(MIC.F.TC-29621)
Harnarine, Harold 1513
(MIC.F.TC-36096)
Harp, Elmer, Jr. 604
Harper, Alexander Maitland 11199
Harper, Charles Woods, Jr. 6557
Harper, Francis 6546
Harper, Irene M. 7234
Harper, Peter Paul 11278
(MIC.TC-7411)
Harries, Hubert W. 2305
Harrill, Ernest Eugene 8619
Harris, Barbara Pritchard 7714
(MIC.F.TC-25525)
Harris, Georgina Bernice 9007
(MIC.F.TC-53825)
Harris, Herbert Raymond 7819
(MIC.F.T-1273)
Harris, Ian McKittrick 5650
(MIC.T-879)
Harris, Joseph John 2867 (MIC.T-464)
Harris, Justine Garwood 4186
(MIC.TC-5094)
Harris, Leonard Stephen 9334
(MIC.F.TC-46357)
Harris, Nancy Jane Adams 9008
(MIC.F.TC-51370)
Harris, Richard Colebrook 4840
(MIC.T-36)
Harris, Robert Clayton 4452
(MIC.F.TC-32950)
Harris, Ronald George 9237
(MIC.F.TC-51979)
Harris, Ronald Sutton 3718
Harris, S.A. 6050

Harris, Simon Richard 2240
(MIC.F.TC-52892)
Harris, Stephen John 7410
(MIC.F.T-1190)
Harrison, Allen Keith 4348
(MIC.F.TC-49862)
Harrison, Brenda Jane 11067
(MIC.F.TC-56614)
Harrison, Deborah Ann 9988
(MIC.F.TC-42138)
Harrison, J.M. 6051
Harrison, John Edward 6052
Harrison, John Keith 8139
(MIC.TC-14462)
Harrison, Linda Faye 1151
(MIC.F.TC-34833)
Harrison, Paul Garth 11953
(MIC.F.TC-22833)
Harrison, Richard Terrence 8005
(MIC.F.TC-24553)
Harrison, Robin Christopher John
Lawrence 2682 (MIC.F.TC-40173)
Harrison, Wilks Douglas 4786
Harrison, William George 4117
Harry, David Gareth 4667
(MIC.F.TC-60221)
Harshenin, Alex Peter 7778
(MIC.T-659)
Hart, Douglas John 1320
(MIC.F.TC-47836)
Hart, John Edward 7394
(MIC.TC-11078)
Hart, John Lawson 11016
(QH1 T68 fol.)
Hart, Josephine Frances Lavinia 11068
Hart, Margaret Elder 6893
Hart, William Charles 5033
(MIC.F.TC-36098)
Hartie, Douglas G. 2183
Hartigan, James Christopher 2365
(MIC.F.T-1062)
Hartleib, Carl John 3681
(MIC.F.TC-38740)
Hartley, Joseph R. 2281
Hartman, Lorne Micheal 9009
(MIC.F.TC-35724)
Hartmann, Bryan Douglas 3221
(MIC.F.TC-34361)
Hartmann, Sister Mary Andrew 7693
Hartney, Patrick Cooper 910
(MIC.F.TC-38741)
Hartwick, Earl Brian 10865
(MIC.F.TC-17182)
Hartwick, John Martin 1350
Harvey, Brian John 11069
(MIC.F.TC-42120)
Harvey, Fernand 2096
Harvey, Gilles 3854
Harvey, Jacqueline 2282
Harvey, Jean Lucien 1780
(MIC.F.TC-48353)
Harvey, John F. 5413
Harvey, Michael Dobbs 9689
(MIC.F.TC-48963)
Harvey, Ray F.E. 2842
Harvey, Roderick Wilson 8006
(MIC.F.TC-24049)
Harvie, Robert 6053
Harwood, John 10793
(MIC.F.TC-24555)
Hasan, Muhammad A. 2206
(MIC.F.TC-32655)
Hasenpusch, Burkhard 10288
Hashimoto, Tsutomu 5703
Hashish, Mahmoud Galal 4545
(MIC.TC-16419)
Haslam, Christopher R.S. 6666
(MIC.F.TC-20728)
Haslett, Earl Allan 1802
(MIC.TC-6313)
Hassard, James Harvey 4187
(MIC.F.T-885)
Hassen, Matthew Robert 3575
(MIC.F.TC-30699)
Hastedt, Glenn Peter 8839
(MIC.F.T-1033)
Hastings, Paul G. 2366
Hatch, Fred J. 8772
Hathaway, Warren Elkanah 2602
(MIC.F.TC-26775)

Hatheway, Glover Gillette 7438
(MIC.T-127)
Hathorn, Ramon 8203
Hathout, Salah Ahmed 4692
(MIC.F.TC-28701)
Hatler, David Francis 10591
Hatt, Fred Kenneth 495 (MIC.T-4937)
Hatter, James 10634
Hauck, Arthur Andrew 2405
(E183.8 C2 H29)
Haug, Elmer Joseph 3160
(MIC.F.TC-19712)
Haugh, John Richard 10743
Haughey, Margaret Lagan 2683
(MIC.F.TC-27660)
Haulman, Clyde Austin 1555
(MIC.T-642)
Hauser, Raymond E. 7428 (MIC.T-605)
Hautecoeur, Jean-Paul 765
(MIC.F.TC-18974)
Havard, Ronald James 3564
(MIC.T-747)
Havas, Magda 11839 (MIC.F.TC-50272)
Havens, J.M. 5020
Haviland, William E. 179
Hawes, David Bruce 10710
(MIC.F.TC-28702)
Hawes, Myrnal Leong 10717
(MIC.F.TC-25179)
Hawke, David Monro 3379
(MIC.F.TC-48964)
Hawkes, Norma Jeanne 3365
Hawkesworth, Earle Kitchner 2829
Hawkins, Freda Elizabeth 7650
(MIC.TC-15397)
Hawkins, Robert Garvin 1605
Hawkins, Terrance Clifford 4066
(MIC.F.TC-35224)
Hawkins, William Maxwell 6356
Hawksley, Oscar 10829
Hawley, Alexander Wilson Lewis 10612
(MIC.F.TC-41286)
Hawley, James P. 2340
(MIC.F.TC-33301)
Hawn, Elmer Joseph 316
Hawthorn, Wayne Rothan 11575
(MIC.TC-14954)
Hay, Alexander Edward 11924
(MIC.F.TC-56770)
Hay, J.E. 4974
Hay, Peter William 5064
Hay, Robert E. 6054
Hay, Thomas Hamilton 538
Hayashitani, Masao 4503
(MIC.F.TC-37280)
Haycock, Ronald Graham 7352
(MIC.F.TC-28241)
Hayduck, Allan Walter 9439
(MIC.F.TC-40423)
Hayes, Albert Orion 5748
Hayes, Bonnie Jean R. 1046
(MIC.F.TC-58972)
Hayes, Francis Joseph 1816
Hayes, Frank Randall 8821
(MIC.F.TC-50273)
Hayes, Helen Elizabeth 4311
(MIC.F.TC-47071)
Hayes, John Jesse 5749
Hayes, Terrance Timothy 4349
(MIC.F.T-1080)
Hayles, Launcellott Barrington 10514
Hayne, David M. 8204
Haynes, Gary Anthony 844
(MIC.F.T-1268)
Haynes, Nancy Jane 1023 (MIC.T-643)
Haynes, Robert Brian 6844
(MIC.F.TC-29625)
Hayter, Roger 1810 (MIC.T-549)
Haythorne, George V. 41
Hayward, Annette Marie 7742
Hayward, Percy Roy 2097
Haywood, Charles 464
(Z5984 U5 H3 fol.)
Head, Clifford Grant 4858
Headon, Christopher Fergus 9833
(MIC.F.TC-23089)
Heads, John 19 (MIC.F.TC-30043)
Hearn, Margaret Therese 4164
(MIC.F.TC-28243)
Heath, Herschel 7446
Heatley, Alistair John 7370

Heaton, Cherrill Paul 8079
Heaver, Trevor David 2254
Hebda, Richard Joseph 6525
(MIC.F.TC-32476)
Hébert, Daryll M. 10636
Hébert, Gérard J. 2139
Hébert, Maria 3910
Hébert, Pierre 8205
Hedden, William Jesse 5065
Hedges, Henry George 3009
(MIC.F.TC-25481)
Hedican, Edward James 539
(MIC.F.TC-39691)
Hedley, Harold Whitfield 4107
(MIC.F.TC-25482)
Hedley, Max Joseph 20
(MIC.F.TC-27663)
Hedley, Robert Lloyd 3454
(MIC.T-178)
Heemsberger, Donald Bastiaan 9440
(MIC.F.TC-48966)
Heeren, Harry Ewald 8530
Heffner, Charles Watson 10048
(MIC.F.TC-58345)
Heger, Ladislav 11688
Heick, Welf Henry 7363 (MIC.T-179)
Heidenreich, Conrad Edmund 4870
Heidenreich, Rosmarin Elfriede 8007
(MIC.F.TC-59885)
Heiken, Diane Ellen Bray 782
(MIC.F.TC-997)
Heilbronn, Marybeth 9690
(MIC.F.TC-29162)
Heimlich, Richard Allen 6055
Hein, Edward Bernard 7066
Hein, Frances Jessie 6357
(MIC.F.TC-46877)
Heinrich, Albert C. 605
Heintzman, Ralph Ripley 7458
(MIC.F.TC-33636)
Heisel, Brian E. 9441
(MIC.F.TC-52970)
Heisler, John Phalen 7385
(MIC.F.TC-19713)
Heit, Michael Joseph James 10460
Heitman, James Herbert 10640
(MIC.F.TC-17543)
Heizer, Robert F. 465
Helbig, James Alfred 11925
(MIC.F.TC-42646)
Heleine, François 7947 (MIC.F-002901)
Helenowski, Vincent 7601
Helgeland, Joseph Douglas 222
(MIC.F.TC-26777)
Helleiner, Frederick Maria 4693
(MIC.TC-12887)
Helleiner, Gerald Karl 2341 (MIC.T-37)
Heller, Monica Sara 7666
(MIC.F.T-1348)
Helling, Rudolf Anton 736
Helliwell, J.F. 1660
Hellkamp, David T. 9172
Hellman, John Leroy 1151
Hellyer, Alan McIntyre 4312
(MIC.F.TC-21836)
Helmer, James Walter 891
(MIC.F.TC-57136)
Helmers, Henrik Olaf 1843
(HD9725 H44)
Helmstaedt, Herwart 5613
(MIC.TC-3635)
Helwig, James Anthony 5750
Hendershot, William Hamilton 235
(MIC.TC-40642)
Henderson, Eric P. 5414
Henderson, Florence Irene 2973
(MIC.F.TC-32911)
Henderson, Gerald Gordon Lewis 5229
Henderson, James Fenwick 5503
Henderson, John Bennett 5842
Henderson, John R. 637 (MIC.T-483)
Henderson, John Russell 6056
Henderson, Jule Ann 9220
(MIC.F.TC-54552)
Henderson, Margaret Carole 8322
(MIC.T-661)
Henderson, Michael Andrew 10944
(MIC.F.TC-63094)
Henderson, Michael Dennis 8807
Henderson, Murray Scott 1405
Henderson, Nancy Elizabeth 10878

Henderson, Robert Brian 8411
Henderson, Susan Wright 6683
Hendrickson, David Calvin 7463
Hendry, Andrew Munn 3582
(MIC.F.TC-21837)
Hennessey, Carol A. 4436
(MIC.F.TC-59734)
Henninger, Polly Johnson 9442
(MIC.F.TC-55748)
Henriquez, Luis Nelson 4476
Henry, John David 10577
(MIC.F.TC-30526)
Henry, Kenneth Albin 10945
Henry, Ralph Marcian 2761
(MIC.TC-13404)
Henry, William Henry 12001
Henry, Zin A. 2207
Henshaw, David Charles 9010
(MIC.F.TC-37856)
Henslowe, Shirley Anne 3958
(MIC.F.TC-40644)
Hepburn, Donald Walter 3817
(MIC.F.TC-31981)
Hepner, Lee Alfred 971 (MIC.T-512)
Heppe, Paul Harry 8653 (MIC.T-79)
Herb, Gregor 5651
Herberg, Edward Norman 9995
(MIC.F.TC-47074)
Herbert, Daryll Marvin 10641
(MIC.F.TC-17184)
Herbert, Yvonne Marie 7823
Herbst, Diana Shawn 3818
(MIC.F.TC-49961)
Herendorf, Charles Edward, III 11790
Herlihy, H. Murray 2159
Herman, Albert 2990 (MIC.T-254)
Herman, Emil Edward 2160
Herman, Frederick Douglas Grant 4136
(MIC.TC-11583)
Herman, Gerald Francis 5021
Herman, Harry Vjekoslav 817
(MIC.F.TC-43654)
Herman, Mary W. 466
Herman, Thomas Bruce 10674
(MIC.F.TC-43435)
Heron, Robert Peter 3629
(MIC.TC-13407)
Heron, W. Craig 7215
(MIC.F.TC-53699)
Héroux, Raymonde 8296
(MIC.F-2M11.155.1)
Héroux, Simon 9895
Héroux, Yvon 6358 (MIC.F-025204)
Herrick, James William 647
Herring, Richard John 1456
(MIC.T-635)
Herring, Robert William 12002
(MIC.F.TC-31594)
Herwig, Aletha Marguerite 109
Herscovics, Nicolas 3333
(MIC.F-2M11.475.4)
Herscovitch, Arthur Gary 3222
(MIC.F.TC-26357)
Herscovitch, Joel A. 9011
(MIC.F.TC-53234)
Hersom, Naomi Louise 2843
(MIC.TC-4938)
Heslegrave, Ronald James 9238
(MIC.F.TC-53074)
Heslop, Louise Annette 2229
(MIC.F.TC-31595)
Hesse, Marta Gudrun 8206
(MIC.F.TC-21391)
Hesslein, Raymond Henry 6057
Hester, Gerald Leroy 4188 (MIC.T-38)
Hetherington, Eugene Douglas 11689
(MIC.F.TC-28704)
Hetherington, Robert William 1626
Hett, Joan Margaret 11746
Hettinger, Loren Robert 11435
(MIC.F.TC-26778)
Hewchuk, Eugene William 9239
(MIC.F.TC-38251)
Hewes, Gordon W. 382
Hewetson, Henry W. 2306
Hewings, John Meredith 4694
(MIC.F.TC-33091)
Hewins, Roger Herbert 6058
(MIC.F-11586)
Hewitson, Malcolm Thomas 4453
(MIC.F.TC-2779)

Hewitt, Donald F. 6059
Hewitt, Jean Dorothy 2991
  (MIC.F.TC-53075)
Heyl, George R. 5751
Heywood, William Walter 5504
Hiatt, Gina Jaccarino 9240
Hickman, George Augustus 4313
  (MIC.F.TC-59735)
Hickox, Charles Frederick., Jr. 5652
Hicks, Douglas Leonard 2742
  (MIC.T-467)
Hicks, Harold Smith 5415
Hicock, Stephen Robert 5230
  (MIC.F.TC-48355)
Hidi, Suzanne Erica 3223
  (MIC.F.TC-30341)
Higgins, Christopher Alan 1152
  (MIC.F.TC-49793)
Higgins, Donald J.H. 8725
  (MIC.TC-16532)
Higgins, John Michael 2603
Higgins, Michael Dennis 6359
  (MIC.F.TC-50547)
Higgins, Neville Charles 5752
  (MIC.F.TC-46746)
High, Norman Hervey 2496
Highland, Jeffrey Ray 2161
  (MIC.F.T-938)
Hilborn, Ray William 10711
  (MIC.F.TC-22104)
Hildebrand, Alexander Anderson 11576
Hildebrand, Robert Shepard 5843
Hildyard, Angela 3224
  (MIC.F.TC-30342)
Hill, Daniel Grafton 744
  (MIC.F.TC-17270)
Hill, David Fred 7528
Hill, Donald 7695 (MIC.F.TC-44064)
Hill, Edmund Russell 1321
Hill, Frederick Irvin 4946
  (MIC.F.TC-38742)
Hill, Gideon Dee, Jr. 11633
Hill, John David 5844
  (MIC.F.TC-48356)
Hill, John Richard 11314
  (MIC.F.TC-31795)
Hill Rix, Marion Elizabeth Ann 2659
  (MIC.F.TC-43710)
Hill, Mary Bulmer Reid 9803
  (MIC.T-321)
Hill, Philip R. 5653 (MIC.F.TC-53701)
Hill, Robert Andrew 7379
  (MIC.TC-7334)
Hiller, Harry Herbert 8663
Hiller, James Kelsey 7167 (MIC.T-913)
Hillier, Robert Melville 9948
Hillmer, George Norman 8813
Hills, Leonard Vincent 5231
Hillyard, Alexander Leonard 3819
  (MIC.F.TC-43439)
Hilts, Joseph Alfred 7350
  (MIC.F.TC-21437)
Hilts, Stewart Garvie 4930
Himelfarb, Alexander 10202
  (MIC.F.TC-32913)
Himes, Mavis Carole 3094
  (MIC.F.TC-36690)
Himes, Mel 8895 (MIC.F.TC-39692)
Himmelman, John Henry 11106
Hindle, Colin James 1713
  (MIC.F.TC-27878)
Hindle, George 2450
Hindmarch, Brian 9296
  (MIC.F.TC-31998)
Hinton, Dallas Edward 999
  (MIC.F.TC-59238)
Hinz, Leo George 7848
Hirabayashi, Gordon K. 759
  (MIC.F.TC-33622)
Hiscott, Richard Nicholas 6360
  (MIC.F.TC-36530)
Hitchin, David Edward 2389
  (MIC.T-130)
Hitchman, Gladys Symons 3682
  (MIC.F.TC-26639)
Hitsman, J. Mackay 7464
Hixon, Sumner Best 6060
Hjartarson, Paul Ivar 8100
Hjortenberg, Erik 6610
Hlasny, Robert G. 9297
  (MIC.F.TC-53308)

Hoadley, John William 5232
Hoag, Peter Lockrie 606
  (MIC.F.T-1139)
Hoag, Roland Boyden, Jr. 6361
  (MIC.F.TC-24340)
Hobbs, Edward Desmond 3312
  (MIC.F.TC-26781)
Hobbs, Gordon A. 11446
Hobbs, J. Brian 1172
Hoch, Peter Coonan 11381
Hochbaum, George Sutton 10767
  (MIC.F.TC-51697)
Hochester, Marilyn Goulden 9538
  (MIC.F.TC-58606)
Hochheimer, Laura 3855 (MIC.T-519)
Hochstein, Alan Peter 6778
  (MIC.F.TC-42941)
Hockin, Margaret L. 795
Hockin, Thomas Alexander 8531
Hocq, Michel 6362
Hodapp, Timothy Victor 1153
  (MIC.F.TC-30343)
Hodder, Robert William 6061
Hodges, David Julian 835
Hodges, Dorothy Jacobsen 2012
Hodges, Jerry Whitfield 9796
Hodges, Lance Thomas 6062
Hodgins, Bruce Willard 7324
  (MIC.T-122)
Hodgins, Cyril D. 1751
  (MIC.F.TC-24584)
Hodgins, Donald Ormond 11926
  (MIC.F.TC-22106)
Hodgins, Larry Edwin 4744
  (MIC.TC-7336)
Hodgins, Thomas Arnold 4395
  (MIC.T-354)
Hodgkins, Gael Atherton 607
Hodgkinson, Christopher Edward 2844
  (MIC.TC-3713)
Hodgson, Christopher John 6363
  (MIC.TC-3960)
Hodgson, Ernest Daniel 2440
Hodgson, J.M.D. 4648
Hodson, Jesse Moroni 11634
Hodgson, John Humphrey 6588
Hodgson, Michael John 2255
  (MIC.F.TC-17272)
Hodgson, Robert David 4884
Hodgson, William Robert 2868
Hodkin, Barbara 9539
  (MIC.F.TC-42824)
Hody, Maud Hazel 2465
  (MIC.F.TC-31371)
Hoe, Ban Seng 752 (MIC.T-781)
Hoebel, Michael Francis 11822
  (MIC.F.TC-62650)
Hoefer, Raymond Henry 11635
Hoefs, Manfred Ernest Gustav 10642
  (MIC.F.TC-28707)
Hoen, Ernst Leon 5845
Hoen, Robert Randolph 2962
  (MIC.F.TC-25183)
Hoeppner, Jo-Ann Bentley 3871
  (MIC.TC-16580)
Hoestlandt-Noël, Christine 9443
  (MIC.F-2M11.607.1)
Hoffer, Jerry Martin 5233
Hofferd, George William 3455
  (OH305.2C3 H64)
Hoffman, Arlene Rochelle 10134
  (MIC.F.TC-21287)
Hoffman, Bernard Gilbert 523
Hoffman, Douglas Weir 208
  (MIC.TC-15734)
Hoffman, Eric Lawrence 6063
  (MIC.F.TC-47075)
Hoffman, Paul F. 5857
Hoffman, Stanley Joel 5234
  (MIC.F.TC-34842)
Hoffmann, Hans 509
Hoffmeister, Donald Frederick 10675
Hoffs, Gordon A. 11436
Hogan, Howard R. 6364
Hogan, James Bennett 8456
Hogan, Sister Mary Ignatia 8207
Hogan, Timothy 3959
Hogg, William Alfred 5089
Hogue, Steve Monroe 11152
Hoiles, Randolph Gerald 6064
Holden, Madronna 674 (MIC.T-718)

Holden, Ronald Robert 9097
  (MIC.F.TC-54098)
Holdsworth, Deryck William 4922
  (MIC.F.TC-56615)
Holladay, James 1429
Holland, R.E. 8822
Holland, Stuart Sawden 5235
Hollbach, Arthur Reiner 1883
Hollick-Kenyon, Timothy Hugh 3583
  (MIC.F.T-1045)
Hollington, Kenneth Charles 3576
Hollibaugh, James T. 11849
  (MIC.F.TC-36104)
Hollister, Lincoln Steffens 5236
Holm, Ernest Harold Sandstedt 8675
  (MIC.F.T-1068)
Holman, Robert Alan 11954
  (MIC.F.TC-44251)
Holman, Roy Paul 10407
Holmberg, Robert George 11214
  (MIC.F.TC-41148)
Holmes, Alfred 3960
Holmes, Barbara Joyce 4226
Holmes, Christopher Patrick 9130
  (MIC.F.TC-36216)
Holmes, James M. 2013
Holmes, Richard Arthur 1661
Holmes, Stanley W. 6365
Holmes, Terence C. 6065
Holroyd, Edmond William, III 5006
Holstein, A. 6066
Holtby, Leslie Blair 11861
  (MIC.F.TC-53079)
Holtzblatt, Karen Asher 9691
  (MIC.F.TC-58348)
Holz, Ronald Walker 956
Home, Alice Marian 10203
  (MIC.F.TC-38744)
Homel, Gene Howard 2551
  (MIC.F.TC-40911)
Honda, Steven Takao 1627
  (MIC.F.T-1164)
Hone, David W. 12003
Honigmann, John Joseph 704
Hood, Peter Jonathan 6067
Honorez, Jean-Marie 9623
Hooper, K. 6516
Hope, Ernest Charles 4800
Hope, Spencer Albert Charles 4695
  (MIC.F.TC-33554)
Hopkins, David William Richard 4377
  (MIC.F.TC-51015)
Hopkins, John Charles 5416
  (MIC.TC-11843)
Hopkins, William Stephen, Jr. 5237
  (MIC.T-757)
Hopkirk, Gerald A. 2684
  (MIC.F.TC-34367)
Hoque, Mozzamel 190
  (MIC.F.TC-49964)
Horan, James Francis 8786
  (MIC.T-429)
Hore, Terence 3025
Horejsi, Brian Louis 10643
  (MIC.F.TC-30531)
Hormisdas, Frère 11765
Horn, David Russell 5847
Horn, Michael Steven Daniel 7148
  (MIC.F.TC-21392)
Horne, Edgar Byron 3428
Horne, Edward P.W. 11955
  (MIC.F.TC-44252)
Horne, Gilbert Richard 1788
Horne, Gregory Stuart 5753
Horne, John MacGregor 1628
  (MIC.F.TC-37345)
Hornick, Joseph Phillip 10124
  (MIC.F.TC-27048)
Hornosty, Jennie Mary 9771
  (MIC.F.TC-40998)
Hornsey, Richard Fraser 8340
  (MIC.F.TC-24057)
Horovatin, Joseph Daniel 2839
Horowitz, Gad 2112 (JL197 N4 H6)
Horscroft, Frank D. 6366
Horsley, Frederick Richard 9103
  (MIC.F.TC-18541)
Horsman, Reginald 7067 (F5073.2H6)
Horth, Raynald 3084
  (MIC.F-2M11.388.7)

Horton, Donald James 7287
(MIC.F.TC-24343)
Horvath, Adam O. 9298
(MIC.F.TC-55037)
Horvath, Peter 9012 (MIC.F.TC-44180)
Horwich, Herbert R. 9996
Horwood, Hereward C. 5505
Hosek, James Charles 9601
(MIC.TC-8621)
Hossé, Hans August 10491
Hostettler, Pierre 1850
Hotson, John Hargrove 1173
Hottel-Burkhart, Nancy Greene 7715
Houde, Denis Bernard 9131
(MIC.F-2M11.475.2)
Hougham, George Millard 8620
(MIC.T-39)
Houghton, Diane 986
Houldin, Barbara Klein 3872
(MIC.F.TC-47077)
Houle, Jocelyne 8916
Houlihan, Patrick Thomas 383
(MIC.T-468)
Houndjahoué, Michel 8879
(MIC.F.TC-59401)
Hourany, Lawrence J. 8917
(MIC.F.TC-28246)
Hourston, Alan Steward 10946
House, Anthony B. 7743
House, John Douglas 10135
(MIC.F.TC-18247)
House, John Hamilton 2845
House, William James 1556
Housego, Ian Edward 2963
Houston, Susan Elizabeth 10289
(MIC.F.TC-27954)
Hovanec, Margret 6716
(MIC.F.TC-50276)
Hover, Gerald Robert 9013
Howard, Benjamin Willis 8140
(MIC.T-312)
Howard, David Lee 10515
Howard, Helen Arlene 7981
Howard, James W. 4108
Howard, Jane Mary 1789
(HD1694 A254 H6)
Howard, Louis Wayne 10260
(MIC.F.TC-21842)
Howard, Theresa C. 3758
(MIC.F.TC-58319)
Howard, Waldorf V. 5614
Howe, Mark LeBas 9540
(MIC.F.TC-54100)
Howe, Robert Crombie 6564
Howe, Ruth J. 8208
Howell, Benita Jankle 467
Howell, Benjamin Franklin 5754
Howell, Colin Desmond 7565
(MIC.T-700)
Howell, David Francis 9799
(MIC.F.TC-44753)
Howell, Gordon P. 957
Howell, John E. 5704
Howells, William C. 5563
Howes, Richard John 9132
(MIC.F.TC-54474)
Howitt, Rhoderick P.E. 9692
(MIC.F.TC-29166)
Howley, Thomas Patrick 4227
(MIC.F.TC-42229)
Howsam, Robert Basil 2905
Hoy, C.H. 2410
Hoy, Elizabeth Ann 3820
(MIC.TC-4114)
Hoy, Helen Elizabeth 8057
(MIC.F.TC-36695)
Hoy, Trygvie 5238 (MIC.F.TC-20249)
Hrestak, Hrvoje Joseph 1000
Hriskevich, Michael Edward 6068
Hromyk, William John 3411
(MIC.T-469)
Hritzuk, John 3225
Hruby, Jiri G. 7591
Hsiao, Stephen I.-Chao 11471
(MIC.TC-10685)
Hsu, Mao-Yang 6069
Huang, Henry Chung-Chi 3429
(MIC.F.TC-49303)
Huard, Michel 958
Hubbard, James Alan 10794

Hubbard, Robert Hamilton 946
Huberman, John 10325 (MIC.TC-2368)
Hubert, Claude M. 6367
Hudak, Janos 11734
Hudon, Christianne 11805
Hudon, Edward Gérard 7898
(MIC.F.TC-35415)
Hudon, Jean-Guy 8308
(MIC.F.TC-60701)
Hudson, Jean-Paul 8267
(MIC.F.TC-44038)
Hudon, Raymond Paul Joseph 1383
(MIC.F.TC-58980)
Hudson, Heather Elizabeth 1154
(MIC.T-665)
Hudson, Herschel C. 468
Hudson, James Edward 11200
(MIC.F.TC-31991)
Hudson, Robert John 6864
(MIC.TC-8305)
Hudson, Samuel C. 68
Hudson, William Anderson 6865
Huel, Raymond Joseph Armand 7246
(MIC.F.TC-24060)
Huff, Harry Bruce 166 (MIC.T-222)
Hufferd, James 4845
Hughes, George Muggah 5417
Hughes, John E. 5239
Hughes, Margaret Ann 3961
(MIC.F.TC-36696)
Hughes, Maxfield Jeffrey 3821
(MIC.F.TC-21844)
Hughes, Norah L. 9861
Hughes, Owen Lloyd 6070
Hughes, Richard D. 5418
Hughes, Terrance Ryan 8115
(MIC.F.TC-50460)
Huhn, Frank Jones 6071
(MIC.F.TC-56990)
Huiner, Harvey Don 974
Hulchanski, John David 10492
(MIC.F.TC-53082)
Hulett, Gary K. 352
Hull, Alexander, Jr. 7744
Hull, Dale Lester 11690
(MIC.F.TC-31798)
Hull, William Henry Miller 1131
Hulmes, Frederick George 8687
(MIC.F-6715)
Hulse, Charles Allen 877
Hum, Andrew 4165 (MIC.F.TC-17555)
Hum, Jennifer Roslyn 11112
Hume, George Sherwood 6072
Hume, Lawrence Pierson Wilson 11382
(MIC.F.TC-48366)
Hume, William Elliot 4454
(LB1731 H85)
Hummelen, Remmelt Carel
Reinder 469 (E7805 H855 fol.)
Humphrey, Gary Keith 9335
(MIC.F.TC-49967)
Humphreys, Carolyn Ann 8918
(MIC.F.TC-43658)
Humphreys, Edward Harold 4263
Humphries, Charles Walter 7388
(MIC.TC-10806)
Hundert, Joel Philip 3226
(MIC.F.TC-28247)
Hundleby, Sigrid Anne 3227
(MIC.F.TC34370)
Hung, Akey Chang-Fu 1153
Hung, David Wai-Kwong 3922
(MIC.F.TC-24571)
Hungr, Oldrich 4477 (MIC.F.TC-53943)
Hunkins, Kenneth Leland 6672
Hunsberger, Bruce Elgin 9959
(MIC.F.TC-17329)
Hunt, Edmund Arthur 10408
(MIC.F.TC-28714)
Hunt, George T. 7429
Hunt, Graham Hugh 5240
Hunt, John W. 12004
Hunt, Larry Ralph 6799 (MIC.T-541)
Hunt, Richard Irving, Jr. 7034
Hunt, Stanley Jack 10409
Hunt, Valerye Agnes 9693
(MIC.F.TC-28715)
Hunt, Wayne Austin 8492
(MIC.F.TC-55723)
Hunte, Keith Donnerson 2529
Hunter, Hugh E. 5506

Hunter, James Alexander M. 6654
(MIC.TC-89917)
Hunter, James Hopkins 11636
Hunter, James Jamison, Jr. 2716
Hunter, John Gerald 11044
(MIC.TC-3149)
Hunter, Michael Arthur 9336
(MIC.F.TC-51021)
Huntington, Hope Davies 5705
(MIC.F.T-1081)
Huntley, Mark Edward 11909
(MIC.F.TC-48200)
Huot, Janine 4410 (MIC.F-2M11.483.3)
Hurlbert, Earl Leroy 2660
(MIC.F.TC-17559)
Hurlich, Marshall Gerald 415
(MIC.T-691)
Hurst, Paul Eugene 3916
(MIC.F.TC-43659)
Hurst, Richard William 5706
Hurwitz, Leon Henry 8441
Husain, Bilal R. 6368
Husain, Syed Shahid 11577
Husby, Philip James 2661
(MIC.TC-3388)
Hussain, Matlub 7656
(MIC.F.TC-39697)
Hussell, David John Trevis 10744
Hussey, Lyman Andrew, Jr. 7558
Hutcheon, Ian E. 5507
(MIC.F.TC-32160)
Hutcheson, Austin E. 7174
Hutchinson, Aleck 302
Hutchinson, Robert D. 5654
Hutchison, Murray Noel 6073
(MIC.F.TC-38747)
Hutson, R. Leighton 3059
Hutton, Harry K. 4396 (MIC.F.T-1300)
Hutton, Miriam Freda 3740
(MIC.F.TC-36698)
Huxley, Christopher Victor 2113
(MIC.F.TC-47080)
Hwang, Chung-Yung 4575
(MIC.F.TC-64374)
Hyatt, Albert Mark John 7411
(MIC.T-1)
Hyatt, Kim Dennis 10947
(MIC.F.TC-51702)
Hyde, Duncan Clark 1514
Hyde, Martin James 1873
Hyde, Naida Denise Dyer 9299
(MIC.F.TC-29177)
Hyde, Richard Stuart 6074
(MIC.F.TC-40359)
Hyde, William Paul 2662
(MIC.F.TC-34846)
Hylander, William Leroy 608
Hyman, Charles 3610 (MIC.TC-13419)
Hyman, Roger Leslie 8153
(MIC.F.TC-35226)
Hymmen, Phyllis Alice 3500
(MIC.F.TC-30344)
Hyndman, Donald William 5241
Hyndman, Richard McCrae 1790
(HF5549.15 T65 fol.)
Hynes, Cecil Vernon 2014

I

Ibele, Oscar H., Jr. 4887
Ichikawa, Hiroo 4901 (MIC.F.TC-5548)
Idle, Dunning 6962
Iga, Masaaki 51 (MIC.TC-6807)
Igartua, José Eduardo 1224
Ignatius, Heikki Gustaf 6075
Igwe, Okay Cyril 70
(MIC.F.TC-32484)
Iida-Miranda, Maria-Lia 9694
Ijaz, Mian Ahmed 3085
(MIC.F.TC-50277)
Ijioma, Chibueze Ibegbu 71
(MIC.F.TC-57989)
Ilori, Joseph Abiodun 8809
Ilsley, Lucretia Little 8823
Imbault, Joseph Paul E. 6076

Imshaug, Henry Andrew 11383
Indra, Doreen Marie 384
　(MIC.F.TC-44912)
Infante-Rivard, Claire 6869
　(MIC.F.T-60911)
Ingalls, Glen Ralph 10290
Ingalls, Karen Ellen 4264
　(MIC.F.T-1011)
Ingerson, Fred E. 5755
Ingham, Walter Norman 6077
Ingle, Robert Alexander 3044
　(MIC.F.TC-16996)
Ingledew, William Albert 2015
　(MIC.F.TC-24572)
Inglis, Gordon Bahan 470
　(MIC.TC-8307)
Ingraham, Diane Verna 11927
　(MIC.F.TC-51704)
Ingraham, Patricia
　Wallace 10112, 8510
Ingram, Earl Glynn 7083 (MIC.T-683)
Ingram, Ernest John 4350
Inkster, Don Robert 5038
　(MIC.F.TC-38256)
Inman, Marianne Elizabeth Pizak 7667
Inman, Mark K. 1430
Innes, Morris J.S. 6589
Innes, Robert John 3604
　(MIC.F.TC-47205)
Innis, Harold Adams 2307
　(HE2810 C2 IS)
Ion, A.H. 9780
Ionescu, Margaret Evelyn 11620
Iqbal, Françoise 8251 (MIC.TC-13230)
Irby, Charles Claude 82
　(MIC.F.TC-41151)
Ireland, Robert John 7716
　(MIC.F.TC-41000)
Irénée-Marie, Frère 11602
Irimoto, Tokashi 562 (MIC.F.TC-44914)
Irish, Ernest J.W. 5419
Irvine, Florence Gladys 3110
　(MIC.TC-14860)
Irvine, Ian Joseph 1174
　(MIC.F.TC-46032)
Irvine, James William 3228
　(MIC.TC-11139)
Irvine, Lorna Marie 8058
　(MIC.F.T-921)
Irvine, Rendel Byron 353
　(MIC.F.TC-36924)
Irvine, William Peter 8576
Irving, Allan 10072 (MIC.F.TC-59802)
Irving, Howard T. 5253
Irving, Howard Harris 10049
　(MIC.TC-8521)
Irving, R.G. 7344
Irwin, Arthur B. 5242
Irwin, Henry Thomas Johnson 703
Irwin, Leonard B. 2308 (HE2807 I78)
Isaacs, Paul 9014 (MIC.F.TC-58858)
Isaacman, Daniel 10434
Isabelle, Laurent A. 3735
Isbester, Alexander Fraser 2129
Ishaque, Muhammad 10516
　(MIC.TC-3294)
Isherwood, Dana Joan 5848
Iskander, Fadel Fawzi 4504
Iskander, Wasby Boulos 4814
　(MIC.T-630)
Islam, Muhammed Nurul 1827
　(MIC.TC-15880)
Islam, Nurul 1531
Islam, Tariq Saiful 21
　(MIC.F.TC-56826)
Issalys, P.F. 7875
Isyumov, Nicholas 4975 (MIC.TC-8998)
Italiano, Joseph Angelo 1431
　(MIC.F.TC-50146)
Itwaru, Arnold Harrichand 8008
　(MIC.F.TC-58747)
Iutcovich, Mark 762
Iyengar, V.K. Sundararaja 11862
Ivers, William Dargan 11910
Ives, Edward Dawson 981 (MIC.T-40)
Ives, Sumner W. 3229

J

Jaakson, Reiner 10461 (MIC.TC-14392)
Jack, Lawrence B. 1499
Jackel, Susan Elizabeth 8009
　(MIC.F.TC-34374)
Jackes, Mary Katheryn 911
　(MIC.F.TC-36699)
Jackman, Harold William 4546
　(MIC.F.TC-17273)
Jackman, Sydney W. 7319
　(F5074.79 H43 J32 fol.)
Jackson, Charles Ian 6639
Jackson, Edgar Lionel 4612
　(MIC.F.TC-27884)
Jackson, Edward Thomas 4027
Jackson, Garth Digby 5707
Jackson, John David 10237
　(MIC.T-185)
Jackson, John James 10326
　(MIC.F.TC-24064)
Jackson, Lionel Eric 5420
Jackson, Michael Wesley 8442
　(MIC.F.TC-29497)
Jackson, Ray W. 12005
Jackson, Richard Ervin 11984
　(MIC.F.TC-42367)
Jackson, Roger Lee 1132 (MIC.T-155)
Jackson, Stewart Albert 5849
　(MIC.TC-8086)
Jackson, Suzanne Fraser 6684
　(MIC.F.TC-53562)
Jackson, William A.D. 4871
Jackson-Whaley, Iris Patricia 9173
　(MIC.F.TC-45986)
Jacob, Jean-Noel 4219
Jacobi, Robert Douglas 5756
Jacobs, John Douglas 5022
Jacobs, Larry Wallace 10378
　(MIC.F.TC-48979)
Jacoby, Russell Stephen 6369
　(MIC.TC-2464)
Jacques, Richard Leo, Jr. 11154
Jaebker, Orville John 7286
　(MIC.T-128)
Jaeger, Martin Jerome 22
Jaenen, Cornelius John 9915
Jaffe, Harold 8076
Jaffe, Peter George 9133
　(MIC.F.TC-20511)
Jahoda, William J. 11059
Jain, Geneviève Laloux 2497
Jain, Hem Chand 1817
Jain, Nirmal 7973
Jakes, Harold Edward 2723
Jamal, Muhammad 2073
　(MIC.F.TC-29861)
Jamart, Bruno M. 11928
Jambor, John Leslie 6078
James, Clifford Rodney 1110
　(MIC.T-186)
James, David Barker 1111
　(MIC.F.T-887)
James, Dorothy Mae Digdon 3962
　(MIC.F.TC-40434)
James, E.O. 471
James, Herman Delano 6800
　(MIC.F.TC-25890)
James, Howard T. 5243
James, Hugh Mackenzie 1205
James, Robert W. 2331 (HC115 J35)
James, Ross David 10745
　(MIC.TC-16636)
James, William 6079
James, William Fleming 6370
Jameson, Elmer 723, 9490
Jamieson, E.R. 5850
Jamieson, Glen Stewart 11215
　(MIC.F.TC-17189)
Jamieson, Margaret S. 3230
　(MIC.F.TC-56827)
Jamieson, Rebecca Anne 5757
　(MIC.F.TC-51125)
Jampolsky, Murray 3774
　(MIC.TC-13422)
Janes, Ethel Mary 3963
Janes, Robert Roy 892
　(MIC.F.TC-28522)

Jansen, Janni Margaretha 1867
　(MIC.F.T-1123)
Jansen, Lyn Ellen 9541
　(MIC.F.TC-48544)
Jansen, William Hugh, II 609
Janzen, Donald Edward 878
Janzen, Eileen Rose 8457
　(MIC.F.T-1182)
Janzen, Henry Lawrence 3683
　(MIC.TC-10093)
Janzen, William 8598
Japp, Robert 2436
Jarrett, John W. 3356
Jarvenpa, Robert Warren 563
Jarvis, Elisabeth Orysia 3964
　(MIC.F.TC-17274)
Jarvis, Eric James 7226
　(MIC.F.TC-48368)
Jarvis, Robert Lee 10795
Jarzen, David MacArthur 5421
　(MIC.F.TC-20569)
Jayasinghe, Nimal Ranjith 5758
　(MIC.F.TC-51126)
Jean, Marguerite 9781
　(BX4220 C2 J42)
Jean, Yves 11031
Jeffares, David 2604
　(MIC.F.TC-17563)
Jeffery, William Gordon 6371
Jeffrey, Walter William 11658
Jeffries, Dean Stuart 6080
　(MIC.F.TC-29641)
Jeglum, John Karl 11621
Jenkins, Alexander William 6779
　(MIC.F.TC-31604)
Jenkins, Allan Laurence 4547
　(MIC.F.TC-42232)
Jenkins, Glenn P. 1533
Jenkins, Harry P.B. 2241
Jenkins, William Angus 4635
Jenks, Leland Hamilton 1244
　(HG186 G7 J4)
Jenness, John L. 4649
Jenness, Stuart E. 5759
Jennings, Daniel Edward 3653
　(MIC.T-156)
Jennings, David Stevane 6081
Jennings, John Nelson 7448
　(MIC.F.TC-42233)
Jensen, Jon Michael 2332 (MIC.T-701)
Jensen, Kenneth Delane 610
　(MIC.T-764)
Jensen, Larry Sigfred 6082
　(MIC.F.TC-49169)
Jensen, Peter Kenneth 3045
　(MIC.F.TC-40435)
Jensen, Peter Michael 849
Jenson, Jane 8621
Jerkic, Sonja Maria 641
　(MIC.F.TC-35228)
Jeroski, Sharon Frances 3393
　(MIC.F.TC-59174)
Jessop, David 1274 (MIC.F.TC-20173)
Jessup, Barton Allen 9015
　(MIC.F.TC-36282)
Jestin, Warren James 1275
　(MIC.F.TC-35229)
Jetté, René 10321 (MIC.F-2M11.561.1)
Jevne, Ronna Fay 4143
　(MIC.F.TC-42525)
Jewell, Cedric Beresford 3995
Jewett, Pauline M. 8560
Jewinski, Edwin 8164
Jida-Miranda, Maria-Lia 815
Joardar, Souro Dyuti 4923
　(MIC.F.TC-34854)
Jobes, Frank Watkins 10912
Jobin, Anthony J. 8209
Jobling, Ian Frank 10341
　(GV585 J62 fol.)
Jobson, Keith Bertram 2432
Jockel, Joseph Thomas 8840
　(MIC.F.T-986)
Johannson, Peter Roff 7549
　(MIC.F.T-993)
Johns, David Paul 10205
　(MIC.F.TC-43443)
Johns, Harold Percival 4189
Johnson, A.T.W. 8521
Johnson, Alan Anthony 1939
　(MIC.F.TC-44497)

Johnson, Alan Packard 1406
Johnson, Albert Wesley 8769
Johnson, Amanda 1225
Johnson, Andrew Frank 1646
Johnson, Arthur L. 2283
Johnson, Bruce Kilgour 4370
  (MIC.TC-9603)
Johnson, Byron Oliver Simpson 1677
  (MIC.T-472)
Johnson, C.G. 8059
Johnson, Caswell Lewington 7657
Johnson, Daniel 1714
Johnson, Daniel Lloyd 320
Johnson, Dennis Brian 10083
  (MIC.TC-13425)
Johnson, Edward Arnold 11540
  (MIC.F.TC-36926)
Johnson, Francis Henry 3105
  (MIC.F.TC-31372)
Johnson, Gilbert Gerald 2208
  (MIC.T-870)
Johnson, Helgi 6083
Johnson, Hugh N. 6372
Johnson, Ivan Charles 1573
Johnson, James Donald 8606
  (MIC.T-553)
Johnson, James Francis 8341
  (MIC.F.TC-51372)
Johnson, Janice Marie 9542
  (MIC.F.TC-56562)
Johnson, John P. 4645
Johnson, Murray Gordon 11797
  (MIC.TC-8524)
Johnson, Neil Alexander 2059
  (MIC.F.T-1025)
Johnson, Norman Gary 989
  (ML410 W668 J68 fol.)
Johnson, Olive Skene 9192
  (MIC.F.TC-51710)
Johnson, Peter Richard 4144
  (MIC.F.TC-44586)
Johnson, Ronald Clifford Arthur 4846
  (MIC.T-534)
Johnson, Ronald Dwight 5244
  (MIC.F.TC-22127)
Johnson, Ross Alfred 8666
  (MIC.F.TC-25889)
Johnson, Ross Eugene 354
Johnson, Stanley C. 7613
Johnson, Stephen Hans 6621
Johnson, Stephen Marshall 7084
  (MIC.F.TC-37802)
Johnson, Stephen Robert 10746
  (MIC.TC-11568)
Johnson, Victor 11155
Johnson, Walter Henry 10879
Johnson, Warren Bertran 7454
Johnson, Wendel John 10578
Johnston C. Celeste Smith 3026
  (MIC.F.TC-47361)
Johnston, Charles Edward 10984
  (MIC.TC-3639)
Johnston, Derek Samuel 7876
  (MIC.F.TC-58363)
Johnston, Edwin Frederick 4210
  (MIC.F.TC-23102)
Johnston, Elizabeth MacLeod 6801
Johnston, James Wilson 1715
Johnston, Janice Louise 6750
  (MIC.F.TC-59738)
Johnston, John A. 9882
Johnston, Kevin James 1577
Johnston, Laura Margaret 6084
  (MIC.F.TC-39500)
Johnston, Marion Campbell 2643
Johnston, Nancy Mary Elizabeth 3027
  (MIC.TC-6832)
Johnston, Richard Barnett 912
  (MIC.T-968)
Johnston, Richard Edward 8553
  (JF751 J65)
Johnston, Richard Gregory
  Chalmers 8622
Johnston, Robert Alexander 1618
  (MIC.T-131)
Johnston, Victor Kenneth 8824
Johnston, William Atchison 10026
  (MIC.F.TC-53497)
Johnston, William G. 6085
Johnstone, Paul Anthony 2424

Johnstone, Wayne David 11659
  (MIC.TC-15127)
Joia, Balbir Singh 11238
  (MIC.F.TC-54403)
Jolicoeur, Catherine 8323 (PS8223 J6)
Jolliffe, Fred T. 5851
Jolly, Nora Patricia 8060 (MIC.T-495)
Jolly, Robert William 23
Jomphe, Gerald E. 2570
Jonah, Brian Austin 9695
  (MIC.F.TC-48369)
Jonason, Jonas Christian 2685
Jonasson, Jonas A. 7375
Jones, Ann-Kailani 8010
  (MIC.F.TC-53951)
Jones, Alexander Gordon 5255
Jones, Anne Marie 9111
  (MIC.F.TC-53237)
Jones, Barry Cyril 10386
  (MIC.F.TC-34385)
Jones, Brian C. 5852 (MIC.F.TC-22403)
Jones, Clarence Fielden 1206
Jones, C.M. 5760
Jones, David Charles 2451
  (MIC.F.TC-37639)
Jones, Edward Austin 4228
Jones, Eldon Lewis 7297
Jones, Elwood Hugh 7085
  (MIC.TC-10206)
Jones, Frank Edward 8773
Jones, Frederick 9896
Jones, Frissell Wagner 3086 (MIC.T-41)
Jones, Islwyn Wyn 5422
Jones, Joan Megan 715 (MIC.T-702)
Jones, John Alfred 8546
Jones, Jonathan Wyn 5246
  (MIC.TC-13883)
Jones, Kevin George 10342
  (MIC.TC-6218)
Jones, M.A. 7631
Jones, Michael Baxter 5247
Jones, Pauline Alice 3060
  (MIC.TC-4943)
Jones, Peter Barrett 5248
Jones, Richard Alan 9818
  (PN4920 A38 J65)
Jones, Robert Alan 5615
Jones, Robert J. 3231 (MIC.TC-16583)
Jones, Robert L. 110
Jones, Rogers 303 (MIC.TC-4735)
Jones, Russell H.B. 5249
Jones, Stephen, B. 4727
Jones, Vernon James 1086
  (MIC.F.TC-25894)
Jones, William 7787
Jones, William Alfred 6086
Jonescu, Margaret Evelyn Chun 11628
Jonish, James Edward 1894
Jooste, René F. 6373
Jordan, Douglas Frederick 851
Jordan, Richard Heath 721
  (MIC.T-841)
Jory, Lisle Thomas 5853
Josaitis, Marvin 3521
Joscelyn, Lela Ames 9696
  (MIC.F.TC-39355)
Joschko, Michael 3783
José, Teresito Adolfo 9337
  (MIC.F.TC-48987)
Josefowitz, Nina 9444
  (MIC.F.TC-50282)
Joseph, Alun Edward 4902
  (MIC.F.TC-29646)
Joseph, Jacob R. 4548 (MIC.TC-10918)
Josephson, Mundi Irvine 3394
  (MIC.F.TC-24071)
Josephson, Wendy Louise 1133
  (MIC.F.TC-54427)
Jost, Tadeusz P. 4728
Journet, Alan R.P. 11315
  (MIC.F.TC-23107)
Joy, Annamma 788 (MIC.F.TC-62965)
Joy, Christopher Stewart 4509
  (MIC.F.TC-19561)
Joyal, Robert 11603
Joyce, Lester D. 3161
Joyce, S. Maureen 3822
  (MIC.F.TC-43910)
Joynt, Carey B. 7566
Jubas, Harry Leib 10231 (MIC.T-666)

Judd, D.C. 7479
Judge, Alan Stephen 6655
Judson, Thomas Andrew 1857
  (MIC.F.TC-1331)
Judy, Robert Dale 8715
Juéry, René 8292
Juhas, Allan Paul 5508
  (MIC.F.TC-17421)
Julia, Sister 1114
Julian, Bruce René 5066
Julian, Paul Roland 5023
Julien, Louise 3764
Julien, Pierre 4576
Julien, Yves Benoit 1432
Junemann, Georgina 9134
Jung, Bong Seo 1914 (MIC.F.TC-35077)
Jure, Albert Edward 5250
Jutlah, Clifford Benjamin 1716
  (MIC.TC-8791)

K

Kaçira, Niyazi 6374 (MIC.TC-11041)
Kadatz, Dennis Melvin 10422
  (MIC.F.T-1082)
Kage, Joseph 7596
Kahn, Joan Yess 4243
  (MIC.F.TC-50468)
Kakela, Peter John 5024
  (MIC.TC-3853)
Kakonge, Sam Atwoki K. 10548
  (MIC.F.TC-21608)
Kalbfleisch, Herbert Karl 1087
  (MIC.T-42)
Kalgutkar, Ramakant Mukundrao 11437
  (MIC.F.TC-17000)
Kalliokoski, Jorma Osmo Kalervo 5509
Kalmar, Ivan 7832 (MIC.F.TC-38752)
Kalmoni-Baassiri, Faika 9445
  (MIC.F.TC-56445)
Kalogeropoulos, Stavros Ilia 5067
  (MIC.F.TC-58296)
Kalpage, Kingsley Samuel
  Perera 11239 (MIC.TC-5542)
Kam, Yee Kiew 11384
  (MIC.F.TC-17190)
Kamineni, Dayananda Choudhari 5854
  (MIC.TC-16812)
Kaminski, Richard Marvin 10768
Kamp, Joseph William 11216
  (MIC.F.TC-17192)
Kamp, Robert Cornelius 1977
  (MIC.TC-16535)
Kanchier, Carole Joyce 9446
  (MIC.F.TC-55364)
Kane, Michael Matthew 11156
Kansky, Robert James 3162
  (MIC.T-224)
Kansup, Wanlop 3501
  (MIC.F.TC-31999)
Kanzler, Eileen McAuliffe 7643
Kao, Ming Hsiung 10996
  (MIC.F.TC-46761)
Kapches, Mima Cora Grant Brown 648
  (MIC.F.TC-53086)
Kaplan, David Jay 4378
Kaplan, Faith Kinaler 3095
  (MIC.F.TC-36708)
Kaplan, Sanford Sandy 5655
Kapoor, Dharam Vir 4425 (MIC.T-865)
Kapoor, Surinder Kumar 3010
Kaprowy, Eugene Anthony 3823
  (MIC.F.TC-26360)
Kapsalis, Constantine 2184
  (MIC.T-833)
Kapuscinski, Sister Bernice
  Phyllis 4455
Karamanski, Theodore John 1245
  (MIC.F.T-1191)
Karan, Mehmet A. 4549
  (MIC.F.TC-33489)
Karaz, Valerie Lynne 4145
  (MIC.F.TC-57174)
Kardasz, Stanley William 1799
  (MIC.F.TC-30170)

Kargbo, Dennis Borboh 3170
Kargianis, Leslie Denis 3873
Kariuki, Priscilla Wanjiru 3046
  (MIC.F.TC-48990)
Karlinsky, Sidney 10291
  (MIC.F.TC-42140)
Karlstrom, Eric Thor 4729
  (MIC.F.TC-52388)
Karniol, Rachel 3232
  (MIC.F.TC-32117)
Karrow, Paul Frederick 6375
Karson, Jeffrey Alan 5761
Karvinen, William O. 6087
  (MIC.F.TC-18543)
Kasensky, Renee Goldsmith 8841
  (DS559.8 D7 K37)
Kasman, Entus Anne 9338
  (MIC.F.TC-39704)
Kassem, Atef M. 4550
  (MIC.F.TC-60201)
Kasurak, Peter Charles 7567
  (MIC.F.T-867)
Kater, John L., Jr. 9834
  (MIC.TC-15890)
Katyal, Krishan L. 3334 (MIC.F.T-888)
Katz, Bruce Allan 361
  (MIC.F.TC-25191)
Katz, Michael Barry 6376
  (MIC.TC-1084)
Katz-Mendelson, Beverley 9213
  (MIC.F.TC-58461)
Katzer, Bruce 665 (MIC.T-508)
Katzko, Michael William 9543
  (MIC.F.TC-48991)
Kaufman, David 3784
  (MIC.F.TC-36409)
Kaufmann, Carol Natalie 638
Kaushik, Narinder Kumar 11863
Kavaliers, Martin Imants 10927
  (MIC.F.TC-36410)
Kavanagh, Oliver F. 3047
  (MIC.F.TC-19716)
Kavanagh, Paul Michael 6377
Kavanaugh, David Henry 11186
  (MIC.F.TC-40438)
Kawecki, Alina 3335 (MIC.F.TC-48551)
Kay, Barry James 8726 (MIC.F.T-943)
Kay, Paul Allan 4668
Kaye, Barry 79
Kazymera, Bohdan 9828
Kealey, Gregory Sean 2098
  (MIC.F.T-968)
Keane, David Ross 3556
  (MIC.F.TC-58365)
Keane, Michael John 4805
  (MIC.F.TC-35930)
Kearney, Michael Sean 11660
  (MIC.F.TC-50616)
Kearsley, Gregory Peter 4250
  (MIC.F.TC-40197)
Keast, Ronald Gordon 9772
  (MIC.F.TC-20311)
Keating, Bernard J. 6378
Keating, Thomas F. 8842
  (MIC.F.TC-57976)
Keddie, Philip Desmond 92
  (MIC.F.TC-27051)
Keddie, Vincent Gordon 10232
  (MIC.F.TC-22626)
Keddy, John Arthur 2981
Keddy, Paul Anthony 11526
  (MIC.F.TC-38389)
Kee, Herbert William 9697
  (MIC.TC-3717)
Keeler, Bernhard Trueman 2931
Keeley, James Francis 1175
  (MIC.F.T-1436)
Keen, Richard Alan 12006
Keenleyside, Hugh Llewellyn 7497
  (F5047 K4)
Keenlyside, David Lane 913
  (MIC.F.TC-37290)
Keep, George Rex Crowley 7632
  (MIC.T-912)
Keeton-Wilson, Anne 3233
  (MIC.TC-16637)
Keevil, Norman Bell, Jr. 4510
  (MIC.T-255)
Keffer, Lowell William 8210
  (MIC.F.TC-59400)
Kehoe, Alice Beck 734

Kehoe, Dalton Anthony 8919
  (MIC.F.TC-17123)
Kehoe, John William 3336
  (MIC.TC-14878)
Keirn, William Clair 10084
  (MIC.TC-13425)
Keirstead, Charles W. 9782
Keith, Eileen Patrick 9339
  (MIC.F.TC-43660)
Keith, Lloyd Burrows 10769
Keith, M. Virginia 2806
Keith, Mackenzie L. 6088
Keitner, Wendy J.R. 8105
  (MIC.TC-16064)
Keleher, Gary Raymond 9098
  (MIC.F.TC-62026)
Kell, John Thompson 10292
  (MIC.F.TC-31607)
Keller, Arnold 4251 (MIC.F.TC-58457)
Keller, Martha Perry Freese 3824
  (MIC.F.TC-33560)
Keller, Rodney Alan 11691
  (MIC.F.TC-17193)
Keller, Sandra M. 10401
  (MIC.F.TC-52665)
Kelley, Danford Greenfield 5656
Kelley, George Thomas 1207
  (MIC.T-346)
Kelley, Henry Edward 7745
Kelley, Maurice Vernon 4028
  (MIC.F.TC-32924)
Kellogg, James Eugene 4860
  (MIC.T-873)
Kelly, Alexander Kenneth 1557
  (MIC.TC-2978)
Kelly, Catherine Elizabeth 8420
  (MIC.F.TC-38084)
Kelly, David Francis 6802
  (BX1759.5 N4 K45)
Kelly, Desmond Aylmer Gratten 3593
Kelly, Donald Wright 1920 (MIC.T-555)
Kelly, Gerald Oliver 3630
  (MIC.F.TC-17569)
Kelly, James Michael 6379
Kelly, John Joseph 7606
  (MIC.F.TC-36992)
Kelly, Kenneth 93 (MIC.TC-2439)
Kelly, Lawrence Alexander 1647
  (MIC.TC-1073)
Kelly, Margaret 9415
  (MIC.F.TC-53238)
Kelner, Merrijoy Sharon 426
  (MIC.TC-4501)
Kelsey, Ian Bruce 3684
Kelsey, John Graham Thornton 3289
  (MIC.F.TC-17570)
Kelsey, John Marvin 10439
Kelso, John Richard Murray 10978
  (MIC.TC-10722)
Kenah, Christopher 5251
Kendall, John Charles 7524
Kendall, Mary Ellen 3096
  (MIC.F.TC-34387)
Kendle, J.E. 7480 (DA18 K43)
Kendrick, Margaret Joan 9016
  (MIC.F.TC-42667)
Keniff, Patrick John 7948
Kennedy, Brian Wayne 191
Kennedy, John Charles 611
  (MIC.T-1021)
Kennedy, John Hopkins 6963
Kennedy, John Robinson 10363
  (MIC.F.T-1140)
Kennedy, Kenneth Francis 1620
Kennedy, Leslie W. 10136
  (MIC.F.TC-32925)
Kennedy, Margaret Sandra Lee 4211
Kennedy, Sister Mary Perputua 4411
Kennedy, Michael Edward 1477
  (MIC.F.TC-30171)
Kennedy, Murray James 11339
  (MIC.F.TC-37648)
Kennedy, Robert Stephen 10517
Kennedy, William Alexander 11017
  (QH1 T68 fol.)
Kennedy, William F.R. 10397
Kennedy, William J. 9487
  (MIC.F.TC-40199)
Kennett, Keith Franklin 9017
  (MIC.TC-11015)

Kennett, Lee Boone 7412 (UA700 K4)
Kenny, Stephen 7086
  (MIC.F.TC-44047)
Kent, Donald M.J. 5564
Kent, Robert Howard 8698
  (MIC.F.TC-25896)
Kenyon, John Peter Blithe 7087
  (MIC.TC-1794)
Kenyon, Susan Mary 700 (MIC.F.T-954)
Kenyon, Walter Andrew 914
  (MIC.TC-1489)
Keown, Lauriston Livingston 6740
  (MIC.F.TC-34391)
Keoyote, Sen 2686 (MIC.F.TC-17571)
Keppie, Daniel MacKenzie 10847
  (MIC.F.TC-26778)
Kepkay, Paul E. 10206
Ker, John William 11692
Ker, Sin Tze 1895 (MIC-TC-14370)
Kerans, Charles 5855
  (MIC.F.TC-59915)
Kerbrat, Dominique Joseph 9773
Kerby, Norma Joann 11541
  (MIC.F.TC-41670)
Kerekes, Joseph Jeno 11834
  (MIC.TC-13143)
Kerfoot, Denis Edward 4669
  (MIC.TC-5819)
Kergin, Dorothy Jean 6915
  (MIC.T-225)
Kern, Alan Steven 8920
  (MIC.TC-15695)
Kernaghan, William David
  Kenneth 8599 (MIC.T-187)
Kerr, Forrest Alexander 6380
Kerr, D.G.G. 7318
Kerr, Donald Peter 4999
Kerr, Janet C.R. 6894
Kerr, William Alexander 192
  (MIC.F.TC-55050)
Kerri, James Nwannukwu 727
  (MIC.T-681)
Kerswill, Charles James 11095
Keschner, Dorothee Anna 3234
Keser, Nurettin 236 (MIC.TC-5820)
Ketchen, Keith Stuart 10948
Ketcheson, John William 261
Ketchum, Edward John Davison 2185
Ketchum, John Anthony Cheyne 2498
  (MIC.F.TC-40921)
Ketner, Keith Brindley 5423
Kevan, Peter Graham 11252
  (MIC.TC-6728)
Kew, John Edward Michael 675
Kewley, Arthur E. 9787
Keyes, Mary Eleanor 10351
Keys, Charles Lawrence 4730
  (MIC.F.TC-24073)
Keys, George Eric Maxwell 4146
Keys, John Erskine 11980
  (MIC.F.TC-35735)
Keyworth, Vida 8414
Khadem, Ramin 1777
Khajavi, Shokooh 2256
  (MIC.F.TC-47086)
Khalidi, Musa Shafiq 10149
  (MIC.TC-15253)
Khalili, Abdolamir 10796
Khan, Emamuddeen 2145
Khan, Mohammed Fashat Ali 223
Khan, Muhammad M.R. 10949
Khan, Nasim Ullah 3011
Khan, Shahamat Ullah 3209
Khan, Takir Raza 6089
  (MIC.F.TC-44411)
Khattat, Abdul-Razzak 11157
  (MIC.F.TC-38267)
Khemani, R.K. 1322
Khondakar, Nezamuddin 4939
  (MIC.F.TC-53828)
Khoo, Hong Woo 10950 (MIC.TC-8310)
Khosla, Vijay Kumar 4577
Kidd, Desmond Fife 4670
Kidd, James R. 2816
Kidd, William Spencer Francis 5762
Kiely, Margaret C. 9698
Kiesekamp, Burkhard 9862
  (MIC.F.TC-31254)
Kilbourn, William Morley 7326
  (F5074.9 M33 K5)
Kilbride, Bernard James 1678

Kilburn, Lionel C. 5068
Kilduff, Vera R.R. 2367
Killan, Gerald 7199 (MIC.F.TC-19416)
Killing, John Peter 1752
Kilpatrick, Doreen Leila 9699
    (MIC.F.TC-29025)
Kim, Bo Kyung 3337
Kim, Chul-Hwan 2342
Kim, Jung-Gun 7658 (MIC.F.TC-59796)
Kim, Jin Woo 1606 (MIC.F.T-1303)
Kim, Moshe 2325 (MIC.F.TC-62110)
Kim, Sang Yoong 1921
    (MIC.F.TC-52253)
Kim, Yung Duk 4551 (MIC.TC-6165)
Kimball, Jeffrey Philip 7068
Kimberley, Mark Harry Dennis 10085
    (MIC.F.TC-36713)
Kimmis, Richard Clark 9300
    (MIC.F.TC-30725)
Kincaid, Patricia Jean 4147
    (MIC.F.TC-55845)
Kinchen, Oscar A. 7465
Kindelan, Kevin M. 9018
Kindle, Cecil Haldane 6381
Kindle, Edward Darwin 6090
Kindt, Lawrence E. 199
King, Alan John Campbell 3298
King, Alfred Richard 4118 (MIC.T-43)
King, Arden R. 472
King, Clement Theodore 3785
    (MIC.F.TC-36413)
King, Elbert Aubrey 5069
King, Floris Ethia 6685
King, Herbert B. 2769
King, Joanne 8342
King, Leonard Henry 3061
    (MIC.F.TC-43448)
King, Lewis H. 5657
King, Marlene Dolores 9135
    (MIC.F.TC-26801)
King, Michael Christopher 9019
    (MIC.F.TC-24351)
King, Richard Alfred 729
King, Robert John 3474
    (MIC.F.TC-26059)
King, Roger Hutton 4671
King, Ruth Elizabeth 7746
    (MIC.F.TC-63592)
King, William L.M. 7599
Kingscote, Barbara F. 10549
    (MIC.TC-7620)
Kingsley, Jack Calvin 1062
    (MIC.T-484)
Kingson, Walter Krulevitch 1155
Kingston, David Russell 5252
Kingston, George Edward 10371
    (MIC.F.TC-34394)
Kingstone, Alan 3631
    (MIC.F.TC-47087)
Kinkaide, Alexandra 3235
    (MIC.F.TC-43450)
Kinney, Edward Coyle, Jr. 10913
Kinoshita, Garry Bing 11279
    (MIC.F.TC-31054)
Kinsley, Brian Leslie 2162
    (MIC.F.TC-41671)
Kirk, Donald W. 4872
Kirkbride, Anna Joan 3786
    (MIC.F.TC-51519)
Kirkham, Peter G. 1695
Kirkham, Rodney Victor 5253
Kirkland, Robert W. 6382
Kirkland, Samuel John Thomas 5565
Kirkpatrick, R.L. 7481
Kirkwood, Kristian John 4275
    (MIC.F.TC-43664)
Kirouac, Jacques 2964
Kirpalani, Vishnu 1896
Kirschvink, Joseph Lynn 6630
Kirsh, Sharon Louise 9700
    (MIC.F.TC-53089)
Kirshenblatt-Gimblett, Barbara 8324
    (MIC.T-481)
Kirton, John James 8843
Kirudja, Charles Mugambi 6780
    (MIC.F.TC-46035)
Kirwan, J.L. 6091
Kish, Laszlo 6383
Kissling, Christopher Charles 2257
    (MIC.TC-921)

Kistler, Ruth Barthold 2412
Kitchell, Jennifer Ann 5856
Kitchen, Brigitte 1323
Kitchen, Hubert William 3338
Kite, Geoffrey W. 6678
    (MIC.TC-16814)
Kivett, Vaden Keith 10695
    (MIC.F.TC-26802)
Klaiman, Stephen 9701
Klapman, Robert B. 10797
Klarreich, Samuel Henry 4166
    (MIC.F.TC-31259)
Klass, Gary Martin 8676
    (MIC.F.T-1084)
Klassen, Bernard Rodney 3395
Klassen, Daniel 9301
Klassen, Henry Cornelius 7321
    (MIC.F.TC-27896)
Klassen, Peter George 9941
    (MIC.F.TC-22337)
Klassen, Rodney Alan 5857
Klassen, Rudolph Waldemar 5510
Klavora, Peter 10327
    (MIC.F.TC-21866)
Kleiber, Nancy Ruth Lewis 385
    (MIC.T-580)
Kleiber, Pierre Maxwell 11823
Klein, Cornelis 5708
Klein, Danny 9544 (MIC.F.TC-25723)
Klein, George Devries 5589
Klein, Gerard 3787 (MIC.F.TC-54102)
Klein, John Frederick 10293
    (MIC.F.TC-21867)
Klein, Juan Luis 4836
    (MIC.F.TC-56326)
Klein, William John 8554
    (MIC.F.TC-31260)
Kleinschmidt, Elko J. 2016
Kleinspehn, Karen Lee 5254
    (MIC.F.T-1286)
Klempay, Mary Janet 4190
Klemplatz, Morrie M. 9624
    (MIC.F.TC-49223)
Kliewer, Erich Victor 737
    (MIC.F.TC-46171)
Klinck, Carl F. 8395 (PS8455 A53 Z73)
Klinck, George A. 8280
    (PS8461 R43 Z6)
Klinka, Jan Antonin 9174
    (MIC.TC-13072)
Klinka, Karel 11693 (MIC.F.TC-29863)
Kloosterman, Bruce 210
    (MIC.TC-10241)
Klopoushak, Edward L. 3430
    (MIC.F.TC-40203)
Klos, Frank William, Jr. 1156
Klostermann, Kerry Julian
    Wolfgang 4412 (MIC.F.TC-46036)
Klotz, Melvin 3775 (MIC.T-667)
Klovan, John Edward 5424
Kluck, Brian Lee 3923
    (MIC.F.TC-45988)
Klug, Leo F. 4148
Klugman, Michael A. 6384
Kluyver, Huybert M. 6385
Klymasz, Robert Bogdan 8325
    (GR113.7 U57 K58)
Knapen, Joseph Mathijs Peter 10150
    (MIC.F.TC-59178)
Knapp, Robert Whelan 2390 (MIC.T-44)
Knapton, Richard W. 10858
    (MIC.F.TC-37804)
Knickle, Harry James 9835
Knight, Colin Joseph 6092
    (MIC.TC-1490)
Knight, David B. 4847 (FC470 K55)
Knight, Dean Humphrey 915
    (MIC.F.TC-36716)
Knight, Graham 10207
    (MIC.TC-37347)
Knight, Ronald John 5658
    (MIC.F.TC-33006)
Kniže, Stanislaw 6622
    (MIC.F.TC-29864)
Knoechel, Roy 11864
Knoepfli, Heather Elizabeth
    Blaine 4029 (MIC.F.TC-55848)
Knoll, Alexander 4212 (MIC.T-795)
Knoll, John Francis 8141 (MIC.T-627)
Knoop, Robert 4314

Knopff, Rainier 8458
Knowles, David Martin 5709
Knowles, Donald Wilson 4119
Knowles, L.C. 8385
Knox, John K. 6386 (MIC.TC-9321)
Knox, John Lewis 4976
    (MIC.F.TC-56600)
Knutson, Franklin Albert 1157
    (BV656 K54)
Knutti, Hans Jakob 272
Knuttila, Kenneth Murray 117
    (MIC.F.TC-58300)
Ko, Ronald Chun Chung 10550
    (MIC.TC-9032)
Ko, Ting Tsz 2163 (H31 C7)
Kobayaski, Nobako 9020
Kobluk, David Ronald 5070
    (MIC.F.TC-36538)
Kobrick, Judi B. 9373
    (MIC.F.TC-35237)
Kobrinsky, Vernon Harris 558
    (MIC.F.TC-17195)
Koch, Carl Fred 6510
Koch, Lyle Ward 335
Koch, William J. 9374
    (MIC.F.TC-58903)
Koch, William Frederick, II 6517
Kodish, Debora Gail 404
    (MIC.F.T-1270)
Koe, George Gerald 4006
    (MIC.F.TC-56607)
Koehler, Wallace Conrad, Jr. 8844
Koelz, Walter 10904
Koenig, Dolores Mary 4120
    (MIC.F.TC-49174)
Koeppe, Clarence Eugene 4977
Koerber, Betty Turner 8142
    (MIC.T-823)
Koerber, Walter Frederick 3996
Koerner, Roy Martindale 5858
    (GB2595 D4 K7 fol.)
Koers, Dirk Antonie 4511
    (MIC.F.TC-46174)
Koester, Charles Beverly 6948
    (FC3217.1 D39 K64)
Koewn, Lauriston Livingston 9447
    (MIC.F.TC-34391)
Koh, Hung-Sun 10676
    (MIC.F.TC-43665)
Koh, Kwang-Lim 1858
Kohler, Larry R. 8845
Kohli, Ulrich Johann Robert 2017
    (MIC.F.TC-28724)
Kojama, Satoru 11472 (MIC.TC-11233)
Koke, Conrad J. 9702
    (MIC.F.TC-41601)
Kolar, J.C. 372
Kolberg, Donald Wayne 5025
Kolesar, Henry 2856
Kolish, Evelyn 7260
    (MIC.F-2M11.583.1)
Kolling, Harold 6978
Kollmeyer, Ronald Charles 11945
Kolt, Stanley Ernest 3605 (MIC.T-634)
Komourdjian, Martin Paul 10985
    (MIC.F.TC-33705)
Konrad, Victor Alexander 4947
    (MIC.F.TC-52255)
Kontos, Donna June Krochman 9545
    (MIC.F.TC-36718)
Konzak, Burt 10126 (MIC.F.TC-35238)
Koo, Jahak 5511
Koolage, William W., Jr. 564
    (MIC.T-974)
Koop, Sandra Jean 9546
    (MIC.F.TC-54553)
Kopec, Richard Joseph 5007
Kopinak, Kathryn Mary 9977
    (MIC.F.TC-36993)
Koppert, Vincent Aloysius 702
Korchinsky, Nestor Nicky 10328
Kord, Dennis 9021 (MIC.F-2M11.395.2)
Kornberg, Allan 8532
Koroscil, Paul Michael 4684
Korpijaakko, Erkki Olavi 11542
Korpijaakko, Maija-Leena 6532
    (MIC.F.TC-30416)
Korteweg, Laurens 3467
    (MIC.TC-13441)
Kosny, Mitchell Ernest 8727
    (MIC.F.TC-37859)

Koster, Emlyn Howard 5919
(MIC.F.TC-33706)
Kothari, Vinay B. 1940
Kotkov, Benjamin 9136
Kotowitz, Yehuda 1753
Kott, Edward 10677 (MIC.TC-90)
Kott, Laima S. 11414
(MIC.F.TC-48757)
Kottman, Richard Norman 7568
(MIC.T-46)
Kovacik, Charles Frank 4848
Kovitz, Karen Elizabeth 9302
(MIC.F.TC-49317)
Kowal, Robert Raymond 11604
Kowalik, Joe 5763
Kowalski, Alvin Edwin 9931
(MIC.TC-11334)
Kowalski, George Jerzy 1902
(MIC.F.TC-39511)
Kozakewick, Edward James 2687
(MIC.F.TC-49004)
Koziar, Andrew 6656
Koziev, Roberta Louise 9448
(MIC.F.TC-27676)
Kraft, Calvin T. 1208
Krahn, Gloria Louise 9022
(MIC.F.TC-47213)
Krahn, John Jacob 9847
Kramer, Edwin Arthur 9023
(MIC.F.TC-47214)
Kramer, John Frank 10423
(MIC.F.TC-40440)
Kranck, Svante Hakan 6387
Krank, Marvin Douglas 9024
(MIC.F.TC-57080)
Krasnor, Linda Doreen Rose 3028
(MIC.F.TC-53569)
Kratzmann, Arthur 4351
Krause, Jerome B. 6093 (MIC.TC-7817)
Krause-Schroeder, Federico
Fernando 5859
Krausher, Randall John Robert 9449
Krauskopf, Frances 6999
Krauter, Joseph Francis 8600
(MIC.T-226)
Kravitz, Joseph Henry 5860
(MIC.F.T-1353)
Krebs, Charles Joseph 10667
Krech, Shepard, III 416
Krecsy, James Patrick 4437
(MIC.F.TC-26362)
Kretz, Ralph 6388
Kreutzwiser, Reid Douglas 4601
(MIC.F.TC-36288)
Krezoski, John Roman 11783
(MIC.F.T-1142)
Krichev, Alan 7694, 9450
(MIC.F.TC-19917)
Krieg, Robert Edward 649
(MIC.F.TC-46037)
Krinsky, Itzhak 1639 (MIC.F.TC-61159)
Krishnan, Thekkey K. 6389
Kristjanson, Baldur H. 120
Kristjanson, G. Albert 4191
(HF5381.5 K7)
Kristjansson, Leo Geir 6640
(MIC.TC-16362)
Kristofferson, Yngve 6631
Krivy, Gary Joseph Paul 2807
(MIC.F.T-1333)
Krogh, Thomas Edward 6094
Krohn, William Barry 10798
Kroller, Eva-Marie 8011
(MIC.F.TC-40209)
Kronenberg, Vernon Joshua 8814, 8846
Kronenberger, Earl J. 9602
Kronitz, Leo 9939
Krueger, Kenneth William 11473
Krueger, Ralph Ray 156
Kruger, Arthur Martin 2164
Krumlik, George Jiri 11694
(MIC.F.TC-42674)
Kruzynski, George Maria 10951
(MIC.F.TC-46176)
Krysowaty, Joyce Bernice 4456
(MIC.F.TC-43457)
Kryzanowski, Lawrence 1692
(MIC.F.TC-29866)
Ku, Lang-fa 11956 (MIC.F.TC-63794)
Kubiski, Walter S. 8476
(MIC.F.TC-33639)

Kucey, Reginald Mathew Nicholas 286
(MIC.F.TC-49175)
Kuchar, Eva 9547 (MIC.F.TC-47091)
Kuchar, Peter 11438 (MIC.F.TC-24077)
Kuczynski, Leon John 9370
Kudar, Randolph Parris 1407
(MIC.F.TC-46038)
Kufeldt, Kathleen Sylvaria 10086
(MIC.F.TC-55368)
Kuhn, Leroy Raymond 9950
(MIC.F.T-1014)
Kuiper, Nicholas A. 9548
(MIC.F.TC-42038)
Kulba, John William 2762 (MIC.T-719)
Kulisek, Larry Lee 7365 (MIC.T-648)
Kulka, Terrence Barratt 4787
(MIC.F.TC-50478)
Kumar, Krishna 3131
(MIC.F.TC-47092)
Kumar, Pradeep 2209
(MIC.F.TC-20257)
Kunin, Roslyn 2242 (MIC.TC-5841)
Kuniyoshi, Shingi 5255 (MIC.T-365)
Kunjbehari, Lalta Lloyd 2688
(MIC.F.TC-51521)
Kunz, Ernest Chen-Tsun 4978
Kunz, Frank Andrew Ferenc 8542
Kuo, Hsiao Yu 6095 (MIC.F.TC-26163)
Kuo, Say Lee 5861 (MIC.F.TC-30730)
Kupfer, George 10261 (MIC.T-169)
Kupp, Theodorus Johannes 6979
(MIC.TC-2317)
Kureth, Elwood John Clark 4824
(MIC.T-498)
Kurialocherry, Anthony J. 2748
Kurland, David Midian 3236
(MIC.F.TC-53093)
Kurland, Leonard T. 6717
Kurtz, Dennis Darl 6096
Kurtz, Larry Robert 1384
(MIC.F.TC-35241)
Kurtz, Morris 10372 (MIC.F.T-1276)
Kurtz, Ronald Douglas 6603
(MIC.F.TC-20583)
Kurtzman, Joseph Balfour 10352
Kuruvilla, P.K. 8557 (MIC.TC-4777)
Kushner, Joseph 6781
Kusy, Martin 1433 (MIC.F.TC-40673)
Kutty, Madasseri Krishnan 10952
Kuz, Tony John 4903 (MIC.T-482)
Kuzynski, Leon 9375 (MIC.F.TC-42240)
Kwak, Teunis A.P. 6097
Kwan, Wan Hing 11316
(MIC.F.TC-18278)
Kwavnick, David 8672 (MIC.TC-4778)
Kwei, John Chi Ber 7961
Kwon, Oh Yul 1478 (MIC.TC-14648)
Kwong, Yan-Tat John 5256
(MIC.F.TC-59343)
Kyle, Jack Leslie 1070
(MIC.F.TC-55897)
Kyle, James Richard 5862
(MIC.F.TC-36290)
Kyle, Neil John 8921
(MIC.F.TC-51722)
Kyriazis, Natalie 10064

L

Laatsch, William Ganfield 4685
(MIC.TC-11143)
Labarrère-Paulé, André 2530
Labelle, Suzanne (Soeur Sainte-Marie)
8299 (BX4705 M36 L25)
Laber, Gene Earle 1978
Labercane, George Donald 3933
(MIC.F.TC-40442)
LaBerge, Gene Ludger 5133
Laberge, Suzanne 766
(MIC.F-2M11.369.3)
Labonté, René 8305 (MIC.F-003304)
Labovitz, Mark Larry 5071
Labreche, Thomas Michael 8922
(MIC.F.TC-58605)

Lacasse, Jean-Paul 7949
(KE1790 Z97 L3)
Lacasse, Madeleine Ladouceur 8211
(MIC.F.TC-37040)
Lacasse, Raynal 3431
(MIC.F-2M11.527.5)
Lachance, André 7905 (KE8809 L32)
Lachance, Paul Émile 1818
Lachapelle, Pierre-Paul 10262
Lacome, Bernard 9703 (MIC.TC-6985)
La Croix, Sister Alida-Marie 3727
Lacroix, Gilles Lucien 10986
(MIC.F.TC-47759)
Lacroix, Guy 11806
Laczko, Leslie Stephen 10179
(MIC.F.TC-58169)
Ladouceur, Gilles 11766
Ladouceur, Jean 2853
(MIC.F.TC-20585)
Lafleur, Normand 7261
La Follette, James E. 7747
(PC3619 L3)
La Forest, Gerard Vincent 1717
Laforest, Lucien 10208
(MIC.F.TC-35432)
Laforest, Marie-Thérèse 8207
Laforet, Andrea Lynne 386
(MIC.F.TC-22142)
Lafortune, Mireille 9704
(MIC.F-005401)
Lafrance, Jeanne 8213
(MIC.F.TC-18985)
Lafrance, Marc R. 6607
Lafrance, Robert Rolland 1434
Lagarac, Daniel 4762
Lagarde, Irénée 7906
Lagier, Pierre Marie 10294
Lagroix, Earl Joseph 2783
(MIC.F.TC-36721)
Laguitlon, Daniel 6390
(MIC.F.TC-26490)
Lahaise, Georges-Pierre 936
Lai, William Louis 3237
(MIC.F.TC-27679)
Laidlaw, Alexander Fraser 4054
(MIC.F.TC-19720)
Laiken, Stanley Norman 1457
(MIC.TC-11403)
Laing, Gordon Wayne 9705
Laing, Lionel H. 2284
Laird, Harry Clarence 6098
Laird, Jo 6391
Lajeunesse, Marcel 7978
Lajoie, Jean 6392
Lajtai, Emery Zoltan 6099
(MIC.TC-648)
Lake, David Wayne 4613 (MIC.T-499)
Lake, Deborah 3874 (MIC.F.TC-49801)
Lake, Philip 2772
Lake, Richard Wallace 4478
(MIC.F.TC-26272)
Lake, Robert Arlington 9706
(MIC.TC-8527)
Lal, Radkey 72
Lal, Ravindra 473
Lal, Ravindra Kumar 6100
(MIC.TC-1027)
Lalancette, Louis-Marie 11018
(MIC.F.TC-23408)
Lalande, Jean-Guy 1088
(MIC.F.TC-58157)
Laliberté, G.-Raymond 8757
(MIC.F.TC-56358)
Lall, Bernard Mohan 2906
Lall, Geeta Rani 4121 (MIC.T-1714)
L'Allier-Sturgess, Louise 9376
Lalonde, André-N. 7184
Lalonde, Bernadette Irene
Dierdre 4192 (MIC.F.TC-40929)
Lalonde, Gilles 9137
Lam, Laurence 7604 (MIC.F.TC-58737)
Lam, Nina Siri-Ngan 4696
(MIC.F.TC-48373)
Lam, Wai Ping 1408 (MIC.T-834)
Lam, Yee Lay Jack 4252
(MIC.TC-11597)
Lamansney, Patrick J. 6964
LaMarche, Luc 9707 (MIC.F-002201)
Lamarche, Robert Y. 6393
Lamarche, Rodolphe H. 4904
(MIC.F.TC-44056)

525

Lamarre, Joseph Léo Paul André 3965
Lamb, Charles William, Jr. 1852
 (MIC.T-842)
Lamb, Eila Mary 3121
 (MIC.F.TC-40676)
Lamb, Henry Francis 5710
Lamb, Robert E. 7376
Lamb, Robert Lee 2808
Lambert, Anthony 11890
Lambert, Carmen 730
 (MIC.F.TC-23124)
Lambert, James 9887
Lambert, John David Hamilton 11543
 (MIC.TC-2375)
Lambert, Leah Rae 3644
 (MIC.F.TC-40930)
Lambert, Maurice Bernard 5257
 (MIC.TC-11001)
Lambert, Pierre D. 2413
Lambert, Roland A. 3339
Lambert, Steven J. 12007
 (MIC.F.TC-33317)
Lambiase, Joseph John 5659
 (MIC.F.TC-33008)
Lamonde, Yvan 2531
Lamont, Daniel R. 8012 (MIC.TC-1508)
Lamont, Donald John 9025
 (MIC.F.TC-44499)
Lamontagne, Jacques 3654
Lamontagne, Léopold 8265
La Montagne, Roland 7293
LaMothe, Dennis Michael 9708
 (MIC.F.TC-40443)
Lamothe, Pierre 3502 (MIC.T-3859)
Lamoureux, Marvin Eugène 4047
 (MIC.F.TC-28728)
Lampard, Dorothy Mary 3396
 (LB1632 L3)
Lamy, Jean-Paul 8214
Lamy, Paul 362 (MIC.F.TC-37981)
Lancaster, Charles F. 9937
Lancaster, M.K. 3966
Lancaster, Jane 4815
Lanclos, Teresa Gloria 7748
Lande, Eric Paul 1607
 (MIC.F.TC-39722)
Landels, Isabel 8261
Landes, Robert W. 5425
Landes, Ronald George 3181
 (MIC.F.TC-17128)
Landes, Ruth 540 (E99 C6 L285)
Landine, Robert Charles 4583
Landino, John Edward 3825
 (MIC.F.TC-49318)
Landry, Burnelle S. 6641
Landry, Joseph Allyn 7749
Landry, Michel 3685 (MIC.F-026709)
Landry, Pauline 9819 (MIC.F.T-1302)
Landry, Réjean 8459 (MIC.F.TC-25725)
Landry, Simon 3655
Landsberg, Dennis Robert 11798
Landsberger, Sheldon 2237
 (MIC.F.TC-58305)
Landuyt, Bernard F. 2018
Landy, Sarah Edith 9340
 (MIC.F.TC-59630)
Lane, Barbara Savadkin 682 (MIC.T-49)
Lane, Robert Brockstedt 561
 (MIC.T-50)
Lanfranconi, Claude Peter 1458
 (MIC.F.TC-28266)
Lang, Arthur Hamilton 5258
Lang, Charles J. 4216
Lang, Frank Alexander 11474
 (MIC.TC-178)
Lang, Ronald William 6877
 (HD9670 C22 L35)
Lang, William Arthur 9625
 (MIC.F.TC-57115)
Langdon, George L. 4697
Lange, James Dubois 9221
 (MIC.F.TC-41227)
Langer, Hans Dieter 9774
Langevin, Marcel 1409 (MIC.F.T-1329)
Langevin, Ronald Lindsay André 3238
 (MIC.TC-9539)
Langford, F.F. 6101
Langford, George Burwash 6102
Langford, Howard David 2817
 (LA418 O6 L3)

Langford, John W. 2258
 (MIC.F.TC-18282)
Langford, Raymond Robert 11084
Langlais, Jacques 8888
 (MIC.F.TC-33009)
Langley, Gerald James 2544
 (MIC.T-51)
Langley, Paul Christopher 2382
 (MIC.F.TC-32661)
Langley, Richard Brian 6657
 (MIC.F.TC-41002)
Langlois, André 4965
Langlois, Hervé Oscar 2788
Lansdell, Clyde Edison 3503
 (MIC.F.TC-47096)
Lansley, Keith Leonard 10353
 (MIC.TC-9608)
Lao, Khedang 6394
Laperrière, René 7877 (HD4933 L36)
Laperrière-Nguyen, Anne 3087
Lapid, Yosef 8577
La Pierre, Laurier, Joseph Lucien 7383
 (MIC.T-52)
Lapierre, René 8252
 (PS8501 Q85 Z765)
Lapkin, Sharon Judith 7750
 (MIC.F.TC-31265)
La Plante, Jacques 10295
Laplante, Serge André 2074
 (MIC.T-606)
Lapp, Janet E. 8923 (MIC.F.TC-50481)
Lappage, Ronald Sidney 10343
 (MIC.F.TC-21050)
Lappin, Allen Ralph 5259
Larbalestier, Paul D.B. 8101
Lardinois, Christian 10472
 (HE131 M55 fol.)
Larin, Gilles 2571 (MIC.F.TC-47376)
Larin, Gilles Normand 1500
Larkin, Edward James 9260
 (MIC.TC-11435)
Larkin, Jill 9026 (MIC.F.TC-38491)
Larner, John William, Jr. 7449
 (MIC.T-491)
Laroche, Jean-Pierre 9603
Larochelle, André, Joseph Edgar 6395
Larochelle, Normand 12008
Larocque, Hubert 8376
Larocque, Paul 1874 (MIC.F.TC-37085)
La Roi, George Henri, III 11644
Larose, Réal 2572 (MIC.F-027202)
Larouche, Georges 7266
Larsen, James Arthur 11544
Larsen, John Knud 10451
Larson, David John 11201
 (MIC.F.TC-19797)
Larson, Douglas William 11578
 (MIC.F.TC-26168)
Larson, Gary Lee 10953
 (MIC.TC-13237)
Larson, Kenneth Louis 2724
Larson, Olaf Peter 4457 (MIC.T-53)
Larson, Vernon Carl 2619
Larter, Sylvia Joan 2573
 (MIC.F.TC-35247)
Laryea, Kofi Budu 262
 (MIC.F.TC-41744)
Lasenby, David Charles 11085
 (MIC.TC-11598)
Laskin, Richard 6845
Lassèrre, Pierre 1176
 (MIC.F.TC-59339)
Last, William Michael 5512
 (MIC.F.TC-47215)
Latham, Allan Brockway 1177
Latheef, Mohamed Abdul 11280
 (MIC.TC-10941)
Latimer, Elspeth Anne 10087
 (MIC.TC-14692)
Latimer, Paul Ross 6846
 (MIC.F.TC-50847)
La Tour, Timothy Earle 6103
 (MIC.F.TC-48375)
Latowsky, Evelyn Kallen 799
 (MIC.F.TC-21395)
Latta, Martha Ann 916
 (MIC.F.TC-35248)
Lattimer, John Ernest 111
Lattin, John Daniel 11158
Lattin, Richard Thomas 3182

Lau, Honkan K. 1351
 (MIC.F.TC-27496)
Lau, Hung-Hay 1844 (MIC.F.TC-17275)
Lau, Ka Ching 4552 (MIC.F.TC-59715)
Laub, Michael Elwood 10440
 (MIC.TC-13238)
Laurence, Gerard 1134
Laurence, Hugh Getty 808
 (MIC.TC-14491)
Laurence, Jean Roch 9549
 (MIC.F.TC-58499)
Laurin, André 6104
Laurin, André-F. 6396
Laurin, Paul 2735
Lauriol, Bernard 4763
 (GB428.5 C2 L39 fol.)
Laursen, Gary A. 11545
Lautard, Emile Hugh 1276
 (MIC.F.TC-40678)
Lauzier, Louis 4578
Lavalée, Alain 3686 (MIC.F-032203)
Lavalée, André 3562
Laver, Alfred Bryan 2574
Lavery, Robert Emmett 2932
 (MIC.F.TC-17592)
Lavi-Levin, Hannah 6762
 (MIC.F.TC-62261)
Lavigne, Gilles 816 (MIC.F-043705)
Lavigne, J. Albert C. 2575
Lavigne, Jean-Claude 4315
 (MIC.F-001009)
Laville, Christian 2533
Law, Kum Tin 4553 (MIC.F.TC-24589)
Law, Norma R. 4276
Law, Tean Chie 4512
 (MIC.F.TC-26815)
Lawani, Stephen Majebi 6847
Lawler, George Herbert 10914
Lawr, Douglas Archie 4098
 (MIC.TC-13789)
Lawrence, Alan Harvey 7088
Lawrence, Thomas Hamel 3475
 (MIC.F.TC-59784)
Lawrie, Bruce Raymond 9943
 (MIC.F.TC-42250)
Lawrie, Neil John 1385
 (MIC.F.TC-35049)
Lawson, Andrew Cowper 6105
Lawson, Glen Allen 9550
 (MIC.F.TC-37902)
Lawson, Murry Grant 1226 (H31 T6 V9)
Lawson, Virginia Kathryn 7801
 (MIC.T-473)
Lawson, William Morse 1679
 (MIC.F.TC-21553)
Lawton, Killip David 6106
Lawton, Murray Shaune 3239
 (MIC.F.TC-40932)
Laxer, Gordon David 1277
 (MIC.F.TC-53096)
Laycock, Arleigh Howard 4731
Laycock, Joseph E. 10127
 (HD7106 C2 L3 fol.)
Layton, Jack G. 1386
 (MIC.F.TC-58751)
Layton, Monique Jacqueline Berthe 738
 (MIC.F.TC-37662)
Lazar, Avrim D. 3397
Lazar, Morty Max 3565
 (MIC.F.TC-25727)
Lazaridis, Panagiotis 1754
 (MIC.F.TC-52668)
Lazarowich, Nicholas Michael B. 10441
 (MIC.F.T-889)
Lazaruk, Walter Andrew 2689
 (MIC.F.T-1321)
Lazer, William 1922
Lazerson, Judith Schoenholtz 9094
 (MIC.F.TC-56605)
Laznička, Petr 5072 (MIC.TC-10359)
Lazure, Hélène 6895
Le, Can Duy 1828 (MIC.F.TC-38764)
Leach, Hamish A. 7505
Leacock, Eleanor Burke 529
 (MIC.T-54)
Leadem, Carole Louise
 Scheuplein 11695 (MIC.F.TC-42678)
Leader, Herman Alexander 1246
Leahy, Jean 10263
Le Anderson, Paul James 6107
 (MIC.F.TC-37518)

Leaper, Richard John 2186
(MIC.T-792)
Leatherbarrow, Robert Wesley 5260
(MIC.F.TC-52794)
Leatt, Peggy 6916 (MIC.F.TC-44766)
Leavitt, Eugene Millidge 5426
Leavy, Normand 441 (MIC.F.TC-56211)
Lebedoff, Victor Richard 9783
Le Bel, Louis 3687
Leblanc, Arthur Joseph 8215
(MIC.F.TC-31612)
LeBlanc, Eugène A. 9626
(MIC.F.TC-29180)
Leblanc, Hugues 10424
(MIC.F.TC-53250)
LeBlanc, Jean-Pierre R. 11317
(MIC.F.TC-60934)
Le Blanc, Lucien Fabuis 11605
Leblanc, Marc 10264
Le Blanc, Raymond Joseph 893
(MIC.F.TC-59782)
Leblanc, Simone 2576
Leblond, André Joseph René 12009
(MIC. F.TC-47379)
Leblond, Paul Henri 11968
Le Cavalier, Patricia
Fitzsimmons 10180
(MIC.F.TC-64620)
Lecker, Robert Allan 8013
(MIC.F.TC-44501)
Leckett, Walter 9303
Leclerc, Jean 7283
Leclerc, Mariel 4438
(MIC.F.TC-18995)
Leclerc, Wilbrod 2309
LeClerc-Chevalier, Denise 11385
Le Couteur, Peter Clifford 5261
(MIC.TC-15132)
Lécuyer, Joseph Edmond André 2831
(MIC.F.TC-35050)
L'Écuyer, René 3240
Lederle, John William 8647
Ledgerwood, Charles Douglas 3366
(MIC.F.TC-26819)
LeDrew, Ellsworth Frank 5026
Leduc, Albert 11606
Le Duc, Lawrence William, Jr. 8623
Leduc, Lucien 9488 (MIC.F-025806)
Leduc, Ronald J. 3566
(MIC.F.TC-1280)
Ledwidge, Michael Barry 9027
(MIC.F.TC-58821)
Lee, Allan Hinglun 11957
Lee, Burdett W. 5711
Lee, Chack Fan 4579 (MIC.TC-12545)
Lee, Chun-Fen 4698
Lee, Chung Hoon 2343
Lee, Chunsun 6511
Lee, Danielle Marie Juteau 8578
(MIC.F.TC-27497)
Lee, Frederic Edward 6965
Lee, Gary Albert 11637
Lee, Hon-Wing 7695 (MIC.F.TC-44064)
Lee, Hurlbert A. 5616
Lee, James W. 5262
Lee, Kenneth 11865 (MIC.F.TC-58302)
Lee, Margaret Naomi 6896
Lee, Peter Ferguson 11579
(MIC.F.TC-43082)
Lee, Robert Kui-Sung 11475
(MIC.TC-179)
Lee, Sai Keung 10518
(MIC.F.TC-35745)
Lee, Sang Man 5863
Lee, Sheng-Shyong 65905
Leech, Geoffrey Bosdin 5263
Leechman, John Douglas 474
Lees, Evert John 5920
Lefebvre, André 1089 (F5072 L44)
Lefebvre, Bernard 9932 (MIC.F-002105)
Lefebvre, Jean-Marie 1966
(MIC.F.T-890)
Lefebvre, Marie-Thérèse 980
Lefevre, Yvon 9416 (MIC.F-034705)
Lefèvre, Esther Riva 9627
(MIC.F.TC-58509)
Leffler, Sanford Ross 11217
Leforest, Marie Thérèse 8207
Lefort, André 7089 (MIC.F.TC-29393)
Le François, Josette 3875
(MIC.F.TC-50486)

Lefrançois, Richard 10296
Lefroy, Donald Arthur 7413, 9297
(MIC.F.TC-54838)
Legault, Gisèle 10088
Legault, Jocelyne Andrée 6108
Legendre, Camille Georges 1819
Legendre, Louis 11807
Léger, Lauraine 7200 (GN494.3 L43)
Leger, Sister Mary Celeste 7430
(E78 M2 L43)
Léger, Raymond Joseph 3118
Legge, Allan Herbert 11439
Leggett, Mary Elizabeth 321
(MIC.F.TC-62318)
Leggett, William Claude 10987
(MIC.TC-5002)
Le Goff, Jean-Pierre 1755
(MIC.F.T-948)
Legris, Renée 8268
Legros, Dominique 576
(MIC.F.TC-56751)
Lehane, Aidan Patrick 9933
(MIC.F.TC-36729)
Lehn, Walter Isaak 7772
Lehr, John Campbell 4876
(MIC.F.TC-37806)
Leicester, John Beauchamp 10442
(MIC.F.TC-45991)
Leigh, Abisogun Olubode 193
(MIC.TC-14008)
Leigh, Gillian Mary 9551
(MIC.F.TC-49806)
Leighton, James Douglas 7450
(MIC.F.TC-24593)
Leiper, Robert Neil 9709
(MIC.F.TC-53450)
Leipziger, Danny Melvin 1534
(MIC.T-608)
Leith, Larry McKenzie 10410
(MIC.F.TC-32014)
Leman, Christopher Kent 8511
Lembeke, Jerry Lee 2152
Lemelin, André 1756
Lemelin, Charles 67
Lemelin, Maurice 2137
(HD8005.2 C2 L46)
Lemelin, Abbé Roméo 7950
Lemieux, André 1047 (P90 L45)
Lemieux, G. 8216
Lemieux, Gérard 8014
Lemieux, Germain 8212
Lemieux, Guy Joseph 11767
Lemieux, Louis 10770
Lemieux, Omer Adrien 112
Lemieux, Pierre Hervé 8293
(PS8515 E16 T63)
Lemieux-Michaud, Denise 8218
(MIC.F.TC-45934)
Lemire, Soeur Antoinette 3132
Lemire, Gilles 7696
Lemire, Maurice Roland 8219
(PS8191 N3 L4)
Lemoine, Roger 7339
Lemmon, Kathlene Sutton 8143
Lemon, Roy Richard Henry 5864
(MIC.F.TC-25488)
Lemonde, André 11159
Lenchyshyn, David Arthur 2982
(MIC.F.T-1312)
Lendenman, Karl Werner 9710
(MIC.F.TC-43670)
Lenk, Cecilia 11607
Lennox, John Watt 8220
(MIC.F.TC-30423)
Lenskyj, Helen 10387
(MIC.F.TC-59828)
Lent, Peter Charles 10616
Lenz, Alfred C. 6547
Leo, Frère Antonio 8307
Leonard, Eric Michael 5427
(MIC.F.T-1223)
Leonard, George Albert 2869
(MIC.F.T-1004)
Leonard, Mortimer Demarest 11160
Leong, Raymond Tak Seng 10551
(MIC.F.TC-26821)
Leong, Wubong-Teck 3876
(MIC.F.TC-59829)
Leonhart, William Boyd 3826
(MIC.F.TC-47216)

Lepage, Ernest 273
Lepicq, Dominique Louise Marie 7697
(MIC.F.TC-47099)
Lepore, Guiseppe 2238
(MIC.F.TC-23126)
Leprohon, Carol Elizabeth 6751
(MIC.F.TC-50293)
Leroy, Perry Eugene 7298 (MIC.T-126)
Lesage, Germain 4816
Lesage, Laurent 11281
(MIC.F.TC-42371)
Lesage, Pierre Bernard 9604
(MIC.T-573)
Leschied, Alan David Winfield 10265
(MIC.F.TC-98377)
LeSieur, Antonio 2749
Lesko, Wayne A. 9711
(MIC.F.TC-39361)
Leslie, Adrian Roy 7822
(MIC.F.TC-42124)
Leslie, Perry Thorold 3877
(MIC.TC-13239)
Leslie, Peter Malcolm 8624
(MIC.TC-1658)
Leslie, Robert James 6548
Lespérance, Pierre Jacques 6397
L'Espérance, Robert L. 6398
Lessard, Claude Robert Théophile 9978
(MIC.F.TC-32934)
Lessard, Francine 9451
Lessard, Victrice 2533
Lessells, C.M. 10799
Lester, Geoffrey Standish 7839
(MIC.F.TC-53499)
Lester, Malcolm 7035 (MIC.T-114)
Létourneau, Gilles 7907 (KE8566 L47)
Létourneau, Jeannette 2534
(MIC.F.TC-44066)
Letourneau, Léo Arthur 4379
(MIC.F.TC-60267)
Létourneau, Marguerite 6897
Létourneau, Pierre 3856
(MIC.F-024208)
Lett, Raymond E.W. 5264
(MIC.F.TC-42682)
Lettau, Bernhard 5027
Leung, Jupian Jupchung 3241
(MIC.F.TC-56603)
Levant, Avrom Victor 8891
Léveillé, Suzanne Michèle 6898
(MIC.F.TC-56457)
Leveillée, Jacques 8758
(MIC.F-031704)
Levesque, Denis R. 2644
Levin, Benjamin Ruvin 1941
(MIC.F.TC-58306)
Levin, Deborah Marcia 8924
(MIC.F.TC-54105)
Levin, E.A. 9377
Levine, Gregory James 9798
(MIC.F.TC-46369)
Levine, Marc Veblen 2793
(MIC.F.T-1208)
Levine, Robert Daigon 7807
(MIC.F.TC-31319)
Lévis, Frère 8373
Levitt, Joseph 7262 (MIC.TC-13792)
Levy, Gary 8443
Levy, Richard Stephen 676
(MIC.F.TC-22152)
Levy, Steven Stanley 10113
(MIC.F.TC-36731)
Levy, Thomas Allen 8493 (MIC.T-657)
Lewandowski, Arthur Joseph 9028
Lewis, Archibald Clifford 4552
(LB2831.656 C3 L49)
Lewis, Charles Frederick Michael 5120
(MIC.TC-1101)
Lewis, Claudia Louise 677 (MIC.T-982)
Lewis, David James 11263
(MIC.F.TC-27556)
Lewis, Edward Dale 2870
Lewis, Elmer N. 3242 (LB1063 L49)
Lewis, George Kinsman 747
(MIC.T-852)
Lewis, Norah Lillian 3097
(MIC.F.TC-51737)
Lewis, Oscar 503 (E99 S54 L4)
Lewis, Terence 237 (MIC.F.TC-29880)

Lewis, Terri Lorraine 9341
(MIC.F.TC-46903)
Lewis, Thomas Leonard 6109
Lewis, Trevor John 6667
(MIC.F.TC-24595)
Lewkowicz, Antoni G. 4672
(MIC.F.TC-53253)
Lewyckyj, Jurij Myroslaw 7780
Leyton-Brown, David Robert 1387
L'Hérault, Pierre 8277
(MIC.F.TC-35753)
Li, Chi-Yen 4521
Li, Lew King 24
Li, Shin-Chai 304 (MIC.F.TC-25209)
Li, Si-Ming 1578 (MIC.F.TC-55955)
Liaw, Wen Kuang 11866
(MIC.F.TC-24736)
Libby, Dorothy 549
Liberakis, Eustace Anatasius 6803
(MIC.F.TC-36903)
Liberty, Bruce Arthur 6110
Libman, Mark Norman 9552
(MIC.F.TC-21554)
Liburd, Rosemary 9305
(MIC.F.TC-49011)
Lichtenberg, Mitchell Palmer 3468
Lichti-Federovich, Sigrid 5105
Lickus, Robert John 6399
Lieff, Bernard Charles 10800
(MIC.TC-16427)
Lieffers, Victor James 11513
(MIC.F.TC-47217)
Lien, San-Lang 4522
Lier, John 25 (MIC.T-210)
Light, Martha Carolyn 3938
(MIC.F.TC-47101)
Lightbody, James William 8699
(MIC.F.TC-32666)
Lightfoot, Lynn O. 9261
(MIC.F.TC-49809)
Lightman, Ernie Stanley 2187
Ligondé, Paultre 10297
Lillegraven, Jason Arthur 6565
Lim, Kiok-Puan 11318
(MIC.F.TC-47380)
Lim, Richard Peter 11086
(MIC.F.TC-28605)
Lima, Oriane A.S. 6848
(MIC.F.TC-53100)
Limages, Thérèse 10266
Limin, Allan Edward 355
Limpert, Roland John C. 10801
Lin, Kwan-Chow 4554
(MIC.F.TC-27907)
Lin, Leon Chin-Shin 180
Linask, Kersti Luhaäär 2437
(MIC.FT-998)
Lincoln, Timothy Nye 5265
Linden, Wolfgang 9029
(MIC.F.TC-52019)
Lindenfield, Rita Graham 1629
Linder, Harold William 5712
Lindgren, Bo Staffan 11218
(MIC.F.TC-53452)
Lindgren, David Treadwell 4888
Lindop, Darla Rhyne 10166
(MIC.F.TC-42304)
Lindquist, Neil Eric 10209
(MIC.F.TC-30744)
Lindquist, Vernon Rolfe 8061
(MIC.F.TC-58686)
Lindsay, Peter Leslie 10343
(MIC.TC-4949)
Lindsay, Stephen Leslie 10696
(MIC.F.T-1219)
Lindsay-Reid, Elizabeth Ann 6694
(MIC.F.TC-42255)
Lindsey, David Allen 6111
Lines, Kenneth 7651 (MIC.T-891)
Ling, Agnes Hamilton 3878
(MIC.TC-15886)
Lingard, Charles Cecil 7185
(JL462 L56)
Link, Peter Karl 5921
Linn, Hilareon Dewell 4745
(MIC.F.TC-36930)
Linnamae, Urve 884 (MIC.F.TC-17008)
Linteau, Paul A. 7271 (MIC.F-021906)
Linton, John Alexander 6668
(MIC.F.TC-30911)
Linzon, Samuel Nathan 11653

Lioy, Michele Louisette 10089
(MIC.F.TC-40683)
Lipman, Marvin Harold 10033
(MIC.TC-7506)
Lippitt, Louis 6112
Lippman-Hand, Abby 4149
(MIC.F.TC-38289)
Lipset, Seymour Martin 8635
(JL197 N4 L5)
Liptak, Dolores Ann 836
Lissey, Allan 11988
Lister, Geoffrey Richard 11476
(MIC.TC-1778)
Lister, William Warwick 972
Lithwick, Carol Louise Appel 4316
Lithwick, Irwin 1209 (MIC.F.TC-23307)
Lithwick, Norman Harvey 1210
(HC115 L3)
Little, Donald Malcolm 3827
(MIC.F.TC-17597)
Little, Heward Wallace 5266
Little, John Irvine 3163
(MIC.F.TC-27689)
Little, John Michael 7576
(MIC.F.TC-32935)
Little, Robert Merle 6870 (MIC.T-651)
Litva, John 12010 (MIC.F.TC-23356)
Litvak, Isaiah 2019 (MIC.T-189)
Liu, Helen Jadwiga 11282
(MIC.F.TC-37430)
Liu, Juanita Ngit Wun 4806
(MIC.F.TC-44931)
Liu, , Kam-Biu 4699 (MIC.F.TC-58265)
Liu, Paul Chi 11902
Liu, Peter Andrew 3029
(MIC.F.TC-53102)
Livada, Valentin Radu 8444
Livermore, John Daniel 7332
(MIC.F.TC-24850)
Livingston, Walter Ross 8710
Llambias, Henry John 8702
(MIC.F.TC-44416)
Lloyd, Andrew Thomas 10582
(MIC.F.T-1296)
Lloyd, Cynthia Brown 1178
(MIC.T-367)
Lloyd, Donald Loftus 90
Lloyd, Trevor 4738
Llull, Georges 3456
(MIC.F-2M11.584.4)
Locat, Jacques 4488 (MIC.F.TC-56083)
Lock, Anthony 10830
(MIC.F.TC-18643)
Lock, Brian Edward 5764
Lock, William Rowland 967
(ML27 O59 L8)
Locke, William Willard, III 5865
(MIC.F.T-1124)
Locker, John Gary 5428 (MIC.TC-3859)
Lockhart, R.A. 9979
Lodha, Ganpat Singh 6591
(MIC.F.TC-36734)
Lodhia-Patel, Vimla 6823
(MIC.F.TC-54843)
Loeb, Nora 3243
Loebel, Peter Bernard 8677
(MIC.F.TC-35052)
Loeber, Magda Southaner 3072
(MIC.F.TC-42529)
Loeffler, E.J. 6549
Loeken, Olav H. 4646
Loft, Genivera Edmunds 4799
Logan, Bayne Stuart 3997
Logan, Harold Amos 2099
Logan, John Edwin 2165 (MIC.T-368)
Logan, Roderick Mackenzie 4700
Logie, Robert Reed 11098
Loh, Wallace Dzu 9712 (MIC.T-330)
Lok, Siepko Hendrik 26
Loken, Joel Obert 3688 (MIC.TC-6735)
Loken, Mark Keith 2020 (MIC.T-428)
Lomasney, Patrick John 9916
Lommen, Paul Warren 12011
London, Anselm Lullellyn 2344
(MIC.F.TC-63127)
Long, Beverly Jean 9342
Long, Bonita Clarice 9104
(MIC.F.TC-17130)
Long, D.V.M. 10519
Long, Darrel Graham Francis 6113
(MIC.F.TC-31616)

Long, Dorothy Elizabeth 7315
Long, John Clifford Anthony 3530
(MIC.F.TC-49014)
Long, John W., Jr. 7525
Long, Larry Howard 10137
Long, Tanya C. 8116
Longley, Ronald S. 7320
Longley, Willard Victor 158
Longley, William W. 6400
Longstaffe, Frederick John 6114
(MIC.F.TC-37987)
Longworth, David John 1608
Lonker, Steven Wayne 6115
Looker, Ellen Diane 10210
(MIC.F.TC-36539)
Loose, Verne William 1862
(MIC.F.TC-40689)
Looy, Anthony Jacobus 7451
(MIC.F.TC-34626)
Lopez, Ramon Eugenio 27
(MIC.F.TC-55063)
Loranger, D.M.L. 6566
Loranger, Michel 3340
Lord, Clifford S. 5513
Loree, Donald James 731
(MIC.F.TC-21889)
Lorimer, Rowland M. 3504
(MIC.TC-5232)
Lorincz, Louis Michael 2690
(MIC.F.TC-49321)
Lorimer, Wesley C. 4397
Lorrain, Jean 9452 (MIC.T-3393)
Lortie, Jeanne d'Arc 8362 (PS8149 L67)
Losey, Timothy Campbell 857
(MIC.F.TC-36422)
Losier, Soeur St. Michael 3469
Lott, Frank Melville 6871
Lotto, David Joshua 9112
(MIC.F.TC-20014)
Loucks, Kenneth Edmond 2075
(MIC.F.TC-20522)
Loucks, Ronald Harold 5008
Louden, Lindsay Warren 2933
(MIC.F.TC-44771)
Loudon, John Russell 5617
Lougheed, Milford Seymour 6642
Loughner-Gillin, Cheryl 9138
(MIC.F.TC-51202)
Loughton, Albert John 3689
(MIC.F.T-995)
Lounsbury, Floyd G. 7809
Lounsbury, Ralph Greenlee 1227
(SH226 L6)
Lousier, Joseph Daniel 224
(MIC.F.TC-44596)
Love, James Hume 2499
Loveridge, Jennifer M. Young 3934
(MIC.F.TC-59774)
Lovering, James Herbert 62
Lovett, Maureen Winnifred 3967
(MIC.F.TC-35757)
Lovink, Johannes Anton
Alexander 8625 (MIC.T-190)
Low, John Hay 6116
Low, Margaret 8226 (MIC.F.TC-39168)
Low, Robert Alan, Jr. 10954
Lowe, Graham Stanley 1278
(MIC.F.TC-40935)
Lowe, Lawrence Edward 274
Lower, Arthur Reginald M. 1279
Lowery, Robert Eugene 2934
(LB2822.5 L6)
Lowes, Brian Edward 5267
Lowry, Douglas Bradley 1179
Lowry, R.B. 475
Lowther, George K. 6401
Lowther, Rachel Mary 3828
(MIC.F.TC-43085)
Loy, William G. 4602
Loyer, Marie des Anges 6879
(MIC.F.TC-56489)
Lozynsky, Artem 8077
Lu, Julin D. 11791
Lu, Wen-Fong 28 (MIC.F.TC-37808)
Lubin, Martin 7157 (MIC.T-582)
Lubitz, Raymond 2391
Lucas, Barry Gillespie 2794
(MIC.T-331)
Lucas, Christine Wooledge 3968
(MIC.F.TC-27200)

Lucas, Margaret Jennifer 5660
Lucas, Rex Archibald 10211
Lucas, Robert Charles 4701
  (MIC.T-703)
Luce, Sally R. 3690
Luck-Allen, Etta Robena 11386
Luckman, Brian Henry 4732
Lucyszyn, Elizabeth Lupien 10520
Ludlow, Wayne Everett 4439
Ludvigsen, Rolf 6550
  (MIC.F.TC-24602)
Ludwig, Daniel Robert 10712
  (MIC.F.TC-55372)
Ludwig, James P. 10831
Luedecke, Barbara Mary 9306
  (MIC.F.TC-44502)
Luk, Shiu Hung 225 (MIC.F.TC-26828)
Lukasevich, Ann 2595
  (MIC.F.TC-29881)
Lumbers, Sydney Blake 6117
Lund, Richard Jacob 5661
Lunde, Magnus 6410
Lundman, Susan Brenda 6782
Lundy, Katharina Lillian Pauline 10212
  (MIC.F.TC-36739)
Lundy, Lawrence Allan 3741
  (MIC.TC-6846)
Lunn, Alice Jean 1228 (MIC.TC-2000)
Lupton, Austin Albert 83
  (MIC.TC-4952)
Lupul, Manoly Robert 9917
Lush, Donald Lawrence 11867
  (MIC.F.TC-19334)
Lusk, John 5627
Lustig, Stephen David 9553
  (MIC.F.TC-39404)
Lusztig, Peter Alfred 1662
  (MIC.T-157)
Luternauer, John Leland 11929
  (MIC.TC-11239)
Luther, Michael Gerard 9554
  (MIC.F.TC-47843)
Lutwick, Laurence E. 287
Lutz, Maija M. 964 (ML3798 L975 fol.)
Luxton, Margaret Joan 422
  (MIC.F.TC-38766)
Lyall, Anil Kumar 5662
Lyall, Harry Bruce 6403
Lynch, Mary Agnes 8469
  (FC626 T7 L95 fol.)
Lynn, James Hugh 1459
  (MIC.F.TC-35055)
Lynott, William John 5268
Lyon, Kenneth Redman Vaughan 8512
  (MIC.F.TC-25212)
Lyon, Noel Adversé 29
Lyons, Helen Ida 9555
  (MIC.F.TC-59129)
Lyons, John Edward 2425
  (MIC.F.TC-49016)
Lyons, Sister Letitia Mary
  Francis 9898
Lyons, Leslie Allan 11319
Lyons, Peter Andrew 9960
  (MIC.F.TC-25770)
Lyons, Renée Felice 10443
  (MIC.F.T-1165)
Lyons, William Elmer 8658
  (MIC.T-132)

M

Ma, Shao Ngang 4253
  (MIC.F.TC-52408)
Ma, Sylvia See-Wai 2230
  (MIC.F.TC-53106)
Maas, Elizabeth 3244
  (MIC.F.TC-29883)
MacArthur, A. Isabel 6752
MacArthur, Robert Allan 10684
  (MIC.F.TC-35855)
Macaulay, Alexander James 11514
  (MIC.F.TC-22548)
Macaulay, James Donald 73
  (MIC.F.TC-25921)

MacAulay, Thomas Gordon 194
  (MIC.F.TC-31077)
MacCharles, Donald Clare 1757
  (MIC.F.TC-38769)
Mac Clean, Alister J. 336
MacDermid, Gordon Edward 9883
  (MIC.T-901)
MacDonald, Alan Stratton 5269
  (MIC.F.TC-17204)
MacDonald, Donald D. 2645
  (HV1626 M33)
MacDonald, George 3367
MacDonald, George Frederick 905
  (MIC.T-980)
MacDonald, Gilbert H. 5566
Macdonald, J. Grant 9262
  (MIC.F.TC-58266)
Macdonald, Helen Grace 7456 (H31 C7)
Mac Donald, Irene Frances 3106
  (MIC.F.TC-30753)
MacDonald, James Andrew 2310
  (MIC.T-587)
MacDonald, John Angus 3341
  (MIC.F.TC-23364)
MacDonald, John Stevenson 10988
  (MIC.F.TC-56137)
MacDonald, Joseph Lorne 559
MacDonald, Mairi Teresa
  St. John 10213
MacDonald, Marilyn Anne 11387
  (MIC.F.TC-31619)
Macdonald, Norman 7466 (MIC.T-868)
MacDonald, Peter Ian 2500
  (MIC.F.TC-47108)
MacDonald, Rae M. 1479
  (MIC.F.TC-28927)
MacDonald, Robert James 8297
MacDonald, Roderick Andrew 4317
  (MIC.F.TC-38771)
MacDonald, Roderick Dickson 5765
MacDonald, Ronald 4413
MacDougall, Edward Bruce 63
  (MIC.TC-1870)
MacDougall, Heather Anne 6695
  (MIC.F.TC-55836)
MacDougall, James Brown 2501
  (LA418 O6 M25)
MacDougall, John Innes 4277
MacDowell, Laurel Sefton 2114
  (MIC.F.TC-50299)
Mace, Pamela Margaret 10955
  (MIC.F.TC-65004)
Mace, Thomas Francis Andrew 11340
  (MIC.F.TC-22711)
MacFadden, Robert James 10090
  (MIC.F.TC-58268)
MacFadyen, Alan James 2021
  (MIC.T-293)
MacFarland, Gertrude Cecile 3656
MacFarland, Roderick Peter 11283
  (MIC.F.TC-20928)
MacFarland, Ronald Oliver 7431
MacGeehan, Patrick John 6404
  (MIC.F.TC-42972)
MacGibbon, Duncan Alexander 2311
  (HE1855 M34)
MacGown, Matthew W. 11161
MacGregor, Hugh A. 4099
MacGregor, Ian Duncan 6118
MacHardy, Fenton V. 195 (MIC.T-869)
Machas, David Lloyd 11850
Machlin, Evangeline L. 3717
MacInnes, Charles Donald 10802
MacInnes, Daniel William 2115
  (MIC.F.TC-39953)
MacInnes, Kaye Lucile 11546
  (MIC.TC-14042)
MacIntosh, Roderick James 8363
  (MIC.F.T-1173)
MacIntyre, Donald George 5270
  (MIC.F.TC-31622)
MacIntyre, Robert John 11053
MacIver, Ian 4702 (TD227 O5 G7)
Mack, Frederich Georg 196
  (MIC.T-760)
Mack, Judith Elaine 9030
  (MIC.F.TC-47844)
Mackas, David Lloyd 11850
  (MIC.F.TC-36128)
MacKay, Bertram Reid 6405
MacKay, David Allister 2857

MacKay, Harry Earle 10181
  (MIC.F.TC-38494)
Mackay, Hector Hugh 11868
MacKay, Kenneth Tod 10994
  (MIC.F.TC-36129)
MacKay, Robert Alexander 8543
  (JL155 M3)
MacKay, Rosemary Joan 11320
  (MIC.TC-11925)
Macken, Catherine Anne 10803
  (MIC.F.T-1015)
MacKenzie, Graham Stewart 6119
MacKenzie, H.M. 1515
Mackenzie, J.A. 7922
MacKenzie, Joan Phillips 3788
  (MIC.F.TC-54854)
MacKenzie, John David 5271
MacKenzie, Marguerite Ellen 7783
  (MIC.F.TC-53109)
MacKenzie, Warren Stuart 5567
  (MIC.TC-99)
MacKenzie, William H. 2712
MacKeracher, Dorothy Margaret 10214
  (MIC.F.TC-55835)
Mackie, Gerald L. 11116
  (MIC.F.TC-19064)
MacKillican, William S. 2663
MacKinnon, Clarence Stuart 7124
  (MIC.TC-7508)
MacKinnon, Francis Perley Taylor 8713
  (JL212 M3)
MacKinnon, I.F. 9788
MacKinnon, Joyce Roberta 6718
  (MIC.F.TC-51749)
MacKinnon, Kenneth Robert 9713
MacKinnon, Malcolm Hector 10022
  (MIC.F.TC-37000)
MacKinnon, Neil Joseph 4030
MacKinnon, Theresa Lucina 1024
  (MIC.T-769)
MacKinnon, Victor Stuart 7878
Mackintosh, William Archibald 118
  (HD1491 C2 M35)
MacKirdy, Kenneth Alexander 6936
Macklin, Evangeline L. 1025
MacLachlan, Donald C. 6120
MacLaggan, Katherine 6899
  (MIC.T-133)
MacLaren, Alexander S. 6406
MacLaurin, Donald L. 2452
  (MIC.T-149)
MacLaury, Bruce King, Jr. 1558
  (MIC.F.TC-21892)
MacLean, Adrian Henry 226
  (MIC.F.TC-21892)
MacLean, Annie Marion 767
MacLean, David Andrew 11732
  (MIC.F.TC-35613)
MacLean, Rev. Donald Alexander 2809
MacLean, Guy Robertson 7125
  (MIC.T-349)
MacLean, Hugh James 5766
MacLean, Margaret Louise 4008
  (MIC.F.TC-58159)
MacLean, Marvin E. 10114
  (MIC.TC-15274)
MacLean, Raymond Angus 7322
  (MIC.TC-15429)
MacLellan, Haidee Patricia 3342
MacLeod, Alan Ross 2992
  (MIC.TC-9615)
Macleod, Betty Belle Robinson 1211
MacLeod, Donald Eric 1280
  (MIC.F.TC-53110)
MacLeod, Donald J. 305
MacLeod, Henry Gordon 9863
  (MIC.F.TC-47111)
MacLeod, Malcolm 7000
MacLeod, Marion J. 130
MacLeod, Nelson B. 4458
Macleod, Roderick Charles 7126
  (F5000 C24)
MacLulich, Duncan Alexander 10660
  (QH1 T68 fol.)
MacLulich, Thomas Donald 8015
  (MIC.TC-26650)
MacMillan, Charles Michael 8463
MacMillan, Cyrus John 962
Macmillan, Michael Roderick 2935
  (MIC.F.TC-17608)
MacNab, Grace Lowe 9997
  (MIC.F.TC-32164)

MacNaughton, Alan Robert 1718
MacNaughton, Bruce Douglas 8513
 (MIC.F.TC-49516)
Macnaughton, William Norman 10644
MacNeil, Donald J. 5429
MacNeil, James Leo 3577
MacNeil, T.B. 3998 (MIC.F.TC-53984)
MacNeish, June H. 550
MacNiven, Hugh Gordon 8678
Macodrum, M.M. 8428
MacPherson, Andrew Hall 10579
MacPherson, Constance Joyce 4764
MacPherson, George R. Ian 7482
 (MIC.TC-7765)
MacPherson, Harry Gordon 6121
MacPherson, Hector 1281
 (HG2051 C38 M2)
Macqueen, Angus 11219
 (MIC.F.TC-19271)
MacQueen, Roger Webb 5430
MacRae, Christopher Frederick 8343
 (MIC.F.TC-33096)
MacRae, Donald Lachlan 4067
 (MIC.F.TC-42261)
MacRae, Neil D. 6122
Macri, Francis Maria 8016
 (MIC.F.TC-51542)
MacRury, Ian MacDonald 9864
 (MIC.F.T-1289)
MacVean, William Campbell 9789
Madak, Paul Richard 3062
 (MIC.F.TC-54530)
Madden, Casey Thomas 6512
Madder, Douglas James 11284
 (MIC.F.TC-48776)
Maddocks, George Raymond 3531
 (MIC.TC-14020)
Maddukuri, C. Subbarao 12012
 (MIC.F.TC-30923)
Madduri, Venkata Bhaskara Narasinha
 Sastry 10313 (MIC.F.TC-43480)
Madge, Ronald Bradley 11162
Madge, S.J. 8825
Madill, Alonzo James 4100
 (S535 O5 M3)
Madore, M. Rose Bernadette 11415
Madrid, Francisco Javier 11321
 (MIC.F.TC-47389)
Maduro, Morris F., Jr. 7929
 (MIC.F.TC-40237)
Maehl, Richard Henry 5663
Maeser, Angelika Maria 8117
 (MIC.F.TC-39743)
Magasi, Laszlo Paul 11580
Magdelenat, Jean-Louis 7908
 (MIC.F.TC-52025)
Mage, Julius Arnold 94
 (MIC.F.TC-21615)
Magee, David J. 10388
 (MIC.F.TC-49028)
Magee, William Henry 8062
 (MIC.F.TC-19723)
Maggs, William Randall 8415
 (MIC.F.TC-41078)
Magidson, Ethel 9343
 (MIC.F-2M11.363.4)
Maguire, Bassett 11547
Magwood, John McLean 7879
 (MIC.F.TC-50303)
Mahalingasivam, Rasiah 1887
 (MIC.TC-6848)
Mahan, Howard F. 7069
Mahen, Robert Gordon 3073
 (MIC.F.TC-34428)
Maher, Christopher Anthony 4948
 (MIC.TC-15415)
Maher, Timothy Francis 9556
 (MIC.F.TC-47113)
Maheu-Latouche, Louise 8221
Mahler, Gregory Steven 8533
 (MIC.F.T-920)
Mahon, Paule Rianne 1388
 (MIC.F.TC-36747)
Mahon, Robin Campbell 11019
 (MIC.F.TC-52527)
Mahoney, Michael Joseph 12013
 (MIC.F.TC-29892)
Maidman, Frank Victor 10034
 (MIC.TC-13062)
Maidstone, Peter 9139
 (MIC.F.TC-59300)

Mailhot, Raymond 7163
 (MIC.F-006502)
Maillet, Antonine 8431 (GR113 M35)
Maillet, Léandre 10298
 (MIC.F-2M11.556.2)
Maillet, Marguerite 8222
Main, Oscar Warren 1282
 (HD9539 N52 C36)
Maine, Star Floyd 9876
Mainemer, Nathan 9222
 (MIC.F.TC-59631)
Maini, Jagmohon S. 11622
Maioni, T.L. 9378
Maister, David Hilton 1803
 (MIC.T-853)
Majcen, Zoran 11768
 ((MIC.F.TC-41431)
Majerus, Yvette Vivian 2535
 (MIC.TC-11417)
Major, Robert 8223 (PN4920 P37 M34)
Makabe, Tomoko 796 (MIC.F.TC-35061)
Makow, Henry 8102 (MIC.F.TC-55852)
Malach, Vernon Walter 1979
Malcuzynski, M. Pierrette 8253
 (MIC.F.TC-58101)
Malecki, Richard Allen 10804
Malenfant, Chanel 8304
Maley, Jean McCanns 1480
 (MIC.T-476)
Malhi, Sukhdev Singh 211
 (MIC.F.TC-36435)
Malik, Hargulshan Singh 9307
 (MIC.TC-9618)
Malik, Muhammad Hussain 1559
Maliyankino, Thadeo Lutatina 2763
 (MIC.F.TC-26840)
Mallet, André L. 11099
 (MIC.F.TC-57982)
Mallett, W. Graham 4122
Mallette, Rolland Roger 9605
 (MIC.F.TC-22320)
Malliah, Holavanahally L. 7235
 (MIC.TC-6223)
Mallinson, Anna Jean 8344
 (MIC.F.TC-51042)
Mallinson, Thomas John 3111
 (MIC.F.TC-31276)
Malloch, Lynette Lockwood 3245
 (MIC.F.TC-40937)
Mallory, Frank Pensom 10668
 ((MIC.F.TC-41749)
Malloy, Brenda Margaret 2552
 (MIC.F.TC-21905)
Maloney, Timothy Lawrence 3657
 (MIC.F.TC-21905)
Malouf, Stanley E. 6407
Maltais, Marie Ludovic 2130
Malus, Avrum 8084 (MIC.F-022204)
Mamandur, Rangarah Chetty 4584
 (MIC.F.TC-34213)
Mamen, Margaret 9377
Mandel, Allan Rudolf 9113
 (MIC.F.TC-51375)
Mandel, Dorothy E. 753
 (MIC.F.T-1217)
Mandelbaum, David Goodman 510
Mandelzys, Nathan 6741
Mandich, Michael M. 9865
Mandziuk, Lucia Marie 3969
 (MIC.F.TC-53399)
Maneckjee, Marie-Claire 7698
Manga, Pranlal 1630 (MIC.F.TC-35062)
Manganas, Antoine 7909
Manhart, George Brown 4841
 (HF3508 T8 R6)
Manley, Ronald Stuart 9031
 (MIC.F.TC-61595)
Manley, Thomas Owen 11969
Mann, Barbara Elizabeth 9557
 (MIC.F.TC-57982)
Mann, Brenda Lynn 9308
 (MIC.F.TC-49031)
Mann, Ernest Leigh 5713
Mann, George Adolf 10233 (MIC.T-809)
Mann, Harvey 1410 (MIC.T-496)
Mann, John Fraser 9558
 (MIC.F.TC-31836)
Mann, Robert Ernest 9263
 (MIC.F.TC-49820)
Mann, William Edward 9967
 (MIC.F.TC-59860)
Manning, Helen Taft 7036 (JV1016 M3)

Manning, William R. 7498
 (F5798 N6 M3)
Mannion, John Joseph 4849
 (MIC.TC-10588)
Manns, Francis Tucker 5272
 (MIC.F.TC-55849)
Manos, James 3088 (MIC.F.TC-26842)
Mansbridge, Francis 8393
Mansell, Robert Leonard 4788
 (MIC.F.TC-24093)
Mansfield, Arthur Walter 10606
Mansfield, Earl Arthur 2846
Manuel, Donald Winsor 4040
 (MIC.F.TC-27700)
Manuel, Paciencia Castello 30
Manuel, Raymond Lewis 11322
 (MIC.F.TC-60936)
Manz, Raymond Leonard 10368
 (MIC.F.TC-40240)
Marano, Louis Anthony 546
Marbach, Joseph F. 9829
Marble, William Oscar 4440
 (MIC.F.TC-53459)
Marceau, Denis 9417
 (MIC.F.TC-39171)
Marceau, Richard 8759
March, Gordon Lorne 10855
 (MIC.TC-8772)
March, Milton Edgar 2664
 (MIC.F.TC-51545)
March, Roman Robert 8534
Marchak, Maureen Patricia 2166
 (MIC.TC-6920)
Marchand, Claude Françoise 4837
 (MIC.F.TC-40938)
Marchand, Michael 5714
Marchant, Cosmo Kenningham 739
 (MIC.F.TC-47846)
Marchylo, Brian Alexander 167
 (MIC.F.TC-37813)
Marcks, Brian Gene 11416
Marcotte, Alexandre 11032
Marcotte, Brian Michael 11082
 (MIC.F.TC-36136)
Marcotte, Gilles 8364
Marcotte, William Arthur 4353
 (MIC.F.TC-43679)
Marcoux, Yves 9628
 (MIC.F-2M11.570.9)
Marcovitch, Howard David 3917
 (MIC.F.TC-43680)
Marcovitch, Sharon Fenton 9380
 (MIC.F.TC-58740)
Marcus, Edward 1324
Margolis, Leo 10552
Margules, Morton 2885
Marie-Diomède, Soeur 8224
Marie-Emmanuel, Soeur 7289
Marie-Médéric, Frère 8432
Marino, Robert Vincent 10091
 (MIC.F.TC-50306)
Marion, Séraphin 8225
Maris, Brian Alan 1481
Marjoribanks, Kevin McLeod 2577
 (MIC.TC-9549)
Mark, Clarence Ellsworth 2502
 (LA419 O8 M3)
Mark, Devon Joy 9309
 (MIC.F.TC-43483)
Markell, H. Keith 9799
Markham, James Wilbur 11477
 (MIC.TC-5108)
Markle, Glen Hugh 3648
 (MIC.F.TC-30348)
Markon, Philippe Joseph Jacques 10389
 (MIC.F.TC-56814)
Markovich, Denise Elizabeth 2345
 (MIC.F.TC-40032)
Marks, C.J.A. 2272
Markus, Nathan 10151
Marlak, Charles F. 2090
Marland, Percy Wilson 4318
 (MIC.F.TC-34435)
Marleau, Alban Raymond 6408
Marliave, Jeffrey Burton 10956
 (MIC.F.TC-28750)
Marois, Claude 10322
Marois, Roger Joseph-Maurice 929
 (MIC.TC-15594)
Marothia, Dinesh Kumar 45
 (MIC.F.TC-53992)

Marquardt, Richard Earl 10805
Marques de Sa, Leticia Lucena 9714
　(MIC.T-3770)
Marquis, Paul-Yvan 7858
　(MIC.TC-15925)
Marr, John Winton 11608
Marr, William Lewis 7659
　(MIC.TC-14043)
Marrin-McConnell, Mary Irene 7699
　(MIC.F.TC-38778)
Mars, Gould 405
Marsan, Jean-Claude 937 (MIC.T-870)
Marsden, Lorna R. 6804 (MIC.T-425)
Marsden, Ralph W. 5134
Marsh, Frank Gene 3432
　(MIC.F.TC-49033)
Marsh, John Stuart 4614
　(MIC.TC-11345)
Marsh, Leonard C. 2116
Marsh, Vernon L. 11422
Marshall, Anna C. 11191
Marshall, Anthony Robert Alfred 3632
　(MIC.F.TC-30761)
Marshall, Christine Mavis 3742
Marshall, David George 2665
　(MIC.F.TC-44777)
Marshall, Elizabeth Anne 4150
　(MIC.F.TC-47116)
Marshall, Ernest Willard 5119
Marshall, John Charles 10373
　(MIC.F.TC-47847)
Marshall, John Urquhart 4703
　(MIC.TC-2482)
Marshall, Joseph Melville 10425
Marshall, Lionel George 2907
Marshall, Malcolm Frederick 3970
　(MIC.F.TC-42696)
Marshall, Michael Anthony 2702
　(MIC.F.TC-37682)
Marshall, Mortimer V. 4398
Marshall, Peter Graham 9715
　(MIC.F.TC-30160)
Marshall, Richard Eugene 8810
　(MIC.T-311)
Marshall, Stephen Archer 11163
Marshall, Valin George K. 11323
Martell, Arthur Melvin 10713
　(MIC.F.TC-24094)
Martell, David Leigh 11747
　(MIC.F.TC-31282)
Martell, J.S. 7175
Marten, Brian Ernest 5715
　(MIC.F.TC-33777)
Martens, Ethel G. 6805 (MIC.T-588)
Martens, Fred Lewis 10402
Martens, Hildegard Margo 809
　(MIC.F.TC-42263)
Martens, James Hart Curry 6409
Martig, Ralph R. 7090
Martin, Alexander Robert 11638
Martin, David Standish 3246
Martin, Fant W. 10806
Martin, Gerald Warren 7467
　(MIC.T-902)
Martin, Jack F. 9453
　(MIC.F.TC-17616)
Martin, Jayne Frances Carney 10521
Martin, Jeanette Helen Price 7784
　(MIC.T-835)
Martin, Leonard John 5866
Martin, Norman Duncan 10734
Martin, Paul-Louis 6937
　(MIC.F.TC-48042)
Martin, Robert Angus 2847
　(MIC.TC-10590)
Martin, Roger Duane 10226
　(MIC.TC-4953)
Martin, Sheilagh Marie 6849
　(MIC.F.TC-34214)
Martin, T.R. 7037
Martin, Terry Homer 8728
　(MIC.F.T-1035)
Martin, Thomas O. 6925
　(MIC.F.TC-44088)
Martin, Victor Leo 2886
Martin, Wilfred Benjamin Weldon 9998
　(MIC.TC-12595)
Martin, William Steward Arnold 2173
　(MIC.F.TC-25493)
Martin, Yvonne Marjorie 2887
　(MIC.F.TC-33334)

Martin-Matthews, Anne
　Elizabeth 10050 (MIC.F.TC-46914)
Martineau, François 8080
Martineau, M.P. 5867
Martinello, Margaret Pappert 8017
　(MIC.F.TC-47848)
Martini, Ireneo Peter 6123
Martini, Janie Lilia 9140
　(MIC.F.TC-33574)
Marton, John Peter 9559
　(MIC.F.TC-49426)
Marton, Katherin 1663 (MIC.T-678)
Martyn, Harold George 3133
　(LB1576 M35)
Maruyama, Allen 1063
Marwick, William Edward 990
　(ML410 W668 M3 fol.)
Marwitz, John 4979 (MIC.TC-9420)
Mary Ignatia, Soeur 8226
Mary Julia, Sister 1105
Mary Madeleine, Sister 3999
Maschino, Sylvette 7281
Mashiach, Asher 10356 (MIC.T-871)
Mason, George David 6410
　(MIC.TC-9313)
Mason, Graham Archdale 9999
　(MIC.TC-15135)
Mason, Gregory Creswell 1389
　(MIC.F.TC-25939)
Mason, Patricia Lynn 3971
　(MIC.F.TC-44461)
Mason, William R.M. 11253
Massami, Bryan Hazlewood 1791
Masse, Denis 4319 (MIC.TC-4954)
Masse, Martin 10267
Massenet, Jean-Marie 7834
　(MIC.F.TC-38779)
Massey, Barbara Jane 4193
　(MIC.F.TC-17619)
Massey, Lucy Alice 8423
Massey, Nicholas William 6124
　(MIC.F.TC-46916)
Massey-Hicks, Mirvene George 3633
　(MIC.F.TC-25036)
Masson, Louis I. 7700
Masson, Paul Robert Leo 1689
Massot, Alain 2983 (MIC.F-042408)
Mastai, Judith Anne F. 800
　(MIC.F.TC-55072)
Masters, Bernard L. 4414
　(MIC.F.TC-17620)
Masters, D.C. 1283 (HF1732 C2 M3)
Masters, Margaret Jean 11515
　(MIC.TC-5776)
Masterson, James Raymond 7001
Masterton, Brooks Alan 3924
　(MIC.F.TC-53117)
Mather, William B. 6125
Matheson, Archie Farquhar 6126
Matheson, George Clifford R. 9105
　(MIC.F.TC-17130)
Matheson, Helen Joyce
　Castleden 2666 (MIC.F.TC-42697)
Matheson, James Evan 9884
Matheson, William Alexander 8522
　(MIC.TC-16542)
Mathewes, Rolf Walter 6526
　(MIC.F.TC-17207)
Mathews, William H. 5273
Mathews, Zena Pearlstone 954
　(F99 S3 M38)
Mathieson, Arthur Curtis 11478
Mathieu, Alfred L. 212
Mathieu, Nicolas Jean 1482
　(MIC.F.TC-52031)
Mathieu, Robert 9606 (MIC.T-3645)
Mathur, Mary Elaine 666 (MIC.T-310)
Matin, Abdul Mohammad 11324
　(MIC.F.TC-64597)
Matossian, Nicolas V. 1180
　(MIC.F.TC-52031)
Matson, William Lawrence 7569
　(MIC.T-638)
Matthew, William Diller 5619
Matthews, Barbara Lee 2436
　(MIC.T-628)
Matthews, David Ralph Lee 7607
Matthews, John C. 2832
Matthews, John Herbert 7541
Matthews, John Pengwerne 8345
Matthews, K. 1229

Matthews, Neville Osborne 2871
Matthews, William David Edison 2503
　(MIC.F.TC-31374)
Matthiasson, John Stephen 612
　(MIC.T-969)
Mattinson, Cyril Rodger 6411
Mattson, Lawrence Garfield 8847
　(MIC.T-854)
Mattson, Margaret Solveig 2273
Matusicky, Carol Ann 4031
Maule, C.J. 1284
Maurice, Louis Jean 7701
　(MIC.TC-6741)
Mavor, James Watt 10888
Mawdsley, James Buckland 6412
Mawer, David Ronald 6949
　(MIC.F.TC-33335)
Maxey, Alva Beatrice 363 (MIC.T-424)
Maxim, Paul Stefan 10268
Maxwell, James Ackley 1525
Maxwell, James Douglas 7127
　(MIC.T-537)
Maxwell, James Kirk 9158
　(MIC.F.TC-52800)
Maxwell, Mary Percival 10000
Maxwell, Thomas Robert 768
　(MIC.TC-11607)
Maxwell, William Anthony 8472
May, Arthur William 10997
　(MIC.TC-442)
May, J. 1483
May, Ronald William 6127
　(MIC.TC-8003)
Mayer, Francine M. 442
　(MIC.F-031602)
Mayer, Janet Judith 2060
　(MIC.F.TC-55620)
Mayer, Lawrence Clark 8535
　(MIC.T-230)
Mayer, Robert 10500
Mayes, Hubert G. 8227
　(MIC.F.TC-35459)
Mayes, Robert Gregory 613
　(MIC.F.TC-39746)
Mayhall, John T. 614
Mayhew, Michael Allen 6632
Maynard, James Edward 6128
Mayne, Seymour 8409 (MIC.TC-11244)
Mayo, H.B. 8706
Mayo, William Leonard 3412
Mayrand, Léon 7930
Mays, Annebelle Marjorie Maude 3505
　(MIC.F.TC-47117)
Mays, Herbert Joseph 131
　(MIC.F.TC-46917)
Mazany, Robin Leigh 10065
　(MIC.F.TC-59309)
McAfee, Rosemary Ann Pickard 10482
　(MIC.F.TC-25215)
McAllister, Arnold L. 5274
McAllister, Barbara Heather 2117
　(MIC.F.TC-58279)
McAllister, James Alexander 8700
　(MIC.F.TC-44418)
McAllister, Ray Scott 11639
McAndrew, Joan Kathleen 4151
　(MIC.F.TC-38768)
McAndrew, William James 7570
　(MIC.F.TC-17203)
McArthur, James Franklin 7751
　(MIC.T-227)
McArthur, Neil Max 4704 (MIC.T-56)
McAuliffe, Angela T.C. 8416
　(MIC.F.TC-44273)
McAvoy, Blanche 11479
McBean, Gordon Almon 11930
　(MIC.TC-6913)
McBeath, Arthur Groat 2965
　(MIC.T-228)
McBride, Billie Eleanor Jean 4320
McBride, Derek Ernest 5620
　(MIC.F.TC-30426)
McBride, Douglas Leonard 11480
　(MIC.TC-13242)
McBride, Stephen Kenneth 2061
　(MIC.F.TC-46908)
McBride, William Allan 52
　(MIC.F.TC-30047)
McBurney, Campbell 4265
　(MIC.F.TC-64026)
McCabe, J.O. 7506

McCabe, Robert Wylie 4905
  (MIC.F.TC-31271)
McCabe, Timothy Lee 11164
McCaffrey, Helen Katherine 8063
McCain, John Charles 11083
McCall, Horace Fillmore 2888
McCalla, Peter Douglas Whitby 2022
  (MIC.T-908)
McCallum, John C.P. 1247
  (MIC.F.TC-33419)
McCallum, John Stuart 1685
  (MIC.F.TC-31272)
Mc Callum, Mary Aletha 4354
  (MIC.F.TC-30346)
McCammon, Helen Mary 5514
McCann, Charles Douglas 9716
  (MIC.F.TC-54107)
McCann, Lawrence Douglas 4906
  (MIC.TC-13461)
McCann, R. 4423
McCann, William Sidney 5275
McCardell, Nora E. 99
  (MIC.F.TC-23411)
McCarl, Robert Smith 8327
  (MIC.F.TC-51135)
McCart, Peter James 10957
  (MIC.F.TC-8316)
McCarthy, Joseph P. 3368
McCarthy, Mary Martha Cecilia 7452
  (MIC.F.TC-54224)
McCarthy, Thomas Noble 9934
McCartney, Allen Papin 894
McCartney, Nancy Glover 895
McCartney, William Douglas 5767
McCarty, J.W. 1285
McCarty, John Myron 1212
McCarty, Mary Anne 3247
  (MIC.F.TC-36743)
McCaskill, Donald Neil 476
  (MIC.F.TC-41003)
McCatty, Cressy Alexander Mayo 2578
  (MIC.TC-16647)
McCauley, Edward 11779
  (MIC.F.TC-64638)
McCauley, Victor John Edmund 11165
  (MIC.F.TC-24086)
McCaw, William Ralph 3829
McCay, Bonnie Jean 406
McClain, Ernest Paul 4993
McClain, Paula Denice 7586
  (MIC.F.T-1026)
McClary, Dan O. 10522
McClellan, Catharine 732
McClelland, Peter Dean 1286
McCloy, James Murl 4686
McCluskey, Kenneth Wilfred 3918
  (MIC.F.TC-47219)
McClymont, Ian 7128 (MIC.T-292)
McCollum, James Freeman 1594
  (MIC.T-744)
McComb, Lloyd Alexander 2259
  (MIC.F.TC-58367)
McCombs, Arthur Rae 4415
  (MIC.F.T-1028)
McConaghy, Gerald Manford 3048
  (MIC.F.TC-53107)
McConnell, Lawrence G. 4152
  (MIC.F.TC-27202)
McConnell, William Howard 8693
McCorkle, David Vernon 11166
McCormack, Andrew Ross 2100
  (MIC.F.TC-20525)
McCormack, James 9717
  (MIC.TC-13462)
McCorquodale, Susan 8707
  (MIC.F.TC-17930)
McCracken, Francis Derwood 10889
McCracken, Kevin William John 4961
  (MIC.TC-15273)
McCready, Douglas Jackson 1325
  (MIC.F.TC-20218)
McCready, John 8679
  (MIC.F.TC-59834)
McCrimmon, Hugh Ross 10880
McCrorie, James Napier 140
  (MIC.T-474)
McCrossan, Robert G. 5431
McCurdy, Sherburne Graham 2810
McCurley, Donna Anne 10066
McCutcheon, Brian Robert 7242
  (MIC.F.TC-19582)

McCutcheon, Wilfred W. 4101
McDaniel, Susan Anderson 10067
  (MIC.F.TC-40227)
McDermott, George Louis 95
McDermott, M. Elizabeth 9032
  (MIC.F.TC-62023)
McDermott, Patricia Catherine 10023
  (MIC.F.TC-58281)
McDermott, William Vincent 3972
  (MIC.F.TC-33205)
McDiarmid, Orville J. 1758
McDonald, Barrie Clifton 6413
McDonald, D.H.I. 2140
McDonald, F.J. 8168
McDonald, Geoffrey Thomas 96
  (MIC.F.TC-18508)
McDonald, Howard 11341
McDonald, James Franklin 4321
  (MIC.F.TC-59833)
McDonald, Jerry Nealon 10613
McDonald, Lawrence Thomas
  Russell 8081 (MIC.F.TC-39525)
McDonald, Linda Mary Olive 3248
  (MIC.F.TC-49018)
McDonald, Mary K. 9381
McDonald, Neil Gerard 2504
  (MIC.F.TC-47107)
McDonald, Robert Arthur John 1287
  (MIC.F.TC-32519)
McDonald, Ronald H. 7499
  (MIC.F.TC-20260)
McDonald, William C. 11516
McDonnell, Roger Francis 573
  (MIC.F.TC-25925)
McDonough, Lawrence Cecil 1664
  (MIC.F.TC-50159)
McDougall, Allen Kerr 8629
  (MIC.TC-16113)
McDougall, Daniel 3506
  (MIC.TC-10116)
McDougall, David J. 6129
McDougall, Duncan Michael 1288
McDougall, Elizabeth Ann 9885
  (MIC.TC-5174)
McDougall, Gordon Hedley
  George 1967 (MIC.TC-8558)
McDougall, John Norman 8561
  (MIC.F.TC-24088)
McDougall, Robert Law 1090
  (MIC.TC-16649)
McDougall, William D. 4459
McDowall, Duncan L. 1289, 1897
  (MIC.F.TC-39042)
McDowell, Clarence Stirling 4355
McDowell, Gloria M. 9175
McDowell, John Parmelee 5123
McDowell, Marilyn Eleanor 4123
  (MIC.T-567)
McEachern, Ronald Alexander 7382
McEachran, John Douglas 11005
McElroy, Ann Poulver 615
McEwen, A.C. 7868
McEwen, Eoin Hall 10617
McEwen, Nelly Zurcher 3405
  (MIC.F.TC-30754)
McFadden, James Douglas 4991
McFadden, Max Wulfsohn 11177
McFadden, Scot Robert 10374
  (MIC.F.TC-55804)
McFadyen, Stuart Malcolm 1501
McFarland, Elsie Marie 10444
  (GV55 M33)
McFarland, Joan Murray 1352
  (MIC.TC-9410)
McFarland, John M. 10345
McFarlane, Samuel H. 10958
McFerran, John Ronald 10299
  (MIC.F.TC-47222)
McFetridge, Donald Grant 1759
  (MIC.TC-13060)
McGahan, Elizabeth Moore Walsh 1290
  (MIC.F.TC-55478)
McGechaen, Alexander 1158
  (MIC.F.TC-37673)
McGaw, R.L. 1853
McGee, Harold Franklin, Jr. 524
  (MIC.T-554)
McGee, John Thomas 530
McGerrigle, Harold W. 6414
McGhee, Robert John 896
  (MIC.TC-2090)

McGill, Ann Carley 9718
  (MIC.F.TC-57190)
McGill, G.W. 4229
McGill, Mary Elizabeth 6783
  (MIC.F.TC-29902)
McGill, Robert Emmett 1026
  (MIC.T-475)
McGillivray, Robert Hilher 3765
McGilly, Francis James 8730
  (MIC.T-366)
McGinn, Roderick Alan 5515
  (MIC.F.TC-43087)
McGinnis, James Harold 9719
  (MIC.F.TC-42373)
McGinnis, Janice Patricia Dickin 7149
  (MIC.F.TC-49021)
McGinnis, Paul St. Clair 4032
  (MIC.F.TC-33094)
McGlade, Jacqueline Myriam 11020
  (MIC.F.TC-52526)
McGlynn, John C. 5516
McGrath, Gerard Michael 6824
  (MIC.F.TC-19801)
McGrath, Patrick John 3691
  (MIC.F.TC-39524)
McGregor, Duncan Colin 5073
McGugan, Blair M. 10553
McGuigan, Derrill Ignatius 2475
McGuigan, Gerald Frederick 136
McGuiness, Norman William 1760
  (MIC.F.TC-36294)
McHenry, Merril Gene 10771
McIlreath, Ian Alexander 5276
McIlwraith, Robert Douglas 1048
  (MIC.F.TC-50938)
McIlwraith, Thomas Forsyth 2023
  (MIC.T-550)
McInnes, Simon M.C. 8514
  (MIC.F.TC-39043)
McInnis, Robert Marvin 1291
McIntosh, Alan Wallace 7387
  (MIC.T-93)
McIntosh, Curtis Emmanuel 146
  (MIC.F.TC-13469)
McIntosh, Herman Whitefield 3692
McIntosh, Janet Christina 4460
  (MIC.F.TC-30347)
McIntosh, William John 4194
McIntyre, Eilene L. Goldberg 10092
  (MIC.F.TC-50300)
McIntyre, Geoffrey R. 2287
McIntyre, Wallace E. 1792
McIvor, N.S. 1516
McIvor, R. Craig 1517
McKague, Ormond Knight 2545
  (MIC.F.T-1259)
McKague, Terence Russell 2858
McKay, Donald Charles 4980
  (MIC.F.TC-31082)
McKay, R. Bruce 1135
  (HE8689.7 C3 M35 fol.)
McKay, William Angus 7158
McKee, Leila Gay Mitchell 7227
  (MIC.F.TC-56573)
McKeen, Wilbert Ezekiel 337
McKee, Janet Doris 10215
  (MIC.F.TC-51373)
McKenna, Isobel Kerwin 8089
  (MIC.F.TC-50161)
McKenna, Mary Olga 2414
McKennan, Robert Addison 616
McKenzie, Rodney Colin 227
  (MIC.F.TC-17605)
McKenzie, Thomas Ross 4068
McKeown, Joseph 12014
McKie, Donald Craig 1942
  (MIC.F.TC-27500)
McKillop, Alexander Brian 7091
  (MIC.F.TC-30155)
McKim, Margaret Kathleen 3098
  (MIC.F.TC-35519)
McKinley, Donald F. 2024
McKinnon, Donald Peter 4048
  (MIC.F.TC-34880)
McKinnon, Sarah Morgan 938
  (HT108 U494 fol.)
McKinnon, Thomas Roy 2025
  (MIC.T-501)
McKinsey, Lauren Stuart 8579
  (MIC.T-583)

McKinstry, Hugh Exton 5277
McKirnan, David James 9264
  (MIC.F.TC-39741)
McKittrick, Edith Patricia 3343
McKone, Warren Douglas 11824
  (MIC.F.TC-25928)
McLachlan, John Francis Clifford 9141
  (MIC.TC-12087)
McLaren, Angus Gordon 8083
McLaren, Digby Johns 5432
McLaren, Ian Alexander 11840
McLaren, Lydia Bernice 8346
McLaren, Patrick 5868
McLaren, Peter Lorimer 10747
  (MIC.F.TC-32938)
McLaren, Walter Wallace 1995
McLarty, James Kenneth 3538
  (MIC.F.T-1063)
McLatchie, Brian Hugh 9265
  (MIC.F.TC-25733)
McLauchlan, Derek George 3249
  (MIC.F.TC-32022)
McLaughlin, John Daniel 11351
  (MIC.F.TC-8218)
McLaughlin, Judith B. 9033
McLaughlin, Kenneth Michael 7129
  (MIC.F.TC-35260)
McLaughlin, Merlyn 7092
McLaughlin, Patsy Ann 11070
McLay, Colin Lindsay 11050
  (MIC.TC-5824)
McLean, Alastair 11481
McLean, Elizabeth M.M. 1091
  (MIC.F.TC-40232)
McLean, Ian Gordon 10697
McLean, James Ross 5568
McLean, John Alexander 11220
  (MIC.F.TC-30285)
McLean, Kenneth Hugh 6938
  (MIC.F.TC-47845)
McLean, Marianne L. 7620
McLean, Mona Marie 9310
  (MIC.F.TC-42266)
McLean, Ruth Winnifred 3658
  (MIC.F.TC-43676)
McLean, Simon James 2312
McLean, Walter Robert 2725
  (MIC.F.T-981)
McLearn, Frank Harris 5664
McLellan, David Ross 8477
McLellan, James Layton 2691
McLeod, Alexander N. 1181
McLeod, Donald 1560
McLeod, Gerald Thomas 2872
  (MIC.F.TC-27697)
McLeod, Gordon Duncan 8018
  (MIC.F.TC-20399)
McLeod, Heleen Julianna 3476
  (MIC.F.TC-49026)
McLeod, John Malcolm 11325
McLeod, Keith Alwyn 2476
  (MIC.F.TC-31373)
McLeod, Leslie Thomas 8347
McLeod, Norman Leslie 3547
  (MIC.TC-7705)
McLeod, Roderick William 3973
  (MIC.F.TC-36431)
McLeod, Stuart Cameron 8680
McLeod, Thomas Hector
  Macdonald 8770
McLernon, Sylvia Grove 8515
McLin, Jon B. 8787 (VA600 M33)
McLintock A.H. 7168 (JL542 M24)
McMahon, James H. 9311
  (MIC.F-2M11.375.1)
McMahon, Peter Casey 10093
  (MIC.F.TC-35261)
McMechan, Margaret Evaline 5278
  (MIC.F.TC-46374)
McMechan, Robert Douglas 5279
  (MIC.F.TC-52910)
McMenemy, John Murray 8848
  (MIC.F.TC-19722)
McMillan, George 4102 (S535 C34 M3)
McMillan, Ronald Hugh 6415
  (MIC.TC-14150)
McMillan, William John 5280
McMinn, Kayron Campbell 7356
  (MIC.F.T-956)
McMinn, Robert Gordon 11482

McMullen, Linda Mae 9142
  (MIC.F.TC-49180)
McMullin, Stanley Edward 3549
  (MIC.F.TC-28917)
McMurchy, Donald J.A. 7366
  (MIC.T-229)
McMurrick, James Playfair 10881
McNab, David Thornton 7093
  (JV171 M4)
McNabb, George Gibbon 3557
  (LA41715 M23)
McNairn, Norman Alexander 9877
McNaughton, K.W.K. 7391
McNaughton, Keith Graham 11696
  (MIC.F.TC-19587)
McNeal, Horace Pitman, Jr. 978
  (MIC.F.T-1034)
McNeary, Stephen A. 685
McNeely, Roger N. 11869
  (MIC.TC-16498)
McNeil, David Harvey 5517
  (MIC.F.TC-36931)
McNeill, John Robert 6966
  (MIC.F.T-1274)
McNicholl, Martin Kell 10848
  (MIC.TC-40234)
McNiven, Christiane Rachel
  Marie 10182 (MIC.T-644)
McPhail, John Donald 11045
McPherson, Alan Locke 879
Mc Pherson, Alfred Angus Murray 2605
  (MIC.T-847)
McPherson, Harold James 4733
  (MIC.TC-1368)
McPherson, John Cecil 4801
  (MIC.T-609)
McPherson, Robert Andrew 5518
  (MIC.TC-6278)
McQuade, Bernard Normand 6416
  (MIC.F.TC-53256)
McQuillan, David Aidan 4850
McRae, Bradley Collins 9312
  (MIC.F.TC-25933)
McRae, Robert Norman 1915
  (MIC.F.TC-32526)
McReynolds, William Peter 2726
  (MIC.TC-7915)
McRoberts, Edward Charles 4505
  (MIC.F.TC-17610)
McRoberts, Hugh Arthur 10216
  (MIC.F.TC-29074)
McRoberts, Kenneth Harvey 8580
McTaggart, Kenneth C. 5281
McTeer, Robert Doyal, Jr. 1609
  (MIC.T-327)
McTiernan, Timothy Patrick John 9720
  (MIC.F.TC-59299)
McVetty, Peter Barclay Edgar 326
  (MIC.F.TC-37810)
Mead, Frank Waldreth 11169
Meade, Edward Simon 4153
  (MIC.F.TC-50312)
Meade, Harlan Donnelly 5282
  (MIC.F.TC-31627)
Meadowcroft, Barbara Wales 8170
  (MIC.F.TC-64603)
Meagher, John William 10426
Meagher, Michael Desmond 11697
  (MIC.F.TC-28754)
Mealing, Francis Mark 8328
  (MIC.T-480)
Meaney, Neville Kingsley 7559
Meany, Edmond Stephen, Jr. 1834
Mechikoff, Robert Alan 8445
Mechling, William Hubbs 519
Medcof, John C. 11096
Meddaugh, William Scott 6130
  (MIC.F.T-1351)
Medford, Gary Allan 5283
  (MIC.TC-28755)
Medjuck, Beth Sheva 395
  (MIC.F.TC-38495)
Medling, James 9034
  (MIC.F.TC-44090)
Medlyn, David Arthur 11483
Mednis, Roberts Janis 4642
Meek, Frederick Ivan 9035
  (MIC.F.TC-57268)
Meek, James Collins 2750
  (MIC.F.TC-40457)
Meek, John James 197 (MIC.T-765)

Meen, Sharon Patricia 7130
  (MIC.F.TC-46208)
Mehmet, Ozay 2188 (MIC.F.TC-19724)
Mehrer, Clifford Francis 10584
Mehrtens, Charlotte Jean 6417
Mehta, Nitin Tarachand 1820
  (MIC.F.T-962)
Meier, Augustine 9176
  (MIC.F.TC-56455)
Meier, Henry Frederick August 306
Meier, Mark Frederick 5433
Meikle, William Duncan 3722
  (LE3 T52 M4)
Meilicke, Carl Alexander 6806
  (MIC.T-191)
Meisel, John 7150 (JL193 M4)
Melbye, Floyd Jerome 880
  (MIC.TC-7919)
Melebamane-Mia-Mucanda,
  Berthollet 10269
Melichercik, John 10128
Melihercsik, Stephen J. 6418
Melik, James Charles 6576
Mellen, Frances Nordlinger 2286
  (MIC.F.TC-31286)
Mellish, Gordon Hartley 1326
  (HG3883 C3 M4)
Mellon, George Barry 5434
Mellor, Gary Edward 11698
  (MIC.TC-13247)
Meloche, John Dennis 5284
  (MIC.F.TC-52979)
Meltz, Noah Moshe 2118 (MIC.T-57)
Melville, Thomas Richard 8774
  (MIC.F.T-1221)
Melvin, Arthur Gordon 4399
Melvin, Scott Merrill 10866
  (MIC.F.T-1305)
Mendels, Roger Pierre 1719 (MIC.T-59)
Mendelson, Beverley Katz 9560
  (MIC.F.TC-58461)
Mendelson, Roslyn 9382
  (MIC.F.TC-61663)
Mendonca, Augustine Rev. 9629
  (MIC.F.TC-56450)
Mendonca, James Dominic 9313
  (MIC.F.TC-23317)
Meneley, William Allison 5569
Mengel, Joseph Torbitt, Jr. 5135
Menig, Paul Henri 7002
Menke, Arnold Stephan Ernst 11170
Menon, Poimplasseri
  Sivaramakrishna 11070
Merbs, Charles Francis 617
  (MIC.T-981)
Mercer, George William 9721
  (MIC.F.TC-25735)
Mercer, John 4907
Mercer, John Hainsworth 4673
Mercer, William 5621
Merchant, David Francis 4195
  (MIC.F.TC-17621)
Merchant, Francis Walter 4230
  (LB3054 C3 M47)
Mercier, Jean Charles 8446
  (MIC.F.T-1328)
Mercier, Jocelyn 3830
  (MIC.F.TC-56487)
Meredith, Don Howard 10698
  (MIC.F.TC-24099)
Meredith, Lindsay Norman 2392
  (MIC.F.TC-51043)
Merk, George Phillip 5136
Merriam, George Henry 7703
Merrill, Lesly I. 9036
  (MIC.F.TC-53260)
Mertz, Elizabeth Ellen 396
  (MIC.F.T-1347)
Merzisen, Yves 8312 (MIC.F.TC-19595)
Meshri, Indurani Dayal 5435
  (MIC.F.T-1166)
Meskill, Michael Francis 2579
Meslow, Edwin Charles 10661
Messieh, Shoukry N. 10895
  (MIC.F.TC-18317)
Messier, Denise 9383
Metcalf, Isaac S.H. 10915
Metcalfe, Janet Ann 9561
  (MIC.F.TC-53119)
Metge, Michel 4555

Metzger, Charles Henry 7038
Metzger, Leonard Paul 10235
Meunier, Jean-Marc 9722
  (MIC.F-2M11.482.6)
Meuser, Dorothy M. 9454
  (MIC.F.TC-44093)
Meuser, Peter Eric 9314
  (MIC.F.TC-44181)
Meyer, Benjamin Stewart 2383
  (MIC.T-521)
Meyer, David Alexander 511
  (MIC.F.TC-56996)
Meyer, Hans K. 11388
Meyer, James Alan 9630
  (MIC.F.TC-50654)
Meyers, Gordon Paterson 3693
  (MIC.F.TC-40940)
Mezei, Kathy 8348 (MIC.F.TC-34632)
Mhun, Henry 1327
Miall, Andrew D. 5869 (MIC.TC-5293)
Michalyna, Walter 250
Michas, Nicholas 1502 (MIC.T-193)
Michaels, Patrick Joseph 3
  (MIC.F.T-1085)
Michaelson, David Rubin 692
Michaud, Lucien Fidèle 3611
  (MIC.T-295)
Michaud, Marguerite Marie 10167
  (FC2499 B69 M52)
Michaud, Pierre 4322
Michaud-Achorn, Aurelda 9037
Michel, Éléanor Louise 8228
  (PS8073.3 M53)
Michel, Frederick Alfred 5870
  (MIC.F.TC-55216)
Michel, Robert 8300
Michelson, Karin Eva 7810
  (MIC.F.T-1362)
Michelson, Peter Glenn 10807
Michener, Charles Edward 6131
Michener, Daniel Ralph 10699
  (MIC.F.TC-12779)
Michone, James Gregory 6419
Middlemiss, Danford William 8849
  (MIC.F.TC-35067)
Middleton, John David 11645
  (MIC.F.TC-59913)
Mierau, Eric 7773
Miers, David Robert 7910
  (MIC.F.TC-30927)
Miezitis, Solveiga Ausma 3030
  (MIC.TC-2483)
Mifflen, Francis James 1292
Migner, Robert-Maurice 137
  (MIC.F-022902)
Migneron, Jean-Gabriel 1943
  (HC10 C34 fol.)
Migue, Jean-Luc 2210 (MIC.T-194)
Mihok, Steven 10714 (MIC.F.TC-43490)
Miklos, Erwin 2936
Milan, Frederick Arthur 551
  (MIC.T-978)
Milburn, Geoffrey 4323
  (MIC.F.TC-58307)
Miles, J.J. 9223 (MIC.F.TC-52416)
Miles, Peter Lomer 1435
  (MIC.TC-2864)
Millar, Frederick David 2119
  (MIC.F.TC-51377)
Millar, James F.V. 897 (MIC.TC-4034)
Millar, John Steven 10662
  (MIC.TC-9621)
Millard, John Rodney Emmett 4479
  (MIC.F.TC-58323)
Millen, Ronald Harold Vincent 1460
  (MIC.F.TC-21715)
Miller, Albert Herman 2505
  (MIC.TC-2384)
Miller, Allan Ross 6420
  (MIC.F.TC-36301)
Miller, Anthony John 8806
  (MIC.TC-9428)
Miller, Barbara 9193 (MIC.TC-15932)
Miller, C.C.I. 7367
Miller, Catherine M.L. 9723
  (MIC.F.TC-57886)
Miller, David Edwin 8165
Miller, Donald Ray 10618
Miller, Edward Henry 10868
  (MIC.F.TC-36142)

Miller, Fern Audrey Rae 2062
  (MIC.F.T-1260)
Miller, Frederick Carl 1484
Miller, Gifford Hubbs 5871
Miller, Gordon Edward 11221
  (MIC.F.TC-58816)
Miller, Herbert E. 2764
Miller, Hugh Gordon 6623
Miller, Ira Ebersole 9942
Miller, James Collins 2667
  (LC5148 C3 M5)
Miller, James Rodger 7131
  (MIC.F.TC-32842)
Miller, John David 11527
  (MIC.F.TC-52729)
Miller, John Pearse 4461
  (MIC.TC-12088)
Miller, Judith Helen 8019
  (MIC.F.TC-51378)
Miller, Larry Arnold 3974
  (MIC.F.TC-27708)
Miller, Marilyn Sue 8925
  (MIC.F.TC-47850)
Miller, Murray Lloyd 6421
Miller, Philip Carl 387
  (MIC.F.TC-40722)
Miller, Richard George 5872
  (MIC.F.TC-56809)
Miller, Richard Brine 11358
Miller, Rickey Shelley 9038
  (MIC.F.TC-58934)
Miller, Robert Edward 1159
  (MIC.TC-10133)
Miller, Robert Edwin 1112
Miller, Robert J.M. 5519
Miller, Selwyn Archibald 2889
  (MIC.F.TC-31288)
Miller, Thomas William 2606
  (MIC.T-479)
Millerd, Francis Webb 65 (MIC.T-493)
Millette, Jean François Gérard 213
Milligan, George Clinton 5520
Millikan, Ross Hamilton 2692
  (MIC.F.TC-40459)
Millman, Thomas R. 9899 (H31 T6 V10)
Milloy, J.S. 7453 (MIC.T-921)
Mills, Allen George 7151
  (MIC.F.TC-28288)
Mills, Antonia Curtze 555
  (MIC.F.T-1283)
Mills, Claudia Eileen 11931
  (MIC.F.TC-58575)
Mills, Hugh Harrison 5436
Mills, Isabelle Margaret 1001
  (MIC.T-379)
Mills, John Edwin 716 (MIC.T-60)
Mills, John Peter 6422
Mills, Kenneth Harold 11021
  (MIC.F.TC-50940)
Mills, Laura Jane 9039
  (MIC.F.TC-54603)
Mills, Michael Irwin 1049
  (MIC.F.TC-50511)
Millward, Hugh Albert 4908
  (MIC.F.TC-24619)
Milne, Louis Johnson 11247
Milne, Victor Gordon 6132
Milne, William George 4480
Milner, Joseph Marc 7414
  (MIC.F.TC-64168)
Milner, Robert L. 6423
Milnor, Andrew Johnson 7247
  (MIC.T-61)
Milot, Victor J. 6967
Milstead, Wayne Lavine 11389
Milstin, Donald Ellis 8788
Minaudo, Vito S. 1160
Minden, Harold Allen 9562
  (MIC.TC-3458)
Minden, Karen Paula 6807
  (MIC.F.TC-51379)
Miner, Horace Mitchell 769 (F5412 M5)
Minghi, Julian Vincent 4615
Mings, Turley Ray 1328
Minkler, Frederick William 3975
Minor, N. Kathleen Mary 4167
  (MIC.F.T-1294)
Minore, James Bruce 364 (MIC.T-713)
Miquelon, Dale Bernard 1230
  (MIC.F.TC-21665)
Miralles-Nobel, Teresa 10217

Mireau, Laurie Jane 4324
  (MIC.F.TC-49040)
Mirynech, Edward 6133
  (MIC.F.TC-17278)
Mischey, Eugene John 9455
  (MIC.F.TC-36759)
Mishler, Craig Wallace 552
  (MIC.F.T-1209)
Mishler, William Thomas Earle, II 8447
  (MIC.T-530)
Mishoff, Willard O. 7439
Misra, B. 7880
Misra, Kailash Chandra 11623
Misra, Kula Chandra 6134
  (MIC.TC-12894)
Mitcham, Elizabeth Allison 8020
  (MIC.TC-16250)
Mitcham, Peter 7468
Mitchell, Beverley Joan 8173
  (MIC.F.TC-30435)
Mitchell, Carlyle L. 1868
  (MIC.F.TC-44095)
Mitchell, Donald Hector 867
Mitchell, Donald W. 7415
Mitchell, Donna Lianne Marie 6719
  (MIC.F.TC-42274)
Mitchell, George Joseph 10611
Mitchell, Lillian Leonora 1010
Mitchell, Marjorie Ruth 678
  (MIC.F.TC-29898)
Mitchell, Myron James 11202
  (MIC.F.TC-21322)
Mitchell, Ormond Glenn 10700
Mitchell, Victor E. 7869
Mitchinson, Wendy Lynn 7094
  (MIC.F.TC-30928)
Mitchner, Ernest Alyn 7373
  (MIC.TC-9624)
Mitra, Rabindranath 6424
Mitterer, John Otto 3976
  (MIC.F.TC-52272)
Mittler, Peter Robert 4631
  (MIC.F.TC-55788)
Miura, Taizo 10959
Moase, Reginald Beverly 4468
  (MIC.F.TC-38783)
Mobley, Jack Arthur 9945
Mock, Dennis Ronald 4949
  (MIC.F.TC-35083)
Mock, Karen Rochelle 2580
  (MIC.F.TC-32849)
Mode, William Niles 5873
  (MIC.F.T-1086)
Moehlman, Arthur Henry 4739
Moeno, Sylvia Ntlantla 740
  (MIC.F.TC-47851)
Moffett, Samuel Erasmus 2333
Mohr, Erich 9040 (MIC.F.TC-58544)
Mohsen, Mohammad Farrukh
  Neyaz 4556 (MIC.F.TC-27061)
Moir, David Ross 11581
Moir, John Sargent 9918
Moir, Robert Oliphant Mathieu 1050
Moisan, Gaston 10772
Moldofsky, Naomi 7660 (MIC.TC-4541)
Molino, Joseph 3831 (MIC.F.TC-56473)
Moll, Nancy Eileen 5768
  (MIC.F.T-1224)
Mollard, John D.A. 74
Molloy, Geoffrey Neale 3089
  (MIC.F.TC-17625)
Molot, Maureen Appel 2346
  (MIC.T-526)
Molto, Joseph Eldon 724
  (MIC.F.TC-47122)
Mommik, Salme 11342
Moncion, Jean 7849 (MIC.F.TC-44097)
Monet, Jacques 7095 (F5029.1 M58)
Monette, Marcel 9724
  (MIC.F-2M11.375.8)
Monette, Marcelle 6900
Money, Peter Lawrence 5570
Mongeau, Jean-Claude 3879
Mongeau, Frère Jean René 11033
Mongeon, Madeleine 9384
  (MIC.F-018805)
Monger, James William Heron 5285
  (MIC.TC-766)
Monk, Patricia 8086 (MIC.F.TC-22526)
Monkman, Leslie Gordon 8064
  (MIC.F.TC-25737)

Monks, Gregory Gerald 868
(MIC.F.TC-34903)
Montague, John Tait 2146
(MIC.F.TC-17279)
Montcalm, Mary Beth 8581
(MIC.F.TC-59906)
Montgometrie, Thomas Craig 2668
(MIC.F.TC-51551)
Montgomery, Joseph H. 5286
(MIC.TC-1821)
Montigny, Louvigny de 8229
(PQ2615 E35 M395)
Montmarquette, Claude 1761
Moodie, Donald Wayne 4842
(MIC.TC-11150)
Moodie, Gordon Eric Edmund 10960
(MIC.TC-6224)
Moodie, Roy Lee 5665
Moody, Barry Morris 7290
(MIC.F.TC-30179)
Moody, Margaret Mary 3115
(MIC.T-751)
Moody, Peter Richard 3107
(MIC.F.TC-49043)
Moody, Robert Earle 6968 (MIC.T-788)
Moogh, Peter Nicholas 2089
(MIC.F.TC-27925)
Mook, Bertha 9177
Moon, David Earle 238
(MIC.F.TC-59310)
Moonay, Sheldon Murray 9725
Mooney, Harold Alfred 11548
Moorcraft, K. 2506
Moore, Andrew 2710
Moore, Basil John 1436
Moore, David Richard 7507
Moore, Debra Lynn 9099
Moore, Dorothy Emma 9980
Moore, Edith Elizabeth 10152
Moore, Elwood S. 6146
Moore, George Albert Baker 4254
(MIC.T-477)
Moore, George Bissland 8789
Moore, James Edward 11090
Moore, James Talmadge 7432
Moore, Jean Louise V. 3759
Moore, John C.G. 5874
Moore, Joseph A.L. 8926
(MIC.TC-11436)
Moore, Joyce Elaine 9456
(MIC.F.TC-47125)
Moore, Mary Candace 9989
(MIC.F.TC-58743)
Moore, Patrick Albert 1878
(MIC.F.TC-19600)
Moore, Peter William 4950
(MIC.F.TC-38787)
Moore, Richard Lewis 6136
(MIC.F.TC-29077)
Moore, Robert Bruce 12015
Moore, Robert John 1071
(MIC.F.TC-23648)
Moore, Russell F. 4325
Moore, T. 5769
Moore, Turrall Adcock 701
Moorhouse, Walter W. 6425
Morah, Benson Chukwuma 10068
(MIC.F.TC-32034)
Moran, Stephen Royse 5571
Morantz, Toby Elaine 512
(MIC.F.TC-47127)
Morchain, Janet Kerr 7514
(MIC.T-350)
Moreau, G.Y. 4231
Moreau, Margaret Ellen 9194
(MIC.F.TC-51044)
Morefield, Roger Dale 1182
(MIC.F.T-969)
Morehouse, F.M.I. 7633
Morel de la Durantaye, Jean-Paul 8377
Morey, Edward Rockendorf 10445
(MIC.F.TC-40732)
Morgan, Catherine E. 10115
(MIC.F.TC-58327)
Morgan, Christopher Llewellyn 263
(MIC.F.TC-42279)
Morgan, Nabil Assad 6679
Morgan, R.L.R. 1854
Morgan, Robert J. 7176
Morganti, John Michael 5922
(MIC.F.TC-50005)

Mori, John Giovanni 10808
(MIC.F.TC-33946)
Moriarty, Richard James 10354
Morin, Fernand 4705 (MIC.F.TC-44100)
Morin, James Arthur 6137
(MIC.F.TC-44387)
Morin, Lise 9385 (MIC.F-2M11.483.1)
Morin, Marcel 6426
Morin, Pierre 10270
Morin, Roger-André 1485 (MIC.T-694)
Morin, Yvon 8263 (MIC.F-003907)
Morison, James Howe 11970
Morissette, Yves-Marie J.R. 7881
(MIC.T-947)
Morissette, Dominique 3344
(MIC.F.TC-48058)
Morissette, Robert 4266
Morlan, Richard Eugene 898
(MIC.T-977)
Morley, John T. 8731
Morley, Lawrence Whitaker 6138
Morley, Mary Louise 3726 (MIC.T-625)
Morphy, David Raymond 3578
Morrall, John Frankland 4557
(HE373 C32 T6 fol.)
Morris, Cerise Darlene 10183
(MIC.F.TC-58106)
Morris, Douglas William 10568
Morris, George Barry 9457
(MIC.F.TC-21914)
Morris, James Robert 11101
(MIC.TC-6225)
Morris, James Thomas 3760
(MIC.F.T-449)
Morris, John Francis 9775
(MIC.F.TC-35271)
Morris, John Louis 7004
Morris, Julius Richard 3063
(MIC.F.TC-42281)
Morris, Mary Laverne 3074
(MIC.F.TC-38788)
Morris, Norman Edward 9195
(MIC.F.TC-35272)
Morris, Raymond Martin 4168
(MIC.F.TC-21667)
Morris, Simon Conway 11343
Morrisey, Francis G. 7840
Morrisey, James Thomas 3171
(MIC.F.T-1167)
Morrison, Alistair 4647 (MIC.TC-930)
Morrison, Allan B. 2717
Morrison, Alvin Hamblen 709
(MIC.T-990)
Morrison, D.A. 417
Morrison, Gregg William 5923
(MIC.F.TC-50621)
Morrison, Hugh M. 7096
Morrison, Kenneth M. 6969
Morrison, Kenneth Leslie 9981
(MIC.F.TC-30929)
Morrison, Michael Lynn 5287
Morrison, Neil Farquharson 4706
Morrison, Philip Scott 4951
(MIC.F.TC-38789)
Morrison, Robert Bruce 375
Morrison, Robert George 11582
(MIC.F.TC-21668)
Morrison, Terrence Robert 7201
(MIC.F.TC-27928)
Morrison, William Robert 7132
(MIC.TC-14964)
Morrissey, Frederic Patric 1793
Morrow, David Watts 5875
Morrow, Ernest Lloyd 9866
Morrow, Harold F. 6139
Morrow, Leslie Donald 2635
(MIC.F.TC-26853)
Morrow, Robert George 2833
(MIC.F.T-1087)
Morse, Norman Harding 159
(MIC.F.TC-22344)
Morse, Robert Harold 6140
(MIC.TC-5738)
Morse, Stearns Anthony 5716
Morse-Chevrier, Jean 3832
(MIC.F-022307)
Mortimore, Richard George Ernest 541
Morton, D.D.P. 7416
Morton, Elizabeth Homer 7968
(MIC.T-873)
Morton, Nelson W. 9607

Morton, Penelope 6141
(MIC.F.TC-59912)
Morton, Ronald Lee 5288
(MIC.F.TC-26603)
Moseley, Frederick Eugene, Jr. 8850
(MIC.F.T-976)
Moses, Barbara Beryl 9315
Mosha, Herme Joseph 3134
(MIC.F.TC-43497)
Moshupi, Matthew Coffat 12016
(MIC.F.TC-34219)
Mosk, Mark David 3833
(MIC.F.TC-52980)
Mosley, James Lawrence 3834
(MIC.TC-6170)
Moss, Alan 11699 (MIC.T-871)
Moss, Albert E. 6427
Moss, John George 8065 (PS8101 I8 M6)
Moss, H. Richard 1479
(MIC.F.TC-28927)
Mossison, Ian Kenneth 11646
(MIC.T.C-3911)
Mossop, Grant Dilworth 5876
Mothersill, John Sydney 5289
(MIC.TC-1211)
Mothersill, Kerry James 9196
(MIC.F.TC-48391)
Mott, Morris Kenneth 10346
(MIC.F.TC-50172)
Mott, Terrance Roger 3507
(MIC.F.TC-26856)
Mottin, James Leon 9266
(MIC.TC-12597)
Mottley, Charles McCammon 10961
Mottus, Leonard Waldemar 10574
(MIC.TC-13492)
Motut, Roger G. 8270 (MIC.T-380)
Moudgil, Ranvir 741
Mougeon, Raymond 7674
(MIC.TC-15938)
Mountain, Dean Clarence 1794
(MIC.F.TC-48392)
Mountjoy, Eric Walter 5437
Mourant, François 10271
(MIC.F-027609)
Mousseau, Yolande 6901
Moussette, Marcel 1762
(MIC.F.TC-48061)
Mover, Joel Leonard 10230
Mowat, Gordon Leslie 2998
Mowbray, James Arthur 7417
(MIC.T-860)
Moyal, Barbara Ruth Roback 9197
(MIC.F.TC-43685)
Moyer, Paul Tyson, Jr. 6428
Moynes, Riley Elgin 2507
(MIC.F.TC-38790)
Mozersky, Kenneth Avrum 4909
Muc, Michael 11549 (MIC.F.TC-27713)
Mudie, Peta J. 5090
Mueller, Claus Curt 10622
(MIC.F.TC-35955)
Mueller-Dombois, Dieter 11700
Muench, Robin Davie 11981
(GC421 M84 fol.)
Muhle, Herman 11417
(MIC.F.TC-17895)
Muir, Barry Sinclair 10882
Muir, Derek C.G. 6 (MIC.F.TC-33343)
Muir, James Douglas 4356
Muir, William Ernest 75
Muir, William Russell 9458
Muise, Delphin Andrew 7177
(MIC.TC-9010)
Mukerji, Mokul Kumar 11326
Mukherjee, Amar Chandra 5521
Mukherjee, Kalyan Kumar 6142
Mulcahy, Robert Francis 3250
(MIC.F.TC-26857)
Mulhall, David Bernard 9900
(MIC.F.TC-42984)
Mullaly, Robert P. 10094
(MIC.F.TC-59855)
Mullen, Gary Richard 10554
Muller-Hehn, Anita 3345 (MIC.T-3913)
Muller, Henry N., III 1248 (MIC.T-539)
Muller, Robert Andrew 1821
(MIC.F.TC-31293)
Muller, Steven 8523
Muller, Thomas Edward 2231
(MIC.F.TC-59306)

Mulligan, Robert 5290
Mullin, D.D. 2669
Mullings, Gloria Elizabeth 3715
  (MIC.F.TC-50320)
Mulvey, Mary Doris 6980
Mumford, Thomas Freuzel, Jr. 11484
Mummery, Robert Craig 6143
  (MIC.TC-14709)
Muncaster, Russell Walton 4940
  (MIC.T-373)
Mundie, John Duncan 1968
Mundy, Ray Allen 2376 (MIC.T-673)
Munn, John Duncan 9041
  (MIC.F.TC-40943)
Munns, Evangeline F. 9042
  (MIC.TC-8373)
Munns, Violet Beatrice 3743
  (MIC.F.TC-35276)
Munro, B.R. 6144
Munro, Barry Cartwright 2581
Munro, David Aird 10809
Munro, Donald Deane 11701
Munro, Donald Scott 5039
  (MIC.F.TC-26181)
Munro, Gary Wayne 8448
  (MIC.F.TC-41674)
Munro, Hugh James 1579
  (MIC.F.TC-52981)
Munro, John Alexander 11735
  (MIC.F.TC-40735)
Munro, John B. 560
Munro, Kenneth 7342
Munro, Peter Fraser 9491
Munro, Ronald Joseph 4069
  (MIC.F.TC-40944)
Munro, William Bennett 6970
Munton, Donald James 8790
  (MIC.T-572)
Munton, Margaret Ann 8349
  (MIC.F.TC-53747)
Murase, Kenneth 3744
Murchie, Robert Welch 123
Murdie, Robert Alexander 4952
  (HB3530 T6 M8)
Murison, William F. 11702
  (MIC.TC-2385)
Murphy, Brendan A. 2026
  (MIC.F.TC-54115)
Murphy, Daniel Lawson 6429
Murphy, E.E. 7882
Murphy, George Joseph 1411
  (MIC.T-308)
Murphy, James Brendan 5666
  (MIC.F.TC-61097)
Murphy, Lawrence Joseph 1574
Murphy, Michael Neil 3594
  (MIC.F.TC-59750)
Murphy, Peter James 3579
  (MIC.F.TC-32828)
Murphy, Raymond John Joseph 4267
  (MIC.F.TC-27504)
Murray, Alan Roderick 11120
Murray, Albert Nelson 6145
Murray, Alexander Lowell 7517
  (MIC.T-112)
Murray, Bruce Churchill 5667
Murray, Charles B. 9043
  (MIC.F.TC-44103)
Murray, Douglas Joseph 8851
  (MIC.F.TC-1193)
Murray, James Wolfe 5438
Murray, Jean E. 1231
Murray, John Alexander 1969
Murray, John David 2347
  (MIC.F.T-1012)
Murray, John Wayne 168
Murray, Leo T. 10729
Murray, Louis G. 6430
Murray, Malcolm Arthur 4931
Murray, Michael Allan 9726
  (MIC.F.TC-58749)
Murray, Stanley Norman 124
Murray, Virginia Elizabeth 3634
  (Z675 U5 M8)
Murray, Yves 9459
Murshid, Abu Hassan 275
  (MIC.F.TC-6403)
Mursky, Gregory 5877
Murthy, Gummulueu S. 6592
  (MIC.TC-4961)
Murty, Grandhi V.R. 1763

Musacckia, Xavier J. 10735
Muskat, Jack S. 3099
  (MIC.F.TC-59857)
Mussalem, Helen 6902
  (RT81 C3 M98 fol.)
Mustello, Anthony J. 9044
Mutch, Robert Alexander 11187
  (MIC.F.TC-55384)
Mutambirwa, Christopher C. 4932
  (MIC.F.TC-17094)
Muttart, David Garth 3108
  (MIC.F.TC-34445)
Mutti, Lawrence J. 5291
Mwamwenda, Tuntufye Selemani 3251
  (MIC.F.TC-51553)
Mwanang'onze, Elimelech H.B. 5522
  (MIC.F.TC-37814)
Mwasa, Joseph 2974
Mwenifumbo, Campbell Jonathan 6658
  (MIC.F.TC-48394)
Myers, Anita Margaret 9727
  (MIC.F.TC-44503)
Myers, Phillip Earl 7608

N

Nacke, Margaret D'Arc 4070
  (MIC.F.TC-42286)
Nadeau, Georges-André 3729
  (MIC.F.T-892)
Nadeau, Jean-Paul 1830
Nadin-Davis, Robert Paul 7911
  (MIC.F.TC-53265)
Nagle, George Shorten 11703
Nag, Chowdhury Deb Kumar 1944
  (MIC.F.TC-62317)
Naiman, Neil 7702 (MIC.F.TC-26077)
Naing, Win 5622
Nair, Murali Dharan 7579
  (MIC.F.T-1013)
Nakamura, Royden 10962
  (MIC.TC-6924)
Nakashima, Brian Shyozo 11882
  (MIC.F.TC-50521)
Nancarrow, Clarke Joanne E. 6808
  (MIC.F.TC-45975)
Nance, Jack Dwain 858
  (MIC.TC-11351)
Nann, Richard C. 10483 (MIC.T-421)
Nanson, Gerald Charles 4616
  (MIC.F.TC-35959)
Nanz, Robert H., Jr. 5115
Napier, Robert E. 9316
  (MIC.TC-44106)
Nappi, Carmine 2027
  (MIC.F.TC-20783)
Naqib, Fadle Mustafa 1535
  (MIC.F.TC-59025)
Narbonne, Guy M. 5523
  (MIC.F.TC-48596)
Nardocchio, Elaine 8230
Narita, Tetsuya 10883 (MIC.TC-6819)
Narod, Brian Barry 6643
  (MIC.F.TC-25228)
Nash, M. Teresa 1113
Nash, Ronald John Thomas 924
  (MIC.TC-2091)
Nashef, Ahmad Adam 9143
  (MIC.F.TC-47131)
Nasmyth, Patrick Walden 11932
  (MIC.TC-6925)
Nason Gerald 4357 (MIC.F.TC-25497)
Nasr, Mostafa Saeed 4585
  (MIC.F.TC-27535)
Nassar, Mohamed Ahmed 4481
  (MIC.F.TC-35627)
Nasser-Bush, Merun Hussein 789
  (MIC.T-770)
Nassichuk, Walter William 5878
Nault, Aimé 2736
Nauratil, Marcia Jeanne 7974
  (MIC.F.TC-58328)
Nauss, Anthony William 5439
Nautiyal, Avinash Chandra 5572
Navarre, Kathleen 9728
  (MIC.F.TC-49236)

Naylor, C.D. 1631
Naylor, George Charles 4278
  (MIC.TC-10932)
Naylor, R.T. 1518
Naysmith, John Kennedy 10485
  (MIC.F.TC-25947)
Neale, Ernest R.W. 6431
Near, Hubert L. 2553 (MIC.T-3)
Neatby, Herbert Blair 7357
  (F5081.9 L3 N4)
Neatby, Hilda M. 7039 (JL255 N4)
Neave, Ferris 10963
Neave, Kendal Gerard 6593
  (MIC.TC-12095)
Needhan, Merrill Arthur, Jr. 6763
  (MIC.T-932)
Needham, Roger David 4603
  (MIC.F.TC-58935)
Needham, William R. 7587
  (MIC.TC-1965)
Needler, Alfred Walker 10890
Neehall, Joan 4071 (MIC.F.TC-59856)
Neff, Thomas Louis 4534
Nehlawi, Joseph 1183
  (MIC.F.TC-28931)
Neil, Kenneth 11264 (MIC.F.TC-53748)
Neill, Garnet Bruce 11240
  (MIC.F.TC-54572)
Neill, Robert Foliet 6950
Neilsen, Gerald Henry 264
  (MIC.TC-33420)
Neilson, James M.H. 6432
Neilson, Murray Morris 11265
Neish, Gordon Arthur 10523
  (MIC.F.TC-32537)
Neish, Iain Charles 10725
  (MIC.F.TC-6926)
Neisser, Albert C. 1845
  (HD9710 C23 N4)
Nelles, Henry Vivian 7202
Nellis, Carl Hansen 10585
Nelson, Alan Robert 5879
Nelson, Ernest 6764 (MIC.F.TC-53266)
Nelson, Gary Stewart 53
  (MIC.F.TC-26371)
Nelson, Geoffrey Brian 9729
  (MIC.F.TC-43089)
Nelson, Janice Edith 9386
  (MIC.F.TC-58149)
Nelson, Joseph Scheiser 10964
  (MIC.TC-186)
Nelson, Karl Douglas 5770
Nelson, John E. 7703
  (MIC.F.TC-50523)
Nelson, Louise Mary 10524
  (MIC.F.TC-30561)
Nelson, Michael Davidson 4358
  (MIC.F.TC-52804)
Nelson, Robert Wayne 10862
Nelson, Samuel J. 5524
Nelson, Susan Hess 10300
  (MIC.F.TC-49524)
Nelson, Wendy Alison 11485
  (MIC.F.TC-55087)
Nemec, Thomas Francis 407
Nemetz, Georgia Helen 9224
  (MIC.F.TC-55088)
Nemetz, Peter Newman 1879
Nemni, Esther Monique 7752
  (MIC.F.TC-27930)
Nephew, James Harold 4416
  (MIC.T-755)
Nepveu, Pierre 8365 (MIC.F-034801)
Neralla, Venkata Rao 5009
  (MIC.F.TC-21619)
Nesbitt, Paul Edward 859
  (MIC.TC-13929)
Ness, Robert Conrad 408
  (MIC.F.T-893)
Netschert, Bruce C. 2368
Netten, John Wilfred 2462
Nettl, Bruno 477
Nettleship, David N. 10748
  (MIC.TC-7107)
Neuendorf, Gwendoline 8478 (JL88 N4)
Neufeld, E.P. 1437 (HG2706 N4 fol.)
Neufeld, Gordon Arthur 3252
  (MIC.F.TC-25232)
Neville, Christine Mary 11022
  (MIC.F.TC-47132)
Nevitte, Neil Hugh 8582

Newberry, Alan John Hesson 2937
(MIC.T-743)
Newberry, John Franklin 3635
(AL.P67 A17 R4 14)
Newbury, Robert William 4527
Newbury, Thomas K. 11353, 11971
(MIC.TC-9436)
Newcombe, Curtis Lakeman 11113
Newcombe, Ervin Ernest 4400
Newcomer, Richard S. 3550
Newell, Dianne Charlotte Elizabeth
10508 (MIC.F.TC-50623)
Newell, Jorge Alfredo 202
(MIC.TC-15294)
Newkirk, Ross Thomas 4558
(MIC.F.TC-28296)
Newman, Albert F. 9267
Newman, Jean Ellen 9563
Newman, Judith Marta 3977
(MIC.F.TC-35089)
Newman, Michael 1945
(MIC.F.TC-55090)
Newman, W.R. 5668
Newman, Warren Oscar 3183
(MIC.TC-8802)
Newman, William Alexander 5669
Newmarch, Charles Bell 5292
Newnham, Robert Montague 11704
Newsome, George Edwin 10979
(MIC.F.TC-26372)
Newsome, Richard Duane 11624
Newton, Donald McKay 10427
(MIC.T-231)
Newton, James Harry 9045
(MIC.F.TC-33459)
Newton, John Lebaron 11891
Newton, Keith 2076 (MIC.TC-30298)
Neysmith-Roy, Jean 3904
(MIC.F.TC-53268)
Ng, Kong Seng 4482 (MIC.F.TC-37694)
Nichol, Diane Sue 8927 (MIC.TC-15702)
Nicholl, George MacKenzie 3253
(MIC.F.TC-32854)
Nicholls, Glen Harvey 2770
(MIC.F.TC-43090)
Nichols, Claude Andrew 478
Nichols, Franklin T. 7005
Nichols, John David 7795
Nichols, Kenneth Hugh 979
(MIC.F.T-1395)
Nichols, Marie A. 4196
Nicholson, Janice E. 7133
(MIC.TC-13100)
Nicholson, Norman Leon 4889
Nickling, William G. 4687
(MIC.F.TC-44790)
Nicks, Gertrude Cecilia 479
Nicol, Andrew James 4124
Nicolson, Murray William Wood 7228
(MIC.F.TC-52538)
Niebauer, Henry Joseph 11906
Nield, John Everson 9776
Nielsen, Erik 5670 (MIC.F.TC-31523)
Nielsen, Grant Leroy 5438
Nielsen, Kent Christopher 5293
(MIC.F.TC-37696)
Nielsen, Peter A. 5880
(MIC.F.TC-32045)
Nielson, Warren Robert 9106
Niemeier, Myra Ann Louise 10867
Niemi, Beth 2189
Nienber, Wilfred 6624
Nietfeld, Patricia Kathleen Linskey 525
(MIC.F.T-1161)
Nimmo, Andrew Peebes 11222
(MIC.TC-6228)
Nish, Cameron 7006
Nish, Margaret Elizabeth 1091
Niskala, Helena 6720
(MIC.F.TC-29910)
Nivoli, Gian Carlo 9178
Nixon, Charles Donald 4513
(MIC.F.TC-43506)
Nixon, Deborah Susan 9144
(MIC.F.TC-47853)
Nixon, Howard R. 10411
Nixon, Mary Theresa 2892
(MIC.F.TC-24104)
Njaa, Lloyd Johan 9418
(MIC.TC-11153)

Nnyamah, Joseph Ugbogu 239
(MIC.F.TC-32538)
Nobbs, Richard Albert 1353
(MIC.TC-11053)
Noble, Edward James 1293
(MIC.F.TC-48795)
Noble, James Peter Allison 5441
Noble, Willa Jane 11486
(MIC.F.TC-65013)
Noble, William Charles 650
(MIC.TC-2092)
Noël, Guy 2737 (MIC.F-033508)
Noël, Jean Claude 8306
Noël, S.J.R. 8708
Nogradi, George Steve 6765
Nokoe, Tertius Sagary 11705
(MIC.F.TC-29911)
Nolan, Francis Michael 3135
(MIC.F.TC-4062)
Nolan, Michael Joseph 1136
(MIC.F.TC-56133)
Nollet, Jean 1946 (MIC.F.TC-58728)
Nolte, William Michael 7634
(MIC.T-766)
Nommik, Salme 6850
Noon, John Alfred 651
Noonan, Barrie Albert 9317
(MIC.F.TC-49052)
Noordeh, Ardeshir 3595
(MIC.F.TC-59905)
Nord, Douglas Charles 7614
(MIC.F.T-1064)
Nordin, Richard Nels 11487
(MIC.F.TC-19604)
Nordin, Vidar John 11748
Norford, Brian Seeley 5294
Norman, David Irwin 6146
Norman, George W.H. 5671
Norman, Jane Margaret 2554
(MIC.TC-6129)
Normandin, Martine Hazel Simard
12017 (MIC.F.TC-42319)
Norrie, Beatrice Irene 3835
(MIC.F.TC-17036)
Norris, Arnold Willy 6521
Norris, Darrell Alan 4825
(MIC.F.TC-29699)
Norris, Donald K. 4483
Norris, Joan Elizabeth 9730
(MIC.F.TC-42379)
Norris, Kenneth Everett 2400
Norris, Kenneth Wayne 8386
(MIC.F.TC-52055)
North, Joseph 3761
Northcote, Kenneth Eugene 5295
(MIC.TC-2387)
Northcote, Thomas Gordon 10965
Northey, Margot Elizabeth 8021
(MIC.F.TC-20020)
Northover, Wallace E. 9820
(MIC.TC-11438)
Northrop, Stuart Alvord 6433
Norton, Margaret T. 1519 (MIC.T-135)
Norton, William 132 (MIC.F.TC-19437)
Norvell, George Michael 1064
Nossal, Kim Richard 8889
(MIC.F.TC-53130)
Nostbakken, David Vinge 1093
(MIC.F.TC-47133)
Notley, Keith Roger 4536
(MIC.F.TC-50176)
Notzke, Claudia 708 (MIC.F.TC-60814)
Nourallah, Fayez Salim 1412
Nourry, Gerard Robert 6612
(MIC.F.TC-28768)
Nourry, Louis 8468 (MIC.F-003906)
Novak, Michael David 240
(MIC.F.TC-56681)
Novakowski, Nicholas Stephen 10654
Novek, Joel Leonard 8583, 10238
(MIC.F.TC-21922)
Nowak, Robert Lars 5442
(MIC.F.TC-51558)
Nowlan, Godfrey 6551
(MIC.F.TC-32133)
Nowlan, James Parker 6147
Noyes, Barbara Ann 3254
(MIC.TC-8375)
Nozdryn-Plotnicki, Michael John 6659
(MIC.F.TC-50177)

Nuckle, Jacques R. 10656
(MIC.F.TC-64150)
Ntunaguza, Gabriel 3012
(MIC.F-2M11.607.4)
Nudds, Thomas David 10773
(MIC.F.TC-48396)
Nuechterlein, Gary Lee 10826
(MIC.FT-1099)
Nunes, Arturo de F. 6434
Nunez, Manuel 12018
(MIC.F.TC-25235)
Nusbaum, D. 618
Nussbaumer, Margaret 3532
(MIC.F.TC-34450)
Nussmann, David George 5137
Nwachukwu, Silas Ogo Okonkwo 5124
Nyborg, Erling Orvald 76
(MIC.TC-5831)
Nygaard, Marvin Hector 2834
Nyland, Agnes Cecilia 8144

O

Oades, Carolyn Diane 4279
Oakes, Jocelyn Diane Eagle 4154
(MIC.F.TC-62292)
Oates, Thomas Raymond 8022
(MIC.F.T-1194)
Obeng-Quaidoo, Isaac 1094
(MIC.F.T-1069)
Oberg, Antoinette Alexander 2607
(MIC.F.TC-26868)
Oberlander, Barbara J. 7644
Oberlander, Henry Peter 8494
Oberle, James Peter 8584 (MIC.T-705)
Obi, Adeniyi Olubunmi 251
(MIC.F.TC-54273)
Obiekwe, Christian Okechukwu 10525
(MIC.F.TC-49053)
O'Brien, C.C. 4155
O'Brien, Gregory Charles 2028
O'Brien, John Egli 1137 (MIC.T-75)
O'Brien, John Wilfred 1778
O'Brien, Margaret Anne 4009
(MIC.F.TC-54008)
O'Bryan, Maureen Hazel 10428
(MIC.F.TC-21674)
Occhietti, Serge 4765 (MIC.F.TC-4414)
Ochitwa, Orest Paul 2848 (MIC.T-761)
O'Connell, Martin Patrick 7338
(MIC.TC-16652)
O'Connell, Mary Sheila 8023
O'Connell, Michael Francis 10998
(MIC.F.TC-63548)
O'Connor, D. 7883
O'Connor, John Joseph William 8024
(MIC.F.TC-35281)
O'Connor, Joseph Francis 11034
(MIC.F.TC-23418)
O'Connor, Kevin Bernard 4910
(MIC.F.TC-22646)
Oczkowski, Gene 9179
(MIC.F.TC-54341)
O'Dell, Leslie Anne 1027
(MIC.TC-55802)
Odell, Noel E. 5717
O'Donald, Peter 10749
O'Donnell, Kathleen 8123
O'Donovan, Joan Elizabeth 8466
O'Driscoll, Denis Christopher 2508
(MIC.T-750)
Odynak, Emily 3184 (MIC.F.TC-5159)
Odynak, Steve Nick 4359
Offenbach, Lilly 10153
Officer, Lawrence Howard 1610
(HG3915 O3)
Offosŭ-Asiedŭ, Albert 11706
Ogilvie, Robert Townley 11661
Ogmundson, Richard Lewis 8449
(MIC.T-452)
Ogram, Ernest William, Jr. 1980
Ogunbadejo, Tajudeen Adetayo 4559
(MIC.TC-14624)
Ogunyomi, Olugbenga 6435
(MIC.F.TC-52057)

Ogwang, Bob Humphrey 11488
(MIC.F.TC-46224)
Oh, Jeung Hoon 2397
Ohan, Farid Emil 2608
(MIC.F.TC-3035)
O'Hara, Norbert W. 6680
(MIC.F.TC-53311)
O'Hara, Thomas John 9564
O'Hearn, Michael James 9967
Ohene-Djan, I.L. 7884
Ohlsson, Karl E. 11489
Ohmoto, Hiroshi 5296
Okello, Lekoboam O. 2693
(MIC.F.TC-40470)
O'Kelly, Morton Edward John 4935
(MIC.F.TC-54193)
Okihiro, Norman Ryukichi 3596
(MIC.F.TC-47855)
O'Kill, Brian Laurence 8145
Okulitch, Andrew Vladimir 5297
(MIC.TC-5110)
Okulitch, Vladimir J. 6436
Olade, Moses A.D. 5298
(MIC.F.TC-25236)
Oladipo, Emmanuel Olukayode 4721
(MIC.F.TC-59749)
Olagbaiye, Joseph Ajiboye 4953
Olakampo, J.O.W. 1438
Olchowecki, Oleksa Alexander 10526
(MIC.TC-12830)
Oldham, Charles H.G. 5299
O'Leary, Jeffrey 5718
O'Leary, Wayne M. 1249
Olenick, Debra Lynn 3836
(MIC.F.TC-43092)
Oleson, Brian Thomas 169
Olfert, Owen Orton 170
(MIC.F.TC-41290)
Olhoeft, Gary Roy 6644
(MIC.F.TC-27938)
Oliva, Frank Daniel 4462
Oliver, Avihai 2077 (MIC.F.TC-42292)
Oliver, Donald Raymond 11254
Oliver, Michael K. 8585
Oliver, Peter Nesbitt 7346
(MIC.TC-4506)
Oliver, Thelma Isabel 8688
(MIC.F.TC-21560)
Oliver, Thomas A. 5525
Ollerenshaw, Neil Campbell 6437
Olley, Robert Edward 1764
(MIC.TC-3518)
Ollivier, Emile 10001
(MIC.F-2M11.535.5)
Ollivier, Maurice 8826
Olmstead, Marvin Lynn 7560
O'Loughlin, Colin Lockhart 11707
(MIC.TC-15141)
Olsen, Dennis 8450 (MIC.F.TC-37357)
Olson, Boyd Edward 9852 (MIC.T-199)
Olson, Franklyn C.W. 11898
Olson, James Murray 9731
(MIC.F.TC-45997)
Olson, Reginald Arthur 5881
(MIC.F.TC-32540)
Olssen, Andrée Lévesque 8636
(MIC.T-531)
Olthorf, Theodorius Hendrikus
Antonius 348
Olzak, Susan Maria Grumich 770
(MIC.F.T-957)
O'Malley, Denis Anthony 3522
(MIC.F.TC-26873)
Omanwar, Pandurang Keraba 228
(MIC.TC-6230)
Omara-Ojungu, Peter Hastings 4797
(MIC.F.TC-49829)
Ommer, Rosemary Elizabeth 1250
(MIC.F.TC-58084)
O'Neil, Emmett Francis 6971
O'Neil, Marion 1251
O'Neil-Lowry, M.K. 6851
O'Neill, Archibald Desmond
Joseph 11986
O'Neill, Florence M. 4053
O'Neill, Gilbert Patrick 3313
(MIC.F.TC-30352)
O'Neill, John Johnston 6438
O'Neill, M.P. 8827
O'Neill, Marie José 3049
(MIC.F.TC-35823)

O'Neill, Mary Elizabeth 1002
(MIC.T-200)
O'Neill, Mora Diane Guthrie 1028
(MIC.T-721)
O'Neill, Patrick Bernard Anthony 1029
(MIC.T-589)
O'Neill, Timothy John 1184
Ong, Sit-Tui 3433 (MIC.F.TC-30786)
Onibokun, Adepoju Gabriel 10493
(MIC.TC-9073)
Onuoha, A.R.A. 6809
(MIC.F.TC-44791)
Oostendorp, Anke 9732
(MIC.F.TC-38800)
Opala, Barbara 8098
(MIC.F-2M11.576.1)
Opheim, Lee Alfred 2287 (MIC.T-369)
Opp, Paul Franklin 3383
Oppenheimer, Robert Jonathon 1947
(MIC.F.TC-50323)
O'Reilly, Robert Richard 4326
O'Riordan, Jonathan 85 (MIC.TC-3729)
Orkin, Mark M. 7841 (MIC.TC-11610)
Orlick, Terrance Douglas 10329
(MIC.TC-13507)
Orlikow, Lionel 2407
Orloci, Laszlo 11490
Orlowski, Duane Edmund 779, 7704
(MIC.T-894)
Ormiston, Allen Roger 6552
Ormsby, Margaret A. 7160
Orpwood, Graham W.F. 2609
(MIC.F.TC-55798)
Orr-Ewing, Alan Lindsay 11708
Ortego, James Brent 10810
(MIC.F.T-1109)
Orton, Larry James 4072
(MIC.F.TC-59811)
Orvig, Svenn 5028
Osachoff, Margaret Gall 8025
(MIC.F.TC-40265)
Osborn, John Edward 11710
(MIC.TC-3054)
Osborne, Dale James 10569
Osborne, Lewis Leroy 11811
(MIC.F.TC-52422)
Osborne, Richard John 8536
Osgood, Cornelius Berrien 567
Oskin, Igbekele 6439
Oss, John Anthony 2938
Ossenberg, Richard J. 7580
(MIC.T-172)
Ossman, Albert John, Jr. 8791
(MIC.T-64)
Ostenso, Ned Allen 6673
Oster, John Edward 4268
(MIC.TC-13508)
Osterberg, Donald 11023
Ostergaard, Karen 7134
Osterman, Lisa Ellen 5882
(MIC.F.T-1288)
Ostrofsky, Milton Lewis 11830
(MIC.F.TC-32134)
O'Sullivan, Julia Therese 9565
(MIC.F.TC-56131)
Otchere-Boateng, Jacob K. 241
(MIC.F.TC-28774)
Otke, Paul Gerald 9608 (MIC.TC-6658)
O'Toole, Padraig 2873
Ott, Edward R. 7007
Otter, Andy Albert Den 7348
(MIC.F.TC-26877)
Ouellet, Fernand 1252 (HC117 Q4 O8)
Ouellet, Gaétan 9733
Ouellet, Henri Roger 10750
(MIC.F.TC-33349)
Ouellet, Marcel 6440
(MIC.F.TC-22416)
Ouellet, Roland 3346 (MIC.F-027709)
Ouellette, Yves 7899
Oukada, Larbi 7753
Oum, Tae Hoon 2260
(MIC.F.TC-42713)
Ourada, Patricia K. 7440 (MIC.T-576)
Outcalt, Samuel Irvine 4924
(MIC.TC-5834)
Ovedovitz, Albert C. 7661 (MIC.T-668)
Ovendale, R. 7571
Ovenshine, Alexander Thomas 5125
Overgaard, Herman Olaf Johan 4826

Overman, William D. 1996
Oviatt, Delmer T. 3112
Oviatt, Sharon Lynn 9344
(MIC.F.TC-42293)
Ovrebo, Clark Ledin 11426
(MIC.F.TC-47136)
Owen, Brian Edward 1390
(MIC.F.TC-28204)
Owen, Clifford Frank 1720
Owen, Stephanie Olive 959
(MIC.T-233)
Owen, Thomas Howard 6686
(MIC.F.T-958)
Owens, Edward Henry 6441
Owens, Ian Francis 4600
(MIC.F.TC-21680)
Owens, Owen E. 6442
Owram, Douglas Robb 7097
(MIC.F.TC-35097)
Oxman, Joel Allan 3925
(MIC.F.TC-51382)
Ozard, John Malcolm 6660
(MIC.TC-5835)
Ozbalt, Marija Ana Irma 8082
(MIC.F.TC-38314)

P

Pace, Danny Roy 10966
(MIC.F.TC-30301)
Pace, James B. 3837
Pachal, Doreen Mae 4169
(MIC.F.TC-59284)
Pacheco, Josephine F. 7040
Pacht, Jory Allen 5300 (MIC.F.T-1102)
Paciga, John Joseph 4560
(MIC.F.TC-32857)
Packer, J.G. 11550
Packer, Katherine Helen 3737
(MIC.T-654)
Packer, Miriam 8118
(MIC.F-2M11.363.1)
Padfield, Clive A.F. 3636
Padgham, William Albert 5573
Paeth, Robert Carl 294
Paetz, Martin Joseph 10928
(MIC.TC-13510)
Paganelli, Yolanda Rafadela 1003
Page, Donald Murray 8800
(MIC.F.TC-31301)
Page, Gordon Graham 2993
(MIC.F.TC-22194)
Page, N.M.G. 7621
Page, R.J.D. 7483
Page, Richard James 5301
Pageau, Gérard 11035
Paillé, Gilbert 11710 (MIC.TC-6933)
Pain, Kerrie Susan 9345
(MIC.F.TC-49064)
Painchaud-Leblanc Gisèle 7705
(MIC.F-2M11.371.1)
Painchaud, Louis 7754 (MIC.F-020801)
Painchaud, Robert Paul 9821
Paine, Frederick Karl 1095
(MIC.F.T-195)
Painter, Susan Lee 9387
(MIC.F.TC-56737)
Pajonas, Patricia Joan 3508
Pakiam, James Edwin 5035
Pal, Hilda Indira 3766
(MIC.F.TC-36775)
Pal, Leslie Alexander 1486
(MIC.F.TC-55971)
Palaniswamy, Pachagounder 11184
(MIC.F.TC-43926)
Palardy, Yvette 9460 (MIC.T-3742)
Palchanis, A.-Eugène 9180
Paley, David Thomas 10095
(MIC.TC-13513)
Palkiewicz, Jan 3284 (MIC.T-3530)
Pallascio, Richard 2596
(MIC.F-043307)
Pallesen, Leonard Carl 4280
(MIC.TC-7713)

Pallotta-Cornick, Maria Angela
    Carvalho 8928 (MIC.F.TC-47230)
Palm, Sister Mary Borgias 7008
    (MIC.T-297)
Palmer, Bryan Douglas 7203
    (MIC.F.T-918)
Palmer, Denise 10435
    (MIC.F.TC-32048)
Palmer, Frederick Cornelius
    Thunde 2939 (MIC.F.TC-27506)
Palmer, Guy Mathew 10429
    (MIC.F.T-1320)
Palmer, Howard Delbert 7236
    (MIC.F.TC-17136)
Palmer, Peter F. 1524
Palmer, Philip Motley 7774
Palmer, Sally Elizabeth 10096
    (MIC.F.TC-59809)
Palonen, Pentti Arnold 5106
    (MIC.F.TC-30565)
Palumbo, Richard Vincent 9046
    (MIC.F.TC-56539)
Pammett, Jon Howard 7398
    (MIC.T-771)
Pandey, Rama Kant 10455
    (MIC.TC-12833)
Pang, Patrick Chi-Kee 252
    (MIC.F.TC-18089)
Pankiewicz, Gerald 3477
    MIC.F.TC-54391)
Pannekoek, Frits 9790
    (MIC.F.TC-22496)
Panneton, Jean 8379 (MIC.F.TC-19017)
Pannu, Gurdial Singh 7982 (Z693 P35)
Pannu, Rajinder Singh 3637
    (MIC.TC-15302)
Panteleyev, Andrejs 5302
    (MIC.F.TC-28775)
Papatola, Kathleen Joan 8929
    (MIC.F.TC-59294)
Papazian, Jack H. 9047
    (MIC.F.TC-44118)
Papen, Jean 8264 (PS8503 U47 Z83)
Papezik, Vladimir Stephen 6148
Paquette, Pierre Jean 1880
Paquin, Jean-Paul 2190
    (MIC.F.TC-44119)
Paquin, Frère Léon Victor 8266
Paradis, Jean-Marc 6981
Paragg, Ralph Ramsarup 1391
    (MIC.F.TC-39542)
Parai, Louis 7581 (MIC.T-234)
Parakulam, George G. 10069
    (MIC.F.TC-38803)
Pardo, Luis Enrique 9982
    (MIC.F.TC-21561)
Parducci, Ronald Edmond 2582
    (MIC.F.TC-38804)
Paré, Eileen Mercedes 6742
    (MIC.F.TC-62017)
Paré, Simone 10160
Parent, Richard 9461
    (MIC.F-2M11.452.2)
Parent, Robert 1884
Parent, Simon Georges 7951
Parenton, Vernon J. 9822
Paret, Marie-Christine 7748
Pargellis, Stanley McCrory 7288
Paribakht, Tahevek 7675
    (MIC.F.TC-58238)
Paris, Ginette 3509 (MIC.F-024705)
Parizeau, J. 2029
Parizek, Richard Rudolph 5574
Park, Frederick Blair 6149
    (MIC.TC-623)
Park, James 4417 (MIC.TC-10753)
Parkash, Barham 6443
Parker, Arthur Kneeland 11711
Parker, George Lawrence 1075
    (MIC.F.TC-18510)
Parker, Keith Alfred 1294 (HC115 P37)
Parker, King Lawrence 7009
Parker, Nora Inez 6926
    (MIC.TC-15441)
Parker, Robert Davis Richard 11427
Parker, Robert Ray 10967
Parker, W.H. 4885
Parkinson, Claire Lucille 4650
Parkos, William George 6721
Parks, Thomas 6150

Parks, William Arthur 6151
    (MIC.F-CC.4)
Parks-Trusz, Sandra Lynn 2426,10002
Parlett, Thomas Arthur Anthony 10301
    (MIC.F.TC-20849)
Parmelee, David Freeland 10736
Parmelee, John Aubrey 11390
Paroschy, John Henry 77
    (MIC.F.TC-38975)
Parr, Gwynth Joy 7645 (MIC.F.T-1044)
Parr, Philip Clayton 1536
Parrish, Randall Richardson 5303
    (MIC.F.TC-59163)
Parrott, Eric George 2583
    (MIC.F.TC-32859)
Parry, John Trevor 4766
Parry, Keith William John 504
Parry, Richard Howell 11171
    (MIC.F.TC-65766)
Parry, Robert John 2940
    (MIC.F.TC-38805)
Parry, Robert Scott 4281
    (MIC.TC-7714)
Parson, Helen Edna 4767
    (MIC.F.T-895)
Parsons, Carl Taylor 11264
Parsons, Clifford Barry 4561
    (MIC.TC-10923)
Parsons, George Llewellyn 2890
Parsons, Myles Lyle 6152
Partin, Charles Arthur 1213
Partlow, Hugh Russell 2631
Partridge, Mary Janice 3031
    (MIC.F.TC-44949)
Parviainen, Esko Atso Nolevi 5126
    (MIC.TC-14970)
Parvin, Viola Elizabeth 4244
    (LB2853 C2 P3)
Pasiciel, Ernest Kurt 9804
Pasko, Stan Joseph 3255
Patchett, Joseph Edmund 6153
Patenaude, Luce 7938 (F5044.3 P38)
Paterson, Colin G. 11870
    (MIC.TC-12621)
Paterson, Donald G. 1665
    (HG5152 P33)
Paterson, Donald Hugh 6852
    (MIC.F.TC-36778)
Paterson, George Morton 9777
    (MIC.F-9923)
Paterson, Ian Arthur 5304
    (MIC.F.TC-17219)
Paterson, Janet Mary 8294
    (MIC.F.TC-58251)
Paterson, William Stanley Bryce 5443
Patil, Arvind Shankar 214
Patmore, William Henry 5305
Paton, James McNidder 4232
Paton, Richard Thurston 9093
    (MIC.TC-3520)
Patrice, Frère 7676
Patrick, Glenda Marie 3558
    (MIC.F.TC-55795)
Patriquin, James Douglas 1632
    (MIC.T-946)
Patsula, Philip James 9489
    (MIC.TC-4966)
Patterson, David Kingsworth, Jr. 917
    (MIC.F.TC-59808)
Patterson, E. Palmer, II 480
    (MIC.T-129)
Patterson, George Cameron 6154
    (MIC.F.TC-49531)
Patterson, Graeme Hazlewood 7204
    (MIC.F.TC-22347)
Patterson, Howard L. 147
Patterson, Ian Wilson 2751
Patterson, James Howard 10774
    (MIC.TC-10949)
Patterson, Laurence P. 9946
Patterson, Lawrence William
    Alexander 1004 (MIC.T-803)
Patterson, Robert Steven 2441
    (MIC.T-202)
Pattison, John Charles 1439
Patton, Donald John 1916 (MIC.T-639)
Patton, Harald Smith 119
    (HD9044 C2 P3)
Patty, John M.V. 3911
    (MIC.F.TC-21562)

Paul, Alexander Humphrey 4707
    (MIC.TC-8111)
Paul, Alix-Herard 8873
Paul, Allen Zachary 11972
Paul, Compton Lawrence 242
    (MIC.F.TC-40749)
Paul, Lorne C. 11334
Paul, Peter Montgomery 11647
    (MIC.T-674)
Paul, Ross Henderson 4282
Paulin, Michel 11841
Pauls, Ronald Walter 10701
    (MIC.F.TC-40042)
Paunonen, Sampo Vilho 9734
    (MIC.F.TC-54116)
Paustian, Shirley Irene 8026
    (MIC.F.TC-24109)
Pautzke, Clarence Greer 11973
Pawaputanon, Kamonporn 10555
    (MIC.F.TC-51772)
Pawlicki, Robert Edward 9566
    (MIC.TC-6780)
Pawlowicz, Richard M. 5444
Payette, L. 7952
Payne, J.G. 6155
Payne, Neil Forrest 10655
Payne, Richard J. 7937
Payne, Robert John 4958
    (MIC.F.TC-34229)
Pazderka, Bohumir 1781
    (MIC.F.TC-30198)
Peach, John Whitmore 3347
    (MIC.TC-6232)
Peach, Peter Angus 6156
Peacock, Adrienne Hazel 11825
    (MIC.F.TC-55099)
Peacock, Andrew Charles 9609
    (MIC.F.TC-53834)
Peale, Rodgers 6444
Pearce, Andrew John 6661
    (MIC.F.TC-18343)
Pearce, John Walter 9214
    (MIC.F.TC-47234)
Pearlman, Sheldon 10051
    (MIC.F.TC-36779)
Pearson, David Arthur 3172
    (MIC.F.TC-30791)
Pearson, George Raymond 6157
Pearson, Philip Michael Lee 2261
Pearson, Roger William 4674
Pearson, Walter John 6169
Pearson, William Chelsie 6625
Pearson, William Norman 6159
    (MIC.F.TC-50180)
Pease, Steven Robert 4604
Peatfield, Giles R. 5306
    (MIC.F.TC-37534)
Peattie, Roderick 4768
Peck, Bryan Trevor 4380
Peddie, Richard 4954
    (MIC.F.TC-36780)
Pederson, Linda Lue 6722
    (MIC.F.TC-48399)
Pedro, Junior Mario José 5046
    (MIC.F.TC-48802)
Peer, Miri 9048 (MIC.F.TC-44504)
Peers, Frank Wayne 1138
    (HE8693 C3 P4)
Pegrum, Reginald H. 6160
Peikert, Ernest William 5445
Peitchinis, Jacquelyn A. 6784
    (MIC.TC-13941)
Peitchinis, S.G. 2211
Pelège, Michael Nicholas 7781
    (MIC.T-529)
Pell, Barbara Helen 8154
Pell, Jerry 5040 (MIC.TC-6032)
Pelland, Flore 9388
Pellegrini, Wayne L. 9198
    (MIC.F.TC-44123)
Pellerin, André R. 9049
Pelletier, Aurèle 3256
    (MIC.F.TC-60188)
Pelletier, Guy 4283
    (MIC.F-2M11.527.4)
Pelletier, J.R. 968
Pelletier, Marc-Lionel 3737
    (MIC.T-3556)
Pelletier, Raymond 100
Pelletier, René A. 6161
Pelosse, Cécile 8366 (MIC.F-016701)

Pelton, Terrance Ronald 10506
(MIC.TC-6935)
Pelzer, Ernest Edward 5446
Pemberton, Carlisle Alexander 54
(MIC.F.TC-30063)
Pemberton, Ian Cleghorn
Blanchard 7010 (MIC.TC-14049)
Pemberton, Stuart George 6162
(MIC.F.TC-46935)
Pencer, Irwin 9225 (MIC.F.TC-48606)
Pendakur, Manjunath 1114
Pendergast, Russell Anthony 7041
Pendle, Frank Ernest, Jr. 7205
Pengelly, David Harvey 11285
Penlington, Norman 7484
Pennanen, Gary Alvin 7542
Pennell, Douglas Gordon 4484
(MIC.TC-3865)
Pennell, William 11057
(MIC.F.TC-18344)
Penner, Norman 8460
(MIC.F.TC-30353)
Penner, Ronald Steven 9567
(MIC.F.TC-58628)
Penner, Rudolph Gerhard 1666
Penner, Wesley Jerry 3348
(MIC.TC-8112)
Penney, Mary Paula 9935
Penta, Gerard Charles 2584
Pentland, David Harry 7788
(MIC.F.TC-62254)
Pentland, Harry Clare 2089
Pépin, Jean-Guy 3314 (MIC.T-478)
Pepler, Debra June 9389
(MIC.F.TC-42383)
Pepperdine, Barbara Joan 6917
(MIC.F.TC-27944)
Percival, John Allan 6163
(MIC.F.TC-52917)
Percy, Michael B. 7662
(MIC.F.TC-32680)
Perdie, Henry S. 6164
Peredery, Walter Volodymyr 6165
(MIC.TC-15444)
Pereira, Cecil Patrick 7603
(MIC.F.T-1175)
Pereira-Mendoza, Lionel 3434
(MIC.F.TC-25964)
Pereira-Da-Rosa, Victor Manuel 7602
(MIC.F.TC-50536)
Perejda, Andrew Daniel 4890
Perin, Robert 9901
Perkett, William Oliver 1838
(MIC.T-65)
Perkins, Marjorie Morrison 4463
(MIC.F.TC-38806)
Perkins, Walter Ethen 11491
(MIC.F.TC-40752)
Perley, Linda 8027
Perlin, George Crosbie 8648
Perner, Josef 9390 (MIC.F.TC-36781)
Perrault, Guy Gilles 5719
(MIC.F.TC-22772)
Perrault, Yvonne L. 3510
Perret, Marie-Solange 1765
Perrier, David Conrad 10302
(MIC.F.TC-30963)
Perron, Marc A. 113 (S417 B25 P45)
Perrotta, Carmine Ann 10687
Perry, David George 6553
(MIC.F.TC-24637)
Perry, Marie-Alphonse 8329
Perry, Raymond Paul 9568
(MIC.TC-10153)
Persky, Joel 1058 (MIC.T-836)
Person, Roland Conrad 7983
(MIC.F.T-1337)
Persson, Diane Iona 4125
(MIC.F.TC-49072)
Peruniak, Geoffrey Stephen 4327
(MIC.F.TC-36782)
Pesonen, Lauri J. 6166 (MIC.F.TC-38807)
Peszat, Lucille Catharine 3721
(MIC.F.TC-42295)
Peter, Karl Andreas 783
Peterman, Edwin Z. 5526
Peterman, Randall Martin 11223
(MIC.F.TC-22200)
Peters, John Ross 1686
Peters, Kenneth Gordon 3889
(MIC.F.TC-36019)

Peters, Mary Alice 2453
Peters, Neil M. 4156
Peters, Ronald George 5771
Peters, Stuart Sanford 10849
Peters, Victor 9842
Petersen, James Otto 1214
Petersen, Richard Randolph 11792
Petersen, Thomas Alfred Steenberg 46
(SB781 P4 fol.)
Petersen, William 7593 (JV7285 D8 P4)
Peterson, Erick James 8586
(MIC.F.TC-896)
Peterson, Everett Bruce 11492
Peterson, Jacqueline Louise 496
(MIC.F.T-1143)
Peterson, James Scott 1721
(MIC.TC-6432)
Peterson, Mayfield 3349
Peterson, Nathan Nelvin 6167
(MIC.TC-3521)
Peterson, Randolph Lee 10635
Peterson, Rex Marion 6168
Peterson, Richard Harry 10989
Peterson, Richard Spencer 10603
Peterson, Robert Emil 5883
Peterson, Wilbur 11391
(MIC.F.TC-44797)
Petherbridge, Douglas Lawrence 443
Petraus Kas, Rymantas 4012
(MIC.F.TC-37162)
Petrie, Brian D. 11958
(MIC.F.TC-22858)
Petrie, J. Richards 1722
Petrimoulx, Catherine 3075
(MIC.F.TC-29220)
Petrone, Serafina Penny 8397
Petruk, William 6445
Petrunik, Michael G. 10218
(MIC.F.TC-36784)
Petryk, Allen Alexander 5447
Petryshyn Jaroslav 2120
(MIC.F.TC-36311)
Pett, H. Gregory 1354
Pettapiece, William Wayne 288
(MIC.TC-6233)
Pettem, Marie Odette Leblanc 3694
(MIC.F.TC-52424)
Pettijohn, Francis John 6169
Pettis, Charles A. 11897
Pettit, George A. 4126 (E51 C15 fol.)
Petzold, Donald Emil 5051
(MIC.F.TC-50539)
Pezer, Vera Rose 8930
(MIC.F.TC-36936)
Pezzetta, John Mario 6170
Pezzot-Pearce, Terry Diane 9145
(MIC.F.TC-47236)
Pfeffer, Helmut William 6171
Pfeiffer, Susan Kay Gosher 373
(MIC.F.TC-36785)
Phair, George 5772
Pharo, Christopher Howard 5307
(MIC.TC-15146)
Pheasant, David Richard 5884
Phemistes, Thomas C. 6172
Phidd, Richard W. 1487
Philbrook, Thomas Vere 4809
(MIC.T-66)
Philippe, Pierre 444 (MIC.F-004403)
Philippon, Donald Joseph 6708
(MIC.F.TC-43521)
Phillips, Alexander James 3164
Phillips, Charles Edward 2623
Phillips, Delores Joan Lavoie 7979
(MIC.F.TC-43699)
Phillips, Dorothy Anne 9735
(MIC.F.TC-21945)
Phillips, Harry John Charles 8613
(MIC.F.TC-28309)
Phillips, John Henry H. 11286
Phillips, Lester Henry 8601
Phillips, Paul Arthur 2121 (MIC.T-903)
Phillips, Samuel Floyd 11517
(MIC.F.TC-26376)
Phillips, William Gregory 31
(HD9486 C22 P5)
Phillips-Riggs, L. 3935
(MIC.F.TC-54014)
Phillipson-Price, Adrienne 6723
(MIC.F.TC-58166)
Philpotts, Anthony R. 6446

Phinney, William Charles 5672
Phipps, Charles V.G. 6173
Phipps, James Benjamin 11933
Picard, Diane 7668
Picard, R.I.C. 1440
Picard-Gerber, Marilen Joy 3939
(MIC.F.TC-49667)
Piccolo, Ornella 9226
(MIC.F.TC-53404)
Piché, Louise 2078 (MIC.F-2M11.399.4)
Pick, Frances Renata 11871
(MIC.F.TC-55778)
Pickard, Brent William 3580
(MIC.F.TC-24116)
Pickard, Lynette Elizabeth 1948
(MIC.F.TC-62981)
Pickett, Eric Elliott 11799
Picklyk, Donald D. 5107
(MIC.TC-15035)
Picman, Jaroslaw D. 10753
(MIC.F.TC-51776)
Piedalue, Gilles 1295 (MIC.F-030802)
Piedalue, Marc 9610 (MIC.F-025304)
Piel, Kenneth Martin 6527
(MIC.TC-8637)
Pienaar, Petrus Johannes 6174
Piene, Harald 11737 (MIC.F.TC-30447)
Pieper, Ezra Henry 7535
Pieper, Richard Edward 11934
(MIC.TC-10259)
Pierce, John T. 4911
Pierce, William David 9736
(MIC.F.TC-25743)
Pierce, William Lloyd 9805
Pieroni, Rita Maria 2191
(MIC.F.TC-44505)
Pierotti, Raymond John 10999
(MIC.F.TC-44316)
Pierson, Donald Fredrick 9146
(MIC.F.TC-40947)
Piette, Alain 8262 (MIC.F-2M11.605.1)
Pigage, Lee Case 5308
(MIC.F.TC-42716)
Pigeon, Richard 9462
Piggott, Glyne Leroy 7796
(MIC.F.TC-27947)
Pijawka, K. David 4592 (MIC.F.T-1344)
Pike, Ruth 3257 (MIC.TC-16657)
Pilcher, Dalton Jefferson 2374
Pilette, Danielle 1949
(MIC.F-2M11.543.1)
Pilkington, Gwendoline 3545
(MIC.F.TC-27948)
Pilon, Jean 4769 (MIC.T-3418)
Pilon, Lise 138
Pilon, Robert 9391 (MIC.F.TC-59015)
Pimlott, Douglas Humphreys 10636
Pinard, Maurice J.L.M. 8664
(JL259 A45 P53)
Pinchin, Hugh McAlester 1997
Pincus, John Alexis 1766
Pinel-Alloul, Bernadette 11119
Ping, Benjamin Leung Kai 3695
Pinkus, Joan 9346 (MIC.F.TC-36788)
Pinnington, J.E. 9836
Pip, Eva 11114 (MIC.F.TC-35862)
Piper, David 3258 (MIC.F.TC-51565)
Piper, Don Courtney 7931
Piper, Edward Harry 481 (HE399 P5)
Pippy, John Herbert Charles 11000
(MIC.F.TC-28124)
Piquette, Roland 4401 (MIC.F-006404)
Pires, Alvaro A. Penna de
Oliveira 10303
Pirie, James 6447 (MIC.TC-9327)
Pirie, Margaret Cameron 801
Pirie, Robert Gordon 6448
Pirot, Michael Alphonse 9569
(MIC.F.TC-29045)
Piscione, Joseph Anthony 2598
(MIC.F.TC-53138)
Pisterman, Susan Jane 9737
(MIC.F.TC-59014)
Pitcher, Max Grow 5091
Pitsel, Patricia Lynne 9318
(MIC.F.TC-51306)
Pitsula, James Michael 7229
(MIC.F.TC-41010)
Pitt, Thomas Kenton 11001
(MIC.F.TC-27570)

Piva, Michael J. 2101
(MIC.F.TC-25349)
Piya-Ajariya, Laeka 3136
(MIC.F.TC-40279)
Plain, Richard Hayward McVicar 2063
(MIC.TC-13527)
Plamondon, André Paul 11712
(MIC.TC-13253)
Plant, Richard Lester 1030
(MIC.F.TC-42297)
Plante, Jean-René 8231
Plante, Lucienne 2537
(MIC.F.TC-19024)
Plate, David R. 9159
(MIC.F.TC-29221)
Plato, William Russell 9867
(MIC.F.TC-25771)
Platt, John Gordon 9050
(MIC.TC-8376)
Platt, Joseph Belnap 10863
(MIC.T-868)
Platt, Thomas Reid 10556
(MIC.F.TC-36459)
Plaxton, Robert Piercy 2966
(MIC.TC-4968)
Plehwe, Rudolf 8732
Plenderleith, William Alexander 2908
Plewes, Doris H. 10398
Pliodzinskas, Algimantas Jonas 11793
Plischke, Elmer O.A. 7900
Ploegaerts, Léon 10501
(MIC.F-020704)
Plotnick, Alan Ralph 1917
Plumb, Jon Michael 10462
(MIC.F.TC-42298)
Pluta, Leonard Andrew 47
(MIC.TC-624)
Pocius, Gerald Lewis 409
Pocklington, Roger 11892
Pocock, Y.P. 5108
Poddar, Arun Kumar 2212
(MIC.F.TC-28310)
Podmore, Christopher John 2415
(MIC.F.TC-38014)
Podrebarac, George R. 2610
(MIC.F.TC-58358)
Poe, Weyland Douglas 1723
Poel, Dale Heeres 8681 (MIC.T-445)
Pohle, Gerhard Werner 11051
(MIC.F.TC-55781)
Pointon, C.R. 5092
Poirier, Pierre Paul 4213
Poirier, Yves 2670
Poisson, Yves 3435
Poitras, Lorraine Rolande 9738
(MIC.F-243304)
Poizner, Sonja 9268 (MIC.TC-15703)
Pojar, James Joseph 11493
Pokotylo, David Leslie 388
(MIC.F.TC-40759)
Poland, Eleanor 7543
Polatajko, Helene J. 3789
(MIC.F.TC-55782)
Polgar, Alexander T. 10097
(MIC.F.TC-55785)
Pollack, Gerald A. 1998
Pollock, C.A. 5448
Pollock, Donald W. 6175
Pollock, Nathan Lionel 9463
(MIC.F.TC-47141)
Pollock, Sheila Joy 6766
(MIC.F.TC-27949)
Polovy, Patricia 9419
(MIC.F.TC-53312)
Polowy, Hannah S. 3032
(MIC.F.TC-40760)
Poloz, Stephen Shawn 1561
(MIC.F.TC-52986)
Polunin, N.V. 11551
Polyzoi, Eleoussa 780
(MIC.F.TC-55783)
Polzin, Paul Elmer 1562 (MIC.T-235)
Pomeroy, John Anthony 869
(MIC.F.TC-51055)
Pomeroy, William Martin 11494
(MIC.F.TC-34924)
Pomfret, Dennis Alan 10003
(MIC.F.TC-50332)
Pomfret, Richard William Thomas 114
(MIC.F.TC-19278)

Pompa, Edward Michael 8884
(MIC.T-236)
Ponak, Allen M. 6918 (MIC.F.T-939)
Pond, George Stephen 4981
(MIC.TC-187)
Ponder, Arthur Aubrey 2967
(MIC.TC-15147)
Ponnuswami, Krishnaswami 7885
(MIC.TC-4595)
Pool, Gail Richard 7590
(MIC.F.TC-43003)
Pool, Jonathan Robert 8587
Poole, Peter 619 (MIC.F.TC-52087)
Poole, William Jr. 1611
Poole, William Hope 5309
Poon, Chung Lam 2313
(MIC.F.TC-28311)
Poon, Wai-Keung 2795
(MIC.F.TC-30354)
Poore, Richard Zell 6518
Pope, Fredrick John 6176
Pope, Glen Robin 4197
(MIC.F.TC-18530)
Pope, Gregory Frederick 11883
(MIC.F.TC-19343)
Pope, Karl Theodore 1031 (MIC.T-542)
Pope, Thomas 2909
Popper, George H.P. 5773
Porteous, Hugh Allengham 7278
(MIC.T-927)
Porter, Carol Anne 9051
(MIC.F.TC-65006)
Porter, Eric Ronald 4127
(MIC.F.TC-53139)
Porter, Fernand 9823 (BX 910 C2 P6)
Porter, Gerald Robert 2941
(MIC.F.T-1088)
Porter, James E. 3790
(MIC.F.TC-49240)
Porter, John Robert 947
(MIC.F-2M11.605.5)
Porter, William Barry 11662
(MIC.F.TC-30569)
Porterfield, Richard Maurice 7485
(MIC.F.T-999)
Posgate, Wilfred Dale 8760
(MIC.T-370)
Posluns, Elaine 4073 (MIC.F.TC-53140)
Posluszny, R. Ushner 11609
(MIC.F.TC-27235)
Posner, Judith Susan 9739
(MIC.F.TC-31305)
Post, George Richard 1767 (MIC.T-67)
Postal, Paul M. 7814
Postner, Harry Haskell 1768
Poston, William Roger 6810
Poteet, Maurice 7582
(MIC.F-2M11.576.2)
Potevin, Eugene 6449
Pothier, Yvonne Marie 3165
(MIC.F.TC-54015)
Potter, Alexander Oberlander 8479
(JL65 J923 P75)
Potter, Christopher John 5310
(MIC.F.T-1345)
Potter, David 11610
Potter, Ralph Richard 6177
(MIC.TC-4783)
Pottinger, Andrew John 8146
(MIC.F.TC-40702)
Pottinger, Robert Peter 11327
(QL552 P6)
Potvin, Robert John Michael 4418
(MIC.F.TC-27507)
Poudrier, Lucien Mark 4074
(MIC.F.TC-38811)
Pouinard, Alfred Antonin 960
Poulin, Ambrose O. 4490
(MIC.TC-11963)
Poulin, Simon Lise 1329
(MIC.F.TC-35785)
Pouliot, Gaston 6450
Poulton, Terence P. 6522
Poupard, Danielle 4441 (MIC.F-014906)
Poupart, Jean 10375 (MIC.F.TC-43005)
Poupeney, Catherine 8028
Powell, Alan Thomas Rees 10169
(MIC.F.TC-27951)
Powell, Barbara Pezalla 8161
(MIC.F.TC-47857)

Powell, Grace Lillian 4636
Powell, John Martin 317
(MIC.TC-3735)
Powell, Keith Raymond 2893
Power, Geoffrey 11046
Power, Graham Clifford 4770
(MIC.F.TC-24644)
Power, Sister Marianita 9392
(MIC.F.TC-21939)
Powers, Sidney 5449
Powles, Percival M. 10896
Powrie, T.L. 1981
Poysa, Vaino Wilhelm 338
(MIC.F.TC-48809)
Poznansky, Ellen 9393 (MIC.F-042404)
Pozniak, Tadeusz D. 3436
Prabhu, Mohan Keshav 6451
(MIC.F.TC-58206)
Prakash, Brahm 3612
(MIC.F.TC-35104)
Prang, Margaret Evelyn 7378
(MIC.F.TC-19729)
Prasher, Shiv Om 78 (MIC.F.TC-62984)
Pratt, David 2585 (MIC.TC-7923)
Pratt, Gary Michael 918
(MIC.F.T-1113)
Pratt, Joyce Barbara 3511
(MIC.F.TC-38812)
Pratt, Julius William 7070 (E713 P895)
Prattis, James Ian 389 (MIC.TC-6937)
Prebble, Thomas Kenneth 2975
(MIC.F.TC-26889)
Precosky, Donald Alexander 8387
(MIC.F.TC-41094)
Prefontaine, Marielle 3523
(MIC.T-211)
Prentice, Alison Leeds 2509
(MIC.F.TC-31306)
Prepas, Ellie Edith 11872
(MIC.F.TC-43702)
Preshing, William Anthony 1139
(MIC.T-137)
Presley, Bobby Joe 5311
Prest, Victor Kent 6178
Preston, Charles Franklyn 3015
Preston, Donald Wesley 7669
(MIC.F.TC-27324)
Preston, Raymond George 4442
(MIC.F.TC-26890)
Preston, Richard Joseph, III 513
(MIC.T-377)
Preston, Valerie Ann 1580
(MIC.F.TC-39972)
Preto, Vittorio A.G. 5312
(MIC.TC-2893)
Prevett, John Paul 10811
(MIC.TC-14627)
Price, Anthony Glynne 4771
(MIC.F.TC-24403)
Price, Jeffrey L. 3259
(MIC.F.TC-29222)
Price, Kenneth Arthur 763
(MIC.F.TC-44507)
Price, Larry Wayne 4688
Price, Peter 6452
Price, Raymond Alex 5313
Price, Trevor 8733 (MIC.F.TC-30204)
Price, William Joseph 9868
(MIC.F.TC-53277)
Priddle, Ruth Evelyn 9394
(MIC.F.TC-49836)
Pride, Cletis Graden 1096
Prince, John Philip 1918
(MIC.F.TC-49080)
Prince, Samuel Henry 10184 (HB31 C7)
Prince, Suzanne 8370
Prince-Falmagne, Thérèse 7284
Prior, Richard Byrvell Leathers 7859
Pritchard, Andrew Lyle 10922
Pritchard, James Stewart 1232
(MIC.F.TC-31308)
Pritchard, John Charles 689
(MIC.F.TC-34927)
Pritchett, John P. 4740
Prives, Moshe Zalman 2138
Prochazka, Antonin 12019
(MIC.TC-11253)
Proctor, Dennis Lester Coor 11256
(MIC.F.TC-43525)
Proctor, Donald John 7042

Proctor, Richard Malcolm 5575
Pross, August Paul 8734
(MIC.TC-1497)
Prosser, Laurence Edwin Keith 10446
Prost, Robert 10502
Proteau, Luc 10330
(MIC.F-2M11.575.9)
Proud, Donald W. 9181
Proudfoot, Alexander James 2874
Proudfoot, Stuart Bradley 8735
(MIC.F.T-989)
Proulx, Gilbert 10685
Proulx, Guy B. 9464
Proulx, J. Roger 10430 (MIC.T-3056)
Proulx, Jean-Pierre 9824
(MIC.F-2M11.502.1)
Proulx, Monique Cécile 3696
(MIC.F.T-898)
Proulx, Ovide 8367
Proulx, Paul Martin 7793
(MIC.F.T-990)
Prout, Peter Francis 2818
(MIC.F.TC-32052)
Provost, Guy 8274
Provost, Marc-André 9241
(MIC.F-023408)
Prucha, Martin John 307
Prueter, Herbert John 3857
Prusti, Bansi D. 5885
Pryke, Kenneth George 7178
(FC2322.4 P79)
Prystowsky, Seymour 9940
Pučat, Amalia Margaret 11328
(MIC.F.TC-23168)
Pucella, Pasquale 3350 (MIC.F-000812)
Puckett, T.C. 2213
Pufahl, Dennis Edward 4491
(MIC.F.TC-30799)
Pugh, George MacLaggan 8931
(MIC.F.TC-36462)
Pulker, Edward A. 1296
Pullen, Harry 3369 (MIC.F.TC-25501)
Pullman, Douglas Robert 10154
(MIC.F.TC-17801)
Pulos, Steven Michael 3260
(MIC.F.TC-41013)
Pulton, Thomas William 3858
(MIC.F.TC-58522)
Punch, Keith Francis 2859
(MIC.TC-1498)
Punter, John Vincent 4955
(MIC.F.TC-27952)
Punugu, Adilakshmamma 11418
(MIC.F.TC-31309)
Pura, Sophie Kathryn 4328
Purchase, Bryne Brock 1769
(MIC.F.TC-53143)
Purdy, Judson Douglas 2555
(MIC.TC-1)
Purdy, John Winston 6179
(MIC.TC-1845)
Putterman, Allan Howard 9182
(MIC.TC-13101)
Pye, Carol Jean 6724
Pye, Edgar George 6180
Pyke, Dale Randolph 6453
(MIC.TC-1399)
Pylypiw, James Alexander 2611
(MIC.F.TC-21945)
Pyrcz, Gregory Emanuel 8451
(MIC.F.TC-43526)

Q

Quarter, Jack Joel 3697
(MIC.TC-9562)
Quashie-Sam, Semion James 339
(MIC.F.TC-41772)
Quay, Paul Douglas 6181
Quealey, Francis Michael 7327
(MIC.TC-15422)
Quenet, Robin Vincent 11495
(MIC.F.TC-17222)
Quenneville, Jean-Guy R. 8588
(MIC.T-848)

Quick, Edison 2626
Quick, Horace Floyd 10570
Quily, Peter Louis 4198
(MIC.TC-15317)
Quinlan, Garry Michael 11944
(MIC.F.TC-53769)
Quinn, Frank Hugh 4523
Quinn, Harold A. 5886
Quinn, Herbert Furlong 8670
(F5430 Q85)
Quinn, Howard Edmond 6182
Quinn, James Joseph 1065
Quinney, Henry Arthur 10390
(MIC.F.TC-21946)
Quirke, Terence Thomas 6183
Quirke, Terence Thomas, Jr. 6454

R

Raabe, Francis Conrad 8890
(MIC.T-298)
Raad, Awni Tewfiq Saleh 265
(MIC.TC-6562)
Rabeau, Yves 1503
Rabie-Azoory, Vera 9631
(MIC.F-031707)
Rabiega, William Albert 2030
(MIC.T-821)
Rabinovitch, Robert 1680 (MIC.T-446)
Rabinowitz, Philip David 6645
Racette, Daniel 1392
(MIC.F.TC-43705)
Racette, Genevieve 2586
(MIC.F-031202)
Racha-Intra, Suparak 3290
(MIC.F.TC-34455)
Rachlis, Lorne Michael 2727
(MIC.F.TC-59820)
Rackowski, Cheryl Stokes 8029
(MIC.F.T-1000)
Radcliffe, Samuel John 2646
(LC46342 O5 R35)
Raddi, Arvind Govind 10623
(MIC.TC-2389)
Radecki, Henry 813 (MIC.F.TC-25745)
Radvanyi, Andrew 10702
Rae, George Ramsay 4861 (MIC.T-69)
Rae, Robert Cameron 148
(MIC.F.TC-54410)
Raeburn, John Maxwell 9347
(MIC.TC-3524)
Raeside, Robert Pollock 5314
Rafati, Mohammad Reza 1612
(MIC.F.TC-46394)
Raffo, Yolanda Adela 7826
(MIC.T-458)
Raghavendra, Bangalore
Gururajachar 1835
(MIC.F.TC-62939)
Rahim, Medhat Hishmat 3437
(MIC.F.TC-54018)
Rahman, K.H. Shafqur 5047
(MIC.F.TC-54117)
Rahmani, Riyadh Abdul Rahim 5450
(MIC.TC-15322)
Rahn, James Jacob 308 (MIC.TC-6563)
Rahn, Sheldon Lloyd 10155
(MIC.F.TC-43706)
Rai, Rama Kant 309 (MIC.TC-6564)
Railton, John Bryan 6558
(MIC.F.TC-18682)
Rains, Robert Bruce 4734
(MIC.TC-4970)
Rainville, Thérèse 6903
(MIC.F.TC-47423)
Rajasekaran, Konnur C. 6455
(MIC.TC-2896)
Rajotte, Freda 4772 (MIC.TC-15975)
Rakhra, Amrik S. 1215
(MIC.F.TC-60184)
Ralph, Diana Sharon 8932
(MIC.F.TC-46599)
Ralph, Edwin George 2711
(MIC.F.TC-43094)
Ralston, Helen 2192 (MIC.TC-16545)

Ralston, Margaret Helen-J. 7608
(MIC.TC-16545)
Ralston, Robert Dean 11519
Ram, Avadh 6646 (MIC.F.TC-28316)
Ramaekers, Paul Peter J. 6184
(MIC.F.TC-31314)
Ramayya, Penumaka Dasaratha 3838
(MIC.F.TC-44803)
Rambaldi, Ermanno Ronaldo 6185
(MIC.TC-8404)
Rambaut, Thomas D. 7422
Ramcharan, Subhas 748
(MIC.F.TC-20024)
Ramer, Donald Gordon 6872
(MIC.F.TC-46241)
Rampton, Glenn Murray 9604
Rampton, Vernon Neil 5924
Ramraj, Victor Jammona 8166
(MIC.F.TC-27429)
Ramsay, Colin Robert 5887
(MIC.F.TC-17665)
Ramsay, Georges Levis 3512
(MIC.F.TC-53501)
Ramsay, Janice Ann 6725
(MIC.F.TC-47239)
Ramsay, Richard Lyon 6767
Ramsden, Peter George 642
(MIC.F.TC-32867)
Ramsey, Julia Havlicek 8828
Ramsoomair, Henry Franklin 4329
(MIC.F.TC-53145)
Rance, Hugh 5527
Rancier, Gordon J. 10156
Randahl, Frances Sylvia 845
(MIC.F.T-1036)
Randall, Robert George 10990
(MIC.F.TC-52735)
Randhawa, Ajit Singh 11496
(MIC.TC-3736)
Randolph, James Collier 10718
(MIC.TC-11729)
Raney, William Francis 7530
Rankin, Douglas Stuart 5673
(MIC.F.TC-20201)
Rankin, Elizabeth Deane 8147
Rannie, William Fraser 11985
(MIC.F.TC-35106)
Ranson, William Albrecht 5720
Rao, Inna Kedage Ravichandra 7984
(MIC.F.TC-50627)
Rao, N.S. Krishna 10557
Rao, Namperumal Baskara 10070
(MIC.TC-15323)
Rao, Ponugoti Someswar 2314
(MIC.TC-32683)
Raphael, Dennis 3315
(MIC.F.TC-82869)
Raphael, Irwin Allan 9465
Rappeport, Martin Steven 8933
(MIC.F.TC-44509)
Rapson, J.E. 5109
Rashid, Khalid Youssef 327
(MIC.F.TC-54385)
Rashid, Muhammad 1537
Rashid, Zenab Fsmat 7043 (D297 R38)
Rasid, Harunur 4746
Rasmussen, Per Gorm 9570
(MIC.F.TC-46243)
Rasmussen, Roy Leonard 10412
(MIC.F.TC-38519)
Rasporich, Anthony Walter 7098
(MIC.TC-5558)
Raspovich, Beverly Jean Matson 8122
(MIC.F.TC-42074)
Rathgerber, Eva-Maria L. 6853
Rathke, David Edwin 11794
Ratner, Dennis P. 6726
Raudsepp, Enn 8103 (MIC.F.TC-35787)
Raudzens, George Karl 7099
(MIC.T-299)
Rauf, Abdur 2587 (MIC.F.TC-38813)
Raup, Hugh Miller 11450
Ravault, René Jean Jacques 1051
Raveling, Dennis Graff 10812
Raveson, Thomas Jay 4817
(MIC.T-734)
Rawlyk, George A. 7011
Rawlyk, Shirley Larson 3762
(MIC.T-669)
Raworth, David Arnold 11224
(MIC.F.TC-59353)

Rawson, Donald Strathern 11873
(QH1 T68 fol.)
Ray, Arthur Joseph, Jr. 4838
(MIC.T-988)
Ray, D.W. 3285
Ray, David Michael 4827
Ray, Eldon Pringle 7179
(MIC.F.TC-19730)
Ray, Verne Frederick 390
Raychaudhuri, Sunil Kumar 6456
Rayko, Donald Stephen 9740
(MIC.F.TC-55796)
Raymond, Charles Forest 5451
Raymond, James Anthony 11006
Raynauld, Jacques 1185
(MIC.F.TC-59040)
Rayside, David Morton 8654
Razaul, Haque M. 811
Rea, James E. 7325
(FC3071.1 M34 R43)
Rea, K.J. 1297
Read, Colin Frederick 7206
(MIC.F.TC-27959)
Read, Edwin Albert 2994
Read, Peter Burland 5315
Ready, Lawrence Maxwell 2910
Reamsbottom, Stanley Baily 5316
(MIC.F.TC-19621)
Reckshow, Kenneth Howland 11780
Record, Stephen Anthony 9227
(MIC.F.TC-33077)
Redding, Forest William, Jr. 8852
(MIC.F.T-1195)
Reddy, Indupuru Kota 12020
(MIC.TC-6750)
Reddy, Jammula Mahenda 1770
(MIC.TC-6751)
Redekop, Clarence George 8880
(MIC.F.TC-42302)
Redekop, Paul Isaac 10052
(MIC.F.TC-38499)
Redfield, James Allen 10850
(MIC.TC-11162)
Redhead, Scott Alan 11392
(MIC.F.TC-42303)
Redish, Angela 1441 (MIC.F.TC-54118)
Redlick, Amy Sands 8589
Redmond, Gerald 10347
(MIC.TC-13538)
Reed, Austin F. 10775
Reed, Debra J. 6753 (MIC.T-3441)
Reed, Edward Brandt 11093
Reed, Paul Bramwell 10012
(MIC.F.TC-35110)
Reeds, Lloyd George 97
(MIC.F.TC-19731)
Reekie, Charles Ian Maxwell 2334
Rees, David L. 4708 (MIC.F.TC-56533)
Rees, Robert E. 2911
Rees, William Ernest 10859
(MIC.TC-16125)
Reese, Craig Eugene 1724
Reesor, Bayard William 8537
(MIC.F.TC-21091)
Reesor, John Elgin 5317
Reeve, Edward John 6186
(MIC.TC-13069)
Reeves, Arthur W. 2442
Reeves, Brian 925 (MIC.TC-6862)
Reeves, William Joseph 7975
(MIC.F.TC-950)
Regan, Joseph James 3880
Regan, Lance 11071 (MIC.TC-3058)
Regan, Ross H. 2703
Regard, Marianne 9160
(MIC.F.TC-58619)
Rege, Udayan Purushottama 1330
(MIC.F.TC-46049)
Regehr, Henry John 9983
(MIC.F.TC-61373)
Regehr, Theodore David 2315
Regenstreif, Samuel Peter 8655
(MIC.T-70)
Reich, Lee Campbell 9395
Reid, Alan Barry 6594 (MIC.TC-13539)
Reid, Allana G. 7275
Reid, André 3543 (MIC.F.TC-56532)
Reid, Angus Edward 6873
(MIC.F.TC-21231)
Reid, Arthur Selbourne Jelf 229
Reid, D.G. 10447

Reid, John Graham 6982 (FC2043 R44)
Reid, Katerina Susanne 693
(MIC.F.TC-29936)
Reid, Martine Jeanne 694
(MIC.F.TC-56729)
Reid, Normand 6743
(MIC.F-2M11.370.10)
Reid, Philippe 1097 (MIC.F.TC-43143)
Reid, Roger Thomas 1186
(MIC.F.TC-26305)
Reid, Roma Marguerite 4419
(MIC.F.TC-32872)
Reid, Stanley Douglas 2031
(MIC.F.TC-47858)
Reik, Gerhard Albert 5452
(MIC.F.TC-35288)
Reilly, J. Nolan 7180
Reilly, Mary Purissima 6951
Reilly, P.M.A. 8096
Reilly, Wayne Gerard 8590
Reimer, Howard James 8030
(MIC.F.TC-26196)
Reinecke, Leopold 5318
Reinertsen, Philip J. 1822
Reinhardt, Edward Wade 6187
Reitan, Clayton Harold 4982
Reiter, David Philip 8031
Reiter, Leon 6595
Reitsma, Hendrik-Jan 80
Reker, Gary Theodore 9052
(MIC.TC-14163)
Relly, Bruce Hamilton 5774
Renaud, Jean 9984 (MIC.F-2M11.491.5)
Renaud, Marc 6702
Renaud, P.E. 7423
Renault, Jacques Roland 5319
Rencz, Andrew Nicholas 295
(MIC.F.TC-38116)
Rencz, Donald Samuel 2079
(MIC.F.T-966)
Rendle, Gary Alan 9319
Renfree, Henry Alexander 9924
Renihan, Patrick Joseph 2875
(MIC.F.TC-34459)
Renouf, Deane 10604
(MIC.F.TC-44328)
Reshetylo, Daniel Allan 376
(MIC.F.TC-51570)
Resnick, Philip 1393 (MIC.F.TC-35111)
Retfalvi, Terez 7706
(MIC.F.TC-60189)
Retty, Joseph Arlington 6457
Retzleff, Marjorie Anne Gilbert 8066
(MIC.F.TC-56008)
Reuber, Grant Louis 2032
(HF3508 C2 R4 fol.)
Reukema, Barbara Ann 2274
(MIC.F.TC-54897)
Revel, Richard David 11497
(MIC.TC-15150)
Reynaud, Aldéo 3261
Reynolds, John Keith 10663
Reynolds, Julian Douglas 11225
(MIC.F.TC-22212)
Reynolds, Lloyd G. 7588
(JV1285 B7 R4)
Reynolds, Peter Herbert 6596
(MIC.TC-2392)
Reynolds, Roy R. 2167
Reynolds, Wynn Robert 7441
Reznicek, Anton Albert 11393
(MIC.F.TC-38815)
Rhéault, Michel 6983
Rheumer, George Alfred 4996
Rhoades, Frederick M. 11425
Rhodes, Ernest Cornell 6811
(MIC.F.T-963)
Rhodes, Richard Alan 7797
(MIC.T-695)
Rhomberg, Rudolph Robert 1613
(MIC.T-238)
Rhyne, Darla Lindop 10013
(MIC.F.TC-42304)
Ribordy, François-Xavier 794
Ricciardelli, Alex Frank 668
Ricciardelli, Catherine Hinckle 669
(MIC.T-158)
Riccio, Luca Michelangelo 5775
(MIC.F.TC-28320)
Rice, Alan William 2942
(MIC.F.TC-36464)

Rice, H.M.A. 5320
Rice, J.J. 8452
Rice, J.R.E. 1253
Rice, Judith Anne 9741
Rice, Keren Dichter 7808
Rice, Marnie Elizabeth 9571
(MIC.F.TC-25747)
Rice, R.E. 2288
Rice, William A. 5127
Rich, Harvey 8736 (MIC.T-675)
Rich, Susan Ann 3262
(MIC.F.TC-58236)
Richard, Bruno 4330
Richard, David Irving 10754
Richard, Fernand 4443
Richard, Hélène 10272
Richard, Joseph Robert Yvon 11769
Richard, Marc M.J. 4199
Richard, Marc-André 9147
(MIC.F-2M11.571.2)
Richard, Pierre 6669
Richards, Albert E. 160
Richards, Barry Charles 5925
(MIC.F.T-1342)
Richards, Donald Marcus 4284
(MIC.TC-9636)
Richards, Gerald Raymond 3406
(MIC.F.TC-30355)
Richards, James Harlan 11654
(MIC.F.TC-51572)
Richards, John Guyon 1904
(MIC.F.T-1317)
Richards, John Howard Byron 4709
(MIC.F.TC-22353)
Richards, Kenneth W. 11203
Richards, Laura Jean 11226
(MIC.F.TC-63047)
Richards, Leonard 10170
(MIC.F.TC-27509)
Richards, Merle Saundra Kazdan 3119
Richards, Thomas Albert 5321
(MIC.TC-10261)
Richardson, Barbara Joan 9320
(MIC.F.TC-48402)
Richardson, Howard Percival 11241
(MIC.TC-214)
Richardson, Joan T. 7272
Richardson, Laurence R. 11036
Richardson, Peter Rodney 1881
(MIC.F.TC-24650)
Richardson, Ralph Percy 4371
(LB2842 R53)
Richardson, Wayne Ronald 3919
Richardson, William John 10737
Richardson, William Leeds 2671
(LB2890 R5)
Richer, Stephen Irwin 3351
Richerson, Jim Vernon 11227
(MIC.TC-10851)
Richert, Jean-Pierre 8591 (MIC.T-520)
Riches, D.J. 620
Richeson, David Randall 7347
(MIC.TC-13541)
Richler, Avrum 6854
(MIC.F.TC-46785)
Richling, Barnett Edward 621
(MIC.F.TC-43013)
Richmond, A.H. 7583
Richmond, William Oliver 5453
Richter, Manfred Martin 7775
(MIC.F.TC-21404)
Richtik, James Morton 4879
(MIC.T-449)
Ricker, Eric William 2796
(MIC.F.TC-58294)
Ricker, Harold Owen 2672
(MIC.F.TC-42384)
Ricker, Léa-Marie 3363
Ricker, William Edwin 10968
Rickett, Olla Goewey 1032 (MIC.T-80)
Ricketts, Alan Stuart 8350
(MIC.F.TC-43535)
Ricketts, Brian David 5888
(MIC.F.TC-44426)
Ricketts, Mac Linscott 482
Ricklefs, John Edward 2292
Ricks, Frances Arlene Souvenir 9742
(MIC.TC-12600)
Rickwood, Roger Ronson 1140
(MIC.F.TC-35112)

Ricord, Ottolene 4444
(MIC.F.TC-56966)
Ricou, Laurence Rodger 8032
(MIC.F.TC-27962)
Ricour, Françoise 4966
Riddell, Brian Everett 10991
Riddell, John E. 6458
Riddell, Walter Alexander 9825
(H31 C7)
Riddell, William Craig 2122
(MIC.F.TC-34647)
Riddle, Bruce Lee 1394
Rider, Peter Edward 7135
(MIC.F.TC-31320)
Ridge, Frank G. 4651
Ridington, William Robbins, Jr. 556
Ridland, George C. 5889
Ridler, Roland Hartley 6188
Ridley, Clifford Keith 9228
(MIC.F.TC-30070)
Ridpath, John Bruce 1520 (MIC.T-710)
Riedel, Dieter Gunter 10558
Riediger, Alfred J. 2193
(MIC.F.TC-43536)
Riendeau, Bruno 2290 (MIC.F.T-872)
Riewe, Roderick Ralph 10715
(MIC.TC-7461)
Rigal, Robert A. 9396 (MIC.F-028303)
Rigaux, L.R. 32
Rigby, Douglas W. 10494
(MIC.F.TC-25603)
Riley, George C. 5890
Riley, Richard Brinton 1795
(MIC.T-815)
Rimmer, David Michael 10992
(MIC.F.TC-47796)
Ringrose, Susan Margaret 4741
Ringuette, Raymond 3728
Riordan, Peter H. 6459
Rioux, Albert 1796 (HD9688 R56)
Ripley, Eleanor Duncan 2393
Ripple, Joe Edward 8592 (MIC.T-341)
Riser, Georges 8371 (MIC.F.TC-56535)
Riske, Morley Edward 10827
(MIC.F.TC-30571)
Ritchie, John Raymond Brent 1970
(MIC.TC-10854)
Ritchie, Myles Houston 4217
Ritchot, Claude 11329
(MIC.F.TC-19359)
Ritchot, Gilles 4773
Rittenhouse, Gordon 6189
Ritter, Charles John 6460
Rivard, Carole 9611 (MIC.F-013709)
Rivard, Jean Yves 1504
Rivard, M. Eugène 7953
Rivard, Reynald 8934
Riverin, Gerald 6461
(MIC.F.TC-34648)
Rivers, Charles James Toby 6190
(MIC.F.TC-29269)
Rivers, Stephen Martin 8935
(MIC.F.TC-49535)
Rix, Marion Elizabeth Ann Hill 2588
(MIC.F.TC-43710)
Rizkalla, Samir 10304 (MIC.F-022203)
Rizvi, Amjad Ali Bahadur 10473
(MIC.TC-8327)
Rizzuto, Malcolm F. 7707
Roach, Paul J. 3166 (MIC.F.TC-29228)
Roald, Jerry Bruce 4360
(MIC.TC-6941)
Roback, Howard B. 9148
(MIC.TC-5621)
Robbins, Edward Herschell 410
(MIC.T-782)
Robbins, John E. 2752
Robbins, Richard Howard 531
Robbins, Stuart G. 4331
(MIC.TC-15327)
Robbins, William Harvey 11024
(MIC.F.TC-24753)
Roberge, Roger Adrian 1823
(MIC.T-492)
Robert, Ginette 11100
(MIC.F.TC-22861)
Robert, Jean Louis 6462
Roberts, Albert Henry 2599
Roberts, Arthur Cecil Batt 881
(MIC.F.TC-56570)

Roberts, Barbara A. 7646
(MIC.F.TC-48615)
Roberts, David Wayne 2102
(MIC.F.TC-38818)
Roberts, Ellis Noel Rees 4912
(MIC.F.TC-35115)
Roberts, Gloria Bernadette 3263
(MIC.F.TC-27729)
Roberts, Guy H. 2033
Roberts, Hayden Wayne 10171
Roberts, Lance William 10172
(MIC.F.TC-32057)
Roberts, Marvin Lee 11419
Roberts, Robert Gwilym 6463
Roberts, Stephen George 7044
(MIC.T-950)
Roberts, William Glyndwr 2876
Robertson, Barbara Mae 771
(MIC.F.T-1089)
Robertson, David S. 5528
Robertson, Elizabeth Irene 9925
Robertson, George Hawthorne 3597
(MIC.T-706)
Robertson, Ian Ross 7364
(MIC.F.TC-27963)
Robertson, Nancy Susan 8593
Robertson, Peter S. 149
Robertson, Robert Allen 1846
Robertson, Roberta Gail 9183
(MIC.F.TC-37816)
Robertson, Robert T. 8033
(MIC.TC-5745)
Robertson, Sharon Elaine 3264
(MIC.TC-4144)
Robichaud, Jean-Bernard 9985
Robillard, Denise 9902
(MIC.F.TC-44134)
Robin, Martin 2103 (HD8108 R6)
Robineault, Pierre G. 4090
Robins, Patrick James 2168, 9612
(MIC.F.TC-57369)
Robinson, Barrie William 3698
Robinson, Brian William 5891
(MIC.TC-8117)
Robinson, Chalfant 7518
Robinson, Donald James 6191
(MIC.F.TC-52988)
Robinson, Edwin George 6464
Robinson, George Carlton 2510
Robinson, Gilbert Adrian 1863
Robinson, Gordon George
   Christopher 11498 (MIC.TC-2393)
Robinson, Ira Miles 4789
Robinson, John Bertram Leonard 4562
(MIC.F.TC-61156)
Robinson, John Bridger 4790
(MIC.F.TC-50337)
Robinson, John L. 4652
Robinson, Joseph Edward 5454
Robinson, Malcolm Campbell 5322
Robinson, Malcolm Emerson 4926
Robinson, Mary Jane 9149
(MIC.F.TC-50949)
Robinson, Norman 2943
Robinson, Peter Cambell 6192
(MIC.F.TC-48405)
Robinson, Peter John 5010
Robinson, Roosevelt Macdonald 2728
(MIC.F.TC-32878)
Robinson, Ross 2291 (MIC.TC-3737)
Robinson, S.C. 6193
Robinson, Samuel Dale 3398
(MIC.F.TC-17671)
Robinson, Sarah Anne 679
Robinson, Thomas Russell 2034
(HF1479 R62)
Robinson, William G. 6465
Robison, Houston T. 7168
Robitaille, Benoît 4675
Robitaille, Gilles 11394
Roby, Dominique 11172
Roby, Yves 2394 (MIC.T-824)
Roche, Laurence 11713 (MIC.TC-2394)
Rocheleau, Michel 6466
(MIC.F-2M11.569.5)
Rochelle, James Arthur 10624
(MIC.F.TC-50035)
Rocher, Guy A.A. 6984
Rochon, Jean A. 6703
Rock, Terrence Walter 200

Rodberg, Gloria John 9466
(MIC.F.TC-60807)
Roddick, James Archibald 5323
Rode, Andris 622 (MIC.F.TC-18516)
Roden, Lethem Sutcliffe 8269
(MIC.F.TC-19732)
Rodgers, Denis Cyril 3839
(MIC.TC-5237)
Rodney, W. 8644
Rodrigue, Denise 948
(GR113.5 Q8 R63)
Rodrigues, Cyril Gerard 5139
(MIC.F.TC-52812)
Rodrigues, Myra Miliza 3840
(MIC.F.TC-55822)
Rodwin, Victor George 6704
(MIC.F.T-1090)
Roed, Murray Anderson 5455
(MIC.TC-3403)
Roeher, Godfrey Allan 3859
Roelofs, Adrienne Kehde 11499
(MIC.F.TC-64874)
Roemer, Hans Ludwig 11500
(MIC.TC-14921)
Roessler, Grayce Maurine 6904
Rogers, Amos Robert 7962 (MIC.T-81)
Rogers, Edward S. 705
Rogers, Garry Colin 6626
Rogers, Jean Hayes 7798
(MIC.F.TC-22357)
Rogers, Kenneth Douglas 1614
Rogers, Robert Spencer 11738
Rogers, S. John 4402
Roggensack, William Dale 4492
(MIC.F.TC-32058)
Rogick, Mary Dora 11795
Rogstad, Barry Kent 1538 (MIC.T-239)
Rohner, Ronald Preston 695
(MIC.T-984)
Roland, Albert Edward 11528
(QK203 N6 R64)
Roliff, W.A. 6467
Rollit, John Buchanan 2316
Rollo, Christopher David 11107
(MIC.F.TC-40771)
Rolph, William K. 7390
(F5704.9 W6 R6)
Roman, D.W. 2317
Romanow, Walter Ivan 1141
(MIC.T-696)
Romney, Paul Martin 7300
(MIC.F.TC-53149)
Roncari, Jean Isobel Dawson 2729
(MIC.F.TC-43713)
Rondeau, Alain 9613
Rondeau, Gilles 10098
Rondeau, Roger 9743
Roon, Leonore M. 6919
Root, Laurence Wilbur 12021
(MIC.TC-19623)
Roots, Ernest Frederick 5324
Rose, Albert 1331
Rose, Bruce 5325
Rose, E.R. 6194
Rose, George Raymond 3699
Rose, Malcolm 9054 (MIC.F.TC-53282)
Rose, Mary J. 1098
Rose, Robert Arthur 9961
(MIC.F.TC-51574)
Rose, Suzanne Maria 7830
(MIC.F.TC-55910)
Roseman, Frank 1804 (MIC.T-203)
Rosemarin, Arno S. 11800
(MIC.F.TC-61686)
Rosen, Harvey Stuart 1615
Rosenberg, David Michael 11204
(MIC.TC-15329)
Rosenberg, Mark Warren 6696
Rosenbluth, Gideon 1771
(HD9734 C2 R6)
Rosencrantz, Eric John 5776
Rosenfeld, Barry David 1298
(MIC.T-447)
Rosenthal, Carolyn Judith 10035
(MIC.F.TC-56999)
Rosoff, Gary H. 7756 (MIC.T-494)
Ross, Aileen D. 772
Ross, Allan Charles Moffat 8309
Ross, Arthur Larry 141
(MIC.F.TC-38823)

Ross, Beatrice Spence 7045
Ross, Bonnie Fay 10157
(MIC.F.TC-51384)
Ross, Campbell John 3478
(MIC.F.TC-30809)
Ross, Carlyle Bonston Albert 10456
(MIC.F.TC-20434)
Ross, Catherine Louise 8398
(MIC.F.TC-28327)
Ross, Douglas Alan 8897
Ross, Douglas Harry 9869
(MIC.F.TC-60190)
Ross, Eric D. 4851 (MIC.T-886)
Ross, George J. 2811
Ross, Gerald Howard Barney 1950
(MIC.F.TC-48406)
Ross, Harry Campbell 3399
(MIC.F.TC-25981)
Ross, Hazel Miriam 369 (MIC.F.T-210)
Ross, Helen Elizabeth 6812
(MIC.F.TC-36799)
Ross, Ian D. 6855 (MIC.F.TC-51575)
Ross, John Arthur 9886
(MIC.F.TC-20334)
Ross, Mary Alexander 6856
Ross, Peter Noble 3559
Ross, Philippe Edward 11884
(MIC.F.TC-49844)
Ross, Stewart H. 6468
Ross, Vincent 4091
Ross, William Bruce 12022
Ross, William Gillies 1299 (MIC.T-896)
Ross, William Michael 4617
(MIC.T-505)
Rossberg-Leipnitz, Elizabeth 7776
Rosser, Frederick Thomas 7207
Rossi, Jean J. 9269
Rossignol, Léo 7268
Rossignol, Philippe Albert 11287
(MIC.F.TC-38824)
Rossiter, James Randall 6597
(MIC.F.TC-36801)
Rostlund, Erhard 483
Rostoker, Mendel David 5590
Rotenberg, Kenneth Jesse 9397
(MIC.F.TC-48407)
Roth, Eric Abella 577
(MIC.F.TC-47150)
Roth, Horst 6469
Roth, John D.T. 8936
(MIC.F.TC-47859)
Roth, Marvin Carson 8937
(MIC.F.TC-17674)
Rothe, John Peter 3370
(MIC.F.TC-42730)
Rothenberg, Stuart 8853 (MIC.F.T-899)
Rothery, M.A. 10099
(MIC.F.TC-59815)
Rothman, Mark David 4128
(MIC.F.T-927)
Rothney, G.O. 1254
Rothschild, Nan Askin 852
Rothwell, David Colin 4618
(MIC.F.TC-25255)
Rothwell, Donald Stuart 1951
(MIC.F.TC-23178)
Rotstein, Abraham 1216
(MIC.TC-13806)
Rouillard, Jacques 2131
(HD6529 Q8 R69)
Rouleau, Ernest 11648
Rouleau, Suzanne 3738 (MIC.F-043805)
Rouse, Glenn Everett 6513
Rouse, Wayne R. 4983
Rousell, Don Herbert 5529
(MIC.TC-37)
Rousseau, Camille 11611
(MIC.TC-14223)
Rousseau, Guildo 8426
Rousseau, Henri Paul 1505
(MIC.F.TC-23338)
Rousseau, Jacques 9986
(MIC.F.TC-45952)
Rousseau, Jacques 11612
(QK1 M8527 fol.)
Rousseau, Marcel 8775 (MIC.T-3471)
Roussin, Marcel 6939
Routh, Charles Joseph 3457
Routledge, Richard Donovan 11395
(MIC.F.TC-28948)

Rovers, Maria Dina 6905
(MIC.F.TC-58234)
Rowat, Donald C. 8711
Rowbotham, Peter Frederick 4593
(MIC.F.TC-41172)
Rowe, Frederick William 2470
(LA418 N4 R6)
Rowe, John Stanley 11520
Rowe, Robert B. 6195
Rowland, Benjamin Moore 7572
Rowlatt, John Donald Foss 10116
(ALH872 A18 W43)
Rowles, Edith 2628
Rowley, Vivienne Wilda 977
(MIC.T-591)
Roxburgh, Kenneth Reid 6613
(MIC.TC-6940)
Roy, Sister Eugéni-De-Rome 6906
Roy, George Ross 8388
Roy, Jean-Louis 7316
(MIC.F.TC-18365)
Roy, Kenneth James 5326
Roy, Patricia Elizabeth 2318
(MIC.TC-15167)
Roy, Paul-Émile 8232
(MIC.F-2M11.598.2)
Roy, Paul Martel 2214
(MIC.F.TC-23180)
Roy, Reginald Herbert 7418
Roy, Robert Thomas 3905
(MIC.F.TC-53284)
Roy, Robert Roger 3407
Roy, Sharat Kumar 6554
Rozario, Wilson Robert 9053
(MIC.F.TC-53286)
Roze, Liga Dace 11228
(MIC.F.TC-55119)
Rozycki, Gaston Raymond 4361
(MIC.F.TC-51576)
Rubenstein, Arnold Hugh 9055
Rubidge, Nicholas Andrew 4049
(MIC.F.TC-50039)
Rubin-Porret, Josianne 9744
(MIC.T-3941)
Rubino, Carl Angelo 8938
(MIC.TC-3927)
Rubins, Charles Curtis 5721
Rubio, Mary Henley 8104
Ruckenstein, Michael 10465
Ruckman, Maribeth Ruth 9056
(MIC.F.TC-50192)
Rudakoff, Judith Debra 1033
(MIC.F.TC-59853)
Rudd, John William McCullagh 11832
(MIC.F.TC-40045)
Ruddel, David-Thiery 7276
Rudersdorf, Ward James 10813
Rudes, Blair Arnold 7815
Rudner, Howard Lawrence 3076
(MIC.F.TC-30811)
Ruff, Norman John 8703
(MIC.TC-15986)
Rugg, Robert D. 10463
Ruggles, R.I. 4843
Ruhly, Sharon Kay 484 (MIC.T-533)
Rumley, Dennis 4891
(MIC.F.TC-25258)
Rumney, George R. 4710
Runcie, N. 2194
Runge, Janis Margaret 2589
(MIC.F.TC-38827)
Rungsinan, Winai 9467
Runyon, Kenneth Lee 11739
(MIC.F.T-1355)
Rusak, Stephen Thaddeus 2458
(MIC.F.TC-24123)
Rusch, Donald Harold 10851
Rushforth, Everett Scott 553
Rusnack, Terrence Anthony 2984
(MIC.F.TC-34079)
Rusnell, Albert Dale 4050
(MIC.F.TC-2220)
Russell, Charles Neil 3606
Russell, Cristine Louise 9398
(MIC.F.TC-53471)
Russell, Frank 623
Russell, H. Harrison 4637
Russell, Loris Shano 5456
Russell, Mary 9321 (MIC.F.TC-53472)
Russell, Susan Jessie 3352
(MIC.F.TC-38828)

Russell, Terence Michael 1898
(MIC.TC-735)
Russell, Thomas Lee 4427
(MIC.F.TC-35122)
Russwurm, Lorne Henry 4933
(MIC.T-83)
Rust, Ronald Stuart 64
Ruth, Jean Bouma 3862 (MIC.TC-6755)
Rutherford, Paul Frederic
William 7136 (MIC.F.TC-43717)
Rutherford, William Herbert 2104
Rutter, Nathaniel Westlund 5457
Ryan, Alan Giffard 3371
(MIC.F.TC-32061)
Ryan, Barry Desmond 5327
(MIC.F.TC-19625)
Ryan, Diane Elizabeth 8167
(MIC.F.T-964)
Ryan, Frances Sheila Ann 9962
(MIC.F.TC-17142)
Ryan, James Kenneth 11257
(MIC.F.TC-34467)
Ryan, Jerry Bill 4892
Ryan, Joan 683 (MIC.F.TC-17229)
Ryan, John 88 (MIC.TC-15987)
Ryan, Sister Marie Margaret 4200
(MIC.T-772)
Ryan, Richard Michael 2944
(MIC.TC-439)
Ryan, S.P. 1255
Ryan, William Francis 1300
Ryant, Joseph Charles 2080
(MIC.F.TC-23184)
Ryckman, Robert M. 4420 (MIC.T-825)
Rydant, Albert Louis 1052
(MIC.F.TC-42131)
Ryder, June Margaret 4619
(MIC.TC-5842)
Ryder, John Pemberton 10814
Ryks, Dolf 9632 (MIC.F.TC-21960)

S

Saad, Randa-Pierre 10755
(MIC.F.TC-56108)
Sabo George, III 899 (MIC.F.T-1150)
Sabourin, Conrad 1187
(MIC.F.TC-46684)
Sabourin, Louis 8495 (MIC.T-579)
Sabourin, Robert J.E. 6470
Sacco, Vincent Frank 10305
(MIC.F.TC-51579)
Saccomanno, Fedel Frank Mario 2262
(MIC.F.TC-38829)
Sackett, Leroy Walter 2590
Sackney, Lawrence Ernest 2849
(MIC.F.TC-30813)
Sacouman, Robert James 10158
(MIC.F.TC-31327)
Sadighian, Masoud 3524
(MIC.F.TC-24124)
Sadig, Riyaz Ahmed 11749
(MIC.F.TC-50341)
Sadler, Herbert Eric 11982
(MIC.F.TC-28950)
Sadler, John Mountford 289
Sadovnick, Adele Delia 6857
(MIC.F.TC-50042)
Safarian, Albert Edward 1332
(HC115 S24 fol.)
Saffer, Barbara 11173
Safran, Jeremy David 9057
(MIC.F.TC-63051)
Safranyik, Laszlo 11229 (MIC.TC-3738)
Sage, Nathaniel M., Jr. 5674
Sage, Walter Noble 7313 (FC172 R8)
Saggar, Surinder Kumar 290
(MIC.F.TC-49186)
Saha, Ajit Kumar 6196
Sahakian, Armen Souren 6471
Saheb, Arlette 8233
Sahi, Ram Kumar 55 (MIC.F.TC-11515)
Sahir, Abul Hasan 171 (MIC.T-584)
Sahoo, Fakir Mohan 9745
(MIC.F.TC-52925)

Said, Galal Mostafa 2263
(MIC.F.TC-49845)
Saif, Saiful Islam 5623
(MIC.F.TC-35647)
Saifullah, Syed Mohammed 11851
(MIC.TC-5009)
St-Arnaud, Robert 4774
St-Arnaud, Roland Joseph 291
St. Clair, Robert Neal 7836
Saint-George, Jean 1099
Saint-Germain, Yves 1100 (MIC.T-646)
St. James, Alice Margaret 2877
St. John, Donald Patrick 652
(MIC.F.T-1243)
St. John, Harold 11613
St-Julien, Pierre 6472
St. Louis, Robert 150
St-Onge, Louise 3700
(MIC.F-2M11.483.2)
St. Onge, Marc Robert 5898
Saint-Pierre, Annette A. 1034
(MIC.F.TC-44141)
Saint-Pierre, Madeleine 7757
(MIC.F-034101)
St-Pierre-Desrosiers, Pauline 9478
(MIC.F.TC-56259)
Saint-Pierre, Yvonne 8034
Sait, Edward McChesney 8761
(FC2920 C38 S34)
Sajid, Muhammad S. 3438
Sakellariou, Dimitri M. 1772
(MIC.TC-14023)
Sakrison, Herbert Charles 6473
(MIC.TC-2240)
Salame, Ramzi F. 3513
(MIC.F-2M11.452.4)
Salameh, Waleed Anthony 9633
(MIC.F-2M11.606.6)
Sales, M. 7758
Salisbury, Matthew Harold 6633
Sallenave, Pierre 8234
(MIC.F.TC-37923)
Salloum, John Duane 340
Sallows, Sharon Heather 1188
Salsedo, André Joseph 742
Salter, Michael Albert 485
(MIC.TC-13557)
Saluzinszky, I.L. 8093
Salway, Anthony Austen 5000
(MIC.F.TC-28796)
Salyzyn, Vladimir 1442
Sam, Edward Rajamony 9887
Samaha, Mohamed Aly 2319
Samarasinghe, Srimathie 11330
Sampson, Edward 5777
Sampson, Geoffrey Alexander 6197
(MIC.TC-15453)
Sampson, Leonard Patrick 2912
Samson, Pierrette 6907
Sanborne, Paul Michael 11174
(MIC.F.TC-61158)
Sanchagrin, Marie U. (Soeur Marie
Ursule) 8330
Sanchez, Arthur Ledda 5328
Sanchez-Craig, Beatriz Martha 3514
(MIC.TC-16097)
Sancton, A.B. 8762
Sandals, Lauran Hayward 3841
(MIC.F.TC-17058)
Sandefur, Bennett T. 6198
Sandercock, Frederick Keith 10969
(MIC.TC-5843)
Sanderman, Llewellyn Arthur 6609
Sanders, Beverly Jean 3265
Sanderson, James Owen Gresham 5458
Sanderson, Marie Elizabeth Lustig 5011
Sanderson, Mary Hildegarde 773
Sanduss, Joachim 1005
Sanford, Robert Morley 3400
(MIC.TC-9641)
Sanford, Thomas Michael 8637
Sangal, Beni Prasad 4711
(MIC.TC-14629)
Sangadasa, Agampodi 10071
(MIC.F.TC-54026)
Sangameshwar, Salem R.R. 5530
Sanger, David 870
Sangster, Alan Lane 6199
(MIC.TC-5503)
Sangster, Donald Frederick 5329

Sankwrathri, Chandra Sekhar 11102
(MIC.F.TC-21961)
Sanson, Robert J. 7850
Santerre, Richard 8235 (MIC.T-917)
Santin, Sylvia Euphrosyne Pegis 3842
(MIC.F.TC-55829)
Santos y de Regla, Benjamin 1581
(MIC.F.TC-22555)
Sargent, Melville Wayne 5110
(MIC.F.TC-28567)
Sargent, Robert John 9903 (MIC.T-204)
Sargent, Thomas Edward Hartley 5330
Sarkar, Eileen 8035 (MIC.F.TC-44143)
Sarkar, Prasanta Kumar 5675
(MIC.F.TC-38503)
Sarlo, Christopher A. 1616
(MIC.F.TC-52926)
Sarrasen, Joanne 4092
Sarty, R.F. 7419
Sarwar, Kaiserruddin 9572
Sas, Anthony 7617
Sas, Louise Dezwirek 10273
(MIC.F.TC-48410)
Sassano, Giampaolo 5576
(MIC.TC-11165)
Sastry, Cherla Bhaskara Rama 11714
(MIC.TC-10264)
Satterly, Jack 5577
Satterthwaite, Donna F. 6528
Saucier, Jean 3731 (MIC.F-2M11.526.2)
Sauder-Trueman, Cynthia 9058
(MIC.F.TC-21564)
Saul, David John 3733
(MIC.F.TC-12112)
Saunders, George S. 1899
Saunders, Jack Kenneth, Jr. 10586
Saunders, Lloyd Harrell 11037
Saunders, Ronald Stanley 2377
Saunders, Stanley Alexander 4807
(HC117 M35 S3)
Saunderson, Houston Clements 4712
(MIC.F.TC-26084)
Sauvé, Pierre 6474
Savage, Hubert William 4332
Savard, Pierre 8318
Savaria, Richard 6768(MIC.T-3870)
Savigny, K. Wayne 4493
Savishinsky, Joel Stephen 571
(MIC.T-979)
Savoie, André 2891
(MIC.F-2M11.370.11)
Savoie, D.J. 8496
Savoie, Mary Leona 6908
(MIC.F.TC-42309)
Sawatzky, Aron 2169 (MIC.T-547)
Sawchyn, William Walter 11175
Sawer, Barbara Jean 4 (MIC.TC-11255)
Sawford, Edward Clayton 6200
(MIC.TC-10950)
Sawula, Lorne William 10391
(MIC.F.TC-32064)
Sawyer, John Arthur 2035
Saxby, Lorie Nelson 9399
(MIC.F.TC-61235)
Saye, Jerry Dale 7963
Sayer, John Leslie, Jr. 7990
(MIC.T-603)
Sayer, Lynda Anne 3316
(MIC.F.TC-47152)
Sayers, Graham Frederick 2443
(MIC.F.TC-55406)
Saywell, John Tupper 8682 (JL198 S3)
Sbar, Marc Lewis 6604
Sbrocchi, Frank Lloyd 1413
(MIC.F.TC-58454)
Scace, Robert Chaston 4802
(MIC.F.TC-21348)
Scaldwell, William Arnold 4445
(MIC.TC-16873)
Scanlan, John Allen, Jr. 8160
Scarfe, Janet Christine 3546
(MIC.F.TC-53126)
Scarth, William Marshall 1595
(MIC.TC-12113)
Schaafsma, Joseph 3613
(MIC.TC-1660)
Schacter, Daniel Lawrence 9573
(MIC.F.TC-55807)
Schaefer, Gordon Peter 1355
(MIC.F.TC-24658)
Schaefer, Wayne Ford 10924

Schaeffer, Claude Everett 671
Schaeffer, Paul William 11246
Schaeffer, Valentin Henry 10719
(MIC.F.TC-41174)
Scharf, Murray Patrick 4362
Schau, Mikkel Paul 5331
(MIC.TC-3742)
Schauff, Michael Eugene 11258
Schaupp, Dietrich Ludwig 1952
(MIC.T-810)
Scheele, Raymond 653 (MIC.T-976)
Schell, Ernest H. 7046
Schenk, Christopher Robert 2215
(MIC.F.TC-59851)
Scheppach, Raymond Carl, Jr. 2378
Scher, Anat 9468 (MIC.F.TC-51316)
Scheu, William John 10138
(MIC.F.TC-25263)
Schiefer, Karl 10897
Schiele, Bernard Eugene 1101
(MIC.F-41501)
Schieman, Ervin 3638
Schier, Lewis 1953 (MIC.T-342)
Schiffer, Marc Evan 7912
Schiller, Edward Alexander 5676
Schimann, Karl 6475 (MIC.F.TC-40300)
Schindeler, Frederick Fernand 8737
(MIC.TC-259)
Schindler, John Norman 5074
(MIC.F.TC-26201)
Schindler, Norman R. 6476
Schirber, Martin Edward 2243
(MIC.TC-5841)
Schledermann, Peter 900
(MIC.F.TC-23778)
Schlegel, J.P.R. 8881
Schlesinger, R.C. 2064
(MIC.F.TC-59776)
Schloss, Brigitte 2624
(MIC.F.TC-43717)
Schlotterer, George Richard 9574
Schluger, Paul Randolph 5624
Schmeider, Allen Arthur 7873
Schmeiser, James A. 9826
Schmidt, Allan D. 9746
Schmidt, David Albert 1395
Schmidt, Erick 8689 (MIC.F.TC-26910)
Schmidt, Jerome Paul 10703
Schmidt, Lanalee Carol 9469
(MIC.TC-15335)
Schmidt, Peter Karl 4446
(MIC.F.TC-50345)
Schmidt, Richard Conrad 569
Schmidt, Ronald G. 5459
Schmidtgoessling, Nancy 9575
Schmitz, Nancy 8236
Schmus, William Randall 6201
Schmutz, Josef Konrad 10776
(MIC.F.TC-55980)
Schneck, Rodney Edward 8461
Schneider, Barry Howard 3100
(MIC.F.TC-36811)
Schneider, Louis Francis 2673
Schneider, Margaret Shari 9206
Schneider, Richard Delmont 9184
Schneider, Saundra Kay 8516
(MIC.F.T-1091)
Schneiderman, Eta Isabel 7677
(MIC.T-855)
Schner, Joseph George 9322
(MIC.F.TC-38831)
Schnitzer, Morris 276
Schoch, Herbert Paul 1414
Schoderboeck, Anna 8237
Schoen, Virginia E. 9059
Schoeneberger, Mary Margaret 3173
(MIC.F.TC-51588)
Schofield, Richard Edward 6202
(MIC.F.T-1285)
Schofield, Stuart James 5332
Scholer, Marc 3413 (MIC.F-031501)
Scholes, A.G. 2427
Schonning, Egil 2149
Schopf, Thomas Joseph Morton 6577
Schoplein, Robert Nicholas 1643
Schotte, Frederick 4129
Schrader, Frederick Mallory 181
Schrank, William E. 2081 (MIC.T-546)
Schreck, David Donald 2244
(MIC.F.TC-37717)

Schreiber, Fred Oscar 4464
(MIC.T-776)
Schreier, Hanspeter 4620
(MIC.F.TC-32570)
Schrodt, Phyllis Barbara 10452
(MIC.F.TC-43543)
Schroeder, Harold John 1189
Schroeter, Elizabeth Arlene 3384
Schueler, Frederick William 10726
(MIC.F.TC-42310)
Schuetz, Charles 8626
Schuh-Kuhlmann, Jeorg 10306
Schulten, Ronald Brendan 11552
Schultz, Harold John 8462
Schultz, John Alfred 8829
(MIC.F.TC-24954)
Schultz, Katherine Joyce 8939
(MIC.F.TC-54449)
Schultz, Lynda Kay 9470
(MIC.F.TC-47241)
Schultz, Richard John 2264
(MIC.F.TC-26662)
Schurman, D.M. 7486
Schuster, E.J.E. 2065
Schuster, Leslie 8854 (MIC.F.T-1005)
Schwantes, Carlos Arnaldo 8667
Schwartz, Arthur Mark 2945
(MIC.F.TC-50346)
Schwartz, Franklin W. 6203
Schwartz, Geraldine Jerri 4000
(MIC.F.TC-29449)
Schwartz, Lawrence Phillip 1396
(MIC.F.TC-928)
Schwartz, Michael 9100
(MIC.F.TC-42311)
Schwartz, Mildred Anne 1072
(MIC.T-160)
Schwartz, Nancy Eileen 172
Schwartzman, David 1301
Schwarz, Edward Richard 9904
Schwass, Rodger Daniel 1102
(MIC.F.TC-27971)
Schweda, Nancy Lee 837
Schwellnus, Jurgen E.G. 6477
Schwert, Donald P. 6519
(MIC.F.TC-36227)
Schwinghamer, Peter 11852
(MIC.F.TC-53779)
Scicluna, Edward John 8453
(MIC.F.TC-58245)
Sciremammano, Frank, Jr. 11912
Scoates, Reginald Francis Jon 6204
(MIC.TC-10990)
Scoggan, Homer J. 11614
Scollie, June Roberta 6927
(MIC.T-426)
Scorsone, Suzanne Rozell 9827
Scott, Anne 6734 (MIC.F.TC-50048)
Scott, Colin H. 514
Scott, Darcy Lon 5333
Scott, David Bruce 5677
(MIC.F.TC-36168)
Scott, David M. 11344
Scott, David Paul 10970
Scott, Douglas Malcolm 2730
(MIC.F.TC-53150)
Scott, Gary Robert 5093
Scott, Harvey Alexander 10369
(MIC.F.TC-17682)
Scott, James Alan Bryson 5334
(MIC.F.TC-19823)
Scott, John Glenn 2946
Scott, John Stanley 5578
Scott, Nolvert Preston, Jr. 10236
Scott, Peter John 11396
(MIC.TC-16381)
Scott, Richard Donald 2216
(MIC.F.TC-46264)
Scott, Seaman Morley 7842
(MIC.T-205)
Scott, Wilfred George 9747
Scott, William Beverley 10916
Scotter, George Wilby 10619
Scratch, Richard Boyd 5625
(MIC.F.TC-50629)
Screenivasa, Bangalore
Annalyappa 6578 (MIC.TC-15755)
Scrimshaw, Ronald Thomas 4130
(MIC.F.T-1108)
Seager, Charles Allen 2105
(MIC.F.TC-56568)

Seah, Hong Ghee 4051
(MIC.F.TC-51064)
Sealy, Nanciellen Davis 774
(MIC.T-861)
Seaman, Lorne Douglas 9471
(MIC.F.TC-51583)
Searle, R. Newell, Jr. 8855
(QH77 Q48 S43)
Searles, William Edward 3458
(MIC.F.TC-44144)
Sears, James Walter 5335
(MIC.F.TC-39560)
Sears, John Tulloch 1567
Seasay, Alieu 2731 (MIC.F.TC-58360)
Seaton, Ean Charles 2694
(MIC.F.TC-42079)
Seaton, Edward Thomas 3167
Seaver, Richard Everett 1035
(MIC.F.T-1145)
Sebastian, Robert Newbold 3137
(MIC.F.TC-36813)
Seccareccia, Mario Sebastiano 1190
Seccombe, Philip Kenneth 6205
(MIC.F.TC-17857)
Seddyk, Esam Abdul-Sattar 277
(MIC.F.TC-50558)
Sedjo, Roger Andrew 2036
See, Katherine O'Sullivan 790
(MIC.T-916)
Segal, Melvyn 3033
Segall, Alexander 6928
(MIC.TC-13072)
Segall, William Edwin 4363
Sego, David Charles Cletus 4494
(MIC.F.TC-44813)
Séguin, Claude-André 8763
(MIC.F.T-1006)
Séguin, Guylaine 9420
Séguin, Jean Joseph 2695
(MIC.F.TC-34473)
Séguin, Jeanne D'Arc 8298
Séguin, Maurice 115
Séguin, Normand 7267
Séguin, Pierre 1066
(MIC.F-2M11.512.3)
Séguin, Robert Lionel 6972
Séguin-Dulude, Louise 2037
Séguinot, Candace Lee Carsen 7717
(MIC.F.TC-35127)
Sehgal, Vinod Kumar 11205
(MIC.TC-6239)
Seidner Kedar, E.H. 8036
Seifried, Neil Robert Michael 4828
(MIC.T-212)
Seigel, Rhonda Sharon 4333
(MIC.F.TC-40305)
Selby, John 2732 (MIC.F.TC-19455)
Selden, Sherman Ward 654
Seldon, James Ralph 1356
Seldon, Zena Katherine 2275
(MIC.F.TC-40047)
Selekman, Ben Morris 2106
(HD5508 A3 S44)
Self, George Doyle 10173
(LC5254.2 N38 S4)
Selinger, Alphonse Daniel 2797
Sellner, Kevin G. 11959
(MIC.F.TC-44346)
Selody, Jack George 1488
(MIC.F.TC-48412)
Semotiuk, Darwin Michael 10336
Semple, Neil Austin Everett 9878
(MIC.F.TC-42315)
Semple, Robert Keith 4934
Semtner, Albert J., Jr. 11974
Senay, Alphonse 7860
Sénécal, André-Joseph 8238
(MIC.F.T-900)
Senior, Elinor Kyte 7273
(MIC.F.TC-29451)
Senneville, Donald Shipley 3301
(MIC.F.T-1304)
Serfaty, Meir 8627 (MIC.F.TC-32178)
Serl, Vernon Claude 784
Serre, Fernand 4093
(MIC.F-2M11.358.7)
Sesay, Chernoh M. 8738
(MIC.F.TC-37362)
Sethi, A.S. 2141
Sethuraman, Kasiviswanathan 6206
(MIC.TC-7190)

Setzer, Vernon G. 2348
Sevenster, Gelshe 7280
Seville, Saturno T. 4201
Sewell, William Robert Derrick 4621
(MIC.T-4)
Sexton, Christine Sophie 9748
(MIC.F.TC-40048)
Sexton, David Lorne 9060
(MIC.F.TC-47243)
Sexton, Jean 2082 (MIC.T-746)
Sexty, Robert William 1773
(MIC.T-756)
Seymour, Norman Reginald 10777
(MIC.F.TC-33378)
Shackleton, David Maxwell 10645
(MIC.F.TC-17062)
Shady, Gary Anthony 6930
(MIC.F.TC-30073)
Shafer, Joseph 7509
Shaffer, Marvin Harold 1357
(MIC.F.TC-22228)
Shaffir, William B.Z. 802
(MIC.TC-15999)
Shafi, Muhammad Iqbal 11583
(MIC.F.TC-17285)
Shafiquillah, Muhammad 6478
(MIC.TC-4784)
Shah, Hemendra 3920
(MIC.F.TC-40958)
Shain, William Arthur 11649
Shalaby, Hany 6479
Shallal, Louis A.Y. 4485
(MIC.F.TC-44430)
Shank, Christopher Cassel 10646
(MIC.F.TC-42081)
Shankel, George Edgar 717
Shannon, Isabelle Louise 2738
(MIC.F.T-901)
Shapiro, Daniel Mark 1667 (MIC.T-682)
Shapiro, David 2765 (MIC.T-371)
Shapiro, Harold Tafler 1489 (MIC.T-85)
Shapiro, Paul L. 9061
Shapiro, Stanley Jack 203
Shapson, Stanley Mark 9576
(MIC.TC-15709)
Sharma, Kamal M. 6480
Sharma, Raghubar D. 7609
(MIC.F.TC-49103)
Sharma, Ram Karan 6697
(MIC.TC-14973)
Sharma, Ram Rachhpal 4381
Sharma, Satish Chandra 4528
(MIC.F.TC-37821)
Sharma, Tribeni Chandra 4563
(MIC.F.TC-33970)
Sharman, George Campbell 8555
Sharman, Vincent Douglas 8067
(MIC.TC-3409)
Sharp, Henry Stephen 565 (MIC.T-796)
Sharp, Patricia Tipton 7985
Sharp, Paul Frederick 7550
(AD1785 S457)
Sharpe, Christopher Andrew 4956
(MIC.F.TC-35129)
Sharpe, Donald Andrew 1333
(MIC.F.TC-58038)
Sharpe, John L. 6481
Sharpe, Robert Friend 2454
Sharples, Brian 2753 (MIC.TC-9646)
Sharratt, Kenneth Orrin 8739
(MIC.T-20535)
Sharum, Elizabeth Louise 9800
Shaw, David Andrew 5336
(MIC.F.TC-52816)
Shaw, David Carvell 1690
Shaw, David Montgomery 4984
Shaw, Donald Elliott 1847
(MIC.F.TC-31683)
Shaw, Ernest William 6207
Shaw, John William 8331
Shaw, Patricia Alice 7828
Shaw, Robert Keith 11441
Shaw, Roderick Wallace 5052
(MIC.TC-7138)
Shawa, M.S. 5892
Shaykewich, Carl Francis 278
(MIC.TC-3216)
Shea, Sidney Ronald 11750
(MIC.F.TC-22780)
Sheane, George Kennedy 2620

Shearer, Ronald Alexander 1668
(MIC.T-206)
Shearing, Clifford Denning 10307
(MIC.F.TC-36816)
Shedd, Stanford 1563 (MIC.T-443)
Shedletsky, Ralph 8940
(MIC.TC-12604)
Sheehan, Carmel Antoinette 2947
(MIC.TC-13073)
Sheehan, Nancy Mary 2444
(MIC.F.TC-49106)
Sheehan, Teresa Danula 9400
(MIC.F.TC-55184)
Sheeran, Francis Burke 8497
Shegelski, Roy Jan 6208
(MIC.F.TC-38837)
Shehata, Shehata Mohamed 11288
(MIC.F.TC-41782)
Shek, Ben-Zion 8239 (MIC.F.TC-18518)
Sheldon, Charles Harvey 8473
Shelton, Georjia Anne 9749
(MIC.F.TC-59324)
Shelton, Kevin Louis 6482
(MIC.F.T-1272)
Shenker, B. 785
Shenker, Leonard J. 9199
(MIC.F.TC-52123)
Shepard, Francis Parker 5337
Shepherd, Norman 6483
Sheppard, David Henry 10704
Sheppard, Deborah Lee 10053
(MIC.F.TC-47861)
Sheppard, Marsha Isabell 215
(MIC.F.TC-33972)
Sheppard, Stephen Charles 253
(MIC.F.TC-54538)
Shepperson, Wilbur S. 7635
Sherbaniuk, James Alexander 1805
(MIC.T-2)
Sheri, Ahmad Nadeem 11025
(SH167 T4 S5 fol.)
Sheridan, Donald Patrick 3701
(MIC.F.TC-44816)
Sheridan, Harold Stanley 4382
(LB1719 C3 S5)
Sheridan, Robert Edmund 6484
Sherk, Harry Gordon 2913 (MIC.T-332)
Sherman, Gregory John 6687
(MIC.F.TC-53153)
Sherman, Jeffrey Stephen 3926
(MIC.F.TC-33656)
Sherman, Michael Eric 8792
Sherrill, Peter Thomas 2459
Sherrin, Phyllis Marilyn 6952
(MIC.F.TC-25750)
Shershen, Eugene D. 9062
Shetler, Stanwyn Gerald 11553
Sherwin, Barbara B. 9242
(MIC.F.TC-58502)
Sherwood, Glen Alan 10815
Sherwood, Herbert Gordon 5075
(MIC.TC-2576)
Sherzer, Joel F. 7785
Sheu, Yi-Tsuei Pai 12023
Shevenell, Raymond H. 3525
Shields, Gerald Bruce 2968
Shields, Robert A. 7487
Shields, Walter Joseph 11751
Shifferd, Patricia Allen 6940
Shilts, William Weimer 6485
Shim, Jae Hyung 11935
(MIC.F.TC-29957)
Shimizu, Kaien Masaru 939
Shiner, Sandra Miriam 3767
(MIC.F.TC-40960)
Shinkwin, Anne Dolores 901
Shinn, Ridgway Foulks, Jr. 8830
(MIC.T-71)
Shipley, Charles M. 4403
Shiry, John David 8740
(MIC.F.TC-32686)
Shkelnyk, Anastasia Maria 486
Shoesmith, Merlin Wendell 10620
(MIC.F.TC-35865)
Shoom-Kirsch, Donna Norma 3890
(MIC.F.TC-26664)
Shore, Bruce Malcolm 9472
(MIC.TC-10169)
Shore, Terence Leckie 11230
(MIC.F.TC-63086)

Shorey, Leonard Ludwig 4075
(MIC.TC-7934)
Short, Frederick W. 157
Short, Judith Ann Catherine 9750
(MIC.F.TC-48414)
Short, Susan Kathleen 6536
Shorthouse, Joseph David 11188
Shortt, Samuel Edward Dole 7137
(MIC.F.TC-22511)
Shouldice, Larry Mason 8037
(PN99 C3 C65)
Shreffler, Jack Henry 11975
Shrive, Frank Norman 8157
Shrofel, Salina Margaret 7799
(MIC.F.TC-53154)
Shulman, Norman 10219
(MIC.TC-13074)
Shulof, Victoria 9185
Shumiatcher, Morris Cyril 7843
Shute, James Carey Miller 3526
(MIC.T-213)
Shuttleworth, Dale Edwin 2819
(MIC.F.TC-38841)
Shy, John Willard 7469
Shymko, Dolores Lillian 9421
(MIC.F.TC-27514)
Siddique, C. Muhammad 10036
(MIC.F.TC-43725)
Siddiqui, Mohammad Fariduddin 2674
(MIC.F.TC-26085)
Sidlofsky, Samuel 7595 (MIC.TC-7935)
Sidney, Kenneth Harry 6727
(MIC.TC-32883)
Sieciechowicz, Krystyna Z. 427
(MIC.F.TC-55726)
Siegel, Arthur 1103 (MIC.F.TC-23195)
Siegel, Sanford Benjamin 2083
(MIC.F.TC-47154)
Siemens, Gerhard J. 803
Siemiatycki, Jack Aaron 6705
(MIC.F.TC-31887)
Sievwright, Eric Colville 1334
Signori, Edro Italo 9614
Sikand, Jagpal Singh 515
(MIC.F.TC-44676)
Sikander, Abdul Hakim 6486
(MIC.TC-1767)
Sikka, Desh Bandu 5460
Siklos, Pierre Leslie 2170
(MIC.F.TC-55632)
Siller, Frederick Howard 1104
(MIC.TC-11065)
Silva, Wanniaratchige Percy
Terrence 4829 (MIC.TC-1065)
Silver, Arthur Isaac 7263
(MIC.F.TC-31335)
Silver, Burr Arthur 5111
Silver, Faith M. 4334
Silver, George Thomas 11529
Silver, Judith Alta 9473
(MIC.F.TC-53155)
Silverman, Carl M. 8148 (MIC.T-509)
Silverman, Jason Howard 7100
(MIC.F.T-1277)
Silverstein, Sanford 8638 (MIC.T-208)
Sim, Soon-Liang 310 (MIC.TC-9816)
Sim, Victor W. 4676
Simard, André 11038
Simard, Jean-Jacques 624
Simard, Lise Monique 9751
(MIC.F.TC-24417)
Simard, Ronald E. 10527
(MIC.TC-6449)
Simard-Trottier, Marie 10100
Simas, Kathleen A. 9615
Simeon, Richard Edmund
Barrington 8498 (MIC.T-241)
Simic, Joan Elaine 3843
(MIC.F.TC-28337)
Simmons, Edwin Craig 5076
Simmons, Joyce Nesker 9474
(MIC.F.TC-53158)
Simmons, Terry Allan 391
Simms, David Arthur 10593
(MIC.F.TC-41014)
Simms, Jeremy Joseph 3138
(MIC.F.TC-40310)
Simon, Pierre 2739 (MIC.F-022302)
Simons, Richard Glyn 173
(MIC.F.TC-48833)

Simonson, Bruce Miller 5094
(MIC.F.T-1291)
Simonson, David Alan 4137
(MIC.F.TC-17688)
Simpson, David 5338
Simpson, Donald George 7208
(MIC.TC-8008)
Simpson, Geoffrey Sedgwick 4893
(MIC.T-906)
Simpson, Samuel John 4677
(MIC.TC-10993)
Simpson, Susanne P. 8776
(MIC.F.TC-60196)
Simpson, Thomas McNider, III 1443
Sims, Herbert Percival 11726
Sims, Richard Allan 11741
(MIC.F.TC-64880)
Sims, William Allen 2239
(MIC.F.TC-36821)
Sinclair, Alasdair MacLean 10314
Sinclair, Alastair James 5339
Sinclair, Carole Mary Jane 9063
(MIC.F.TC-17144)
Sinclair, Donald Michael 2195
(MIC.F.TC-42320)
Sinclair, Glenn William 2675
(MIC.F.TC-40313)
Sinclair, John Earl 8607 (MIC.T-571)
Sinclair, Mark Lanham 9348
(MIC.F.TC-46399)
Sinclair, Michael Mackay 11913
Sinclair, Peter Rayment 8639
(MIC.T-880)
Sinclair, Peter Wilson 133
(MIC.F.TC-50352)
Sinclair, Pierrette 7861
(MIC.F.TC-33384)
Singer, Charles 568 (MIC.F.TC-47155)
Singer, Howard Lewis 8594
(MIC.F.T-916)
Singer, Jacques Joachim 1829
Singh, Amarjit 10004 (MIC.T-444)
Singh, Bhawan 5053 (MIC.F.TC-31888)
Singh, Chaitanya 5470
Singh, Harshendra Kumar 1999
(MIC.TC-18382)
Singh, Indu Bhushan 8856
(MIC.F.T-952)
Singh, Karnail 1982 (MIC.TC-14976)
Singh, Noreen 11335 (MIC.TC-11025)
Singh, Raj Kumar 4033
(MIC.F.TC-43727)
Singh, Ranbir 1444
Singh, Ranjit Harry 33
(MIC.F.TC-40051)
Singh, Sudesh Kumar 5722
(MIC.TC-14181)
Singhawisal, Wilars 2948
Singleton, Glen Allen 5340
(MIC.F.TC-42742)
Sinha, Ravindra Prasad 5678
Siperko, Gloria M.B., Burima 3266
(MIC.F.TC-27738)
Sippell, William Lloyd 11289
Sirken, Irving A. 1983
Sirridge, Agnes T. 7047
Sirois-Berliss, Michelle 9064
(MIC.F.TC-48636)
Sitwell, Oswald, Francis George 4638
Sivarajasingam, Sittampalam 151
(MIC.F.TC-43846)
Sivaramayya, Bhamidipati 7886
(MIC.TC-9819)
Skarsten, Steinar Stan 10101
(MIC.F.TC-35302)
Skelton, Robert Allen 973
(ML418 J6 S62 fol.)
Skene, R.R. 1036
Skey, Boris Peter 134
Skidmore, Wilfred B. 6487
Skinner, Daniel T. 8281
Skinner, Ralph 5626
Skinner, Robert Gerald 6209
Skinner-Gardner, Eleanor
Jo-Anne 9752 (MIC.F.TC-25751)
Sklash, Michael Gregory 11893
(MIC.F.TC-36230)
Skogstad, Grace Darlene 8628
(MIC.F.TC-32577)
Skolko, Arthur John 11176

Skolrood, Arthur Harold 4364
(MIC.T-252)
Skoulas, Nicholas 2196 (MIC.TC-15489)
Skuba, Michael 2999
Slack, Brian 2292 (MIC.TC-12047)
Slack, Naomi Enid 8741
(MIC.F.TC-36822)
Slater, David Walker 2038
Slater, John Morton 2369
Slatterie, Elinor Faith 9065
(MIC.TC-11444)
Slattery, Brian 7837 (E98 L3 S44)
Slingsby, Judith Marion 9243
(MIC.F.TC-27539)
Slipp, Robert M. 6488
Sloan, Leroy Vincent 2416
(MIC.F.TC-49111)
Sloan, William Neville 838
(MIC.F.TC-61110)
Sloane, Morton Joseph 392
Slobodin, Richard 578
Slonim, Leon 8421 (MIC.F.TC-43729)
Slutsky, B.V. 1954
Sly, Hildreth Francis 2995
Small, Helen F. 9969
(MIC.F.TC-19459)
Small, James Matthew 3533
(MIC.T-432)
Small, Lawrence George 411
Small, Michael Willouhby 3534
(MIC.F.TC-44819)
Smallbone, Barry W. 10528
(MIC.F.TC-56480)
Smart, Carolyne Faith 1955
(MIC.F.TC-50056)
Smart, Patricia Purcell 8254
Smeiris, Fred Eldon 328
Smereka, Edward Peter 11290
Smetanka, John Andrew 1956
Smiley, Calvin Lindsay 8068
(MIC.F.TC-42321)
Smiley, Donald Victor 8547
Smiley, Wesley Carson 10274
(MIC.F.TC-31652)
Smit, Barry Edward 2197
(MIC.F.TC-33056)
Smit, David Ernst 5778
Smitkin, John Nichols 1648
Smith, Alexander 2335 (HF3228 U3 S6)
Smith, Alice Margaret Gullen 7964
Smith, Allan Charles Lethbridge 7500
(MIC.F.TC-31339)
Smith, Annette Louise 10597
Smith, Archibald Ian 1957
(MIC.F.TC-48417)
Smith, Bennett Lawrence 6210
Smith, Bryan James 1958
(MIC.F.TC-55786)
Smith, Charles H. 5779
Smith, Courtney David Campbell 10239
Smith, David J. 10392
(MIC.F.TC-54036)
Smith, David Chadwick 1490
Smith, David Edward 8480 (MIC.T-180)
Smith, David William 341
(MIC.TC-1091)
Smith, Denis C. 2704
Smith, Derald Glen 4735 (MIC.T-733)
Smith, Derek George 625
Smith, Donald 8278 (MIC.F.TC-44149)
Smith, Donald Boyd 527
(MIC.F.TC-31340)
Smith, Donald Leigh 5341 (MIC.T-761)
Smith, Doreen Lucille 10005, 10037
(MIC.F.TC-44821)
Smith, Douglas Allister 2384
Smith, Douglas Lane 9066
Smith, Douglas Wilson 393
(MIC.F.TC-38341)
Smith, Edgar E.N. 5579
Smith, Edward Hanson 5893
Smith, Emmett Hughes 10450
Smith, Eric Alden 626 (MIC.F.T-1092)
Smith, Gaddis 7488
Smith, Garry John 10331
(MIC.F.TC-21973)
Smith, Geoffrey Charles 4936
Smith, Geoffrey Wayne 5342
Smith, Gerald P. 9067
Smith, Gerald Ray 10901
Smith, Gordon Ward 4894 (MIC.T-87)

Smith, Harry Douglas 8282
Smith, Ian Michael 11291
(MIC.F.TC-22367)
Smith, Iola 4233 (MIC.F.TC-47156)
Smith, J. 7862
Smith, J.P. 7526
Smith, James G.E. 542
Smith, Jason Wallace 902
Smith, Jennifer Irene 7101
(MIC.F.TC-53786)
Smith, June Margaret M. 8941
Smith, L.A.H. 7048
Smith, L.E. 9871
Smith, L. Graham 1797
Smith, Lawrence Berk 1588
(HD7305 A3 S63 fol.)
Smith, Marc J. 7442
Smith, Martin Sherer 8942
(MIC.F.TC-51386)
Smith, Mary Dolores 7218
(MIC.F.T-1100)
Smith, Matthew Eliot 8668
(MIC.F.T-1007)
Smith, Michael William 4678
(MIC.F.TC-17235)
Smith, Morland Ellis 6211
Smith, Murray Cameron 10664
(MIC.F.TC-33977)
Smith, Nancy Johnson 6858
Smith, Neal Griffith 10832
Smith, Ned Philip 11907
Smith, Patrick Joseph 8629
Smith, Paul Hubert 7622
Smith, Peter Henderson 5894
Smith, Philip Marvin 1900
(MIC.F.TC-26315)
Smith, Ralph Elliott Henry 11885
(MIC.F.TC-54918)
Smith, Richard Barrie 11715
Smith, Richard Byron 342
(MIC.TC-7180)
Smith, Richard David 6698
(MIC.F.TC-47157)
Smith, Robert Bell 9951
(MIC.F.TC-35135)
Smith, Robert Frederick 9839
(MIC.T-592)
Smith, Roberta Katherine 5343
(MIC.TC-775)
Smith, Roger Francis C. 10705
(MIC.F.TC-17696)
Smith, Roy Edward 6555
Smith, Stephen Murray 11259
(MIC.TC-5562)
Smith, Stuart Boland 10971
Smith, Thomas Donald 11331
Smith, Thomas G. 10605
(MIC.TC-9484)
Smith, Trevor Vincent Goldhawk 8943
(MIC.F.TC-42523)
Smith, Victor E. 1848
Smith, William 101 (MIC.F.TC-52132)
Smith, William Donald 10385
Smith, William Randy 2265
(MIC.F.TC-38503)
Smith-Evenden, Roberta
Katherine 6529 (MIC.TC-775)
Smitheringale, William Vickers 5591
Smithman, Harold Henry 3064
Smol, John Paul 11874
(MIC.F.TC-58975)
Smye, Marti Diane 754
Smyth, Delmar McCormack 3639
(MIC.F.TC-17287)
Smyth, Frances E. 3702
(MIC.F.TC-44151)
Smyth, Michael 9753
(MIC.F.TC-25753)
Smyth, Walter Ronald 5780
(MIC.F.TC-17405)
Smyth, William John 2996
(MIC.F.TC-40498)
Snead, David Edward 4514
(MIC.TC-6946)
Snead, Robert Garland 5462
Sneddon, James Ian 243
(MIC.F.TC-19634)
Sneddon, Richard 4830
Snelgrove, Alfred Kitchener 5781
Snell, James Grant 7527
(MIC.TC-7574)

Snider, Dawn Laureen 7913
(MIC.F.TC-36825)
Snow, William Garfield 9244
(MIC.F.TC-30947)
Snowdon, Lloyd R. 5895
Snyder, Richard C. 2000
Snyderman, George S. 655
Socken, Paul Gerald 8313
(MIC.F.TC-31341)
Socknat, Thomas Paul 7138
(MIC.F.TC-52298)
Soe, Lin 34
Sohn, Herbert Alvin 8538
Sokoloff, Elliott 9754 (MIC.F-006509)
Solberg, Patricia A. 9616
Solomon, Elizabeth Theresa
Echlin 8944 (MIC.F.TC-46403)
Solomon, Susan Linda Zener 9755
(MIC.TC-8817)
Soltesz, Joseph Attila 7759
(MIC.TC-10903)
Solyom, Carol Anne Elizabeth 9068
(MIC.F.TC-49694)
Somers, Bertram Alexander 1644
Somers, Hugh Joseph 9905
Sommer, Daniel 9107 (MIC.T-3809)
Sommer, Frank Henry, III 696
Sommerfield, Howard Bruno 125
Song, Dae Hee 174
Soper, James Herbert 11584
Soper, Nancy E. 10117
(MIC.F.TC-49545)
Soper, Robert Joseph 216
Sophocleous, Marios 5463
(MIC.F.TC-40317)
Sopp, Trudy Jane 10006
(MIC.F.TC-62169)
Sopuck, Vladimir Joseph 5077
(MIC.F.TC-32688)
Sordoni, Carl Richard 9069
(MIC.F.TC-42389)
Soregaroli, Arthur Earl 5344
(MIC.TC-2396)
Sorenson, Curtis James 4599
Sorfleet, John Robert 8069
(MIC.F.TC-27441)
Sorg, Marcella Harnish 839
(MIC.F.T-1037)
Sorge, Walter Felix 949
Sorochty, Roger W. 4202
Soroka, Lewis Arthur 1725
(MIC.TC-7144)
Soubrier, Robert 10466
Souch, Stanley Grant 9475
(MIC.TC-6241)
Soucie, Daniel G. 10431 (MIC.T-777)
South, David Merrill 566
Southall, Russell Melvin 11397
Souther, Jack Gordon 5345
Southey, Clive 1358 (MIC.TC-5117)
Southmayd, Stephen Eric 9200
(MIC.F.TC-59078)
Southon, Frank Charles Gray 12024
(MIC.F.TC-17865)
Southward, Glen Morris 1859
Souto-Maior, Joel 8857
(MIC.F.TC-55137)
Sowder, Ellie Mae 4055
Spangler, George Russell 10920
(MIC.F.TC-27982)
Sparby, Harry Theodore A. 2445
(MIC.T-88)
Sparham, Donald Cauthers 2401
(MIC.F.TC-30948)
Sparks, Jared, Jr. 1726
Spaulding, Philip Taft 497
Speagle, Richard Ernest 1575
Speare, Allan Denley 3065
Spearman, Donald 9617
Spector, Norman 1142
Speer, John Alexander 5723
Speers, Elmer Clarence 6212
Speirs, Rosemary Ellen Jane 2123
(MIC.F.TC-27516)
Speisman, Stephen Alan 804
(MIC.F.TC-42322)
Spekkens, André 1633
Spell, Lota M.H. 2634
Speller, Stanley Wayne 10580
Spence, Andrée F. 6489
(MIC.F.TC-35137)

Spence, C.G. 9422
Spence, Edward Smith 4722
  (MIC.TC-8126)
Spence, Ernest J.H. 1335
Spence, Graeme 9070
Spence, John Andrew 11292
  (MIC.TC-8631)
Spence, John Richard 11231
  (MIC.F.TC-42751)
Spence, Ruth Elizabeth 2511
Spence, William Henry 6213
Spencer, Byron Grant 1727
Spencer, Hildreth Houston 2433
Spensley, Philip John 1037
Sperrazzo, Gerald 9186
Spettigue, Douglas Odell 8070
  (MIC.TC-10824)
Spevack, Michael G. 3286
  (MIC.TC-16007)
Spicer, James Keith 8793
Spieker, John Oscar 10816
Spiess, Arthur Eliot 846
Spigelman, Martin Samuel 7139
  (MIC.F.TC-28956)
Spina, Joseph M. 8595
Spinaris, Caterina Georgia 9577
  (MIC.F.TC-57163)
Spinner, Barry 9756 (MIC.F.TC-43102)
Spiro, Solomon Joseph 8403
  (MIC.F.TC-50570)
Spittlehouse, David Leslie 11936
  (MIC.F.TC-55138)
Splane, Richard Beverley 10118
Spongberg, Stephen A. 11554
Spradley, James Phillips 697
Spragge, George Warburton 2434
Spreng, Alfred C. 5464
Spricer, Rosa 9476
Springate, David John Victor 1669
  (MIC.T-436)
Springer, Stephen Alan 3881
  (MIC.F.TC-33658)
Sproule, John Campbell 6214
Sprules, William Memberg 11293
Squair, H. 5896
Squires, Benjamin M. 2107
Sreenivasa, Mannada Rani 11585
Sreenivasan, Uma 9401
  (MIC.F.TC-53353)
Srivastava, Satish Kumar 5465
Stabler, Jack Carr 1302 (MIC.T-560)
Stace, Michael Vincent 7914
  (MIC.F.TC-47862)
Stace-Smith, Richard 10529
Stacey, Charles Perry 7420 (F5076 S72)
Stacey, Rosalind 9477
  (MIC.F.TC-31653)
Stacy, Maurice C. 5679
Stafford, James Dale 10014
Stager, David Arnold Albert 3614
  (MIC.T-267)
Stager, John K. 4862 (MIC.T-881)
Stagg, James M. 12025
Stagg, Ronald John 7230
  (MIC.F.TC-35138)
Stahl, William Austin 9990
  (MIC.F.T-1262)
Stainer, John Evelyn Randall 11177
  (MIC.F.TC-39804)
Stairs, Arlene 3267 (MIC.F.TC-44431)
Stairs, Denis Winfield 8894
  (MIC.TC-4511)
Stalker, Archibald M. 5466
Stalwick, H.N. 7102
Stam, Henderikus Johannes 9245
  (MIC.F.TC-59923)
Stamatelopoulou-Seymour, Karen
  Catherine 6490 (MIC.F.TC-60977)
Stamm, Sharon Winston 3978
  (MIC.F.TC-39805)
Stamp, Robert Miles 2512
  (MIC.TC-6181)
Stanbury, William Thomas 1303
Standen, Sydney Dale 7277
  (MIC.F.TC-35303)
Stanek, Walter Karl Leopold 11716
Stange, Karl Henry 3745
Staniforth, Richard John 11586
  (MIC.F.TC-24673)
Stanislawski, Howard Jerry 8885
  (MIC.F.T-1177)

Stanley, Alan David 5467
  (MIC.TC-484)
Stanley, Della Margaret Maude 7396
  (MIC.F.TC-55491)
Stanley, G.F.G. 7377
Stanley, George D., Jr. 6530
Stanley, Thomas Brock 6785
  (MIC.F.TC-78618)
Stannard, Stanley Adam 3598
Stanton, John Ormond 10054
  (MIC.TC-14693)
Stanton. Stephen B. 7515 (MIC.F.CC4)
Stanworth, C.W. 5897
Staples, Edward A. 9270
  (MIC.F.TC-32143)
Staples, Richard Brian 4447
Stapleton, John James 2798
  (MIC.F.TC-35304)
Staranczak, Genio Alexander 10119
Stark, Frank 8499
Stark, Ronald William 11198
Starkes, Janet Lynn 10367
  (MIC.F.TC-46010)
Starling, Robert Neale 11530
  (MIC.F.TC-39569)
Starr, Gerald Frank 2217
  (MIC.F.TC-17288)
Stater, John Morton 2373
Stauble, Vernon Ronald 10357
Staveley, Michael 10317
  (MIC.F.TC-20222)
Stearn, Colin W. 5531
Stearns, Mary Lee 639 (MIC.T-593)
Stearns-Seidner, Anna 764
Stebbins, Lucius Lebaron 10651
  (MIC.TC-3414)
Steck, Francis Borgia 6985 (F352 S84)
Steckler, Gerard George 9906
  (MIC.T-89)
Steele, Charles Reginald 8389
  (MIC.F.TC-23343)
Steele, Donald Harold 11054
Steele, Marion Louise 1304
  (MIC.F.TC-31343)
Steele, Robert Gordon 11026
  (MIC.F.TC-23344)
Steenburgh, William Elgin 11294
Steeves, Robin Roy 12026
  (MIC.F.TC-55492)
Steibe, Susan 9071 (MIC.F.TC-53290)
Steiger, A. 8240
Stein, Barry Michael 9072
  (MIC.F.TC-36328)
Stein, Dominique Shuly 7760
  (MIC.T-783)
Stein, Leonard Milton 10220
  (MIC.F.TC-31654)
Stein, Marsha L. 9578
  (MIC.F.TC-28347)
Stein, Michael Bernard 8665
Stein, Steven J. 9757
  (MIC.F.TC-35528)
Steinberg, Charles 2171 (MIC.T-789)
Steinberg, Rhona Hinda 4138
  (MIC.F.TC-20359)
Steiner, William Wayne, II 11005
Steinert, Yvonne 4421
Steinhorson, Dallas H. 1359
Steinthorsson, Sigurdur 5078
Stelck, Charles R. 6523
Stelfox, John Glyde 10647
Stene, Lawrence Paul 4736
  (MIC.F.TC-28348)
Steneker, Gustav Adolf 11727
Stenger, Alfred 1869
Stephens, Carl Edmund 3844
  (MIC.F.TC-22559)
Stephens, George Christopher 5346
Stephens, William Eldon 8858
Stephenson, John Francis 5532
  (MIC.TC-11631)
Stephenson, Marylee Grace 10185
  (MIC.F.TC-25998)
Stephenson, Peter Hayford 786
  (MIC.F.TC-38849)
Stephenson, Peter John 9618
  (MIC.F.TC-55728)
Stephenson, Randall Alexander 5079
  (MIC.F.TC-53792)
Stepney, Philip Harold Robert 10756
  (MIC.F.TC-42325)

Stermac, Lana Elizabeth 9229
  (MIC.F.TC-58336)
Sternberg, Ben Kollock 6598
Stevens, Carey 9073
Stevens, Roderick D. 11717
Stevens, Kenneth Ray 7510
Stevens, Paul Douglas 7358
  (MIC.TC-10826)
Stevens, Peter S. 8351 (MIC.T-543)
Stevens, René Paley 3268
  (MIC.F.TC-47448)
Stevens, Robert Keith 5782
  (MIC.F.TC-28380)
Stevens, Ward Earl 10686
Stevens, Wayne Edson 7049
  (HD9944 U45 S8)
Stevenson, David 627 (MIC.TC-11261)
Stevenson, Ira M. 5680
Stevenson, James Cameron 10972
Stevenson, James Smith 5468
Stevenson, John S. 6491
Stewart, Alfred Neil 2969
Stewart, Alice R. 7362
Stewart, Brinsley Elford Alister 8241
  (MIC.F.TC-28814)
Stewart, Bryce Morrison 2174
  (HD7838 S7)
Stewart, Charles Lockwood 7050
Stewart, Dermot Michael 9579
  (MIC.F.TC-25754)
Stewart, Donald Alexander, Jr. 445
  (MIC.F.TC-52137)
Stewart, Edward Emslie 3560
Stewart, Ian Affleck 1336 (MIC.T-162)
Stewart, Ian Hampton 7934
  (MIC.F.TC-61617)
Stewart, James Smith 5468
Stewart, John Benjamin 8524
  (MIC.T-90)
Stewart, Lorne Duncan 4465
Stewart, Max Douglas 1837
Stewart, Moira Anne 6813
  (MIC.F.TC-24675)
Stewart, Robert Arthur 6215
  (MIC.F.TC-54123)
Stewart, Robert Bruce 4985
  (MIC.F.TC-26208)
Stewart, Robert Earl, Jr. 10778
Stewart-Patterson, Cleveland 1539
  (MIC.F.TC-50572)
Steyn, Douw Gerbrand 4925
  (MIC.F.TC-51804)
Stich, Klaus Peter 8038
  (MIC.F.TC-21566)
Sticht, John H.H. 5926
Stier, Jeffrey Charles 10817
Stiles, Ralph Geoffrey 1872
  (MIC.F.TC-18387)
Stilgenbauer, Floyd Adlai 4640
Stillwell, Le Vern Henry 1038
Stirling, Alexander 4214
Stirling, Paul Hunter 9074
  (MIC.F.TC-48422)
Stites, Sara Henry 656 (F99 I7 S85)
Stoakes, Franklin Arthur 5469
  (MIC.F.TC-57169)
Stobbe, Peter C. 266
Stober, Stephen Robert 9580
  (MIC.F.TC-58465)
Stockdale, John 8039
Stockdale, Peter Howard Gough 11359
  (MIC.TC-7629)
Stocking, Kenneth M. 11398
Stocks, Anthony Howarth 1506
  (MIC.T-91)
Stockton, Donald Alan 2949
Stockwell, Clifford Howard 5533
Stoddart, Gregory Lloyd 6814
  (MIC.F.TC-26000)
Stoddart, William Brunton 3768
Stoker, Richard Glen 3882
Stokes, Allen 10852
Stokes, Ernest Ball 1582
  (MIC.F.TC-42528)
Stokes, Milton Lonsdal 1445
  (HG2706 S76)
Stolar, Robert William 1415
Stolle, Dieter Franz Eugen 4538
  (MIC.F.TC-57087)
Stollery, Kenneth Robert 1903
  (MIC.F.TC-46405)

Stone, Blair Francis 1067 (MIC.T-552)
Stone, David Philip 11072
 (MIC.F.TC-37729)
Stone, Denver Cedrill 5534
 (MIC.F.TC-53162)
Stone, Donald Norman George 121
 (MIC.F.TC-49189)
Stone, Frederick L. 10917
Stonehouse, David Peter 198
 (MIC.F.TC-30075)
Storer, John Edgar, III 6571
 (MIC.TC-9930)
Storey, Arthur George 4001
Storey, Keith John 4810
 (MIC.F.TC-31657)
Storey, Robert Henry 2124
 (MIC.F.TC-62089)
Storey, Vernon James 2950
 (MIC.F.TC-40792)
Story, Donald Clarke 8801
 (MIC.F.TC-40965)
Stortz, Thomas Gerald John 9907
 (MIC.F.TC-43851)
Stothers, C.E. 2914 (LB2845 S86)
Stothers, David Marvyn 725
Stott, Donald Franklin 5470
Stouffer, Allen Philip 7528
Stouge, Svend Sandbergh 5783
 (MIC.F.TC-51166)
Stoughton, Herbert Warren 4524
Stout, Samuel Darrel 847
Stovel, John A. 1984 (HF1479 S7)
Strain, Allan Richard 3845
 (MIC.F.TC-49358)
Strand, William Eugene 7359
Strang, John Douglas 3791
 (MIC.F.TC-51212)
Strangway, David William 5080
Strasburger, Erich Leopold 3703
 (MIC.F.TC-48423)
Straus, Melvin Potter 8602
Strauss, Dennis Lyle 3372 (MIC.T-856)
Strauss, Hans Ernst Hermann 1728
 (MIC.F.TC-39808)
Strauss, Esther Helen 9581
 (MIC.F.TC-43732)
Strauss, H. Peter 3979
 (MIC.F.TC-25755)
Strawn, Robertson L. 657
Strayer, Barry Lee 8539
Strempel, Ulrich 8874
 (MIC.F.TC-56948)
Strevig, Jennie May 9801
Strick, John Charles 1491
Striegel, James Finley 1068
 (MIC.F.T-1020)
Strilaeff, Florence 6920
 (MIC.F.TC-27984)
Stringer, Guy 2538
Stringer, Paul William 11442
 (MIC.TC-4978)
Stringer, Y. 1493
Stringham, Bryant Louis 2799
 (MIC.F.TC-21986)
Stroetmann, Karl Antonius 2349
 (MIC.F.TC-19642)
Stromberg, Paul Charles 10918
Stronach, James Alexander 11937
 (MIC.F.TC-37730)
Stronach, Nicholas John 5112
 (MIC.F.TC-57188)
Strong, Frederick Blakeney 4076
 (MIC.F.TC-36832)
Strong, Kirkpatrick Margaret 10120
Strong-Boag, Veronica Jane 7140
 (MIC.F.TC-31347)
Struik, Lambertus Cornelis 5347
 (MIC.F.TC-51321)
Strum, Harvey Joel 7071
Struthers, James Edward 2198
 (MIC.F.TC-40966)
Struthers, John Russell Tim 8071
Struthers, Park H. 10688
Stryd, Arnold Henri 871
 (MIC.F.TC-17069)
Stryde, Sherman James 2676
 (MIC.F.TC-17701)
Stryker, Josiah Dirck 2039
Stuart, Euan Ross 1039
 (MIC.F.TC-27517)
Stuart, Roy Armstrong 5348

Stubbs, G.M. 423
Stuckey, Ronald Lewis 11399
Stuckler-Gropper, Anna Sophia 9215
 (MIC.F.TC-53503)
Studemeister, Paul Alexander 6216
 (MIC.F.TC-52990)
Studnicki-Gizbert, Konrad W. 2276
Stuebing, William Kenneth 10221
 (MIC.F.TC-32833)
Sturgess, Philip John Moore 8149
 (MIC.T-874)
Sturino, Franc 7647 (MIC.F.TC-53163)
Stutz, Reuben Craig 11555
 (MIC.TC-15360)
Stykolt, Stefan 1971 (HD9162 C22 S8)
Stymeist, David Harold 428
Suarez, Frère 3139
Subasinghe, S.M. Chandrasiri 11242
 (MIC.F.TC-54387)
Subins, Gunar 4713 (MIC.F.TC-20540)
Subramandam, Indira Anne 761
 (MIC.F.TC-36833)
Suckling, Philip Wayne 4622
 (MIC.F.TC-34958)
Sue, Hiroko 572
Suensilpong, S. 5627
Suffling, Roger Charles 11752
 (MIC.F.TC-31128)
Sugar, Judith Ann 9582
 (MIC.F.TC-51387)
Sugden, Lawson Gordon 10779
Sugges, Peter R., Jr. 1191
 (MIC.F.T-902)
Sugrue, Dennis Patrick 9201
Suguitan, Lynda Santos 5077
Sullivan, Ann Dolores 6754
 (MIC.F.TC-51806)
Sullivan, Barbara Koster 11894
Sullivan, Brian Edward 2266
 (MIC.T-671)
Sullivan, Elizabeth Michelle 6859
 (MIC.F.TC-56125)
Sullivan, Kathryn Dwyer 5784
 (MIC.F.TC-38407)
Sullivan, Keith Charles 2850
 (MIC.F.TC-32834)
Sullivan, Patricia L. 6735
 (MIC.F.TC-30840)
Sullivan, Thomas Priestley 10678
 (MIC.F.TC-42760)
Sumagaysay, Lourdes S. 3168
 (MIC.TC-9933)
Summers, Harold Angus Charles 4791
 (MIC.T-268)
Summers, Peter 12027
Summers, Randal William 1959
 (MIC.F.TC-44827)
Summers, William F. 10318
Sumner, Alfred R. 4986
Sun, Shih-Ping 35 (MIC.F.TC-30076)
Sunday, E.P.M. 3066
Sundstrom, Marvin Thomas 1806
 (MIC.F.TC-29748)
Surdam, Ronald Clarence 5349
Surgenor, Brian William 4564
 (MIC.F.TC-61620)
Surkes, Jean Kathleen 9402
 (MIC.F.TC-49454)
Surkes, Steven 4234 (MIC.F.TC-44539)
Surplis, David William 8649
 (MIC.F.TC-36834)
Surrey, David Sterling 7584
 (MIC.F.T-1094)
Sussman, Edmond 1446
Sutherland, David Alexander 7181
 (MIC.F.TC-27985)
Sutherland, E. Ann 3269
 (MIC.TC-16009)
Sutherland, John Neil 2438
 (MIC.T-596)
Sutherland, Patrick K. 5350
Sutherland, S.L. 3704
Sutherland-Brown, Atholl 5351
Sutherland de Merlis, Doris 3906
Sutterlin, Peter George 5471
Suttles, Wayne 680
Sutton, George Miksch 10738
Svoboda, Josef 11556
 (MIC.F.TC-21988)
Swadesh, Morris 7831
Swailes, George Edward 11443

Swain, Wayland Roger 11784
Swaine, James Malcolm 11178
Swaine, John Ronald 9075
 (MIC.F.TC-53295)
Swainson, Donald Wayne 7209
 (MIC.F.TC-18520)
Swainson, Neil Alexander 8859
 (MIC.T-585)
Swales, William E. 11345
Swan, G.R. 7264
Swan, John Marcus Allan 11625
Swann, Francis Richard 7237
 (MIC.T-314)
Swanson, Carl Eliot 7012
 (MIC.F.TC-48424)
Swanson, Clarence Otto 5352
Swanson, Roger Frank 8860
Swanson, Stella Marie 11336
 (MIC.F.TC-38520)
Sweeney, James Ernest 3140
 (MIC.F.TC-33218)
Sweet, Arthur Richard 6514
 (MIC.TC-13970)
Sweet, Robert Arthur 3980
 (MIC.F.TC-34960)
Sweetman, E. 7309
Swidinsky, Robert 2199 (MIC.T-650)
Swift, Michael Crane 11826
 (MIC.F.TC-19644)
Swiger, Ernest Cullimore, Jr. 1305
Swinbanks, David Donald 5353
 (MIC.F.TC-42764)
Switzer, Kennee B. 7648
Swygard, Kline Ruthwen 1855
Sydor, Leon Paul 2293
Syed, Aftab Ali 1192
 (MIC.F.TC-30319)
Syer, David Dirk 9150 (MIC.TC-12607)
Sykes, Clark Mansfield 919
 (MIC.F.TC-59839)
Sykes, Donald Henry 3891
 (MIC.TC-5401)
Sykes, Susan E. 6744 (MIC.F.TC-36232)
Sylvestre, Abbé Lucien 7851
Sylvestre, R.F. 11615
Symons, David Thorburn Arthur 5138
 (MIC.TC-265)
Syms, Edward Leigh 424
 (MIC.F.TC-30846)
Symyrozum, Lloyd Edwin 2696
 (MIC.F.TC-54048)
Synghal, Krishnan N. 230
Syrotuik, John M. 9583
 (MIC.F.TC-34569)
Syvitski, James Patrick Michael 5354
 (MIC.F.TC-40794)
Szablowski, George Jerzy 8481
 (MIC.F.TC-43038)
Szabo, Nicholas Louis 5628
 (MIC.F.TC-27445)
Szalai, John Paul 9076
 (MIC.F.TC-53504)
Szathmary, Emoke Jolan Erzsebet 543
 (MIC.F.TC-27518)
Szczawinski, Adam F. 11501
Szijj, Laszlo Josef 10751
Sziklai, Oscar 11718
Szmidt, Yvette 7761 (MIC.F.TC-36837)
Szplett, Elizabeth Schmehl 4798
 (MIC.F.TC-57122)
Szwed, John Francis 412
 (HN110 N4 S98)

T

Tabba, Mohammad Myassar 4580
 (MIC.F.TC-43039)
Taenzer, Paul 9246 (MIC.F.TC-64506)
Taerum, Terry Verne 4255
 (MIC.F.TC-42088)
Tagg, Melvin Salway 9849 (MIC.T-92)
Tahir, Sayyid 1360 (MIC.F.TC-52304)
Tait, George Edward 2621
 (MIC.F.TC-25508)

Taitt, Mary Joan 10679
(MIC.F.TC-40795)
Talarico, Joseph Frank 2370
(MIC.T-93)
Talkington, Raymond Willis 5785
(MIC.F.TC-51167)
Tallman, Ann Marie 5355
Tallman, Erika Jansic 10869
Tallman, Richard Sensor 8332
(MIC.F.TC-21510)
Tallman, Ronald Duea 7529
(MIC.T-528)
Talman, James John 7210
(MIC.F.TC-21411)
Talpis, Jeffrey Alan 7932
Tam, Cham-Kan 1540
Tam, Chung-Ngoh Isaac 9202
(MIC.F.TC-49121)
Tamilia, Robert Dominique 1053
(MIC.F.T-917)
Tamplin, Morgan John 926 (MIC.T-903)
Tan, Benito Ching 11502
(MIC.F.TC-55144)
Tan, Chin-Sheng 244
(MIC.F.TC-32600)
Tan, Jee-Theng Tony 5899
(MIC.F.TC-42089)
Tan, Siang-Yang 9077 (RC331 B85 fol.)
Tan, Wai Koon Lau 11444
(MIC.F.TC-40323)
Tanaszi, M.J. 8072
Tandon, Bankey Behari 2218
(MIC.F.TC-32691)
Tang, Fay C.F. 3846 (MIC.F.TC-44155)
Tanghe, Raymond 4775 (FS449 M6 T35)
Tanguay, Yolande 9403
(MIC.F.TC-35144)
Tanner, Adrian 706
Tanner, Christopher Jean
Eugene 11503 (MIC.F.TC-46284)
Tanser, Harry Ambrose 9492
(F5033 N3 T35)
Tansill, Charles Callan 7519 (H31 J6)
Tant, Judy Louise 3892
(MIC.F.TC-39810)
Taplin, John Harold Eaton 175
(MIC.T-242)
Tapper, Gerald Oscar 4714
Tarasoff, Frederick John 10598
(MIC.TC-16015)
Tarasofsky, Abraham 1493
(MIC.TC-3229)
Tardif, Guy 7915 (HV7994 T37)
Tardif, Marie Marthe 10222
Tari, Andor Joseph 3101
(MIC.TC-9652)
Tarnovecky, Joseph 7539
Taruvinga, Peter Pangarirai 4594
Tarzi, Joseph Gergy 6217
(MIC.F.TC-31131)
Tassie, James Stewart 7762
Taube, Eva 8040 (MIC.T-727)
Tauber, Maurice Falcolm 7986
Tauran, Rouland Herman 3981
Tauthong, Pensook 11243
(MIC.F.TC-26383)
Tautz, Arthur Frederick 10973
(MIC.F.TC-34963)
Tax, Joel Perry 9991
(MIC.F.TC-53505)
Tay, Andrew Joo-Hwa 4565
(MIC.F.TC-35146)
Taylor, Allan Ross 7790
Taylor, Andrew 4679
Taylor, Andrew Ronald Argo 11400
Taylor, Beatrice Elizabeth 5029
(MIC.F.TC-23209)
Taylor, Bruce Wayne 11244
(MIC.F.TC-50954)
Taylor, Colin Hubert 4776
(MIC.TC-14576)
Taylor, Donald Maclean 365
Taylor, Frederick C. 6218
Taylor, Gerald Dale 4157
(MIC.F.TC-38856)
Taylor, Gilbert Frederick 2976
Taylor, Iain Duncan Stewart 4566
(MIC.F.TC-35147)
Taylor, James Addison 4715
(MIC.T-707)

Taylor, James Garth 628
(MIC.TC-15427)
Taylor, John Leonard 7186
(MIC.F.TC-30227)
Taylor, Kenneth Gordon 11827
Taylor, Malcolm G. 1634 (RA411 T39 fol.)
Taylor, Margaret Jane Whatman 3769
(MIC.F.TC-58361)
Taylor, Margo Jane 9584
(MIC.F.TC-52144)
Taylor, Marilyn Margaret 4034
(MIC.F.TC-40968)
Taylor, Martin Edward 1416
(MIC.T-745)
Taylor, Mitchell Kerry 10572
(MIC.TC-1318)
Taylor, Nancy Douglas 9585
(MIC.F.TC-4765)
Taylor, Norman William 1217
Taylor, Reed David 1807
Taylor, Robert Gordon 11295
(MIC.F.TC-41680)
Taylor, Robert John 7141
(MIC.F.TC-29756)
Taylor, Ronald Maxwell 11420
(MIC.T-757)
Taylor, Stanley James 2622
(MIC.F.TC-56785)
Taylor, Stuart Martin 4623
(MIC.F.TC-22244)
Taylor, William David 11875
(MIC.F.TC-36841)
Taylor, William Ewart, Jr. 903
(E78 C2 T3)
Taylor, William Harold 3640
(MIC.F.TC-49122)
Teal, Philip Rae 6219
(MIC.F.TC-42863)
Teale, Arthur Ernest 9947
Teare, Jane Lake 9271
(MIC.F.TC-35148)
Teboul, Albert Victor 8289
Tedla, Shibru 11027
Teicher, Morton Irving 547
(MIC.F.TC-17813)
Telford, William M. 12028
Te Linde, Derek John 9586
(MIC.F.TC-50632)
Telka, Eugene 9323 (MIC.F.TC-53296)
Teller, Hans Leo 11719
Tellier, Yvan 10275
Telschow, Frederick H. 991
(ML410 W668 T26 fol.)
Tempalski, Jerry 2040
Temple, Anna 3561 (MIC.F.T-1147)
Temple, Peter G. 5900
Templeman, Wilfred 11077
Templeman-Klint, Dirk Jacob 5927
(MIC.TC-395)
Tener, John Simpson 10638
Tennant, Alan D. 10530
Tennant, Paul 2878
Tennant, Paul Richard 8525
Tennyson, B.D. 8882
Tennyson, Marilyn Elizabeth 5356
Tenove, S. C. 6921 (MIC.F.TC-56940)
Terasmae, Joan 6220
Terroux, Georges 7708
Terry, Christopher Stephen 1461
(MIC.T-862)
Terry, John Charles Joseph 8683
(MIC.F.TC-33661)
Teskey, Dennis James 6599
(MIC.F.TC-39812)
Teskey, Herbert Joseph 11296
(QL535.1 T4 fol.)
Tessier, Jules Jacques 7763
(MIC.F.TC-55805)
Tester, Albert Louis 10974
Teta, Diana C. 9324
Têtu, Michel 2132
Tevis, Raymond Harry 7051
Textor, Lucy Elizabeth 7623
(H31 T6 V3)
Thachenkary, Cherian Sebastian 1193
(MIC.F.TC-49861)
Thacker, Robert William 8041
(MIC.F.TC-50955)
Thakur, Ramesh Chandra 8794
(MIC.F.TC-37550)

Thaler, Gary Ross 11587
(MIC.F.TC-27992)
Tharin, James C. 5472
Thatcher, Max B. 8764 (MIC.T-94)
Theeuwes, Julius Jacobus Maria 2084
(MIC.F.TC-26006)
Theis, John Peter 10308
(MIC.F.TC-51215)
Theis, Nicholas J. 6221
(MIC.F.TC-30229)
Théoret, Raymond 1447
(HB31 R332 fol.)
Thériault, Adrien 8279 (PN4913 F6 T4)
Thériault, Alma 8242
Thériault, Serge A. 8295
(MIC.F.TC-44158)
Thériault-Pitre, Jacqueline 3034
Théroux, Charles Paul-Émile 9108
(MIC.F.TC-47248)
Therriault, Jean-Claude 11853
(MIC.F.TC-36186)
Therrien, Susan Alice 3067
(MIC.F.TC-26933)
Thevenon, Michael Jean 1824
Thexton, James David 4235
(MIC.T-722)
Thibaudeau, Guy 4236
(LB1131 T55 fol.)
Thibault, André 4094 (MIC.F-027206)
Thibault, André 10467
(MIC.F.TC-48131)
Thibault, Claude J. 8795 (MIC.T-601)
Thibault, J. Robert 11770
Thibeau, Patrick Wilfred 2473
Thibert, Gilles 3459
Thiede, David Steven 5580
Thielman, George G. 810
Thiessen, G.G. 1670
Thiessen, Jack 7777
Thiessen, Richard Leigh 5535
(MIC.F.T-1095)
Thiffault, Charles 10376 (MIC.T-579)
Thirkell, Peter Creswell 2232
(MIC.F.TC-50631)
Thirkettle, Frank William 1076
(MIC.F.TC-26666)
Thivierge, Nicole 2539
(MIC.F.TC-56268)
Thom, Douglas John 2733
(MIC.F.TC-38858)
Thomae, Richard Bruce 3982
Thomas, Amos Gordon 11588
(MIC.TC-12641)
Thomas, Alain Maurice Georges 7764
(MIC.F.TC-58341)
Thomas, Alan Miller 1059
Thomas, Anthony William 11206
(MIC.TC-9654)
Thomas, Barry 10680 (MIC.TC-10274)
Thomas, Charles Eugene 11720
(MIC.F.TC-51810)
Thomas, Clara Eileen 8111
Thomas, Donald Charles 10625
(MIC.TC-5847)
Thomas, Dwight Robert 1972
Thomas, Earle Schwartz 7303
(MIC.F.TC-43257)
Thomas, George Philip 11721
Thomas, Gerald Rowland 8333
(MIC.F.TC-33792)
Thomas, Hartley Munro 6973
Thomas, Howard H. 10681
(MIC.F.T-1313)
Thomas, James B. 11185
Thomas, John Morris 4372
Thomas, Lewis G. 7238 (F5729 T48)
Thomas, Lewis Herbert 7187
(JL462 T5)
Thomas, Martin Lewis Hall 11961
Thomas, Paul French 4077
(MIC.F.TC-36846)
Thomas, Paul Griffith 8548
(MIC.F.TC-35149)
Thomas, Prentice M., Jr. 487
Thomas, Robert Francis 2915
(MIC.F.TC-36848)
Thomas, Theodore Elia 9919
(MIC.T-448)
Thomas, Veslof 3141 (MIC.T-164)
Thomlison, Raymond John 10102
(MIC.F.TC-17291)

Thompson, Andrew Royden 7887
Thompson, Arthur N. 9837
Thompson, Dwayne Thomas 8867
(MIC.T-123)
Thompson, Edward Gerald 4365
(MIC.F.TC-42326)
Thompson, Eric Callum 8042
(MIC.F.TC-22987)
Thompson, Frederic F. 7169
Thompson, Gail 872 (LB5 R46 fol.)
Thompson, Hugh R. 4680
Thompson, J. Wayne 9479
(MIC.F.TC-40331)
Thompson, John 7232
(MIC.F.TC-24891)
Thompson, Joyce Lesley 8043
(MIC.F.TC-24892)
Thompson, Lynda Marion 3893
(MIC.F.TC-40969)
Thompson, Peter Hamilton 6222
(MIC.TC-14100)
Thompson, R.W. 1985
Thompson, Richard Henry 755
(MIC.F.T-1023)
Thompson, Robert I. 5357
Thompson, Roderick Ross 4957
(MIC.F.TC-34087)
Thompson, Thomas Luman 5368
Thompson, William Paul 940
Thomson, Colin Argyle 2556
(MIC.TC-13599)
Thomson, Ellis 6223
Thomson, James Edgar 6224
Thomson, John Gray 2951
Thomson, Lisle Alexander 10436
(MIC.F.TC-64017)
Thomson, Richard Edward 5030
(MIC.TC-8336)
Thomson, Robert 6225
Thong, Cyril How Sik 11232
(MIC.F.TC-19295)
Thorburn, Hugh Garnet 8704
(JL235 T47)
Thorn, Frank Molyneux 4237
(LB1131 T58)
Thornton, David Andrew 9992
(MIC.F.TC-27070)
Thornton, Patricia Elizabeth 4859
(MIC.F.TC-30471)
Thorpe, Frederick John 7013
Thorpe, Ralph Irving 5359
Thorsell, James Westvick 10453
(MIC.TC-10275)
Thorsteinson, Raymond 5901
Thurlow, John Geoffrey 5786
(MIC.F.TC-51169)
Thurston, Phillips Cole 6226
(MIC.F.TC-56139)
Thusu, Bindraban 6579
Thwaites, James Douglas 2540
Tibbetts, Bruce Hamilton 8150
(MIC.T-709)
Tiberius, Richard Gordon 6825
(MIC.F.TC-32889)
Tierney, Mary C. 9404
(MIC.F.TC-34571)
Tiessen, Holm 292 (MIC.F.TC-60499)
Tiffany, Orrin Edward 7511 (F5074 T5)
Tiffin, Donald Lloyd 6627
(MIC.TC-5848)
Tihany, Eva 3615
Tilby, Penelope Jean 9078
(MIC.F.TC-24893)
Tillman, John Robert 6227
Tilly, George Anthony 7718
(MIC.F.TC-47863)
Timko, Paul Joseph 9936
Timleck, Derry Gray 4035
Timmer, Victor Robert 11740
(MIC.F.T-1256)
Timmis, Roger 11722
(MIC.F.TC-17238)
Timmins, Marie A. L. 8381
(PS8526 E38 Z79)
Timofeeff, Nicolay Peter 102
Tindale, Joseph Arthur 4285
(MIC.F.TC-51388)
Tindall, William Norman 6878
(MIC.T-214)
Tindill, Arthur Sidney 2705
(MIC.F.T-1131)

Tipnis, Ravindra S. 5902
(MIC.F.TC-40332)
Tipper, Howard W. 5360
Tippett, Clinton Raymond 5903
(MIC.F.TC-46407)
Tippett, Maria W. 7142
Tisdale, Edwin W. 11504
Tisdall, Douglas Michael 8390
(MIC.F.TC-27994)
Titman, Roger Donaldson 10780
(MIC.F.TC-18874)
Todd, Arlen Wesley 10575
(MIC.F.TC-1307)
Todd, Daniel 4811 (HC117 N8 T63)
Todd, Evelyn Mary 7800 (MIC.T-535)
Todres, Elaine Meller 8500
(MIC.F.T-906)
Toews, Henry 4428 (MIC.T-784)
Toews, Laurette Kathleen Woolsly
3705 (MIC.TC-16156)
Toker, Mia Beer 3077
(MIC.F.TC-29473)
Tolderlund, Douglas Stanley 5095
Tollefson, E.A. 7916
Tollenaar, Matthijs 343
(MIC.F.TC-31134)
Tolman, Carl 6228
Tolsma, Catherine Colette 4007
(MIC.F.TC-59272)
Tomkins, George Strong 4587
Tomkins, Muriel Winnifred 3401
(MIC.T-257)
Tomlinson, Peter 9405 (MIC.TC-12229)
Tomović, Vadislav A. 3746
(MIC.F.TC-27071)
Tompa, Frank Stephen 10860
Toner, Brenda Bernadette 8945
(MIC.F.TC-59726)
Tones, Patricia Isabel 11887
(MIC.F.TC-31685)
Toogood, Alexander Featherston 1143
(HE8699 C2 T5)
Toohey, Kelleen Ann 7709
(MIC.F.TC-55716)
Tookey, Herbert Barton 9079
Toombs, Morley Preston 2477
(MIC.T-96)
Toombs, Wilbert Nelson 2754
Tootle, James Roger 7443 (MIC.T-442)
Topley, Derrick Norman 4366
Topping, Coral Wesley 10309
(HV9504 T6)
Topping, Milton Stanlee 11233
(MIC.TC-5122)
Torbit, Gary Edward 3515
(MIC.TC-15366)
Torrance, George Murray 6786
(MIC.F.TC-36852)
Torrance, Judy Margaret Curtis 8596
(MIC.F.TC-25758)
Torrance, Robert Joseph 4036
Torrence, Lois Evelyn 8630
Tosterud, Robert James 42
(MIC.F.TC-16922)
Touchette, Claude Joseph René 4095
(MIC.F.TC-31353)
Toussignant, Pierre 7052
Touzin-St-Pierre, Lloyd Cécile 2960
(MIC.F-2M11.608.4)
Tovell, Walter Massey 5473
Tower, Gael Welles 3567
(MIC.F.T-1197)
Townes, Henry K., Jr. 11260
Townsend, Thomas William 10626
(MIC.TC-16335)
Toxey, Walter William, Jr. 8831
Tozer, Edward Timothy 6567
Tracey, Kevin 4286 (MIC.T-244)
Tracie, Carl Joseph 84 (MIC.TC-6243)
Tracy, Martin Booth 2066
(MIC.F.T-1211)
Traill, R.J. 6229
Trask, Maxwell 2879
Trauger, David Lee 10781
Traves, Thomas Donald 1306
(MIC.F.TC-26667)
Travis, Keith I. 9080 (MIC.TC-9941)
Travis, Leroy Douglas 3706
(MIC.F.TC-26938)
Treasure, Morris Ralph 3353
(MIC.F.TC-26939)

Treddenick, John Macauley 2784
(MIC.TC-3527)
Trehub, Sandra E. 9587
(MIC.F.TC-18396)
Treiman, Allan Harvey 6492
Treleaven, Harvey Leroy 2697
Tremaine, Ruth V. 3142
Tremblay, Bernard 4335
Tremblay, Christianne 1115
Tremblay, Doris 1619 (MIC.T-253)
Tremblay, J.J. 8597
Tremblay, Jean 2591
(MIC.F-2M11.527.7)
Tremblay, Jean Paul 8255
Tremblay, Léo-Paul 6493
Tremblay, Louis-Marie 1361
Tremblay, Marc-Adélard 10174
(MIC.T-97)
Tremblay, Nicole 4037 (MIC.T-3147)
Trempe, Pierre-Léon 3174
(MIC.F-2M11.560.2)
Trenton, Thomas Norman 3707
(MIC.F.TC-36853)
Trépanier, Pierre 7361 (S417 L47 T74)
Trescott, Peter Chapin 5681
Treslan, Dennis Liv 3357
(MIC.F.TC-34089)
Trettin, Hans Peter 5361
Trevithick, Morris Henry 1589
(MIC.F.T-904)
Trevor-Deutsch, Burleigh 10650
Triantis, Stephen George 2041
Trick, Charles Gordon 11938
(MIC.F.TC-62878)
Trigg, Charles M. 5581
Trigg, Linda Joyce 3270
(MIC.F.TC-47249)
Trimble, William Joseph 1307
(TN23 T7)
Trimnell, Frank Owen 1448
(MIC.F.TC-52306)
Trinh, Hieu Nghia 2350 (MIC.T-545)
Trites, Ronald Wilmot 11939
Trnavskis, Boris 10478
(MIC.F.TC-21362)
Troelsen, Johannes C. 5787
Troop, William Hamilton 7489
(FC243 T76)
Troper, Harold Martin 7585
(MIC.F.TC-31354)
Trosky, Odarka Savella 4336
(MIC.TC-9942)
Trotter, Reginald George 7103
Trottier, Claude René 2800
(MIC.F.TC-43735)
Trottier, Robert 11297 (MIC.TC-9943)
Trowsdale, George Campbell 1006
(MIC.F.TC-21416)
Troxler, Carole Watterson 7624
(MIC.T-749)
Truavskis, Boris 2277
(MIC.F.TC-21362)
Trucco, Ramiro 11886
(MIC.F.TC-60178)
Trudeau, Claudette Suzanne Marie 1040
(MIC.F.TC-58335)
Trudeau, Jean 516 (MIC.T-182)
Trudeau, Nicole 1007 (MIC.T-3948)
Trudel, François 629 (MIC.F.T-1201)
Trudel, Marcel 8243 (PS8073 T8)
Trudel, Pierre 6494
Trueman, David Lawrence 5536
(MIC.F.TC-47250)
Trueman, George Johnstone 2786
(LB2891 Q8 T7)
Trussler, Terrence Andrew 4038
(MIC.F.TC-55787)
Trusz, Andrew Richard 3539
Truszka, Mary Gregory 4002
Trute, Barry 10103 (MIC.T-790)
Tryphonopoulos, Jeannie Hager 7710
(MIC.F.TC-56565)
Trzcienski, Walter Edward, Jr. 6230
(MIC.TC-9508)
Tsai, Hui-Liang 1564 (MIC.F.T-905)
Tsao, Fei 3271
Tsong, Chin-Fong 6647
(MIC.F.TC-21127)
Tsuchiyama, Tamie 8334
Tuchmaier, Henri Samuel 8244

Tuck, Joseph Hugh 2108
(MIC.F.TC-28365)
Tuck, Ralph 6231
Tucker, Christopher Marshall 4643
(MIC.F.TC-46963)
Tucker, David Harold 9325
Tucker, David John 10104
(MIC.F.TC-38862)
Tucker, Gilbert N. 1256 (HC114 T8)
Tucker, Michael John 8796
(MIC.F.TC-40970)
Tucker, Otto George 2715
Tucker, William Allen 11904
Tuckwell, Neil Brian 4337
(MIC.F.TC-44836)
Tudiver, Judith Gail 9230
Tufuor, Joseph Kwame 3730
(MIC.F.TC-59357)
Tuggle, Benjamin Noel 10818
Tugwell, Stephen Maurice 1870
(MIC.F.TC-20275)
Tuke, Michael Francis 5788
(MIC.TC-1829)
Tulchinsky, Gerald Jacob Joseph 1257
(MIC.F.TC-28003)
Tully, John P. 11940
Tunell, George Gerard 2294
(MIC.F-CC-4)
Tung, Fu-Lai 56 (MIC.F.TC-22564)
Tunstall, Kenneth Wilfred J.R. 4256
(MIC.TC-8535)
Tuohy, Carolyn Joy 6815 (MIC.T-811)
Tuokko, Holly Anna 9081
(MIC.F.TC-58590)
Tupper, Allan James 8454
(MIC.F.TC-34668)
Tupper, David Edward 9406
(MIC.F.TC-58550)
Tupper, William MacGregor 5629
Turk, James Leonard 10038
(MIC.TC-10600)
Turnbull, Allen A. 9758
Turnbull, Christopher John 873
(MIC.TC-15618)
Turnbull, Jane Mason 8368
(PS8141 T87)
Turnbull, Sarah Louise 4338
(MIC.F.TC-55714)
Turnbull, Stuart McLean 1462
(MIC.F.TC-19654)
Turner, Andrew Allan 10394
(MIC.F.TC-56954)
Turner, Arthur C. 7392
Turner, Christy Gentry, II 488
Turner, Douglas Jack 10395
(MIC.F.TC-1319)
Turner, Gordon Philip 8044
(MIC.F.TC-42769)
Turner, Howard 4595
(MIC.F.TC-25614)
Turner, Lorne Craig 6728
(MIC.F.TC-50959)
Turner, Nancy Jean 11505
(MIC.F.TC-17239)
Turner, Wesley Barry 7470 (MIC.T-324)
Turtle, John Patrick 1362 (MIC.T-785)
Tushingham, Gary Warren 2977
(MIC.T-725)
Tusko, Frank Ferenc 11723
Tuthill, Robert Joseph 9207
(MIC.F.TC-38864)
Tway, Duane Converse 7143
(MIC.T-99)
Tweedle, Dean Frederick 3439
(MIC.F.TC-40339)
Twenhofel, William Henry 6495
Twidale, Charles Rowland 4777
Twyman, James DeWitt 6232
(MIC.F.TC-59867)
Tyler, Albert Vincent 10993
(MIC.TC-3568)
Tyler, Barrington Michael John 11298
(MIC.F.TC-39012)
Tyler, Thomas Lee 3712 (MIC.T-773)
Tyler, W.P.N. 7471
Tyman, John Langton 89 (MIC.T-907)
Tymko, Joseph Lawrence 2985
(MIC.F.TC-43576)
Tynan, Thomas Martin 8861

Tywoniuk, Nick 4567
(MIC.F.TC-48646)
Tzuk, Yogev 9844

U

Ubbelohde, Carl W., Jr. 7053
Uhlaner, Carole Jean 8455
Uhlman, Charles Clarence 4287
(MIC.TC-13608)
Uhlman, H.J. 2766
Ujimoto, Koji Victor 7600
(MIC.TC-15158)
Ukaga, Gabriel Chidi 2952
(MIC.F.TC-25080)
Ulke, Titus 11506
Ullman, Stephen Hayes 722
(MIC.T-586)
Ullman, Walter 7265
Ulrych, Tadeusz Jan 12029
Umar, Pervez Akhtar 6496
(MIC.F.TC-38353)
Umstead, Kenneth H.H. 6974
Umoren, Uduakobong E., Rev. 446
Underhill, Harold F. 2175
Underwood, Lawrence Stratton 10581
Underwood, Thomas Joseph 4913
(MIC.F.TC-24689)
Unsoy, Jeelee 10495 (MIC.F.TC-55267)
Upadhyay, Hansa Datt 5789
(MIC.F.TC-17411)
Upson, Roger Ballard 1541
Upton, Leslie F.S. 7292
Urbain, Frère Marie 3143
Urbas, Jeannette 8245
(MIC.F.TC-38865)
Ure, George Brian 11245
(MIC.F.TC-50960)
Urich, Max Albert 176
Urion, Carl Armand 517
(MIC.F.TC-40340)
Urquhart, Frederick Albert 11299
Usher, Brian Robert 4170
(MIC.F.TC-27520)
Usher, Jean Edwards 9908
(MIC.TC-3748)
Usher, John L. 5362
Usher, Peter Joseph, Jr. 4818
(MIC.TC-5849)
Usher, Sarah 9082 (MIC.F.TC-33665)
Uthe, Richard Edward 5630
(MIC.F.TC-38138)
Uyeno, Thomas Tadashi 6568

V

Vachon, Jacques 10105 (MIC.F.T-1018)
Vachon, Mary L. Suslak 10055
(MIC.F.TC-42147)
Vagners, Uldis Janis 6233
(MIC.TC-6184)
Vaid, Jyotsna 7711 (MIC.F.TC-58165)
Vail, Barry Richard 4269
Vaillancourt, François 2219
(MIC.F.TC-39578)
Vaillancourt, Raymond F. 2986
Valaskakis, Gail Guthrie 1054
(MIC.F.TC43049)
Valdés, Maria Elena de 3747
(MIC.F.TC-30350)
Valhappan, Palaniappan 4529
Valiquette, Guy 6497
Valiquette, John Edmund 3847
(MIC.F.T-1336)
Vallely, Lois Mary 7397
Valley, Victoria 9247
(MIC.F.TC-48648)
Valliant, Robert Irwin 6498
(MIC.F.TC-50634)
Vallières, Marc Georges 1528
(MIC.F.TC-48144)

Vallis, Terrance Michael 9083
(MIC.F.TC-56146)
Van Alstine, Ralph Erskine 5790
Van Alstyne, R.W. 7520
Vanasse, Alfred Rowland 7014
Van Camp, Keven Robert 2460
Vance, James Hinman 3440
(MIC.TC-4986)
Vandenberghe, Hilde M. 6860
(MIC.F.TC-59869)
Vanderhill, Burke Gordon 4723
(MIC.T-79)
Vanderkamp, J. 1363
Vander Kloet, Samuel P. 11401
(MIC.TC-14073)
Van der Krabben, Jacobus Johannes
Maria 10106 (MIC.F.TC-36856)
Van der Merwe, Hendrik Willem 10175
(MIC.T-100)
Van der Merwe, Marina Suzanne 6736
(MIC.F.T-1263)
Van Dromme, Huguette Ruimy 3013
(MIC.F-003606)
Van Dyke, Edward William 366
(MIC.TC-13613)
Van Hesteren, Francis Nicholas 4158
Van Hoff, Howard S. 3983
Van Horn, Lawrence Franklin 526
(MIC.F.T-907)
Vanier, Guy 9084 (MIC.T-3162)
Van Kirk, Sylvia M. 7015
Van Lierop, Johannes Henricus 1583
(MIC.F.TC-47170)
Van Lierop, William 279
Van Loo, Mary Frances 1671
Van Loon, Richard Jerome 8482
(MIC.TC-2345)
Van Nus, Walter 10474
(MIC.F.TC-35311)
Van Oosten, John 10921
Van Raamsdonk, Renée Giselle 3641
(MIC.F.TC-49367)
Van Roey-Roux, Françoise 8246
(MIC.T-3024)
Van Ryswyk, Albert Leonard 245
Van Vliet, Maurice L. 10399
Van Vliet, Willem 10015
(MIC.F.TC-47171)
Van Wagner, Judy Kay Collischan 950
Van Zinderen Bakker, Eduard
Meine 11663 (MIC.F.TC-22014)
Van Zull de Jong, Constantinus
Gerhard 10599 (MIC.TC-3908)
Van Zyl, François David Wallace 1041
(MIC.F.TC-19356)
Varma, Premlata 8169
(MIC.F.TC-48649)
Vascotto, Gian L. 11781
(MIC.F.TC-30081)
Vastokas, Joan Marie 489 (MIC.T-991)
Vastokas, Romas 719
Vaucamps, Françoise 7457
Vaughan, Maurice Stephen 4424
Vaughan, Michael Bryan 2042
Vaughan, Ronald Frederick 8483
Veatch, Richard 8802
(JX1975.5 C2 V44)
Vecsey, Christopher Thomas 544
Veevers, Jean Eleanor 10056
Veitch, Douglas W. 8151
Venkataraman, Sundaram 267
(MIC.TC-7888)
Venkitasubramanyan, Calicut S. 6234
(MIC.TC-4568)
Vennum, Thomas 545 (F99 C6 V43)
Venugopal, Virinchipuram R. 12030
(MIC.TC-5124)
Verdet, Paula 10176
Verduyn, Christl 8247
(MIC.F.TC-44165)
Verge, Pierre 7935
Verma, Dhirendra 2474
(MIC.F.TC-37882)
Verma, Tika Ram 231 (MIC.TC-3418)
Vermeer, Rees 10833
Verniero, Sharon Anne 3713
Vernon, Foster 4078 (MIC.TC-16136)
Vernon, Howard A., Jr. 6727
Véronneau, Denise 1116
(MIC.F-029705)

Verreault, Claude 7765
(MIC.F.TC-59437)
Verreault, René 9407
(MIC.F-2M11.388.4)
Verriour, Patrick St. George 3035
(MIC.F.TC-40522)
Vicero, Ralph Dominic 4852
Vichman, Gustaf T. 9806
Vickery, Vernon R. 11179
Vickery, William Lloyd 10682
(MIC.F.TC-31910)
Victor, Peter Alan 1364 (MIC.TC-8340)
Vienneau, Jean-Guy 10338
(MIC.F.T-1327)
Vigod, Bernard L. 7384
(MIC.F.TC-24896)
Vigoda, Deborah V.F. 4079
(MIC.F.TC-47174)
Viguie, Francis 9272
Vij, Kewal Kishore 12031
(MIC.F.TC-17079)
Vilks, Gustavs 11976 (MIC.F.TC-18722)
Villagonzalo, Paulino Iriarte 3708
(MIC.TC-4988)
Villeneuve, Georges O. 11771
Villeneuve, Paul Yvon 4917
Villeneuve, Richard 9408, 9759
Villeneuve, Abbé Rudolph 10107
Villiers-Westfall, William
Edward de 9791 (MIC.F.TC-35160)
Villmow, Jack R. 5036
Vine, William George 10139
(MIC.F.TC-43741)
Vineberg, Solomon 1729 (H31 C7)
Viner, Jacob 1986
Vinet, Alain 9101
Vinette, Roland 3144
Viney, Bonnie 2880 (MIC.F.TC-48650)
Vintar, John 4367 (MIC.F.TC-50363)
Violato, Claudio 9634
Vipond, Mary Jean 7152
(MIC.F.TC-27521)
Virgin, Albert Edward 2953
Visscher, Adrian 9760
(MIC.F-2M11.169.7)
Vitaro, Frank 9480 (MIC.T-3436)
Vitt, Dale Hadley 11402
Vivian, Robert Evans 4568
Vocke, Robert Donald 5724
Voege, Marion Pexrise 4080
(MIC.F.TC-59844)
Vogan, Nancy Fraser 1008
Vogel, Claude L. 9792 (BX3109 L68 V6)
Vogel, Hal 7153
Voisey, Paul Leonard 7239
(MIC.F.TC-59870)
Voisine, Nive 9909
Volge, M.P. 9761
Von Baeyer, Carl Lucius 9085
(MIC.F.TC-37876)
Von Fange, Erick Alvin 2894
Vonhof, Jan Albert 5582
Von Zur-Muehlen, Max 3659
Votaw, Robert Barnett 6235
(MIC.T-372)
Vowinchel, Thomas 11616
(MIC.F.TC-24444)
Vox, Vicki Elaine 8631 (MIC.F.T-941)
Voyce, Stanley 4257 (MIC.F.TC-40972)
Vraa, Calvin Woodrow 3709
Vrsic, Gabriel 818
Vuorinen, Saara Sofia 749
(MIC.F.TC-19358)

W

Waddell, Christopher Robb 1337
(MIC.F.TC-51390)
Waddington, Edwin Donald 6600
(MIC.F.TC-59354)
Waddington, John 11521
(MIC.TC-3311)
Wade, Gwendolyn Gibbs 9762
(MIC.T-441)
Wadland, John Henry 951
(MIC.F.TC-30954)

Wagenberg, R.H. 8883
Waggoner, Marion Arthur 8640
Wagner, David Henry 11507
Wagner, Frances Joan Estelle 5363
Wagner, James Richard 8862
(MIC.T-165)
Wagner, Roy M.K. 3710
(MIC.F.TC-54089)
Wagner, Rudolph 3068
Wagner, William James 3272
(MIC.F.TC-53170)
Wagner, William Philip 5474
Wahab, Abdul 1672 (MIC.F.TC-37749)
Wahl, Donald Frederick 2043
Wahl, John Lesslie 5631
(MIC.F.TC-38141)
Wahl, William G. 6499
Wahlstrom, Wanda Louise 3984
(MIC.F.TC-58343)
Wahn, Michael Brian 1194
(MIC.F.TC-49129)
Waide, Frederick Gordon 2513
Wain, Olev Martin 6930
(MIC.F.TC-53171)
Wainwright, John Andrew 8045
(MIC.F.TC-38411)
Waiser, William Andrew 5082
(MIC.F.TC-60530)
Waite, Don T. 11876 (MIC.TC-15762)
Waite, Peter Busby 7104
Wake, Akio 4525
Waksman, Mary 3776
(MIC.F.TC-31360)
Walawender, Michael John 5054
Walden, Keith 8073 (MIC.F.TC-50208)
Waldenberger, Robert Wesley 10432
Waldichuk, Michael 11941
Waldie, Valerie Lynn 9619
(MIC.TC-12612)
Waldon, Freda F. 8109
Wales, Bertram Edwards 4052
Wali, Mohan Kishen 11508
(MIC.TC-5855)
Walker, Bernal Ernest 2446
(MIC.T-101)
Walker, Brian Harrison 11626
Walker, David Charles 8742
Walker, David Frank 4792
(MIC.TC-12959)
Walker, David G. 11445
(MIC.F.TC-40525)
Walker, Edward Robert 5001
Walker, Ernest Gordon 927
(MIC.F.T-1111)
Walker, H.V.H. 57
Walker, Harley Jesse 4653
Walker, J.C. 9888
Walker, James William 7625
(MIC.F.TC-18724)
Walker, Jennifer Mary 11522
(MIC.TC-218)
Walker, John Fortune 5364
Walker, John Roger 4203
(MIC.F.TC-43105)
Walker, John W. 6236
Walker, Keith Donald 9273
(MIC.F.TC-42336)
Walker, Laurence John 3273
(MIC.F.TC-38867)
Walker, Mabel G. 7536
Walker, Michael Angus 1365
(MIC.TC-7604)
Walker, Robert William 3527
(MIC.F.TC-37552)
Walker, Wilfred 5083
(MIC.F.TC-33735)
Walkington, Albert Hodgson 3616
(MIC.F.TC-24154)
Wall, Albert Edward 3848
(MIC.F.TC-40346)
Wall, John Hallett 5583
Wall, Robert David 920 (MIC.F.T-1112)
Wall, Robert E. 6681
Wallace, Carl Murray 7386
(MIC.TC-13621)
Wallace, Elizabeth 8684
Wallace, H.N. 7472
Wallace, Kenneth Walter Anthony 4383
(MIC.TC-6764)
Wallace, Mary Elisabeth 8540
(JL651949 W3 fol.)

Wallace, Myles Stuart 2351
Wallace, Reginald Stanley 2278
(HE9788 W53)
Wallace, Ronald Richard 11332
Wallach, Joseph Leonard 6237
(MIC.TC-14198)
Wallen, Donald George 11828
(MIC.TC-6854)
Wallens, Stanley Gerald 698
(MIC.F.T-935)
Walles, M.J.S. 8864
Wallis, Peter Malcolm 11987
(MIC.F.TC-37878)
Wallot, Albert 3274
Wallot, Jean Pierre 7055
(MIC.F-2M11.142.3)
Walls, Richard Alan 5475
(MIC.F.TC-38356)
Wallschlaeger, Michael John 2773
Walpole, Robert Leonard 5476
Walsh, Anne 976
Walsh, David Francis 8765 (MIC.T-826)
Walsh, Gerald 3470 (MIC.TC-488)
Walsh, John A. 4339
Walsh, John J. 7852
Walsh, Robert James Patrick 7360
Walters, Jean Elizabeth Maddox 3275
(MIC.F.TC-42536)
Walters, Martin 6500
(MIC.F-2M11.533.1)
Walters, Vladimir 11047
Walthier, Thomas N. 5791
Walton, Grant Fontain 296
Walton, Jonathan William 7213
(MIC.F.T-1027)
Wanamaker, Murray 7719 (MIC.T-139)
Wandesforde-Smith, Geoffrey
Albert 8863
Wang, Der-Hsiung 1860
(MIC.F.TC-909)
Wang, Hong-Cheng 1521
(MIC.F.TC-50585)
Wang, I-Chen 11655 (MIC.F.TC-55163)
Wang, Shin 6501
Wang, Ying Thomason 10819
Wangerin, Walter Martin 3287
Waniewicz, Ignacy 4081
(MIC.F.TC-47175)
Wankiewicz, Anthony Cyril 4624
(MIC.F.TC-28830)
Wann, Phillip Daley 9588
Wanzel, Robert Stewart 10396
(MIC.F.TC-21133)
Ward, Daniel Bertram 11589
Ward, Frederick James 10975
Ward, Harold B. 4831
Ward, James Stanley 4914 (MIC.T-557)
Ward, John Gordon 10834
(MIC.F.TC-17241)
Ward, Norman McQueen 8549
(JL167 W3)
Ward, Peter Douglas 5365
Ward, William P. 7636
(MIC.F.TC-21172)
Wardell, Nancy Needham 2371
Wardhaugh, Ronald 4238
Wardle, Richard Julian 5632
(MIC.F.TC-38142)
Ware, Dennis William 36
Ware, Martin Peter 8391
(MIC.F.TC-48276)
Wareham, Wilfred William 413
(MIC.F.T-1212)
Warescha, Blaine Eugene 10276
Wargny, Nancy J. 3036
(MIC.F.TC-33406)
Warkentin, John Henry 4880
(MIC.F.TC-17817)
Warnaars, Benjamin Caspar 280
(MIC.TC-16039)
Warner, Alan 3276 (MIC.F.TC-63705)
Warner, Charles 5041
(MIC.TC-9515)
Warner, Donald F. 7516
Warner, James Lawrence 11960
Warner, M.M. 6689
Warner, Ronald Earl 9495
(MIC.F.TC-36862)
Warnes, Carl Edward 10531
Warnock, John William, Jr. 8797
(MIC.T-315)

Warren, Catharine Elizabeth 10223
(MIC.T-953)
Warren, Edward Gillingham, III 8712
Warren, Percival Sydney 5477
Warren, Philip John 2774
Warren, Sharon Ann 6816
(MIC.F.TC-17102)
Warren, Wendy Kaye 2612
(MIC.F.TC-55773)
Warren, William John 3792
(MIC.F.TC-49369)
Warrington, Patrick Douglas 11403
(MIC.TC-4856)
Warwick, Jack 8248
Warwick, Susan Jane 8119
(MIC.F.TC-58755)
Warwick, William Frank 11801
(MIC.F.TC-37831)
Wasescha, Blaine Eugene 9481
Washavsky, Jacob 37
Washburn, Albert Lincoln 5904
Wasilewski, Bohdan Kazimierz 3516
(MIC.F.TC-20850)
Wasserman, D.A. 4041
Wasson, Avtar Singh 9482
Wasteneys, Hortense Catherine
Fordell 10159 (MIC.F.TC-31363)
Watanabe, Roy Yoshinobu 5478
Waterhouse, Michael Francis 10475
(MIC.F.TC-49867)
Waterman, Larry William 3037
(MIC.F.TC-49257)
Waters, Gloria Sydna 9589
(MIC.F.TC-52701)
Waters, John William 4832
Waters, Joseph St. Clair 4368
Waters, Nigel Michael 4941
(MIC.F.TC-33615)
Watkin, Janis Kathryn 8392
(MIC.F.TC-51602)
Watkins, Donald 7824 (MIC.TC-6766)
Watkins, Glenn Gregory 10359
(MIC.TC-11620)
Watson, Alexander John 1060
(MIC.F.TC-53172)
Watson, Catherine Margaret 10310
Watson, Donald Whitman 6238
Watson, George Lee 8632
(MIC.F.T-1065)
Watson, Glenn Aubrey 2954
(MIC.F.TC-35319)
Watson, Graham Martin Wallett 9203
(MIC.F.TC-54462)
Watson, James W. 4716
Watson, Kenneth Depencier 5792
Watson, Kenneth Frank 1397
Watson, Raymond Kevin 4340
(MIC.F.TC-51330)
Watson, Rita Patricia May 3145
(MIC.F.TC-58342)
Watson, Roy Ernest Love 4369
Watson, Russell Anne M. 3038
(MIC.F.TC-59845)
Watson, William George 1730
Watt, Frank William 8074
(MIC.F.TC-25510)
Watt, John Alexander 4857
(MIC.F.TC-58850)
Watt, Mary Susan 10108 (MIC.F.T-929)
Watt, Theodore Marvin 4486
Watts, Floyd E. 7490
Watts, Howard Norman 4384
(MIC.TC-11176)
Watts, Martin John 1366
(MIC.F.TC-29980)
Waxer, Peter Harold 9086
(MIC.TC-4180)
Way, Harold G. 6239 (MIC.T-593)
Way, Jacob Edson, III 630
(MIC.F.TC-36863)
Waylen, Peter Robert 4625
(MIC.F.TC-57008)
Wayne, Jack 10016 (MIC.TC-12235)
Weale, David Emrys 9910
(MIC.F.TC-30235)
Wearing, J. 7105
Weary, Bettina 10007
Weary, Gregory Charles 11753
(MIC.F.TC-21233)
Weatherhead, Patrick James 10861
(MIC.F.TC-37553)

Weaver, Jeffrey Stephen 4495
Weaver, John Charles 7561
(MIC.T-574)
Weaver, Robert Kent 2320
(MIC.F.T-1311)
Weaver, Sally Mae 658 (MIC.TC-1864)
Weaver, Susan Emerson 11590
(MIC.F.TC-46055)
Weaver, Wendy Clifton 6909
(MIC.F.TC-36864)
Webb, David Charles 3603 (MIC.T-358)
Webb, Douglas John 987
Webb, Ross Allan 2321 (MIC.T-79)
Webber, Patrick John 11557
(MIC.TC-8717)
Weber, Gerald Irwin 1565 (MIC.T-103)
Weber, Joann Cynthia 659
Weber, Wilfred William Louis 5479
Weber, Yvonne B. 10630
Webster, Clara Margaret 9922
(MIC.F.TC-31364)
Webster, Douglas Richard 10479
(MIC.T-873)
Webster, Edward 4204
Webster, Gary Stewart 660
(MIC.F.T-1350)
Webster, Loyola Cathleen 4082
(MIC.F.TC-53174)
Webster, Terry Richard 11404
Webster, Thomas Stewart 7056
Wedel, George John 3302 (MIC.T-742)
Weeden, Robert B. 10853
Weeks, Donald Ralph 3599
Weeks, Harold L. 2706
Weeks, Peter Alan Donald 1009
(MIC.F.TC-58325)
Wege, Michael Lane 10820
Wegner, Rogert Edward Chesley 7610
(MIC.F.TC-1049)
Wehr, Nancy Reed 11785
Wehrkamp, Timothy Lee 7311
(MIC.F.T-911)
Weightman, Barbara Ann 490
(MIC.T-450)
Weil, Edward Benjamin 853
(MIC.F.T-1252)
Weinberger, Alex S. 3277
(MIC.F.TC-49259)
Weiner, John Louis 5480
Weinhauer, Carlin Eugene 3528
(MIC.F.TC-43584)
Weinfeld, Mortan Irwin 805
Weinstein, Edwin Lawrence 3600
(MIC.F.TC-43944)
Weinstein, Martin Sunny 10560
(MIC.TC-16042)
Weinstein, Pauline Smith 2632
(MIC.T-506)
Weinzweig, Paul Alan 10008
(MIC.F.TC-28015)
Weir, Collin Coke 254
Weir, John Angus 2245
(MIC.F.TC-37717)
Weir, Robin Elizabeth 6699
(MIC.F.TC-43743)
Weir, Thomas R. 86
Weirich, Frank A. 4626
(MIC.F.TC-62140)
Weisbart, Melvin 10976 (MIC.TC-1166)
Weise, Selene Harding Card 7144
(MIC.T-857)
Weiss, David Maurice 6688
Weiss, David Shlomo 3985
(MIC.F.TC-47178)
Weitz, Jacqueline Marie 491
Weitz, Joseph Leonard 5793
Welbourne, Arthur James 3517
Welch, Cecil Allan 4171
(MIC.F.TC-31918)
Welch, David Michael 4717
(MIC.TC-12561)
Weleschuk, Marian Alfred 3535
(MIC.F.TC-34513)
Wellington, Norman David 9423
(MIC.F.TC-39326)
Wells, Alan W. 10891
(MIC.F.TC-40348)
Wells, Bertram Whittier 313
Wells, Gary Seven 6240
(MIC.F.TC-46413)
Wells, James Ralph 631

Wells, T.A.G. 81
Wells, Ward M. 10380
Welsh, David Albert 10596
(MIC.F.TC-28974)
Welt, F. 7888
Welton, Mary Amedeus 8314
(BX4705 R7255 W4)
Wendte, John Curtis 5481
Wenker, Jerome Richard 963
(MIC.F.T-1024)
Wentholt, H. 812
Wenzel, George William 632
Wenzlau, Thomas Eugene 1494
Werker, Janet Feldman 7817
(MIC.F.TC-63100)
Wernecke, Hanns Bertram 2428
Werner, Antony Boris Tracy 1882
(MIC.T-812)
Werner, Harry Jay 5794
Werth, Elizabeth Marie 9151
(MIC.F.TC-42538)
Wertimer, S. 7652
Wesche, Marjorie Anne Birgham 4083
(MIC.F.TC-32900)
Weseloh, Datlaf Vaughn 10835
(MIC.F.TC-25585)
Wessel, James M. 5795
West, Douglas Scott 1973
(MIC.F.TC-46303)
West, Kenneth Ernest 4987
(MIC.TC-11177)
West, Lloyd Wilbert 9424
West, Nels Oscar 10627
(MIC.F.TC-26021)
West, Norman William 3409
West, Peter Michael 3536
(MIC.F.TC-56970)
West, Peter Templar 9274
(MIC.F.TC-48439)
West, Roy 6729 (MIC.F.TC-47468)
Westbury, Robert Clifton 6817
Westerman, Christopher John 6241
(MIC.F.TC-38040)
Westermark, Tory I. 3185
Westervelt, Thomas N. 5366
Westfall, William Edward 7211
(MIC.F.TC-35160)
Westgate, John Arthur 5482
Westhues, Anne 10186
(MIC.F.T-1403)
Westley, Frances R. 9970 (BL60 W48)
Westlund, Knut B. 6861
Westmacott, Martin William 2267
(MIC.TC-11178)
Westra, Robert 10631
(MIC.F.TC-40349)
Westrom, Marvin Lawton 4258
(MIC.F.TC-17729)
Westwater, Robert 2820
Westwood, Marvin James 10109
(MIC.TC-11179)
Wetherell, Albert Anthony 7016
Wetherell, Donald Grant 7145
(MIC.F.TC-50211)
Wexler, Mark N. 10224
(MIC.F.TC-37027)
Weyer, Edward Moffat, Jr. 633
(E99 E7 W48)
Weyl, Shalom 8433
Whale, Kathleen Bailie 3146
(MIC.F.TC-43747)
Whebell, C.F. J. 4895
Wheeler, Alan Edmund 3460
(MIC.TC-30865)
Wheeler, Everett P. 5725
Wheeler, John Oliver 5928
Whetten, Nathan Laselle 1308
Whitaker, Reginald Alan 8656
(JL197 L5 W47)
Whitaker, Roy Alexander 4627, 6931
(MIC.TC-8342)
Whitaker, Sidney Hopkins 5584
Whitaker, W.R. 10884
White, Antony 6601
White, Clinton Oliver 7248
White, Donald E. 5796
White, Douglas Perry 8087
(MIC.F.TC-42539)
White, Edwin Theodore 4245
White, Graham George 8743

White, Ivan Floyd 2613
(MIC.F.TC-55707)
White, James Murray 874
(MIC.F.TC-62359)
White, Joseph Clancy 6242
(MIC.F.TC-48440)
White, Lewis Theodore 11754
White, Lloyd 3381
White, Noel David George 11180
(MIC.F.TC-43106)
White, Owen Lester 6243
White, Patrick C.T. 7057
White, Randall Craig 8744
White, Ronald George 9409
(MIC.F.TC-23579)
White, Terrence Harold 2067
White, Walter Leroy 8526 (MIC.T-140)
White, William Alan 4833 (MIC.T-774)
White, William Gar 2614
White, William Hart 10458
White, William Robert Hugh 6628
Whitehead, LeRoy Ezra 2835
(MIC.F.TC-34094)
Whitehead, Ritchie George 4239
(MIC.T-565)
Whitehead, Robert Edgar 5633
(MIC.F.TC-18885)
Whitelaw, William Menzies 7162
(F5197.2 N4)
Whiteley, Hugh Russell 4569
(MIC.F.TC-22734)
Whitfield, Agnes Jane 8249
(MIC.F.TC-56246)
Whitlock, G.L. 7965
Whitman, Alfred Russell 6244
Whitmore, Duncan R. E. 5726
Whitney, Harriet E. 7562
Whitridge, Margaret E. 8112
Whittaker, Walter Leslie 1042
(MIC.T-141)
Whittick, Alan 11421
(MIC.F.TC-17419)
Whittinger, Julius Edward 965
Whittingham, Frank J. 2085
(MIC.TC-10681)
Whittingham, Michael David 10311
(MIC.F.TC-50281)
Whittle, Robert MacLean 3986
Whyte, Kenneth James 4131
(MIC.F.T-910)
Wilbberley, G.P. 182
Wickenden, Robert Thomas
Daubigny 5375
Wickett, Reginald Ernest
Yeatman 4039 (MIC.F.TC-36868)
Wicklund, Reuben Edward 217
Widden, Paul Rodney 11650
(MIC.TC-10195)
Widdowson, John David Allison 8335
(MIC.F.TC-43193)
Widmer, Kemble 5797
Wiedrick, Laurence George 7980
(MIC.T-504)
Wieland, James Murray 8404
(MIC.F.TC-37556)
Wiener, Melvin H. 9087
(MIC.F.TC-44173)
Wiens, John 2978
Wier, Richard Anthony 6818
Wiget, Andrew O. 634 (MIC.F.T-924)
Wiggin, Gladys A. 2546
Wiggs, Alfred James 10885
Wightman, Daryl M. 5682
(MIC.F.TC-48280)
Wightman, John Roaf 7766
Wigley, Philip George Edward 8815
Wike, Joyce Annabel 492 (MIC.T-104)
Wilce, Robert Thayer 11617
Wilchesky, Marc H. 3793
(MIC.F.TC-47869)
Wilcox, John Carman 161
Wilcox, William Roy 3518
(MIC.TC-15378)
Wildman, Howard Geoffrey 11446
(MIC.F.TC-42103)
Wilensky, Marshall Shimon 2592
(MIC.F.TC-42340)
Wilkins, Cecil J. 4003
Wilkinson, Bruce William 2755
Wilkinson, John Provost 7987
(MIC.T-876)

Wilkinson, Michael 3278
(MIC.F.TC-30868)
Wilkinson, Paul Frank 4718
(MIC.F.TC-27513)
Wilks, Arthur Garland 2851
(MIC.F.TC-49378)
Willard, Joseph William 10129
Willems, Jane Sisk 6706
(MIC.F.TC-29483)
Williams, Carole C. 10433
Williams, Charles Brian 2125
(MIC.T-105)
Williams, Christopher John 152
(MIC.F.TC-17244)
Williams, Constance Elaine Jayne 4132
(MIC.F.TC-1214)
Williams, Dana Adrienne 9763
(MIC.F.TC-47870)
Williams, David Dudley 11877
(MIC.F.TC-23435)
Williams, David Rees 3584
(MIC.F.TC-50086)
Williams, David Robert 4570
(MIC.F.TC-42541)
Williams, Douglas Harold 11724
(MIC.F.TC-32615)
Williams, Edgar Roland 3441
(MIC.F.TC-40534)
Williams, Edwin Philip 5483
Williams, Gary Wayne 38
Williams, Glen Sutherland 1398
(MIC.F.TC-38505)
Williams, Glyndwr 4844 (G640 W5)
Williams, Gordon Donald
Clarence 5484
Williams, Harold 5537
Williams, John 1774 (MIC.T-831)
Williams, John Edwin 10821
Williams, John Ryan 8650
(JL197 P7 W5)
Williams, L.D. 5031
Williams, Leonard Edward 2955
(MIC.F.T-1297)
Williams, Lowell Leavitt 2698
(MIC.TC-13988)
Williams, Mary-Jo 4341
(MIC.F.TC-54079)
Williams, Merton Yarwood 5683
Williams, Noel Henry 3794
(MIC.F.TC-30870)
Williams, Richard Lee 3461
Williams, Robert James 8745
(MIC.F.TC-17294)
Williams, Rosemary Janet 3113
(MIC.F.TC-55742)
Williams, Sharon Anne Clare 7889
(K3791 W54 fol.)
Williams, Sharon Mona 9152
(MIC.F.TC-46415)
Williams, Thomas Bowerman 5367
Williams, Trevor Hugh 9493
(MIC.F.TC-17295)
Williams, W. Blair 5 (MIC.F.TC-20099)
Williams, Wilfred Lawrence 3849
Williams-Jones, Anthony Eric 6502
(MIC.F.TC-17948)
Williamson, David Lee 11181
Williamson, David Robert 2220
(MIC.TC-16464)
Williamson, John Peter 1693
Williamson, John T. 6503
Willinsky, John M. 3402
(MIC.F.TC-57918)
Willis, Arthur L. 268
Willis, Charles Barwick 4240
Willis, Kathleen Diane 9764
(MIC.F.TC-58624)
Willis, Kenneth Richard 3358
Williston, Robert Horace 2987
(MIC.F.TC-53178)
Willms, Walter David 10628
Willoughby, Ernest Ross Floyd 4241
Willoughby, William Reid 7551
Willows, Dale Marjorie 3987
(MIC.TC-10930)
Willox, P. 2068 (HD8408 W54)
Willson, Katherine Joan 4259
(MIC.F.T-1301)
Willson, Sheila Catharine 9590
(MIC.F.TC-36870)

Willson, Stanley 4288
(MIC.F.TC-30872)
Wilmot, L.H. 8832
Wilmot, Marilyn Susan 10225
(MIC.F.TC-17149)
Wilson, Allan Cecil 2836
Wilson, Alexander Meade 3279
(MIC.F.TC-34095)
Wilson, Alfred William Gunning 6245
Wilson, Alice Evelyn 6246
Wilson, Arlene E. Lange 1987
Wilson, Arthur Grenville 183
(MIC.TC-2457)
Wilson, Bruce Gordon 7058
Wilson, Bruce Hamilton 8659
Wilson, Charles F. 116
Wilson, Christopher Richard
MacLean 1960
Wilson, Cynthia 5055
Wilson, David A. 2044
Wilson, David Thomas 1775
(MIC.TC-7246)
Wilson, Donald Cathcart 3471
(MIC.F.TC-30873)
Wilson, Doreen Edith 11405
Wilson, Edna C. 7615
Wilson, Franklin 3280
(MIC.F.TC-40977)
Wilson, George Alan 9793
Wilson, George Earl 7308
(F5076.9 B3 W5)
Wilson, Harold Alexander 3281
(MIC.F.TC-30361)
Wilson, Harold Arnold 7336
(F5086 B67 W5)
Wilson, Harold Fisher 840
Wilson, Harry Rex 7720
Wilson, James Albert 7589
Wilson, John A.R. 4205
Wilson, John Donald 2514
(MIC.TC-7850)
Wilson, John W., III 10571
Wilson, Keith 2461 (MIC.T-209)
Wilson, Kevin Arthur 2767
(MIC.TC-6768)
Wilson, LeRoy John 4103
(MIC.F.TC-26956)
Wilson, Llewellyn Lee 3749
Wilson, Lon Ervin 9963
Wilson, Malcolm Alan 11627
(MIC.F.TC-49190)
Wilson, Mary Louise Lewis 8336
Wilson, Mark V.H. 6531
(MIC.F.TC-30362)
Wilson, Michael 860
Wilson, Morley Evans 6504
Wilson, Nadine 10977 (MIC.TC-3065)
Wilson, Norman L. 6505
Wilson, Richard Garth 4988
Wilson, Robert Jeremy 8694
(MIC.F.TC-40817)
Wilson, Susannah Jane Foster 1106
(MIC.F.TC-36871)
Wilson, Sybil Everesta 4466
(MIC.TC-13086)
Wilson, Thomas Frederick 1195
(MIC.F.T-1215)
Wilson, Thomas H. 9838
(MIC.F.TC-48056)
Wilson, Vincent Seymour 8558
(MIC.TC-7585)
Wilson, William Edgar 8864
Wilson, William Warren 2322
(MIC.F.TC-47253)
Wilton, Arthur C. 11406 (MIC.TC-157)
Wilton, David Arthur 1849
(HB171 Q8 fol.)
Wilton, Murray Thomas 7678
(MIC.F.TC-38472)
Winakor, Arthur H. 1449
Windal, Pierre Bernard Marie 2233
(MIC.F.TC-37762)
Winder, Charles G. 6247
Winer, Stanley Lewis 1495
Wingert, Paul Stover 681
(E78 N78 W6 A76 fol.)
Wingfield, Alexander Hamilton 9494
(BF341 W5)
Winks, Robin William 7531
Winn, Conrad Leslie James 8633
(MIC.T-454)

Winn, William Edwin 7393
Winner, William Eugene 11447
  (MIC.F.TC-34273)
Winsor, Elizabeth Joan Townsend 6862
  (MIC.F.TC-18732)
Winter, Carol Florence 2615
  (MIC.F.TC-42343)
Winter, Carl G. 7552
Winter, George Robert 1196
Winterhalder, Bruce Paul 518
Winters, George Henry 10898
  (MIC.F.TC-28979)
Winters, Tobey Lee 10476
Wintre, Maxine Ann Gallander 3039
  (MIC.F.TC-37028)
Wintsobe, Ronald Stephen 1399
  (MIC.F.TC-35162)
Winzer, Margaret Ann 2647
  (MIC.F.TC-53181)
Winzer, Stephen Randolph 5368
  (MIC.F.TC-17737)
Winzerling, Oscar W. 7626
Wirick, Ronald Guy 153
  (MIC.F.TC-46056)
Wise, Daniel Lewis 5012
Wiseman, Henry 8798 (MIC.TC-7839)
Wiseman, Nelson 8641
  (MIC.F.TC-32904)
Wishart, James S. 5684
Wisniewski, Lawrence John 2086
  (MIC.F.TC-36572)
Witten, Alan Joel 11905
Wittier, Glen Eric 1888
Wobeser, Gary Arthur 6866
Wodlinger, Michael George 4342
  (MIC.F.TC-49135)
Wolbeer, Hendrick Jan 5043
Wolcott, Harry Fletcher 699
  (MIC.T-985)
Wold, Ivor Peterson 1338
Wolf, Frank Michael 1417
  (MIC.F.TC-20089)
Wolf, Morris 661
Wolfart, Hans Christoph 7792
  (MIC.T-536)
Wolfe, David Allan 1400
Wolfe, Jacqueline Susan 4896
  (MIC.F.TC-38041)
Wolfe, Lila F. 3175 (MIC.F.TC-59770)
Wolfe, Norbert Joseph 2447
  (MIC.F.TC-49379)
Wolfe, Roy Israel 4719
Wolfe, Stephen Howard 6506
Wolfe, William Brian 4289
  (MIC.F.TC-47181)
Wolfe, William John 5369
Wolff, Anthony Bernard 9088
  (MIC.F.TC-43057)
Wolfgang, Robert W. 11350
Wolforth, John Raymond 4681
  (MIC.TC-8559)
Wolfson, Alan David 6819
Wolfus, Beverly Bella 3912
  (MIC.F.TC-53182)
Wonders, William Clare 5032
  (MIC.F.TC-22799)
Wong, Angelina Teresa 4084
Wong, William Ho-Ching 7663
  (MIC.F.TC-40536)
Wong, Yuwa 367 (MIC.F.TC-51089)
Wong-Rieger, Durhane 9765
  (MIC.F.TC-58150)
Wonnacott, Gordon Paul 1566
  (HG3915 W65 fol.)
Wonnacott, Ronald Johnston 2336
Woo, Ming-Ko 11942 (MIC.TC-11274)
Woo, Patrick Tung Kee 10561
  (MIC.TC-7630)
Wood, Anne 2557
Wood, Benjamin William 11407
Wood, Colin James Barry 4598
Wood, H. Diane 3078
  (MIC.F.TC-29249)
Wood, Jack Maxwell 2699
  (MIC.F.TC-32090)
Wood, Jack Sheehan 10822
Wood, James Douglas 3359
  (MIC.F.TC-35322)
Wood, Kenneth George 11796
Wood, Linda Adele 9766
  (MIC.F.TC-30961)

Wood, Nancy L. 10413
  (MIC.F.TC-49136)
Wood, Susan Joan 8046
  (MIC.F.TC-32905)
Wood, V. Alfred 48
Wood, William Donald 2147
Wood-Dauphinee, Sharon Lee 6863
  (MIC.F.TC-57991)
Woodburn, Robert Harrison 2616
  (MIC.F.T-1411)
Woodhouse, Charles Douglas, Jr. 11073
  (MIC.TC-8344)
Woodley, William John Richard 1988
Woodliffe, Helen Mae 3069
Woodman, Joseph Edmund 5685
Woodrow, James 2707
  (MIC.F.TC-19672)
Woodrow, Robert Brian 8517
  (MIC.F.TC-42347)
Woodruff, James Frederick 4720
Woods, Carter 493
Woods, David S. 2771
Woods, Howard Bruce 7721
  (MIC.F.TC-46311)
Woods, Marvin J. 1731
Woods, Stuart B. 12032
Woodside, Kenneth E.B. 1732
Woodsworth, Glenn James 1218
Woodward, Harold W. 5113
Woodward, James Brian 9483
  (MIC.F.TC-39331)
Woolard, Louis Clyde 4246
Woolcott, Donna Myles 6755
  (MIC.F.TC-41802)
Woolner, Paul Allan 2677
  (MIC.F.TC-58362)
Woolstencroft, Robert Peter 8614
  (MIC.F.TC-40355)
Woolverton, Ralph S. 5370
Worden, Otis Osborne 3770
Workman, William Bates 904
  (MIC.T-816)
Workman, William Laurence 3585
  (MIC.F.TC-24163)
Wormsbecker, John Henry 2455
Woroby, Tamara M. 1309
  (MIC.F.TC-52941)
Woussen, Gerard 6507
Wray, Lyle Dwight 3850
  (MIC.F.TC-47254)
Wren, Christopher D. 5084
  (MIC.F.TC-63475)
Wrenn, Phyllis Margaret 7767
  (MIC.F.TC-27524)
Wright, Anna Margaret 7106
  (MIC.F.TC-25517)
Wright, Annette Eileen 2801
  (MIC.F.TC-42788)
Wright, Aubrey Willis 4467
Wright, Charles Malcolm 5538
  (MIC.TC-16517)
Wright, Claudia Frances Ayres 8556
  (MIC.T-645)
Wright, Donald Kenneth 1107
  (MIC.F.558)
Wright, Gerald Campbell Vaughan 2352
Wright, Grant M. 5905
Wright, Harold Douglas 6248
Wright, Ian Michael 3079
  (MIC.F.TC-26959)
Wright, James Douglas 6249
Wright, James R. 255
Wright, James Valliere 662
  (MIC.T-107)
Wright, Jeffrey 6662
  (MIC.F.TC-36874)
Wright, John Frank 6250
Wright, John Ross 10503
  (MIC.TC-15764)
Wright, Kathleen L. 3040
Wright, Mary Jean 3771
Wright, Philip Alan 344
Wright, Richard Kyle 11990
  (MIC.F.TC-52186)
Wright, Ruth Lynne 2617
  (MIC.F.TC-56424)
Wright, William Josiah 5686
Wrighton, Patricia Ann 9591
  (MIC.F.TC-37832)
Wrigley, Robert Ernest 10683
  (KL737 R688 W75)

Wrona, Frederick John 11349
  (MIC.F.TC-60830)
Wu, Liang-Yu 11360
Wuorinen, Vilho 4927
  (MIC.F.TC-44543)
Wyatt, David John 7426 (MIC.T-451)
Wyatt, Frank Leopold 3988
  (MIC.F.TC-23971)
Wybourn, Edbrooke Sidney 2821
Wycoco, Remedios Santiago 8337
Wyder, John Ernest 5585
Wydra, Alina E. 9231
  (MIC.F.TC-52942)
Wylie, Mary Eileen 11448
Wylie, William Newman Thomas 7059
  (MIC.F.TC-50217)
Wyndham, Robert Campbell 10532
  (MIC.F.TC-57128)
Wynn, Graeme Clifford 4853
  (MIC.F.TC-20598)
Wynne, Robert Edward 7161
  (F855.2 C5 W96)
Wynne-Edwards, Hugh Robert 6251
Wyphema, Ronald Conrad Peter 11300
  (MIC.F.TC-59106)

Y

Yaciuk, Gordon 4487
  (MIC.F.TC-18108)
Yackulic, Richard Alan 9484
  (MIC.F.TC-51611)
Yadav, Gopal Ji 2045 (HB31 B7 fol.)
Yaeger, Malcah 7768 (MIC.F.TC-1046)
Yagil, Joseph 1463 (MIC.F.TC-43751)
Yamanaka, Koji 322 (MIC.F.TC-62953)
Yang, C.N. 8833
Yang, Richard Chun-Hsiung 11725
  (MIC.F.TC-40823)
Yap, David Hamilton 4628
  (MIC.TC-15164)
Yardley, Donald H. 5906
Yarie, John Anthony 11509
  (MIC.F.TC-37767)
Yarnal, Brenton Murray 4997
  (MIC.F.TC-58812)
Yarnell, Richard Asa 720
Yates, Alan 1144 (MIC.F.TC-47471)
Yates, Elizabeth Prewitt 9232
  (MIC.F.TC-50218)
Ycas, Martynas Albert 7679
  (MIC.F.TC-24456)
Yee, Paul Him-Ngar 9485
Yeh, Martin H. 24
Yeh, Ming-che 756 (MIC.F.TC-47185)
Yellin, Carole Susan 4206
  (MIC.F.TC-35323)
Yerbury, John Collin 554
  (MIC.F.TC-51090)
Yerles, Magdaleine 10332
  (MIC.F.T-1096)
Yewchuk, Carolyn Rose 3851
  (MIC.TC-13635)
Yingst, Larry Ronald 3711
  (MIC.F.TC-17086)
Yitzhak, Varda 3852 (MIC.F.TC-53187)
Yole, Raymond William 5371
Yorath, Christopher J. 6252
  (MIC.TC-1098)
Yorgason, Vernon Wayne 39
  (MIC.T-319)
York, James Earl 6605
York, Mary Neris 9089
York, Thomas Lee 8152
Younce, Gordon Baldwin 5798
Young, Brian J. 2323
  (MIC.F.TC-17953)
Young, D.M. 7473
Young, David George 3642
  (MIC.F.TC-43601)
Young, Duane Eugene 10856
Young, Frank Wilbur 370 (MIC.T-72)
Young, Frederick Griffin 5372
  (MIC.TC-6062)
Young, George Albert 6508

Young, Gerald 3989 (MIC.TC-5066)
Young, Gerald C. 9349
    (MIC.F-2M11.141.1)
Young, Gerald Loren 154
Young, Gordon James 4596
    (MIC.F.TC-23238)
Young, Harvey Ray 5539
Young, John Ernest McKim 3354
Young, J.H. 1197
Young, James Albert 9275
    (MIC.F.TC-52191)
Young, James Walton 2126
    (MIC.F.TC-27292)
Young, John Geoffrey 1776
Young, Mary McPherson 371
    (MIC.F.TC-22012)
Young, Richard Anthony 4159
    (MIC.F.TC-33410)
Young, Robert Hume 4207 (MIC.T-246)
Young, Roger Adams 6663
    (MIC.F.TC-43752)
Young, Walter Douglas 8642
    (MIC.T-7517)
Young, William Curtis 1043
Young, William L. 6253
Young, William Robert 1073
    (MIC.F.TC-37770)
Younger, Jonathan Cole 9767
    (MIC.F.TC-38878)
Younkin, Walter Erwin 11558
    (MIC.F.TC-22013)
Youson, John Harold 10905
    (MIC.TC-5338)
Yu, Agnes Yinling 3282
    (MIC.F.TC-51613)
Yu, Kwang-Hwa Andrew 11899
Yu, Shaw-Lei 4526
Yuen, Clement Ming-Kai 4571
    (MIC.F.TC-48447)
Yuill, Thomas Mackay 6867
Yule, David Lloyd George 4042
    (MIC.F.TC-40981)
Yungblut, Douglas Harold 155
    (MIC.F.TC-41809)
Yuzyk, Paul 9830 (BX743.3 Y89)

Z

Zaccano, Joseph Peter, Jr. 7017
    (MIC.T-110)
Zach, Reto 10752
Zaharchuk, Ted Michael 3643
    (MIC.TC-12242)
Zaidi, Mahmood Ahmed 2221
    (MIC.T-146)
Zajac, Ihor Stephan 5799
Zakuta, Leo 8643 (JL197 N4 Z3)
Zales, William Milton 11408
    (MIC.TC-15165)
Zammuto, Richard Michael 10706
    (MIC.F.TC-56122)
Zandi, Farokh-Reza 1198
    (MIC.F.TC-55641)
Zanes, John Page 3551
Zanuncio, José Cola 11234
    (MIC.F.TC-50788)
Zarb, Janet Mary 10277
    (MIC.F.TC-36877)
Zaremba, Alois Louis 1989 (MIC.T-256)
Zarley, Arvid M. 2046
Zarnke, Randall Lee 10533
Zarnovican, Richard 11772
    (MIC.F.TC-64333)
Zarull, Michael Anthony 11878
    (MIC.F.TC-42874)
Zasada, Donald 40 (MIC.F.TC-54583)
Zaslow, Morris 4819 (MIC.F.TC-19736)
Zebroski, James Thomas 3147
Zechetmayr, Monika 10400
    (MIC.F.TC-51614)
Zegura, Stephen Luke 635
Zeichner, Amos 9276
    (MIC.F.TC-39842)
Zeitz, Mordecai 7274 (HV17 Z24)
Zelmer, Amy Elliott 4043 (MIC.T-804)

Zeman, Lubomir John 11943
    (MIC.F.TC-17249)
Zenger, Dixie Robson 961
Zenoff, David Brossell 2353
Zentner, Robert Paul 177
    (MIC.F.T-1287)
Zerker, Sally Friedberg 2151
    (MIC.TC-13091)
Zezulka, Joseph Martin 8155
    (MIC.TC-13053)
Zicha, Victor George 3714 (MIC.T-264)
Zicus, Michael Chester 10823
Ziebarth, Robert E. 7018
Zieber, George Henry 4959
    (MIC.TC-9662)
Ziegel, J.S. 7890
Zielinski, Wasyl Gregory 4133
Ziemkiewicz, Paul Frank 11510
    (MIC.F.TC-53519)
Zilke, Samuel 11640
Ziller, Wolf Gunther 324
Zimmer, Ramon Clemence 345
    (MIC.TC-2019)
Zimmerly, David William 414
    (MIC.T-843)
Zimmermann, Robert Allen 6254
Zin, Michael 1418
Zins, Michel A. 2234
Zipp, John Francis 8615
    (MIC.F.T-1019)
Zittin, David 11074 (MIC.F.TC-46316)
Ziv, Liora 4085
Zlotkin, Stanley Howard 6756
    (MIC.F.TC-50371)
Zmurkevych, Stephanie 8352
Znaniecki, Barbara A.R. 9592
    (MIC.F.TC-44179)
Zodgekar, Arvind V. 10315 (MIC.T-433)
Zollo, Tancredi 4793 (MIC.F.TC-37122)
Zoltvany, Yves-François 7294
    (F5063.1 V3 Z6)
Zucker, Kenneth Jay 9350
Zucy, James B. 9090 (MIC.F.TC-48661)
Zuk, William Michael 2593 (MIC.T-680)
Zussman, David R. 9593
    (MIC.F.TC-24786)
Zwack, Peter P. 4989 (MIC.TC-16054)
Zwanzig, Herman V. 5373
    (MIC.TC-16090)
Zwickel, Fred Charles 10854
    (MIC.TC-196)
Zycher, Benjamin 1635 (MIC.F.T-1041)